The cover of this textbook
captures the increasing importance
of technology in the retail industry.
Retailers use sophisticated
communications and information
systems and analytical models to
increase their operating efficiencies,
improve customer service, and increase
customer value. Even small, local retailers
are now offering their customers the
opportunity to shop online as well as
in their stores. Integrated supply chain
management systems and RFID
technology is being used to reduce the
cost and back up inventory involved in
moving merchandise from vendor
manufacturing plants to retail stores.
In addition to selling merchandise,
retailers are using the Internet to build
brand images, provide customer service,
and manage their employees. Retailers
are using advanced analytical techniques
and models to tailor promotions to
individual customers, evaluate locations
for stores, plan assortments, and make
pricing and markdown decisions. This
textbook captures the exciting changes
that are occurring in retailing and offers
a view of the future for students as
shoppers and retail managers.

RETAILING MANAGEMENT

SIXTH EDITION

Michael Levy, PhD
Babson College

Barton A. Weitz, PhD
University of Florida

McGraw-Hill
Irwin

Boston   Burr Ridge, IL   Dubuque, IA   Madison, WI   New York   San Francisco   St. Louis
Bangkok   Bogotá   Caracas   Kuala Lumpur   Lisbon   London   Madrid   Mexico City
Milan   Montreal   New Delhi   Santiago   Seoul   Singapore   Sydney   Taipei   Toronto

**McGraw-Hill
Irwin**

RETAILING MANAGEMENT
Published by McGraw-Hill/Irwin, a business unit of The McGraw-Hill Companies, Inc., 1221
Avenue of the Americas, New York, NY, 10020. Copyright © 2007 by The McGraw-Hill
Companies, Inc. All rights reserved. No part of this publication may be reproduced or distributed
in any form or by any means, or stored in a database or retrieval system, without the prior written
consent of The McGraw-Hill Companies, Inc., including, but not limited to, in any network or
other electronic storage or transmission, or broadcast for distance learning.

Some ancillaries, including electronic and print components, may not be available to customers
outside the United States.

This book is printed on acid-free paper.

3 4 5 6 7 8 9 0 DOW/DOW 0 9 8 7

ISBN-13: 978-0-07-301978-9
ISBN-10: 0-07-301978-X

Editorial director: *John E. Biernat*
Publisher: *Andy Winston*
Managing developmental editor: *Nancy Barbour*
Executive marketing manager: *Rhonda Seelinger*
Producer, Media technology: *Janna Martin*
Project manager: *Harvey Yep*
Manager, New book production: *Heather D. Burbridge*
Director of design BR: *Keith J. McPherson*
Senior photo research coordinator: *Jeremy Cheshareck*
Photo researcher: *Keri Johnson*
Senior media project manager: *Susan Lombardi*
Cover design: *Keith McPherson*
Cover illustrator: *Randy Lyhus*
Interior design: *Maureen McCutcheon*
Typeface: *10.5/12 Janson*
Compositor: *Techbooks*
Printer: *R. R. Donnelley*

Library of Congress Control Number: 2006922628

To Norman and Jacquie Levy, whose enduring love for each other is an inspiration to all.

To Shirley Weitz, whose love, patience, and understanding support are cherished.

ABOUT THE AUTHORS

Michael Levy, PhD, is the Charles Clarke Reynolds Professor of Marketing at Babson College and co-editor of *Journal of Retailing.* He received his PhD in business administration from The Ohio State University and his undergraduate and MS degrees in business administration from the University of Colorado at Boulder. He taught at Southern Methodist University before joining the faculty as professor and chair of the marketing department at the University of Miami. He has taught retailing management for 25 years.

Professor Levy has developed a strong stream of research in retailing, business logistics, financial retailing strategy, pricing, and sales management that has been published in over 45 articles in leading marketing and logistics journals, including the *Journal of Retailing, Journal of Marketing,* and *Journal of Marketing Research.* He currently serves on the editorial review board of the *Journal of Retailing, Journal of the Academy of Marketing Science, International Journal of Logistics Management, International Journal of Logistics and Materials Management, ECR Journal,* and *European Business Review.*

Professor Levy has worked in retailing and related disciplines throughout his professional life. Prior to his academic career, he worked for several retailers and a housewares distributor in Colorado. He has performed research projects with many retailers and retail technology firms, including Accenture, Burdines Department Stores, Khimetrics, Mervyn's, Neiman Marcus, ProfitLogic, and Zale Corporation.

Michael Levy, PhD
Babson College
mlevy@babson.edu

Barton A. Weitz, PhD, received an undergraduate degree in electrical engineering from MIT and an MBA and a PhD in business administration from Stanford University. He has been a member of the faculty at the UCLA Graduate School of Business and the Wharton School at the University of Pennsylvania and is presently the JCPenney Eminent Scholar Chair in Retail Management in the Warrington College of Business Administration at the University of Florida.

Professor Weitz is the executive director of the David F. Miller Center for Retailing Education and Research at the University of Florida. The activities of the center are supported by contributions from 30 national and regional retailers, including JCPenney, Sears, Macy's, Wal-Mart, Famous Footwear, Build-A-Bear, Bealls, City Furniture, and Office Depot. Each year the center places over 200 undergraduates in paid summer internships and management trainee positions with retail firms and funds research on retailing issues and problems.

Professor Weitz has won awards for teaching excellence and has made numerous presentations to industry and academic groups. He has published over 50 articles in leading academic journals on channel relationships, electronic retailing, store design, salesperson effectiveness, and sales force and human resource management. He is on the editorial review boards of the *Journal of Retailing, Journal of Marketing, International Journal of Research in Marketing, Marketing Science,* and *Journal of Marketing Research.* He is a former editor of the *Journal of Marketing Research* and is presently co-editor of *Marketing Letters.*

Professor Weitz was the chair of the American Marketing Association and a member of the board of directors of the National Retail Federation, the National Retail Foundation, and the American Marketing Association. In 1989 he was honored as the AMA/Irwin Educator of the Year in recognition of his contributions to the marketing discipline.

Barton A. Weitz, PhD
University of Florida
bart_weitz@cba.ufl.edu

PREFACE

Our objective in preparing this sixth edition is to stimulate student interest in retailing courses and careers by capturing the exciting and challenging opportunities facing the retailing industry, an industry that plays a vital economic role in society. The textbook continues to be a "good read" for students with a focus on the strategic issues facing retailers.

NEW FEATURES

In preparing the sixth edition of *Retailing Management*, we have revised the textbook to address three important developments in retailing: (1) the increased use of technology and analytical methods, (2) the globalization of the retail industry, and (3) the growing importance of ethical and legal considerations.

 Use of Technology in Retailing   Retailing is evolving into a high-tech industry as retailers increasingly use communications and information systems technologies and analytical models to increase operating efficiencies and improve customer service. Some of these new technology applications, identified with a technology icon in the margin and discussed in the sixth edition, are:

- Use of Web sites to sell products and services to customers (Chapter 3).
- Provide a seamless multichannel (stores, Web sites, and catalogs) interface so that customers can interact with retailers anytime, anywhere (Chapter 3).
- Store of the future using technology to provide a more rewarding shopping experience (Chapter 3).
- Application of geographic information system (GIS) technology for store location decisions (Chapter 8).
- Internet applications for effective human resource management (Chapter 9).
- Integrated supply chain management systems (Chapter 10).
- RFID (radio frequency identification) technology to improve supply chain efficiency (Chapter 10).
- Analysis of customer databases to determine customer lifetime value, target promotions toward a retailer's best customers, and undertake market basket analyses (Chapter 11).
- Implementation of marketing programs to increase customer share of wallet (Chapter 11).
- CPFR (collaboration, planning, forecasting, and replenishment) systems for coordinating vendors and retailer activities (Chapter 12).
- Sophisticated inventory management systems (Chapter 13).
- Reverse auctions for buying merchandise (Chapter 14).
- Use of profit-optimization decision support systems for setting prices in different markets and taking markdowns (Chapter 15).
- Development of targeted promotions using customer databases (Chapter 16).
- Internet-based training for store employees (Chapter 17).
- Decision support systems for scheduling sales associates (Chapter 17).
- EAS technology to reduce shoplifting (Chapter 17).
- Creation of planograms to optimize the sales and profits from merchandise categories (Chapter 18).

- Digital signage to reduce cost and increase message flexibility (Chapter 18).
- In-store kiosks, mobile devices, and the Internet to improve customer service (Chapter 19).
- Instant chat for servicing online customers (Chapter 19)

Globalization of the Retail Industry   Retailing is a global industry. With a greater emphasis being placed on private-label merchandise, retailers are working with manufacturers located throughout the world to acquire merchandise. In addition, retailers are increasingly looking to international markets for growth opportunities. For instance, Carrefour, France's hypermarket chain and the second-largest retailer in the world, is focusing its growth investments in 25 countries but not in France. Some of the global retailing issues, identified with an icon in the margin, examined in this edition are:

- Retail efficiencies in different economies (Chapter 1).
- Illustrations of global expansion by retailers (Chapter 2).
- Cultural impacts on customer buying behavior (Chapter 4).
- Keys to successful entry into international markets (Chapter 5).
- Evaluation of international growth opportunities (Chapter 5).
- Differences in location opportunities in global markets (Chapter 7).
- Regulations affecting customer data collection in world markets (Chapter 10).
- Employee management issues in international markets (Chapters 9 and 17).
- Global sourcing of private-label merchandise (Chapter 14).
- Cultural differences in customer service needs (Chapter 19).

Legal and Ethical Issues Confronting Retailers   Retail institutions are pervasive in our society and thus have a major impact on the welfare of their customers, suppliers, and employees. Given the importance of their societal role, retailers need to consider the impact of their decisions on a broad range of stakeholders. Some of the social welfare, ethical, and legal issues we examine in this sixth edition are:

- Framework for ethical decision making (Chapter 1).
- Managing diversity and the glass ceiling (Chapter 9).
- Privacy considerations in collecting and using customer data (Chapter 11).
- Legal issues affecting purchasing and pricing merchandise (Chapters 14 and 15).
- Sexual harassment and discrimination in hiring and promotions (Chapter 17).
- Provision of employee benefits (Chapter 17).
- Ecologically friendly store design and operations (Chapter 18).
- Store design in light of the American with Disabilities Act (ADA) (Chapter 18).
- Three new cases that deal with legal, ethical, and social welfare issues.

OTHER UNIQUE ASPECTS OF LEVY AND WEITZ'S *RETAILING MANAGEMENT* TEXTBOOK

Chapter on Customer Relationship Management   Chapter 11 examines how retailers are using customer databases to build repeat business and realize a greater share of wallet from key customers. These customer relationship management activities exploit the 80–20 rule—20 percent of the customers account for 80 percent of the sales and profits. In this chapter, we discuss how retailers identify their best customers and target these customers with special promotions and customer services.

Chapter on Multichannel Retailing   Chapter 3 describes the opportunities and challenges retailers face interacting with customers through multiple channels—stores, catalogs, and the Internet. While markets for Internet-only retailers have stabilized, traditional retailers are investing in using the Internet to complement their stores. This chapter discusses how multichannel retailers can and do provide more value to their customers.

Expanded Treatment of Brand Development Issues   To differentiate their offering and build a competitive advantage, retailers are placing more emphasis on developing their brand image, building a strong image for their private-label merchandise, and extending their image to new retail formats. Issues related to the development of brand images and private-label merchandise are discussed in more detail from both a merchandise management and a communications perspective.

Get Out and Do It! Exercises   Found at the end of each chapter, these exercises suggest projects that students can undertake by visiting local retail stores, surfing the Internet, or using the student Web site. A continuing assignment exercise is included so that students can engage in an exercise involving the same retailer throughout the course. The exercises are designed to provide a hands-on learning experience for students.

Monthly Newsletter with Short Cases   These cases are based on recent retailing articles appearing in the business and trade press. Instructors can use these short cases to stimulate class discussions on current issues confronting retailers. The newsletter is e-mailed to instructors and archived on the text's Web page.

Eleven New Cases   These include cases on Wal-Mart's image, Abercrombie & Fitch's hiring practices, retailing to teens and college students, Yankee Candle's private-label development process, customer buying behavior affecting the design of supermarkets, Men's Wearhouse's training programs, and sustainable retail development in the United Kingdom. All 37 cases in the textbook are either new or updated with current information. A number of the cases, such as Build-A-Bear, Rainforest Café, and Wal-Mart, have videos complementing the written case.

Ten New Videos   Twenty-nine video segments are available to illustrate issues addressed in the text. The topics addressed by the new videos include Internet shopping behavior, supply chain management, pricing, management information systems, and suburban and lifestyle shopping centers. Some of the retailers featured in the videos are YUM Brands (Pizza Hut, Taco Bell, and KFC), 1-800-Flowers, Marsh Supermarkets, Marks & Spencer, Wal-Mart, Home Depot, Starbucks, JCPenney, Walgreens, and Jos. A. Banks.

Completely Redesigned Student Web Site   The student Web site has a number of experiential learning exercises, including evaluating international market growth opportunities, examining the financial performance of a retailer, evaluating retail location opportunities, editing the assortment in a merchandise category, developing a merchandise budget plan, and evaluating various markdown strategies.

STUDENT-FRIENDLY TEXTBOOK

This sixth edition creates interest and involves students in the course and the industry by making the textbook a "good read" for students by using Refacts (retailing factoids), Retailing Views, and retail manager profiles at the beginning of each chapter.

Refacts We have updated and added more interesting facts about retailing, called Refacts, in the margins of each chapter. Did you know that a Montgomery Ward buyer created Rudolph the Red-Nosed Reindeer as a Christmas promotion in 1939? Or that the teabag was developed by a Macy's buyer and pantyhose was developed by a JCPenney buyer?

Retailing Views Each chapter contains either new or updated vignettes called Retailing Views to relate concepts to activities and decisions made by retailers. The vignettes look at major retailers, like Wal-Mart, Walgreens, Sears, JCPenney, Neiman Marcus, and Macy's, that interview students on campus for management training positions. They also discuss innovative retailers like REI, Starbucks, The Container Store, Sephora, Harry Rosen, Curves, Chico's, and Bass Pro Shops. Finally, a number of Retailing Views focus on entrepreneurial retailers competing effectively against national chains.

Profiles of Retail Managers To illustrate the challenges and opportunities in retailing, each chapter in the sixth edition begins with a brief profile in their own words from a manager or industry expert whose job or expertise is related to the material in the chapter. These profiles range from Jim Wright and Bill Moran, CEOs of Tractor Supply Co. and Sav-A-Lot, respectively, to Jennifer O'Neil, a senior assistant buyer at Dillard's, and Sybil Jackson, a store manager at PETsMART. They include people who have extensive experience in a specific aspect of retailing like Bari Harlam (vice president of customer relationship management for CVS) and Scott Jennerich (vice president of retail estate for Famous Footwear). The profiles illustrate how senior executives view the industry and suggest career opportunities for college students. They provide students with firsthand information about what people in retailing do and their rewards and challenges.

Web Site for Students and Instructors (www.mhhe.com/levy6e) Just as retailers are using the Internet to help their customers, we have developed a Web site to help students and instructors use the sixth edition of this textbook effectively. Some of the features on the Web site are:

- Multiple-choice questions on the student site.
- Experiential exercises for students.
- Chapter-by-chapter Instructor Manual coverage.
- Case and video notes.
- Retailing trade publications and professional associations.
- News articles about current events in retailing.
- PowerPoint slides summarizing key issues in each chapter.
- Hot links to retailing news sites and sites associated with the Internet exercises in the textbook.
- Additional cases about retailers.

BASIC PHILOSOPHY

The sixth edition of *Retailing Management* maintains the basic philosophy of the previous five editions. We continue to focus on the broad spectrum of retailers, both large and small, selling merchandise and services. The text examines key strategic issues with an emphasis on financial considerations and store management issues. We include descriptive, how-to, and conceptual material.

Broad Spectrum of Retailing In this text, we define retailing as the set of business activities that adds value to the products and services sold to consumers for their personal or family use. Thus, in addition to the products in stores, this text examines the issues facing service retailers like Starbucks and Curves and non-store retailers like eBay and Avon.

Critical Issues in Retailing   Strategic thinking and the consideration of financial implications are critical for success in the present dynamic, highly competitive retail environments. In addition, operations and store management are playing an increasingly important role.

Strategic Perspective   The entire textbook is organized around a model of strategic decision making outlined in Exhibit 1–5 in Chapter 1. Each section and chapter is related back to this overarching strategic framework. In addition, the second section of the book focuses exclusively on critical strategic decisions such as selecting target markets, developing a sustainable competitive advantage, and building an organizational structure and information and distribution systems to support the strategic direction.

Financial Analysis   The financial aspects of retailing are becoming increasingly important. The financial problems experienced by some of the largest retail firms like Kmart highlight the need for a thorough understanding of the financial implications of retail decisions. Financial analysis is emphasized in selected chapters, such as Chapter 6 on the overall strategy of the firm, Chapter 11 on the evaluation of customer lifetime value, and Chapter 13 on retail buying systems. Financial issues are also raised in the sections on negotiating leases, bargaining with suppliers, pricing merchandise, developing a communication budget, and compensating salespeople.

Operations and Store Management   Traditionally, retailers have exalted the merchant prince—the buyer who knew what the hot trends were going to be. This text, by devoting an entire chapter to information systems and supply chain management and an entire section to store management, reflects the changes that have occurred over the past 10 years—the shift in emphasis from merchandise management to the block and tackling of getting merchandise to the stores and customers and providing excellent customer service and an exciting shopping experience. Due to this shift toward store management, most students embarking on retail careers go into store management rather than merchandise buying.

Balanced Approach   The sixth edition continues to offer a balanced approach for teaching an introductory retailing course by including descriptive, how-to, and conceptual information in a highly readable format.

Descriptive Information   Students can learn about the vocabulary and practice of retailing from the descriptive information throughout the text. Examples of this material are:

- Leading U.S. and international retailers (Chapter 1).
- Management decisions made by retailers (Chapter 1).
- Types of store-based and nonstore retailers (Chapter 2).
- Approaches for entering international markets (Chapter 5).
- Locations (Chapter 7).
- Lease terms (Chapter 8)
- Organization structure of typical retailers (Chapter 9).
- Flow of information and merchandise (Chapter 10).
- Branding strategies (Chapter 14).
- Methods for communicating with customers (Chapter 16).
- Store layout options and merchandise display equipment (Chapter 18).
- Career opportunities (Appendix 1A to Chapter 1).

How-to Information   *Retailing Management* goes beyond this descriptive information to illustrate how and why retailers, large and small, make decisions. Step-by-step procedures with examples are provided for making the following decisions:

- Comparison shopping (Appendix 2A to Chapter 2).
- Managing a multichannel outreach to customers (Chapter 3).
- Scanning the environment and developing a retail strategy (Chapter 5).
- Analyzing the financial implications of retail strategy (Chapter 6).
- Evaluating location decisions (Chapter 8).
- Developing a merchandise assortment and budget plan (Chapters 12 and 13).
- Negotiating with vendors (Chapter 14).
- Pricing merchandise (Chapter 15).
- Recruiting, selecting, training, evaluating, and compensating sales associates (Chapter 17).
- Designing the layout for a store (Chapter 18).
- Providing superior customer service (Chapter 19).

Conceptual Information   *Retailing Management* also includes conceptual information that enables students to understand why decisions are made as outlined in the text. As Mark Twain said, "There is nothing as practical as a good theory." Students need to know these basic concepts so they can make effective decisions in new situations. Examples of this conceptual information in the sixth edition are:

- Customers' decision-making process (Chapter 4).
- Market attractiveness/competitive position matrix for evaluating strategic alternatives (Appendix 5A to Chapter 5).
- The strategic profit model and approach for evaluating financial performance (Chapter 6).
- Price theory and marginal analysis (Chapters 15 and 16).
- Motivation of employees (Chapter 17).
- In-store shopping behaviors (Chapter 18)
- The Gaps model for service quality management (Chapter 19).

Supplemental Materials   To improve the student learning experience, the sixth edition includes new cases and videos illustrating state-of-the-art retail practices, a Web-based computer exercise package for students, and a comprehensive online instructor's manual with additional cases and teaching suggestions.

ACKNOWLEDGMENTS

Throughout the development of this text, several outstanding individuals were integrally involved and made substantial contributions. First and foremost, we recognize the invaluable contributions of Hope Bober Corrigan (Loyola College in Maryland) for providing constructive comments and suggestions on the revised chapters, editing the cases and video package, and providing many useful teaching activities found in the Instructor's Manual. We wish to express our sincere appreciation to Amy Tomas (University of Vermont) for preparing the Instructor's Manual and Cecilia Schulz (University of Florida) for preparing the PowerPoint slides and Test Bank.

We'd like especially to acknowledge the contribution of Retail Forward, Inc. Their daily news briefing and research reports facilitated the research that has gone into this text.

We also appreciate the contributions of Margaret Jones and Betsy Trobaugh (David F. Miller Center for Retailing Education and Research, University of Florida) and Morgan Wolters (Babson College) who provided invaluable assistance in preparing the manuscript.

The support, expertise, and occasional coercion from our Sponsoring Editor, Andy Winston, and Managing Developmental Editor, Nancy Barbour, are greatly appreciated. The book would also never have come together without the editorial and production staff at McGraw-Hill/Irwin: Harvey Yep, Trent Whatcott, Janna Martin, Sue Lombardi, Jeremy Cheshareck, Keith McPherson, and Heather Burbridge.

Retailing Management has also benefited significantly from contributions by several leading executives and scholars in retailing and related fields. We would like to thank:

William Alcorn
JCPenney

Mark Blakeley
Oracle

Cynthia Cohen
Strategic Mindshare

Paul Freddo
JCPenney

Scott C. Friend
Oracle

John Gremer
Walgreens

Dhruv Grewal
Babson College

James Hughes
JCPenney

Linda Hyde
Retail Forward

Howard Kimpel
JCPenney

Steve Knopik
Beall's Inc.

Doug Koch
Famous Footwear

Bradley Macullum
ESRI

Bruce Mager
Macy's

Richard A. McAllister
Florida Retail Federation

William Moran
Sav-A-Lot

Tracey Mullins
National Retail Federation

Steven Keith Platt
Platt Retail Institute

Susan Reda
Stores Magazine

Ann Rupert
Burdines

Ron Sacino
Sacino's Formalwear

Lori Schafer
SAS Retail

John Thomas
Pinch-A-Penny

Suzanne Voorhees
The Grapevine Group

The sixth edition of *Retailing Management* has benefited from the reviews by several leading scholars and many teachers of retailing and related disciplines. Together, these reviewers spent hundreds of hours reading and critiquing the manuscript. We gratefully acknowledge:

Stephen J. Anderson
Austin Peay State University

David Blanchette
Rhode Island College

Sylvia Clark
St. John's University

Angela D'Auria-Stanton
Radford University

Kathleen Debevic Witz
University of Massachusetts

David Erickson
Angelo University

Sally Harmon
Purdue University

Joshua Holt
Brigham Young University

Barbara Mihm
University of Wisconsin–Stevens Point

Dorothy M. Oppenheim
Bridgewater State University

Michael M. Pearson
Loyola University, New Orleans

Linda Pettijohn
Southern Missouri State University

Amy Tomas
University of Vermont

Sandy White
Greenville Tech College

We also thank the following reviewers for their diligence and insight in helping us prepare previous editions:

Kevin Fertig
University of Illinois

David M. Georgoff
Florida Atlantic University

Peter Gordon
Southeast Missouri State University

Larry Gresham
Texas A&M University

Tom Gross
University of Wisconsin

Michael D. Hartline
Louisana State University

Tony L. Henthorne
University of Southern Mississippi

Eugene J. Kangas
Winona State University

Herbert Katzenstein
St. John's University

Terrence Kroeten
North Dakota State University

Elizabeth Mariotz
Philadelphia College of Textiles and Science

Harold McCoy
Virginia Commonwealth University

Kim McKeage
University of Maine

Robert Miller
Central Michigan University

Mary Anne Milward
University of Arizona

John J. Porter
West Virginia University

Nick Saratakes
Austin Community College

Laura Scroggins
California State University–Chico

Shirley M. Stretch
California State University–LA

William R. Swinyard
Brigham Young University

Janet Wagner
University of Maryland

Ron Zallocco
University of Toledo

Mary Barry
Auburn University

Lance A. Bettencourt
Indiana University

Jeff Blodgett
University of Mississippi

George W. Boulware
Lipscomb University

Leroy M. Buckner
Florida Atlantic University

David J. Burns
Purdue University

Lon Camomile
Colorado State University

J. Joseph Cronin, Jr.
Florida State University

Irene J. Dickey
University of Dayton

Ann DuPont
University of Texas

Chloe I. Elmgren
Mankato State University

Richard L. Entrikin
George Mason University

Kenneth R. Evans
University of Missouri–Columbia

Richard Feinberg
Purdue University

Mark Abel
Kirkwood Community College

Jill Attaway
Illinois State University

Willard Broucek
Northern State University

Donald W. Caudill
Bluefield State College

James Clark
Northeastern State University

Drew Ehrlich
Fulton-Montgomery Community College

Susan Harmon
Middle Tennessee State University

Kae Hineline
McLennan Community College

David Horne
California State University–Long Beach

Michael Jones
Auburn University

Ann Lucht
Milwaukee Area Technical College

Tony Mayo
George Mason University

Michael McGinnis
University of South Alabama

Phyliss McGinnis
Boston University

Cheryl O'Hara
Kings College

Janis Petronis
Tarleton State University

Sue Riha
University of Texas–Austin

Steve Solesbee
Aiken Technical College

Janet Wagner
University of Maryland

Gary Walk
Lima Technical College

Mary Weber
University of New Mexico

Fred T. Whitman
Mary Washington College

Merv Yeagle
University of Maryland

We received cases from professors all over the world. Although we would like to have used more cases in the text and the Instructor's Manual, space was limited. We would like to thank all who contributed but are especially appreciative of the following authors whose cases were used in *Retailing Management* or in the Instructor's Manual:

Ronald Adams
University of North Florida

Laura Bliss
Stephens College

Valerie Bryan
University of Florida

James Camerius
Northern Michigan University

Daphne Comfort
University of Gloucestershire

Hope Bober Corrigan
Loyola College in Maryland

Sue Cullers
Tarleton State University

David Ehrlich
Marymount University

Sunil Erevelles
University of North Carolina, Charlotte

Ann Fairhurst
Indiana University

Linda F. Felicetti
Clarion University

Susan Fournier
Boston University

Joseph P. Grunewald
Clarion University

Peter Jones
University of Gloucestershire

David Hillier
University of Glamorgan

K. Douglas Hoffman
*University of North
Carolina–Wilmington*

Kirthi Kalyanam
Santa Clara University

Dilip Karer
University of North Florida

Hean Tat Keh
National University, Singapore

Robert Kenny
Saint Michael's College

Alison T. Knott
University of Florida

Nirmalya Kumar
London Business School

Robert Letovsky
Saint Michael's College

Alicia Lueddemann
The Management Mind Group

Gordon H. G. McDougall
Wilfrid Laurier University

Debra Murphy
Saint Michael's College

Jan Owens
University of Wisconsin

Kristina Pacca
University of Florida

Michael Pearce
University of Western Ontario

Pirkko Peterson
University of Florida

Catherine Porter
University of Massachusetts

Richard Rausch
Hofstra University

Teresa Scott
University of Florida

William R. Swinyard
Brigham Young University

Stephen Vitucci
Tarleton State University

William Walsch
University of Florida

Vidya Sundari
National University, Singapore

Elizabeth J. Wilson
Suffolk University

Irvin Zaenglein
Northern Michigan University

Heather Zuilkoski
University of Florida

ABOUT *RETAILING MANAGEMENT, 6e*

For five editions, Levy & Weitz's **Retailing Management** has been known for its strategic focus, decision-making emphasis, applications orientation, and readability. The authors and McGraw-Hill/Irwin are proud to introduce the sixth edition and invite you to see how this edition captures the exciting, dynamic nature of retailing.

Retailers are **using technology** to increase operating efficiencies and improve customer service. Some of these new technology applications are identified with a technology icon in the margin and discussed in the sixth edition are:

Use of **RFID** by retailers to increase inventory turnover, reduce stockouts, and improve supply chain efficiency

Geographic information systems for store location

Self-checkout to provide better customer service and increase labor productivity

Digital signage for targeting in-store messaging

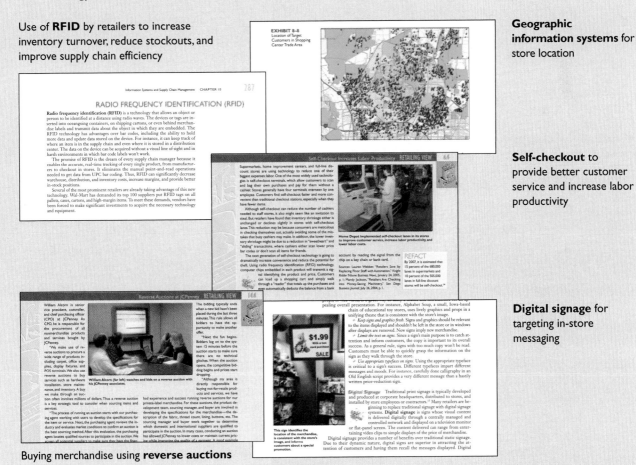

Buying merchandise using **reverse auctions**

Other important developments reviewed in the text are the **globalization** of the retail industry and heightened need to consider **ethical, legal and social responsibility** issues in decision-making.

Retail is now a **global** industry with retailers working with manufacturers located throughout the world to acquire merchandise. In addition, retailers are increasingly looking to international markets for growth opportunities.

Retailing is a pervasive element in our society and has a major impact on the welfare of their customers, suppliers, and employees. Thus retailers need to consider the impact of their decisions on a broad range of stakeholders. The text included expanded treatment of how **ethical and legal issues** should affect decision making.

Using 3-D and zoom technology, Coach.com converts "touch and feel" into "look and see" information.

Consider branded merchandise like Nautica perfume or Levi's 501 jeans. Even though you can't smell a sample of the perfume before buying it, you know that it will smell like your last bottle when you buy it electronically because the manufacturer of Nautica makes sure each bottle smells the same. Similarly, if you wear a size 30-inch waist/32-inch model Levi's 501 jeans, you know they will fit when you buy them electronically.

The retailer's brand can also provide information about the consistency and quality of merchandise. For example, consumers might be reluctant to buy produce using an electronic channel because they cannot see the fruits and vegetables before purchasing. However, the same consumers would likely feel comfortable buying fruit from Harry and David catalogs or its Internet site, because Harry and David has established a strong reputation for selling only the highest quality fruit.

Using Technology Retailers with electronic channels are using technology to convert touch-and-feel information into look-and-see information that can be communicated through the Internet. Web sites are going beyond offering the basic image to giving customers the opportunity to view merchandise from different angles and perspectives using 3D imaging and/or zoom technology. The use of these image-enhancing technologies has increased **conversion rates** (the percentage of consumers who buy the product after viewing it) and reduced returns.

To overcome the limitations for trying on clothing, apparel retailers have started to use virtual models on their Web sites. These virtual models enable consumers to see how selected merchandise looks on an image with similar proportions to their own and then rotate the model to the "fit" can be evaluated from all angles. The virtual models are either selected from set of "prebuilt" models or constructed on the basis of the shopper's response to questions about his or her height, weight, and other dimensions.[4]

For example, at Landsend.com, online shoppers choose a model that looks like them. Customers then dress the model using a "click and drag" interface. Items are suggested while the customer is "trying on" the apparel. Lands' End reports that customers using the virtual model feature were 28 percent more likely to make a purchase and spent 13 percent more on their average purchases. When JCPenney offered this feature on its Web site, over 100,000 customers saved their model for future visits.

Lands' End virtual model on its Web site lets customers "try on" its apparel at home.

These applications are harbingers of future applications in which customers can use a personal, 3D, digitized body scan to serve as an actual model rather than a virtual model. In addition, the measurements for the body scan could be input, along with information about the garment, to a predictive model that would advise customers on how well a specific item will fit using a five-star rating system and then suggest the appropriate size.

Even though it is limited in its ability to provide look-and-see information, in some situations, the Internet channel might be able to provide superior information than stores can. For example, Judy, before she started to shop electronically, wanted to see toys before buying one for her son Dave. So she went to stores to look at the toys. But in the stores, the toys were not displayed; all she could see was a picture on the side of the box containing the toy. Now that Judy shops electronically, she can get superior information from the full-motion video clip showing a child playing with the toy.

Gifts In some situations, touch-and-feel information might be important, but the information in a store is not much better than the information provided electronically. For example, suppose you're buying a bottle of perfume for your mother. Even if you go to the store and smell the samples of all the new scents, you might not get much information to help you determine which one your mother would like. In this situation, stores offer little benefit over an electronic channel in terms of useful information provided about the merchandise. But buying gifts electronically offers the benefit of saving you the time and effort of packing and sending the gift to your mother. For this reason, gifts represent a substantial portion of sales made through the Internet channel. Retailing View 3.3 describes how RedEnvelope uses the Internet and its catalog to focus on the gift market.

REFACT

Orvis, a catalog retailer, had a 60–70 percent increase in sales after adding 3D technology to display merchandise on its Web site.[5]

EXHIBIT 11–2
The Customer Pyramid

SOURCE: Valarie Zeithaml, Roland Rust, and Katherine Lemon, "The Customer Pyramid: Creating and Serving Profitable Customers," California Management Review 43 (Summer 2001), p. 125. Reprinted by permission.

develop more appropriate strategies for each of the segments. Each of the four segments is described below.

• *Platinum segment* This segment is composed of the retailer's customers with the top 25 percent LTVs. Typically, these are the most loyal customers who are not overly concerned about merchandise price and place more value on customer service.

• *Gold segment* The next 25 percent of customers in terms of their LTV make up the gold segment. These customers have a lower LTV than platinum customers because they are more price sensitive. Even though they buy a significant amount of merchandise from the retailer, they are not as loyal as platinum customers and probably patronize some of the retailer's competitors.

• *Iron segment* Customers in this third tier probably do not deserve much special attention from the retailer due to their modest LTV.

• *Lead segment* Customers in the lowest segment can cost the company money. They often demand a lot of attention but do not buy much from the retailer. For example, real estate agents often encounter people who want to spend their weekends looking at houses but are really not interested in buying one.

This segmentation scheme differs, for example, from the segments of passengers in airline frequent flier programs because it is based on LTV rather than miles flown. Thus, it recognizes that some customers who fly a lot of miles might be taking low-cost flights, whereas other customers, though flying the same number of miles, might be much more profitable because they fly first class and don't seek discount fares.

RFM Analysis An **RFM** (recency, frequency, monetary) **analysis**, often used by catalog retailers and direct marketers, is a scheme for segmenting customers according to how recently they have made a purchase, how frequently they make purchases, and how much they have bought. Exhibit 11–3 is an example of an RFM analysis done by a catalog apparel retailer that mails a catalog each month to its customers.

The catalog retailer divides its customers into 32 groups or segments on the basis of how many orders the customer has placed during the last year, how much merchandise the customer has purchased, and the last time the customer placed an order. Each segment is represented by one cell in Exhibit 11–3. For example, the customers

---

EXHIBIT 11–1
The CRM Process Cycle

Overview of the CRM Process

Exhibit 11–1 illustrates that CRM is an iterative process that turns customer data into customer loyalty through four activities: (1) collecting customer data, (2) analyzing the customer data and identifying target customers, (3) developing CRM programs, and (4) implementing CRM programs. The process begins with the collection and analysis of data about a retailer's customers and the identification of target customers. The analysis translates the customer information into activities that offer value to the targeted customers. Then those activities are executed through communication programs undertaken by the marketing department and customer service programs implemented by customer contact employees, typically sales associates. Each of the four activities in the CRM process is discussed in the following sections.

COLLECTING CUSTOMER DATA

The first step in the CRM process is to construct a **customer database**. This database is part of the data warehouse described in Chapter 10. It contains all of the data the firm has collected about its customers and is the foundation for subsequent CRM activities.

Customer Database

Ideally, the database should contain the following information:

• *Transactions*—a complete history of the purchases made by the customer, including the purchase date, the price paid, the SKUs purchased, and whether the merchandise was purchased in response to a special promotion or marketing activity.

• *Customer contacts*—a record of the interactions that the customer has had with the retailer, including visits to the retailer's Web site, inquiries made through in-store kiosks, and telephone calls made to the retailer's call center, plus information about contacts initiated by the retailer, such as catalogs and direct mail sent to the customer.

• *Customer preferences*—what the customer likes, such as favorite colors, brands, fabrics, and flavors, as well as apparel sizes. As the beginning of this chapter, we described Shari Ast's experience checking into the Boston Ritz-Carlton. The Ritz-Carlton did not learn about Shari's preferences by asking her to complete a questionnaire; instead, it collected this information by recording each

---

Expanded treatment of **multi-channel retailing** describes the challenges and opportunities for store-based retailers as they add an Internet channel to provide information about products and services and sell merchandise.

Includes a chapter devoted to **customer relationship management (CRM)** that includes methods of determining customer lifetime value and developing programs to increase loyalty and build share-of-wallet from a retailer's best customers.

This edition continues the emphasis placed on **creating interest and involving students** in the course and the industry. Refacts, Retailing Views, and retail manager profiles at the beginning of each chapter make the textbook a **"good read"** for students.

Refacts (retailing factoids) are interesting facts about retailing, related to the textual material, that are placed in the margin.

Retailing Views are vignettes in each chapter that relate concepts developed in the text to issues and problems confronting retailers.

To illustrate the opportunities and rewards from a career in retailing, each chapter begins with a **profile** of a retail manager—either a senior executive or recent college graduate—discussing their area of decision-making and their career path.

Buying Merchandise

EXECUTIVE BRIEFING
Jennifer O'Neill, Buyer, Dillard's

Information Systems and Supply Chain Management

EXECUTIVE BRIEFING
Jim LaBounty, Senior Vice President and Director of Supply Chain Management, JCPenney

The end of the chapter Get Out and Do It exercises and the online learning center involve students in the course and the material covered in the text.

Get Out and Do It! Exercises Found at the end of each chapter, these exercises suggest projects that students can undertake by either visiting local retail stores, surfing the Internet, or using the student website. The exercises are designed to provide a hands-on learning experience for students. A continuing exercise is included in each chapter so that students can be involved in an experiential exercise involving the same retailer throughout the course.

To **stimulate class discussion** about issues confronting retail managers, the text contains 36 cases, including Wal-Mart's social responsibility activities, retailing to teens and college students, Yankee Candle's private label development process, how customer buying behavior affects the design of supermarkets, and Mens Wearhouse's training programs.

Twenty-nine video segments are available to illustrate issues addressed in the text. Topics addressed in the video include Rainforest Café's and Build-A-Bear's retail strategy, Internet shopping behavior, supply chain management, pricing, management information systems, and suburban and lifestyle shopping centers. A number of the videos complement the cases.

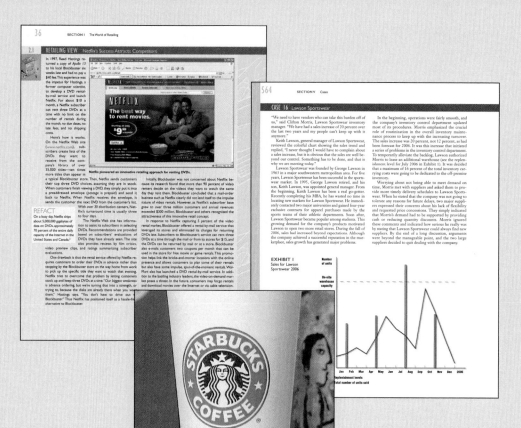

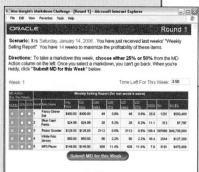

The **Online Learning Center** is a website that includes Instructor and Student materials. The Instructors side contains the Instructor's Manual, the PageOut course management system, PowerPoint slides, and the archived Retailing Newsletter.

The **online learning center** provides students with exercises to evaluate international expansion opportunities, examine financial performance of retailers, analyze potential store locations, develop a merchandise budget plan, make pricing and markdown decisions, and determine break-even sales levels. The **online learning center** also contains an exciting simulation in which students make weekly markdown decisions and compare their results with Oracle's Markdown Optimization software. Sample test questions and flash cards are provided for each chapter to aid student learning.

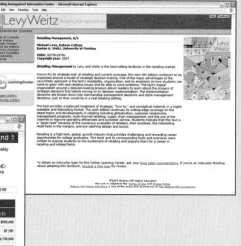

Each month, the authors prepare and distribute through email a Retailing Newsletter. The newsletters contain ten to twelve abstracts of articles appearing in the business or trade press about current issues facing retailers specifically and the industry in general.

BRIEF CONTENTS

CONTENTS

CHAPTER 4 CUSTOMER BUYING BEHAVIOR 92

SECTION II RETAILING STRATEGY

CHAPTER 5 RETAIL MARKET STRATEGY 126

CHAPTER 9   HUMAN RESOURCE MANAGEMENT   236

CHAPTER 10   INFORMATION SYSTEMS AND SUPPLY CHAIN MANAGEMENT   266

SECTION V   CASES

RETAILING MANAGEMENT

THANK YOU FOR SHOPPING AT **ASDA**

Happy to Help

The World of Retailing

The chapters in Section I provide the background information about retail customers and competitors that you need to understand the world of retailing and develop and effectively implement a retail strategy.

Chapter 1 describes the functions retailers perform and the variety of decisions they make to satisfy customers' needs in rapidly changing, highly competitive retail environments. The remaining chapters in this section give you background information to understand the world of retailing.

Chapter 2 describes the different types of retailers.

Chapter 3 examines how retailers are using multiple selling channels—stores, the Internet, and catalogs—to reach their customers.

Chapter 4 discusses factors consumers consider when choosing stores and buying merchandise.

The chapters in Section II focus on the strategic decisions retailers make.

The chapters in Sections III and IV explore tactical decisions involving merchandise and store management.

Introduction to the World of Retailing → Retailing Strategy → Merchandise Management, Store Management

Introduction to the World of Retailing

TRACTOR SUPPLY C° **MISSION**

To work hard, have fun and make money by providing legendary service and great products at everyday low prices.

OUR BUSINESS:
We are committed to be the most dependable supplier of basic maintenance products to farm, ranch and rural customers.

OUR PEOPLE:
We value honesty, integrity, mutual respect and teamwork above all else.

We are an open company where everyone has the information and tools to grow and excel.

We encourage risk taking, celebrate initiative

TRACTOR SUPPLY C° **VALUES**

ETHICS
Do the "right thing" and always encourage others to do the right, honest and ethical things.

RESPECT
Treat others with the same personal and professional consideration we expect for ourselves.

BALANCE
Manage your time for both business and personal success.

WINNING ATTITUDE
Have a "can-do" attitude. Be positive, upbeat, and focused. We are winners!

COMMUNICATION
Share information, ask questions, listen effectively, speak thoughtfully, and let ideas live.

DEVELOPMENT
Learn from each other. Teach, coach, and listen. Create an environment where everyone can be a "star".

TEAMWORK
Value different viewpoints. Execute the agreed-upon plans. Together, everyone achieves more!

CHANGE
race it. Initiate it. Do everything r, faster, and cheaper.

INITIATIVE
unities. Use good judgement. gent risks. Champion ideas.

EXECUTIVE BRIEFING
Jim Wright, CEO, Tractor Supply

Retail has the quickest cycle time from idea, to implementation, to assessment and refinement of any industry. The pace is exhilarating. In the stores feedback is instantaneous; customers buy or not, they are pleased or not, and team members can have an immediate impact. Even at senior levels the feedback is real-time.

I enjoy the people side of retail. More than most industries, the opportunity to mentor and develop young team members is limitless. As I look back over my career there are numerous examples of cashiers who became store managers—store managers who today are in multi-unit management, merchants, or operating executives. A true joy has been in discovering bright, hard-working, and dedicated people and giving them a chance to build a career. For those who step up to the opportunity, the results are very rewarding for them and their mentor.

I began my retail career working part time in a Kmart Auto Center while in college. Full-time assistant and store manager positions followed while still in school. My career

with Kmart progressed to district manager, a national operating position, and several buying positions. I left in 1988 to become the vice president of store operations for Western Auto and enjoyed several promotions before leaving in 1996 to become the CEO of an underperforming turnaround company, Tire Kingdom.

After we successfully completed the turnaround, I sold the company and considered a number of opportunities. I wanted to stay in retail to be involved in a growth company that had a solid foundation of mission and values. Tractor Supply proved to be a great fit. The foundation was solid, the niche defined, and the skill set I had acquired over the previous 30 years proved to be applicable. Our team has built the business from $759 million to over $2 billion in the last 5 years. Tractor Supply Co. (TSCO) is the leading farm and ranch store chain in the U.S. Our target customer is the do-it-yourselfer involved in the rural renaissance. They tend to own land, pickup trucks, dogs, cats, horses, and some livestock. We also

What is retailing?

What do retailers do?

Why is retailing important in our society?

What career and entrepreneurial opportunities does retailing offer?

What types of decisions do retail managers make?

Most consumers shopping in their local stores don't realize that retailing is a high-tech, global industry. To illustrate the sophisticated technologies used by retailers consider the following: If you are interested in buying an MP3 player, Best Buy provides a Web site (www.bestbuy.com) you can access to learn about the features of the different models and even which models are in stock at your local store. You can order the player from the Web site and have it delivered to your home or pick it up at the local store. If you decide to go to the store, Best Buy has Web-enabled kiosks that you can use to review information on its Web site.

When you decide to buy an iPod at the store, the point-of-sales (POS) terminal transmits data about the transaction to Best Buy's distribution center and then on to the manufacturer, Apple Computer. When the in-store inventory level drops below a prespecified level, an electronic notice is automatically transmitted authorizing the shipment of more units to the distribution center and then to the store. The movements of the iPod shipment are tracked from Apple Computer's manufacturing facility to Best Buy's distribution center to your local store through the radio waves generated by microchips embedded in the shipping container. Data about your purchase are also transmitted to a buyer at Best Buy who analyzes the information to determine how many and which types of units should stocked in your local store and what price should be charged. Finally, the data about your purchase are stored in Best Buy's data warehouse and used to design special promotions for you.

serve suburban home owners, small contractors, and municipalities.

While the growth potential was attractive, the values and mission were even more appealing. Every decision we make is based on our values and mission statement, which you can see at our Web site. Everyone in our company carries a card with these guiding principles and every office has a copy on the wall. When I meet our new employees at the store support center each Monday morning, the first thing I talk about is our values and mission statement. A lot of companies have these types of statements, but at TSC, we walk the talk. We believe that being a great place to work enables us to be a great place to shop and invest.

Sony, Toyota, and Toshiba are well known around the world as industry leaders but another retailer, 7-Eleven, though less well known, is as much a high-tech business success story and has probably had a greater impact on Japanese culture. In Japan, 7-Eleven has over 10,000 convenience stores (called *combini*) that have changed the way people shop and eat. Weary commuters leaving the train station often go to 7-Eleven before heading home. Some simply buy magazines, cigarettes, or soft drinks, but many buy dinner from an array of *bento* boxes and *onigiri* rice balls delivered fresh only hours earlier. Others use the kiosks in the stores to pay bills, buy tickets for events, or print photos from their digital cameras. The stores have become the focal point in many urban Japanese communities—the place where teenagers try to buy their first cigarettes, executives drop their golf bags for delivery to the course on Sunday, wives pick up the laundry, and grandmothers buy their buckwheat noodles instead of making them by hand.

REFACT

Wal-Mart's data warehouse contains over 425 terabytes of data, almost twice as much data as contained in the World Wide Web.[1]

Stores in Japan offer fresh fruits, vegetables and seafood, meat, tofu, pickled and canned food, dairy products, and high-appetite appeal instant meals based on traditional foodstuffs.

Each 7-Eleven store gets 10 deliveries a day. The entire food offering changes three times a day for breakfast, lunch, and dinner. 7-Eleven employs one of the most sophisticated data management systems in the world to make sure the right merchandise is in the right place at the right time. The information system also is used to tailor merchandise assortments to the local markets. "In Hokkaido, we make *bento* boxes with local scallops and sea urchin," says a 7-Eleven executive, Minoru Matsumoto. "But in Sendai, the specialty is cow's tongue, so we cater to that taste there." Weather conditions are closely monitored so that more cold noodles are stocked on warm days and more fresh produce on rainy days to accommodate customers who decide to shop at the convenient *combini* rather than travel to the grocery store.[2]

Historically, the retail landscape has been dominated by local retailers buying and reselling merchandise from local suppliers. Thirty years ago, some of the largest retailers in the United States—Wal-Mart, The Gap, Home Depot, and Best Buy—either were small start-ups or did not even exist. Now most retail sales are made by large national and international chains that buy merchandise from all over the world. Wal-Mart is the world's largest corporation. French-based Carrefour, the world's second-largest retailer, operates hypermarkets in 24 countries (but not in the United States). Some of the largest retailers in the United States, such as A&P, Food Lion, Stop & Shop, and 7-Eleven, are owned by companies with headquarters in Europe and Japan.

REFACT

Wal-Mart buys merchandise from over 5,000 different factories located in 60 countries.[3]

Retailing is such a common part of our everyday lives that it's often taken for granted. Retail managers make complex decisions in selecting their target markets and retail locations; determining what merchandise and services to offer; negotiating with suppliers; distributing merchandise to stores; training and motivating sales associates; and deciding how to price, promote, and present merchandise. Considerable skill and knowledge are required to make these decisions effectively. Working in this highly competitive, rapidly changing environment is challenging and exciting and offers significant financial rewards.

This book describes the world of retailing and offers principles for effectively managing retail businesses in highly competitive environments. Knowledge of retailing principles and practices will help you develop management skills for many business contexts. For example, Procter & Gamble and Hewlett-Packard managers need to have a thorough understanding of how retailers operate and make money so they can get their products on retail shelves and work with retailers to sell them to consumers. Financial and health care institutions use retail principles to develop their offerings, improve customer service, and provide convenient, easy access for their customers. Thus, students interested in professional selling, marketing, and finance will find this book useful.

WHAT IS RETAILING?

Retailing is the set of business activities that adds value to the products and services sold to consumers for their personal or family use. Often people think of retailing only as the sale of products in stores, but retailing also involves the sale of services: overnight lodging in a motel, a doctor's exam, a haircut, a DVD rental, or a home-delivered pizza. Not all retailing is done in stores. Examples of nonstore retailing include Internet sales of hot sauces (www.firehotsauces.com), the direct sales of cosmetics by Avon, and catalog sales by L.L. Bean and Patagonia.

A Retailer's Role in a Distribution Channel

A **retailer** is a business that sells products and/or services to consumers for their personal or family use. Retailers are the final business in a distribution channel that links manufacturers to consumers. A **distribution channel** is a set of firms that facilitate the movement of products from the point of production to the point of sale to the ultimate consumer. Exhibit 1–1 shows the retailer's position within a distribution channel.[4]

Manufacturers typically make products and sell them to retailers or wholesalers. When manufacturers like Ralph Lauren and Dell sell directly to consumers, they are performing both production and retailing business activities. Wholesalers buy products from manufacturers and resell these products to retailers, and retailers resell products to consumers. Wholesalers and retailers may perform many of the same functions described in the next section. But wholesalers satisfy retailers' needs, whereas retailers direct their efforts to satisfying the needs of ultimate consumers. Some retail chains, like Home Depot and Office Depot, function as both retailers and wholesalers. They're performing retailing activities when they sell to consumers but wholesaling activities when they sell to other businesses, like building contractors or small business owners.

In some distribution channels, the manufacturing, wholesaling, and retailing activities are performed by independent firms, but most distribution channels have some vertical integration. **Vertical integration** means that a firm performs more than one set of activities in the channel, such as investments by retailers in wholesaling or manufacturing. **Backward integration** arises when a retailer performs some distribution and manufacturing activities, such as operating warehouses or designing private label merchandise. **Forward integration** is when a manufacturer undertakes retailing activities, such as Ralph Lauren operating its own retail stores.

For example, most large retailers—such as Safeway, Wal-Mart, and Lowe's—engage in both wholesaling and retailing activities. They buy directly from manufacturers, have merchandise shipped to their warehouses for storage, and then

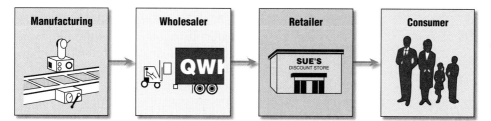

EXHIBIT I–I
Example of a Distribution Channel

distribute the merchandise to their stores. Other retailers, such as The Gap and Victoria's Secret, are even more vertically integrated. They design the merchandise they sell and then contract with manufacturers to produce it exclusively for them.

Functions Performed by Retailers

Why are retailers needed? Wouldn't it be easier and cheaper to buy directly from companies that manufacture the products? The answer is generally no. Although there are situations in which it is easier and cheaper to buy directly from manufacturers, such as at a local farmer's market or from Dell Computer, retailers provide important functions that increase the value of the products and services they sell to consumers and facilitate the distribution of those products and services for those who produce them. These value-creating functions are

1. Providing an assortment of products and services.
2. Breaking bulk.
3. Holding inventory.
4. Providing services.

Providing Assortments   Supermarkets typically carry 20,000 to 30,000 different items made by over 500 companies. Offering an assortment enables their customers to choose from a wide selection of brands, designs, sizes, colors, and prices at one location. Manufacturers specialize in producing specific types of products. For example, Campbell's makes soup, Kraft makes dairy products, Kellogg makes breakfast cereals, and McCormick makes spices. If each of these manufacturers had its own stores that only sold its own products, consumers would have to go to many different stores to buy the groceries needed to prepare a single meal.

All retailers offer assortments of products, but they specialize in the assortments they offer. Supermarkets provide assortments of food, health and beauty care, and household products, while Abercrombie & Fitch provides assortments of clothing and accessories. Most consumers are well aware of the product assortments retailers offer; even small children tend to know where to buy different types of products. But new types of retailers offering unique assortments appear each year, such as Play It Again Sports (used sporting goods), Auntie's Beads (www.auntiesbeads. com) (beads), and PODS (portable, on-demand storage service).

Breaking Bulk   To reduce transportation costs, manufacturers and wholesalers typically ship cases of frozen dinners or cartons of blouses to retailers. Retailers then offer the products in smaller quantities tailored to individual consumers' and households' consumption patterns. This is called **breaking bulk.** Breaking bulk is important to both manufacturers and consumers. Whereas it is cost effective for manufacturers to package and ship merchandise in larger, rather than smaller, quantities, consumers want to purchase merchandise in smaller, more manageable quantities.

Holding Inventory   A major function of retailers is to keep inventory that is already broken into user-friendly sizes so that products will be available when consumers want them. Thus, consumers can keep a smaller inventory of products at home because they know local retailers will have the products available when they need more. By maintaining an inventory, retailers provide a benefit to consumers; they reduce the consumers' cost of storing products. This is particularly important to consumers with limited storage space and who want to purchase perishable merchandise like meat and produce.

A Bass Pro Shops sporting goods store in Gurnee Mills Mall near Chicago lets customers try out archery. Bows and arrows are on display nearby.

Providing Services   Retailers provide services that make it easier for customers to buy and use products. They offer credit so consumers can have a product now and pay for it later. They display products so consumers can see and test them before buying. Some retailers have salespeople in stores or use their Web sites to answer questions and provide additional information about products.

Increasing the Value of Products and Services   By providing assortments, breaking bulk, holding inventory, and providing services, retailers increase the value consumers receive from their products and services. To illustrate, consider a door in a shipping crate in an Iowa manufacturer's warehouse. The door won't

---

Home Depot's commitment to its social responsibilities is reflected in two of its five core values:

- *Giving back to our communities:* An important part of the fabric of The Home Depot is giving our time, talents, energy and resources to worthwhile causes in our communities and society.
- *Doing the right thing:* We exercise good judgment by "doing the right thing" instead of just "doing things right." We strive to understand the impact of our decisions, and we accept responsibility for our actions.

These values encourage Home Depot's 300,000 associates to be as committed to their communities as they are to the company. Every year, Home Depot employees contribute more than 7 million hours of service through Team Depot, its volunteer corps. In addition, the corporation donates more than $25 million to four target areas: affordable housing, at-risk youth, the environment, and disaster preparedness and relief.

A large portion of Home Depot associates' volunteer time is spent constructing and repairing affordable housing. The company has worked with over 350 Habitat for Humanity affiliates to help make the dream of home ownership a reality for low-income families. In addition to building homes from the ground up, Home Depot partners with Rebuilding Together, a nonprofit organization, to rehabilitate housing for the elderly and disabled. What began as a single weekend project has flourished into an annual commitment with thousands of associates volunteering their time to mend leaky roofs, replace threadbare carpet, and fix broken staircases.

Home Depot associates also help people face emergencies before, during, and after disasters. They work with relief organizations to provide supplies and volunteers to confront natural disasters and severe weather. For example, when dry weather and high temperatures sparked Colorado wildfires, Home Depot, working with its vendors, provided thousands of supply kits. Clean-up kits were distributed to homeowners whose homes were affected by smoke and fire, and mitigation kits were distributed to those preparing for evacuation. These kits included tools such as hoses and sprinklers for wetting down landscapes and rooftops, shovels and rakes for clearing lawn debris from the perimeter of homes, gloves, masks, and safety goggles.

As the world's largest retailer of lumber, Home Depot also recognizes its responsibility to preserve the world's forests. The company recently appointed Ron Jarvis to a newly created executive position, environmental global project manager. Jarvis has the authority to sever logging contracts with any supplier whose practices

Home Depot donated $1 million in tools and materials to the U.S. military to support their efforts in rebuilding Iraq. Employees, along with U.S. Army soldiers and Marines, are loading a truck with donated tools.

harm endangered forests or otherwise hurt the environment. In Indonesia, Home Depot's main supplier was cutting trees using a slash-and-burn technique that destroyed entire swaths of the country's rain forest. "We asked them to stop, but they said they would continue," he recalls. In response, Jarvis cut 90 percent of Home Depot's purchases of Indonesian lumber. The remaining purchases came from suppliers that didn't slash and burn. Jarvis also successfully mediated in the acrimonious relationship between Chilean environmentalists and Chile's two largest timber producers.

Sources: Bob Nardelli, "Good Citizenship Builds Strong Culture," *Chief Executive*, April 2004, p. 14; Jim Carleton, "New Leaf: Once Targeted by Protestors, Home Depot Plays Green Role," *The Wall Street Journal*, August 6, 2004, pp. A1, A15; Home Depot, *Social Responsibility Report*, http://www.homedepot.com.

satisfy the needs of a do-it-yourselfer (DIYer) who wants to replace a closet door today. For the DIYer, a conveniently located home improvement center like Home Depot or Lowe's offers one door that is available when the DIYer wants it. The home improvement center helps the customer select the door by displaying doors so they can be examined before they're purchased. An employee is available to explain which door is best for closets and how the door should be hung. The center also has an assortment of hardware, paint, and tools that the DIYer will need to complete the job. In this way, retailers increase the value of products and services bought by their customers.

SOCIAL AND ECONOMIC SIGNIFICANCE OF RETAILING

Support for Community

Retailing View 1.1 on the previous page illustrates how retailers provide value to their communities and society, as well as to their customers. Retailers are also responsible for developing many innovative products and services. For example, a Macy's buyer designed the first tea bag, and a JCPenney buyer invented panty hose.

Retail Sales

Retailing affects every facet of life. Just think of how many daily contacts you have with retailers when you eat meals, furnish your apartment, have your car fixed, and buy clothing for a party or job interview. American retail sales in 2003 were $3.4 trillion—more than 9 percent of the U.S. gross domestic product.[5] However, this sales level underestimates the impact of retailing because it does not include the retail sales of services to consumers, such as movie tickets, automobile services and repairs, hotel rooms, or legal assistance.

While the majority of retail sales are made by large retail chains, most retailers are small businesses. There are over 1,000,000 retail firms in the United States, and 95 percent of these firms have only one store. Less than 1 percent of U.S. retail firms have over 100 stores.[6]

Employment

Retailing also is one of the nation's largest industries in terms of employment. As Exhibit 1–2 indicates, over 27 million people were employed in retailing in 2003—approximately 21 percent of the nonagricultural U.S. workforce. Between 2004

EXHIBIT 1–2
U.S. Employment by Industry 2003

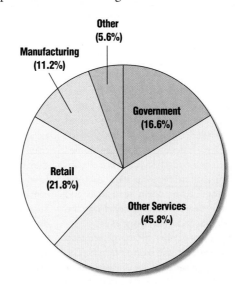

SOURCE: *Retail Industry Indicators,* Washington, DC: National Retail Foundation, August 2004, p. 17. Courtesy of the NRF Foundation.

and 2012, the retail industry expects to add 2.1 million jobs, making it one of the largest sectors for job growth in the United States.[8]

Global Retailers

Exhibit 1–3 lists the 20 largest global retailers in 2004. With worldwide retail sales estimated at $8 trillion, the 20 largest retailers represent a 12 percent share of the world market. Combined, the 200 largest retailers capture 29 percent of worldwide sales. Wal-Mart remains the undisputed leader in the retail world, with sales almost three times as large as those of Carrefour, the second-largest retailer. Home Depot also has made significant sales gains over the last several years. Its fourth-place ranking in 2004 was up from 24th in 1996.

Food retailing continues to dominate among the largest retailers. Eight of the ten largest retailers sell food, and slightly over 50 percent of the 200 largest retailers have supermarket, warehouse, hypermarket, or cash-and-carry formats, or some combination of them. The dominance of food retailing would be even more pronounced if U.S. drug store chains, which place more emphasis on convenience food, were included as food retailers.

Of the top 2004 global retailers, 42.5 percent are headquartered in the United States, 39 percent in Europe, and 13 percent in Japan. Large retailers headquartered in the United States tend to concentrate on the United States and operate fewer formats than their global counterparts. American retailers in the top 50 list operate, on average, two formats in 3.5 countries, while top 50 retailers headquartered outside the United States operate twice as many formats in three times more countries.[9]

Rank	Retailer	Headquarters	2003 Retail Sales ($ millions)	Number of Formats	Number of Countries	Five-Year *CAGR%
1	Wal-Mart	U.S.	229,617	5	11	14.2%
2	Carrefour	France	85,011	6	31	18.7
3	Home Depot	U.S.	58,247	2	4	19.2
4	Kroger	U.S.	51,760	5	1	14.3
5	Metro	Germany	48,349	6	26	12.4
6	Target	U.S.	42,722	3	1	9.0
7	Ahold	Netherlands	40,755	7	17	12.5
8	Tesco	U.K.	40,071	5	10	9.7
9	Costco	U.S.	37,993	1	8	9.8
10	Sears	U.S.	35,698	1	3	−2.9
11	Albertsons	U.S.	35,626	3	1	19.4
12	Aldi Einkauf	Germany	33,837	2	12	15.2
13	Safeway	U.S.	32,398	1	3	7.6
14	JCPenney	U.S.	32,347	2	3	1.8
15	Intermarche	France	31,688	8	7	9.2
16	Rewe	Germany	31,404	7	12	7.4
17	Kmart	U.S.	30,762	2	1	−0.9
18	Walgreens	U.S.	28,281	1	1	16.5
19	Edeka/AVA	Germany	26,514	5	6	17.2
20	Lowe's	U.S.	26,491	1	1	21.2

EXHIBIT 1–3
20 Largest Retailers Worldwide

*Compound annual growth rate.

SOURCE: "2004 Global Powers of Retailing," *Stores*, January 2004, pp. G11–12. Courtesy of STORES Magazine/Deloitte.

Structure of Retailing and Distribution Channels around the World

The nature of retailing and distribution channels in the United States is quite unique. Some critical differences among U.S., European, and Japanese retailing and distribution systems are summarized in Exhibit 1–4.

The U.S. distribution system has the greatest retail density and the greatest concentration of large retail firms. Some people think that the United States is overstored. Many U.S. retail firms are large enough to operate their own warehouses, eliminating the need for wholesalers. The fastest growing types of U.S. retailers sell through large stores with over 20,000 square feet. The combination of large stores and large firms results in a very efficient distribution system.

In contrast, the Japanese distribution system is characterized by small stores operated by relatively small firms and a large independent wholesale industry. To make daily deliveries to these small retailers efficient, merchandise often might pass through three distributors between the manufacturer and retailer. This difference in efficiency results in a much larger percentage of the Japanese labor force being employed in distribution and retailing than in the United States.

The European distribution system falls between the U.S. and Japanese systems on this continuum of efficiency and scale, but the northern, southern, and central parts of Europe have to be distinguished, with northern European retailing being the most similar to the U.S. system. In northern Europe, concentration levels are high; in some national markets, 80 percent or more of sales in a sector such as food or home improvements are accounted for by five or fewer firms. Southern European retailing is more fragmented across all sectors. For example, traditional farmers' market retailing is still important in some sectors, operating alongside large, "big box" formats. In central Europe, the privatization of retail trade has resulted in a change from a previously highly concentrated, government-controlled structure to one of extreme fragmentation characterized, by many small, family-owned retailers.

Some factors that have created these differences in distribution systems in the major markets are (1) social and political objectives, (2) geography, and (3) market size. First, an important priority of the Japanese economic policy is to reduce

EXHIBIT 1–4   Comparison of Retailing and Distribution Channels across the World

Characteristic	U.S.	EUROPE								Japan
		NORTH				**SOUTHERN**		**CENTRAL**		
		U.K.	Belgium	France	Germany	Spain	Italy	Hungary	Czech	
Concentration (% of retail sales in category by top three firms)	High	High				Low		Very low		Medium
Number of outlets per 1,000 people	Medium	Medium				High		Low		High
Retail density (sq. ft. of retail space per person)	High	Medium				Low		Low		Medium
Store size (% of retail sales made in stores over 10,000 sq. ft.)	High	Medium				Low		Low		Low
Role of wholesaling (wholesale sales as a % of retail sales)	Low	Medium				Medium		High		High
Distribution inefficiency (average maintained markup—distribution costs as a % of retail price)	Low	Medium				High		High		High

unemployment by protecting small businesses like neighborhood retailers. The Japanese Large Scale Retail Stores Law regulates the locations and openings of stores of over 5,000 square feet. Several European countries have also passed laws protecting small retailers. For example, in 1996, France tightened its existing laws to constrain the opening of stores of over 3,000 square feet. European governments have also passed strict zoning laws to preserve green spaces, protect town centers, and inhibit the development of large-scale retailing in the suburbs.

Second, the population density in the United States is much lower than in Europe or Japan. Thus, Europe and Japan have less low-cost real estate available for building large stores.

Third, the U.S. retail market is larger than that of Japan or any single European country. In Europe, distribution centers and retail chains typically operate within a single country and are therefore not able to achieve the scale economies of U.S. firms, which serve a broader customer base. Even with the euro and other initiatives designed to make trade among European countries easier and more efficient, barriers to trade still exist that are not found in the United States.

Due to government restrictions on large stores, small, independent retailers flourish in Europe.

OPPORTUNITIES IN RETAILING

Management Opportunities

To cope with a highly competitive and challenging environment, retailers are hiring and promoting people with a wide range of skills and interests. Students often view retailing as a part of marketing because the management of distribution channels is part of a manufacturer's marketing function. But retailers operate businesses and, like manufacturers, undertake most traditional business activities. Retailers raise capital from financial institutions; purchase goods and services; develop accounting and management information systems to control operations; manage warehouses and distribution systems; design and develop new products; and undertake marketing activities such as advertising, promotions, sales force management, and market research. Thus, retailers employ people with expertise and interest in finance, accounting, human resource management, logistics, and computer systems, as well as marketing.

Retail managers are often given considerable responsibility early in their careers. Retail management is also financially rewarding. After completing a management trainee program in retailing, managers can double their starting salary in three to five years if they perform well. The typical buyer in a department store earns $50,000 to $60,000 per year. Store managers working for department or discount store chains often make over $100,000. (See Appendix 1A at the end of this chapter.)

Entrepreneurial Opportunities

Retailing also provides opportunities for people who wish to start their own business. Some of the world's richest people are retailing entrepreneurs. Many are well known because their names appear over the stores' door; others you may not

There are entrepreneurial opportunities in retailing. Jeff Bezos, founder of Amazon.com, pecked out a business plan for his new company on his laptop in 1994 while driving across the U.S. with his wife.

recognize.[10] Retailing View 1.2 examines the life of one of the world's greatest entrepreneurs, Sam Walton. Some other innovative retail entrepreneurs include Jeff Bezos, Donald Fisher, and Dave Thomas.

Jeff Bezos (Amazon.com)   After his research uncovered that Internet usage was growing at a 2,300 percent annual rate in 1994, Jeffrey Bezos, the 30-year-old son of a Cuban refugee, quit his job on Wall Street and left behind a hefty bonus to start an Internet business. While his wife MacKenzie was driving their car across country, Jeff pecked out his business plan on a laptop computer. By the time they reached Seattle, he had rounded up the investment

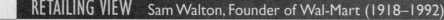

1.2   RETAILING VIEW   Sam Walton, Founder of Wal-Mart (1918–1992)

"Like Henry Ford with his Model T," said a professor of rural sociology at the University of Missouri, "Sam Walton and his Wal-Marts, for better or for worse, transformed small-town America." Others think he transformed the entire nation and the global retail industry.

After graduating from the University of Missouri in 1940, Walton began working at a JCPenney store in Des Moines, Iowa. He served in the Army during World War II and then purchased a Ben Franklin variety store franchise in Newport, Arkansas. He boosted sales by finding suppliers who would sell to him lower than he could buy from Ben Franklin.

Walton lost his store, however, in 1950 when the landlord refused to renew his lease. He then moved to Bentonville, Arkansas, where he and a younger brother franchised another Ben Franklin store. Walton employed a new self-service system, one he had discovered at two Ben Franklin stores in Minnesota: no clerks or cash registers around the store, only checkout lanes in the front. By 1960, Walton had 15 stores in Arkansas and Missouri that laid the foundation for his own discount chain.

By the early 1960s, retailers had developed the discount superstore concept using self-service, a limited assortment, low overhead costs, and massive parking lots. Walton joined them in 1962 when he opened his first Wal-Mart Discount City in Rogers, Arkansas. At least one observer called it a mess—with donkey rides and watermelons mixed together outside under the boiling sun and merchandise haphazardly arranged inside.

But Walton quickly brought order to his enterprise and pursued an innovative strategy: large discount stores in small towns. Walton felt cities were saturated with retailers and believed he could prosper in towns that the larger companies had ignored. By the 1980s, Walton started building stores in larger suburbs. Walton then started Sam's Clubs, warehouse-style stores that sold bulk merchandise at discount prices. Next came Wal-Mart Supercenters, ranging from 100,000 to 200,000 square feet, that featured a supermarket and a regular Wal-Mart under one roof. As a result of their success, Wal-Mart is now the largest food retailer in the United States.

Walton often visited his stores, dropping in unannounced to check the merchandise presentation or financial performance and talk to his "associates." He prided himself on a

Sam Walton believed in "Management by Walking Around."

profit-sharing program and a friendly, open atmosphere, business practices he had learned when working for JCPenney. He often led his workers in a cheer that some called corny, others uplifting. He once described it: "Give me a W! Give me an A! Give me an L! Give me a Squiggly! (Here, everybody sort of does the twist.) Give me an M! Give me an A! Give me an R! Give me a T! What's that spell? Wal-Mart! What's that spell? Wal-Mart! Who's number one? THE CUSTOMER!"

He offered his own formula for how a large company must operate: "Think one store at a time. That sounds easy enough, but it's something we've constantly had to stay on top of. Communicate, communicate, communicate: What good is figuring out a better way to sell beach towels if you aren't going to tell everybody in your company about it? Keep your ear to the ground: A computer is not—and will never be—a substitute for getting out in your stores and learning what's going on."

In 1991, due to the success of his concept and management practices, Walton became America's wealthiest person. He died of leukemia in 1992. Wal-Mart is now the world's largest corporation.

Sources: Wendy Zellner, "Sam Walton: King of the Discounters," *BusinessWeek*, August 9, 2004, p. 12; "Sam Walton," *American Business Leaders*, January 1, 2001. See also Andy Serwer, "The Waltons: Inside America's Richest Family," *Fortune*, November 15, 2004, pp. 86–101.

capital to launch the first Internet book retailer. The company, Amazon.com, is named after the river that carries the greatest amount of water, symbolizing Bezos's objective of achieving the greatest volume of Internet sales. He was one of the few dot.com leaders to recognize that sweating the details was critical to success. Under his leadership, Amazon developed technologies to make shopping on the Internet faster, easier, and more personal than shopping in stores by offering personalized recommendations and home pages. Amazon.com has become more than a bookstore. It now provides its Web site and fulfillment services for major retailers like Office Depot, Borders, and Toys "R" Us in addition to hosting storefronts for thousands of smaller retailers.[11]

Donald Fisher (The Gap)   Donald Fisher was a finance major and star swimmer at the University of California, Berkeley. After graduating in 1950, he entered his family's real estate development business. He cofounded The Gap with his wife in 1969 out of his frustration at not being able to find blue jeans that would fit his normally proportioned, 6′1″, 34-inch waist frame. The Gap stores were unique in offering every size and style of Levi's, arranged by size for convenience. When the teen-jean craze slowed in the mid-1970s, stores were repositioned for a more mature customer. Now The Gap sells only private-label merchandise under its own brand name. Reminiscent of the founding of The Gap, GapKids was started when the former chief operating officer Mickey Drexler couldn't find comfortable clothing for his children. Drexler also developed Old Navy to cater to the new lifestyle trend in which being hip means not spending lots of money on clothing.[12]

Dave Thomas (Wendy's)   Dave Thomas appeared in over 300 televisions commercials and became the most well-known restaurateur in the United States. His unassuming persona conveyed an image that the chain was owned by a caring grandfather rather than a faceless corporation, a lesson he learned from Colonel Sanders, founder of KFC. His personal appeal was so great that he continued to be used in commercials even after his death in 2002. Thomas never knew his parents, and his adoptive mother died when he was five. His involvement in the restaurant business began at the age of 12. After dropping out of high school and completing service in the army, he bought a run-down KFC franchise. Even with these challenges, at the age of 35, Thomas became a millionaire when he sold his KFC franchises. He soon decided to open some fast-food restaurants to pay for his children's college educations. Wendy's success is attributed to his focusing on young adults and offering them sandwiches made to order with the condiments selected by the customer.[14]

Under Jeff Bezos's vision and leadership, Amazon.com has become an influential force in retailing.

REFACT

After working with consultants to develop a name for his new retail concept, Mickey Drexler settled on Old Navy after seeing it on a building during a walk around Paris.[13]

REFACT

Wendy's International was named after one of Dave Thomas's daughters, Melinda Sue, whose nickname is Wendy. She graduated from the University of Florida with a major in psychology.[15]

THE RETAIL MANAGEMENT DECISION PROCESS

This book is organized around the management decisions retailers make to provide value to their customers and develop an advantage over their competitors. Exhibit 1–5 identifies the chapters in this book associated with each type of decision.

Understanding the World of Retailing—Section I

The first step in the retail management decision process, as Exhibit 1–5 shows, is understanding the world of retailing. Retail managers need to know the environment in which they operate before they can develop and implement effective strategies. The first section of this book provides a general overview of the retailing industry and its customers.

REFACT

Fred Lazarus Jr., founder of the Lazarus department stores, now part of Macy's, promoted the idea of fixing Thanksgiving on the fourth weekend of November to expand the Christmas shopping season. Congress adopted his proposal in 1941.[16]

EXHIBIT 1–5
Retail Management
Decision Process

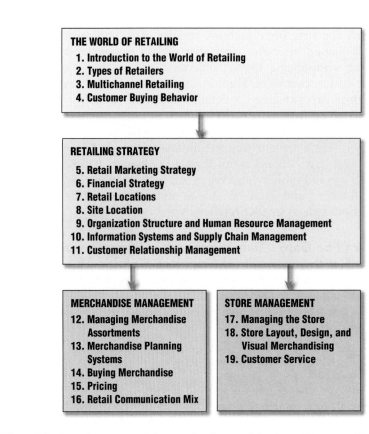

THE WORLD OF RETAILING
1. Introduction to the World of Retailing
2. Types of Retailers
3. Multichannel Retailing
4. Customer Buying Behavior

RETAILING STRATEGY
5. Retail Marketing Strategy
6. Financial Strategy
7. Retail Locations
8. Site Location
9. Organization Structure and Human Resource Management
10. Information Systems and Supply Chain Management
11. Customer Relationship Management

MERCHANDISE MANAGEMENT
12. Managing Merchandise Assortments
13. Merchandise Planning Systems
14. Buying Merchandise
15. Pricing
16. Retail Communication Mix

STORE MANAGEMENT
17. Managing the Store
18. Store Layout, Design, and Visual Merchandising
19. Customer Service

The critical environmental factors in the world of retailing are (1) the macroenvironment and (2) the microenvironment. The impacts of the macroenvironment—including technological, social, and ethical/legal/political factors—on retailing are discussed throughout the book. For example, the influence of technology on the rise of multichannel retailing is reviewed in Chapter 3; the use of new information and supply chain technologies is examined in Chapters 10 and 11; ethical, legal, and public policy issues are discussed throughout the book.

The retailer's microenvironment focuses on its competitors and customers.

Competitors   At first glance, identifying competitors appears easy. A retailer's primary competitors are other retailers using the same format. Thus, department stores compete against other department stores and supermarkets against other supermarkets. This competition between the same type of retailers is called **intratype competition.**

To appeal to a broader group of consumers, many retailers are increasing the variety of their merchandise. **Variety** is the number of different merchandise categories within a store or department. By offering greater variety in one store, retailers can offer one-stop shopping to satisfy more of the needs of their target market. For example, clothing and food are now available in grocery, department, discount, and drug stores. Fast food is available at McDonald's and 7-Eleven convenience stores. The offering of merchandise not typically associated with the store type, such as clothing in a drug store, is called **scrambled merchandising.** Scrambled merchandising increases **intertype competition,** or competition between retailers that sell similar merchandise using different formats, such as discount and department stores.

Increasing intertype competition has made it harder for retailers to identify and monitor their competition. In one sense, all retailers compete against one another for the dollars consumers spend on goods and services. But the intensity of competition is greatest among retailers located near each other who sell offerings that are viewed as very similar.

Because the convenience of a location is important in store choice, a store's proximity to competitors is a critical factor in identifying competition. Consider two DVD rental stores, Blockbuster and Harry's Video, in two suburbs 10 miles

Netflix developed an innovative approach for satisfying the needs of movie renters, and others are following in its footstep, hoping to overtake it.

apart. The stores are the only specialty DVD rental retailers within 50 miles, but a grocery store also rents a more limited selection of DVDs in the same strip center as Blockbuster. Due to the distance between Blockbuster and Harry's Video, they probably don't compete against each other intensely. Customers who live near Harry's Video will rent tapes there, whereas customers close to Blockbuster will rent DVDs at Blockbuster or the grocery store. In this case, Harry's major competition may be movie theaters, cable TV, and Netflix, a mail-order rental service, because it's too inconvenient for customers close to Harry's to rent DVDs elsewhere. In contrast, Blockbuster might compete most intensely with the grocery store.

Management's view of competition also can differ depending on the manager's position within the retail firm. For example, the manager of the Saks Fifth Avenue women's sportswear department in Bergen County, New Jersey, views the other women's sportswear specialty stores in the Riverside Square mall (www. shopriverside.com) as her major competitors. But the Saks store manager views the Bloomingdale's store in a nearby mall as her strongest competitor. These differences in perspective arise because the department sales manager is primarily concerned with customers for a specific category of merchandise, whereas the store manager is concerned with customers seeking the entire selection of all merchandise and services offered by a department store.

The CEO of a retail chain, in contrast, views competition from a much broader geographic perspective. For example, Nordstrom might identify its strongest competitor as Macy's in the Northwest, Saks in northern California, and Bloomingdale's in northern Virginia. The CEO may also take a broader strategic perspective and recognize that other activities compete for consumers' disposable income. For example, Blockbuster's CEO takes the consumer's perspective and recognizes that DVD rental stores are competing in the entertainment industry with other DVD rental stores, other retailers that rent DVDs (such as grocery and convenience stores), movie theaters, regular and cable TV, mail-order DVD services, theater, opera, ballet, nightclubs, and restaurants.

Retailing is intensely competitive. Understanding the different types of retailers and how they compete with one another is critical to developing and implementing a retail strategy. Chapter 2 discusses various types of retailers and retail strategies, and Chapter 3 concentrates on how many retailers have adopted multichannel strategies to give them a competitive edge.

Customers   The second factor in the microenvironment is customers. Customer needs are changing at an ever-increasing rate. Retailers must respond to broad demographic and lifestyle trends in our society, such as the growth in the elderly and minority segments of the U.S. population and the importance of shopping convenience to the rising number of two-income families. To develop and implement an effective strategy, retailers need to understand why customers shop, how they select a store, and how they select among that store's merchandise—the information found in Chapter 4.

Developing a Retail Strategy—Section II

The next stages in the retail management decision-making process, formulating and implementing a retail strategy, are based on an understanding of the macro- and microenvironments developed in the first section. Section II focuses on decisions related to developing a retail strategy, wheras Sections III and IV concern decisions surrounding the implementation of the strategy.

The **retail strategy** indicates how the firm plans to focus its resources to accomplish its objectives. It identifies (1) the target market, or markets, toward which the retailer will direct its efforts; (2) the nature of the merchandise and services the retailer will offer to satisfy the needs of the target market; and (3) how the retailer will build a long-term advantage over its competitors.

The nature of a retail strategy can be illustrated by comparing the strategies of Wal-Mart and Circuit City. Initially Wal-Mart identified its target market as small towns (under 35,000 in population) in Arkansas, Texas, and Oklahoma. It offers name-brand merchandise at low prices in a broad array of categories, ranging from laundry detergent to girls' dresses. Although Wal-Mart stores have many different categories of merchandise, selection in each category is limited. A store might have only three models of TV sets, whereas an electronic category specialist might have 30 models.

In contrast to Wal-Mart, Circuit City identified its target as consumers living in suburban areas of large cities. Rather than carrying a broad array of merchandise categories, Circuit City stores specialize in consumer electronics and carry most of the types and brands currently available in the market. Both Wal-Mart and Circuit City emphasize self-service. Customers select their merchandise, bring it to the checkout line, and then carry it to their cars. Customers may even assemble the merchandise at home. Because both Wal-Mart and Circuit City emphasize low prices, they've made strategic decisions to develop a cost advantage over competitors. Both firms have sophisticated distribution and management information systems to manage inventory. Their strong relationships with suppliers enable them to buy merchandise at low prices.

Strategic Decision Areas   The key strategic decision areas for a firm involve determining its market, financial, location, organizational structure and human resource, information systems and supply chain, and customer relationship management strategies.

Chapter 5 discusses how selection of a retail market strategy is based on analyzing the environment and the firm's strengths and weaknesses. When major environmental changes occur, the current strategy and the reasoning behind it must be reexamined. The retailer then decides what, if any, strategy changes are needed to take advantage of new opportunities or avoid new threats in the environment.

The retailer's market strategy must be consistent with the firm's financial objectives. Chapter 6 reviews how financial variables such as sales, costs, expenses, profits, assets, and liabilities are used to evaluate the market strategy and its implementation.

Decisions concerning location strategy (reviewed in Chapters 7 and 8) are important for both consumer and competitive reasons. First, location is typically consumers' top consideration when selecting a store. Generally consumers buy gas at the closest service station and patronize the shopping mall that's most convenient to their home or office. Second, location offers an opportunity to gain a long-term advantage over competition. When a retailer has the best location, a competing retailer must settle for the second-best location.

A retailer's organization design and human resource management strategies are intimately related to its market strategy. For example, retailers that attempt to serve national or regional markets must make trade-offs between the efficiency of centralized buying and their need to tailor merchandise and services to local demands. Retailers that focus on customer segments seeking high-quality customer service must motivate and enable sales associates to provide the expected levels of service. The organization structure and human resources policies discussed in Chapter 9 coordinate the implementation of the retailing strategy by buyers, store managers, and sales associates.

Retail information and supply chain management systems will offer a significant opportunity for retailers to gain strategic advantage in the coming decade. Chapter 10 reviews how some retailers are developing sophisticated computer and distribution systems to monitor flows of information and merchandise from vendors to retail distribution centers to retail stores. Point-of-sale (POS) terminals read price and product information coded into Universal Product Codes (UPCs) affixed to the merchandise. This information is then transmitted electronically to distribution centers or directly to vendors, computer to computer. These technologies are part of an overall inventory management system that enables retailers to (1) give customers a more complete selection of merchandise and (2) decrease their inventory investment.

Basic to any strategy is understanding the customers to provide them with the goods and services they want. And even more important is to understand and cater to the wants of the retailer's most valued customers. After all, these customers account for the lion's share of a retailer's sales and profits. Chapter 11 examines customer relationship management from a retailer-to-consumer perspective, including the process used by retailers to identify, design programs for, increase their share of wallet of, and build loyalty with their best customers.

JCPenney Moves from Main Street to the Mall

The interrelationships among these retail strategy decisions—market strategy, financial strategy, organization structure and human resource strategies, and location strategy—are illustrated by the strategic changes JCPenney has undertaken to cope with changes in the retail landscape.[17]

In the late 1950s, Penney was one of the most profitable national retailers. Its target market was middle-income consumers living in small towns. In its Main Street locations, Penney sold staple soft goods—underwear, socks, basic clothing, sheets, tablecloths, and so forth—at low prices with friendly service. All sales were cash; the company didn't offer credit to its customers. Penney had considerable expertise in the design and purchase of private label soft goods—brands developed by the retailer and sold exclusively at its stores.

Its organization structure was decentralized. Each store manager controlled the type of merchandise sold, the pricing of merchandise, and the management of store employees. Promotional efforts were limited and also controlled by store managers. Penney store managers were active participants in their community's social and political activities.

Although Penney was a highly successful retailer, there was a growing awareness among company executives that macroenvironmental trends would have a negative impact on the firm. First, as the nation's levels of education and disposable income rose, consumers grew more interested in fashionable rather than staple merchandise. Second, with the development of a national highway system, the growth of suburbs, and the rise of regional malls, small-town residents were attracted to conveniently located, large, regional shopping malls. Third, Sears (the nation's largest retailer) was beginning to locate stores and auto centers in regional malls. These trends suggested a decline in small-town markets for staple soft goods.

In the early 1960s, Penney changed its strategy in response to these changes in its environment. All new Penney stores were located in regional malls across the United States. Penney opened several mall locations in each metropolitan area to

Over the last 40 years, JCPenney has made dramatic strategic changes, moving from Main Street in small towns to suburban malls (left) and now to stand-alone, off-mall locations (right).

create significant presence in each market. (Of course, as JCPenney was moving from small towns to suburban malls, Wal-Mart began opening discount stores in small towns.) The firm began to offer credit to its customers and added new merchandise lines: appliances, auto supplies, paint, hardware, sporting goods, consumer electronics, and moderately priced fashionable clothing.

To effectively control its 1,150 department stores, Penney installed a national communication network. Store managers could monitor daily sales of each type of merchandise in their store and every other store in the chain. Buyers at corporate headquarters in New York and then Dallas communicated daily with merchandise managers in each store over a satellite TV link, but store managers continued to make merchandise decisions for their stores.

In response to the increased time pressure on two-income and single–head-of household families, Penney launched its catalog operation and now is the largest catalog retailer in the United States. Penney has used its catalog distribution capability to aggressively move into selling merchandise over the Internet (www. jcpenney.com), a multichannel strategy that has been very successful.

The success of discount stores poses a growing threat for JCPenney. Department stores targeting middle-income families such as JCPenney and Sears are caught in the middle between higher-priced, fashion-oriented department store chains like Macy's that are lowering their prices through sales and lower-cost stores such as Kohl's, Target, and Wal-Mart that are offering more fashionable merchandise.

To compete effectively with the retailers targeting JCPenney's middle-income customers, the company has made some radical changes in how it operates, its organizational structure, and where it locates its stores. First, JCPenney is reducing its distribution costs by shipping merchandise through distribution centers rather than using direct delivery from vendors to stores. Second, it also has centralized merchandise management; rather than store managers making the merchandise decisions, buyers at corporate headquarters manage them. Centralization of merchandise decisions enables JCPenney to use its size to buy merchandise at a lower cost and respond more quickly to changing fashions. Third, to increase customer convenience, JCPenney is building new stores away from malls in stand-alone locations and designing the stores with centralized checkout counters rather than checkout counters in each area of the store. To develop and implement these relatively radical changes in a 100-year old company, in 1999, JCPenney apppointed Alan Questrom as its first CEO who had not been promoted to the position from the company's internal management team. Myron Ullman followed Questrom as the second outsider to be appointed CEO in 2005.

Implementing the Retail Strategy—Sections III and IV

To implement a retail strategy, management develops a retail mix that satisfies the needs of its target market better than that of its competitors. The **retail mix** is the decision variables retailers use to satisfy customer needs and influence their

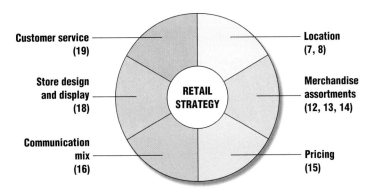

EXHIBIT 1–6
Elements in the Retail Mix

purchase decisions. Elements in the retail mix (Exhibit 1–6) include the types of merchandise and services offered, merchandise pricing, advertising and promotional programs, store design, merchandise display, assistance to customers provided by salespeople, and convenience of the store's location. Section III reviews the implementation decisions made by buyers, and Section IV focuses on decisions made by store managers.

Managers in the buying organization must decide how much and what types of merchandise to buy (Chapters 12 and 13), the vendors to use and the purchase terms (Chapter 14), the retail prices to set (Chapter 15), and how to advertise and promote merchandise (Chapter 16).

Store managers must determine how to recruit, select, and motivate sales associates (Chapter 17), where and how merchandise will be displayed (Chapter 18), and the nature of services to provide customers (Chapter 19).

Whole Foods Market: An Organic and Natural Food Supermarket Chain

Whole Foods Market, one of the fastest-growing supermarket chains, illustrates the use of merchandise and store management activities to implement its retail strategy of providing a supermarket offering that targets health- and environmentally conscious consumers. Its stores are twice as productive as the typical supermarket.[19]

It is easy to mistake John Mackey for an aging hippie rather than the founder and CEO of a retailer with over $4.0 billion in annual sales. At the University of Texas in Austin, Mackey developed a passion for philosophy and religion. When he found that textbooks weren't going to provide the answers he was looking for, he dropped out of college, lived in a vegetarian housing co-op, worked in an Austin natural food store, and eventually opened his own health food store and restaurant. Unlike other veggie joints, Mackey's store catered to a broad clientele by carrying items typically not found at health food stores, such as refined sugar and eggs. Then he teamed up with a local organic grocer to open the first Whole Foods, which was an instant success.

The 140 Whole Foods stores take up 25,000 to 60,000 square feet and carry a much broader assortment than the typical natural and organic grocery store. The stores sell vegetarian no-nos, such as red meat and coffee, so that even health-conscious nonvegetarians can have a one-stop shopping experience. The assortment also includes three lines of private-brand products that are free of artificial sweeteners, colorings, artificial flavorings, and preservatives. Buyers work with artisan food producers and organic farmers to attain products sold under the superpremium Authentic Food Artisan brand. Its core private brands are called Whole Catch, Whole Ranch, Whole Kitchen, Whole Treats, and Whole Kids. The 365 Day Value line provides natural products at value prices. To ensure the

REFACT

A survey of U.S. households found that 58 percent had purchased a food item labeled organic, and 32 percent said it was somewhat or very important that their food is organic.[20]

Whole Foods has a retail mix that supports its strategy of targeting health conscious consumers.

quality of its private labels, a fleet of inspectors fly over 100,000 miles a year visiting farms and checking the crops.

After spending three months reading about modern factory farming, Mackey did two things. First, he changed his vegetarian diet to vegan (he no longer eats food produced from animals, including dairy products). Second, the company started to use its influence and buying power to demand that the meat it sells comes from animals that have been treated with a measure of dignity before being slaughtered.

The company communicates openly with its customers about issues related to the food it sells. Stores display placards detailing test results for PCB contamination in the chain's farm-raised and wild salmon, along with FDA limits. Curious about the life of a chicken in the display case? It comes with a 16-page booklet and an invitation to visit the live chickens at the company's Pennsylvania farm.

The flower power of the 1960s is reflected in Mackey's guiding management principles: love, trust, and employee empowerment. Walking the aisles, the staff is constantly high-fiving and cheering. Employees can look up one another's earnings, and 93 percent of stock options awarded last year went to nonexecutives.

All employees are organized into self-managed teams that meet regularly to discuss issues and solve problems. Almost all team members have stock options in the firm. To ensure that employees are compensated equitably, the company has a cap on salaries so that no employee's total compensation, including executives', can be more than 14 times the average compensation of any employee.[21]

Whole Foods is waving goodbye to its standard, 31,000-square-foot stores and opening new, exciting 50,000-square-foot versions.[22] "Americans love to eat. And Americans love to shop. But we don't like to shop for food. It's a chore, like doing laundry," laments John Mackey. "Whole Foods thinks shopping should be fun. With this store, we're pioneering a new lifestyle that synthesizes health and pleasure. We don't see a contradiction." Some of the elements in the new concept are

- **Candy Island**, where you can dip fresh strawberries in a flowing chocolate fountain for $1.59 each.

- **Lamar Street Greens**, where you can sit among the organic produce and have a salad handmade for you to enjoy with a glass of Chardonnay.

- **Fifth Street Seafood**, a version of Seattle's Pike Place Market, where you can have any of 150 fresh seafood items cooked, sliced, smoked, or fried for instant eating.

- **Whole Body**, where a massage therapist will work the kinks out with a 25-minute deep-tissue massage for $50.

Each of the sections is designed with self-contained architecture that is curved inward to feel intimate—and to encourage shoppers to linger. Pleasure is woven into every crevice of the new flagship store: The guy who hawks fresh hot doughnuts—with no artificial ingredients, of course. A walk-in beer cooler (bring your mittens) and 800 kinds of beer. And 14 pastry chefs, any of whom will be happy to whip up a baked Alaska on the spot. The lighting for the produce is the kind used in art galleries. The music is classical. Walk by the hot nut section, and special fans waft that tummy-teasing smell of roasting nuts your way. Even the store signs and displays aren't plastic and particle board but a more eco-friendly, woodlike product made from wheat straw.

Ethical and Legal Considerations

When making the strategic and tactical decisions discussed previously, managers need to consider the ethical and legal implications of their decisions in addition to the effects those decisions have on the profitability of their firms and the satisfaction of their customers. **Ethics** are the principles governing the behavior of individuals and companies to establish appropriate behavior and indicate what is right and wrong. Defining the term is easy, but determining what the principles are is difficult. What one person thinks is right another may consider wrong.

What is ethical can vary from country to country and from industry to industry. For example, offering bribes to overcome bureaucratic roadblocks is an accepted practice in Middle Eastern countries but is considered unethical, and even illegal, in the United States. An ethical principle also can change over time. For example, some years ago, doctors and lawyers who advertised their services were considered unethical. Today such advertising is accepted as common practice.

Some examples of difficult situations that retail manager face are

- Should a retailer sell merchandise that it suspects was made using child labor?

- Should a retailer advertise that its prices are the lowest available in the market even though some items are not?

- Should a retail buyer accept an expensive gift from a vendor?

- Should retail salespeople use a high-pressure sales approach when they know the product is not the best for the customer's needs?

- Should a retailer give preference to minorities when making promotion decisions?

- Should a retailer treat some customers better than others?

Laws dictate which activities society has deemed to be clearly wrong, those activities for which retailers and their employee will be punished through the federal or state legal systems. However, most business decisions are not regulated by laws. Often retail managers have to rely on their firms' and industries' codes of ethics and/or their own codes of ethics to determine the right thing to do.

Many companies have codes of ethics to provide guidelines for their employees in making their ethical decisions. These ethical policies provide a clear sense of right and wrong so that companies and their customers can depend on their employees when questionable situations arise. However, in many situations, retail managers need to rely on their personal code of ethics—their personal sense of what is right or wrong.

EXHIBIT 1–7
Checklist for Making
Ethical Decisions

1. Would I be embarrassed if a customer found out about this behavior?
2. Would my supervisor disapprove of this behavior?
3. Would most coworkers feel that this behavior is unusual?
4. Am I about to do this because I think I can get away with it?
5. Would I be upset if a company did this to me?
6. Would my family or friends think less of me if I told them about engaging in this activity?
7. Am I concerned about the possible consequences of this behavior?
8. Would I be upset if this behavior or activity were publicized in a newspaper article?
9. Would society be worse off if everyone engaged in this behavior or activity?

Exhibit 1.7 lists some questions you can ask yourself to determine whether a behavior or activity is unethical. The questions emphasize that ethical behavior is determined by widely accepted views of what is right and wrong. Thus, you should engage only in activities about which you would be proud to tell your family, friends, employer, and customers.

If the answer to any of these questions is yes, the behavior or activity is probably unethical, and you should not do it.

Your firm can strongly affect the ethical choices you will have to make. When you view your firm's polices or requests as improper, you have three choices:

1. Ignore your personal values and do what your company asks you to do. Self-respect suffers when you have to compromise your principles to please an employer. If you take this path, you will probably feel guilty and be dissatisfied with your job in the long run.

2. Take a stand and tell your employer what you think. Try to influence the decisions and policies of your company and supervisors.

3. Refuse to compromise your principles. Taking this path may mean you will get fired or be forced to quit.

You should not take a job with a company whose products, policies, and conduct conflict with your standards. Before taking a job, investigate the company's procedures and selling approach to see if they conflict with your personal ethical standards. Throughout this text, we will highlight the legal and ethical issues associated with the retail decisions made by managers.

SUMMARY

Retailing is evolving into a global, high-tech industry that plays a major role in the global economy. More than 60 percent of U.S. economic activity is affected by retailing, and about one in five U.S. workers is employed by retailers. Although most people identify retailers as stores selling products, retailers are also involved with selling products over the Internet and through catalogs. Firms selling services to consumers, such as dry cleaning and automobile repairs, are also retailers.

Retailing is defined as a set of business activities that add value to the products and services sold to consumers for their personal or family use. These value-added activities include providing assortments, breaking bulk, holding inventory, and providing services.

The retail management decision process involves developing a strategy for creating a competitive advantage in the marketplace and then developing a retail mix to implement that strategy. The strategic decisions, discussed in the first section of this textbook, involve

selecting a target market, defining the nature of the retailer's offering, and building a competitive advantage through locations, human resource management, information and supply chain management systems, and customer relationship management programs. The tactical decisions for implementing the strategy, discussed in the second half of this textbook, involve selecting a merchandise assortment, buying merchandise, setting prices, communicating with customers, managing the store, presenting merchandise in stores, and providing customer service. Large retail chains use sophisticated information systems to analyze business opportunities and make these decisions about how to operate their businesses in multiple countries.

Retailing offers opportunities for exciting, challenging careers, either working for a retail firm or starting your own business. Aspects of retail careers are discussed in Appendix 1A, and Appendix 1B provides some sources of information about the retail industry.

KEY TERMS

backward integration, *7*

breaking bulk, *8*

distribution channel, *7*

ethics, *23*

forward integration, *7*

intertype competition, *16*

intratype competition, *16*

retailer, *7*

retailing, *7*

retail mix, *20*

retail strategy, *18*

scrambled merchandising, *16*

variety, *16*

vertical integration, *7*

GET OUT AND DO IT!

CONTINUING CASE ASSIGNMENT In most chapters of this textbook, there will be a GET OUT AND DO IT! assignment that will give you an opportunity to examine the strategy and tactics of one retailer. Your first assignment is to select a retailer and prepare a report of the retailer's history, including when it was founded and how it has evolved over time. To ensure that you can get information about the retailer for subsequent Continuing Case Assignments, the retailer you select should

- Be a publicly held company so that you can access its financial statements and annual reports. Do not select a retailer that is owned by another company. For example, since Office Max is owned by Boise Cascade, you can only get financial information about Boise Cascade and not the individual companies it owns, such as Office Max.

- Focus on one type of retailing. For example, Abercrombie & Fitch just operates one type of specialty stores and thus would be a good choice. However, Wal-Mart operates discount stores, warehouse club stores, and supercenters and thus would not be a good choice

- Choose a store that you can visit easily and collect information about. Some retailers and store managers may not allow you to interview them about the store, take pictures of the store, talk with sales associates, or analyze the merchandise assortment in the store. Try to pick a retailer with a local store manager who can help you complete the assignments.

Some examples of retailers that meet the first two criteria are: Whole Foods Market, Dress Barn, Burlington Coat Factory, Ross Stores, Ann Taylor, Cato, Chico's, Finish Line, Foot Locker, Brookstone, Claire's, CVS, Walgreens, Staples, Office Depot, Borders, American Eagle Outfitter, Pacific Sunwear, Abercrombie & Fitch, Tiffany & Co., Zales, Autozone, Pep Boys, Hot Topic, Wet Seal, Best Buy, Family Dollar, Dollar General, Circuit City, Michaels, PETsMART, Federated Department Stores, Dillard's, Pier 1 Imports, Home Depot, Lowe's, Bed Bath & Beyond, Men's Warehouse, Kroger, Kohl's, Radio Shack, Safeway, and Target.

1. **GO SHOPPING** Visit a local retail store and describe each of the elements in its retail mix.

2. **INTERNET EXERCISE** Data on U.S. retail sales are available at the U.S. Bureau of the Census Internet site at http://www.census.gov/mrts/www/mrts.html. Look at the unadjusted monthly sales by type of retailer. In which quarter are sales the highest? Which types of retailers have their greatest sales in the fourth quarter?

3. **INTERNET EXERCISE** Go to the Federated Department Store Web site, which provides information about a retail career with the company (www.retailology.com). Review the information about the different positions in the company. In which positions would you be interested? Which positions are not of interest to you? Why?

DISCUSSION QUESTIONS AND PROBLEMS

1. What is your favorite retailer? Why do you like this retailer? What would a competitive retailer have to do to get your patronage?

2. From your perspective, what are the benefits and limitations of purchasing a pair of jeans directly from a manufacturer rather than from a retailer?

3. What retailers would be considered intratype competitors for a convenience store chain such as 7-Eleven? What firms would be intertype competitors?

4. Does Wal-Mart contribute to or detract from the communities in which it operates stores?

5. What are some differences between the retail environment in the United States and that in Japan? Why do these differences result in lower costs and retail prices in the United States?

6. Why do retail managers need to consider ethical issues in making decisions?

7. Choose one of the top 20 retailers (Exhibit 1–3). Go to the company's Web site and find out how the company started and how it has changed over time.

8. From a personal perspective, how does retailing rate as a potential career compared with others you are considering?

9. How might managers at different levels of a retail organization define their competition?

10. Retailing View 1.1 describes some socially responsible activities in which Home Depot and its employees are involved. Take the perspective of a stockholder in the company. What effect will these activities have on the value of Home Depot stock? Why might they have a positive or negative effect?

SUGGESTED READINGS

Hardwick, M. Jeffrey. *Mall Maker: Victor Gruen, Architect of an American Dream.* Philadelphia: University of Pennsylvania Press, 2004.

Kahn, Barbara, and Leigh McAllister. *The Grocery Revolution.* Reading, MA: Addison-Wesley, 1997.

Ishikawa, Akira, and Tai Nejo. *The Success of 7-Eleven Japan: Discovering the Secrets of the World's Best-Run Convenience Chain Stores.* Singapore: World Scientific, 2002.

Marcus, Bernard, and Arthur Blank. *Built from Scratch: How a Couple of Regular Guys Grew the Home Depot from Nothing into $30 Billion.* New York: Random House, 1999.

Plunkett, Jack (ed). *Plunkett's Retail Almanac.* Houston: Plunkett Research, Ltd., 2005.

Retail Industry: Top Ten Issues 2004–2005. New York: Deloitte, 2004.

Schultz, Howard, and Dori Jones Lang. *Pour Your Heart into It: How Starbucks Built a Company One Cup at a Time.* New York: Hyperion, 1997.

Spector, Robert, and Patrick McCarthy. *The Nordstrom Way: The Inside Story of America's #1 Customer Service Company.* New York: Wiley, 1995.

Slater, Robert. *The Wal-Mart Decade: How a New Generation of Leaders Turned Sam Walton's Legacy into the World's #1 Company.* New York: Portfolio, 2003.

"2004 Global Powers of Retailing," *Stores,* January 2004, pp. G1–45.

APPENDIX 1A   Careers in Retailing

Retailing offers exciting and challenging career opportunities. Few other industries grant as many responsibilities to young managers. When students asked Dave Fuente, former CEO of Office Depot, what they needed to become a CEO someday, he responded, "You need to have profit and loss responsibility and the experience of managing people early in your career." Entry-level retail jobs for college graduates offer both of these opportunities. Most college graduates begin their retail careers as assistant buyers or department managers, in which positions you have the responsibility for the profitability of a line of merchandise or an area of the store, and you manage people who work for you.

Even if you work for a large company, retailing provides an opportunity for you to do your own thing and be rewarded. You can come with an idea, execute it almost immediately, and see how well it is doing by reviewing the sales data at the end of the day.

Retailing offers a variety of career paths, such as buying, store management, sales promotion and advertising, personnel, operations/distribution, loss prevention, and finance, in several different corporate forms, such as department stores, specialty stores, food stores, and discount stores.

In addition, retailing offers almost immediate accountability for talented people so they can reach key management positions within a decade. Starting salaries are competitive, and the compensation of top management ranks among the highest in any industry.

CAREER OPPORTUNITIES

In retail firms, career opportunities occur among the merchandising/buying, store management, and corporate staff functions. Corporate positions are found in such areas as accounting, finance, promotions and advertising, computer and distribution systems, and human resources.

The primary entry-level opportunities for a retailing career are in the areas of buying and store management. Buying positions are more numbers oriented, whereas store management positions are more people oriented. Entry-level positions on the corporate staff are limited. Retailers typically want all of their employees to understand their customers and their merchandise. Therefore, most executives and corporate staff managers begin their careers in store management or buying.

Store Management

Successful store managers must have the ability to lead and motivate employees. They also need to be sensitive to the customers' needs by making sure that merchandise is available and neatly displayed.

Store management involves all the discipline necessary to run a successful business: sales planning and goal setting, overall store image and merchandise presentation, budgets and expense control, customer service and sales supervision, personnel administration and development, and community relations.

Store managers work directly in the local market, often at quite a distance from the home office, which means they have limited direct supervision. Their hours generally mirror their store's and can therefore include some weekends and evenings. In addition, they spend time during nonoperating hours tending to administrative responsibilities.

The typical entry-level store management position is a department manager with responsibility for merchandise presentation, customer service, and inventory control for an area of the store. The next level is an area or group manager with responsibility for executing merchandising plans and achieving sales goals for several areas, as well as supervising, training, and developing department managers. Beyond these positions, you might be promoted store manager, then a district manager responsible for a group of stores, and then regional manager responsible for a group of districts. Retailing View 1.3 describes James McClain's experience in store management.

Merchandise Management

Merchandise management attracts people with strong analytical capabilities, an ability to predict what merchandise will appeal to their target markets, and a skill for negotiating with vendors as well as store management to get things done. Many retailers have broken the merchandising management activities into two different yet parallel career paths: buying and merchandise planning.

Retail merchandise buyers are similar to financial portfolio managers. They invest in a portfolio of merchandise, monitor the performance (sales) of the merchandise, and, on the basis of the sales, either decide to buy more merchandise that is selling well or get rid of (discount) merchandise that is selling poorly. Buyers are responsible for selecting the type and amount of merchandise to buy, negotiating the wholesale price and payment terms with suppliers, setting the initial retail

price for the merchandise, monitoring merchandise sales, and making appropriate retail price adjustments. Thus buyers need to have good financial planning skills, knowledge of their customers' needs and wants and competitive activities, and the ability to develop good working relationships with vendors. To develop a better understanding of their customers, buyers typically stay in contact with their stores by visiting them, talking to sales associates and managers, and monitoring the sales data available through their merchandise management systems.

Planners have an even more analytical role than buyers. Their primary responsibility is to determine the assortment of merchandise sent to each store—how many styles, colors, sizes, and individual items to purchase for each store. Planners also are responsible for allocating merchandise to stores. Once the merchandise is in the stores, planners closely monitor sales and work with buyers on decisions such as how much additional merchandise to purchase if the merchandise is doing well or when to mark down the merchandise if sales are below expectations.

The typical entry-level position of college graduates interested in merchandise management is either assistant buyer or assistant planner in a merchandise category such as men's athletic shoes or accessories for consumer electronics. In these positions, you will do the sales analysis

---

James McClain–District Manager, Bridgestone Firestone **RETAILING VIEW** **1.3**

"My job is anything but boring. Every day is different. Some days I work with the corporate office, other days I have one-on-one sessions with sales associates and customers. I interact with a lot of different people, and each one has specific problems that must be dealt with. These situations range from customer service problems to various technical and equipment changes. One thing I have learned is that when a problem arises, you need to deal with it in a fast and timely fashion.

"My goal as an assistant district manager is to reach and satisfy the needs of our target market—value-conscious consumers who value their time and money. At the beginning of the day, I go through the sales numbers to see how the stores are doing compared to their budgeted expectations. Then I visit selected stores to look over the overall operation. My goal is to make car care easier for our customers and to fix it right the first time. During the course of a day, some of our busier stores will work with 70 to 80 customers. We listen to find out each customer's needs and suggest the best products or services for their car and driving lifestyle.

James McClain, District Manager, Bridgestone/Firestone, loves his job because every day is different.

"An important aspect of my job is selecting and hiring associates and store managers. No matter what the job is, I look for someone who is outgoing and personable—people who have a natural tendency to smile. This is an important quality that can't be taught and is really critical when dealing with customers. At Bridgestone/Firestone, the customer is number one, and Bridgestone/Firestone searches for those people who will treat customers the right way."

After graduating from the University of Alabama at Birmingham, James McClain started as a management trainee for Toys "R" Us. He then accepted a management trainee position with Bridgestone/Firestone. Through his hard work and dedication, he worked his way up to his present position. He feels that the major factor in convincing him to stay with Bridgestone/Firestone for eight years is the company rewards. The company acknowledges employees' hard work through promotions, rather than focusing promotions on the seniority of an employee.

needed to support the decisions eventually made by the planner or buyer for whom you work. From this entry-level position, you could be promoted to buyer and then divisional merchandise manager, responsible for a number of merchandise categories. Most retailers believe that merchandise management skills are not category specific. Thus, as you are promoted in the buying organization, you will probably work in various merchandise categories. Retailing View 1.4 provides a buyer's perspective on her job.

Corporate Staff

The corporate staff positions in retail firms involve activities and require knowledge, skills, and abilities similar to comparable positions in nonretail firms. Thus many managers in these positions identify with their profession rather than the retail industry. For example, accountants in retail firms view themselves as accountant, not retailers.

Management Information Systems (MIS)   Employees in this area are involved with applications for capturing data and developing and maintaining inventory, as well as the management of store systems such as POS terminals, self-checkout systems, and in-store kiosks.

Operations/Distribution   Operations employees are responsible for operating and maintaining the store's physical plant; providing various customer services; the receipt, ticketing, warehousing, and distribution of a store's inventory; and buying and maintaining store supplies and operating equipment. Students in operations and MIS typically major in production, operations, or computer information systems.

Promotions/Advertising   Promotion's many aspects include public relations, advertising, visual merchandising, and special events. This department attempts to build the retail firm's brand image and encourage customers to visit the retailer's stores and/or Web site. Managers in this area typically major in marketing or mass communications.

Loss Prevention   Loss prevention employees are responsible for protecting the retailer's assets. They develop systems and procedures to minimize employee theft and shoplifting. Managers in this area often major in sociology or criminology, though, as we discuss in Chapters 9 and 16, loss prevention is beginning to be viewed as a human resource management issue.

1.4   RETAILING VIEW   Debbie Harvey, Director of Merchandise Buying, Ron Jon Surf Shop

Debbie Harvey, Director of Merchandise Buying, Ron Jon Surf Shop, looks at what her customers are wearing to spot fashion trends.

"One of the exciting challenges in my job is trying to figure out what merchandise customers are going to buy. The big swimwear markets for us are Miami in July and Surf Expo in September. So we need to place our bet nine months before most of the merchandise arrives in the stores. Ron Jon Surf Shop is known worldwide for its extensive selection of active lifestyle apparel, board sports equipment, and dive apparatus. Our 52,000-square-foot Coco Beach, Florida, store is open 24 hours a day, 365 days a year—just like the beach. We also have stores in Ft. Lauderdale; Orange, California; and Long Beach Island, New Jersey.

"To keep on top of the fashion trends, our buyers read the trade publications like *WWD* and *DNR,* look through teen magazines and surf magazines, and watch MTV. But the best source of information is looking at what our customers are wearing. We find that the fashion trends typically start on the West Coast and move East. However, these fashion waves are spreading a lot faster due to the Internet and MTV.

"Even though we have to place our orders months before the season, we negotiate with our vendors to reduce the risk of making a bad choice. With our longtime vendors, we are able to reduce the size of an order if the merchandise is not selling or switch our commitment to better-selling items. We have relationships with these vendors, and we can generally work out problems. Dealing with the new vendors with hot merchandise is more problematic. Their merchandise is in demand, and they are not very flexible.

"The key to buying is staying on top of things. If we have merchandise that isn't selling, we mark it down to get rid of it so we can get faster-selling merchandise in the stores. I really feel a sense of accomplishment when we can get all aspects of the business—sportswear, shoes, hardgoods, swimwear, and accessories—to do well at the same time."

Finance/Control   Many retailers are large businesses involved in complicated corporate structures. Most retailers also operate with a tight net profit margin. With such a fine line between success and failure, retailers continue to require top financial experts—and they compensate them generously. The finance/control division is responsible for the financial health of the company. They prepare financial reports for all aspects of the business, including long-range forecasting and planning, economic trend analysis and budgeting, shortage control and internal audits, gross and net profit, accounts payable to vendors, and accounts receivable from charge customers. In addition, they manage the retailer's relationship with the financial community. Students interested in this area often major in finance or accounting.

Real Estate   Employees in the real estate division are responsible for selecting locations for stores, negotiating leases and land purchases, and managing the leasehold costs. Students entering this area typically major in real estate or finance.

Store Design   Employees working in this area are responsible for designing the store and presenting merchandise and fixtures in the store. Talented, creative students in business, architecture, art, and other related fields will have innumerable opportunities for growth in the area of retail store design.

Human Resource Management   Human resource management is responsible for the effective selection, training, placement, advancement, and welfare of employees. Because there are seasonal peaks in retailing (such as Christmas, when many extra people must be hired), human resource personnel must be flexible and highly efficient.

The National Retail Federation Foundation (http://www.nrf.com/content/foundation/rcp/main.htm) and Federated Department Stores (http://www.retailology.com) provide more information about retail careers and profiles of people in the wide variety of positions offered by retail firms.

MYTHS ABOUT RETAILING

Sales Clerk Is the Entry-Level Job in Retailing

Most students and their parents think that people working in retailing have jobs as sales clerks and cashiers. They hold this view because, as customers in retail stores, they typically only interact with sales associates, not their managers. But, as we have discussed in this chapter, retail firms are large, sophisticated corporations that employ managers with a wide variety of knowledge, skills, and abilities. Entry-level positions for college and university graduates are typically management trainees in the buying or store organization, not sales associates.

Management trainees in retailing are given more responsibility more quickly than in other industries. Buyers are responsible for choosing, promoting, pricing, distributing, and selling millions of dollars worth of merchandise

each season. The department manager, generally the first position after a training program, is often responsible for merchandising one or more departments, as well as managing 10 or more full- and part-time sales associates.

College and University Degrees Are Not Needed to Succeed in Retailing

While some employees are promoted on the basis of their retail experience, a college degree is needed for most retail management positions ranging from store manager to CEO. Over 150 colleges and universities offer programs of study and degrees or majors in retailing.

REFACT

Forty-seven percent of all retail employees have some college education, and 27.1 percent have college degrees.[23]

Retail Jobs Are Low Paying

Starting salaries for management trainees with a college degree range from $25,000 to $45,000 a year, and the compensation of top management ranks with the highest in industry. For example, store managers with only a few years of experience can earn up to $100,000 or more, depending on their performance bonuses. A senior buyer for a department store earns from $50,000 to $90,000 or more. A department store manager can earn from $50,000 to $150,000; a discount store manager makes from $70,000 to $100,000 or more; and a specialty store manager earns from $35,000 to $60,000 or more.

Compensation varies according to the amount of responsibility. Specialty store managers are generally paid less than department store managers because their annual sales volume is lower. But advancements in this area can be faster. Aggressive specialty store managers often are promoted to district managers and run 8 to 15 units after a few years so that they quickly move into higher pay brackets.

Because information systems enable retailers to assess the sales and profit performance of each manager, and even each sales associate, the compensation of retail managers is closely linked to objective measures of their performance. As a result, in addition to salaries, retail managers are generally given strong monetary incentives based on the sales they create.

A compensation package consists of more than salary alone. In retailing, the benefits package is often substantial and may include a profit-sharing plan, savings plan, stock options, medical and dental insurance, life insurance, long-term disability protection and income protection plans, and paid vacations and holidays. Two additional benefits of retailing careers are that most retailers offer employees valuable discounts on the merchandise that they sell, and some buying positions include extensive foreign travel.

Retailing Is a Low Growth Industry with Little Opportunity for Advancement

While the growth rate of retail parallels the growth rate of the overall economy, many opportunities for rapid advancement exist simply because of the sheer size of the retail industry. With so many retail firms, there is always a large number of firms that are experiencing a high growth rate, opening many new stores, and needing store managers and support staff positions.

Working in Retailing Requires Long Hours and Frequent Relocation

Retailing has an often exaggerated reputation of demanding long and unusual hours. Superficially, this reputation is true. Store managers do work some evenings and weekends. But many progressive retailers have realized that if the unusual hours aren't offset by time off at other periods during the week, many managers become inefficient, angry, and resentful—in other words, burned out. It's also important to put the concept of long hours into perspective. Most professional careers require more than 40 hours per week for the person to succeed. In a new job with new tasks and responsibilities, the time commitment is even greater.

Depending on the type of retailer and the specific firm, retailing enables executives to change locations often or not at all. In general, a career path in store management has more opportunity for relocation than paths in buying/merchandising or corporate. Because buying and corporate offices are usually centrally located, these positions generally aren't subject to frequent moves. In addition, employees in corporate positions and merchandise management tend to work during normal business hours.

Retailing Doesn't Provide Opportunities for Women and Minorities

Many people consider retailing to be among the most race- and gender-blind industries. Retailers typically think that their managers and executives will make better decisions if they mirror their customers. Since most purchases are made by women and because minorities are becoming an increasingly important factor in the market, most retailers have active programs designed to provide the experiences and support that will enable women and minorities to be promoted to top management positions.

APPENDIX 1B   Sources of Information about Retailing

Retail Trade Publications

Apparel Merchandising Reports, forecasts, and interprets apparel merchandising trends and strategies in women's, men's, and children's wear. www. dsnretailingtoday.com

Chain Store Age Monthly magazine for retail headquarters executives and shopping center developers. Deals with management, operations, construction, modernization, store equipment, maintenance, real estate, financing, materials handling, and advertising. More oriented to operations than stores. www. chainstoreage.com

CS News Monthly magazine for convenience store and oil retailing executives, managers, and franchisees. Covers industry trends, news, and merchandising techniques. www.csnews.com

DNR (formerly *Daily News Record*) Daily newspaper about retail fashion, products, merchandising, and marketing for men's and boy's wear. Geared to retailers, wholesalers, and manufacturers. www. dnrnews.com

Dealerscope Monthly publication for retailers of consumer electronics, appliances, and computers. www.dealerscope.com

DSN Retailing Today Biweekly national newspaper describing marketing developments and productivity reports from executives in full-line discount stores, warehouse clubs, and specialty discount chains. www.dsnretailingtoday.com

Drug Store News Biweekly publication covering chain drug and combination store retailing. www. drugstorenews.com

Fairchild's Executive Technology Monthly publication with executive interviews, feature reports, show coverage, international news, and analysis. Retail classes of trade, from specialty apparel, department, and discount to supermarket, drug, and convenience. www.executivetechnology.com

Furniture/Today Weekly newspaper for retail executives in furniture and department stores and for executives in manufacturing firms. www. furnituretoday.com

Hobby Merchandiser Monthly publication for suppliers and retailers in the model hobby industry. www.hobbymerchandiser.com

Hotel and Motel Management Bimonthly magazine reports news and trends affecting the lodging industry. www.advanstar.com

Internet Retailer Monthly magazine devoted to electronic retailing issues. www.internetretailer.com

Mass Market Retailers Biweekly newspaper for executives in supermarket, chain drug, and chain discount headquarters. Reports news and interprets its effects on mass merchandisers. www. massmarketretailers.com

Modern Grocer Weekly newspaper covers regional and national news current events relating to food retailing. http://griffcomm.net

Modern Jeweler Monthly magazine for jewelry retailers. Looks at trends in jewelry, gems, and watches. www.modernjeweler.com

NACS Magazine Monthly publication for convenience stores. www.cstorecentral.com

Private Label Bimonthly magazine for buyers, merchandisers, and executives involved in purchasing private, controlled packer, and generic labeled products for chain supermarkets and drug, discount, convenience, and department stores. www.privatelabelmag.com

Progressive Grocer Monthly magazine reporting on the supermarket industry. In-depth features offer insights into trends in store development, technology, marketing, logistics, international retailing, human resources, and consumer purchasing patterns. www.grocerynetwork.com

Retail Info Systems News Monthly magazine addressing system solutions for corporate/financial, operations, MIS, and merchandising management in retail. www.risnews.com

Retail Merchandiser Published monthly for retail buyers, CEOs, financial investors, visual merchandisers, and consultants. www.retail-merchandiser.com

Retailtech Magazine Monthly magazine reporting on and interpreting technologies available for all levels of the fashion distribution chain from manufacturers to retailers. Includes computers, retail POS systems, computer-aided design and manufacturing, software, electronic retailing, credit systems, visual merchandising, and factory automation. www.retailtech.com

Retail Traffic Monthly magazine for managers involved in real estate and location decisions. www.retailtraffic.com

Shopping Center World Monthly magazine on new center developments and leasing, redevelopments and releasing, management, operations, marketing, design, construction, and financing of shopping centers. www.intertec.com

Shopping Centers Today Monthly publication on the development of new shopping centers and the expansion of existing ones. www.icsc.org

Store Planning Design and Review Monthly publication describing new trends and techniques in store design and merchandise presentation. www.retailreporting.com

Stores Monthly magazine published by the National Retail Federation (NRF). Aimed at retail executives in department and specialty stores, it emphasizes broad trends in customer behavior, management practices, and technology. www.stores.org

VM/SD (Visual Merchandising/Store Design) Monthly magazine for people involved in merchandise display, store interior design and planning, and manufacturing of equipment used by display and store designers. http://www.stmediagroup.com/index.php3?d=pubs&p=vm

WWD (formerly *Women's Wear Daily*) Daily newspaper reports fashion and industry news on women's and children's ready-to-wear, sportswear, innerwear, accessories, and cosmetics. www.wwd.com

Retail Trade Associations

Food Marketing Institute
Membership includes 1,600 grocery retailers and wholesalers. Maintains liaisons with government and consumers and conducts research programs. Publishes *Facts About Supermarket Development* and *Supermarket Industry Financial Review*. Formed by the merger of the National Association of Food Chains and Supermarket Institute. www.fmi.org

International Council of Shopping Centers
Represents 35,000 owners, developers, retailers, and managers of shopping centers; architects, engineers, contractors, leasing brokers, promotion agencies, and others who provide services and products for shopping center owners, shopping center merchant associations, retailers, and public and academic organizations. Promotes professional standards of performance in the development, construction, financing, leasing, management, and operation of shopping centers throughout the world. Engages in research and data gathering on all aspects of shopping centers; compiles statistics. www.icsc.org

Retail Industry Leaders Association
Formerly the International Mass Retailer Association. Membership includes 750 mass retailing (discount) chains. Conducts research and educational programs on every phase of self-service general merchandise retailing. Publishes *Operating Results of Mass Retail Stores/Mass Retailers' Merchandising and Operating Results* annually. www.rila.org

National Association of Chain Drug Stores
Membership includes 1,163 chain drug retailers plus manufacturers, publishers, and advertising agencies. Interprets actions by government agencies in such areas as drugs, public health, federal trade, labor, and excise taxes. www.nacds.org

National Association of Convenience Stores
Membership includes 4,000 retail stores that sell gasoline, fast foods, soft drinks, dairy products, beer, cigarettes, publications, grocery items, snacks, and nonfood items and are usually open seven days per week. www.cstorecentral.com

National Retail Federation (NRF)
Formed by a merger of the American Retail Federation (ARF), with a membership of 1,500,000 smaller retailers, and the National Retail Merchants Association (NRMA), with a membership of 55,000 department, specialty, and discount chain stores. The ARF was primarily concerned with the effect of legislation and government regulation on retailers. The NRF conducts extensive conferences and educational programs for retailers, provides statistical information and publishes *Stores Magazine*. www.nrf.com

Shop.org
The only trade association to focus exclusively on Internet retailing. Its 300 members represent all segments of online retailing, including virtual retailers, conventional retailers, catalogers, manufacturers, and companies providing products and services for online retailers. Sponsors studies on electronic retailing. A division of the NRF. www.shop.org

Types of Retailers

EXECUTIVE BRIEFING
Maxine Clark, Founder and Chief Executive Bear, Build-A-Bear Workshop

became President of Payless Shoe Stores, then a division of May Department Store with over 4,500 stores and $2 billion plus in annual sales at the time.

In early 1997, I decided to launch a retail concept I had been thinking about—Build-A-Bear Workshop®. While most retailers are merchandise driven, Build-A-Bear Workshop® offers highly interactive experiences like a theme park. It combines the universal appeal of plush animals with an interactive assembly line that allows children of all ages to create and accessorize their own huggable companions. We opened the first Build-A-Bear Workshop in St. Louis in the fall of 1997 and have now grown to over 200 stores and in 2003, $300 million in annual sales.

The keys to our success are great merchandise, great people, and great store execution. These three factors combine to create an environment where families share quality time and form irreplaceable memories. Our passion for serving our guests is emulated by our dedicated associates, known as "Master Bear Builders," who make every effort to ensure that each visit is memorable and enjoyable. Employees are empowered to make sure that

I had a passion for retailing even when I was a young girl. At an early age, I recognized the importance of having exciting merchandise and providing an engaging store experience for customers. But I never realized how significant these feelings would be in my life. I started my retail career, like many college graduates going into retailing, as an executive trainee at May Department Stores Company. Over the next 20 years I held a variety of store and merchandise positions of increasing responsibility. In 1992, I

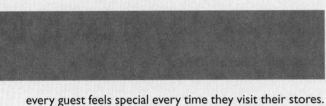

CHAPTER 2

QUESTIONS

What trends are shaping today's retailers?

What are the different types of retailers?

How do retailers differ in terms of how they meet the needs of their customers?

How do services retailers differ from merchandise retailers?

What are the types of ownership for retail firms?

every guest feels special every time they visit their stores. We have a company culture where great service and recognition are a daily occurrence. Ninety percent of guests rate the quality of experience in the highest two categories and 76 percent indicate that nothing could be done to improve their store experience.

We also believe strongly that we need to give back to the communities in which we have stores. For example, as part of our ongoing commitment to children's health and wellness, we introduced a series of Nikki's Bears to honor Nikki Giampolo, a young girl who lost her life to cancer. A portion of proceeds from the sale of Nikki's is donated to support programs that help children maintain normal lives while they struggle with difficult health issues including cancer, diabetes, and autism. To date, the program has raised nearly $700,000 for important children's health and wellness causes.

You want to have a good cup of coffee in the morning, not instant, but you don't want to bother with grinding coffee beans, boiling water, pouring it through ground coffee in a filter, and waiting. Think of all of the different retailers that could help you satisfy this need. You could get your cup of brewed coffee from the drive-through window at the local Starbucks, or you could decide to buy an automatic coffeemaker with a timer so your coffee will be ready when you wake up. You could purchase the coffeemaker at a discount store like Wal-Mart or Target, a department store like Macy's, a drugstore like Walgreens, or a category specialist like Circuit City. If you want to buy the coffeemaker without taking the time to visit a store, you could order it from the JCPenney catalog or go to www.shopping.yahoo.com, search for "coffeemaker," and review the information on 270 models sold by more than 60 Internet retailers.

All these retailers are competing against one another to satisfy your need for a hassle-free, good cup of coffee. Many are selling the same brands, but they offer different services, prices, atmospheres, and convenience. For example, if you want to buy a low-price, basic coffeemaker, you might go to a discount store. But if you are interested in a coffeemaker with more features and want to have someone explain the different features, you might visit a department store or a category specialist.

To develop and implement a retail strategy, retailers need to understand the nature of competition in the retail marketplace. This chapter describes the different types of retailers—both store and nonstore—and how they compete against one another by offering different benefits to consumers. These benefits are reflected in the nature of the retail mixes used by the retailers to satisfy customer needs: the types of merchandise and services offered, the degree to which their offerings emphasize services versus merchandise, and the prices charged (see Exhibit 1–6).

RETAILER CHARACTERISTICS

The 1.5 million U.S. store-based retailers range from street vendors selling hot dogs to large corporations such as Sears that have become an integral part of American culture. Each retailer survives and prospers when it satisfies a group of consumers' needs more effectively than its competitors can. The different types of retailers offer unique benefits, so consumers patronize different retail types when they have different needs. For example, you might value the convenience of buying a tee shirt from a catalog as a gift for a friend in another city but buy from a local store when making a purchase for yourself so you can try the shirt on. You might go to a discount store to buy an inexpensive tee shirt for a camping trip, or go to a sporting goods specialty store to buy a tee shirt with the insignia of your favorite football team.

As consumer needs and competition have changed, new retail formats have been created and continue to evolve. The initial category specialists in toys, consumer electronics, and home improvement supplies have been joined by a host of new specialists, including Guitar Center (musical instruments), Bed Bath & Beyond (home furnishings), and PETsMART (pet supplies). Wal-Mart is closing its traditional discount stores to open supercenters—large stores that combine a discount store with a supermarket. CarMax competes with traditional automobile dealers that sell used cars using traditional retailing methods. Travelocity and Expedia use the Internet to provide many of the services offered by traditional travel agents.

As these new formats emerge and prosper, they attract competitors. Retailing View 2.1 describes how Netflix has attracted many customers who had patronized Blockbuster by offering a unique service, mail-order DVD rentals, but also has attracted a number of competitors.

The most basic characteristics used to describe different types of retailers is the retail mix, the elements used by retailers to satisfy their customers' needs (see Exhibit 1–6). Four elements of the retail mix are particularly useful for classifying retailers: the type of merchandise and/or services sold, the variety and assortment of merchandise sold, the level of customer service, and the price of the merchandise.

Type of Merchandise

REFACT

NAICS replaces the Standard Industrial Classification (SIC) system that had been used by the U.S. Census Bureau since the 1930s.

The United States, Canada, and Mexico have developed a classification scheme, called the **North American Industry Classification System (NAICS),** to collect data on business activity in each country. Every business is assigned a hierarchical, six-digit code based on the type of products and services it produces and sells. The first two digits identify the firm's business sector, and the remaining four digits identify various subsectors.

The classifications for retail firms selling merchandise, based largely on the type of merchandise sold, are illustrated in Exhibit 2–1. Merchandise retailers constitute sectors 44 and 45, and the third digit breaks down these retailers further. For example, retailers selling clothing and clothing accessories are in classification 448, whereas general merchandise retailers are in classification 452. The fourth and fifth digits provide a finer classification. As shown in Exhibit 2–1, the fourth digit subdivides clothing and accessory retailers (448) into clothing stores (4481), shoe stores (4482), and jewelry and luggage stores (4483). The fifth digit provides a further breakdown into men's clothing stores (44811) and women's clothing stores (44812). The sixth digit, not illustrated in Exhibit 2–1, is used to capture differences in the three North American countries using the classification scheme.

Most services retailers appear in sectors 71 (arts, entertainment, and recreation) and 72 (accommodation and food services). For example, food services and drinking places are in category (722), subdivided into full-service restaurants (7221) and limited-service eating places like fast-food restaurants (7222).

EXHIBIT 2–1
NAICS Codes for Retailers

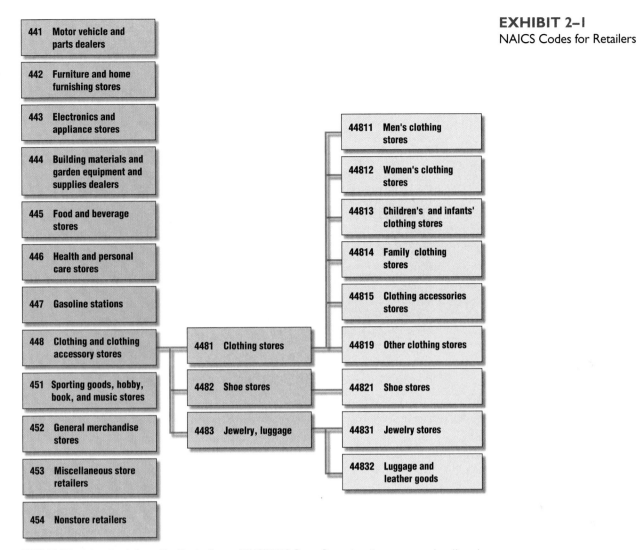

441	Motor vehicle and parts dealers
442	Furniture and home furnishing stores
443	Electronics and appliance stores
444	Building materials and garden equipment and supplies dealers
445	Food and beverage stores
446	Health and personal care stores
447	Gasoline stations
448	Clothing and clothing accessory stores
451	Sporting goods, hobby, book, and music stores
452	General merchandise stores
453	Miscellaneous store retailers
454	Nonstore retailers

4481	Clothing stores
4482	Shoe stores
4483	Jewelry, luggage

44811	Men's clothing stores
44812	Women's clothing stores
44813	Children's and infants' clothing stores
44814	Family clothing stores
44815	Clothing accessories stores
44819	Other clothing stores
44821	Shoe stores
44831	Jewelry stores
44832	Luggage and leather goods

SOURCE: "North American Industry Classification System (NAICS)," U.S. Census Bureau, http://www.census.gov/ epcd/www/ naics.html.

Variety and Assortment

Even if retailers sell the same type of merchandise, they might not compete directly against each other. For example, the primary classification for retailers selling clothing is 448. But clothing can be purchased in sporting goods stores (45111), department stores (4521), warehouse clubs and superstores (45291), and electronic shopping and mail-order houses (4541). These different types of retailers do not compete directly because they appeal to different customer needs due to the differences in the assortments and variety of merchandise and services they offer.

Variety represents the number of merchandise categories a retailer offers. **Assortment** is the number of different items in a merchandise category. Variety is often referred to as the **breadth of merchandise** carried by a retailer; assortment is referred to as the **depth of merchandise.** Each different item of merchandise is called an **SKU (stockkeeping unit).** Some examples of SKUs are an original scent, 33-ounce box of Tide laundry detergent with bleach or a blue, long-sleeved, button-down-collar Ralph Lauren shirt, size 16–33.

Warehouse club stores, discount stores, and toy stores all sell toys. However, warehouse clubs and discount stores sell many other categories of merchandise in addition to toys (i.e., they have greater variety). Stores specializing in toys stock

REFACT

A quarter of all U.S. retail sales are for motor vehicles and parts (441), whereas department stores (4521) account for less than 7 percent.[1]

2.1 RETAILING VIEW   Netflix's Success Attracts Competitors

In 1997, Reed Hastings returned a copy of *Apollo 13* to his local Blockbuster six weeks late and had to pay a $40 fee. This experience was the impetus for Hastings, a former computer scientist, to develop a DVD rental-by-mail service and launch Netflix. For about $10 a month, a Netflix subscriber can rent three DVDs at a time with no limit on the number of rentals during the month, no due dates, no late fees, and no shipping costs.

Here's how it works. On the Netflix Web site (www.netflix.com), subscribers create lists of the DVDs they want to receive from the company's library of over 35,000 titles—ten times more titles than appear in

Netflix pioneered an innovative retailing approach for renting DVDs.

a typical Blockbuster store. Then, Netflix sends customers their top three DVD choices, assuming they are in stock. When customers finish viewing a DVD, they simply put it into a preaddressed envelope (postage is prepaid) and send it back to Netflix. When Netflix receives the envelope, it sends the customer the next DVD from the customer's list.

With over 30 distribution centers, Netflix's turnaround time is usually three to four days.

The Netflix Web site has information to assist its subscribers in selecting DVDs. Recommendations are provided based on subscribers' evaluations of DVDs they have already seen. The site also provides reviews by film critics, video preview clips, and ratings summarizing subscriber evaluations.

One drawback is that the rental service offered by Netflix requires customers to order their DVDs in advance rather than stopping by the Blockbuster store on the way home from work to pick up the specific title they want to watch that evening. Netflix tries to overcome that problem by letting customers stock up and keep three DVDs at a time. "Our biggest weakness is advance ordering, but we're turning that into a strength, or trying to, because the disks are already there when you want them," Hastings says. "You don't have to drive out to Blockbuster." Thus Netflix has positioned itself as a hassle-free alternative to Blockbuster.

REFACT

On a busy day, Netflix ships about 5,000,000 gigabytes of data on DVDs, approximately 70 percent of the entire daily capacity of the Internet in the United States and Canada.[2]

Initially, Blockbuster was not concerned about Netflix because its research found that more than 90 percent of video renters decide on the videos they want to watch the same day they rent them. Blockbuster concluded that a mail-order business such as Netflix clearly did not lend itself to the impulse nature of video rentals. However, as Netflix's subscriber base grew to over three million customers and annual revenues exceeded $300 million, Blockbuster and others recognized the attractiveness of this innovative retail concept.

In response to Netflix capturing 5 percent of the video rental market, Blockbuster offered a rental-by-mail service that leveraged its stores and eliminated its charges for returning DVDs late. Subscribers to Blockbuster's service can rent three DVDs at a time through the mail or from its stores for $15, and the DVDs can be returned by mail or at a store. Blockbuster also e-mails customers two coupons per month that can be used in the store for free movie or game rentals. This promotion helps link the bricks-and-mortar locations with the online presence and allows customers to plan some of their rentals but also have some impulse, spur-of-the-moment rentals. Wal-Mart also has launched a DVD rental-by-mail service. In addition to the battling industry leaders, the video-on-demand market poses a threat. In the future, consumers may forgo rentals and download movies over the Internet or via cable television.

Sources: Gary Rivlin, "Does the Kid Stay in the Picture?" *New York Times*, February 22, 2005, p. B1; Betsy Streisand, "No Pause in DVD Rental Wars," *U.S. News & World Report*, October 18, 2004, pp. 54–56.

The local bike shop (left) offers the deepest assortment of bicycles. Toys "R" Us (right) is in the middle of the assortment/ variety dimension.

more types of toys (more SKUs). For each type of toy, such as dolls, the specialty toy retailer offers a greater assortment (more models, sizes, and brands) than full-line discount stores or warehouse clubs.

Exhibit 2–2 shows the breadth and depth of bicycles carried by Gator Cycle, a local bicycle shop in Gainesville, Florida (a specialty store), Toys "R" Us (a category specialist), and Wal-Mart (a discount store). Toys "R" Us carries three basic types and has a narrower variety than the specialty store, which carries four types. But Toys "R" Us also has the greatest assortment in children's bicycles. Wal-Mart has the lowest number of total SKUs (83) compared with Toys "R" Us (118) and Gator Cycle (130). Note that Wal-Mart and Toys "R" Us carry some of the same brands, but Gator Cycle offers a completely different set of brands.

Services Offered

Retailers also differ in the services they offer customers. For example, Gator Cycle offers assistance in selecting the appropriate bicycle, adjusting the bicycle to fit the individual, and repairing bicycles. Toys "R" Us and Wal-Mart don't provide any of these services. Customers expect almost all retailers to provide certain services:

EXHIBIT 2–2
Variety and Assortment of Bicycles in Different Retail Outlets

	Adult Road	Adult Hybrid	Mountain	Child
Gator Cycle	Trek, Lemond, Klein	Gary Fisher, Trek 800	Gary Fisher, Trek, Klein Attitude	Gary Fisher, Trek
	60 SKUs	15 SKUs	40 SKUs	15 SKUs
	$630–9500	$260–1500	$240–5000	$110–600
Toys"R"Us	Murray, Schwinn, Mongoose, Pacific, Huffy	—	Mongoose, Schwinn, Pacific, Dynacraft, Kent	Pacific, Huffy, Radio Flyer, Dynacraft, Rand Int'l, Kent, Schwinn, Murray, Mongoose
	23 SKUs		13 SKUs	82 SKUs
	$59.99–179.99		$79.99–249.99	$29.99–179.99
Wal-Mart	Huffy, Kent Int'l	—	Roadmaster, Next, Mongoose, Schwinn	Roadmaster, Next, Schwinn, Mongoose, Huffy, Barbie
	14 SKUs		19 SKUs	50 SKUs
	$59.99–379.74		$53.73–237.82	$29.88–177.63

displaying merchandise, accepting credit cards, providing parking, and being open at convenient hours. Some retailers charge customers for other services, such as home delivery and gift wrapping. Retailers that cater to service-oriented consumers offer customers most of these services at no charge.

Prices and the Cost of Offering Breadth and Depth of Merchandise and Services

Stocking a deep and broad assortment like Gator Cycle's offering in bicycles is appealing to customers but costly for retailers. When a retailer offers customers many SKUs, its inventory investment increases because the retailer must have backup stock for each SKU.

Similarly, services attract customers to the retailer, but they're also costly. More salespeople are needed to provide information and assist customers, alter merchandise to meet customers' needs, and demonstrate merchandise. Child care facilities, rest rooms, dressing rooms, and check rooms take up valuable store space that could be used to stock and display merchandise. Offering delayed billing, credit, or installment payments requires a financial investment that could be used to buy more merchandise.

EXHIBIT 2–3

Sales and Growth Rate for Retail Sectors

	Estimated Sales 2005 $ Millions	Estimated % Sales Compounded Sales Growth 2003–2008
Food Retailers		
Conventional supermarkets	$ 482,597	2.5%
Supercenters	206,591	15.0
Warehouse clubs	87,718	6.0
Convenience stores	380,513	5.0
General Merchandise Retailers		
Department stores	84,232	–1.0
Apparel and accessory specialty stores	141,614	4.4
Jewelry stores	32,201	5.8
Shoe stores	22,904	1.4
Furniture stores	58,513	4.9
Home furnishing stores	52,243	5.8
Office supply stores	26,073	3.8
Sporting goods stores	30,595	5.2
Book stores	17,794	4.5
Building material, hardware, and garden supply stores	373,662	6.2
Consumer electronics and appliance stores	106,700	5.7
Drug stores	187,729	6.9
Full-line discount stores	130,647	1.0
Food and general merchandise extreme value stores	45,229	6.2
Nonstore retailers		
Nonstore retailing	144,413	9.2
E-commerce	85,000	26.8

SOURCES: *Softgoods Economic Forecast: Outlook to 2008,* Columbus, OH: Retail Forward, May 2004; *Hardgoods Economic Forecast: Outlook to 2008,* Columbus, OH.: Retail Forward, May 2004; *Food Drug Mass Economic Forecast: Outlook to 2008,* Columbus, OH: Retail Forward, May 2004.

To make a profit, retailers that offer broader and deeper assortments and services need to charge higher prices. For example, department stores have higher prices because they have higher costs due to stocking a lot of fashionable merchandise, discounting merchandise when errors are made in forecasting consumer tastes, providing some personal sales service, and having expensive mall locations. In contrast, discount stores appeal to customers who are looking for lower prices and are less interested in services but want to see a wide range of merchandise brands and models. Thus, a critical retail decision involves the trade-off between the costs and benefits of maintaining additional inventory or providing additional services. Chapters 6 and 12 address the considerations required in making this trade-off.

To compare their offering with competitive offerings, retailers often shop their competitors' stores. Appendix 2A provides a template used by retailers for their comparison shopping. In the next section, we discuss the different types of food retailers, then general merchandise and nonstore retailers. Exhibit 2–3 contains information about the size and growth rates for each of these retail sectors.

FOOD RETAILERS

The food retailing landscape is changing dramatically. Twenty years ago, consumers purchased food primarily at conventional supermarkets. Now conventional supermarkets account for only 61 percent of food sales. The fastest growing segment of the food retail market is the remaining 39 percent of food sales made by supercenters, warehouse clubs, convenience stores, and new concepts such as limited assortment supermarkets (see Exhibit 2–4).[3] While Wal-Mart and other general merchandise retailers are offering more food items, traditional supermarkets are carrying more nonfood items, and many offer pharmacies, photo processing centers, banks, and cafés.

The world's largest food retailer is Wal-Mart, with over $100 billion sales of supermarket-type merchandise, followed by Kroger (U.S. corporate headquarters), Carrefour (France), Ahold (Netherlands), and Albertson's (U.S.). Most of Wal-Mart's food sales are generated from its supercenter format, whereas Carrefour garners most of its sales using the hypermarket format that

Primary Shopping Format for Food and Sales Growth Rates of Food by Retail Format **EXHIBIT 2–4**

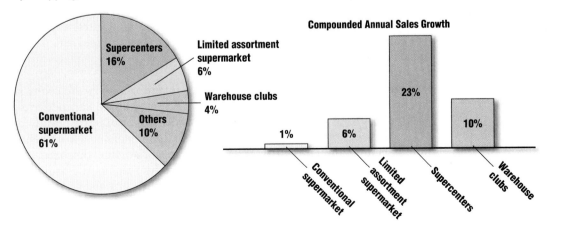

SOURCE: *Industry Outlook: Food Channel*, Columbus, OH: Retail Forward, February 2004, p. 7; *Industry Outlook: Warehouse Club*, Columbus, OH: Retail Forward, October 2004, p. 3.

EXHIBIT 2–5   Characteristics of Food Retailers

	Conventional Supermarket	Limited Assortment Supermarket	Supercenter	Warehouse Club	Convenience Store
Percentage food	70–80	80–90	30–40	60	90
Size (000 sq ft)	20–30	7–10	150–220	100–150	2–3
SKUs (000)	20–40	1–1.5	100–150	20	2–3
Variety	average	narrow	broad	broad	narrow
Assortment	average	shallow	deep	shallow	shallow
Ambience	pleasant	minimal	average	minimal	average
Service	modest	limited	limited	limited	limited
Prices	average	lowest	low	low	high
Gross margin (%)	20–22	10–12	15–18	12–15	25–30

it developed. The remaining larger food retailers primarily sell through conventional supermarkets. Exhibit 2–5 shows the retail mixes for different types of food retailers.

Supermarkets

A **conventional supermarket** is a self-service food store offering groceries, meat, and produce with limited sales of nonfood items, such as health and beauty aids and general merchandise.[4] Perishables like meat and produce account for 44 percent of supermarket sales and typically have higher margins than packaged goods.[5] The largest supermarket chains in the United States are Kroger, Albertson's, Safeway, Ahold USA, and Publix.

Whereas conventional supermarkets carry about 30,000 SKUs, **limited assortment supermarkets,** also called **extreme value food retailers,** only stock 1,250 SKUs. The two largest limited assortment supermarket chains in the United States are Save-A-Lot and ALDI. Retailing View 2.2 describes how ALDI, a German retail firm, competes effectively against Wal-Mart in both the United States and Germany.

Rather than carrying twenty brands of laundry detergent, limited assortment stores offer one or two brands and sizes, one of which is a store brand. Stores are designed to maximize efficiency and reduce costs. For example, merchandise is shipped in cartons that can serve as displays so that no unloading is needed. Some costly services that consumers take for granted, such as free bags and paying with credit cards, are not provided. Stores are typically located in second- or third-tier shopping centers with low rents. By trimming costs, limited assortment supermarkets can offer merchandise at 40 percent lower prices than conventional supermarkets.[7]

Trends in Food Retailing   Although conventional supermarkets still sell a majority of food merchandise, they are under substantial competitive pressure. Everyone wants a piece of the food pie. Supercenters are rapidly attracting conventional supermarket customers with their broader assortments of food and general merchandise at attractive prices. Full-line discount chains, like Target and Wal-Mart, and dollar stores are increasing the amount of space they devote to consumables. Convenience stores are also selling more fresh merchandise.

Low-cost competitors, supercenters, and warehouse clubs are particularly troublesome for supermarkets because of their superior operating efficiencies. A study commissioned by an industry task force in the early 1990s found that the supermarket industry had over $30 billion in excess inventory due to its failure to employ the just-in-time inventory practices adopted by Wal-Mart and other low-cost competitors. The report indicated that by managing inventory more efficiently, supermarkets could reduce their prices by 10 to 14 percent. [8] The set of programs supermarket chains have undertaken to achieve these inventory reductions is called **efficient customer response (ECR)** and includes just-in-time inventory management and better assortment planning. These activities are discussed in more detail in Chapters 10 and 12.

The supermarket format, however, continues to be more costly than supercenters. To compete successfully against intrusions by other food retailing formats, conventional supermarkets are differentiating their offering by (1) emphasizing fresh perishables, (2) targeting health-conscious and ethnic consumers, (3) providing a better in-store experience, and (4) offering more private label brands. For example, fresh merchandise categories, the areas around the outside walls known as the **"power perimeter,"** have long been the mainstays of conventional supermarkets. These include the dairy, bakery, meats, florist, produce, deli, and coffee bar departments—high traffic, profitable departments

ALDI Meets Wal-Mart's Challenge   RETAILING VIEW   2.2

At first glance, an ALDI store in Germany reminds you of the sparse retail stores in Eastern Europe in 1975. Jars of asparagus and cans of beans are displayed in cardboard boxes piled on top of pallets. There are only two brands of toilet paper and one brand of pickles. The line at the cash registers is 10 customers deep. But the prices are really low—three frozen pizzas for $3.24, a $2.36 bottle of decent Cabernet, and a trench coat for $21.

Aldi provides quality merchandise at low prices by reducing its assortment to control store operating expenses.

on display is an ALDI exclusive label, such as Millville Raisin Bran at $1.49 a box and Sweet Valley root beer for $1.89 a 12 pack. However, the quality of the store brands is comparable to that of nationally advertised brands like Nestlé and Kraft. Because it sells so few products, ALDI can exert strong control over quality and price and simplify shipping and handling.

ALDI reduces its labor costs by keeping limited store staff. Its stores typically have four or five workers compared with about fifteen at a normal supermarket. Meat and bakery items are shipped to stores to eliminate the need for costly "specialist" clerks, such as butchers or bakers. Time and effort spent arranging products on shelves is minimized. Food gets stacked in its original packing boxes with the tops removed, piled high either on top of pallets against the walls or on simple shelving units. Prices are plainly listed on paper signs attached to molding hung from the ceiling, and shoppers bag their own groceries. Due to this mode of operations, ALDI's labor cost are only 6 percent of sales compared with 12 to 16 percent for the typical supermarket.

ALDI stores are found not only in working-class neighborhoods but also in wealthy communities. An astonishing 89 percent of German households shopped at least once at ALDI during the year. ALDI, short for "Albrecht Discount," has a cult following, including a Web site for fans of the retailer. Karl Albrecht, the cofounder, is the world's third-richest man, with a fortune estimated at $23 billion by *Forbes* magazine.

 Like Wal-Mart, ALDI focuses relentlessly on reducing costs, has huge market clout, is very profitable, and seems to enjoy unstoppable growth. Although ALDI, with its annual sales of over $40 billion, is only one-seventh the size of Wal-Mart, it is still one of the world's biggest retailers and a major force in Europe.

ALDI has a simple but highly effective strategy. A typical ALDI store stocks less than 1,000 products, compared with as many as 150,000 at a Wal-Mart Supercenter. Almost everything

Sources: Erin White and Susanna Ray, "Bare Bones Shopping: Germany's Discount Retailers Are Among the World's Most Successful," *The Wall Street Journal*, May 10, 2004, p. R6; Jack Ewing, Andrea Zammert, Wendy Zellner, Rachel Tiplady, Ellen Groves, and Michael Eidam, "The Next Wal-Mart?" *BusinessWeek*, April 26, 2004, pp. 38–40.

that help pull shoppers through the store. The dairy and produce sections in particular are high need items and, if of high quality and priced competitively, can increase store loyalty among customers. Conventional supermarkets are building on this strength by devoting more space to fresh merchandise with cooking exhibitions and "action" stations such as store-made sushi and freshly grilled meat.[9]

Another example of the emphasis on "fresh" is meal solutions offered to time-pressured consumers. At Wegmans (an upstate New York–based supermarket chain), customers can eat lunch overlooking the European-style Market Cafe or buy prepared meals to take home. Chefs in monogrammed white jackets and tall pleated paper hats staff the separate pizza, deli, and fresh-baked bread stations. Along one wall, Caesar salads are made to order. At another station, customers have a choice of Alfredo, marinara, or vodka sauce on their hot pasta. At a station called the Outer Loop, the store offers open-face sandwiches of crab cakes and grilled salmon criss-crossed with bacon. Turkey chili is served in a hollowed-out round loaf of crusty bread. Folks who keep kosher have their own area for, say, meat-stuffed cabbage and potato pancakes or a Waldorf salad.[10]

Conventional supermarkets also are offering more natural, organic, low-fat, low-sugar, and low-salt merchandise for the growing segment of consumers who are health conscious or have dietary restrictions that they must follow. Sales at Whole Earth and Wild Oats, two national supermarket chains that focus on natural/organic food, are growing at 20 percent per year.[11]

Furthermore, conventional supermarkets are adjusting their merchandise mix to attract more ethnic shoppers. Hispanics, who now constitute 13 percent of the U.S. population, have significantly different shopping and eating patterns than does the general population. They are more likely to prepare meals from scratch, spend more on groceries, prefer stores with bilingual staff and signage, and place importance on fresh food.[12] President Supermarkets in Little Havana in Miami feel like home for Latinos. Merengue or mariachi music plays over the store's audio system, not the Moody Blues or Neil Diamond. Molleja en salsa, tamal en hojas, and Cuban sandwiches are available at a lunch counter to go with your café con leche. Abundant heaps of exotic produce are on display, labeled "Malangas," "Boniato Americano," "Haitian Mangoes," "Fresh Cassavas," and "Jamaican Yellow Yams." And the grocery clerks are Cuban, Mexican, Haitian, Colombian, and Peruvian.[13]

Private label brands (discussed in Chapter 14) are a benefit to both customers and retailers. The benefits to customers include having more choices, finding the same ingredients and quality as in national brands, relying on the reputation of the store, enjoying availability in many categories, and saving 5 to 15 percent without coupons. The benefits of private label brands to retailers include increased store loyalty, the ability to differentiate themselves from the competition, high customer awareness and acceptance of store brands, minimal promotional costs, and higher gross margins compared with national brands. Private label brands account for approximately 20 percent of total U.S. sales by food retailers.[14]

Creating an enjoyable shopping experience through store ambiance and customer service is another key approach that supermarket chains use to differentiate themselves from low-cost, low-price competitors. Supermarkets are increasingly incorporating "food as theatre" concepts, such as open-air market designs, cooking classes, demos, and food tasting. For example, H.E. Butt's (a Texas-based supermarket chain) Central Market concept includes a Bulk Bar with prepared sauces, Grab & Go meals, and outstanding customer service.

At EatZi's, time-pressured consumers find fresh meal alternatives to restaurants.

Supercenters

Supercenters, the fastest growing retail category, are large stores (150,000–220,000 square feet) that combine a supermarket with a full-line discount store. Wal-Mart operates over 2,000 supercenters in the United States—four times more than its leading competitors Meijer, Kmart, Fred Meyer (a division of Kroger), and Target combined. By offering broad assortments of grocery and general merchandise products under one roof, supercenters provide a one-stop shopping experience. Customers will typically drive farther to shop at these stores than to visit conventional supermarkets (which offer a smaller selection).

General merchandise (nonfood) items are often purchased on impulse when customers' primary reason for coming to the supercenter is to buy groceries. The general merchandise has higher margins, enabling the supercenters to price food items more aggressively. However, because supercenters are very large, some customers find them inconvenient because it can take a long time to find the items they want.

Hypermarkets are also large (100,000–300,000 square feet) combination food (60–70 percent) and general merchandise (30–40 percent) stores. Hypermarkets typically stock fewer SKUs than supercenters—between 40,000 and 60,000 items ranging from groceries, hardware, and sports equipment to furniture and appliances to computers and electronics.

Hypermarkets were created in France after World War II. By building large stores on the outskirts of metropolitan areas, French retailers could attract customers and not violate strict land-use laws. They have spread throughout Europe and become popular in some South American countries such as Argentina and Brazil.

Hypermarkets are not common in the United States, though hypermarkets and supercenters are similar. Both hypermarkets and supercenters are large, carry grocery and general merchandise categories, offer self-service, and are located in warehouse-type structures with large parking facilities. However, hypermarkets carry a larger proportion of food items than supercenters with a greater emphasis placed on perishables—produce, meat, fish, and bakery. Supercenters, on the other hand, have a larger percentage of nonfood items and focus more on dry groceries, such as breakfast cereal and canned goods, instead of fresh items.

Although supercenters and hypermarkets are the fastest growing segments in food retailing, they face challenges in finding locations for new big box stores. In Europe and Japan, land for building large stores is limited and expensive. New supercenters and hypermarkets in these areas often have to be multistory, which increases operating costs and reduces shopper convenience. Furthermore, some countries place restrictions on the size of new retail outlets. In the United States, there has been a backlash against large retail stores, particularly Wal-Mart stores. These opposing sentiments are based on local views that big box stores drive local retailers out of business, offer low wages, are nonunion jobs, have unfair labor practices, threaten U.S. workers due to their purchase of imported merchandise, and cause excessive automobile and delivery truck traffic.

Warehouse Clubs

Warehouse clubs are retailers that offer a limited and irregular assortment of food and general merchandise with little service at low prices for ultimate consumers and small businesses. The largest warehouse club chains are Costco, Sam's Club (a division of Wal-Mart), and BJ's Wholesale Club, a distant third. Costco differentiates itself by offering unique upscale merchandise not available elsewhere at low prices. For example, Costco began selling fine art priced from $450 to $15,000 on its Web site. Sam's Club focuses more on small businesses, providing services such as group health insurance as well as products.

REFACT

Supermarket shoppers make 6.8 trips per month, whereas supercenter shoppers make only 3.3 trips per month.[15]

Costco lures its more affluent clientele with warehouse prices for gourmet foods and upscale brands such as Waterford crystal, Raymond Weil watches and Ralph Lauren clothing.

Warehouse clubs are large (at least 100,000–150,000 square feet) and typically located in low-rent districts. They have simple interiors and concrete floors. Aisles are wide so forklifts can pick up pallets of merchandise and arrange them on the selling floor. Little service is offered. Customers pick merchandise off shipping pallets, take it to checkout lines in the front of the store, and usually pay with cash. Warehouse clubs can offer low prices because they use low-cost locations, inexpensive store designs, and little customer service and keep inventory holding costs low by carrying a limited assortment of fast selling items. In addition, they buy merchandise opportunistically. For example, if Hewlett-Packard is introducing new models of its printers, warehouse clubs will buy the inventory of the older models at a significant discount and then offer them for sale until the inventory is depleted.

Most warehouse clubs have two types of members: wholesale members who own small businesses and individual members who purchase for their own use. For example, many small restaurants are wholesale customers who buy their supplies, food ingredients, and desserts from a warehouse club rather than from food distributors. To cater to their business customers, warehouse clubs sell food items in very large containers and packages—sizes that also appeal to larger families.

Typically, members must pay an annual fee of $25–45. In some stores, individual members pay no fee but pay 5 percent over an item's ticketed price. Wholesale members typically represent less than 30 percent of the customer base but account for over 70 percent of sales.

Convenience Stores

Convenience stores provide a limited variety and assortment of merchandise at a convenient location in 2,000–3,000 square foot stores with speedy checkout. They are the modern version of the neighborhood mom-and-pop grocery/general store. Convenience stores enable consumers to make purchases quickly, without having to search through a large store and wait in a long checkout line. Over half the items bought are consumed within 30 minutes of purchase.

Due to their small size and high sales, convenience stores typically receive deliveries every day. Convenience stores only offer limited assortments and variety, and they charge higher prices than supermarkets. Milk, eggs, and bread once represented the majority of their sales, but now almost all convenience stores sell gasoline, which accounts for over 66 percent of annual sales. The second-highest selling item is cigarettes, accounting for 14 percent of sales.[17]

Convenience stores also are facing increased competition from other formats. Sales increase during periods of rising gasoline prices, but their dependency on gasoline sales is a problem because gasoline sales have low margins. In addition, supercenter and supermarket chains are attempting to increase customer store visits by offering gasoline and tying gasoline sales into their frequent shopper programs. Drugstores and full-line discount stores also are setting up easily accessed areas of their stores with convenience store merchandise.

In response to these competitive pressures, convenience stores are taking steps to decrease their dependency on gasoline sales, tailoring assortments to local markets, and making their stores even more convenient to shop. To get gasoline customers to spend more on other merchandise and services, convenience stores are offering more fresh food and healthy fast food that appeals to today's on-the-go consumers, especially women and young adults. Some convenience stores are adding fast causal restaurants, like BP's Wild Bean Cafe. 7-Eleven is exploring ways to bring its successful fresh-food strategy to the United States. Finally, convenience stores are also adding new services such as financial service kiosks that give customers the opportunity to cash checks, pay bills, and buy prepaid telephone minutes, theatre tickets, and gift cards.

Convenience store operators also are tailoring their merchandise assortments to cater to the needs of local markets. Couche-Tard, operating over 2,500 convenience stores in Canada and the Midwestern United States, tailors both its product selection and its interior design to the local market. Stores have themes to match the local demographics or blend in with the neighborhood. One outlet, in suburban Montreal, has what Alain Bouchard calls a NASA motif, with a model of a spaceship in one corner of the store and employee uniforms that resemble spacesuits. Although 70 percent of the items it offers are common across its stores, stores in upscale neighborhoods stock a higher proportion of imported European beers, while those with a big Hispanic customer base sell Latin American brands.[20]

To increase convenience, convenience stores are opening smaller stores close to where consumers shop and work. For example, 7-Eleven has stores in airports, office buildings, and schools. Easy access, storefront parking, and quick in-and-out access are key benefits offered by convenience stores. They also are exploring the use of technology to increase shopping convenience. For example, Sheetz, a Pennsylvania-based convenience store chain, has self-service food-ordering kiosks at its gasoline pumps. Customers can order a custom-made sandwich while filling their tank and pick it up in the store when they are finished.[21]

GENERAL MERCHANDISE RETAILERS

The major types of general merchandise retailers are department stores, full-line discount stores, specialty stores, category specialists, home improvement centers, off-price retailers, and extreme value retailers. Exhibit 2–6 summarizes the characteristics of general merchandise retailers that sell through stores.

Department Stores

Department stores are retailers that carry a broad variety and deep assortment, offer customer services, and organize their stores into distinctly separate departments for displaying merchandise. The largest department store chains in the United States are Macy's (part of Federated Department Stores), Sears, JCPenney, and Kohl's.

REFACT

T. Stewart was the first U.S. department store, opening in 1847 in New York.[22]

Characteristics of General Merchandise Retailers   **EXHIBIT 2–6**

Type	Variety	Assortment	Service	Prices	Size (000 sq. ft.)	SKUs (000)	Location
Department stores	Broad	Deep to average	Average to high	Average to high	100–200	100	Regional malls
Discount stores	Broad	Average to shallow	Low	Low	60–80	30	Stand alone, power strip centers
Specialty stores	Narrow	Deep	High	High	4–12	5	Regional malls
Category specialists	Narrow	Very deep	Low to high	Low	50–120	20–40	Stand alone, power strip centers
Home improvement centers	Narrow	Very deep	Low to high	Low	80–120	20–40	Stand alone, power strip centers
Drugstores	Narrow	Very deep	Average	Average to high	3–15	10–20	Stand alone, strip centers
Off-price stores	Average	Deep but varying	Low	Low	20–30	50	Outlet malls
Extreme value retailers	Average	Average and varying	Low	Low	7–15	3–4	Urban, strip

Traditionally, department stores attracted customers by offering a pleasing ambience, attentive service, and a wide variety of merchandise under one roof. They sold both soft goods (apparel and bedding) and hard goods (appliances, furniture, and consumer electronics). But now most department stores focus almost exclusively on soft goods. The major departments are women's, men's, and children's apparel and accessories; home furnishings; cosmetics; and kitchenware and small appliances. Each department within the store has a specific selling space allocated to it, a POS terminal to transact and record sales, and salespeople to assist customers. The department store often resembles a collection of specialty shops.

Department store chains can be categorized into three tiers. The first tier includes upscale, high fashion chains with exclusive designer merchandise and excellent customer service, such as Neiman Marcus, Bloomingdale's (part of Federated Department Stores), and Saks Fifth Avenue (part of Saks). Macy's (also part of Federated Department Stores) is in the second tier of upscale traditional department stores, in which retailers sell more modestly priced merchandise with less customer service. The value-oriented third tier—Sears, JCPenney, and Kohl's—caters to more price-conscious consumers. The retail chains in the first tier have established a clearly differentiated position and are producing strong financial results, while the value-oriented tier is facing significant competitive challenges from discount stores, particularly Target. Retailing View 2.3 describes the innovative strategy of Kohl's, a successful value-oriented department store chain.

Department stores still account for some of retailing's traditions—multistoried downtown stores, special events and parades, Santa Claus lands, holiday decorations—and offer designer brands that are not available from other retailers. But many consumers are questioning the benefits and costs of shopping at department stores. Department stores are not as convenient as discount stores because they are located in large regional malls rather than local neighborhoods. Customer service has diminished due to cutbacks in labor costs. In addition, department stores have not been as successful as discount stores and food retailers in reducing costs by working with their vendors to establish just-in-time inventory systems, so prices are relatively high.

The performance of department stores is linked to the strengths of the brands they sell, such as Liz Claibourne, Tommy Hilfiger, Ralph Lauren, and Estée Lauder. In light of the decline in department store patronage, many of these brands, previously sold exclusively through department stores, are pursuing other growth opportunities. For example, Estée Lauder, a cosmetic brand sold at first-tier department stores, has developed an exclusive private label cosmetics line for Kohl's. Levi Strauss created the Levi Straus Signature line for Wal-Mart and other discount stores.[24]

To deal with their eroding market share, department stores are (1) attempting to increase the amount of exclusive merchandise they sell, (2) undertaking marketing campaigns to develop strong images for their stores and brands, and (3) building better relationships with their key customers.[25] To differentiate their merchandise offering and strengthen their image, department stores are aggressively seeking exclusive arrangements with nationally recognized brands. For example, Macy's negotiated with Tommy Hilfiger to launch its new H line exclusively, with supporting advertising featuring Iman and David Bowie. JCPenney became the exclusive retailer for Bisou Bisou, a contemporary apparel brand that was previously sold through better specialty stores and upscale department stores.[26]

In addition, department stores are placing more emphasis on developing their own private label brands. For example, Macy's has been very successful in developing a strong image for its private label brands, such as INC (women's clothing) and Tools of the Trade (housewares). Macy's intends to increase the percentage of exclusive merchandise it offers, from the present 20 percent to over 50 percent.

In recent years, department stores' discount sales events have increased dramatically to the point that consumers have been trained to wait for items to be placed on sale rather than buy them at full price. Department stores are shifting their marketing activities from promotional sales to brand-building activities involving television advertising and specialty publications such as Saks Fifth Avenue's *S* magazine.

Finally, department stores are using technology and information systems to improve customer service in a cost-effective manner. Wireless devices used on the selling floor provide sales associates with customer and merchandise information. Department stores are collecting and analyzing information to identify their best customers and target promotions to these customers. In Chapter 11, we discuss these customer relationship management (CRM) programs in more detail.

Kohl's—A Rapidly Growing Department Store Chain   RETAILING VIEW   2.3

Max Kohl and his family (Herbert Kohl, the Senator from Wisconsin, is a family member) pioneered the supermarket concept in Wisconsin, opening their first store in 1942. In 1962, the family started a chain of discount stores also named Kohl's. The Kohls sold their retail business to British American Tobacco (BATUS) in 1972, which then closed the supermarkets and eventually sold the discount store chain in 1986 to its executives in a

Kohl's department stores place the checkout counters in a convenient centralized location near the store entrances.

fixture spacings are wider than those of the typical department store so that customers pushing a shopping cart or baby stroller can easily navigate the store. Rather than having POS terminals in each department, the stores have centralized cash wraps (checkout stations) near the store entrances so that customers can select merchandise from different areas of the store and pay for it all at once when they are ready to leave.

leveraged buyout. These executives developed a novel concept, combining a department and a discount store, that has produced one of the fastest growing retail firms in the United States.

Kohl's formula for success is offering shopping convenience for time-pressured soccer moms interested in buying national brand apparel and soft home merchandise at reasonable prices. Some of the national brands it sells are Sag Harbor women's wear, Dockers and Arrow men's wear, Healthtex and Oshkosh children's clothing, KitchenAid appliances, and Nike and Sketchers footwear. In addition, it has exclusive sub-brand arrangements with some national brands sold at second-tier department stores such as Estée Lauder cosmetics and Laura Ashley home textile and bedroom accessories.

But the key to Kohl's success is convenience. Its stores, located in suburban neighborhood centers, are easy to shop. The stores are smaller (80,000 square feet) than traditional, mall-based department stores and are on one floor. The aisles and

Since Kohl's does not carry designer brands that require "store within a store" displays, it groups different brands by the type of item rather than brand. Kohl's avoids a cluttered look by positioning display racks in amphitheater style, making all the merchandise visible. Colors are displayed from light to dark, a pattern that is most appealing to the eye. And unlike most stores, which try to straighten up merchandise all day, Kohl's keeps presentations sharp with a daily 2:00 p.m. "recovery period," when everyone in the store—from secretaries to store managers—is called upon to straighten up displays. Night crews do something similar. The total effect is to allow salesclerks to concentrate solely on customers.

From 76 stores in 1992, Kohl's has grown to over 600 stores in 45 states. Its format has proved to be so attractive to shoppers that JCPenney and Sears are opening off-the-mall stores with shopping carts and centralized cash wraps.

Source: www.kohls.com.

REFACT

Hudson's Bay Company, the oldest retailer in North America, conquered the Canadian wilderness by trading furs over 300 years ago. Today, it is one of the largest retailers in Canada, operating chains of discount, department, and home stores. [28]

Full-Line Discount Stores

Full-line discount stores are retailers that offer a broad variety of merchandise, limited service, and low prices. Discount stores offer both private labels and national brands, but these brands are typically less fashion oriented than the brands in department stores. The big three full-line discount store chains are Wal-Mart, Kmart, and Target, which account for 84 percent of the sales in this retail format.[27]

Since Wal-Mart alone accounts for over 58 percent of full-line discount store retail sales, the most significant trend in this sector is Wal-Mart's conversion of discount stores to supercenters. Wal-Mart is planning to open 220 new supercenters each year, two-thirds of which will be conversions of current discount stores. In 2008, it is estimated that Wal-Mart will be operating over 2,300 supercenters and less than 1,200 traditional discount stores.[29] This change in emphasis is the result of the increased competition faced by full-line discount stores and the operating efficiencies of supercenters. Full-line discount stores confront intense competition from discount specialty stores that focus on a single category of merchandise, such as Old Navy, Circuit City, Bed Bath & Beyond, Sports Authority, and Lowe's.

While Wal-Mart is closing its full-line discount stores, Target is becoming one of the most successful retailers in terms of sales growth and profitability. Target succeeds because its stores offer fashionable merchandise at low prices in a pleasant shopping environment. It has developed an image of "cheap chic" by teaming with designers such as Michael Graves, Isaac Mizrahi, and Giannulli Mossimo to produce inexpensive, exclusive merchandise.

Specialty Stores

Specialty stores concentrate on a limited number of complementary merchandise categories and provide a high level of service in relatively small stores. Exhibit 2–7 lists some of the largest U.S. specialty store chains.

Specialty stores tailor their retail strategy toward a very specific market segment by offering deep but narrow assortments and sales associate expertise. For example, Hot Topics focuses on selling licensed, music-inspired apparel to teenagers in mall-based stores. Its sales associates know what's new on the radio, in record stores, on concert tours and among pop culture. Its licensing, design, and sourcing processes are designed so that it can move hot rock stars' fashions and logos from the concert stage to store shelves in 90 days.[30]

Sephora, France's leading cosmetic chain and a division of the luxury goods conglomerate LVMH (Louis Vuitton–Moet Hennessy), is another example of an innovative specialty store concept. In the United States, prestige cosmetics are typically sold in department stores. In contrast, Sephora is a cosmetic and

EXHIBIT 2–7
Specialty Store Retailers

Accessories	Electronics/Software/Gifts	Jewelry
Claire's	Radio Shack	Zales
	Electronics Boutique	Tiffany
Apparel	Sharper Image	
The Gap		**Optical**
The Limited	**Food Supplements**	Cole National
Victoria's Secret	GNC	
Charming Shop		**Shoes**
Abercrombie & Fitch	**Furniture**	Foot Locker
JoAnn Stores	Ethan Alllen	Payless Shoes
Talbots	Havertys	Famous Footware
Auto Parts	**Housewares**	**Sporting Goods**
AutoZone	Williams–Sonoma	Dick's
Advanced Auto Parts	Crate & Barrel	Hibbett
Pep Boys		

perfume specialty store offering a deep assortment in a self-service, 5,000 square foot format. The 100-plus U.S. stores (over 500 in 14 other countries) have more than 13,000 SKUs. Merchandise is grouped by product category, with the fragrance brands displayed alphabetically so customers can locate them easily. Each brand has a separate counter with a salesperson stationed there to help customers. Video walls and interactive kiosks provide extensive product and use information. Customers are free to shop and experiment on their own. Sampling is encouraged, and salespeople are available to assist customers. However, unlike in department stores, the salespeople are paid a salary by Sephora, not a commission by the manufacturer. The low-key atmosphere results in customers spending more time shopping.

Sephora offers a unique shopping experience differentiating it from other specialty stores selling beauty products.

Because specialty retailers focus on specific market segments, they are vulnerable to shifts in consumer tastes and preferences. For example, mall-based specialty retailers are affected by consumers who prefer the convenience of shopping in off-mall stores. Apparel and footwear specialty retailers are capturing less of consumers' total spending because consumers are spending more on necessities involving health and home, as well as "everyday" luxuries such as concert tickets and eating out.

Drugstores

Drugstores are specialty stores that concentrate on health and personal grooming merchandise. Pharmaceuticals often represent over 50 percent of drugstore sales and an even greater percentage of their profits. The largest drugstore chains in the United States are Walgreens, CVS, Rite Aid, and Albertson's. The four chains account for over 69 percent of U.S. drug store sales.

Drugstores, particularly the national chains, are experiencing sustained sales growth because the aging population requires more prescription drugs. Although the profit margins for prescription pharmaceuticals are higher than for other drugstore merchandise, these margins are shrinking due to government health care policies, HMOs, and public outcry over lower prices in other countries, especially Canada.

Drugstores are also being squeezed by considerable competition from pharmacies in discount stores and supermarkets, as well as from prescription mail-order retailers. In response, the major drugstore chains are building larger stand-alone stores to offer a wider assortment of merchandise, more frequently purchased food items, and the convenience of drive-through windows for picking up prescriptions. To build customer loyalty, the chains are also changing the role of their pharmacists from simply dispensing pills (referred to as count, pour, lick, and stick) to providing health care assistance such as explaining how to use a nebulizer.

Drugstore retailers are using systems to allow pharmacists time to provide personalized service. For example, at Walgreens, customers can order prescription refills via the phone and receive automatic notification when the prescription is ready. Based on the time customers plan to pick up the prescription, a computer system automatically schedules the workload in the pharmacy. The systems also monitor the frequency of refilling

Walgreens offers drive-through prescription pickup as a value-added customer service.

REFACT

Wal-Mart is the third-largest pharmacy operator in the United States (behind Walgreens and CVS).

REFACT

Forty-four percent of customers picking up a prescription at a drug store do not buy other merchandise.[31]

Apparel	Crafts	Musical Instruments
Men's Warehouse	Michaels	Guitar Center
Kids "R" Us	**Furniture**	**Office Supply**
Appliances	IKEA	Office Depot
Brandsmart	Pier 1	Staples
Books	**Home**	Office Max
Barnes & Noble	Bed Bath & Beyond	**Pet Supplies**
Borders	Linens 'n Things	PETsMART
Computers	**Home Improvement**	Petco
Comp USA	Home Depot	**Sporting Goods**
Consumer Electronics	Lowe's	Sports Authority
Best Buy	Menards	Gart
Circuit City		Big 5

prescriptions so the pharmacist can make phone calls or send e-mails to ensure patient drug compliance.[32]

Category Specialists

Category specialists are big box discount stores that offer a narrow but deep assortment of merchandise. Exhibit 2–8 lists the largest category specialists in the United States.

These retailers are basically discount specialty stores. Most category specialists use a self-service approach, but some specialists in consumer durables offer assistance to customers. For example, Office Depot stores have a warehouse atmosphere, with cartons of copying paper stacked on pallets plus equipment in boxes on shelves. However, some departments, such as computers and other high-tech products, have salespeople in the display area available to answer questions and make suggestions.

By offering a complete assortment in a category at low prices, category specialists can "kill" a category of merchandise for other retailers and thus are frequently called **category killers.** Due their category dominance, they use their buying power to negotiate low prices and are assured of supply when items are scarce. Department stores and full-line discount stores located near category specialists often have to reduce their offerings in the category because consumers are drawn to the deep assortment and low prices at the category killer. Retailing View 2.4 describes Bass Pro Shop, a category specialist targeting fishing and hunting enthusiasts.

One of the largest and most successful types of category specialist is the home improvement center. A **home improvement center** is a category specialist offering equipment and material used by do-it-yourselfers and contractors to make home improvements. The largest U.S. home improvement chains are Home Depot and Lowe's. Like warehouse clubs and office supply category specialists, home improvement centers operate as retailers when they sell merchandise to consumers and as wholesalers when they sell to contractors and other businesses. Although merchandise in home improvement centers is displayed in a warehouse atmosphere, salespeople are available to assist customers in selecting merchandise and to tell them how to use it.

Most category specialist chains started in one region of the country and saturated that region before expanding to other regions. For example, Office Depot started in Florida and expanded throughout the Southeast and Southwest, and Staples started in Boston and expanded through New England and the Midwest. During this period of expansion, competition between specialists in a category was limited. As the firms expanded into the regions originally dominated by another firm, competition in each category became very intense. In most merchandise categories, the major firms are now in direct competition across the nation.

This direct competition focuses on price, resulting in reduced profits because the competitors have difficulty differentiating themselves on other elements of the retail mix. All the competitors in a category provide similar assortments since they have similar access to national brands, and they all provide the same level of service. In response to this increasing competitive intensity, the category killers continue to concentrate on reducing costs by increasing their operating efficiency and acquiring smaller chains to gain scale economies. Due to this consolidation, two or three firms dominate each category.

Some category specialists are attempting to differentiate themselves with service. For example, both Staples and Office Depot have specialized sales associates dedicated to selling electronic office equipment. Home Depot and Lowe's hire licensed contractors as sales associates to help customers with electrical and plumbing repairs. They also provide classes to train home owners in tiling, painting, and other tasks to give shoppers the confidence to tackle their DIY projects.

The Big Fish Story—Bass Pro Shops   **RETAILING VIEW**   2.4

The first and largest Bass Pro Shops Outdoor World Showroom, located in Springfield, Missouri, may be the most visited store in the country. Every year, the 300,000 square foot showroom attracts more than 4 million visitors, making it the number one tourist attraction in Missouri. It has a four-story waterfall, rifle and archery ranges, four aquariums, an indoor driving range, a putting green, and a 250-seat auditorium and conference room for fish-feeding shows and workshops. Visitors can also get a haircut or dine at McDonald's or Hemingway's Blue Water Café, which has a 30,000 gallon saltwater aquarium.

Category killers, like the Bass Pro Shops, offer a deep assortment of merchandise at low prices.

By early 2005, Bass Pro Shops had 27 stores, including 1 in Canada, with 6 more slotted to open by the end of the year. These stores are smaller (though still over 250,000 square feet) yet also highly interactive and entertaining. The average customer travels two hours to its stores and shops for more than three hours. (Other retailers typically see averages of 15 minute drives and 30 minute visits.) The stores offer everything a person needs for hunting and fishing—from 27-cent plastic bait to boats. The merchandise and services include fishing tackle, shooting and hunting equipment, camping gear, boats and marine accessories, a taxidermy studio, cutlery, rod and reel repair, gifts, outdoor-related books and videos, and sportswear and footwear.

Sales associates are knowledgeable outdoors people. Each is hired for a particular department that matches that person's expertise. Private branded products are field tested by Bass Pro Shops' professional teams: Redhead Pro Hunting Team and Tracker Pro Fishing Team.

A syndicated radio show, *Bass Pro Shops Outdoor World,* is heard on 450 radio stations in 48 states and 139 foreign countries. A television show of the same name can be seen weekly on The Outdoor Channel, which reaches over 24 million households a year and has already won many top industry awards for its fresh approaches to hunting, fishing, and conservation. Bass Pro Shops also puts on a Fall Hunting Classic and Spring Fishing Classic, and its many other weekend events include a free outdoor skills workshop for adults, kids, and families.

Sources: Bridget Finn, "Luring 'Em In, Who Cares About Prices? Bass Pro Shop Hooks Customers with Tuna and Taxidermy," *Business 2.0,* March 2005, pp. 44–45; Bob Carr, "The Outdoor Business Keeps Evolving," *Sporting Goods Business,* September 2004, p. 14.

Dollar General is in one of the fastest growth retail industry segments—extreme value retailing.

Extreme Value Retailers

Extreme value retailers are small, full-line discount stores that offer a limited merchandise assortment at very low prices. The largest extreme value retailers are Dollar General and Family Dollar Stores. Extreme value retailers are one of the fastest growing segments in retailing.[36]

Like limited assortment food retailers, extreme value full-line retailers reduce costs and maintain low prices by offering a limited assortment and operating in low-rent, urban, or rural locations. Many value retailers, particularly Family Dollar and Dollar General, target low-income consumers, whose shopping behavior differs from typical discount store or warehouse club customers. For instance, though these consumers demand well-known national brands, they often can't afford to buy large-size packages. Because this segment of the retail industry is growing rapidly, vendors often create special smaller packages just for them.[37]

Extreme value retailers follow a variety of business models. Dollar Tree, Greenbacks, and 99 Cents Only stores draw from multiple income groups and are generally located in suburban strip malls. They specialize in giftware, party, and craft items rather than consumables. Despite some of these chains' names, few just sell merchandise for a dollar. In fact, the two largest—Family Dollar and Dollar General—don't employ a strict dollar limit. The $1 price is the focus for Dollar General; however, merchandise is sold at other points. Prices at Family Dollar go up to $20. The names imply a *good value* while not limiting the customer to the arbitrary dollar price point.

In the past, extreme value retailers were considered low-status retailers that catered to lower-income consumers. Today, however, higher-income consumers are increasingly patronizing dollar stores for the thrill of the hunt. Some shoppers see extreme value retailers as an opportunity to find some hidden treasure among the bric-a-brac. To capitalize on this attraction for unusual items, many supermarkets and full-line discount stores are adding dollar aisles to their stores.

Off-Price Retailers

Off-price retailers offer an inconsistent assortment of brand name merchandise at low prices. America's largest off-price retail chains are TJX Companies (which operates T.J. Maxx and Marshalls), Ross Stores, and Burlington Coat Factory. Off-price retailers sell brand name and even designer label merchandise at low prices through their unique buying and merchandising practices. Most merchandise is bought opportunistically from manufacturers or other retailers with excess inventory at the end of the season. The merchandise might be in odd sizes or unpopular colors and styles, or it may be irregulars (having minor mistakes in construction). Typically, merchandise is purchased at one-fifth to one-fourth of the original wholesale price. Off-price retailers can buy at low prices because they don't ask suppliers for advertising allowances, return privileges, markdown adjustments, or delayed payments. (Terms and conditions associated with buying merchandise are detailed in Chapter 14.)

Due to this pattern of opportunistic buying, customers can't be confident that the same type of merchandise will be in stock each time they visit the store. Different bargains will be available on each visit. To improve their offerings' consistency, some off-price retailers complement their opportunistically bought merchandise with merchandise purchased at regular wholesale prices. Two special types of off-price retailers are closeout and outlet stores.

Closeout retailers are off-price retailers that sell a broad but inconsistent assortment of general merchandise as well as apparel and soft home goods. The largest closeout chains are Big Lots Inc. (Big Lots, Big Lots furniture, MacFrugal's Bargain Close-Outs, Odd Lots, Odd Lots furniture, and Pic'N Save) and Tuesday Morning. **Outlet stores** are off-price retailers owned by manufacturers or department or specialty store chains. Those owned by manufacturers are frequently referred to as **factory outlets.** Outlet stores are typically found in one of the fastest growing types of malls—the outlet mall, discussed in Chapter 7.

Manufacturers view outlet stores as an opportunity to improve their revenues from irregulars, production overruns, and merchandise returned by retailers. Outlet stores also allow manufacturers some control over where their branded merchandise is sold at discount prices. Retailers with strong brand names such as Saks (Saks Off Fifth) and Brooks Brothers operate outlet stores too. By selling excess merchandise in outlet stores rather than at markdown prices in their primary stores, these department and specialty store chains can maintain an image of offering desirable merchandise at full price.

NONSTORE RETAILERS

In the preceding sections, we examined retailers whose *primary* channel is their stores. In this section, we will discuss types of retailers that operate primarily through nonstore channels. The major nonstore channels are the Internet, catalogs and direct mail, direct selling, television home shopping, and vending machines.

Electronic Retailers

Electronic retailing (also called **e-tailing, online retailing,** and **Internet retailing**) is a retail format in which the retailers communicate with customers and offer products and services for sale over the Internet. Perspectives on electronic retailing have changed dramatically over the last 10 years. In 1998, most retail experts were predicting that a new breed of high-tech, Web-savvy entrepreneurs would dominate the retail industry. Everyone would be doing their shopping over the Internet in the future; stores would close due to lack of traffic, and paper catalogs would become obsolete. The prospects for electronic retailing were so bright that billions of dollars were invested, and lost, in Internet retail entrepreneurial ventures like Webvan, eToys, and Garden.com—companies that no longer appear in the retail landscape.

Even though online retail sales continue to grow much faster than retail sales through stores and catalogs, we now realize the Internet is not a revolutionary new retail format that will replace stores and catalogs. While the Internet continues to provide opportunities for entrepreneurs in the retail industry, it is now primarily used by traditional retailers as a tool to complement their store and catalog offerings, grow their revenues, and provide more value for their customers. In Chapter 3 we discuss how traditional store-based retailers are using the Internet to evolve into multichannel retailers.

Some of the most well-known Internet-based companies associated with retailing, Amazon.com and eBay, are not really retailers. While Amazon does sell merchandise to consumers, a significant portion of its revenues is generated by providing Web site development and fulfillment services for other retailers, ranging from individual consumers selling used books to large, store-based retailers such as Toys "R" Us and Borders. eBay is not directly involved in the transactions between buyers and sellers who participate in the auctions on its Web site. Thus, eBay is more like a mall or shopping center operator providing a place for buyers and sellers to interact with each other.

Most of the retailers that sell merchandise exclusively over the Internet target niche markets—markets that are so small and dispersed that they cannot be economically serviced by stores. For example, Dilmah's (www.dilmahtea.com) sells teas from the plantations in the highlands of Ceylon, Steel of the Night (www.steelofthenight.com) offers a complete line of steel drums, and Zappos (www.zappos.com) sells a very deep selection of shoes in a complete range of sizes and colors.

Catalog and Direct-Mail Retailers

Catalog retailing is a nonstore retail format in which the retail offering is communicated to a customer through a catalog, whereas **direct-mail retailers** communicate with their customers using letters and brochures. Historically, catalog and direct-mail retailing were most successful with rural consumers who lacked ready access to retail stores. With the growth of two-income and single-head-of-household families, however, consumers are finding catalogs to be convenient and a time-saving shopping alternative. Nineteen percent of the U.S. population orders merchandise and/or services by mail.[40] Exhibit 2–9 lists the nation's largest catalog retailers

In 2003, $125 billion of merchandise and services were sold through catalogs, and over 17 billion catalogs were distributed in the United States.[42] The merchandise categories with the greatest catalog sales are apparel, gifts, books, and home décor.[43] The Internet has become a natural extension to most catalogers' selling strategy. Ninety-five percent of catalogers describe themselves as multichannel retailers, with 53 percent defining their companies as catalog/Internet/retail and 42 percent as catalog/Internet.[44]

REFACT

Mail-order catalogs began in 1856 when Orvis began selling fishing gear. In 1872, Aaron Montgomery Ward made an arrangement with the National Grange—America's largest farming organization—to offer 163 items of merchandise under the title "The Original Wholesale Grange Supply House." Ward's catalog was followed by one published by Richard Warren Sears, who in 1886 began a mail-order business selling watches.[41]

EXHIBIT 2–9
Largest Catalog Retailers

	2002 Sales $000	Merchandise Sold
JCPenney	$ 3,349	general merchandise
Sears	1,793	general merchandise
Brylane	1,540	apparel, home
L.L.Bean	1,400	outdoor
Spiegel	1,203	general merchandise
Limited Brands	938	apparel
Cabela's	775	outdoor
Williams-Sonoma	798	home décor
Blair	580	apparel and home
Bear Creek	500	food, gifts

SOURCE: *Statistical Fact Book.* Washington, DC: Direct Marketing Association, 2004, pp. 74–75. Reprinted with the permission of Primedia Business Magazines & Media. Copyright 2004. All rights reserved.

Types of Catalog and Direct-Mail Retailers

Two types of firms selling products through the mail are (1) general merchandise and specialty catalog retailers and (2) direct-mail retailers. **General merchandise catalog retailers** offer a broad variety of merchandise in catalogs that are periodically mailed to their customers. For example, JCPenney distributes a 1,200-page catalog to over 14 million people.[45] In addition to its general merchandise catalog, Penney distributes 70 specialty catalogs each year.

Specialty catalog retailers focus on specific categories of merchandise, such as fruit (Harry and David), gardening tools (Smith & Hawken), and

Specialty-catalog retailers focus on specific categories of merchandise such as fruit (Harry and David), sporting goods (REI and Bass Pro Shops), seeds (Burpee), and home furnishings (Restoration Hardware).

seeds and plants (Burpee). Direct-mail retailers typically mail brochures and pamphlets to sell a specific product or service to customers at one point in time. For example, USAA sells a broad array of financial services targeted to the military community.[46] In addition to their focus on a specific product or service, most direct-mail retailers are primarily interested in making a single sale from a specific mailing, whereas catalog retailers typically maintain relationships with customers over time.

Catalog retailing is very challenging. First, it is difficult for smaller catalog and direct-mail retailers to compete with large, well-established firms with sophisticated CRM and fulfillment systems. Second, the mailing and printing costs are high and increasing. Third, it is difficult to get consumers' attention as they are mailed so many catalogs and direct-mail promotions. Fourth, the length of time required to design, develop, and distribute catalogs makes it difficult for catalog and direct-mail retailers to respond quickly to new trends and fashions.

Direct Selling

Direct selling is a retail format in which salespeople, frequently independent businesspeople, contact customers directly in a convenient location, either at the customer's home or at work; demonstrate merchandise benefits and/or explain a service; take an order; and deliver the merchandise or perform the service. Direct selling is a highly interactive form of retailing in which considerable information is conveyed to customers through face-to-face discussions with salespeople. However, providing this high level of information, including extensive demonstrations, is costly.

Annual U.S. sales for direct selling are over $25 billion and more than $100 billion worldwide. The largest categories of merchandise sold through direct selling are home/family care (e.g., cooking and kitchenware), personal care (e.g., cosmetics and fragrances), services, wellness, and leisure/educational items. Similar to catalog retailers and television shopping networks, direct sellers are using the Internet to complement face-to-face selling. About 70 percent of all direct sales are made face to face, mostly in homes.[47]

Almost all of the 13 million salespeople who work in direct sales are independent agents. They aren't employed by the direct sales firm but act as independent distributors, buying merchandise from the firms and then reselling it to consumers. Over 80 percent of the salespeople work part time (less than 30 hours per week). In most cases, direct salespeople may sell their merchandise to anyone, but some companies, such as Avon, assign territories to salespeople who regularly contact households in their territory.

Two special types of direct selling are the party plan and multilevel selling. About 30 percent of all direct sales are made using a **party plan system,** in which salespeople encourage customers to act as hosts and invite friends or coworkers to a "party" at which the merchandise is demonstrated. Sales made at the party are influenced by the social relationship of the people attending with the host or hostess, who receives a gift or commission for arranging the meeting. A party plan system can be, but does not have to be, used in a multilevel network.

About 80 percent of direct sales are made through multilevel networks. In a **multilevel network,** people serve as master distributors, recruiting other people to become distributors in their network. The master distributors either buy merchandise from the firm and resell it to their distributors or receive a commission on all merchandise purchased by the distributors in their network. In addition to selling merchandise themselves, the master distributors are involved in recruiting and training other distributors.

Some multilevel direct-selling firms are illegal pyramid schemes. A **pyramid scheme** develops when the firm and its program are designed to sell merchandise and services to other distributors rather than to end users. The founders and initial distributors in pyramid schemes profit from the inventory bought by later participants, but little merchandise is sold to consumers who use it.

Television Home Shopping

Television home shopping is a retail format in which customers watch a TV program that demonstrates merchandise and then place orders for the merchandise by telephone. The three forms of electronic home shopping retailing are (1) cable channels dedicated to television shopping, (2) infomercials, and (3) direct-response advertising. **Direct-response advertising** includes advertisements on TV and radio that describe products and provide an opportunity for consumers to order them. **Infomercials** are TV programs, typically 30 minutes long, that mix entertainment with product demonstrations and then solicit orders placed by telephone.

Television home shopping is a $10 billion business in the United States. The two largest home shopping networks are QVC and HSN. Although all Americans with cable television have access to a television shopping channel, relatively few watch on a regular basis. Furthermore, most of the purchases are made by a relatively small proportion of viewers. Like catalogs, TV home shopping networks are embracing the Internet; the major home shopping networks all have Internet operations. Further growth in this shopping venue will depend on how quickly interactive TV becomes available and the degree to which it is adopted by consumers.

The major advantage of TV home shopping compared with catalog retailing is that customers can see the merchandise demonstrated on their TV screen. However, customers can't examine a particular type of merchandise or a specific item when they want to, as they can with catalogs, but instead must wait for the time when the merchandise shows up on the screen. To address this limitation, home shopping networks schedule categories of merchandise for specific times so customers looking for specific merchandise can plan their viewing time. Television home shopping retailers appeal primarily to lower-income consumers. Forty percent of TV home shopping sales are inexpensive jewelry, and other major categories include apparel, cosmetics, kitchenware, and exercise equipment.

Vending Machine Retailing

Vending machine retailing is a nonstore format in which merchandise or services are stored in a machine and dispensed to customers when they deposit cash or use a credit card. Vending machines are placed at convenient, high-traffic locations, such as in the workplace or on university campuses, and primarily contain snacks or drinks.

While $16 billion in goods are sold annually through vending machines in the United States, vending machine sales growth has been declining over the last few years.[49] Due to increasing labor and gasoline costs, vending machine operators are

REFACT

The Greek mathematician Hero invented the first vending machine in 215 BC to vend holy water in Egyptian temples. The first commercial coin-operated vending machines were introduced in London, England, in the early 1880s to dispense post cards.[48]

increasing their prices and retrofitting machines to accept higher denomination bills. However, the price increases are not covering the increases in costs. The vast majority of vending machine sales are cold beverages, candy, and snacks, but sales in these categories are being adversely affected by growing concerns among consumers about healthy eating habits.

Technological developments in vending machine designs may result in long-term sales growth. New video kiosk vending machines enable consumers to see the merchandise in use, get information about it, and use their credit cards to make a purchase. The new vending machine designs also enable retailers to increase the productivity of the machines. Electronic systems in the machine keep track of inventory, cash, and other operating conditions, then radio devices transmit the data back to a host computer. These data are analyzed, and communications are sent to route drivers telling them when stockouts and malfunctions occur. Many vending machine operators, however, do not have the resources to make investments in these new technologies.

There are 5.4 million *jidoohambaiki* (vending machines) in Japan—one machine for every 23 people. Unlike the packaged food and soft drink offerings in the United States, products in Japan range from rice crackers and eyebrow shapers to micro radios and condoms. Some reasons for the prevalence of vending machines in Japan are consumers' interest in gadgets, the large number of people commuting by subway and train rather than by automobile, and the low rate of crime and vandalism in Japan.[50]

Some retailers are experimenting with vending machines as another channel to service their customers. For example, Staples has installed vending machines at Boston's Logan International Airport and a handful of college campuses, hoping to learn whether captive consumers in need of emergency office supplies will pay a premium for computer mice, pens, headphones, batteries, and travel-sized Monopoly games. Staples is just one of many retailers now experimenting with so-called nontraditional vending to sell products at higher prices with lower overhead. The ability of vending machines to accept credit cards is driving the trend, as is the appeal of being able to reach consumers at times when traditional retail stores aren't open.[51]

SERVICES RETAILING

The retail firms discussed in the previous sections sell products to consumers. However, **services retailers**, firms selling primarily services rather than merchandise, are a large and growing part of the retail industry. Consider a typical Saturday. After a bagel and cup of coffee at a nearby Einstein Bros. Bagels, you go to the laundromat to wash and dry your clothes, drop a suit off at a dry cleaner, leave film to be developed at a Walgreens drugstore, and make your way to the Jiffy Lube to have your car's oil changed. Since you are in a hurry, you drive through a Taco Bell so you can eat lunch quickly and not be late for your haircut at 1:00 p.m. By midafternoon, you're ready for a workout at your health club. After stopping at home for a change of clothes, you're off to dinner, a movie, and dancing with a friend. Finally, you end your day with a café latte at Starbucks, having interacted with 10 different services retailers during the day.

Service providers, like this automobile oil change service, are retailers too.

There are several trends that suggest considerable future growth in services retailing. For example, the aging population will increase demand for health care services. Younger people are also spending more time and money on health and fitness. Busy parents in two-income families are willing to pay to have their homes cleaned, lawns maintained, clothes washed and pressed, and meals prepared so they can spend more time with their families.

EXHIBIT 2–10
Services Retailers

Type of Service	Service Retail Firms
Airlines	American, Delta, British Airways, Singapore Airway
Automobile maintenance and repair	Jiffy Lube, Midas, AAMCO
Automobile rental	Hertz, Avis, Budget, Enterprise
Banks	Citibank, NCNB, Bank of America
Child care centers	Kindercare, Gymboree
Credit cards	American Express, VISA, MasterCard
Education	Babson College, University of Florida
Entertainment parks	Disney, Universal Studios, Six Flags
Express package delivery	Federal Express, UPS, U.S. Postal Service
Financial services	Merrill Lynch, Dean Witter
Fitness	Jazzercise, Bally's, Gold's Gym
Health care	Humana, HCA, Kaiser
Home maintenance	Chemlawn, Mini Maid, Roto-Rooter
Hotels and motels	Hyatt, Sheraton, Marriott, Days Inn
Income tax preparation	H&R Block
Insurance	Allstate, State Farm
Internet access/electronic information	America Online
Movie theaters	AMC, Odeon/Cineplex
Real estate	Century 21, Coldwell Banker
Restaurants	TGI Friday's, Wendy's, Pizza Hut
Truck rentals	U-Haul, Ryder
Weight loss	Weight Watchers, Jenny Craig
Video rental	Blockbuster, Hollywood Video
Vision centers	Lenscrafters, Pearle

Exhibit 2–10 shows the wide variety of services retailers, along with the national companies that provide these services. These companies are retailers because they sell goods and services to consumers. However, some are not just retailers. For example, airlines, banks, hotels, and insurance and express mail companies sell their services to businesses as well as consumers. Also, a large number of services retailers, such as lawyers, doctors, and dry cleaners, do not appear in the exhibit because they focus on local markets and do not have a national presence.

Many organizations such as banks, hospitals, health spas, legal clinics, entertainment firms, and universities that offer services to consumers traditionally haven't considered themselves retailers. Due to increased competition, these organizations are adopting retailing principles to attract customers and satisfy their needs. For example, Zoots is a dry cleaning chain in the Boston area. Founded by a former Staples executive, Zoots has adopted many retailing best practices. It has several convenient locations, plus it offers pickup and delivery service. Zoots stores have extended hours, are open on weekends, and offer a drop-off option for those who cannot get to the store during operating hours. The stores are bright and clean. Clerks are taught to always welcome customers and acknowledge their presence if there is a line.[52]

All retailers provide goods and services for their customers. However, the emphasis placed on the merchandise versus the services differs across retail formats, as Exhibit 2–11 shows. On the left side of the exhibit are supermarkets and warehouse clubs. These retail formats consist of self-service stores that offer very few services, except perhaps for displaying merchandise, cashing checks, and assisting customers. Moving along the continuum from left to right, department and specialty stores provide even higher levels of service. In addition to assistance from sales associates, these stores offer services such as gift wrapping,

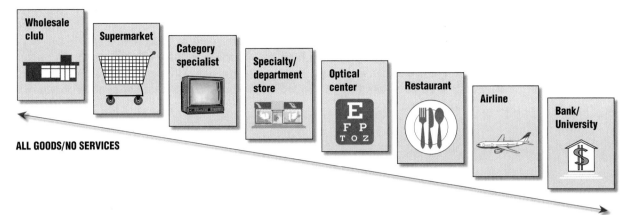

bridal registries, and alterations. Optical centers and restaurants lie somewhere in the middle of the merchandise/service continuum. In addition to selling frames, eyeglasses, and contact lenses, optical centers also provide important services like eye examinations and eyeglasses fittings. Similarly, restaurants offer food plus a place to eat, music in the background, a pleasant ambience, and table service. As we move to the right end of the continuum, we encounter retailers whose offering is primarily services. However, even these retailers have some products associated with the services offered, such as a meal on the airplane or a checkbook at a bank.

Differences between Services and Merchandise Retailers

Four important differences in the nature of the offering provided by services and merchandise retailers are (1) intangibility, (2) simultaneous production and consumption, (3) perishability, and (4) inconsistency of the offering to customers.[53]

Intangibility   Services are generally intangible—customers cannot see, touch, or feel them. They are performances or actions rather than objects. For example, health care services cannot be seen or touched by a patient. Intangibility introduces challenges for services retailers. Since customers can't touch and feel services, it's difficult for them to evaluate services before they buy them or even after they buy and consume them. Due to the intangibility of their offering, services retailers often use tangible symbols to inform customers about the quality of their services. For example, lawyers frequently have elegant, carpeted offices with expensive antique furniture. Services retailers also have difficulty evaluating the quality of services they are providing. For example, it's hard for a law firm to evaluate how well its lawyers are performing their jobs. To evaluate the quality of their offering, services retailers often solicit customer evaluations and complaints.

Simultaneous Production and Consumption   Products are typically made in a factory, stored and sold by a retailer, and then used by consumers in their homes. Service providers, however, create and deliver the service as the customer is consuming it. For example, when you eat at a restaurant, the meal is prepared and consumed almost at the same time. The simultaneity of production and consumption also creates some special problems for services retailers. First, the customers are present when the service is produced, may even have an opportunity to see it produced, and in some cases may be part of the production process, as in making their own salad at a salad bar. Second, other customers consuming the service at the same time can affect the quality of the service provided. For example, an obnoxious passenger next to you on an airplane can make the flight very unpleasant. Third, the services retailer often does not get a second chance to satisfy the needs of its customers. Whereas customers can return damaged merchandise to a store, customers that are dissatisfied with services have limited recourse. Thus, it is critical for services retailers to get it right the first time.

Because services are produced and consumed at the same time, it is difficult to reduce costs through mass production. For this reason, most services retailers are small, local firms. Large national retailers are able to reduce costs by "industrializing" the services they offer. They make substantial investments in equipment and training to provide a uniform service. For example, McDonald's has a detailed procedure for cooking French fries and hamburgers to make sure they come out the same whether cooked in Paris, France, or Paris, Illinois.

Perishability   Because the creation and consumption of services are inseparable, services are perishable. They can't be saved, stored, or resold. Once an airplane takes off with an empty seat, the sale is lost forever. This is in contrast to merchandise that can be held in inventory until a customer is ready to buy it. Due to the perishability of services, an important aspect of services retailing is matching supply and demand. Most services retailers have a capacity constraint, and the capacity cannot be changed easily. There are a fixed number of tables in a restaurant, seats in a classroom, beds in a hospital, and electricity that can be generated by a power plant. To increase capacity, services retailers need to make major investments such as buying more airplanes or building an addition to increase the size of the hospital or restaurant. In addition, demand for service varies considerably over time. Consumers are most likely to fly on airplanes during holidays and the summer, eat in restaurants at lunch and dinner time, and use electricity in the evening rather than earlier in the day.

Thus, services retailers often have times when their services are underutilized and other times when they have to turn customers away because they can't accommodate them. Services retailers use a variety of programs to match demand and supply. For example, airlines and hotels set lower prices on weekends when they have excessive capacity because businesspeople aren't traveling. To achieve more capacity flexibility, health clinics stay open longer during flu season, and tax preparation services are open on weekends during March and April. Restaurants increase staffing on weekends, may not open until dinner time, and use a reservation system to guarantee service delivery at a specific time. Finally, services retailers attempt to make customers' waiting time more enjoyable. For example, videos and park employees entertain customers while they wait in line at Disney theme parks.

Inconsistency   Products can be produced by machines with very tight quality control so customers are reasonably assured that all boxes of Cheerios will be identical. Because services are performances produced by people (employees and customers), no two services will be identical. For example, tax accountants can have different knowledge and skills for preparing tax returns. The waiter at the Olive Garden can be in a bad mood and make your dining experience a disaster. Thus, an important challenge for services retailers is providing consistently high-quality services. Many factors that determine service quality are beyond the control of the retailers; however, services retailers expend considerable time and effort selecting, training, managing, and motivating their service providers.

This Chinese restaurant adjusts its capacity by having more waiters during lunch and dinner time, but fewer waiters at other times during the day.

TYPES OF OWNERSHIP

Previous sections of this chapter discussed how retailers are classified in terms of their retail mix and the merchandise and services they sell. Another way to classify retailers is by their ownership. The major classifications of retail ownership are (1) independent, single-store establishments, (2) corporate chains, and (3) franchises.

Independent, Single-Store Establishments

Retailing is one of the few sectors in our economy in which entrepreneurial activity is extensive. Over 100,000 new retail businesses are started in the United States each year. Many of these retail start-ups are owner managed, which means management has direct contact with customers and can respond quickly to their needs. Small retailers are also very flexible and can therefore react quickly to market changes and customer needs. They aren't bound by the bureaucracies inherent in large retail organizations.

Whereas single-store retailers can tailor their offerings to their customers' needs, corporate chains can more effectively negotiate lower prices for merchandise and advertising due to their larger size. In addition, corporate chains have a broader management base, with people who specialize in specific retail activities. Single-store retailers typically have to rely on their owner–managers' capabilities to make the broad range of necessary retail decisions. Retailing View 2.5 describes how a small, independently owned drug store competes in a sector dominated by giants.

To better compete against corporate chains, some independent retailers join a **wholesale-sponsored voluntary cooperative group,** which is an organization operated by a wholesaler offering a merchandising program to small, independent retailers on a voluntary basis. Independent Grocers Alliance (IGA), Tru Serv (supplier to True Value Hardware), and Ace Hardware are wholesale-sponsored voluntary cooperative groups. In addition to buying, warehousing, and distribution, these groups offer members services such as advice on store design and layout, site selection, bookkeeping and inventory management systems, and employee training programs.

Corporate Retail Chains

A **retail chain** is a company that operates multiple retail units under common ownership and usually has centralized decision making for defining and implementing its strategy. Retail chains can range in size from a drugstore with two stores to retailers with over 1,000 stores, such as Safeway, Wal-Mart, Target, and JCPenney. Some retail chains are divisions of larger corporations or holding companies. For example, Limited Brands owns The Limited, Express, Victoria's Secret, Bath & Body Works, The White Barn Candle Co., and Henri Bendel. The Gap owns Old Navy, Baby Gap, GapKids, and Banana Republic.

Franchising

Franchising is a contractual agreement between a franchisor and a franchisee that allows the franchisee to operate a retail outlet using a name and format developed and supported by the franchisor. Approximately one-third of all U.S. retail sales

---

2.5   RETAILING VIEW   Elephant Pharmacy Takes On the National Chains

Stuart Skorman recognizes the benefits his New Age outlook has for Elephant Pharmacy, a 10,000 square foot store that blends a traditional prescription pharmacy with herbal remedies and other alternative medicines, health-related books, upscale beauty products, organic foods, and flowers. Although CVS and Walgreens drugstores are popping up around his store, he remains relaxed knowing he has "...really invented a whole new model."

The first Elephant Pharmacy opened in 2002 in Berkeley, California, and is showing rapid growth with an expected $11 million in sales this year. Critics wonder if Skorman and Elephant Pharmacy will be able to sell homeopathic medicine to the masses, but he sees the health-conscious, affluent slice of the population as willing to pay higher prices for better quality, selection, and theater in the aisles.

Skorman is no newbie to the dog-eat-dog world of retailing. After two years, he dropped out of college to manage a blues band, travel, and drive a cab. In 1977, he signed on as a marketing manager with Bread & Circus, an upscale natural foods grocery store that was eventually sold to Whole Foods. He then put his entire inheritance of $100,000 into a video business that he ultimately sold to Blockbuster for $6 million. Skorman then decided to start up Reel.com, which he sold to Hollywood Video for $100 million. The investments from his last venture went into Elephant Pharmacy.

Elephant Pharmacy offers a reading room with over 2,500 book titles, as well as classes on-site each month in subjects ranging from infant massage and communication to Ayurvedic bliss therapy. Aging, affluent Baby Boomers are welcoming the relief that Skorman offers them. Megadoses of sea kelp and Siberian ginseng to forestall illness are only a few of the odd products that keep the customers coming back more frequently than customers at national chains.

Three-quarters of Elephant's business comes from higher-margin, nonprescription business in areas such as gifts, videos, and health and beauty aids, unlike the typical drugstore that generates as much as 75 percent of its revenue from prescriptions only to end up with gross margins less than 20 percent. Skorman keeps himself ahead of mass retailers in other ways as well. His 80 employees include herbalists and degree-holding specialists in Chinese medicine and homeopathy. Flowers are sold under an outside awning, and the food section offers organic produce and

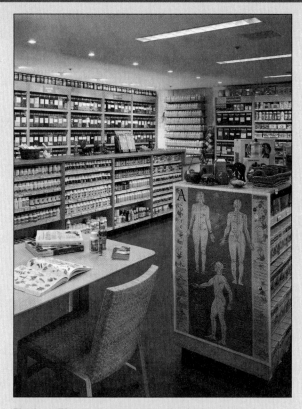

Elephant Pharmacy competes effectively against the national drug store chains by offering a unique assortment of homeopathic remedies.

dairy products. With all that said, Elephant Pharmacy boasts a whopping storewide gross margin of around 40 percent, though the industry average is below 30 percent. Based on the success of Elephant's concept, Saks Fifth Avenue is opening 1,000 square foot Elephant boutiques in 10 of its stores.

Sources: Michael Johnsen, "Elephant Finds Upscale Partner in Saks," *Drug Store News,* October 25, 2004, pp. 3–4; Ed Welles, "Can California Startup Elephant Pharmacy Really Compete with the Drugstore Chains by Selling Herbs, Potions, Supplements—And Even a Few Prescriptions?" *Fortune,* September 1, 2004, p. 61.

Food Retailers	Services Retailers
Arby's	AAMCO
Baskin Robbins	Coldwell Banker
Ben & Jerry's	Century 21
Denny's	Curves
Domino's Pizza	Days Inn
Dunkin' Donuts	Hampton Inn
KFC	InterContinental hotels
McDonald's	Jackson Hewitt Tax Service
Panera Bread	Jazzercise
7-Eleven	Jani-King
Subway	Jiffy Lube
Taco Bell	Lawn Doctor
Merchandise Retailers	Midas
Culligan	Payless Car Rental
GNC	RE/MAX
Matco Tools	Rent-a-Wreck
Merle Norman	UPS stores
Pearle Vision	
Sign-A-Rama	

EXHIBIT 2–12
Retailers Using Franchise
Business Model

are made by franchisees. Exhibit 2–12 lists some retailers governed by franchise agreements.

In a franchise contract, the franchisee pays a lump sum plus a royalty on all sales for the right to operate a store in a specific location. The franchisee also agrees to operate the outlet in accordance with procedures prescribed by the franchisor. The franchisor provides assistance in locating and building the store, developing the products or services sold, training managers, and advertising. To maintain each franchisee's reputation, the franchisor also makes sure that all outlets provide the same quality of services and products.

The franchise ownership format attempts to combine the advantages of owner-managed businesses with the efficiencies of centralized decision making of chain store operations. Franchisees are motivated to make their store successful because they receive the profits (after the royalty is paid). The franchisor is motivated to develop new products and systems and to promote the franchise because it receives a royalty on all sales. Advertising, product development, and system development are efficiently done by the franchisor, with costs shared by all franchisees.

SUMMARY

This chapter has explained different types of retailers and how they compete with different retail mixes to sell merchandise and services to customers. To collect statistics about retailing, the federal government classifies retailers by the type of merchandise and services sold. But this classification method may not be useful in determining a retailer's major competitors. A more useful approach for understanding the retail marketplace is classifying retailers on the basis of their retail mix, merchandise variety and assortment, services, location, pricing, and promotion decisions made to attract customers.

Over the past 30 years, U.S. retail markets have been characterized by the emergence of many new retail institutions. Traditional institutions (supermarkets, convenience, department, discount, and specialty stores) have been joined by category specialists, superstores, hypermarkets, convenience stores, warehouse clubs, off-price retailers, catalogers, and nonstore retailers. In addition, there has been substantial growth in services retailing.

The inherent differences between services and merchandise result in services retailers emphasizing store management while merchandise retailers emphasize inventory control issues. Traditional retail institutions have changed in response to these new retailers. For example, department stores have increased their emphasis on fashion-oriented apparel and improved the services they offer. Supermarkets are focusing more attention on meal solutions and perishables.

KEY TERMS

assortment, *35*

breadth of merchandise, *35*

catalog retailing, *54*

category killers, *50*

category specialist, *50*

closeout retailer, *53*

convenience store, *44*

conventional supermarket, *40*

department store, *45*

depth of merchandise, *35*

direct-mail retailer, *54*

direct-response advertising, *56*

direct selling, *55*

drugstore, *49*

efficient customer response, *41*

electronic retailing, *53*

e-tailing, *53*

extreme value food retailers, *40*

extreme value retailers, *52*

factory outlet, *53*

franchising, *62*

full-line discount store, *48*

general merchandise catalog
  retailer, *55*

home improvement center, *50*

hypermarket, *43*

infomercial, *56*

Internet retailing, *53*

limited assortment
  supermarket, *40*

multilevel network, *56*

NAICS (North American Industry
  Classification System), *34*

off-price retailer, *52*

online retailing, *53*

outlet store, *53*

party plan system, *55*

power perimeter, *41*

pyramid scheme, *56*

retail chain, *62*

services retailer, *57*

SKU (stockkeeping unit), *35*

specialty catalog retailer, *55*

specialty store, *48*

supercenter, *43*

television home shopping, *56*

variety, *35*

vending machine retailing, *56*

warehouse club, *43*

wholesale-sponsored voluntary
  cooperative group, *61*

GET OUT AND DO IT!

1. **CONTINUING CASE ASSIGNMENT: GO SHOPPING** The Comparison Shopping Exercise in Appendix 2A gives you the opportunity to see a retail store through the eyes of a retailer instead of a consumer. The objective of this assignment is to have you take the retailer's perspective and think about the different strategies that the retailer you selected and another retailer might have, as well as how these strategies result in different retail mixes. The assignment is to conduct a comparison of the retail offering for a specific merchandise category, such as camcorders, men's suits, country/western CDs, women's athletic shoes, or house paint, for two different retailers. The other retailer selected might be a direct competitor using the same format or a retailer selling similar merchandise with a different format.

   Your comparison should include the following:

   • The strategy pursued by the two retailers—each retailer's target market and general approach toward satisfying the needs of that target market.

   • The retail mixes (store location, merchandise, pricing, advertising and promotion, location of merchandise category in store, store design, customer service) used by each of the retailers.

   • With respect to the merchandise category, a detailed comparison of the variety and depth of assortment. In comparing the merchandise offering, use the table and questions in Appendix 2A.

   To prepare this comparison, you need to visit the stores, observe the retail mixes in the stores, and play the role of a customer to observe the service.

2. **GO SHOPPING** Go to an athletic footwear specialty store such as Foot Locker, a department store, and a discount store. Analyze their variety and assortment of athletic footwear by creating a table similar to that in Exhibit 2–2.

3. **GO SHOPPING** Keep a diary of where you shop, what you buy, and how much you spend for two weeks. Get your parents to do the same thing. Tabulate your results by type of retailer. Are your shopping habits significantly different from those of your parents? Do your and your parents' shopping habits coincide with the trends discussed in this chapter? Why or why not?

4. **INTERNET EXERCISE** Data on U.S. retail sales are available from the U.S. Bureau of the Census Internet site at www.census.gov/mrts/www/mrts.html. Look at the unadjusted monthly sales by NAICS. Which categories of retailers have the largest percentage of sales in the fourth quarter (the holiday season)?

5. **INTERNET EXERCISE** Four large associations of retailers are the National Retail Federation (www.nrf.com), the Food Marketing Institute (www.fmi.org), the National Association of Chain Drug Stores (www.nacds.org), and the National Association of Convenience Stores (www.nacsonline.com). Visit these sites and report on the latest retail developments and issues confronting the industry.

6. **INTERNET EXERCISE** Go to *Entrepreneur Magazine*'s Franchise Zone Web page at http://www.entrepreneur.com/franchise500 and view the top 500 franchises for the past year. How many of the retailers in the top ten have you patronized as a customer? Did you know that they were operated as a franchise? Look at the lists from previous years to see changes in the rankings. Click on the link "About the Franchise 500" and describe what factors were used to develop the list. Finally, what is the nature of the businesses that seem to lend themselves to franchising?

DISCUSSION QUESTIONS AND PROBLEMS

1. Distinguish between variety and assortment. Why are these important elements of the retail market structure?

2. How can small, independent retailers compete against large national chains?

3. What do off-price retailers need to do to compete against other formats in the future?

4. Compare and contrast the retail mixes of convenience stores, traditional supermarkets, supercenters, and warehouse stores. Can all of these food retail institutions survive over the long run? How? Why?

5. Why are retailers in the limited assortment supermarket and extreme value discount store sectors growing so rapidly?

6. The same brand and model of a personal computer is sold by specialty computer stores, discount stores, category specialists, and warehouse stores. Why would a customer choose one store over the others?

7. Choose a product category that both you and your parents purchase (e.g., clothing, CDs, electronic equipment). In which type of store do you typically purchase this merchandise? What about your parents? Explain why there is, or is not, a difference in your store choices.

8. At many optical stores, you can get your eyes checked *and* purchase glasses or contact lenses. How is the shopping experience different for the service as compared to the product? Design a strategy designed to get customers to purchase both the service and the product. In so doing, delineate specific actions that should be taken to acquire and retain optical customers.

9. Which of the store-based retail formats discussed in this chapter is most vulnerable to competition from Internet retailers? Why? Which is least vulnerable? Why?

10. Many experts believe that customer service is one of retailing's most important issues. How can retailers that emphasize price (such as discount stores, category specialists, and off-price retailers) improve customer service without increasing costs and, thus, prices?

SUGGESTED READINGS

Bond, Ronald L. *Retail in Detail: How to Start and Manage a Small Retail Business.* 2nd ed. PSI Research/The Oasis Press, 2001.

Dant, Rajiv, and Patrick Kaufman. "Structural and Strategic Dynamics in Franchising," *Journal of Retailing* 79, no. 2 (2003), pp. 63–76.

Goldman, Arieh; S. Ramaswami; and Robert Krider. "Barriers to the Advancement of Modern Food Retail Formats: Theory and Measurement," *Journal of Retailing* 78 (Winter 2002), pp. 281–297.

Granger, Michele, and Tina Sterling. *Fashion Entrepreneurship.* New York: Fairchild, 2003.

Howe, Stuart (ed). *Retailing in the European Union.* New York: Routledge, 2003.

Quinn, Bill. *Specialty Stores: Marketing Triumphs and Blunders.* Westport, CT: Quorum Books, 2001.

Schroeder, Carol. *Specialty Shop Retailing: How to Run Your Own Store.* New York: Wiley, 2002.

Spector, Robert. *Category Killers: The Retail Revolution and its Impact on Consumer Culture.* Boston: Harvard Business School, 2005.

"Top 100 Retailers," *Stores,* August 2005.

APPENDIX 2A   Comparison Shopping

All retailers learn about their competitors through comparison shopping. Comparison shopping might be as informal as walking through a competitor's store and looking around, but a structured analysis is more helpful in developing a retail offering that will attract consumers from a competitor's store.

The first step in the process is to define the scope of the comparison. For example, the comparison might be between two retail chains, two specific stores, two departments, or two categories of merchandise. The appropriate scope depends on the responsibilities of the person undertaking the comparison. For example, CEOs of retail chains would be interested in comparing their chain with a competitor's. Such comparisons might focus on the chains' financial resources, inventory levels, number of stores and employees, store locations, merchandise sold, employee compensation programs, and return policies. Thus, CEOs would examine factors for which the corporate office is responsible. In contrast, store managers would be interested in comparing their store with a competing store. For example, department store managers would want to know more about other department stores anchoring the mall in which they're located. Buyers and department managers would focus on specific areas of merchandise for which they're responsible.

Exhibit 2–13 lists questions to consider when comparison shopping. Exhibit 2–14 suggests a format for comparing merchandise, in this case lugsole shoes in JCPenney and a men's shoe store.

EXHIBIT 2–13
Example of Issues to
Address in Comparison
Shopping

Merchandise Presentation

1. How is the selling floor laid out? What selling areas are devoted to specific types of merchandise? How many square feet are devoted to each area?

2. Where are the different selling areas located? Are they in heavy traffic areas? By restrooms? On the main aisle? On a secondary aisle? How does this location affect sales volume for merchandise in the area?

3. What kind of fixtures are used in each selling area (faceouts, rounders, cubes, bunkers, tables, gondolas)?

4. Are aisles, walls, and columns used to display merchandise?

5. What is the lighting for sales areas (focus, overhead, bright, toned down)? How is the merchandise organized in the selling areas (by type, price point, vendor, style, color)?

7. Evaluate the housekeeping of the selling areas. Are they cluttered or messy? Are they well maintained and organized?

8. What's the overall atmosphere or image of the selling areas? What effect does the lighting, fixturing, spacing, and visual merchandising have on customers?

9. What type of customer (age, income, fashion orientation) would be attracted to the store and each selling area within it?

Sales Support/Customer Services

1. How many salespeople are in each department? Is the department adequately staffed?

2. How are salespeople dressed? Do they have an appropriate appearance?

3. Do salespeople approach customers promptly? How soon after entering a selling area is a customer greeted? How do customers respond to the level of service?

4. Evaluate salespeople's product knowledge.

5. Do salespeople suggest add-on merchandise?

6. Where, if applicable, are fitting rooms in relation to the selling floor? In what condition are they? Are they supervised? Are there enough fitting rooms to meet demand?

7. How many registers are on the selling floor? Are they well staffed and well stocked with supplies?

8. What services (credit card acceptance, gift wrapping, delivery, special ordering, bridal registry, alterations, other) does the store offer?

9. What level of customer service is provided in the selling area?

Merchandise (Each Category)

1. Who are the key vendors?

2. How deep are the assortments for each vendor?

3. What are the private labels and how important are they?

4. What are the low, average, and top prices for merchandise in the category?

Summary and Conclusions

1. Who is the store's target customer?

2. What are the competitor's strengths and weaknesses?

3. How can we capture more business from the competitor?

Format for Merchandise Comparison   **EXHIBIT 2–14**

Retailer	Factors	Lug sole casual shoes			Comments
JC Penney	Style	3 eyelet oxford			
	Brands	St. Johns Bay (private)			
	Price	$35			
	% mix	5%			
	SKUs	36 pair			
Father/Son Shoes	Style	3 eyelet oxford	Tie suede	Chakka suede	
	Brands	British Knights Private	Private	Private	
	Price	$38.99–39.99	$29.99	$37.95	
	% mix	10%	5%	5%	
	SKUs	24 pairs	36 pairs	12 pairs	
Harwyns	Style	2 eyelet oxford	Tie suede		
	Brands	British Knights	Private		
	Price	$39.99	$29.95		
	% mix	5%	5%		
	SKUs	36 pairs	36 pairs		

Style For clothing, style might be the fabric or cut. For example, sweater styles might be split into wool, cotton, or polyblend and V-neck, crewneck, or cardigan.

Brands The identifying label. Indicate whether or not the brand is a national brand or store brand.

Price The price marked on the merchandise. If the item has been marked down, indicate the original price and the marked-down price.

Percent mix The percentage of the total assortment devoted to this style of merchandise.

SKUs The number of different items in this subcategory.

Multichannel Retailing

My career path is a bit unusual. After graduating from the U.S. Military Academy and serving a number of years in the U.S. Army, I earned an MBA from Harvard Business School and went to work as a consultant for McKinsey. After awhile, I realized that I wanted to be in a position of developing and implementing strategies, rather than just analyzing situations and making recommendations. Through my consulting experience, I recognized that retailing offered exciting challenges and opportunities. Over the past twenty years, I have had senior management positions at May Department Stores, Home Shopping Network, Payless Shoes, and now JCPenney.

More and more we find that consumers want the convenience of shopping through different channels. Sometimes they want to go to our stores, see the merchandise before buying it, and get it immediately. Other times they

EXECUTIVE BRIEFING
Ken Hicks, President and Chief Merchandising Officer, JCPenney

find the 7/24 access and deep assortment at our Web site and catalogs appealing.

JCPenney is ideally positioned to provide a multichannel offering for our customers. We have over 1,000 stores and distribute over 380 million catalogs a year. We have been operating a catalog business for over fifty years and thus we have a very efficient fulfillment system and distribution centers to also support our Internet channel.

We work at coordinating the operations and merchandise assortments of the three channels so customers see a seamless interface. Using our POS terminals, sales associates can order merchandise for customers from our Web site. For example, we stock 20 colors of bath towels in the store, but offer 32 colors at our Web site. If a customer doesn't find the color she wants in the store, a sales associate will order the towels from the Web site and have it delivered to her home, or she can pick it up at the store.

Coordinating the merchandise assortments is challenging because the channels appeal to different customers and the merchandise they buy differs. Our catalog cus-

What are the unique customer benefits offered by the three retail channels: stores, catalogs, and the Internet?

Why are retailers moving toward using all three channels?

How do multichannel retailers provide more value to their customers?

What are the key success factors in multichannel retailing?

How might technology affect the future shopping experience?

Even though sales over the Internet are growing at more than 25 percent per year, more than five times faster than store or catalog sales, Internet sales are expected to represent only 6 percent of total retail sales by 2008.[1] However, the Internet has and will continue to have a substantial influence on consumer store choice and purchase decisions. For example, more than 40 percent of U.S. consumers review information on Web sites before buying automobiles, consumer electronics, or books. The Internet has become a place to shop as well as buy.

In this chapter, we take a strategic perspective in our discussion of three different channels—stores, catalogs, and the Internet—through which retailers can communicate with and sell merchandise and services to their customers. Then we look at how retailers can increase revenues and improve their customers' shopping experience by using all of these channels to interact with their customers. At the end of the chapter, we illustrate how integrating these channels and using new technologies will create a compelling shopping experience in the future.

In other chapters, we examine how retailers use the Internet in specific applications, including managing employees, buying merchandise, managing customer relationships, advertising and promoting merchandise, and providing customer service.

tomers tend to be older, while Internet customers are younger. Hard goods and toys sell better through non-store channels than in the stores, but apparel sells better in stores. In addition, the channels have different planning cycles—the merchandise and prices in the catalog are set for six months, but changes to our Internet offering can be made instantaneously.

Retailing is a high-tech, high-touch growth industry that offers opportunities for people to make profit and loss decisions early in their careers. There are opportunities in store management for those who like working with people, while the buying organization provides jobs appealing to the more analytical people.

RETAIL CHANNELS FOR INTERACTING WITH CUSTOMERS

Chapter 2 categorized retailers by their offering—food, general merchandise, or services—and then by the channel they used to reach their customers, whether store- or nonstore-based (electronic, catalog/direct mail, direct selling, TV home shopping, vending machine). However, most retail firms are now using more than one channel to reach their customers. For example, almost all large store-based and catalog retailers, such as JCPenney, sell merchandise from their Web sites as well as in their stores. Two of the most successful electronic retail-

---

3.1   RETAILING VIEW   Recreational Equipment Inc. (REI)—A Leader in Multichannel Retailing

In 1938, mountain climbers Lloyd and Mary Anderson joined with 21 fellow northwestern climbers to found Recreational Equipment Inc. (REI) so that high-quality, European ice axes and climbing equipment could be purchased locally. REI develops its own outdoor gear and apparel in addition to selling national brands. Products are evaluated in one of the industry's most complete quality assurance labs and tested extensively in the most important laboratory of them all: the outdoors. REI's product quality assurance team is made up of avid outdoor people who test products in all types of conditions.

The company, based in Kent, Washington, is a 77-store category specialist in

Customers at REI get to enjoy the excitement of rock climbing and trying the equipment when visiting the store. This experience cannot be duplicated with their other retail channels.

outdoor gear and clothing. Its stores provide an exciting place for outdoor enthusiasts to shop. For example, the Seattle flagship store has a 65 foot high, freestanding climbing rock; mountain bike trails; camp stove demonstration tables; and "rain rooms" so customers can test all their equipment before buying it. REI also sells merchandise domestically and internationally through catalogs and its three Web sites (www.rei.com, www.rei-outlet.com, and www.japan.rei.com). The company also operates REI Adventures, a full-service travel agency for outdoor adventures.

REI was a pioneer in electronic retailing when, in 1996, it started selling merchandise over the Internet. The Internet offered a way for REI to "deliver any product, any time, any place, and answer any question."

- *Any product:* a larger selection on the Internet.
- *Any time:* 24 hours/seven days a week.
- *Any place:* Internet/stores/catalog, domestic and international.
- *Any question:* rich product information on the Web.

By using all three channels synergistically, REI increases its sales to customers. For example, 35 percent of the products bought over the Internet are picked up in stores. When

customers come to pick up their orders, one-third of them spend more than $90 buying additional merchandise.

REI brings the Internet into its stores by linking its point-of-sale (POS) terminals to the Internet. Through the connection, cashiers gain Internet access and additional product-search functionality. Since the in-store kiosks are linked to the Internet, even its smallest stores are able to offer the company's full assortment.

REI also uses its Web site to build loyalty by creating a community of outdoor enthusiasts who, through dozens of message boards, exchange stories about their adventures, seek guidance on products, and post snapshots of their travels. The site also includes primers written by expert users, covering topics such as how to choose gear and what to do "If You Become Lost." When REI opened its first overseas store in Tokyo, the company already had 80,000 Japanese customers, thanks to its decade-old catalog operation and a year-old Japanese Web site (www.rei.co.jp).

Sources: www.rei.com; Laurie Sullivan, "E-Commerce: Promise Fulfilled," *Information Week*, November 8, 2004, pp. 70–73; Megan Santosus, "How REI Scaled E-Commerce Mountain," *CIO*, May 15, 2004, pp. 1–3.

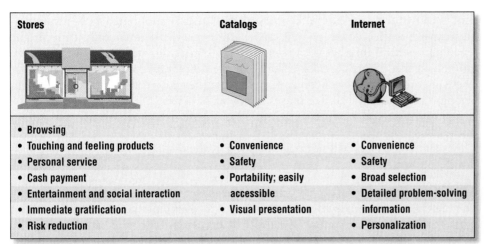

ers, Travelocity.com and Expedia, are opening stores to complement their Internet offerings of travel services.[2] Thus, most retailers are evolving from focusing on a single channel to becoming multichannel retailers.

Multichannel retailers are those retailers that sell merchandise or services through more than one channel. By using a combination of channels, retailers can leverage the unique benefits provided by each to attract and satisfy more customers. Retailing View 3.1 illustrates how REI, a chain that sells outdoor equipment and apparel, uses all three channels to interact with its customers. In addition, Exhibit 3–1 lists the unique benefits of stores, catalogs, and the Internet to illustrate how the channels can be used to complement one another.

Store Channel

Stores offer a number of benefits to customers that they cannot get when shopping through catalogs or on the Internet.

Browsing Shoppers often have only a general sense of what they want (e.g., a sweater, something for dinner, a gift) but don't know the specific item they want. They go to a store to see what is available before they decide what to buy. While many consumers surf the Internet and look through catalogs for ideas, most consumers still prefer browsing in stores.

Touching and Feeling Products Perhaps the greatest benefit offered by stores is the opportunity for customers to use all five of their senses—touching, smelling, tasting, seeing, and hearing—when examining products. Although new technologies can provide 3D representations on a CRT screen, these visual improvements do not provide the same level of information you get when actually trying on a swimsuit or smelling the fragrance of a candle.

Personal Service Although shoppers might be critical of the personal service they get in stores, sales associates still have the capability of providing meaningful, personalized information. They can tell you if a suit looks good on you, suggest a tie to go with a dress shirt, or answer questions you might have about what is appropriate to wear at a business-casual event. Customers for durable goods such as appliances report that salespeople are the most useful information source, more useful than *Consumer Reports*, advertising, or friends.[4]

Cash Payment Stores are the only channel that accept cash payments. Many customers prefer to pay with cash because it is easy, resolves the transaction immediately, and does not result in potential interest payments.

Entertainment and Social Experience   In-store shopping can be a stimulating experience for some people, providing a break in their daily routine and enabling them to interact with friends. Paco Underhill, author of *How We Shop*, points out that "Stores are a social experience. I don't care how many chat rooms there are on a site, they will never provide what the experience of brick-and-mortar shopping provides for all five senses, if not six or seven."[6]

All nonstore retail formats are limited in the degree to which they can satisfy these entertainment and social needs. Even the most attractive and inventive Web pages and video clips will not be as exciting as the displays and activities in a Bass Pro Shop or REI store.

Immediate Gratification   Stores have the advantage of allowing customers to get the merchandise immediately after they buy it. If your child has a fever, you are not going to wait a day or two for the delivery of a prescription from Drugstore.com.

Risk Reduction   When customers purchase merchandise in stores, the physical presence of the store assures them that any problems with the merchandise will be corrected. The store will be there to receive defective or unsuitable merchandise and issue you a credit for it. Consumers do not have this same level of confidence when buying merchandise from catalogs or through the Internet.

Catalog Channel

The catalog channel provides some benefits to customers that are not available from the store or Internet channels.

Convenience   Catalogs, like all nonstore formats, offer the convenience of looking at merchandise and placing an order on any day at any time from almost anywhere. With a catalog, consumers have the added convenience of not being restricted to a place with Internet access and a computer; they can look through a catalog on the beach or propped up in bed. Finally, the information in a catalog is easily accessible for a long period of time. Consumers can refer to the information in a catalog anytime by simply picking it up from the coffee table. The development of **"magalogs,"** catalogs with magazine-type editorial content, enhances consumers' desire to keep catalogs readily available.

Safety   Security in malls and shopping areas is becoming an important concern for many shoppers, particularly the elderly. Nonstore retail formats have an advantage over store-based retailers in that they enable customers to review merchandise and place orders from a safe environment—their homes.

In some situations, catalogs are much more convenient than shopping in stores or over the Internet.

Quality of Visual Presentation   The photographs of merchandise in catalogs, while not as useful as in-store presentations, are superior to the visual information that can be displayed on a CRT screen.

REFACT

E-commerce was born on August 11, 1994, when a CD by Sting was sold by Net-Market over the Internet.[7]

Internet Channel

Shopping over the Internet provides the convenience and safety benefits offered by catalogs and other nonstore formats. However, the Internet, compared with store and catalog channels, also has the potential to offer a greater selection of products and more personalized information about products and services.

Broader Selection   One benefit of the Internet channel, compared with the other two channels, is the vast number of alternatives available to consumers. By shopping on the Internet, consumers can easily "visit" and select merchandise from a broader array of retailers. People living in Columbus, Ohio, can shop electronically at Harrod's in London in less time than it takes them to visit their local supermarket.

Retail Web sites typically offer deeper assortments of merchandise (more colors, brands, and sizes) than are available in stores.

More Information to Evaluate Merchandise   An important service offered by retailers is the provision of information to help customers make better purchase decisions. The retail channels differ in terms of how much information they provide and whether customers can format the information to compare different brands easily. For instance, some catalogs provide only a few facts about each item, such as price, weight, and brand/model, along with a photograph. Other catalogs offer much more detail about each item carried. For many clothing items, Lands' End not only provides color pictures but often gives extensive information about the construction process, stitching, and materials.

Stores also differ in the information they make available to consumers. Specialty and department stores typically have trained, knowledgeable sales associates, whereas most discount stores do not. However, the personal knowledge of sales associates is often limited. The space available in self-service stores and catalogs to provide information is constrained by the size of a printed page, a sign, or a package on a shelf.

Using an Internet channel, retailers have the capability to provide as much information as each customer wants and more information than they can get through store or catalog channels.[9] Customers shopping electronically can drill down through Web pages until they have enough information to make a purchase decision. Unlike in catalogs, the information on an electronic channel database can be frequently updated and will always be available—24/7, 365 days per year. Furthermore, retaining knowledgeable sales associates is difficult and, in many cases, not cost effective. The cost of adding information to an Internet channel is likely to be far less than the cost of continually training thousands of sales associates.

In addition, when using the Internet channel, customers can format the information so that they can effectively use it when evaluating products. Exhibit 3–2 illustrates how Circuit City provides information in a side-by-side comparison

REFACT

In the U.S., visits to shopping Web sites accounted for almost 10 percent of all Internet visits.[8]

EXHIBIT 3–2
Side-By-Side Comparison Offered by the Internet Channel

	Apple® 4GB iPod® mini (M9800LL/A)	Apple® 1GB iPod® shuffle (M9725LL/A)	Apple® 4GB iPod® mini (M9806LL/A)
Price	$199.99 add to cart	$149.99 add to cart	$199.99 add to cart
Availability	Availability ✓ Shipping ✓ Pick up in most stores	Availability ✓ Shipping ✓ Pick up in most stores	Availability ✓ Shipping ✓ Pick up in most stores
Customer rating	4.6	4.6	4.4
Memory			
Built-in memory	4GB	1GB	4GB
Maximum memory	4GB	1GB	4GB
Expandable memory	No	No	No
Memory media/type	Hard Drive	Internal Flash Memory	Hard Drive
Storage capacity	1,000 songs in 128-Kbps AAC format	240 songs in 128-Kbps AAC format	1,000 songs in 128-Kbps AAC format
Note:	MB = megabytes, GB = gigabytes; actual formatted capacity may vary.	MB = megabytes, GB = gigabytes; actual formatted capacity may vary.	MB = megabytes, GB = gigabytes; actual formatted capacity may vary.
File formats supported			
WMA	No	No	No
WAV	Yes	Yes	Yes
OGG	No	No	No
Radio			
Digital tuner	No	No	No
# of AM/FM tuner presets	N/A	N/A	N/A
Music data transfer			

format. In contrast, customers in stores usually have to inspect each brand, one item at a time, and then remember the different attributes to make a comparison.[10]

The Internet channel also offers retailers an opportunity to go beyond the traditional product information available in stores to provide tools and information for solving customer problems. **Virtual communities,** networks of people who seek information, products, and services and communicate with one another about specific issues, are examples of these problem-solving sites. For example, iVillage (www.ivillage.com) is a virtual community for women, with subcommunities for pregnant women, women with babies, and working women. The site for pregnant women offers information and advice on morning sickness, birth options, and body changes; books and apparel for pregnant women; and chat rooms in which community members can express their views and ask and answer questions. Retailers are ideally suited to offer these problem-solving sites for customers because they have the skills to put together merchandise assortments, services, and information to attract members. Chat rooms are discussed in more detail in Chapter 19. Retailing View 3.2 describes how Web sites can help couples plan their wedding.

Personalization The most significant potential benefit of the Internet channel is its ability to personalize the information for each customer economically. Catalogers cannot economically tailor their merchandise and information to the needs

---

3.2 RETAILING VIEW The Wedding Channel Helps Couples Get Ready for the Big Day

The typical engagement/wedding planning process lasts for 14 months, costs almost $20,000, and involves many emotionally charged decisions, such as how many people and whom to invite, what print style to use on the invitations, where to hold the reception, what music to play during the ceremony, and what gifts to list in the registry. Traditionally the bride's family managed the wedding planning process. But with more couples getting married when they are older, both work, and do not live near their parents, wedding planning is more challenging.

Internet wedding sites, such as Wedding Channel. com (www.weddingchannel. com), which is partially owned by Federated Department Stores, offer couples and their families planning guides, tips, and an opportunity to chat with other couples getting married. Gift registries can be created at different retailers and broadcast to guests through e-mail. The couple can collect information from home rather than by making appointments with different suppliers. Potential places for the reception can be ruled out by looking at photos on the Web, and instead of going to hear different bands, audio clips also

The WeddingChannel.com offers merchandise, services, and information for couples planning their wedding.

can be downloaded from the Web. Hotel reservations for out-of-town guests can be made over the Internet, and maps can be created to show those guests how to get to the hotel and reception. Finally, couples can have their own personal site on which they post their wedding pictures.

Sources: www.weddingchannel.com; www.theknot.com.

and preferences of all individual consumers. To be cost effective, they have to send the same catalog to a large segment of customers.

Sales associates in service-oriented retailers like department and specialty stores can provide this benefit however. They know what their preferred customers want. They can select a few outfits and arrange to show these outfits before the store opens or even take the outfits to the customer's office or home. However, store-based retailers can only provide this benefit when their sales associates are working, and even then, providing it is costly. The Internet offers an opportunity to provide "personal" service at a low cost.

Personalized Customer Service   Traditional Internet channel approaches for responding to customer questions—such as FAQ (frequently asked questions) pages and offering an 800 number or e-mail address to ask questions—often do not provide the timely information customers are seeking. To improve customer service from an electronic channel, many retailers are offering live, online chats. An **online chat** provides customers with the opportunity to click a button at anytime and have an instant messaging e-mail or voice conversation with a customer service representative. This technology also enables electronic retailers to automatically send a proactive chat invitation to customers on the site. The timing of these invitations can be based on the time the visitor has spent on the site, the specific page the customer is viewing, or a product on which the customer has clicked. For example, an instant message asking "Do you need any additional information?" might be sent when a customer has spent more than five minutes looking at the specifications for MP3 players.

Offering online chats is economically attractive for retailers. The average cost per electronic customer service session is $7.80 for a live chat compared with $9.99 for e-mail and $33.00 for a telephone customer session. Retailers vary in how they make the trade-off between stimulating sales and increasing customer satisfaction versus the cost of providing online instant chat services. Some retailers elect to

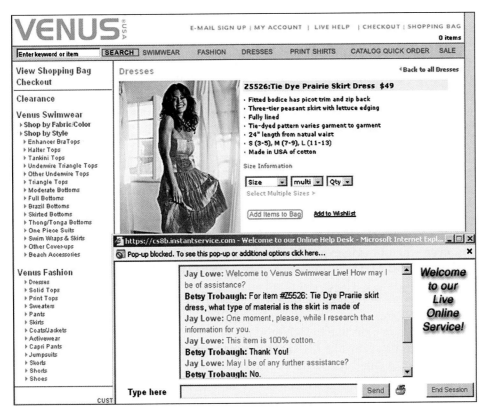

Venus Swimwear uses live chat to provide customer service on its web site.

make this service option available and highly visible on the home page and all highly trafficked pages, while others deliberately make these services hard to find to encourage customers to use less costly options like FAQs.

Personalized Offering   The interactive nature of the Internet provides an opportunity for retailers to personalize their offerings for each of their customers. For example, at many Web sites, you can create a personal home page, like myYahoo, that is tailored to your individual needs. Using a cookie (a small computer program that provides identifying information installed on your hard drive), Amazon serves you a personalized home page with information about books and other products of interest based on your past purchases. Amazon.com will also send customers who are interested customized e-mail messages that notify them that their favorite author or recording artist has published a new book or released a new CD. Another personalized offering that online retailers are able to present to customers is recommendations of complementary merchandise. Just as a well-trained salesperson would make recommendations to customers prior to checkout, an interactive Web page can make suggestions to the shopper about items that he or she might like to see, such as what other customers who bought the same item also purchased.

Bluefly.com is an electronic off-price retailer that sells end-of-season and excess production designer clothing from such elite design houses as Donna Karan and BCBG at discounts up to 75 percent. Bluefly.com exploits the ability of an electronic retailer to personalize its offering and thereby overcomes the common frustration of the size-12 off-price shopper finding a garment she really wants and then discovering it is only available in a size 2. Its "MyCatalog" service allows customers to enter their sizes and preferences. When they go to the site, the clothing they view has been preselected. They don't have to look through pages of merchandise that they don't like or that isn't available in their size. The registered users are also notified by e-mail when their favorite clothing is posted on the site.

Personalization in the Future   The scenario in Exhibit 3–3 illustrates the personalization benefits that will be available to consumers shopping via the Internet in the future.

FRED is an **electronic agent,** a computer program that locates and selects alternatives on the basis of some predetermined characteristics.[11] In the future, electronic agents may be computer software programs bought by consumers or offered as a service to customers by retailers or third parties. The agent could learn about a consumer's tastes by asking questions when it is installed on the consumer's computer or when the consumer goes to the retailer's Web site. For example, when Judy added the FRED software to her home electronic systems, the software asked her questions to learn about her tastes and preferences.

Electronic agents like FRED unleash the interactive benefits of Internet shopping. For example, one benefit of the Internet channel is access to more retailers and deeper merchandise assortments. However, having a lot more alternatives to consider is not that much of a benefit. Consumers rarely visit more than two outlets, even when buying expensive consumer durables.[12] Consider Judy Jamison's search with FRED. Does Judy really care if FRED initially found 10 or 121 toys? Having identified 121 Internet retail sites selling a product you might like, how many sites would you take the time to visit? The advantages of having a lot of alternatives is only meaningful if you have FRED to search through them and find a few items you might like to look at in detail.

An electronic agent like FRED also can search through a wide range of alternatives, select a small set for the customer to look at in detail, and provide the information that the customer typically considers. In addition, FRED never is in

Personalization Potential for Internet Shopping   **EXHIBIT 3–3**

Judy Jamison wants to buy a present for her son Dave, whose birthday is in several weeks. She goes to her home computer, accesses her personal shopper program called FRED, and has the following interactive dialogue:

FRED: Do you wish to browse, go to a specific store, or buy a specific item?

Judy: Specific item

FRED: Occasion? [Menu appears and Judy selects.]

Judy: Gift

FRED: For whom? [Menu appears on screen.]

Judy: Dave

FRED: Type of gift? [Menu appears.]

Judy: Toy/Game

FRED: Price range? [Menu appears.]

Judy: $75–100

[Now Fred goes out and literally shops the world electronically, visiting servers for companies selling toys and games in Europe, Asia, Africa, Australia, and North and South America.]

FRED: 121 items have been identified. How many do you want to review? [Menu appears.]

Judy: Just five

[FRED selects the five best alternatives based on information about Dave's age and preference for toys and Judy's preference for

nonviolent, educational toys. The five toys appear on the screen with the price, brand name, and retailer listed beneath each one. Judy clicks on each toy to get more information about the toy. With another click, she sees a full-motion video of a child Dave's age playing with the toy. She selects the toy she finds most appealing.]

FRED: How would you like to pay for this? [Menu appears.]

Judy: American Express

FRED: Toys "R" Us [the firm selling the toy Judy selected] suggests several books that appeal to children who like the toy you have selected. Do you want to review these books?

Judy: Yes

[The books are displayed on the screen. Judy reviews each of the books and decides to order one.]

FRED: Would you like this gift wrapped?

Judy: Yes

[The different designs for wrapping paper are displayed on the screen and Judy selects paper with a baseball motif.]

FRED: The product you ordered is available at the stores listed below. Do you want to pick up the product at the store, have it sent to your home, or sent to your office?

Judy: [Selects pickup at a store close to her office.]

a bad mood, is not paid anything to do its job, and is always available. These agents function like a super sales associate in a department store, helping customers locate merchandise they might like. For example, Netflix has an electronic agent that recommends DVD rentals based on the customer's previous rentals.

The Internet channel has the capability of offering some unique benefits to consumers; however, this channel, like all nonstore channels, has some important limitations. The interactive capabilities of the Internet result in some unique approaches for addressing these limitations.

Selling Merchandise with "Touch-and-Feel" Attributes   When you buy products, some critical information might be "look-and-see" attributes like color, style, and grams of carbohydrates or "touch-and-feel" attributes like how the shirt fits, the ice cream flavor tastes, or the perfume smells. Fit can only be predicted well if the apparel has consistent sizing and the consumer has learned over time what size to buy from a particular brand. Due to the problems of providing touch-and-feel information, apparel retailers experience return rates of more than 20 percent on purchases made through an electronic channel but only 10 percent for purchases made in stores.

Role of Brands   Brands provide a consistent experience for customers that helps overcome the difficulty of not being able to touch and feel merchandise prior to purchase online. Because consumers trust familiar brands, products with important touch-and-feel attributes, such as clothing, perfume, flowers, and food, with well-known name brands are being sold successfully through nonstore channels including the Internet, catalogs, and TV home shopping.

REFACT

Travel services, apparel, CDs, videos, and computer software are the best selling product categories on the Internet.[13]

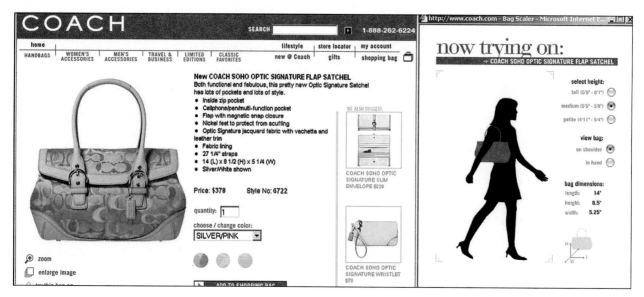

Using 3-D and zoom technology, Coach.com converts "touch and feel" into "look and see" information.

Consider branded merchandise like Nautica perfume or Levi's 501 jeans. Even though you can't smell a sample of the perfume before buying it, you know that it will smell like your last bottle when you buy it electronically because the manufacturer of Nautica makes sure each bottle smells the same. Similarly, if you wear a size 30-inch waist/32-inch inseam Levi's 501 jeans, you know they will fit when you buy them electronically.

The retailer's brand can also provide information about the consistency and quality of merchandise. For example, consumers might be reluctant to buy produce using an electronic channel because they cannot see the fruits and vegetables before purchasing. However, the same consumers would likely feel comfortable buying fruit from Harry and David catalogs or its Internet site, because Harry and David has established a strong reputation for selling only the highest quality fruit.

Using Technology   Retailers with electronic channels are using technology to convert touch-and-feel information into look-and-see information that can be communicated through the Internet. Web sites are going beyond offering the basic image to giving customers the opportunity to view merchandise from different angles and perspectives using 3D imaging and/or zoom technology. The use of these image-enhancing technologies has increased **conversion rates** (the percentage of consumers who buy the product after viewing it) and reduced returns.

To overcome the limitations for trying on clothing, apparel retailers have started to use virtual models on their Web sites. These virtual models enable consumers to see how selected merchandise looks on an image with similar proportions to their own and then rotate the model so the "fit" can be evaluated from all angles. The virtual models are either selected from set of "prebuilt" models or constructed on the basis of the shopper's response to questions about his or her height, weight, and other dimensions.[14]

For example, at Landsend.com, online shoppers choose a model that looks like them. Customers then dress the model using a "click and drag" interface. Items are suggested while the customer is "trying on" the apparel. Lands' End reports that customers using the virtual model feature were 28 percent more likely to make a purchase and spent 13 percent more on their average purchases. When JCPenney offered this feature on its Web site, over 100,000 customers saved their model for future visits.

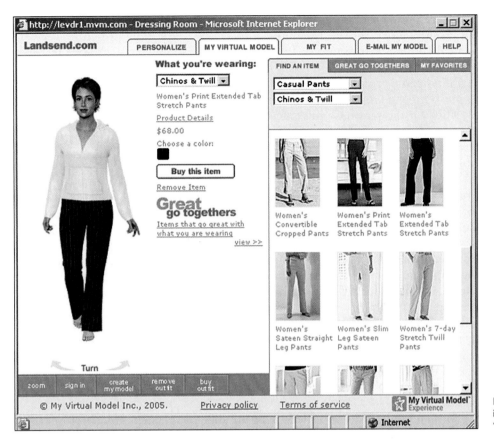

Lands' End virtual model on its Web site lets customers "try on" its apparel at home.

These applications are harbingers of future applications in which customers can use a personal, 3D, digitized body scan to serve as an actual model rather than a virtual model. In addition, the measurements for the body scan could be input, along with information about the garment, to a predictive model that would advise customers on how well a specific item will fit using a five-star rating system and then suggest the appropriate size.

Even though it is limited in its ability to provide look-and-see information, in some situations, the Internet channel might be able to provide superior information than stores can. For example, Judy, before she started to shop electronically, wanted to see toys before buying one for her son Dave, so she went to stores to look at the toys. But in the stores, the toys were not displayed; all she could see was a picture on the side of the box containing the toy. Now that Judy shops electronically, she can get superior information from the full-motion video clip showing a child playing with the toy.

Gifts   In some situations, touch-and-feel information might be important, but the information in a store is not much better than the information provided electronically. For example, suppose you're buying a bottle of perfume for your mother. Even if you go to the store and smell the samples of all the new scents, you might not get much information to help you determine which one your mother would like. In this situation, stores offer little benefit over an electronic channel in terms of useful information provided about the merchandise. But buying gifts electronically offers the benefit of saving you the time and effort of packing and sending the gift to your mother. For this reason, gifts represent a substantial portion of sales made through the Internet channel. Retailing View 3.3 describes how RedEnvelope uses the Internet and its catalog to focus on the gift market.

REFACT

Orvis, a catalog retailer, had a 60–70 percent increase in sales after adding 3D technology to display merchandise on its Web site.[15]

Services   Some services retailers have been very successful over the Internet, because the look-and-see attributes in their offering can be presented very effectively online. For example, Travelocity (www.travelocity.com) is an Internet travel planning service. After you go to the Internet site and fill in an online form indicating your destination and preferred departure time, the electronic agent locates the lowest-cost fare for that flight. To purchase a ticket, you simply click on the purchase ticket icon, enter your credit card information, and get an e-ticket confirmation number. Travel service providers like Travelocity and Expedia (www.expedia.com) provide detailed information about destinations, like the locations of hotels on a map. Chat rooms provide an opportunity for travelers to share their experiences in hotels and restaurants—a benefit they cannot get through the other channels.[16] Due to the appeal of the Internet for providing services, many banks are making major investments to provide banking services online.[17]

Perceived Risks in Electronic Shopping   Although most consumers have had the opportunity to try out electronic shopping, they also have some concerns about buying products through an electronic channel. The two critical perceived risks are (1) the security of credit card transactions on the Internet and (2) potential privacy violations. While many consumers are concerned about credit card security, extensive security problems have not arisen in actual usage. Almost all retailers use sophisticated technologies to encrypt communications. The perception of risk also is diminishing as credit card companies promote the use of their cards on the Internet and inform customers that they will not be responsible for security lapses.[18]

Consumers also are concerned about the ability of retailers to collect information about their purchase history, personal information, and search behavior on the Internet. Consumers may be worried about how this information will be used in the future. Will it be sold to other retailers, or will the consumer receive unwanted promotional materials online or in the mail? Issues related to privacy, and

REFACT

When asked what attributes are critical in selecting a Web site for shopping, 25 percent of consumers said credit card security, 22 percent cited fast download speed, 20 percent named the availability of customer service, 7 percent answered deep price discounts, and 7 percent said privacy.[19]

3.3   RETAILING VIEW   RedEnvelope Makes Gift Giving Easy

Launched in 1999, RedEnvelope's mission has been to make gift giving—no matter what the occasion or circumstance—simple and fun. The name RedEnvelope comes from an Asian tradition in which gifts are often presented in a simple red envelope, a symbol of good fortune, love, and appreciation.

Its Web site and seasonal catalogs offer a unique assortment of upscale gifts, such as a $90 cashmere baby sweater and a $129 set of kids' golf clubs. Many items are created exclusively for RedEnvelope. RedEnvelope's merchandising group works directly with domestic manufacturers, importers, and overseas agents to design and manufacture products. About 25 percent of their products come from overseas. By working directly with overseas agents and manufacturers, RedEnvelope can effectively manage its product development and quality.

Customers can choose to shop the site by purchase occasion such as Mother's Day, a wedding, or "just because"; by recipient such as father, son, daughter, or business associate; or by shops (product categories) such as home and garden, gadgets, or flowers and plants.

Personalization is a big part of its business. For example, the company has a product that lets customers send in a digitized photo and then have it printed and inserted into a picture frame that can be sent as a gift. Or a customer can write a three-line poem or verse and have it engraved on a box. Songs can be uploaded and burned on a CD that is put in a monogrammed CD holder.

A number of services are offered to make gift giving easier. Need help choosing a gift? Customers can get answers to their questions and suggestions in real time by clicking on the Personal Shopper icon and using the pop-up window to chat with a customer service representative. Want to buy a gift fast? The gift search feature makes finding the perfect gift quick and easy. RedEnvelope also offers a complimentary reminder service to help customers remember their family and friends on special days. Customers are reminded of special occasions in advance with an e-mail that includes a list of gift suggestions. Every time customers send someone a gift, the recipient's name and vital information is saved so the next time they purchase, they see all their past recipients in a convenient pull-down address book on the product information page.

Sources: www.redenvelope.com; "Online Extra: Pushing the RedEnvelope," *Business Week*, January 10, 2005, p. 30.

the steps that retailers are taking to allay these concerns, are discussed in more detail in Chapter 11.

EVOLUTION TOWARD MULTICHANNEL RETAILING

Traditional store-based and catalog retailers are placing more emphasis on their electronic channels and evolving into multichannel retailers for four reasons. First, the electronic channel gives them an opportunity to overcome the limitations of their primary existing format. Second, by using an electronic channel, retailers can reach out to new markets. Third, providing a multichannel offering builds "**share of wallet**," or the percentage of total purchases made by a customer from that retailer. Fourth, an electronic channel enables retailers to gain valuable insights into their customers' shopping behavior.

Overcoming Limitations of an Existing Format

One of the greatest constraints facing store-based retailers is the size of their stores. The amount of merchandise that can be displayed and offered for sale in stores is limited. By blending stores with Internet-enabled kiosks, retailers can dramatically expand the assortment offered to their customers. For example, Wal-Mart and Home Depot have a limited number of major appliance floor models in their stores, but customers can used a Web-enabled kiosk to look at an expanded selection of appliances, get more detailed information, and place orders.

Another limitation that store-based retailers face is inconsistent execution. The availability and knowledge of sales associates can vary considerably across stores or even within a store at different times during the day. This inconsistency is most problematic for retailers selling new, complex merchandise. For example, consumer electronic retailers such as Best Buy find it difficult to communicate the features and benefits of the newest products to all of their sales associates. To address this problem, Best Buy installed kiosks designed to be used by sales associates and customers to obtain product information.[20]

A catalog retailer also can use its electronic channel to overcome the limitations of its catalog. Once a catalog is printed, it can't be updated with price changes and new merchandise. Therefore, Lands' End uses its Internet site to provide customers with real-time information about stock availability and price reductions on clearance merchandise.

Expanding Market Presence

Adding an electronic channel is particularly attractive to firms with strong brand names but limited locations and distribution. For example, retailers such as Tiffany's, Harrod's, Saks Fifth Avenue, Bloomingdale's, and Neiman Marcus are widely known for offering unique, high-quality merchandise, but they require customers to travel to England or major U.S. cities to buy many of the items they carry. Interestingly, most of these store-based retailers currently are multichannel retailers through their successful catalog offerings. Retailing View 3.4 illustrates how small retailers can also expand their markets using the Internet.

Increasing Share of Wallet[21]

Although offering an electronic channel may lead to some cannibalization, using it synergistically with other channels can result in consumers making more purchases from a retailer. Exhibit 3–4 illustrates the multichannel shopping behavior of customers. Forty-three percent of customers visiting a retailer's Web site and 19 percent of those looking at a retailer's catalog make purchases in the retailer's store. Thus, the electronic and catalog channels drive more purchases from the

EXHIBIT 3–4
Percentage of Cross-
Channel Shoppers

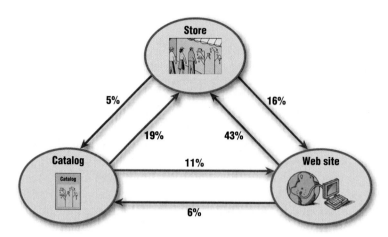

SOURCE: *Statistical Fact Book 2004.* Washington, DC: Direct Marketing Association, p. 131.

stores, and the stores drive more purchases from the Web site. Eddie Bauer, a retailer supporting all three channels, finds that single-channel customers spend $100–200 per year, dual-channel customers spend $300–500 per year, and tri-channel customers spend $800–1,000 per year.[22]

Traditional single-channel retailers can use one channel to promote services offered by other channels. For example, the URL of their Web site can be advertised on in-store signs, shopping bags, credit card billing statements, POS receipts, and print or broadcast advertising used to promote their stores. The physical stores and catalogs are also advertisements for all of the retailer's channels. The retailer's electronic channel can be used to stimulate store visits by announcing special store events and promotions. Store-based retailers can also leverage their stores to lower the cost of fulfilling orders and processing returned merchandise if they use the stores as "warehouses" for gathering merchandise for delivery to customers. Customers also can be offered the opportunity to pick up and return merchandise at the retailer's stores rather than pay shipping charges. Some retailers, such as L.L. Bean, will waive shipping charges when orders are placed online or through the catalog if the customer physically comes in the store.

REFACT

Consumers report that information about the availability of merchandise in a local store is the most useful feature on a retail Web site.[23]

3.4   **RETAILING VIEW**   Reaching Global Markets by Peddling on the Web

Harris Cyclery, a small bicycle shop in West Newton, Massachusetts, has built an international reputation and increased its store sales by selling parts and providing information on its Web site (www.harriscyclery.com). The bicycle shop stumbled on this opportunity through the interests of one of its employees, Sheldon Brown, a longtime mechanic at various shops in the Boston area. In 1995, Brown suggested that the shop spend $30 a month to host a Web site that initially included just a picture of the shop with its address. Brown taught himself HTML, the computer language for creating Web pages, and created hundreds of pages listing hard-to-find parts with prices. Other pages contain technical explanations on topics like maintaining freewheeling or adjusting cantilever brakes.

The site now generates 300 e-mails and 20 parts orders a day. Harris Cyclery operates its parts business in a low-tech, low-cost manner. E-mail orders are pasted into a Word file, and

then Brown goes to the stockroom to find and package the parts. "Inventory control" means turning over an empty box in the stockroom to indicate it is time to reorder the part. In addition to generating one-third of the shop's sales, the Web site draws in a lot of traffic to the shop—enough to employ a staff of five mechanics year round.

Aaron Harris, the owner of the shop, is surprised at how many customers come to the store from elsewhere in Massachusetts because they were impressed with the hard-to-find parts posted on the Web site and the personal service offered by Brown.

Source: Ross Kerber, "Dot-Coms May Be Dead, but Small Businesses Are Still Using the Internet to Extend Their Reach Peddling on the Web," *Boston Globe*, April 15, 2002, p. C1. Copyright 2002 by Globe Newspaper Co. (MA). Reproduced with permission of Globe Newspaper Co. (MA) via Copyright Clearance Center.

Insights into Customer Shopping Behavior

An electronic channel can provide valuable insights into how and why customers shop and are dissatisfied or satisfied with their experiences. For example, information on how customers shop a merchandise category would be useful for designing a store or a Web site.

The store and Web site layouts need to reflect whether customers shop by brands, size, color, or price point. Customer willingness to substitute one brand for another, for example, is valuable information for assortment planning. To collect this information from store or catalog shoppers would be quite difficult; someone would have to follow them around the store or observe them going through catalog pages. However, collecting data as customers navigate through a Web site is quite easy.[24]

The Internet channel offers the opportunity to collect more detailed information about customer preferences. For example, the Lands' End Web site offers a feature called My Personal Shopper. Customers are exposed to pairs of outfits and asked to choose which one they prefer. A market research technique called conjoint analysis is used to understand the customer's overall preferences from these choices. This information is then used to offer personalized recommendations on the first page customers see when they go to the Lands' End site.

Finally, an electronic channel can be used to get both positive and negative feedback from customers. Most customers are more inclined to provide feedback through an electronic channel because it is quick, easy, and less personal.

Saks Fifth Avenue, a multichannel retailer, uses its shopping bags to promote its Internet channel.

CAPABILITIES NEEDED FOR MULTICHANNEL RETAILING

Until the turn of the twenty-first century, most consumer goods were sold to consumers through stores or catalogs. There was no Internet, and manufacturers generally did not want their store and catalog customers to compete, nor did they have the expertise or general inclination to enable them to do so.

The Internet changed all that. As we noted in Chapter 2, in the late 1990s, there was a large group of new Internet-only retailers that ultimately failed. Many traditional retailers and catalog firms moved into electronic retailing very cautiously. Today, except for a few notable exceptions such as Amazon.com, most Internet-only retailers are niche players that sell hard-to-find products and services, hobbies, and collectables. The rest of electronic retailing activity is controlled by retailers that have their roots in either traditional stores or catalogs. Such retailers have found, however, that substantial opportunities exist for growing their businesses by integrating the electronic channel into their operations and becoming multichannel retailers.

To effectively operate and realize the benefits of multichannel retailing, firms need to have skills in (1) developing assortments and managing inventory—the basic merchandise management activities; managing store operations including (2) managing employees in distant locations and (3) distributing merchandise efficiently from distribution centers to stores; undertaking nonstore retail activities including presenting merchandise in (4) catalogs and (5) Web sites, (6) processing orders electronically, and (7) efficiently distributing individual orders to homes; and finally (8) operating communications and information systems that provide a seamless interface with customers throughout all channels. Some retailer types and merchandise manufacturers are better at these skills than others. Exhibit 3–5 provides an assessment of the degree to which the different types of retailers and merchandise manufacturers possess these skills.

EXHIBIT 3–5
Capabilities Needed for
Multichannel Retailing

Capabilities	Store-Based Retailers	Catalog Retailers	Niche Electronic Retailers	Merchandise Manufacturers
Develop assortments and manage inventory	High	High	Low	Low
Manage people in remote locations	High	Low	Low	Low
Efficiently distribute merchandise to stores	High	Low	Low	High
Present merchandise effectively in a printed format and distribute catalogs	Medium	High	Low	Low
Present merchandise effectively on a Web site	Medium	High	High	Low
Process orders from individual customers electronically	Medium	High	High	Low
Efficiently distribute merchandise to homes and accept returns	Medium	High	Low	Low
Integrate information systems to provide a seamless customer experience across channels	Low	Medium	High	Low

Who Has These Critical Resources?

As indicated in Exhibit 3–5, catalog retailers are best positioned to add an electronic channel offering. They have very efficient systems for taking orders from individual customers, packaging the merchandise ordered for shipping, delivering it to homes, and handling returned merchandise. They also have extensive information about their customers and the database management skills needed to effectively personalize their service. For example, many catalog retailers presently have systems that their telephone operators use to search their customer databases and make suggestions for complementary merchandise. Finally, the visual merchandising skills necessary for preparing catalogs are similar to those needed in setting up an effective Web site.

Store-based and catalog retailers both are ideally suited to offer assortments and efficiently manage merchandise inventories. Typically, they have more experience and greater skills in putting together merchandise assortments, a skill that most manufacturers and pure electronic retailers lack. In addition, store-based and catalog retailers typically have more credibility than manufacturers when suggesting merchandise since they offer an assortment of brands from multiple suppliers. These traditional retailers also have relationships with vendors, purchasing power, and information/distribution systems in place to manage the supply chain from vendors to distribution centers. However, most store-based retailers and manufacturers lack the appropriate systems for shipping individual orders to households. Their distribution center systems are designed to fill large orders from retail firms or stores and deliver truckloads of goods to retailers' distribution centers or stores. However, store-based retailers with broad market coverage can use their stores as convenient places for Internet shoppers to pick up their merchandise and return unsatisfactory purchases.

Whereas electronic-only retail entrepreneurs were, at one time, highly valued by investors, Exhibit 3–5 suggests that most of them did not possess sufficient resources to evolve into multichannel retailers. These pure electronic retailers were immersed in Internet technology and had considerable skills in designing Web sites and developing systems to manage transactions. They also had the opportunity to exploit this unique interactive feature of the Internet, but they lacked the brand recognition and retailing skills necessary to create consumer trust, build merchandise assortments, manage inventory, and fulfill small orders to households.

Over time, the remaining electronic retail entrepreneurs have recognized the importance of these retailing skills and distribution systems. They have hired executives from traditional retailers to undertake the merchandise management tasks and build their own warehouses.[25]

To illustrate the differences in resources possessed by pure electronic retailers and traditional store-based retailers, let's compare the electronic drugstores Drugstore.com and Soma.com with Walgreens.[26] Walgreens had the following resources to build on when it introduced its electronic channel:

- Three thousand conveniently located stores in the United States with drive-through windows for picking up prescriptions and merchandise.

- A distribution system in place for picking, packing, and shipping prescription pharmaceuticals and merchandise presently ordered by phone.

- A strong brand reputation for being trustworthy and helping customers with health-related decisions.

- Agreements in place with third-party payers (HMOs and insurance companies) to accept and provide pharmaceutical benefits for its customers.

Recognizing these synergies between store-based and electronic retailing, CVS acquired Soma.com, and Rite-Aid bought a 25 percent interest in Drugstore.com.[27] Most of the other electronic drugstores were either acquired or went bankrupt. Electronic-only retailers that pioneered selling merchandise and service over the Internet had a difficult time defending their initial success when store-based retailers became "bricks-and-clicks" retailers by launching their own electronic channels.

Do Manufacturers Use the Electronic Channel to Sell Their Products?

Disintermediation occurs when a manufacturer sells directly to consumers, bypassing retailers. Retailers are concerned about disintermediation because manufacturers can get direct access to their consumers by establishing a retail site on the Internet. But as indicated in Exhibit 3–5, manufacturers lack many of the critical skills necessary to sell merchandise electronically, and retailers are more efficient in dealing with customers directly than are manufacturers. They have considerably more experience than manufacturers in distributing merchandise directly to customers, providing complementary assortments, and collecting and using information about customers. Retailers also have an advantage because they can provide a broader array of products and services to solve customer problems. For example, if consumers want to buy a dress shirt and tie directly from the manufacturers of those items, they must go to two different Internet sites and still can't be sure that the shirt and tie will go together. Finally, if manufacturers start selling direct, they risk losing the support of the retailers they bypass.

Which Channel Is the Most Profitable?

Many people thought that the electronic channel would enable retailers to sell products at a lower price because they would not have to incur the costs of building and operating stores and compensating sales associates working in those stores. However, the electronic channel involves significant costs to design, maintain, and refresh a Web site; attract customers to the site; maintain distribution systems and warehouses dedicated to selling to individual customers; and deal with a high level of returns. These costs associated with operating an electronic channel may even be greater than the costs of operating physical stores.

REFACT

Merchandise returns can be as high as 40 percent for sales made through an electronic channel, compared with 6 percent for catalogs and even less for store sales.[28]

ISSUES IN MULTICHANNEL RETAILING

Customers want to be recognized by a retailer, whether they interact with a sales associate or kiosk in a store, log on to the retailer's Web site, or contact the retailer's call center by telephone. JCPenney provides this type of customer interface through its "threetailing" strategy: "Come in, call in, log on." In Penney's new flagship store in Frisco, Texas, shoppers can walk the aisles or browse and buy through a Web kiosk, which gives them access to all the merchandise in Penney's catalog. Catalog items can be purchased in the store as well, and merchandise received at home can be returned to the store.[29]

However, to provide a consistent face to customers across multiple channels, retailers need to integrate their customer databases and the systems used to support each channel. In addition to the information technology issues, other critical issues facing retailers that desire to provide an integrated, customer-centric offering include brand image, merchandise assortment, and pricing.

Integrated Shopping Experience

When retailers initially went online, they simply displayed products for sale on their Web sites. Now, to get ahead of the competition, multichannel retailers need to provide features and services that enhance the customer's experience across channels. Some of these features and services are listed in Exhibit 3–6.

Many retailers are still struggling to integrate the shopping experience across all their channels. Legacy systems (systems that were first installed long ago) and disconnected customer and inventory databases hamper retailers' ability to maintain consistency across channels. For some large department stores with a large array of inventory, it's impossible to mirror online exactly what is offered in stores. What's more, the expensive technology upgrades needed are a tough sell in today's budget-conscious retail environment, especially when online sales still account for such a small fraction of all sales. Many retailers are finding it easier to offer integration one step at a time rather than trying to link everything from the start, which could be financially and technologically daunting for them and alienate consumers if things don't go well.

One of the earliest integration success stories has been giving customers the ability to visit stores to return items purchased online. Once customers are in the store, they also are more likely to buy something than they would be if they only saw an item on the Web. While in the store, many customers are tempted to make

EXHIBIT 3–6

Multichannel Services and Features

- A liberal return policy in which the store accepts products purchased online.
- Web site features the retailer's promotions and sales.
- Store receipts contain the URL for retailer's Web site.
- Store associates direct customers to Web site for out-of-stock items.
- Customers can place orders online for store pickup.
- Stores have kiosks enabling customers to access retailer's Web site.
- Web sites offer inventory information (what merchandise is available in local stores).
- In-store kiosks allow customers to order merchandise not carried in stores.
- Web site offers the ability to prepare and print out a shopping list for store visit.
- Web site offers store coupons and other promotions.
- Web site lists information about in-store events.
- Store associates direct shoppers to Web site for postpurchase information.
- Retailer offers free shipping of products bought from Web site but picked up at the store.
- Shoppers can pay cash in store for products purchased from Web site.
- Store offers coupons for online purchases.

SOURCE: *Industry Outlook: Multichannel Retailing: Benchmarks and Practices.* Columbus, OH: Retail Forward, May 2004, p. 6. Used by permission of Retail Forward, Inc.

other purchases. About 30 percent of those who buy something online but pick it up from the store in person spend more when they arrive in the store.[30]

Brand Image

Multichannel retailers need to project the same image to their customers across all channels. For example, Talbots reinforces its image of classic-style apparel and excellent customer service in its stores, catalogs, and Web site. Customers enter the Web site (www.talbots.com) through an image of the red doors used in its stores and are greeted by the

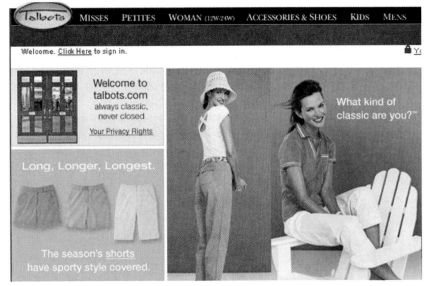

Talbots' Web site uses design elements from its stores to provide a consistant brand image.

phrase "Always classic, never closed." On the site, customers can consult an online style guide offering seasonal fashion tips and articles about how to buy the right size swimsuit, the art of layering, and petite sizing. Talbots' commitment to "friendly" service is reinforced by the availability of 24-hour personal service.

Merchandise Assortment

Typically, customers expect that everything they see in a retailer's store will also be available on its Web site. A significant product overlap across channels reinforces the brand image in the customer's mind.

However, the amount of product overlap across channels varies dramatically across retailers. Some retailers, like Wal-Mart, Kmart, Macy's, and Barnes & Noble, operated their electronic and catalog channels as separate businesses or independent divisions during the dot-com boom, which resulted in uncoordinated merchandise offerings. The trend now is to integrate merchandise offerings across channels. Issues related to the organization of multichannel retail firms are discussed in Chapter 9.

Other multichannel retailers use their Internet channel to increase revenues by expanding the assortment they can offer to customers. For example, Gap.com sells more colors and sizes for some merchandise categories than are available in Gap stores. The implications of multichannel capability for merchandise assortments are discussed in Chapter 12.

Finally, many multichannel retailers have tailored the assortments sold on their Web site to include only products their customers are likely to buy over the Internet. For example, Walmart.com discontinued offering low-price cosmetics and apparel items because the shipping costs were greater than the value of the merchandise.

Pricing

Pricing represents another difficult decision for a multichannel retailer. Customers expect pricing consistency across channels (excluding shipping charges and sales tax). However, in some cases, retailers need to adjust their pricing strategy because of the competition they face in different channels. For example, Barnes & Noble.com offers lower prices through its electronic channel to compete effectively against Amazon.com.

Retailers with stores in multiple markets often set different prices for the same merchandise to deal with differences in local competition. Typical customers do not realize these price differences because they are only exposed to the prices in their local markets. However, multichannel retailers may have difficulties sustaining these regional price differences when customers can easily check prices on the Internet.

Multichannel retailers are beginning to offer new types of pricing, like auctions, that take advantage of the unique properties of the Internet. We discuss these pricing alternatives in Chapter 15.

In conclusion, there is a growing expectation among customers that they should be able to interact with retailers anytime, anywhere, any place and that the retailer should recognize them and their transaction history, regardless of the channel used to contact the retailer. Multichannel retailers face a difficult challenge in providing the seamless interface that their customers expect. In the next section, we illustrate the benefits to customers that multichannel retailers can provide.

SHOPPING IN THE FUTURE

The following scenario illustrates the seamless interface across channels that customers in the future may experience.

Shopping Experience

It's Tuesday morning, and Judy Jamison is eating breakfast and flipping through a catalog from her local department store chain. She sees some attractive dresses and decides to buy a new dress for the cocktail party and dinner she'll be attending this Friday night for the Cancer Society. The event is being held at the Ritz Carlton and will be attended by a lot of movers and shakers in town. She goes to the department store's Web site to look at more dresses and then decides to visit the store after work.

Shortly after Judy walks into the store, a chip in her credit card signals her presence and status as a frequent shopper to a PDA (personal digital assistant) held by the store sales associate responsible for preferred clients. Information about items in which Judy might be interested, including the items she viewed on the Web site earlier in the day, is downloaded from the store server to Judy's and the sales associate's PDAs.

A sales associate approaches Judy and says, "Hello, Ms. Jamison. My name is Joan Bradford. How can I help you?" Judy tells the associate she needs to buy a dress for a cocktail party. She has seen some dresses on the store's Web site and would like to look at them in the store. The sales associate takes Judy to a virtual dressing room.

In the dressing room, Judy sits in a comfortable chair and views the dresses displayed on her image, which has been drawn from a body scan stored in Judy's customer file. Information about Judy's recent visit to the retailer's Web site and past purchases is used to select the dresses displayed.

Using her PDA, Judy shares this personalized viewing with her friend, who is still at work in California. They discuss which dress looks best on Judy. Then using her PDA again, Judy drills down more information about the dress—the fabric, cleaning instructions, and so forth. Finally she selects a dress and purchases it with one click.

Using information displayed on her PDA, the sales associate Joan suggests a handbag and scarf that would complement the dress. These accessories are added to the image of Judy in the dress. Judy decides to buy the scarf but not the handbag. Finally, Judy is told about the minor alterations needed to make the dress a perfect fit. She can check the retailer's Web site to find out when the alterations are completed and then indicate whether she wants the dress delivered to her home or if she will pick it up at the store.

Judy sits in a virtual dressing room reviewing dress selections based on her preferences shown on her virtual image.

Judy shares this shopping experience electronically with her friend using a PDA

As Judy passes through the cosmetics department on her way to her car, she sees an appealing new lipstick shade. She purchases the lipstick and a three-ounce bottle of her favorite perfume and walks out of the store. The store systems sense her departure, and the merchandise she has selected is automatically charged to her account through the use of an RFID (radio frequency identification) chip.

Supporting the Shopping Experience

This scenario illustrates the advantages of having a customer database shared by all channels and integrated systems. The sales associate and the store systems are able to draw on this database for information about Judy's body scan image, her interaction with the retailer's Web site, and her past purchases and preferences.

Judy's interest in buying a new dress was stimulated by a catalog, and then she interacted with the retailer's Web site to review the available merchandise before she went to the store, check the status of her alterations, and decide about having the merchandise delivered to her home. The scenario also includes some new technologies that will exist in the store of the future, such as RFID, self-checkout, and personalized virtual reality displays.

SUMMARY

Traditional store-based and catalog retailers are adding electronic channels and evolving into integrated, customer-centric, multichannel retailers. This evolution toward multichannel retailing has been driven by the increasing desire of customers to communicate with retailers anytime, anywhere, anyplace.

Each of the channels (stores, catalogs, and Web sites) offers unique benefits to customers. The store channel enables customers to touch and feel merchandise and use the products immediately after they are purchased. Catalogs enable customers to browse through a retailer's offering anytime and anyplace. A unique benefit offered by the electronic channel is the opportunity for consumers to search across a broad range of alternatives, develop a smaller set of alternatives based on their needs, and get specific information about the alternatives they want.

By offering multiple channels, retailers overcome the limitations of each channel. Thus, Web sites can be used to extend the geographical presence and assortment offered by the store channel or to update the information provided in catalogs. Stores can be used to provide a multiple sensory experience and an economical distribution capability in support of the electronic channel.

The type of merchandise sold most effectively through the Internet channel depends on delivery costs, the consumer's need for immediacy, and the degree to which electronic retailers can provide prepurchase information that helps customers determine whether they will be satisfied with the merchandise. The successful use of an electronic channel will overcome its limitations by offering testimonials from other buyers, providing video information about experience with the merchandise, or using information about brand–size combinations that fit specific members of the household. For consumers who have previously purchased a branded product, brand name alone may be enough information to predict their satisfaction with the purchase decision.

Some critical resources needed for successful multichannel retailing include operating each of the channels efficiently and then having the systems needed to provide a seamless customer experience across channels. Traditional store-based and catalog retailers possess most of these assets and thus are better positioned to evolve into multichannel retailers than are the entrepreneurial electronic retailers that first started using the Internet to reach customers. Disintermediation by manufacturers is unlikely because most manufacturers do not have the capability to distribute merchandise efficiently to individual consumers or provide sufficient assortments.

Providing a seamless interface across channels is very challenging for multichannel retailers. Meeting the shopper's expectations will require the development and use of common customer databases and integrated systems. In addition, multichannel retailers will have to make decisions about how to use the different channels to support the retailer's brand image, as well as how to present consistent merchandise assortments and pricing across channels.

KEY TERMS

conversion rate, *78*

disintermediation, *85*

electronic agent, *76*

magalogs, *72*

multichannel retailer, *71*

online chat, *75*

share of wallet, *81*

virtual communities, *74*

GET OUT AND DO IT!

1. **CONTINUING CASE ASSIGNMENT: GO SHOPPING.** Assume that you are shopping on the Internet for an item in the same merchandise category you analyzed for the Comparison Shopping exercise in Chapter 2. Go to the retailer's Web site and compare the merchandise assortment offered, the prices, and the shopping experience in the store and on the store's Web site. How easy was it to locate what you were looking for? What were the assortment and pricing like? What was the checkout like? What are features of the sites you like and dislike, such as the look and feel of the site, navigation, special features, etc.?

2. **INTERNET EXERCISE** Go to the Web sites of The Gap (www.gap.com), JCPenney (www.jcpenney. com), and Lands' End (www.landsend.com) and shop for a pair of khaki pants. Evaluate your shopping experience at each site. Compare and contrast the sites and your experiences on the basis of characteristics you think are important to consumers.

3. **INTERNET EXERCISE** Assume that you are getting married and planning your wedding. Compare and contrast the usefulness of www.theknot.com and www.weddingchannel.com for planning your wedding. What features of the sites do you like and dislike? Indicate the specific services offered by these sites that you would use.

4. **INTERNET EXERCISE** Go to the Center for Democracy and Technology's homepage at http://www.cdt.org/ and click on Consumer Privacy. Why is privacy a concern for Internet shoppers? What are the top ten recommended ways for consumers to protect their privacy online? How many of these recommendations have you employed when using the Internet?

5. **INTERNET EXERCISE** Go to the Internet Retailer's homepage at http://www.internetretailer.com/ and type in "Internet Retailer Best of the Web" in the search box. How are online retailers improving the multichannel shopping experience? Look at the list of Top 50 Retailing Sites. Which of these Internet retailers have you visited in the past? Which would you add to the list? Why should they be included in the list of top retail Web sites?

DISCUSSION QUESTIONS AND PROBLEMS

1. Why are store-based retailers aggressively pursuing sales through electronic channels?

2. What capabilities are needed to be an effective multichannel retailer?

3. From a customer's perspective, what are the benefits and limitations of stores? Catalogs? Retail Web sites?

4. Do you think sales through an electronic channel will eventually achieve annual sales greater than catalog sales? Why or why not?

5. Why are the electronic and catalog channels frequently patronized for gift giving?

6. Should a multichannel retailer offer the same assortment of merchandise for sale on its Web site at the same price as it sells in its stores? Why or why not?

7. Which of the following categories of merchandise do you think could be sold effectively through an electronic channel: jewelry, TV sets, computer software, high-fashion apparel, pharmaceuticals, and health care products such as toothpaste, shampoo, and cold remedies? Why?

8. What is an electronic agent? What benefits does it offer consumers?

9. Assume you are interested in investing in a virtual community targeting people who enjoy active outdoor recreation, such as hiking, rock climbing, and kayaking. What merchandise and information would you offer on the site? What type of a entity do you think would be most effective in running the site: a well-known outdoors person, a magazine targeting outdoor activity, or a retailer selling outdoor merchandise? Why?

10. Outline a strategy for an electronic-only retail business that is involved in selling merchandise or services in your town. Outline your strategy in terms of your target market and the offering available on your Internet site. Who are your competitors in providing the merchandise or service? What advantages and disadvantages do you have over your competitors?

SUGGESTED READINGS

Duffy, Dennis. "Using On-Line Retailing as a Springboard for Catalog Marketing," *Journal of Consumer Marketing* 2/3 (2004), pp. 221–35.

Evanschitzky, Heiner; Gopalkrishnan Iyer; Josef Hesse; and Dieter Ahlert. "E-Satisfaction: A Re-Examination," *Journal of Retailing* (Fall 2004), pp. 239–51.

Ganesh, Jai. "Managing Customer Preferences in a Multi-Channel Environment Using Web Services," *International Journal of Retail & Distribution Management* 2/3 (2005), pp. 140–51.

Gerht, Kenneth, and Ruoh-Nan Yan. "Situational, Consumer, and Retailer Factors Affecting Internet, Catalog, and Store Shopping," *International Journal of Retail & Distribution Management* 1 (2004), pp. 5–21.

Hoffman, Donna; Thomas Novak; and Alladi Venkatesh. "Has the Internet Become Indispensable?" *Communications of the ACM* (July 2004), pp. 37–44.

Lindstrom, Marty; Martha Rodgers; and Don Pepper. *Clicks, Bricks, and Brands.* Dover, NH: DualBook, 2001.

Min, Sungwook, and Mary Wolfinbarger. "Market Share, Profit Margin, and Marketing Efficiency of Early Movers, Bricks and Clicks, and Specialists in E-Commerce," *Journal of Business Research* (August 2004), pp. 5–19.

Nicholson, Michael; Ian Clarke; and Michael Blakemore. "'One Brand, Three Ways to Shop': Situational Variables and Multichannel Consumer Behaviour," *International Review of Retail, Distribution & Consumer Research* (April 2002), pp. 131–49.

Porter, Michael. "Strategy and Internet," *Harvard Business Review* (March 2001), pp. 63–78.

Stringer, Kortney. "Style & Substance: Shoppers Who Blend Store, Catalogue and Web Spend More," *The Wall Street Journal*, September 3, 2004.

Tedeschi, Bob. "No Longer a Niche Marketing Outlet, the Internet Is Now Attracting Shoppers from Almost All Walks of Life," *New York Times*, March 29, 2004.

2005 Online Shopping Directory for Dummies. Hobokan, NJ: Wiley, 2005.

Customer Buying Behavior

EXECUTIVE BRIEFING
Andrea Learned
President, Learned On Women

For a good part of my business career I worked in male dominated industries. Eventually I realized that women and men approach problems and make decisions differently, and that got me thinking about how women buy as opposed to men. Since women make most household purchases, I decided to develop a career in educating companies on how to market products and services specifically to them.

In the book I co-authored which published in 2004, *Don't Think Pink: What Really Makes Women Buy—And How to Increase Your Share of This Crucial Market*, I emphasize marketing transparently to women, which means taking inspiration from the women who are your customers, themselves, rather than making assumptions based on stereotypes of "what women want." Narrowing your focus, inviting and utilizing regular feedback, and maintaining brand authenticity along the way are all keys to the transparent approach.

My Web blog (www.learnedonwomen.com) and presentations now often center on a topic I call "humanizing," which includes the many ways to connect with customers in an effort to maintain that crucial authenticity. Women, especially, are looking to forge relationships with brands, and so are very interested in the human-scale stories with which they can relate around any given product or service. Elements like copy style, photographs or images used, and even the causes sponsored by a brand can all be developed to more authentically reflect the company's roots and be more relevant to core passionate customers. There is real power in inspiring and empowering customer connection through these pretty grass-roots methods.

The bonus of transparent marketing, authenticity and humanization overall is that, though you conduct all the research and do the work to better connect with the women in your market, the reality is you will likely better

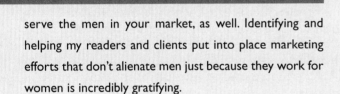

serve the men in your market, as well. Identifying and helping my readers and clients put into place marketing efforts that don't alienate men just because they work for women is incredibly gratifying.

A s discussed in Chapter 1, an effective retail strategy satisfies customer needs better than do competitors' strategies. Thus, understanding customer needs and buying behavior is critical for effective retail decision making. When Dennis Pence (cofounder and CEO of Coldwater Creek, a northern Idaho catalog retailer) was asked about his company being the highest-performing retailer in a consumer survey, he responded, "Our success has everything to do with our intense customer focus. We have never allowed ourselves to think that we are smarter than the customer is and can anticipate what she wants. We take all our cues from her."

This chapter focuses on the needs and buying behavior of customers and groups of customers, or market segments. It describes the stages customers go through to purchase merchandise and the factors that influence the buying process. We then use information about the buying process to discuss how consumers can be grouped into market segments.[1] The appendix to this chapter examines special aspects of consumer behavior that concern retailers selling fashion merchandise.

THE BUYING PROCESS

The following scenario illustrates the steps consumers go through when purchasing merchandise. Jennifer Sanchez, a student at San Francisco State University, is beginning to interview for jobs. For the first interviews on campus, Jennifer had planned to wear the blue suit her parents bought her three years ago. But looking at her suit, she realizes that it's not very stylish and that the jacket is beginning to show signs of wear. Wanting to make a good first impression during her interviews, she decides to buy a new suit.

Jennifer surfs the Internet for tips on dressing for interviews (www.collegegrad.com and www.jobsearch.about.com) and looks through some catalogs to see the styles being offered. But she decides to go to a retail store so she can try on the suit and have it for her first interview next week. She likes to shop at Abercrombie & Fitch and American Eagle Outfitters, but neither sells business suits. She remembers an ad in the *San Francisco Chronicle* for women's suits at Macy's. She decides to go to Macy's in the mall close to her apartment and asks her friend Brenda to come along. Jennifer values Brenda's opinion because Brenda is interested in fashion and has good taste.

Walking through the store, they see some DKNY suits. Jennifer looks at them briefly and decides they're too expensive for her budget and too trendy. She wants to interview in the banking industry and thinks she needs a more conservative suit.

Jennifer and Brenda are approached by a salesperson in the career women's department. After asking Jennifer what type of suit she wants and her size, the salesperson shows her three suits. Jennifer asks Brenda what she thinks about the suits and then tries on all three.

When Jennifer comes out of the dressing room, she is unsure which suit to select, but Brenda and the salesperson think the second suit is the most attractive and appropriate for interviewing. Jennifer is happy with the color, fit, fabric, and length of the suit but is concerned that it will require dry cleaning and that she is spending more than she had planned. Jennifer decides to buy the suit after another customer in the store tells her she looks very professional in the suit

Jennifer doesn't have a Macy's charge card, so she asks if she can pay with a personal check. The salesperson says yes, but the store also takes Visa and Master-Card. Jennifer decides to pay with her Visa card. As the salesperson walks with Jennifer and Brenda to the cash register, they pass a display of scarves. The salesperson stops, picks up a scarf, and shows Jennifer how well the scarf complements the suit. Jennifer decides to buy the scarf also.

Consider Jennifer's shopping trip as we describe the customer buying process. The **buying process,** the steps consumers go through when buying a product or service, begins when customers recognize an unsatisfied need. They seek information about how to satisfy the need, such as what products might be useful and how they can be bought. Customers evaluate the alternative retailers and channels available for purchasing the merchandise, such as stores, catalogs, and the Internet, and then choose a store or Internet site to visit or a catalog to review. This encounter with a retailer provides more information and may alert customers to additional needs. After evaluating the retailer's merchandise offering by weighing both objective and subjective criteria, customers may make a purchase or go to another retailer to collect more information. Eventually, customers make a purchase, use the product, and then decide whether the product satisfies their needs during the postpurchase evaluation stage of the customer buying process.

Exhibit 4–1 outlines the buying process—the stages in selecting a retailer and buying merchandise. Retailers attempt to influence consumers as they go through the buying process to encourage them to buy the retailer's merchandise and services. Each stage in the buying process is addressed in the following sections.

As we discuss the stages in the buying process, you should recognize that customers may not go through the stages in the same order shown in Exhibit 4–1. For example, a person might learn about the Kodak EasyShare 740 digital camera at a Web site like www.dcresource.com, decide to buy the camera, and then search for

REFACT

Two out of three shoppers are willing to spend more than they normally would for clothing that is comfortable and fits well.[2]

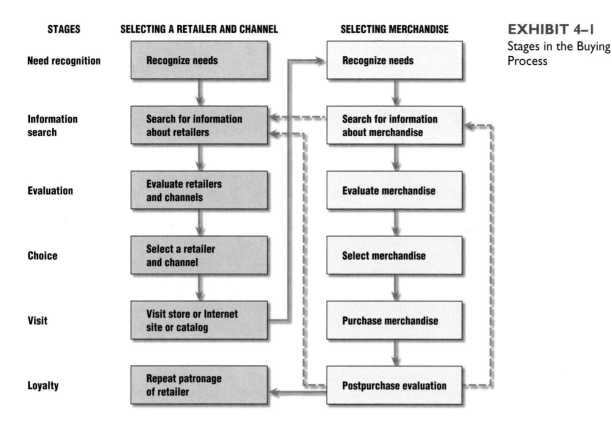

STAGES	SELECTING A RETAILER AND CHANNEL	SELECTING MERCHANDISE
Need recognition	Recognize needs	Recognize needs
Information search	Search for information about retailers	Search for information about merchandise
Evaluation	Evaluate retailers and channels	Evaluate merchandise
Choice	Select a retailer and channel	Select merchandise
Visit	Visit store or Internet site or catalog	Purchase merchandise
Loyalty	Repeat patronage of retailer	Postpurchase evaluation

EXHIBIT 4–1
Stages in the Buying Process

a retailer that sells the camera. In this case, the customer decides what product he or she wants and then selects the specific retailer. Alternatively, customers might decide they want to buy an iPod on the Internet, go to shopping Web site such as www.mysimon.com, and then buy the iPod from the retailer with the lowest price.

Need Recognition

The buying process is triggered when consumers recognize they have an unsatisfied need. An unsatisfied need arises when a customer's desired level of satisfaction differs from his or her present level of satisfaction. For example, Jennifer Sanchez recognized that she had a need when she was faced with interviewing for jobs in her blue suit. She needed a suit that would make a good impression and realized her worn, outdated blue suit wouldn't satisfy this need. Need recognition can be as straightforward as realizing you need a haircut or as ambiguous as feeling the need for an uplifting experience after a final exam. Visiting stores, surfing the Internet, and purchasing products are approaches to satisfying different types of needs.

Window displays and free samples can stimulate need recognition and start the buying process.

Types of Needs   The needs that motivate customers to go shopping and purchase merchandise can be classified as utilitarian or hedonic. When consumers go shopping to accomplish a specific task, such as Jennifer buying a suit for job interviews, they are seeking to satisfy **utilitarian needs.** When consumers go shopping for pleasure, they are seeking to satisfy their **hedonic needs**—their needs for an entertaining, emotional, and recreational experience. Thus, from the consumer's perspective, utilitarian needs are associated with work, whereas hedonic needs are associated with fun.[3]

Successful retailers attempt to satisfy both the utilitarian and hedonic needs of their customers. Consumers motivated by utilitarian needs typically shop in a more deliberate and efficient manner; thus, retailers need to make the shopping experience easy and effortless for utilitarian shoppers by providing the desired merchandise so that it can be easily located and purchased. Some hedonic needs that retailers can satisfy include stimulation, social experience, learning new trends, status and power, self-reward, and adventure.[4]

1. *Stimulation.* Retailers and mall managers use background music, visual displays, scents, and demonstrations in stores and malls to create a carnival-like, stimulating experience for their customers. These environments encourage consumers to take a break from their everyday lives and visit these stores. Retailers also attempt to stimulate customers with exciting graphics and photography in their catalogs and on their Web sites.

2. *Social experience.* Marketplaces have traditionally been centers of social activity, places where people could meet friends and develop new relationships.[5] Regional shopping malls in many communities have replaced open markets as social meeting places, especially for teenagers. Mall developers satisfy the need for social experiences by providing places for people to sit and talk in food courts. Barnes & Noble bookstores have cafés where customers can discuss novels while sipping a latte. Online retailers provide similar social experiences through chat rooms. For example, visitors to Amazon.com (www.amazon.com) can share information and opinions about books with other readers.

3. *Learning new trends.* By visiting retailers, people learn about new trends and ideas. These visits satisfy customers' needs to be informed about their environment. For example, teens might go to the Apple store to learn about new computer and iPod technologies.

4. *Status and power.* For some people, a store or a service provider is one of the few places where they get attention and respect. Canyon Ranch offers upscale health resorts in Tucson, Arizona, and Lenox, Massachusetts, as well as spa clubs in Las Vegas and Kissimmee, Florida. All Canyon Ranch resorts and spas make the customer the center of attention with spa services, medical and nutritional consultations and workshops, spiritual pursuits, and healthy gourmet cuisine.

5. *Self-reward.* Customers frequently purchase merchandise to reward themselves when they have accomplished something or want to dispel depression. Perfume and cosmetics are common self-gifts. Retailers satisfy these needs by "treating" customers to personalized makeovers while they are in the store.[6]

While shopping for cosmetics, this woman experiences the benefits of a new skin care product during an enjoyable makeover.

6. *Adventure*. Often consumers go shopping because they enjoy finding bargains, looking for sales, and finding discounts or low prices. They treat shopping as a game to be "won." Off-price retailers cater to this need by putting merchandise haphazardly in bins so that customers have an opportunity to go hunting for a bargain.

Conflicting Needs   Most customers have multiple needs. Moreover, these needs often conflict. For example, Jennifer Sanchez would like to wear a DKNY suit, which would enhance her self-image, earn her the admiration of her college friends, and be appropriate for her upcoming job interviews. But this hedonic need conflicts with her budget and her utilitarian need to get a job. Employers might feel that she's not responsible if she wears an expensive suit to an interview for an entry-level position. Typically, customers make trade-offs between their conflicting needs. Later in this chapter, we will discuss a model of how customers make such trade-offs.

Because needs often cannot be satisfied in one store or by one product, consumers may appear to be inconsistent in their shopping behavior. For example, an executive might own an expensive Mercedes-Benz automobile and buy gas from a discount service station. A grocery shopper might buy an inexpensive store brand of paper towels and a premium national brand of orange juice. The pattern of buying both premium and low-priced merchandise or patronizing both expensive, status-oriented retailers and price-oriented retailers is called **cross-shopping.**

Although all cross-shoppers seek value, their perception of value varies across product classes. Thus, a cross-shopper might feel it is worth the money to buy an expensive sweater in a boutique but believe there is little quality difference between jeans at Kmart and designer brands at a boutique. Similarly, consumers may cut back on their dining occasions at an expensive restaurant but still want to treat themselves to expensive, high-quality jams, mustards, and olive oils from the supermarket. While retailers might think the buying patterns of cross-shoppers do not make sense, they make sense to their customers.[7]

Stimulating Need Recognition   As we have said, customers must recognize unsatisfied needs before they are motivated to visit a store or go online to buy merchandise. Sometimes these needs are stimulated by an event in a person's life. For example, Jennifer's department store visit to buy a suit was stimulated by her impending interview and her examination of her blue suit, and an ad motivated her to look for the suit at Macy's. Retailers use a variety of approaches to stimulate problem recognition and motivate customers to visit their stores and buy merchandise. Advertising, direct mail, publicity, and special events communicate the availability of merchandise or special prices. Within the store, visual merchandising and salespeople can stimulate need recognition. For example, a salesperson showed Jennifer a scarf to stimulate her need for an accessory to complement her new suit.

One of the oldest methods for stimulating needs and attracting customers is still one of the most effective. The Saks Fifth Avenue store in Manhattan has 310 feet of store frontage along 49th and 50th streets and the famed Fifth Avenue. Each day at lunchtime, about 3,000 people walk by the 31 window displays. Saks produces 1,200 different window displays each year, with the Fifth Avenue windows changing each week. These displays can dramatically impact sales by catalyzing need recognition in the many potential customers that see them daily.

Information Search

Once customers identify a need, they may seek information about retailers or products to help them satisfy that need. Jennifer's search was limited to the three suits shown her by the salesperson at Macy's. She was satisfied with this level of information search because she and her friend Brenda had confidence in Macy's merchandise and pricing, and she was pleased with the selection of suits presented to her. More extended buying processes may involve collecting a lot of information, visiting several retailers, or deliberating a long time before making a purchase.[8]

Amount of Information Searched   In general, the amount of **information search** depends on the value customers feel they'll gain from searching versus the cost of searching. The value of the search stems from how it improves the customer's purchase decision. Will the search help the customer find a lower-price product or one that will give superior performance? The costs of search include both time and money. Traveling from store to store can cost money for gas and parking, but the major cost incurred is the customer's time.

The Internet can dramatically reduce the cost of information search. Information about merchandise sold across the world is just a mouse click away. Retailing View 4.1 describes how readily available information on the Web is affecting the automobile buying process.

Factors influencing the amount of information search include (1) the nature and use of the product being purchased, (2) characteristics of the individual customer, and (3) aspects of the market and buying situation in which the purchase is made.[9] Some people search more than others. For example, customers who enjoy shopping search more than those who don't like to shop. Also, customers who are self-confident or have prior experience purchasing and using the product or service tend to search less.

Marketplace and situational factors affecting information search include (1) the number of competing brands and retail outlets and (2) the time pressure under which the purchase must be made. When competition is greater and there are more alternatives to consider, the amount of information search increases. However, the amount decreases as time pressure increases.

Sources of Information   Customers have two sources of information: internal and external. **Internal sources** are information in a customer's memory such as names, images, and past experiences with different stores. For example, Jennifer relied on an internal source (her memory of an ad) when choosing to visit Macy's.

External sources are information provided by ads and other people. Customers see hundreds of ads in print and the electronic media; they notice signs for many retail outlets each day. In addition, customers get information about products and retailers from friends and family members.

The major source of internal information is the customer's past shopping experience. Even if they remember only a small fraction of the information they are exposed to, customers have an extensive internal information bank to draw upon when deciding where to shop and what to buy.[10]

When customers feel that their internal information is inadequate, they turn to external information sources. Remember how Jennifer Sanchez asked a respected friend to help her make the purchase decision? External sources of information play a major role in the acceptance of fashions, as discussed in the appendix to this chapter.

Reducing the Information Search   The retailer's objective at the information search stage of the buying process is to limit the customer's search to its store or Web site. Each element of the retailing mix can be used to achieve this objective.

Primarily, retailers must provide a good selection of merchandise so customers can find something to satisfy their needs within the store. Providing a wide variety of products and a broad assortment of brands, colors, and sizes increases the chances that customers will find what they want. For example, Best Buy uses Web-enabled in-store kiosks to increase the selection of merchandise available to customers, giving them the opportunity to purchase merchandise not available in the store, such as custom-designed computers.

Services provided by retailers can also limit search to the retailer's location. The availability of credit and delivery may be important for consumers who want to purchase large durable goods, such as furniture and appliances. And salespeople can provide enough information to customers so they won't feel the need to collect additional information by visiting other stores. For example, the mail-order retailer of sportswear and sports equipment L.L. Bean gives employees 40 hours of training before they interact with their first customer. Due to this extensive training, people across the United States call L.L. Bean for advice on such subjects as what to wear for cross-country skiing and what to take on a trip to Alaska. If the employee answering the phone can't provide the information, the customer is switched to an expert within the company. Thanks to L.L. Bean's reputation for expertise in sportswear and sporting goods, customers feel they can collect all the information they need to make a purchase decision from this one retailer.

Buying a Car in the Internet Age **RETAILING VIEW** **4.1**

Ten years ago, if consumers wanted to buy a car, they would visit several dealers, look at different models, test drive the cars sold by each dealer, and then negotiate price and financing with the dealer. Many consumers viewed this traditional process of buying a car as about as pleasurable as a visit to the dentist. But now the Internet is changing this experience, as well as the nature of automobile retailing.

The Internet is giving consumers more control over the car-buying process. Consumers can go to Web sites such as www.autobytel.com, www.cars.com, or www.edmunds.com; access a wealth of information, including the dealer's costs for cars and options; compare

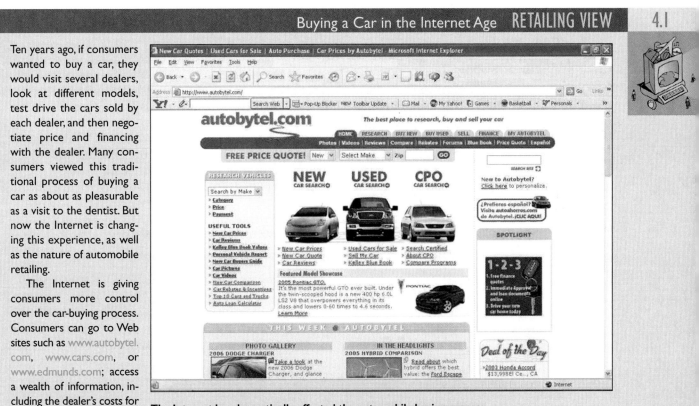

The Internet has dramatically affected the automobile buying process.

vehicles in a side-by-side chart that lists their price, features, horsepower, mileage, legroom, and options; read multiple reviews for most models; and even take a 360-degree photo tour of car interiors that gives them an idea of what the view looks like from the driver's seat. Through the sites' relationships with car dealers, you can request prices from retailers in your area. A handy calculator tells you how much your monthly payment would be if you were to buy a car on credit. The sites also have calculators to help you figure out how much you can afford to spend on a car, whether you should buy a new or used car, and whether you should lease or buy.

This information enables consumers to walk into a dealership knowing as much or more than the dealer's salespeople.

Sources: James Butters, "More Car Dealers Are Embracing Internet," *Knight Ridder Tribune Business News*, February 2, 2005, p. 1; Lisa Klein and Gary Ford, "Consumer Search for Information in the Digital Age: An Empirical Study of Prepurchase Search for Automobiles," *Journal of Interactive Marketing*, 17 (Summer 2003), pp. 29–41.

REFACT

Fifty percent of new car buyers base their purchase decisions on research they began on the Internet. The typical auto shopper who uses the Internet spends nearly five hours online and visits seven Web sites to gather information.[11]

Everyday low pricing is another way retailers increase the chance that customers will buy in their store and not search for a better price elsewhere. An **everyday low pricing strategy** emphasizes the continuity of retail prices at a level somewhere between the regular nonsale price and the deep discount sale price of the retailer's competitors. Since Wal-Mart and Best Buy have everyday low pricing policies, customers can feel confident that they won't find that merchandise at a lower price at another retailer. Many stores with everyday low pricing offer money-back guarantees if a competitor offers the same merchandise at a lower price. Chapter 15 talks about benefits and limitations of this and other pricing strategies.

Evaluation of Alternatives: The Multiattribute Model

The multiattribute attitude model provides a useful way to summarize how customers use the information they have about alternative products, evaluate the alternatives, and select the one that best satisfies their needs. We will discuss it in detail because it offers a framework for developing a retailing strategy.[12]

The **multiattribute attitude model** is based on the notion that customers see a retailer, a product, or a service as a collection of attributes or characteristics. The model is designed to predict a customer's evaluation of a product, service, or retailer based on (1) its performance on relevant attributes and (2) the importance of those attributes to the customer. Retail buyers can also use the multiattribute model to evaluate merchandise and vendors (see Chapter 14).

Beliefs about Performance   To illustrate this model, consider the store choice decision confronting a young, single, professional, Minneapolis woman who needs groceries. She considers three alternatives: a supercenter in the next suburb, her local supermarket, or an Internet grocery retailer such as SimonDelivers (www.simondelivers.com), as compared in Exhibit 4–2.

The customer mentally processes Exhibit 4–2A's "objective" information about each grocery retailer and forms an impression of the benefits it provides. Exhibit 4–2B shows her beliefs about these benefits. Notice that some benefits combine several objective characteristics. For example, the convenience benefit

EXHIBIT 4–2
Characteristics of Food Retailers

A. INFORMATION ABOUT STORES SELLING GROCERIES			
Store Characteristics	**Supercenter**	**Supermarket**	**Internet Grocer**
Grocery prices	20% below average	average	10% above average
Delivery cost ($)	0	0	10
Total travel time (minutes)	30	15	0
Typical checkout time (minutes)	10	5	2
Number of products, brands, and sizes	40,000	25,000	20,000
Fresh produce	Yes	Yes	Yes
Fresh fish	Yes	Yes	No
Ease of finding products	Difficult	Easy	Easy
Ease of collecting nutritional information about products	Difficult	Difficult	Easy

B. BELIEFS ABOUT STORES' PERFORMANCE BENEFITS*			
Performance Benefits	**Supercenter**	**Supermarket**	**Internet Grocer**
Economy	10	8	6
Convenience	3	5	10
Assoriment	9	7	5
Availability of product Information	4	4	8

*10 = excellent; I = poor.

	IMPORTANCE WEIGHTS*		PERFORMANCE BELIEFS		
Characteristic	Young Single Woman	Parent with Four Children	Supercenter	Supermarket	Internet Grocer
Economy	4	10	10	8	6
Convenience	10	4	3	5	10
Assortment	5	8	9	7	5
Availability of product information	9	2	4	4	8
OVERALL EVALUATION					
Young single woman			151	153	221
Parent with four children			192	164	156

EXHIBIT 4–3
Evaluation of Retailers

*10 = very important; 1 = very unimportant.

combines travel time, checkout time, and ease of finding products. Grocery prices and delivery cost affect the customer's beliefs about the economy of shopping at the retail outlets.

The degree to which each retailer provides the benefit is represented on a 10-point scale: 10 means the retailer performs well in providing the benefit; 1 means it performs poorly. Here, no retailer has superior performance on all benefits. The supercenter performs well on economy and assortment but is low on convenience. The Internet grocer offers the best convenience but is weak on economy and assortment.

Importance Weights   The young woman in the preceding example forms an overall evaluation of each alternative based on the importance she places on each benefit the stores provide. The importance she places on a benefit can also be represented using a 10-point rating scale, with 10 indicating the benefit is very important and 1 indicating it's very unimportant. Using this rating scale, the importance of the retailer benefits for the young woman and a parent with four children are shown in Exhibit 4–3, along with the performance beliefs previously discussed. Notice that the single woman values convenience and the availability of product information much more than economy and assortment. But the parent places a lot of importance on economy, assortment is moderately important, and convenience and product information aren't very important. The importance of a retailer's benefits differs for each customer and may also differ for each shopping trip.[13] For example, the parent with four children may stress economy for major shopping trips but place more importance on convenience for a fill-in trip.

In Exhibit 4–3, the single woman and parent have the same beliefs about each retailer's performance, but they differ in the importance they place on the benefits the retailers offer. In general, customers can differ in their beliefs about the retailers' performance as well as in their importance weights.

Evaluating Stores   Research has shown that a customer's overall evaluation of an alternative (in this situation, two stores and the Internet channel) is closely related to the sum of the performance beliefs multiplied by the importance weights.[14] Thus, we calculate the young, single woman's overall evaluation or score for the supercenter as follows:

$$4 \times 10 = 40$$
$$10 \times 3 = 30$$
$$5 \times 9 = 45$$
$$9 \times 4 = \underline{36}$$
$$151$$

EXHIBIT 4–4
Information Jennifer
Sanchez Used in Buying a
Suit

Benefits Provided by Suits	Importance Weights	BELIEFS ABOUT PERFORMANCE		
		Suit A	Suit B	Suit C
Economy	6	6	5	8
Quality	6	10	7	5
Conservative look	8	6	6	10
Complement to wardrobe	8	7	6	9
Fashion	4	7	10	5
Fit	10	?	?	8
Overall evaluation				330

Exhibit 4–3 shows the overall evaluations of the three retailers using the importance weights of the single woman and the parent. For the single woman, the Internet grocer has the highest score, 221, and thus the most favorable evaluation. She would probably select this retailer for most of her grocery shopping. On the other hand, the supercenter has the highest score, 192, for the parent, who'd probably buy the family's weekly groceries there.

When customers are about to select a retailer, they don't actually go through the process of listing store characteristics, evaluating retailers' performances on these characteristics, determining each characteristic's importance, calculating each store's overall score, and then patronizing the retailer with the highest score! The multiattribute attitude model doesn't reflect customers' actual decision process, but it does predict their evaluation of alternatives and their choice.[15] In addition, the model provides useful information for designing a retail offering. For example, if the supermarket could increase its performance rating on assortment from 7 to 10 (perhaps by adding a bakery and a wide selection of prepared meals), customers like the parent might shop at the supermarket more often than at the supercenter. Later in this chapter, we'll discuss how retailers can use the multiattribute attitude model to improve their store's evaluation.

The application of the multiattribute attitude model in Exhibit 4–3 deals with a customer who's evaluating and selecting a retail store. The same model can also be used to describe how a customer evaluates and selects which channel to use (store, Internet, or catalog) or what merchandise to buy from a retailer. For example, Exhibit 4–4 shows Jennifer Sanchez's beliefs and importance weights about the three suits shown to her by the salesperson. Jennifer evaluated only three suits at one store and bought suit "C" because it met most of her original needs, even though she didn't bother to fully evaluate "A" and "B" to assess the fit. Its overall evaluation passed some minimum threshold (which in terms of this multiattribute attitude model might be a score of 330).

Customers often make choices as Jennifer did. They don't thoroughly evaluate all alternatives, as is suggested by the multiattribute attitude model. They simply buy merchandise that's good enough or very good on one particular attribute. In general, customers don't spend the time necessary to find the very best product. Once they've found a product that satisfies their need, they stop searching.[16]

Implications for Retailers   How can a retailer use the multiattribute attitude model to encourage customers to shop at it more frequently? First, the model indicates what information customers use to decide which retailer to patronize and which channel to use. Second, it suggests tactics that retailers can take to influence customer store choice and merchandise selection.

Thus, to develop a program for attracting customers, the retailer must do market research to collect the following information:

1. Alternative retailers that customers consider.

2. Characteristics or benefits that customers consider when evaluating and choosing a retailer.

3. Customers' ratings of each retailer's performance on the characteristics.

4. The importance weights that customers attach to the characteristics.

Armed with this information, the retailer can use several approaches to influence customers to patronize their store or Internet site.

Getting into the Consideration Set

The retailer must make sure that it is included in the customer's **consideration set,** or the set of alternatives the customer evaluates when making a selection.[17] To be included in the consideration set, the retailer must develop programs to increase the likelihood that customers will remember it when they're about to go shopping. The retailer can influence this top-of-the-mind awareness through advertising and location strategies. Heavy advertising expenditures that stress the retailer's name can increase top-of-the-mind awareness. When a retailer such as Starbucks locates several stores in the same area, customers are exposed more frequently to the store name as they drive through the area.[18] A major factor contributing to the failure of many pure Internet retailers has been the high cost of creating awareness and getting into consumer consideration sets.

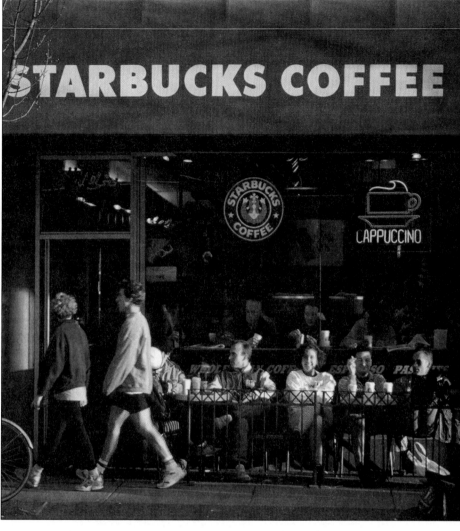

Starbucks uses a saturation strategy to increase brand awareness when selecting locations.

After ensuring that it is in the consideration set, the retailer can use four methods to increase the chances that customers will select its store for a visit:

1. Increase beliefs about the store's performance.

2. Decrease the performance belief for competing stores in the consideration set.

3. Increase customers' importance weights.

4. Add a new benefit.

Changing Performance Beliefs   The first approach involves altering customers' beliefs about the retailer's performance by increasing the retailer's performance rating on a characteristic. For example, the supermarket in Exhibit 4–3 would want to increase its overall rating by improving its rating on all four benefits. The supermarket could improve its rating on economy by lowering prices and its rating on assortment by stocking more gourmet and ethnic foods.[19] Retailing View 4.2 illustrates how Home Depot is altering its offering to appeal more to women.

It's costly for a retailer to improve its performance on all benefits. Thus, a retailer should focus its efforts on improving its performance on those benefits that are important to customers in its target market. For example, 7-Eleven's market research found that women avoid convenience stores because they view them as dingy and unsafe. To attract more women, 7-Eleven has improved the shopping environment in a number of its stores. To create a sense of space, brighter lighting was installed, and aisles were widened. Cigarette racks and other clutter were cleared off checkout counters, and colorful signage was used to designate merchandise areas.

A change in the performance belief concerning an important benefit results in a large change in customers' overall evaluation. In Exhibit 4–3's situation, the supermarket should attempt to improve its convenience ratings if it wants to attract more young, single women who presently shop on the Internet. If its convenience rating rose from 5 to 8, its overall evaluation for young, single women would increase from 153 to 183 and thus be much higher than the young women's evaluation of supercenters. Note that an increase in the rating from 8 to 10 for a less important benefit, such as economy, would have less effect on the store's overall evaluation. The supermarket might try to improve its rating on convenience by increasing the number of

---

4.2   RETAILING VIEW   Do It Herself at Home Depot

You probably think that home improvement centers are a retail recreation destination for men. Men go there on the weekends to check out the new tools and buy material for their do-it-yourself (DIY) projects. But over 50 percent of the sales at home improvement centers are made to women. Women not only make the decisions about what materials are used for home improvement projects but also end up doing much of the work themselves.

Home Depot's primary competitor, Lowe's, was early to recognize the importance of female customers. It redesigned its stores to be brighter, minimize the warehouse look, and feature departments more appealing to women. Aisles were widened to help eliminate "butt brush," the uncomfortable contact that can occur as customers navigate narrow, crowded aisles and something that women particularly dislike.

Home Depot has implemented merchandising concepts to attract more female shoppers.

Historically, home improvement centers have overmarketed to men and undermarketed to women. Now Home Depot is altering its retail mix to cater more to women. Home Depot found that women wanted clean and tidy stores that offered all the nuts and bolts of a home improvement store and lots of information about how to tackle renovations. To make the store feel less intimidating, Home Depot has made the shelves shorter and beige instead of orange. Aisle markers mimic those in grocery stores, and maps help customers find products. Polished concrete floors reflect light, making them less industrial-looking than those in older stores. Home Depot also has overhauled its catalog and Web site to make them more appealing to women, offering decorating ideas alongside images of the tools needed for the projects. This retailer has also increased its television sponsorship of home renovation television programs like *Trading Spaces,* which are extremely popular with women.

However, Home Depot must balance the performance beliefs and importance weights that women have about their store with those of men. Its core male customers might shun stores if they feel they are too feminine. Home Depot found that women held the same negative view of overly feminine home improvement stores as men, so it decided to teach women about tools rather than carrying tools specifically designed for women. They now hold Tuesday night Do-It-Herself clinics to teach women how to make such things as a mosaic table or a wood-frame display box, as well as install carpeting and perform basic plumbing tasks, to help women successfully implement DIY projects at home.

Sources: Bethany Clough, "Home-Improvement Store Empowers Female Customers with Do-It-Herself Tools," *Knight Ridder Tribune Business Service,* March 20, 2005, p. 1; Fara Warner, "Yes, Women Spend (And Saw and Sand)," *New York Times,* February 29, 2004, p. C1.

REFACT

The importance of women to retailers has grown in part because more households are headed by women—27 percent at last count, a fourfold increase since 1950.[20]

checkout stations, using customer scanning to reduce checkout time, or providing more in-store information so customers could locate merchandise more easily.

Research suggests that consumers in Germany, France, and the United Kingdom place different weights on three important attributes—price/value, service/quality, and relationships—when selecting a retailer to patronize. German consumers tend to place more weight on price/value, whereas customer service and product quality are more important for French consumers, and affinity benefits such as loyalty cards and preferred customer programs are more important for English consumers. Thus, in general, retailers that emphasize price and good value will be more successful in Germany than in France or the United Kingdom.[21]

Another approach is to try to decrease customers' performance ratings of a competing store. This approach may be illegal and usually isn't very effective, because customers typically don't believe a firm's negative comments about its competitors.

Changing Importance Weights   Altering customers' importance weights is another approach to influencing store choice. A retailer would want to increase the importance customers place on benefits for which its performance is superior and decrease the importance of benefits for which it has inferior performance.

For example, if the supermarket in Exhibit 4–3 tried to attract families who shop at supercenters, it could increase the importance of convenience for them. Typically, changing importance weights is harder than changing performance beliefs because importance weights reflect customers' personal values.[22]

Adding a New Benefit   Finally, retailers might try to add a new benefit to the set of benefits customers consider when selecting a store. Because JCPenney is a national department store, a customer can purchase a gift at a local Penney store or from its Web site and send it to a friend in another part of the country knowing that, if necessary, the recipient can exchange it at his or her local Penney store. Normally, customers wouldn't consider this benefit when selecting a retailer. The approach of adding a new benefit is often effective because it's easier to change customer evaluations of new benefits than of old benefits.

Purchasing the Merchandise or Service

Customers don't always purchase a brand or item of merchandise with the highest overall evaluation. The item or service offering the greatest benefits (having the highest evaluation) may not be available in the store, or the customer may feel that its risks outweigh the potential benefits. Some of the steps that retailers take to increase the chances that customers can easily convert their positive merchandise or service evaluations into purchases are

1. Don't stock out of popular merchandise. Have a complete assortment of sizes and colors for customers to buy. For services retailers, have service providers available when customers are ready to place orders.

2. Reduce the risk of purchasing merchandise or services by offering liberal return policies, money-back guarantees, and refunds if the same merchandise is available at a lower price from another retailer.

3. Offer credit.

4. Make it easy to purchase merchandise by having convenient checkout terminals.

5. Reduce the actual and perceived waiting time in lines at checkout terminals.[23]

Postpurchase Evaluation

The buying process doesn't end when a customer purchases a product. After making a purchase, the customer uses the product and then evaluates the experience to determine whether it was satisfactory or unsatisfactory. **Satisfaction** is a postconsumption evaluation of how well a store or product meets or exceeds customer expectations. This **postpurchase evaluation** then becomes part of the customer's

REFACT

More than **67 percent** of consumers who begin shopping on retail Web sites abandon their carts without making a purchase.[24]

internal information that affects future store and product decisions. Unsatisfactory experiences can motivate customers to complain to the retailer, patronize other stores, and select different brands in the future.[25] Consistently high levels of satisfaction build store and brand loyalty, important sources of competitive advantage for retailers. Chapters 17 and 19 discuss some means to increase customer satisfaction, such as offering quality merchandise, providing accurate information about merchandise, and contacting customers after a sale.

TYPES OF BUYING DECISIONS

In some situations, customers like Jennifer spend considerable time and effort selecting a retailer and evaluating the merchandise—going through all the steps in the buying process described in the preceding section. In other situations, buying decisions are made automatically with little thought. Three types of customer decision-making processes are extended problem solving, limited problem solving, and habitual decision making.

Extended Problem Solving

Extended problem solving is a purchase decision process in which customers devote considerable time and effort to analyzing their alternatives. Customers typically engage in extended problem solving when the purchase decision involves a lot of risk and uncertainty. Financial risks arise when customers purchase an expensive product or service. Physical risks are important when customers feel that a product or service may affect their health or safety. Social risks arise when customers believe a product will affect how others view them. Lasik eye surgery, for instance, involves all three types of risks: It can be expensive, potentially damage the eyes, and change a person's appearance.

Consumers engage in extended problem solving when they are making a buying decision to satisfy an important need or when they have little knowledge about the product or service. Due to the high risk in these situations, customers go beyond their personal knowledge to consult with friends, family members, or experts. They may visit several retailers before making a purchase decision.

Consumers enjoy the convenience of shopping online using the Internet to search for information and order merchandise.

Retailers stimulate sales from customers engaged in extended problem solving by providing the necessary information in a readily available and easily understood manner and by offering money-back guarantees. For example, retailers that sell merchandise involving extended problem solving provide information on their Web site describing the merchandise and its specifications, have informational displays in the store (such as a sofa cut in half to show its construction), and use salespeople to demonstrate features and answer questions.

Limited Problem Solving

Limited problem solving is a purchase decision process involving a moderate amount of effort and time. Customers engage in this type of buying process when they have had some prior experience with the product or service and their risk is moderate. In these situations, customers tend to rely more on personal knowledge than on external information. They usually choose a retailer they have shopped at before and select merchandise they have bought in the past. The majority of customer decisions involve limited problem solving.

Retailers attempt to reinforce this buying pattern when customers are buying merchandise from them. If customers are shopping elsewhere, however, retailers need to break this buying pattern by introducing new information or offering different merchandise or services.

Jennifer Sanchez's buying process illustrates both limited and extended problem solving. Her store choice decision was based on her prior knowledge of the merchandise in various stores she had shopped in and an ad in the *San Francisco Chronicle*. Considering this information, she felt the store choice decision was not very risky; thus, she engaged in limited problem solving when deciding to visit Macy's. But her buying process for the suit was extended. This decision was important to her; thus, she spent time acquiring information from a friend, the salesperson, and another shopper to evaluate and select a suit.

One common type of limited problem solving is **impulse buying**, which is a buying decision made by customers on the spot after seeing the merchandise.[27] Jennifer's decision to buy the scarf was an impulse purchase.

Retailers encourage impulse buying behavior by using prominent point-of-purchase or point-of-sale (POP or POS) displays to attract customers' attention. For example, sales of a grocery item are greatly increased when the item is featured in an end cap or other special display, when a "Best Buy" shelf-talker sign is placed on display with the item, when the merchandise is placed at eye level (typically on the third shelf from the bottom), or when items are placed at the checkout counters so customers can see them as they wait in line. Supermarkets use these displays and prime locations for profitable items that customers tend to buy on impulse, such as gourmet food, rather than commodities such as flour and sugar, which are usually planned purchases. Impulse purchases by electronic shoppers are stimulated by putting special merchandise on the retailer's homepage and suggesting complementary merchandise.[28]

Habitual Decision Making

Habitual decision making is a purchase decision process involving little or no conscious effort. Today's customers have many demands on their time. One way they cope with these time pressures is by simplifying their decision-making process. When a need arises, customers may automatically respond with, "I'll buy the same thing I bought last time from the same store." Typically, this habitual decision-making process is used when decisions aren't very important to customers and involve familiar merchandise they have bought in the past. When customers are loyal to a brand or a store, they are involved in habitual decision making.

Brand loyalty means that customers like and consistently buy a specific brand in a product category. They are reluctant to switch to other brands if their favorite brand isn't available. Thus, retailers can satisfy these customers' needs only if they offer the specific brands desired.

Brand loyalty creates both opportunities and problems for retailers. Customers are attracted to stores that carry popular brands, but since retailers must carry these high-loyalty brands, they may not be able to negotiate favorable terms with the supplier of the popular national brands. If, however, the high-loyalty brands are private label brands, (i.e., brands owned by the retailer), both brand and store loyalty is heightened. Chapter 14 covers buying and stocking branded and private label merchandise.

Supermarkets use a variety of approaches to increase impulse buying, including in-store coupons.

Store loyalty means that customers like and habitually visit the same store to purchase a type of merchandise. All retailers would like to increase their customers' store loyalty and might do so by selecting a convenient location (see Chapters 7 and 8), offering complete assortments of national and private label brands (Chapter 11), reducing the number of stockouts (Chapter 13), rewarding customers for frequent purchases (Chapters 11 and 16), and providing good customer service (Chapter 19).

SOCIAL FACTORS INFLUENCING THE BUYING PROCESS

Exhibit 4–5 illustrates that customer buying decisions are influenced by the customer's social environment: the family, reference groups, and culture.

Family

REFACT

Seventy-six percent of consumers say their child's preference is either very or somewhat important in deciding on a full-service restaurant.[32]

Many purchase decisions are made for products that the entire family will consume or use. Thus, retailers must understand how families make purchase decisions and how various family members influence these decisions. The previous discussion of the buying decision process focused on how one person makes a decision—how Jennifer purchases a suit for herself. When families make purchase decisions, they often consider the needs of all family members.[31] In a situation such as choosing a vacation site, all family members may participate in the decision making. In other situations, one member of the family may assume the decision-making role. For example, the husband might buy the groceries, which the wife then uses to prepare their child's lunch, which the child consumes in school. In this situation, the store choice decision might be made by the husband, but the brand choice decision might be made by the mother, though it likely is greatly influenced by the child.

Children play an important role in family buying decisions. Satisfying the needs of children is particularly important for many Baby Boomers who decide to have children late in life. They often have more disposable income and want to stay in luxury resorts, but they still want to take their children on vacations. Resort hotels now realize they must satisfy children's needs as well as those of adults. For example, Hyatt hotels greet families by offering books and games tailored to the children's ages. Parents checking in with infants receive a first-day supply of baby food or formula and diapers at no charge. Baby-sitting and escort services to attractions for children are offered.[33]

Retailers can attract consumers who shop with other family members by satisfying the needs of all family members. For example, IKEA, the Swedish furniture store chain, has a "ball pit" in which children can play while their

EXHIBIT 4–5
Social Factors Affecting
Buying Decisions

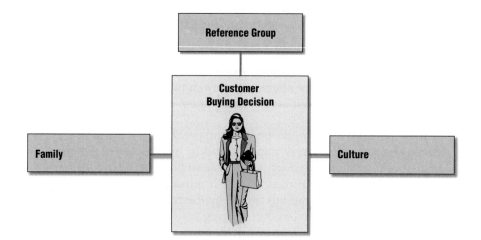

parents shop. Nordstrom provides sitting areas in its store and pubs where men can have a beer and watch a football game while their wives shop. By accommodating the needs of men and children who might not be interested in shopping, the retailer keeps the family in the stores longer and thereby encourages them to buy more merchandise.

Retailing View 4.3 profiles some retailers that are targeting "tween" shoppers who visit stores with their parents.

Reference Groups

A **reference group** is one or more people whom a person uses as a basis of comparison for beliefs, feelings, and behaviors. A consumer might have a number of different reference groups, though the most important is the family, as we discussed in the previous section. These reference groups affect buying decisions by (1) offering information, (2) providing rewards for specific purchasing behaviors, and (3) enhancing a consumer's self-image.

Many purchase decisions consider the needs of family members other than the shopper.

Tween shoppers, those between the ages of 8 and 12 years, are the fastest growing age segment in the United States. The 20 million U.S. tweens spend $6 billion annually on apparel using their own money and influence the $175 billion that their parents spend on them. A tween girl may want to emulate her older sister, but sex and romance are not part of her life yet—she is still a little girl at heart. She likes fun, frilly, glittery, sensory environments that tap into the kid in her. She wants to be treated as young but not babyish.

Two Inc., with 575 stores, is a market leader in the tween segment. It realizes that the tween girl might want to look like a 15 year old but that apparel assortments need to be fine tuned to a younger body type and to be more modest and sensible. Two's stores create a mood of power and excitement for the tween girl with their colorful storefront windows, light displays, photographic sticker booths, ear-piercing stations, and gumball machines. Special fixtures are placed at eye level for younger girls, even though the girls will be visiting the store with a parent, because here, the tweens choose and the parents pay.

Club Libby Lu, a division of Saks Inc., offers a more interactive format for the tween girl. By joining the club (membership is free), girls—whom the chain calls VIPs, or "very important princesses"—get access to what Saks describes as "a fun, funky atmosphere to hang out and interact." At the center of the activities are birthday parties, during which the girls can dress up, get makeovers, and, of course, buy things. At Club Libby Lu, girls can dress up in costumes, make their own jewelry, create personalized T-shirts, or receive a "princess" makeover. Or they can cover themselves in glitter and make their own lotions. However mature today's young girls may act, fantasy still has huge appeal for this age group. The retailer also develops its own merchandise targeted to tweens, such as scented sleepwear and complete sleep-over kits.

Retailers like Two Inc. target tween shoppers.

Sources: Kate Fitzgerald, "Club Libby Lu," *Advertising Age*, Nov. 1, 2004, p. S4; Maureen Wallenfang, "Preteens Wield Economic Strength in Family's Purchasing Decisions," *Knight Ridder Tribune Business News*, October 12, 2003, p. 1; Dave Siegel, Tim Coffy, and Greg Livingstone, *The Great Tween Buying Machine: Marketing to Today's Tweens* (Ithaca, NY: Paramount Marketing Publications, 2001).

Reference groups provide information to consumers directly through conversation or indirectly through observation. For example, Jennifer received valuable information from her friend about the suits she was considering. On other occasions, Jennifer might look to women like soccer player Mia Hamm and tennis player Maria Sharapova to guide her selection of athletic apparel. The role of reference groups in creating fashion is discussed in the appendix to this chapter.

Some reference groups influence purchase behaviors by rewarding behavior that meets with their approval. For example, the reference group of employees in a company might define the appropriate dress style and criticize fellow workers who violate this standard.

By identifying and affiliating with reference groups, consumers create, enhance, and maintain their self-image. Customers who want to be seen as members of an elite social class may shop at prestige retailers, whereas others who want to create an image of an outdoors person might buy merchandise from the L.L. Bean Web site.

Some retailers use teen boards, a select group of students who serve as a sounding board for merchandise and service offerings, to provide a reference group influence on teenage shoppers. The teen board members are selected because they represent a group of students whom other students would like to emulate. By buying apparel worn by teen board members, other students can identify with these student leaders.

Culture

Culture is the meaning, beliefs, morals, and values shared by most members of a society. For example, an important value in most Western cultures is individualism; people should only look out for themselves and their immediate family. Thus, consumers in individualistic cultures rely on their own inner standards and beliefs when making decisions. However, Eastern cultures value collectivism, which emphasizes that considerations of others should guide behavior. Thus, social relationships are more important and material goods less important to consumers in collectivist cultures.

The shopping behavior of customers in collectivistic cultures (Eastern) differs from that of people in individualistic cultures (Western).

Research has found that collectivists are more price sensitive than individualistic consumers about private goods (products and services consumed privately) but less price sensitive about public goods. For example, supermarkets patronized by Chinese consumers, compared with mainstream American supermarkets in southern California, have 37 percent lower prices for packaged goods of the same brand and size and more than 100 percent lower prices for meats and seafood of the same type and description.[34]

In addition, research reports that Chinese shoppers spend more time selecting products and make greater use of their five senses in evaluating products. For example, a sample of Chinese shoppers took four times longer to select bananas and touched four times more bunches before making a selection than consumers in an American sample in the same store. In addition, significantly more Chinese customers smelled the fruit than did other customers.[35]

Subcultures are distinctive groups of people within a culture. Members of a subculture share some customs and norms with the overall society but also have some unique perspectives.[36] Subcultures can be based on geography (southerners), age (Gen Y), ethnicity (Asian Americans), or lifestyle (preppies).

REFACT

In 1994, the Swedish furniture retailer IKEA aired the first mainstream TV ad targeted toward the gay subculture by featuring a gay relationship.[37]

MARKET SEGMENTATION

The preceding discussion focused on (1) how individual customers evaluate and select stores and merchandise and (2) the factors affecting their decision making. To be cost effective, retailers identify groups of these customers (market segments) and target their offerings to meet the needs of typical customers in that segment rather than the needs of a specific customer.

A **retail market segment** is a group of customers whose needs are satisfied by the same retail mix because they have similar needs. For example, families traveling on a vacation have different needs than executives on business trips. Thus, Marriott offers hotels with different retail mixes for each of these segments. The Internet enables retailers to target individual customers efficiently and market products to them on a one-to-one basis. This one-to-one marketing concept is discussed in Chapter 11 as it pertains to customer relationship management.

Criteria for Evaluating Market Segments

Customers are grouped into segments in many different ways. Exhibit 4–6 shows some different methods for segmenting retail markets. There's no simple way to determine which method is best, though four criteria useful for evaluating whether

Segmentation Descriptor	Example of Categories
GEOGRAPHIC	
Region	Pacific, Mountain, Central, South, Mid-Atlantic, Northeast
Population density	Rural, suburban, urban
Climate	Cold, warm
DEMOGRAPHIC	
Age	Under 6, 6–12, 13–19, 20–29, 30–49, 50–65, over 65
Gender	Male, female
Family life cycle	Single, married with no children, married with youngest child under 6, married with youngest child over 6, married with children no longer living at home, widowed
Family income	Under $19,999, $20,000–29,999, $30,000–49,999, $50,000–$74,999, over $75,000
Occupation	Professional, clerical, sales, craftsperson, retired, student, homemaker
Education	Some high school, high school graduate, some college, college graduate, graduate degree
Religion	Catholic, Protestant, Jewish, Muslim
Race	Caucasian, African American, Hispanic, Asian
Nationality	American, Japanese, British, French, German, Italian, Chinese
PSYCHOSOCIAL	
Social class	Lower, middle, upper
Lifestyle	Striver, driver, devoted, intimate, altruist, fun seeker, creative
Personality	Aggressive, shy, emotional
FEELINGS AND BEHAVIORS	
Attitudes	Positive, neutral, negative
Benefit sought	Convenience, economy, prestige
Stage in decision process	Unaware, aware, informed, interested, intend to buy, bought previously
Perceived risk	High, medium, low
Innovativeness	Innovator, early adopter, early majority, late majority, laggard
Loyalty	None, some, completely
Usage rate	None, light, medium, heavy
Usage situation	Home, work, vacation, leisure
User status	Nonuser, ex-user, potential user, current user

EXHIBIT 4–6
Methods for Segmenting Retail Markets

a retail segment is a viable target market are actionability, identifiability, accessibility, and size.

Actionability   The fundamental criteria for evaluating a retail market segment are as follows: (1) customers in the segment must have similar needs, seek similar benefits, and be satisfied by a similar retail offering and (2) those customers' needs must be different from the needs of customers in other segments. **Actionability** means that the definition of a segment clearly indicates what the retailer should do to satisfy its needs. According to this criterion, it makes sense for Lane Bryant (a division of Charming Shoppes that caters to full-figured women) to segment the apparel market on the basis of the demographic characteristic physical size. Customers who wear large sizes have different needs than those who wear small sizes, so they are attracted to a store offering a unique merchandise mix. In the context of the multiattribute attitude model discussed previously, women who wear large sizes place more importance on fit and fashion because it's relatively hard for them to satisfy these needs.

In contrast, it wouldn't make sense for a supermarket to segment its market on the basis of customer size. Large and small men and women probably have the same needs, seek the same benefits, and go through the same buying process for groceries. This segmentation approach wouldn't be actionable for a supermarket retailer because the retailer couldn't develop unique mixes for large and small customers. Thus, supermarkets usually segment markets using demographics such as income or ethnic origin to develop their retail mix.

Identifiability   Retailers must be able to identify the customers in a target segment. **Identifiability** permits the retailer to determine (1) the segment's size and (2) with whom the retailer should communicate when promoting its retail offering. It is important for retailers to be able to identify their customers so they can access them for communication purposes, the third market segmentation criterion.

Accessibility   **Accessibility** refers to the ability of the retailer to target its communications to customers in a segment. Customers of Marriott convention hotels and resort hotels access information in different ways. Convention hotel customers are best reached through newspapers such as *USA Today* and *The Wall Street Journal*, whereas resort hotel customers are best reached through ads on TV and in travel and leisure magazines.

Size   A target segment must be large enough to support a unique retailing mix. For example, the market for pet pharmaceuticals is probably not large enough in a local area to support a unique segmentation strategy, but a national market could be serviced through the Internet channel.

Approaches for Segmenting Markets

Exhibit 4–6 illustrates the wide variety of approaches for segmenting retail markets. No one approach is best for all retailers. Instead, they must explore various factors that affect customer buying behavior and determine which factors are most important for them.

Geographic Segmentation   **Geographic segmentation** groups customers according to where they live. A retail market can be segmented by countries (Japan, Mexico) or by areas within a country, such as states, cities, and neighborhoods. Because customers typically shop at stores convenient to where they live and work, individual retail outlets usually focus on the customer segment reasonably close to the outlet.

In the United States, many food retailers concentrate on regions of the country. For example, Publix concentrates on Florida and Georgia, HEB concentrates on Texas, and Wegmans concentrates on western New York. However, in the United Kingdom, supermarket retailing is dominated by national firms such as Tesco, Sainsbury, and ASADA.

Even though national retailers such as The Gap and Sears have no geographic focus, they do tailor their merchandise selections to different regions of the country. Snow sleds don't sell well in Florida, and surfboards don't sell well in Colorado. Even within a metropolitan area, stores in a chain must adjust to the unique needs of customers in different neighborhoods. For example, supermarkets in affluent neighborhoods typically have more gourmet foods than stores in less affluent neighborhoods.

Segments based on geography are identifiable, accessible, and substantial. It's easy to determine who lives in a geographic segment such as the Paris metropolitan area and to target communications and locate retail outlets for customers in Paris. However, when customers in different geographic segments have similar needs, it would be inappropriate to develop unique retail offerings by geographic markets. For example, a fast-food customer in Detroit probably seeks the same benefits as a fast-food customer in Los Angeles. Thus, it wouldn't be useful to segment the U.S. fast-food market geographically.

Demographic Segmentation **Demographic segmentation** groups consumers on the basis of easily measured, objective characteristics such as age, gender, income, and education. Demographic variables are the most common means to define segments because consumers in these segments can be easily identified and accessed. The media used by retailers to communicate with customers are defined in terms of demographic profiles.

Older consumers are the fastest growing age segment. Between 2000 and 2010, the 50–69-year-old segment is projected to increase by 37 percent—3.5 times the growth rate of the general U.S. population.[38] Retailing View 4.4 describes how a German supermarket retailer targets its offering to this segment.

However, demographics may not be useful for defining segments for some retailers. For example, demographics are poor predictors of users of activewear such as jogging suits and running shoes. At one time, retailers assumed that activewear would be purchased exclusively by young people, but the health and fitness trend has led people of all ages to buy this merchandise. Relatively inactive consumers also find activewear to be comfortable.

Aging Baby Boomers are an attractive target market for retailers.

Geodemographic Segmentation **Geodemographic segmentation** uses both geographic and demographic characteristics to classify consumers. This segmentation scheme is based on the principle that "birds of a feather flock together."[39] Consumers in the same neighborhoods tend to buy the same types of cars, appliances, and apparel and shop at the same types of retailers.

One widely used tool for geographic segmentation is PRIZM (Potential Rating Index by Zip Market) developed by Claritas (www.claritas.com). Claritas identified 62 geodemographic segments, called neighborhoods or clusters, using detailed demographic and consumption information and data on the media habits of the people who live in each U.S. block tract (zip code + 4).

In addition to providing demographic information about each cluster, Claritas provides indexes comparing the buying behavior and media habits of consumers in each cluster to the national average, which is set to 100. Thus, an index of 155 for a cluster indicates that the cluster is 55 percent higher than the national average for those variables. The information in the table below describes three PRIZM clusters:

Cluster name	Town & Gown	Gray Collars	Latino American
Cluster number	31	42	44
Description	College-town singles	Aging couples in near suburbs	Hispanic middle class
Lifestyle/products	Foreign videos (551)*	Lottery tickets (169)	Boxing (443)
	Online services (216)	Six-month CDs (140)	Dance music (194)
	Dogs (54)	Museums (68)	Campers (45)
	Sewing (35)	Tennis (42)	Barbecuing (57)
Food and drink	Tequila (183)	Fresh cold cuts (136)	Avocado (230)
	Coca-Cola (145)	Fast food (134)	Pita bread (115)
	Pasta salad (141)	Frozen dinners (130)	Chewing gum (105)
	Fast food (105)	Non-alcoholic beer (129)	Coca-Cola (108)
Media used	*Cosmopolitan* (183)	*Ebony* (159)	*Cosmopolitan* (228)
	Sports Illustrated (182)	*McCall's* (141)	*Touched by an Angel* (193)
	Friends (222)	*Good Morning*	*Court TV* (156)
	Face the Nation (164)	*America* (139)	*Seventeen* (117)
		TV Wrestling (137)	

*Index based on 100 = average.

These neighborhoods, with their similar demographics and buying behaviors, can be any place in the United States. For example, Exhibit 4–7 outlines the location of gray-collar areas in the United States.

4.4 RETAILING VIEW   Selling Groceries to Older Germans

The Adeg Aktiv Markt 50+, Europe's first supermarket designed for shoppers over age 50 years, targets Europe's aging population. The median age in Europe is 37.7, but it is expected to rise to 52.3 by 2050 because of a plummeting birth rate and longer life expectancies. In addition to its growing size, this market segment has a lot of buying power. These consumers have already paid off their homes and cars. Their children are out of the house, and their disposable income is higher than that of younger groups.

Some of the store's appealing differences, which would hardly surprise American shoppers, are neatly stocked shelves with attractive goods, a contrast to many European supermarkets where products are slid onto shelves in jagged-edged cardboard trays. Other changes are more subtle. The signs and labels are big; the aisles are wide; the floors are nonskid, even when wet; and there are plenty of places to sit down. The lights are specially calibrated to reduce glare on elderly customers' more sensitive eyes. The shelves are lower so products are within easy reach. In addition to regular shopping carts, there are carts that hook onto wheelchairs and carts that double as seats for the weary—as soon as a shopper sits down, the wheels lock. There is even a machine to check blood pressure, something a shopper of any age might appreciate after waiting in the checkout line on a Saturday afternoon. Because the elderly tend to buy for only one or two people, small-sized packages dominate the merchandise mix.

The employees are older as well. They are highly motivated, more so than the younger generation, because they came of age with a different work ethic. The staff falls into two categories: women who dropped out of the work force when they had children and middle-age workers who lost their jobs and have had difficulty finding employment because of their age. The workers are paid about 10 percent more than their younger counterparts, but the additional cost pays off because there is less turnover and the older workers rarely call in sick.

Even the parking lot strives to make the experience more convenient by featuring wider-than-average parking spaces. This feature has had the added benefit of appealing to other shoppers, such as mothers with small children. In fact, Adeg discovered its new format has broad appeal and that about half of its customers are under 50 years of age.

Sources: Shellee Fitzgerald, "Shaking Up the Box," *Canadian Grocer*, February 2005, p. 43; John Seewer, "Stores Sit Up and Take Notice as Older Shoppers Speak, Win Recognition When They Adjust," *Houston Chronicle*, July 26, 2004; Tania Ralli, "As Europe Ages, a Grocery Chain Extends a Hand," *Chain Store Age*, February 2004, pp. 31–32.

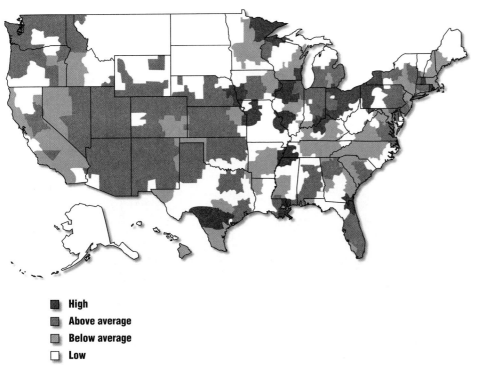

EXHIBIT 4–7
Location of Gray-Collar
Neighborhoods

■ **High**
■ **Above average**
■ **Below average**
□ **Low**

SOURCE: Michael J. Weiss, *The Clustered World* (Boston: Little, Brown, 2000), p. 262. Reprinted by permission.

Geodemographic segmentation is particularly appealing to store-based retailers, because customers typically patronize stores close to their neighborhood. Thus, retailers can use geodemographic segmentation to select locations for their stores and tailor the assortment in the stores to the preferences of the local community. In Chapter 8, we illustrate how geodemographic segmentation is used to make store location decisions.

Lifestyle Segmentation   **Lifestyle,** or **psychographics,** refers to how people live, how they spend their time and money, what activities they pursue, and their attitudes and opinions about the world in which they live. The segments are identified through consumer surveys that ask respondents to indicate whether they agree or disagree with statements such as "My idea of fun in a national park would be to stay in an expensive lodge and dress up for dinner," "I often crave excitement," or "I could not stand to skin a dead animal." Retailers today are placing more emphasis on lifestyles than on demographics to define a target segment.

One of the most widely used tools for **lifestyle segmentation** is **VALS**™ developed by SRI Consulting Business Intelligence (www.sric-bi.com/VALS).[40] On the basis of responses to the VALS survey, consumers are classified into the eight segments shown in Exhibit 4–8.

The segments are described by two dimensions: (1) the consumers' resources, including their income, education, health, and energy level, and (2) their primary consumer motivation—ideals, achievement, self-expression, and ideas-motivated consumption. Achievement-motivated consumers strive to win the approval of others, and self-expressive–motivated people make choices that emphasize individuality and a sense of adventure. Lifestyle segmentation is useful because it identifies what motivates buying behavior, but it is difficult to identify and access consumers in specific lifestyle segments.

EXHIBIT 4–8
VALS™ American Lifestyle
Segments

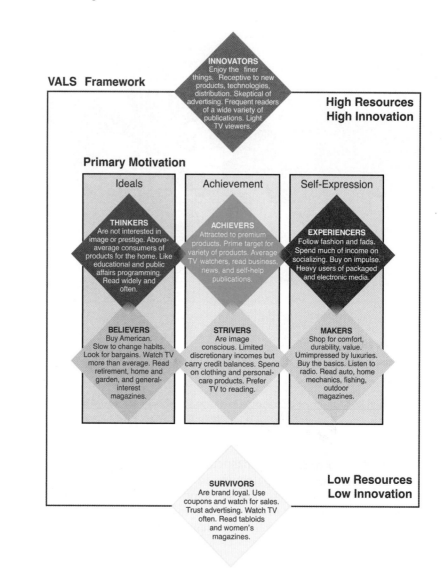

Buying Situation Segmentation   The buying behavior of customers with the same demographics or lifestyle can differ depending on their buying situation. Thus, retailers may use **buying situations,** such as fill-in versus weekly shopping, to segment a market. For example, in Exhibit 4–3, the parent with four children evaluated the supercenter higher than the Internet grocer or supermarket for weekly grocery purchases. But if the parent ran out of milk during the week, he or she would probably go to the convenience store rather than the wholesale club for this fill-in shopping. In terms of Exhibit 4–3's multiattribute attitude model, convenience would be more important than assortment in the fill-in shopping situation. Similarly, an executive will stay at a convention hotel on a business trip and a resort during a family vacation.

Buying situation segmentation rates high among the criteria for evaluating market segments. The segments are actionable because it is relatively easy to determine what a marketer should do to satisfy the needs of a particular segment. They are identifiable and accessible because the retailer or service provider can determine who the customers are on the basis of who has purchased the product or service and under what circumstances. Once they have identified the customer segment, they can assess its size.

Which of Best Buy's Customer Centricity segments does this customer belong to: "Barrys," "Jills," "Buzzes," or "Rays"?

Benefit Segmentation   Another approach for defining a target segment is to group customers seeking similar benefits; this is called **benefit segmentation.** In the multiattribute attitude model, customers in the same benefit segment would have a similar set of importance weights for the attributes of a store or product.

For example, customers who place high importance on fashion and style and low importance on price might form a fashion segment, whereas customers who place more importance on price would form a price segment.

Benefit segments are very actionable. The benefits sought by customers in the target segment clearly indicate how retailers should design their offerings to appeal to those customers. But customers in benefit segments aren't easily identified or accessed; it's hard to look at a person and determine what benefits he or she is seeking. Typically, the audience for the media used by retailers is described by demographics rather than by the benefits they seek.

Composite Segmentation Approaches

As we've seen, no one approach meets all the criteria for useful customer segmentation. For example, segmenting by demographics and geography is ideal for identifying and accessing customers, but these characteristics often are unrelated to customers' needs, which means these approaches may not indicate the actions necessary to attract customers in these segments. On the other hand, knowing what benefits customers are seeking is useful for designing an effective retail offering; the problem is identifying which customers are seeking these benefits. For these reasons, **composite segmentation** plans use multiple variables to identify customers in the target segment. They define target customers by their benefits sought, lifestyles, and demographics.

Best Buy has introduced its "Customer Centricity" program, which involves targeting five composite segments.[41] Each of these segments, referred to by a first name, has its own manager responsible for developing a retail strategy for that market segment. "Barrys" are the best customers. They are affluent professional males, 30–60 years old, who make a minimum of $150,000 a year and drive luxury cars. Barry is the kind of guy who walks into Best Buy, sees a $30,000 home theater system, and says, "I'll take it." "Jills" are busy suburban moms. "Buzzes" are focused, active, younger men, and "Rays" are family men who like their technology practical. The fifth segment is composed of small businesses that buy their consumer electronics at Best Buy.

A group of stores has been redesigned to focus on the specific segment or two that has significant representation in the local area. For example, Jill stores have areas for children to play while "Jill" shops. The soundtrack playing in the background is often children's music. Stores catering to Barrys promote high-end entertainment systems; stores for Jills dedicate more inventory to things like learning software and feature softer colors, a children's technology department, and personal shopping services. The Buzz-oriented stores, in contrast, feature the very latest technologies and comfortable places in which to sample them, complete with sofas and flat-screen TVs for testing video games and consoles.

SUMMARY

To satisfy customer needs, retailers must thoroughly understand how customers make store choice and purchase decisions and the factors they consider when deciding. This chapter describes the six stages in the buying process (need recognition, information search, evaluation of alternatives, choice of alternatives, purchase, and postpurchase evaluations) and how retailers can influence their customers at each stage.

The importance of the stages depends on the nature of the customer's decision. When decisions are important and risky, the buying process is longer because customers spend more time and effort on information search and evaluating alternatives. When buying decisions are less important to customers, they spend little time in the buying process, and their buying behavior may become habitual.

The buying process of consumers is influenced by their personal beliefs, attitudes, and values and by their social environmental. The primary social influences are provided by the consumers' families, reference groups, and culture.

To develop cost-effective retail programs, retailers group customers into segments. Some approaches for segmenting markets are based on geography, demographics, geodemographics, lifestyles, usage situations, and benefits sought. Because each approach has its advantages and disadvantages, retailers typically define their target segment by several characteristics.

KEY TERMS

accessibility, *112*
actionability, *112*
benefit segmentation, *117*
brand loyalty, *107*
buying process, *94*
buying situations, *116*
compatibility, *122*
complexity, *122*
composite segmentation, *117*
consideration set, *103*
cross-shopping, *97*
culture, *110*
demographic segmentation, *113*
everyday low pricing strategy, *100*
extended problem solving, *106*

external sources of information, *98*
fashion, *120*
geodemographic segmentation, *113*
geographic segmentation, *112*
habitual decision making, *107*
hedonic needs, *96*
identifiability, *112*
impulse buying, *107*
information search, *98*
internal sources of information, *98*
knockoff, *121*
lifestyle, *115*
lifestyle segmentation, *115*
limited problem solving, *106*
mass-market theory, *121*

multiattribute attitude model, *100*
observability, *123*
postpurchase evaluation, *105*
psychographics, *115*
reference group, *109*
retail market segment, *111*
satisfaction, *105*
store loyalty, *108*
subculture, *110*
subculture theory, *122*
trialability, *123*
trickledown theory, *121*
utilitarian needs, *96*
VALS™, *115*

GET OUT AND DO IT!

1. **CONTINUING CASE ASSIGNMENT: GO SHOPPING** Visit the retail store operated by the target firm for your continuing assignment. Pretend that you are looking to buy something sold at the store. Write down all of the things that the store does to try to stimulate you to buy merchandise.

2. **GO SHOPPING** Go to a supermarket and watch people selecting products to put in their shopping carts. How much time do they spend selecting products? Do some people spend more time than others?

3. **Web OLC EXERCISE** Go to the student side of the book's Web site to develop a multiattribute model describing your evaluation and decision concerning some relatively expensive product you bought recently, such as a car or a consumer electronics product. Open the multiattribute model exercise. List the attributes you considered in the left-hand column. List the alternatives you considered in the top row. Now fill in the importance weights for each attribute in the second column (10-very important, 1-very unimportant). Now fill in your evaluation of each product on each attribute (10-excellent performance, 1-poor performance). Based on your importance weights and performance beliefs, the evaluation of each product is shown in the bottom row. Did you buy the product with the highest evaluation?

4. **INTERNET EXERCISE** To better understand the segmentation classification of consumers, SRI Business Consulting Intelligence has developed the VALS tool that uses psychology to segment people according to their distinct personality traits. Go to the firm's homepage at http://www.sric-bi.com/VALS/presurvey. shtml and take the survey to identify your VALS profile based on your values, attitudes, and lifestyle. According to the results, what is your VALS profile type? Do you agree with your consumer profile? Why or why not? How can retailers effectively use the results of this survey when planning and implementing their business strategies?

5. **INTERNET EXERCISE** Retailers want to segment the market on the basis of the geographic classification of customers to select the best site for their businesses. Go to the ESRI Business Information Solutions homepage at http://www.esribis.com/index. html and type in the zip code for your hometown or your campus and read the results. How would a retailer, such as a local restaurant, use the information in this report when making a decision about whether to open a location in this zip code?

6. **INTERNET EXERCISE Go to the following Internet sites offering information about the latest fashions:** www.style.com *(Vogue)*, www.fashioninformation.com (U.K.), www.fashion.telegraph.co.uk (U.K.), www.t-style.com (Japan), and www.infomat. com/information/trends. Write a report describing the latest apparel fashions that are being shown by designers. Which of these fashions do you think will be popular? Why?

DISCUSSION QUESTIONS AND PROBLEMS

1. Does the customer buying process end when a customer buys some merchandise? Explain your answer.

2. What would make a consumer switch from making a habitual choice decision to eat at Wendy's to making a limited or extended choice decision?

3. Using the steps in the consumer buying process (Exhibit 4–1), describe how you (and your family) used this process to select your college/university. How many schools did you consider? How much time did you invest in this purchase decision? When you were deciding on which college to attend, what objective and subjective criteria did you use in the alternative evaluation portion of the consumer buying process?

4. Why is geodemographic segmentation used by retailers to locate stores?

5. Any retailer's goal is to get a customer in its store to stop searching and buy a product at its outlet. How can a sporting goods retailer ensure that the customer buys athletic equipment at its outlet?

6. A family-owned used record store across the street from a major university campus wants to identify the various segments in its market. What approaches might the store owner use to segment its market? List two potential target market segments based on this segmentation approach. Then contrast the retail mix that would be most appropriate for the two potential target segments.

7. How would you expect the buying decision process to differ when shopping on the Internet compared with shopping in a store?

8. Using the multiattribute attitude model, identify the probable choice of a local car dealer for a young, single woman and for a retired couple with limited income (see the table on p. 120). What can the national retail chain do to increase the chances of the retired couple patronizing its dealership? You can use the multiattribute model template on the student side of the book's Web site to analyze this information.

Performance Attributres	IMPORTANCE WEIGHTS		PERFORMANCE BELIEFS		
	Young, Single Woman	Retired Couple	Local Gas Station	National Service Chain	Local Car Dealer
Price	2	10	9	10	3
Time to complete repair	8	5	5	9	7
Reliability	2	9	2	7	10
Convenience	8	3	3	6	5

SUGGESTED READINGS

Black, Pam; Molly Knight; and David Koch. "Meet the Shoppers: How, Why and Where They Buy," *Retail Traffic* 33 (November 2004), pp. 24–31.

Curtis, Eleanor. *Fashion Retail*. Chichester, West Sussex: Wiley-Academy, 2004.

Fox, Edward; Alan Montogmery; and Leonard Lodish. "Consumer Shopping and Spending across Retail Formats," *Journal of Business* 77 (April 2004), pp. S25–61.

Ha, Young, and Leslie Stoel. "Internet Apparel Shopping Behaviors: The Influence of General Innovativeness," *International Journal of Retail & Distribution Management* 32 no. 8/9 (2004), pp. 377–91.

"Inside the Consuming Mind; HFN, in an Exclusive Study with the NPD Group, Looks at What Drives Shoppers' Buying Habits," *HFN*, January 31, 2005, pp. 1–8.

Keen, Cherie; Martin Wetzels; Ko de Ruyer; and Richard Feinberg. "E-Tailers versus Retailers: Which Factors Determine Consumer Preferences?" *Journal of Business Research* 57 (July 2004), pp. 685–701.

Mangleburg, Tamara; Patricia Doney; and Terry Bristol. "Shopping with Friends and Teens' Susceptability to Peer Influence," *Journal of Retailing* 80, no. 2 (2004), pp. 101–23.

Mummalaneu, Venkatapparao. "An Empirical Investigation of Web Site Characteristics, Consumer Emotional States and On-Line Shopping Behaviors," *Journal of Business Research* 58 (April 2005), pp. 526–45.

Pooler, Jim. *Why We Shop: Emotional Rewards and Retail Strategies*. Westport, CT: Praeger, 2003.

Underhill, Paco. *Why We Buy: The Science of Shopping*. New York: Simon & Schuster, 1999.

William, Colin. "A Lifestyle Choice? Evaluating the Motives of Do-It-Yourself (DIY) Consumers," *International Journal of Retail & Distribution Management* 32, no. 4/5, (2004), pp. 270–85.

APPENDIX 4A   Customer Buying Behavior and Fashion

Many retailers, particularly department and specialty stores, sell fashionable merchandise. To sell this type of merchandise profitably, retailers need to (1) understand how fashions develop and diffuse throughout the marketplace and (2) use operating systems that enable them to match supply and demand for this volatile merchandise. This appendix reviews the consumer behavior aspects of fashion; the operating systems for matching supply and demand for fashion merchandise are discussed in Chapter 13.

Fashion is a type of product or a way of behaving that is temporarily adopted by a large number of consumers because the product, service, or behavior is considered socially appropriate for the time and place.[42] For example, in some social groups, it is or has been fashionable to have brightly colored hair, play golf, wear a coat made from animal fur, have a beard, or go to an expensive health spa for a vacation. In many retail environments, however, the term *fashion* is associated with apparel and accessories.

CUSTOMER NEEDS SATISFIED BY FASHION

Fashion gives people an opportunity to satisfy many emotional and practical needs. Through fashions, people develop their own identity. They also can use fashions to manage their appearance, express their self-image and feelings, enhance their egos, and make an impression on others. Through the years, fashions have become associated with specific lifestyles or the roles people play. You wear different clothing styles when you are attending class, going out on a date, or interviewing for a job.

Fashion also can be used to communicate with others. For example, a salesperson might wear a classic business suit when calling on a buyer at Best Buy but more informal and fashion-forward attire when calling on Abercrombie & Fitch. These different dress styles indicate the salesperson's understanding of the differences in the cultures of these firms.

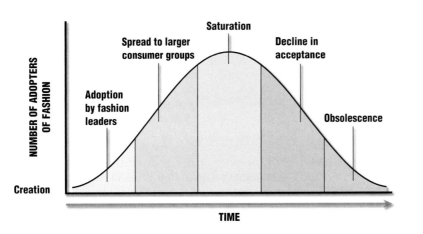

EXHIBIT 4–9
Stages in the Fashion
Life Cycle

People use fashions to both develop their own identity and gain acceptance from others. These two benefits of fashion can be opposing forces. If you choose to wear something radically different, you will achieve recognition for your individuality but might not be accepted by your peers. To satisfy these conflicting needs, manufacturers and retailers offer a variety and combination of designs that are fashionable and still enable consumers to express their individuality.

Consumers also adopt fashions to overcome boredom. People get tired of wearing the same clothing and seeing the same furniture in their living room. They seek changes in their lifestyles by buying new clothes or redecorating their houses to meet their changing tastes, preferences, and income.

HOW DO FASHIONS DEVELOP AND SPREAD?

Fashions are not universal. A fashion might be accepted in one geographic region, country, or age group and not in another. Consider how your idea of "fashionable" differs from your parents'. Many of you might have a hard time imagining them dressed in distressed, hip-hugging jeans and a tight tee-shirt. Well, they might have just as much trouble picturing you in a double-breasted business suit. One interesting sports fashion trend has been the uniforms for college and NBA basketball players. Thirty years ago, they sported long hair and wore tight, short shorts and Converse shoes. Now they have short hair and wear baggy shorts and Nike shoes. See http://www.nba.com/photostore/.

The stages in the fashion life cycle are shown in Exhibit 4–9. The cycle begins with the creation of a new design or style. Then some consumers recognized as fashion leaders or innovators adopt the fashion and start a trend in their social group. The fashion spreads from the leaders to others and is accepted widely as a fashion. Eventually, the fashion is accepted by most people in the social group and can become overused. Saturation and overuse set the stage for the decline in popularity and the creation of new fashions.

Creation

New fashions arise from a number of sources. Couture fashion designers are one source of creative inspirations, but fashions are also developed by creative consumers, celebri-

ties, and even retailers. When high-profile actors, performers, and athletes wear the latest styles in television shows and movies, on stage, or on the red carpet, consumers interested in fashion often adopt and follow these trends.

Adoption by Fashion Leaders

The fashion life cycle really starts when the fashion is adopted by leading consumers. These initial adopters of a new fashion are called *fashion leaders, innovators, or trend-setters,* and they are the first people to display the new fashion in their social group. If the fashion is too innovative or very different from currently accepted fashion, the style might not be accepted by the social group, thus prematurely ending its life cycle.

Three theories have been proposed to explain how fashion spreads within a society. The **trickle-down theory** suggests that fashion leaders are consumers with the highest social status—wealthy, well-educated consumers. After they adopt a fashion, the fashion trickles down to consumers in lower social classes. When the fashion is accepted in the lowest social class, it is no longer acceptable to the fashion leaders in the highest social class. Manufacturers and retailers stimulate this trickledown process by copying the latest styles displayed at designer fashion shows and sold in exclusive specialty stores. These copies, referred to as **knockoffs,** are sold at lower prices through retailers targeting a broader market. For example, shortly after the models walk down the runway at Prada's annual fashion show in Milan, Italy, displaying the latest designs on a slim silhouette, sewing machines are whirring 6,000 miles away in Hong Kong, churning out similar apparel. As little as six weeks later, clothing that looks a lot like Prada's latest designs appears in catalogs and stores that sell these items for an affordable price. Sometimes the knockoffs even beat the originals to the stores.[43]

The second theory, the **mass-market theory,** suggests that fashions spread across social classes. Each social class has its own fashion leaders who play key roles in their own social networks. Fashion information trickles across social classes rather than down from the upper classes to the lower classes. Some retailers use teen boards to stimulate diffusion of fashion across social classes. Social leaders are selected to be members of the board and promote the retailer and the merchandise sold in its stores.

The third theory, the **subculture theory,** is based on the development of recent fashions. Subcultures of mostly young and less affluent consumers, such as motorcycle riders or urban rappers, started fashions for such things as colorful fabrics, tee-shirts, sneakers, jeans, black leather jackets, and surplus military clothing. These fashions started with people in lower-income consumer groups and trickled up to mainstream consumer classes. Nike employs "cool hunters" to canvas subcultures and find out what will be the next hot sneaker. The goth scene is an example of a subculture that has developed a unique style. It revolves around dark fashion and even darker, moody music performed by artists like Marilyn Manson. Hot Topics, a Pomona-based mall retailer, sells clothing and accessories that reflect a variety of music-related lifestyles, which include street wear, retro-influenced lounge, punk, club, and gothic. Many fashions worn by bands such as Korn, Linkin Park, and Good Charlotte have often appeared in Hot Topic stores prior to their widespread popularity.[45]

These theories of fashion development indicate that fashion leaders can come from many different places and social groups. In our diverse society, many types of consumers have the opportunity to be the leaders in setting fashion trends.

Spread to Large Consumer Groups

During this stage, the fashion is accepted by a wider group of consumers referred to as *early adopters.* The fashion becomes increasingly visible, receives greater publicity and media attention, and is readily available in retail stores. The relative advantage, compatibility, complexity, trialability, and observability of a fashion affect the time it takes the fashion to spread through a social group. New fashions that provide more benefits have a higher relative advantage compared with existing fashions, and these new fashions spread faster. Fashions are often adopted by consumers because they make people feel special. Thus, more exclusive fashions like expensive clothing are adopted more quickly in an affluent target market. On a more utilitarian level, clothing that is easy to maintain, such as wrinkle-free pants, will diffuse quickly in the general population.

Compatibility is the degree to which the fashion is consistent with existing norms, values, and behaviors. When new fashions aren't consistent with existing norms, the number of adopters and the speed of adoption are lower. Since the mid-1960s, the fashion industry has repeatedly attempted to revive the miniskirt. It has had only moderate success because the group of women with the most disposable income to spend on fashion are Baby Boomers, many of whom no longer find the miniskirt a relevant fashion for their family-oriented lifestyles.

Complexity refers to how easy it is to understand and use the new fashion. Consumers have to learn how to incorporate a new fashion into their lifestyle. For example, at times, tie manufacturers have tried to stimulate sales of

Fashion trends change rapidly. Designers may be featuring animal prints and full long skirts one season and a completely different silhouette the next season.

bow ties but were unsuccessful because men had difficulty tying the knot.

Trialability refers to the costs and commitment required to adopt the fashion initially. For example, when consumers need to spend a lot of money buying a new type of expensive apparel to be in fashion, the rate of adoption is slower than if the consumers can see how it looks on them without having to buy it.

Observability is the degree to which the new fashion is visible and easily communicated to others in the social group. Clothing fashions are very observable compared with fashions for the home, such as sheets and towels. It is therefore likely that a fashion in clothing will spread more quickly than a new color scheme or style for the bedroom.

Fashion retailers engage in many activities to increase the adoption and spread of a new fashion throughout their target market. Compatibility is increased and complexity is decreased by showing consumers how to coordinate a new article of fashion clothing with other items the consumer already owns. Trialability is increased by providing dressing rooms so customers can try on clothing and see how it looks on them. Providing opportunities for customers to return merchandise also increases trialability. Retailers increase observability by displaying fashion merchandise in their stores and advertising it in the media.

Saturation

In this stage, the fashion achieves its highest level of social acceptance. Almost all consumers in the target market are aware of the fashion and have decided to either accept or reject it. At this point, the fashion has become old and boring to many people.

Decline in Acceptance and Obsolescence

When fashions reach saturation, they have become less appealing to consumers. Because most people have already adopted the fashion, it no longer provides an opportunity for people to express their individuality. Fashion creators and leaders thus are beginning to experiment with new fashions. The introduction of a new fashion speeds the decline of the preceding fashion.

Retailing Strategy

Section I described retail management decisions; the different types of retailers, including how retailers use multiple selling channels—stores, the Internet, and catalogs—to reach their customers; and factors that affect consumers' choices of retailers, channels, and merchandise. This broad overview of retailing provided the background information needed to develop and implement an effective retail strategy.

Section II discusses strategic decisions made by retailers.

Chapter 5 describes the development of a retail market strategy.

Chapter 6 examines the financial strategy associated with the market strategy.

Chapters 7 and 8 discuss the location strategy for retail outlets.

Chapter 9 looks at the firm's organization and human resource strategy.

Chapter 10 examines systems used to control the flow of information and merchandise.

Chapter 11 details approaches that retailers take to manage relationships with their customers.

As outlined in Chapter 1, these decisions are strategic rather than tactical because they involve committing significant resources to developing long-term advantages over the competition in a target market segment.

Sections III and IV review tactical decisions regarding merchandise and store management to implement the retail strategy. These implementation or tactical decisions affect a retailer's efficiency, but their impact is shorter term than the strategic decisions reviewed in Section II.

Retail Market Strategy

With annual sales approaching $20 billion, Publix Super Markets, Inc., is one of the 10 largest supermarket chains in the United States. We operate over 860 stores, primarily in Florida, but also have stores in Georgia, Alabama, South Carolina, and Tennessee.

My background began in operations, with my first job out of college being a production supervisor at Frito Lay. I also spent time in the software consulting industry prior to joining Publix in 1994. Since coming to Publix, I've spent time in a wide variety of business areas including Manufacturing, Distribution, Fresh Products,

EXECUTIVE BRIEFING
Jim Cossin, Director of Strategy Support
Publix Super Markets, Inc.

Engineering, and Strategic Planning. I also was Director of Fulfillment for PublixDirect, our online shopping and home delivery test.

As Director of Strategy Support, my primary responsibility is to support and facilitate the development and implementation of strategy at Publix. Each year, our various business areas are required to update their annual business plan. My department is responsible for assisting these business units through a rigorous process of strategy development and helping them to define the initiatives that will best achieve their desired goals. We also assist with implementation by providing project management support for these initiatives, and by measuring and reporting progress.

Another area of responsibility is to facilitate the development of our corporate business plan. I constantly monitor and evaluate the supermarket industry, and gather information that helps to identify potential opportunities and threats facing Publix. I provide this information to our president, CEO, and CFO, and work with them to determine our best course of action.

In addition to supporting strategic planning and implementation, I am also responsible for the Process

CHAPTER 5

QUESTIONS

What is a retail strategy?

How can a retailer build a sustainable competitive advantage?

What steps do retailers go through to develop a strategy?

What different strategic growth opportunities can retailers pursue?

What retailers are best positioned to become global retailers?

Improvement team (a group of 12 industrial engineers) as well as our Continuous Quality Improvement programs.

At Publix, our strategy centers on customer service. We have a 75-year tradition of providing premier service to our customers. We continually look for ways to improve this service, as well as ways to improve our operations so we can continue to provide the products and services our customers want at a good value.

Being part of the Strategy Support group at Publix has allowed me to be involved in many new and promising opportunities we are investigating. Publix is currently testing our "Pix" convenience stores and gas kiosks, "Publix Liquors," "Publix Sabor" (our format geared at meeting the needs of our Hispanic customers), as well as our recently announced "Publix Greenwise Market" (our natural and organic format). These are just a few of the exciting opportunities that we experience every day. It's an aspect of retail that I never knew existed prior to my coming to Publix.

The growing intensity of retail competition—due to the emergence of new competitors, formats, and technologies, as well as shifts in customer needs—is forcing retailers to devote more attention to long-term strategic planning. As the retail management decision-making process (discussed in Chapter 1) indicates, retailing strategy (Section II) is the bridge between understanding the world of retailing—that is, the analysis of the retail environment (Section I)—and the more tactical merchandise management and store operations activities (Sections III and IV) undertaken to implement the retail strategy. The retail strategy provides the direction retailers need to deal effectively with their environment, customers, and competitors.[1]

The first part of this chapter defines the term *retail strategy* and discusses three important elements of retail strategy: the target market segment, retail format, and sustainable competitive advantage. Next, we outline approaches for building a sustainable competitive advantage. The chapter concludes with a discussion of the strategic retail planning process.

REFACT

The word *strategy* comes from the Greek word meaning the "art of the general."[2]

WHAT IS A RETAIL STRATEGY?

The term *strategy* is frequently used in retailing. For example, retailers talk about their merchandise strategy, promotion strategy, location strategy, and private brand strategy. The term is used so commonly it appears that all retailing decisions are strategic decisions, but in truth, retail strategy isn't just another expression for retail management.

Definition of Retail Market Strategy

A **retail strategy** is a statement identifying (1) the retailer's target market, (2) the format the retailer plans to use to satisfy the target market's needs, and (3) the bases upon which the retailer plans to build a sustainable competitive advantage.[3] The **target market** is the market segment(s) toward which the retailer plans to focus its resources and retail mix. A **retail format** suggests the type of retail mix (nature of merchandise and services offered, pricing policy, advertising and promotion program, approach to store design and visual merchandising, typical location) used by the retailer to satisfy the needs of its target market. A **sustainable competitive advantage** is an advantage over the competition that is not easily copied and thus can be maintained over a long period of time. Here are a few examples of retail strategies.

- Curves has grown to more than 8,400 franchises in all 50 states and 28 countries, making it by far the world's top fitness center in terms of number of clubs. One in every four fitness clubs in the United States is a Curves. While other clubs go after the prized 18-to-34-year-old demographic segment, Curves' customers are aging Baby Boomers, typically living in small towns. This retailer's fitness centers don't have treadmills, saunas, locker rooms, mirrors, aerobics classes, or free weights. Members work out on 8 to 12 hydraulic resistance machines, stopping between stations to walk or jog in place. The clubs' standard routine is finished in 30 minutes and designed to burn 500 calories. Club members usually pay $29 a month, far less than conventional fitness clubs. Rather than attract customers from other clubs, Curves generates customers who haven't considered joining a fitness club before.[4]

While most fitness centers target the 18–34-year-old segment, Curves' retail offering appeals to aging Baby Boomers.

- Magazine Luiza, Brazil's third-largest nonfood retailer, targets low-income consumers by selling consumer electronics and appliances on installment payment plans and offering affordable credit in a country with some of the world's highest interest rates. The company requires customers to return to the store each month to make payments in person, enticing many of the customers to make new purchases when they see the appealing new merchandise on sale. In a country where almost half the population does not have a checking account, the retailer also provides services—including personal loans and insurance policies—that would otherwise be out of reach to many customers. Even though 80 percent of its sales are paid for in installments, its default rate is 50 percent lower than that of other Brazilian retailers.[5]

- Chico's, with its more than 300 specialty stores, sells apparel that is fashionable but clearly designed for a woman between 35 and 55 years of age. Chico's apparel flatters more mature women with active lifestyles. The company sells only its own private label brands and handles everything from sourcing to designing to supervising merchandise manufacturing and delivery. This retailer has over 1.2 million members enrolled in its loyalty program who account for 80 percent of the company's sales. The average transaction for loyalty club members is more than $130, compared with less than $90 for those not enrolled in the program. Chico's also delivers high-quality customer service and devotes considerable time and effort to training its sales associates to establish a personal relationship with each of its customers.[6]

• From a single store in 1977, Save-A-Lot, a wholly owned subsidiary of SuperValu, has grown to more than 1000 stores, making it the United States' 13th largest supermarket chain. Save-A-Lot stores offer an edited assortment of only 1,250 SKUs compared with 20,000–30,000 SKUs in a conventional supermarket. By offering only the most popular items, most of which are private label merchandise, Save-A-Lot reduces its costs and is able to price its merchandise 40 percent lower than conventional supermarkets. Due to its buying power, Save-A-Lot also is able to develop customized product specifications to provide high-quality private label merchandise at low prices.[7]

Each of these retail strategies involves (1) selecting target market segment(s), (2) selecting a retail format (the elements in a retail mix), and (3) developing a sustainable competitive advantage that enables the retailer to reduce the level of competition it faces. Now let's examine these central concepts of a retail strategy.

TARGET MARKET AND RETAIL FORMAT

The **retailing concept** is a management orientation that focuses a retailer on determining the needs of its target market and satisfying those needs more effectively and efficiently than its competitors do. The selection of a target market concentrates the retailer on a group of consumers whose needs it will attempt to satisfy, and the selection of a retail format outlines the retail mix to be used to satisfy the needs of those customers. Successful retailers satisfy the needs of customers in their target segment better than their competition does.

A **retail market** is a group of consumers with similar needs (a market segment) that is serviced by a group of retailers using a similar retail format to satisfy them.[8] Exhibit 5–1 illustrates a set of retail markets for women's clothing and lists various retail formats in the left-hand column. Each format offers a different retail mix to its customers. Market segments are listed in the exhibit's top row. As mentioned in Chapter 4, these segments could be defined in terms of the customers' geographic location, demographics, lifestyle, buying situation, or benefits sought. In this exhibit, we divide the market into three fashion-related segments: conservative, or consumers who place little importance on fashion; traditional, or those who want classic styles; and fashion-forward, or those who want the latest fashions.

Each square of the matrix shown in Exhibit 5–1 describes a potential retail market in which retailers compete. For example, Wal-Mart and Kmart stores in the same geographic area compete with each other using a discount store format targeting conservative customers, while Bloomingdale's and Neiman Marcus compete against each other using a department store format targeting the fashion-forward segment. Each fashion segment—conservative, traditional, and fashion-forward—is likely to shop multiple formats. For instance, a fashion-forward customer might shop Urban Outfitters for casual wear and Neiman Marcus for business attire.

The women's clothing market in Exhibit 5–1 is just one of several representations that could have been used. Retail formats might be expanded to include outlet stores and category specialists. Rather than being segmented by fashion

EXHIBIT 5–1   Retail Markets for Women's Apparel

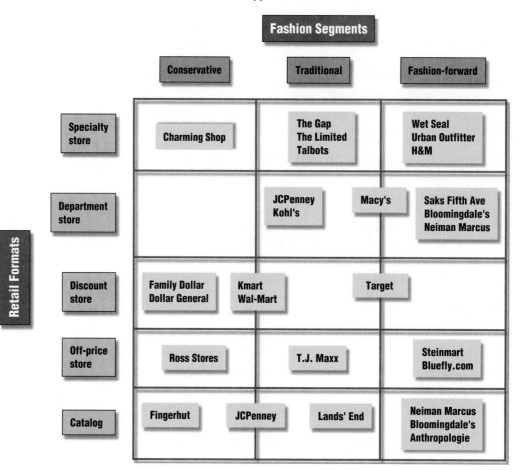

orientation, the market could be segmented using the other approaches described in Chapter 4. Although Exhibit 5–1 isn't the only way to describe the women's retail clothing market, it does illustrate how retail markets are defined in terms of retail format and customer market segment and portrays a retail market in each square.

Exhibit 5–1's matrix also describes the battlefields on which women's apparel retailers compete. The position in each battlefield (cell in the matrix) indicates the first two elements of a retailer's strategy: the fashion segment (the x-axis) and retail format (the y-axis).

Consider the situation confronting The Gap as it develops a retail strategy for the women's clothing market. Should The Gap compete in all 15 retail markets shown in Exhibit 5–1, or should it focus on a limited set of markets? If The Gap decides to focus on a limited set of markets, which should it pursue? The Gap's answers to these questions define its retail strategy and indicate how it should focus its resources.

BUILDING A SUSTAINABLE COMPETITIVE ADVANTAGE

The final element in a retail strategy is the retailer's approach to building a sustainable competitive advantage. Any business activity that a retailer engages in can be the basis for a competitive advantage, but some advantages are sustainable over a long period of time, whereas others can be duplicated by competitors almost immediately.[9] For example, it would be hard for Starbucks to establish a long-term

Sources of Advantage	SUSTAINABILITY OF ADVANTAGE	
	Less Sustainable	More Sustainable
Customer loyalty (Chapters 11 and 16)	Habitual repeat purchasing; repeat purchases because of limited competition in the local area	Building a brand image with an emotional connection with customers; using databases to develop and utilize a deeper understanding of customers
Location (Chapters 7 and 8)		Convenient locations
Human resource management (Chapter 9)	More employees	Committed, knowledgeable employees
Distribution and information systems (Chapter 10)	Bigger warehouses; automated warehouses	Shared systems with vendors
Unique merchandise (Chapters 12 to 14)	More merchandise; greater assortment; lower price; higher advertising budgets; more sales promotions	Exclusive merchandise
Vendor relations (Chapter 14)	Repeat purchases from vendor due to limited alternatives	Coordination of procurement efforts; ability to get scarce merchandise
Customer service (Chapter 19)	Hours of operation	Knowledgeable and helpful salespeople

EXHIBIT 5–2

Methods of Developing Sustainable Competitive Advantage

advantage over Seattle's Best Coffee by simply offering the same coffee specialties at lower prices. If Starbucks' lower prices were successful in attracting customers, Seattle's Best would know what Starbucks had done and quickly match the price reduction. Similarly, it's hard for retailers to develop a long-term advantage by offering broader or deeper merchandise assortments. If broader and deeper assortments attract a lot of customers, competitors will simply go out and buy the same merchandise for their stores.

Establishing a competitive advantage means that the retailer, in effect, builds a wall around its position in a retail market. When the wall is high, it will be hard for competitors outside the wall (i.e., operating in other markets or entrepreneurs) to enter the market and compete for the retailer's target customers.

Over time, all advantages will be eroded due to competitive forces, but by building high, thick walls, retailers can sustain their advantage, minimize competitive pressure, and boost profits for a longer time. Thus, establishing a sustainable competitive advantage is the key to positive long-term financial performance.

Seven important opportunities for retailers to develop sustainable competitive advantages are as follows: (1) customer loyalty, (2) location, (3) human resource management, (4) distribution and information systems, (5) unique merchandise, (6) vendor relations, and (7) customer service. Exhibit 5–2 shows the aspects of these sources of competitive advantage that are more and less sustainable. Let's look at each of these approaches.

Customer Loyalty

Customer loyalty means that customers are committed to buying merchandise and services from a particular retailer. Other bases for sustainable competitive advantage discussed in this section help attract and maintain loyal customers; for instance, having dedicated employees, unique merchandise, and superior customer service all help solidify a loyal customer base. But having loyal customers is, in and of itself, an important method of sustaining an advantage over competitors.

Loyalty is more than simply liking one retailer over another.[10] Loyalty means that customers will be reluctant to patronize competitive retailers. For example, loyal customers will continue to shop at Magazine Luiza even if a competitor opens a store nearby and provides slightly lower prices. Some ways that retailers build loyalty are by (1) developing a strong brand for the store or store brands, (2) developing clear and precise positioning strategies, and (3) creating an emotional attachment with customers through loyalty programs.[11]

Retail Branding   Stores use brands to build loyalty in much the same way that manufacturers do. In retailing, however, a store's brand may be the name over the door, such as Tiffany's or Wal-Mart. Stores often have merchandise with their store's name on it, such as Banana Republic, or a name that is found exclusively at that store, such as Kenmore appliances at Sears. These store brands are also known as private label brands and are discussed in Chapter 14.

A retail brand, whether it is the name of the retailer or a private label, can create an emotional tie with customers that builds their trust and loyalty. People know, for instance, that when they buy the L.L. Bean brand, they can be assured that the products are "guaranteed to give 100% satisfaction in every way."[12] Retail brands also facilitate store loyalty because they stand for a predictable level of quality that customers feel comfortable with and often seek. Retail branding is discussed in Chapter 16. A strong retail brand also becomes part of a retailer's positioning strategy, the topic discussed next.

Positioning   A retailer builds customer loyalty by developing a clear, distinctive image of its retail offering and consistently reinforcing that image through its merchandise and service. **Positioning** involves the design and implementation of a retail mix to create an image of the retailer in the customer's mind relative to its competitors.[13]

Furthermore, positioning emphasizes that the image in the customer's mind (not the retail manager's mind) is critical. Thus, the retailer needs to research what its image is and make sure that it is consistent with what customers in its target market want. A perceptual map is frequently used to represent the customer's held image and preferences for retailers.

Exhibit 5–3 offers a hypothetical perceptual map of retailers selling women's clothing in the Washington, DC, area. The two dimensions in this map, fashion/style and service, represent the two primary characteristics that consumers in this example use in forming their impressions of retail stores. Perceptual maps are developed so that the distance between two retailers' positions on the map indicates how similar the stores appear to consumers. For example, Neiman Marcus and Bloomingdale's are very close to each other on the map because consumers in this illustration see them as offering similar service and fashion. In contrast, Nordstrom and Kmart are far apart, indicating consumers think they're quite different. Note that stores close to each other compete vigorously because consumers feel they provide similar benefits.

According to this example, The Gap has an image of offering moderately priced, fashionable women's clothing with good service. T.J. Maxx offers more fashionable clothing with less service. Sears is viewed as a retailer offering women's clothing that is not fashionable and relatively limited service.

The ideal points (marked by red dots on the map) indicate the characteristics of an ideal retailer for consumers in different market segments. For example, consumers in segment 3 prefer a retailer that offers high-fashion merchandise with low service, whereas consumers in segment 1 want more traditional apparel and aren't concerned about service. The ideal points are

Hypothetical Perceptual Map of Women's Apparel Market in Washington, DC   **EXHIBIT 5–3**

located so that the distance between a retailer's position (marked with a blue "x") and the ideal point indicates how consumers in the segment evaluate that retailer.

Retailers that are closer to an ideal point are evaluated more favorably by the consumers in the segment than are retailers located farther away. Thus, consumers in segment 6 prefer Wet Seal and Hot Topics to Neiman Marcus because they are more fashion forward and their target customers do not require such high service levels.

Loyalty Programs   Loyalty programs are part of an overall customer relationship management (CRM) program that is examined in Chapter 11. These programs are prevalent in retailing, from department stores to the local pizza shop.

Customer loyalty programs work hand-in-hand with CRM. Members of loyalty programs are identified when they buy because they use some type of loyalty card. Their purchase information then is stored in a huge database known as a **data warehouse.** From this data warehouse, analysts determine what types of merchandise and services certain groups of customers are buying. Using this information, retailers can tailor their offerings to better meet the needs of their loyal customers.

For instance, by analyzing its database, Safeway might identify those customers who buy expensive wines and gourmet food. Having identified these customers, Safeway could develop a special promotion focusing on preparing a gourmet meal and offer recipes, a list of ingredients, and coupons for some of the products. Retailing View 5.1 describes how a Canadian menswear chain uses customer information to build store loyalty through customer service and targeting its promotional activities to improve customer satisfaction.

Location

The classic response to the question "What are the three most important things in retailing?" is "location, location, location." Location is the critical factor in consumers' selection of a store. For example, most people shop at the super-market closest to where they live. A competitive advantage based on location is sustainable because it is not easily duplicated. For instance, once Walgreens has put a store at the best location at an intersection, CVS is relegated to the second-best location.

5.1   RETAILING VIEW   Loyalty to Harry

Harry Rosen operates 16 stores in Canada, where it sells high-end clothing from Ermenegildo Zegna, J.P. Tilford by Samuelsohn, Hugo Boss, Canali, Armani Collezioni, and others, in addition to nine Hugo Boss boutiques across the United States. This retailer, with its annual sales of $150 million Canadian, uses information systems to improve cus-tomer service and build long-term relationships.

Each Harry Rosen sales-person can access the firm's data warehouse with customer information from any point-of-sale (POS) terminal in any store. The database describes what the customer has bought in the past and provides his or her personal informa-

Harry Rosen builds loyalty and competitive advantage by using its customer database to tailor its promotional offerings.

tion. All sales associates are urged to contribute to the data-base. If a wife buys a birthday gift for her husband, salespeople are encouraged to find out his birthday and how old he is and then include this information in the system rather than in their personal notebook.

The information system improves customer service and the targeting of retail promotions. For example, when garments are left in the store for alterations, the system tracks their progress and electronically notifies the salesperson of any delay so the salesperson can relay this information to the customer. Heavy spenders are easily identified and invited to special promotional events. The system is also used to sell slow-moving merchandise.

For example, a particular store may have too many size 44-short suits. A salesperson can go to a terminal, generate a list of all customers who have bought 44-short suits in the past few months, and contact them. When new merchandise arrives, the salesperson can identify the customers who have bought that type of merchandise in the past and inform them of the new merchandise.

Sources: Ed McHinley, "Custom Fit Solutions," *Stores*, June 2005, p. 23; Luba Krekhovetsky, "Harry Rosen," *Canadian Business*, February 16, 2004, p. 98; Brian Dunn, "A Half-Century of Harry; After 50 Years of Service, Harry Rosen Hasn't Lost a Step," *DNR*, March 8, 2004, p. 7.

Starbucks has developed a strong competitive advantage with its location selection. It conquers one area of the city at a time and then expands in the region, saturating a major market before entering a new market. For example, there were over 100 Starbucks outlets in the Seattle area before the company expanded to a new region. Starbucks will frequently open several stores close to one another, such as its two stores on the corners of the intersection of Robson and Thurlow streets in Vancouver. Starbucks has such a high density of stores that it lets the storefront promote the company and does very little media advertising. Approaches for evaluating and selecting locations are discussed in Chapters 7 and 8.

Starbucks creates a competitive advantage by picking good locations that saturate an area.

Human Resource Management

Retailing is a labor-intensive business, in which employees play a major role in providing services for customers and building customer loyalty. Knowledgeable and skilled employees committed to the retailer's objectives are critical assets that support the success of companies such as Southwest Airlines, Whole Foods, Home Depot, and Men's Wearhouse.[14]

Recruiting and retaining great employees does not come easy. Chapter 9 examines how retailers gain a sustainable competitive advantage by developing programs to motivate and coordinate employee efforts, providing appropriate incentives, fostering a strong and positive organizational culture and environment, and managing diversity.

Distribution and Information Systems

All retailers strive to reduce operating costs—the costs associated with running the business—and make sure the merchandise that customers want is available. Then retailers can decide how to use the cost savings they achieve. They could offer even better service, increase the breath and depth of their merchandise assortments, or lower prices to differentiate themselves from competition.

Retailers achieve these efficiencies by developing sophisticated distribution and information systems and sharing information with vendors.[15] For instance, merchandise sales information flows seamlessly from Wal-Mart to its vendors, like Procter & Gamble, to facilitate quick and efficient merchandise replenishment that avoids costly stockouts. Wal-Mart has the largest data warehouse in the world, enabling the company to fine-tune its merchandise assortments on a store-by-store, category-by-category basis. Wal-Mart's distribution and information systems have enabled this retailer to be the lowest cost provider of merchandise in every market in which it competes.

Unique Merchandise

It is difficult for retailers to develop a competitive advantage through merchandise because most competitors can purchase and sell the same popular national brands. But many retailers realize a sustainable competitive advantage by developing **private label brands** (also called *store brands*), which are products developed and marketed by a retailer and available only from that retailer.[16] For example, if you want to buy Craftsman tools, you have to buy them from Sears. Store brands now account for one of every five items sold every day in U.S. supermarkets, drug chains, and mass merchandisers. They represent more than $50 billion in annual

Sears has a strong private label program. If you want to buy Craftsman tools or Kenmore appliances, you have to purchase them from Sears or Kmart.

sales in the United States and are achieving new levels of growth every year.[17] Issues pertaining to the development of store brand merchandise are discussed in Chapter 14.

Vendor Relations

By developing strong relations with vendors, retailers may gain exclusive rights to (1) sell merchandise in a specific region, (2) obtain special terms of purchase that are not available to competitors who lack such relationships, or (3) receive popular merchandise in short supply. Relationships with vendors, like relationships with customers, are developed over a long time and may not be easily offset by a competitor.[18] For example, Ahold, the Holland-based food retailer, works very closely with Swiss food giant Nestlé to bring its customers products that are tailored to meet their local tastes.[19] Chapter 14 examines how retailers work with their vendors to build mutually beneficial, long-term relationships.

Customer Service

Retailers also can build a sustainable competitive advantage by offering excellent customer service.[20] Offering good service consistently is difficult because customer service is provided by retail employees, and humans are less consistent than machines. The quality of service can vary from person to person and from day to day. Retailers that offer good customer service instill its importance in their employees over a long period of time through coaching and training. In this way, customer service becomes part of the retailer's organizational culture, a topic examined in Chapter 9.

It takes considerable time and effort to build a tradition and reputation for customer service, but good service is a valuable strategic asset. Once a retailer has earned a service reputation, it can sustain this advantage for a long time because it's hard for a competitor to develop a comparable reputation. Chapter 19 discusses how retailers develop a service advantage.

Multiple Sources of Advantage

To build a sustainable competitive advantage, retailers typically don't rely on a single approach, such as low cost or excellent service.[21] Instead, they need multiple approaches to build as high a wall around their position as possible. For example, McDonald's success is based on providing customers with a good value that meets their expectations, having good customer service, possessing a strong brand name, and offering great locations. By pursuing all of these strategies correctly, McDonald's has developed a strong competitive position in the quick service restaurant market.

McDonald's has always positioned itself as providing a good value—customers get a lot for not much money. Its customers don't have extraordinary expectations; they don't expect a meal prepared to their specific tastes. But customers do expect and get hot, fresh food that is reasonably priced.

McDonald's customers also don't expect friendly table service with linen table cloths and sterling silverware. Their service expectations, which are typically met, are simple. By developing a system for producing its food and using extensive training for its store employees, McDonald's reduces customers' waiting time.

Furthermore, McDonald's has a strong brand name with very high levels of awareness around the world. When most people think of fast food, they think of McDonald's. The brand also has a number of favorable brand associations, such as Ronald McDonald, fast, clean, and french fries.

Finally, McDonald's has a large number of great locations, which is very important for convenience products such as fast food. Given its market power, it has been successful in finding and opening stores in prime retail locations. In every great city in which it operates around the world, McDonald's has outstanding locations.

By developing these unique capabilities in a number of areas, McDonald's has built a high wall around its position as a service retailer, using a fast-food format directed toward families with young children. Each of the retail strategies outlined at the beginning of the chapter involves multiple sources of advantage. For example, Chico's has developed a strong competitive position through its unique merchandise, strong brand name, high-quality service provided by committed employees, and effective loyalty program. Retailing View 5.2 describes The Container Store, a retail chain that built a sustainable competitive advantage through unique merchandise, excellent customer service, and strong customer relations.

The Container Store—Selling Products that Make Life Simpler   RETAILING VIEW   5.2

Customers go to The Container Store to solve a problem. For example, when approached by salesperson, a customer may say, "My wife loves romance novels. She's got them scattered all over the house. I need something to keep them in." And the salesperson helps the customer solve the problem, or challenge, as the company likes to call them.

The Container Store sells products to help people organize their lives. Multipurpose shelving and garment bags are available to organize closets. Portable file cabinets and magazine holders create order in home offices. Backpacks, modular shelving, and CD holders can make dorm rooms less cluttered. Recipe holders, bottles, jars, and recycling bins bring harmony to kitchens.

Its 33 stores range in size from 22,000 to 29,000 square feet and showcase more than 10,000 innovative products. The stores are divided into lifestyle sections marked with brightly colored banners, such as Closet, Kitchen, Office, and Laundry. Wherever you look in the store, there's always someone in a blue apron ready to help solve everything from the tiniest of storage problems to the most intimidating organizational challenges. The annual sales per square foot for this retailer are an impressive $400, more than two times the industry average.

Although many of the stores' items are available elsewhere, few competitors offer such an extensive assortment under one roof, coupled with great customer service. Considerable time is spent educating sales associates about the merchandise, who are then empowered to use their own intuition and creativity to solve customer problems.

Over the years, the company has developed strong vendor relations. Most of its vendors' primary focus has been to

The Container Store spends considerable time educating sales associates about its unique merchandise that simplifies its customers' lives.

manufacture products for industrial use. Yet over time, the company has worked closely with its vendors to develop products that are appropriate for the home.

Sources: Maria Halkias, "Container Store Sees Growing Interest from Customers, Investors," *Knight Ridder Tribune Business News,* January 29, 2005, p. 1; Eilene Zimmerman, "Stores Find Good Workers Among Devoted Customers," *New York Times,* January 2, 2005, pp. 10–11; "Kip Tindell," *Chain Store Age,* August 2004, pp. 28–29.

GROWTH STRATEGIES

Four types of growth opportunities that retailers may pursue—market penetration, market expansion, retail format development, and diversification—are shown in Exhibit 5–4.[22] The vertical axis indicates the synergies between the retailer's present markets and the growth opportunity—whether the opportunity involves markets the retailer is presently pursuing or new markets. The horizontal axis indicates the synergies between the retailer's present retail mix and the retail mix of the growth opportunity—whether the opportunity exploits the retailer's present format or requires a new format.

Market Penetration

A **market penetration growth opportunity** involves realizing growth by directing efforts toward existing customers using the retailer's present retailing format. These opportunities involve either attracting consumers from its current target market who don't patronize the retailer currently or devising approaches that get current customers to visit the retailer more often or buy more merchandise on each visit.

Market penetration approaches include opening more stores in the target market and keeping existing stores open for longer hours. Other approaches involve displaying merchandise to increase impulse purchases and training salespeople to cross-sell. **Cross-selling** means that sales associates in one department attempt to sell complementary merchandise from other departments to their customers. For example, a sales associate who has just sold a DVD player to a customer will take the customer to the accessories department to sell special cables to improve the performance of the player.

Market Expansion

A **market expansion growth opportunity** involves using the existing retail format in new market segments. For example, Abercrombie & Fitch (A&F) Co.'s primary target market is college students, not high schoolers. Since college students don't particularly like to hang out with younger teens, A&F has opened a new, lower-priced chain called Hollister Co. to appeal to high schoolers. Although the merchandise and ambience are slightly different than those of A&F, the retail format is essentially the same.[24] When the French hypermarket chain Carrefour

REFACT

A 4 percent increase in weekly store visits by customers can result in a 58 percent increase in profits for a typical grocery store.[23]

EXHIBIT 5–4
Growth Opportunities

expanded into other European and South American countries, it was exploiting a market expansion growth strategy because it was entering a new geographic market segment with essentially the same retail format.[25]

Retail Format Development

A **retail format development growth opportunity** is an opportunity in which a retailer develops a new retail format—a format with a different retail mix—for the same target market. For example, Barnes & Noble, a specialty book, store-based retailer, exploited a format development opportunity when it began selling books to its present target market over the Internet (www.barnesandnoble.com).

Another example of a retail format development opportunity is Best Buy offering professional services to install new high-tech electronic equipment for consumers. Best Buy offers a Geek Squad to customers with 24-hour computer support and service. Although this growth opportunity is directed toward the same customers who buy merchandise in its stores, it involves running a service rather than a merchandise-based retail business.[26]

Diversification

A **diversification growth opportunity** is one in which a retailer introduces a new retail format directed toward a market segment that's not currently served by the retailer. Diversification opportunities are either related or unrelated.

Related versus Unrelated Diversification In a **related diversification growth opportunity,** the retailer's present target market or retail format shares something in common with the new opportunity. This commonality might entail purchasing from the same vendors, operating in similar locations, using the same distribution or management information system, or advertising in the same newspapers to similar target markets. In contrast, an **unrelated diversification** lacks any commonality between the present business and the new business.

Foot Locker, the world's largest retailer of athletic footwear and apparel (formerly known as Venator), became involved in several unrelated diversification endeavors in the 1990s. For instance, it owned some Burger King franchises and Afterthoughts accessory stores. After realizing that athletic apparel and footwear

After several attempts at unrelated diversification, Foot Locker decided to stick to its core business, athletic shoes.

was its core business and had the greatest profit potential, it sold the businesses that were not synergistic with its core capabilities. Foot Locker now operates Foot Locker, Lady Foot Locker, Kids Foot Locker, Champs Sports, Foot action, and Foot Locker stores in Europe, plus a highly profitable Internet and catalog business, footlocker.com.

Unrelated diversifications are considered very risky and often are not successful, as was the case with Foot Locker. As a result, most retailers apply the old adage "stick to your knitting" and seek growth opportunities that are closer in nature to their current operations. For example, JCPenney sold the Eckerd drug store chain to focus on its multichannel, department store–based market, and Target sold its department stores to focus on its discount stores.

Vertical Integration   **Vertical integration** is diversification by retailers into wholesaling or manufacturing.[27] Examples of vertical integration include The Limited's acquisition of Mast Industries (a trading company that contracts for private label manufacturing) and Zales Corporation designing jewelry. When retailers integrate by manufacturing products, they are making risky investments because the requisite skills to make products are different from those associated with retailing them.

In addition, retailers and manufacturers have different customers; the immediate customers for a manufacturer's merchandise are retailers, whereas a retailer's customers are consumers. Thus, a manufacturer's marketing activities are very different from those of a retailer. Note that designing private label merchandise is a related diversification because it builds on the retailer's knowledge of its customers, but actually making the merchandise is considered an unrelated diversification.

Strategic Opportunities and Competitive Advantage

Typically, retailers have the greatest competitive advantage when they engage in opportunities that are similar to their present retail strategy. Thus, retailers would be most successful engaging in market penetration opportunities that don't involve entering new, unfamiliar markets or operating new, unfamiliar retail formats.

When retailers pursue market expansion opportunities, they build on their strengths in operating a retail format and apply this competitive advantage in a new market. Those retailers that successfully expand globally are able to translate what they do best—their core competencies—to a new culture and market.

A retail format development opportunity builds on the retailer's reputation and success with its present customers. Even if a retailer doesn't have experience and skills in operating the new format, it hopes to attract its loyal customers to it. For example, as discussed in Chapter 3, some retailers have successfully developed multichannel strategies by seamlessly integrating stores, the Internet, and catalogs to provide extra convenience and multiple opportunities for their current customers to shop.

Retailers have the least competitive advantage when they pursue diversification opportunities. Thus, these opportunities are generally risky and often don't work, as was the case with Venator/Foot Locker.

GLOBAL GROWTH OPPORTUNITIES

International expansion is a market expansion growth opportunity that many retailers find attractive. Of the 50 largest global retailers, 37 operate in more than one country.[29] But international expansion can be risky because retailers must deal with different government regulations, cultural traditions, supply chain considerations, and languages. We first discuss the types of retailers that successfully compete globally, followed by a look at some of the pitfalls of global expansion. Then we examine the key success factors for global expansion, and finally, evaluate the strategies for entering a nondomestic market.

Who Is Successful and Who Isn't?

Retailers with an offering that has universal appeal, such as distinctive merchandise or low cost, are the most successful at exploiting global markets. For example, some of the most successful global retailers are specialty store retailers with strong brand images and/or unique merchandise such as Starbucks, McDonald's, The Gap, and IKEA; category specialists such as Home Depot and Toys "R" Us that offer broad assortments and low prices, which appeal to consumers in different cultures; and discount and food retailers with low prices such as Wal-Mart, Carrefour, Royal Ahold, and Metro AG. Retailing View 5.3 discusses some of the successes and problems IKEA has encountered on its way to being a global retailer.

REFACT

The top 50 global retailers operate in an average of 9.1 countries. Eleven of the 13 retailers in the top 50 that operate in only one country are headquartered in the United States.[30]

IKEA: Bringing Its Philosophy to a World Market RETAILING VIEW 5.3

IKEA has adjusted its unique furniture retail offering to satisfy the needs of U.S. consumers.

As it expands globally, IKEA is not just selling products, it's also selling its philosophy: This is how things are done in Sweden. The IKEA concept is based on offering unique, well-designed, functional furniture at low prices. Home furnishing solutions and products are displayed in realistic room settings. Customers are encouraged to get actively involved in the shopping experience by sitting on the sofas and opening and closing drawers. Price and product information is clearly marked on large, easy-to-read tags, making it easier for customers to serve themselves. Merchandise is purchased in unassembled flat packs. The guiding philosophy is: "You do your part. We do our part. Together, we save money."

Store openings generate tremendous excitement and large crowds. In September 2004, two men were trampled to death and 16 shoppers were injured in a rush by 20,000 people to claim vouchers at the first IKEA in Saudi Arabia. In February 2005, a riot at the opening of a new IKEA in North London forced the store to close just 30 minutes after opening. IKEA currently operates 130 stores in 29 countries.

While other global retailers like McDonald's make changes to adapt to local preferences, IKEA is less willing to make

concessions. For example, there is only one set of instructions to assemble a piece of IKEA furniture, wherever you are in the world. Every store opening begins in the same way: a Swedish breakfast and a traditional log sawing ceremony, which founder Ingvar Kamprad often attends. Every store is decorated in blue and yellow, the colors of Sweden's flag, with a complex layout. One of the most frequently asked questions is how to get out of the store.

When IKEA entered the United States in 1987, it discovered that U.S. consumers were not buying into its "one size fits all" philosophy, and it had to make some changes. For example, IKEA initially tried to sell its Scandinavian beds in the United States before discovering they were the wrong size for American bed linens. Its Scandinavian-styled bookshelves were too small to hold a TV for Americans who wanted shelving for an entertainment system. Even IKEA's European-style bath towels were too small and thin, and its glasses were deemed too small for the super-sized thirsts of Americans. The European-style sofas were too hard for American bottoms, and the IKEA dining room tables weren't big enough to fit a turkey in the center on Thanksgiving.

IKEA's system of self-service, self-assembly, and consumer involvement in the whole retail process also did not appeal to many Americans. However, rather than deviate from its philosophy and sell assembled merchandise, IKEA decided to improve its instructions and offer an assembly service.

REFACT

The name IKEA was derived from the founder's initials plus the first letters of the farm and village where he grew up.

Sources: Elen Lewis, "Is IKEA for Everyone?" *Brandchannel.com*, March 28, 2005; James Scully, "IKEA," *Time*, Summer 2004, pp. 16–17; http://www.IKEA.com.

Category specialists and supercenter retailers may be particularly suited to succeed globally because of their operating efficiencies. First, these retailers are leaders in their use of technology to manage inventories, control global logistical systems, and tailor merchandise assortments to local needs. Second, retailers like Wal-Mart and Carrefour have scale economies for buying merchandise globally. Third, despite idiosyncrasies in the global environment, category specialists and supercenter retailers have developed unique systems and standardized formats that facilitate control over multiple stores. Fourth, at one time, U.S.-based retailers believed that consumers outside the United States who were used to high levels of personalized service would not embrace the self-service concept employed by category killers and supercenter retailers. However, the experience of chains such as Carrefour (France) and ALDI (Germany) has shown that consumers around the globe are willing to forgo service for lower prices.[31]

Some U.S. retailers have a competitive advantage in global markets because American culture is emulated in many countries, particularly among young people. Due to rising prosperity and the rapidly increasing access to cable TV with American programming, fashion trends in the United States are spreading to young people in emerging countries. The global MTV generation prefers Coke to tea, athletic shoes to sandals, Chicken McNuggets to rice, and credit cards to cash. In the last few years, China's major cities have sprouted American stores and restaurants, including KFC, Pizza Hut, and McDonald's. Shanghai and Beijing each have more than two dozen Starbucks, where coffee was not the drink of choice until Starbucks came to town. But these Chinese urban dwellers go there to impress a friend or because it's a symbol of a new kind of lifestyle. Although Western products and stores have gained a reputation for high quality and good service in China, in some ways, it is the American culture that many Chinese consumers want.[32]

On the other hand, some large European and Japanese retailers offer considerably more local products and hire and train local managers, thus passing the power and authority to locals quickly. Even though Wal-Mart has a more efficient distribution system, Carrefour has competed effectively against it in Brazil and Argentina.

Keys to Success

Four characteristics of retailers that have successfully exploited international growth opportunities are (1) a globally sustainable competitive advantage, (2) adaptability, (3) global culture, and (4) financial resources.[33] A hypothetical evaluation of international growth opportunities is described in the appendix to this chapter.

Globally Sustainable Competitive Advantage   Entry into nondomestic markets is most successful when the expansion opportunity is consistent with the retailer's core bases of competitive advantage. Some core competitive advantages for global retailers are shown in the following table:

Core Advantage	Global Retailer Example
Low-cost, efficient operations	Wal-Mart, Carrefour
Strong private brands	IKEA, Starbucks
Fashion reputation	The Gap, Zara, H&M
Category dominance	Office Depot, Toys "R" Us

Thus, Wal-Mart and Carrefour are successful in international markets where price plays an important role in consumer decision making and a distribution infrastructure is available to enable these firms to exploit their logistical capabilities.

In contrast, The Gap and Zara are successful in international markets that value fashionable merchandise.

Adaptability   While successful global retailers build on their core competencies, they also recognize cultural differences and adapt their core strategy to the needs of local markets.[34] Color preferences, the preferred cut of apparel, and sizes differ across cultures. For example, in China, white is the color of mourning and brides wear red dresses. Food probably has the greatest diversity of tastes around the world.

Selling seasons also vary across countries. The Gap's major U.S. selling season is the back-to-school period in August; however, this is one of the slowest sales periods in Europe because most people are on vacation. Back-to-school season in Japan occurs in April.

Store designs and layouts often need to be adjusted in different parts of the world. In the United States, for instance, discount stores are usually quite large and on one level. In other parts of the world, such as Europe and parts of Asia, where space is at a premium, stores must be designed to fit a smaller space and are often housed in multiple levels. In some cultures, social norms dictate that men's and women's clothing cannot be displayed next to each other.

Cultural values and government regulations can also affect store operations. Some differences, such as holidays, hours of operation, and regulations governing part-time employees and terminations, are easy to identify. Other factors require a deeper understanding. For example, Latin American culture is very family oriented, so traditional U.S. work schedules would need to be adjusted so that Latin American employees could have more time with their families. Boots, a U.K. drugstore chain, has the checkout clerks in its Japanese stores standing up because it discovered that Japanese shoppers found it offensive to pay money to a seated clerk, but retailers have to provide seating for checkout clerks in Germany. Retailers in Germany also must recycle packaging materials sold in their stores. Also in Germany, seasonal sales can be held only during specific weeks and apply only to specific product categories, and the amount of the discounts are limited.

Starbucks has been pleasantly surprised at how quickly consumers around the world have accepted the products it sells in the United States. It isn't just the lattes or cappuccinos; the Frappuccino is also extremely popular. For example, the company thought that its U.S. beverages would be too sweet for the palate of many Asians—not true. People are a lot more alike than they thought.

In terms of assortment, there isn't great variation from country to country. Outside the United States, food is a bigger part of business, much more important in China, Japan, and the United Kingdom than it is in the United States. Frappuccino-type products, however, are popular everywhere, though Starbucks has developed some unique drinks for different markets. For example, the green tea Frappuccino, sold only in Taiwan and Japan, is the best selling Frappuccino in those countries, and a strawberries-and-cream Frappuccino was developed for the United Kingdom.[35]

Global Culture   To be global, retailers must think globally. It is not sufficient to transplant a home-country culture and infrastructure into another country. In this regard, Carrefour is truly global. In the early years of its international expansion, it started in each country slowly, which reduced the company's ethnocentrism. Further enriching its global perspective, Carrefour has always encouraged the rapid development of local management and retains few expatriates in its overseas operations. Carrefour's management ranks are truly international. One is just as likely to run across a Portuguese regional manager in Hong Kong as a French or Chinese one. Finally, Carrefour discourages the

Coffee was not the drink of choice until Starbucks came to China. But now Shanghai and Beijing each have more than two dozen Starbucks.

classic overseas "tour of duty" mentality often found in U.S. firms. International assignments are important in themselves, not just as stepping stones to ultimate career advancement back in France. The globalization of Carrefour's culture is perhaps most evident in the speed with which ideas flow throughout the organization. A global management structure of regional "committees," which meet regularly, advances the awareness and implementation of global best practices. The proof of Carrefour's global commitment lies in the numbers. It has had almost 30 years of international experience in 21 countries, both developed and developing.[36]

Financial Resources   Expansion into international markets requires a long-term commitment and considerable upfront planning. Retailers find it very difficult to generate short-term profits when they make the transition to global retailing.[37]

Entry Strategies

Four approaches that retailers can take when entering nondomestic markets are direct investment, joint venture, strategic alliance, and franchising.[38]

Direct Investment   **Direct investment** involves a retail firm investing in and owning a division or subsidiary that operates in a foreign country. This entry strategy requires the highest level of investment and exposes the retailer to significant risks, but it also has the highest potential returns. One advantage of direct investment is that the retailer has complete control of the operations. For example, McDonald's chose this entry strategy for the U.K. market, building a plant to produce buns when local suppliers could not meet its specifications.

Joint Venture   A **joint venture** is formed when the entering retailer pools its resources with a local retailer to form a new company in which ownership, control, and profits are shared. Examples of successful joint ventures include Royal Ahold (the Netherlands) and Velox Holdings (Argentina); Metro AG (Germany) and Koc Group's Migros (Turkey); Carrefour and Sabanci Holding (Turkey); Metro AG (Germany) and Marubeni (Japan); and Monsoon (United Kingdom) and Charming Shoppes (United States).

A joint venture reduces the entrant's risks. Besides sharing the financial burden, the local partner provides an understanding of the market and has access to local resources, such as vendors and real estate. Many foreign countries, such as China, require joint ownership, though these restrictions may loosen as a result of World Trade Organization (WTO) negotiations. Problems with this entry approach can arise if the partners disagree or the government places restrictions on the repatriation of profits.

Strategic Alliance   A **strategic alliance** is a collaborative relationship between independent firms. For example, a retailer might enter an international market through direct investment but use DHL or UPS to facilitate its local logistical and warehousing activities.

Franchising   **Franchising** offers the lowest risk and requires the least investment. However, the entrant has limited control over the retail operations in the foreign country, potential profit is reduced, and the risk of assisting in the creation of a local domestic competitor is increased. The U.K.-based Marks & Spencer, for example, has franchised stores in 29 countries.[39]

THE STRATEGIC RETAIL PLANNING PROCESS

The **strategic retail planning process** entails the set of steps a retailer goes through to develop a strategic retail plan[40] (see Exhibit 5–5). It describes how retailers select target market segments, determine the appropriate retail format, and build sustainable competitive advantages. As indicated in Exhibit 5–5, it is not always necessary to go through the entire process each time an evaluation is performed (step 7). For instance, a retailer could evaluate its performance and go directly to step 2 to conduct a situation audit.

The planning process can be used to formulate strategic plans at different levels within a retail corporation. For example, the corporate strategic plan of The Gap indicates how resources are to be allocated across the corporation's various divisions, such as The Gap, Old Navy, Banana Republic, GapKids, and Baby Gap. Each division, in turn, develops its own strategic plan. As we discuss the steps in the retail planning process, we will apply each step to the planning process Kelly Bradford is undertaking. Kelly owns Gifts To Go, a small, two-store chain in the Chicago area. One of her 1,000 square foot stores is located in the downtown area; the other is in an upscale suburban mall. The target market for Gifts To Go is upper-income men and women looking for gifts in the $50–500 price range. The stores have an eclectic selection of merchandise, including handmade jewelry and crafts, fine china and glassware, perfume, watches, writing instruments, and a variety of one-of-a-kind items. Gifts To Go also has developed a number of loyal customers who are contacted by sales associates when family anniversaries and birthdays come up. In many cases, customers have a close relationship with a sales associate and enough confidence in the associate's judgment that they tell the associate to pick out an appropriate gift. The turnover of Gifts To Go sales associates is low for the industry, because Kelly treats associates as part of the family.

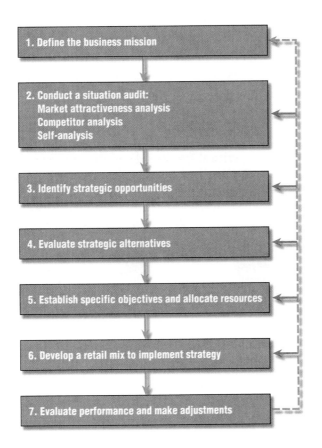

EXHIBIT 5–5

Stages in the Strategic Retail Planning Process

The company pays for medical insurance for all associates, and they share in the profits of the firm.

Step 1: Define the Business Mission

The first step in the strategic retail planning process is to define the business mission. The **mission statement** is a broad description of a retailer's objectives and the scope of activities it plans to undertake.[41] Whereas the objective of a publicly held firm is to maximize its stockholders' wealth by increasing the value of its stock and paying dividends,[42] owners of small, privately held firms frequently have other objectives, such as achieving a specific level of income and avoiding risks rather than maximizing income.

The mission statement defines the general nature of the target segments and retail formats on which the firm will focus. For example, the mission statement of an office supply category specialist, "Serve the customer, build value for shareholders, and create opportunities for associates," is too broad. It fails to provide a sense of strategic direction.

In developing the mission statement, managers need to answer five questions: (1) What business are we in? (2) What should be our business in the future? (3) Who are our customers? (4) What are our capabilities? (5) What do we want to accomplish? Gifts To Go's mission statement is "The mission of Gifts To Go is to be the leading retailer of higher-priced gifts in Chicago and provide a stable income of $100,000 per year for the owner."

Because the mission statement defines the retailer's objectives and the scope of activities it plans to undertake, Gifts To Go's mission statement clarifies that its management won't consider retail opportunities outside the Chicago area, for selling low-priced gifts, or that would jeopardize its ability to generate $100,000 in annual income.[43]

Step 2: Conduct a Situation Audit

After developing a mission statement and setting objectives, the next step in the strategic planning process is to conduct a **situation audit,** an analysis of the opportunities and threats in the retail environment and the strengths and weaknesses of the retail business relative to its competitors. The elements in the situation analysis are shown in Exhibit 5–6.[44]

Market Factors   Some critical factors related to consumers and their buying patterns are the target market size and growth, sales cyclicity, and seasonality. Market size, typically measured in retail sales dollars, is important because it

EXHIBIT 5–6

Elements in a Situation Audit

MARKET FACTORS

Size

Growth

Seasonality

Business cycles

COMPETITIVE FACTORS

Barriers to entry

Bargaining power of vendors

Competitive rivalry

ENVIRONMENTAL FACTORS

Technology

Economic

Regulatory

Social

ANALYSIS OF STRENGTHS AND WEAKNESSES

Management capabilities

Financial resources

Locations

Operations

Merchandise

Store management

Customer loyalty

indicates a retailer's opportunity to generate revenues to cover its investment. Large markets are attractive to large retail firms, but they are also attractive to small entrepreneurs because they offer more opportunities to focus on a market segment. Some retailers, however, prefer to concentrate on smaller markets. Cato, for instance, sells value-priced women's fashion in 950 stores located in 30 U.S. states, primarily in small towns.[45]

Growing markets are typically more attractive than mature or declining markets. For example, retail markets for limited assortment, extreme value retailers are growing faster than are those for department stores. Typically, the return on investment is higher in growing markets because competition is less intense than in mature markets. Because new customers are just beginning to patronize stores in growing markets, they may not have developed strong store loyalties and thus might be easier to attract to new outlets.

Firms are often interested in minimizing the business cycle's impact on their sales. Thus, those retail markets for merchandise affected by economic conditions (such as cars and major appliances) are less attractive than retail markets unaffected by economic conditions (such as food).

In general, markets with highly seasonal sales are unattractive because a lot of resources are needed to accommodate the peak season, but then resources are underutilized the rest of the year. To minimize problems due to seasonality, ski resorts promote summer vacations to generate sales during all four seasons.

To conduct an analysis of the market factors for Gifts To Go, Kelly Bradford went on the Internet to get information about the size, growth, and cyclical and seasonal nature of the gift market in general and, more specifically, in Chicago. On the basis of her analysis, she concluded that the market factors were attractive; the market for more expensive gifts was large, growing, and not vulnerable to business cycles. The only negative aspect was the high seasonality of gifts, with peaks at Valentine's Day, June (due to weddings), Christmas, and other holidays.

Competitive Factors   The nature of the competition in retail markets is affected by barriers to entry, the bargaining power of vendors, and competitive rivalry.[46] Retail markets are more attractive when competitive entry is costly. **Barriers to entry** institute conditions in a retail market that make it difficult for other firms to enter the market, such as scale economies, customer loyalty, and the availability of great locations.

Scale economies are cost advantages due to a retailer's size. Markets dominated by large competitors with scale economies are typically unattractive. For example, a small entrepreneur might avoid becoming an office supply category specialist because the market is an oligopoly dominated by three large firms: Staples, Office Depot, and OfficeMax. These firms have a considerable cost advantage over the entrepreneur because they can buy merchandise cheaper and operate more efficiently by investing in the latest technology and spreading their overhead across more stores. However, Retailing View 5.4 discusses how some small retailers develop sustainable advantages over national chains with significant scale economies.

Retail markets dominated by a well-established retailer that has developed a loyal group of customers also are unattractive. For example, Home Depot's high customer loyalty in Atlanta makes it hard for a competing home improvement center to enter the Atlanta market.

Finally, the availability of locations may impede competitive entry. Staples, for instance, attributes part of its success over its rivals in the northeastern United States to its first-mover advantage. Since the Northeast has a preponderance of mature but stable retail markets, finding new locations is more difficult there than it is in most of the rest of the United States. Staples started in the Northeast and was therefore able to open stores in the best available locations.

Entry barriers are a double-edged sword. A retail market with high entry barriers is very attractive for retailers presently competing in that market, because those barriers limit competition. However, markets with high entry barriers are unattractive for retailers not already in the market. For example, the lack of good retail locations in Hong Kong makes this market attractive for retailers already in the region but less attractive for retailers desiring to enter the market.

Another competitive factor is the **bargaining power of vendors.** Markets are less attractive when only a few vendors control the merchandise sold in it. In these situations, vendors have the opportunity to dictate prices and other terms (like delivery dates), reducing the retailer's profits. For example, the market for retailing fashionable cosmetics is less attractive because two suppliers, Estée Lauder (Estée

5.4 RETAILING VIEW   Competing against the Giants

Dave Umber owns three hardware stores in Ft. Wayne, Indiana (population 200,000), and competes against two Home Depots, two Menards (a Midwestern chain of home improvement centers), three Lowe's, and three Wal-Marts. Each time one of them opens, the customer count at Umber's nearest store falls at least 10 percent for the next year. The majority of customers eventually come back for at least some of their needs, but some don't. "You keep working a little harder and a little harder, and yet you see profits slowly eroding," says Umber, the third generation to run Umber's Ace Hardware.

Umber was able to start growing his business

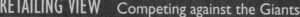

To compete against Home Depot and Lowe's, Dave Umber's Ace Hardware offers personalized service and an assortment tailored to the local community.

and turn a profit by working with an Ace Hardware consultant to reduce his costs and offer products and services that many of the big box stores don't, such as smaller cans of paint thinner and chain by the foot, along with free delivery. After conducting one of his annual exit surveys, Umber learned that his customers were interested in bird feeders. Two weeks later, he had 24 feet of shelving devoted to them. He also stays in tune with the community. At science-fair time, he stocks extra bell wire, batteries, mousetraps, springs, and magnets. When the Cub Scouts hold their annual Pinewood Derby, he has not only graphite lubricant in stock but advice as well: "We'll show them the best way to weight the wood," he says. "I'll even pull out my son's car from a few years ago and show them."

Still, the biggest challenge for any independent fighting superstore competition is pricing. Umber's rule of thumb is to keep his prices within 10 percent of the competition's. Because Umber buys 90 percent of his inventory through Ace, he can remain competitive on price and also know which products sell best nationally. Virtually all independent hardware stores buy from a major supplier, whether a co-op such as Ace or True Value or a

wholesaler such as Orgill. The co-ops also provide advice on what works for other members and, for around $2,500 a month in Umber's case, national advertising of the Ace brand.

To make sure his prices are right, Umber regularly shops the competition. One morning while checking out toilet parts at Home Depot, Umber met Tim Stinson, a longtime customer, who asked, "What are you doing here?" "I'm spying on the competition," Umber said with a smile. "What are you doing here?" "Well, there are things on my list that you just don't have," says Stinson, citing Rustoleum chalkboard paint. But Stinson says he still prefers to shop at Umber's Ace, where "people help you a lot quicker. I know if I buy a shovel there, and it breaks, all I have to do is bring it back and he'll replace it, no questions asked. Here you've got to find someone to help you and fill out lots of forms. And at Ace they always have a big smile." "Nice to see you, Tim," says Umber, shaking his hand before leaving. "See?" says Stinson. "Nobody at Home Depot knows my name."

Source: Julie Sloane, "Beat the Beast," *FSB: Fortune Small Business*, September 2004, pp. 44–45. Time Inc. All rights reserved.

Lauder, Clinique, Prescriptives, Aramis, Tommy Hilfiger, M·A·C, and Origins) and L'Oréal (Maybelline, Giorgio Armani, Helena Rubinstein, Lancôme, Lanvin, and Ralph Lauren), provide very desirable premium brands. Because department stores need these brands to support a fashionable image, the suppliers have the power to sell their products to retailers at high prices.

The final industry factor is the level of competitive rivalry in the retail market. **Competitive rivalry** defines the frequency and intensity of reactions to actions undertaken by competitors. When rivalry is high, price wars erupt, employee raids occur, advertising and promotion expenses increase, and profit potential falls. Conditions that may lead to intense rivalry include (1) a large number of competitors that are all about the same size, (2) slow growth, (3) high fixed costs, and (4) a lack of perceived differences between competing retailers.

When Kelly Bradford started to analyze the competitive factors for Gifts To Go, she realized that identifying her competitors wasn't easy. While there were no gift stores carrying similar merchandise and price points in the Chicago area, there were a number of other retailers from which a customer could buy gifts. She identified her primary competitors as department stores, craft galleries, catalogs, and Internet retailers. Kelly felt there were some scale economies in developing customer databases to support gift retailing. The lack of large suppliers meant that vendors' bargaining power wasn't a problem, and competitive rivalry was minimal because the gift business was not a critical part of the department store's overall business. In addition, merchandise carried by the various retailers offered considerable differentiation opportunities.

Environmental Factors   Environmental factors that can affect market attractiveness span technological, economic, regulatory, and social changes. When a retail market is going through significant changes in technology, existing competitors are vulnerable to new entrants that are skilled at using the new technology.

Some retailers may be more affected by economic conditions than others. High-end department stores employ well-paid salespeople to provide customer service. When unemployment is low, their costs may increase significantly, as salespeople's wages rise due to the difficulty of hiring qualified people. But retailers like Wal-Mart that provide little service and have much lower labor costs as a percentage of sales may be less affected by low unemployment.

Government regulations can reduce the attractiveness of a retail market. For example, it is difficult for large retailers to open new stores in France due to size restrictions placed on new stores. Also, many local governments within the United States have tried to stop Wal-Mart from entering their markets in an attempt to protect locally owned retailers.

Finally, trends in demographics, lifestyles, attitudes, and personal values affect retail markets' attractiveness. Brooks Brothers, for example, has been struggling with several trends simultaneously. Known for its traditional suits and button-down shirts, the company has not learned how to appeal to younger customers and businesspeople who prefer to dress casually without alienating its traditional customer base.[47]

Retailers need to answer three questions about each environmental factor:

1. What new developments or changes might occur, such as new technologies and regulations or different social factors and economic conditions?

2. What is the likelihood that these environmental changes will occur? What key factors affect whether these changes will occur?

3. How will these changes impact each retail market, the firm, and its competitors?

Kelly Bradford's primary concern when she did an environmental analysis was the potential growth of Internet gift retailers such as RedEnvelope. Gifts seem ideal for an electronic channel, because customers can order the item over the

EXHIBIT 5–7

Elements in a Strengths and Weaknesses Analysis

In performing a self-analysis, the retailer considers the potential areas for developing a competitive advantage listed below and answers the following questions:

At what is our company good?

In which of these areas is our company better than our competitors?

In which of these areas does our company's unique capabilities provide a sustainable competitive advantage or a basis for developing one?

 MANAGEMENT CAPABILITY

Capabilities and experience of top management

Depth of management—capabilities of middle management

Management's commitment to firm

 MERCHANDISING CAPABILITIES

Knowledge and skills of buyers

Relationships with vendors

Capabilities in developing private brands

Advertising and promotion capabilities

 FINANCIAL RESOURCES

Cash flow from existing business

Ability to raise debt or equity financing

 STORE MANAGEMENT CAPABILITIES

Management capabilities

Quality of sales associates

Commitment of sales associates to firm

 OPERATIONS

Overhead cost structure

Quality of operating systems

Distribution capabilities

Management information systems

Loss prevention systems

Inventory control systems

 LOCATIONS

 CUSTOMERS

Loyalty of customers

Internet and have it shipped directly to the gift recipient. Kelly also recognized that the electronic channel could effectively collect information about customers and then target promotions and suggestions to them when future gift-giving occasions arose.

Strengths and Weaknesses Analysis   The most critical aspect of the situation audit is for a retailer to determine its unique capabilities in terms of its strengths and weaknesses relative to the competition. A **strengths and weaknesses analysis** indicates how well the business can seize opportunities and avoid harm from threats in the environment. Exhibit 5–7 outlines some issues to consider in performing a strength and weakness analysis.

Here is Kelly Bradford's analysis of Gifts To Go's strengths and weaknesses:

Management capability	Limited—Two excellent store managers and a relatively inexperienced person helped Kelly buy merchandise. An accounting firm kept the financial records for the business but had no skills in developing and utilizing customer databases.
Financial resources	Good—Gifts To Go had no debt and a good relationship with a bank. Kelly had saved $255,000 that she had in liquid securities.
Operations	Poor—While Kelly felt Gifts To Go had relatively low overhead, the company did not have a computer-based inventory control system or management and customer information systems. Her competitors (local department stores, catalog and Internet retailers) certainly had superior systems.
Merchandising capabilities	Good—Kelly had a flair for selecting unique gifts, and she had excellent relationships with vendors providing one-of-a-kind merchandise.
Store management capabilities	Excellent—The store managers and sales associates were excellent. They were very attentive to customers and loyal to the firm. Employee and customer theft were kept to a minimum.
Locations	Excellent—Both of Gifts To Go's locations were excellent. The downtown location was convenient for office workers. The suburban mall location was at a heavily trafficked juncture.
Customers	Good—While Gifts To Go did not achieve the sales volume in gifts done in department stores, the company had a loyal base of customers.

Step 3: Identify Strategic Opportunities

After completing the situation audit, the next step is to identify opportunities for increasing retail sales. Kelly Bradford presently competes in gift retailing using a specialty store format. The strategic alternatives she is considering are defined in terms of growth opportunities in Exhibit 5–4. Note that some of these growth strategies involve a redefinition of her mission.

Market penetration	1. Increase size of present stores and amount of merchandise in stores.
	2. Open additional gift stores in Chicago area.
Market expansion	1. Open gift stores outside the Chicago area (new geographic segment).
	2. Sell lower-priced gifts in present stores or open new stores selling low-priced gifts (new benefit segment).
Format development	1. Sell apparel and other nongift merchandise to same customers in same or new stores.
	2. Sell similar gift merchandise to same market segment using the Internet.
Diversification	1. Manufacture craft gifts.
	2. Open apparel stores targeted toward teenagers.
	3. Open a category specialist selling low-priced gifts.

Step 4: Evaluate Strategic Opportunities

The fourth step in the strategic planning progress is to evaluate opportunities that have been identified in the situation audit. The evaluation determines the retailer's potential to establish a sustainable competitive advantage and reap long-term profits from the opportunities being evaluated. Thus, a retailer must focus on opportunities that utilize its strengths and its competitive advantage.

Both the market attractiveness and the strengths and weaknesses of the retailer need to be considered in evaluating strategic opportunities. The greatest investments should be made in market opportunities where the retailer has a strong competitive position. A formal method for performing such an analysis is described in the appendix to this chapter. Here's Kelly's informal analysis:

Growth Opportunity	Market Attractiveness	Competitive Position
Increase size of present stores and amount of merchandise in stores	Low	High
Open additional gift stores in Chicago area	Medium	Medium
Open gift stores outside the Chicago area (new geographic segment)	Medium	Low
Sell lower-priced gifts in present stores or open new stores selling low-priced gifts (new benefit segment)	Medium	Low
Sell apparel and other nongift merchandise to same customers in same or new stores	High	Medium
Sell similar gift merchandise to same market segment using the Internet	High	Low
Open apparel stores targeted at teenagers	High	Low
Open a category specialist selling low-priced gifts	High	Low

Step 5: Establish Specific Objectives and Allocate Resources

After evaluating the strategic investment opportunities, the next step in the strategic planning process is to establish a specific objective for each opportunity. The retailer's overall objective is included in the mission statement; the specific objectives are goals against which progress toward the overall objective can be measured. Thus, these specific objectives have three components: (1) the performance sought, including a numerical index against which progress may be measured; (2) a time frame within which the goal is to be achieved; and (3) the level of investment needed to achieve the objective. Typically, the performance levels are financial criteria such as return on investment, sales, or profits. Kelly's objective is to increase profits by 20 percent in each of the next five years. She expects she will need to invest an additional $25,000 in her apparel and other nongift merchandise inventory.

Step 6: Develop a Retail Mix to Implement Strategy

The sixth step in the planning process is to develop a retail mix for each opportunity in which an investment will be made and control and evaluate performance. Decisions related to the elements in the retail mix are discussed subsequently in Sections III and IV.

Step 7: Evaluate Performance and Make Adjustments

The final step in the planning process is to evaluate the results of the strategy and implementation program. If the retailer is meeting or exceeding its objectives, changes aren't needed. But if the retailer fails to meet its objectives, reanalysis is required. Typically, this reanalysis starts with reviewing the implementation programs, but it may indicate that the strategy (or even the mission statement) needs to be reconsidered. This conclusion would result in starting a new planning process, including a new situation audit. Retailing View 5.5 illustrates how changes in the environment forced bowling alley operators to reevaluate their strategy, target a new market segment, and tailor their offering to meet the needs of this new segment.

5.5   RETAILING VIEW   Cosmic Bowling

Although bowling is a popular sport for Baby Boomers, it does not have as much appeal for younger generations. Without an enthusiastic new generation of bowlers to look forward to, bowling centers seemed ready for the history books.

In today's bowling centers, laser lights, neon, glow-in-the-dark alleys, fog machines, and a top-quality sound system are as important as bowling balls and pins. Turn down the lights, turn on the special effects, and the center is transformed into a nightclub. DJs with portable microphones work the crowd. Video cameras are installed so customers can see all the action by watching monitors placed throughout the center, or the same monitors can show music videos.

REFACT

Bowling is the number one participant sport in the United States.[48]

Brunswick developed the "cosmic bowling" concept to attract young people to its centers. The nightclub atmosphere draws lots of high school students who aren't old enough to attend clubs, but it also appeals to youngsters and oldsters. Theme nights are used to attract different segments by varying the type of music played—retro, rap, country. The increased revenues from cosmic bowling are due to more efficient space utilization, as well as attracting a new market segment. Typically, bowling centers had few customers from 10:00 p.m. to 2:00 a.m., but cosmic bowling enthusiasts fill the centers during this dead time with people who pay a premium to party.

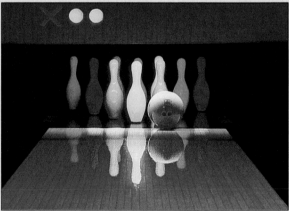

Brunswick developed cosmic bowling to attract a younger generation to bowling when its target market of league bowlers declined.

Sources: Robyn Lamb, "'Cosmic Bowling' Offers Fun Night Out," *Baltimore Daily Record,* May 8, 2004, p. 1; Douglas Trattner, "Late-Night Bowling That's Out of This World," *Cleveland Plain Dealer,* April 26, 2002, p. 12.

Strategic Planning in the Real World

The planning process in Exhibit 5–5 suggests that strategic decisions are made in a sequential manner. After the business mission is defined, the situation audit is performed, strategic opportunities are identified, alternatives are evaluated, objectives are set, resources are allocated, the implementation plan is developed, and, finally, performance is evaluated and adjustments are made. But actual planning processes have interactions among the steps. For example, the situation audit may uncover a logical alternative for the firm to consider, even though this alternative isn't included in the mission statement. Thus, the mission statement may need to be reformulated. The development of the implementation plan might reveal that the resources allocated to a particular opportunity are insufficient to achieve the objective. In that case, the objective would need to be changed, the resources would need to be increased, or the retailer might consider not investing in the opportunity at all.

SUMMARY

Strategic planning is an ongoing process. Every day, retailers audit their situations, examine consumer trends, study new technologies, and monitor competitive activities. But the retail strategy statement isn't changed every year or every six months; the strategy statement is reviewed and altered only when major changes in the retailer's environment or capabilities occur.

When a retailer undertakes a major reexamination of its strategy, the process for developing a new strategy statement may take a year or two. Potential strategic directions are generated by people at all levels of the organization, then evaluated by senior executives and operating personnel to ensure that the eventual strategic direction is profitable in the long run and can be implemented.

A retailer's long-term performance is largely determined by its strategy. A strategy coordinates employees' activities and communicates the direction the retailer plans to take. Thus, retail market strategy describes both the strategic direction and the process by which the strategy is to be developed.

The retail strategy statement includes an identification of a target market and the retail format (its offering) to be directed toward that target market. The statement also needs to indicate the retailer's methods to build a sustainable competitive advantage. Seven important opportunities for retailers to develop sustainable competitive advantages are (1) customer loyalty, (2) location, (3) human resource management, (4) distribution and information systems, (5) unique merchandise, (6) vendor relations, (7) and customer service.

The strategic planning process consists of a sequence of steps, including (1) defining the business mission, (2) conducting a situation audit, (3) identifying strategic opportunities, (4) evaluating the alternatives, (5) establishing specific objectives and allocating resources, (6) developing a retail mix to implement strategy, and (7) evaluating performance and making adjustments.

KEY TERMS

bargaining power of vendors, *148*

barriers to entry, *147*

competitive rivalry, *149*

cross-selling, *138*

customer loyalty, *131*

data warehouse, *133*

direct investment, *144*

diversification growth opportunity, *139*

franchising, *144*

joint venture, *144*

market attractiveness/competitive position matrix, *155*

market expansion growth opportunity, *138*

market penetration growth opportunity, *138*

mission statement, *146*

positioning, *132*

private label brands, *135*

related diversification growth opportunity, *139*

retail format, *128*

retail format development growth opportunity, *139*

retailing concept, *129*

retail market, *129*

retail strategy, *128*

scale economies, *147*

situation audit, *146*

strategic alliance, *144*

strategic retail planning process, *145*

strengths and weaknesses analysis, *150*

sustainable competitive advantage, *128*

target market, *128*

unrelated diversification, *139*

vertical integration, *140*

GET OUT AND DO IT!

1. **CONTINUING CASE ASSIGNMENT** Prepare an analysis of the company you selected for the continuing assignment. Identify its direct competitors, its target market and positioning, its strategy with respect to its competitors, its retail format (the elements in its retail mix—merchandise variety and assortment, pricing, locations), and its bases for developing a competitive advantage relative to its competitors. Outline the retailer's strengths, weaknesses, opportunities, and threats relative to its competitors. Pick a specific country in which the firm does not operate and make a recommendation of whether the retailer should enter the country and, if so, how it should do so.

2. **INTERNET EXERCISE** Visit the Web sites for IKEA (www.ikea.com) and Curves (www.curves.com). Do these Internet sites reflect the way these companies' strategies have been portrayed in the chapter?

3. **INTERNET EXERCISE** Go to the Web sites for Wal-Mart (www.walmartstores.com), Carrefour (www.carrefour.com), Royal Ahold (www.ahold.com), and Metro AG (www.metro.de). Which chain has the most global strategy? Justify your answer.

4. **GO SHOPPING** Visit two stores that sell similar merchandise categories and cater to the same target segment(s). How are their retail formats (the elements in their retail mixes) similar? Dissimilar? On what bases do they have a sustainable competitive advantage? Explain which you believe has a stronger position.

5. **Web OLC EXERCISE** Go to the student side of the book's Web site and click on Market Position Matrix. Exercise 1: This spread sheet reproduces the analysis of international growth opportunities discussed in the appendix to Chapter 5. What numbers in the matrices would have to change to make China and France more attractive opportunities? To make Brazil and Mexico less attractive opportunities? Change the numbers in the matrices and see what effect it has on the overall position of the opportunity in the grid. Exercise 2: The market attractiveness/ competitive position matrix can also be used by a department store to evaluate its merchandise categories and determine how much investment should be made in each category. Fill in the importance weights (10 = very important, 1 = not very important) and the evaluations of the merchandise categories (10 = excellent, 1 = poor) and then see what is recommended by the plot on the opportunity matrix. Exercise 3: Think of another investment decision that a retailer might make and analyze it using the strategic analysis matrix. List the alternatives and the characteristics of the alternatives, and then put in the importance weights for the characteristics (10 = very important, 1 = not very important) and the evaluation of each alternative on each characteristic (10 = excellent, 1 = poor).

DISCUSSION QUESTIONS AND PROBLEMS

1. For each of the four retailers discussed at the beginning of the chapter, describe their strategy and the basis of their competitive advantage.

2. Choose a retailer and describe how it has developed a competitive strategic advantage.

3. Give an example of a market penetration, a retail format development, a market expansion, and a diversification growth strategy that Best Buy might use.

4. Choose your favorite retailer. Draw and explain a positioning map, like that shown in Exhibit 5–3, that includes your retailer, retailers that sell the same types of merchandise, and the customer segments (ideal points).

5. Do a situation analysis for McDonald's. What is its mission? What are its strengths and weaknesses? What environmental threats might it face over the next 10 years? How could it prepare for these threats?

6. What are Neiman Marcus's and Save-A-Lot's bases for sustainable competitive advantage? Are they really sustainable?

7. Assume you are interested in opening a restaurant in your town. Go through the steps in the strategic planning process shown in Exhibit 5–5. Focus on conducting a situation audit of the local restaurant market, identifying and evaluating alternatives, and selecting a target market and a retail mix for the restaurant.

8. Chico's acquired the White House/Black Market chain, a specialty store selling private label apparel to women aged 18 to 25 years, and launched its own concept of an intimate store targeting Baby Boomer women, a Victoria's Secret for women 35 to 55 years old. What type of growth opportunities are each of these retail concepts? Which is most synergistic with the Chico's store chain?

9. Identify a store or service provider that you believe has an effective loyalty program. Explain why it is effective.

10. Choose a retailer that you believe could be, but is not yet, successful in other countries. Explain why you think it could be successful.

11. Amazon.com started as an Internet retailer selling books. Then it expanded to music, DVDs, electronics, software, and travel services. Evaluate these growth opportunities in terms of the probability that they will be profitable businesses for Amazon.com. What competitive advantages does Amazon.com bring to each of these businesses?

SUGGESTED READINGS

Aaker, David. *Strategic Market Management.* 7th ed. New York: Wiley, 2004.

Ander, Willard, and Neil Stern. *Winning at Retail: Developing a Sustained Model for Retail Success.* Hoboken, NJ: Wiley, 2004.

Kumar, Nirmalya. "The Global Retail Challenge," *Business Strategy Review* 16 (Spring 2005), pp. 5–14.

Landry, John. "The Art of the Advantage: 36 Strategies to Seize the Competitive Edge," *Harvard Business Review*, March 2004, pp. 26–30.

Lehmann, Donald and Russell Winer. *Analysis for Marketing Planning.* 6th ed. Burr Ridge, IL: McGraw-Hill/Irwin, 2004.

Reynolds, Jonathan, and Christine Cuthbertson (eds). *Retail Strategy: The View from the Bridge.* Boston: Butterworth Heinemann, 2003.

Rigby, Darrell, and Dan Haas. "Outsmarting Wal-Mart," *Harvard Business Review*, December 2004, pp. 22–24.

Samli, A. Coskun. *Up Against the Retail Giants: Targeting Weakness, Gaining an Edge.* Mason, OH: Thomson, 2004.

Sternquist, Brenda. *International Retailing.* New York: Fairchild Publications, 1998.

Toftoy, Charles, and Joydeep Chatterjee. "Mission Statements and Small Business," *Business Strategy Review*, Autumn 2004, pp. 41–50.

APPENDIX 5A   Using the Market Attractiveness/Competitive Position Matrix

The following example illustrates an application of the **market attractiveness/competitive position matrix.**[49] The matrix (Exhibit 5–8) provides a method for analyzing opportunities that explicitly considers both the retailer's capabilities and the retail market's attractiveness. Its underlying premise is that a market's attractiveness determines its long-term profit potential for the opportunity, and the retailer's competitive position indicates the long-term profit potential for the opportunity. That is, the matrix indicates that the greatest investments should be made in opportunities where the retailer has a strong competitive position.

There are six steps in using the matrix to evaluate opportunities for strategic investments:

1. Define the strategic opportunities to be evaluated. For example, a store manager could use the matrix to evaluate departments in a store; a vice president of stores

for a specialty store chain could use it to evaluate stores or potential store sites; a merchandise vice president could use it to evaluate merchandise categories sold by the retailer; or a retail holding company's CEO could use it to evaluate international growth opportunities.

2. Identify key factors determining market attractiveness and the retailer's competitive position. Factors that might be selected are discussed in the market attractiveness, competitor analysis, and self-analysis sections of the situation audit.

3. Assign weights to each factor used to determine market attractiveness and competitive position to indicate that factor's importance. Typically, weights are selected so they add up to 100.

4. Rate each strategic investment opportunity on (a) the attractiveness of its market and (b) the retailer's

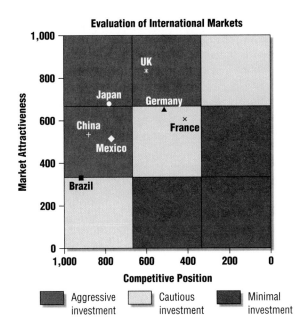

Evaluation of International Markets

EXHIBIT 5–8
Market Attractiveness/
Competitive Position
Matrix

EXHIBIT 5–9 Data on International Markets

	U.S.	Mexico	Brazil	Germany	France	U.K.	Japan	China
Population, 2004 (Millions)	293.6	106.2	179.1	82.6	60	59.7	127.6	1300.1
Projected population change 2004–2050 (%)	16	41	24	−9	7	10	−21	11
Gross domestic product (GDP), 2002 (Billions)	10446	621	452	1992	1439	1564	4146	1287
Per capita GDP, 2002 ($)	36406	6257	2570	24301	24018	26010	31408	1002
Projected GDP annual growth rate 2003–2007 (%)	2.9	3	2.9	1.5	1.8	2.1	0.6	7.8
Per capita retail sales, 2002 (%)	8347	1998	839	3640	5187	5227	8522	367
Internet usage (%)	65	3	8	53	36	57	44	5
Population density (per sq. mile)	79	140	54	599	282	630	875	352
% living in urban areas	79	75	81	88	74	89	48	41
Business environment ranking	4	33	37	15	13	5	27	38

SOURCES: http://www.stores.org/pdf/GlobalRetail04.pdf; "2004 World Population Data Sheet," *Stores*, 2004 Global Powers of Retailing. Courtesy of STORES Magazine/Deloitte.

competitive position in that market. Typically, opportunities are rated on a 1-to-10 scale, with 10 indicating a very attractive market or very strong competitive position and 1 indicating a very unattractive market or very weak competitive position.

5. Calculate each opportunity's score for market attractiveness and competitive position. Scores are calculated by (a) multiplying the weights by each factor's rating and (b) adding across the factors.

6. Plot each opportunity on the matrix in Exhibit 5–8.

In this example, a fashion-oriented U.S. women's apparel retailer is evaluating seven countries for international expansion: Mexico, Brazil, Germany, France, the United Kingdom, Japan, and China. Some information about the markets appears in Exhibit 5–9.

To evaluate each country's market attractiveness, the retailer's management identified five market factors, assigned a weight to each factor, rated the markets on each factor, and calculated a market attractiveness score for each alternative (Exhibit 5–10). Here, management

assigned the highest weight to the attitude that consumers in the country have toward the United States (30) and gave the lowest weight to market growth (10). Ratings for market size and market growth are based on country data; the firm also had to consider size of its target market—middle-class women between the ages of 25 and 50. For this reason, Brazil and Mexico had low ratings on market size. These countries are also low on economic stability; however, the retailer did not find that factor particularly important because the buying power of its target segment is relatively insensitive to the country's economy. The business climate factor includes an assessment of the degree to which the government supports business and foreign investment. The European countries and Japan are high on this dimension.

Exhibit 5–11 shows the factors, weights, and ratings used to evaluate the retailer's position in each country versus the competition. In evaluating the competitive position, management felt that its brand name was the most critical aspect because image is particularly important in selling fashionable merchandise. Since cost was viewed as

EXHIBIT 5–10 Market Attractiveness Ratings for International Growth Opportunities

	Weight	Mexico	Brazil	Germany	France	U.K.	Japan	China
Market size	20	2	2	7	6	5	10	4
Market growth	10	10	7	3	3	3	2	6
Economic stability	15	2	2	10	9	9	5	2
Business climate	25	4	2	7	7	10	6	2
Attitude toward U.S.	30	7	5	8	3	10	10	2
Total	100	480	340	735	550	815	745	280

EXHIBIT 5–11   Competitive Position for International Growth Opportunities

	Weight	Mexico	Brazil	Germany	France	U.K.	Japan	China
Cost	10	9	10	5	5	5	7	10
Brand image	30	8	10	4	3	7	9	6
Vendor relations	20	7	7	4	4	3	8	8
Locations	20	6	8	6	5	7	6	10
Marketing	20	8	8	6	3	6	8	10
Total	100	750	860	490	380	630	780	840

the least important factor in determining the competitive position of a high-fashion retailer, it received a weight of only 10.

In terms of the retailer's competitive position within each country, the firm believed its brand name was very well known in Japan and Brazil but not in France or Germany. Brazil, Mexico, and China offer the best opportunities to operate efficiently due to the low labor costs in these countries. Evaluations of each of the countries are plotted on the market attractiveness/competitive position matrix shown in Exhibit 5–8. Based on the recommended investment level and objectives associated with each cell in the exhibit, the retailer should invest substantially in Japan, the United Kingdom, Mexico, and China and be cautious about investments in Brazil, Germany, and France.

Financial Strategy

EXECUTIVE BRIEFING
Bill Moran, Founder and CEO, Save-A-Lot

In 1977, I was the Vice President of Sales for a food wholesaler in St. Louis. Our customers, independent grocers, were facing a weak economy and stiff competition from the growth of regional supermarket chains. I developed an extreme value, limited assortment concept to give small grocery stores a way to compete. We tested the concept with several stores. Even though the concept worked in the test stores, the wholesaler felt the concept would not work when the economy improved. I disagreed, left the company, got an SBA loan and opened three stores. Now we have over 1,200 stores across the United States with consistent double-digit sales growth.

We target a value and convenience-oriented, psychographic segment. The consumers in this segment are looking for a good value—quality merchandise at low prices.

They don't want to park a half a mile from the storefront and search for merchandise in a 100,000 square foot store.

Our financial model produces a high ROI with high inventory turnover and low margins. Our inventory turnover is high because our stores stock 1,250 SKUs compared to 30,000 SKUs in a traditional supermarket. To offer quality merchandise at low prices and be profitable, we need to tightly control our costs. Offering a limited assortment of high quality, primarily private label merchandise combined with highly efficient distribution systems is critical to our success. We also reduce our cost of goods sold by being a low maintenance customer for our vendors. Our vendors give us low prices because we don't ask for advertising allowance, fees for stocking items, merchandise return privileges, or chargebacks.

When we started, we focused simply on providing value to our customers by selling the basics—bread, eggs, milk, flour, sugar, canned goods—at low prices in a bare bones atmosphere. Over time, our market research revealed that our customers' concept of value was changing. Our customers are like all consumers. They might not

CHAPTER 6

QUESTIONS

How is a retail strategy reflected in retailers' financial objectives?

Why do retailers need to evaluate their performance?

What is the strategic profit model, and how is it used?

What measures do retailers use to assess their performance?

have high incomes, but they want to treat themselves to something special. So we have added special items to our assortment. For example, frozen shrimp is now one of our best selling items. At half the price charged by traditional supermarkets, our customers can have that special meal at a reasonable price.

Our success has attracted competitors. For example, the extreme value general merchandise chains are now offering more food items. But controlling costs and developing an efficient distribution system like ours for food is not easy, so we feel we can maintain our competitive advantage.

Financial objectives and goals are an integral part of a retailer's market strategy. In Chapter 5, we examined how retailers develop their strategy and build a sustainable competitive advantage to generate a continuing stream of profits. In this chapter, we look at how financial analysis can be used to assess the retailer's market strategy—to monitor the retailer's performance, assess the reasons its performance is above or below expectations, and provide insights into appropriate actions that can be taken if performance falls short of those expectations.

For example, Kelly Bradford, the owner of Gifts To Go whom we described in Chapter 5, needs to know how well she is doing because she wants to stay in business, be successful, increase the profitability of her company, and realize her goal of generating an annual income over $100,000. To assess her performance, she can count the number of customers who buy something at her stores and total the receipts at the end of the day. But these simple measures don't indicate how well her business is doing. For instance, she might find that sales are good, and her accountant tells her the business is profitable, but she doesn't have the cash to buy new merchandise. When this happens, Kelly needs to analyze her business to determine the cause of the problem and what can be done to overcome it.

In this chapter, we first review the importance of establishing objectives and measuring performance against specific goals. After considering the various objectives retailers might have, we introduce the strategic profit model, which was developed by DuPont to analyze the factors affecting the financial performance of a firm. To illustrate the use of this model, we examine and compare the factors affecting the performance of Federated Department Stores (Macy's and Bloomingdale's) and Costco, the largest warehouse club chain. Then we demonstrate how the model can be used to evaluate one of the growth opportunities Kelly Bradford is considering. In the last part of this chapter, we examine productivity measures that assess the performance of retail activities, merchandise management, and store operations.

OBJECTIVES AND GOALS

As we discussed in Chapter 5, the first step in the strategic planning process involves articulating the retailer's objectives and the scope of activities it plans to undertake. These objectives guide the development of the retailer's strategy,[1] and specific performance goals determine whether the retailer's objectives are being achieved. When the goals are not being achieved, the retailer knows that it must take corrective actions. Three types of objectives that a retailer might have are (1) financial, (2) societal, and (3) personal.[2]

Financial Objectives

When assessing financial performance, most people focus on profits: What were the retailer's profits or profit margin (profit as a percentage of sales) last year, and what will they be this year and into the future? But the appropriate financial performance measure is not profits but rather return on investment (ROI). Kelly Bradford set a financial objective of making a profit of at least $100,000 a year, but she really needs to consider how much she needs to invest to make the $100,000, the profit she desires from her investment.

Think of the decisions you might make when planning how to invest some money you might have. In making this investment, you want to determine the highest percentage return you can—the highest interest rate or greatest percentage increase in stock price—not the absolute amount of the return. You can always get a greater absolute return by investing more money. For example, Kelly Bradford would be delighted if she made $100,000 and only needed to invest $500,000 (a 20 percent ROI) in the business but disappointed if she had to invest $2,000,000 to make $100,000 profit (a 5 percent ROI). A commonly used measure of the return on investment is **return on assets (ROA),** or the profit return on all the assets possessed by the firm.

Societal Objectives

Societal objectives are related to broader issues about providing benefits to society—making the world a better place to live. For example, retailers might be concerned about providing employment opportunities for people in a particular area or more specifically for minorities or the handicapped. Other societal objectives might include offering people unique merchandise, such as environmentally sensitive products, providing an innovative service to improve personal health, such as weight reduction programs, or sponsoring community events.

For example, McDonald's values diversity among its employees and suppliers. The company ensures diversity among its corporate employees by including it in the business planning process. "As business units and corporate departments put together their business plans, diversity is included in them. We have diversity business planning guidelines that we provide to the McDonald's leadership, so that they're incorporated in the strategic planning process," explains chief diversity officer Pat Harris. McDonald's also values diversity in its supply chain and has been recognized by *Fortune* magazine as the "top purchaser from minority suppliers, spending more than $3 billion a year, or 27 percent of its total, at minority-owned firms."[3]

Performance with respect to societal objectives is more difficult to measure than financial objectives. But explicit societal goals can be set, such as the percentage of executives or store managers that are women or minorities or the percentage of profits donated to worthy charities.

This store owner/manager develops a retail strategy and coordinates the day-to-day operations to ensure that financial objectives are being met.

Personal Objectives

Many retailers, particularly owners of small, independent businesses, have important personal objectives, including self-gratification, status, and respect. For example, the owner/operator of a book store may find it rewarding to interact with others who like reading and authors that visit the store for book-signing promotions. By operating a popular store, a retailer might be recognized as a well-respected business leader in the community.

Whereas societal and personal objectives are important to some retailers, financial objectives should be the primary focus of managers of publicly held retailers—retailers whose stocks are listed on and bought through a stock market. Investors in publicly held companies, namely, the people who buy stock in a company, are primarily interested in getting a return on their investment, and the managers of these companies must have the same objectives as the investors. Therefore, the remaining sections of this chapter focus on financial objectives and the factors affecting a retailer's ability to achieve financial goals.

STRATEGIC PROFIT MODEL

The **strategic profit model,** illustrated in Exhibit 6–1, is a method for summarizing the factors that affect a firm's financial performance as measured by ROA. The model decomposes ROA into two components: (1) net profit margin and (2) asset turnover. The **net profit margin** is simply how much profit (after tax) a firm makes divided by its net sales. Thus, it reflects the profits generated from each dollar of sales. If a retailer's net profit margin is 5 percent, it makes $.05 for every dollar of merchandise or services it sells.

Asset turnover is the retailer's net sales divided by its assets. This financial measure assesses the productivity of a firm's investment in its assets and indicates how many sales dollars are generated by each dollar of assets. Thus, if a retailer's asset turnover is 3.0, it generates $3 in sales for each dollar invested in the firm's assets.

EXHIBIT 6–1
Components of the
Strategic Profit Model

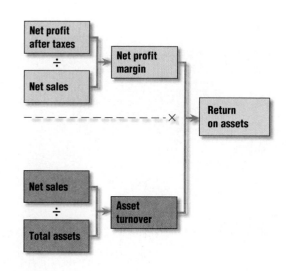

The retailer's ROA is determined by multiplying the two components together:

Net profit margin   ×   Asset turnover   =   Return on assets (ROA)

$$\frac{\text{Net profit}}{\text{Net sales}} \times \frac{\text{Net sales}}{\text{Total assets}} = \frac{\text{Net profit}}{\text{Total assets}}$$

These two components of the strategic profit model illustrate that ROA is determined by two sets of activities, profit margin management and asset management, and that a high ROA can be achieved by various combinations of net profit margin and asset turnover.

To illustrate the different approaches for achieving a high ROA, consider the financial performance of two very different hypothetical retailers in Exhibit 6–2. La Madeline Bakery has a net profit margin of only 1 percent and asset turnover of 10, resulting in an ROA of 10 percent. Its profit margin is low due to the highly competitive nature of its business. Consumers can buy baked goods from a wide variety of retailers, as well as from the other bakeries in the area. However, its asset turnover is relatively high, because the firm has a very low level of inventory assets. It has very little inventory because it sells everything the same day it is baked.

On the other hand, Kalame Jewelry Store has a net profit margin of 10 percent—ten times higher than that of the bakery. Even though it has a much higher net profit margin, the jewelry store has the same ROA because it has a very low asset turnover of 1. Kalame's asset turnover is low compared with the bakery's because Kalame has a high level of inventory; it stocks a lot of items that take many months to sell. In addition, the jewelry store offers liberal credit to customers, increasing its assets in accounts receivable.

Thus, La Madeline is achieving its 10 percent ROA by having a relatively high asset turnover—the asset management path. Kalame Jewelry Store, in contrast, achieves its same ROA with a relatively high net profit margin—the profit margin management path.

In the next section, we take a close look at these two components of ROA. Specifically, we examine the relationship between these ratios and a firm's retail strategy and describe how these financial measures can be used to assess

EXHIBIT 6–2

Different Approaches for
Achieving an Acceptable
ROA—A Bakery and
Jewelry Store

	Net Profit Margin	×	Asset Turnover	=	Return on Assets
La Madeline Bakery	1%		10 times		10%
Kalame Jewelry	10%		1 time		10%

performance with traditional accounting information. To illustrate the financial implications of different retail strategies, we compare the financial performance of Federated Department Stores and Costco.

Federated Department Stores, described in Retailing View 6.1, operates two national department store chains, Macy's and Bloomingdale's. Like other department store chains, Federated offers a wide variety of fashionable apparel and home furnishings, a relatively high level of customer service provided by its sales associates, and an attractive shopping environment. Costco's warehouse stores, in contrast, offer a limited assortment of food and general merchandise in a self-service, warehouse environment. Retailing View 6.2 provides some background information about Costco.

Federated Department Stores, Inc. · RETAILING VIEW · 6.1

Federated Department Stores was founded in 1929 as a holding company by several family-owned, regional department store chains, including Shillito's, founded in 1830 in Cincinnati, Ohio; Bloomingdale's, founded in 1885 in New York; Jordan Marsh, founded in 1841 in Boston; F&R Lazarus, founded in 1851 in Columbus, Ohio; and Abraham & Straus, founded in 1865 in New York. Over the next 30 years, Bon Marche (Seattle), Rike's (Dayton, Ohio), Goldsmith's (Memphis), Burdines (Miami), and Rich's (Atlanta) joined Federated. In addition, the company started Filene's Basement (an off-price retailer) and Gold Circle (a full-line discounter) and acquired Ralph's (a West Coast supermarket chain). Each of these chains was operated as an independent division with its own buying office, distribution center, corporate offices, and human resource policies.

Although the divisions were profitable, the stock price was low. In 1986, Robert Campeau, a successful Canadian real estate developer, felt that the stock for retail conglomerate companies like Federated was undervalued and bought Allied, a similar holding company, for $3.5 billion. In April 1988, he bought Federated for $6.6 billion. To finance these acquisitions, he sold off over 25 chains owned by the two holding companies, including Brooks Brothers, Ann Taylor, Ralph's, Filene's, Joske's, Miller's, Bonwit Teller, and Gold Circle, and attempted to cut operating costs. However, most of the acquisition was financed by issuing bonds and taking out loans. On January 15, 1990, the retail subsidiaries could not pay the interest on the debt and filed for bankruptcy, the largest bankruptcy in U.S. history at that time.

Under the protection of the bankruptcy court, Federated's new management team closed unprofitable stores, sold divisions unrelated to its core department store activities, and reduced operating costs dramatically by developing centralized information, distribution, and buying systems used by most of the department store divisions. In 1992, Federated emerged from bankruptcy as one of the largest and best managed retail chains. The company has since acquired four department store chains—Macy's, Horne's (Pittsburgh), The Broadway (Los Angeles), and Liberty House (Hawaii)—and has continued to develop synergies among its regional chains so it can exploit its scale economies.

It 2005, it completed its implementation of a long-term strategy of operating two national retail chains (Bloomingdale's and Macy's) positioned at different points on the price/quality continuum. All regional chains were renamed Macy's, and the Macy's stores were organized into four regions: East, Florida, Central, and West.

The Macy's store located at Herald Square in New York City is the United States' largest department store.

Macy's and Bloomingdale's are two of retailing's strongest brand names. The core customer shopping at Macy's 420 department stores is female; is between 25 and 54 years old; typically works outside the house; has children and an average family income over $75,000; and spends $5,000 on merchandise sold at Macy's for herself, her family, and gifts. Macy's has been particularly effective in developing private label merchandise such as I.N.C., Charter Club, The Cellar, Alfani, Greendog, and Tools of the Trade. These private labels presently account for 17 percent of sales, and Macy's plans to increase their share to over 20 percent.

The Bloomingdale's chain of 34 stores targets fashion-forward women who are interested in the latest styles in designer apparel and accessories. In addition to offering exclusive designer merchandise, Bloomingdale's provides a high level of personalized customer service. Sales associates regularly contact their top customers to announce new merchandise, invite them to store events, and follow up to ensure high levels of customer satisfaction.

REFACT

Federated Department Stores was named one of the top 30 companies for executive women by the National Association of Female Executives and one of the top 100 companies providing the best opportunities for Latinos by *Hispanic Magazine*.[4]

Sources: Georgia Lee, "Future Is Now for Macy's New Nameplates," *WWD*, March 8, 2005, p. 16; Thomas Hine, "Once, We Knew Our Cities by Their Department Stores," *The Washington Post*, March 6, 2005, p. B.03; *2004 Fact Book* (Cincinnati, OH: Federated Department Stores, 2004).

Profit Margin Management Path

Information used to examine the profit margin management path comes from the retailer's income statement, which summarizes a firm's financial performance over a period of time. For example, the income statement in a retailer's annual report provides a summary of the retailer's performance during the previous fiscal year. To capture all the sales and returns from the Christmas season, most retailers define their fiscal year as beginning on February 1 and ending January 31.

Exhibit 6–3 shows income statements adapted from the annual reports of Federated Department Stores and Costco. The profit margin management path portion of the strategic profit model that summarizes these data appears in Exhibit 6–4. In the following sections, we consider each element in the profit margin management path.

Net Sales   The term **net sales** refers to the total revenue received by a retailer after all refunds have been paid to customers for returned merchandise. Sales are an important measure of performance because they indicate the activity level of

---

Income Statement ($ millions)	Federated Department Stores	Costco
Net sales	$15,630	$48,107
Less: Cost of goods sold	9,297	42,093
Gross margin	6,333	6,014
Less: Operating expenses	4,933	4,629
Less: Interest expenses/income	284	−15
Total expenses	5,217	4,614
Net profit, pre-tax	1,116	1,400
Less: Taxes	427	518
Net profit after taxes	689	882
Gross margin %	40.5%	12.5%
Operating expenses % of sales	31.6	9.6
Net profit % after taxes	4.4	1.8
Net profit % before interest and taxes	9.0	2.9

EXHIBIT 6–3
Income Statement for Federated Department Stores and Costco

the merchandising function. Costco's net sales are more than three times greater than Federated's.

Net sales = Gross amount of sales + Promotional allowances − Customer return

Customer returns represent the value of merchandise that customers return and for which they receive a refund of cash or a credit. **Promotional allowances** are payments made by vendors to retailers in exchange for the retailer promoting the vendor's merchandise. For example, consumer packaged good manufacturers will frequently pay supermarket chains to stock a new product (called slotting fees)

Profit Management Path for Federated and Costco   **EXHIBIT 6–4**

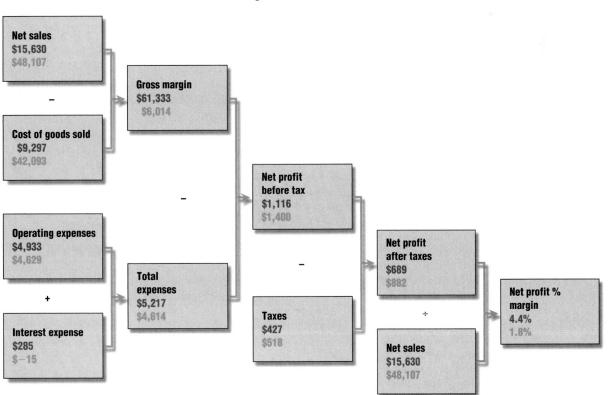

Federated Department Stores
Costco

or advertise a product. Retailing View 6.3 describes the impact of these promotional allowances on a retailer's reported net sales. For warehouse clubs such as Costco, membership fees are an additional source of revenue. About 4 percent of Costco's $48 billion in sales are from membership fees.

Gross Margin   The **gross margin,** also called **gross profit,** is net sales minus the cost of the goods sold. It is an important measure in retailing because it indicates how much profit the retailer is making on merchandise sales without considering the expenses associated with operating the store.

$$\text{Gross margin} = \text{Net sales} - \text{Cost of goods sold}$$

Gross margin, like other performance measures, is also expressed as a percentage of net sales so retailers can compare (1) the performances of various types of merchandise and (2) their own performance with other retailers with higher or lower levels of sales.

$$\frac{\text{Gross margin}}{\text{Net sales}} = \text{Gross margin \%}$$

$$\text{Federated: } \frac{\$6,333}{\$15,630} = 40.5\%$$

$$\text{Costco: } \frac{\$6,014}{\$48,107} = 12.5\%$$

(Throughout the chapter, these dollar figures are expressed in millions.)

Even though Costco has more than three times the sales of Federated, both retailers have about the same gross margin, and Federated has a much higher gross margin percentage. This difference in gross margin percentage can be traced back to the retail strategies of the companies. Warehouse clubs generally have lower gross margin percentages than department stores because they target cost-oriented consumers, sell merchandise at low prices, and provide minimal service. Department stores, on the other hand, carry brands that their customers

---

6.3   RETAILING VIEW   Accounting for Promotional Allowances Can Provide Misleading Information about Retail Sales

Manufacturers of branded consumer products pay promotional allowances, also called rebates, to retailers for a variety of actions, such as to get them to meet sales targets, stock new products in their stores, or place products in prime store locations (known as slotting allowances)— even to compensate for damaged goods. For example, rather than have the supermarket chain return damaged merchandise for credit, the vendor simply gives the supermarket chain an allowance of 3 percent of the merchandise bought.

These promotional allowances can have a significant impact on reported sales. A typical manufacturer may spend 20 percent of its sales with a retailer on promotional allowances; a $50 million contract for cookies or tomato sauce thus would include a $10 million promotional allowance. The payments are usually made upfront but can also take the form of volume-based bonuses. If a retailer fails to deliver the volume, the bonus is not paid or may have to be renegotiated.

The effect of these promotional allowances on a retailer's reported sales and profit have made headlines in the business press. In 2003, vendors such as Sara Lee Corp. and ConAgra Foods Inc. paid U.S. Foodservice rebates that executives recog-

nized as sales before the sales goals were realized. U.S. Foodservice is a division of Ahold, one of the largest global supermarket retailers, headquartered in The Netherlands. By inflating sales and earnings, the executives met their annual goals and received significant bonuses. In response to an SEC (Securities and Exchange Commission) complaint, two U.S. Foodservice executives pleaded guilty to criminal charges in the matter, while two others are fighting the charges.

In response to this scandal, an accounting task force was established by the Federal Accounting Standards Board (FASB) to define how promotional allowances should be treated in financial statements. While Safeway Inc. discloses vendor allowances in detail—breaking them down into promotional and stocking allowances on a quarterly basis—many other companies disclose little new information and describe minimal effects on earnings because they feel the information is propriety.

Sources: Diya Gullapalli, "In the Grocery World, Rebates Remain the Mystery Meat," *The Wall Street Journal,* August 9, 2004, p. C.1; Constance L. Hays, "Reliance on Promotional Allowances Can Result in Shortfalls," *New York Times,* February 25, 2003, p. C.8.

recognize and are loyal to, some of which are very prestigious. This merchandise, coupled with higher service than other retail formats, makes their customers less price sensitive and enables them to achieve a higher gross margin. It is important for department stores to achieve a relatively high gross margin because their operating expenses are also higher than those of some other retail formats.

Operating Expenses   **Operating expenses** are costs, other than the cost of merchandise, incurred in the normal course of doing business, such as salaries for sales associates and managers, advertising, utilities, office supplies, and rent. Another major expense category, interest, includes the cost of borrowing money to finance everything from inventory to the purchase of a new store location.

Like the gross margin, operating expenses are expressed as a percentage of net sales to facilitate comparisons across items and departments within firms. Federated has significantly higher operating expenses as a percentage of net sales than Costco does.

$$\frac{\text{Operating expenses}}{\text{Net sales}} = \text{Operating expenses \%}$$

$$\text{Federated:} \frac{\$4,933}{\$15,630} = 31.6\%$$

$$\text{Costco:} \frac{\$4,629}{\$48,107} = 9.6\%$$

The operating expenses percentage for Costco is about one-third as large as that for Federated because Costco has lower selling expenses. Also, it incurs lower costs in maintaining the appearance of its stores. Finally, warehouse club stores operate with a smaller administrative staff than do department stores. For instance, Costco's buying expenses are much lower because fewer buyers are needed in the simpler buying process for commodity-type merchandise, like packaged foods and fresh meat and produce, than for fashion apparel. Also, its buyers don't have to travel to fashion markets around the world like department store buyers do.

Net Profit   **Net profit** (after taxes) is the gross margin minus operating expenses and taxes:

Net profit = Gross margin − Expenses − Taxes

It is a measure of overall performance with respect to the profit margin management path and can also be expressed before taxes. Net profit margin, like gross margin, is often expressed as a percentage of net sales:

$$\frac{\text{Net profit}}{\text{Net sales}} = \text{Net profit \%}$$

$$\text{Federated:} \frac{\$689}{\$15,630} = 4.4\%$$

$$\text{Costco:} \frac{\$882}{\$48,107} = 1.8\%$$

A commonly used overall profit measure is the profit percentage before interest and taxes. This measure is used because operating managers have little control over interest and tax expenses, so these expenses do not reflect the performance of operating managers or the retailer's operating effectiveness. Profit percentage before interest and taxes for Federated is 7.1 percent and only 2.9 percent for Costco.

In an examination of their profit management paths, it appears that even though Costco has more than four times greater sales than Federated, both companies generate about the same level of absolute profits, and Federated has a much

REFACT

Over 40 percent of supermarket executives think Wal-Mart is a formidable competitor. To counter this threat, they plan to drive profits by penetrating new markets (39 percent), lowering operating expenses (18 percent), investing in new technology (17 percent), and improving customer service (16 percent).[6]

EXHIBIT 6–5
Asset Information from
Federated's and Costco's
Balance Sheets

	Federated Department Stores	Costco
Accounts receivable	$ 3,418	$ 335
Merchandise inventory	3,120	3,644
Cash	868	2,823
Other current assets	104	467
Total current assets	7,510	7,269
Fixed assets	7,375	7,824
Total assets	$14,885	$15,093
Inventory turnover	3.0	11.6
Asset turnover	1.1	3.2
ROA	4.6%	5.8%

higher profit percentage before interest and taxes. Thus, this component of the strategic profit model suggests that Federated is outperforming Costco, but the following examination of the asset management path tells a different story.

Asset Management Path

The information used to analyze a retailer's asset management path primarily comes from the firm's balance sheet. Whereas the income statement summarizes the financial performance over a period of time (usually a year or quarter), the balance sheet summarizes a retailer's financial position at a given point in time, typically at the end of its fiscal year. The information about Federated's and Costco's assets from their balance sheets is shown in Exhibit 6–5, and the asset management path components in the strategic profit model are shown in Exhibit 6–6.

EXHIBIT 6–6
Asset Management Path
for Federated and Costco

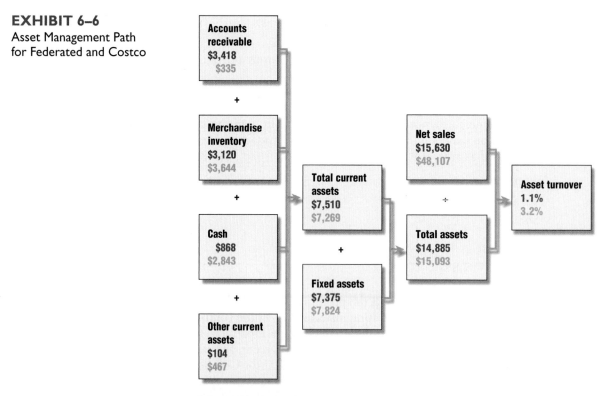

Federated Department Store
Costco

Assets are economic resources (such as inventory or store fixtures) owned or controlled by a firm. There are two types of assets, current and fixed.

Current Assets   By accounting definition, **current assets** are assets that can normally be converted to cash within one year. In retailing, current assets are primarily cash, accounts receivable, and merchandise inventory. **Accounts receivable** are primarily monies owed to the retailer from selling merchandise on credit to customers.

Current assets = Cash + Accounts receivable + Merchandise inventory + Other current assets

Current assets are substantial for some retailers. For example, Federated has more of its assets in accounts receivable than in merchandise inventory and ten times more accounts receivable than Costco even though Costco has four times more sales. Costco's investment in accounts receivable is proportionately much smaller than Federated's because Costco's customers have a higher propensity to pay cash, whereas a significant number of Federated's customers use their Macy's or Bloomingdale's credit cards.

From a marketing perspective, the accounts receivable generated from credit sales provides an important service to customers. The retailer's ability to provide credit, particularly at low interest rates, can make the difference between making or losing a sale because paying cash for a sizable purchase like a diamond engagement ring or car may be difficult for many people. But offering this service is costly because it increases accounts receivable and thus the level of assets needed by the retailer. When merchandise is sold on credit, proceeds of the sale are tied up in accounts receivable until collection is made. The money invested in accounts receivable costs the retailer interest expense and keeps the retailer from investing the money generated by a sale elsewhere. To ease the financial burden of carrying accounts receivable, retailers use third-party credit cards, such as Visa or MasterCard, and collect from delinquent accounts quicker.

Merchandise inventory is a retailer's lifeblood. The principle benefit retailers offer customers is having the right merchandise inventory available at the right time and place. **Inventory turnover,** a ratio like gross margin, is used to evaluate how effectively retailers utilize their investment in inventory and reflects the cost of goods sold from the income statement divided by the average inventory level from the balance sheet. Note that the inventory level reported on the balance sheet is the level on the last day of the fiscal year, not the average level. To measure the average inventory level more accurately, you would have to measure the level on each day of the year and divide by 365 or each month and divide by 12.

$$\frac{\text{Cost of goods}}{\text{Average inventory}} = \text{Inventory turnover}$$

Federated: $\dfrac{\$9,297}{\$3,120}$ = 3.0

Costco: $\dfrac{\$42,093}{\$3,644}$ = 11.6

Inventory turnover is a measure of the productivity of inventory. It shows how many times, on average, inventory cycles through the store during a specific period of time (usually a year). Costco's higher inventory turnover is expected due to the nature of its retail strategy and the merchandise it sells. That is, most items in Costco are commodities and staples such as food, batteries, housewares, and basic apparel items. Unlike apparel fashions that are the mainstay for department stores like Federated, these staples can be replenished quickly. Costco stores also have

REFACT

Zara, Spain's fashion specialty store chain, believes that in a perfect world a store would never have anything in it that it wasn't going to sell that very day. Zara isn't perfect, but its inventory turnover is three times as fast as that of The Gap.[7]

only have 4,000 SKUs in total; for example, it may only offer one brand of ketchup in two different sizes, which represents two inventory items. Department stores, on the other hand, may stock 500 SKUs of just men's dress shirts (different colors, sizes, styles, and brands). Larger assortments, like those in department stores, require relatively higher inventory investments, which slows inventory turnover. Finally, Federated sells a lot of private label merchandise that is made in other countries, requiring buyers to place orders many months in advance of delivery. Costco orders readily available products and has them delivered in days.

Fixed Assets   Fixed assets are those assets that require more than a year to convert to cash. In retailing, the principal fixed assets are buildings (if store property is owned rather than leased), fixtures (such as display racks), equipment (such as computers or delivery trucks), and other long-term investments such as stock in other supplier firms.

Fixed assets are more difficult to manage than current assets such as inventory. However, when a retailer remodels a store, for example, old fixtures, carpeting, and lights are removed and replaced with new ones. Thus, like inventory, these assets cycle through the store. The difference is that the process is a lot slower. The life of a fixture in a Federated store may

To provide a more attractive store environment, department store retailers (top) accept higher fixed costs than wholesale club retailers (bottom).

be five years (instead of two months, as it might be for a Polo shirt), yet the concept of turnover is the same. When a retailer decides to invest in a fixed asset, it should determine how many sales dollars can be generated from that asset.

Suppose that Federated is considering the purchase of a new fixture for displaying dinnerware. It has a choice of buying an expensive antique display cabinet for $20,000 or having a simple plywood display constructed for $5,000. Using the expensive antique, it forecasts incremental sales of $50,000 in the first year, whereas the plywood display is expected to generate only $25,000. Ignoring all other assets for a moment,

$$\frac{\text{Net sales}}{\text{Fixed assets}} = \text{Fixed asset turnover}$$

Antique cabinet: $\dfrac{\$50,000}{\$20,000} = 2.5$

Plywood cabinet: $\dfrac{\$25,000}{\$5,000} = 5.0$

The antique cabinet will certainly help create an atmosphere conducive to selling expensive dinnerware. Exclusively from a marketing perspective, the antique cabinet would thus appear appropriate. But it costs much more than the plywood shelves. Clearly, by considering only asset turnover, the plywood shelves are the way to go. In the end, a combination of marketing and financial factors should be considered when making the appropriate asset purchase decision.[8]

Asset Turnover   **Asset turnover** is an overall performance measure from the asset management component in the strategic profit model.

$$\frac{\text{Net sales}}{\text{Total assets}} = \text{Asset turnover}$$

$$\text{Federated:} \frac{\$15,630}{\$14,885} = 1.1$$

$$\text{Costco:} \frac{\$48,107}{\$15,093} = 3.2$$

Costco's asset turnover thus is three times greater than Federated's. Again, this difference reflects the different retail strategies pursued by the companies. Costco targets consumers who are more interested in low prices than in an extensive assortment of merchandise from which to select. Thus, Costco stocks a small number of SKUs, has limited inventory, and has high inventory turnover. In addition, fewer fixed assets (such as fixtures, lighting, and mannequins) are used in its stores compared with in Federated stores.

On the other hand, Federated targets a market segment interested in buying fashionable apparel. Consumers in its target segment are less price conscious; want to choose from a broad assortment of colors, sizes, and brands; and like to shop in a more attractive environment, certainly not a warehouse. Thus, Federated needs to invest in more current assets (merchandise inventory) and fixed assets (store design elements) and therefore has a lower asset turnover.

Return on Assets

In terms of the profit margin management path, Federated performs better than Costco, but Costco has a higher asset turnover and thus performs better on the asset management path. But overall performance, as measured by ROA, is determined by considering the effects of both paths by multiplying the net profit margin by asset turnover:

	Net profit margin	×	Asset turnover	=	Return on assets
Federated:	4.41	×	1.05	=	4.63%
Costco:	1.83	×	3.29	=	5.84%

In the end, the two firm's ROAs are fairly close. Federated has the higher net profit margin; Costco has the higher asset turnover. Return on assets is a very important performance measure, because it shows how much money the retailer is making on its investment in assets and how good that return is relative to other investments. For instance, if a retailer can achieve a 9 percent ROA by opening a new store and 10 percent by investing in a risk-free Treasury bill, the retailer should make the higher-yield, lower-risk investment.

The strategic profit model illustrates two important issues. First, retailers and investors need to consider both net profit margin and asset turnover when evaluating their financial performance. Firms can achieve high performance (high ROA) by effectively managing both net profit margins and asset turnover. Second, retailers need to consider the implications of strategic decisions on both components of the strategic profit model. For example, simply increasing prices will increase the gross margin and net profit margins (the profit margin management path). However, increasing prices will result in fewer sales, and assuming the level of assets stays the same, asset turnover will decrease. Thus profit margin increases, assets turnover decreases, and the effect on ROA depends on how much the profit margin increases compared to the decrease in asset turnover.

REFACT

Gas stations, on average, have a gross margin of only 15.5 percent but have an inventory turnover of 39.3.[9]

EXHIBIT 6–7
Strategic Profit Model
Ratios for Selected
Retailers

	Net Profit Margin	Asset Turnover	Return on Assets
Category specialists			
Best Buy*	2.87%	2.84	8.15%
Home Depot	6.84	1.88	12.85
Lowe's	5.97	1.72	10.26
PETsMART	5.08	2.03	10.33
Michaels	5.92	1.61	9.52
Barnes & Noble	2.93	1.48	4.33
Borders	3.40	1.48	5.02
Specialty stores			
The Gap	7.07%	1.62	11.45%
Chico's	15.86	1.24	19.72
Abercrombie & Fitch	10.69	1.50	16.04
The Limited Brands	7.49	1.55	11.58
Urban Outfitters	10.88	1.48	16.16
CVS	3.00	2.10	6.32
Walgreens	3.60	2.81	10.12
Discount			
Family Dollar	4.88%	2.38	11.60%
Dollar General	4.49	2.70	12.11
Wal-Mart	3.60	2.37	8.54
Target	6.83	1.45	9.90
Supermarket			
Safeway	1.56%	2.33	3.64%
Albertson's	1.11	2.18	2.42

SOURCE: 2005 annual reports.

* 2004 annual report.

Exhibit 6–7 shows the strategic profit model ratios for a variety of retailers. The exhibit illustrates that supermarket and discount chains typically have higher asset turnovers and lower net profit margin percentages. However, Target is unusual with its higher net profit margin percentage and lower asset turnover ratio, which reflects its "cheap chic" strategy of offering more fashionable merchandise with a heavy emphasis on private labels. The apparel specialty stores have lower asset turnovers and higher net profit margin percentages; however, the drug store chains are just the opposite. Note also the range in ROA ratios among specialty stores, with Chico's, Urban Outfitters, and Abercrombie & Fitch at the top and supermarkets Safeway and Albertson's at the bottom.

Illustration: Kelly Bradford's Evaluation of the Gifts_To_Go.com Growth Opportunity

To illustrate the use of the strategic profit model for evaluating a growth opportunity, let's look at the opportunity that Kelly Bradford, from Chapter 5, is considering. Recall that Kelly Bradford owns Gifts To Go, a two-store chain in the Chicago area. She's considering several growth options, one of which is to open a new Internet channel called Gifts_To_Go.com. She determined that the market size for this channel is high but very competitive. Now she needs to conduct a financial analysis for the proposed online channel, compare the projections with Gifts To Go stores, and determine the financial performance of the combined businesses. We'll first look at the profit margin management path, followed by the asset turnover management path. Exhibit 6–8 shows income statement information for Kelly's Gifts To Go stores, her estimates for Gifts_To_Go.com, and the combined businesses.

Income Statement	Gifts To Go Stores	Gifts_To_Go.com (Projected)	Businesses Combined
Net sales	$700,000	$440,000	$1,140,000
Less: Cost of goods sold	350,000	220,000	570,000
Gross margin	350,000	220,000	570,000
Less: Operating expenses	250,000	150,000	400,000
Less: Interest expenses/income	8,000	0	8,000
Total expenses	258,000	150,000	408,000
Net profit, pre-tax	92,000	70,000	162,000
Less: Taxes	32,200	24,500	56,700
Net profit after taxes	59,800	45,500	105,300
Gross margin %	50.0%	50.0%	50.0%
Operating expenses % of sales	35.7	34.1	35.1
Net profit % after taxes	8.54	10.34	9.2
Net profit % before interest and taxes	14.3	15.9	14.9

EXHIBIT 6–8

Income Statement Information for Gifts To Go Stores and Proposed Gifts_To_Go.com Internet Channel

Profit Margin Management Path   Kelly thinks she can develop Gifts_To_Go.com into a business generating annual sales of $440,000. She anticipates some cannibalization of her store sales by the Internet channel; some customers who will buy merchandise at Gifts_To_Go.com will no longer go into her stores to make their purchases. On the other hand, she thinks the Internet channel will stimulate some store sales; customers who see gift items on her Web site will visit the stores and make their purchases there. Thus, she decided to do the analysis with the assumption that her store sales will remain the same after the introduction of the Internet channel.

Gross Margin Percentage   Kelly plans to charge the same prices and sell basically the same merchandise with an extended assortment at Gifts_To_Go.com as she sells in her stores. Thus, she expects the gross margin percentage for store sales will be the same as the gross margin percentage for Gifts_To_Go.com sales.

$$\frac{\text{Gross margin}}{\text{Net sales}} = \text{Gross margin \%}$$

Stores: $\dfrac{\$350,000}{\$700,000} = 50\%$

Gifts_To_Go.com: $\dfrac{\$220,000}{\$440,000} = 50\%$

Operating Expenses   Initially, Kelly thought that her operating expenses as a percentage of sales would be lower for Gifts_To_Go.com because she would not need to pay rent or highly trained salespeople. But she discovered that her operating expenses as a percentage of sales will be only slightly lower for Gifts_To_Go.com because she needs to hire a firm to maintain the Web site, process orders, and get orders ready for shipment. Also, Gifts To Go stores have an established clientele and highly trafficked locations with good visibility. Although some of her current customers will learn about the Web site from her in-store promotions, Kelly will have to invest in advertising and promotion to create awareness for her new channel and inform people who are unfamiliar with her stores.

$$\frac{\text{Operating expenses}}{\text{Net sales}} = \text{Operating expenses \%}$$

Stores: $\dfrac{\$250,000}{\$700,000} = 35.7\%$

Gifts_To_Go.com: $\dfrac{\$150,000}{\$440,000} = 34.1\%$

Net Profit Margins   Because the gross margin and operating expenses as a percentage of sales for the two operations are projected to be the same, Gifts_To_Go.com is expected to generate a slightly higher net profit margin percentage:

$$\frac{\text{Net profit}}{\text{Net sales}} = \text{Net profit \%}$$

Stores: $\dfrac{\$59,800}{\$700,000} = 8.5\%$

Gifts_To_Go.com: $\dfrac{\$45,500}{\$440,000} = 10.3\%$

Asset Turnover Management Path   Now let's compare the two operations using the asset turnover management path with the balance sheet information from Exhibit 6–9.

Accounts Receivable   Like Gifts To Go, Gifts_To_Go.com will have accounts receivable because many customers use credit cards to buy gifts. Since the percentage of credit card sales is higher over the Internet channel than in stores, Kelly expects that the accounts receivable for the Internet channel will be higher than for the store channel.

Inventory Turnover   Kelly estimates that Gifts_To_Go.com will have a higher inventory turnover than Gifts To Go because it will consolidate the inventory at one centralized distribution center that services a large sales volume, as opposed to Gifts to Go, which has inventory sitting in several stores with relatively lower sales volumes.

$$\frac{\text{Cost of goods}}{\text{Average inventory}} = \text{Inventory turnover}$$

Stores: $\dfrac{\$350,000}{\$175,000} = 2.0$

Gifts_To_Go.com: $\dfrac{\$220,000}{\$70,000} = 3.1$

Fixed Assets   Gifts To Go's store space is rented. Thus, Kelly's fixed assets consist of the fixtures, lighting, and other leasehold improvements for her stores, as well as equipment such as POS terminals. Kelly also has invested in assets that make her stores aesthetically pleasing. Gifts_To_Go.com is outsourcing its fulfillment of orders placed on its Web site so it has no warehouse assets. Thus, its fixed assets are its Web site and order processing computer system.

EXHIBIT 6–9

Balance Sheet Information for Gifts To Go stores and Proposed Internet Channel

Balance Sheet Information	Gifts to Go Stores	Gifts_To_Go.com (Projected)	Businesses Combined
Accounts receivable	$140,000	$120,000	$260,000
Merchandise inventory	175,000	70,000	245,000
Cash	35,000	11,000	46,000
Total current assets	350,000	201,000	551,000
Fixed assets	30,000	10,000	40,000
Total assets	380,000	211,000	591,000
Inventory turnover	2.0	3.1	2.3
Asset turnover	1.84	2.09	1.93
ROA	15.7%	21.6%	17.8%

Asset Turnover   As she expects, Gifts_To_Go.com's projected asset turnover is higher than Gifts To Go's stores because Kelly estimates that Gifts_To_Go.com will have a higher inventory turnover, and its other assets are lower.

$$\frac{\text{Net sales}}{\text{Total assets}} = \text{Asset turnover}$$

Stores: $\dfrac{\$700,000}{\$380,000} = 1.84$

Gifts_To_Go.com: $\dfrac{\$440,000}{\$211,000} = 2.09$

Return on Assets   Because Kelly's estimates for the net profit margin and asset turnover for Gifts_To_Go.com are higher than those for her stores, Gifts_To_ Go.com has a higher ROA. Thus, this strategic profit model analysis indicates that Gifts_To_Go.com is a financially viable growth opportunity for Kelly.

	Net profit margin	×	Asset turnover	=	Return on assets
Stores:	8.54	×	1.84	=	15.7%
Gifts_To_Go.com:	10.3	×	2.09	=	21.3%

Using the Strategic Profit Model to Analyze Other Decisions

The strategic profit model is useful to retailers because it combines two decision-making areas: profit margin management and asset turnover management. Managers can use the model to examine interrelationships between the components. For example, Kelly might consider an investment in a computerized inventory control system that would help her make better decisions about what merchandise to order, when to reorder merchandise, and when to lower prices on merchandise that is not being bought.

If she buys the system, her sales will increase because she will have a greater percentage of merchandise that is selling well and fewer stockouts. However, her cost of goods sold will increase but not proportionally, because she will have fewer price discounts to sell slow-moving merchandise.

Looking at the asset turnover management path, the purchase of the computer system will increase her fixed assets by the amount of the system, but her inventory turnover will increase and the level of inventory assets will decrease because she is able to buy more efficiently. Thus her asset turnover will probably increase because sales will increase at a larger percentage than the total assets. In fact, total assets may actually decrease if the additional cost of the inventory system is less than the reduction in inventory.

SETTING AND MEASURING PERFORMANCE OBJECTIVES

Setting performance objectives is a necessary component of any firm's strategic planning process. How would a retailer know how it has performed if it doesn't have specific objectives in mind to compare actual performance against? Performance objectives should include (1) a numerical index of the performance desired against which progress may be measured, (2) a time frame within which the objective is to be achieved, and (3) the resources needed to achieve the objective. For example, "earning reasonable profits" isn't a good objective. It doesn't provide specific goals that can be used to evaluate performance. What's reasonable? When do you want to realize the profits? A better objective would be "earning $100,000 in profit during calendar year 2007 on $500,000 investment in inventory and building."

Top-Down versus Bottom-Up Process

Setting objectives in large retail organizations entails a combination of the top-down and bottom-up approaches to planning.

Top-down planning means that goals are set at the top of the organization and passed down to the lower operating levels. In a retailing organization, top-down planning involves corporate officers developing an overall retail strategy and assessing broad economic, competitive, and consumer trends. With this information, they develop performance objectives for the corporation. These overall objectives are then broken down into specific objectives for each buyer and merchandise category and for each region, store, and even departments within stores and the sales associates working in the departments.

The overall strategy determines the merchandise variety, assortment, and product availability, plus the store size, location, and level of customer service. Then the merchandise vice presidents decide which types of merchandise are expected to grow, stay the same, or shrink. Next, performance goals are established for each buyer and merchandise manager. This process is reviewed in Chapters 12 and 13.

Similarly, regional store vice presidents translate the company's performance objectives into objectives for each district manager, who then develop objectives with their store managers. The process then trickles down to department managers in the stores and individual sales associates. The process of setting objectives for sales associates in stores is discussed in Chapter 17.

This top-down planning is complemented by a bottom-up planning approach. **Bottom-up planning** involves lower levels in the company developing performance objectives that are aggregated up to develop overall company objectives. Buyers and store managers estimate what they can achieve, and their estimates are transmitted up the organization to the corporate executives.

Frequently there are disagreements between the goals that have trickled down from the top and those set by lower-level employees of the organization. For example, a store manager may not be able to achieve the 10 percent sales growth set for his or her region because a major employer in the area has announced plans to lay off 2,000 employees. These differences between bottom-up and top-down plans are resolved through a negotiation process involving corporate executives and operating managers. If the operating managers aren't involved in the objective-setting process, they won't accept the objectives and thus will be less motivated to achieve them.

Accountability

At each level of the retail organization, the business unit and its manager should be held accountable only for the revenues, expenses, and contribution to ROA that they can control. Thus, expenses that affect several levels of the organization (such as the labor and capital expenses associated with operating a corporate headquarters) shouldn't be arbitrarily assigned to lower levels. In the case of a store, for example, it may be appropriate to set performance objectives based on sales, sales associate productivity, store inventory shrinkage due to employee theft and shoplifting, and energy costs. If the buyer lowers prices to get rid of merchandise and therefore profits suffer, then it's not fair to assess a store manager's performance based on the resulting decline in store profit.

Performance objectives and measures are used to pinpoint problem areas. Reasons performance may be above or below planned levels must be examined. Perhaps the managers involved in setting the objectives aren't very good at making estimates. If so, they may need to be trained in forecasting. Also, buyers may misrepresent their business unit's ability to contribute to the firm's financial goals to get a larger inventory budget than is warranted and consequently earn a higher bonus. In either case, investment funds would be misallocated.

Actual performance may be different than the plan predicts due to circumstances beyond the manager's control. For example, there may have been a recession. Assuming the recession wasn't predicted, or was more severe or lasted longer than anticipated, there are several relevant questions: How quickly were plans adjusted? How rapidly and appropriately were pricing and promotional policies modified? In short, did the manager react to salvage an adverse situation, or did those reactions worsen the situation?

Performance Objectives and Measures

Many factors contribute to a retailer's overall performance, which makes it hard to find a single measure to evaluate performance. For instance, sales is a global measure of a retail store's activity level. However, a store manager could easily increase sales by lowering prices, but the profit realized on that merchandise (gross margin) would suffer as a result. Clearly, an attempt to maximize one measure may lower another. Managers must therefore understand how their actions affect multiple performance measures. It's usually unwise to use only one measure because it rarely tells the whole story.

The measures used to evaluate retail operations vary depending on (1) the level of the organization at which the decision is made and (2) the resources the manager controls. For example, the principal resources controlled by store managers are space and money for operating expenses (such as wages for sales associates and utility payments to light and heat the store). Thus, store managers focus on performance measures like sales per square foot and employee costs.

Types of Measures

Exhibit 6–10 breaks down a variety of retailers' performance measures into three types: output measures, input measures, and productivity measures. **Input measures** assess the amount of resources or money used by the retailer to achieve outputs such as sales. **Output measures** assess the results of a retailer's investment decisions. For example, sales revenue results from decisions about how many stores to build, how much inventory to have in the stores, and how much to spend on advertising. A **productivity measure** (the ratio of an output to an input) determines how effectively retailers use their resource—what return they get on their investments.

In general, since productivity measures are a ratio of outputs to inputs, they are very useful for comparing the performance of different business units. Suppose Kelly Bradford's two stores are different sizes: One has 5,000 square feet, and the other has 10,000 square feet. It's hard to compare the stores' performances using just output or input measures, because the larger store will probably generate more sales and have higher expenses. But if the larger store has lower space productivity because it generates $210 net sales per square foot and the smaller store

Performance Objectives and Measures Used by Retailers   **EXHIBIT 6–10**

Level of Organization	Output	Input	Productivity (output/input)
Corporate (measures for entire corporation)	Net sales Net profits Growth in sales, profits, same store sales	Square feet of store space Number of employees Inventory Advertising expenditures	Return on assets Asset turnover Sales per employee Sales per square foot
Merchandise management (measures for a merchandise category)	Net sales Gross margin Growth in sales	Inventory level Markdowns Advertising expenses Cost of merchandise	Gross margin return on investment (GMROI) Inventory turnover Advertising as a percentage of sales* Markdown as a percentage of sales*
Store operations (measures for a store or department within a store)	Net sales Gross margin Growth in sales	Square feet of selling areas Expenses for utilities Number of sales associates	Net sales per square foot Net sales per sales associate or per selling hour Utility expenses as a percentage of sales* Inventory shrinkage*

*These productivity measures are commonly expressed as an input/output.

generates $350 per square foot, Kelly knows that the smaller store is operating more efficiently even though it's generating lower sales.

Corporate Performance   At a corporate level, retail executive have three critical resources (inputs)—merchandise inventory, store space, and employees—that they can manage to generate sales and profits (output). Thus, effective productivity measures of the utilization of these assets are asset and inventory turnover, sales per square foot of selling space, and sales per employee.

As we have discussed, ROA is an overall productivity measure combining the profit margin percentage and asset turnover management. Another commonly used measure of overall performance is **same store sales growth,** or the growth in stores that have been open for over one year. Growth in sales can come from increasing the sales generated per store or the number of stores. Growth in same store sales assesses the first component in sales growth and thus is an indicator of how well the retailer is doing with its core business concept. A decrease in same store sales indicates the retailer's fundamental business approach is not being well received by its customers, even if overall sales are growing because the retailer is opening more new stores.

Merchandise Management Measures   The critical resource (input) controlled by merchandise managers is merchandise inventory. Merchandise managers also have the authority to set initial prices and lower prices when merchandise is not selling (take a markdown). Finally, they negotiate with vendors on the price paid for merchandise.

Inventory turnover is a productivity measure of the management of inventory; higher turnover means greater inventory management productivity. Gross margin percentage indicates the performance of merchandise managers in negotiating with vendors and buying merchandise that can generate a profit. Discounts (markdowns) as a percentage of sales are also a measure of the quality of the merchandise buying decisions. If merchandise managers have a high percentage of markdowns, they may not be buying the right merchandise or the right quantities since they weren't able to sell some of it at its original retail price. Note that gross margin and discount percentages are productivity measures, but they are typically expressed as an input divided by an output as opposed to the typical productivity measures that are outputs divided by inputs.

REFACT

Between 1995 and 2002, the annual labor productivity growth for the entire retail industry was 3.8 percent, more than 50 percent higher than the productivity growth for all U.S. businesses.[12]

Store Operations Measures   The critical assets controlled by store managers are the use of the store space and the management of the store's employees. Thus, measures of store operations productivity include sales per square foot of selling space and sales per employee (or sales per employee per working hour, to take into account that some employees work part-time). Store management is also responsible for controlling theft by employees and customers (referred to as inventory shrinkage), store maintenance, and energy costs (lighting, heating, and air conditioning). Thus, some other productivity measures used to assess the performance of store managers are inventory shrinkage and energy costs as a percentage of sales. Retailing View 6.4 describes how self-checkout increases labor productivity.

Assessing Performance: The Role of Benchmarks

As we have discussed, the financial measures used to assess performance reflect the retailer's market strategy. For example, because Costco targets a more price-sensitive market segment than Federated, it has a lower profit margin. But it gets an acceptable ROA because it increases its inventory and asset turnovers by stocking a more limited merchandise assortment of less fashionable, more staple items. On the other hand, Federated targets a market segment that wants to select from a broad merchandise assortment. Thus, it has lower inventory and asset turnovers but achieves an acceptable ROA by having higher profit margins. In other words, the performance of a retailer cannot be accurately assessed by simply looking at

Federated Department Stores and Costco Financial Performance over Three Years   **EXHIBIT 6–11**

	FEDERATED DEPARTMENT STORES			COSTCO		
	2004	2003	2002	2004	2003	2002
Gross margin %	40.5%	40.4%	40.0%	12.5%	12.5%	12.3%
Operating expenses % of sales	31.6%	31.6%	31.3%	9.6%	9.8%	9.4%
Profit % pre-tax	7.1%	7.1%	6.8%	2.9%	2.7%	2.9%
Profit % after taxes	4.4%	4.5%	4.1%	1.8%	1.7%	1.8%
Asset turnover	1.05	1.05	1.07	3.19	3.23	3.34
ROA	4.6%	4.8%	4.4%	5.8%	5.5%	6.0%
Sales per square feet	$188	$182	$185	$826	$771	$751
Inventory turnover	2.98	2.83	2.76	11.55	11.15	10.87
Sales per employee	$139,553	$137,513	$136,593	$436,277	$413,763	$395,567
Percentage increase in competitor store sales	2.6%	−0.9%	−3.0%	6.0%	5.0%	10.0%

SOURCE: Used by permission of Federated Department Stores and Costco Wholesale Corporation. Annual reports for the calendar years.

isolated measures because they are affected by the retailer's strategy. To get a better assessment of a retailer's performance, you need to compare it to a benchmark. Two commonly used benchmarks are (1) the performance of the retailer over time and (2) the performance of the retailer compared with that of its competitors.

Performance over Time   One useful approach for assessing a retailer's performance is to compare its recent performance with its performance in preceding months, quarters, or years. Exhibit 6–11 shows performance measures for Federated Department Stores and Costco over a three-year period.

REFACT

On average, the annual sales per square foot for supermarkets is $451, and the annual sales per labor hour is $79.77.[13]

Self-Checkout Increases Labor Productivity   **RETAILING VIEW**   **6.4**

Supermarkets, home improvement centers, and full-line discount stores are using technology to reduce one of their biggest expenses: labor. One of the most widely used technologies is self-checkout terminals, which allow customers to scan and bag their own purchases and pay for them without a cashier. Stores generally have four terminals overseen by one employee. Customers find self-checkout faster and more convenient than traditional checkout stations, especially when they have fewer items.

Although self-checkout can reduce the number of cashiers needed to staff stores, it also might seem like an invitation to steal. But retailers have found that inventory shrinkage either is unchanged or declines slightly in stores with self-checkout lanes. This reduction may be because consumers are meticulous in checking themselves out, actually avoiding some of the mistakes that busy cashiers may make. In addition, the lower inventory shrinkage might be due to a reduction in "sweetheart" and "sliding" transactions, where cashiers either scan lower price bar codes or don't scan all items for friends.

The next generation of self-checkout technology is going to dramatically increase convenience and reduce the potential for theft. Using radio frequency identification (RFID) technology, computer chips embedded in each product will transmit a signal identifying the product and price. Customers can load up a shopping cart and simply walk through a "reader" that totals up the purchases and even automatically deducts the balance from a bank

Home Depot implemented self-checkout lanes in its stores to improve customer service, increase labor productivity, and lower labor costs.

account by reading the signal from the chip on a key chain or bank card.

Sources: Lauren Webber, "Retailers Save by Replacing Floor Staff with Automation," *Knight Ridder Tribune Business News*, January 24, 2005, p. 1; Mandy Jackson, "Retailers Are Checking into Money-Saving Machinery," *San Diego Business Journal*, July 26, 2004, p. 1.

REFACT

By 2007, it is estimated that 15 percent of the 680,000 lanes in supermarkets and 10 percent of the 505,000 lanes in full-line discount stores will be self-checkout.[14]

EXHIBIT 6–12   Financial Performance of Federated Department Stores and Other National Department Store Chains

	Federated	JCPenney	May	Dillard's	Nordstrom	Kohl's
Net sales (millions $)	15,630	18,424	14,441	7,528	7,131	11,700
Gross margin %	40.52%	38.75%	29.28%	37.17%	36.07%	35.16%
Net profit % thousands	4.41%	2.84%	3.63%	1.56%	5.52%	6.24%
Asset turnover	1.05	1.30	0.95	1.32	1.55	1.47
Return on assets	4.63%	3.71%	3.46%	2.07%	8.53%	9.15%
Inventory turnover	2.98	3.56	3.30	2.90	4.97	3.90
Sales per employee	140	122	206	140	143	585
Sales per square foot (sq ft selling space)	186	150	165	136	327	255
Same store sales % change	2.6	5.0	−2.4	−1.0	4.3	0.3

SOURCES: 2005 Annual Reports.

Costco's financial performance dipped a bit in 2003, while 2003 was a better year for Federated. However, for both retailers, gross margin percentages and pre-tax profit margin percentages are improving over time. Inventory turnover, sales per square foot, and sales per employee are also improving for Costco. While Federated is achieving improvements in inventory turnover, sales per square foot and sales per employee are not improving. The difference in comparable store sales growth is dramatically different. Costco is achieving significant gains in comparable store sales growth, while Federated's comparable store sales growth is actually declining. Thus, Federated is improving its performance over time on key productivity measures but suffering, as other department store retailers are, from declining customer interest in department store shopping.

Performance Compared to Competitors   A second approach for assessing a retailer's performance is to compare it with its competitors. Exhibit 6–12 compares the performance of Federated Department Stores with other national department store chains.

Federated has the highest gross margin, but due to its higher operating expenses and interest payment, its net profit margin is lower than Nordstrom and Kohl's. In terms of its asset and inventory turnover, Federated is not doing as well as the other department store chains, and thus, its ROA is low compared with that of the other department store chains. Kohl's and Nordstrom have the best labor and space productivity. However, a concern for Kohl's, as well as for May and Dillard's, is the lower percentage increase in same store sales.

SUMMARY

This chapter explains some basic elements of the retailing financial strategy and examines how retailing strategy affects the financial performance of a firm. We use the strategic profit model as a vehicle for understanding the complex interrelations between financial ratios and retailing strategy. We also note that different types of retailers have different financial operating characteristics. Specifically, department store chains like Federated generally have higher profit margins and lower turnover ratios than warehouse clubs like Costco. Yet, when margin and turnover are combined into return on assets, we show that it's possible to achieve similar financial performance.

We also describe some financial performance measures used to evaluate different aspects of a retailing organization. Although the return on assets ratio in the strategic profit model is appropriate for evaluating the performance of the retail executives responsible for managing the firm, other measures are more appropriate for more specific activities. For instance, inventory turnover and gross margin are appropriate for buyers, whereas store managers should be concerned with sales or gross margin per square foot or per employee.

KEY TERMS

accounts receivable, *169*
assets, *169*
asset turnover, *161, 171*
bottom-up planning, *176*
current assets, *169*
customer returns, *165*
fixed assets, *170*
gross margin, *166*

gross profit, *166*
input measures, *177*
inventory turnover, *169*
net profit, *167*
net profit margin, *161*
net sales, *164*
operating expenses, *167*
output measures, *177*

productivity measures, *177*
promotional allowances, *165*
return on assets, *160*
same store sales growth, *178*
strategic profit model, *161*
top-down planning, *176*

GET OUT AND DO IT!

1. **CONTINUING CASE ASSIGNMENT** Evaluate the financial performance of the retailer you have selected for the continuing case assignment and another store that sells similar merchandise categories but to a very different target market. If yours is a high margin/low turnover store, compare it with a low margin/high turnover store. You can get this information from its latest annual report, available either in the "investor relations" area of its Web site or in the Edgar files at www.sec.gov. Explain, from a marketing perspective, why you would expect the gross margin percentage, operating expenses-to-sales ratio, net profit margin, inventory turnover, asset turnover, sales per square foot, and sales per employee to be different for the two stores. Assess which chain has better overall financial performance.

2. **INTERNET EXERCISE** Go to the latest annual reports and use the financial information to update the numbers in the net profit margin management model and the asset turnover management models for Federated Department Stores and Costco. Have

there been any significant changes in their financial performance? Why are the key financial ratios for these two retailers so different?

3. **GO SHOPPING** Go to your favorite store and interview the manager. Determine how the retailer sets its performance objectives. Evaluate its procedures relative to the procedures presented in the text.

4. **Web OLC EXERCISE** Go to the Strategic Profit Model (SPM) on the student side of the book's Web site. The SPM tutorial was designed to provide a refresher for the basic financial ratios leading to return on assets and walks you through the process step-by-step. A "calculation page" is also included that will calculate all the ratios. You can type in the numbers from a firm's balance sheet and income statement to see the financial results produced with the current financial figures. You can also access an Excel spreadsheet for SPM calculations. The calculation page or the Excel spreadsheet can be used for Case 9: Best Buy and Radio Shack: Comparing Strategic Profit Models, page 551.

DISCUSSION QUESTIONS AND PROBLEMS

1. Why does a retailer need to use multiple performance measures to evaluate its performance?

2. Describe how a multiple-store retailer might set its annual performance objectives.

3. Buyers' performance is often measured by their gross margin percentage. Why is this measure more appropriate than net profit percentage?

4. How does the strategic profit model assist retailers in planning and evaluating their marketing and financial strategies?

5. Neiman Marcus (a chain of high-service department stores) and Wal-Mart target different customer segments. Which retailer would you expect to have a higher asset turnover? Net profit margin percentage? Why?

6. What elements in the strategic model are affected if a retailer decides to build and open 10 new stores?

7. What differences would you expect to see when comparing Gifts To Go's specialty store strategic profit model with that of two dry cleaning service businesses?

8. Using the following information taken from Lowe's 2005 annual report, determine its asset turnover, net profit margin percentage, and ROA. (Figures are in $ millions.)

Net sales	$36,464
Total assets	$21,209
Net profit	$ 2,176

9. Using the following information taken from the 2005 balance sheet and 2005 income statement for Urban Outfitters, develop a strategic profit model. (Figures are in $000.) You can access an Excel spreadsheet for SPM calculations on the student side of the book's Web site.

Net sales	$827,750
Cost of goods sold	489,000

Operating expenses	198,384
Interest expenses	0
Inventory	98,996
Accounts receivable	8,364
Other current assets	171,508
Fixed assets	271,776

SUGGESTED READINGS

Athanassopoulos, Antreas. "Strategic Groups, Frontier Benchmarking and Performance Differences: Evidence from the UK Retail Grocery Industry," *Journal of Management Studies* 40 (June 2003), pp. 921–54.

Brealey, Richard; Stewart C. Myers; and Franklin Allen. *Principles of Corporate Finance*, 8th ed. New York: McGraw-Hill, 2006.

Brewer, Peter; Ray Garrison; and Eric Noreen. *Introduction to Managerial Accounting* 2nd ed. New York; McGraw-Hill, 2005.

Castellano, Joseph; Saul Young; and Harper Roehm. "The Seven Fatal Flaws of Performance Measurement," *The CPA Journal* 74 (June 2004), pp. 32–36.

Dawson, John, and Roy Larke. "Japanese Retailing through the 1990s: Retailer Performance in a Decade of Slow Growth," *British Journal of Management* 15 (March 2004), pp. 73–95.

Devan, Janamitra; Anna Kristina Millan; and Pranav Shirke. "Balancing Short- and Long-Term Performance," *McKinsey Quarterly* 1 (2005), pp. 31–35.

Finn, Adam. "A Reassessment of the Dimensionality of Retail Performance," *Journal of Retailing & Consumer Services* 11 (July 2004), pp. 235–46.

Ittner, Christopher, and David Larcker. "Coming Up Short on Nonfinancial Performance Measurement," *Harvard Business Review*, November 2003, pp. 88–90.

Ratchford, Brian. "Has the Productivity of Retail Food Stores Really Declined?" *Journal of Retailing* 79 (Fall 2003), pp. 171–92.

Scheumann, Jon. "Defining Productivity," *Cost Management Update*, no. 126 (April 2002) p. 1.

Successful Retail Business. Irvine, CA: Entrepreneur Press, 2003.

Swamy, Ramesh. "Strategic Performance Measurement in the New Millennium," *CMA Management* 76, no. 3 (May 2002), pp. 44–47.

Retail Locations

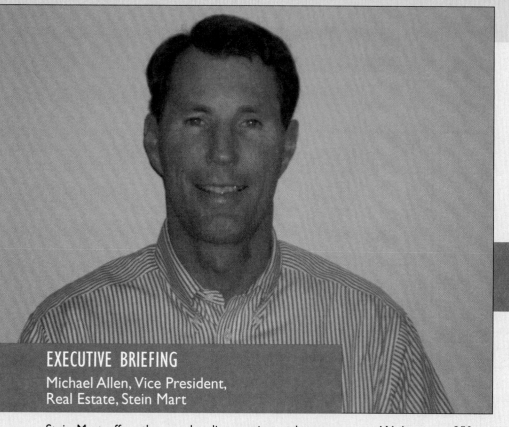

EXECUTIVE BRIEFING
Michael Allen, Vice President,
Real Estate, Stein Mart

Stein Mart offers the merchandise, service, and presentation of a traditional better department/specialty store at prices competitive with off-price retail chains. Our Ladies' Boutique features a strong current season fashion assortment of casual, career, and evening wear. We also have a full selection of ladies sportswear including women's and petite sizes, as well as intimate apparel.

In our Men's Department, customers find luxury fiber sport coats, classic khakis and shirts from the designers who made khakis famous, and golf sportswear bearing the names of the guys who win the tournaments. The Home Department has merchandise ranging from unusual housewares and French crystal to Egyptian cotton towels and goose down pillows. Our customers say, "If I need a gift for a wedding, a hostess, a new baby or a birthday, I simply stop at Stein Mart on the way because I always know that I will find something unique and wonderful."

We have over 250 stores in 30 states and the District of Columbia from California to Florida to New York and are adding approximately 20 new stores a year. Stein Mart's customers have very high taste levels. Thus we like locations near the highest average household incomes/demographics we can find in any appropriately sized MSA, preferably with 300,000 people or more, high ($1.0 billion plus) retail sales and carriage trading residential areas near the site.

Our best locations are upscale shopping centers near affluent residential markets. We do well in neighborhood centers anchored by a service-oriented supermarket. However, we also consider lifestyle or community centers and some regional malls. Higher-end supermarkets, bookstores, Target, Blockbuster, sporting good stores, drug stores, and nicer restaurants are good co-tenants for us.

I am responsible for evaluating new location opportunities and negotiating the leases for the properties we

CHAPTER 7

QUESTIONS

What types of locations are available to retailers?

What are the relative advantages of each location type?

Why are some locations particularly well suited to specific retail strategies?

Which types of locations are growing in popularity with retailers?

select. After graduating from law school, I went to work for a real estate developer for 12 years and then took my present position at Stein Mart. Each year I evaluate hundreds of proposals from real estate brokers and developers. Much of my time is spent negotiating lease terms. Retail real estate leases need to address a wide range of issues ranging from the rental fee and insurance to the tenant mix and potential asbestos removal during remodeling. Developing lease terms and conditions that benefit both us and the developer can be challenging.

The oft-referenced response to the question "What are the three most things in retailing?" is "Location, location, location." Why is store location such an important decision for a retailer? First, location is typically the prime consideration in a customer's store choice decision. For instance, when choosing where you're going to have your car washed, you usually pick the location closest to your home or work. Most consumers similarly shop at the supermarket closest to them. Second, location decisions have strategic importance because they can be used to develop a sustainable competitive advantage. If a retailer has the best location, that is, the location that is most attractive to its customers, competitors can't easily copy this advantage and are relegated to occupying the second-best location. Third, location decisions are risky. Typically, when retailers select a location, they must either make a substantial investment to buy and develop the real estate or commit to a long-term lease with developers. It's not unusual for national chains to sign leases for 7 to 10 years.

As you will see, in the United States, there are a wide variety of locations available for retailers, ranging from a renovated historical building such as Faneuil Hall in Boston to enclosed malls. However, location decisions are more restricted in Western Europe and Asia. These areas of the world have higher population densities and more people living and shopping in urban environments. Thus, less space is available for retailing, and the space that is available is costly. In addition, many Western European countries restrict retailing to specific areas and then restrict the sizes of the stores that can be built.

REFACT

In 2005, the United States had 20 square feet of retail space in shopping centers for every person, up from 11 square feet in 1980. The second-highest country in retail space per citizen is Sweden with 3.1 square feet per person.[1]

In the first part of this chapter, we discuss the types and relative advantages of locations available to retailers. We then examine how the location decision fits into the retailer's strategy. For example, the best locations for a 7-Eleven convenience store are not the best locations for a category specialist such as a Lowe's home improvement center. In the next chapter, we discuss the issues involved in selecting areas of the country in which to locate stores and how to evaluate specific locations and negotiate leases.

TYPES OF LOCATIONS

Many types of locations are available for retail stores, each with its own strengths and weaknesses. Retailers have three basic types of locations to choose from: free-standing, city or town business district, or shopping center. Retailers can also locate in a nontraditional location like an airport or within another store.

Choosing a particular location type involves evaluating a series of trade-offs. These trade-offs generally involve the size of the trade area, the occupancy cost of the location, the pedestrian and vehicle customer traffic generated in association with the location, the restrictions placed on store operations by the property managers, and the convenience of the location for customers. The **trade area** is the geographic area encompassing most of the customers who would patronize a specific retail site.

The following sections describe the characteristics of each type of location, which are summarized in Exhibit 7–1. The first two types of locations are unplanned areas occupied by retail stores, whereas the remaining locations are planned and managed shopping center developments.

EXHIBIT 7–1   Types of Locations

	Size (000 sq. ft.)	Trading Area (Miles)	Annual Occupancy Cost ($ per sq. ft.)	Shopping Convenience	Pedestrian Traffic	Vehicular Traffic	Restrictions on Operations	Typical Tenants
UNPLANNED AREAS								
Free standing	Varies	3–7	15–30	High	Low	High	Limited	Convenience, drug stores, category specialists
Urban locations/ Central business district	Varies	Varies	8–20	Low	High	Low	Limited to medium	Specialty stores
SHOPPING CENTERS								
Neighborhood and community shopping centers	30–350	3–7	8–20	High	Low	High	Medium	Supermarkets, discount stores
Power centers	250–600	5–10	10–20	Medium	Medium	Medium	Limited	Category specialists
Enclosed malls	400–1,000+	5–25	10–70	Low	High	Low	High	Department and specialty apparel stores
Lifestyle centers	150–500	5–15	15–35	Medium	Medium	Medium	Medium to high	Specialty apparel and home stores, restaurants
Fashion/specialty centers	80–250	5–15	10–70	Medium	High	Low	High	High-end fashion-oriented specialty stores
Outlet centers	50–400	25–75	8–15	Low	High	High	Limited	Off-price retailers and factory outlets
Theme/festival centers	80–250	N/A	20–70	Low	High	Low	Highest	Specialty stores and restaurants

SOURCE: Personal communications with industry executives.

UNPLANNED RETAIL LOCATIONS

Some retailers put their stores in unplanned locations for which there is not centralized management to determine where specific stores are and how they are operated. Two types of unplanned retail locations are freestanding sites and city or town locations.

Freestanding Sites

Freestanding sites are retail locations for an individual, isolated store unconnected to other retailers; however, they might be near other freestanding retailers, a shopping center, or, in the case of a kiosk, inside an office building or shopping center. Advantages of freestanding locations are their convenience for customers (easy access and parking); high vehicular traffic and visibility to attract customers driving by; modest occupancy costs; separation from direct competition; and fewer restrictions on signs, hours, or merchandise, as are typically imposed in shopping centers. However, freestanding locations have a limited trade area because there are no other nearby retailers to attract customers interested in shopping at multiple outlets on one trip. In addition, freestanding locations have higher occupancy costs than strip centers because they do not have other retailers to share the cost of outside lighting, parking lot maintenance, or trash collection. Finally, freestanding locations generally appear in areas with little pedestrian traffic, limiting the number of customers who might drop in because they are walking by.

Although most U.S. retailers locate in shopping centers, freestanding locations are, due to the convenience they offer customers, becoming more popular. For example, based on Kohl's success with its freestanding locations, JCPenney and Sears are opening off-the-mall stores.[2] The three major drugstore chains have shifted their emphasis to freestanding locations because they want drive-through windows for pharmacies and more floor space to offer convenience store–type merchandise at the front end of their stores. Walgreens stores that have moved to freestanding sites, away from strip centers, attract 10 percent more customers and achieve 30 percent higher revenues than they did in their strip center locations.[3]

Some Sears stores are located in freestanding structures away from the mall to provide easy parking and convenience for customers.

Merchandise Kiosks **Merchandise kiosks** are small, temporary selling spaces typically located in the walkways of enclosed malls, airports, train stations, or office building lobbies. These spaces typically run between 40 and 500 square feet. They usually have short-term leases and often are operated seasonally. For example, James and Marilyn Raines operate a business called Ornaments Galore in three mall locations. Their booth features small teddy bears dressed in white sailor suits and other service uniforms. Dangling from red ribbons, glazed bears and other Christmas tree ornaments can be personalized with the names of family members or friends for prices that range from $7.99 to $11.99 each. They open their carts on November 1 and will close the last day of December.[4]

For mall operators, kiosks are an opportunity to generate rental income in otherwise vacant space and offer a broad assortment of merchandise for visitors. They also can generate excitement, leading to additional sales for the entire mall. For instance, Woodbridge Center in Woodbridge, New Jersey, typically offers several kiosks selling ethnic merchandise such as clothing and art made by Africans and Native Americans.

Kiosks offer developers an opportunity to generate revenue from unused space and provide additional services to visitors.

Mall operators are sensitive to their regular mall tenants' needs. When planning the locations of kiosks, they are careful to avoid kiosks that block any store fronts, create an incompatible image, or actually compete directly with permanent tenants by selling similar merchandise.

Office building managers view kiosks as a way to provide services for people working in the building. Thus, kiosks in office lobbies often sell newspapers, flowers, or snacks.

City or Town Locations

Most retailers have followed U.S. families as they have moved from the inner city to the surrounding suburbs. However, some retailers are finding urban locations attractive, particularly in cities that are redeveloping their downtowns and surrounding urban areas. Many urban areas are going through a process of gentrification—the renewal and rebuilding of offices, housing, and retailers in deteriorating areas—coupled with an influx of more affluent people that often displaces earlier, usually poorer residents. Young professionals and retired empty-nesters are moving into these areas to enjoy the convenience of shopping, restaurants, and entertainment near where they live. Cities often provide significant incentives for retailers to locate in gentrified and other urban areas. Not only do these retailers bring needed goods and services to the area, they also bring jobs. Retailing View 7.1 describes how Magic Johnson has brought retailing to the inner city.

In general, urban locations have low occupancy costs, and locations in the central business district often have high pedestrian traffic. However, vehicular traffic is limited due to congestion in the inner city, and parking problems reduce consumer convenience. Unlike freestanding locations, such locations are restricted in their signage, and store operations are limited.

Central Business District   The **central business district (CBD)** is the traditional downtown business area in a city or town. Due to its daily activity, it draws many people and employees into the area during business hours. The CBD is also

7.1   RETAILING VIEW   Magic Johnson Brings Retailing to the Inner City

In 13 unparalleled years in the National Basketball Association, Earvin "Magic" Johnson rewrote the record books and dazzled fans with his no-look passes and clutch jump shots. He led the Los Angeles Lakers to five championships. After he announced to the world in 1991 that he had contracted HIV, many thought he would retire from public life. Instead, for Johnson, basketball was just the beginning. "People thought I was going to go away," he says. "But I never planned on going anywhere."

Rather, he took his game to a different arena, one in which the obstacles are higher and the challenges greater. His new career began with a relatively modest partnership with Loews Cineplex Entertainment, formerly Sony Retail Entertainment. After doing some research, Magic and his partners realized that minorities make up approximately 32 to 35 percent of the nationwide movie audience, but there were few theaters in minority neighborhoods. Minorities living in the inner city were driving 30 to 40 minutes to get to a theater. So it seemed natural to build movie theaters in urban neighborhoods across the country.

With the theaters in place, the next step was finding other businesses that would complement these theatres. What they found was most casual sit-down restaurants targeted similar demographics and market conditions. Because of either the franchise holders or the companies in charge, eateries weren't willing to commit to urban locations. Magic and his parters had customers coming in saying they loved the theaters, but they

No longer a presence on the basketball court, Magic Johnson has become a leader in urban retail developments.

had to go all the way across town if they wanted to get something to eat. So next Magic collaborated with Starbucks and TGI Fridays. Now he is also developing shopping centers and malls in African American neighborhoods around the country.

Sources: Roger Vincent, "More Real Estate Investors Believe in Magic in Inner City," *Los Angeles Times*, March 23, 2005, p. C1; "Magic Johnson," *Jet* 101, no. 3 (January 7, 2002), pp. 54–59.

the hub for public transportation, and there is a high level of pedestrian traffic. Finally, many CBDs have a large number of residents living in the area.

But CBD locations in the United States have been declining in popularity with retailers and their customers for years. Retailers are concerned about CBDs because high security may be required, shoplifting can be especially common, and parking is often limited. Parking problems and drive times can discourage shoppers from the suburbs from patronizing stores in the CBD. Shopping in the evening and on weekends is also slow in many CBDs. Finally, unlike shopping centers, CBDs tend to suffer from a lack of planning. One block may contain upscale boutiques, while the next may be populated with low-income housing, which means consumers may not have enough interesting retailers that they can visit on a shopping trip.

Main Street   Another city or town location alternative is **Main Street,** the traditional shopping area of smaller towns or a secondary business district in a suburb or within a larger city. Often streets in these areas have been converted into pedestrian walkways. They represent an effort by cities to draw people from the suburbs and revitalize the downtown area as a destination for shopping and recreation.

Main Streets share most of the characteristics of the primary CBD, but their occupancy costs are generally lower. They do not draw as many people as the primary CBD because fewer people work in the area, and fewer stores generally mean a smaller overall selection. In addition, Main Streets typically don't offer the range of entertainment and recreational activities available in the more successful primary CBDs. Finally, the planning organization for the town or redevelopment often imposes some restrictions on store operations.

In the United Kingdom, 80 percent of retail sales are made by small retailers in Main Street (referred to in the United Kingdom as High Street) locations.[7] Yet there and in most of Europe, the number of small- and medium-sized stores has declined over the last 10 years. In the United Kingdom, for example, shopping centers are growing twice as fast as retail sales as a whole. Less than one-third of consumers describe the High Street retailers as their preferred shopping location. High Street locations are also threatened by large supermarket and hypermarkets located in the suburbs and exurbs.

REFACT

The most expensive retail locations are Fifth Avenue in New York City, which costs $950 per square foot annually; Causeway Bay in Hong Kong, which costs $569 a square foot; and Avenue des Champs-Elysées in Paris, which rents for $569 a square foot.[5]

REFACT

The annual cost for The Gap's 19,000 square foot flagship store on the Champs-Elysées in Paris is over $10 million.[6]

In the United Kingdom, small retailers with inner-city, High Street locations remain popular but face competition from larger retailers such as supermarkets and hypermarkets.

Local governments are trying to restrain superstores' growth by limiting their size and subsidizing the redevelopment of downtown areas to help local retailers compete. For instance, in metropolitan Norwich, the downtown now has more than 500 shops and 200 restaurants, an open-air market, and a new mall that lures one-quarter of a million shoppers into the city center each week.

The preservation of the downtown areas is more successful in European cities such as Norwich than in the United States. Europe has greater population density and less space, and strict planning and greenbelt laws provide a sharp division between town and country. Suburbs are few with no urban areas to sprawl. But preservation comes at a cost for Europe. The limits on out-of-town, big-box retailing reduce competition and retailing efficiency, causing higher prices.[9]

Inner City   The **inner city** in the United States is a high-density urban area consisting of apartment buildings populated primarily by lower-income consumers. There are about 8 million households in America's inner cities. Conservatively, inner-city consumers constitute $85 billion in annual retail buying power—far more than the entire country of Mexico. Unmet demand tops 25 percent in many inner-city markets and reaches 60 percent in others.[10]

Inner-city customers desire to buy branded merchandise from nationally recognized retailers in the neighborhoods where they live.[11] Although income levels are lower in inner cities than in other neighborhoods, most inner-city retailers achieve a higher sales volume and often higher margins, resulting in higher profits.

Due to the potential of this untapped market and incentives from local governments, developers are increasing their focus on opportunities in the inner city. Often the local government will use its right of eminent domain to buy buildings and land that is then sold to developers at an attractive price. In other cases, developers have built on so-called brownfields—former industrial locations with a history of chemical pollutants. In the 1980s, most developers avoided abandoned industrial sites, but investors and their lenders are taking a second look at such sites because of changes in environmental law in the mid-1990s and increased protection from legal complications. Liability insurance is increasingly available to developers who clean up industrial sites, and local governments have increasingly offered guarantees to shield developers against future lawsuits.[12]

Retailing plays an important role in inner-city redevelopment activities by providing needed services and jobs for inner-city residents, as well as property taxes to support the redevelopment. However, inner-city redevelopments can be controversial. For instance, people are concerned about the residents displaced by the development, increased traffic, and parking difficulties.[13] Although we have discussed these urban developments in terms of unplanned locations, they also may be managed shopping centers, as discussed in the following section.

SHOPPING CENTERS

A **shopping center** is a group of retail and other commercial establishments that is planned, developed, owned, and managed as a single property. From the 1950s through the 1980s, suburban shopping centers grew as populations shifted to the suburbs. By combining many stores at one location, disproportionately more consumers are attracted to the shopping center than if the stores were at separate locations. It's not uncommon, for instance, for a store's sales to increase after a competing store enters a shopping center. However, the developer and shopping center management carefully select a set of retailers that are complementary to provide consumers with a one-stop shopping experience with a well-balanced assortment of merchandise.

The shopping center management maintains the common facilities (referred to as common area maintenance [CAM]), such as the parking area, and is responsible for activities such as providing security, parking lot lighting, outdoor signage for the center, and advertising and special events to attract consumers. The stores in the center typically pay a negotiated annual fee based on their size to cover the CMA costs. The shopping center management can also place restrictions on the operating hours, signage, and even the type of merchandise sold in the stores.

Most shopping centers have at least one or two major retailers, referred to as **anchors**. These retailers are courted by the center developer because they attract a significant number of consumers and consequently make the center more appealing for other retailers. To get these anchor retailers to locate in a center, developers frequently make special deals, such as reduced lease costs, for the anchor tenants. For example, the median rental cost is less than $2 per square foot for anchors in an enclosed mall but $20 for nonanchor retailers.[15]

In strip centers, supermarkets are typically anchors, while department stores traditionally anchor shopping malls. However, a lifestyle center may not have anchors, whereas power centers are composed primarily of multiple "anchor" stores. The different types of shopping centers are discussed next.

Neighborhood and Community Shopping Centers

Neighborhood and **community centers** (also called **strip shopping centers**) are an attached row of stores managed as a unit, with onsite parking usually located in the front of the stores. Since the common areas are not enclosed, these centers are often referred to as "open air centers." The most common layouts are linear, L-shaped, and inverted U-shaped. Historically, the term "strip center" has applied to the linear configuration.

Smaller centers (**neighborhood centers**) are typically anchored by a supermarket or a drugstore; the larger centers (**community centers**) have additional anchors such as discount stores, off-price stores, or category specialists selling such items as apparel, home improvement/furnishings, shoes, pet supplies, electronics, and sporting goods. These anchors are supported by smaller specialty stores offering hardware, flowers, and a variety of personal services such as barber shops and dry cleaners.

Supermarkets typically locate in convenient strip centers near residential neighborhoods with other complementary retailers.

The primary advantages of these centers are that they offer customers convenient locations and easy parking, and they have relatively low occupancy costs. The primary disadvantage is that smaller centers have a limited trade area due to their size and lack entertainment and restaurants. In addition, there is no protection from the weather. As a result, neighborhood and community centers do not attract as many customers as larger, enclosed malls.

Now neighborhood and community centers have fewer local, independent stores than in the past. National chains such as Children's Place, Borders, Charming Shop, Kohl's, Radio Shack, and Blockbuster Video compete effectively against their rival mall-based stores by offering the convenience of a neighborhood or community center. In these locations, they can offer lower prices, partly because of the lower occupancy cost, plus their customers can drive right up to the door.

These centers also have started to take on nontraditional, service-oriented tenants. For example, 80 percent of Orthodontics Centers of America's patients are children. Thus, it looks to locate in neighborhood and community centers or professional buildings near retailers with a complementary consumer base, such as Toy "R" Us and Home Depot.

Power Centers

Power centers are shopping centers that consist primarily of collections of big-box retail stores, such as discount stores (Target), off-price stores (Marshalls), warehouse clubs (Costco), and category specialists (Lowe's, Staples, Michaels, Barnes & Noble, Circuit City, Sports Authority, Toys "R" Us). While these centers are "open air," unlike traditional strip centers, power centers often include several freestanding (unconnected) anchors and only a minimum number of small specialty tenants. Many power centers are located near an enclosed shopping mall.

Power centers were virtually unknown before the 1990s, but they have steadily grown in number as the sales of category specialists have grown. Many are now larger than some regional malls and have trade areas as large as regional malls. Power centers offer low occupancy costs and modest levels of consumer convenience and vehicular and pedestrian traffic.

Shopping Malls

Shopping malls are enclosed, climate controlled, lighted shopping centers with retail stores on one or both sides of an enclosed walkway. Parking is usually provided around the perimeter of the mall. Shopping malls are classified as either regional (less than 1 million square feet) or super regional (more than 1 million square feet). Super regional centers are similar to regional centers, but because of their larger size, they have more anchors, specialty stores, and recreational opportunities and draw from a larger geographic area. They often are considered tourist attractions.[19] Retailing View 7.2 describes the South China Mall, the largest shopping center in the world.

Shopping malls have several advantages over alternative locations. First, because of the many different types of stores, the merchandise assortments available within those stores, and the opportunity to combine shopping with entertainment, shopping malls attract many shoppers and have a large trade area. They have become the Main Street for today's shoppers, generating significant pedestrian traffic in front of the mall stores. Teenagers hang out and meet friends, older citizens in Nikes get their exercise by walking the malls, and families make trips to the mall an inexpensive form of entertainment.

Second, retailers and their customers don't have to worry about their external environment. The mall's management takes care of maintaining common areas and marketing the mall to attract consumers. Mall tenants can look forward to a strong level of homogeneous operations with the other stores. For instance, most major malls enforce uniform hours of operation. Since most shopping malls are enclosed, customers are protected from the weather.

Malls also have some disadvantages. First, for most retailers, mall occupancy costs are higher than those of strip centers, freestanding sites, and most central business districts. Second, some tenants may not like mall management's control of their operations. For example, most malls have strict rules governing window displays and signage. Third, competition within shopping centers can be intense. Several specialty and department stores might sell very similar merchandise and be located in close proximity.

In addition, shopping malls are facing several challenges. First, shopping malls appeal to consumers who have the time to enjoy wandering through stores, punctuated by a leisurely lunch or an afternoon movie. The increasing number of two-income families and families with a single household head is creating more time pressures for consumers, limiting the time they can devote to shopping. Freestanding locations, strip centers, and power centers are more convenient because customers can park in front of a store, go in and buy what they want, and go about their other errands.

According to the *Guiness Book of Records*, the world's largest shopping, amusement, and recreation center is the West Edmonton Mall in Alberta, Canada, with over 5.2 million square feet of covered space.

The World's Largest Shopping Center   RETAILING VIEW   7.2

When completed in 2007, the South China Mall in Dongguan City, just north of Hong Kong, will be the world's biggest shopping center at 6.5 million square feet. The mall has seven "zones" modeled on international cities, nations, and regions: Amsterdam, Paris, Rome, Venice, Egypt, the Caribbean, and California. Considerable attention is paid to details so the areas feel like the real thing. For example, the security guards in the Parisian section will dress as gendarmes.

The first phase of the $1 billion development opened in 2005, with space for 600 shops. The second and third phases will bring the mall to 5.2 million square feet of gross leasable area, with 1,500 stores and 11 anchors. At its total of 6.5 million square feet of leasable and nonleasable space, it beats out the West Edmonton Mall in Edmonton, Alberta, which houses only 3.8 million square feet of retail space and covers 5.3 million square feet, counting its amusement parks

The South China Mall is an indoor and outdoor center spread over about 100 acres, with some stores facing sidewalks along the streets. Most of the space is on two or three levels, but department store anchors rise to five stories. The designers have taken the principles of the best malls of North America—the way they flow, the way the parking is laid out, and the position of the anchors. But some unusual elements have been added. For example, shoppers can circumnavigate the perimeter by gondolas and water taxis on a Venetian-inspired canal that stretches more than a mile. The mall's entertainment component includes roller coasters and water slides, an IMAX cinema, and some Warner Bros. movie theaters.

But retail is what the center is about. Shoppers will find stores from retail chains based in China, Hong Kong, Taiwan, Japan, Singapore, and Europe but few stores other than Wal-Mart from retailers based in North America. Parking spaces are expected to number about 8,000—far short of the more than 20,000 spaces that earned West Edmonton Mall a place in the *Guinness Book of World Records*—but car ownership in China is far below Western levels. Many shoppers will arrive at the South China Mall on public transportation or on foot.

However they choose to arrive, the area's burgeoning population will provide a huge audience. About 4 million people live within 6 miles, 9 million within 12 miles, and 40 million within 60. Those millions have money to spend. The center lies in the Pearl River Delta, one of the wealthiest areas in China, where 90 percent of the world's computers are assembled and where phone maker Nokia employs 90,000 workers.

Source: "South China Mall, World's Biggest, to Open by Year's End," Copyright © 2005, International Council of Shopping Centers, Inc., New York, New York. Published in *Shopping Centers Today*, October 2004. Reprinted with permission.

Second, most retailers in shopping malls sell fashionable apparel, a merchandise category that has seen limited growth in the last 10 years due to more casual lifestyles and a shift in taste from fashion to traditional styles. Third, many malls were built more than 30 years ago, which often makes them rundown and therefore unappealing to shoppers. Furthermore, these older malls are now located in areas with unfavorable demographics, because the population has shifted from the near suburbs to outer suburbs and exerbs. Finally, the consolidation in retailing, particularly in the department store segment, has decreased the number of potential anchor tenants, leaving some malls with diminished drawing power.

While many malls are having problems, some remain good locations. Mall trips have increased from about 77 minutes in 1996 to 82 minutes in 2003. Average spending has increased from $28.40 a trip in 1996 to $42.20 in 2003, and enclosed malls report increasing sales per square foot for nonanchor tenants—$366 in 2004, a 12 percent increase compared with 2003.[22] However, these averages don't tell the entire story. Two hundred of the 1200 malls in the United States are doing very well, while 400 malls are doing so poorly that they are likely to close soon.[23] Retailing View 7.3 describes a program undertaken by a large shopping center developer to revitalize its troubled malls.

Mall Renovation and Redevelopment   While few new shopping malls are being built, considerable investment is being made in renovating and redeveloping existing malls. For example, the 1.3 million square foot SouthPark Mall in Charlotte, North Carolina, could be a candidate for the reality show *Extreme Makeover*. The owners of the 30-year-old mall started in 2000 on a plan to remake SouthPark from a typical regional mall into a destination retail center that would attract discriminating shoppers who patronize upscale stores in Atlanta. The makeover cost $100 million.

The first step was getting the Charlotte City Council to approve a rezoning that allowed the mall to nearly double in size. The new zoning enabled the mall to add a new anchor department store, Nordstrom; 40 specialty retailers; a 123,000 square foot expansion of the two existing department stores; and 85,000 square feet for restaurants and shops around the center. The new zoning also made way for Symphony Park, an amphitheater for the Charlotte Symphony Orchestra's summer pops series.

The area previously occupied by a Sears store was converted into a lifestyle center anchored by an 84,000 square foot, two-story Dick's (formerly Galyan's Sporting Goods) store and an outdoor food court. Leading from the mall to the food

REFACT

At least 300 older malls in the United States, each with one or two anchor stores, have shut down since the mid-1990s. Only five new malls per year were opened between 2000 and 2005.[24]

7.3   RETAILING VIEW   Giving Away Retail Space to Generate New Tenants

General Growth Properties, a major shopping center developer, is trying to turn its most troubled malls around by giving away retail space. Through a new program called Project Startup, the company offers to pay the inventory and equipment costs for new tenants and even to build their stores at no charge.

The 11 malls participating in the program have unleased space, are experiencing market shifts, or are undergoing renovation. Of the 11, the 29-year-old Century Plaza, in Birmingham, Alabama, best represents the problems facing these and other malls across the country. Shopper traffic slowed after anchor Rich's-Macy's shut its doors in May 2004. Competition from newer malls and lifestyle centers contributed to the closures of over a dozen specialty stores, and there is a limited pool of potential new tenants. Most of the national chains are taking space only in newer and larger properties. So General Growth started a program to find new tenants.

The 11 mall managers in the program gave interviews to local media, placed ads, passed out brochures, and attended community business meetings to hunt for savvy entrepreneurs with the potential to be long-term tenants. At General Growth's Chicago headquarters, a committee reviews the applications. The individuals selected must sign a five-year lease. General Growth pays for inventory, equipment, store fixtures, and furniture. If a national franchise is involved, General Growth will even pay the franchise fee.

Source: Brannon Boswell and Jo Ellen Meyers Sharp, "GGP Program Nurtures Fresh Retail Concepts," Copyright © 2005, International Council of Shopping Centers, Inc., New York, New York. Published in *Shopping Centers Today*, November 2004. Reprinted with permission.

court is a wing aimed at younger shoppers with such attractions as Ann Taylor Loft, Pottery Barn Kids, Hollister & Co., Finish Line, American Eagle, Abercrombie & Fitch, Puma, and Urban Outfitters. A freestanding CVS drugstore occupies the former Sears Automotive Center site.[25]

But renovating poorly performing shopping malls is challenging and costly. Frequently these malls cannot be supported entirely by retailers and have to be converted into mixed use developments, which are developments that combine several uses into one complex.[26] For example, the Boca Mall, a 430,000 square foot regional shopping mall in Boca Raton, Florida, opened in 1974. Decades later, the mall was plagued by two trends: Population growth was occurring west of the city, and competing malls, such as the 1.3 million square foot Town Center Mall, were attracting most of its patrons. The original anchors and many of the specialty stores departed.

The city government created the Boca Raton Community Redevelopment Agency, a group of civic and business leaders and private citizens. The mall was demolished and replaced with a mixed use development called Mizner Park. Mizner Park has commercial office space located above the ground-floor retail space on one side of the street, and residential units sit above the retail space on the opposite side. In all, 272 apartments and townhouses are on the site. The retail space now generates sales of $556 per square foot, twice the national average.

Mizner Park stands out even among mixed use projects because two-thirds of the site is devoted to public areas. The public areas are owned by the city of Boca Raton and have become a gathering space for its residents. The amphitheater on the north end of the development draws anywhere from 3,000 to 5,000 people for events.[27]

Mizner Park in Boca Raton combines retail, residential, and entertainment offerings in one location with unique boutiques, eateries, music, movies, and art galleries conveniently located close to ocean-front apartments and condos.

Lifestyle Centers

Lifestyle centers are shopping centers with an open-air configuration of upscale specialty stores, entertainment, and restaurants with design ambience and amenities such as fountains and street furniture. Lifestyle centers are typically located near affluent neighborhoods and cater to the "lifestyles" of consumers in their trade areas. Some retailers frequently located in lifestyle centers include Talbots, Chico's, Banana Republic, Williams-Sonoma, The Bombay Store, Barnes & Noble, and Restoration Hardware. Some lifestyle centers are anchored by upscale department stores such as Neiman Marcus or Saks Fifth Avenue.

Due to the ease of parking, lifestyle centers are very convenient for shoppers. But they are smaller than enclosed malls and thus have a smaller trade area and attract fewer customers than enclosed malls. Like Main Street locations, shoppers go to lifestyle centers because they are attractive, energetic places to meet their friends and have fun. Thus, pedestrian traffic is greater than at strip malls. Finally, occupancy costs and operating restrictions are less than those of enclosed malls but greater than those of strip centers.

Although exposure to the weather may be a disadvantage, lifestyle centers have grown from just a few dozen based in mostly warm climates to over 150 centers all over the United States. For example, Chapel View lifestyle center in Cranston, Rhode Island, transformed a historic old school and church into a village-style retail, residential, and office complex.

Aspen Grove Lifestyle Center is located in Littleton, Colorado. The location has outstanding demographics; nearly 730,209 people with an average household income of $85,966 live within 10 miles of the site. More than 75,000 vehicles pass by this location each day.

The seven-building complex that formally housed the Sockanosset Boys Training School, a state-owned correctional and educational facility not unlike the one immortalized in the 1938 movie *Boys Town*, was converted into a lifestyle center. The Sockanosset school, founded in 1898, closed in 1995. To preserve its historical features, the developer worked closely with both the Cranston Historical Society and the Rhode Island Historic Preservation & Heritage Commission to transform the facility into retail and residential space.

The heart of the site is the granite Victorian chapel whose interior will be converted into an upscale restaurant. Among the architectural challenges was the joining of three former dormitories into a single facility with both retail and residential space. With the exception of the Shaw's supermarket anchor and the chapel, the buildings will combine ground-floor retail with residential and/or office space above. The residences, ranging from 700 to 2,200 square feet, will sell for $300,000 to $1.5 million. The retail space includes five restaurants and such high-end merchants as Bombay Co. All the tenants except Shaw's are adapting their storefronts to the Victorian design.[28]

Fashion/Specialty Centers

Fashion/specialty centers are shopping centers composed mainly of upscale apparel shops, boutiques, and gift shops carrying selected fashions or unique merchandise of high quality and price. These centers need not be anchored, though sometimes upscale department stores, gourmet restaurants, drinking establishments, and theaters can function as anchors. The physical design of these centers is very elegant, emphasizing a rich decor and high-quality landscaping.

Fashion/specialty centers usually are found in trade areas with high income levels, in tourist areas, or in some central business districts. These centers' trade areas are larger than the typical enclosed mall because of the distinctive nature of the tenants and their products. Occupancy costs are also higher than those of the typical enclosed mall because the common areas are more elegant.

An example of a fashion/specialty center is Phipps Plaza. Located in the exclusive Buckhead area of Atlanta, Phipps Plaza was named a "Southern Best" in *Southern Living* magazine's Readers' Choice Awards. This fashion/specialty mall is anchored by Nordstrom, Parisian, and Saks Fifth Avenue. As Atlanta's premier upscale shopping center, Phipps Plaza is home to more than 100 specialty stores including Tiffany, Gucci, Max Mara, Barney's New York, Giorgio Armani, and Tommy Bahama.

Outlet Centers

Outlet centers are shopping centers that contain mostly manufacturers' and retailers' outlet stores, though they sometimes include off-price retailers such as T.J. Maxx and Burlington Coat Factory. Outlet centers have progressed from no-frills warehouses to well-designed buildings with landscaping, gardens, and food courts that make them hard to distinguish from more traditional shopping centers.

Compared with the other types of shopping centers, outlet centers are a relatively new phenomenon. In 1970, the VF Outlet opened in Reading, Pennsylvania, on the site of the Berkshire Knitting Mills hosiery factory, to sell not only hosiery but also surplus Vanity Fair lingerie and sleepwear. In 1996, the number of outlet centers peaked at 329 and has since dwindled to 230. Although fewer in number, outlet centers today are larger in size than they were a decade ago—up from 148,000 square feet of gross leasing space to 338,000 square feet. In addition, the number of retail chains operating stores in outlet centers has declined from 446 in 2000 to 363 in 2004. However, manufacturers find that outlet stores are quite profitable because the occupancy costs are generally 6 to 8 percent of sales, compared with 12 to 15 percent for enclosed malls.[30]

Phipps Plaza is a successful fashion/specialty enclosed mall in Atlanta.

The newest outlet centers have a strong entertainment component, including movie theaters and theme restaurants, comprising about 15 to 20 percent of the leasable area.[31] Mall developers believe that these entertainment concepts help keep people on the premises longer. Outlet center tenants have also upgraded their offerings by adding credit, dressing rooms, high-quality fixtures and lighting, and other ammenities.

Outlet centers are often located some distance from shopping centers so that the manufacturers' brands sold at discount prices in their outlet stores will not compete for the customers buying the same brands in department stores. In addition to the geographic separation, manufacturer outlet stores offer assortments that do not overlap with department store assortments.

Outlet centers are often located in tourist areas, because shopping is a favorite vacation pastime. For instance, the 1.2 million square foot Factory Outlet Mega Mall in Niagara Falls, New York, offers an interesting diversion for the 15 million tourists per year who visit Niagara Falls. Some center developers actually organize bus tours to bring people hundreds of miles to their malls. As a result, the primary trade area for some outlet centers is 50 miles or more.

While there may be a downturn in outlet centers in the United States, their popularity is beginning to take off in other areas like Japan and Europe. Japan is particularly attractive given its large population, interest in American brands, and growing consumer enthusiasm for value retailing concepts. Although its employment and income situation deteriorated after the collapse of Japan's bubble economy, consumer tastes for brand name goods remain strong. So, at the foot of Mount Fuji, the Gotemba Premium Outlet is flooded with people, young and old, seeking brand name items. This outlet center, Japan's largest, covers an area seven times that of the Tokyo Dome and houses 165 shops. Many of the visitors to the Gotemba Outlet come from Hong Kong on packaged tours that include visits to

(Tokyo) Disneyland and Hakone, a famous sightseeing spot west of Tokyo, where the outlet is located. On weekends, more than 10,000 vehicles and 100 buses arrive at the outlet center, and the number of visitors on each Saturday and Sunday is estimated at about 30,000.[32]

Theme/Festival Centers

Theme/festival centers are shopping centers that typically employ a unifying theme carried by the individual shops in their architectural design and, to an extent, in their merchandise. The biggest appeal of these centers is for tourists. The centers typically contain tenants similar to those in the specialty centers, except that there are usually no large specialty stores or department stores. Theme/festival centers can be anchored by restaurants and entertainment facilities.

A theme/festival center might be located in a place of historical interest, such as Quincy Market and Faneuil Hall in Boston or Ghirardelli Square in San Francisco. Alternatively, they may attempt to replicate a historical place (such as the Old Mill Center in Mountain View, California) or create a unique shopping environment (like MCA's CityWalk in Los Angeles).

Other Types of Shopping Centers

Many shopping centers combine elements of these different types. For example, enclosed malls often appear next to a power center. Dillard's, Sam's Club, JCPenney, and Best Buy normally would not occur in the same shopping center, but you'll find them all at the Yuma Palms (Arizona) Regional Center, outside Phoenix, which combines mall, lifestyle, and power center components in a unified, open-air layout. Although centers of this type do not have an official name, they may be referred to as **omnicenters.**

Omnicenters are responding to several trends in retailing, including the desire of tenants for lower common-area maintenance charges and the growing tendency of consumers to cross-shop, such as when a Target customer also patronizes the Cheesecake Factory, J. Crew, and Nordstrom. To accommodate cross-shopping, the 1.3 million square foot St. John's Town Center in Jacksonville, Florida, is divided into three components: a lifestyle center with a Dillard's department store anchor, a community center anchored by Dick's Sporting Goods and a Barnes & Noble bookstore, and a Main Street with Cheesecake Factory and P.F. Chang's restaurants as anchors.

Unifying these different concepts so that the project still resembles a cohesive whole is accomplished through the use of similar architectural themes and elements. Parking is another issue. Big-box retailers require large parking fields in front, the antithesis of an urban street. Thus Yuma's Main Street, the power center, and Sam's Club occupy distinctly different areas, so cars can be kept away from the places they're not wanted.[33]

OTHER LOCATION OPPORTUNITIIES

Mixed use developments, airports, resorts, hospitals, and stores within a store are other location alternatives for many retailers.

Mixed Use Developments

Mixed use developments (MXDs) combine several different uses in one complex, including shopping centers, office towers, hotels, residential complexes, civic centers, and convention centers. MXDs are popular with retailers because they bring additional shoppers to their stores. Developers also like MXDs because they use space productively. For instance, land costs the same whether a developer builds a shopping mall by itself or an office tower on top of the mall or parking structure.

Airports are good locations for Borders book stores because pedestrian traffic is high and travelers are good customers for books.

An example of an MXD is found in Kansas City with Missouri's Country Club Plaza. Originally developed in the 1920s, "the Plaza" is home to many of Kansas City's toniest stores and restaurants. Surrounded by offices and apartments, the Plaza draws tourists and residents to stores like Saks Fifth Avenue, Restoration Hardware, and Tommy Bahama and restaurants like Cheesecake Factory, Ruth's Chris Steakhouse, and Capital Grille.[34]

Airports

A high-pedestrian area that has become popular with national retail chains is airports. After all, what better way to spend waiting time than to have a Starbucks coffee or buy a gift at Brookstone? Sales per square foot at airport malls are often three to four times as high as at regular mall stores.[35] However, rents are at least 20 percent higher. Also, costs can be higher—hours are longer, and since the location is often inconvenient for workers, the businesses have to pay higher wages. The best airport locations tend to be ones where there are many connecting flights (Atlanta and Frankfurt) and international flights (Washington Dulles and London Heathrow). The best-selling products are those that make good gifts, necessities, and easy-to-pack items.

REFACT

About 25 percent of air traffic is delayed. There are 670 million U.S. air passengers per year, and the 20 busiest airports see 55 percent of all air traffic. That is a lot of potential shoppers![36]

Resorts

Retailers view resorts as prime location opportunities. There is a captive audience of well-to-do customers with time on their hands. As we noted previously, outlet malls are popular in tourist areas. In fact, some outlet malls, such as Sawgrass Mills in Sunrise, Florida, or Silver Sands Factory Stores of Destin, Florida, actually draw tourists to the area. Resort retailing also attracts small, unique, local retailers and premium national brands like Starbucks or Polo. Resorts like Beaver Creek in Colorado can support dozens of art galleries and fashion retailers with high-end designers. After all, it isn't unusual for visitors at such places to have a net worth of several million dollars.[37]

Hospitals

Hospitals are an increasingly popular location alternative. Both patients and their guests often have time to shop. Necessities are important for patients since they can't readily leave, and gift-giving opportunities abound. At the University Pointe hospital in West Chester, Ohio, there are 75,000 square feet of retail space filled with restaurants serving healthy fare and a host of health-related stores and services, such as a day spa.[38]

Store within a Store

Another nontraditional location for retailers is within other, larger stores. Retailers, particularly department stores, have traditionally leased space to other retailers, such as sellers of fine jewelry or furs. Grocery stores have been experimenting with the store-within-a-store concept for years with service providers like dry cleaners, coffee bars, banks, film processors, and video outlets. Wal-Mart had been putting McDonald's and independently owned coffee shops in some of its new stores. Radio Shack has put stores inside Blockbuster Video locations.

LOCATION AND RETAIL STRATEGY

The selection of a location type must reinforce the retailer's strategy. Thus, the location type decision needs to be consistent with the shopping behavior and size of its target market and the retailer's positioning in its target market. Each of these factors is discussed next. In Retailing View 7.4, Steve Knopik, President of Bealls,

7.4 RETAILING VIEW   Bealls Locations Support Its Strategy

"In addition to our Florida-based department stores, we operate over 500 Bealls Outlet and Burke's Outlet stores in Sunbelt states from South and North Carolina to California. Our strategy is to sell to price-sensitive customers, value-priced apparel in 12,000 to 40,000 square foot stores. To service these customers, we need to keep our prices and costs down. In 2000, we eliminated all advertising. That decision had a very positive impact on our costs and profits. However, our 'no-ad' strategy increased the importance of attracting customers by locating our stores in heavily trafficked intersections or strip shopping centers. Some experts say you can't pay too much for a good location, but the results show that in our business, controlling rent cost is critical to profitability.

"We use a geodemographic service to identify and evaluate potential markets. We know the clusters that our customers are in, and our goal is to locate our stores where those clusters are overrepresented. Once we identify a community that meets our criteria, the next step is to find a specific location in the area. Our best locations are in strip shopping centers with a cotenant like Wal-Mart, Target, or a grocer that attracts a lot of shoppers.

"Bankruptcies, store closings, and the strategy of the drug store chains to move from in-line to stand-alone stores have opened up a number of economical location opportunities for us. Sometimes we find an appealing site that is 30,000 to 40,000 square feet—often too big for us. To take advantage of these opportunities, we sometimes partner with a complementary retailer, like Big Lots [an off-price, hardlines retailer] and approach the property owner together.

"One of our competitors is taking an interesting approach in smaller, more rural markets where there is no vacant shopping center space available. They are putting up low-cost, metal buildings with concrete-block fronts on stand-alone sites. The stores are finished on the inside such that the interior is indistinguishable from a regular store. While the traffic patterns aren't the same as those expected in shopping centers, this approach has promise as a cost-effective way to break into a new market, particularly if the location is on an outparcel of a good center or a heavily trafficked street."

Top: Steve Knopik, president of Bealls, Inc., visits one of the Bealls locations. Bottom: Bealls Outlet attracts customers by locating stores in heavily trafficked strip shopping centers with trade areas that match the profile of its target market.

a value-oriented, off-price retailer, describes how the company's location decisions fit into its retail strategy.

Shopping Behavior of Consumers in Retailer's Target Market

A critical factor affecting the location consumers select to visit is the shopping situation in which they are involved. Three types of shopping situations are convenience shopping, comparison shopping, and specialty shopping.

Convenience Shopping   When consumers are engaged in **convenience shopping situations**, they are primarily concerned with minimizing their effort to get the product or service they want. They are indifferent about which brands to buy or the retailer's image and are somewhat insensitive to price. Thus, they don't spend much time evaluating different brands or retailers; they simply want to make the purchase as quickly and easily as possible. Examples of convenience shopping situations are getting a cup of coffee during a work break or buying milk for breakfast in the morning.

Retailers targeting customers involved in convenience shopping, such as convenience stores, usually locate their stores close to where their customers are and make it easy for them to park, find what they want, and go about their other business. Thus, convenience stores should and generally do locate in neighborhood strip centers, freestanding spots, and city and town locations. Drugstores and fast-food restaurants also cater to convenience shoppers and thus select locations with easy access, parking, and locations that enable them to offer the additional convenience of a drive-through window. Convenience also plays an important role for supermarkets and full-line discount stores. Generally, shoppers at these stores are not particularly brand or store loyal and do not find shopping in these stores enjoyable. Thus, these stores typically are also located in neighborhood strip centers and freestanding locations.

Comparison Shopping   Consumers involved in **comparison shopping situations** have a general idea about the type of product or service they want, but they do not have a strong preference for a brand, model, or specific retailer to patronize. Similar to many convenience shopping situations, consumers are not particularly brand or store loyal. However, the purchase decisions are more important to them, so they seek information and are willing to expend considerable effort planning and making their purchase decisions. Consumers typically engage in this type of shopping behavior when buying furniture, appliances, apparel, consumer electronics, hand tools, and cameras.

Furniture retailers, for instance, often locate next to each other to create a "furniture row." In New York City, a number of retailers selling houseplants and flowers are all located in Chelsea between 27th and 30th streets on 6th Avenue, and diamond dealers are located on West 47th Street between 5th and 6th avenues. These competing retailers locate near one another because doing so facilitates comparison shopping and thus attracts customers to the locations. To compare different types of houseplants and prices, New Yorkers just need to walk from store to store on 6th Avenue, and they know they will see most types of houseplants. Similarly, the advantage of attracting a large number of shoppers to West 47th Street outweighs the disadvantage of sharing these customers with other jewelers.

Enclosed malls offer the same benefits to consumers interested in comparison shopping for fashionable apparel. For example, Jennifer Sanchez, the student described in Chapter 4 who was looking for a business suit for job interviews, could easily compare the suits offered at JCPenney and Ann Taylor with the suits she saw at Macy's by simply walking to these other stores located in the same mall. Thus, department stores and specialty apparel retailers locate in enclosed malls for the

As a destination store, Best Buy offers many brands of merchandise to give consumers the opportunity to comparison shop for consumer electronics.

same reason that houseplant retailers locate together on 6th Avenue in New York City. By co-locating in the same mall, they attract more potential customers interested in comparison shopping for fashionable apparel. Even though the enclosed mall might be inconvenient compared with a freestanding location, comparison shopping is easier after the customers have arrived.

Category specialists offer the same benefit of comparison shopping as a collection of co-located specialty stores like those described previously. Rather than going to a set of specialty stores when comparison shopping for consumer electronics, consumers know they can see almost all of the brands and models they would want to buy in either Best Buy or Circuit City. Thus, category specialists are **destination stores,** places where consumers will go even if it is inconvenient, just like enclosed malls are destination locations for fashionable apparel comparison shopping. Category specialists locate in power centers primarily to reduce their costs and create awareness of their location and secondarily to benefit from the multiple retailers attracting more consumers and the potential for cross-shopping. Basically, power centers are a collection of destination stores.

Specialty Shopping   When consumers are going **specialty shopping,** they know what they want and will not accept a substitute. They are brand and/or retailer loyal and will pay a premium or spend extra effort, if necessary, to get exactly what they want. Examples of these shopping occasions include buying an expensive designer brand perfume, adopting a dog from the animal shelter, or buying a dress made by a specific designer. The retailer they patronize when specialty shopping also becomes a destination store. Thus, consumers are willing to travel to an inconvenient location to patronize a unique gourmet restaurant or a health food store that specializes in organic vegetables. Having a convenient location is not as important for retailers selling unique merchandise or services.

Density of Target Market

A second, but closely related factor that affects the choice of location type is the density of the retailer's target market in relation to the location. A good location has many people in the target market that are drawn to it. So, a convenience store located in a CBD can be sustained by customers living or working in fairly close proximity to the store. Similarly, a comparison shopping store located next to a Wal-Mart is a potentially good location because Wal-Mart draws lots of customers from a very large area. It is not as important to have high customer density near a store that sells specialty merchandise because people are willing to search out this type of merchandise. A Porsche dealer, for instance, need not be near other car dealers or in close proximity to its target market because those seeking this luxury car will drive to wherever the dealer may be.

Uniqueness of Retail Offering

Finally, the convenience of their locations is less important for retailers with unique, differentiated offerings than for retailers with an offering similar to other retailers. For example, Bass Pro Shops provide a unique merchandise assortment and store atmosphere. Customers will travel to wherever the store is located, and its location will become a destination.

LEGAL CONSIDERATIONS

Legal considerations need to be examined when evaluating different location types. Laws regarding how land is used have become so important that they should be a retailer's first consideration in a site search. Legal issues that affect the location decision include environmental issues, zoning, building codes, signs, and licensing requirements.

Environmental Issues

The Environmental Protection Agency, as well as state and local agencies, has become increasingly involved with issues that could affect retail stores. Two environmental issues have received particular attention in recent years. The first is above-ground risks such as asbestos-containing materials or lead pipes used in construction. These materials can be removed relatively easily.

The second issue is hazardous materials that have been stored in the ground. This consideration can be particularly important for a dry cleaner because of the chemicals it uses or for an auto repair shop because of its disposal of used motor oil and battery fluid. The costs of cleaning up hazardous materials can range from several thousand to many millions of dollars per site.

Real estate transactions almost always require an environmental impact statement on the property. But relying on past public filings of buried tanks and other potential hazards can be unreliable and do not provide protection in court. Retailers have two remedies to protect themselves from these environmental hazards. The best option at their disposal is to stipulate in the lease that the lessor is responsible for the removal and disposal of any such material if it is found. Alternatively, the retailer can buy insurance that specifically protects it from these risks.

Zoning and Building Codes

Zoning determines how a particular site can be used. For instance, some parts of a city are zoned for residential use only; others are zoned for light industrial and retail uses. Building codes are similar legal restrictions that specify the type of building, signs, size and type of parking lot, and so forth that can be used at a particular location. Some building codes require a certain sized parking lot or a particular architectural design. In Santa Fe, New Mexico, for instance, building codes require buildings to keep a traditional mud stucco (adobe) style.

Signs

Restrictions on the use of signs can also impact a particular site's desirability. Sign size and style may be restricted by building codes, zoning ordinances, or even the shopping center management. At the Bal Harbour Shops in North Miami Beach, for example, all signs (even sale signs) must be approved by the shopping center management prior to implementation by the individual retailer.

Licensing Requirements

Licensing requirements may vary in different parts of a region. For instance, some Dallas neighborhoods are dry, meaning no alcoholic beverages can be sold; in other areas, only wine and beer can be sold. Such restrictions can affect retailers other than restaurants and bars. For instance, a theme/festival shopping center that restricts the use of alcoholic beverages may find its clientele limited at night.

Legal issues such as those mentioned here can discourage a retailer from pursuing a particular site. These restrictions aren't always permanent, however. Although difficult, time consuming, and possibly expensive, lobbying efforts and court battles can change these legal restrictions.

SUMMARY

Decisions about where to locate a store are critical to any retailer's success. Location decisions are particularly important because of their high-cost, long-term commitment and impact on customer patronage. Choosing a particular location type involves evaluating a series of trade-offs. These trade-offs generally include the occupancy cost of the location, the pedestrian and vehicle customer traffic associated with the location, the restrictions placed on store operations by the property managers, and the convenience of the location for customers. In addition, legal issues need to be considered when selecting a site.

Retailers have a plethora of types of sites from which to choose. Each type of location has advantages and disadvantages. Many central business districts, inner-city, and Main Street locations have become more viable options than in the past due to gentrification of the areas, tax incentives, and the lack of competition. There also are a wide variety of shopping center types for retailers. They can locate in a strip or power center, or they can go into an enclosed mall or a lifestyle, fashion/specialty, theme/festival, or outlet center. Other nontraditional sites are mixed use developments, airports, resorts, hospitals, and stores within a store.

KEY TERMS

anchor, *191*

central business district (CBD), *188*

community center, *191*

comparison shopping situation, *201*

convenience shopping situation, *201*

destination store, *202*

fashion/specialty center, *196*

freestanding site, *187*

inner city, *190*

merchandise kiosk, *187*

lifestyle center, *195*

Main Street, *189*

mixed use development (MXD), *198*

neighborhood center, *191*

omnicenter, *198*

outlet center, *197*

power center, *192*

shopping center, *190*

shopping mall, *192*

specialty shopping, *202*

strip shopping center, *191*

theme/festival center, *198*

trade area, *186*

GET OUT AND DO IT!

1. **CONTINUING CASE ASSIGNMENT** Interview the manager of the shopping center in which the retailer you selected for the continuing assignment is located. Write a report summarizing which retailers the shopping center manager thinks are his best tenants and why they are valued. How does he rate the retailer you have selected? What criteria does he use?

2. **INTERNET EXERCISE** Go to www.faneuilhallmarketplace.com and www.cocowalk.com. What kind of center are these? What are their similarities and differences?

3. **GO SHOPPING** Go to your favorite shopping center and analyze the tenant mix. Do the tenants appear to complement one another? What changes would you make in the tenant mix to increase the overall health of the center?

4. **GO SHOPPING** Go to a theme/festival center, a lifestyle center, and a fashion/specialty center either

in your area or, if that is not possible, on the Internet. Explain why you believe your chosen locations deserve the designation you have given them. How are they different or similar?

5. **INTERNET EXERCISE** Go to the homepage of your favorite fashion mall and describe it in terms of the following characteristics: number of anchor stores, number and categories of specialty stores, number of sit-down and quick service restaurants, and types of entertainment offered. What are the strengths and weaknesses of this assortment of retailers?

6. **GO SHOPPING** Visit a power center near your home or college where there is a Target, Staples, Sports Authority, Home Depot, or other category specialist. What other retailers are in the same location? How is this mix of stores beneficial to both shoppers and retailers?

DISCUSSION QUESTIONS AND PROBLEMS

1. Why is store location such an important decision for retailers?

2. Pick your favorite store. Describe the advantages and disadvantages of its current location, given its target market.

3. Home Depot, a rapidly growing chain of large home improvement centers, typically locates in either a power center or a freestanding site. What are the strengths of each location for a store like Home Depot?

4. As a consultant to 7-Eleven convenience stores, American Eagle Outfitters, and Porsche of America, what would you say is the single most important factor in choosing a site for these three very different types of stores?

5. Retailers are developing shopping centers and freestanding locations in central business districts that have suffered decay. Some people have questioned the ethical and social ramifications of this process, which is known as gentrification. What are the benefits and problems associated with gentrification?

6. Staples and Office Depot both have strong multichannel strategies. How does the Internet affect their strategies for locating stores?

7. In many malls, fast-food retailers are located together in an area known as a food court. What are this arrangement's advantages and disadvantages to the fast-food retailers?

8. Why would a Payless ShoeSource store locate in a neighborhood shopping center instead of a regional shopping mall?

9. How does the mall that you shop at frequently combine the shopping and entertainment experience?

10. Consider a big city that has invested in an urban renaissance. What components of the gentrification project attract both local residents and visiting tourists to spend time shopping, eating, and sightseeing in this location?

11. How will retail consolidation, such as Kmart merging with Sears or Federated Department Stores merging with May Department Stores, impact the anchor space in enclosed regional malls?

12. Different brands of car dealerships are usually located near one another on the same street. What are the pros and cons of this strategy?

SUGGESTED READINGS

Cohen, Nancy. *America's Marketplace: The History of Shopping Centers.* Lyme, CT: Greenwich Publishing Group, 2002.

Halebsky, Stephen. "Superstores and the Politics of Retail Development," *City & Community* 3 (June 2004), pp. 115–35.

Hardwick, M. Jeffrey. *Mall Maker: Victor Gruen, Architect of an American Dream.* Philadelphia: University of Pennsylvania, 2004.

ICSC Research Quarterly. New York: International Council of Shopping Centers.

Karande, Kiran, and John Lombard. "Location Strategies of Broad-Line Retailers: An Empirical Investigation," *Journal of Business Research* 58 (2005), pp. 687–95.

Retail Traffic Magazine. New York: Primedia Business Magazines and Media, http://retailtrafficmag.com/.

Ruiz, Jean-Paul; Jean-Charles Chebat; and Pierre Hansen. "Another Trip to the Mall: A Segmentation Study of Customers Based on Their Activities," *Journal of Retailing & Consumer Services* 11(November 2004), pp. 333–51.

Shopping Centers Today Magazine. International Council of Shopping Centers, http://www.icsc.org/srch/sct/.

Smiley, David J. *Sprawl and Public Space: Redressing the Mall.* New York: Princeton Architectural Press, 2002.

Underhill, Paco. *The Call of the Mall.* New York: Simon & Schuster, 2004.

Warnaby, Gary; David Bennison; Barry Davies; and Howard Hughes. "People and Partnerships Marketing Urban Retailing," *International Journal of Retail & Distribution Management* 32, no. 11 (2004), pp. 545–57.

Retail Site Location

EXECUTIVE BRIEFING

Scott Jennerich, Vice President for Real Estate,
Brown Shoe Company, Famous Footwear

Brown Shoe owns and operates two footwear retail chains—Famous Footwear and Naturalizer. Famous Footwear is the largest brand-name, value-priced family shoe store chain in the United States with more than 900 stores in 50 states. Naturalizer is our flagship brand of women's shoes. Recognized for comfort and its range of sizes, Naturalizer offers more fashionable footwear in 350 retail stores in the United States and Canada.

Our location strategy for Famous Footwear stores has changed to support the changes in our retail strategy. When we were focusing on 4,000- to 5,000-square-foot stores, we located our stores in neighborhood centers typically anchored by supermarkets and regional malls. With the shift in our emphasis to larger, category killer stores, with an 8,000-square-foot format, our preferred locations are power centers. These centers are typically anchored by a discount department store and a home improvement store (Lowe's or Home Depot). We look for centers that also have major soft goods anchors such as T.J. Maxx, Marshall's, Old Navy, Ross, Bed Bath & Beyond, and Linens-N-Things because these stores attract customers also interested in buying shoes for the family.

Typically, to fully develop a market, we will have one store per 50,000 households that meet our customer profile. Our bottom line is profitable market optimization. To select the trading area, we use a variety of data to analyze potential sites, including GIS data, the brand development index, the population index, PRIZM clusters, comparable store analysis, and the Famous Footwear customer profile. We evaluate the population density, household income levels, education levels, household size, households with children, median age, lifestyle interests, and numerous other variables to determine whether a trade area meets our criteria. But site selection is really a combination of science and art. Even with all of the analysis, sometimes you have to draw upon your own past

QUESTIONS

What factors do retailers consider when determining where to locate their stores?

What is a trade area for a store, and how do retailers determine the trade area?

What factors do retailers consider when deciding on a particular site?

How do retailers forecast sales for new store locations?

Where can retailers get information to evaluate potential store locations?

What issues are involved in negotiating leases?

experience when the data may contradict what your gut tells you!

After graduating from college with a finance degree, I went to work for a developer for three years. Then I took a position at McDonald's. Before coming to Famous Footwear, I had been promoted to regional real estate manager responsible for new store development, relocations, remodels, and asset management for the New Jersey, New York City, and Hartford districts. Real estate decisions are a long-term commitment by our company and have a tremendous impact on our resources, sales, profits, and shareholder value. I understand the magnitude of these decisions and enjoy my role in the complex analysis in making these decisions.

Chapter 7 reviewed the different types of locations available to retailers and why certain types of retailers gravitate toward particular locations. This chapter takes a closer look at how retailers choose specific sites for locating stores.

Chapter 5 emphasized the strategic importance of location decisions. Although location decisions can create strategic advantage, like all strategic decisions, they are also risky because they involve a significant commitment of resources. Opening a store at a site often involves committing to a lease of five years or more or purchasing land and building a store. If the store's performance is below expectations, the retailer may not be able to recover its investment easily by having another party move in and assume the lease or buy the building.

Selecting retail locations involves the analysis of a lot of data and the use of sophisticated statistical models. Because most retailers make these decisions infrequently, it is not economical for them to employ full-time real estate analysts with state-of-the-art skills. Thus, retailers often use firms that provide the geographic and demographic data and consulting services needed to evaluate specific sites. However, there continues to be an element of art in making these location decisions.

This chapter reviews the steps retailers go through in selecting their store locations and negotiating leases. The first part of the chapter examines the factors retailers consider in selecting a general area for locating stores and determining the number of stores to operate in an area. Next, the chapter reviews different approaches used to evaluate specific sites and estimate the expected sales if and when a store is located at that site. Finally, the chapter looks at the various terms that are negotiated when a retailer commits to leasing space for its store.

EVALUATING SPECIFIC AREAS FOR LOCATIONS

Areas that retailers consider for locating stores might be countries, areas within a country such as a province in France or a state in the United States, particular cities, or areas within cities. In the United States, retailers often focus their analysis on a **metropolitan statistical area (MSA)** because consumers tend to shop within an MSA, and media coverage and demographic data for analyzing location opportunities often are organized by MSA.

An MSA is a core urban area containing a population of more than 50,000 inhabitants, together with adjacent communities that have a high degree of economic and social integration with the core community. For example, many people in an MSA commute to work in the urban core but live in the surrounding areas. An MSA can consist of one or several counties and usually is named after the major urban area in the MSA. For example, the Cincinnati–Middleton MSA consists of sixteen counties (four in Indiana, seven in Kentucky, and five in Ohio) with a population of 2,009,632; the Missoula, Montana, MSA consists of one county with a population of 95,802. A **micropolitan statistical area** is a smaller unit of analysis with only 10,000 inhabitants in its core urban area.[1]

The best areas for locating stores are those that generate the highest long-term profits for a retailer. Some factors affecting the long-term profit generated by stores that should be considered when evaluating an area include (1) the economic conditions, (2) competition, (3) the strategic fit of the area's population with the retailer's target market, and (4) the costs of operating stores (see Exhibit 8–1). Note that these factors are similar to those that retailers consider when evaluating an investment in a new business growth opportunity or entry into a foreign market, as discussed in Chapter 5.

Economic Conditions

Because locations involve a commitment of resources over a long time horizon, it is important to examine an area's level and growth of population and employment. A large, fully employed population means high purchasing power and high levels of retail sales. Exhibit 8–2 shows the population growth for MSAs in the United States.

But population and employment growth alone aren't enough to ensure a strong retail environment in the future. Retail location analysts must determine how long such growth will continue and how it will affect demand for merchandise sold in

EXHIBIT 8–1

Factors Affecting the Demand for a Region or Trade Area

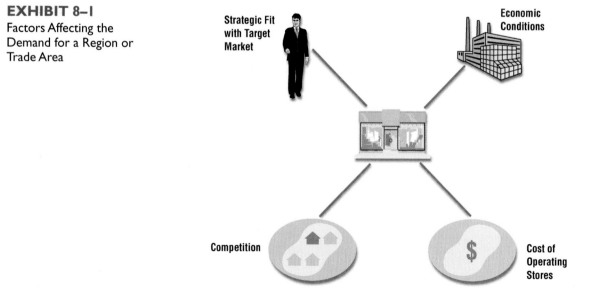

Strategic Fit with Target Market

Economic Conditions

Competition

Cost of Operating Stores

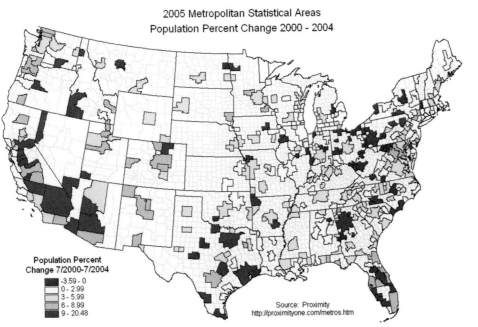

2005 Metropolitan Statistical Areas
Population Percent Change 2000 - 2004

Population Percent
Change 7/2000-7/2004
- -3.59 - 0
- 0 - 2.99
- 3 - 5.99
- 6 - 8.99
- 9 - 20.48

Source: Proximity
http://proximityone.com/metros.htm

EXHIBIT 8–2
Population Growth of
Metropolitan Statistical
Areas

SOURCE: http://www.proximityone.com/metros.htm.

stores. For instance, the economies of some Rust Belt cities like Flint, Michigan, experience greater peaks and valleys due to their dependence on specific industries such as automobiles. If growth is not diversified in various industries, the area may be unattractive because of extreme cyclical trends. However, many areas that have been traditionally dependent on agriculture, a declining industry, have attempted to bring in new industries, such as manufacturing and high-tech, to help diversify their economies.

Also, it is useful to determine which areas are growing quickly and why. For instance, the east side of Seattle, Washington, has become a desirable retail location because of its proximity to Microsoft's corporate headquarters. But the performance of these retail locations is inextricably linked to the financial performance of Microsoft.

In most cases, areas where the population is large and growing are preferable to those with declining populations. However, some retailers, such as Subway, often go into new strip shopping centers with few nearby households with the anticipation that the surrounding suburban area will eventually be built up enough to support the stores.

Competition

The level of competition in an area clearly affects demand for a retailer's merchandise. Wal-Mart's early success was based on a location strategy of opening stores in small towns that were relatively **understored,** a condition in which an area has too few stores to satisfy the needs of local consumers for specific merchandise and services. Wal-Mart stores offered consumers in small towns merchandise at prices that they previously could only acquire by driving to and shopping in much larger towns.

Whereas they once viewed them as undesirable areas, full-service restaurant chains now are opening locations in inner-city neighborhoods. Full-service operators like IHOP, T.G.I. Friday's, Chili's, and Denny's are moving into urban areas from Oakland, California, to New York. They are discovering that that these previously underserved markets are attractive because of their lack of competition, the relatively high level of disposable income of the residents, and their large, untapped labor force.

REFACT

The first Wal-Mart Discount City was opened in Rogers, Arkansas, in 1962.[3]

The IHOP unit in Harlem, New York's historic black community in Manhattan is an interesting example. Harlem has seen an extraordinary retail and residential rebirth since the early 1990s. The 5,000 square foot, 180-seat IHOP fills to capacity during breakfast, lunch, dinner, and late-night hours. One of the best new stores in the 1,167-unit chain, the unit occupies the same remodeled five-story building that formerly housed Small's Paradise, a famous 1920s bebop-era jazz club once co-owned by the late basketball legend Wilt Chamberlain.[4] Retailing View 8.1 describes how Whole Foods caters to a different urban market segment.

Strategic Fit

Population level, growth, and competition alone don't tell the whole story. The area needs to have consumers who are in the retailer's target market—who are attracted to the retailer's offering and interested in patronizing its stores. Thus, the area must have the right demographic and lifestyle profile. The size and composition of households in an area can be an important determinant of success. For instance, Ann Taylor (a chain specializing in traditional and business apparel for women) generally locates in areas with high-income, dual-career families and tourist areas. Household size, however, is not a particularly critical issue. Toys "R" Us, in contrast, is interested in locations with heavy concentrations of families with young children.

Finally, lifestyle characteristics of the population may be relevant, depending on the target market(s) that a particular retailer is pursuing. For example, areas with consumers interested in outdoor activities are attractive for REI and Bass Pro Shops.

Operating Costs

Finally, the cost of operating stores can vary across areas. For example, store rental and advertising costs in the Missoula, Montana, MSA are significantly lower than those in the Cincinnati–Midland MSA. But of course, the potential sales and

---

8.1 RETAILING VIEW Whole Foods Market Is Just Downstairs

The sheer size and glamour of the 74-story Met 3 condominium tower in Miami should be enough to attract buyers. But with more than 50,000 condos in development in the city, what really differentiates Met 3 is the Whole Foods Market that occupies its ground floor. Whole Foods has joined the gym and the concierge as a must-have amenity in luxury condominium towers being built in cities across the country.

Most Whole Foods supermarkets are located in stand-alone sites. But these mixed use locations offer a win-win situation for Whole Foods and the condominium developer. Ron Bond, a real estate developer, says the Whole Foods store in a 160-unit apartment complex that he built in San Francisco has helped push occupancy higher than the rest of the market. "Their stores are happenings," Bond says. "They're having cooking stations, prepared foods, and tastings. They're making the shopping experience an event."

The target market for the condominiums is similar to Whole Foods' target market— higher income households that have sophisticated tastes. Due to the limited number of supermarkets in urban areas, Whole Foods can dominate its primary trade area by offering these city dwellers a very convenient location with an appealing merchandise mix and store environment.

Upscale supermarkets in condominium developments are popular with urban residents and attractive locations for Whole Foods Markets.

Source: Ryan Chittum, "If Whole Foods Market Is Part of a Retail/Condo Complex, New Apartments Sell Briskly," *The Wall Street Journal*, May 11, 2005, p. B1. Used by permission of Dow Jones Inc. via The Copyright Clearance Center.

profits from stores located in the Cincinnati–Midland MSA are substantially greater due to its larger population.

Operating costs are also affected by the proximity of the area being considered to other areas in which the retailer operates stores. For example, if a store is located near other stores and the retailer's distribution centers, the cost of shipping merchandise to the store is lower, as is the cost and travel time spent by the district manager supervising the stores' operations.

Lastly, the local and state legal and regulatory environment can have a significant effect on operating stores. Some retailers are reluctant to locate stores in California because they feel that the state and local governments, its political process of vote-initiated referendums, and a legal environment that fosters class-action lawsuits result in higher operating costs. For example, the California legislature has considered or passed laws requiring employers to pay for health care benefits, lowering requirements for workman's compensation claims, requiring the payment of overtime wages to employees classified as managers but who do some of the same activities as hourly employees, and making it easier for employees to sue employers for wage and work condition violations. In addition, the state court and legal system has supported class-action suits affecting retail operations, such as making retail stores more accessible to the handicapped. Various cities have passed "living wage" laws raising the minimum wage above the national law. Although these political and legal activities provide benefits to employees and consumers, they also increase the operating costs for retailers and eventually increase the prices consumers pay for merchandise.

NUMBER OF STORES IN AN AREA

Having selected an area in which to locate its stores, a retailer's next decision is how many stores to operate in the area. At first glance, you might think that a retailer should choose the one best location in each MSA, but clearly, larger MSAs can support more stores than smaller MSAs. But there is a limit to how many stores can be operated in even the largest MSAs. When making the decision about how many stores to open in an area, retailers must consider the trade-offs between lower operating costs and potential sales cannibalization from having multiple stores in an area.

Economies of Scale from Multiple Stores

Most retail chains open multiple stores in an area because promotion and distribution economies of scale can be achieved. A retailer's total promotional costs are the same for newspaper advertising that promotes 20 stores in an area or only one store. Multiple stores in an area are needed to justify the cost of building a new distribution center. Thus, chains like Wal-Mart expand into areas only where they have a distribution center in place to support the stores. When Kohl's entered the Florida market, it opened 14 stores in Jacksonville and Orlando on the same day.

Opening multiple stores in an area can increase sales per store as well as reduce costs. For instance, Davenport, Iowa–based Von Maur (www.vonmaur.com) is a family-owned, 22-store regional department store chain. Although it cannot compete with larger, national chains on costs due to its smaller scale economies, one of its advantages stems from its regional orientation. It maintains a loyal customer base that identifies with the local communities. Moreover, its merchandising, pricing, and promotional strategies specifically target the needs of a regional rather than a national market. Finally, the management team can have greater span of control over a regional market; managers can easily visit the stores and assess competitive situations.

Cannibalization

While there are scale economies gained from opening multiple locations in an area, there also are diminishing returns associated with locating too many additional stores in an area. For example, suppose the first four stores opened in an MSA by a specialty store retailer generate sales of $2 million each. Because they are located far apart from one another, customers only consider patronizing the store nearest to them, and there is no cannibalization. When the retailer opens a fifth store close to one of the existing stores, it anticipates a net sales increase for the area of $2 million; the new store should generate the same sales level as the four existing stores. Instead, the increase in sales is only $1.5 million because the sales in the nearest existing store drop to $1.7 million, and sales from the new store are only $1.8 million because its location is only the fifth best in the area Thus, because the new store cannibalizes sales from the closest store, it only contributes sales of $1.5 million.

Because a primary retailing objective is to maximize profits for the entire chain, retailers should continue to open stores only as long as profits continue to increase or, in economic terms, as long as the marginal revenues achieved by opening a new store are greater than the marginal costs. Wal-Mart opens over 200 supercenters a year in the United States. When Wal-Mart analyzes a potential new location, it takes into account the impact that new store will have on existing store sales—the cannibalized sales. However, Wal-Mart has found that it can profitably put supercenters closer together than it originally thought. It deliberately plans to cannibalize sales in existing stores when those stores reach annual sales volumes of $100 million or more. Basically, Wal-Mart prefers operating two supercenters, each with annual sales of $80 million, to one location with annual sales over $100 million. The cannibalization that results from opening new stores near existing stores reduces its sales growth potential for stores that are currently open by a percentage point or two. In the long run, however, this intentional cannibalization builds a competitive advantage because the shopping experience for customers is enhanced—two stores, less congestion. In addition, having multiple stores in an area makes it less attractive for a competitor to enter the area and increases the retailer's market share.[5]

Cannibalization from outlets located too close to one another is an important issue for franchisees like Subway.

For franchise retail operations, the objectives of the franchisor and franchisee differ, and thus, disputes can arise over the number of locations in an area. The franchisor is interested in maximizing the sales of all stores because it earns a royalty based on total store sales. The franchisee is interested in just the sales and profits from its store(s). Thus, the franchisor is not as concerned about cannibalization as the franchisee is. To reduce the level of conflict, most franchise agreements grant franchisees an exclusive territory to protect them from another franchisee cannibalizing their sales.

EVALUATING A SITE FOR LOCATING A RETAIL STORE

Having decided to locate stores in an area, the retailer's next step is to evaluate and select a specific site. In making this decision, retailers consider three factors: (1) the characteristics of the site, (2) the characteristics of the trading area for a store at the site, and (3) the estimated potential sales that can be generated by a store at the site. The first two sets of factors are typically considered in an initial screening of potential sites. The methods used to forecast store sales, the third factor, can involve a more complex analytical approach. Each of these factors is discussed in the following section.

SITE CHARACTERISTICS

Some characteristics of a site that affect store sales and thus are considered in selecting a site are (1) the traffic flow past the site and accessibility to the site, (2) the characteristics of the location, and (3) the costs associated with locating at the site (see Exhibit 8–3). The section at the end of the chapter on negotiating a lease reviews the cost factors associated with sites.

Traffic Flow and Accessibility

One of the most important factors affecting store sales is the number of vehicles and pedestrians that pass by the site, or the **traffic flow.** When the traffic is greater, more consumers are likely to stop in and shop at the store. Thus, retailers often use traffic count measures to assess a site's attractiveness. Traffic counts are particularly important for retailers offering merchandise and services bought on impulse, such as convenience stores and car washes, but less important for destination retailers.

For example, Wireless Toyz is a specialty retailer that provides a one-stop shopping destination for all brands of cell phone service, equipment, and accessories. When it evaluates new sites, it looks for locations in middle-class, predominantly blue-collar neighborhoods, with a minimum population of 50,000 people, that are positioned at intersections with daily traffic counts of at least 50,000 vehicles. Of course, many retailers are looking for similar freestanding sites. However, Wireless Toyz is willing to consider small parcels with dilapidated buildings and then builds new, inviting retail destinations.[7]

More traffic flow is not always better; rather, traffic flow is a question of balance. The site should have a substantial number of cars per day but not so many cars that traffic congestion impedes access to the store.

To assess the level of vehicular traffic, the retailer can either perform site visits or commission a specialized firm to do the study. The number of vehicles going by the site may not tell the whole story, however. For instance, the data may need to be adjusted for the time of day. Areas congested during rush hours may have a good traffic flow during the rest of the day when most shopping takes place.

The **accessibility** of the site, which can be as important as traffic flow, is the ease with which customers can get into and out of the site. Accessibility is greater for sites located near major highways, on uncongested highways, and with traffic

Traffic Flow and Accessibility	Restrictions
vehicular traffic	zoning
ease of vehicular access	signage
access to major highways	restrictions on tenant mix
street congestion	safety code restrictions
pedestrian traffic	
availability of mass transit	
Location Characteristics	**Costs**
parking spaces	rental fee
access to store entrance and exit	common area maintenance cost
visibility of store from street	local taxes
access for deliveries	advertising and promotion fees
size and shape of store	length of lease
condition of building	
adjacent retailers	

EXHIBIT 8–3
Site Characteristics

lights and lanes that enable turns into the site. Retailing View 8.2 describes the importance of accessibility to a retailer's business.

Natural barriers, such as rivers or mountains, and **artificial barriers,** such as railroad tracks, divided or limited access highways, or parks, may also affect accessibility. These barriers' impact on a particular site primarily depends on whether the merchandise or services will appeal to customers so strongly that they cross the barrier. For example, a supermarket on one side of a divided highway with no convenient cross-over point will only appeal to consumers going in one direction.

In the United States, most consumers drive to shopping centers, and thus, vehicular traffic is an important consideration when evaluating a site. However, pedestrian traffic flow and access by public transportation is more important for site analysis in a country where consumers do not drive to shop or for evaluating urban sites and sites within an enclosed mall.

Location Characteristics

Some factors associated with specific locations that retailers consider when evaluating a site are (1) parking, (2) store visibility, and (3) adjacent retailers.

Parking   The amount and quality of parking facilities are critical for evaluating a shopping center and specific site within the center. On the one hand, if there aren't enough spaces or the spaces are too far from the store, customers will be discouraged from patronizing the site and the store. On the other hand, if there are too many open spaces, the shopping center may be perceived as having unpopular stores. A standard rule of thumb is 5.5:1,000 (five and a half spaces per thousand square feet of retail store space) for a shopping center and 10 to 15 spaces per 1,000 square feet for a supermarket.

Retailers need to observe the shopping center at various times of the day, week, and season. They also must consider the availability of employee parking, the proportion of shoppers using cars, parking by nonshoppers, and the typical length of a shopping trip.

8.2   RETAILING VIEW   The Importance of a Right Turn

One retailer's demise can be another retailer's opportunity. Jones Hardware & Building Supply in Wake Forest, North Carolina, survived the Great Depression and the relocation of the town's largest employer, so it believed it could "survive Home Depot coming to town." However, the traffic pattern near the store was changed to accommodate new Home Depot and Target stores. The hardware store's once-accessible, prized corner lot location was crippled by a new intersection that prevented a left turn into the store's parking lot. Customers turning left into the store were forced to make a U-turn and access Jones Hardware through an adjoining Winn-Dixie parking lot. Whether it was this inconvenience or the arrival of Lowe's Home Improvement across from Home Depot, the fate of the smaller retailer was sealed, and within two years, Jones Hardware closed.

That same corner lot soon became the site of the market's first Walgreens because the location satisfies Walgreens' fundamental real estate strategy: to be easily accessible for residents as they return home from work. Walgreens positions its stores so that evening commuter traffic can make an easy right turn into the store's parking lot. The former Jones Hardware store fronts a key artery for afternoon commuter traffic, and the CVS store in the shopping center across from the Walgreens has to

Walgreens selects locations that enable it to offer drive-through prescription pickup—a value-added customer service.

rely on customer loyalty to motivate those same commuters to make the less convenient left-hand turn into its parking area.

Source: Connie Gentry, "Science Validates Art." Reprinted by permission from *Chain Store Age*, April 2005, pp. 83–84. Copyright Lebhar-Friedman, Inc., 425 Park Avenue, New York, NY 10022.

An issue closely related to the amount of available parking facilities but extended into the shopping center itself is the relative congestion of the area. **Congestion** can refer to the amount of crowding of either cars or people. There is some optimal level of congestion for customers. Too much congestion can make shopping slow, irritate customers, and generally discourage sales. However, a relatively high level of activity in a shopping center creates excitement and can stimulate sales.[8]

Available parking is an important consideration in the evaluation of locations.

Visibility   **Visibility** refers to customers' ability to see the store from the street. Good visibility is less important for stores with a well-established and loyal customer base, but most retailers still want a direct, unimpeded view of their store. In an area with a highly transient population, such as a tourist center or large city, good visibility from the road is particularly important.

Adjacent Tenants   Locations with complementary, as well as competing, adjacent retailers have the potential to build traffic. Complementary retailers target the same market segment but have a different, noncompeting merchandise offering. For example, Save-A-Lot, a limited assortment supermarket targeting price-sensitive consumers, prefers to be co-located with other retailers targeting price-sensitive consumers, such as Family Dollar or even Wal-Mart.

Have you ever noticed that competing fast-food restaurants, automobile dealerships, antique dealers, and even shoe and apparel stores in a mall are located next to one another? Consumers looking for these types of merchandise are involved in convenience or comparison shopping situations, as we described in Chapter 7. They want to be able to make their choice easily in the case of convenience shopping or to have a good assortment so they can "shop around."

This location approach is based on the principle of **cumulative attraction,** in which a cluster of similar and complementary retailing activities will generally have greater drawing power than isolated stores that engage in the same retailing activities.

Restrictions and Costs

As we will learn later in this chapter, retailers may place restrictions on the type of tenants that are allowed in a shopping center in their lease agreement. Some of these restrictions can make the shopping center more attractive for a retailer. For example, a specialty men's apparel retailer may prefer a lease agreement that precludes other men's specialty apparel retailers from locating in the same center. A florist in a strip center may specify that if the grocery anchor tenant vacates the center, it can be released from its lease. Retailers would look unfavorably on a shopping center with a sign size restriction that prevented easy visibility of the store's name from the street. At the end of the chapter, we discuss some other restrictions and cost issues involved in negotiating a lease.

Locations within a Shopping Center

Location within a shopping center affects both sales and occupancy costs, in that the better locations have higher occupancy costs. In a strip shopping center, the more expensive locations are closest to the supermarket, so a drug store or flower shop that may attract impulse buyers should be close to the supermarket. But a shoe repair store, which does not cater to customers shopping on impulse, could be in an inferior location farther away from the supermarket because customers in need of this service will seek out the store. In other words, it is a destination store.

The same issues apply to evaluating locations within a multilevel, enclosed shopping mall. Stores that cater to consumers engaging in comparison shopping, such as shoppers buying fashionable apparel, benefit from being located in more expensive locations near the department store anchors, which are destinations for comparison apparel shoppers. As apparel shoppers enter and leave the department store, they walk by and may be attracted to neighboring specialty store retailers. In contrast, a retailer such as Foot Locker, another destination store, need not be in the most expensive location, because many of its customers know they're in the market for this type of product before they even go shopping.

Another consideration is how to locate stores that appeal to similar target markets. In essence, customers want to shop where they'll find a good assortment of merchandise. The principle of cumulative attraction applies to both stores that sell complementary merchandise and those that compete directly with one another. Consider Exhibit 8–4, a map of the Columbia Mall, the centerpiece of the planned community of Columbia, Maryland. The mall's trade area includes 753,000 people located in wealthy Howard County, which is positioned halfway between Baltimore, Marlyland, and Washington, DC. This mall underwent a major expansion, completed in 2003, that added 80,000 square feet of new merchandise space and entertainment venues. The new tenants include three restaurants located along the perimeter of the center: P.F. Chang's, Uno Chicago Grill, and Champs; a 14-screen, state-of-the-art, stadium-seating cinema; and L.L. Bean, Domain, Restoration Hardware, Banana Republic, bebe, Build-A-Bear Workshop, Abercrombie & Fitch, Starbucks, J. Crew, and GUESS? Stores.

EXHIBIT 8–4

Grouping Retailers in an Enclosed Mall

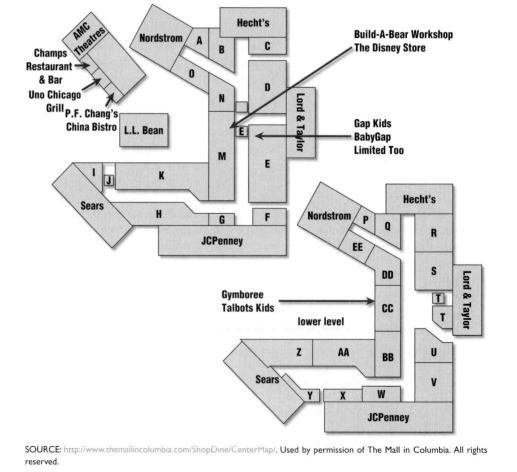

During the expansion, many tenants were repositioned within the mall into category zones to better match their target audience. A good example of this is the location of retailers selling children's apparel and related merchandise. Looking at the map in Exhibit 8–4, note that Gymboree and Talbots Kids are located side-by-side in section CC on the lower level. A short escalator ride to the upper level takes busy parents and their children to the Build-A-Bear Workshop and The Disney Store, both located in Section M. Directly across the walkway, shoppers can visit GapKids, BabyGap, and Limited Too for more children's clothing and accessories.

TRADE AREA CHARACTERISTICS

After identifying several sites that have acceptable traffic flow, accessibility, and other location characteristics, the next step is to collect information about the trade area that can be used to forecast sales for a store located at the site. The retailer first needs to define the trade area for the site. Once the trade area is defined, the retailer can use a number of different information sources to develop a detailed understanding of the nature of consumers in the site's trade area.

Trade Area Definition

A **trade area** is a contiguous geographic area that accounts for the majority of a store's sales and customers. Trade areas can be divided into three zones, as shown in Exhibit 8–5. The exhibit of the trade area for a shopping center located at the red square shows the five-minute drive time zone (light brown), the ten-minute zone (blue), and the fifteen-minute zone (green).

The zones' exact definitions are flexible to account for particular retailers and geographic areas. Thus, the trade area zones shown in Exhibit 8–5 are not concentric circles based on distance from the store but rather are irregular polygons based on the location of roads, highways, and natural barriers, like rivers and valleys, that affect the driving time to the store. The location of competitive stores can also affect the actual trade area configuration.

The **primary trading area** is the geographic area from which the shopping center or store site derives 50–70 percent of its customers. The **secondary trading area** is the geographic area of secondary importance in terms of

EXHIBIT 8–5
Zones in a Trade Area

customer sales, generating about 20–30 percent of the site's customers. The **tertiary trading area** or **fringe** (the outermost area) includes the remaining customers who shop at the site but come from widely dispersed areas. These customers might travel an unusually long distance because they do not have comparable retail facilities closer to home, or they may drive near the store or center on their way to or from work.

The appropriate definition of the three zones should be driving time. Thus, the primary trading might be defined as customers within five minutes' driving time of the site; the secondary trading area, customers with a fifteen minute drive, and the tertiary zone, customers more than fifteen minutes away from the site by car. However, it is much easier to collect information about the number of people and their characteristics in the different zones by geographical distance than driving time. Thus, retailers often define the zones by distance—such as three, five, and ten miles from the site—rather than driving time.

Factors Affecting the Size of the Trade Area

The actual boundaries of a trade area are determined by the store's accessibility, natural and physical barriers, and level of competition, which we discussed earlier in this chapter. The boundaries are also affected by the type of shopping area and type of store.

Trade area size is influenced by the type of store or shopping area. A 7-Eleven convenience store's trade area, for example, may extend less than 1 mile; a category specialist like Best Buy may draw customers from 10 miles away; and a Wal-Mart Supercenter in a rural area might draw customers from 30 miles away. The size of the trading area is determined by the nature of the merchandise sold, the assortment offered, and the location of alternative sources for the merchandise. Convenience stores are popular because customers can buy products like milk and bread quickly and easily, but if customers must drive great distances, the store is no longer more convenient than a supermarket. Category specialists offer a large choice of brands and products for which customers are engaged in comparison shopping. Thus, customers will generally drive some distance to shop at a category specialist.

A **destination store** is one in which the merchandise, selection, presentation, pricing, or other unique features attract customers to the store regardless of other neighboring stores. In general, destination stores have a large trade area—people are willing to drive farther to shop there. Examples of destination stores are anchor stores in shopping malls such as department stores, certain exclusive specialty stores such as Polo/Ralph Lauren, category killers such as Staples and Office Depot, and some service providers such as IMAX theaters.

A **parasite store** is one that does not create its own traffic and whose trade area is determined by the dominant retailer in the shopping center or retail area. A co-located dry cleaner would be a parasite store to a Wal-Mart store because people tend to stop at the dry cleaner on the way to or from Wal-Mart and other stores. Its business is thus derived from Wal-Mart and other businesses in the area. Some retail experts have noted that Wal-Mart can be a destructive force to competition in a trade area because it is so dominant. Yet some parasite stores and stores that have learned to provide product/service offerings that complement, rather than compete with, Wal-Mart actually benefit from its presence.

For example, Party City, America's largest party-goods chain store, has 249 company-owned outlets and 257 franchised stores in 41 states. They offer a wide selection of merchandise for celebratory occasions, such as birthdays and anniversaries, as well as for seasonal events, such as Halloween and Thanksgiving. The party-goods market is estimated at $12 billion, including crossover categories such as candy and sweets. Party City looks for locations close to Wal-Mart and Target for three reasons. First, it carries a wider selection of party stuff than

Wal-Mart or Target. Second, the giant discount stores bring customers to the shopping center. Third, the discount stores attract customers who buy lots of party merchandise.[10] Other examples of parasite stores are food court restaurants and kiosks in a mall.

Measuring the Trade Area for a Retail Site

Retailers can determine the trade area for their existing stores by customer spotting. **Customer spotting** is the process of locating the residences of customers for a store on a map and displaying their positions relative to the store location. The addresses for locating the customers' residences usually are obtained by asking the customers, recording the information from a check or Internet channel purchases, or collecting the information from customer loyalty programs. An older method observes automobile license plates in the parking lot and traces them to the owner by purchasing the information from state governments or private research companies. However, this method is not believed to be very accurate and is illegal in some states, though if may be the easiest way to understand competitors' trade areas. The data collected from customer spotting can be processed in two ways: manually plotting the location of each customer on a map or using a geographic information system like those described later in this chapter. Retailing View 8.3 describes how multichannel retailers use their nonsales data to spot customers and potential store locations.

It is more challenging to estimate the trade area for a new store location than for existing locations. However, retailers typically use information about the trade areas for existing stores to estimate the trade areas for new stores. For example, a sporting goods retail chain with 7,000 square foot stores located in neighborhood shopping centers might find that the primary trading area for its stores is a drive of less than 10 minutes, the secondary trade area is a drive of 10–20 minutes, and the tertiary trade zone is more than a 20-minute drive. Assuming the site under consideration is located in an area that has similar demographic and lifestyle characteristics, the retailer assumes the trade areas for the new site will be defined by same 10- and 20-minute drive times.

Sources of Information about the Trade Area

To further analyze the attractiveness of a potential store site, a retailer needs information about both the consumers and the competitors in the site's trade area. Two widely used sources of information about the nature of consumers in the trade area are (1) data published by the U.S. Census Bureau based on the *Decennial Census of the United States* and (2) data from GIS (geographic information systems) provided by several commercial firms.

Demographic Data from U.S. Census Bureau   A **census** is a count of the population of a country as of a specified date. The first U.S. decennial census was undertaken in 1790 as part of a constitutional mandate to periodically reapportion state representation in the House of Representatives on the basis of state population.

Every ten years, census takers attempt to gather demographic information (sex, age, ethnicity, education, marital status, etc.) from every household in the United States. Many questions on the decennial census are mandated by federal law, and questions change over time to reflect changes in data needs and national interests. For example, current census questionnaires no longer ask about household use of electric lights and television ownership, but they do ask about foster children and stepchildren, the presence of solar heat in the home, and, most recently, grandparents as primary caregivers of children. The decennial census is more than just a head count; it provides a snapshot of the country's demographic, social, and economic characteristics.

The U.S. Census Bureau prepares periodic reports summarizing the data from two sources: the census demographics for each person and additional data collected from a sample of the population. The smallest geographic entity for which census data is available is the **census block,** an area bounded on all sides by visible (roads, rivers, etc.) and/or invisible (county, state boundaries) features. There are seven million census blocks in the United States, each containing the residences of about 40 people. The smallest unit for the sample data is the **block group,** a collection of adjacent blocks that contain between 300 and 3,000 people. Data are also available at higher levels of aggregation, including zip code, census tract (collections of adjacent block groups), county, state, and region.[12]

Although the data from the U.S. Census Bureau can be used to develop a better understanding of the nature of consumers in a region or trade area, it has several limitations. First, because it is based on data collected every ten years, it is not very current, though its projections are reasonably accurate. Second, only demographic data about an area are available. As we discussed in Chapter 4, demographics are not always the best predictor of buying behavior. Third, the data are not particularly user friendly. It is difficult to utilize census data to examine the trade areas for various locations for specific products or services. Thus, most retailers rely on GIS data offered by a number of companies to examine trade areas for potential stores.

Geographic Information System (GIS) Suppliers   **GIS** is a system of hardware and software used to store, retrieve, map, and analyze geographic data, along with the operating personnel and the data that go into the system. The key feature

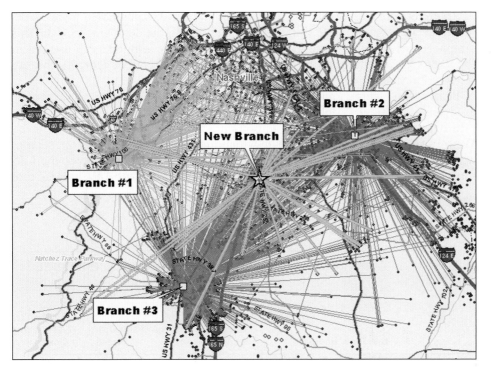

EXHIBIT 8–6
GIS Map for Bank Trade
Areas in an MSA

of GIS data is that they are identified with a coordinate system (latitude/longitude) that references a particular place on Earth. The data in the systems include spatial features such as rivers and roads, as well as descriptive information associated with the spatial features such as the street address and characteristics of the household at the address.

Firms such as ESRI (www.esri.com), Claritas (www.claritas.com), and MapInfo (www.mapinfo.com) that construct and offer services involving GIS combine updated demographic census data with data from other sources that describe consumer spending patterns and lifestyles in a geographic area. In addition, they provide a user-friendly interface so the data can be accessed and analyzed easily. Frequently, the outputs from the system are maps that enable retailers to visualize the implications of the data quickly. For example, the map in Exhibit 8–6 shows the trading areas for three branch banks that a retailer has in an MSA and a fourth branch it is considering, as well as the residences of its customers relative to the branch at which they bank. This map suggests that people bank near their work, and thus, the new location might cannibalize from the other branches.

For example, a retailer interested in developing a deeper understanding of the trade areas for several sites can provide the ESRI GIS with the latitude and longitude or street addresses for the sites under consideration. The system then provides the data shown below for 2007 and projected for 2012 on the people living within a three-, five-, and 10-mile radius from the sites.

gender	occupation
income	travel time to work
disposable income	transportation mode to work
net worth	household composition
education	household expenditures by NAICS categories
age	geodemographic market segment
race/ethnicity	market potential index
employment status	spending potential index

An example of a report on the retail goods and services purchased by residents in a trade area is shown in Exhibit 8–7. In addition to the demographic data, this sample report contains some special data—the lifestyle segments represented in the trade area and the spending power index for various retail categories—that are discussed next.

Before Rob George joined Wendy's as manager of GIS services, the company used demographic data only to make site selection decisions. Now Wendy's uses GIS data that go well beyond basic household income. At the corporate level, Wendy's uses a model to help decide which macro markets to focus on, such as whether to concentrate on Miami or Salt Lake City. On a micro level, the GIS tools help Wendy's select a site within the market. Working with a Web-based tool

EXHIBIT 8–7   Data from GIS on Retail Expenditures in Trade Area

Retail Goods and Services Expenditures
Sample

123 Main Street
Any City, USA   **Site Type: Radius**

		Latitude:	38.8828
		Longitude:	-77.1175
		Radius:	1.0 miles

Top Tapestry Segments:		**Demographic Summary**	**2005**	**2010**
Metro Renters	42.0%	Population	33,753	35,478
Trendsetters	14.9%	Households	16,184	17,159
Old and Newcomers	14.0%	Families	6,422	6,423
Urban Chic	11.7%	Median Age	36.3	39.1
Wealthy Seaboard Suburbs	8.8%	Median Household Income	$88,053	$111,040

	Spending Potential Index	Average Amount Spent	Total
Apparel and Services			
Men's	173	$4,784.07	$77,425,416
Women's	171	$893.18	$14,455,151
Children's	173	$1,563.72	$25,307,319
Footwear	184	$710.48	$11,498,376
Watches & Jewelry	180	$900.79	$14,578,346
	181	$454.26	$7,351,743
Apparel Products and Services	180	$261.65	$4,234,481
Computer			
Computers and hardware for Home Use	176	$433.43	$7,014,696
Software and Accessories for Home Use	175	$51.33	$830,718
Food	168	$13,321.86	$215,600,940
Food at Home	166	$7,882.64	$127,572,631
Bakery and Cereal Products	166	$1,178.88	$19,079,020
Meat, Poultry, Fish, and Eggs	165	$2,094.91	$33,904,094
Dairy Products	165	$848.78	$13,736,682
Fruits and Vegetables	171	$1,422.83	$23,027,067
	164	$2,337.23	$37,825,768
Snacks and Other Food at Home			
Food Away from Home	172	$5,439.43	$88,028,309
Alcoholic Beverages	187	$958.43	$15,511,283
Nonalcoholic Beverages at Home	164	$850.73	$10,531,477
Health			
Nonprescription Drugs	155	$153.81	$2,489,307
Prescription Drugs	131	$707.64	$11,452,487
Eyeglasses and Contact Lenses	152	$130.42	$2,110,794

from Claritas, which we described in Chapter 4, George can access data on Wendy's existing stores to create projected sales forecasts for new sites. "It takes less than a minute for one of our real estate directors to compare a potential location with four of our restaurants that have the most similar characteristics," explains George.

"The Web-based GIS maps are great because of the level of detail that can be viewed," he continues. "Our real estate directors in the field can see traffic counts, shopping center locations, competitors, and surrounding neighborhoods on their screens. Also, the information is updated whenever the market changes. This is so much better than having to work from a wall map with color-coded sticky dots—and there was no telling where those sticky dots might get displaced any time the map got folded."[14]

Tapestry Segments   ESRI and other GIS suppliers have developed schemes for classifying geographical areas in the United States by combining census and survey data about people's lifestyles and purchasing behavior with the mapping capabilities of GIS. The analysis is based on the premise that "birds of a feather flock together." Specifically, people that live in the same neighborhoods tend to have similar lifestyle and consumer behavior patterns.

The ESRI Community Tapestry segmentation scheme classifies neighborhoods into 65 categories. The largest segment—metro renters—in the trade area report in Exhibit 8–7 is described next.[15]

Metro renters are young (approximately 30 percent are in their 20s), well-educated singles beginning their professional careers in the largest cities, such as New York, Chicago, and Los Angeles. Their median household income of $50,400 has been increasing faster than most market segments. A majority are renters, often in older high-rise units. They live alone or share with roommates. *Metro renters* spend money on themselves, buying women's designer jeans, ski apparel, and workout clothing. They also enjoy time with friends and entertain at home. For leisure, they attend rock concerts, go to the movies, and go dancing, as well as play racquetball and tennis, practice yoga, work out regularly, ski, and jog. Surfing the Internet is an important part of their lives; they go online to search for jobs, listen to the radio, and order airline and concert tickets.

Several similar and competing GIS are currently commercially available, including PRIZM (Potential Rating Index for Zip Markets), which was developed by Claritas and is described in Chapter 4.

Spending Potential Index   The **spending potential index (SPI)** report, also shown in Exhibit 8–7, compares the average expenditure for a particular product or service to the amount spent on that product or service nationally. The average expenditure across the United States is indexed to 100 so the 173 SPI for men's apparel in Exhibit 8–7 means that men in the trade area spend 73 percent more than the average for the rest of the United States. This particular trading area is higher than the national average for all merchandise and service categories.

Exhibit 8–8 shows the location of customers who have the desired geodemographic profile on a trade area map for a shopping center. Note that most of the retailer's desirable customers are not in the primary trade area; thus, this shopping center would not be a desirable location.

Competition in the Trade Area

In addition to information about the residents in a trade area, retailers need to know about the amount and type of competition in the trade area. Although GIS vendors provide data on the location of competitive retailers, there are other sources for this information. For example, most retailer Web sites list not only all

EXHIBIT 8–8
Location of Target
Customers in Shopping
Center Trade Area

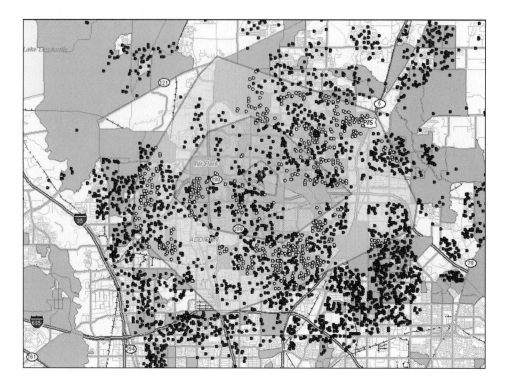

current store locations but future sites as well. A more traditional method of accessing competitive information is to look through the Yellow Pages of the telephone book. Other sources of competitive information include directories published by trade associations, chambers of commerce, *Chain Store Guide* (published by CSG Information Services, www.csgis.com), and municipal and county governments.

ESTIMATING POTENTIAL SALES FOR A STORE SITE

Three approaches for using the information about the trade area to estimate the potential sales for a store at the location are (1) the Huff gravity model, (2) regression analysis, and (3) the analog method.

Huff Gravity Model

The **Huff gravity model**[16] for estimating the sales of a retail store is based on the concept of gravity: Consumers are attracted to a store location just like Newton's falling apple was attracted to the Earth. In this model, the force of the attraction is based on two factors: the size of the store (larger stores have more pulling power) and the time it takes to travel to the store (stores that take more time to get to have less pulling power). The mathematical formula to predict the probability of a customer going to a specific store location is as follows:

$$P_{ij} = \frac{S_j/T_{ij}^{\lambda}}{\sum S_j/T_{ij}^{\lambda}}$$

where

P_{ij} = probability that customer i shops at location j,
S_j = size of the store at location j, and
T_{ij} = travel time for customer i to get to location j.

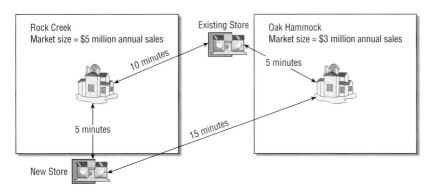

The formula indicates that the larger the size (S_j) of the store compared with competing stores' sizes, the greater the probability that a customer will shop at the location. A larger size is generally more attractive in consumers' eyes because it means more merchandise assortment and variety. Travel time or distance (T_{ij}) has the opposite effect on the probability that a consumer will shop at a location. The greater the travel time or distance from the consumer, compared with that of competing locations, the lower the probability that the consumer will shop at the location. Generally, customers would rather shop at a close store rather than a distant one.

The exponent λ reflects the relative effect of travel time versus store size. When λ is equal to 1, store size and travel time have an equal but opposite effect on the probability of a consumer shopping at a store location. When λ is greater than 1, travel time has a greater effect, and when λ is less than 1, store size has a greater effect. The value of λ is affected by the nature of the shopping trips consumers generally take when visiting the specific type of store. For instance, travel time or distance is generally more important for convenience goods than for shopping goods because people are less willing to travel a great distance for a quart of milk than they are for a new pair of shoes. Thus, a larger value for λ is assigned if the store being studied specializes in convenience shopping trips rather than comparison shopping trips. The value of λ is usually estimated statistically using data that describe shopping patterns at existing stores.

To illustrate the use of the Huff model, consider the situations shown in Exhibit 8–9. A small town has two communities, Rock Creek and Oak Hammock. The town currently has one 5,000 square foot drugstore with annual sales of $8 million, $3 million of which come from Oak Hammock residents and $5 million from Rock Creek residents. A competitive chain is considering opening a 10,000 square foot store. As the exhibit illustrates, the driving time for the average Rock Creek resident to the existing store is ten minutes but would only be five minutes to the new store. In contrast, the driving time for the typical Oak Hammock resident to the existing drug store is five minutes and would be fifteen minutes to the new store. Based on its past experience, the drug store chain has found that λ equals 2 for its store locations. Using the Huff formula, the probability of a Rock Creek resident shopping at the new location, P_{RC}, is

$$P_{RC} = \frac{10{,}000/5^2}{10{,}000/5^2 + 5{,}000/10^2} = .889.$$

The probability of Oak Hammock residents shopping at the new location, P_{OH}, is

$$P_{OH} = \frac{10{,}000/15^2}{10{,}000/15^2 + 5{,}000/5^2} = .182.$$

The expected sales (probability of patronage times market size) for the new location thus would be

$.889 \times \$3$ million $+ .182 \times \$5$ million $= \$4{,}910{,}000.$

This simple application assumes that the market size for drug stores in the community will remain the same at $8 million with the addition of the new store. We also could have considered that two drug stores would increase the total size of the market. In addition, rather than do the calculations for the average customer located in the middle of each community, we could have calculated the probabilities that each customer in the two communities would go to the new location.

Even though the Huff gravity model only considers two factors affecting store sales—travel time and store size—its predictions are quite accurate because these two factors typically have the greatest effect on store choice.[17] The regression approach discussed in the next section provides a way to incorporate additional factors into the sales forecast for a store under consideration.

Regression Analysis

The **regression analysis** approach is based on the assumption that factors that affect the sales of existing stores in a chain will have the same impact on stores located at new sites being considered. When using this approach, the retailer employs a technique called multiple regression to estimate a statistical model that predicts sales at existing store locations. The technique can consider the effects of the wide range of factors discussed in this chapter, including site characteristics such as visibility and access and characteristics of the trade area such as demographics and lifestyle segments represented.

Consider the following example. A chain of sporting goods stores has analyzed the factors affecting sales in its existing stores and found that the following model is the best predictor of store sales (the weights for the factors, such as 275 for the number of households, are estimated using multiple regression):

Stores sales = 275 × number of households in trade area (15-minute drive time)
+ 1,800,000 × percentage of households in trade area with children under 15 years of age
+ 2,000,000 × percentage of households in trade area in Tapestry segment "aspiring young"
+ 8 × shopping center square feet
+ 250,000 if visible from street
+ 300,000 if Wal-Mart in center.

The sporting goods chain is considering the following two locations:

Variable	Location A	Location B
Households within 15 minute drive time	11,000	15,000
% of households with children under 15 years old	70%	20%
% of households in aspiring young geodemographic segment	60%	10%
Sq ft of shopping center	200,000	250,000
Visible from street	yes	no
Wal-Mart in shopping center	yes	no

Using the statistical model, the forecasted sales for location A are:

Stores sales at location A = $7,635,000 = 275 × 11,000
+ 1,800,000 × .7
+ 2,000,000 × .6
+ 8 × 200,000
+ 250,000
+ 300,000,

and forecasted sales for location B are:

Stores sales at location B = \$6,685,000 = 275 × 15,000
+ 1,800,000 × .2
+ 2,000,000 × .1
+ 8 × 250,000.

Note that location A has greater forecasted sales, even though it has a smaller trading area population and shopping center size, because the profile of its target market fits the profile of the trade area better.

Analog Approach

To develop a regression model, a retailer needs data about the trade area and site characteristics from a large number of stores. Because small chains cannot use the regression approach, they use the similar but more subjective analog approach. When using the **analog approach,** the retailer simply describes the site and trade area characteristics for its most successful stores and attempts to find a site with similar characteristics. The use of this approach is described in the following illustration.

ILLUSTRATION OF SITE SELECTION: EDWARD BEINER OPTICAL

Edward Beiner Optical is a South Miami, Florida, store specializing in upper-end, high-fashion eyewear. Its store is in a Main Street location. Although a Main Street location does not draw from a trade area as large as a central business district or a shopping center, it serves the people working and living in the area.

The retailers in this Main Street location recognize that their location lacks the entertainment and recreation found in shopping centers, so they sponsor art and music festivals to bring people to the area. On Halloween, each store provides candy to its future customers and their parents.

Edward Beiner Optical specializes in high-fashion eyewear and targets affluent consumers.

Edward Beiner Optical recognizes other issues that make its South Miami Main Street location less than perfect. There's no protection against the heavy rains that characterize the area's subtropical climate. Security also could be an issue, though most stores are closed at night (when most of their customers have time to shop). Although most of the stores in the area cater to upscale customers living in surrounding neighborhoods, the tenant mix is not always balanced. For instance, Edward Beiner shares its block with a secondhand clothing store and an inexpensive diner. Finally, parking is often a problem.

In general though, Edward Beiner finds its Main Street location attractive. The rent is much less than it would be in a shopping mall. There is usually good pedestrian traffic. Because the properties in the Main Street location are owned by several individuals, the landlords have less control over the tenants than they would in a planned shopping center. Finally, though there are other optical stores in the area, the competition is not intense due to the exclusive lines Edward Beiner carries.

Edward Beiner Optical wants to open a new location. Because its present location in South Miami has been very successful, it would like to find a location whose trade area has similar characteristics. It has identified several potential locations that it is evaluating.

Using the analog approach, Edward Beiner undertakes the following steps:

1. Do a competitive analysis.
2. Define present trade area.
3. Analyze trade area characteristics.
4. Match characteristics of present trade area with potential sites.

Competitive Analysis

The competitive analysis of the four potential sites being considered by Edward Beiner is shown in Exhibit 8–10. To perform the analysis, Edward Beiner first estimated the number of eyeglasses sold per year per person (column 2), obtained from industry sources. Then the area population was taken from information provided by ESRI (column 3). Column 4 is an estimate of the trade area potential reached by multiplying column 2 times column 3.

The estimates of the number of eyeglasses sold in the trade areas, column 5, are based on visits to competitive stores. Column 6 represents the unit sales potential for eyeglasses in the trade areas, or column 4 minus column 5. Then the trade area potential penetration is calculated by dividing column 6 by column 4. For instance, because the total eyeglasses potential for the South Miami store trade area is 17,196 pairs and an additional 9,646 pairs could be sold in that trade area, 56.09 percent of the eyeglasses market in this area remains untapped. The bigger the number, the lower the competition. Column 8, the relative level of competition, is subjectively estimated on the basis of column 7.

EXHIBIT 8–10   Competitive Analysis of Potential Locations

Trade Area (1)	Eyeglasses/ Year/ Person (2)	Trade Area Population (3)	Total Eyeglasses Potential (4)	Estimated Eyeglasses Sold (5)	Trade Area Potential Units (6)	Trade Area Potential Percentage (7)	Relative Level of Competition (8)
South Miami	0.2	85,979	17,196	7,550	9,646	56.09%	Low
Site A	0.2	91,683	18,337	15,800	2,537	13.83	Medium
Site B	0.2	101,972	20,394	12,580	7,814	38.32	Low
Site C	0.2	60,200	12,040	11,300	740	6.15	High
Site D	0.2	81,390	16,278	13,300	2,978	18.29	Medium

Trade Area for Edward Beiner Optical   **EXHIBIT 8–11**

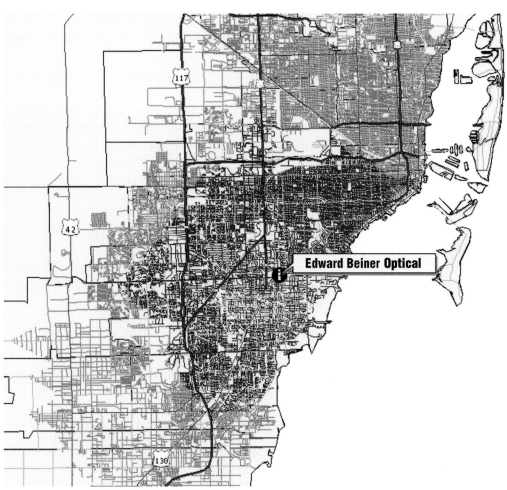

Edward Beiner Optical

Unlike other optical stores in the trade area, Edward Beiner Optical carries a very exclusive merchandise selection. In general, however, the higher the trade area potential, the lower the relative competition will be.

On the basis of the information in Exhibit 8–10, Edward Beiner Optical should locate its new store at site B. The trade area potential is high, and competition is relatively low. Of course, relative competition is only one issue to consider. Later in this section, we'll consider competition along with other issues to determine which is the best new location for Edward Beiner Optical.

Define Present Trade Area

On the basis of customer spotting data gathered from its data warehouse of current customers, the trade area map in Exhibit 8–11 was generated using ESRI's GIS. The zones are based on drive times: 5 minutes for the primary trade area (red), 10 minutes for the secondary trade area (blue), and 20 minutes for the tertiary trade area (green). Note that the trade area boundaries are oblong because the major highways, especially U.S. 1, run north and south. Not only do the north–south highways bring traffic to the area, but heavy traffic often makes them difficult to cross. Biscayne Bay also limits the trade area on the east.

Because Edward Beiner Optical has a Main Street location, its trade area is smaller than it would be if it were located in a regional shopping mall. However, Edward Beiner Optical is one of several optical shops in this business district.

Having similar shopping goods stores in the same vicinity expands its trade area boundaries; more people are drawn to the area to shop because of its expanded selection. In addition, Edward Beiner Optical's trade area is limited on the south by a large regional shopping center that has several stores carrying similar merchandise.

Trade Area Characteristics

Having defined its trade area, Edward Beiner Optical reviewed a number of reports describing the characteristics of its trade area according to the ESRI GIS. Some of interesting findings from these reports were

* The average household income is $92,653, 27.6 percent of the households have incomes between $75,000 and $149,000, and 13.7 percent have incomes over $150,000. The three-mile ring surrounding Edward Beiner Optical is very affluent.
* The area surrounding Edward Beiner Optical has a population that is 53.1 percent Hispanic.
* The major geodemographic segments in the trade area are High-Rise Renters, Thriving Immigrants, Top One Percenters, and Wealthy Seaboard Suburbs.

Match Characteristics of Present Trade Area with Potential Sites

Edward Beiner Optical feels that the profile of its current trade area is high income, predominantly white-collar occupations, a relatively large percentage of older residents, upscale geodemographic segments, and relatively low competition for expensive, high-fashion eyewear. Exhibit 8–12 compares Edward Beiner's current location with four potential locations on these five factors.

Although the potential customers of site A typically have white-collar occupations, they also have relatively low incomes and are comparatively young. Young Immigrant Families also tend to have young families, so expensive eyewear may not be a priority purchase. Finally, there's a medium level of competition in the area.

The Gray Power residents surrounding site B have moderate incomes and are mostly retired. Even though competition would be low and most residents need glasses, these customers are more interested in value than in fashion.

Site C has strong potential because the Young Literate residents in the area are young and have a strong interest in fashion. Although working, they are busy furnishing their first homes and apartments and paying off college loans. They probably would appreciate Edward Beiner's fashionable assortment, but they won't appreciate the high prices. Also, other high-end optical stores are entrenched in the area.

EXHIBIT 8–12   Four Potential Locations for a New Edward Beiner Optical Store

Store Location	Average Household Income	White-Collar Occupations	Percentage Residents Age 45 and Over	Predominant Geodemographic Segments	Level of Competition
Edward Beiner Optical	$100,000	High	37%	Top One Percent	Low
Site A	60,000	High	25	Young Immigrant Families	Medium
Site B	70,000	Low	80	Gray Power	Low
Site C	100,000	High	30	Young Literate	High
Site D	120,000	High	50	Upper-Income Empty-Nesters	Medium

Site D is the best location for Edward Beiner. The residents are older professionals or early retirees with high incomes. Upper-Income Empty-Nesters are sophisticated consumers of adult luxuries like high-fashion eyewear. Importantly, this geodemographic segment is similar to Top One Percenters and Wealthy Seaboard Suburbs—two large segments in Edward Beiner's current location.

Unfortunately, finding analogous situations isn't always as easy as in this example. The weaker the analogy, the more difficult the location decision will be. When a retailer has a relatively small number of outlets (say, 20 or fewer), the analog approach is often best. Even retailers with just one outlet like Edward Beiner Optical can use the analog approach. As the number of stores increases, it becomes more difficult for the analyst to organize the data in a meaningful way. More analytical approaches, such as regression analysis, then are necessary.

NEGOTIATING A LEASE

Once a particular site is chosen, retailers still face a multitude of decisions, including the types and terms of the lease.

Types of Leases

Most retailers lease store sites. Although there are advantages to owning a store site (such as stable mortgage payments and freedom from lease covenants), most retailers don't wish to tie up their capital by owning real estate. Also, most of the best locations—such as in shopping malls—are only available by leasing. There are two basic types of leases: percentage and fixed-rate.

Percentage Leases   Although there are many combinations within each type of lease, the most common form is a **percentage lease,** in which rent is based on a percentage of sales. In addition to the percentage of sales, retailers also typically pay a maintenance fee based on a percentage of their square footage of leased space. Most malls use some form of percentage lease. Since retail leases typically run from 5 to 10 years, they appear to be equitable to both parties if rents go up (or down) with sales and inflation.

A percentage lease with a specified maximum is a lease that pays the lessor, or landlord, a percentage of sales up to a maximum amount. This type of lease rewards good retailer performance by allowing the retailer to hold rent constant above a certain level of sales. A similar variation, the percentage lease with a specified minimum, specifies that the retailer must pay a minimum rent no matter how low sales are.

Another type of percentage lease is a sliding scale lease in which the percentage of sales paid as rent decreases as sales go up. For instance, a retailer may pay 4 percent on the first $200,000 in sales and 3 percent on sales greater than $200,000. Like the percentage lease with a specified maximum, the sliding scale rewards high-performing retailers.

Fixed-Rate Leases   The second basic type of lease is a **fixed-rate lease,** most commonly used by community and neighborhood centers. Here a retailer pays a fixed amount per month over the life of the lease. With a fixed-rate lease, the retailer and landlord know exactly how much will be paid in rent, but, as we noted earlier, this type doesn't appear to be as popular as the various forms of percentage leases.

A variation of the fixed-rate lease is the graduated lease, in which rent increases by a fixed amount over a specified period of time. For instance, rent may be $1,000 per month for the first three years and $1,250 for the next five years.

A maintenance-increase–recoupment lease can be used with either a percentage or fixed-rate lease. This type of lease allows the landlord to increase the rent if insurance, property taxes, or utility bills increase beyond a certain point.

Terms of the Lease

Although leases are formal contracts, they can be changed to reflect the relative power and specific needs of the retailer. Because the basic format of most leases is developed by the lessor (the property owner), the lease's terms may be slanted in favor of the lessor. It is therefore up to the lessee (the party signing the lease, in this case the retailer) to be certain that the lease reflects the lessee's needs. Let's look at some clauses retailers may wish to include in a lease.

Prohibited Use Clause   A prohibited use clause limits the landlord from leasing to certain kinds of tenants. Many retailers don't want the landlord to lease space to establishments that take up parking spaces but do not bring in shoppers, such as a bowling alley, skating rink, meeting hall, dentist, or real estate office. Retailers may also wish to restrict the use of space from those establishments that could harm the shopping center's wholesome image. Prohibited use clauses often specify that bars, pool halls, game parlors, off-track betting establishments, massage parlors, and pornography retailers are unacceptable.

Exclusive Use Clause   An exclusive use clause prohibits the landlord from leasing to retailers selling competing products. For example, a discount store's lease may specify that the landlord cannot lease to other discount stores, variety stores, extreme value stores, or discount clothing outlet stores.

Some retailers also are particular about how the storefront appears. For instance, a women's specialty store may specify that the storefront must have floor-to-ceiling glass to maximize window displays to improve customers' ability to see into the store. Other retailers believe it is important that nothing blocks the view of the store from the street, so they specify that the landlord cannot place any outparcels in the parking lot. An **outparcel** is a building (like a bank or McDonald's) or kiosk (like an automatic teller machine) that sits in the parking lot of a shopping center but is not physically attached to the center.

It is crucial to some retailers that they be in shopping centers with specific types of tenants. For instance, a chain of moderately priced women's apparel shops benefits from the traffic flow of Kmart and Wal-Mart stores. It therefore specifies in its leases that if the major retailer leaves the shopping center, it has the option of canceling its lease or paying a reduced rent.

Escape Clause   An interesting feature that any retailer would want to have in a lease, if it could get away with it, is an escape clause. An escape clause allows the retailer to terminate its lease if sales don't reach a certain level after a specified number of years or if a specific cotenant in the center terminates its lease.

SUMMARY

Location decisions have great strategic importance because they have a significant effect on store choice and are difficult advantages for competitors to duplicate. Picking good sites for locating stores is part science and part art.

Some factors retailers consider when evaluating an area to locate stores are (1) the economic conditions, (2) competition, (3) the strategic fit of the area's population with the retailer's target market, and (4) the costs of operating stores. Having selected an area to locate stores, the next decision is how many stores to operate in that area.

When making the decision about how many stores to open in an area, retailers have to consider the trade-offs between lower operating costs and potential cannibalization from multiple stores in an area. Most retail chains open multiple stores in an area because promotion and distribution economies of scale can be achieved. Although scale economies can be gained from opening multiple locations in an area, there also are diminishing returns associated with locating too many additional stores in an area due to cannibalization.

The next step for a retailer is to evaluate and select a specific site. In making this decision, retailers consider three factors: (1) the characteristic of the site, (2) the characteristics of the trading area for a store at the site, and (3) the estimated potential sales that can be generated by a store at the site.

Trade areas are typically divided into primary, secondary, and tertiary zones. The boundaries of a trade area are determined by how accessible it is to customers, the natural and physical barriers that exist in the area, the type of shopping area in which the store is located, the type of store, and the level of competition.

Once retailers have the data that describe their trade areas, they use several analytical techniques to estimate demand. The Huff model predicts the probability that a customer will choose a particular store in a trade area, based on the premise that customers are more likely to shop at a given store or shopping center if it is conveniently located and offers a large selection. Regression analysis is a statistically based model that estimates the effects of a variety of factors on existing store sales and uses that information to predict sales for a new site. The analog approach—one of the easiest to use—can be particularly useful for smaller retailers. Using the same logic as regression analysis, the retailer can make predictions about sales by a new store based on sales in stores in similar areas.

Finally, retailers need to negotiate the terms of a lease. These lease terms affect the cost of the location and may restrict retailing activities.

KEY TERMS

accessibility, *213*
analog approach, *227*
artificial barrier, *214*
block group, *220*
census, *220*
census block, *220*
congestion, *215*
cumulative attraction, *215*
customer spotting, *219*
destination store, *218*
fixed-rate lease, *231*

fringe, *218*
geographic information system (GIS), *220*
Huff gravity model, *224*
metro renters, *223*
metropolitan statistical area (MSA), *208*
micropolitan statistical area, *208*
natural barrier, *214*
outparcel, *232*
parasite store, *218*

percentage lease, *231*
primary trading area, *217*
regression analysis, *226*
secondary trading area, *217*
spending potential index (SPI), *223*
tertiary trading area, *218*
trade area, *217*
traffic flow, *213*
understored, *209*
visibility, *215*

GET OUT AND DO IT!

1. **CONTINUING CASE ASSIGNMENT** Evaluate the location of a store operated by the retailer you have selected for the continuing case assignment. What is the size and shape of the retailer's trade area? Describe the positive and negative aspects of its location. Compare the store's location with the locations of its competitors.

2. **INTERNET EXERCISE** See if the expression "birds of a feather flock together" really is true and if similar groups are clustered together by going to www.claritas.com and clicking on "You are where you live." Type in the zip code for your home or school address and the access code. Does the information you get accurately describe you and your family? Compare the Claritas description to the one provided by ESRI at http://www.gis.com/index.html under "Zip Code Fast Facts." Note the similarities and differences in these two reports for the same zip code.

3. **INTERNET EXERCISE** Go to http://www.gis.com/index.html, the homepage for ESRI Geographical Information Systems, and click on "Demo: What is GIS?" After watching the three-minute video, explain how retailers can make better decisions with GIS.

4. **GO SHOPPING** Go to a shopping mall. Get or draw a map of the stores. Analyze whether the stores are clustered in some logical manner. For instance, are all the high-end stores together? Is there a good mix of retailers catering to the comparison shoppers near one another?

5. **GO SHOPPING** Visit a jewelry store in an enclosed mall and one in a neighborhood strip shopping center. List the pros and cons for each location. Which location is the most desirable?

6. **Web OLC EXERCISE** Go to the student side of the book's Web site and click on "Location." You will see an Excel spreadsheet that contains the sales for 45 retail locations of a sporting goods retail chain, plus the characteristics of each location: number of households in trading area, percentage of households with children under 15 years old, percentage of households in appropriate Tapestry segments that the retailer is targeting, distance from a Wal-Mart store, and distance from a Sports Authority store. Estimate a multiple regression model that predicts sales as a function of the site characteristics, and use the estimate weights to evaluate the two sites at the bottom of the spreadsheet.

DISCUSSION QUESTIONS AND PROBLEMS

1. What factors do retailers consider when evaluating an area of the country to locate stores? How do retailers determine the trade area for a store?

2. When measuring trade areas, why is the analog approach not a good choice for a retailer with several hundred outlets?

3. True Value Hardware plans to open a new store. Two sites are available, both in middle-income neighborhood centers. One neighborhood is 20 years old and has been well maintained. The other was recently built in a newly planned community. Which site is preferable for True Value? Why?

4. Trade areas are often described as concentric circles emanating from the store or shopping center. Why is this practice used? Suggest an alternative method. Which would you use if you owned a store in need of a trade area analysis?

5. Under what circumstances would a retailer use the analog approach for estimating demand for a new store? What about regression?

6. Some specialty stores prefer to locate next to or close to an anchor store. But Little Caesars, a takeout pizza retailer typically found in strip centers, wants to be at the end of the center away from the supermarket anchor. Why?

7. Retailers have a choice of locating on a mall's main floor or second or third level. Typically, the main floor offers the best, but most expensive, locations. Why would specialty stores such as Radio Shack and Foot Locker choose the second or third floor?

8. What retail locations are best for department stores, consumer electronics category killers, specialty apparel stores, and warehouse stores? Discuss your rationale.

9. If you were considering the ownership of a Taco Bell franchise, what would you want to know about the location in terms of traffic, population, income, employment, and competition? What else would need to be researched about a potential location?

10. P. F. Chang's China Bistro Inc. will launch a new Japanese restaurant concept in the first quarter of 2006. The restaurant will have higher prices than P. F. Chang's China Bistro. What locations should be considered for the Japanese restaurant concept to attract the desired target audience and avoid cannibalizing sales from the China Bistros?

11. Consider the merger of Sears and Kmart stores. Company executives are considering converting hundreds of Kmarts into Sears stores. This strategy would move Sears out of malls and into freestanding or strip center locations. What are the pros and cons of this decision? How would this move impact a consumer shopping for appliances, tools, or apparel?

12. A drugstore is considering opening a new location at shopping center A, with hopes of capturing sales from a new neighborhood under construction. Two nearby shopping centers, B and C, will provide competition. Using the following information and the Huff gravity model, determine the probability that residents of the new neighborhood will shop at shopping center A:

Shopping center	Size (000's sq. ft.)	Distance from new neighborhood (miles)
A	3,500	4
B	1,500	5
C	300	3

Assume that $\lambda = 2$.

SUGGESTED READINGS

Birkin, Mark; Graham Clarke; and Martin Clarke. *Retail Geography and Intelligent Network Planning*. Chichester, U.K.: Wiley, 2002.

Clark, Bruce. "Using Multiple Regression for Site Selection: A Marketing Exercise That Uses Secondary Data to Prioritize Areas for New Construction Efforts," *Marketing Education Review*, Spring 2004, pp. 1–10.

Gentry, Connie. "Science Validates Art," *Chain Store Age*, April 2005, pp. 83–84.

González-Benito, Óscar, and Javier González-Benito. "The Role of Geodemographic Segmentation in Retail Location Strategy," *International Journal of Market Research* 3 (2005), pp. 295–317.

Groebe, Janet. "How Close Is Too Far?" *Stores*, December 2004, p. 60.

Karande, Kiran, and John Lombard. "Location Strategies of Broad-Line Retailers: An Empirical Investigation," *Journal of Business Research* 58 (May 2005), pp. 687–91.

Mendes, A., and I. Themado. "Multi-Outlet Retail Site Assessment," *International Transactions in Operations Research* 11 (2004), pp. 1–18.

O'Kelly, Morton. "Retail Market Share and Saturation," *Journal of Retailing and Consumer Services* 8, no. 1 (2001), pp. 37–45.

Peterson, Keith (ed). *The Power of Place: Advanced Customer and Location Analytics for Market Planning*. San Diego: Integras, 2004.

Smith, Douglas, and Susan Sanchez. "Assessment of Business Potential at Retail Sites: Empirical Findings from a U.S.

Supermarket Chain," *International Review of Retail, Distribution & Consumer Research* 13 (January 2003), pp. 37–59.

Tsao Amy. "Better Sites through Science," *Retail Traffic*, June 2003, p. 32.

Human Resource Management

EXECUTIVE BRIEFING

Sherry Hollock, Divisional Vice President of
Organization Development at Federated
Department Stores

I am responsible for organizational development, executive and career development, succession planning, college relations, selling services, and executive staffing for Federated Department Stores (Macy's, Bloomingdales)—the largest department store chain in the world.

One of the biggest challenges facing Federated and most other retail chains is hiring and retaining managers to lead our company in the coming years. The changing demographics are working against us. Over the next ten years, a lot of our senior managers, members of the Baby Boomer generation, will be retiring. So we are going to be competing with other retailers and firms in other industries for a smaller pool of available managers in the generations behind the Boomers. In addition, retailing is becoming a much more sophisticated business. Our managers need to be comfortable with new technologies, information and supply chain management systems, and

international business as well as managing a diverse workforce and buying merchandise.

We have developed a number of initiatives to help us deal with this challenge. First, we created the Federated Leadership Institute in 1998, which currently serves as the corporate university for the top 1200 executives in the corporation for store managers, DMMs, and above. A key objective of the Institute is to develop leadership skills. At the institute we emphasize the need for participating managers to prepare the people who work for them toward advancement. We have incorporated this training and development emphasis in many of our processes including the annual reviews of our managers. Every manager is evaluated on how well they are developing their subordinates.

A second initiative we have undertaken is developing a Web site (www.retailogy.com) to stimulate interest in retailing careers and help us recruit the best and brightest on college campuses. Retailing does not get the press coverage that high-tech businesses get, but running a retail business is just as exciting and complex. Students have a

CHAPTER 9

QUESTIONS

In what way does the management of human resources play a vital role in a retailer's performance?

How do retailers build a sustainable competitive advantage by developing and managing their human resources?

What activities do retail employees undertake, and how are they typically organized?

How does a retailer coordinate employees' activities and motivate them to work toward the retailer's goals?

What are the human resource management programs for building a committed workforce?

How and why do retailers manage diversity among their employees?

lot of choices when they graduate and many of them don't really know much about retailing. Their experience with our industry is shopping in our stores and at our Web site and working as sales associates during the holidays. Students don't realize that if they enter our management training program when they graduate, they can be in charge of a $5 million department with 20 employees or buying and managing $50 million of merchandise in several years. At our retailogy Web site, students can learn about the wide range of retail careers and the opportunities for advancement and "meet" our executives and hear their stories.

Retailers achieve their financial objectives by effectively managing their five critical assets: locations, merchandise inventory, stores, employees, and customers. This chapter focuses on the organization and management of employees—the retailer's human resources. Howard Schultz, chairman and chief global strategist of Starbucks, emphasizes that "the relationship that we have with our people and the culture of our company is our most sustainable competitive advantage."[1]

Human resource management is particularly important in retailing because employees play a major role in performing its critical business functions. In manufacturing firms, capital equipment (machinery, computer systems, robotics, etc.) often is used to perform the jobs employees once did. But retailing and other service businesses remain labor intensive. Retailers still rely on people to perform the basic retailing activities, such as buying and displaying merchandise and providing service to customers.

Two chapters in this text are devoted to human resource management because it is such an important issue for the performance of retail firms. This chapter focuses on the broad strategic issues involving organization structure; the general approaches used for motivating and coordinating employee activities; and the management practices for building an effective, committed workforce and reducing turnover. The activities undertaken to implement the retailer's human resource strategy, including recruiting, selecting, training, supervising, evaluating, and compensating sales associates, are typically undertaken by store management. Such operational issues will be discussed in more detail in Chapter 17 in the Store Management section of this textbook.

GAINING COMPETITIVE ADVANTAGE THROUGH HUMAN RESOURCE MANAGEMENT

REFACT

Labor costs typically are more than 25 percent of sales and 50 percent of operating costs in service-oriented department and specialty stores.[2]

REFACT

A study of Sears' employees found that a 5 percent increase in employee satisfaction resulted in a 1.3 percent increase in customer satisfaction, which led to a 0.5 percent growth in sales.[3]

Human resource management can be the basis of a sustainable competitive advantage for three reasons. First, labor costs account for a significant percentage of a retailer's total expenses. Thus, the effective management of employees can produce a cost advantage. Second, the experience that most customers have with a retailer is determined by the activities of employees who select merchandise, provide information and assistance, and stock displays and shelves. Thus, employees can play a major role in differentiating a retailer's offering from its competitor's. Third, these potential advantages are difficult for competitors to duplicate. For example, every department store executive knows that Nordstrom employees provide outstanding customer service; however, they are not able to develop the same customer-oriented culture in their firms. Retailing View 9.1 describes how Men's Wearhouse built a competitive advantage through effective human resource management.

Objectives of Human Resource Management

The strategic objective of human resource management is to align the capabilities and behaviors of employees with the short- and long-term goals of the retail firm. One human resource management performance measure is **employee productivity**—the

---

9.1   RETAILING VIEW   The Men's Wearhouse: Using Human Resources to Build a Competitive Advantage

Men's tailored apparel has been a declining market since George Zimmer, at the age of 24, opened his first Men's Wearhouse store in Houston in 1973. While the sale of men's tailored clothing has declined over the last 30 years, Men's Wearhouse has continued to gain market share, becoming one of the largest specialty retailers of men's apparel in North America. Men's Wearhouse sales have grown to over $1.5 billion with over 700 retail store locations in the United States and Canada.

The core of the company's strategy is to offer superior customer service delivered by knowledgeable, caring salespeople, called wardrobe consultants. The term *wardrobe consultant* was chosen intentionally to emphasize that sales associates are professionals like physicians or attorneys.

George Zimmer believes in a win–win–win philosophy, in which the customer, the wardrobe consultant, and the company all do well. Because the company believes that its job is to develop the untapped human potential in its employees, it devotes considerable attention to training. Some of Men's Wearhouse's core philosophies include the following:

Fulfillment at Work   Job satisfaction—everyone wants to have it. So how does Men's Wearhouse help its employees find it? It all starts with trust and respect.

Don't Be Afraid of Mistakes   You can tell a lot about a company by observing the way they handle mistakes. Men's Wearhouse focuses on the learning opportunities that mistakes provide. It likes to say that it celebrates its successes and its failures.

Balancing Work and Family Life   Men's Wearhouse encourages employees to balance the worlds inside and outside of the workplace.

Having Fun at Work with Friends   A workplace filled with fun amongst friends is GOOD for business.

Extensive training and teamwork enable Men's Wearhouse sales personnel to provide excellent customer service and build a competitive advantage for the firm.

Celebrate Individual and Team Success   Men's Wearhouse recognizes that individual and team excellence are interrelated—they support each other. That's why it celebrates both individual and team achievements.

Promote from Within   Skills and experience at a job are only part of the picture. When picking its leaders, it looks for people who care about others, take the time to listen, and show enthusiasm when working toward team and individual goals. That's why it promotes people it already knows.

Sources: 2005 Men's Wearhouse Annual Report; http://www.menswearhouse.com. Used by permission of The Men's Wearhouse.

retailer's sales or profit divided by the number of employees. Employee productivity can be improved by increasing the sales generated by employees, reducing the number of employees, or both.

Whereas employee productivity is directly related to the retailer's short-term profits, employee attitudes such as job satisfaction and commitment have important effects on customer satisfaction and the subsequent long-term performance of the retailer. In addition to survey measures of these attitudes, a behavioral measure of these attitudes is employee turnover. **Employee turnover** equals

$$\frac{\text{Number of employees leaving their job during the year}}{\text{Number of positions}}$$

So if a store owner had five sales associate positions and three left and were replaced during the year, the turnover would be $3/5 = 60$ percent. Note that turnover can be greater than 100 percent if a substantial number of people are replaced more than once during the year. In our example, if the replacements for the three employees that left also left during the year, the turnover would be $6/5 = 120$ percent.

A failure to consider both long- and short-term objectives can result in the mismanagement of human resources and a downward performance spiral, as shown in Exhibit 9–1. Often, when retailers' sales and profits decline due to increased competition, they respond by decreasing labor costs. They reduce the number of sales associates in stores, hire more part-timers, and spend less on training. Although these actions may increase short-term productivity and profits, they have an adverse effect on long-term performance because employee morale and customer service decline.[4]

The Human Resource Triad

Retailers such as Home Depot, Wegmans, Men's Wearhouse, and The Container Store believe that human resources are too important to be left to the human resources (HR) department. The full potential of a retailer's human resources is realized when three elements of the HR triad work together—HR professionals, store managers, and employees.

Human resources professionals, who typically work out of the corporate office, have specialized knowledge of HR practices and labor laws. They are responsible for establishing HR policies that enforce the retailer's strategy and provide the tools and training used by line managers and employees to implement those policies. Store or line managers, who primarily work in the stores, are responsible

EXHIBIT 9–1
Downward Performance Spiral

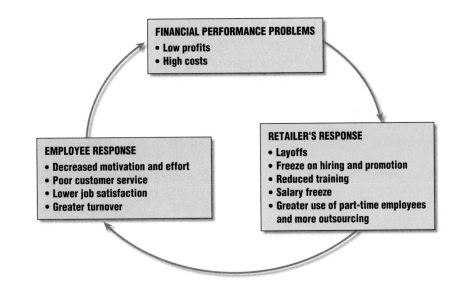

EXHIBIT 9–2
Human Resource Triad

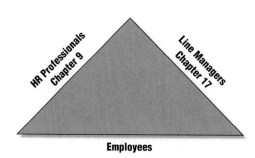

HR Professionals Chapter 9

Line Managers Chapter 17

Employees

for bringing the policies to life through their daily management of the employees who work for them. The issues confronting HR professionals are discussed in this chapter; Chapter 17, in the Store Management section of this book, reviews the responsibilities of line managers. Finally, the employees also share in the management of human resources. They can play an active role by providing feedback on the policies, managing their own careers, defining their job functions, and evaluating the performance of their managers and coworkers. These three elements of the HR triad are illustrated in Exhibit 9–2.

Special HR Conditions Facing Retailers

Human resource management in retailing is very challenging due to (1) the need to use part-time employees, (2) the emphasis on expense control, and (3) the changing demographics of the workforce. Retailers operating in international markets face additional challenges.

Part-Time Employees   Most retailers are open long hours and weekends to respond to the needs of family shoppers and working people. In addition, peak shopping periods occur during lunch hours, at night, and during sales. To deal with these peak periods and long hours, retailers have to complement their one or two shifts of full-time (40 hours per week) store employees with part-time workers. Part-time workers can be more difficult to manage than full-time employees because they often are less committed to the company and their jobs and more likely to quit than full-time employees.

Expense Control   Retailers often operate on thin margins and must control their expenses. Thus, they are cautious about paying high wages to hourly employees who perform low-skill jobs. To control costs, retailers often hire people with little or no experience to work as sales associates, bank tellers, and waiters. High turnover, absenteeism, and poor performance often result from this use of inexperienced, low-wage employees.

The lack of experience and motivation among many retail employees is particularly troublesome because these employees are often in direct contact with customers. Unlike manufacturing workers on an assembly line, the lowest-paid retail employees work in areas that are highly visible to customers. Poor appearance, manners, and attitudes can have a negative effect on sales and customer loyalty.

Employee Demographics   The changing demographic pattern will result in a chronic shortage of qualified sales associates. Annual percentage growth in the U.S. labor market in 1980 was 14 percent. In 2010, it is forecasted to be only 4 percent and then drop to 2 percent in 2020. Thus, retailers need to explore various approaches for operating effectively in a tight labor market—increase retention; recruit, train, and manage minority, handicapped, and mature workers; and use incentives and technology to increase productivity.

REFACT

Thirty-five percent of all retail employees work part-time, and more than 500,000 employees are added to the retail workforce during the holiday season.[5]

REFACT

Approximately one-third of retail employees are 24 years old or younger.[6]

To satisfy their HR needs, retailers are increasing the diversity of their workforces, employing more minorities, handicapped people, and elderly. The work values of young employees are quite different than those of their Baby Boomer supervisors, which causes many older managers to feel that younger employees have poor work ethics. Younger employees respond by saying, "Get a life," as they strive to balance their personal and professional lives. Managing this growing diversity and the changing values in the retail workforce creates both opportunities and problems for human resource managers.[7]

More and more retailers are encouraging older workers to work for them, because older workers prove to be more reliable employees. The attraction of older workers stems from their lower turnover rates and often better work performance. Home Depot even offers winter work in Florida and summer work in Maine. By building relationships with groups like the American Association of Retired Persons (AARP), Home Depot hopes to help people like military retirees find jobs in the future. Training and recruitment costs are much lower for older people, evening out any increased costs in missed days for medical problems.[8]

International Human Resource Issues   Finally, the management of employees working for international retailers is especially challenging.[9] Differences in work values, economic systems, and labor laws mean that HR practices that are effective in one country might not be effective in another. For example, U.S. retailers rely heavily on individual performance appraisals and rewards tied to individual performance—a practice consistent with the individualistic U.S. culture. However, in countries with a collectivist culture, such as China and Japan, employees downplay individual desires and focus on the needs of the group. Thus, group-based evaluations and incentives are more effective in those countries.

The legal/political system in countries often dictates the human resource management practices that retailers can use. For example, the United States has led the world in eliminating workplace discrimination. However, in Singapore, it is perfectly legal to place an employment ad specifying that candidates must be male, between the ages of 25 and 40 years, and ethnic Chinese. In the Netherlands, a retailer can make a substantial reduction in its workforce only if it demonstrates to the government that the cutback is absolutely necessary. In addition, a Dutch retailer must develop a plan for the cutback, which must then be approved by unions and other involved parties.[10]

Finally, the staffing of management positions in foreign countries raises a wide set of issues. Should management be local, or should expatriates be used? How should the local managers or expatriates be selected, trained, and compensated? For example, Wal-Mart makes every effort to replace expatriates with locals. Yet it is expanding faster than it can train people internally and has lost high-quality local managers to rivals.

The following sections of this chapter examine three important strategic issues facing retail HR professionals: (1) the design of the organization structure for assigning responsibility and authority for tasks to people and business units, (2) the approaches used to coordinate the activities of the firm's departments and employees and motivate employees to work toward achieving company goals, and (3) the programs used to build employee commitment and retain valuable human resources.

REFACT

It costs U.S. retailers 6 weeks of wages to fire an employee. The cost in China is 90 weeks of wages and 165 weeks in Brazil.[11]

DESIGNING THE ORGANIZATION STRUCTURE FOR A RETAIL FIRM

The **organization structure** identifies the activities to be performed by specific employees and determines the lines of authority and responsibility in the firm. The first step in developing an organization structure is to determine the tasks that must be performed. Exhibit 9–3 shows tasks typically performed in a retail firm.

EXHIBIT 9–3   Tasks Performed by a Typical Retail Firm

STRATEGIC MANAGEMENT
- Develop a retail strategy
- Identify the target market
- Determine the retail format
- Design organizational structure
- Select locations

MERCHANDISE MANAGEMENT
- Buy merchandise
    Locate vendors
    Evaluate vendors
    Negotiate with vendors
    Place orders
- Control merchandise inventory
    Develop merchandise budget plans
    Allocate merchandise to stores
    Review open-to-buy and stock position
- Price merchandise
    Set initial prices
    Adjust prices

STORE MANAGEMENT
- Recruit, hire, and train store personnel
- Plan work schedules
- Evaluate performance of store personnel
- Maintain store facilities
- Locate and display merchandise
- Sell merchandise to customers
- Repair and alter merchandise
- Provide services such as gift wrapping and delivery
- Handle customer complaints
- Take physical inventory
- Prevent inventory shrinkage

ADMINISTRATIVE MANAGEMENT (OPERATIONS)
- Promote the firm, its merchandise, and its services
    Plan communication programs
    Develop communication budget
    Select media
    Plan special promotions
    Design special displays
    Manage public relations
- Manage human resources
    Develop policies for managing store personnel
    Recruit, hire, and train managers
    Plan career paths
    Keep employee records
- Distribute merchandise
    Locate warehouses
    Receive merchandise
    Mark and label merchandise
    Store merchandise
    Ship merchandise to stores
    Return merchandise to vendors
- Establish financial control
    Provide timely information on financial performance
    Forecast sales, cash flow, and profits
    Raise capital from investors
    Bill customers
    Provide credit

These tasks are divided into four major categories in retail firms: strategic management, administrative management (operations), merchandise management, and store management. The organization of this textbook is based on these tasks and the managers who perform them.

Section II of this text focuses on strategic and administrative tasks. Strategic market and finance decisions (discussed in Chapters 5 and 6) are undertaken primarily by senior management: the CEO, chief operating officer, vice presidents, and the board of directors that represents shareholders in publicly held firms. Administrative tasks (discussed in Chapters 7–11) are performed by corporate staff employees who have specialized skills in human resource management, finance, accounting, real estate, distribution, and management information systems. People in these administrative functions develop plans, procedures, and information to assist operating managers in implementing the retailer's strategy.

In retail firms, the primary operating or line managers are involved in merchandise management (Section III) and store management (Section IV). These operating managers implement the strategic plans with the assistance of administrative personnel. They make the day-to-day decisions that directly affect the retailer's performance.

To illustrate the connection between the tasks performed and the organization structure in Exhibit 9–3, the tasks are color coded. Brown represents the strategic tasks, gold the merchandise management, green store management, and blue administrative management tasks.

Matching Organization Structure to Retail Strategy

The design of the organization structure needs to match the firm's retail strategy.[12] For example, category specialists and warehouse clubs such as Best Buy and Costco target price-sensitive customers and thus are very concerned about building a competitive advantage based on low cost. They minimize the number of employees by assigning decisions to a few people at corporate headquarters. These centralized organization structures are very effective when there are limited regional or local differences in customer needs.

In contrast, high-fashion clothing customers often aren't very price sensitive, and their tastes vary across the country. Retailers targeting these segments tend to have more managers and make decisions at the local store level. When more decisions are made at the local store level, human resource costs are higher, but sales also increase because the merchandise and services are tailored to meet the needs of local markets. Retailing View 9.2 illustrates how all of the elements of the human resource strategy, including the organization structure, are used to reinforce PETsMART's strategy.

PETsMART's HR Practices Support Its Retail Strategy   RETAILING VIEW   9.2

When PETsMART launched its concept for a pet supply category killer in 1988, it followed the lead of other category killers and emphasized its low prices, broad product assortment, limited customer service, and warehouse atmosphere. But it discovered that pet owners wanted more. They viewed their pets as part of the family, not just animals that needed to be fed. They wanted to be good "pet parents" and deal with a company that was as concerned about their pets' health and well-being as they were. Thus, PETsMART undertook a strategy to reposition its brand from category killer to a caring and trusted source of products and service for pets.

To implement this new positioning, PETsMART started to provide some new services in the stores such as pet styling, veterinary services, and training classes. Rather than hire veterinarians, PETsMART arranged to have the clinics operated by Banfield, The Pet Hospital, a trusted source of "human"-quality medical care for pets. PETsMART also decided to provide facilities and space for shelters to make homeless pets available rather than sell dogs and cats. Finally, the company changed its marketing communications to be less price oriented and more service driven, with all messages highlighting that pets are as welcome in the store as the rest of their family is. Promotional tie-ins with major animal shelters and pet rescue services became major focal points nationally and at the local store level.

PETsMART also recognized that its employees would play a crucial role in the development of a new brand image. Its front-line employees have to understand and accept the brand's values and the promise the brand is making to its customers. To develop these values in its employees, PETsMART changed the criteria it used for selecting sales associates. The company no longer looks for people who could just stock the shelves; it now hires people who have a deep love for dogs or cats or tropical fish. The groomers in its styling salons love making a

PETsMART hires caring pet groomers and trainers to offer complementary services to pet owners in one convenient location.

pet look beautiful. To develop its employees, PETsMART provides extensive training so that the store employees can become even more knowledgeable about the pets with whom they work.

Sources: *PETsMART 2005 Annual Report;* Darrell Rigby and Dan Haas, "Outsmarting Wal-Mart," *Harvard Business Review,* December 2004, pp. 22–25.

EXHIBIT 9–4 Organization Structure for a Small Retailer

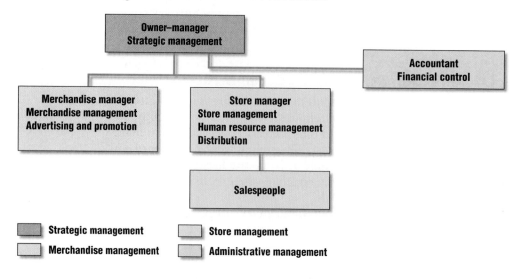

Organization of a Single-Store Retailer

Initially, the owner–manager of a single store may be the entire organization. When he or she goes to lunch or heads home, the store closes. As sales grow, the owner–manager hires employees. Coordinating and controlling employee activities is easier in a small store than in a large chain of stores; the owner–manager simply assigns tasks to each employee and watches to see that these tasks are performed properly. Because the number of employees is limited, single-store retailers have little **specialization.** Each employee must perform a wide range of activities, and the owner–manager is responsible for all management tasks.

As sales continue to increase, specialization in management may occur when the owner–manager hires additional management employees. Exhibit 9–4 illustrates the common division of management responsibilities into merchandise and store management. The owner–manager continues to perform strategic management tasks. The store manager may be responsible for administrative tasks associated with receiving and shipping merchandising and managing the employees. The merchandise manager or buyer may handle the advertising and promotion tasks, as well as merchandise selection and inventory management tasks. Often the owner–manager contracts with an accounting firm to perform financial control tasks for a fee.

Organization of a National Chain Store

Compared with the management of a single store, managing a national retail chain is much more complex because managers must supervise units that are geographically distant from one another. In this section, we use JCPenney to illustrate the organization of a national, multichannel retail company.

Traditionally, retail businesses were family owned and managed. The organization of these firms was governed by family circumstances. Executive positions were designed to accommodate family members involved in the business. Then, in 1927, Paul Mazur proposed a functional organization plan that has been adopted by most retailers.[15] The organization structures of retail chains continue to reflect principles of the Mazur plan, such as separating buying and store management tasks into different divisions.

Exhibit 9–5 shows JCPenney's corporate organization. Most retail chains such as The Gap, Home Depot, and Best Buy have similar organization structures. Vice presidents responsible for administrative tasks (blue), merchandise management (gold), and store operations (green) report to the chairperson/CEO (brown). Most managers and employees in the store operations area work in stores. Merchandise,

EXHIBIT 9–5
Organization of JCPenney
Corporation

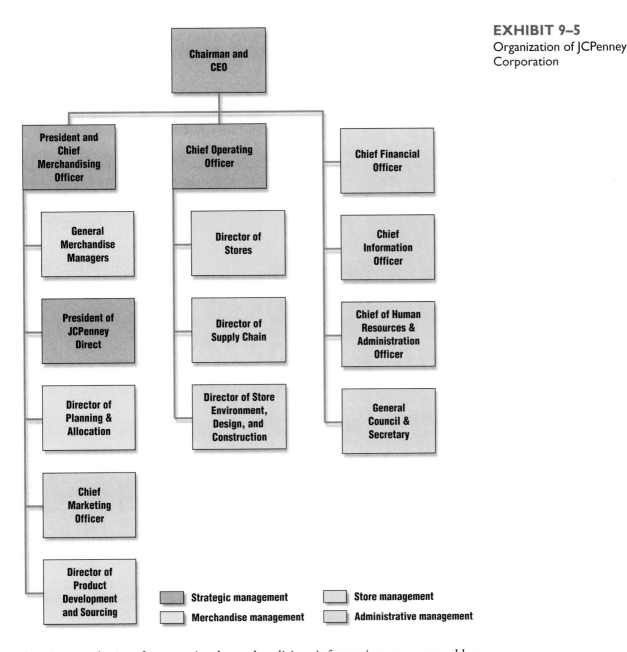

planning, marketing, finance, visual merchandising, information systems, and human resource managers and employees work at corporate headquarters.

The Chief Operating Officer (COO) is responsible for managing managers and sales associates in more than 1,000 JCPenney's stores across the United States. In addition, the COO manages the supply chain activities that ship merchandise to the stores, as well as store design, visual merchandising, and store construction.

The President and Chief Merchandising Officer is responsible for developing merchandising strategies, buying and pricing merchandise, determining what merchandise is allocated to specific stores, coordinating relationships with vendors, and designing and sourcing private-label merchandise. Some of JCPenney's private-label brands include Hunt Club, Stafford, Worthington, Arizona, St. John's Bay, and Chris Madden.

In addition to the merchandise management staff, the Chief Marketing Officer responsible for JCPenney's brand-building and advertising programs and the President of JCPenney Direct report to the President and Chief Merchandising Officer. The President of JCPenney Direct is responsible for Penney's catalog and Internet channels, which generate over $2.7 billion in annual sales. The President of JCPenney Direct receives reports from both merchandise management and operations staff. To be an effective multichannel retailer, JCPenney closely coordinates the merchandise and operations of its two direct channels with its stores.

Merchandise Management

The merchandise division is responsible for procuring the merchandise sold in the stores and ensuring that the quality, fashionability, assortment, and pricing of that merchandise is consistent with the firm's strategy. Chapters 12–15 discuss major activities performed in the merchandise division.

Exhibit 9–6 shows a detailed organization structure of JCPenney's merchandise management, with a separate merchandise management structure for catalog/Internet. This exhibit provides a more detailed view of the gold boxes in the left column of Exhibit 9–5.

EXHIBIT 9–6  JCPenney Store Merchandising

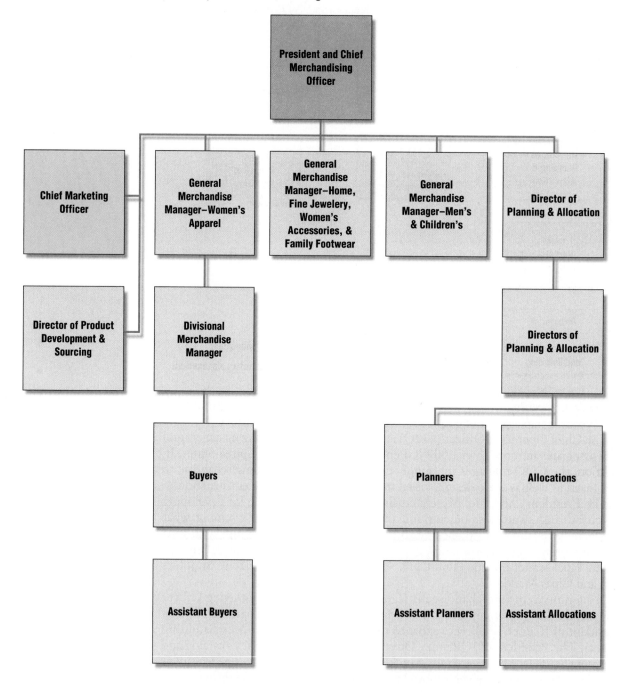

Buying Organization at Typical Department Store Chain   **EXHIBIT 9–7**

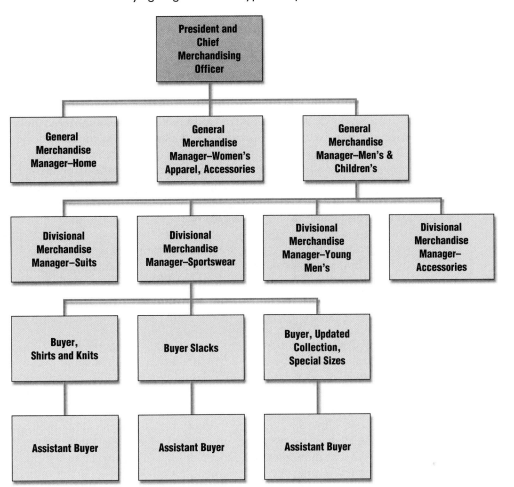

The buyer, allocator, and planner for each merchandise category form a merchandise action team (MAT) that is responsible for managing the merchandise category. Basically, it has the profit and loss responsibility for "running a business" associated with the merchandise category. Team members sit near one another in an open office environment with a convenient conference table so they can exchange information easily and make inventory management decisions.

Although MATs are given considerable autonomy to "run their own business," they must adhere to an inventory budget that varies from season to season. The budget is the result of a negotiation among the team and its superiors, divisional and general merchandise managers, planners, and allocators. The issues involved in managing the inventory budget are discussed in Chapters 12 and 13, and merchandise buying activities are reviewed in Chapter 14.

Exhibit 9–7 provides even more detail to describe how the buying function is organized by product category in a typical department store. This organization chart does not reflect the organization of JCPenney's merchandising area.

Buyers   **Buyers** are responsible for procuring merchandise and building and maintaining relationships with vendors. They attend trade and fashion shows and negotiate with vendors on prices, quantities, assortments, delivery dates, and payment terms. In addition, they might specify private-label merchandise or request modifications to tailor the merchandise to the retailer's target market and differentiate it from competitive offerings.

Allocators   Traditionally, buyers were also responsible for developing merchandise budget plans, monitoring the financial performance of the merchandise category, determining the assortment stocked in each store, allocating merchandise to the stores, monitoring sales, and placing reorders. Giving this responsibility solely to buyers meant that the merchandise strategy within a store might not be coordinated. For example, some buyers might allocate more expensive merchandise to a store in high-income areas, but others wouldn't make this adjustment.

To address these problems, most retail chains created merchandise allocators, with a senior executive of planning and allocation, at the same level as the merchandise managers in the buying organization. Each merchandise **allocator** is responsible for allocating merchandise and tailoring the assortment in several categories for specific stores in a geographic area. For example, the planner at The Limited would alter the basic assortment of sweaters for the different climates of south Florida and the Pacific Northwest.

Planners   JCPenney has divided the traditional activities performed by buyers by including a planner position. The **planner** is responsible for financial planning and analysis of the merchandise category. Planners develop the merchandise budget plan and monitor performance with respect to the plan for several merchandise categories.

Buying in Supermarkets   In recent years, the buyer's role in supermarket chains has evolved into a category manager. Traditional supermarket buyers were vendor focused. For example, they would be responsible for buying merchandise only from a specific vendor, such as Campbell or Kraft. They developed close relationships with vendors and were more concerned with maintaining these vendor relationships than selling products to customers. This focus was partially caused by evaluation systems that rewarded supermarket buyers more for securing price discounts than for sales, gross margins, or inventory turns.

Category managers are responsible for a set of products that are viewed as substitutes by customers. For example, a category manager might be in charge of all pastas—fresh, frozen, packaged, or canned. Category managers are evaluated on the profitability of their category and thus are motivated to eliminate "me-too" products and keep essential niche products. Note that buyers in most other types of retail firms have always been responsible for merchandise categories. Thus, the term *category manager* is used primarily by supermarket retailers.

Store Operations

At JCPenney, managers responsible for regions of the country report to the Director of Stores. District managers report to the regional managers, and store managers report to the district managers. The managers responsible for loss prevention, real estate, and styling salons also report to the Director of Stores.

Exhibit 9–8 shows the organization chart of a JCPenney store. Store managers in large stores have an assistant manager, department managers, and loss prevention and visual merchandise managers. The senior department managers and shoe and jewelry managers manage their sales associates and the presentation of merchandise in their areas of the store. The senior visual manager is responsible for the presentation of the merchandise in the store. The assistant store manager is responsible for selecting, training, and evaluating employees; the catalog and Internet kiosk areas; customer service activities, such as returns, complaints, and gift wrapping; the receiving, shipping, and storage areas of the store; and the styling salon.

JCPenney's Store Organization **EXHIBIT 9–8**

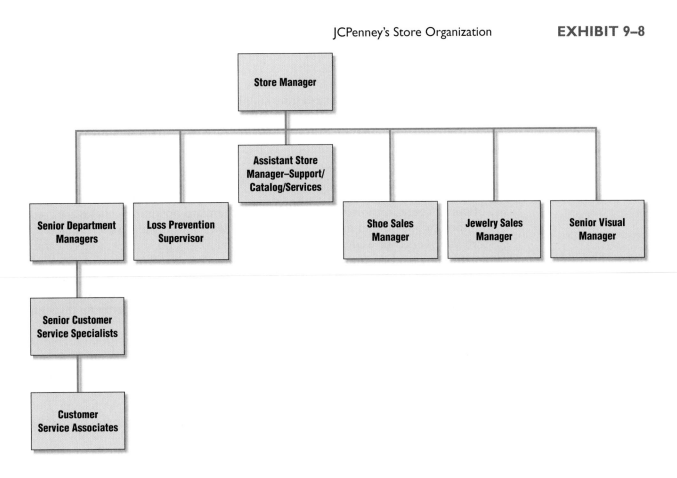

RETAIL ORGANIZATION DESIGN ISSUES

Two important issues in the design of a retail organization are (1) the degree to which decision making is centralized or decentralized and (2) the approaches used to coordinate merchandise and store management. The first issue translates into whether the decisions concerning activities such as merchandise management, information and distributions systems, and human resource management are made by regional, district, or store managers or by managers in the corporate headquarters. The second issue arises because retailers divide merchandise and store management activities into different organizations within the firm. Thus, they need to develop ways to coordinate these interdependent activities.

Centralization versus Decentralization

Centralization is when authority for retailing decisions is delegated to corporate managers rather than to geographically dispersed managers; **decentralization** is when authority for retail decisions is assigned to lower levels in the organization. JCPenney is an example of a retail corporation that has migrated from geographically decentralized decision making to centralized decision making. Now most retailing management decisions are made by corporate managers.

Retailers reduce costs when decision making is centralized in corporate management. First, overhead falls because fewer managers are required to make the merchandise, human resource, marketing, and financial decisions. For example, Federated Department Stores operates four regional Macy's department store chains—Florida, Central, East, and West—plus the Bloomingdale's chain. Thus, it has six women's blouse buyers (four in the Macy's regional offices, one for Bloomingdale's, and a corporate buyer coordinating the regional chains and buying private-label blouses). In contrast, JCPenney has one buyer for women's blouses at the corporate headquarters. Centralized retail organizations can similarly reduce personnel in administrative functions such as marketing, real estate, information systems, and human resources.

Second, by coordinating buying across geographically dispersed stores, the company can achieve lower prices from suppliers. The retailer can negotiate better purchasing terms by placing one large order rather than a number of smaller orders. Third, centralization provides an opportunity to have the best people make decisions for the entire corporation. For example, in a centralized organization, people with the greatest expertise in areas such as management information systems (MIS), buying, store design, and visual merchandise can have all stores benefit from their skills.

Fourth, centralization increases efficiency. Standard operating policies are used for store and personnel management; these policies limit the decisions made by store managers. For example, corporate merchandisers do considerable research to determine the best method for presenting merchandise. They provide detailed guides for displaying merchandise to each store manager so that all stores look the same throughout the country. Because they offer the same core merchandise in all stores, centralized retailers can achieve economies of scale by advertising through national media rather than more costly local media.

Although centralization has advantages in reducing costs, its disadvantage is that it makes it more difficult for a retailer to adapt to local market conditions. For example, Gainesville is located in central Florida, and thus, the manager in charge of the fishing category at the Sports Authority corporate office might think that the Gainesville store customers primarily engage in freshwater lake fishing. But the local store manager knows that most of his customers drive 90 miles to go saltwater fishing in either the Gulf of Mexico or the Atlantic Ocean.

In addition to problems with tailoring its merchandise to local needs, a centralized retailer may have difficulty responding to local competition and labor markets. Since pricing is established centrally, individual stores may not be able to respond quickly to competition in their market. Finally, centralized personnel policies may make it hard for local managers to pay competitive wages in their area or hire appropriate types of salespeople.

However, centralized retailers are relying more on their information systems to react to local market conditions. For example, American Drug Stores buyers at the division's headquarters use data collected by point-of-sale terminals to understand local conditions. Most drugstore chains are cutting back on the space devoted to automotive supplies, but American Drug sales data indicated that people in the inner city are more likely to change their own oil, so it maintains its automotive supply offering in these stores. By looking at buying patterns across a large number of stores, the centralized buyer might uncover opportunities that local managers would not see.

Coordinating Merchandise and Store Management

Small independent retailers have little difficulty coordinating their stores' buying and selling activities. Owner–managers typically buy the merchandise and work with their salespeople to sell it. In close contact with customers, the owner–managers know what their customers want.

In contrast, large retail firms organize the buying and selling functions into separate divisions. Buyers specialize in buying merchandise and have limited contact with the store management responsible for selling it. While this specialization increases buyers' skills and expertise, it makes it harder for them

This buyer frequently visits stores to get feedback from customers and sales associates.

to understand customers' needs. Three approaches large retailers use to coordinate buying and selling are (1) improving buyers' appreciation for the store environment, (2) making store visits, and (3) assigning employees to coordinating roles.

Improving Appreciation for the Store Environment   Fashion-oriented retailers use several methods to increase buyers' contact with customers and improve informal communication between buyers and the store personnel who sell the merchandise they buy. Management trainees, who eventually become buyers, are required by most retailers to work in the stores before they enter the buying office. During this 6–10-month training period, prospective buyers gain appreciation for the activities performed in the stores, the problems salespeople and department managers encounter, and the needs of customers.

Making Store Visits   Another approach to increasing customer contact and communication is to have buyers visit the stores and work with the departments for which they buy. At Wal-Mart, all managers (not just the buyers) are required to visit stores frequently and practice the company philosophy of CBWA (coaching by wandering around). Managers leave corporate headquarters in Bentonville, Arkansas, on Sunday night and return to share their experiences at the traditional Saturday morning meetings.[16] This face-to-face communication provides managers with a richer view of store and customer needs than they could get from impersonal sales reports from the company's management information system. Spending time in the stores improves buyers' understanding of customer needs, but this approach is costly because it reduces the time the buyer has to review sales patterns, plan promotions, manage inventory, and locate new sources of merchandise.

Assigning Employees to Coordinating Roles   Some retailers, like JCPenney, maintain people in the merchandise division (planners and allocators who work with buyers) and stores who are responsible for coordinating buying and selling activities. Many national retail chains have regional and even district personnel to coordinate buying and selling activities. For example, Target's regional merchandise managers in Chicago work with stores in the north-central U.S. region to translate plans developed by corporate buyers into programs that meet the regional needs of consumers.

In addition to developing an organization structure, HR management undertakes a number of activities to improve employee performance, build commitment among employees, and reduce turnover. In the following two sections of this chapter, we examine these human resource management activities.

MOTIVATING RETAIL EMPLOYEES

A critical task of human resource management is to motivate employees to work toward achieving the firm's goals and implementing its strategy. This task is often difficult because the employees' goals may differ from those of the firm. For example, a sales associate might find it more personally rewarding to arrange a display creatively than to help a customer. Retailers generally use three methods to motivate their employees' activities: (1) written policies and supervision, (2) incentives, and (3) organization culture.[17]

Policies and Supervision

Perhaps the most fundamental method of coordination is to (1) prepare written policies that indicate what employees should do and (2) have supervisors enforce these policies. For example, retailers may set policies about when and how merchandise can be returned by customers. If employees use the written policies to make these decisions, their actions will be consistent with the retailer's strategy. But strict reliance on written policies also can reduce employee motivation because employees have little opportunity to use their own initiative to improve performance of their areas of responsibility. As a result, they eventually might find their jobs uninteresting.

Relying on rules as a method of coordination leads to a lot of red tape. Situations will arise that aren't covered by a rule, in which case employees will need to talk to a supervisor or wait for a new policy before they can deal with a new situation.

Incentives

The second method of motivating and coordinating employees uses incentives to encourage them to perform activities consistent with the retailer's objectives. For example, buyers will be motivated to focus on the firm's profits if they receive a bonus based on the profitability of the merchandise they buy.

Types of Incentive Compensation
Two types of incentives are commissions and bonuses. A commission is compensation based on a fixed formula, such as 2 percent of sales. Many retail salespeople's compensation is based on a fixed percentage of the merchandise they sell.

A bonus is additional compensation awarded periodically on the basis of an evaluation of the employee's performance. For example, store managers often receive bonuses at the end of the year based on their store's performance relative to its budgeted sales and profits. Chapter 17 details the advantages and disadvantages of compensation plans compared with other nonfinancial incentives like recognition and promotions.

In addition to incentives based on individual performance, retail managers often receive income based on their firm's performance. These profit-sharing arrangements can be offered as a cash bonus based on the firm's profits or a grant of stock options that link additional income to the performance of the firm's stock.

Retailers such as Starbucks, Wal-Mart, and Home Depot use stock incentives to motivate and reward all employees, including sales associates. Employees are encouraged to buy shares in their companies at discounted prices through payroll deduction plans. These stock incentives align employees' interests with those of the company and can be very rewarding when the company does well. However, if growth in the company's stock price declines, employee morale declines too, corporate culture is threatened, and demands for higher wages and more benefits develop.

Drawbacks of Incentives
Incentives are very effective at motivating employees to perform the activities on which the incentives are based. But incentives also may cause employees to ignore other activities. For example, salespeople whose compensation is based entirely on their sales may be reluctant to spend time restocking the fixtures and shelves. Excessive use of incentives to motivate employees also can reduce employee commitment. Company loyalty falls because employees feel that the firm hasn't made a commitment to them (since it's unwilling to guarantee their compensation). Thus, if a competitor offers to pay a higher commission rate, they'll feel free to leave.[20]

Organization Culture

The final method for motivating and coordinating employees is to develop a strong organization culture. An **organization culture** is the set of values, traditions, and customs of a firm that guides employee behavior. These guidelines aren't written down as a set of policies and procedures; they are traditions passed along by experienced employees to new employees.

REFACT

The late Mary Kay Ash, founder of Mary Kay Cosmetics, was fond of saying, "There are two things that people want more than sex and money—recognition and praise."[18]

REFACT

Until recently, Japanese companies were not permitted to issue their stock as compensation.[19]

REFACT

An employee who paid $1,650 for 100 shares of Wal-Mart stock when the company went public in 1970 would now own stock worth over $5 million.

Many retail firms have strong organization cultures that give employees a sense of what they ought to do on their jobs and how they should behave to be consistent with the firm's strategy. For example, Nordstrom's strong organization culture emphasizes customer service, whereas Wal-Mart's focuses on reducing costs so the firm can provide low prices to its customers.

An organization culture often has a much stronger effect on employees' actions than do rewards offered through compensation plans, directions provided by supervisors, or written company policies. Nordstrom emphasizes the strength of its organization culture in the policy manual given to new employees. The manual has one rule: Use your best judgment to do anything you can to provide service to our customers. Lack of written rules doesn't mean that Nordstrom employees have no guidelines or restrictions on their behavior; rather, its organization culture guides employees' behavior. New salespeople learn from other employees that they should always wear clothes sold at Nordstrom, that they should park their cars at the outskirts of the parking lot so customers can park in more convenient locations, that they should approach customers who enter their department, that they should accept any merchandise returned by a customer even if the merchandise wasn't purchased at a Nordstrom store, and that they should offer to carry packages to the customer's car.

Developing and Maintaining a Culture

Organization cultures are developed and maintained through stories and symbols.[21] Values in an organization culture are often explained to new employees and reinforced to present employees through stories. For example, Nordstrom's service culture is emphasized by stories describing the "heroic" service undertaken by its salespeople. Salespeople will relate how a fellow salesperson went across the mall and bought a green, extra-large Ralph Lauren/Polo shirt for a customer who was upset because Nordstrom didn't have the shirt in his size. Department sales managers encourage storytelling by holding contests in which the salesperson with the best hero story for the week wins a prize.

The Container Store emphasizes the importance of add-on sales using the "man in the desert" story. A man crawling through the desert, gasping for water, is offered water by a retailer at the oasis. But if The Container Store were at the oasis, the salesperson would have said, "Here's some water, but how about some food? I see you're wearing a wedding ring. Can we call your family to let them know you are here?"[22]

Using symbols is another technique for managing organization culture and conveying its underlying values. Symbols are an effective means of communicating with employees because the values they represent can be remembered easily. Wal-Mart makes extensive use of symbols and symbolic behavior to reinforce its emphasis on controlling costs and keeping in contact with its customers. Photocopy machines at corporate headquarters have cups on them for employees to use to pay for any personal copying. At the traditional Saturday morning executive meeting, employees present information on the cost-control measures they've recently undertaken. Managers who have been traveling in the field report on what they've seen, unique programs undertaken in the stores, and promising merchandise. Headquarters are Spartan. Founder Sam Walton, one of the world's wealthiest people before he died, lived in a modest house and drove a pickup truck to work.

Sam Walton, founder of Wal-Mart, symbolized Wal-Mart's corporate culture of providing value to customers by controlling costs.

Disney strengthens its organization culture through the labels it uses for its employees and by steeping employees in the culture during the selection process. Management and employees view themselves as part of a team whose job is to produce a very large show. Applicants are trying out for a role in the cast rather than being hired for a job. For hourly jobs, the casting director (the person in charge of recruiting) interviews applicants to determine if they can adapt to the company's strong organizational culture. Do they understand and accept the fact that Disney has strict grooming requirements (no facial hair for men, little makeup for women)? Is the applicant willing to work on holidays? After the initial screening, the remaining applicants are judged on how well they might fit in with the show. Current employees participate in the entire process; they assess the applicant's behaviors and attitudes while providing firsthand information about their role in the "production."

BUILDING EMPLOYEE COMMITMENT

REFACT

The voluntary annual turnover in the retail industry is 31.4 percent, but among hourly retail employees, it approaches 100 percent per year.[24]

As mentioned previously, an important challenge in retailing is to reduce turnover.[23] High turnover reduces sales and increases costs. Sales are lost because inexperienced employees lack the skills and knowledge about company policies and merchandise to interact effectively with customers; costs increase due to the need to continually recruit and train new employees. Retailing View 9.3 illustrates how IKEA has built a committed workforce.

Consider what happens when Bob Roberts, meat department manager in a supermarket chain, leaves the company. His employer promotes a meat manager from a smaller store to take Bob's position, promotes an assistant department manager to the position in the smaller store, promotes a meat department trainee to the assistant manager's position, and hires a new trainee. Now the supermarket chain needs to train two meat department managers and one assistant manager and hire and train one trainee. The estimated cost for replacing Bob Roberts thus is almost $10,000.

To reduce turnover, retailers need to build an atmosphere of mutual commitment in their firms. When a retailer demonstrates its commitment, employees respond by developing loyalty to the company. Employees improve their skills and work hard for the company when they feel the company is committed to them over the long run, through thick and thin. Some approaches that retailers take to build mutual commitment are (1) developing employee skills through selection and training, (2) empowering employees, and (3) creating a partnering relationship with employees.[25] Research indicates that engaging in these human resource management practices increases the firm's financial performance.[26]

Developing Skills

Two activities that retailers undertake to develop knowledge, skills, and abilities in their human resources are selection and training. Retailers that build a competitive advantage through their human resources are very selective in hiring people and make significant investments in training.

Selective Hiring   The first step in building a committed workforce is recruiting the right people. Singapore Airlines, one of Asia's most admired companies, is consistently ranked among the top airlines in terms of service quality. Since its flight attendants are the critical point of contact with its customers, senior management is personally involved in their selection. Only 10 percent of the applicants make it through the initial screen, and only 2 percent are eventually hired.

The job requirements and firm strategy dictate the type of people hired. Simply seeking the best and the brightest often may not be the most effective approach. For example, at Recreational Equipment Inc. (REI), a category specialist in outdoor gear, the motto is "You live what you sell." Outdoor enthusiasts are hired as sales associates so they can help customers and serve as a resource for the buying staff. Borders Books and Music similarly wants avid readers in its workforce.[27]

Training   Training is particularly important in retailing because more than 60 percent of retail employees have direct contact with customers, which means they are responsible for helping customers satisfy their needs and resolve their problems. A key to the success of the Men's Wearhouse is how it treats its employees and its emphasis on training. All wardrobe consultants and store managers go through a five-day training program at "Suits University," the

REFACT

Averaging only seven hours per employee per year, the retail industry spends less time on training than all other industries.[28]

The IKEA Way   RETAILING VIEW   9.3

Employees gather around Pernille Spiers-Lopez, CEO of IKEA North America (left), and Jim Tilley, store manager, IKEA San Francisco (right), to witness a log-sawing ceremony held to celebrate the opening of a new IKEA store in San Francisco. These IKEA executives support the company culture that prizes developing employees.

of subjects such as driving a forklift. And then there is the cafeteria, where employees can get anything on the menu for $2.

IKEA supports its employees. When Pernille Spiers-Lopez, CEO of IKEA North America, hires a "coworker," as IKEA terms its employees, her plan is to help the person through his or her slumps. One of her greatest rewards is to see a worker she has worked with excel, and she believes all supervisors and managers should serve as mentors. "It's easy to be committed to the coworker who's doing great," she said. "The [real] commitment is when she's struggling. When I hire you, I am there until you don't want to do it anymore."

A key part of her job

When IKEA announces the opening of a store, job candidates line up outside the store for a chance to work for this retailer that is keenly interested in the development and well-being of its employees. New management hires start their jobs with paid health insurance coverage, life insurance, and three weeks paid leave during their first year. Many employees find themselves, for the first time, eligible for long- and short-term disability pay. While only 15 percent of the part-time retail employees in this industry have health benefits, all of IKEA's do.

Store managers and sales assistants all dress in the same uniform, and executive perks are shunned. To keep management positions "within the IKEA family," the company has begun its own personnel development program called "Paddle Your Own Canoe," in which workers sit down with their bosses and plot out their future with the company. Employees make plans to become store managers, and if they need more education, the company reimburses their tuition. Some employees elect to take special training courses to earn certificates in the practical mastery

is to convince her managers to find ways to match their stores' needs with those of employees, using flexible work schedules, job sharing, compressed work weeks, and other techniques. IKEA North America routinely surveys employees to gauge morale and spot issues that need to be addressed.

The company's philosophy seems simple enough: Workers tend to be more productive and engaged in what they do when their basic needs are taken care of. IKEA's grateful employees, in return, are committed to making their career working for IKEA. IKEA's profit margin is estimated at 6 percent, almost double the margin of other furniture retailers, and its turnover is the lowest in the retail category.

Sources: Julie Forster, "IKEA's Ideas: The Swedish Retailer's Worker Benefits and Attitudes Are Unusual," *Minneapolis Pioneer Press*, July 11, 2004; "IKEA: Furnishing Good Employee Benefits Along with Dining Room Sets," *Knowledge@Wharton*, April 2004; Susan Reda, "Nice Guys Finish First," *Stores*, June 2004, pp. 28–31.

company's 35,000 square foot training center in Fremont, California. The training program emphasizes "clienteling," a process designed to foster a strong relationship between the wardrobe consultants and their customers. Periodically, experienced store personnel come back to the training center for three- and four-day retraining sessions. The employee commitment Men's Wearhouse builds through its training investment is reflected in its low inventory shrinkage rate. Its employees watch out for the company: They don't steal, and they stop others from shoplifting.

Investing in developing employee skills tells employees that the firm considers them important. In response to the difficulty of finding qualified service workers, Marriott has made a considerable investment in recruiting and training entry-level workers. The training goes beyond the basics of doing the job to include grooming habits and basic business etiquette, like calling when you can't come to work. Employees involved in this program have a strong commitment to Marriott. For example, Sara Redwell started working at Marriott as a housekeeper after emigrating from Mexico. She's now a housekeeping manager supervising 20 employees and mentoring other Mexican immigrants. "What Marriott gave to me, I want to give to others," she says. Tom Lee, a bartender at the Seattle Marriott, proudly proclaims, "Every day I put on this uniform just like an NBA player."[29] Walgreen's, Wal-Mart, and T.J. Maxx also have active programs for hiring people who do not possess entry-level skills. Retailing View 9.4 illustrates how Starbucks creates strong commitment among its employees.

9.4 RETAILING VIEW   Starbucks' *Baristas* Are Committed to Providing the Perfect Cup of Coffee

Starbucks develops a passion for coffee in its customers by providing the perfect cup in an entertaining atmosphere. Recognizing that its frontline employees are critical to providing the perfect cup, the company has built an organization culture based on two principles: (1) strict standards for how coffee should be prepared and delivered to customers and (2) a laid-back, supportive, empowering attitude toward employees.

All new hires go through a 24-hour training program that instills in them a sense of purpose, commitment, and enthusiasm. The new staff are treated with dignity and respect that goes along with their title as *baristas* (Italian for bartender). To emphasize their responsibility to please customers, they're presented with a scenario in which a customer complains that a pound of beans was ground incorrectly. The preferred response is to replace the beans on the spot without checking with the manager or someone with greater authority.

So the firm can hold on to these motivated, well-trained employees, all employees, both full- and part-time, are eligible for health benefits and a stock option plan called "Bean Stock." Baristas know about and are encouraged to apply for promotion to store management positions. Due to its training, empowerment, benefits, and opportunities, Starbucks' turnover is only 60 percent of its store employees, considerably less than the 300 percent average turnover experienced by similar food service firms.

Starbucks' human resource practices also have facilitated its entry into foreign markets. For example, its joint venture partner Mei Da Coffee Company faced a challenge hiring local managers for its first four restaurants in Beijing. Even though the demand for good managers was far greater than the supply,

Starbucks' corporate culture supports this barista's role in providing customers with a satisfying experience.

Starbucks was viewed as an attractive employer because of its corporate culture and opportunities for career development and advancement. Candidates were impressed with the casual atmosphere and the respect employees show for one another. One recruit stated, "People are looking for a good working environment where they can learn, and they are looking for dignity." The new recruits were trained in Seattle so they could experience the corporate culture and learn how to make the different coffee drinks.

Sources: Gretchen Weber, "Preserving the Counter Culture," *Workforce Management,* February 2005, pp. 28–34; Craig S. Smith, "Globalization Puts a Starbucks into the Forbidden City in Beijing," *New York Times,* November 25, 2000, p. B1.

REFACT

Across the world each day, Starbucks opens four stores and hires 200 employees.[30]

Empowering Employees

Empowerment is a process in which managers share power and decision-making authority with employees. When employees have the authority to make decisions, they are more confident in their abilities, have greater opportunity to provide service to customers, and are more committed to the firm's success.[31]

The first step in empowering employees is reviewing those employee activities that require a manager's approval. For example, Parisian, a regional department store chain owned by Saks, changed its check authorization policy, thereby empowering sales associates to accept personal checks of up to $1,000 without a manager's approval. Under the old policy, a customer often had to wait more than 10 minutes for the sales associate to locate a manager. Then the busy manager simply signed the check without reviewing the customer's identification. When the sales associates were empowered to make approvals, service improved and the number of bad checks decreased because the sales associates felt personally responsible and checked the identification carefully.

Each store in the Whole Foods chain is a profit center with the store employees empowered by their organization into 10 self-managed teams. The teams are responsible and accountable for the store's performance. For example, the store manager recommends new hires, but it takes a two-thirds vote of the team to actually hire the candidate. The team members pool their ideas and come up with creative solutions to problems.

Empowerment of retail employees transfers authority and responsibility for making decisions to lower levels in the organization. These employees are closer to the customers and in a good position to know what it takes to satisfy these customers. For empowerment to work, managers must have an attitude of respect and trust, not control and distrust.

Creating Partnering Relationships

Three HR management activities that build commitment by developing partnering relationships with employees are (1) reducing status differences, (2) promoting from within, and (3) enabling employees to balance their careers and families.

Reducing Status Differences   Many retailers attempt to reduce status differences among employees. With limited status differences, employees feel that they play an important role in the firm's ability to achieve its goals and that their contributions are valued.

Status differences can be reduced symbolically through the use of language and substantively by lowering wage differences and increasing communications among managers at different levels in the company. For example, hourly workers at JCPenney are referred to as associates and managers are called partners, a practice that Sam Walton adopted when he started Wal-Mart.

Whole Foods has a policy of limiting executive compensation to less than eight times the compensation of the average full-time salaried employee. When Herb Kelleher was CEO of Southwest Airlines, he negotiated a five-year wage freeze for his employees in exchange for stock options. He also agreed to freeze his base salary at $380,000. Sam Walton typically appeared on lists of the most underpaid CEOs.

All Home Depot senior executives spend time in the stores, wearing the orange apron, talking with customers and employees. This "management by walking around" makes employees feel that their inputs are valued by the company and reinforces the customer service culture at Home Depot.[33]

Promotion from Within   **Promotion from within** is a staffing policy that involves hiring new employees only for positions at the lowest level in the job hierarchy and then promoting those experienced employees for openings at higher

REFACT

Sam Walton, Wal-Mart's founder and one of the wealthiest people in the world when he passed away, flew first-class only once in his life, on a trip to Africa.[32]

levels in the hierarchy. Nordstrom, Home Depot, and Wal-Mart all have used promotion-from-within policies, whereas others frequently hire people from competitors when management positions open up.

Promotion-from-within policies establish a sense of fairness. When employees do an outstanding job and then outsiders are brought in over them, the employees feel that the company doesn't care about them. Promotion-from-within policies also commit the retailer to developing its employees.[34]

Balancing Careers and Families   The increasing number of two-income and single-parent families makes it difficult for employees to effectively do their jobs and manage their households. Retailers can build employee commitment by offering services like job sharing, childcare, and employee assistance programs to help their employees manage these problems.

Flextime is a job scheduling system that enables employees to choose the times they work. With **job sharing,** two employees voluntarily are responsible for a job that was previously held by one person. Both programs let employees accommodate their work schedules to other demands in their life, such as being home when their children return from school.[35]

Many retailers offer childcare assistance. Sears' corporate headquarters near Chicago has a 20,000 square foot day care center. At Eddie Bauer in Seattle, the corporate headquarters cafeteria stays open late and prepares takeout meals for time-pressed employees. Some companies will even arrange for a person to be at an employee's home waiting for the cable guy to come or pick up and drop off dry cleaning.

ISSUES IN RETAIL HUMAN RESOURCE MANAGEMENT

In this final section, we discuss three trends in HR management: (1) the increasing importance of a diverse workforce, (2) the growth in legal restrictions on HR practices, and (3) the use of technology to increase employee productivity.

Managing Diversity

Managing diversity is a human resource management activity designed to realize the benefits of a diverse workforce. Today, diversity means more than differences in skin color, nationality, or gender, but managing a diverse workforce isn't a new issue for retailers. In the late 1800s and early 1900s, waves of immigrants entering America went to work in retail stores. The traditional approach for dealing with these diverse groups was to blend them into the "melting pot." Minority employees were encouraged to adopt the values of the majority, white, male-oriented culture. To keep their jobs and get promoted, employees abandoned their ethnic or racial distinctiveness.

But times have changed. Minority groups now embrace their differences and want employers to accept them for who they are. The appropriate metaphor now is a salad bowl, not a melting pot. Each ingredient in the salad is distinctive, preserving its own identity, but the mixture of ingredients improves the combined taste of the individual elements.[36]

Some legal restrictions promote diversity in the workplace by preventing retailers from practicing discrimination based on non–performance-related employee characteristics. But retailers now recognize that promoting employee diversity also can improve financial performance. By encouraging diversity in their workforce, retailers can better understand and respond to the needs of their customers and deal with the shrinking labor market.

Retailers are increasing the diversity of their workforce to match the diversity among their customers.

To compete in this changing marketplace, retailers need management staffs that match the characteristics of their target markets. For example, the majority of merchandise sold in department stores and home improvement centers is bought by women. To better understand customer needs, department stores and home improvement retailers feel that they must have women in senior management positions—people who really understand their female customers' needs.

Besides gaining greater insight into customer needs, retailers must deal with the reality that their employees will become more diverse in the future. Many retailers have found that these emerging groups are more productive than their traditional employees. After renovating its national reservation center to accommodate workers with disabilities, Days Inn found that turnover among disabled workers was only 1 percent annually compared with 30 percent for its entire staff. Lowe's, a home improvement center chain, changed floor employees' responsibilities so they wouldn't have to lift heavy merchandise. By assigning these tasks to the night crew, the firm was able to shift its floor personnel from male teenagers to older employees who provided better customer service and had personal experience with do-it-yourself projects. Effectively managing a diverse workforce isn't just morally correct, it's necessary for business success.[37]

The fundamental principle behind managing diversity is the recognition that employees have different needs and require different approaches for accommodating those needs. Managing diversity goes beyond meeting equal employment opportunity laws. It means accepting and valuing differences. Some programs that retailers use to manage diversity involve offering diversity training, providing support groups and mentoring, and managing career development and promotions.

Diversity Training   Diversity training typically consists of two components: developing cultural awareness and building competencies. The cultural awareness component teaches people about how their own culture differs from the culture of other employees and how the stereotypes they hold influence the way they treat people, often in subtle ways that they might not realize. Then role-playing is used to help employees develop their competencies, such as better interpersonal skills that enable them to show respect and treat people as equals.

Support Groups and Mentoring   **Mentoring programs** assign higher-level managers to help lower-level managers learn the firm's values and meet other senior executives.[38] Many retailers help form minority networks to exchange information and provide emotional and career support for members who traditionally haven't been included in the majority's networks. In addition, mentors are often assigned to minority managers. At Giant Foods, a Maryland-based supermarket chain, the mentoring program has reduced turnover of minorities by making them more aware of the resources available to them and giving them practical advice for solving problems that arise on their jobs.

Career Development and Promotions   Although laws provide entry-level opportunities for women and minority groups, these employees often encounter a glass ceiling as they move through the corporation. A **glass ceiling** is an invisible barrier that makes it difficult for minorities and women to be promoted beyond a certain level. To help employees break through this glass ceiling, JCPenney monitors high-potential minority and female employees and makes sure they have opportunities for store and merchandise management positions that are critical for their eventual promotion to senior management.

Similarly, women in the supermarket business have traditionally been assigned to peripheral departments like the bakery and deli, while men were assigned to the critical departments in the store like meat and grocery. Even in the supermarket chain corporate office, women traditionally have been in staff-support areas like HR management, finance, and accounting, whereas men have been more involved

REFACT

In 1866, Macy's employed the first female executive in retailing when Margaret Getchell was promoted to the position of store superintendent.[39]

in store operations and buying. To make sure that more women have an opportunity to break through the glass ceiling in the supermarket industry, more firms are placing them in positions critical to the firm's success.[40]

Legal and Regulatory Issues in Human Resource Management

The proliferation of laws and regulations affecting employment practices in the 1960s was a major reason for the emergence of human resource management as an important organization function. Managing in this complex regulatory environment required expertise in labor laws and skills in helping other managers comply with those laws. The major legal and regulatory issues involving the management of retail employees are (1) equal employment opportunity, (2) compensation, (3) labor relations, (4) employee safety and health, (5) sexual harassment, and (6) employee privacy.

Equal Employment Opportunity   The basic goal of equal employment opportunity regulations is to protect employees from unfair discrimination in the workplace. **Illegal discrimination** refers to the actions of a company or its managers that result in members of a protected class being treated unfairly and differently than others. A protected class is a group of individuals who share a common characteristic as defined by the law. Companies cannot treat employees differently simply on the basis of their race, color, religion, sex, national origin, age, or disability status. There are a very limited set of circumstances in which employees can be treated differently. For example, it is illegal for a restaurant to hire young, attractive servers because that is what its customers prefer. Such discrimination must be absolutely necessary, not simply preferred.

In addition, it is illegal to engage in a practice that disproportionately excludes a protected group, even though it might seem nondiscriminatory. For example, suppose that a retailer uses scores on a test to make hiring decisions. If a protected group systematically performs worse on the test, the retailer is illegally discriminating even if there was no intention to discriminate.

Compensation   Laws relating to compensation define the 40-hour workweek, the pay rate for working overtime, and the minimum wage, and they protect employee investments in their pensions. In addition, they require that firms provide the same pay for men and women who are doing equal work.

A recent issue related to compensation is the criteria used to classify employees as managers who are paid a salary and not eligible for overtime pay. A number of lawsuits have been filed by assistant managers claiming that they do the same job as hourly employees but are classified as managers so that their retail employer can avoid paying them overtime wages. For example, one lawsuit claimed Wal-Mart's district managers frequently encourage store managers to send hourly workers home before their shift is over to avoid overtime pay and then cause assistant managers to continue working to compensate for the absence of hourly workers.

These lawsuits point out the difficulty in distinguishing the tasks of assistant managers and hourly workers. Federal law requires that managers be paid overtime if more than 40 percent of their time is not spent supervising or if their jobs do not include decision making. However, many retailers feel managers perform other activities, such as interviewing job candidates, making schedules, and handling other supervisory duties. Because so many lawsuits regarding overtime pay are filed each year, the Labor Department has developed overtime rules and regulations, such as defining specific jobs as managerial and paying overtime to managers who earn less than $23,660 a year but denying overtime to employees who earn more than $100,000 annually.[41]

United Food and Commercial Workers Union members strike to maintain wages and benefits earned from southern California supermarkets that are facing stiff competition from nonunion retailers.

Labor Relations   Labor relations laws describe the process by which unions can be formed and the ways in which companies must deal with the unions. They precisely indicate how negotiations with unions must take place and what the parties can and cannot do.

Wal-Mart has vigorously challenged attempts by unions to represent their employees. Supermarket chains with unionized employees believe they have a labor cost disadvantage that makes it difficult for them to compete effectively with Wal-Mart. In 2003, the three major super market chains in Southern California—Ralphs, Albertson's, and Vons—failed to get concessions during contract negotiations with the United Food and Commercial Workers union, which then initiated a strike. The 20-week strike and lockout idled 59,000 workers, inconvenienced millions of shoppers, and cost the chains $2 billion in lost sales.

The key issues were healthcare and pension costs. The contract that was eventually ratified created a lower pay scale for all new hires and virtually ended the supermarket chains' responsibility for new workers' health coverage. Employers agreed to contribute $4.60 hourly for current workers. While the contract produced savings in labor costs, it has also made entry-level supermarket jobs less attractive to potential workers.[42]

Employee Safety and Health   The basic premise of these laws is that the employer is obligated to provide each employee with an environment that is free from hazards that are likely to cause death or serious injury. Compliance officers from the Department of Labor enforce the Occupational Safety and Health Act (OSHA) by conducting inspections to ensure that employers are providing such an environment for their workers.[43]

Sexual Harassment   Sexual harassment includes unwelcome sexual advances, requests for sexual favors, and other inappropriate verbal and physical conduct. Harassment isn't confined to requests for sexual favors in exchange for job considerations such as a raise or promotion. Simply creating a hostile work environment can be considered sexual harassment. For example, actions considered sexual harassment include lewd comments, joking, and graffiti, as well as showing obscene photographs, staring at a coworker in a sexual manner, alleging that an employee got rewards by engaging in sexual acts, and commenting on an employee's moral reputation.[44]

Customers can engage in sexual harassment as much as supervisors and coworkers. For example, female pharmacists find that some male customers demand lengthy discussions when they buy condoms. Pharmacists have difficulty dealing with these situations because they want to keep the person as a customer but also protect themselves from abuse.

Employee Privacy   Employees' privacy protection is very limited. For example, employers can monitor e-mail and telephone communications, search an employee's work space and handbag, and require drug testing. However, employers cannot discriminate among employees when undertaking these activities unless they have a strong suspicion that specific employees are acting inappropriately.

Developing Policies   The HR department is responsible for developing programs and policies to make sure that managers and employees are aware of these legal restrictions and know how to deal with potential violations. These legal and regulatory requirements are basically designed to treat people fairly. Employees want to be treated fairly, and companies want to be perceived as treating their employees fairly. The perception of fairness encourages people to join a company and leads to the trust and commitment of employees to a firm. When employees believe they are not being treated fairly, they can complain internally, stay and accept the situation, stay but engage in negative behavior, quit, or complain to an external authority or even sue the employer.

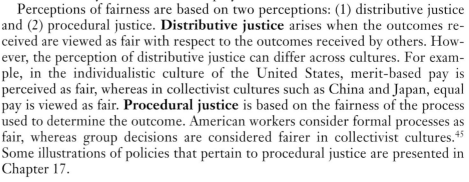

Perceptions of fairness are based on two perceptions: (1) distributive justice and (2) procedural justice. **Distributive justice** arises when the outcomes received are viewed as fair with respect to the outcomes received by others. However, the perception of distributive justice can differ across cultures. For example, in the individualistic culture of the United States, merit-based pay is perceived as fair, whereas in collectivist cultures such as China and Japan, equal pay is viewed as fair. **Procedural justice** is based on the fairness of the process used to determine the outcome. American workers consider formal processes as fair, whereas group decisions are considered fairer in collectivist cultures.[45] Some illustrations of policies that pertain to procedural justice are presented in Chapter 17.

Use of Technology

Retail chains are using intranets to automate and streamline their HR operations. For example, Penney's 150,000 employees use kiosks in the 1,200 Penney stores to make changes in their personnel records, request time off, register for training classes, review the company's policies and procedures manual, and request services such as direct deposit of their paychecks. These self-service kiosks are also used by job applicants to review open positions, submit applications, and take prescreening tests. The use of these kiosks, connected through an intranet to a centralized database, dramatically reduces the time human resources administrators spend on paperwork.[46]

REFACT

It costs a retailer $20 to $30 to process a paper HR form, but processing the form over an intranet costs only $.05 to $.10.[47]

SUMMARY

Human resource management plays a vital role in supporting a retailing strategy. The organization structure defines supervisory relationships and employees' responsibilities. The four primary groups of tasks performed by retailers are strategic decisions by the corporate officers, administrative tasks by the corporate staff, merchandise management by the buying organization, and store management.

In developing an organization structure, retailers must make trade-offs between the cost savings gained through centralized decision making and the benefits of tailoring the merchandise offering to local markets—benefits that arise when decisions are made in a decentralized manner.

Two critical human resource management issues are the development of a committed workforce and the effective management of a diverse workforce. Building a committed workforce is critical in retailing because high turnover has a major impact on profitability. A key factor in reducing turnover is developing an atmosphere of mutual commitment.

Managing diversity also is important in retailing because customers are becoming more diverse, and new entrants into the retail workforce will come largely from the ranks of women and minorities. Programs for managing diversity include diversity training, support groups and mentors, and promotion management.

The human resource department is also responsible for making sure that its firm complies with the laws and regulations that prevent discriminatory practices against employees and making sure that employees have a safe and harassment-free work environment.

KEY TERMS

allocator, *248*

buyer, *247*

category manager, *248*

centralization, *249*

decentralization, *249*

distributive justice, *262*

employee productivity, *238*

employee turnover, *239*

empowerment, *257*

flextime, *258*

glass ceiling, *259*

illegal discrimination, *260*

job sharing, *258*

managing diversity, *258*

mentoring program, *259*

organization culture, *252*

organization structure, *241*

planner, *248*

procedural justice, *262*

promotion from within, *257*

specialization, *244*

GET OUT AND DO IT!

1. **CONTINUING CASE ASSIGNMENT** Meet with the store manager of the retailer you have chosen for this continuing assignment. Ask the store manager which company HR policies he or she feels are very effective and which are not effective. Why? Also ask the manager about the store's policies concerning the legal and regulatory issues discussed in the chapter. Does the retailer have written policies that enable the manager to deal effectively with any situations that arise? Have situations arisen that were not covered by the policies? How was the situation addressed? To what degree does the manager feel he or she is empowered to make decisions that affect the performance of the store? Would the manager like more or less decision-making authority? Why?

2. **INTERNET EXERCISE** Go to the Society of Human Resource Management's home page, www. shrm.org. An organization of human resource professionals, SHRM publishes *HR Magazine*, with articles available online at www.workforceonline.com. Find and summarize the conclusions of articles addressing the HR challenges that retailers are facing, such as the management of a diverse workforce, international expansion, and the use of technology to increase productivity.

3. **INTERNET EXERCISE** The Fair Measures Law Consulting Group provides training and legal services for employers. Go to its Web site,

www.fairmeasures.com, and choose one of the legal areas to investigate (sexual harassment, wrongful termination, and so forth). Another source of information about legal issues regarding employees is www.law.cornell.edu/topics/employment.html. Read the most recent court opinions and articles about employment issues, and summarize the implications for human resource management in retailing.

4. **INTERNET EXERCISE** Go to Club Med's recruitment home page at http://www.clubmed-jobs.com/en/index.php. Take a few minutes and become familiar with the information offered about the interview process, job descriptions, and the competencies that this global leisure company is looking for when hiring. What are some of the unique challenges that this employer faces when hiring internationally?

5. **INTERNET EXERCISE** Go to the National Retail Federation's Retail Careers & Advancement home page at http://www.nrf.com/RetailCareers/ and click on "Is retail for me?" Read about the different career paths in Marketing/Advertising, Store Operations, Loss Prevention, Store Management, Finance, Human Resources, IT and E-Commerce, Sales and Sales-Related, Distribution/Logistics/Supply Chain Management, Merchandise Buying/Planning, and Entrepreneurship. Which area(s) appeals to you the most? Why is this the case?

6. **GO SHOPPING** Talk with a salesperson in a store. Ask him or her how committed he or she is to working for the retailer. Why does the salesperson feel that way? What could the retailer do to build a great sense of commitment?

7. **Web OLC EXERCISE**

   A. Go to the student side of the book's Web site and review the student resumes. Which resumes do you think are effective? Ineffective? Why?

   B. Update your resume and prepare for an interview for a Manager Training program with a large lumber and building supply retailer. This full-time position promises rapid advancement upon completion of the training period. A college degree and experience in retail, sales, and marketing are preferred. The base pay is between $28,000 and $34,000 per year. This retailer promotes from within, and a new Manager Trainee can become a Store Manager within two to three years, with an earning potential of $100,000 or more. The benefits package is generous, including medical/hospitalization/dental/disability/life insurance, a 401k plan, profit sharing, awards and incentives, paid vacations, and holidays. Your resume should include your contact information, education and training, skills, experience and accomplishments, and honors and awards.

   C. Role play a practice interview for this position. Pair up with another student and read each others' resumes; then spend 20 to 30 minutes on each side of the interview. One student should be the Human Resource Manager screening applicants, and the other person should be the candidate for the Manager Training program. Here are some questions to use in the role-play scenario:

   • Why are you applying for this position?
   • What are your strengths and weaknesses for this position?
   • Why should this organization consider you for this position?
   • Why are you interested in working for this company?
   • What are your career goals for the next five to ten years?
   • Describe your skills when working in a team setting.
   • What questions do you have about the company?

DISCUSSION QUESTIONS AND PROBLEMS

1. Why is human resource management more important in retailing than in manufacturing firms?

2. Describe the similarities and differences between the organization of small and large retail companies. Why do these similarities and differences exist?

3. Some retailers have specific employees (merchandise assistants) assigned to restock the shelves and maintain the appearance of the store. Other retailers have sales associates perform these tasks. What are the advantages and disadvantages of each approach?

4. How can national retailers like Best Buy and Victoria's Secret, which both use a centralized buying system, make sure that their buyers are aware of the local differences in consumer needs?

5. What are the positive and negative aspects of employee turnover? How can a retailer reduce the turnover of its sales associates?

6. To motivate employees, several major department stores are experimenting with incentive compensation plans, though frequently, compensation plans with a lot of incentives don't promote good customer service. How can retailers motivate employees to sell merchandise aggressively and at the same time not jeopardize customer service?

7. Assume that you're starting a new restaurant that caters to college students and plan to use college students as servers. What human resource management problems would you expect to have? How could you build a strong organization culture in your restaurant to provide outstanding customer service?

8. Three approaches for motivating and coordinating employee activities are policies and supervision, incentives, and organization culture. What are the advantages and disadvantages of each?

9. Why should retailers be concerned about the needs of their employees? What can retailers do to satisfy these needs?

10. You've been promoted to manage a general merchandise discount store. Your assistant managers are an African-American male, a Hispanic male, a white female, and a female who has worked for the company for 35 years. What are the strengths of your management group, and what problems do you foresee arising?

11. What HR trends are helping meet employees' needs, increase job satisfaction, and lower turnover?

SUGGESTED READINGS

Bendapudi, Neeli. "Creating the Living Brand," *Harvard Business Review*, May 2005, pp. 124–31.

Burke, Ronald, and Cary Cooper (eds). *Reinventing Human Resource Management: Challenges and New Directions.* London: Routledge, 2005.

Duff, Mike. "Top-Shelf Employees Keep Container Store on Track," *DSN Retailing Today*, March 8, 2004, pp. 7–9.

Ivancevich, John. *Human Resource Management.* 9th ed. Boston: McGraw-Hill/Irwin, 2004.

Noe, Raymond; John Hollenbeck; Barry Gerhart; and Patrick Wright. *Human Resource Management.* 4th ed. Burr Ridge, IL: McGraw-Hill Irwin, 2003.

Reda, Susan. "Nice Guys Finish First," *Stores*, June 2004, pp. 28–31.

Rothwell, William. *Beyond Training and Development: The Groundbreaking Classic on Human Performance Enhancement.* 2nd ed. New York: American Management Association, 2005.

Silverthorne, Colin. *Organizational Psychology in Cross-Cultural Perspective.* New York: New York University Press, 2005.

"The 100 Best Companies to Work For," *Fortune*, January 10, 2005, pp. 148–68.

Information Systems and Supply Chain Management

EXECUTIVE BRIEFING

Jim LaBounty, Senior Vice President and
Director of Supply Chain Management,
JCPenney

Jim LaBounty (center) with Marie Lacertosa (left), Vice President and Director of Supply
Chain Operations, and Marice McNeal (right), Operations/Inventory Manager for the Alliance
Distribution Center near Fort Worth, Texas.

At JCPenney, I provide the strategic and operational leadership for managing the pipeline that moves merchandise from our vendors around the world to our stores and Internet/catalog customers. Over 8,000 Penney's associates and $1 billion in annual expenses are involved in these supply chain activities to ensure that we have the right product at the right place at the right time.

Before joining JCPenney, I served over 28 years in the U.S. Army. Prior to my retirement from the military, I was the Commander (CEO/COO) of the Defense Distribution Region West. I learned how to move people and material quickly and efficiently during my military career, but the most important thing I learned in the military was leadership—how to provide a vision of what needs to be done, organize and motivate people to do it effectively, and respond quickly to changes in the environment.

Shortly before I arrived at JCPenney in 2001, the company made a strategic decision to change its supply chain management approach from having vendors ship merchandise directly to stores (direct store delivery) to using distribution centers for storing inventory and consolidating merchandise for store shipments. The old approach got the merchandise to the stores slightly faster but resulted in excess inventory in the supply chain and greater labor costs. Store employees had to receive deliveries from a lot of different vendors and then get it ready to be displayed on the sales floor. We can do these "floor ready" activities much more efficiently in our distribution centers and have just one delivery to the store each day.

Even though most of what my colleagues and I do is behind the scenes, it's very important for us to visit the stores to understand how we can better service them.

CHAPTER 10

QUESTIONS

How do merchandise and information flow from the vendor to the retailer to consumers?

What information technology (IT) developments are facilitating vendor–retailer communications?

How do retailers and vendors collaborate to make sure the right merchandise is available when customers are ready to buy it?

What are the benefits to vendors and retailers of collaborating on supply chain management?

What is RFID, and how will it affect retailing?

For example, during some visits I made when I first joined Penney's, store associates told me they spent a lot of time taking plastic wrappers off apparel. The vendors wrap each garment in plastic so they will remain clean during shipment. A test we conducted revealed that we could take the plastic wrap off in the distribution center for all garments except suits and white apparel and the garments would remain clean. By removing the wrappers in the distribution centers, we saved a lot of labor hours for store associates, hours they now spend on providing customer service, and generated some revenue by gathering and recycling the plastic.

Retailing is an exciting business. New problems and challenges come up every day. One day we are helping a buyer get hot merchandise from China into our stores faster and the next day we have to deal with a longshoremen's strike at a major port. There's never a dull moment.

Joe Jackson wakes up in the morning, takes a shower, dresses, and goes to his kitchen to make a cup of coffee and toast a bagel. He slices the bagel and puts it in his toaster oven, and to his dismay, the toaster oven is not working. As he reads the newspaper and eats his untoasted bagel with his coffee, he notices that Target is having a sale on Michael Graves toaster ovens. The toaster ovens look great. So, on his way home from work, he stops at a Target store to buy one. He finds the advertised Michael Graves model on the shelf and buys it.

Joe expects to find a Michael Graves and other toaster oven models available at Target, but he probably doesn't realize that Target uses sophisticated information and supply chain management systems to make sure that the Michael Graves toaster ovens and other brands are available in stores whenever he and other customers want them. When Joe bought the toaster oven, the information about his transaction was automatically forwarded to computers at Target's regional distribution center, the home appliance planner at Target's corporate headquarters in Minneapolis, and the manufacturer in China. A computer information system monitors all toaster oven sales and inventory levels in every Target store and decides when to have toaster ovens shipped from the manufacturer in China to the regional distribution centers and then from the centers to the stores. Shipments to the distribution centers and stores are monitored using a satellite tracking system that locates the ships and trucks transporting the toaster ovens.

Of course, Target could ensure the availability of toaster ovens and other merchandise by simply keeping a large number of units in the stores at all times. But stocking a large number of each stock keeping unit (SKU) would require much more space to store the items and a significant investment in additional inventory. So the challenge for Target is to limit its inventory investment but still make sure products are always available when customers want them.

This chapter begins by outlining how retailers can gain a strategic advantage through supply chain management and information systems. Then the chapter describes supply chain information and product flows and the activities undertaken in distribution centers. Next it examines how vendors and retailers work together to efficiently manage the movement of merchandise from the vendor through the retailer's distribution centers to its stores. The chapter concludes with a discussion of a new technology, radio frequency identification (RFID), being used to improve supply chain efficiency.

CREATING STRATEGIC ADVANTAGE THROUGH SUPPLY MANAGEMENT AND INFORMATION SYSTEMS

As discussed in Chapter 1, retailers connect customers with vendors who provide the merchandise. It is the retailers' responsibility to gauge customers' wants and needs and work with the other members of the supply chain—distributors, vendors, and transportation companies—to make sure the merchandise that customers want is available when they want it. A simplified supply chain is illustrated in Exhibit 10–1. Vendors ship merchandise either to a **distribution center** operated by a retailer (as is the case for vendors V1 and V3) or directly to stores (as is the case for vendor V2). The relative advantages of shipping directly to stores versus to distribution centers are discussed later in this chapter.

EXHIBIT 10–1   Illustration of a Supply Chain

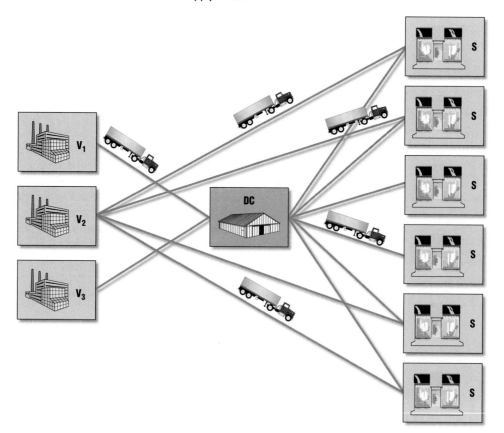

In a retailing context, **supply chain management** is the delivery of economic value to customers through the management of the flow of physical goods and associated information from vendors to customers.[1] Thus, supply chain management is a set of business activities that manages the movement of products to retail distribution centers and stores and the exchange of information between retailers and vendors.

Retailers are increasingly taking a leadership role in managing their respective supply chains. When retailers were predominantly small, family-owned businesses, larger manufacturers and distributors dictated when, where, and how merchandise was delivered. But with the consolidation and emergence of larger, national retail chains, retailers now play an active role in coordinating supply chain management activities. The size of these national retailers typically makes them more powerful than their vendors and thus better able to control their supply chains. In addition, retailers are more knowledgeable about their customers. They are in the unique position to collect purchase information customer by customer, transaction by transaction. As we will discuss later in the chapter, this information is being shared with suppliers to plan production, promotions, deliveries, assortments, and inventory levels.

Improved Product Availability

Efficient supply chain management provides two benefits to customers: (1) reduced stockouts, and (2) tailored assortments. These benefits translate into greater sales, lower costs, higher inventory turnover, and lower markdowns for retailers.

Reduced Stockouts A **stockout** occurs when an SKU that a customer wants is not available. What would happen if Joe went to the Target store and the store had stocked out of Michael Graves toaster ovens because the distribution center did not ship enough to the store? The store would give Joe a rain check so he could come back and still pay the sale price when the store received a new shipment, but Joe would have made a wasted trip to the store. As a result of the stockout, Joe might decide to buy another model, or he might go to a nearby Wal-Mart to buy a toaster oven. While at Wal-Mart, he could purchase other items in addition to the toaster oven. He also might be reluctant to shop at Target in the future and tell all of his friends about the negative experience he had. This bad experience could have been avoided if Target had done a better job of managing its supply chain.[2]

Tailored Assortments   Another benefit provided by information systems that support supply chain management is making sure that the right merchandise is available at the right store. National retail chains have long adjusted assortments in their stores on the basis of climate—stocking more wool sweaters in northern stores and cotton sweaters in southern stores during the winter. Now retailers use sophisticated statistical methods to analyze sales transaction data and adjust store assortments for a wide range of merchandise on the basis of the customer demand characteristics of the store's local market. For example, Meijer, a regional supercenter chain, analyzed its sales data and discovered that its private label water softening tablets sold well in some stores, but the national brands sold better in other stores. So it adjusted its private label stock to be higher in one set of stores.[4]

Higher Return on Investment

From the retailer's perspective, an efficient supply chain and information system can improve its return on investment because it increases sales, net profit margins, and assets (inventory turnover). Net sales increase because customers are offered more attractive assortments that are in stock. Consider Joe Jackson's toaster oven purchase. Target, with its excellent information systems, could accurately estimate

REFACT

Supermarkets lose 43 percent of intended purchases when a product is out of stock. Thirty-seven percent of shoppers go to another store, and 6 percent do not buy at all when confronted with a stockout.[3]

REFACT

Forty-six percent of shoppers have experienced empty shelves "often" or "sometimes" in their supermarkets.[5]

how many Michael Graves toaster ovens each store would sell during the special promotion. Using its supply management system, it made sure sufficient stock was available at Joe's store so all of the customers wanting to buy one could.

Net profit margin is improved by increasing the gross margin and lowering expenses. An information system that coordinates among the buying staff and vendors allows retailers to take advantage of special buying opportunities and obtain the merchandise at a lower cost, thus improving their gross margin. Retailers also can lower their operating expenses by coordinating deliveries, thus reducing transportation expenses. With more efficient distribution centers, merchandise can be received, prepared for sale, and shipped to stores with minimum handling, further reducing expenses.

By efficiently managing their supply chain, retailers can carry less backup inventory to stay in stock. Thus, inventory levels are lower, and with a lower inventory investment, the total assets are also lower, so the asset and inventory turnovers are both higher. Retailing View 10.1 describes how 7-Eleven is transforming its business operations through information technology.

Strategic Advantage

Of course, all retailers would strive to increase sales and reduce costs by using high-performance information systems and efficient supply chain management. But not all retailers can develop a competitive advantage from their information and supply chain systems. However, if they do develop an advantage, the advantage is sustainable; that is, it is difficult for competitors to duplicate. For

---

10.1   RETAILING VIEW   7-Eleven Serves a Big Gulp of Technology

By investing over $100 million in information technology, 7-Eleven, the Dallas-based convenience store chain, is redefining the convenience store concept. This ambitious makeover is powered by technology systems that, analysts say, rival those of Wal-Mart. The majority of 7-Eleven's technology investments focus on enhancing its proprietary retail information system. 7-Eleven's three objectives for these investments are to (1) automate and simplify store operations, (2) use technology to improve customer service and the customer experience, and (3) deliver quality information across the different areas of the business to enable fact-based decision making.

7-Eleven is emerging as a leader in efficient supply chain management, matching customer demand with supply and weeding out slow-moving items in favor of fast-moving SKUs. Information technology is enabling 7-Eleven to transform its business. Now store managers can reorder fresh foods in the morning and replenish their shelves that night. Using the company's sophisticated systems, store managers know what's selling, item-by-item and hour-by-hour. They can monitor customers' buying patterns, react to changing weather forecasts, and capitalize on neighborhood happenings. For example, a store manager who finds out on Thursday about the local high school's "big game" can have enough soda and hot dogs to satisfy customers by kick-off Friday night.

7-Eleven's Retail Information System collects data from POS terminals and transmits it in real time to a data warehouse (a data warehouse is a collection of databases and mechanisms to access the data designed to support decision making in organizations). The data are analyzed to better understand customer preferences, pricing, and new product launches. The system not only improves in-stock performance, it also allows

Shelves at 7-Eleven are replenished frequently with the best-selling merchandise based on local customer buying patterns.

entrepreneurial-minded store managers to tailor their assortments in an effort to maximize sales. "It's about giving those in the stores the ability to make decisions rather than having decisions made for them by someone off in an ivory tower," says Keith Morrow, 7-Eleven's CIO. "They're the ones listening to and interacting with the customer. Our goal is to provide the information they need at the time they need it to make decisions store by store and item by item."

Sources: Susan Reda, "Slurpee Power: 7-Eleven Serves Convenience with a Big Gulp of Technology," *Stores*, May 2005, pp. 23–27; Christopher Koch, "Who's Minding the Store?" *CIO*, May 15, 2005, pp. 1–6.

example, a critical factor in Wal-Mart's success is its information and supply chain management systems. Even though competitors recognize this advantage, they have difficulty achieving the same level of performance as Wal-Mart's systems for two reasons. First, Wal-Mart has made a substantial investment in developing its systems and has the scale economies to justify this investment. Second, its systems are not simply some software any firm can buy from a supplier. Through experience and learning, small changes are always being made to improve the performance of these systems. In addition, the effective use of these systems requires the coordinated effort of employees and functional areas throughout the company.

To illustrate the complexity of the tasks performed by these systems and the need for coordinated efforts, consider the various factors that can cause stockouts, as shown below:[7]

Store forecasting (ineffective algorithms, long forecasting cycles)	33%
Store stocking (inadequate/incorrect shelf space, shelf stocking frequency, congested backroom)	22%
Store ordering (late/no orders, inappropriate replenishment intervals)	18%
Management errors (last-minute price/promotion decisions, inaccurate/obsolete product information)	13%
Warehousing (poor ordering policies, data accuracy)	11%
Manufacturer availability (packaging/raw materials, capacity issues)	3%

To minimize stockouts, retailers need to forecast demand accurately. But they also need to make sure the merchandise in the store's stockroom is put on the shelves in the right place; buyers place orders with vendors at the right time; the stores place accurate, timely orders with the distribution center; the distribution center sends the right merchandise quantities to the stores; and the marketing managers provide enough lead time for the delivery of merchandise subject to special sales and promotional materials.

The complexities of the merchandise and information flows in a typical multi-store chain are illustrated in Exhibit 10–2. Although information and merchandise flows are intertwined, in the following sections, we describe first how information about customer demand is captured at the store, which triggers a series of

REFACT

The retail industry spends $20 billion annually on software.[6]

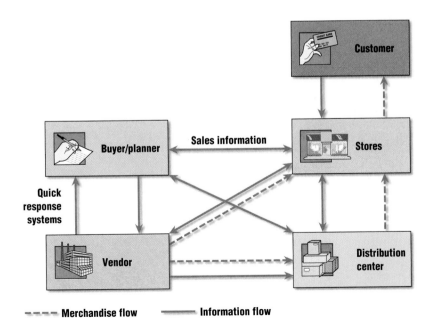

EXHIBIT 10–2
Information and Merchandise Flows

responses from buyers and planners, distribution centers, and vendors that is designed to ensure that merchandise is available at the store when the customer wants it. Then, we discuss the physical movement of merchandise from vendors through distribution centers to the stores.

INFORMATION FLOWS

When Joe Jackson bought his toaster oven at Target, he initiated the following information flows illustrated in Exhibit 10–3 (the numbers in parentheses refer to the path in the exhibit):

The Target cashier scans the **Universal Product Code (UPC)** tag on the toaster oven box (1), and a sales receipt is generated for Joe. The UPC tag is a black-and-white bar code containing a 13-digit code that indicates the manufacturer of the item, a description of the item, and information about special packaging, such as cents-off promotions.[8] The codes for all products are issued by GS1 US (www.gs1us.org), formerly the Uniform Code Council.

The information about the transaction is captured at the point-of-sale (POS) terminal and sent to Target's computer system, where it can be accessed by the planner for the toaster oven product category (2). The planner uses this information to monitor and analyze sales and decide to reorder more toaster ovens or reduce their prices if sales are below expectations.

The sales transaction data also are sent to the distribution center (6). When the store inventory drops to a specified level, more toaster ovens are shipped to the store, and the shipment information is sent to the Target computer system (5) so the planner knows the inventory level that remains in the distribution center.

When the inventory drops to a specified level in the distribution center (4), the planner negotiates terms and shipping dates and places an order with the manufacturer of the toaster ovens. The planner then informs the distribution centers about the new order and when they can expect delivery (5).

When the manufacturer ships the toaster ovens to the Target distribution centers, it sends an advanced shipping notice to the distribution centers (7). An **advanced shipping notice (ASN)** is a document that tells the distribution center what specifically is being shipped and when it will be delivered. The distribution center then makes appointments for trucks to make the delivery at a specific time, date, and loading dock.

REFACT

By analyzing its customer database, Wal-Mart knows that sales of strawberry Pop Tarts increase by 700 percent in areas facing the arrival of a hurricane.[9]

EXHIBIT 10–3
Information Flows

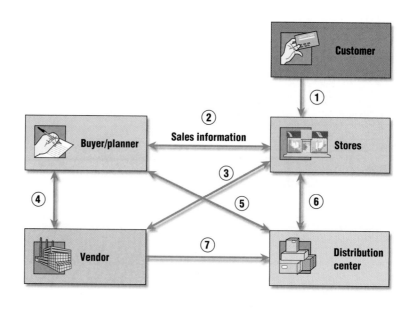

When the shipment is received at the distribution center, the planner is notified (5) and then authorizes payment to the vendor.

In some situations that will be discussed later in the chapter, the sales transaction data are sent directly from the store to the vendor (3), and the vendor decides when to ship more merchandise to the distribution centers and stores. In other situations, especially when merchandise is reordered frequently, the ordering process is done automatically, bypassing the planners.[10]

Data Warehouse

Purchase data collected at the point of sale goes into a huge database known as a data warehouse. The information stored in the data warehouse is accessible on various dimensions and levels, as depicted in the data cube in Exhibit 10–4.

As shown on the horizontal axis, data can be accessed according to the level of merchandise aggregation—SKU (item), vendor, category (dresses), department (women's apparel), or all merchandise. Along the vertical axis, data can be accessed by level of the company—store, division, or the total company. Finally, along the third dimension, data can be accessed by point in time—day, season, or year.

The CEO might be interested in how the corporation is generally doing and could look at the data aggregated by quarter for a merchandise division, a region of the country, or the total corporation. A buyer may be more interested in a particular vendor in a certain store on a particular day. Analysts from various levels of the retail operation extract information from the data warehouse to make a plethora of marketing decisions about developing and replenishing merchandise assortments.

Data warehouses also contain detailed information about customers, which is used to target promotions and group products together in stores. These applications are discussed in Chapter 11.

REFACT
Shortly after 8:00 a.m. on June 26, 1974, the first UPC tag was scanned in Troy, Ohio, when Clyde Dawson bought a ten-pack of Wrigley's Juicy Fruit gum for 67 cents in a Marsh Supermarket. Now, over 10 billion items are scanned each day.[11]

Retail Data Warehouse   **EXHIBIT 10–4**

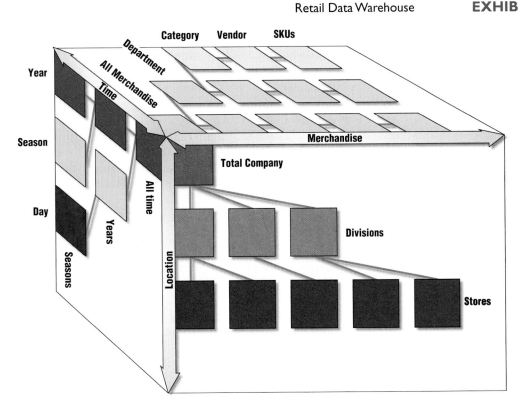

SOURCE: SAS Retail.

Electronic Data Interchange

In the past, the information flows described above were accomplished by sending handwritten or typed documents through the mail or by fax. Now most communications between vendors and retailers occur via electronic data interchange. **Electronic data interchange (EDI)** is the computer-to-computer exchange of business documents in a structured format, which means that the data transmissions use a standard format to communicate the data. For example, specific symbols are used to delineate the purchase order number, the vendor's name, the address the merchandise is being shipped to, and so forth.

Standards   In the retail industry, two data transmission standards are used: (1) the Uniform Communication Standard (UCS), used primarily by the grocery sector, and (2) the Voluntary Interindustry Commerce Standard (VICS), used by the general merchandise retailing sector. Using these standards, retailers and vendors can exchange information about purchase order changes, order status, transportation routings, advance shipping notices, on-hand inventory status, and vendor promotions, as well as information that enables vendors to put price tags on merchandise. The development and use of these standards is critical to the use of EDI because they enable all retailers to use the same format when transmitting data to their vendors.[12]

Transmission Systems   In larger retail firms, communications among employees within a company, such as the communications between store managers, planners, and distribution center employees, are done through an intranet. An **intranet** is a local area network (LAN) that employs Internet technology in an organization to facilitate communication and access to information internally.

To communicate with people outside the organization, such as vendors and transportation companies, large retailers like Wal-Mart initially developed their own propriety transmission systems. But now EDI transmissions between retailers and vendors occur over the Internet through extranets. An **extranet** is a collaborative network that uses Internet technology to link businesses with their suppliers, customers, or other businesses. Extranets are typically private and secure and can be accessed only by authorized parties.

An extranet is generally an extension of a company's intranet, modified to allow access to specified external users. The shift from a propriety transmission network to Internet-based networks enables small retailers and vendors to take advantage of EDI economically. For example, Target Corporation has shifted its propriety EDI network to an extranet system called Partners Online, and Wal-Mart's extranet is called Retail Link. These companies make certain time-sensitive procedures, confidential information, and general supplier information, such as shipping requirements and prerequisites for packing cartons, available to vendors via the extranet.

Security   Because the Internet is a publicly accessible network, its use to communicate internally and externally with vendors and customers raises security issues. Some potential implications of security failures are the loss of business data essential to conducting business, disputes with vendors and customers, loss of public confidence and its effect on brand image, bad publicity, and the loss of revenue from customers using an electronic channel.[13]

Security has become a bigger challenge in recent years as a result of EDI using extranets and the operation of Internet retail channels. Now vendors and customers all need some form of access to the retailer's information system. In addition, the control of retail information is slipping away from centralized information systems to systems housed in the functional areas of the business, such as buying and distribution.

To help control this changing information environment, retailers have incorporated security policies. A **security policy** is the set of rules that apply to activities involving computer and communications resources that belong to an organization. However, in addition to instituting these policies, retailers train employees and add the necessary software and hardware to enforce the rules. The objectives of the security policy are:

- *Authentication.* The system assures or verifies that the person or computer at the other end of the session really is who or what it claims to be.
- *Authorization.* The system assures that the person or computer at the other end of the session has permission to carry out the request.
- *Integrity.* The system assures that the arriving information is the same as that sent, which means that the data have been protected from unauthorized changes or tampering (data integrity).

Benefits of EDI   The use of EDI provides three main benefits to retailers and their vendors. First, EDI reduces cycle time, or the time between the decision to place an order and the receipt of merchandise. Information just flows quicker using EDI, which means that inventory turnover is higher. Second, EDI improves the overall quality of communications through better record keeping; fewer errors in inputting order, order receipt, and ASNs; and less human error in the interpretation of data. Third, the data transmitted by EDI are in a computer-readable format that can be easily analyzed and used for a variety of tasks ranging from evaluating vendor delivery performance to automating reorder processes.

Due to these benefits, many retailers are asking their vendors to interface with them using EDI. However, small-to medium-sized vendors and retailers face significant barriers, specifically, cost and the lack of information technology (IT) expertise, to become EDI enabled. For example, in late 2003, Greg Kieler, co-president of Worktools International, an $8 million specialty paintbrush company, got a letter from Lowe's requesting that his firm adopt a new EDI system that would let Lowe's track inventory more easily. Worktools' deadline: April 2005. This notification presented a challenge because Worktools doesn't have an IT department, and none of its 40 employees has real computer expertise. But Kieler didn't have a choice; Lowe's is his largest customer.

Kieler hired consultants that had worked with Lowe's. They upgraded Worktools' software, charging a $1,000 set-up fee and $125 a month in ongoing support. Worktools also paid $600 a year to have its products listed in UCCnet, a registry run by the Uniform Code Council. When Lowe's went live with the system, Kieler was ready. "Now we hopefully have an inside track on making Lowe's happy," he says.[14]

Pull and Push Supply Chains

Information flows such as that described above illustrate a **pull supply chain**—a supply chain in which orders for merchandise are generated at the store level on the basis of sales data captured by POS terminals. Basically, in this type of supply chain, the demand for an item pulls it though the supply chain. An alternative and less sophisticated approach is a **push supply chain,** in which merchandise is allocated to stores on the basis of forecasted demand. Once a forecast is developed, specified quantities of merchandise are shipped (pushed) to distribution centers and stores at predetermined time intervals.

Because inventory at the store is based on consumer demand, in a pull supply chain, there is less likelihood of being overstocked or out of stock. Also, a pull approach increases inventory turnover and is more responsive to changes in customer demand. A pull approach becomes even more efficient than a push approach when demand is uncertain and difficult to forecast.

Although generally more desirable, a pull approach is not the most effective in all situations.[15] First, a pull approach requires a more costly and sophisticated information system to support it. Second, for some merchandise, retailers do not have the flexibility to adjust inventory levels on the basis of demand. For example, commitments must be made months in advance for fashion and private label apparel. Since these commitments cannot be easily changed, the merchandise has to be preallocated to the stores at the time the orders are formulated. Third, push supply chains are efficient for merchandise that has steady, predictable demand, such as milk and eggs, basic men's underwear, and bath towels. Because both pull and push supply chains have their advantages, most retailers use a combination of these approaches.

THE PHYSICAL FLOW OF MERCHANDISE—LOGISTICS

Exhibit 10–5 illustrates the physical flow of merchandise within the supply chain:

1. Merchandise flows from vendor to distribution center.
2. Merchandise goes from distribution center to stores.
3. Alternatively, merchandise can go from vendor directly to stores.

REFACT

Logistics accounts for about 10 percent of the U.S. gross domestic product.[17]

Logistics is the aspect of supply chain management that refers to the planning, implementation, and control of the efficient flow and storage of goods, services, and related information from the point of origin to the point of consumption to meet customers' requirements.[16] In addition to managing the inbound and outbound transportation, logistics involves the activities undertaken in the retailer's distribution center. For example, sometimes merchandise is temporarily stored at the distribution center; other times it is immediately prepared for shipment to individual stores. This preparation may include breaking received shipping cartons into smaller quantities that can be more readily utilized by the individual stores (breaking bulk), as well as affixing price tags or stickers, UPC codes, and the store's label.

Distribution Centers versus Direct Store Delivery

As indicated in Exhibit 10–5, retailers can have merchandise shipped directly to their stores—direct store delivery (path 3)—or to their distribution centers (paths 1 and 2). The appropriate decision depends on the characteristics of the merchandise and the nature of demand. To determine which distribution system—distribution

EXHIBIT 10–5
Merchandise Flow

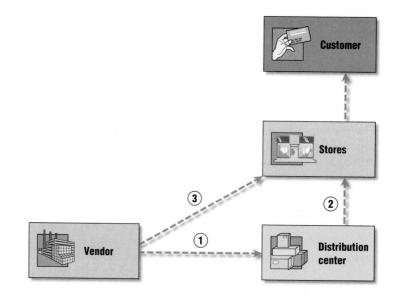

centers or direct store delivery—is better, retailers consider the total cost associated with each alternative and the customer service criterion of having the right merchandise at the store when the customer wants to buy it.

There are several advantages to using a distribution center:

• More accurate sales forecasts are possible when retailers combine forecasts for many stores serviced by one distribution center rather than doing a forecast for each store. Consider a set of 50 Target stores, serviced by a single distribution center, that each carry Michael Graves toasters. Each store normally stocks 5 units for a total of 250 units in the system. By carrying the item at each store, the retailer must develop 50 individual forecasts, each with the possibility of errors that could result in either too much or too little merchandise. Alternatively, by delivering most of the inventory to a distribution center and feeding the stores additional toasters as they need them, the effects of forecast errors for the individual stores are minimized, and less backup inventory is needed to prevent stockouts.

• Distribution centers enable the retailer to carry less merchandise in the individual stores, which results in lower inventory investments systemwide. If the stores get frequent deliveries from the distribution center, they need to carry relatively less extra merchandise as backup stock.

• It's easier to avoid running out of stock or having too much stock in any particular store since merchandise is ordered from the distribution center as needed.

• Retail store space is typically much more expensive than space at a distribution center, and distribution centers are better equipped than stores to prepare merchandise for sale. As a result, many retailers find it cost effective to store merchandise and get it ready for sale at a distribution center rather than in individual stores.

But distribution centers aren't appropriate for all retailers. If a retailer has only a few outlets, the expense of a distribution center is probably unwarranted. Also, if many outlets are concentrated in metropolitan areas, merchandise can be consolidated and delivered by the vendor directly to all the stores in one area economically. Finally, direct store delivery gets merchandise to the stores faster and thus is used for perishable goods (meat and produce), items that help create the retailer's image of being the first to sell the latest product (e.g., video games), or fads. For example, by developing a supply chain that bypasses the distribution center, ProFlowers reduced the delivery time from flower cutting to store delivery from 12 to 3 days.[18]

Thus, the types of retail stores that are most efficiently supplied through distribution centers are those:

• Selling nonperishable merchandise.

• Offering merchandise that has highly uncertain demand, such as fashionable apparel, because more accurate sales forecasts are possible when demand from many stores is aggregated at distribution centers.

• Selling merchandise that needs to be replenished frequently, like grocery items, because a direct store delivery system requires stores to spend too much time receiving and processing deliveries from many vendors.

• That carry a relatively large number of items that are shipped to stores in less than full-case quantities, such as drug stores.

• With a large number of outlets that aren't geographically concentrated within a metropolitan area but are within 150 to 200 miles of a distribution center.

Some vendors provide direct store delivery for retailers to ensure that their products are on the store's shelves, properly displayed, and fresh. For example,

REFACT

About half of a video game's sales are made within three days of its release, and 70 percent are rung up within the first week.[19]

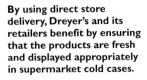

By using direct store delivery, Dreyer's and its retailers benefit by ensuring that the products are fresh and displayed appropriately in supermarket cold cases.

employees delivering Frito-Lay snacks directly to supermarkets replace products that have been on the shelf too long and are stale, replenish products that have been sold, and arrange products so they are neatly displayed.

THE DISTRIBUTION CENTER

The distribution center performs the following activities: coordinating inbound transportation; receiving, checking, storing, and crossdocking; getting merchandise "floor-ready"; and coordinating outbound transportation.[20] To illustrate these activities being undertaken in a distribution center, consider a shipment of Sony MP3 players arriving at a Sears distribution center.

Activities Managed by Distribution Centers

Management of Inbound Transportation   Traditionally, buyers focused their efforts when working with vendors on developing merchandise assortments, negotiating prices, and arranging joint promotions. Now, buyers and planners are much more involved in coordinating the physical flow of merchandise to the stores. The Sears MP3 buyer has arranged for a truckload of MP3 players to be delivered to its Warren, Ohio, distribution center on Monday between 1:00 and 3:00 p.m. The buyer also specifies how the merchandise should be placed on pallets for easy unloading.

The truck must arrive within the specified time because the distribution center has all of its 100 receiving docks allocated throughout the day, and much of the merchandise on this particular truck is going to be shipped to stores that evening. Unfortunately, the truck was delayed in a snow storm. The **dispatcher**—the person who coordinates deliveries to the distribution center—reassigns the Sony truck to a Wednesday morning delivery slot and charges the firm several hundred dollars for missing its delivery time. Although many manufacturers pay transportation expenses, some retailers negotiate with their vendors to absorb this expense. These retailers believe they can lower their net merchandise cost and better control merchandise flow if they negotiate directly with trucking companies and consolidate shipments from many vendors.

Receiving and Checking   **Receiving** is the process of recording the receipt of merchandise as it arrives at a distribution center. **Checking** is the process of going through the goods upon receipt to make sure they arrived undamaged and that the merchandise ordered was the merchandise received.

In the past, checking merchandise was a very labor-intensive and time-consuming process. Today, however, many distribution systems using EDI are designed to minimize, if not eliminate, these processes. The advance shipping notice tells the distribution center what should be in each carton. A UPC label on the shipping carton that identifies the carton's contents and the number of each type of Sony MP3 player is scanned and automatically counted as it is being received and checked.

Storing and Crossdocking   After the merchandise is received and checked, it is either stored or crossdocked. When merchandise is stored, the cartons are transported by a conveyor system and forklift trucks to racks that go from the distribution center's floor to its ceiling. Then, when the merchandise is needed in the stores, a forklift driver goes to the rack, picks up the carton, and places it on a conveyor system that routes the carton to the loading dock of a truck going to the store.

Merchandise cartons that are **crossdocked** are prepackaged by the vendor for a specific store. The UPC labels on the carton indicate the store to which it is to be sent. The vendor also may affix price tags to each item in the carton. Since the merchandise is ready for sale, it is placed on a conveyor system that routes it from the unloading dock at which it was received to the loading dock for the truck going to the specific store. The cartons are routed on the conveyor system automatically by sensors that read the UPC label on the cartons. Crossdocked merchandise is only in the distribution center for a few hours before it is shipped to the stores.

Merchandise size and the sales rate typically determine whether cartons are crossdocked or stored. For instance, due to their small size, MP3 players are shipped in cartons with 48 players, but a Sears store can only display and hold 12 players at a time. So the Sony MP3 player shipment needs to be stored in a "break pack" area where the carton of 48 players is opened and 12 players are removed, put in another carton with other items being sent to the store, and sent to the specific Sears store. However, the Sears MP3 buyer might negotiate with Sony to have MP3 players shipped to Sears distribution centers in cartons of 12 units so they could be crossdocked, thus avoiding the additional cost of breaking the carton and repacking them.

REFACT

Crossdocking can cut 35 to 45 cents off a vendor's total cost of 60 to 70 cents per case to deliver products to a supermarket chain.[21]

Getting Merchandise Floor Ready For some merchandise, additional tasks are undertaken in the distribution center to make the merchandise floor ready. **Floor-ready merchandise** is merchandise that is ready to be placed on the selling floor. Getting merchandise floor ready entails ticketing, marking, and, in the case of some apparel, placing garments on hangers.

Ticketing and marking refers to affixing price and identification labels to the merchandise. It is more efficient for a retailer to perform these activities at a distribution center than in its stores. In a distribution center, an area can be set aside and a process implemented to efficiently add labels and put apparel on hangers. Conversely, getting merchandise floor ready in stores can block aisles and divert salespeople's attention from their customers. An even better approach from the retailer's perspective is to get vendors to ship floor-ready merchandise, thus totally eliminating the expensive, time-consuming ticketing and marking process.

Preparing to Ship Merchandise to a Store At the beginning of the day, the computer system in the distribution center generates a list of items to be shipped to each store on that day. For each item, a pick ticket and shipping label is generated. The **pick ticket** is a document or display on a screen in a forklift truck indicating how much of each item to get from specific storage areas. The forklift driver goes to the storage area, picks up the number of cartons indicated on the pick ticket, places UPC shipping labels on the cartons indicating the stores to which the items are to be shipped, and puts the cartons on the conveyor system, where they are automatically routed to the loading dock for the truck going to the stores.

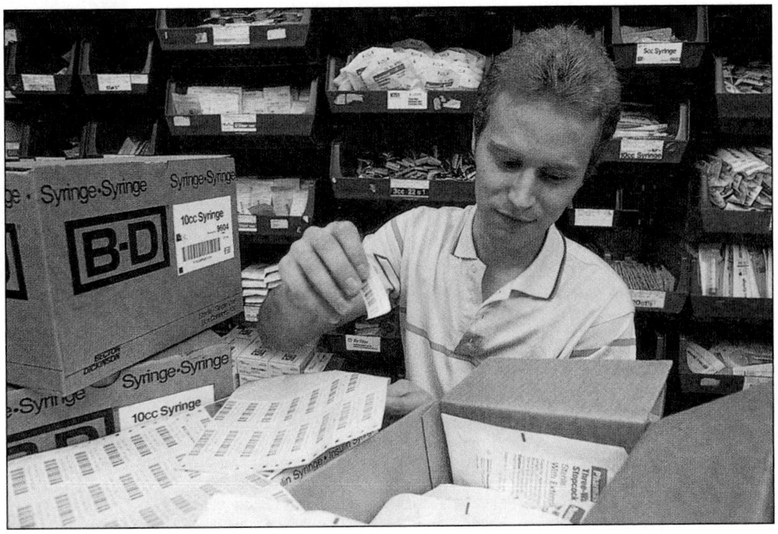

An important activity undertaken in distribution centers is ticketing and marketing merchandise so it is "floor ready."

Pick tickets and labels are also generated for the break pack area. In the break pack area, the number of items for a store are selected by employees from the open cartons and put into a new carton. Then shipping labels indicating the store destinations are attached to the cartons, and the cartons are placed on the conveyor system and routed to the appropriate loading dock.

So the conveyor system feeds cartons from three sources to the loading dock for a truck going to a specific store: (1) crossdocked cartons directly from the vendor's delivery trucks, (2) cartons stored in the distribution center, and (3) cartons from the break pack area. These cartons are then loaded onto the trucks by employees.

Management of Outbound Transportation   The management of outbound transportation from distribution center to stores has become increasingly complex. Most distribution centers run 50–100 outbound truck routes in one day. To handle this complex transportation problem, the centers use sophisticated routing and scheduling computer systems that consider the locations of the stores, road conditions, and transportation operating constraints to develop the most efficient routes possible. As a result, stores are provided with an accurate estimated time of arrival, and vehicle utilization is maximized.

Retailing View 10.2 describes these activities in Wal-Mart's distribution centers.

10.2   RETAILING VIEW   Wal-Mart's Muscle: Its Distribution Centers

The untold story behind Wal-Mart's success is a squat, gray building on the outskirts of Bentonville, Arkansas. Wal-Mart Distribution Center (DC) No. 6094 is dedicated to replenishing the general merchandise of 120 stores, primarily across Arkansas, Missouri, and Oklahoma. At 1.2 million square feet, DC No. 6094 stores more than $55 million in merchandise of 50,000 items. The receiving, processing, and shipping operations that occur there are repeated at 173 other facilities the world over.

Whereas founder Sam Walton used to transport merchandise from the DCs to the stores in his own station wagon, DC No. 6094 dispatches and receives 200–250 trucks daily. Lower-volume stores receive four or five truckloads of merchandise in a week, while busy stores may receive that many in a single day. Wal-Mart's DCs ship more than 2.5 billion cartons annually. Wal-Mart also maintains four DCs for imports.

Half of the merchandise that DC No. 6094 processes is crossdocked and ships out less than 24 hours after it arrives. The other half, called "pull stock," is stored at the DC. Eighty-five percent of the pull stock is processed through the facility's approximately 20 miles worth of conveyors. Automated, conveyor-mounted shoes push cartons off the lane and down one of the facility's 100 chutes to a waiting truck at a rate of 200 cartons per minute.

The remaining 15 percent of pull stock consists of "non-conveyables": merchandise that is too bulky to be carried on the conveyors, such as Christmas trees or home gyms. These are transported to the waiting trucks by forklift. A voice-based guidance system directs the forklift drivers to the right trucking bay. The drivers can typically operate their battery-powered forklifts six to eight hours between charges.

Less than 10 percent of the pull stock is break pack merchandise. For efficiency and ergonomic reasons, merchandise at the break pack area is segregated by product category. The fastest-moving merchandise is stored at waist level so workers don't have to stretch or bend any more than is necessary. Wal-Mart's famed thriftiness can be seen on every break pack carton the DC ships: On each cardboard carton is printed a reminder for the store associates: "This box cost Wal-Mart 75¢ to

State-of-the-art technology helps move merchandise efficiently through Wal-Mart's 80 distribution centers, keeping its 8,000 stores well stocked.

make." Store associates are encouraged to return the boxes to the DC so they can be reused in the break pack area.

Source: Dan Scheraga, "Distribution Centers: Wal-Mart's Muscle," *Stores*, June 2005, pp. 34–36.

Reverse Logistics

Reverse logistics is the flow of returned merchandise back through the channel, from the customer back to the stores, distribution centers, and vendors. Reverse logistics can be an important issue. For instance, returns of apparel bought from catalogs range from 12 to 35 percent of sales, depending on the product's characteristics.[22] Tailored, fashion-forward apparel has a higher return rate than does traditional casual apparel.

Reverse logistics systems are challenging. The returned items may be damaged or lack the original shipping carton and thus require special handling. Transportation costs can be high because items are shipped back in small quantities.

To recover the cost of returned merchandise, Sears and other retailers sell returned merchandise through online auctions.[24] Sears has sold thousands of items at auction on eBay and recovered an average of two to three times more than it would have using other liquidation channels. A third-party distribution facilitator, Genco Distribution Systems, collects the merchandise to be auctioned from Sears, inspects it, and, following criteria set by Sears, lists the items on eBay without identifying the Sears brand name. After the auction, Genco packs and ships the merchandise to the consumer.

REFACT

Returns cost retailers from .2 to 25 percent of their sales.[23]

Logistics for Fulfilling Catalog and Internet Orders

Fulfilling Internet and catalog orders from customers is very different than distributing merchandise to stores. The typical retail distribution center is designed to ship a large number of cartons in truckloads to a relatively small number of stores. These distribution centers typically have automated material-handling equipment and warehouse-management software. In contrast, when fulfilling orders from individual consumers, retailers ship small packages with one or two items to a large number of different places. Thus, a completely different distribution center design is required for supplying Internet and catalog channels compared with that for a store channel.

Catalog retailers use distribution centers designed to pick and pack orders for individual consumers. Traditional store-based retailers, as they evolve into multichannel retailers, have had to either redesign their distribution centers or outsource the fulfillment. Some multichannel retailers, like Staples, use different distribution centers to service stores and Internet and catalog customers. Sharper Image, which started as a catalog merchant and now operates almost 100 stores in the United States, uses one distribution center to service all three retail formats. Borders is partnering with Amazon.com to assist it with its online fulfillment needs.

Amazon.com is so efficient at fulfilling orders for shipment to individual customers that it provides this function for other retailers.

Outsourcing Logistics

To streamline their operations and make more productive use of their assets and personnel, retailers consider **outsourcing** logistical functions if those functions can be performed better or less expensively by third-party logistics companies. **Third-party logistics companies** are firms that facilitate the movement of merchandise from manufacturer to retailer but are independently owned. Specifically, they provide transportation, warehousing, consolidation of orders, and documentation.

Transportation   Retailers are careful in choosing their shippers. They demand reliable, customized services because, to a large extent, the retailer's cycle time and its variations are determined by the transportation company. Also, many retailers are finding that it is worth the added cost of airfreight to get merchandise into stores quicker.

One cost advantage of independent transportation companies is they are better able to fill trucks on the return trip (backhaul) than the retailer. By arranging a productive round-trip, they can offer their services at a lower cost than most retailers can achieve themselves.

Some retailers mix modes of transportation to reduce overall costs and time delays. For example, many Japanese shippers send Europe-bound cargo by ship to the U.S. West Coast. From there, the cargo is flown to its final destination in Europe. By combining the two modes of transport, sea and air, the entire trip takes about two weeks, as opposed to four or five weeks with an all-water route, and the cost is about half that of an all-air route.

Warehousing   To meet the increasingly stringent demands retailers are placing on their vendors to meet specific delivery times for floor-ready merchandise, many vendors must store merchandise close to their retail customers. Rather than owning these warehouses themselves, vendors typically use **public warehouses** that are owned and operated by a third party. By using public warehouses, vendors can provide their retailers with the level of service demanded without having to invest in warehousing facilities.

Freight Forwarders   **Freight forwarders** are companies that purchase transport services. They then consolidate small shipments from a number of shippers into large shipments that move at a lower freight rate. These companies offer shippers lower rates than the shippers could obtain directly from transportation companies because small shipments generally cost more per pound to transport than do large shipments.[25]

One of the most daunting tasks for a retailer involved in importing merchandise to the United States is government bureaucracy. International freight forwarders not only purchase transportation services but also prepare and expedite all documentation, such as government-required export declarations and consular and shipping documents.

Integrated Third-Party Logistics Services   Traditional definitions distinguishing among transportation, warehousing, and freight forwarding have become blurred in recent years. Some of the best transportation firms, for example, now provide public warehousing and freight forwarding. The same diversification strategy is being used by other types of third-party logistics providers. Retailers are finding this one-stop shopping quite useful.

COLLABORATION BETWEEN RETAILERS AND VENDORS IN SUPPLY CHAIN MANAGEMENT

As we discussed previously, retailers' and vendors' objectives for supply chain management are to make sure that merchandise is available in the stores when customers want it (minimize stockouts) and to accomplish this task with the minimum investment in inventory and costs. Supply chain efficiency dramatically improves when vendors and retailers share information and work together. By collaborating, vendors can plan their purchases of raw materials and production process to match the retailer's merchandise needs. Thus vendors can make sure that the merchandise is available "just in time," when the retailer needs it, without having to stock excessive inventory in the vendor's warehouse or the retailer's distribution centers or stores.

When retailers and vendors do not coordinate their supply chain management activities, excess inventory builds up in the system even if the retail sales rate for the merchandise is relatively constant. This buildup of inventory in an uncoordinated channel is called the **bullwhip effect.** The effect was first discovered by Procter & Gamble, which saw that its orders from retailers for Pampers disposable diapers were shaped like a bullwhip even though retail sales were relatively constant (see Exhibit 10–6). Since it is more cost effective for Procter & Gamble to manufacture disposable diapers at a continuous rate, the company or its retailers had to maintain an inventory of a lot of diapers to meet the "irregular" demand it saw.[26]

Research has found that the bullwhip effect in an *uncoordinated supply chain* is caused by the following factors:

* *Delays in transmitting orders and receiving merchandise.* Even when retailers can forecast sales accurately, there are delays in getting orders to the vendor and receiving those orders from the vendor. In an uncoordinated supply chain, retailers might not know how fast they can get the merchandise, and thus, they overorder to prevent stockouts. When the retailers overorder, the vendors think demand is higher than it really is, and they overproduce.

* *Overreacting to shortages.* When retailers find it difficult to get the merchandise they want, they begin to play the shortage game. They order more than they need to prevent stockouts, hoping they will receive a larger partial shipment. These overorders again lead the vendor to think demand is higher than it really is.

* *Ordering in batches.* Rather than generating a number of small orders, retailers wait and place larger orders to reduce order processing and transportation costs and take advantage of quantity discounts. This ordering pattern leads the vendor to think that sales are more irregular than they really are.

These factors cause the bullwhip effect even when sales are fairly constant. However, for many retailers, sales are not constant; they go up dramatically when retailers put merchandise on sale and during special gift-giving times of the year. These irregularities in sales heighten the bullwhip effect and the buildup of inventory in the supply chain.

Vendors and retailers have found that by working together they can reduce the level of inventory in the supply chain and the number of stockouts in the stores. Four approaches for coordinating supply chain activities, in order of the level of collaboration, are (1) using EDI; (2) exchanging information; (3) using vendor-managed inventory; and (4) employing collaborative planning,

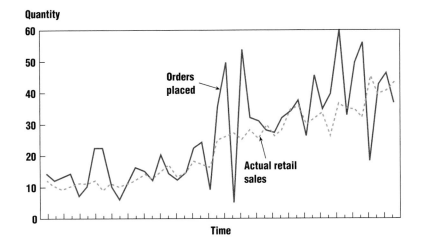

EXHIBIT 10–6
Bullwhip Effect in an Uncoordinated Supply Chain

forecasting, and replenishment (CPFR).[27] Retailing View 10.3 describes the historical forces motivating retailers and vendors to collaborate on supply chain management.

Using EDI

The use of EDI to transmit purchase order information reduces the time it takes for retailers to place orders and for vendors to acknowledge the receipt of orders and communicate delivery information about those orders. In addition, EDI facilitates the implementation of other collaborative approaches discussed in the following sections. However, the use of EDI without other collaborative approaches only addresses one factor discussed previously, the delay in transmitting and receiving orders, that causes the buildup of inventory in the supply chain.

Sharing Information

One of the major factors causing excessive inventory in the supply chain is the inability of vendors to know what the actual level of retail store sales are. If vendors knew that sales were increasing, they could produce more merchandise and prevent shortages and stockouts. With information that sales are decreasing, vendors could cut back on production and prevent excessive inventory buildup.[28]

Wal-Mart's Retail Link is a data warehouse and decision support system that provides vendors with a two-year sales history and inventory levels for each of their products in each of Wal-Mart's 5,000 stores worldwide. The data warehouse

---

10.3   RETAILING VIEW   Quick Response and Efficient Consumer Response (ECR)

Retailer–vendor collaboration in supply chain management grew out of activities undertaken by apparel manufacturers and retailers, called quick response (QR), and consumer package goods (CPG) manufacturers and supermarket retailers, called efficient consumer response (ECR). In the mid-1980s, Milliken, a U.S. textile manufacturer facing severe price competition from imports, developed a strategy to compete on its speed to market rather than price. At the time, it took 66 weeks for the apparel industry to go from yarn at the manufacturer to clothing on a retail store fixture. But since no one in the supply chain knew what would be selling in a month, much less a year, the cost of that lengthy supply cycle was devastating. The apparel industry as a whole lost billions of dollars each year through price reductions on items customers didn't want and because they did not have enough of what they did want.

To address this supply chain inefficiency, Milliken joined with The Warren Featherbone Company, a children's apparel maker, and Mercantile Stores, a large retail chain, to compete through what they called quick response. Quick response was modeled after the just-in-time (JIT) initiatives undertaken by manufacturers and adapted to retailing. Mercantile developed a sales forecast for a season. Milliken manufactured the fabric to meet the forecast but kept most of the fabric as "grey goods" that could be dyed different colors when orders for the specific colors came in. Featherbone cut and sewed a small initial assortment of garments and shipped them to Mercantile. Mercantile monitored the initial sales of colors and sizes, then transmitted this information to Featherbone and Milliken so the remaining fabric could be dyed, cut, and sewed in the colors and sizes that consumers were buying.

Wal-Mart and other discount store chains were the motivating force for collaboration between CPG manufacturers and supermarket retailers. Through the Food Marketing Institute, supermarkets, facing price competition from discount stores, commissioned Kurt Salmon Associates (KSA) to find out how they could compete more effectively. KSA found that the supermarkets had a significant cost disadvantage due to their inefficient supply chains. When CPG manufacturers held special trade promotions (discounted the wholesale price), supermarket chains would buy a six-month supply of the products, leaving them with $30 billion of excess inventory in their distribution centers. In 1993, the KSA report recommended a multipronged approach called ECR that involved collaboration between manufacturers and retailers to achieve efficient replenishment and promotions.[29]

Since these initiatives were launched, the grocery industry has made greater strides in improving supply chain efficiencies than the apparel industry because the manufacturing process for apparel is more complex and the number of SKUs is significantly greater.

Sources: Goran Svensson, "Efficient Consumer Response—Its Origin and Evolution in the History of Marketing," *Management Decision* 40 (2002), pp. 508–20; Barbara Kahn and Leigh McAlister, *Grocery Revolution: The New Focus on the Consumer* (Reading, MA: Longman, Addison-Wesley, 1997).

available from Retail Link is so rich in information that many vendors hire analysts and buy third-party software to uncover patterns that can help them improve sales forecasts and the assortments to allocate to specific stores. Wal-Mart solicits input from vendors on how to improve the system. It sponsors Retail Link User Groups that meet regularly around the country, in which participating vendors can share tips and strategies for increasing the effectiveness of the system. Wal-Mart also has a Retail Link steering committee comprised of members of the vendor community that meets quarterly and is able to share suggestions on how to improve the functionality of the system.[30]

Sharing sales data with vendors is an important first step in improving supply chain efficiency. With these sales data, vendors can improve their sales forecasts, improve production efficiency, and reduce the need for excessive backup inventory. But additional levels of collaboration are needed to use this information effectively. The sales data reflect historical data, not what the retailer's plans are for the future. For example, the retailer might decide to delete a vendor's SKU from its assortment—a decision that clearly affects future sales.

Vendor-Managed Inventory

Vendor-managed inventory (VMI) is an approach for improving supply chain efficiency in which the vendor is responsible for maintaining the retailer's inventory levels in each of its stores.[31] As illustrated in Exhibit 10–7, the vendor determines a reorder point—a level of inventory at which more merchandise is required. The retailer shares sales data with the vendor via EDI. When inventory drops to the order point, the vendor generates the order (i.e., a reverse purchase order) and delivers the merchandise. While VMI can be used to replenish inventory at retail stores, the approach is usually applied to replenish inventories at the retailer's distribution center.[32]

In ideal conditions, the vendor replenishes inventories in quantities that meet the retailer's immediate demand, reducing stockouts with minimal inventory. In addition to better matching retail demand to supply, VMI can reduce the vendor's and retailer's costs. Vendor salespeople no longer need to spend time selling products, and their role shifts to maintaining relationships. Retail buyers and planners no longer need to monitor inventory levels and place orders.

For example, TAL Apparel Ltd., a Hong Kong shirt maker, manages JCPenney's men's dress shirt inventory. TAL collects POS data for Penney's shirts directly from its stores in North America and then runs the numbers through a computer

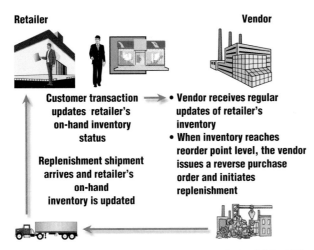

Retailer

Vendor

Customer transaction updates retailer's on-hand inventory status ⟶ • Vendor receives regular updates of retailer's inventory
• When inventory reaches reorder point level, the vendor issues a reverse purchase order and initiates replenishment

Replenishment shipment arrives and retailer's on-hand inventory is updated

EXHIBIT 10–7
Vendor-Managed Inventory

SOURCE: Adapted from Terrance L. Pohlen and Thomas J. Goldsby, "VMI and SMI Programs," *International Journal of Physical Distribution & Logistics Management* 33, no. 7 (2003), p. 567.

model it designed. The Hong Kong company, now the manufacturer of one-seventh of all dress shirts sold in the United States, decides how many shirts to make and in what styles, colors, and sizes. It sends the shirts directly to each Penney store, bypassing the retailer's distribution centers and merchandise managers. Because TAL manages the entire process, from design to ordering yarn, it can bring a new style from the testing stage to full retail rollout in four months, much faster than Penney could on its own. The system, in effect, lets consumers, not merchandise managers, pick the styles.[33]

The use of VMI is not a new approach. Frito-Lay and other snack food, candy, and beverage vendors have managed the stocks of their products on supermarket shelves for a long time. However, technological advances have increased the sophistication of VMI. The sharing of POS transaction data, for instance, allows vendors to sell merchandise on **consignment;** they own the merchandise until it is sold by the retailer, at which time the retailer pays for the merchandise. Consignment selling provides an incentive for the vendor to pick SKUs and inventory levels that will minimize inventory and generate sales. Due to these incentives, when merchandise is sold on consignment, retailers might let the vendor be responsible for determining the inventory plan and appropriate assortment for each store in some cases.[34]

Although it is a more advanced level of collaboration than simply using EDI and sharing information, VMI has its limitations. Whereas the vendor coordinates the supply chain for its specific products, it does not know what other actions the retailer is taking that might affect the sales of its products in the future. For example, Pepsi might not know that a supermarket will be having a big promotion in three weeks for a new beverage introduced by Coca-Cola. Without this knowledge, Pepsi would ship too much merchandise to the supermarket.

Collaborative Planning, Forecasting, and Replenishment

Collaborative planning, forecasting, and replenishment (CPFR) is the sharing of forecast and related business information and collaborative planning between retailers and vendors to improve supply chain efficiency and product replenishment.[35] While retailers share sales and inventory data when using a VMI approach, the vendor is responsible for managing the inventory. In contrast, CPFR is a more advanced form of retailer–vendor collaboration that involves sharing proprietary information such as business strategies, promotion plans, new product developments and introductions, production schedules, and lead time information.

The first CPFR application was in 1987 when Wal-Mart and Procter & Gamble forged a groundbreaking partnership to cooperate more fully. The partnership required trust and commitment instead of the traditional adversarial price negotiation process between retailers and their suppliers. The partnership program improved product availability, decreased inventory, and reduced costs, which Wal-Mart passed on as savings to its customers in the form of lower prices.

Now the CPFR methodology (www.cpfr.org)—developed by Voluntary Interindustry Commerce Standards, or VICS (www.vics.org), and adopted by ECR Europe (www.ecrnet.org)—is a nine-step process that enhances the coordination of all trading parties in a supply chain. Because the necessary software is Internet based, it is more easily and inexpensively accessible to all parties. Retail exchanges such as WorldWide Retail Exchange (www.worldwideretailexchange.org) and Global NetXchange (www.gnx.com) now offer CPFR software to their members. Retailing View 10.4 illustrates how collaborative planning between Zara and its private label suppliers builds a competitive advantage.

RADIO FREQUENCY IDENTIFICATION (RFID)

Radio frequency identification (RFID) is a technology that allows an object or person to be identified at a distance using radio waves. The devices or tags are inserted into oceangoing containers, on shipping cartons, or even behind merchandise labels and transmit data about the object in which they are embedded. The RFID technology has advantages over bar codes, including the ability to hold more data and update data stored on the device. For instance, it can keep track of where an item is in the supply chain and even where it is stored in a distribution center. The data on the device can be acquired without a visual line of sight and in harsh environments in which bar code labels won't work.

The promise of RFID is the dream of every supply chain manager because it enables the accurate, real-time tracking of every single product, from manufacturers to checkout in stores. It eliminates the manual point-and-read operations needed to get data from UPC bar coding. Thus, RFID can significantly decrease warehouse, distribution, and inventory costs, increase margins, and provide better in-stock positions.

Several of the most prominent retailers are already taking advantage of this new technology. Wal-Mart has demanded its top 100 suppliers put RFID tags on all pallets, cases, cartons, and high-margin items. To meet these demands, vendors have been forced to make significant investments to acquire the necessary technology and equipment.

Zara Delivers Fashion Fast   RETAILING VIEW   10.4

Zara, located in La Coruna, Spain, is now the third-largest clothing retailer in the world, with profits growing at 30 percent per year. It operates over 800 stores in 55 countries. Its supply chain management process begins with the store managers, who are equipped with handheld devices linked directly to the company's design rooms in Spain. They report daily on what customers are buying and not buying and what they are asking for but not finding. For instance, when buyers found that customers were requesting a purple shirt that was similar to one they were selling in pink, they passed this information on to the designers in Spain.

Fabrics are cut and dyed by robots in the company's 23 highly automated factories in Spain. The final assembly is entrusted to a network of 300 or so small suppliers that are located near the factories in Galicia and northern Portugal.

Because Zara controls the entire production and design process, it can make products in small lots. By so doing, it can see how the first few hundred items are selling before making more. Instead of shipping new products once a season like many fashion retailers, Zara makes deliveries to each of its stores every few days. The purple shirts were in stores in two weeks—compared with the several months it would take for most department stores and other specialty apparel stores to accomplish the same feat.

Zara successfully reduces lead time by communicating electronically with the factory, using automated equipment, employing assemblers who are in close proximity to the factory, and using premium transportation such as airfreight to get merchandise to the stores. For instance, if a Zara store is running low on a medium kelly-green sweater, its supply chain management system ensures a shorter lead time than that of more traditional retailers. As a result, it's less likely that the Zara store will be out of stock before the next sweater shipment arrives.

Zara gains competitive advantage by carefully coordinating its production, design, and distribution process so that the most current fashions are available when they are in high demand, which increases the percentage of merchandise sold at full price.

Due to the efficiency of its supply chain, Zara does not have to discount merchandise that is not selling as much as other specialty store apparel retailers do. Zara's sales are 85 percent of the initial sales prices, while The Gap's sales are 60–70 percent of the initial price. Zara is able to achieve these results and still design 40,000 new SKUs each year.

Sources: Susan Reda, "Retail's Great Race Getting Fashion to the Finish Line," *Stores,* March 2004, pp. 36–40; Kasra Ferdows, Michael Lewis, and Jose Machuca, "Rapid-Fire Fulfillment," *Harvard Business Review,* November 2004, pp.104–10.

Benefits of RFID

Some of the benefits of RFID include

Reduced warehouse and distribution labor costs Warehouse and distribution costs typically represent 2–4 percent of operating expenses for retailers. Replacing point-and-read, labor-intensive operations with sensors that track pallets, cases, cartons, and individual products anywhere in the facility can significantly reduce labor costs by as much as 30 percent.

Reduced point-of-sale labor costs Using RFID at the product level can help retailers reduce the labor costs needed for checking shelf inventory. In addition, RFID-enabled products will improve self-scan checkouts and increase the use of self-scans, thus shortening checkout times and reducing employee fraud.

Inventory savings RFID reduces inventory errors, ensuring that the inventory recorded is actually available. By tracking pieces more exactly, companies have more accurate information about what was sold and what inventory is actually needed.

Reduced theft With RFID, products can be tracked through the supply chain to pinpoint where a product is at all times, which helps reduce theft in transportation, at the distribution centers, or in the stores. RFID has already been successfully deployed in stores, particularly on costly items prone to theft, such as Gillette Mach 3 razor blades.

Reduced out-of-stock conditions Since RFID facilitates accurate product tracking, forecasts are more accurate, which decreases stockouts. Using RFID, store managers can be automatically notified when specific SKUs are not on the shelves and need to be stocked.[37]

Impediments to the Adoption of RFID

A major obstacle to the widespread adoption of RFID is the high costs, which make the present return on investment low. The cost of RFID tags is 25 to 30 cents per tag, down from 40 cents in 2002. Even though the cost is dropping, it still only makes economic sense to put tags on pallets, cartons, expensive merchandise, or high theft items. However, with demand increasing and tag production costs declining, the tags are expected to reach 5 cents per tag.

Another reason RFID has not been adopted by more retailers is that it generates more data than can be efficiently processed, and therefore, retailers find it difficult to justify the implementation costs. Most retailers are not capable of transmiting, storing, and processing the data that would be available about the location of pallets, cases, cartons, totes, and individual products in the supply chain.

SUMMARY

Supply chain management and information systems have become important tools for achieving a sustainable competitive advantage. Developing more efficient methods of distributing merchandise creates an opportunity to reduce expenses and improve customer service levels.

The systems used to control the flow of information to buyers and then on to vendors have become quite sophisticated. Retailers have developed data warehouses that provide them with intimate knowledge of who their customers are and what they like to buy. These data warehouses are being used to strengthen the relationships with their customers and improve the productivity of their marketing and inventory management efforts.

Some retailers are using distribution centers for crossdocking instead of storing merchandise. Others have their vendors supply them with floor-ready merchandise and adhere to strict delivery schedules. Still other retailers are having vendors deliver merchandise directly to their stores and use pull supply chains that base inventory policies on consumer demand. Retailers are outsourcing many of these logistics functions to third-party logistics companies.

Retailers and vendors are collaborating to improve supply chain efficiency. Electronic data interchange enables retailers to communicate electronically with their vendors. The Internet has accelerated the adoption of EDI, especially among smaller, less sophisticated vendors. Other more involving and effective collaborative approaches include information sharing, VMI, and CPFR. These approaches represent the nexus of information systems and logistics management. They reduce lead time, increase product availability, lower inventory investment, and reduce overall logistics expenses.

Finally, RFID has the potential of further streamlining the supply chain. These small devices are affixed to pallets, cartons, and individual items and can be used to track merchandise through the supply chain and store information such as when an item was shipped to a distribution center. Although still relatively expensive to be placed on all items, RFID technology can reduce labor, theft, and inventory costs.

KEY TERMS

advanced shipping notice (ASN), *272*

bullwhip effect, *283*

checking, *278*

collaborative planning, forecasting, and replenishment (CPFR), *286*

consignment, *286*

crossdocked, *278*

dispatcher, *278*

distribution center, *268*

electronic data interchange (EDI), *274*

extranet, *274*

floor-ready merchandise, *279*

freight forwarders, *282*

intranet, *274*

logistics, *276*

outsourcing, *281*

pick ticket, *279*

public warehouse, *282*

pull supply chain, *275*

push supply chain, *275*

radio frequency identification (RFID), *287*

receiving, *278*

reverse logistics, *281*

security policy, *275*

stockout, *269*

supply chain management, *269*

third-party logistics companies, *281*

ticketing and marking, *279*

Universal Product Code (UPC), *272*

vendor-managed inventory (VMI), *285*

GET OUT AND DO IT!

1. **CONTINUING ASSIGNMENT** Interview the store manager working for the retailer you have selected for the continuing assignment. Write a report that describes and evaluates the retailer's information and supply chain systems. Use this chapter as a basis for developing a set of questions to ask the manager. Some of the questions might include: Where is the store's distribution center? Does the retailer use direct store delivery from vendors? How frequently are deliveries made to the store? Does the merchandise come in ready for sale? What is the store's percentage of stockouts? Does the retailer use a push or pull system? Does the store get involved in determining what merchandise is in the store and in what quantities? Does the retailer use VMI, EDI, CPFR, or RFID?

2. **INTERNET EXERCISE** The Council of Supply Chain Management Professionals is the premier industry organization in the logistics area. Go to its Web site, http://www.cscmp.org/, and find out about new trends in logistics.

3. **INTERNET EXERCISE** Go to EPCglobal's home page at http://www.epcglobalinc.org/index.html and click on the video, "The Basics of RFID and EPC." After watching the short video clip, describe how electronic product codes and radio frequency identification can make the shopping experience better for consumers and improve efficiency in the supply chain.

4. **INTERNET EXERCISE** Go to the GS1 US (www.gs1us.org) (formerly named the Uniform Code Council) home page. What are the goals and mission of this organization? What is its role in the area of UPC bar codes?

DISCUSSION QUESTIONS AND PROBLEMS

1. Retail system acronyms include VMI, EDI, CPFR, and RFID. How are these terms related to one another?

2. Explain how an efficient supply chain system can increase a retailer's level of product availability and decrease its inventory investment.

3. This chapter has presented trends in logistics and information systems that benefit retailers. How do vendors benefit from these trends?

4. Evaluate the options retailers have for dealing with returned merchandise.

5. Why haven't more fashion retailers adopted an integrated supply chain system similar to Zara's?

6. Explain the differences between pull and push supply chains.

7. Why is global logistics much more complicated than domestic logistics?

8. Consumers have five key reactions to stockouts: buy the item at another store (31 percent), substitute a different brand (26 percent), substitute same brand (19 percent), delay purchase (15 percent), or do not purchase the item (9 percent). Consider your own purchasing behavior and describe how various categories of merchandise would result in different reactions to a stockout.

9. Abandoned purchases as a result of stockouts can mean millions of dollars a year in lost sales. How are retailers and manufacturers using technology to reduce stockouts and improve sales?

10. In the past, manufacturers dominated the relationship between vendors and retailers. Today, retailers have more leverage, and both parties are investing in and seeing the benefits of a more trusting relationship with two-way communication. How has the emergence of mega formats, mergers and acquisitions, and technology enabled this shift to greater cooperation between retailers and manufacturers?

SUGGESTED READINGS

Birtwistle, Grete; Noreen Siddiqui; and Susan Fiorito. "Quick Response: Perceptions of UK Fashion Retailers," *International Journal of Retail & Distribution Management* 31 (2003), pp. 119–29.

Bowersox, Donald; M. Bixby Cooper; and David Closs. *Supply Chain Logistics Management*. New York: McGraw-Hill, 2002.

Chopra, Sunil, and Peter Meindl. *Supply Chain Management*. 3rd ed. Englewood Cliffs, NJ: Prentice Hall, 2006.

Coyle, John; Edward Bardi; and C. John Langley. *Management of Business Logistics: A Supply Chain Perspective*. Cincinnati, OH: Thomson Learning, 2002.

Maltz, Arnold, and Nichole Denoratius. *Warehousing: The Evolution Continues*. Oakbrook, IL: Warehousing Education and Research Council, 2004, www.werc.com.

Murphy, Paul, and Donald Wood. *Contemporary Logistics*. 9th ed. Englewood Cliffs, NJ: Prentice Hall, 2006.

Seifert, Dick. *Collaborative Planning, Forecasting, and Replenishment: How to Create a Supply Chain Advantage*. New York: American Management Association, 2003.

Stock, James, and Douglas Lambert. *Strategic Logistics Management*. 5th ed. New York: McGraw-Hill, 2003.

Customer Relationship Management

EXECUTIVE BRIEFING
Bari Harlam, Vice President, Marketing
Intelligence, CVS, Inc.

Our group is responsible for analyzing the purchasing data we have on our customers and developing programs and promotions that increase CVS's share of wallet. These customer relationship management activities drive off the data we collect from the 40 million active customers enrolled in our ExtraCare® program. Customers in the program earn ExtraBucks®—2 percent on most in-store and online purchases and $1 for every two prescriptions purchased—that can be used when shopping in our stores or online. ExtraCare® customers also receive e-mails and direct mailings with helpful health and beauty insights, new product information, and valuable coupons in addition to free merchandise when we have special vendor promotions.

By analyzing the buying behavior of our ExtraCare® customers, we discover some interesting opportunities for cross-promotions. For example, about two-thirds of our customers buying toothpaste did not buy tooth-brushes from us. To encourage these customers to buy toothbrushes as well as toothpaste, we target these customers for a special tooth brush promotion.

We also use targeted special promotions to increase the average size of a customer's market basket. For example, we offer $4 coupons when customers with an average market basket of $15 buy $25. Customers who normally purchase $25 of merchandise get a $10 coupon if they make a $50 purchase.

Each quarter we distribute over five million messages to our customers. These messages contain information and offers tailored to the customers' buying behavior. Like most drugstore chains, over 20 percent of our sales involve some form of promotion. These promotions increase sales but can lower our gross margin. We experiment with different messaging and offerings and then analyze customer buying behavior to determine which promotions are more profitable.

We are very concerned about our customers' privacy. Our program is an opt-in one and therefore we only send

CHAPTER II

QUESTIONS

What is customer relationship management?

Why do retailers want to treat customers differently?

How do retailers determine who their best customers are?

How can retailers build customer loyalty?

What can retailers do to increase their share of wallet?

What can retailers do to alleviate the privacy concerns of their customers?

mailings to customers who give us permission to do so. At times, we use outside processing companies as our agents to help print and send mailings. But these agents never receive any personal customer information beyond name and address. We value our customers' privacy and never give or sell any specific information about them to any manufacturer or direct marketers.

Ms. Harlam earned a Ph.D. in marketing from the Wharton School at the University of Pennsylvania. Prior to joining CVS, she was a marketing professor at the University of Rhode Island and Columbia University's Graduate School of Business.

The business press and companies are talking a lot about the importance of managing customer relationships. Companies are spending billions of dollars on computer systems to help them collect and analyze data about their customers. With all of this buzz, you'd think that the customer is a popular new kid in the neighborhood. However, the customer is more like an old friend who's been taken for granted—until now.

Consider the following example. Shari Ast is on her third business trip this month. She takes a cab from Boston Logan airport to the Ritz-Carlton, her favorite hotel. As the doorman opens the car door for her, he greets her with, "Welcome back to the Ritz-Carlton, Ms. Ast." When she goes to the registration desk, the receptionist gives her a room key and asks if she would like to have her stay charged to her American Express card. Then she goes to her room and finds just what she prefers—a room with a view of the Boston Commons, a single queen-size bed, an extra pillow and blanket, a fax machine connected to her telephone, and a basket with her favorite fruits and snacks.

Shari Ast's experience is an example of the Ritz-Carlton's customer relationship management program. **Customer relationship management (CRM)** is a business philosophy and set of strategies, programs, and systems that focuses on identifying and building loyalty with a retailer's most valued customers. Based on the philosophy that retailers can increase their profitability by building relationships with their better customers, the goal of CRM is to develop a base of loyal customers who patronize the retailer frequently. In the following sections of this chapter, we discuss in more depth the objective of CRM programs and the elements of the CRM process.

THE CRM PROCESS

Traditionally, retailers have focused their attention on encouraging customers to visit their stores, look through their catalogs, and visit their Web sites. To accomplish this objective, they have used mass media advertising and sales promotions, treating all of their customers the same. Now retailers are beginning to concentrate on providing more value to their best customers using targeted promotions and services to increase their **share of wallet**—the percentage of the customers' purchases made from the retailer—from these customers. This change in perspective is supported by research indicating that it costs three to six times more to sell products and services to new customers than to existing customers and that small increases in customer retention can lead to dramatic increases in profits.[1] For instance, at the furniture retailer Domain, the typical first-time purchase by a customer is about $1,500. Repeat purchasers with Domain spend 3.5 times what a one-time-only customer purchases. Their "most valuable" customers have spent over $140,000.[2]

What Is Loyalty?

REFACT

Fifty-five percent of consumers aged 25 years and older are not truly loyal to the stores at which they shop most frequently.[4]

Customer loyalty, the objective of CRM, is more than having customers make repeat visits to a retailer and being satisfied with their experiences. **Customer loyalty** to a retailer means that customers are committed to purchasing merchandise and services from the retailer and will resist the activities of competitors attempting to attract their patronage. They have a bond with the retailer, and the bond is based on more than a positive feeling about the retailer.[3] Retailing View 11.1 describes how Neiman Marcus builds loyalty with its best customers.

Loyal customers have an emotional connection with the retailer. Their reasons for continuing to patronize a retailer go beyond the convenience of the retailer's store or the low prices and specific brands offered by the retailer. They feel such goodwill toward the retailer that they will encourage their friends and family to buy from it.

Programs that encourage repeat buying by simply offering price discounts can be easily copied by competitors. In addition, these types of price-promotion programs encourage customers to always look for the best deal rather than develop a relationship with one retailer. However, when a retailer develops an emotional connection with a customer, it is difficult for a competitor to attract that customer.[5]

Emotional connections develop when customers receive personal attention. For example, many small, independent restaurants build loyalty by functioning as neighborhood cafés, where waiters and waitresses recognize customers by name and know their preferences. Dorothy Lane Market in Dayton, Ohio, for example, uses a sophisticated customer database management system to lavish attention on its customers. Loyalty club members who spent the most over the previous year receive a handwritten note from the CEO. When a major roadway slowed business from customers living in a particular area, Dorothy Lane mailed out maps to affected residents detailing a detour to help encourage customers to return.[6]

Unusual positive experiences also build emotional connections. For example, a family was shopping for shoes for their teenage daughter who was going through a growth spurt. One of her feet was a size 10, and the other was a 10½. The salesperson broke up two pairs of shoes to make the sale and ensure a satisfied customer. The gesture paid off—that day the family purchased five pairs of shoes and have remained loyal customers ever since.[7] Providing such memorable experiences is an important avenue for building customer loyalty.[8]

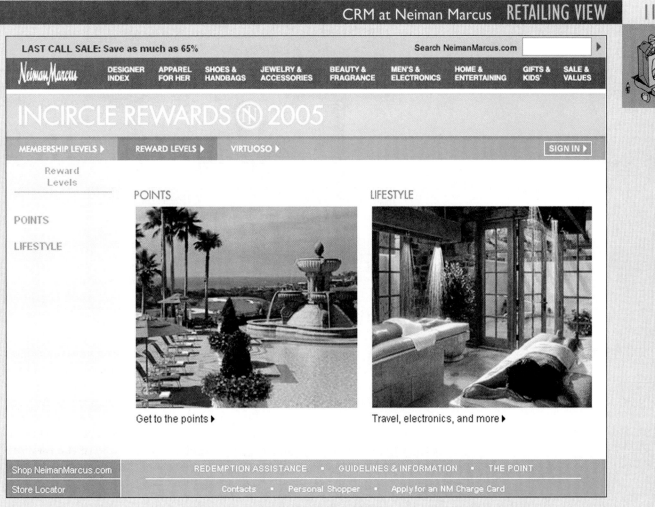

Neiman Marcus's InCircle program provides special benefits to build its share of wallet with its best customers.

One of the best examples of a CRM activity designed to build customer loyalty is Neiman Marcus's InCircle program. The program is designed to develop more customers like Brandi Bloodworth, a 24-year-old Dallas resident, who said while shopping at the downtown Dallas store for a new hat to wear to the Kentucky Derby, "Since I was an infant, I have been wearing Neiman's."

Customers spending more than $5,000 annually are enrolled in the program and get special gifts, awards, and services. Customers whose higher spending levels place them in the "Passport" and "Platinum" categories generate additional rewards and services for themselves. There are currently 100,000 InCircle members, whose median household income is $285,000 and who spend an average of $11,000 per year.

Customers earn one point for each dollar charged on a Neiman Marcus credit card. The points can be redeemed for prizes ranging from a limited-edition Emilio Pucci silk scarf to an eight-night excursion through India to a complete Sony home movie theater. Reward options are refined and expanded annually, but the options are designed to enhance Neiman's exclusive image and reputation for uniqueness.

InCircle members receive frequent communications from Neiman Marcus throughout the year, including the quarterly InCircle newsletter and the semiannual InCircle *Entrée* magazine, a quality publication produced by the creators of *Southern Living* and *Southern Accents*.

Customer relationships are also nurtured at the store level. Neiman's sales associates can tap into information about customers' past purchases and shopping behaviors and are encouraged to contact these customers personally. Sales associates have the freedom to be creative in helping InCircle customers shop in multiple departments and use the various services Neiman Marcus offers, from gift wrapping to travel services. Store managers invite InCircle members to free luncheons on their birthdays.

Recognizing the value of these preferred customers, Neiman invites InCircle members to sit on a board that provides feedback and suggestions as to how Neiman can improve its customers' shopping experience and enhance and broaden its role in the community. These board meetings help Neiman Marcus maintain a genuine, ongoing dialogue with its best customers and make these customers feel that the company respects them and values their opinions.

> **REFACT**
> In 1984, Neiman Marcus launched the first frequent shopper program sponsored by a retailer.[9]

Sources: Ellen Bryon, "Sale of Neiman's Is Latest Sign of Luxury Halo," *The Wall Street Journal*, May 2005, p. B1; Maria Halkias, "Customers Who Spend a Lot at Neiman Marcus Wonder about New Owners," *Knight Ridder Tribune Business News*, May 3, 2005, p. 1.

EXHIBIT 11–1
The CRM Process Cycle

Overview of the CRM Process

Exhibit 11–1 illustrates that CRM is an iterative process that turns customer data into customer loyalty through four activities: (1) collecting customer data, (2) analyzing the customer data and identifying target customers, (3) developing CRM programs, and (4) implementing CRM programs. The process begins with the collection and analysis of data about a retailer's customers and the identification of target customers. The analysis translates the customer information into activities that offer value to the targeted customers. Then these activities are executed through communication programs undertaken by the marketing department and customer service programs implemented by customer contact employees, typically sales associates. Each of the four activities in the CRM process is discussed in the following sections.

COLLECTING CUSTOMER DATA

The first step in the CRM process is to construct a **customer database.** This database is part of the data warehouse described in Chapter 10. It contains all of the data the firm has collected about its customers and is the foundation for subsequent CRM activities.

Customer Database

Ideally, the database should contain the following information:

* *Transactions*—a complete history of the purchases made by the customer, including the purchase date, the price paid, the SKUs purchased, and whether the merchandise was purchased in response to a special promotion or marketing activity.
* *Customer contacts*—a record of the interactions that the customer has had with the retailer, including visits to the retailer's Web site, inquiries made through in-store kiosks, and telephone calls made to the retailer's call center, plus information about contacts initiated by the retailer, such as catalogs and direct mail sent to the customer.
* *Customer preferences*—what the customer likes, such as favorite colors, brands, fabrics, and flavors, as well as apparel sizes. As the beginning of this chapter, we described Shari Ast's experience checking into the Boston Ritz-Carlton. The Ritz-Carlton did not learn about Shari's preferences by asking her to complete a questionnaire; instead, it collected this information by recording each

request she made during her previous stays at Ritz-Carlton hotels into her customer file.

- *Descriptive information*—demographic and psychographic data describing the customer that can be used in developing market segments.
- *Responses to marketing activities*—the analysis of transaction and contact data provides information about the customer's responsiveness to marketing activities.

Different members of the same household also might also have interactions with a retailer. Thus, to get a complete view of the customer, retailers need to be able to combine individual customer data from each member of a household. For example, at Mitchells/Richards, a family-owned apparel chain in Westport and Greenwich, Connecticut, husbands and wives buy things for each other. The chain's database keeps track of both household-level purchases and individual purchases so sales associates can help one spouse buy a gift for the other. The database also keeps track of spending changes and habits. Anniversaries, birthdays, and even divorces and second marriages are tracked along with style, brand, size, and color preferences; hobbies; and sometimes pets' names and golf handicaps.[10] Retailing View 11.2 describes how Harrah's uses its customer database for its loyalty program.

With today's technology, independent companies are able to network with their larger suppliers to increase sales. For example, George Matick Chevrolet in Redford, Michigan, doubled its sales when it installed a CRM program that helped it keep track of potential sales leads. The leads originate both from its own and General Motors' Web site.[11]

Harrah's Bets on CRM RETAILING VIEW 11.2

Many retailers and service providers alike maintain loyalty programs, but Harrah's leads the pack with its profitable Total Rewards loyalty card program. With 26 casinos in 13 states, customers have many chances to accumulate points. When a gamer—casino lingo for a customer—gambles, he or she swipes the card through the slot machine or a pit boss estimates his or her bets at a table. As the points total, card holders earn new status titles: 3,000 points earns a gamer platinum status and a few privileges such as having to wait in shorter lines. With 10,000 points, a gamer earns the diamond card, which entitles him or her to benefits such as free valet parking, room upgrades, and free weekend reservations. Harrah's is unapologetic for their customer discrimination policy based on how much customers spend. Gamers are rewarded on the basis of their value to the hotel chain and encouraged to earn the next loyalty card status level. Harrah's Total Rewards program, which began in 1997, now has six million active members and accounts for 76 percent of the chain's gaming revenues.

Before its CRM program was implemented, Harrah's would base the perks given to customers on the amount they spent on a particular visit. So, if they spent $100, they might get a free parking pass. Now Harrah's uses decision science

Harrah's best customers earn points toward benefits and upgrades based on how much they spend through the Total Rewards loyalty card program. The program helps Harrah's determine the lifetime value of each customer.

models that analyze demographic and behavioral data gathered from customers and project the potential value of a customer. If a customer spends $10 on one visit but the models predict he or she could be a "high roller," Harrah's markets to that person aggressively.

Each reservation and CRM system in each hotel is integrated to store and share all information among its casinos. Loyalty card data are blended with information from the hotel reservation system, giving associates the tools to determine whether a room upgrade or discount is in order. Marketing executives use the data to develop one-to-one marketing programs. Customer service representatives use the system to reward valued customers with on-the-spot perks, such as complimentary meals or event tickets.

Sources: Edward McKinley, "Betting on Better Customer Information," *Credit Card Management* 18, no. 1 (April 2005), pp. 46–48; Christina Brinkley, "Numbers Game: Taking Retailers' Cues, Harrah's Taps into Science of Gambling; Others Focus on High Rollers While Casino Giant Prefers Telemarketing, Databases; From East Chicago to Caesar's," *The Wall Street Journal*, November 22, 2004, p. A1.

Identifying Information

Constructing a database for catalog and Internet shoppers and customers who use the retailer's credit card when buying merchandise in stores is relatively easy. Customers buying merchandise through nonstore channels must provide their contact information, name, and address so that the purchases can be sent to them. When retailers issue their own credit cards, they can collect the contact information for billing when customers apply for the card. In these cases, the identification of the customer is linked to the transaction. However, identifying most customers who are making in-store transactions is more difficult because they often pay for the merchandise with a check, cash, or a third-party credit card such as Visa and MasterCard.

Three approaches that store-based retailers use to overcome this problem are (1) asking customers for their identifying information, (2) offering frequent shopper cards, and (3) connecting Internet purchasing data with the stores.

Asking for Identifying Information   Some retailers such as M.A.C, New England's Christmas Tree Shops, and The Container Store have their sales associates ask customers for identifying information, such as their phone number or name and address, when they ring up a sale.[12] This information is then used to create a transaction database for the customer. However, this approach has two limitations. First, some customers may be reluctant to provide the information and feel that the sales associates are violating their privacy. Second, sales associates might forget to ask for the information or decide not to spend the time getting and recording it during a busy period.

Offering a Frequent Shopper Card   **Frequent shopper programs,** also called **loyalty programs,** are programs that identify and provide rewards to customers who patronize a retailer. When customers enroll in one of these programs, they provide some descriptive information about themselves or their household and are issued a card with an identifying number. The customers then are offered an incentive to use the card when they make purchases from the retailer. As we saw in Retailing Views 11.1 and 11.2, Neiman Marcus and Harrah's both give points for every dollar spent or gambled. At Neiman Marcus, the points are redeemed for special gifts, whereas Harrah's customers get special privileges and complementary food, drinks, and even rooms.

From the retailer's perspective, frequent shopper programs offer two benefits: (1) customers provide demographic and other information when they sign up for the program and then are motivated to identify themselves at each transaction and (2) customers are motivated by the rewards offered to increase the number of visits and the amount purchased on each visit to the retailer.

The major problems with using frequent shopper cards for identification are that the card is often squeezed out of the customer's wallet by other cards, the customer might forget to bring it to the store when shopping, or the customer might decide not to show it if he or she is in a hurry. Retailers overcome this problem by informing customers that if they forget their membership card, their phone number will suffice.

Other retailers are experimenting with technology to increase customer loyalty and spending but eliminate cards. The Interactive Loyalty Card (ILC) is a miniature optical scanner with two-way communication ability that stores and transmits data. This small piece of equipment attaches to a key chain and integrates current store loyalty programs with

Frequent shopper cards are becoming so common that consumers cannot carry all their many cards.

the retailer's and manufacturers' promotions. Customers can simply scan print coupons or download Internet discounts. The eligible coupon codes are integrated with the customer's personal loyalty account, and deductions are taken from the total. Kiosks can allow customers to view and sort their coupons. This technology has been pilot tested at Green Hills Farms in Syracuse, New York, with promising success. The store saw an increase across the board in year-to-year sales, frequency of visits, and manufacturer coupon redemption.[15]

Rather than asking for identifying information or requiring a frequent shopper card, some retailers, especially those in the services sector, use a cardless, cashless payment and loyalty system. Using a preregistered fingerprint, a customer can pay efficiently, and the company can store the customer information quickly and accurately.

The Piggly Wiggly grocery chain has implemented this biometric technology in over 100 grocery stores in South Carolina. Once the fingerprint is recognized and the customer enters a "search" number (usually a phone number), the customer's loyalty account is opened, and a list of payment options appears such as checking, debit, or credit. This system eliminates all cards, completely and fully integrates loyalty programs and customer data, and makes rewards easily available with the simple act of a fingerprint scan.[16]

Connecting Internet Purchasing Data with the Stores   If a customer has used a credit card while shopping on a multichannel retailer's Internet site or from its catalog, and then uses the same card to make a purchase in the retailer's store, the retailer can update the customer's purchase record and capture information about where the customer lives or works from the shipping information. For instance, if a customer purchases a computer at staples.com using a credit card and then uses the same credit card to purchase supplies at a store, Staples can capture the customer's name and shipping address and update the purchase record.

Privacy and CRM Programs

While detailed information about individual customers helps retailers provide more benefits to their better customers, consumers are concerned about retailers violating their privacy when they collect this information. For example, Amazon caused considerable concerns among its customers when it e-mailed them to say it was changing its privacy rules. The new rules indicated that Amazon would no longer allow its customers to preclude Amazon from sharing the information about the customers' purchases with third parties. The adverse public reaction spurred on by two online privacy organizations—Junkbusters (www.junkbusters.com) and the Electronic Privacy Information Center (www.epic.org)—created such an uproar that Amazon altered its policy.

Since that time, other retailers have been criticized for failing to respect consumers' privacy. For instance, the Federal Trade Commission (FTC) charged BJ's Wholesale Club with failing to encrypt consumer information when transmitting or storing data at its outlets and taking "unnecessary risks" by storing data for more than 30 days. The FTC also charged that BJ's stored data in files that could be accessed "using commonly known default user IDs and passwords." As a result, BJ's settled a consent agreement with the FTC that requires much tighter security at BJ's, as well as an independent audit of the chain's computer security system every two years for the next 20 years.[17]

Privacy Concerns   The degree to which consumers feel their privacy has been violated depends on

• Their control over their personal information when engaging in marketplace transactions. Do they feel they can decide on the amount and type of information collected by the retailer?

REFACT

In 2005, there were an estimated 25 million victims of identity theft.[18]

REFACT

Seventy-one percent of consumers believe that protecting personal information and privacy is more of a concern now than a few years ago.[20]

• Their knowledge about the collection and use of personal information. Do they know what information is being collected and how the retailer will be using it? Will the retailer be sharing the information with other parties?[19]

These concerns are particularly acute for customers using an electronic channel because many of them do not realize the extensive amount of information that can be collected without their knowledge. In addition to collecting transaction data, electronic retailers can collect information by placing cookies on visitor's hard drives. **Cookies** are text files that identify visitors when they return to a Web site. Due to the data in the cookies, customers do not have to identify themselves or use passwords every time they visit a site. However, the cookies also collect information about other sites the person has visited and what pages they have downloaded.

Protecting Customer Privacy   What is personal information? The definition is debatable. Some people define personal information as all information that is not publicly available; others include both public (e.g., driver's license, mortgage data) and private (hobbies, income) information.

Who is responsible for ensuring consumer privacy? In the United States, legal protection for individual privacy is limited.[21] Existing legislation is restricted to the protection of information in a few specific contexts, including government functions and practices in credit reporting, video rentals, banking, and health care.[22] However, the European Union (EU) and Canada[23] are much more aggressive in protecting consumer privacy. Some of the provisions of the EU directive on consumer privacy include the following:

• Businesses can collect consumer information only if they have clearly defined the purpose, such as completing the transaction.

• The purpose must be disclosed to the consumer from whom the information is being collected.

• The information can only be used for that specific purpose.

• The business can only keep the information for the stated purpose. If the business wants to use the information for another purpose, it must initiate a new collection process.

• Businesses operating in Europe can only export information from the 25 EU countries to importing countries with similar privacy policies. Thus, U.S. retailers, hotel chains, airlines, and banks cannot transfer information from Europe to the United States because the United States does not have similar privacy policies.

Basically, the EU perspective is that consumers own their personal information and retailers must get consumers to explicitly agree to share this personal information. This agreement is referred to as an **opt in.** In contrast, personal information in the United States is generally viewed as being in the public domain, and retailers can use it in any way they desire. American consumers must explicitly tell retailers not to use their personal information—they must **opt out.**[24]

The EU has delayed enforcement of its directive. The United States is currently negotiating a safe harbor program that would enable U.S. companies abiding by the EU directives to export information. However, due to increasing concerns about consumer privacy, Congress is considering new legislation on consumer privacy. The Federal Trade Commission has developed the following set of principles for fair information practices:

• *Notice and awareness*—covers the disclosure of information practices, including a comprehensive statement of information use such as information storage, manipulation, and dissemination.

• *Choice/consent*—includes both opt out and opt in options and allows consumers the opportunity to trade information for benefits.

- *Access/participation*—allows for the confirmation of information accuracy by consumers.
- *Integrity/security*—controls for the theft of and tampering with personal information.
- *Enforcement/redress*—provides a mechanism to ensure compliance by participating companies.

In summary, there is growing consensus that personal information must be fairly collected, that the collection must be purposeful, and that the data should be relevant, maintained as accurate, essential to the business, subject to the rights of the owning individual, kept reasonably secure, and transferred only with the permission of the consumer. To address these concerns, many retailers that collect customer information have privacy policies. The Electronic Privacy Information Center (www.epic.org) recommends that privacy policies clearly state what information is collected from each visitor and how it will be used, give consumers a choice as to whether they give information, and allow them to view and correct any personal information held by an online retail site. Retailers need to ensure their customers that information about them is held securely and not passed on to other companies without the customer's permission.[25]

ANALYZING CUSTOMER DATA AND IDENTIFYING TARGET CUSTOMERS

The next step in the CRM process is to analyze the customer database and convert the data into information that will help retailers develop programs for building customer loyalty. **Data mining,** one approach commonly used to develop this information, identifies patterns in data, typically those that the analyst is unaware of prior to searching through the data. For example, an electronic retailer in London discovered that customers who had bought portable DVD players typically commuted to work by train. Using this information, the retailer experienced a 43 percent increase in portable DVD player sales when it redirected most of its communication budget from daytime television commercials to newspapers and billboards along the train tracks.[26]

Market basket analysis is a specific type of data analysis that focuses on the composition of the basket, or bundle, of products purchased by a household during a single shopping occasion. This analysis is often useful for suggesting where to place merchandise in a store. For example, on the basis of market basket analyses, Wal-Mart changed the traditional location of several items:

- Because bananas are the most common item in Americans' grocery carts, Wal-Mart Supercenters sell bananas next to the corn flakes, as well as in the produce section.
- Kleenex tissues are in the paper goods aisle and also mixed in with cold medicine.
- Measuring spoons appear in housewares and also hang next to Crisco shortening.
- Flashlights are in the hardware aisle and with the Halloween costumes.
- Little Debbie snack cakes are next to the coffee.
- Bug spray is merchandised with the hunting gear.

Identifying Market Segments

Traditionally, customer data analysis has focused on identifying market segments—groups of customers who have similar needs, purchase similar merchandise, and respond in a similar manner to marketing activities.

For example, when Eddie Bauer analyzed its customer database, it discovered two types of shoppers. One group it calls "professional shoppers"—people who love fashion and value good customer service. The other group it calls "too busy to shop people"—people who want the shopping experience over as quickly as possible. The professional shoppers tended to use the alteration service, call the customer service desk, and seek out the same salesperson when they make purchases in the stores. In contrast, the people too busy to shop typically shop from the catalog and Web site. Eddie Bauer uses this information to develop unique advertising programs targeting each of these segments.

Eddie Bauer also discovered that morning shoppers are more price sensitive and like to buy products on sale more than do evening shoppers, who tended to be in the professional shopper segment. Using this information, Eddie Bauer installed electronic window posters in some test stores that allowed different images to be displayed at different times of the day. In the morning, the displays featured lower-priced merchandise and items on sale, whereas in the evening, the more expensive and fashionable merchandise was displayed.[27]

Identifying Best Customers

Using information in the customer database, retailers can develop a score or number indicating how valuable customers are to the firm. This score can then be used to determine which customers to target.

Lifetime Value   A commonly used measure to score each customer is called lifetime customer value. **Lifetime customer value (LTV)** is the expected contribution from the customer to the retailer's profits over his or her entire relationship with the retailer.

To estimate LTV, retailers use past behaviors to forecast future purchases, the gross margin from these purchases, and the costs associated with servicing the customers. Some of the costs associated with a customer include the costs of advertising, promotions used to acquire the customer, and processing merchandise that the customer has returned. Thus, a customer who purchases $200 of groceries from a supermarket every other month would have a lower LTV for the supermarket than a customer who buys $30 on each visit and shops at the store three times a week. Similarly, a customer who buys apparel only when it is on sale in a department store would have a lower LTV than a customer who typically pays full price and buys the same amount of merchandise.

These assessments of LTV are based on the assumption that the customer's future purchase behaviors will be the same as they have been in the past. Sophisticated statistical methods are typically used to estimate the future contributions from past purchases. For example, these methods might consider how recent purchases have occurred. The expected LTV of a customer who purchased $600 on one visit six months ago is probably less than the LTV of a customer who has been purchasing $100 of merchandise every month for the last six months.

Customer Pyramid   Most retailers realize that their customers differ in terms of their profitability or LTV. In particular, they know that a relatively small number of customers account for the majority of their profits. This realization is often called the **80–20 rule**—80 percent of the sales or profits come from 20 percent of the customers. Thus, retailers could group their customers into two groups on the basis of the LTV scores. One group would be the 20 percent of the customers with the highest LTV scores, and the other group would be the rest. However, this two-segment scheme, "best" and "rest," does not consider important differences among the 80 percent of customers in the "rest" segment.[29] A commonly used segmentation scheme divides customers into four segments, as illustrated in Exhibit 11–2. This scheme allows retailers to

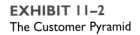

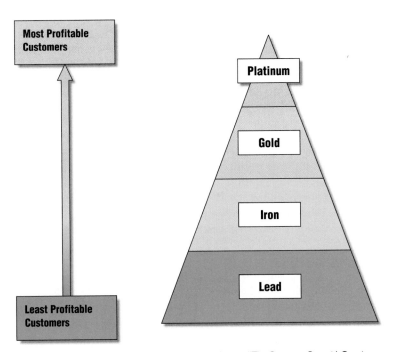

EXHIBIT 11–2
The Customer Pyramid

SOURCE: Valarie Zeithaml, Roland Rust, and Katherine Lemon, "The Customer Pyramid: Creating and Serving Profitable Customers," *California Management Review* 43 (Summer 2001), p. 125. Reprinted by permission.

develop more appropriate strategies for each of the segments. Each of the four segments is described below.

- *Platinum segment* This segment is composed of the retailer's customers with the top 25 percent LTVs. Typically, these are the most loyal customers who are not overly concerned about merchandise price and place more value on customer service.
- *Gold segment* The next 25 percent of customers in terms of their LTV make up the gold segment. These customers have a lower LTV than platinum customers because they are more price sensitive. Even though they buy a significant amount of merchandise from the retailer, they are not as loyal as platinum customers and probably patronize some of the retailer's competitors.
- *Iron segment* Customers in this third tier probably do not deserve much special attention from the retailer due to their modest LTV.
- *Lead segment* Customers in the lowest segment can cost the company money. They often demand a lot of attention but do not buy much from the retailer. For example, real estate agents often encounter people who want to spend their weekends looking at houses but are really not interested in buying one.

This segmentation scheme differs, for example, from the segments of passengers in airline frequent flier programs because it is based on LTV rather than miles flown. Thus, it recognizes that some customers who fly a lot of miles might be taking low-cost flights, whereas other customers, though flying the same number of miles, might be much more profitable because they fly first class and don't seek discount fares.

RFM Analysis   An **RFM** (recency, frequency, monetary) **analysis,** often used by catalog retailers and direct marketers, is a scheme for segmenting customers according to how recently they have made a purchase, how frequently they make purchases, and how much they have bought. Exhibit 11–3 is an example of an RFM analysis done by a catalog apparel retailer that mails a catalog each month to its customers.

The catalog retailer divides its customers into 32 groups or segments on the basis of how many orders the customer has placed during the last year, how much merchandise the customer has purchased, and the last time the customer placed an order. Each segment is represented by one cell in Exhibit 11–3. For example, the customers

EXHIBIT 11–3
RFM Analysis for a
Catalog Retailer

Frequency	Monetary	RECENCY			
		0–2 months	3–4 months	5–6 months	Over 6 months
1–2	<$50	0.050*	0.035	0.010	0.001
1–2	Over $50	0.050	0.036	0.011	0.001
3–4	<$50	0.080	0.050	0.015	0.006
3–4	Over $150	0.090	0.050	0.017	0.008
5–6	<$300	0.100	0.060	0.025	0.010
5–6	Over $300	0.120	0.080	0.027	0.012
Over 6	<$450	0.150	0.100	0.035	0.180
Over 6	Over $450	0.160	0.110	0.040	0.020

*Percent of customers in the cell who made a purchase from the last catalog mailed to them.

SOURCE: Reprinted by permission of Harvard Business School Press. Adapted from Robert Blattberg, Gary Getz, and Jacquelyn Thomas, *Customer Equity: Building and Managing Relationships as Valuable Assets* (Boston: Harvard Business School Press, 2001), p. 18. Copyright © 2001 by the Harvard Business School Publishing Corporation; all rights reserved.

in the upper-left cell have made one or two purchases in the last year, made a purchase within the last two months, and purchased less than $50 of merchandise.

Catalog retailers often use this type of analysis to determine which customer groups should be sent catalogs. For each of the RFM groups, they will determine the percentage of customers in the group who made a purchase from the last catalog sent to them. For example, 5 percent of the customers in the upper-left corner of Exhibit 11–3 placed an order from the last catalog sent to them. With information about the response rate and the average gross margin from orders placed by customers in each cell, the catalog retailer can calculate the expected profit from sending catalogs to different customers. For example, if the average gross margin from orders placed by customers in the upper-left cell is $20 and the cost of sending a catalog to customers in the cell is $.75, the catalog would make $.25 per customer from each catalog mailed to those customers.

$20 contribution × .05 response
= $1.00 expected contribution − $.75 cost
= $.25 per customer.

Thus, RFM analysis is basically a method of estimating the LTV of a customer using the recency, frequency, and monetary value of his or her past purchases. Exhibit 11–4 illustrates how RFM can be used for developing customer target strategies.

Customers who have made infrequent, small purchases recently are considered first-time customers. The objective of CRM programs directed toward this segment of customers is to convert them into early repeat customers and eventually

EXHIBIT 11–4
RFM Target Strategies

Frequency	Monetary	RECENCY			
		0–2 months	3–4 months	5–6 months	Over 6 months
1–2	<$50	First-time customers		Low-value customers	
1–2	Over $50				
3–4	<$150	Early repeat customers		Defectors	
3–4	Over $150				
5–6	<$300	High-value customers		Core defectors	
5–6	Over $300				
Over 6	<$450				
Over 6	Over $450				

SOURCE: Reprinted by permission of Harvard Business School Press. Adapted from Robert Blattberg, Gary Getz, and Jacquelyn Thomas, *Customer Equity: Building and Managing Relationships as Valuable Assets* (Boston: Harvard Business School Press, 2001), p. 18. Copyright © 2001 by the Harvard Business School Publishing Corporation; all rights reserved.

high-value customers. Customer relationship management programs directed toward customers in the high-value segment (high RFM value) attempt to maintain loyalty, increase retention, and gain a greater share of wallet by selling more merchandise to them. However, customers who have not purchased recently either have a low lifetime value and therefore are not worth pursuing or are committed to another retailer and may be difficult to recapture. The CRM programs designed to realize objectives related to these different segments are discussed in the following section.

DEVELOPING CRM PROGRAMS

Having segmented customers according to their future profit potential, the next step in the CRM process (see Exhibit 11–1) is to develop programs for the different customer segments. In the following sections, we discuss programs retailers use for (1) retaining their best customers, (2) converting good customers into high-LTV customers, and (3) getting rid of unprofitable customers.

Customer Retention

Four approaches that retailers use to retain their best customers are (1) frequent shopper programs, (2) special customer services, (3) personalization, and (4) community.

Frequent Shopper Programs   As mentioned previously, frequent shopper programs are used to both build a customer database by identifying customers by their transactions and encourage repeat purchase behavior and retailer loyalty.[30] Retailers provide incentives to encourage customers to enroll in the program and use the card. These incentives are either discounts on purchases made from the retailer or points for every dollar of merchandise purchased. The points are then redeemable for special rewards. Some recommendations concerning the nature of the rewards offered are as follows:

- *Tiered* Rewards should be tiered according to the volume of purchase to motivate customers to increase the level of their purchases. These tiers can be based on individual or cumulative transactions. Some programs combine both approaches by offering a $5 discount on purchases between $100 and $149.99, $10 dollars off purchases from $150 to $249.99, and $15 off purchases of $250 or more. In addition, for every $100 of cumulative discounts, customers earn an additional $10 of savings. Customers generally accept the idea that people who spend more should receive greater rewards.
- *Offer choices* Not all customers value the same rewards. Thus, the most effective frequent shopper programs offer customers choices. For example, Coles Myer, a leading Australian retailer, originally offered customers air miles but shifted to a menu of rewards when it discovered that many customers did not value air miles. Tesco, a U.K. supermarket chain, lets customers cash in points for special discounts on entertainment, vacation packages, or sporting events. Sainsbury, a competitor, allows customers to use their points for vouchers at a variety of retail partners such as Blockbuster and British Gas. Nonmonetary incentives also are very attractive to some customers. For example, Neiman Marcus's InCircle program offers customers the opportunity to redeem points for an invitation to a cocktail party and Sotheby's auction or an underwater expedition to see the Titanic.

Some retailers link their frequent shopper programs to charitable causes. For example, Target donates 1 percent of all purchases charged to Target's Guest Card to a program that benefits local schools. Although these altruistic rewards can be an effective part of a frequent shopper program, such incentives probably should not be the focal point of the program. Research indicates that the most effective incentives benefit the recipient directly, not indirectly, as is the case with charitable contributions.

- *Reward all transactions* To ensure the collection of all customer transaction data and encourage repeat purchases, programs need to reward all purchases, not just purchases of selected merchandise.

- *Transparency and simplicity* Customers need to be able to quickly and easily understand when they will receive rewards, what the rewards are, how much they have earned, and how they can redeem the points they have accumulated. The ground rules need to be clearly stated. There should be no surprises or confusion.[31]

Four factors limit the effectiveness of frequent shopping programs. First, they can be expensive. For example, a 1 percent price discount can cost large retailers over $100 million a year. In addition, for a large retailer, the initial launch and maintenance investments (store training, marketing, fulfillment support, and information technology and systems costs) can be as high as $30 million. Annual maintenance costs can reach $5–$10 million when marketing, program support, offer fulfillment, customer service, and IT infrastructure costs are included. Then there are the marketing support costs needed to maintain awareness of the program.[33]

Second, it is difficult to make corrections in programs when problems arise. Programs become part of the customer's shopping experience, so customers must be informed about even the smallest changes in programs. They react negatively to any perceived "take away" once a program is in place, even if they are not actively involved in it. The more successful the program is, the greater the customer reaction to changes are, and these negative reactions can reduce customer trust in and loyalty toward the retailer.

Third, it is not clear that these programs increase customer spending behavior and loyalty toward the retailer.[34] For example, the Wisconsin-based Sun Prairie grocery store polled shoppers throughout its 39 stores regarding its frequent shopper program. Over 80 percent of those surveyed would rather not use a card to receive the discounts on their purchases.[35]

Fourth, and perhaps most important, it is difficult to gain a competitive advantage based on frequent shopper programs. Because the programs are visible, they can be easily duplicated by competitors. Between 50 and 70 percent of all grocery retailers offer a loyalty card to their customers, and 80 percent of households have at least one of these grocery stores' cards in their wallets. Yet the perceived value of the cards is low. Supermarkets' loyalty cards allow customers access to price discounts, which encourages the low-price shopper but not the loyal customer. Consumers see little difference between the programs when they all provide a discount of $.50 on detergent.[36]

To avoid this problem, retailers are offering more personalized benefits to their best customers based on their unique knowledge of the customer; these benefits thus are more "invisible" to competitors.

Special Customer Services   Retailers provide unusually high-quality customer service to build and maintain the loyalty of their best customers. At Mitchells/Richards in Connecticut, it is not unusual for a salesperson to open the store after hours or bring an item to a customer's home. It is this type of special attention that facilitates success in a retail sector that has seen difficult times in recent years.[37]

Personalization   An important limitation of CRM strategies developed for market segments, such as a platinum segment in the customer pyramid (Exhibit 11–2) or early repeat customers in the RFM analysis (Exhibit 11–3), is that each segment is composed of a large number of customers who are not identical. Thus, any strategy will be most appealing for only the typical customer and not as appealing to the majority of customers in the segment. For example, customers in the platinum segment with the highest LTVs might include a 25-year-old single woman who has quite different needs than a 49-year-old working mother with two children.

With the availability of customer-level data and analysis tools, retailers can now economically offer unique benefits and target messages to individual customers. They have the ability to develop programs for small groups of customers and even specific individuals. For example, at Harry Rosen, a Canadian men's apparel specialty retailer, customers are occasionally contacted by the salesperson with whom they have developed a personal relationship. If Harry Rosen receives a new shipment of Armani suits, the sales clerk will contact customers who have purchased Armani in the past. If a customer has been relatively inactive, the retailer might send him a $100 certificate on something he has not bought in a while.[38]

Developing retail programs for small groups or individual customers is referred to as **1-to-1 retailing.** Many small, local retailers have always practiced 1-to-1 retailing. They know each of their customers, greet them by name when they walk in the store, and then recommend merchandise they know the customers will like. These local store owners do not need customer databases and data mining tools; they have the information in their heads. But most large retail chains and their employees do not have this intimate knowledge of their customers. Thus, the CRM process enables larger retailers to efficiently develop relationships similar to those that many small local retailers have with customers.

The Internet channel provides an opportunity for retailers to automate the practice of 1-to-1 retailing. When registered customers log on to Amazon.com, the first page they see is personalized for them. Their name is displayed in a greeting, and the products displayed are based on an analysis of their past purchase behavior. For example, if a customer has bought mystery novels from Amazon.com in the past, the latest books from mystery book authors whose novels he or she has bought are presented. Some privacy experts believe that some personalization efforts have crossed the line, however. For instance, Amazon has launched a Web search engine, called A9, that can remember everything the customer has ever searched for, and the site reserves the right to share the information with its retailing arm. Amazon also funds a Web site called 43 Things that seeks to link people with similar goals, such as getting out of debt.[39]

The personalized rewards or benefits that customers receive are based on unique information possessed by the retailer and its sales associates. This information, in the retailer's customer database, cannot be accessed or used by competitors. Thus, it provides an opportunity to develop a sustainable competitive advantage.

The effective use of this information creates the positive feedback cycle in the CRM process (see Exhibit 11–1). Increasing repeat purchases from a retailer increases the amount of data collected from the customer, which enables the retailer to provide more personalized benefits, which in turn increases the customer's purchases from the retailer.

Amazon.com provides personalized recommendations based on the past purchases of its customers.

Community   A fourth approach for building customer retention and loyalty is to develop a sense of community among customers. The Internet channel offers an opportunity for customers to exchange information using bulletin boards and develop more personal relationships with one another and the retailer. By participating in such a community, customers are more reluctant to leave the "family" of other people patronizing the retailer.

For example, in addition to offering merchandise for sale, a sporting goods retailer could provide an opportunity for organizers of local sporting events to post information about these events on its Web site. The volunteers organizing youth soccer and little league baseball teams and tennis and golf tournaments could provide information about meetings and game dates, times, and places. Then the retailer could collect information about the participants in local leagues and offer discounts to encourage teams to buy their uniforms and equipment from its store and facilitate these transactions. Retailing View 11.3 describes a retailer that has builts a community of boaters.

Converting Good Customers into Best Customers

In the context of the customer pyramid (Exhibit 11–2), increasing the sales made to good customers is referred to as *customer alchemy*—converting iron and gold customers into platinum customers.[40] Customer alchemy involves offering and selling more products and services to existing customers and increasing the retailer's share of wallet with these customers.

Tesco, the U.K. supermarket chain, added a second tier to its frequent shopper program to increase its share of wallet. The first tier has a traditional design to gather customer data. The second tier, targeted at its better customers, is more innovative. Customers earn a "key" when they spend $38 or more in a single transaction. Fifty keys make the customer a "keyholder," 100 keys a "premium keyholder." When customers achieve these higher levels, they get discounts on popular entertainment events, theater tickets, sporting events, and hotel vacations. The key program seeks to convert iron and gold customers into platinum customers. In the four years since starting its key program, Tesco has raised its market share from 13 percent to more than 17 percent.

The retailer's customer database also reveals opportunities for cross selling and add-on selling. **Cross selling** refers to selling a complementary product or service in a specific transaction, such as selling a customer a printer when he or she has decided to buy a computer. For example, Stop & Shop Co. equipped some of its grocery stores in the Boston area with a "shopping buddy," a wireless computer device attached to shopping carts. It utilizes the retailer's loyalty card and the shopping history it collects to alert customers of sale items that they previously

---

11.3   **RETAILING VIEW**   Building a Community of Boaters

MarineMax, the world's largest recreational boat retailer, based in Clearwater, Florida, offers a number of programs to help its customers reject the cliché that the two best days in boating are the day you buy your boat and the day you sell it. The company organizes hundreds of "Getaways" annually that give their customers an opportunity to take trips with other boaters. The trips range from weekend runs to two-week voyages to the Bahamas. Each of the Getaways is led by a MarineMax pilot. Thus, the boat owners can feel comfortable doing something more adventuresome than they might normally do. In addition to enjoying an exciting boating experience, boaters can meet and share experiences with others on the trip.

Beyond sponsoring the Getaways, MarineMax provides other services that ensure its customers have good boating experiences and are motivated to trade up to larger and more

MarineMax organizes boat outings for its customers to develop their sense of community, enhance the boating experience, and build customer loyalty.

expensive crafts. For example, the retailer provides hands-on training for all new "Captains," including the fundamentals of boat operations, safety, and docking, right down to tying to the cleat.

MarineMax takes on all other aspects of the boating life including financing, insurance, and operating a brokerage for used boats when someone decides to sell or upgrade. "Our focus is on the boating experience, not just selling boats," says Dawna Stone, chief marketing officer. "When we get a customer, we tend to keep that customer for as long as they're in boating." Moreover, she adds, "One of our most powerful selling tools is word of mouth. We count our existing customers among our best salespeople."

Sources: 2004 MarineMax Annual Report; Don Peppers, "Building Relationships across the Product Lifecycle," *Inside 1to1*, March 11, 2002, p. 2.

purchased and might want to buy again while they are on sale. If the customer's history shows she frequently purchases hamburgers but not ketchup, the shopping buddy might provide her with a special coupon for each.[41]

Add-on selling involves selling additional new products and services to existing customers, such as a bank encouraging a customer with a checking account to apply for a home improvement loan.

Oprah Winfrey is a master of add-on selling. She has capitalized on her popularity by building on her daytime television show *(The Oprah Winfrey Show)* to sell and promote books, movies, and television specials (Harpo Productions), a cable channel (Oxygen Media), a Web site (www.oprah.com), and a widely read magazine *(O)* to her target audience—women interested in self-improvement and empowerment. For viewers of the television show, each of these products provides additional value. For example, when a respected celebrity appears on her television show, an article with more detailed information about the celebrity will be published in *O*. Winfrey builds community by using her television show and magazine to encourage her customers to exchange experiences with her and others through her Web site. For example, a customer reading an article on volunteering with a nonprofit organization can go online and share her interests and experiences with others interested in volunteering.[42]

The Shopping Buddy, created by Cuesol Inc., is a wireless computer device attached to shopping carts. Consumers scan items on their grocery list as they shop to keep track of their spending.

Dealing with Unprofitable Customers

In many cases, the bottom tier of customers actually has a negative LTV. Retailers lose money on every sale they make to these customers. For example, catalog retailers have customers who repeatedly buy three or four items and return all but one of them. The cost of processing two or three returned items is much greater than the profits coming from the one item

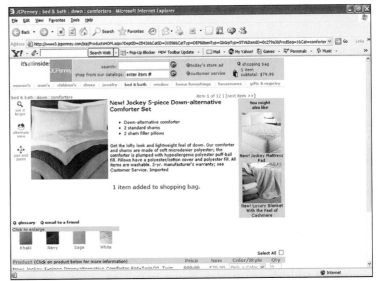

JCPenney's Web site builds add-on sales by providing suggestions for items that complement the merchandise customers are considering and decide to buy.

that the customer kept. Customers in the bottom tier may also be there as a result of vanishing and reappearing. For example, customers may vanish because a competitor is offering a more attractive offer or they are dissatisfied, and then return months or years later as a new customer. The costs of their (re)acquisition make them unprofitable. The process of no longer selling to these unprofitable customers can be referred to as "getting the lead out," in terms of the customer pyramid.[43] Retailing View 11.4 describes how Limited Express and Best Buy are dealing with undesirable customers.

Other approaches for getting the lead out are (1) offering less costly approaches for satisfying the needs of lead customers and (2) charging customers for the services they are abusing. Fidelity Investments has about 550,000 Web site visits a day and more than 700,000 daily calls, about three-quarters of which go to automated systems that cost the company less than a $1 each. The remaining calls are handled by call center agents, who cost $13 per call. Fidelity contacted 25,000 lower-tier customers who placed a lot of calls to agents and told them they must use the Web site or automated calls for simple account and price information. Each name was flagged and routed to a special representative who would direct callers back to automated services and tell them how to use it. "If all our customers chose to go through live reps, it would be cost prohibitive," said a Fidelity spokeswoman.

IMPLEMENTING CRM PROGRAMS

Increasing sales and profits through CRM programs is a challenge. For example, according to a study, 52 percent of retailers indicated that they were engaged in some type of data mining, but 76 percent of those retailers undertaking data mining indicated that the activity had made no contribution to their bottom line.[44]

This experience of retailers emphasizes that effective CRM requires more than appointing a CRM manager, installing a computer system to manage and analyze a customer database, and making speeches about the importance of customers. The effective implementation of CRM programs requires the close coordination of activities by different functions in a retailer's organization. The MIS department needs to collect, analyze, and make the relevant information readily accessible to the employees implementing the programs—the frontline service providers and sales associates and the marketers responsible for communicating with customers through impersonal channels (mass advertising, direct mail, e-mail). Store operations and human resource management needs to hire, train, and motivate the employees who will be using the information to deliver personalized services.

Most retailers are product-centric, not customer-centric; as shown in Chapter 9, buyers in a retail firm are organized by type of product. Typically, there is no area of a retail firm organized by customer type and responsible for delivering products and services to different types of customers. Perhaps in the future, retailers will have market managers to perform this coordinating function.

11.4   RETAILING VIEW   Getting the Lead Out

Return fraud costs retailers over $15 billion each year. Some examples of these costly returns are people buying a large screen Television for a Super Bowl party and then returning it after the game or buying an expensive dress for a special occasion and then returning it afterward. Professional returners are now using the Internet to make money on fraudulent returns. Some people steal merchandise from a store, return it for credit slips, and then turn the credit slips into cash by selling them at a discount on eBay or other online auction sites.

Retailers like The Limited and Best Buy are fighting back against such high-tech fraud with high-tech defenses. Limited Express's return policy says consumers have up to 60 days to return items. However, the company's return policy also notes that it uses an industrywide service operated by Return Exchange to authorize returns and that "under certain circumstances we reserve the right to deny returns." Return Exchange, based in Irvine, California, analyzes Express's customer database and identifies customers who have an unusually high propensity to return merchandise. When these customers return merchandise, the POS terminal generates a slip of paper that says "RETURN DECLINED," and the sales associate tells the customer to call the toll-free number at the bottom for more information.

Best Buy is undertaking a strategy to focus on gold and platinum customers and get rid of lead customers. To lure high spenders, it is providing more effective customer service. To discourage undesirable customers, it is reducing promotions that tend to draw them into the store and removing them from direct marketing lists. The trickiest challenge may be to deter bad customers without turning off good ones.

Best Buy's campaign against undesirable customers pits it against dozens of Web sites like FatWallet.com, SlickDeals.net, and TechBargains.com that trade electronic coupons and tips from former clerks and insiders, hoping to gain extra advantages against the stores. At SlickDeals.net, whose subscribers boast about techniques for gaining hefty discounts, a visitor recently bragged about his practice of shopping at Best Buy only when he thinks he can buy at below the retailer's cost.

Best Buy cannot bar undesirable customers from its stores, but it is taking steps to put a stop to their most damaging practices. It's enforcing a restocking fee of 15 percent of the purchase price on returned merchandise. To discourage customers who return items with the intention of repurchasing them at a "returned merchandise" discount, it is experimenting with reselling returned merchandise over the Internet, so the goods don't reappear in the store where they were originally purchased. Best Buy also cut ties to FatWallet.com, an online "affiliate" that had collected referral fees for delivering customers to Best Buy's Web site.

Rejecting customers is a delicate business. Filene's Basement was criticized on television and in newspapers for asking two Massachusetts customers not to shop at its stores because of their frequent returns and complaints. Best Buy's CEO apologized in writing to students at a Washington, DC, school after employees at one store barred a group of black students while admitting a group of white students.

Sources: Ariana Cha, "Some Shoppers Find Fewer Happy Returns," *Washington Post*, November 7, 2004, p. A01; Gary McWilliams, "Minding The Store," *The Wall Street Journal*, November 8, 2004, p. A1.

SUMMARY

To develop a strategic advantage, retailers must effectively manage their critical resources—their finances (Chapter 6), human resources (Chapter 9), real estate and locations (Chapters 7 and 8), inventory and information (Chapter 10), and customers (Chapter 11). This chapter focuses on activities that retailers are undertaking now and will undertake in the future to increase the sales and profits they get from their better customers. Customer relationship management is a business philosophy and set of strategies, programs, and systems that focuses on identifying and building loyalty with a retailer's most valued customers. Loyal customers are committed to patronizing a retailer and are not prone to switch to a competitor. In addition to building loyalty, CRM programs are designed to increase the share of wallet from the retailer's best customers.

Customer relationship management is an iterative process that turns customer data into customer loyalty through four activities: (1) collecting customer data, (2) analyzing the customer data and identifying target customers, (3) developing CRM programs, and (4) implementing CRM programs. The first step of the process is to collect and store data about customers. One of the challenges in collecting customer data is identifying the customer in connection with each transaction and contact.

Retailers use a variety of approaches to overcome this challenge.

The second step is to analyze the data to identify the most profitable customers. Two approaches used to rank customers according to their profitability are calculating the customer's lifetime value and categorizing customers on the basis of characteristics of their buying behavior—their recency, frequency, and monetary value.

Using this information about customers, retailers can develop programs to build loyalty in their best customers, increase their share of wallet with better customers (e.g., converting gold customers into platinum customers), and deal with unprofitable customers (getting the lead out). Four approaches that retailers use to build loyalty and retain their best customers are (1) launching frequent shopper programs, (2) offering special customer services, (3) personalizing the services they provide, and (4) building a sense of community. Retailers also increase share of wallet through cross selling and add-on selling. Unprofitable customers are dealt with by developing lower-cost approaches for servicing them. Effectively implementing CRM programs is difficult because it requires coordinating a number of different areas in a retailer's organization.

KEY TERMS

add-on selling, *309*
cookies, *300*
cross selling, *308*
customer database, *296*
customer loyalty, *294*
customer relationship management (CRM), *293*

data mining, *301*
80–20 rule, *302*
frequent shopper program, *298*
lifetime customer value (LTV), *302*
loyalty program, *298*
market basket analysis, *301*

1-to-1 retailing, *307*
opt in, *300*
opt out, *300*
RFM analysis, *303*
share of wallet, *294*

GET OUT AND DO IT!

1. **CONTINUING ASSIGNMENT** Interview the store manager working for the retailer you have selected for the continuing assignment. Ask the manager if the store offers a frequent shopper program and how effective it is in terms of increasing the store's sales and profits. Find out why the manager has these views and what could be done to increase the effectiveness of the program. Then talk to some customers in the store. Ask them why they are members or not. Find out how membership in the program affects their shopping behavior and loyalty toward the retailer.

2. **INTERNET EXERCISE** Go to some of the retail sites that you frequent and compare their privacy policies. Which policies make you less concerned about violations of your privacy? Why? Which policies, or lack of policies, raise your concern? Why?

3. **INTERNET EXERCISE** Go to the Web site for the Electronic Privacy Information Center (www.epic.org)

and review the issues raised by the organization. What does this watchdog organization feel are the most important issues? How will these issues affect retailers and their customers?

4. **INTERNET EXERCISE** Go to Pier 1 Imports' home page at http://www.pier1.com/ and click on the link for Credit Cards. Read about the different levels of membership for this customer card program and describe how Pier 1 Imports is using the customer pyramid (Exhibit 11–2) in their CRM program to target and classify customers.

5. **INTERNET EXERCISE** Go to the home page for the Peppers & Rodgers Consulting Group at http://www.1to1.com/home.aspx. Take a few minutes to see what this site has to offer. What is 1-to-1 marketing? How can retailers use 1-to-1 marketing? How does this concept tie into CRM?

DISCUSSION QUESTIONS AND PROBLEMS

1. What is CRM?

2. Why do retailers want to determine the lifetime value of their customers?

3. Why do customers have privacy concerns about the frequent shopper programs that supermarkets offer, and what can supermarkets do to minimize these concerns?

4. What are examples of opportunities for add-on selling that might be pursued by (a) travel agents, (b) jewelry stores, and (c) dry cleaners?

5. Which of the following types of retailers do you think would benefit most from instituting CRM: (a) supermarkets, (b) banks, (c) automobile dealers, or (d) consumer electronic retailers? Why?

6. Develop a CRM program for a local store that sells apparel with your college's or university's logo. What type of information would you collect about your customers, and how would you use this information to increase the sales and profits of the store?

7. What are the different approaches retailers can use to identify customers with their transactions? What are the advantages and disadvantages of each approach?

8. A CRM program focuses on building relationships with a retailer's better customers. Some customers who do not receive the same benefits as the retailer's best customers may be upset because they are treated differently. What can retailers do to minimize this negative reaction?

9. Think of one of your favorite places to shop. How does this retailer create customer loyalty and satisfaction, encourage repeat visits, establish an emotional bond between the customer and the retailer, know the customer's preferences, and provide personal attention and memorable experiences to their "best customers"?

10. How would a retailer use transactions, customer contacts, customer preferences, descriptive information, and responses to marketing activities in its customer database?

SUGGESTED READINGS

Bell, Simon; Seigyoung Auh; and Karen Smalley. "Customer Relationship Dynamics: Service Quality and Customer Loyalty in the Context of Varying Levels of Customer Expertise and Switching Costs," *Journal of the Academy of Marketing Science* 33 (Spring 2005), pp. 169–84.

Blattberg, Robert C.; Gary Getz; and Jacquelyn S. Thomas. *Customer Equity: Building and Managing Relationships as Valuable Assets.* Boston: Harvard Business School Press, 2001.

Bligh, Philip, and Douglas Turk. *CRM Unplugged: Releasing CRM's Strategic Value.* Hoboken, NJ: Wiley, 2004.

Budman, Matthew. "Customer Loyalty: Are You Satisfying the Right Ones?" *Across the Board* 42, no. 2 (2005), pp. 51–52.

Buttle, Francis. Customer *Relationship Management: Concepts and Tools.* Oxford: Butterworth-Heinemann, 2004.

Greenberg, Paul. *CRM at the Speed of Light: Capturing and Keeping Customers in Internet Real Time.* 3d ed. New York: Osborne/McGraw-Hill, 2004.

Kumar, V., and Denish Shah. "Building and Sustaining Profitable Customer Loyalty for the 21st Century," *Journal of Retailing* 80, no. 4 (2004), pp. 317–30.

Magi, Anne. "Share of Wallet in Retailing: The Effects of Customer Satisfaction, Loyalty Cards, and Shopper Characteristics," *Journal of Retailing* 79, no. 2 (2003), pp. 97–106.

Peppers, Don, and Martha Rogers. *Managing Customer Relationships: A Strategic Framework.* New York: Wiley, 2004.

Noble, Stephanie, and Joanna Phillips. "Relationship Hindrance: Why Would Consumers Not Want a Relationship with a Retailer?" *Journal of Retailing* 80, no. 4 (2004), pp. 289–303.

Rigby, Darrell, and Dianne Ledingham. "CRM Done Right," *Harvard Business Review,* November 2004, pp. 118–28.

Rust, Roland; Valerie Zeithaml; and Katherine Lemon. *Driving Customer Equity.* New York: Free Press, 2002.

Shugan, Steven. "Brand Loyalty Programs: Are They Shams?" *Marketing Science* 24 (Spring 2005), pp. 185–94.

Venkatesan, Rajkumar, and V. Kumar. "A Customer Lifetime Value Framework for Customer Selection and Resource Allocation Strategy," *Journal of Marketing* 68 (October 2004), pp. 106–26.

Wallace, David; Joan Giese; and Jean Johnson. "Customer Retailer Loyalty in the Context of Multiple Channel Strategies," *Journal of Retailing* 80, no. 4 (2004), pp. 249–61.

Merchandise Management

Section II reviewed the strategic decisions made by retailers—the development of their retail market strategy, their financial strategy associated with the market strategy, their store location opportunities and choices, their organization and human resource strategy, the systems they use to control the flow of information and merchandise, and the approaches they take to manage relationships with their customers. These decisions are strategic rather than tactical because they involve committing significant resources to developing long-term advantages over the competition in a target retail market segment.

This section, Section III, examines the tactical merchandise management decisions undertaken to implement the retail strategy.

> Chapter 12 provides an overview of how retailers manage their merchandise inventory—how they organize the merchandise planning process, evaluate their performance, forecast sales, establish an assortment plan, and determine the appropriate inventory levels.
>
> Chapter 13 examines the buying systems used to manage basic and fashion merchandise inventories.
>
> Chapter 14 explores how retailers buy merchandise from vendors—their branding options, negotiating processes, and vendor relationship-building activities.
>
> Chapter 15 addresses the question of how retailers set and adjust prices.
>
> Chapter 16 looks at the approaches that retailers take to build their brand image and communicate with their customers.

The following section, Section IV, focuses on store management implementation decisions.

Managing Merchandise Assortments

Three years ago I graduated from the University of Illinois–Champaign with a BA degree, majoring in Marketing. I have been on an exciting rollercoaster ride since I accepted a position in the Sears' buying office in Hoffman Estates, a suburb of Chicago.

At Sears, each buying team is composed of Inventory Analysts, an Inventory Manager, and Buyers. My initial job was as an Inventory Analyst for the Denim and Workwear Apparel team. My primary responsibility on the team was to propose the model stock plans for each of the different categories of denim, in the varying sized stores. In determining the assortment, I would analyze brands, styles, colors, sizes, and selling history across the different store volume classifications. Then, I used our merchandise planning systems to monitor sales and suggest a course of action to ensure we had the right amount of inventory—in the right stores—at the right time. While the sales of staple programs such as Levi 501s are easy to forecast, the challenge is predicting the impact of new cuts and washes that vendors are introducing each season, in order to react to the current trend.

After a year, I was promoted to Senior Inventory Analyst for the Men's Underwear and Hosiery team. As a Senior Analyst, I became more involved in the decisions regarding how much of each product to buy (for regular and promotional sales). In addition, I was more involved in setting and achieving the financial goals for the merchandise categories. You might think that underwear is pretty mundane, but men are making fashion statements with patterned boxer briefs. We must make good choices and keep on top of inventory levels to ensure our financial success.

Then, last year I was promoted to my present position as Associate Buyer for Men's Furnishings. Even though I am an Associate Buyer, I am still responsible for making

QUESTIONS

How is the merchandise management process organized?

Why do the merchandise management processes differ for staple and fashion merchandise?

How do retailers evaluate the quality of their merchandise management decisions?

How do retailers forecast sales for merchandise classifications?

How do retailers plan their assortments and determine the appropriate inventory levels?

What trade-offs must buyers make in developing merchandise assortments?

buying decisions as it relates to belts and wallets, cold weather accessories, and holiday gifts—a portion of my senior buyer's total business. I meet with national brand and private label vendors to review their product lines, pick out items we want to carry in our assortment, and negotiate the price and terms. I am an integral part of running a business valued at over $50 million annually.

Each promotion has involved more responsibilities and given me the opportunity to further develop my merchandise management skills. I really enjoy my job and continue to develop my career at Sears. I am given all the responsibility I can handle and the support I need to be successful. I like the fast pace of retailing. There are new challenges and opportunities everyday. It is really exciting to come to work, turn on the computer, and track how well the merchandise decisions you made relate to the customer (as measured by sales). It is rewarding to work in an atmosphere where I am committed to improving the lives of our customers by providing quality services, products, and solutions that earn their trust and build lifetime relationships.

Merchandise management activities are undertaken primarily by buyers and their superiors, divisional merchandise managers (DMMs) and general merchandise managers (GMMs). Many people view these jobs as very exciting and glamorous. They think that buyers spend most of their time trying to identify the latest fashions and trends, attending designer shows replete with celebrities in Paris and Milan, and going to rock concerts and other glamorous events to see what the trendsetters are wearing. But in reality, the lives of retail buyers are more like Wall Street investment bankers than globe-trotting trend gurus.

Investment bankers manage a portfolio of stocks. They buy stock in companies they think will increase in value and sell stocks in companies they believe do not have a promising future. They continuously monitor the performance of the stocks they own and might buy to see which are increasing in value and which are decreasing. Sometimes they make mistakes and invest in companies that do not perform well. So they sell their stock in these companies and lose money, but they use the money from the sold stocks to buy more attractive stocks. Other times, the stocks they buy increase dramatically in price, and they wish they had bought more shares.

Rather than managing a portfolio of stocks, retail buyers manage a portfolio of merchandise inventory. They buy merchandise they think will be popular with their customers. Like investment bankers, they use their retailer's information system to monitor the performance of their merchandise portfolio—to see what is selling and what is not. Retail buyers also make mistakes. When the merchandise they bought is not selling well, they get

rid of it by putting it on sale so they can use the money to buy better selling merchandise. However, they also might make a risky decision and buy a lot of a new product and be rewarded when it sells well, whereas competitors, who were more conservative, don't have enough of the product.

Merchandise management refers to the process by which a retailer attempts to offer the right quantity of the right merchandise in the right place at the right time and meet the company's financial goals. Buyers need to be in touch with and anticipate what customers will want to buy, but this ability to sense market trends is just one skill needed to manage merchandise inventory effectively. Perhaps an even more important skill is the ability to continually analyze sales data and make appropriate adjustments in prices and inventory levels.

The first section of this chapter outlines the process retailers use to manage their merchandise assortments. Then, several steps in the process—forecasting sales, formulating an assortment plan, and determining the appropriate inventory level—are examined in more detail. Other steps in the merchandise management process reviewed in subsequent chapters are merchandise management planning (Chapter 13), buying merchandise (Chapter 14), and pricing (Chapter 15).

Traders on the stock exchange floor manage a portfolio of stocks, and retail buyers manage a portfolio of merchandise inventory. Both continually assess the risks associated with their purchase decisions.

MERCHANDISE MANAGEMENT PROCESS OVERVIEW

This section provides an overview of the merchandise management process, including the organization of a retailer's merchandise management activities and the objectives and measures used to evaluate merchandise management performance. The section concludes with an outline of the steps in the merchandise management process and a discussion of the differences in the process for managing fashion and seasonal merchandise versus basic merchandise.

The Buying Organization

Every retailer has its own system for grouping categories of merchandise, but the basic structure of the buying organization is similar for most retailers. Exhibit 12–1 illustrates this basic structure by depicting the organization of the merchandise division for a department store chain such as Macy's, Belk, or Dillard's. Exhibit 12–1 shows the organization of buyers in the merchandise division, but a similar structure for planners and assorters parallels the structure for buyers.

Merchandise Group   The highest classification level is the **merchandise group.** The organization chart shown in Exhibit 12–1 has four merchandise groups: women's apparel; men's, children's, and intimate apparel; cosmetics, shoes, jewelry, and accessories; and home and kitchen. Each of the four merchandise groups is managed by a general merchandise manager (GMM), who is often a senior vice president in the firm. Each of these GMMs is responsible for several departments. For example, the GMM for men's, children's, and intimate apparel makes decisions about how the merchandise inventory is managed in five departments: men's dress apparel, men's sportswear, young men's apparel, children's apparel, and intimate apparel.

Illustration of Merchandise Classifications and Organization   **EXHIBIT 12–1**

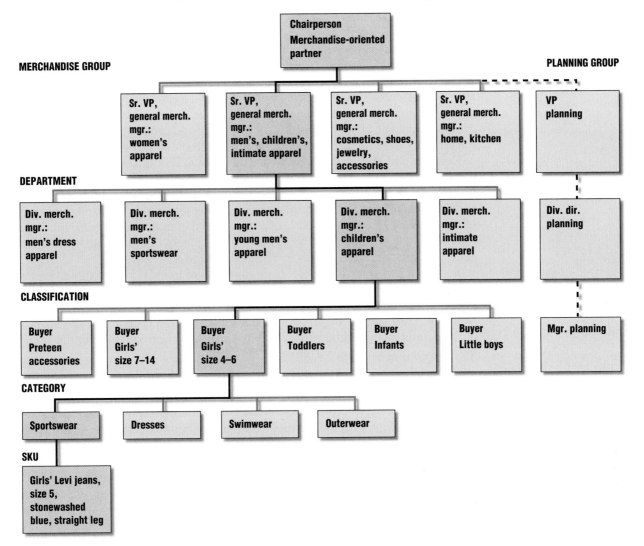

Department   The second level in the merchandise classification scheme is the **department.** Departments are managed by divisional merchandise managers (DMMs). For example, the DMM highlighted in Exhibit 12–1 is in charge of children's apparel and manages the buyers responsible for six merchandise classifications: preteen accessories, girls' sizes 7 to 14, girls' sizes 4 to 6, toddlers, infants, and little boys.

Classification   The classification is the third level for categorizing merchandise and organizing merchandise management activities. A **classification** is a group of items targeting the same customer type, such as girls' sizes 4 to 6.

Categories   Categories are the next lower level in the classification scheme. Each buyer manages several merchandise categories. For example, the girls' sizes 4 to 6 buyer manages the sportswear, dresses, swimwear, and outerwear categories for girls who wear sizes 4 to 6.

Stock-Keeping Unit   A **stock-keeping unit (SKU)** is the smallest unit available for inventory control. In soft goods merchandise, for instance, a SKU usually means size, color, and style. For example, a pair of size 5, stonewashed, blue, straight-legged Levis is an SKU.

Merchandise Category—The Planning Unit

The merchandise category is the basic unit of analysis for making merchandising management decisions. A **merchandise category** is an assortment of items that customers see as substitutes for one another. For example, a department store might offer a wide variety of girls' dresses sizes 4 to 6 in different colors, styles, and brand names. But a mother buying a dress for her daughter might consider the entire set of dresses when making her purchase decision. Lowering the price on one dress may increase the sales of that dress but also decrease the sales of other dresses. Thus, the buyers' decisions about pricing and promoting specific SKUs in the category will affect the sales of other SKUs in the same category.

Retailers and their vendors may have different definitions of a category. A vendor might assign shampoos and conditioners, for example, to different categories, on the basis of their significant differences in product attributes. However, a grocery store might put them and other combination shampoo–conditioner products into a single category on the basis of consumers' common buying behavior. Paper towels could be assigned to a "paper products" category or combined with detergent, paper tissues, and napkins in a "cleaning products" category.

Some retailers may define categories in terms of brands. For example, Tommy Hilfiger might be one category and Estée Lauder and Polo/Ralph Lauren each another because the retailer feels that the brands are not substitutes for each other. A "Tommy" customer buys Tommy and not Ralph. Also, it is easier for the buyer to purchase merchandise and plan distribution and promotions if the entire line of branded merchandise is coordinated.

Category Management   Whereas department stores, in general, manage merchandise at the category level, supermarkets and other general merchandise retailers traditionally have organized their merchandise around brands or vendors. For instance, in a supermarket chain, three different buyers—one each for Kellogg's, General Mills, and General Foods—might buy breakfast cereal.

Managing merchandise within a category by brands can lead to inefficiencies because it fails to consider the interdependencies between SKUs in the category. For example, a breakfast cereal category manager might make the decision to stock specific SKUs for corn flakes from Kellogg's, General Mills, General Foods, a private-label vendor, and a popular locally produced brand. An analysis might indicate that there is relatively little demand for the giant-sized box of corn flakes, so the category manager would decide to stock only one giant-sized corn flakes SKU. But if the decision were being made by each of the three buyers, the supermarket chain might stock three giant-sized corn flakes SKUs, one from each vendor. The analysis might also indicate that though the locally produced brand is not a top seller, it has a strong following among customers that have a high lifetime value. If the retailer drops the local brand, it may lose some very good customers. Finally, the supermarket chain might make a greater profit by setting three different prices (high, medium, and low) for the corn flakes offered by the three vendors rather than pricing them all at the same level.

Thus, the **category management** approach to managing breakfast cereals should have one buyer or category manager who oversees all merchandising activities for the entire category. Managing by category can help ensure that the store's assortment includes the "best" combination of sizes and vendors—the one that will get the most profit from the allocated space.

REFACT

The grocery retailers that are best at category management are Wal-Mart, Safeway, and HEB.[1]

Should the dairy aisle be managed by category or by brand for optimum efficiency?

Category Captain   Some retailers turn to a preferred vendor to help them manage a particular category. The vendor, known as the **category captain,** works with the retailer to develop a better understanding of customer behavior, create assortments that satisfy consumer needs, and improve the profitability of the merchandise category. Vendors are often in a better position to manage a category than retailers because they gain superior information through their focus on a specific category and their insights from working with different retailers.

For example, Kraft acts as a category captain for many retail chains.[2] To help Kraft manage a category, supermarket chains give Kraft access to their market and store information, including their costs and the sales of their competitors. In return, Kraft works with the supermarkets' category managers to make decisions about assortments, product placement on shelves, promotions, and pricing for all brands in the category. Before category management, these decisions were often based on whichever vendor was able to make the best argument to the buyer. Shelf space allocation, for instance, could change daily, depending on which vendor's salesperson offered a promotional price to a buyer that day.

Appointing vendors as category captains has its advantages for retailers. It makes merchandise management tasks easier and can increase profits. But retailers are becoming increasingly reluctant to turn over these important decisions to their vendors. They have found that working with their vendors and carefully evaluating their suggestions is a much more prudent approach.[4]

A potential problem with establishing a vendor as a category captain is that vendors could take advantage of their position. It is somewhat like "letting the fox into the henhouse." Suppose, for example, that Kraft chose to maximize its own sales at the expense of its competition. It could suggest an assortment plan that included most of its SKUs and exclude SKUs that contributed to the retailer's profit, such as high margin, private-label SKUs.[5]

There are also antitrust considerations. The vendor category captain could collude with the retailer to fix prices. It could also block other brands, particularly smaller ones, from access to shelf space. Category captains need to temper their zeal for control over retailers as well. Some actions that vendor category captains can take to avoid antitrust problems are

- Divulge all information obtained from the retailer to the other brands in the category.
- Appoint another large brand as a "category adviser" to oversee the captain's decisions.
- To circumvent potential collusion in price setting, refuse to serve as captain for two retailers in the same market.[6]

Evaluating Merchandise Management Performance—GMROI

As we discussed in Chapter 6, a good performance measure for evaluating a retail firm is ROI. Return on investment is composed of two components, asset turnover and net profit margin. But ROI is not a good measure for evaluating the performance of merchandise managers because they do not have control over all of the retailer's assets or all the expenses that the retailer incurs. Merchandise managers only have control over the merchandise they buy (the retailer's merchandise inventory assets), the price at which the merchandise is sold, and the cost of the merchandise. Thus, buyers generally have control over the gross margin but not operating expenses, such as store operations, human resources, real estate, and supply chain management and information systems.

A financial ratio that assesses a buyer's ROI performance on the basis of the factors that the buyer can control is gross margin return on inventory investment (GMROI, typically pronounced *jim-roy*).[7] It measures how many gross margin dollars are earned on every dollar of inventory investment made by the buyer.

REFACT

From the perspective of retailers, the best manufacturers that practice category management are Kraft, Procter & Gamble, and General Mills.[3]

Thus, GMROI is a similar concept to ROI, except that its components are under the control of the buyer rather than other managers in the firm. Instead of combining net profit margin and asset turnover, GMROI combines gross margin percentage and the sales-to-stock ratio, which is similar to inventory turnover.

$$
\begin{aligned}
\text{GMROI} &= \text{Gross margin percentage} \times \text{Sales-to-stock ratio} \\
&= \frac{\text{Gross margin}}{\text{Net sales}} \times \frac{\text{Net sales}}{\text{Average inventory at cost}} \\
&= \frac{\text{Gross margin}}{\text{Average inventory at cost}}
\end{aligned}
$$

When calculating the sales-to-stock ratio, the numerator is net sales; when calculating inventory turnover, the numerator is the cost of goods sold. Thus, when measuring inventory turnover, both the "sales" and the average inventory are measured at cost. Sales-to-stock ratio is used to measure GMROI instead of inventory turnover because GMROI is an ROI measure, and investments are expressed at cost. To convert the sales-to-stock ratio to inventory turnover, simply multiply the sales-to-stock ratio by $(1 -$ gross margin percentage). Thus, if the sales-to-stock ratio is 9.0 and the gross margin percentage is .40, the inventory turnover for the category is 5.4:

$$
\begin{aligned}
\text{Inventory turnover} &= (1 - \text{Gross margin percentage}) \times \text{Sales-to-stock ratio} \\
5.4 &= (1 - .4) \times 9.0
\end{aligned}
$$

Buyers have control over both components of GMROI. The gross margin component is affected by the prices they set and the prices they negotiate with vendors when buying merchandise, whereas the sales-to-stock ratio is affected by the popularity of the merchandise they buy. If they buy merchandise that customers want, it sells quickly, and the sales-to-stock ratio is high.

Like ROI, GMROI assesses not just the profitability of merchandise decisions but also how effectively the merchandise assets (inventory) are used. Thus, merchandise categories with different margin/turnover profiles can be compared and evaluated. For instance, within a supermarket, some categories (such as wine) are high margin/low turnover, whereas other categories (such as milk) are low margin/high turnover. If the wine category's performance is compared to that of milk using inventory turnover alone, the contribution of wine to the supermarket's performance will be undervalued. In contrast, if only gross margin is used, wine's contribution will be overvalued.

Consider the situation in Exhibit 12–2 in which a supermarket wants to evaluate the performance of two categories: bread and ready-to-eat prepared foods. If evaluated on gross margin percentage or sales alone, prepared foods is certainly the winner with a 50 percent gross margin and sales of $300,000 compared with

EXHIBIT 12–2
Illustration of GMROI

			Bread	**Prepared Foods**
	Gross margin		$2,000	$150,000
	Sales		$150,000	$300,000
	Average inventory		$1,000	$75,000
	GMROI $=$ $\dfrac{\text{Gross margin}}{\text{Net sales}}$ $\times$ $\dfrac{\text{Net sales}}{\text{Average inventory}}$ $=$ $\dfrac{\text{Gross margin}}{\text{Average inventory}}$			
Bread	GMROI $=$ $\dfrac{\$2,000}{\$150,000}$ $\times$ $\dfrac{\$150,000}{\$1,000}$ $=$ $\dfrac{\$2,000}{\$1,000}$			
	$=$ 1.333% $\times$ 150 times $=$ 200%			
Prepared Foods	GMROI $=$ $\dfrac{\$150,000}{\$300,000}$ $\times$ $\dfrac{\$300,000}{\$75,000}$ $=$ $\dfrac{\$150,000}{\$75,000}$			
	$=$ 50% $\times$ 4 $=$ 200%			

Department	Gross Margin %	Sales-to-Stock Ratio	GMROI
Apparel	37	6.35	235
Housewares	35	4.63	162
Food	20	8.75	175
Jewelry	38	3.24	123
Furniture	31	4.09	90
Health and beauty supplies	22	5.14	113
Consumer electronics	21	5.05	106

EXHIBIT 12–3
GMROI for Selected Departments in Discount Stores

bread's gross margin of 1.33 percent and sales of $150,000. Yet prepared foods' sales-to-stock ratio is only four times a year, whereas bread turns 150 times a year. Using GMROI, both classifications achieve a GMROI of 200 percent and so are equal performers from an ROI perspective.

Exhibit 12–3 shows the GMROI percentages for selected departments in discount stores. Jewelry, apparel, and housewares have the highest gross margin percentages. Their sales-to-stock ratios range from 8.75 (food) to 3.24 (jewelry). We might expect food to have the highest sales-to-stock ratio because it is perishable; it is either sold quickly or spoils. However, as a luxury item, jewelry has a relatively low sales-to-stock ratio. Furniture also has a low sales-to-stock ratio because a relatively large assortment of costly items is needed to support the sales level.

In this case, GMROI ranges from 235 (apparel) to 90 (furniture). Thus, it's not surprising that Wal-Mart and Target are emphasizing apparel and have deemphasized furniture. They continue to carry consumer electronics and health and beauty products—both with low GMROIs—because these categories have traditionally brought customers into the store. The retailers hope that while customers buying products from these categories are in the store, they will also purchase higher GMROI items.

Measuring Sales-to-Stock Ratio   Retailers normally express sales-to-stock ratios (and inventory turnover) on an annual basis rather than for part of a year. If the sales-to-stock ratio for a three-month season equals 2.3, the annual sales-to-stock ratio will be four times that number (9.2). Thus, to convert a sales-to-stock ratio based on part of a year to an annual figure, multiply it by the number of such time periods in the year.

The most accurate measure of average inventory is to measure the inventory level at the end of each day and divide the sum by 365. Most retailers can use their information systems to get accurate average inventory estimates by averaging the inventory in stores and distribution centers at the end each day. Another method is to take the end-of-month (EOM) inventories for several months and divide by the number of months. For example,

Month	End of Month Inventory at Retail Prices
January	$22,000
February	33,000
March	38,000
Total inventory	93,000
Average inventory	31,000

This approach is adequate only if the EOM figure does not differ in any appreciable or systematic way from any other day. For instance, January's EOM inventory is significantly lower than that of February or March because it assesses the inventory position at the end of the winter clearance sale and before the spring buildup.

Managing Inventory Turnover

As we discussed at the beginning of the chapter, buyers are responsible for investing in and managing merchandise inventory. Inventory turnover and the sales-to-stock ratio help assess the buyer's performance in managing this asset. Retailers want to achieve a high inventory turnover, but just focusing on increasing inventory turnover can actually decrease GMROI. Thus, buyers need to consider the trade-offs associated with managing their inventory turnover.

Benefits of High Turnover   Increasing inventory turnover can increase sales volume, improve salesperson morale, reduce the risk of obsolescence and markdowns, and provide more resources to take advantage of new buying opportunities.

Higher inventory turnover increases sales because new merchandise is continually available to customers, and new merchandise sells better and faster than old merchandise. New merchandise attracts customers to visit the store more frequently because they see new things. When inventory turnover is low, the merchandise begins to look worn out. Increasing the amount of new merchandise also improves sales associate morale. Salespeople are excited about and more motivated to sell the new merchandise, and thus, sales increase, increasing inventory turnover even further.

The value of fashion and other perishable merchandise starts declining as soon as it is placed on display. When inventory is selling quickly, merchandise isn't in the store long enough to become obsolete. As a result, sale price discounts are reduced, and gross margins increase.

Finally, when inventory turnover increases, more money previously invested in inventory is available to buy new merchandise. Having money available to buy merchandise late in a fashion season can open up profit opportunities.

Potential Problems with Approaches for Improving Inventory Turnover
Retailers need to strike a balance in their rate of inventory turnover. Some approaches for improving inventory turnover can lower GMROI by lowering sales volume, increasing the cost of goods sold, and increasing operating expenses.

One approach to increase turnover is to reduce the number of merchandise categories, the number of SKUs within a category, or the number of items within an SKU. But if customers can't find the size or color they seek—or even worse, if they can't find the brand or product line at all—patronage and sales can decrease. Customers who are disappointed on a regular basis will shop elsewhere and possibly urge their friends to do the same.

Another approach for increasing inventory turnover is to buy merchandise more often and in smaller quantities, which reduces average inventory without reducing sales. But by buying smaller quantities, the gross margin decreases because buyers can't take advantage of quantity discounts and transportation economies of scale. Buying merchandise frequently in small quantities can also increase operating expenses, in that buyers spend more time placing orders and monitoring deliveries.

Merchandise Management Process

Exhibit 12–4 outlines the activities and decisions that are involved in the merchandise management process. First, buyers forecast category sales, develop an assortment plan for merchandise in the category, and determine the amount of inventory needed to support the forecasted sales and assortment plan. Each of these activities is discussed the remaining sections of this chapter.

Second, buyers develop a plan outlining the sales expected for each month, the inventory needed to support the sales, and the money that can be spent on replenishing sold merchandise and buying new merchandise. Along with the plan, the buyer or planners/assorters decide what type and how much merchandise should be allocated to each store. The development of these merchandise plans is discussed in Chapter 13.

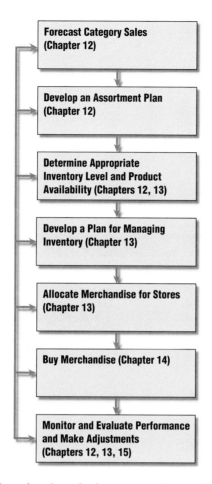

EXHIBIT 12–4
Merchandise Planning
Process

Third, having developed a plan, the buyer negotiates with vendors and buys the merchandise. These merchandise buying activities are reviewed in Chapter 14.

Buyers continually monitor the sales of merchandise in the category and make adjustments. For example, if category sales are less than the forecast in the plan and the projected GMROI for the category falls below the buyer's goal, the buyer may decide to dispose of some merchandise by putting it on sale and using the money generated to buy merchandise with greater sales potential or to reduce the number of SKUs in the assortment to increase the inventory turnover.

Although Exhibit 12–4 suggests that these decisions follow each other sequentially, in practice, some decisions may be made at the same time or in a different order. For example, a buyer might first decide on the amount of inventory to invest in the category, and this decision might determine the number of SKUs that can be offered in the category.

Types of Merchandise Management Planning Processes

Retailers use two distinct types of merchandise management planning systems for managing (1) staple and (2) fashion merchandise categories. **Staple merchandise categories,** also called **basic merchandise categories,** consist of items that are in continuous demand over an extended time period. The number of new product introductions in these categories is limited. Some examples of staple merchandise categories are most categories sold in supermarkets, housewares, white paint, copy paper, hosiery, inexpensive watches, basic causal apparel such as tee shirts, and men's underwear.

Because sales of staple merchandise are relatively steady from day to day, it is relatively easy to forecast demand, and the consequences of making mistakes in forecasting are not great. For example, if a buyer overestimates the demand for canned soup and buys too much, the retailer will have excess inventory for a short period of time, but eventually the canned soup will be sold without having to resort to discounts or special marketing efforts. Because the demand for basic merchandise is predictable, merchandise planning systems for staple categories focus on continuous replenishment. These systems involve continuously monitoring merchandise sales and generating replacement orders, often automatically, when inventory levels drop below predetermined levels.

Fashion merchandise consists of items that are only in demand for a relatively short period of time. New products are continually introduced into these categories, making the existing products obsolete. In some cases, the basic product does not change, but the colors and styles change to reflect what is "hot" that season. Some examples of fashion merchandise categories are athletic shoes, laptop computers, and women's apparel. Retailing View 12.1 describes how Mango creates and manages fashion merchandise.

12.1   RETAILING VIEW   Fast Fashion at Mango

With the opening of *The Matrix: Reloaded*, designers at the European specialty store retailer Mango planned a series of women's styles inspired by the third film in the *Matrix* trilogy. The designs were heavy on black, with lots of leather and high necklines. But the film was not the anticipated blockbuster; softer, more feminine clothes appeared on European runways; and the sci-fi look was doomed. So the company dropped the entire line.

"We know how to improvise," says David Egea, Mango's merchandising director and a top executive. "To react and have what people want, we have to break some rules." Mango/MNG Holding SL, with over 700 stores in 72 countries, typifies the new retail trend of "fast fashion," pioneered by Spain's Zara and Sweden's H&M. These chains fill their racks with a steady stream of new, gotta-have-it merchandise. Their retail strategy combines stylistic and technological resources built on flexibility and speed from design sketch to the store shelf.

Mango is famous for an eclectic mix of body-hugging styles; a black pinstriped jacket sells for $60 and a tight black minidress for $40. It maintains tight controls over the design and manufacturing of its private-label merchandise. Last minute changes, like substituting a fabric or dropping a hemline, are a built-in part of the creative process. So long as the company has fabric in stock, it can move a design from sketchpad to store in four weeks.

Mango's merchandise planning cycle begins every three months when designers meet to discuss important new trends for each of its main collections, which contain five or six minicollections. So shops receive a near-constant stream of merchandise, ranging from clingy short dresses to work wear and sparkly evening gowns. New items are sent to its stores once a week, roughly six times as often as the typical American clothing chain.

To get ideas for each collection, designers attend the traditional fashion shows and trade fairs. But they also stay close to the customer. They take photos of stylish young women and note what people are wearing on the streets and in nightclubs. "To see what everyone's going to do for next season is very easy," says Egea. "But that doesn't mean this is the thing that is going to catch on." Hoping to stay au courant, design teams meet each week to adjust to ever-changing trends.

When collection designs are set, Mango's product management and distribution team assigns them personality traits, denoting SKUs as trendy, dressy, or suitable for hot weather. Depending on an item's personality, it heads to one of Mango's 731 stores, which also has its own set of traits, such as the climate, where the shop is located, and whether large or small

Mango stocks high-fashion, trendy merchandise to attract its target shoppers.

sizes sell best. A proprietary computer program then matches compatible shops and styles.

Orders get programmed into a large distribution machine, surrounded by a rotating ring of cardboard boxes on hooks. Clothes are scanned and dropped into one of 466 store-specific slots. Then they're boxed and shipped to shops, where managers can adjust store layouts daily on the basis of input from regional supervisors and headquarters.

Mango stores only display a limited merchandise assortment. On each rack, only one size per item is hung. This policy encourages a sense of urgency by playing on customers' worst fear: Maybe your size is going to run out.

Sources: Erin White, "For Retailer Mango, Frenzied 'Fast Fashion' Proves Sweet," *The Wall Street Journal*, May 28, 2004, p. B1; and Leonie Barrie, "Making a Mark: Some of the Issues to Watch in 2004: Fast Fashion Continues to Speed Up," *Just—Style*, January 2004, pp. 17–20.

Forecasting the sales for fashion merchandise categories is much more challenging than for staple goods. Buyers for fashion merchandise categories have much less flexibility in correcting forecasting errors. For example, if the laptop computer buyer for COMPUSA buys too many units of a particular model, the excess inventory cannot be easily sold when a new replacement model is introduced. Due to the short life cycle of fashion merchandise, buyers often do not have a chance to reorder additional merchandise after an initial order is placed. So if buyers initially order too little fashion merchandise, the retailer may not be able to satisfy the demand for the merchandise and will develop a reputation for not having the most popular merchandise in stock. Thus, an important objective of merchandise planning systems for fashion merchandise categories is to be as close to out of stock as possible at the same time that the SKUs become out of fashion.

Seasonal merchandise, such as Christmas tree ornaments, is prominently displayed before the holiday to help shoppers find decorations for their homes and gifts for their friends and family members.

Seasonal merchandise categories consist of items whose sales fluctuate dramatically depending on the time of year. Some examples of seasonal merchandise are Halloween candy, Christmas ornaments, swimwear, and snow shovels. Both staple and fashion merchandise can be seasonal categories. For example, swimwear is a fashion merchandise category, while snow shovels are a staple merchandise category. However, from a merchandise planning perspective, retailers buy seasonal merchandise in much the same way that they buy fashion merchandise. Retailers could store unsold snow shovels at the end of the winter season and sell them the next winter, but it is typically better to sell the shovels at a steep discount near the end of the season rather than incur the cost of carrying this excess inventory until the beginning of the next season. Thus, buyers for seasonal merchandise develop plans for getting rid of all of their merchandise at the end of the season.

These two different merchandise planning systems are discussed in more detail in Chapter 13. The remaining sections in this chapter examine three elements in the merchandise management process: (1) forecasting sales, (2) developing an assortment plan, and (3) determining the appropriate inventory level.

FORECASTING SALES

As indicated in Exhibit 12–4, the first step in merchandise management planning is to develop a forecast for category sales. To develop a category forecast, one needs to understand the nature of category life cycles and the factors that might affect the shape of the life cycle in the future. The methods and information used for forecasting basic and fashion merchandise categories are also discussed in this section.

Category Life Cycles

Merchandise categories typically follow a predictable sales pattern: Sales start off low, increase, plateau, and then ultimately decline. This sales pattern, referred to as the **category life cycle** (Exhibit 12–5), is divided into four stages: introduction, growth, maturity, and decline. Knowing where a category is in its life cycle is important in developing a sales forecast and merchandising strategy.

EXHIBIT 12–5
The Category Product
Life Cycle

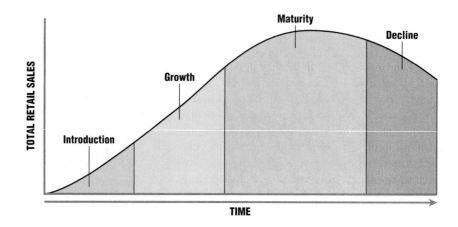

For example, when personal digital assistants (PDAs) were first introduced in 1996, the target market was businesspeople who were high-tech aficionados, people who wanted to be the first to adopt an innovation and were willing to pay for the convenience of having a very small, handheld computer.[8] Compared with address and appointment books, PDAs were very expensive, and they weren't available at most stores that normally sold office supplies or computers. Then PDAs were marketed to doctors, stockbrokers, and business executives, who used them for access to medical databases, stock markets, and e-mail. As this category reached its growth and maturity stages, it appealed to a broader, mass-market customer who patronized discount stores and category specialists.

However, the shape of the life cycle is affected by the activities undertaken by retailers and vendors. For instance, a vendor might set a low introductory price for a new product to increase the adoption rate of the product or a high price to increase profits even though sales might not grow as fast.

Care must be taken, however, when using the category life cycle as a predictive tool. If a product is classified as being in the decline stage of its product life cycle, it's likely that retailers will stock less variety and limit promotions. Naturally, sales will go down. Thus, the declining classification may actually become a self-fulfilling prophesy. Many products have been successfully maintained at the maturity stage because their buyers have maintained innovative strategies to market the mature product.

Variations in Category Life Cycles   The characteristics of common variations of the category life cycle—fad, fashion, and staple—are shown in Exhibit 12–6. The distinguishing characteristics between these variations are the number of seasons sales are sustained, whether specific styles also

EXHIBIT 12–6
Variations in Category
Life Cycles

	FAD	FASHION	STAPLE
Sales over many seasons	No	Yes	Yes
Sales of a specific style over many seasons	No	No	Yes
Sales vary dramatically from one season to the next	No	Yes	No
Illustration (Sales against Time)	Sales / Time	Sales / Time	Sales / Time

sell for many seasons, and whether sales vary dramatically from one season to the next.

A **fad** is a merchandise category that generates a lot of sales for a relatively short time, often less than a season. Examples are Pokémon, pet rocks, some licensed characters like Star Wars action figures, and some electronic games. The art of retailing a fad comes in recognizing the fad in its earliest stages, taking a significant inventory position, and having it available in stores nationwide before the competition does. However, retailing fads is risky because even if the company properly identifies a fad, it must still know when the peak occurs so it isn't stuck with a warehouse full of merchandise.

Unlike a fad, fashion categories typically last several seasons; however, like fads, sales of specific SKUs (styles and colors) can vary dramatically from one season to the next. For instance, black apparel might be popular one year, and the same style in purple is popular the next year. Some questions that help buyers distinguish between fads and more enduring fashions are

- *Is it compatible with a change in consumer lifestyles?* Innovations that are consistent with lifestyles are more enduring. For example, denim jeans are an enduring fashion because they are comfortable to wear, are easily laundered, and can be worn on multiple occasions. Leather pants, in contrast, are uncomfortable and expensive to clean and thus more fadish.
- *Does the innovation provide real benefits?* The switch to poultry and fish from beef is not a fad because it provides real benefits to a health-conscious society.
- *Is the innovation compatible with other changes in the marketplace?* For example, cell phones are more enduring because they are compatible with a more mobile, time-pressured society.
- *Who is adopting the trend?* If the product is being adopted by a large and growing segment, such as working mothers, Baby Boomers, Generation Y, or the elderly, it is more likely to endure.[9]

In the early 1980s, when Cabbage Patch Dolls were first introduced, they were such a popular fad that only a few shoppers were allowed in toy stores at a time to prevent parents from fighting over the dolls during the Christmas season. The dolls are still sold today, but they only enjoyed such high demand for a short period of time.

Staple merchandise categories experience relatively steady sales over an extended period of time. However, even staple merchandise categories go into decline eventually. For example, changing technology resulted in the eventual decline of VCR sales with the growth in demand for DVD players.

Forecasting Staple Merchandise Categories

The sales of staple merchandise categories are relatively constant from year to year. Thus, forecasts are typically based on extrapolating historical sales. Because there are substantial sales data available, statistical techniques can be used to forecast future sales. Exhibit 12–7 illustrates the analysis of past unit sales data for paperback mystery novels at a bookstore chain to forecast sales for 2007.

Exhibit 12–7a contains the sales data by quarter over the last eight years. These quarterly sales data are plotted in Exhibit 12–7b, and the annual sales data are plotted in Exhibit 12–7c. The annual sales pattern reveals a slight annual growth in sales. Average annual growth has been 3.6 percent; however, sales actually decreased in 2005 and then jumped 7.6 percent in 2006.

The graph of quarterly sales shows a seasonal pattern, with sales greatest during the fourth quarter and lowest during the third quarter. The average percentage of annual sales for each quarter is 21 percent for the first quarter, 26 percent second

EXHIBIT 12–7   Sales of Paperback Mystery Novels at a Bookstore Chain

EXHIBIT 12–7a   Units Sales by Quarter

Year	Quarter	Sales by Quarter	Annual Sales	Annual Sales Growth Rate	% Annual Sales by Quarter
1999	1	21,074			23%
	2	24,123			26
	3	16,066			17
	4	32,145	93,408		34
2000	1	20,728			23
	2	23,656			26
	3	15,867			18
	4	30,135	90,387	−3.2%	33
2001	1	21,076			22
	2	25,259			26
	3	18,585			19
	4	33,064	97,984	8.4	34
2002	1	20,617			21
	2	26,084			26
	3	18,308			18
	4	34,921	99,931	2.0	35
2003	1	21,464			20
	2	27,568			26
	3	18,996			18
	4	38,163	106,192	6.3	36
2004	1	24,401			21
	2	28,057			25
	3	21,092			18
	4	40,843	114,394	7.7	36
2005	1	23,859			22
	2	27,441			25
	3	19,537			18
	4	39,726	110,562	−3.3	36
2006	1	24,588			21
	2	30,788			26
	3	19,869			17
	4	43,718	118,963	7.6	37

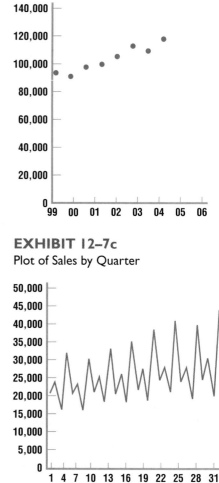

EXHIBIT 12–7b
Plot of Sales by Year

EXHIBIT 12–7c
Plot of Sales by Quarter

quarter, 18 percent third quarter, and 35 percent fourth quarter. Even though summer book sales are typically higher than average, they are lower for this Florida chain because many people who live near the stores spend their summers in North Carolina to escape the high temperatures and humidity.

On the basis of these past unit sales data, the buyer could simply project the sales data and estimate the annual unit sales for paperback mystery books for 2007 as

2007 annual sales = 1.036 (3.6 percent growth) × 118,963 (2006 annual sales)
= 123,245

The estimated quarterly sales would be

First-quarter sales   = 123,245 × .21 = 25,881
Second-quarter sales = 123,245 × .26 = 32,044
Third-quarter sales   = 123,245 × .18 = 22,184
Fourth-quarter sales = 123,245 × .35 = 43,136

However, these projections are based on the assumption that the factors affecting paperback mystery book sales in 2007 will be the same and have the same effect as they have had for the past eight years. Even though sales for staple merchandise categories such as paperback mystery novels are relatively predictable, controllable and uncontrollable factors can have a significant impact on them.

Controllable factors include openings and closings of stores, the price set for the merchandise in the category, special promotions for the category, pricing and promotion of complementary categories, and the placement of the merchandise categories in the stores. Some factors beyond the retailer's control are the weather, general economic conditions, special promotions and new product introductions by vendors, the availability of products, pricing, and promotional activities by competitors. Retailing View 12.2 illustrates how retailers use long-range weather forecasts to improve their merchandise planning.

In this case, the buyer might adjust the annual unit sales projection downward for paperback mystery books because publishers, and thus the retailer, are increasing their prices for paperback books in 2007. Also, third-quarter sales might be adjusted upward because the chain, for the first time, is holding a series of in-store promotions featuring visits and a book signing by Tony Hillerman, a noted mystery novel writer.

Forecasting Fashion Merchandise Categories

Forecasting sales for fashion merchandise categories is challenging because some or all of the items in the category are new and different than units offered in previous years. Some sources of information that retailers use to develop forecasts

REFACT

Men in New York get inspired to buy a winter coat when the temperature drops to 51 degrees Fahrenheit. But in Chicago, it has to drop to 41 degrees.[10]

Forecasting the Weather   **RETAILING VIEW**   **12.2**

Tractor Supply Company was prepared when hurricanes Charley, Frances, Ivan, and Jeanne hit Florida in August and September 2004. Its weather weapon was Planalytics' long-range weather forecasting models that projected an active 2004 hurricane season in November 2003. Using the models, Tractor Supply beefed up its emergency response inventory and was able to deploy it to the right store locations before, during, and after the storms hit.

Long-range weather forecasting helps retailers manage severe weather events, but these models are most valuable in providing retail executives, buyers, planners, and allocators with the data and expertise needed to manage noncatastrophic weather,

Tropical storms, hurricanes, thunderstorms, and other severe weather can cause serious damage to homes and property. Retailers should stock merchandise that homeowners and contractors need to make repairs and help get the community back to normal after the damage caused by catastrophic weather events.

like the fluctuations in temperature that translate into risks or opportunities for many merchandise categories. The data are especially useful for apparel merchants whose decisions about the timing of supply chain flow, promotions, and price discounts can have huge gross margin implications. For example, one of Planalytics' apparel retailer clients paid attention to the forecast of warmer temperatures in September and kept some shorts on reserve—resisting the urge to take markdowns of 40 to 60 percent in August—and managed to eek out some postseason profits in a category that competitors had already cleared from their shelves.

It is also important to understand when not to use weather forecasts. In October and November, weather affects what shoppers choose to purchase, but by December, Planalytic's analysis revealed that weather is more likely to influence store traffic issues.

When analyzing the effects of weather, one needs to recognize that it is relative. What's cold to a Texan is very different from what cold feels like to someone who lives in Buffalo. Another good example is Los Angeles. If it's cloudy and rainy in L.A. in November, consumers react as if winter is upon them and start buying fleece and Duraflame logs, even though the temperature is still in the 60s.

REFACT

Research in the United Kingdom reports that for every degree Celsius increase in temperature between 18 (64.4 degrees F) and 24 degrees (75.2 degrees F), sales of carbonated soft drinks rise fourfold. Once the temperature exceeds 24 degrees Celsius, soft drink sales drop off as people drink more water. Brand preferences also change as thirsty consumers seek lower priced beverages.[11]

Source: Susan Reda, "Whither Forecasting?" *Stores*, December 2004, pp. 23–27.

for fashion merchandise categories are (1) previous sales data, (2) personal aware-ness, (3) fashion and trend services, (4) vendors, and (5) traditional market research.

Previous Sales Data   Although items in fashion merchandise categories might be new each season, the basic merchandise in many categories is the same, and thus, accurate forecasts might be generated by simply projecting past sales data. For example, women's fashion dresses might change from season to season with new colors, styles, and fabrics. Whereas the SKUs are different each season, the total number of fashion dresses sold each year might be relatively constant and very predictable.

Personal Awareness   Buyers for fashion merchandise categories need to be aware of trends that can affect their category sales. To find out what customers are going to want in the future, they immerse themselves in the customers' world: go into Internet chat rooms and blogs, look in their closets, attend soccer games and rock concerts. They visit hot spots around town like restaurants and nightclubs and attend football games and concerts. Some suggestions to help buyers keep abreast of what teenage customers will want to buy are shop, converse, act, and notice (SCAN).[12]

- *Shop* retail stores, Web sites and catalogs as a customer would. When visiting your own stores, don't identify yourself. When store employees know you are coming, they are on their best behavior. Surprise them: Watch how your staff interacts with shoppers. Pretend to be a customer. The key is to open your eyes to things that are new and different.
- *Converse* with consumers, sales clerks, neighbors, your children. Ask them, What are your favorite bands? Why are you buying a $16 Gap tee shirt to wear with a $200 suit? What TV and radio shows are you tuning in to? What do you do in your spare time? Talk to vendors and other people who are close to consumers, such as beauticians and real estate agents.
- *Act* like your customer. For one weekend, become your customer and see your merchandise or stores through the eyes of the consumer. Buy yourself a pair of cut-up jeans, Saucony shoes, and a bowling shirt. Spend the day in a mall, pick

Although specific notebook computer types and models go in and out of fashion, the overall sales for the product category can be forecasted using historical sales data.

up a copy of *Teen People*, listen to Linkin Park and Sum 41, go to a trendy nightclub (the ones that get going at midnight or later). Check out online teen Web sites such as Alloy.com and Bolt.com's coolhunting polls to see how teens feel about reality shows, belly-button rings, and inflatable furniture.

 • *Notice*, notice, notice. Become a cultural sleuth by noticing the things that make you uncomfortable or seem strange and different. What movies are hits at the box office? Who is going to see them? What books and albums are on the top 10 lists? What magazines are consumers purchasing? Become an information junkie and read voraciously. Are there themes that keep popping up? All of these clues are cultural trend posts that can become an on-ramp into the mainstream.

Fashion and Trend Services   There are many services such as Trendzine (www.FashionInformation.com), Doneger Creative Services (www.Doneger.com), and Fashion Snoops (www.fashionsnoops.com) that buyers, particularly buyers of apparel categories, can subscribe to that forecast the latest fashions, colors, and styles. For example, Doneger Creative Services offers a range of services related to trend and color forecasting and analysis for apparel, accessories, and lifestyle markets in the women's, men's, and youth merchandise categories through its print publications, online content, and live presentations. Its color forecast service provides color direction for each season using dyed-to-specification color standards plus suggested color combinations and applications for specific categories. Its online clipboard reports present actionable information and style news from the runways to the streets.[13]

Kim Hastreiter, the cofounder and editor of *Paper* magazine, is a cool hunter. To most people, *Paper* is just a glossy magazine filled with clothes they can't imagine ever wearing. But exploring the underground has been *Paper*'s mission for 20 years—discovering and documenting provocateurs, places, and ideas in their

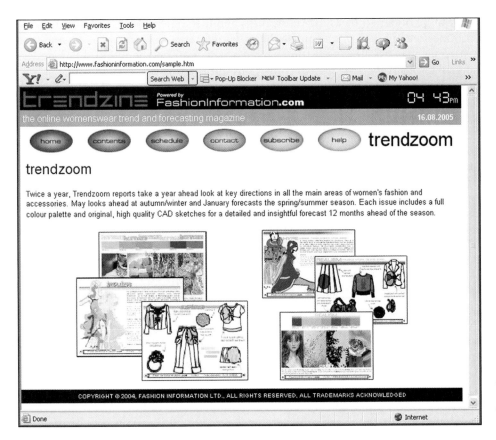

Fashion services like Trendzine provide apparel buyers information about the latest fashions, colors, and styles.

earliest, rawest, and often most disconcerting form. *Paper* doesn't pride itself on being trendy. It is pretrendy.

"Trends don't start with trendy people," Hastreiter says. So you won't find Hastreiter dining at the latest restaurant where reservations require a secret number. Hastreiter will be at the restaurant off the alley behind a seedy street. "We prefer to write about things when they're still in garages, when they're more rough," Hastreiter says. "Years ago we put a local waitress with tattoos all over her body on the cover of the magazine. We lost ads because of it. But we had never seen that before." Now, of course, tattoos or body piercings are common, and their wearers are models for such mainstream brands as The Gap and Pepsi.[14]

Vendors   Vendors have proprietary information about their marketing plans, such as new product launches and special promotions that can have a significant impact on retail sales for their products and the entire merchandise category. In addition, vendors tend to be knowledgeable about market trends for merchandise categories because they typically specialize in fewer merchandise categories than retailers. Thus, information from vendors about their plans and market research about merchandise categories is very useful to buyers as they develop category sales forecasts.

A systematic approach for incorporating vendor information in merchandise planning is the collaborative planning, forecasting, and replenishment (CPFR) discussed in Chapter 10. For example, the CVS drugstore chain implemented CPFR with 11 key vendors. Through this formal process of sharing information with one vendor, sales forecast accuracy improved by 8.2 percent, which led to a 7.5 percent reduction in out-of-stocks, an 18 percent decrease in over-stocks, and an 18 percent improvement in inventory turnover.[15] Retailing View 12.3 describes how a Macy's buyer worked with a vendor to build sales for a merchandise category.

Market Research   Information on how customers will react to new merchandise can be obtained by asking customers about the merchandise and measuring customer reactions to merchandise through sales tests. For example, a cashier at a restaurant may ask how a customer liked a new item on the menu. But retailers need to have a systematic way to collect this information and relay it to the appropriate buyers. Some retailers have their salespeople maintain **want books** in which out-of-stock and requested merchandise is recorded. This information is then collected by buyers for making forecasts and purchasing decisions.

Customer information also can be collected through traditional forms of marketing research like depth interviews and focus groups. The **depth interview** is an unstructured personal interview in which the interviewer uses extensive probing to get individual respondents to talk in detail about a subject. For example, one grocery store chain goes through the personal checks received each day and selects all customers with large purchases of groceries and several with small purchases. Representatives from the chain call these customers and interview them to find out what they like and don't like about the store.

A more informal method of interviewing customers is to require buyers to spend some time on the selling floor waiting on customers. In most national retail chains, buyers are physically isolated from their customers. For example, buying offices for Target and The Gap are in northern California and Minnesota, respectively, yet their stores are throughout America. It has become increasingly hard for buyers in large chains to be attuned to local customer demand. Frequent store visits help the situation. Some retailers require their buyers to spend a specified period of time, like one day a week, in a store.

A **focus group** is a small group of respondents interviewed by a moderator using a loosely structured format. Participants are encouraged to express their views and comment on the views of others in the group. To keep abreast of the teen market, for instance, some stores have teen boards comprised of opinion leaders that meet to discuss merchandising and other store issues.[16]

Finally, many retailers have a program of conducting merchandise experiments. For example, Claire's, an international specialty accessory retail chain targeting teens, continually runs tests to determine whether new merchandise concepts will produce adequate sales. It introduces the new merchandise into a representative group of stores and sees what sales are generated for the items. Multichannel retailers often run similar tests by offering new items on their Web sites before making a decision to stock them in their stores.

Sales Forecasting for Service Retailers

Due to the perishable nature of services, service retailers face a more extreme problem than fashion retailers. Their offering perishes at the end of day, not at the end of the season. If there are empty seats when a plane takes off or the rock concert is over, the revenue that might have been generated from these seats is lost forever. However, if more people are interested in dining at a restaurant than there are tables available, a revenue opportunity also is lost. So service retailers have devised approaches for managing demand for their offering so that it meets but does not exceed capacity.[17]

Some service retailers attempt to match supply and demand by taking reservations or making appointments. Physicians often overbook their appointments so many patients have to wait. They do this so they will always fill their capacity and not have unproductive, non–revenue-generating time. Restaurants take reservations so that customers will not have to wait for a table. In addition, the reservations indicate the staffing levels needed for that meal. Another approach is selling advance tickets for a service.[18]

DEVELOPING AN ASSORTMENT PLAN

After forecasting sales for the category, the next step in the merchandise management planning process is to develop an assortment plan. An **assortment plan** is a list of the SKUs that a retailer will offer in a merchandise category. The assortment plan thus reflects the variety and assortment that the retailer plans to offer in a merchandise category.

Macy's DMM Talks about Catching the Wave   **RETAILING VIEW**   12.3

Chris Manning was the women's swimwear and casual weekend wear buyer for Macy's in Atlanta and is now the DMM for men's accessories.

"My job finding fashion trends is like surfing. Sometimes you catch a big wave [trend] and it's exhilarating and sometimes you think you've caught a good wave and brown turns out not to be the color this season. But the real fun is getting the most out of the wave you can. Let me give you an example of how I worked a big wave when I was the swimwear buyer.

"At the swimwear marts, they started to show tankinis— womens' bathing suits with bikini bottoms and tank tops. My customers were women in their 40s that had a couple of kids. I thought they would really go for this new style because it had the advantages of a two-piece bathing suit but wasn't much more revealing than a one-piece suit. I bought a wide color assortment— bright reds, yellows, pink, and black—and put them in our fashion-forward stores in January for a test. The initial sales were good, but our customers thought they were a little too skimpy. Then I started to work the wave. I went back to the vendor and got them to recut the top so that the suit was less revealing, and

I placed a big order for the colors that were selling best. We launched an advertising campaign presenting the tankini as the suit of the season. Sales were so good that the other Macy's divisions picked up on it, but we rode the wave the longest and had the best swimwear sales of all of the Federated divisions.

"I feel like I am an entrepreneur running Chris Manning.com. The men's accessory business is now my business. I use my finance background to analyze investments in inventory, my management skills in supervising buyers and coordinating activities with our planners and the men's department managers in the stores, and my marketing knowledge to develop promotions and advertising. The key to success in my business is speed and reaction. You need to move quickly. Everyday I come in, turn on the computer, and get a scorecard on how much we sold yesterday. I look over the trends, talk to people in the stores, and go to work on getting some more out of the wave."

Source: Personal communication.

Category Variety and Assortment

In Chapter 2, the **variety** or breadth of a retailer's merchandise was defined as the number of different merchandising categories offered, and the retailer's **assortment** or depth of merchandise was defined as the number of SKUs within a category. For example, Target, a full-line discount store chain, offers a wide variety of merchandise categories ranging from consumer electronics to women's dresses but only a limited number of the most popular SKUs in each category. Thus, Target's merchandise offering is high on variety (broad) and low on assortment (shallow). A category specialist such as Circuit City, in contrast, focuses on consumer electronics and thus sells fewer merchandise categories (less variety or breadth) but has a greater assortment of merchandise in each category (depth).

Services retailers also make assortment decisions. For example, some health clubs offer a large variety of activities and equipment from exercise machines to swimming, wellness programs, and New Age lectures. Others, like Gold's Gym, don't offer much variety but have deep assortments of body-building equipment and programs. Some hospitals, such as big municipal hospitals found in most urban areas, offer a large variety of medical services, whereas others specialize in services such as trauma or prenatal care.

In the context of merchandise planning, the concepts of variety and assortment are applied to a merchandise category rather than a retail firm. At the category level, variety reflects the number of different types of merchandise, and assortment is the number of SKUs per type. For example, the assortment plan for girls' jeans in Exhibit 12–8 includes 10 types or varieties (traditional boot cut, regular denim stonewashed, and three price points reflecting different brands). For each type, there are 81 SKUs (3 colors × 9 sizes × 3 lengths). Thus, this retailer plans to offer 810 SKUs in girls' jeans.

Determining Variety and Assortment

In attempting to determine the variety and assortment for a category like jeans, the buyer considers the following factors: the firm's retail strategy, GMROI of the merchandise mix, physical characteristics of the store, trade-off between too much versus too little assortment, and the degree to which categories of merchandise complement one another.

Retail Strategy　　The number of SKUs to offer in a merchandise category is a strategic decision. Target focuses on customers who value a one-stop shopping experience and are not interested in comparing different brands and models within

EXHIBIT 12–8　　　　Assortment Plan for Girls' Jeans

Styles	Traditional	Traditional	Traditional	Traditional	Traditional	Traditional
Price levels	$20	$20	$35	$35	$45	$45
Fabric composition	Regular denim	Stonewashed	Regular denim	Stonewashed	Regular denim	Stonewashed
Colors	Light blue	Light blue	Light blue	Light blue	Light blue	Light blue
	Indigo	Indigo	Indigo	Indigo	Indigo	Indigo
	Black	Black	Black	Black	Black	Black

Styles	Boot-Cut	Boot-Cut	Boot-Cut	Boot-Cut
Price levels	$25	$25	$45	$45
Fabric composition	Regular denim	Stonewashed	Regular denim	Stonewashed
Colors	Light blue	Light blue	Light blue	Light blue
	Indigo	Indigo	Indigo	Indigo
	Black	Black	Black	Black

a category. Thus, it offers fewer SKUs per category. In contrast, Circuit City focuses on consumers interested in comparing alternatives for specific consumer electronic categories and thus offers more SKUs per category.

The breath and depth of the assortment in a merchandise category can affect the retailer's brand image. In general, retailers need to offer enough SKUs to satisfy the customers' needs and maintain their brand image with respect to the merchandise category but not too many so that their image is compromised. Selecting the right assortment is referred to as "editing the assortment."

dELiAs, for instance, is a multichannel retailer that targets teenage girls. Its brand image is very strong in its target market. Suppose that dELiAs began to expand the variety and assortment of casual dresses in its stores, catalogs, and Internet site. It decides to offer twelve casual dress styles instead of six. In the past, the casual dress buyer was able to choose the styles that fit perfectly with the customers' preferences. As the buyer expands the assortment, the buyer might start including items that don't have the same appeal to the target customers. Increasing its assortment could adversely affect dELiAs's customers in two ways. First, customers may become confused by the additional choices, resulting in lost patronage. Second, a diluted product selection may cause customers to lose sight of what dELiAs is all about. It may no longer be the top-of-mind place for these customers to shop. The business would, in essence, have lost its distinctive competence.

Recent research has shown that customers actually buy more if there are modest reductions of redundant items in assortments, such as different sizes of ketchup and low-share brands in a supermarket.[19] Deep cuts in the assortment size, however, probably lead to sales declines.

GMROI of Merchandise Assortment   Buyers are constrained by the amount of money they have to invest in a merchandise category and the store space available to display the merchandise. They must deal with the trade-off of increasing sales by offering more breadth and depth but potentially reducing inventory turnover and GMROI by stocking more SKUs.

The depth of dELiAs assortment in a merchandise category can affect its brand image.

Increasing breadth and depth also can increase the need to put merchandise on sale and thus negatively affect the gross margin. For example, the more SKUs offered, the greater the chance of **breaking sizes**—that is, stocking out of a specific size SKU. If a stockout occurs for a popular SKU in a fashion merchandise category and the buyer cannot reorder during the season, the buyer will typically discount the entire merchandise type. The buyer's objective is to remove the merchandise type from the assortment altogether so that customers will not be disappointed when they don't find the size and color they want.

Physical Characteristics of the Store   Retailers must consider how much space to devote to the category. If many styles and colors are in the assortment, more space will be required to display and store the merchandise properly. However, a rack may hold 300 pairs of jeans. It wouldn't be aesthetically pleasing to display only 100 units on the rack or to mix the jeans with another merchandise category.

For some merchandise categories, a lot of space is needed to display individual items, limiting the number of SKUs that can be offered in stores. For example, furniture takes up a lot of space, and thus, furniture retailers typically display one model of a chair or sofa and then have photographs and cloth swatches to show how the furniture would look with different upholstery.

Multichannel retailers address the space limitations in stores by offering a greater assortment through their Internet and catalog channels than they do in stores. For example, JCPenney offers more sizes and colors for knit shirts in its special casual clothing catalog and Internet site than it stocks in its stores. If customers do not find the size and color they want in the store, sales associates direct them to the company's Internet site and can even order the merchandise for them from a POS terminal.

Complementary Merchandise   When retailers plan to alter their assortment, they must consider whether the merchandise under consideration complements other merchandise in the department. For instance, DVD players may stimulate the sales of DVDs, accessories, and cables. Whereas the DVD players might have a low GMROI that does not justify a significant assortment, the complementary accessories might have very high GMROIs. Thus, retailers may decide to carry more DVD player SKUs to build up accessory sales.

SETTING INVENTORY AND PRODUCT AVAILABILITY LEVELS

Assortment plans typically include the inventory levels of each SKU stocked in the store, as illustrated in Exhibit 12–9. This summary of the typical store inventory support for a merchandise category is referred to as the **model stock plan.** For example, the model stock plan in Exhibit 12–9 includes nine units of size 1, short,

EXHIBIT 12–9
Model Stock Plan

LENGTH		SIZE									
	1	**2**	**4**	**5**	**6**	**8**	**10**	**12**	**14**		
Short	2	4	7	6	8	5	7	4	2	%	
	9	17	30	26	34	21	30	17	9	units	
Medium	2	4	7	6	8	5	7	4	2	%	
	9	17	30	26	34	21	30	17	9	units	
Long	0	2	2	2	3	2	2	1	0	%	
	0	9	9	9	12	9	9	4	0	units	
								Total		100%	
										429 units	

which represent 2 percent of the 429 total units for girls' traditional $20 denim jeans in light blue. Note that there is more stock for more popular sizes.

The retailer might have a model stock plan for each type in a merchandise category and for different store sizes. For example, retailers typically classify their stores as A, B, and C stores on the basis of their sales volume. The basic assortment in a category is stocked in C stores. For the larger stores, more space is available, and thus, the number of SKUs is increased. The larger A and B stores may have more brands, colors, styles, and sizes of apparel or more models for hard goods such as appliances and consumer electronics.

This supermarket sauce section reflects the category manager's model stock plan.

Product Availability

The backup stock in the model stock plan determines product availability. **Product availability** is defined as the percentage of demand for a particular SKU that is satisfied. For instance, if 100 people go into a Macy's department store to purchase a pair of traditional, light blue, denim jeans, and only 90 people can make the purchase before the stock in the store is depleted, product availability for that SKU is 90 percent. Product availability is also referred to as the **level of support** or **service level.**

The higher the product availability, the higher the amount of backup stock, or **buffer stock,** necessary to ensure that the retailer won't be out of stock on a particular SKU when customers demand it. Choosing an appropriate amount of backup stock is critical to successful assortment planning because if the backup stock is too low, the retailer will lose sales, and possibly customers too. If the level is too high, scarce financial resources will be wasted on needless inventory that could be more profitably invested in more variety or assortment.

Exhibit 12–10 shows the trade-off between inventory investment and product availability. Although the actual inventory investment varies in different situations, the general relationship is that a very high level of service results in a prohibitively high inventory investment.

Several factors need to be considered to determine the appropriate level of buffer stock and thus the product availability for each SKU. Retailers often

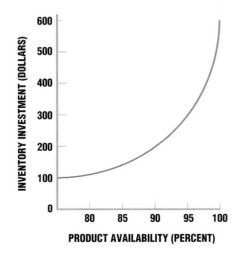

EXHIBIT 12–10
Inventory Investment and Product Availability

classify merchandise categories or individual SKUs as A, B, or C items, reflecting the product availability the retailer wants to offer. For A items, the retailer rarely wants to risk stockout, whereas lower product availability is acceptable for C items. For example, white paint is an A item for Sherwin Williams, and copy paper is an A item for Office Depot. Stocking out of these SKUs would diminish the image of these retailers.

Some other factors considered in determining backup stock levels and product availability are the fluctuations in demand, the lead time for delivery from the vendor, fluctuations in vendor lead time, and the frequency of store deliveries. These factors are discussed in more detail in Chapter 13, along with the merchandising planning systems for staple and fashion merchandise categories, the allocation of merchandise to stores, and the performance evaluation for merchandise categories.

The trade-off among variety, assortment, and product availability is a crucial issue in determining a retailer's merchandising strategy. Buyers have a limited budget for the inventory investments they can make in a category. Thus, they are forced to sacrifice breadth of merchandise if they opt to increase depth or reduce both depth and breadth to increase product availability.

SUMMARY

This chapter provides an overview of the merchandise management planning process and examines sales forecasting and assortment planning in more detail. Merchandise is broken down into categories for planning purposes. Buyers and their partners, merchandise planners and assorters, manage these categories, often with the help of their major vendors.

Performance measures used to assess merchandise management are GMROI, sales-to-stock ratios and inventory turnover, and gross margin. Retailers use GMROI to plan and evaluate merchandise performance. The GMROI planned for a particular merchandise category is derived from the firm's overall financial goals, broken down to the category level. Gross margin percentage and inventory turnover work together to form this useful merchandise management tool.

High inventory turnover is important for a retailer's financial success. But if the retailer attempts to push inventory turnover to its limit, stockouts and increased costs may result.

When developing a sales forecast, retailers need to know what stage of the life cycle a particular category is in and whether the product is a fad, fashion, or staple item so they can plan their merchandising activities accordingly. Creating a sales forecast involves such sources of information as (1) previous sales data, (2) personal awareness, (3) fashion and trend services, (4) vendors, and (5) traditional market research.

The next step in the merchandise planning process is developing an assortment plan and model stock list. The assortment plan reflects the retailer's merchandise strategy with respect to the depth and breadth of merchandise carried in the category.

KEY TERMS

GET OUT AND DO IT!

1. **CONTINUING EXERCISE** Go to a retailer's store and audit the variety and assortment for a specific merchandise category. Record the breadth and depth of the assortment and the backup inventory levels. Compare the variety and assortment for the same category in a competing retail store.

2. **INTERNET EXERCISE** Go to www.badfads.com. Choose some fads. Ask the four questions we listed on page 329 in this chapter. Based on your answers, did these fads deserve a sudden and quick death?

3. **INTERNET EXERCISE** InfoScan's Web site is located at www.infores.com. Go to its site and describe the services it offers retailers.

4. **INTERNET EXERCISE** Go to www.macys.com and www.jcpenney.com. Which seems to have the largest variety? Choose a merchandise category and determine which retailer offers the largest assortment.

5. **INTERNET EXERCISE**. Go to Oracle Retail Merchandise Planning at www.oracle.com/applications/retail/MP/index.html and read about their merchandise planning software. How does the software use sales and inventory data to help retailers make more informed merchandise planning decisions?

6. **INTERNET EXERCISE**. Go to the home page for the following three retail trade publications: *WWD* at http://www.wwd.com/, *Chain Store Age* at http://www.chainstoreage.com/, and *Discount Store News* at http://www.dsnretailingtoday.com/. How can the articles found in these sources assist retailers with merchandise planning decisions?

DISCUSSION QUESTIONS AND PROBLEMS

1. What are the differences among a fashion, a fad, and a staple? How should a merchandise planner manage these types of merchandise differently?

2. How and why would you expect variety and assortment to differ between a traditional bricks-and-mortar store and its Internet counterpart?

3. Simply speaking, increasing inventory turnover is an important goal for a retail manager. What are the consequences of turnover that's too slow? Too fast?

4. Assume you are the grocery buyer for canned fruits and vegetables at a five-store supermarket chain. Del Monte has told you and your boss that it would be responsible for making all inventory decisions for those merchandise categories. It would determine how much to order and when shipments should be made. It promises a 10 percent increase in gross margin dollars in the coming year. Would you take Del Monte up on its offer? Justify your answer.

5. A buyer has received a number of customer complaints that he has been out of stock on a certain category of merchandise. The buyer subsequently decides to increase this category's product availability from 80 percent to 90 percent. What will be the impact on backup stock and inventory turnover?

Will your answer be the same if the buyer is implementing an efficient supply chain inventory system?

6. Variety, assortment, and product availability are the cornerstones of the merchandise planning process. Provide examples of retailers that have done an outstanding job of positioning their stores on the basis of one or more of these issues.

7. The fine jewelry department in a department store has the same GMROI as the small appliances department, even though characteristics of the merchandise are quite different. Explain this situation.

8. Calculate the GMROI and inventory turnover given annual sales of $20,000, average inventory (at cost) of $4,000 and a gross margin of 45 percent.

9. How does Home Depot change its merchandise inventory on a seasonal basis? How has this retailer used its merchandise offerings to attract more female customers?

10. Give examples of products that you have purchased that are fad, fashion, and staple items according to the category life cycle. How does each item fit the definitions given in Exhibit 12–6?

11. As the athletic shoe buyer for Sports Authority, how would you go about forecasting sales for a new Nike running shoe?

SUGGESTED READINGS

Basuroy, Suman; Murali K. Mantrala; and Rockney G. Walters. "The Impact of Category Management on Retailer Prices and Performance: Theory and Evidence," *Journal of Marketing* 65, no. 4 (October 2001), pp. 16–32.

Bohlinger, Maryanne. *Merchandise Buying.* 5th ed. New York: Fairchild, 2001.

Brannon, Evelyn. *Fashion Forecasting: Research, Analysis and Presentation.* 2nd ed. New York: Fairchild, 2005.

Charness, Peter. "Back to the Future: A Renaissance for Buyers?" *Stores,* March 2005, p. 103.

Coldfelter, Richard. *Retail Buying: From Basics to Fashion.* New York: Fairchild, 2002.

Dhar, Sanjay; Stephen Hoch; and Nanda Kumar. "Effective Category Management Depends on the Role of the Category," *Journal of Retailing,* Summer 2001, pp. 165–84.

Diamond, Jay. *Retail Buying.* 7th ed. New York: Prentice Hall, 2004.

Donnellan, John. *Merchandise Buying and Management,* 2nd ed. New York: Fairchild, 2002.

Dupre, Kyle, and Thomas Gruen. "The Use of Category Management Practices to Obtain a Sustainable Competitive Advantage in the Fast-Moving Consumer-Goods Industry," *Journal of Business & Industrial Marketing* 19 (2004), pp. 444–60.

Gruen, Thomas, and Reshma Shah. "Determinants and Outcomes of Plan Objectivity and Implementation in Category Management Relationships," *Journal of Retailing* 76, no. 4 (Winter 2000), pp. 483–511.

Thomas, Chris. *Management of Retail Buying.* New York: Wiley, 2005.

Varley, Rosemary. *Retail Product Management: Buying and Merchandising.* 2nd ed. New York: Routledge, 2005.

Merchandise Planning Systems

EXECUTIVE BRIEFING
Bill Lucas,
President, NPD Retail Business Group

The NPD Group provides global sales and market data that help our clients, both retailers and vendors, make better, fact-based decisions. The reports provided by our system are derived from two databases—POS sales data and consumer panel data.

The POS data are supplied by over 600 retail clients around the world, detailing sales in over 150,000 stores. The database provides sales for discrete products and their price across a broad cross-section of nonfood retailers including department, discount, and specialty store industry segments.

The online consumer panel consists of 2.5 million people who have agreed to participate in surveys and provide in-

formation on their purchase behavior. In addition to sales by product and retailer, the database includes demographic and other information about the panel members including customer satisfaction evaluations following specific purchase occasions. This database allows sales tracking across all industry segments, by demographic segments. We use statistical techniques to ensure that the consumer sample is representative of the population.

Our systems are designed to make it easy for retailers to get the data that help them analyze market performance and make fact-based decisions. A variety of reports are available drawing on both databases. For example, a specialty store buyer for athletic shoes can find out what his market share is for different athletic shoe subcategories such as running, basketball, and cross-trainer shoes, as well as specific brands and items within each subcategory. With this data, he might undertake additional analyses to determine why his share is below average in some subcategories. He might then look at his

share by age or other segmentation variables. He can also find out the specialty store sales for different brands and SKUs and with this data discover brands and SKUs that are selling well at competing retailers and need to be added to his assortment plan.

Recently, an automotive parts retailer reviewed a fair share report that compared their market share in each merchandise category to their overall market share and discovered some areas in which they were not getting their fair share—they had a market share of 8 percent in the category compared to their overall market share of 11 percent. By drilling down into the data, the buyer for the category adjusted her assortment plan, changing the emphasis placed on specific brands and SKUs. The result was an increase in annual sales of $3 million and a promotion.

Chapter 12 provided an overview of the process for managing inventory for a merchandise category and the measures—GMROI, gross margin, and inventory turnover—used to evaluate the performance of buyers in managing their inventory investments. Issues related to forecasting sales and developing assortment plans indicated in very general terms what and how much inventory should be carried in a particular merchandise category. But the actual management of a retail inventory on a daily basis is quite complex. For example, Sears' buyers have to place orders and keep track of inventory levels for 500,000 SKUs.

Retailers employ computer-based, information, and planning support systems to assist buyers in this challenging management task. These systems help buyers, planners, and assorters determine when and how much to buy and what adjustments might be needed in the pricing and allocation of merchandise to specific stores.

As discussed in Chapter 12, retailers use two different merchandise planning systems—one for staple merchandise categories and the other for fashion merchandise categories. Because staple merchandise items are continuously sold over a number of years, there is a sales history of each SKU, and standard statistical techniques can be used to forecast sales. In addition, the risks associated with inaccurate forecasts are minimal because excess inventory can be sold during subsequent time periods. Thus, staple merchandise planning systems manage inventory at the level of the SKU.

In contrast, fashion merchandise categories typically consist of many SKUs that are new products without a sales history available for accurate forecasts. In addition, the potential losses from forecasting errors are significant because, if the merchandise does not sell during the season, it can no longer be sold because it will be out of fashion. Therefore, fashion merchandise planning systems manage inventory at the category level. After determining the appropriate inventory levels in dollars, buyers for fashion merchandise categories then develop assortment plans to determine the quantity of specific SKUs to purchase. The open-to-buy systems keep track of merchandise flow (orders, sales, and merchandise receipts) so buyers don't spend too much or too little.

Some retailers have developed their own merchandise planning systems, whereas others use systems developed by software companies such as Marketmax, a subsidiary of SAS; Retek, a division of Oracle; JDA; and GERS. In some retail firms, these merchandise planning systems are part of the firm's enterprise resource planning (ERP) system, which integrates merchandise planning with systems for managing supply chains and other business activities. In small retail firms, the software for merchandise planning might be installed on the owner's personal computer. Retailing View 13.1 describes how Office Depot is making a major change to upgrade its merchandise management systems.

This chapter begins with a look at buying systems for staple merchandise. Buying systems for fashion merchandise are examined next, followed by an examination of open-to-buy systems. The Marketmax systems are used to illustrate the

---

13.1 RETAILING VIEW Office Depot Launches Magellan

Office Depot is undertaking a major project to upgrade its merchandise and supply chain management planning processes. The project is called Magellan because, like that of the mission of the sixteenth century Portuguese explorer, Office Depot's goal is to have a larger, more detailed view of its world. Before launching the Magellan project, most of Office Depot's merchandise planning was done on Excel spreadsheets. Using these spreadsheets required a lot of manual entries that decreased their accuracy. In addition, the spreadsheets were not integrated with the company's inventory control and supply chain management systems. While its journey is not over yet, Office Depot has already increased its annual inventory turns to 7.6 from 6.9 compared with the preceding year. Also, its in-stock position now is 99 percent. Some elements of the new system provided by Retek, a subsidiary of Oracle, are as follows:

Using the Magellan planning system, Office Depot is now better able to track and plan inventory and to more accurately forecast future customer demand in all of its stores.

Demand forecasting   With the new forecasting application, buyers can adjust an extensive range of parameters to reflect changes in customer demand or the business climate and thus make more accurate forecasts than the simple projection made with spreadsheets.

Merchandise financial planning   The new system enables top-down and bottom-up financial planning that is integrated with Office Depot's merchandise planning solutions and provides buyers with critical inventory and financial metrics, such as inventory shrink and return-to-vendor merchandise, as well as inventory turns and GMROI.

Merchandise data warehouse   Central to the Magellan project was the creation of a merchandise data warehouse that provides a unified view of Office Depot's

merchandise inventory position at its stores and distribution centers in real time.

Assortment planning   Before implementing Retek's assortment planning system, Office Depot had no standardized processes for assortment planning. The few processes the retailer did have were detached from its SKU life cycle forecasting and inventory management processes. Implementation of the new assortment planning solution connected those processes and gave buyers a greater ability to measure the performance of their assortments using key financial, inventory, and space productivity metrics.

Sources: Dan Scherga, "Viability Venture," *Chain Store Age,* July 2005, pp. 45–46; Mike Troy, "Office Depot Resurges Amid Merchandising Makeover," *DSN Retailing Today,* June 7, 2004, pp. 20–21.

functions of reports generated by these systems. The chapter then discusses how multistore retailers allocate merchandise among stores and how merchandise management performance is evaluated. At the end of this chapter, Appendix 13A describes the retail inventory method (RIM).

STAPLE MERCHANDISE MANAGEMENT SYSTEMS

Exhibit 13–1 illustrates the function of a staple merchandise management system. In the left panel of the figure, the inventory of an SKU in a retailer's distribution center or store is depicted as a container. Orders received from the vendor fill up the container and increase the inventory level, whereas sales of the SKU to customers decrease the level of inventory in the container. The level of inventory in the container is shown in the right panel of the exhibit.

At the beginning of week 1, the retailer had 150 units of the SKU in inventory. At that time, the buyer placed an order for 96 units. During the next two weeks, customers purchased the SKU, and the inventory level decreased to 20 units. At the end of week 2, the 96-unit order from the vendor arrived, and the inventory level jumped up to 116 units. The buyer places another order with the vendor that will arrive two weeks later, before customer sales decrease the inventory level to 0 and the retailer stocks out.

Inventory that goes up and down due to the replenishment process is called **cycle stock,** or **base stock.** The retailer would like to reduce the base stock inventory to keep its inventory investment low. One approach for reducing the base stock is to reorder and receive merchandise from the vendor more often instead of once every other week. But more frequent ordering and shipments would increase administrative and transportation costs.

Because sales of the SKU and receipts of orders from the vendor cannot be predicted with perfect accuracy, the retailer has to carry **backup stock,** also known as **safety stock** or **buffer stock,** as a cushion so it doesn't stock out before the next order arrives. Backup stock is shown in yellow in Exhibit 13–1.

Several factors determine the level of required backup stock. First, it depends on the product availability the retailer wishes to provide. If Lowe's wants to rarely stock out of white paint, it needs to have a higher level of backup stock. However, if it is willing to accept a 75 percent product availability for melon-colored paint, a lower level of buffer stock is needed for that SKU.

Second, the greater the fluctuation in demand, the more backup stock is needed. Suppose a Lowe's store sells an average of 30 gallons of purple paint in

EXHIBIT 13–1
Inventory Levels for Staple Merchandise

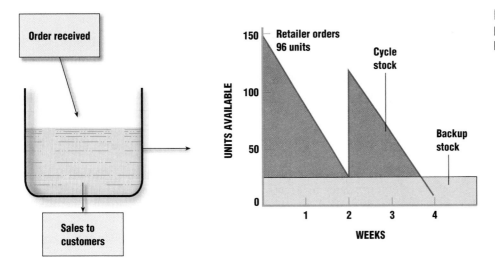

When planning the amount of inventory to order for a staple merchandise category, such as paint, Lowe's buyers must consider current inventory, customer demand, lead time for replenishment, and backup stock needed to avoid stockouts in the department.

two weeks. Yet, in some weeks, sales are 50 gallons, and some weeks they are only 10 gallons. When sales are less than average, the store ends up carrying a little more merchandise than it needs. But when sales are much more than average, there must be more backup stock to ensure that the store does not stock out. Note in Exhibit 13–1 that during week 4, sales were greater than average so the retailer had to dip into its backup stock to avoid a stockout.

Third, the amount of backup stock needed is affected by the lead time from the vendor. **Lead time** is the amount of time between the recognition that an order needs to be placed and the point at which the merchandise arrives in the store and is ready for sale. If it took two months to receive a shipment of purple paint, the possibility of running out of stock is greater than if lead time were only two weeks, because the Lowe's store would have to forecast for a longer period. The shorter lead times inherent in collaborative supply chain management systems (described in Chapter 10) result in a lower level of backup stock required to maintain the same level of product availability.

Fourth, fluctuations in lead time also affect the amount of backup stock. If Lowe's knows that lead time for purple paint is always two weeks, plus or minus one day, it can more accurately plan its inventory levels. But if the lead time is plus or minus one day on one shipment and then plus or minus five days on the next shipment, the stores must carry additional backup stock to cover the uncertainty in lead time. Many retailers using collaborative supply chain management systems require their vendors to deliver merchandise within a very narrow window— sometimes two or three hours—to reduce the fluctuations in lead time and thus the amount of required backup stock.

Fifth, the vendor's product availability also affects the retailer's backup stock requirements. For example, Lowe's can more easily plan its inventory requirements if the vendor normally ships every item that is ordered. If, however, the vendor only ships 75 percent of the ordered items, Lowe's must maintain more backup stock to be certain that the paint availability for their customers isn't adversely affected. The percentage of complete orders received from a vendor is called the **fill rate.**

Staple merchandise planning systems provide the information needed to determine how much to order and when to place orders for SKUs. These systems assist buyers by performing three functions:

- Monitoring and measuring current sales for items at the SKU level.
- Forecasting future SKU demand with allowances made for seasonal variations and changes in trends.
- Developing ordering decision rules for optimum restocking.

The inventory management report, discussed in the next section, provides the information to perform these functions.

The Inventory Management Report

The inventory management report provides information about the current sales rate or velocity, sales forecasts, inventory availability, the amount on order, decision variables such as product availability, the backup stock needed to provide the product availability desired, performance measures such as planned and actual inventory turnover, and the appropriate ordering decisions for each SKU.

Inventory Management Report for Rubbermaid SKUs   **EXHIBIT 13–2**

Marketmax - In-Season Management - Worksheet: Inventory Mangement - Rubbermaid (Business View: 'Inventory Management : Global')

Worksheet   In-Season Management

Plan   Edit   View   Tools   Help

Skip To   Style

	Quantity On Hand	Quantity On Order	Sales Last 4 Wks	Sales Last 12 Wks	Forecast Next 4 Wks	Forecast Next 8 Wks	Product Availability	Backup Stock	Turnover Planned	Turnover Actual	Order Point	Order Quantity
RM- Bath												
RM Bath Mat - Avacado	30	60	72	215	152	229	99	18	12	11	132	42
RM Bath Mat - Blue	36	36	56	130	115	173	95	12	9	10	98	26
RM Bath Mat - Gold	41	72	117	325	243	355	99	35	12	13	217	104
RM Bath Mat - Pink	10	12	15	41	13	25	90	3	7	7	13	0

Exhibit 13–2 shows a retailer's inventory management report for Rubbermaid SKUs. Rubbermaid is a large manufacturer of household plastic products. The suggested order point and quantity are the critical decisions the buyer for a staple merchandise category needs to make. They indicate when and how much to order.

The first five columns of Exhibit 13–2 contain the descriptions of each item, how many items are on hand and on order, and sales for the past 4 and 12 weeks. The first row SKU is a Rubbermaid bath mat in avocado green. There are 30 units on hand and 60 on order. Thus, the quantity available of this SKU is 90. (Quantity on hand + quantity on order = quantity available.) Sales for the past 4 and 12 weeks were 72 and 215 units, respectively.

Sales forecasts for the next four and eight weeks are determined by the system using a statistical model that considers the trend in past sales and the seasonal pattern for the SKU. However, in this case, the buyer made an adjustment in the forecast for the next four weeks to reflect a special promotion for avocado, blue, and gold bath mats in two weeks.

The product availability is a decision variable input by the buyer. For the avocado bath mat SKU, the buyer wants 99 out of every 100 customers to find it in stock. But the buyer is less concerned about stocking out of pink bath mats and thus sets its product availability at 90 percent. The system then calculates the necessary backup stock for the avocado bath mat—18 units. This number is determined by the system on the basis of the specified product availability, the variability in demand, the vendor delivery lead time, and the variability in the lead time.

The planned inventory turnover for the SKU, 12 times, is a decision variable also set by the buyer on the basis of the retailer's overall financial goals; it drives the inventory management system. For this SKU, the system determined that the actual turnover, based on the cost of goods sold and average inventory, is 11.

Order Point   The **order point** is the amount of inventory below which the quantity available shouldn't go or the item will be out of stock before the next order arrives. This number tells the buyer that when the inventory level drops to this point, additional merchandise should be ordered. The order point is defined as

Order point = Sales/Day × (Lead time + Review time) + Backup stock

Lead time is the time between the recognition that an order needs to be placed and the receipt of merchandise in stores ready for sale. However, buyers might not review each SKU every day; **review time** is the maximum time between reviews of the SKU. In a situation in which the lead time is two weeks, the buyer reviews the SKU once a week, 18 units of backup stock are needed to maintain the product availability desired, and the sales rate forecasted for the next four weeks is 5.5 units per day, the order point is

Order point = [(5.4 units) × (14 + 7 days)] + (18 units) = 132 units

For this SKU, the buyer needs to place an order if the quantity in inventory falls to 132 or fewer units to produce the desired product availability.

Order Quantity   When inventory reaches the order point, the buyer needs to order enough units so the cycle stock isn't depleted and sales dip into backup stock before the next order arrives. This order quantity is the difference between the quantity available and the order point. Using the avocado bath mats in Exhibit 13–2, since quantity available is 90, the buyer orders 42 units, because the order point is 132 (i.e., $132 - 90 = 42$).

Using this system to calculate order points and order quantities for staple merchandise SKUs, orders can be transmitted directly to vendors such as Rubbermaid using electronic data interchange (EDI) without needing to involve the buyer. The buyer would only need to set the decision variables desired, such as product availability, make adjustments for special promotions, and monitor the performance of the SKUs in terms of inventory turnover and GMROI.

FASHION MERCHANDISE MANAGEMENT SYSTEMS

The system for managing fashion merchandise categories is typically called a merchandise budget plan. The **merchandise budget plan** specifies the planned inventory investment in dollars in a fashion merchandise category over time. It is a financial plan that specifies how much money will be spent each month to support sales and achieve the desired inventory turnover and GMROI objectives. However, it isn't a complete buying plan because it doesn't indicate the specific assortment of SKUs to buy or the quantities.

Exhibit 13–3 shows a six-month merchandise budget plan for men's casual slacks at a national specialty store chain. For a category like this, the buyer probably completes the plan in the fall for the following spring and summer. The buyer needs to plan how much merchandise should be delivered in each month to achieve the financial goals for the period.

Actual sales might differ from the sales forecasted in the merchandise budget plan. Even with this uncertainty though, the plan is used to coordinate the supply and demand for merchandise and ensure that the financial goals are realized.

The remaining part of this section describes the steps in developing the merchandise budget plan and determining the bottom line, line 8, the "Monthly Additions to Stock," in Exhibit 13–3. The "Monthly Additions to Stock" tells the buyer how much merchandise in retail dollars he or she needs to have arriving in the stores and available for sale each month for the retailer's financial goals to be met.

EXHIBIT 13–3   Six-Month Merchandise Budget Plan for Women's Casual Slacks

	Spring	April	May	June	July	August	September
1. Sales % Distribution to Season	100.00%	21.00%	12.00%	12.00%	19.00%	21.00%	15.00%
2. Monthly Sales	$130,000	$27,300	$15,600	$15,600	$24,700	$27,300	$19,500
3. Reduc % Distribution to Season	100.00%	40.00%	14.00%	16.00%	12.00%	10.00%	8.00%
4. Monthly Reductions	$16,500	$6,600	$2,310	$2,640	$1,980	$1,650	$1,320
5. BOM Stock to Sales Ratio	4.00	3.60	4.40	4.40	4.00	3.60	4.00
6. BOM Inventory	$98,280	$98,280	$68,640	$68,640	$98,800	$98,280	$78,000
7. EOM Inventory	$65,600	$68,640	$68,640	$98,800	$98,280	$78,000	$65,600
8. Monthly Additions to Stock	$113,820	$4,260	$17,910	$48,400	$26,160	$8,670	$8,420

Window title: Marketmax - Financial Planning - Worksheet: Men's Tailored Suits - Budget Plan (Business View: 'Merchandise Budget Plan : Global')

Worksheet   Financial Planning

Plan Edit View Tools Help

Skip To

Monthly Sales Percentage Distribution to Season (Line 1)

Line 1 of the plan projects what percentage of the total sales is expected to be sold in each month. In Exhibit 13–3, 21 percent of the six-month sales are expected to occur in April.

	Six-Month Data	SPRING			SUMMER		
		April	May	June	July	August	September
Sales % Distribution to 1 Month	100.00%	21.00%	12.00%	12.00%	19.00%	21.00%	15.00%

Historical sales data provide the starting point for determining the percentage distribution of sales by month. The percentage of total category sales that occurs in a particular month doesn't vary much from year to year. However, the buyer might adjust the historical percentages to reflect changes in buying patterns and special promotions. For instance, the buyer might feel that the autumn selling season for men's casual slacks continues to be pushed further back into summer and thus increase the percentages for July and decrease the percentages for August and September. The buyer might also decide to hold a special Easter sale promotion, increasing the April percentage and decreasing the other percentages.

Monthly Sales (Line 2)

Monthly sales are the forecasted total sales for the six-month period in the first column ($130,000) multiplied by each monthly sales percentage (line 1). In Exhibit 13–3, monthly sales for April = $130,000 × 21% = $27,300.

	Six-Month Data	SPRING			SUMMER		
		April	May	June	July	August	September
Sales % Distribution to 1 Month	100.00%	21.00%	12.00%	12.00%	19.00%	21.00%	15.00%
2 Monthly sales	$130,000	$27,300	$15,600	$15,600	$24,700	$27,300	$19,500

Monthly Reductions Percentage Distribution to Season (Line 3)

To have enough merchandise every month to support the monthly sales forecast, the buyer needs to consider other factors that reduce the inventory level in addition to sales made to customers. Although sales are the primary reduction, the value of the inventory is also reduced by markdowns (sales discounts), shrinkage, and discounts to employees. The merchandise budget planning process builds these additional reductions into the planned purchases. If these reductions were not considered, the category would always be understocked. Note that in Exhibit 13–3, 40 percent of the season's total reductions occur in April as a result of price discounts (markdowns) during end-of-season sales.

	Six-Month Data	SPRING			SUMMER		
		April	May	June	July	August	September
3 Reduction % Distribution to Season	100.00%	40.00%	14.00%	16.00%	12.00%	10.00%	8.00%

Clothing in this children's apparel store is marked down at the end of the spring season to make room for summer merchandise.

Markdowns also can be forecasted from historical records. However, changes in markdown strategies—or changes in the environment, such as competition or general economic activity—must be taken into consideration when forecasting markdowns.

Discounts to employees are like markdowns, except that they are given to employees rather than to customers. The level of the employee discount is tied fairly closely to the sales level and number of employees. Thus, employee discounts can be forecasted from historical records.

Shrinkage refers to inventory losses caused by shoplifting, employee theft, merchandise being misplaced or damaged, and poor bookkeeping. Retailers measure shrinkage by taking the difference between (1) the inventory's recorded value based on merchandise bought and received and (2) the physical inventory actually in stores and distribution centers. Shrinkage varies by department and season and typically directly with sales as well. So if sales of women's casual slacks rise 10 percent, then the buyer can expect a 10 percent increase in shrinkage.

Monthly Reductions (Line 4)

Monthly reductions are calculated in the same way as monthly sales. The total reductions are multiplied by each percentage in line 3. In Exhibit 13–3, April reductions = $16,500 × 40% = $6,600.

			SPRING			SUMMER	
	Six-Month Data	April	May	June	July	August	September
3 Reduction % Distribution to Season	100.00%	40.00%	14.00%	16.00%	12.00%	10.00%	8.00%
4 Monthly reductions	$16,500	$6,600	$2,310	$2,640	$1,980	$1,650	$1,320

BOM (Beginning-of-Month) Stock-to-Sales Ratio (Line 5)

The **stock-to-sales ratio,** listed in line 5, specifies the amount of inventory that should be on hand at the beginning of the month to support the sales forecast and maintain the inventory turnover objective for the category. Thus, a stock-to-sales ratio of two means that the retailer plans to have twice as much inventory on hand at the beginning of the month as there are forecasted sales for the month. Both the BOM stock and forecasted sales for the month are expressed in retail dollars.

			SPRING			SUMMER	
	Six-Month Data	April	May	June	July	August	September
5 BOM stock-to-sales ratio	4.0	3.6	4.4	4.4	4.0	3.6	4.0

Rather than specifying the stock-to-sales ratio, many retailers specify a related measure, weeks of inventory. A stock-to-sales ratio of 4 means there are 16 weeks of inventory, or approximately 112 days, on hand at the beginning of the month. A stock-to-sales ratio of 1/2 indicates a two-week supply of merchandise, or approximately 14 days. The stock-to-sales ratio is determined so the merchandise category achieves its targeted performance—its planned GMROI and inventory turnover. The steps in determining the stock-to-sales ratio for the category are shown next.

Step 1: Calculate Sales-to-Stock Ratio

GMROI is equal to the gross margin percentage times the sales-to-stock ratio. The sales-to-stock ratio is conceptually similar to inventory turnover except the denominator in the stock-to-sales ratio is expressed in retail sales dollars, whereas the denominator in inventory turnover is the cost of goods sold (sales at cost). The buyer's target GMROI for the category is 123 percent, and the buyer feels the category will produce a gross margin of 45 percent. Thus,

GMROI = Gross margin % × Sales-to-stock ratio
Sales-to-stock ratio = GMROI / Gross margin percent = 123 / 45 = 2.73

Because this illustration of a merchandise budget plan is for a six-month period rather than a year, the sales-to-stock ratio is based on six months rather than annual sales. So for this six-month period, sales must be 2.73 times the inventory at cost to meet the targeted GMROI.

Step 2: Convert the Sales-to-Stock Ratio to Inventory Turnover

Inventory turnover is

Inventory turnover = Sales-to-stock ratio × (1.00 − Gross margin % / 100)
                   =   2.73   × (1.00 − 45/100)
1.50   =   2.73   ×   .55

This adjustment is necessary because the sales-to-stock ratio defines sales at retail and inventory at cost, whereas inventory turnover defines both sales and inventory at cost. Like the sales-to-stock ratio, this inventory turnover is based on a six-month period.

Step 3: Calculate Average Stock-to-Sales Ratio

The average stock-to-sales ratio is

Average stock-to-sales ratio = 6 months / Inventory turnover
4   = 6 / 1.5

If preparing a 12-month plan, the buyer divides 12 by the annual inventory turnover. Since the merchandise budget plan in Exhibit 13–3 is based on retail dollars, it's easiest to think of the numerator as BOM retail inventory and the denominator as sales for that month. Thus, to achieve a six-month inventory turnover of 1.5, on average, the buyer must plan to have a BOM inventory that equals four times the amount of sales for a given month, which is equivalent to four months, or 16 weeks, of supply.

One needs to be careful when thinking about the average *stock-to-sales ratio*, which can be easily confused with the *sales-to-stock ratio*. These ratios are not the inverse of each other. Sales are the same in both ratios, but stock in the sales-to-stock ratio is the average inventory at cost over all days in the period, whereas stock in the stock-to-sales ratio is the average BOM inventory at retail. Also, the BOM stock-to-sales ratio is an average for all months. Adjustments are made to this average in line 5 to account for seasonal variation in sales.

Step 4: Calculate Monthly Stock-to-Sales Ratios

The monthly stock-to-sales ratios in line 5 must average the stock-to-sales ratio calculated previously to achieve the planned inventory turnover. Generally, monthly stock-to-sales ratios vary in the opposite direction of sales. That is, in months when sales are larger, stock-to-sales ratios are smaller, and vice versa.

To make this adjustment, the buyer needs to consider the seasonal pattern for men's casual slacks in determining the monthly stock-to-sales ratios. In the ideal

REFACT

Supermarkets apprehend approximately 253,000 shoplifters annually in the United States, an average of 50 per store, with an average value of merchandise recovered of about $27. Cigarettes, health and beauty care items, meat, liquor, and analgesics rank as the most frequently stolen items. Employees are even better at stealing than customers. They were attempting to steal an average of over $400 in cash or merchandise for each discovered theft.[3]

Retail sales are very seasonal. The Christmas season often accounts for more than 40 percent of a retailer's annual sales.

situation, men's casual slacks would arrive in the store the same day and in the same quantity that customers demand them. Unfortunately, the real-life retailing world isn't this simple. Note in Exhibit 13–3 (line 8) that men's casual slacks for the spring season start arriving slowly in April ($4,260 for the month), yet demand lags behind these arrivals until the weather starts getting warmer. Monthly sales then jump from 12 percent of annual sales in May and June to 19 percent in July (line 1). But the stock-to-sales ratio (line 5) decreased from 4.4 in May and June to 4.0 in July. Thus, in months when sales increase (e.g., July), the BOM inventory also increases (line 6) but at a slower rate, which causes the stock-to-sales ratios to decrease. Likewise, in months when sales decrease dramatically, like in May (line 1), inventory also decreases (line 6), again at a slower rate, causing the stock-to-sales ratios to increase (line 5).

When creating a merchandise budget plan for a category such as men's casual slacks with a sales history, the buyer also examines previous years' stock-to-sales ratios. To judge how adequate these past ratios were, the buyer determines if inventory levels were exceedingly high or low in any months. Then the buyer makes minor corrections to adjust for a previous imbalance in inventory levels, as well as for changes in the current environment. For instance, assume the buyer is planning a promotion for Memorial Day. Since this promotion has never been done before, the stock-to-sales ratio for that May should be adjusted downward to allow for the expected increase in sales. Note that monthly stock-to-sales ratios don't change by the same percentage as the percentage distribution of sales by month is changing. In months when sales increase, stock-to-sales ratios decrease but at a slower rate. Because there is no exact method of making these adjustments, the buyer must make some subjective judgments.

BOM Stock (Line 6)

The amount of inventory planned for the beginning-of-the-month (BOM) inventory for April equals

BOM inventory = Monthly sales (line 2) × BOM stock-to-sales ratio (line 5)
$98,280   = $27,300   × 3.6

	Six-Month Data	SPRING			SUMMER		
		April	May	June	July	August	September
6 BOM inventory	$98,280	$98,280	$68,640	$68,640	$98,800	$98,280	$78,000

EOM (End-of-Month) Stock (Line 7)

The BOM stock for the current month is the same as the EOM (end-of-month) stock in the previous month. That is, BOM stock in line 6 is simply EOM inventory in line 7 from the previous month. Thus, in Exhibit 13–3, the EOM stock for April is the same as the BOM stock for May, $68,640. Forecasting the ending inventory for the last month in the plan is the next step in the merchandise budget plan. Note that EOM inventory for June is high, planning for a substantial sales increase in July.

	Six-Month Data	SPRING			SUMMER		
		April	May	June	July	August	September
7 EOM inventory	$85,600	$68,640	$68,640	$275,080	$98,280	$78,000	$65,600

Monthly Additions to Stock (Line 8)

The monthly additions to stock needed is the amount to be ordered for delivery in each month to meet the inventory turnover and sales objectives.

$$\text{Additions to stock} = \text{Sales (line 2)} + \text{Reductions (line 4)}$$
$$+ \text{ EOM inventory (line 7)} - \text{BOM inventory (line 6)}$$
$$\text{Additions to stock (April)} = \$27,300 + 6,600 + 68,640 - 98,280 = \$4,260$$

At the beginning of the month, the inventory level equals BOM stock. During the month, merchandise is sold, and various inventory reductions affecting the retail sales level occur, such as markdowns and theft. So BOM stock minus monthly sales minus reductions equals EOM stock if nothing is purchased. But something must be purchased to get back up to the forecast EOM stock. The difference between EOM stock if nothing is purchased (BOM stock – sales – reductions) and the forecast EOM stock is the additions to stock.

	Six-Month Data	SPRING			SUMMER		
		April	May	June	July	August	September
8 Monthly additions to stock	$113,820	$4,260	$17,910	$48,406	$26,180	$8,670	$8,420

Evaluating the Merchandise Budget Plan

Inventory turnover, GMROI, and the sales forecast are used for both planning and control. The previous sections have described how they all fit together in planning the merchandise budget. Buyers negotiate GMROI, inventory turnover, and sales forecast goals with their superiors, the GMMs and DMMs. Then merchandise budgets are developed to meet these goals. Well before the season, buyers purchase the amount of merchandise found in the last line of the merchandise budget plan to be delivered in those specific months—the monthly additions to stock.

After the selling season, the buyer must determine how the category actually performed compared with the plan. If the actual GMROI, turnover, and forecast are greater than those in the plan, performance is better than expected. However, performance evaluations should not be based just on any one of these measures. Several additional questions should be answered to evaluate the buyer's performance: Why did the performance exceed or fall short of the plan? Was the deviation from the plan due to something under the buyer's control? (For instance, was too much merchandise purchased?) Did the buyer react quickly to changes in demand by either purchasing more or having a sale? Was the deviation instead due to some external factor, such as a change in competitive level or economic activity? Every attempt should be made to discover answers to these questions. Later in this chapter, several additional tools used to evaluate merchandise performance will be examined.

OPEN-TO-BUY SYSTEM

The open-to-buy system is used after the merchandise is purchased and is based on the merchandise budget plan or staple merchandise management system. The merchandise management systems discussed previously provide buyers with a plan for purchasing merchandise. The **open-to-buy** system keeps track of merchandise flows while they're occurring. It keeps a record of how much is actually spent purchasing merchandise each month and how much is left to spend.

In the same way that you must keep track of the checks you write, buyers need to keep track of the merchandise they purchase and when it is to be delivered. Without the open-to-buy system keeping track of merchandise flows, buyers might buy too much or too little. Merchandise could be delivered when it isn't needed and be unavailable when it is needed. Thus, sales and inventory turnover would suffer. For consistency, we will continue this example of an open-to-buy system with the merchandise budget plan previously discussed, though the open-to-buy system is also applicable to staple goods merchandise management systems.

To make the merchandise budget plan successful (i.e., meet the sales, inventory turnover, and GMROI goals for a category), the buyer attempts to buy merchandise in quantities with delivery dates such that the actual EOM stock for a month will be the same as the projected or forecasted EOM stock. For example, at the end of September, which is the end of the spring/summer season, the buyer would like to be completely sold out of spring/summer women's casual slacks so there will be room for the fall styles. Thus, the buyer would want the projected EOM stock and the actual EOM stock for this fashion and/or seasonal merchandise to both equal zero.

Calculating Open-to-Buy for the Current Period

Buyers develop plans indicating how much inventory for the merchandise category will be available at the end of the month. However, these plans might be inaccurate. Shipments might not arrive on time, sales might be greater than expected, and/or reductions (price discounts due to sales) might be less than expected. The open-to-buy is the difference between the projected EOM inventory and the planned EOM inventory. Thus, open-to-buy for a month is:

Open-to-buy = Actual EOM planned inventory − Projected EOM inventory

The EOM planned inventory is taken from the merchandise budget plan, and the EOM projected inventory is calculated as follows:

Projected EOM inventory = Actual BOM inventory
+ Monthly additions actual
  (received new merchandise)
+ On order (merchandise to be delivered)
− Sales plan (merchandise sold)
− Monthly reductions plan

Six-Month Open-to-Buy System Report **EXHIBIT 13–4**

Loc - 10	Spring					
Merch - Aged Soft	April	May	June	July	August	September
EOM Stock Plan	$68,640	$68,640	$98,800	$98,280	$78,000	$65,600
EOM Actuals	$59,500					
BOM Stock Plan	$98,280	$68,640	$68,640	$98,800	$98,280	$78,000
BOM Stock Actual	$95,000	$59,500				
Monthly Additions Plan	$4,260	$17,910	$48,400	$26,160	$8,670	$8,420
Monthly Additions Actuals	$3,500	$7,000				
OnOrder	$45,000	$18,000	$48,400			
Sales Plan	$27,300	$15,600	$15,600	$24,700	$27,300	$19,500
Sales Actuals	$26,900					
Monthly Reductions Plan	$6,600	$2,310	$2,640	$1,980	$1,650	$1,320
Monthly Reductions Actuals	$1,650					
Projected EOM Stock Plan	$59,500	$66,590	$96,750	$70,070	$41,120	$20,300
Projected BOM Stock Plan	$24,570	$59,500	$66,500	$96,750	$70,070	$41,120
OTB	$0.00	$2,050	$2,050	$28,210	$36,880	$45,300

Thus, the projected EOM inventory will be less than the planned EOM inventory if sales or reductions are greater than the merchandise budget plan or less merchandise is delivered than planned.

Exhibit 13–4 presents the six-month open-to-buy for the same category of men's casual slacks discussed in the fashion merchandise planning section of this chapter. Consider May as the current month. The BOM stock (inventory) actual level is $59,500, but there is no EOM actual inventory yet because the month hasn't finished. When calculating the open-to-buy for the current month, the projected EOM stock plan comes into play. Think of the projected EOM stock plan as a new and improved estimate of the planned EOM stock from the merchandise budget plan. This new and improved version takes information into account that wasn't available when the merchandise budget plan was made. The formula for projected EOM inventory for the category is

Projected EOM inventory = Actual BOM inventory	$59,500
+ Monthly additions actual	+7,000
+ On order	+18,000
− Sales plan	−15,600
− Monthly reductions plan	−2,310
=	$66,590

The open-to-buy for the current month is:

Open-to-buy plan = EOM inventory planned − Projected EOM inventory
$2,050 = $68,640 − $66,590

Therefore, the buyer has $2,050 left to spend in May to reach the planned EOM stock of $68,640. This is a relatively small amount, so we can conclude that the buyer's plan is right on target. But if the open-to-buy for May were $20,000, the buyer could then go back into the market and look for some great buys. If one of the vendors had too much stock of men's casual slacks, the buyer might be able to use the $20,000 to pick up some bargains that could be passed on to customers.

If, however, the open-to-buy was a negative $20,000, the buyer would have overspent the budget. Similar to overspending your checkbook, the buyer would have to cut back on spending in future months so the total purchases would be within the merchandise budget. Alternatively, if the buyer believed that the overspending was justified because of changes in the marketplace, a negotiation could take place between the buyer and the DMM to get more open-to-buy.

ALLOCATING MERCHANDISE TO STORES

After developing a plan for managing merchandise inventory in a category, the next step in the merchandise management process is to allocate the merchandise purchased and received to the retailer's stores (see Exhibit 12–4). Research has found that these allocation decisions have a much bigger impact on profitability than does the decision about the quantity of merchandise to purchase.[4] In other words, buying too little or too much merchandise has less impact on category profit than making mistakes in allocating the right amount and type of merchandise to stores. Thus, many retailers have created positions called either "allocators" or "planners" to specialize in making store allocation decisions. Allocating merchandise to stores involves three decisions: (1) how much merchandise to allocate to each store, (2) what type of merchandise to allocate, and (3) when to allocate the merchandise to different stores.

Amount of Merchandise Allocated to Each Store

One approach for allocating the amount of merchandise to stores is to make the allocation proportional to the forecasted sales for each store. Thus, if a store represents 10 percent of the merchandise categories sales, it is allocated 10 percent of the merchandise inventory. The process for making allocations on the basis of this decision rule is illustrated in Exhibit 13–5.

In this example, the buyer is allocating $150,000 of merchandise across a chain of 15 stores. The chain classifies its stores into three size categories: A stores are forecasted to each sell $15,000 for the merchandise category, B stores with a $10,000 forecast, and C stores with a $7,500 forecast. Thus, the buyer might allocate $15,000 of merchandise to each A store, $10,000 to each B store, and $7,500 to each C store.

However, a core assortment is necessary to maintain the image of the chain. If the chain were to cut back the assortment too far in smaller stores, customers would perceive the smaller stores, and the chain, as having an inferior assortment. Hence, smaller stores require a higher-than-average stock-to-sales ratio. The opposite is true for stores with larger-than-average sales. The actual allocation made by the planner is shown in column 5.

EXHIBIT 13–5
Allocation Based on Sales Volume

1 Type of store	2 Number of Stores	3 Sales per Store	4 Sales by Type (col. 2 × 3)	5 Actual Allocation per Store	6 Allocation by Type
A	4	$15,000	$ 60,000	$14,000	$ 56,000
B	3	10,000	30,000	10,000	30,000
C	8	7,500	60,000	8,000	64,000
Total			150,000		150,000

EXHIBIT 13–6
Example of Different
Geodemographic Segments

Laptops and Lattes	Rustbelt Retirees
Laptops and Lattes are affluent, single, and still renting. They are educated, professional, and partial to city life, favoring major metropolitan areas such as New York, Boston, Chicago, Los Angeles, and San Francisco. Median household income is more than $87,000; median age is 38 years. Technologically savvy, the Laptops and Lattes segment is the top market for notebook PCs and PDAs. They use the Internet on a daily basis to trade stocks and make purchases and travel plans. They are health conscious and physically fit; they take vitamins, use organic products, and exercise in the gym. They embrace liberal philosophies and work for environmental causes.	As the name implies, most of these residents live in the Northeast or Midwest, especially in Pennsylvania and areas around the Great Lakes. Although many residents are still working, labor force participation is below average. More than 40 percent of these households draw retirement income. Their neighborhoods are typically found in older, industrial cities. Residents live in owner-occupied, single-family houses with a current market value of $111,000. Unlike many retirees, those in the Rustbelt are not inclined to move. These settled, hard-working residents are loyal to their communities and country; they make an effort to vote in elections and participate in volunteer activities and fund-raising. They serve on church boards; some are members of veterans' clubs. Rustbelt Retirees watch their pennies and search for bargains at discount stores and warehouse clubs. They drive older, domestic vehicles; prefer renting movies over attending the cinema; and dine out only occasionally.

Type of Merchandise Allocated to Stores

In addition to classifying stores on the basis of their size and sales volume, retailers classify stores according to the characteristics of the stores' trading area. As discussed in Chapter 8, the profiles of trading areas are used in making store location decisions. Store trade area geodemographics are also used to develop merchandise assortments for specific stores. Consider the allocation decision of a national supermarket for its ready-to-eat cereal assortment. Some stores are located in areas dominated by segments called "Rustbelt Retirees," and other areas are dominated by the "Laptops and Lattes segment," as described in Exhibit 13–6.

The ready-to-eat breakfast cereal buyer would certainly want to offer different assortments for stores in these two areas. Stores with a high proportion of Rustbelt Retirees in their trading areas would have better results with an assortment of lower priced, well-known brands and more private-label cereals. Stores in areas dominated by the Laptops and Lattes geodemographic segment would do better with an assortment with higher priced brands that were low in sugar, organic, and whole wheat. Private-label cereals would be deemphasized.

Even the sales of different apparel sizes can vary dramatically from store to store in the same chain. Exhibit 13–7 illustrates this point. Notice that Store X sells significantly more large sizes and fewer small sizes than is average for the chain. If the buyer allocated the same size distribution of merchandise to all stores in the chain, Store X would stock out of large sizes, have an oversupply of small sizes, or be out of some sizes sooner than other stores in the chain.

The assortment offered in a ready-to-eat cereal aisle should match the demands of the demographics of shoppers in the local area.

EXHIBIT 13–7
Apparel Size Difference for Store X and Chain's Average

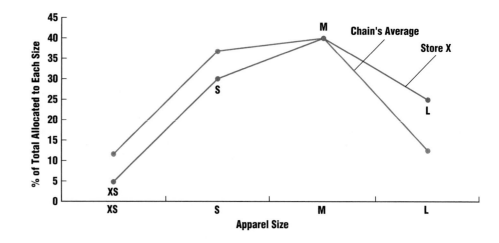

Timing of Merchandise Allocation to Stores

In addition to the need to allocate different inventory levels and types of merchandise across stores, differences in the timing of category purchases across stores need to be considered. Exhibit 13–8 illustrates these differences by plotting sales data over time for capri pants in different regions of the United States. Comparing regions, capri sales peak in late July in the Midwest and at the beginning of September in the West due to seasonality differences and differences in consumer demand. Buyers need to recognize these regional differences and arrange for merchandise to be shipped to the appropriate regions when customers are ready to buy to increase inventory turnover in the category.

The issues involved in allocating the merchandise inventory to stores, as just described, are particularly important for both fashion merchandise and new staple items. If these types of merchandise sell and evolve into staple merchandise, they get replenished over time, either by the vendor or through distribution centers. As we discussed in Chapter 10, retailers use either a pull or a push distribution strategy to replenish merchandise. With a pull distribution strategy, orders for merchandise are generated at the store level on the basis of sales data captured by point-of-sale terminals. With a push distribution strategy, merchandise is allocated to the stores on the basis of historical demand, the inventory position at the distribution center, and the needs of the stores. As Chapter 10 noted, a pull strategy is more sophisticated and more responsive to customer demand and can correct initial misallocations.

EXHIBIT 13–8
Sales of Capri Pants by Region

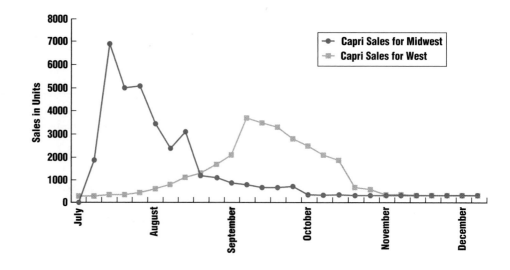

ANALYZING MERCHANDISE MANAGEMENT PERFORMANCE

The next step in the merchandise planning process is to analyze the performance of the process and make adjustments, such as ordering more or less merchandise, lowering prices to increase sales, allocating different assortments to specific stores, or changing the assortment and model stock plans. Three types of analyses related to the monitoring and adjustment step are (1) sell-through analysis, (2) ABC analysis of assortments, and (3) multiattribute analysis of vendors. The first analysis provides an ongoing evaluation of the merchandise management plan compared with actual sales. The remaining two analyses offer approaches for evaluating and altering the assortment plan using the specific SKUs in the plan and the vendors that provide the merchandise to support the plan.

Sell-Through Analysis Evaluating Merchandise Plan

A **sell-through analysis** compares actual and planned sales to determine whether more merchandise is needed to satisfy demand or price reductions (markdowns) are required. Exhibit 13–9 shows a sell-through analysis for blouses for the first two weeks of the season.

Blouses are high fashion items that experience significant uncertainty in sales. Thus, after two weeks in the stores, the buyer reviews sales and determines if adjustments are needed. The need to make adjustments depends on a variety of factors, including experience with the merchandise in the past, plans for featuring the merchandise in advertising, and the availability of **markdown money** from vendors (funds a vendor gives a retailer to cover lost gross margin dollars that result from markdowns).

In this case, the white blouses are selling significantly less than planned. Therefore, the buyer makes an early price reduction to ensure that the merchandise isn't left unsold at the end of the season. The decision regarding the blue blouses isn't as clear. The small blue blouses are selling slightly ahead of the plan, and the medium blue blouses are also selling well, but the large blue blouses are selling ahead of plan only in the second week. In this case, the buyer decides to wait another week or two before taking any action. If actual sales stay significantly ahead of planned sales, a reorder might be appropriate.

Evaluating the Assortment Plan and Vendors

ABC Analysis   An **ABC analysis** identifies the performance of individual SKUs in the assortment plan. It is used to determine what SKUs should be in the plan and how much backup stock and resulting product availability is provided for each SKU in the plan. In an ABC analysis, the SKUs in a merchandise category are rank ordered by several performance measures, such as sales, gross margin, inventory turnover, and GMROI. Typically, this rank order reveals the general 80–20 principle; namely, approximately 80 percent of a retailer's sales or profits come

Stock Number		Description	WEEK 1			WEEK 2		
			Plan	Actual-to-Plan Actual	Percentage	Plan	Actual-to-Plan Actual	Percentage
1011	Small	White silk V-neck	20	15	−25%	20	10	−50%
1011	Medium	White silk V-neck	30	25	−16.6	30	20	−33
1011	Large	White silk V-neck	20	16	−20	20	16	−20
1012	Small	Blue silk V-neck	25	26	4	25	27	8
1012	Medium	Blue silk V-neck	35	45	29	35	40	14
1012	Large	Blue silk V-neck	25	25	0	25	30	20

EXHIBIT 13–9
Example of a Sell-Through Analysis

from 20 percent of the products. This principle suggests that retailers should concentrate on products that provide the biggest returns.

After rank ordering the SKUs, the next step is to classify the items; on the basis of the classification, determine whether to maintain the item in the assortment plan; and, if so, what level of product availability to offer. For example, a men's dress shirt buyer might identify the A, B, C, and D SKUs by rank ordering them by sales volume. The A items account for only 5 percent of the SKUs in the category but represent 70 percent of sales. The buyer decides that these SKU items should never be out of stock and thus plans to maintain more backup stock for A items, such as keeping more sizes of long- and short-sleeved white and blue dress shirts than of the B and C items.

The B items represent 10 percent of the SKUs and 20 percent of sales. These items include some of the other better-selling colors and patterned shirts and contribute to the retailer's image of having fashionable merchandise. Occasionally, the retailer will run out of some SKUs in the B category because it does not carry the same amount of backup stock as for A items.

The C items account for 65 percent of SKUs but contribute to only 10 percent of sales. The planner may plan to carry some C items only in very small or very large sizes of the most basic shirts, with special orders used to satisfy customer demand.

Finally, the buyer discovers that the remaining 20 percent of the SKUs, D items, have virtually no sales until they are marked down. Not only are these items excess merchandise and an unproductive investment, but they also distract from the rest of the inventory and clutter the store shelves. The buyer decides to eliminate most of these items from the assortment plan. Retailing View 13.2 looks

13.2   RETAILING VIEW   Evaluating Victoria's Secret's Bra Assortment

In a busy Victoria's Secret store in New York's SoHo district, Amanda White, 27, picks up a matching set of a leopard-print bra and underwear, a black negligee, a turquoise lace bra, and three simple cotton bras in pale blue, white, and yellow. After about a half-hour in the fitting room, she walks out of the store carrying three items: the simple cotton bras. "My boyfriend won't love these, but I need something I can wear everyday," she says.

Victoria's Secret has more bad news for Ms. White's boyfriend. The chain, which built its image as a sexy lingerie retailer with expensive ad campaigns featuring famous models, wants to include more basic, less expensive styles of lingerie. American women seem to prefer them. The move carries risks but has a clear business logic: A large majority of the bras sold at Victoria's Secret fall into the so-called "glamour" category with lace or push-up features. But according to analysts, between 70 to 80 percent of the total bra market in the United States still consists of what some women call "workhorse" bras—simple styles that are comfortable and durable.

Victoria's Secret wants a larger "share of drawer" in its customers' dressers and hopes to grab a good chunk of the everyday market currently dominated by other lingerie players and away from retailers such as The Gap and J. Crew, which have their own lingerie lines.

Adjusting an assortment from sexy to practical is a tricky business. So far, however, the strategy is working: When the company launched its "Body by Victoria" collection in 1999, a simple line of bras in nylon and spandex that promised its wearers, "all you see is curves," it quickly became a best seller.

The move to plainer styles is risky because the company could smudge its image as a purveyor of fancy lingerie. Its brand

Victoria's Secret is continually adjusting its lingerie assortment to attract more customers and increase sales to each of those customers.

says "sexy," but being too sexy has given the company problems in the past, such as when Victoria's Secret made a misstep in its sleepwear. It offered a lot of see-through negligees and too few flannel pajamas. Sales fell.

Also, if it is going to continue to grow, the company must expand its market. Although its image is still "26 and sexy," not every Victoria's Secret client fits that image anymore. To broaden its appeal, instead of featuring models in black lace, thigh-high stockings on the cover, one recent catalog touted, "NEW! SEXY SUPPORT." Underneath, in smaller print, was written, "Sizes 34B–40DD."

Sources: Margaret Pressler, "Under Where? Retail's Unmentionable Is What She Won't Put On," *Washington Post*, February 8, 2004, p. F.06; Sarah Ellison, "Is Less Risque Risky for Victoria's Secret?" *The Wall Street Journal*, May 20, 2002, p. B1.

EXHIBIT 13–10
Multiattribute Model for
Evaluating Vendors

Issues (1)	Importance Evaluation of Issues (I) (2)	Brand A (P_a) (3)	Brand B (P_b) (4)	Brand C (P_c) (5)	Brand D (P_d) (6)
	PERFORMANCE EVALUATIONS OF INDIVIDUAL BRANDS ACROSS ISSUES				
Vendor reputation	9	5	9	4	8
Service	8	6	6	4	6
Meets delivery dates	6	5	7	4	4
Merchandise quality	5	5	4	6	5
Markup opportunity	5	5	4	4	5
Country of origin	6	5	3	3	8
Product fashionability	7	6	6	3	8
Selling history	3	5	5	5	5
Promotional assistance	4	5	3	4	7
Overall evaluation $\sum_{i=1}^{n} I_j \times P_{ij}$		290	298	212	341

$\sum_{i=1}^{n}$ = Sum of the expression.

I_j = Importance weight assigned to the ith dimension.

P_{ij} = Performance evaluation for jth brand alternative on the ith issue.

1 = Not important.

10 = Very important.

at the tough decisions that Victoria's Secret has to deal with in evaluating its assortment of bras.

Multiattribute Method for Evaluating Vendors   The **multiattribute analysis** method for evaluating vendors uses a weighted average score for each vendor. The score is based on the importance of various issues and the vendor's performance on those issues. This method is similar to the multiattribute approach that can be used to understand how customers evaluate stores and merchandise, as we discussed in Chapter 4.

To illustrate the multiattribute method for evaluating vendors, either current or proposed, consider the example in Exhibit 13–10 for a vendor of women's casual slacks. A buyer can evaluate vendors using the following five steps:

1. Develop a list of issues to consider in the evaluation (column 1).

2. Importance weights for each issue in column 1 are determined by the buyer/ planner in conjunction with the GMM (column 2) on a 1–10 scale, where 1 equals not important and 10 equals very important. For instance, the buyer and the merchandise manager believe that vendor reputation should receive a 9 because it's very important to the retailer's image. Merchandise quality receives a 5 because it's moderately important. Finally, a vendor's selling history is less important, so it could be rated 3.

3. Make judgments about each individual brand's performance on each issue (remaining columns). Note that some brands have high ratings on some issues but not on others.

4. Develop an overall score by multiplying the importance of each issue by the performance of each brand or its vendor. For instance, vendor reputation importance (9) multiplied by the performance rating (5) for brand A is 45. Promotional assistance importance (4) multiplied by the performance rating (7) for vendor D is 28. This type of analysis illustrates an important point: It doesn't pay to perform well on issues that retailers don't believe are very

important. Although vendor D performed well on promotional assistance, the buyer didn't rate this issue highly in importance, so the resulting score was still low.

5. To determine a vendor's overall rating, add the products for each brand for all issues. In Exhibit 13–10, brand D has the highest overall rating (341), so D is the preferred vendor.

SUMMARY

This chapter reviews the merchandise planning and buying systems for staple and fashion merchandise. Buying systems for staple merchandise are very different from those for fashion merchandise. Because information is available about past sales for each SKU, it is relatively straightforward to forecast future merchandise needs.

The sales forecast and inventory turnover described in Chapter 12 work together to drive the merchandise budget plan for fashion merchandise. The sales forecast is broken down by month, based on historical seasonality patterns. It is necessary to purchase more in months when sales are forecast to be higher than average. Planned inventory turnover is converted to stock-to-sales ratios and used in the merchandise budget plan to determine the inventory level necessary to support sales. Monthly stock-to-sales ratios are then adjusted to reflect seasonal sales patterns. The end product of the merchandise budget planning process is the dollar amount of merchandise a buyer should purchase each month for a category if the sales forecast and inventory turnover goals are to be met.

The open-to-buy system begins where the merchandise budget plan and staple goods inventory management systems leave off. It tracks how much merchandise is purchased for delivery in each month. Using an open-to-buy system, buyers know exactly how much money they've spent compared with how much they plan to spend.

Once the merchandise is purchased, merchandise buyers in multistore chains must allocate the merchandise to stores. Buyers must look at the differences in not only sales potential among stores but also the characteristics of the customer base.

In the end, the performance of buyers, vendors, and individual SKUs must be determined. Three different approaches can evaluate merchandise performance. The sell-through analysis is more useful for examining the performance of individual SKUs in the merchandise plan. The buyer compares actual with planned sales to determine whether more merchandise needs to be ordered or if the merchandise should be put on sale. In an ABC analysis, merchandise is rank ordered from highest to lowest. The merchandising team uses this information to set inventory management policies. For example, the most productive SKUs should carry sufficient backup stock to never be out of stock. Finally, the multiattribute method is most useful for evaluating vendors' performance. This chapter concludes with Appendix 13A, in which we examine the retail inventory method.

KEY TERMS

ABC analysis, *361*
backup stock, *347*
base stock, *347*
buffer stock, *347*
cycle stock, *347*
fill rate, *348*

lead time, *348*
markdown money, *361*
merchandise budget plan, *350*
multiattribute analysis, *363*
open-to-buy, *356*
order point, *349*

review time, *349*
safety stock, *347*
sell-through analysis, *361*
shrinkage, *352*
stock-to-sales ratio, *352*
weeks of supply, *352*

GET OUT AND DO IT!

1. **INTERNET EXERCISE** Go to www.oracle.com/retex/index.html. How are Oracle Retex products being used by retailers today?

2. **INTERNET EXERCISE** Go to www.sas.com/industry/retail/merchandise/index.html, the SAS Merchandise Intelligence group Web site. How are

their products different from Retex's? Who would you hire, Retex or SAS?

3. **WEB OLC EXERCISE** The merchandise budget plan determines how much merchandise should be purchased in each month of a fashion buying season (in dollars), given the sales and reduction forecast,

inventory turnover goals, and seasonal monthly fluctuations in sales. Go to the student side of the Online Learning Center and click on Merchandise Budget Plan. The merchandise budget plan generally covers one fashion season for one merchandise category. This application presents both a one-month and a six-month example. In addition, practice calculations are presented for the one-month example. Have your calculator ready! In the calculation section, you have access to an Excel-based six-month merchandise budget plan that can be used to complete Case number 22 (McFadden's Department Store) in the text.

4. **WEB OLC EXERCISE** The vendor evaluation model utilizes the multiattribute method for evaluating vendors described in the chapter. Go to the student side of the Online Learning Center and click on Vendor Evaluation Model. There are two spreadsheets. Open the first spreadsheet, vendor evaluation 1.xls. This spreadsheet is the same as Exhibit 13–10. If you were selling Brand A to the retailer, which numbers would change? Change the numbers in the matrix and see the effect of that change on the overall evaluation. Go to the second spreadsheet, labeled

evaluation 2.xls. This spreadsheet can be used to evaluate brands or merchandise you might stock in your store. Assume you own a bicycle shop. List the brands you might consider stocking and the issues you would consider in selecting the brands to stock. Fill in the importance of the issues (10 = very important, 1 = not very important) and the evaluation of each brand on each characteristic (10 = excellent, 1 = poor). Determine which is the best brand for your store.

5. **INTERNET EXERCISE.** According to Target's home page, available at http://www.targetcorp.com/, the company has a "Merchandise Focus with an emphasis on basic merchandise—staple, everyday items that consumers use and need most. Combined with an aggressive fashion strategy, this foundation in basics enables Target to compete as a life-style trend merchandiser in all merchandise categories, from apparel to personal care, home decor to automotive." Based on this statement, how does this discounter manage a buying system to ensure that both staple and fashion merchandise are properly stocked to meet customer demand?

DISCUSSION QUESTIONS AND PROBLEMS

1. Inventory shrinkage can be a problem for many retailers. How does the merchandise budget planning process account for inventory shrinkage?

2. Using the following information, calculate additions to stock:

    Sales $24,000

    EOM stock $90,000

    BOM stock $80,000

3. Using the following information, calculate the average BOM stock-to-sales ratio for a six-month merchandise budget plan:

    GMROI 150%

    Gross margin 40%

4. Today is July 19. A buyer is attempting to assess his current open-to-buy given the following information:

    Actual BOM stock $50,000

    Monthly additions actual $25,000

    Merchandise on order to be delivered $10,000

    Planned monthly sales $30,000

    Planned reductions $5,000

    Planned EOM stock $65,000

    What is the open-to-buy on July 19? What does this number mean to you?

5. Now it is July 31, and we need to calculate the open-to-buy for August given the following information:

    Planned monthly sales $20,000

    Monthly additions actual $40,000

    Planned markdowns $5,000

    Projected BOM stock $50,000

    Projected EOM stock $30,000

    Calculate the open-to-buy and explain what the number means to you.

6. Typically, August school supply sales are relatively low. In September, sales increase tremendously. How does the September stock-to-sales ratio differ from the August ratio?

7. Using the 80–20 principle, how can a retailer make certain it has enough inventory of fast selling merchandise and a minimal amount of slow selling merchandise?

8. What is the order point and how many units should be reordered if a food retailer has an item with a 7-day lead time, 10-day review time, and daily demand of 8 units? Say 65 units are on hand, and the retailer must maintain a backup stock of 20 units to maintain a 95 percent service level.

9. A buyer at a sporting goods store in Denver receives a shipment of 400 ski parkas on October 1 and expects to sell out by January 31. On November 1, the buyer still has 375 parkas left. What issues should the buyer consider in evaluating the selling season's progress?

10. If you have a stock-to-sales ratio of 2, how many months of supply do you have? How many weeks of supply?

11. A buyer is trying to decide from which vendor to buy a certain item. Using the information on the next page, determine from which vendor the buyer should buy:

	VENDOR PERFORMANCE		
	Importance Weight	Vendor A	Vendor B
Reputation for collaboration	8	9	8
Service	7	8	7
Meets delivery dates	9	7	8
Merchandise quality	7	8	4
Gross margin	6	4	8
Brand name recognition	5	7	5
Promotional assistance	3	8	8

SUGGESTED READINGS

Belcher, Leslie. "Inventory Management: Measure, Plan and Optimize," *Stores Magazine*, May 2005, p. 146.

Bragg, Steven. *Inventory Best Practices*. Hoboken, NJ: Wiley, 2004.

Bragg, Steven. *Inventory Accounting: A Comprehensive Guide*. Hoboken, NJ: Wiley, 2005.

Corsten, Daniel, and Thomas Gruen. "Stock-Outs Cause Walkouts," *Harvard Business Review*, May 2004, pp. 26–30.

Dandeo, Lisa; Susan Fiorito; Larry Giunipero; and Dawn Pearcy. "Determining Retail Buyers' Negotiation Willingness for Automatic Replenishment Programs," *Journal of Fashion Marketing & Management* 8 (2004), pp. 27–41.

Grewal, Dhruv; Michael Levy; Anuj Mehrotra; and Arun Sharma. "Planning Merchandising Decisions to Account for Regional and Product Assortment Differences," *Journal of Retailing* 75, no. 3 (Fall 1999), pp. 405–24.

Muller, Max. *Essentials of Inventory Management*. New York: AMACOM, 2003. "The New Crystal Ball," *Chain Store Age*, September 2004, pp. 4A–6A.

Scheraga, Dan. "Sounds like a Plan," *Chain Store Age*, March 2005, pp. 65–67.

Tepper, Bette K. *Mathematics for Retail Buying*. 5th ed. New York: Fairchild Books, 2002.

Varley, Rosemary. *Retail Product Management: Buying and Merchandising*. 2nd ed. New York: Routledge, 2005.

APPENDIX 13A   Retail Inventory Method

Similar to firms in most industries, retailers can value their inventory at cost—and some retailers do just that. Yet many retailers find it advantageous to value their inventory at retail and use the retail inventory method (RIM), which has two objectives:

1. To maintain a perpetual or book inventory in terms of retail dollar amounts.
2. To maintain records that make it possible to determine the cost value of the inventory at any time without taking a physical inventory.

THE PROBLEM

Retailers generally think of their inventory at retail price levels rather than at cost. They take their initial markups, markdowns, and so forth as percentages of retail. (These terms are thoroughly defined in Chapter 15.) When retailers compare their prices with competitors', they compare retail prices. The problem is that when retailers design their financial plans, evaluate performance, and prepare financial statements, they also need to know the cost value of their inventory.

One way to keep abreast of their inventory cost is to take physical inventories. Anyone who has worked in retailing knows that this process is time consuming, costly, and not much fun. So retailers usually only take physical inventories once or twice a year. By the time management receives the results of these physical inventories, it's often too late to make any changes.

Many retailers use POS terminals that easily keep track of every item sold, its original cost, and its final selling price. The rest of the retail world faces the problem of not knowing the cost value of its inventory at any one time. Therefore, RIM can be used by retailers with either computerized or manual systems.

ADVANTAGES OF RIM

The RIM has five advantages over a system of evaluating inventory at cost.

* The retailer doesn't have to "cost" each time. For retailers with many SKUs, keeping track of each item at cost is expensive and time consuming, and it increases the cost of errors. It's easier to determine the value of inventory with the retail prices marked on the merchandise than with unmarked or coded cost prices.

* It follows the accepted accounting practice of valuing assets at cost or market, whichever is lower. The system lowers the value of inventory when markdowns are taken but doesn't allow the inventory's value to increase with additional markups.

* As a by-product of RIM, the amounts and percentages of initial markups, additional markups, markdowns, and shrinkage can be identified. This information can

then be compared with historical records or industry norms.

- It is useful for determining shrinkage. The difference between the book inventory and the physical inventory can be attributed to shrinkage.

- The book inventory determined by RIM can be used in an insurance claim in case of a loss (e.g., due to fire).

DISADVANTAGES OF RIM

However, RIM is a system that uses an average markup. When markup percentages change substantially during a period or when the inventory on hand at a particular time isn't representative of the total goods handled in terms of markups, the resulting cost figure may be distorted. As with inventory turnover, merchandise budget planning, and open-to-buy, RIM should be applied on a category basis to avoid this problem.

The record-keeping process involved in RIM is burdensome. Buyers must take care so that changes made to the cost and retail inventories are properly recorded.

STEPS IN RIM

Exhibit 13–11 is an example of RIM in action. The following discussion, which outlines the steps in RIM, is based on this exhibit.

Calculate Total Goods Handled at Cost and Retail

To determine the total goods handled at cost and retail, retailers take the following steps:

1. *Record beginning inventory at cost* ($60,000) *and at retail* ($84,000). The initial markup is reflected in the retail inventory.

2. *Calculate net purchases* ($39,000 at cost and $54,600 at retail) by recording gross purchases ($50,000 at cost and $70,000 at retail) and adjusting for merchandise returned to vendor ($11,000 at cost and $15,400 at retail).

3. *Calculate net additional markups* ($2,000) by adjusting gross additional markups ($4,000) by any additional markup cancellations ($2,000). (An additional markup is a markup that occurs in addition to the normal markup for an item. A markup cancellation occurs if an item has an additional markup, and then the price is reduced. The price reduction is a markup cancellation until it reaches the initial markup price. Any reduction below the initial markup price is a markdown.) Note: These figures are recorded only at retail because markups affect only the retail value of inventory.

4. *Record transportation expenses* ($1,000). Transportation is recorded at cost because it affects only the cost of the inventory.

5. *Calculate net transfers* ($714 at cost and $1,000 at retail) by recording the amount of transfers in and out. A transfer can be from one department to another or from

EXHIBIT 13–11
RIM Example

Total Goods Handled	Cost		Retail	
Beginning Inventory		$60,000		$84,000
Purchases	$50,000		$70,000	
– Return to vendor	(11,000)		(15,400)	
Net purchases		39,000		54,600
Additional markups			4,000	
– Markup cancellations			(2,000)	
Net markups				2,000
Additional transportation		1,000		
Transfers in	1,428		2,000	
– Transfers out	(714)		(1,000)	
Net transfers		714		1,000
Total goods handled		$100,714		$141,600

Reductions	Retail	
Gross sales	$82,000	
– Customer returns and allowances	(4,000)	
Net sales		$78,000
Markdowns	6,000	
– Markdown cancellations	(3,000)	
Net markdowns		3,000
Employee discounts		3,000
Discounts to customers		500
Estimated shrinkage		1,500
Total reductions		$86,000

store to store. Transfers are generally made to help adjust inventory to fit demand. For instance, a sweater may be selling well at one store but not at another. A transfer is, in effect, just like a purchase (transfer in) or a return (transfer out). Thus, it's recorded at both cost and retail.

6. *Calculate the sum as the total goods handled* ($100,714 at cost and $141,600 at retail).

Calculate Retail Reductions

Reductions are the transactions that reduce the value of inventory at retail (except additional markup cancellations, which were included as part of the total goods handled). Reductions are calculated as follows:

1. *Record net sales.* The largest reduction in inventory is sales. Gross sales ($82,000) are reduced to net sales ($78,000) by deducting customer returns and allowances ($4,000).

2. *Calculate markdowns.* Net markdowns ($3,000) are derived by subtracting any markdown cancellations ($3,000) from gross markdowns ($6,000). (A markdown cancellation is the amount by which the price of an item increases after a markdown is applied, such as when a weekend sale occurs and the price goes back up after the weekend.)

3. *Record discounts to employees* ($3,000) *and customers* ($500).

4. *Record estimated shrinkage* ($1,500). Estimated shrinkage is used to determine the ending book inventory if the buyer is preparing an interim financial statement. The estimate is based on historical records and presented as a percentage of sales. Estimated shrinkage wouldn't be included, however, if a physical inventory was taken at the time the statement was being prepared. In this case, the difference between the physical inventory and the book inventory would be the amount of shrinkage due to loss, shoplifting, and so forth.

5. *Calculate the sum as the total reductions* ($86,000).

Calculate the Cumulative Markup and Cost Multiplier

The cumulative markup is the average percentage markup for the period. It's calculated the same way the markup for an item is calculated:

$$\text{Cumulative markup} = \frac{\text{Total retail} - \text{Total cost}}{\text{Total retail}}$$

$$28.87\% = \frac{\$141,600 - \$100,714}{\$141,600}$$

The cumulative markup can be used as a comparison against the planned initial markup. If the cumulative markup is higher than planned, the category is doing better than planned.

The cost multiplier is similar to the cost of goods sold percentage, also called the cost complement.

$$\text{Cost multiplier} = (100\% - \text{Cumulative markup \%})$$

$$71.13\% = 100\% - 28.7\%$$

$$\frac{\text{Total cost}}{\text{Total retail}} = \frac{\$100,714}{\$141,600} = 71.13\%$$

The cost multiplier is used in the next step to determine the ending book inventory at retail.

Determine Ending Book Inventory at Cost and Retail

$$\text{Ending book} = \text{Total goods handled at retail inventory at retail} - \text{Total reductions}$$

$$\$55,600 = \$141,600 - \$86,000$$

The ending book inventory at cost is determined in the same way that retail has been changed to cost in other situations—by multiplying the retail times (100% − gross margin).

$$\text{Ending book inventory} = \text{Ending book inventory at cost at retail} \times \text{Cost multiplier}$$

$$\$39,548 = \$55,600 \times 71.13\%$$

Buying Merchandise

EXECUTIVE BRIEFING
Jennifer O'Neill, Buyer, Dillard's

My first exposure into the management side of retailing was after my junior year at the University of Florida when I had a summer internship at a Dillard's department store in Central Florida. I liked the fast pace of retailing and the satisfaction of seeing the results of your efforts almost immediately. So when I graduated, I took a job in store management with Dillard's.

During my first two years with Dillard's, I had a variety of jobs culminating in managing the ladies' and juniors' areas in the Sanford store—a $12 million business. In this position I supervised an assistant area sales manager and over fifty sales associates, and I worked with the buyers to make sure we had the right assortments for our market.

I then transferred to our buying office in Fort Worth, Texas, as an assistant buyer of ladies' bridge apparel—a category including brands like Dana Buchman and Eileen Fisher. Recently, I was promoted to associate buyer for men's Polo Ralph Lauren—a $200 million business.

I really look forward to reviewing our daily financial results, the report cards that track the sales generated by my category. It's a great experience to see the merchandise I bought selling well and the strategies we implemented being so successful. And even when sales are below expectations, I am excited about the challenge of turning things around.

I really enjoy using our merchandise management systems to analyze what's selling and where, and making sure we have the right merchandise in the right stores. For example, I recently analyzed the sales patterns in our stores close to the Mexican border and discovered that we needed to change the assortment plan for these stores to increase the amount of smaller sizes, cut back on shorts, and increase woven shirts.

CHAPTER 14

QUESTIONS

What branding options are available to retailers?

How do retailers buy national brands?

How do retailers prepare for and conduct negotiations with their vendors?

What legal and ethical issues are involved in buying merchandise?

What issues do retailers consider when buying and sourcing private-label merchandise internationally?

Why are retailers building strategic relationships with their vendors?

I am really happy that I decided to go into retailing. My job is exciting and challenging. It keeps me busy every day. And it's rewarding, both personally and financially. With my recent promotion, my compensation is now double what it was when I started with Dillard's.

The preceding two chapters outlined the merchandise management process and the steps in the process that buyers go through to determine what and how much merchandise to buy. After creating an assortment plan for the category, forecasting sales, and developing a plan outlining the flow of merchandise (how much merchandise needs to be ordered and when it needs to be delivered), the next step in the merchandise management process is to buy the merchandise.

The first strategic decision that needs to be made is the type of merchandise to buy for the category—well-known national brands or private-label brands that are available exclusively from the retailer. When buying national brands, buyers meet with vendors at retail markets or in their offices and negotiate many issues such as prices, delivery dates, payment terms, and advertising and markdown support.

When retailers decide to offer private-label merchandise, their buyers work with other people in the company to develop specifications for the private-label products and negotiate with manufacturers to produce the merchandise. Most private-label merchandise is manufactured outside the United States, and thus, retailers need to deal with the complexities of international business transactions.

Although buyers meet and negotiate with national-brand vendors and private-label manufacturers each season concerning new merchandise, there is a trend toward developing long-term strategic relationships with key suppliers. These partnerships enable the collaboration needed to develop the efficient supply chains discussed in Chapter 10, as well as joint merchandise and marketing programs.

This chapter begins with a description of the different merchandise branding alternatives. Then the issues involved in buying national brands and private-label merchandise are reviewed. The chapter concludes with a discussion of the development of strategic partnering relationships between retailers and their suppliers.

BRAND ALTERNATIVES

Retailers and their buyers face a strategic decision about the mix of national and private-label brands to offer in a product category. The advantages and disadvantages of these branding alternatives are discussed in this section.

Types of Brands

National Brands

National brands, also known as **manufacturer brands,** are products designed, produced, and marketed by a vendor and sold to many different retailers. The vendor is responsible for developing the merchandise, producing it with consistent quality, and undertaking a marketing program to establish an appealing brand image. In some cases, vendors use an umbrella or family brand associated with their company and a subbrand associated with the product, such as Kellogg's (family brand) Corn Flakes (subbrand) or Ralph Lauren/Polo shirts. In other cases, vendors use individual brand names for different product categories and don't associate the brands with their companies. For example, most consumers probably don't know that Procter & Gamble makes Iams pet food, Crest toothpaste, Ivory soap, Max Factor cosmetics, Folgers coffee, Hugo Boss cologne, and Pringles potato chips.

Some retailers organize their buying activities around national brands that cut across merchandise categories. For instance, buyers in department stores may be responsible for all cosmetic brands offered by Estée Lauder (Estée Lauder, Origins, Clinique, and Prescriptives) rather than for a product category such as skin care, eye makeup, and so forth. Managing merchandise by national brand,

REFACT

The world's 10 most valuable company brands are Coca-Cola, Microsoft, GE, IBM, Intel, Disney, McDonald's, Nokia, Toyota, and Marlboro.[1]

By offering these national brands, retailers attract customers to their stores and Web sites and therefore do not have to incur the cost of developing and promoting the brand's image and associated merchandise.

rather than by category, gives retailers more clout when dealing with vendors. However, as indicated in Chapter 12, there are inefficiencies associated with managing merchandise at the brand rather than the category level.

Private-Label Brands   **Private-label brands,** also called **store brands, house brands,** or **own brands,** are products developed and managed by retailers. Retailers typically develop the specifications for their private-label products and then contract with manufacturers, often located in countries with developing economies, to produce the products. But the retailers, not manufacturers, are responsible for promoting the brand. Retailing View 14.1 describes Asada's private-label strategy.

Private-label merchandise is available for sale only from the retailer that develops the brand. However, some private-label brands, such as Kenmore appliances and Craftsman tools, are so well known and highly regarded that many consumers may think they are national brands sold at retailers other than Sears.

George Is Number 1 in the U.K. but Not the U.S.   RETAILING VIEW   14.1

The British supermarket retailer Asada, acquired by Wal-Mart, has a private-label portfolio that accounts for 45 percent of its grocery and 50 percent of its nonfood sales. Asada has extended its own label into such categories as healthy eating, organics, and food for kids and now is placing more emphasis on developing premium-priced private labels.

Asada offers six private-label brands in the food, health and beauty, and household categories. In addition, it has its successful George private-label clothing brand and a selection of Asada-branded financial services including home, motor, and life insurance. The six brands are

Asada, a U.K. chain owned by Wal-Mart, developed George, a private-label apparel and accessories brand. The brand has been so successful in the United Kingdom that Wal-Mart is now selling George merchandise in its U.S. stores.

- Smartprice—economy-value food and general merchandise essentials.
- The standard Asada-owned label—"best in market" everyday food and general merchandise items at low prices.
- Good for you!—foods with lower fat content than standard Asada brand alternatives.
- Organic—best value organic "everyday" products.
- Extra Special—Asada's premium private-label food brand.
- More for Kids—healthier, fun products for kids across the food and health and beauty categories.

The Extra Special premium private-label brand was launched in October 2000 with 40 lines. By mid-2004, the brand had been increased to 650 lines across categories including confectionery, soft drinks, snacks, trifles, specialty breads, prepared meat and fish meals, and a wide range of cheeses and sliced meats. The criteria for an Extra Special brand include better tastes than standard alternatives or national premium equivalents but still affordable at a 10–15 percent lower price than competitors' premium private-label equivalents. Other key criteria are a better shelf look and products that are innovative and bring new ingredients and cooking methods to customers who appreciate good food.

In July 2004, Asada's private-label clothing and footwear brand, George, became the best-selling brand by volume in the United Kingdom for the first time, eclipsing the mighty Marks & Spencer. Created by George Davies, the former owner of a successful chain of British apparel stores, George merchandise comprises sleek but inexpensive clothing, accessories, and undergarments for women and men.

Wal-Mart is importing George merchandise and selling it in its U.S. stores as part of its effort to upgrade its apparel offering. But George merchandise has not been as successful in the United States. The problem might be with Wal-Mart's merchandising of the products rather than the products themselves. In-store displays are small and often hard to find. Some feel it has suffered from a lack of advertising in a heavily promotional industry.

REFACT

In the United Kingdom, private-label brands account for 40–44 percent of sales; in the United States, private-label brands range between 10 and 20 percent of sales depending on the retail format and product category.[2]

Sources: Stephen Foster, "Asada Grows PL Portfolio," *Private-label Magazine,* November/December 2004, pp. 13–26; Ann Zimmerman and Sally Beatty, "Wal-Mart's Fashion Fade; Buy George? Retailer Learns that Chic and Cheap Are Tough to Mix 'n Match," *The Wall Street Journal,* July 2, 2004, p. B1.

REFACT

Macy's was among the first department stores to pioneer the concept of private-label brands for fashion goods. In the 1890s, its "Macy's" and "Red Star" brands were the rage in New York.[3]

Retailers' use of private labels represented a relatively small portion of their total sales in the past. National brands were developed and maintained by vendors through heavy advertising on TV and other media. It was difficult for smaller local and regional retailers to gain the economies of scale in design, production, and promotion needed to develop well-known brands.

In recent years, as the size of retail firms has increased through consolidation, private labels have assumed a new level of significance because of their ability to establish distinctive identities among retailers. Private-label products now account for an average of 25 percent of the purchases in the United States and roughly 45 percent in Europe.[4] Private-label dollar volume in supermarkets, drug chains, and mass merchandisers is increasing twice as fast as that of national brands.

Traditionally, private-label merchandise has been viewed by consumers as being lower quality than national-brand merchandise. However, in "double blind" taste tests, 51 percent of consumers preferred the taste of the private-label product over the national brand version in 12 popular categories.[5] Consumers also find the quality and style of private-label fashion apparel sold by stores like Macy's (INC) and Banana Republic to be superior to many national brand manufacturers with which they compete.

REFACT

Private-label product sales are growing faster than their national-brand counterparts. Between 1997 and 2002, private-label consumer goods grew 38 percent, compared with the 19 percent growth of national-brand products.[6]

In addition, there is a trend for national-brand manufacturers to develop private-label brands for specific retailers. For example, cosmetics powerhouse Estée Lauder sells three brands of cosmetics and skin care products—American Beauty, Flirt, and Good Skin—exclusively at Kohl's. The products are priced between mass-market brands such as Cover Girl or Maybelline, which are sold mainly in drugstores, discount stores, and supermarkets, and Lauder's higher-end brands, sold mainly in more fashion-forward department stores such as Macy's and Dillard's. Levi's has also developed Signature brand jeans for sale at Wal-Mart.[7]

Similar to national-brand manufacturers, retailers can use their name to create a private label for merchandise in many different categories or develop category-specific private brands. For example, The Gap and Victoria's Secret use a family brand approach, in which all of their private-label merchandise is associated with their name. In contrast, Macy's has a portfolio of private-label brands associated with different merchandise types, such as Charter Club, First Impressions, Greendog, INC, The Cellar, and Tools of the Trade.

EquiTrend, developed by Harris Interactive, is a measurement and comparison tool for brands. Its brand value measure is based on five factors: familiarity, quality, purchase intention, brand expectations, and distinctiveness. The top product brands, according to EquiTrend, are Reynolds Wrap aluminum foil, Hershey's milk chocolate candy bars, Ziploc food bags, Heinz ketchup, and Duracell batteries. The top retailer brands are shown in Exhibit 14–1.

Licensed Brands   **Licensed brands** are brands for which the owner of a well-known brand name (licensor) enters into a contract with a licensee to develop, produce, and sell the branded merchandise. Licensees may be either (1) retailers who license

EXHIBIT 14–1
Value of Retail Brands

Brand	Rank	EquiTrend Score
Wal-Mart discount stores	1	70.8
Home Depot	2	68.9
Target stores	3	68.0
Barnes & Noble book stores	4	67.2
Best Buy	5	66.1
Lowe's Home Improvement	6	65.5
Borders book stores	7	63.9
Office Depot	8	63.8
Sam's Club	9	63.1
Toys "R" Us stores	10	62.5

SOURCE: Harris Interactive, 2004. Spring 2004 EquiTrend® Brand study by Harris Interactive®. Used by permission.

	TYPE OF VENDOR	
Impact on Store	**Manufacturer Brands**	**Private-Label Brands**
Store loyalty	?	+
Store image	+	+
Traffic flow	+	+
Selling and promotional expenses	+	−
Restrictions	−	+
Differential advantages	−	+
Margins	?	?

EXHIBIT 14–2
Relative Advantages of Manufacturer versus Private Brands

+ advantage to the retailer, − disadvantage to the retailer, ? depends on circumstances.

the name and then contract with manufacturers to produce the licensed products or (2) a third party that has the merchandise produced and then sells it to retailers.

Licensed brands' market share has grown increasingly in recent years. Owners of trade names not typically associated with manufacturing have also gotten into the licensing business. For instance, the manufacturer of a sweatshirt or baseball cap emblazoned with your university's logo pays your school a licensing fee. If it didn't, it would be infringing on the university's logo (a trademark) and therefore be involved in counterfeiting.

National or Private-Label Brands?

Exhibit 14–2 outlines the advantages and disadvantages of national and private-label brands. Buying from vendors of national brands can help retailers build their image and traffic flow and reduce their selling/promotional expenses. Retailers buy national brands because the retailers' customers have some loyalty to the brand and thus patronize retailers selling the branded merchandise and ask for it by name. This loyalty toward the brand develops because customers know what to expect from the products, like them, and trust them.

Vendors devote considerable resources to create images of their brands that build customer loyalty. As a result, retailers need to spend relatively less money selling and promoting national brands. For instance, Sony attempts to communicate a constant and focused message about the quality and performance of its products to its customers by coordinating advertising with in-store promotions and displays. Thus, Best Buy and Circuit City do not need to engage in image advertising for Sony products.

But since vendors of national brands assume the expenses of designing, manufacturing, distributing, and promoting the brand, retailers typically realize lower gross margins for them compared with those for their private-label brands. Also, since national brands are sold by other retailers, competition can be intense. Customers compare prices for these brands across stores, which means retailers often

Macy's has developed the I.N.C. private-label brand, which provides Macy's with the opportunity to offer exclusive merchandise and realize higher margins.

have to offer significant discounts on some national brands to attract customers to their stores, further reducing their gross margins.

To encourage retailer support, some national-brand vendors make variations of their branded merchandise for specific retailers. For example, a Canon digital camera sold at Best Buy might have a different model number than a Canon digital camera with similar features available at Circuit City. Different model numbers and, for some products, different exterior features make it difficult for consumers to compare prices for virtually the same camera sold by different retailers. Thus, the retailers are less likely to compete on price when selling these unique brand variations, their margins for the products will be higher, and they will be motivated to devote more resources toward selling the national-brand products.[8]

Stocking national brands may increase or decrease store loyalty. If the national brand is available through a limited number of retail outlets (e.g., Nike shoes, Diesel jeans), customers loyal to the brand will also become loyal to the limited number of stores selling the brand. If, however, manufacturer brands are readily available from many retailers in a market, customer loyalty may decrease because the retailer can't differentiate itself from its competition.

Another problem with manufacturer brands is that they can limit a retailer's flexibility. Vendors of strong brands can dictate how their products are displayed, advertised, and priced. Jockey underwear, for instance, tells retailers exactly when and how its products should be advertised.

14.2   RETAILING VIEW   Target Uses Private-Label Designer Brands to Create Its Cheap Chic Image

Part of Target's strategy for differentiating itself from other discount stores is to develop partnerships with designers. Target's most recent arrangement is with fashion designer Isaac Mizrahi. Mizrahi, when he ran his own fashion house, had little patience for the details of the business. His job was to come up with "a new, bold, crazy look every six months, making something fabulous and pretty for my friends and the models." Now he gets excited over how well his clothes sell to ordinary women. "I did this blended wool toggle coat with a pink quilted lining for $50 and Target sold something like 17,000 of them!" stated Mizrahi. He gets satisfaction from tracking sales and weeks of inventory of individual items.

Target has long sought to position itself as a slightly higher-end discounter than Wal-Mart or Kmart. In addition to having cleaner and better-lit stores, Target's strategy involves selling designer products. Mizrahi joins Target's stable of designers who create exclusive merchandise that bolsters Target's "cheap chic" image. Other designers include Todd Oldham, Michael Graves, and Mossimo Giannulli, a young designer whose star had faded but then came back through his exclusive association with Target.

The retailer has done an excellent job of integrating its designer brands through marketing and store layout so that they add to Target's cachet. Target's more upscale marketing and product message appeals to shoppers at a time when they're more willing to trade down to save money. Thus, Target's more upscale image helps attract higher-income shoppers.

Source: Teri Agins, "The Lessons of Isaac: What Mr. Mizrahi Learned Moving from Class to Mass," *The Wall Street Journal*, February 7, 2005, p. B1; Walter Loeb, "Isaac Mizrahi, a Designer for Class and Mass Customers," *Stores*, February 2004, p. 73.

Target reinforces its cheap chic brand image by offering merchandise developed by well-known designers such as Liz Lange (left) and Isaac Mizrahi (right). Hope (middle), Target's mascot, along with the target, are used as symbols to enhance its brand recognition.

Offering private labels also has its pluses and minuses, as shown in Exhibit 14–2. First, the exclusivity of strong private labels boosts store loyalty. For instance, Target's designer brands, as discussed in Retailing View 14.2, are not available from its competitors.

Well-known and highly desirable private labels can enhance the retailer's image and draw customers to the store. Another reason private labels are attractive to customers is their lower prices—10 to 18 percent less expensive than national brands in the United States and as much as 25 percent cheaper in Europe.[9] In addition, private-label brands don't have restrictions on their display, promotion, or price imposed by the national-brand vendor, which might conflict with the retailer's strategy and profits. Finally, gross margin opportunities may be greater.

But there are drawbacks to private-label brands. Although gross margins may be higher for private-label brands than for manufacturer brands, there are other expenses that aren't readily apparent. Retailers must make significant investments to design merchandise, manage global manufacturers, create customer awareness, and develop a favorable image for their private-label brands. If the private-label merchandise doesn't sell, the retailer can't return the merchandise to the vendor or resell it to an off-price retailer.

REFACT

Private labels are big business in Europe: ALDI's private brands account for 95 percent of its sales; Lidl, 80 percent; Sainsbury, 60 percent; Tesco, 40 percent; Wal-Mart in Europe, 40 percent; and Carrefour, 33 percent.[10]

BUYING NATIONAL-BRAND MERCHANDISE

After developing a merchandise budget plan and determining how much merchandise needs to be bought, the next step is to buy the merchandise. Buyers of fashion apparel and accessory categories typically make major merchandise buying decisions five or six times a year, six months before the beginning of a season, and then make minor adjustments to these decisions during the season. Buyers of staple merchandise categories make decisions about buying new merchandise items less frequently, but they replenish the merchandise on a continuous basis, sometimes daily. This section reviews how retail buyers of national-brand merchandise meet with vendors, review the merchandise they have to offer, and negotiate the terms of the purchase. The section concludes with a review of the legal and ethical issues involved in buying merchandise.

Meeting with Vendors

Buyers "go to market" to see the variety of available merchandise and make buying decisions. A **wholesale market** for retail buyers is a concentration of vendors within a specific geographic location, perhaps even under one roof or over the Internet. These markets may be permanent wholesale market centers or annual trade shows or trade fairs. Retailers also interact with vendors at their corporate headquarters. A listing of over 3,000 trade shows and market weeks for the fashion industry can be viewed at Infomat (http://www.infomat.com).

Wholesale Market Centers For many types of merchandise, particularly fashion apparel and accessories, buyers regularly visit with vendors in established market centers. Wholesale market centers have permanent vendor showrooms that retailers can visit throughout the year. At specific times during the year, these wholesale centers host **market weeks** during which buyers make appointments to visit the various vendor showrooms. Vendors that do not have permanent showrooms at the market center lease temporary space to participate in market weeks.

Probably the world's most well-known wholesale market center for many merchandise categories is in New York City. The Fashion Center, also known as the Garment District, is located from Fifth to Ninth avenues and from 35th to 41st streets. An estimated 22,000 apparel buyers visit every year for five market weeks and

65 annual trade shows. The Garment District has 5,100 showrooms and 4,500 factories.[11] There are also major wholesale markets in London, Milan, Paris, and Tokyo.

The United States also has a number of regional wholesale market centers. The Dallas Market Center, the world's largest, is a 6.9-million-square-foot complex of six buildings.[12] Over 26,000 manufacturers and importers display their international products in its 2,200 permanent showrooms and 460,000 square feet of temporary spaces. The Dallas Market Center conducts 50 markets annually, attended by more than 130,000 buyers for products ranging from floor coverings to toys, apparel, jewelry, and gifts.

These regional merchandise marts are used by smaller retailers to view and purchase merchandise. For example, the owner of a gift shop in Birmingham, Alabama, might go to the Atlanta Merchandise Mart several times a year to buy merchandise for his store. Some regional centers have developed into national markets for specific merchandise categories. For example, the Miami Merchandise Mart is now an international market for swimwear.

Trade Shows   **Trade shows** provide an opportunity for buyers to see the latest products and styles and interact with vendors. For example, consumer electronics buyers attend the annual International Consumer Electronics Show (CES) in Las Vegas, the world's largest trade show for consumer technology (www.cesweb.org). The trade show, like most, is closed to the public, but manufacturers, developers, and suppliers of consumer technology hardware, content, technology delivery systems, and related products and services are among the more than 130,000 attendees from over 110 countries. Nearly 2,500 vendor exhibits take up 1.5 million net square feet of exhibit space, showcasing their latest products and services. Vendors often use CES to introduce new products such as the first camcorder (1981), high definition television (HDTV) (1998), and Internet protocol television (IP TV) (2004). In addition to providing an opportunity for retail buyers to see the latest products, CES has a conference program featuring prominent speakers from the technology sector, such as Bill Gates.

Buyers for sporting equipment and apparel attend The Super Show® (www.thesupershow.com), sponsored by the Sporting Goods Manufacturers Association. One of the features of this trade show is that world-renowned athletes participate to promote their licensed merchandise. Everyone who is anyone in the book industry attends the Frankfurt Book Fair (www.frankfurter-buchmesse.de)—authors and publishers, book retailers and librarians, art dealers and illustrators, agents and journalists, information brokers and readers. Not only is the Frankfurt Book Fair the meeting place for the business, it is also the world's largest marketplace for trading in publishing rights and licenses.

Trade shows are typically staged at convention centers not associated with wholesale market centers. McCormick Place in Chicago (the nation's largest convention complex, with more than 2.2 million square feet) hosts over 65 meetings and trade shows per year, including the National Hardware Show and National Housewares Manufacturers Association International Exposition.[14] At these trade shows, the vendors display their merchandise in designated areas and have sales representatives, company executives, and sometime celebrities available to talk with buyers as they walk through the exhibit area.

When attending market weeks or trade shows, buyers and their superiors typically make a series of appointments with key vendors. During these meetings, the buyers discuss

REFACT

An estimated $7.5 billion of wholesale transactions are conducted within the Dallas Market Center complex annually.[13]

These buyers from a sporting goods retail chain meet with a vendor in its display area at the Super Show to review the vender's product line for next season.

the performance of the vendor's merchandise during the previous season, review the vendor's offering for the coming season, and possibly place orders for the coming season. These meetings take place in conference rooms in the vendors' showrooms at wholesale market centers, whereas they likely are less formal during trade shows. The meetings during market weeks offer an opportunity for an in-depth discussion, whereas trade shows have the advantage of providing the opportunity for buyers to see merchandise offered by a broader array of vendors and gauge the reactions to the merchandise by observing the level of activity in the vendor's display area.

Often buyers do not negotiate with vendors and place orders, referred to as "writing paper," during the market week or trade show. They typically want to see what merchandise and prices are available from all the potential vendors before deciding on what items to buy. So after attending a market week or trade show, buyers return to their offices, meet with their superiors to review the available merchandise, make decisions on what items are most attractive, and then negotiate with the vendors before placing an order.

Negotiating with Vendors

To describe how buyers negotiate with vendors, consider the hypothetical situation in which Carolyn Swigler, women's jeans buyer at Bloomingdale's, is preparing to meet with Dario Carvel, the salesperson from Juicy Couture, in her office in Pacoima, California. Swigler, after reviewing the merchandise during the womenswear market week in New York, is ready to buy Juicy Couture's spring line, but she has some merchandising problems that have yet to be resolved from last season.

Knowledge Is Power   The more Swigler knows about her situation and Juicy Couture's, the more effective she will be during the negotiations. First, Swigler assesses the relationship she has with the vendor. Although Swigler and Carvel have only met a few times in the past, their companies have had a long, profitable relationship. A sense of trust and mutual respect has been established, which Swigler feels will lead to a productive meeting

Although Juicy Couture jeans have been profitable for Bloomingdale's in the past, three styles sold poorly last season. Swigler plans to ask Carvel to let her return some merchandise. Swigler knows from past experience that Juicy Couture normally doesn't allow merchandise to be returned but does provide **markdown money**—funds vendors give retailers to cover lost gross margin dollars due to markdowns needed to sell unpopular merchandise. Retailing View 14.3 describes how book publishers (vendors) routinely take back unsold merchandise— a practice that creates inefficiencies and leads to high prices.

A buyer calls her planner to decide about the quantity of an order after reviewing Juicy Couture's new merchandise line in its showroom.

Vendors and their representatives are excellent sources of market information. They generally know what is and isn't selling. Providing good, timely information about the market is an indispensable and inexpensive marketing research tool. So Swigler plans to spend at least part of the meeting talking to Carvel about market trends.

Just as Carvel can provide market information to Swigler, she can provide information to him. For example, on one of her buying trips to England, she found a great new wash made by a small English firm. She bought a pair and gave it to Carvel, who passed it along to Juicy Couture's designers. They used the jeans to develop a new wash that was a big success.

Swigler also knows that Carvel will want her to buy some of the newest and most avant-garde designs in Juicy Couture's spring product line. Carvel knows that many U.S. buyers go to market in New York and that most stop at Bloomingdale's to see what's new, what's selling, and how it's displayed. Thus, Carvel wants to make sure that Juicy Couture is well represented at Bloomingdale's.

Issues   Besides taking care of last season's leftover merchandise, Swigler is prepared to discuss six issues during the upcoming meeting: (1) prices and gross margin, (2) special margin-enhancing opportunities, (3) terms of purchase, (4) delivery and exclusivity, (5) advertising allowances, and (6) transportation.

Price and Gross Margin   Of course, Sigler wants to buy the merchandise at a low price so she will have a high gross margin. In contrast, Carvel wants sell the jeans at a higher price because he is concerned about Juicy Couture's profits.

Additional Markup Opportunities   At times in the past, Juicy Couture has offered Swigler discounted prices to take excess merchandise. This excessive merchandise arises from order cancellations, returned merchandise from other retailers, or simply an overly optimistic sales forecast. While Swigler can realize higher-than-normal

---

14.3   RETAILING VIEW   Book Returns Pile Up

In most retail sectors, retailers have to negotiate with vendors to return merchandise. In general, vendors don't have to take back products that don't sell. However, book publishers have a tradition of accepting returns, a system that traces its origins to the Depression, when publishers told struggling bookstores they could return unwanted books as long as they kept ordering new titles. Unlimited returns are also common for DVDs, music CDs, and, to a lesser extent, videogames.

Approximately one out of every three adult hardcover books sent to book stores is returned unsold. This tidal wave of unsold merchandise creates great inefficiencies. Publishers have to process the returns and then deeply discount the price and ship them back to retailers. Books that can't be sold at any price are processed into recycled paper for a total loss. So many books come back that publishers have raised prices to compensate for the high cost of transporting and processing returns. As book returns increased between 1985 and 2003, hardcover book prices rose 118 percent, far outpacing the 71 percent gain in the Consumer Price Index during that period.

The book returns problem has escalated as category specialists and discount stores have increased the size of their orders. These stores sell a few hundred titles in massive numbers and constantly replace slow-selling books with newer titles. Most stores promote new books for only one or two weeks. Books that might have remained on the best-seller list 10 to 12 weeks a decade ago now often stay only 6 to 8 weeks. Because potential bestsellers have only a short time to get established, publishers say they need towering stacks at the front of stores to ensure their titles get noticed and to make sure they don't miss any sales. The principle is similar to movie studios wanting to get their films in as many theaters as possible on opening weekend.

Retailers, who pay millions in freight and handling for returns every year, have mixed feelings about the present system. "There is no doubt it gives us too much confidence," says Gregory P. Josefowicz, CEO of Borders Group, the nation's second-largest book retailer. "Without that umbrella, we might be more analytical" in what books are bought. Steve Riggio, CEO of Barnes & Noble, the United States' top bookstore chain, says he has a solution: He wants Barnes & Noble to start

In the book industry, publishers ship large quantities of best sellers like the *Harry Potter* series to retailers and then allow those retailers to return unsold books.

marking down books and selling them on the spot. Customers would appreciate the bargains, publishers would generate more sales, and costs would be cut. He says that eliminating returns "would revolutionize… and revitalize the book business."

Sources: Jeffrey A. Trachtenberg, "Quest for Best Seller Creates a Pileup of Returned Books," *The Wall Street Journal*, June 3, 2005, p. A1; "Shops Urge Returns Rethink," *Music Week*, March 19, 2005, p. 1.

gross margins on this merchandise or put the merchandise on sale and pass the savings on to customers, Bloomingdale's has to preserve its image as a fashion leader, and thus, Swigler is not very interested in any excess inventory that Juicy Couture has to offer.

Terms of Purchase   Swigler would like to negotiate for a long time period in which to pay for merchandise. A long payment period improves Bloomindale's cash flow, lowers its liabilities (accounts payable), and can reduce its interest expense if it's borrowing money from financial institutions to pay for its inventory. But Juicy Couture also has its own financial objectives it wants to accomplish and thus would like to be paid soon after it delivers the merchandise.

Delivery and Exclusivity   In fashion merchandise categories, timely delivery and having exclusive merchandise are important. Being the first or only retailer in a market to carry certain products helps a retailer hold a fashion-leader image and achieve a differential advantage. Swigler wants her shipment of the new spring line to arrive as early in the season as possible and would like to have some jeans styles and washes that won't be sold to competing retailers. On the other hand, Juicy Couture wants to have its products sold by many different retailers to maximize its sales.

Advertising Allowances   Retailers often share the cost of advertising through a cooperative arrangement with vendors known as **co-op (cooperative) advertising**— a program undertaken by a vendor in which the vendor agrees to pay for all or part of a pricing promotion. As a fashion leader, Bloomingdale's advertises heavily. Swigler would like Juicy Couture to support an advertising program with a generous advertising allowance.

Transportation   Transportation costs can be substantial, though this isn't a big issue for the Juicy Couture jeans due to their high unit price and low weight and size. Nonetheless, the question of who pays for shipping merchandise from vendor to retailer will be a significant negotiating point.

Tips for Effective Negotiating[15]

Have at Least as Many Negotiators as the Vendor   Retailers have a psychological advantage at the negotiating table if the vendor is outnumbered. At the very least, the negotiating teams should be of equal number. Swigler plans to invite her DMM (divisional merchandise manager) into the discussion if Carvel comes with his sales manager.

Choose a Good Place to Negotiate   Swigler may have an advantage in the upcoming meeting since it will be in her office. She'll have ready access to information, plus secretarial and supervisory assistance. From a psychological perspective, people generally feel more comfortable and confident in familiar surroundings. However, Swigler also might get more out of the negotiation if Carvel feels comfortable. In the end, selecting the location for a negotiation is an important decision.

Be Aware of Real Deadlines   Swigler recognizes that Carvel must go back to his office with an order in hand since he has a quota to meet by the end of the month. She also knows that she must get markdown money or permission to return the unsold jeans by the end of the week or she won't have sufficient open-to-buy to cover the orders she wishes to place. Recognizing these deadlines will help Swigler come to closure quickly in the upcoming negotiation.

Separate People from the Problem   Suppose Swigler starts the meeting with, "Dario, you know we've been friends for a long time. I have a personal favor to ask. Would you mind taking back $10,000 in shirts?" This personal plea puts Carvel in an uncomfortable situation. Swigler's personal relationship with Carvel isn't the issue here and shouldn't become part of the negotiation. An equally detrimental scenario would be for Swigler to say, "Dario, your line is terrible. I can hardly give the stuff away. I want you to take back $10,000 in jeans. After all, you're dealing with Bloomingdale's. If you don't take this junk back, you can forget about ever doing business with us again." Threats usually don't work in negotiations. They put the other party on the defensive. Threats may actually cause negotiations to break down, in which case no one wins.

Insist on Objective Information   The best way to separate people from the business issues is to rely on objective information. Swigler must know exactly how many shirts need to be returned to Juicy Couture or how much markdown money is necessary to maintain her gross margin. If Carvel argues from an emotional perspective, Swigler will stick to the numbers. For instance, suppose that after Swigler presents her position, Carvel says that he'll get into trouble if he takes back the merchandise or provides markdown money. With the knowledge that Juicy Couture has provided relief in similar situations in the past, Swigler should ask what Juicy Couture's policy is regarding customer overstock problems. She should also show Carvel a summary of Bloomingdale's buying activity with Juicy Couture over the past few seasons. Using this approach, Carvel is forced to acknowledge that providing assistance in this overstock situation—especially if it has been done in the past—is a small price to pay for a long-term profitable relationship.

One approach that this buyer (right) uses to negotiate with the designer (left) is to create innovative, mutually beneficial alternatives, such as an exclusive version of some items in the designer's product line.

Invent Options for Mutual Gain   Inventing multiple options is part of the planning process, but knowing when and how much to give, or give up, requires quick thinking at the bargaining table. Consider Swigler's overstock problem. Her objective is to get the merchandise out of her inventory without significantly hurting her gross margin. Carvel's objective is to maintain a healthy yet profitable relationship with Bloomingdale's. Thus, Swigler must invent options that could satisfy both parties, such as offering to buy some of Juicy Couture's most avant-guard jeans in return for markdown money for her excess inventory.

Let Them Do the Talking   There's a natural tendency for one person to continue to talk if the other person involved in the conversation doesn't respond. If used properly, this phenomenon can work to the negotiator's advantage. Suppose Swigler asks Carvel for special financial support for Bloomingdale's Christmas catalog. Carvel begins with a qualified no and cites all the reasons he can't cooperate. But Swigler doesn't say a word. Although Carvel appears nervous, he continues to talk. Eventually, he comes around to a yes. In negotiations, those who break the silence first lose.

Know How Far to Go   There's a fine line between negotiating too hard and walking away from the table with less than necessary. If Swigler overnegotiates by getting the markdown money, better terms of purchase, and a strong advertising allowance, the management of Juicy Couture may decide that other retailers are more worthy of early deliveries and the best styles. Carvel may not be afraid to say no if Swigler pushes him beyond a legal, ethical, profitable relationship.

Don't Burn Bridges   Even if Swigler gets few additional concessions from Carvel, she shouldn't be abusive or resort to threats. Bloomingdale's may not wish to stop doing business with Juicy Couture on the basis of this one encounter. From a personal perspective, the world of retailing is relatively small. Swigler and Carvel may meet at the negotiating table again, possibly both working for different companies. Neither can afford to be known in the trade as unfair, rude, or worse.

Don't Assume   Many issues are raised and resolved in any negotiating session. To be certain there are no misunderstandings, participants should orally review the outcomes at the end of the session. Swigler and Carvel should both summarize the session in writing as soon as possible after the meeting.

Legal and Ethical Issues

Given the large number of negotiations and interactions between retail buyers and vendors, ethical and legal issues are bound to arise. This section reviews some practices that arise in buyer–vendor negotiations that may have legal and/or ethical implications.

Terms and Conditions of Purchase   The Robinson-Patman Act, passed by the U.S. Congress in 1936, potentially restricts the prices and terms that vendors can offer to retailers. The Act forbids vendors from offering different terms and conditions to different retailers for the same merchandise and quantity. Sometimes called the "Anti-Chain-Store Act," it was passed to protect independent retailers from chain-store competition. Thus, if a vendor negotiates a good deal on the issues discussed in the previous section (price, advertising allowance, markdown money, transportation), the Robinson-Patman Act requires the vendor to offer the same terms and conditions to other retailers.

However, vendors can offer different terms to retailers for the same merchandise and quantities if the costs of manufacturing, selling, or delivery are different. The cost of manufacturing is usually the same, but selling and delivery could be more expensive for some retailers. For example, vendors may incur larger transportation expenses due to smaller shipments to independent retailers.

Different prices can also be offered if the retailers are providing different functions. For example, a large retailer can get a lower price if its distribution centers store the merchandise or its stores provide different services valued by customers. In addition, lower prices can be offered to meet competition and dispose of perishable merchandise.[16]

Resale Price Maintenance   **Resale price maintenance (RPM)** is a requirement imposed by a vendor that a retailer cannot sell an item for less than a specific price—the **manufacturer's suggested retail price (MSRP).** Vendors place this restriction on retail prices so that the retailers will have adequate margin to provide the services needed to sell the vendors' products.

For example, suppose Bose feels that its retailers need to have a specially designed soundproof room to demonstrate the quality of its speakers to customers. However, an audio specialty retailer might incur the additional cost of building and maintaining this special room in its stores but not make more sales to customers.

A specialty audio retailer will be reluctant to offer this listening room service if customers eventually buy the audio equipment at a discount store that does not bear the cost of providing a listening room.

Consumers may experience the quality of Bose speakers in the specialty store and then buy the speakers at a discount store that can sell the speakers at a lower cost because it did not have to incur the costs of building and maintaining the special room.

In this situation, the discount store is **free riding** on the specialty store's services; it is taking more than its fair share of the benefits but not incurring its fair share of the costs. Thus, RPM is an approach for reducing free riding. If all retailers are required to charge the same price for Bose speakers, they will have an incentive to compete on service rather than price, which will enable Bose to demonstrate the superior quality of its speakers to consumers. Although RPM has been viewed as a restraint of competition and thus illegal in the past, it is now legal. If any of its retailers violate that policy, the vendor can terminate its relationship with the discounters. In this way, the vendor exercises its right to choose with whom it will sell.

Some retailers, however, do not appreciate RPM. Their position is that since they own the merchandise, they should be able to sell it for whatever they like, even if it is at very low prices. Suppose Best Buy purchased more Toshiba computers than it really needed or possibly purchased a lot on purpose for the back-to-school season. It would want the flexibility to reduce the price below the MSRP to either get rid of the excess or generate traffic into the store.

Commercial Bribery   **Commercial bribery** occurs when a vendor or its agent offers or a buyer asks for "something of value" to influence purchase decisions. Say a salesperson for a ski manufacturer takes a sporting goods retail buyer to lunch at a fancy private club and then proposes a ski weekend in Vail. These gifts could be construed as bribes or kickbacks, which are illegal unless the buyer's manager is informed of them. To avoid these problems, many retailers forbid employees to accept any gifts from vendors. Other retailers have a policy that it is fine to accept limited entertainment or token gifts, such as flowers or wine for the holidays. In either case, they want their buyers to decide on purchases solely on the basis of what is best for the retailer.[17]

Chargebacks   A **chargeback** is a practice used by retailers in which they deduct money from the amount they owe a vendor. Retailers use two rationales for these deductions: (1) the merchandise isn't selling or (2) the vendor did not meet the agreed upon terms, such as improperly applied labels to shipping containers or merchandise, missing items in the shipments, or late shipments. Chargebacks are especially difficult for vendors because once the money is deducted from an invoice and the invoice is marked "paid," it is difficult to dispute the claim and get the missing amount back. Some retailers take chargebacks that are not justifiable, a highly unethical practice.[18]

Slotting Allowances   **Slotting allowances,** also called **slotting fees,** are charges imposed by a retailer to stock an item. For example, when Kraft wants to introduce a new product, supermarket chains might charge between $3,000 and $40,000 per store to stock the product. The fee varies depending on the nature of the product and the relative power of the retailer. Products with low brand loyalty pay the highest slotting allowances. Likewise, large supermarket chains can demand higher slotting allowances than small independent retailers.

Retailers, and some economists, argue that slotting allowances are a reasonable method for ensuring that their valuable space is used efficiently.[19] Such fees cover the costs of adding a new SKU to their computerized system of inventory, especially knowing that most new products fail and the SKU must later be removed. Payment of the slotting fee also signals the vendors' confidence in the sales potential for the product. However, many vendors view slotting allowances as extortion, and small vendors feel these fees preclude their access to retail stores. However, it is legal for retailers to charge slotting fees.

Buybacks   Similar to slotting allowances, **buybacks,** also known as **stocklifts** or **lift-outs,** are activities engaged in by vendors and retailers to get products into retail stores. Specifically, in a buyback situation, a retailer either allows a vendor to create space for its merchandise by "buying back" a competitor's inventory and removing it from a retailer's system, or the retailer forces a vendor to buy back slow-moving merchandise. A vendor with significant market power can violate federal antitrust laws if it stocklifts from a competitor so often as to shut it out of a market, but such cases are difficult to prove.

Exclusives   Retailers often negotiate with vendors for an exclusive arrangement so no other retailer can sell the item or brand. Through these exclusive arrangements, retailers can differentiate themselves from competitors and realize higher margins due to reduced price competition. In some cases, vendors also benefit by making sure that the image of retailers selling their merchandise is consistent with their brand image. For example, Prada might want to give an exclusive for its apparel to only one store in a major market, such as Neiman Marcus. In addition, an exclusive offers a monopoly to the retailer and, thus, a strong incentive to promote the item.

Granting exclusives is legal as long as consumers have alternative sources for similar products. For example, exclusive Ferrari dealers wouldn't be viewed as anticompetitive because other luxury cars are readily available to the public. In contrast, if De Beers, the South African diamond cartel, granted an exclusive to one jewelry store chain, diamonds wouldn't be readily available through other sources.

Counterfeit Merchandise Selling counterfeit merchandise can negatively affect a retailer's image and its relationship with the vendor of the legitimate brand. **Counterfeit merchandise** includes goods made and sold without the permission of the owner of a trademark or copyright. Trademarks and copyrights are **intellectual property,** that is, intangible and created by intellectual (mental) effort as opposed to physical effort. A **trademark** is any mark, word, picture, device, or nonfunctional design associated with certain merchandise (for instance, the crown on a Rolex watch and the GE on General Electric products). A **copyright** protects the original work of authors, painters, sculptors, musicians,

It is illegal for this "street retailer" to sell counterfeit watches, because it violates the watch manufacturers' rights to control the use of their trademarks.

and others who produce works of artistic or intellectual merit. This book is copy-righted, so these sentences cannot be used by anyone without the consent of the copyright owners.

The nature of counterfeiting has changed over the past decade. Although vendors of strong brand-name consumer goods are still affected by counterfeiters, there's now a thriving business in counterfeit information products such as software, CDs, and CD-ROMs. This type of merchandise is attractive to counterfeiters because it has a high unit value, is relatively easy to duplicate and transport, and has high consumer demand. The ease of illegally downloading and distributing music means that neither the record label nor the artist receives any money for their investment, work, or talent, and thus, both are less motivated to develop and produce music.

Gray Markets and Diverted Merchandise   **Gray-market goods** are products with a U.S. registered trademark made by a foreign manufacturer but imported into the United States without permission of the U.S. trademark owner. For example, to increase its profits, McGraw-Hill, the publisher of this textbook, charges a higher wholesale price for this textbook in the United States than in other countries. An importer can buy textbooks at a low price in other countries, import them into the United States, and sell them at a price lower than U.S. bookstores'. Selling gray-market merchandise is legal in the United States, but the European Court of Justice decided to limit gray-market imports only to those from one member-state to another and not from outside the European Union.[20]

Diverted merchandise is similar to gray-market merchandise except there need not be distribution across international boundaries. Suppose, for instance, the fragrance manufacturer Givenchy grants an exclusive to Saks Fifth Avenue. The Saks buyer has excess inventory and sells the excess inventory at a low price to a discount store. Thus, the merchandise is diverted from its legitimate channel of distribution, and Saks in this case would be referred to as the diverter.

Discount store retailers argue that customers benefit from the lack of restriction on gray-market and diverted goods because it lowers prices. Other retailers and vendors argue that competition from retailers selling gray-market and diverted merchandise forces them to cut their prices, offer less service, and suffer a degraded brand image.

Vendors engage in a number of activities to avoid gray-market/diverting problems. They require all of their retail and wholesale customers to sign a contract stipulating that they will not engage in gray marketing. If a retailer is found in violation of the agreement, the vendor will refuse to deal with it in the future. Another strategy is to produce different versions of products for different markets. For instance, McGraw-Hill sells a different version of this textbook in other countries than it sells in the United States.

Exclusive Dealing Agreements   **Exclusive dealing agreements** occur when a vendor restricts a retailer to carrying only its products and nothing from competing vendors. The effect of these arrangements on competition determines their legality. For instance, suppose a retailer signs an agreement with Lee to sell only its jeans. There's no real harm done to competition because other manufacturers have many alternative retail outlets, and Lee's market share isn't large enough to approach monopolistic levels. However, suppose Safeway signed a contract with Coca-Cola to only sell Coke products. Since Coca-Cola has a relatively large market share and Safeway is a very large grocery chain, smaller competitors could be severely hurt, and the agreement therefore would be considered anticompetitive.

Tying Contract   A **tying contract** exists when a vendor requires a retailer to take a product it doesn't necessarily desire (the tied product) to ensure that it can buy a product it does desire (the tying product). Tying contracts are illegal if they may substantially lessen competition or tend to create a monopoly, but the complaining party has the burden of proof. Thus, it is typically legal for a vendor to require a buyer to buy all items in its product line.

Refusal to Deal   The practice of refusing to deal (buy or sell to) can be viewed from both vendors' and retailers' perspectives. Generally, both vendors and retailers have the right to deal or refuse to deal with anyone they choose. But there are exceptions to this general rule when there's evidence of anticompetitive conduct by one or more firms that wield market power. A vendor may refuse to sell to a particular retailer, but it can't do so for the sole purpose of benefiting a competing retailer. For example, Mattel decided not to offer certain popular Barbie packages to wholesale clubs. This action in itself would have been legal. However, it was determined that Mattel agreed to do so as part of a conspiracy among 10 toy manufacturers orchestrated by Toys "R" Us to prevent wholesale clubs from underselling the same toy packages that Toys "R" Us sold. The refusal to deal then became an illegal group boycott.[22]

In summary, any time buyers and vendors interact, there's a potential for ethical and legal problems. Buyers face issues such as how much to charge a vendor for shelf space in their stores or whether they should accept a gift or favor from a vendor with no strings attached. An eye toward fairness and the desire to maintain a strong relationship should dictate behavior in these areas. Retailers must also be concerned with the origin of their merchandise. Specifically, is it counterfeit or gray-market merchandise?

BUYING PRIVATE-LABEL MERCHANDISE

Buying and selling private-label merchandise is a strategic decision that can involve a significant investment. Retailers that offer a significant amount of private-label merchandise, such as JCPenney, Macy's, The Gap, and American Eagle Outfitters, have large departments with people specializing in identifying trends, designing and specifying products, selecting manufacturers to make the products, maintaining a worldwide staff to monitor the conditions under which the products are made, and managing facilities to test the quality of the manufactured products.

Most retailers do not own and operate manufacturing facilities. However, Limited Brands acquired MAST Industries in 1978. MAST is now one of the world's biggest contract manufacturers, importers, and distributors of apparel, with manufacturing operations and joint ventures in more than a dozen countries including China, Israel, Mexico, and Sri Lanka. In addition to being a major private-label supplier of Limited Brands (Victoria's Secret, Bath & Body Works, and Express), it provides private-label merchandise for Abercrombie & Fitch, Lane Bryant, New York & Company, and Saks Fifth Avenue. More than one-quarter of Limited Brands merchandise is sourced through MAST.

Smaller retail chains can offer private-label merchandise without making a significant investment in the supporting infrastructure. Many national brands will modify their national brand merchandise and put the store's label on the products. In addition, firms specializing in producing private labels can provide private-label merchandise just as national brand vendors do. For example, when Costco wanted to launch a promotion of "Two pillows for $10," it called Leo and Jeff Hollander, the father-and-son team that owns Hollander

Home Fashions. When Laura Ashley decided to introduce its own branded pillows, down comforters, and mattress pads, it also bought the products from Hollander.

Hollander makes 150,000 pillows a day, but for most of its 50-year history, it has kept a low profile with its products being sold under other brand names, such as Eddie Bauer or Simmons Beautyrest. It has managed to compete against billion-dollar domestic mills, as well as an onslaught of cheap foreign imports, in part because it shifted some manufacturing to China years before its competitors.[23]

Reverse Auctions

Retailers buying significant quantities of private-label merchandise have departments responsible for designing and specifying the merchandise. Rather than negotiating with manufacturers to produce the merchandise, many retailers are now using reverse auctions to get quality private-label merchandise at low prices. For example, Bashas', a privately held supermarket chain based in Chandler, Arizona, uses reverse auctions to purchase about 70 percent of its meat. Twice weekly, seven competing suppliers bid for the business.[24]

In traditional auctions like those conducted by eBay, there is one seller and many buyers. Auctions conducted by retailer buyers of private-label merchandise are called **reverse auctions** because there is one buyer, the retailer, and many potential sellers, the manufacturing firms. In reverse auctions, retail buyers provide a specification for what they want a group of potential vendors to bid on. The competing vendors then bid on the price at which they are willing to sell until the auction is over. However, the retailer is not required to place an order with the lowest bidder. The retailer can choose to place an order at the price from that vendor the retailer feels will provide the merchandise in a timely manner and at the specified quality.[25]

Reverse auctions have not been very popular with vendors. Few want to be anonymous contestants in bidding wars where price alone, not service or quality, seems to be the sole basis for winning the business. Strategic relationships are also difficult to nurture when the primary interactions with vendors are through electronic auctions.[26]

The most common use of reverse auctions is to buy the products and services used in retail operations rather than merchandise for resale. Some operating materials that are frequently bought through reverse auctions are store carpeting, fixtures, and supplies. However, now reverse auctions can also be used by retailers to procure private-label merchandise, commodities (like meat), and seasonal merchandise like lawn furniture. In Retailing View 14.4, William Alcorn, the chief purchasing officer at JCPenney, describes Penney's experience with reverse auctions.

In some cases, a number of retailers have worked together to develop a specification for POS terminal paper tape and then pooled their buying power to run a reverse auction and find a low-cost supplier that would meet all of their needs. However, some retailers have found that the cost savings do not justify the time and effort needed to develop a jointly agreed upon specification.

Global Sourcing

An important issue facing large retailers that design and contract for the production of private-label merchandise is to select a manufacturer. Barriers to international trade are diminishing, which means that retailers can consider sources of production from across the globe. In this section, factors affecting global sourcing costs and human rights and child-labor violations are examined.

Retailing View 14.5 describes how Chinese manufacturers achieve low costs by developing economies of scale, not exploiting workers.

Costs Associated with Global Sourcing Decisions   Retailers use production facilities located in developing economies for much of their private-label merchandise because of the very low labor costs in these countries. To counterbalance the lower acquisition costs, however, there are other more subtle expenses that increase the costs of sourcing private-label merchandise from other countries. These costs include foreign currency fluctuations, tariffs, longer lead times, and increased transportation costs.

Fluctuations in currency exchange rates can increase costs. For example, if the Indian rupee increases relative to the U.S. dollar, the cost of private-label merchandise produced in India and imported for sale into the United States will increase. If this increase occurs between the time the order is placed and when it is delivered, U.S. retailers will have to pay more for the merchandise than planned. Most retailers use financial instruments such as options and futures contracts to minimize the effects of currency fluctuations.

REFACT

Workers in China cost about 92 cents an hour compared with $1.20 in Thailand, $1.70 in Mexico, and about $21.80 in the United States. Only India among the major export countries, at about 70 cents an hour, is cheaper.[27]

Reverse Auctions at JCPenney   RETAILING VIEW   14.4

William Alcorn is senior vice president, controller, and chief purchasing officer (CPO) at JCPenney. As CPO, he is responsible for the procurement of all nonmerchandise products and services bought by JCPenney.

"We make use of reverse auctions to procure a wide range of products including carpet, office supplies, display fixtures, and POS terminals. We also use reverse auctions to buy services such as hardware installation, store maintenance, and inventory. A buy we make through an auction often involves millions of dollars. Thus a reverse auction is a key strategic tool to consider when sourcing items and services.

"The process of running an auction starts with our purchasing agent working with users to develop the specifications for the item or service. Next, the purchasing agent reviews the industry and evaluates market conditions to confirm an auction is the best sourcing method. After this evaluation, the purchasing agent locates qualified sources to participate in the auction. We screen all potential suppliers to make sure they have the financial resources and capabilities to provide products and services that meet our standards. We also make sure that women and minority-owned businesses are among the set of bidders whenever possible. Usually, we open the bidding to between three and seven suppliers.

"Then the rules for the auction are established—such as, the minimum decrement for a new bid versus the previous low bid, whether bidders will see the amount of the lowest bid or just their rank, and when the auction will open and close.

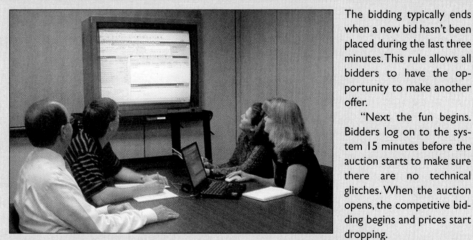

William Alcorn (far left) watches and bids on a reverse auction with his JCPenney associates.

The bidding typically ends when a new bid hasn't been placed during the last three minutes. This rule allows all bidders to have the opportunity to make another offer.

"Next the fun begins. Bidders log on to the system 15 minutes before the auction starts to make sure there are no technical glitches. When the auction opens, the competitive bidding begins and prices start dropping.

"Although my area is directly responsible for buying not-for-resale products and services, we have had experience and success running reverse auctions for our private-label merchandise. For these auctions, the product development team, sourcing manager, and buyer are involved in developing the specifications for the merchandise—the description of the fabric, thread count, lining, buttons, etc. The sourcing manager and buyer work together to determine which domestic and international suppliers are qualified to participate in the auction. In many cases, conducting an auction has allowed JCPenney to lower costs or maintain current pricing while improving the quality of a garment. A good example involves two auctions that were conducted for one type of men's pants. The first auction was for the fabric, which was being upgraded. The second auction was for the construction of the pants. Both auctions resulted in savings of more than $1 per pair while providing an improved quality garment to our customers."

Source: Personal communication.

Tariffs, also known as **duties,** are taxes placed by a government on imports that increase the cost of merchandise imported from international sources. Import tariffs have been used to shield domestic manufacturers from foreign competition. Because tariffs raise the cost of imported merchandise, retailers have a strong incentive to use their political clout to reduce them.

Inventory turnover is likely to be lower when purchasing from suppliers outside the United States than from domestic suppliers, which will result in higher inventory carrying costs. Consider The Spoke bicycle store in Aspen, Colorado, which is buying Moots bicycles manufactured in Steamboat Springs, Colorado. The Spoke buyer knows that the lead time—the amount of time between the recognition that an order needs to be placed and the point at which the merchandise arrives in the store and is ready for sale—is usually two weeks, plus or minus three days. But if The Spoke ordered bikes from Italy, the lead time might be three months, plus or minus three weeks. Since lead times are longer, retailers using foreign sources must maintain larger inventories to ensure that merchandise is available when the customer wants it. Larger inventories mean larger inventory carrying costs.

14.5   RETAILING VIEW   Datang, China, Is Sock City

Datang, China, is called Sock City because nine billion pairs of socks, more than one set for every person in the world, are produced there each year. Its annual trade fair attracts 100,000 buyers from around the world. Southeast of Datang is Shenzhou, which is the world's necktie capital; to the west is Sweater City and Kids' Clothing City; and to the south is Underwear City.

This specialization creates the economies of scale that have made Chinese businesses the world's leading garment manufacturers. Buyers from New York to Tokyo can now place orders for 500,000 pairs of socks all at once—or 300,000 neckties, 100,000 children's jackets, or 50,000 size 36B bras—in China's giant new specialty cities.

Textile production is a prime example of how the Chinese government guides development indirectly through local planning instead of state ownership. In the late 1970s, Datang was a rice-farming village with 1,000 people, who gathered in small groups and stitched socks together at home and then sold them in baskets along the highway. But the government designated Datang's sock makers as producers and ordered them to stop retailing socks. Now, they produce over one-third of the world's output. Due to the policy, there are many rags-to-riches tales in Datang, such as that of Dong Ying

As a result of government and private investment, China has become the leading manufacturer of private-label and national-brand merchandise.

Hong, who in the 1970s gave up a $9-a-month job as an elementary-school teacher to make socks at home. Now, she is the owner of Zhejiang Socks and a sock millionaire.

The Chinese government has also designated large areas for development, formed giant industrial parks, given tax benefits, and developed the infrastructure and transportation networks needed to move products quickly to market. It has created networks of support businesses located near one another, such as the button capital that furnishes most of the buttons on the world's shirts, pants, and jackets. Private companies, with the support of the government, have built huge textile factory complexes, complete with dormitories and hospitals, that provide food, shelter, and health care, along with close supervision.

Huafang Group, one of China's largest textile companies, has over 100 factory buildings, 30,000 employees, and round-the-clock operations. More than 20,000 workers live free of charge in Huafang's dormitories. Conditions aren't great, but they are often better than the conditions in the inland provinces from which the workers come. Many women go there after high school, stay for a few years, and then return home to be married. As they return home, another 10,000 are bused in from the countryside.

Sources: David Barboza, "In Roaring China, Sweaters Are West of Socks City," *New York Times,* December 24, 2004, p. C2; David Francis, "Will China Clothe the World?" *Christian Science Monitor,* August 5, 2004, p. 1.

REFACT

Twelve percent of China's exports to the United States are sent to Wal-Mart. Wal-Mart's purchases account for 1 percent of China's gross domestic product.[28]

It is also more difficult to predict exactly how long the lead time will be when sourcing globally. When the bicycle goes from Steamboat Springs to Aspen, the worst that could happen is it getting caught in a snowstorm for a day or two. In contrast, the bicycle from Italy might be significantly delayed because of multiple handlings at sea or in airports, customs, strikes of carriers, poor weather, or bureaucratic problems. Similar to long lead times, inconsistent lead times require the retailer to maintain high levels of backup stock, which increases the inventory carrying costs.

Finally, transportation costs are higher when merchandise is produced in foreign countries. In general, the farther merchandise has to travel, the higher the transportation cost will be. For instance, the cost of shipping a container of merchandise by ship from China to New York is significantly higher than the cost from Cleveland to New York.

Managerial Issues Associated with Global Sourcing Decisions   While the cost factors associated with global sourcing are easy to quantify, some more subjective issues are quality control, time to market, and social/political factors.

When sourcing globally, it's harder to maintain consistent quality standards than when sourcing domestically. Quality control problems can cause delays in shipment and adversely affect a retailer's image. Suppose Banana Republic is having pants made in Haiti. Before the pants leave the factory, Banana Republic representatives find that the workmanship is so poor that the pants need to be remade. Banana Republic would need extra backup stock to carry it through until the pants can be remade. More likely, however, it won't have advance warning of the problem, so the stores will be out of stock. A more serious problem arises if the pants are delivered to the stores without the problem having been detected. This scenario could happen if the defect is subtle, such as inaccurate sizing. Customers can become irritated and question merchandise quality.

In addition, the collaborative supply chain management approaches described in Chapter 10 are more difficult to implement when sourcing globally. Collaborative systems are based on short and consistent lead times. Vendors provide frequent deliveries of smaller quantities. For a collaborative system to work properly, there must be a strong alliance between the vendor and the retailer that is based on trust and sharing of information. These activities are more difficult to perform globally than domestically. Furthermore, the level of difficulty increases with distance and the vendor's sophistication. Catalog and Internet retailer Coldwater Creek (www.coldwatercreek.com), for instance, sources about 75 percent of its merchandise from North America so it can purchase relatively small orders and receive quick delivery.[29]

A final issue with global sourcing is the problem of policing potential violations of human rights and child labor laws. Sears, Wal-Mart, Ralph Lauren, The Gap, Nordstrom, J. Crew, The Limited, and others have had to publicly defend themselves from allegations about human rights, child labor, or other abuses involving factories and countries where their goods are made.[30]

Due to the efforts of U.S. retailers, few imported goods are produced in sweatshop conditions. In the early 1990s, Wal-Mart required its suppliers to sign a code of basic labor standards. After exposés in the mid-1990s of abuses in factories making Kathie Lee products, which the chain carries, Wal-Mart and Kathie Lee Gifford both began hiring outside auditing firms to inspect supplier factories to ensure their compliance with the code.

Many other companies that produce or sell goods made in low-wage countries do similar self-policing, from Toys "R" Us to Nike to The Gap. While no company suggests that its auditing systems are perfect, most say they catch major abuses and either force suppliers to fix them or yank production. Self-policing allows companies to avoid painful public revelations about them. For example, in 2005, The Gap Inc. released a 40-page "social-responsibility report" that detailed the problems it found in the 3,000 factories it contracted with to produce clothing for its outlets. The company discovered persistent wage, health, and safety violations in most regions where it does business, including China, Africa, India, and Central and South America. None of the findings was especially surprising; labor abuses are a fact of life in the global apparel industry, where intense price competition continually drives factories to produce more clothing for less money. However, The Gap's willingness to go public and reveal, in exceptional detail, its responses to these conditions is unusual. Even some of The Gap's harshest critics say the company's candor will drive industry changes that ultimately improve the lives of factory workers.[31]

SUPPORT SERVICES FOR THE BUYING PROCESS

Two services available to buyers that can help them more effectively acquire merchandise are resident buying offices and Internet exchanges.

Resident Buying Offices

Resident buying offices are organizations located in major market centers that provide services to help retailers buy merchandise. As retailers have become larger and more sophisticated, the third-party resident buying offices have become less important. Retailers simply perform the services formerly provided by these buying offices themselves.

To illustrate how buying offices operate, consider how David Smith of Pockets Men's Store in Dallas utilizes his resident buying offices when he goes to market in Milan. Smith meets with market representative Alain Bordat of the Doneger Group. Bordat, an English-speaking Italian, knows Smith's store and his upscale customers, so in advance of Smith's visit, he sets up appointments with Italian vendors he believes will fit Pockets' image.

When Smith is in Italy, Bordat accompanies him to the appointments and acts as a translator, negotiator, and accountant. Bordat informs Smith of the cost of importing the merchandise into the United States, taking into account duty, freight, insurance, processing costs, and so forth.

Once the orders are placed, Bordat writes the contracts and follows up on delivery and quality control. The Doneger Group also acts as a home base for buyers like Smith, providing office space and services, travel advisers, and emergency aid. Bordat and his association continue to keep Smith abreast of what's happening on the Italian fashion scene through reports and constant communication. Without the help of a resident buying office, it would be difficult, if not impossible, for Smith to penetrate the Italian wholesale market.

Internet Exchanges

Retail exchanges are providers of Internet-based solutions and services for retailers. The software and services offered by exchanges help retailers, manufacturers, and their trading partners reduce costs and improve efficiency by streamlining and automating sourcing and supply chain processes. They provide an opportunity for vendors and retailers to interact electronically rather than meet face-to-face in a physical market. Retail exchanges can increase the efficiency of the buying process by offering software to support several of the systems discussed in previous chapters, such as reverse auctions; supply chain management; and collaborative planning, forecasting, and replenishment.

Two major retail exchanges, WorldWide Retail Exchange (WWRE) (www. wwre.org) and GlobalNetXchange (GNX) (www.gnx.com), were launched in 2000 as nonprofit organizations owned and supported by groups of large retailers. The objective of these exchanges was to promote collaboration between retailers and

Retail exchanges like GNX provide services to buyers, such as platforms for conducting reverse auctions and engaging in collaborative planning with vendors.

vendors. They planned to provide a single, central hub that connected trading partners. Retailers would have unlimited access to their vendors' production data, and vendors would have instant access to retailers' sales projections.

The original vision of GNX and WWRE had a number of flaws. First, the exchanges underestimated the technological complexity of building such an exchange. Although some companies such as Wal-Mart and Liz Claibourne had built effective private exchanges, they were designed to connect one trading partner to many, not many to many, as GNX and WWRE envisioned. Second, the cost of the software to provide some services, such as reverse auctions, dropped in price to the point that individual retailers could afford to administer their own reverse auctions. Third, the retail industry is extremely competitive, and retailers are reluctant to share information, preferring instead to keep their data and plans secret.[32]

In 2005, the two exchanges merged. The combined entity includes about 50 food, drug, and apparel retailers, including Carrefour SA, Sears Holdings Corp., Walgreen Co., Kroger Co., and Federated Department Stores Inc. Executives of the newly merged exchanges continue to hope that by creating a bigger and more sophisticated marketplace, retailers will be better equipped to face off against Wal-Mart. The combined exchange will facilitate transactions for a retail group with about $1 trillion in combined annual sales.[33]

STRATEGIC RELATIONSHIPS

Chapter 5 emphasized that maintaining strong vendor relationships is an important method of developing a sustainable competitive advantage. Chapters 10 and 12 discussed some of the ways partnering relations can improve information exchange, planning, and the management of supply chains. For example, collaborative planning, forecasting, and replenishment (CPFR) systems cannot operate effectively without the vendor and retailer making a commitment to work together and invest in the relationship. In this section, we examine how retailers can develop strategic relationships and the characteristics of successful long-term relationships.

Defining Strategic Relationships

Traditionally, relationships between retailers and vendors have focused on haggling over how to split up a profit pie.[34] The relationships were basically win–lose encounters because when one party got a larger portion of the pie, the other party got a smaller portion. Both parties were interested exclusively in their own profits and unconcerned about the other party's welfare. These relationships continue to be common, especially when the products being bought are commodities and have no major impact on the retailers' performance. Thus, there is no benefit to the retailer to enter into a strategic relationship.

A **strategic relationship,** also called a **partnering relationship,** emerges when a retailer and vendor are committed to maintaining the relationship over the long term and investing in opportunities that are mutually beneficial to the parties. In these relationships, it's important for the partners to take risks to expand the profit pie to give the relationship a strategic advantage over other companies. In addition, the parties have a long-term perspective. They are willing to make short-term sacrifices because they know that they will get their fair share in the long run.

Strategic relationships are win–win relationships. Both parties benefit because the size of the profit pie increases—both the retailer and vendor increase their sales and profits—because the parties in strategic relationships focus on uncovering and exploiting joint opportunities. They depend on and trust each other heavily; they share goals and agree on how to accomplish those goals; and they thus reduce the risks of investing in the relationship and sharing confidential information.

A strategic relationship is like a marriage. When businesses enter strategic relationships, they're wedded to their partners for better or worse. For example, the U.K.'s Marks & Spencer had jointly developed a kitchen product with a vendor.[35] Four months after the product's introduction, the manufacturer realized that it had miscalculated the product's cost and, as a result, had underpriced the product and was losing money on the deal. It was a big hit at Marks & Spencer because it was underpriced. Marks & Spencer decided not to raise the price because the product was already listed in its catalog. Instead, it worked with the vendor to reengineer the product at a lower cost, cut its own gross margin, and gave that money to the manufacturer. It took a profit hit to maintain the relationship. Retailing View 14.6 examines how two big, tough companies, Wal-Mart and Procter & Gamble, have learned to work together.

Maintaining Strategic Relationships

The four foundations of successful strategic relationships are mutual trust, open communication, common goals, and credible commitments.

Mutual Trust   The glue in a strategic relationship is trust. **Trust** is a belief that a partner is honest (reliable, stands by its word, sincere, fulfills obligations) and benevolent (concerned about the other party's welfare).[36] When vendors and buyers trust one another, they're more willing to share relevant ideas, clarify goals and problems, and communicate efficiently. Information shared between the parties becomes increasingly comprehensive, accurate, and timely. There's less need for the vendor and buyer to constantly monitor and check up on each other's actions because each believes the other won't take advantage, even given the opportunity.[37]

Strategic relationships and trust are often developed initially between the leaders of organizations. For example, when Wal-Mart started to work with Procter & Gamble to coordinate its buying activities, Sam Walton got together with P&G's vice president of sales on a canoeing trip (see Retailing View 14.6). They discussed the mutual benefits of cooperating and the potential risks associated with altering their normal business practices. In the end, they must have concluded that the potential long-term gains were worth the additional risks and short-term setbacks that would probably occur as they developed the new systems.

Open Communication   To share information, develop sales forecasts together, and coordinate deliveries, Wal-Mart and P&G have to have open and honest communication. This requirement may sound easy in principle, but most businesses don't like to share information with their business partners. They believe it is none of the other's business. But open, honest communication is a key to developing successful relationships. Buyers and vendors in a relationship need to understand what's driving each other's business, their roles in the relationship, each firm's strategies, and any problems that arise over the course of the relationship.

Common Goals   Vendors and buyers must have common goals for a successful relationship to develop. Shared goals give both members of the relationship an incentive to pool their strengths and abilities and exploit potential opportunities between them. There's also assurance that the other partner won't do anything to hinder goal achievement within the relationship.

For example, Wal-Mart and P&G recognized that it was in their common interest to remain business partners—they needed each other—and to do so, both had to be allowed to make profitable transactions. Wal-Mart can't demand prices so low that P&G can't make money, and P&G must be flexible enough to accommodate the needs of its biggest customer. With a common goal, both firms have an incentive to cooperate because they know that by doing so, each can boost sales. Common goals also help sustain the relationship when expected

---

Procter & Gamble and Wal-Mart Are Partners   RETAILING VIEW   14.6

Historically, Procter & Gamble (P&G) has had enormous leverage and dominated its relationship with retailers. Its brands, such as Crest toothpaste, Folgers coffee, Pepto-Bismol, and Pampers, are so popular that every retailer must carry them. But, with consolidation in the retail industry, large retailers such as Wal-Mart have the power to demand low prices and great service from their vendors.

Today, Wal-Mart and P&G have a relationship that is emulated throughout the industry. But it wasn't always that way. In the mid-1980s, Sam Walton went on a canoe trip with Lou Pritchett, P&G's vice president for sales. On this trip, they started a process of examining how the two firms could mutually profit by working together. In the old days, there was no sharing of information, no joint planning, and no systems coordination. Today, they use a sophisticated EDI system coupled with CPFR that enables P&G to work with Wal-Mart to establish sales forecasts and replenishment goals for products like Crest. P&G receives continual data on sales, inventory, and prices for its products at individual Wal-Mart stores. This information allows P&G to anticipate, say, Crest sales and automatically ship orders. Electronic invoicing and electronic transfer of funds complete the transaction cycle.

The companies work together when problems arise. For example, Wal-Mart discovered a downside to P&G's pricier products like Crest Whitestrips and Mach3 razors—these products were the most popular to steal. So executives from the firms met and developed a solution. P&G altered its packaging to make its products harder to steal. It changed its Olay package from a box to a clear plastic container with a flat piece of cardboard, known as a "clamshell" because it is so difficult to open. It made the Crest Whitestrips package larger and added an extra layer of plastic. It assumed the extra cost. Gillette also adopted clamshell packaging for its razor packs. For the blade refills, it created a clear-front, plastic dispenser system fitted with drawers that let customers take just one package at a time.

This relationship benefits all parties. Customers get lower prices and high product availability. P&G has reduced order-processing costs and inventory shrinkage. P&G produces according to demand, thereby lowering the need for backup stock. Wal-Mart needs less inventory as well. By working together, the two have turned what used to be a sometimes adversarial relationship into a win–win proposition.

REFACT

The population of Bentonville, Arkansas, the corporate headquarters for Wal-Mart, is 17,000, with 7,000 of these people working for Wal-Mart. Another 7,000 people represent vendors that call on Wal-Mart every month. More than 100 companies that are suppliers to Wal-Mart have opened offices in Bentonville, including Hewlett-Packard, Clorox, Nabisco, and Procter & Gamble.[38]

Sources: Sarah Ellison, Ann Zimmerman, and Charles Forelle, "P&G's Gillette Edge: The Playbook It Honed at Wal-Mart," *The Wall Street Journal*, January 31, 2005, p. A1; Mike Troy, "Working with Wal-Mart: America's Most Powerful Partnership," DSN *Retailing Today*, June 2004, pp. 4–9.

benefit flows aren't realized. If one P&G shipment fails to reach a Wal-Mart store on time due to an uncontrollable event like misrouting by a trucking firm, Wal-Mart won't suddenly call off the whole arrangement. Instead, Wal-Mart is likely to view the incident as a simple mistake and remain in the relationship. This is because Wal-Mart knows it and P&G are committed to the same goals in the long run.

Credible Commitments   Successful relationships develop because both parties make credible commitments. Credible commitments are tangible investments in the relationship. They go beyond just making the hollow statement, "I want to be a partner." Credible commitments involve spending money to improve the supplier's products or services provided to the customer.[39] For example, one of the strengths of the Wal-Mart/P&G partnership is the obvious and significant investments both parties have made in CPFR systems and material handling equipment.

Building Partnering Relationships

Although not all retailer–vendor relationships should or do become strategic partnerships, the development of strategic partnerships tends to go through a series of phases characterized by increasing levels of commitment: (1) awareness, (2) exploration, (3) expansion, and (4) commitment.

In the awarenss stage, no transactions have taken place. This phase might begin with the buyer seeing some interesting merchandise at a retail market or an ad in a trade magazine. The reputation and image of the vendor can play an important role in determining if the buyer moves to the next stage.

During the exploration phase, the buyer and vendor begin to explore the potential benefits and costs of a partnership. At this point, the buyer may make a small purchase and try to test the demand for the merchandise in several stores. In addition, the buyer will get information about how easy it is to work with the vendor. Eventually, the buyer has collected enough information about the vendor to consider developing a longer-term relationship. The buyer and the vendor determine if there is potential for a win–win relationship. They begin to work on joint promotional programs, and the amount of merchandise sold increases. If both parties continue to find the relationship mutually beneficial, it moves to the commitment stage and becomes a strategic relationship. The buyer and vendor then make significant investments in the relationship and develop a long-term perspective toward it.

It is difficult for retailer–vendor relationships to be as committed as some supplier–manufacturer relationships. Manufacturers can enter into monogamous (sole source) relationships with other manufacturers. However, an important function of retailers is to provide an assortment of merchandise for their customers. Thus, they must always deal with multiple, sometimes competing suppliers.

SUMMARY

This chapter has examined issues surrounding purchasing merchandise and vendor relations. Retailers can purchase either manufacturers' brands or private-label brands. Each type has its own relative advantages. Choosing appropriate brands and a branding strategy is an integral component of a firm's merchandise and assortment planning process.

Buyers of national brands attend trade shows and wholesale market centers to meet with vendors, view new merchandise, and place orders. Virtually every merchandise category has at least one annual trade show at which retailers and vendors meet. They negotiate the wholesale price as well as other issues, including return privileges, markdown money, advertising allowances, payment terms, and transportation costs. Successful vendor relationships depend on planning for and being adept at negotiations.

Buyers need to be aware of ethical and legal issues to guide them in these negotiations and purchase decisions. There are also problems associated with counterfeit and gray-market merchandise and issues that vendors face when selling to retailers, such as exclusive territories and tying contracts. Care should be taken when placing restrictions on which retailers they will sell to, what merchandise, how much, and at what price.

Two factors involved in buying private-label merchandise are global sourcing and the use of reverse auctions. A large percentage of private-label merchandise is manufactured outside of the United States. The cost, managerial, and ethical issues surrounding global sourcing decisions must be considered.

Buying merchandise sometimes is facilitated by resident buying offices. Market representatives of these resident buying offices facilitate merchandising purchases in foreign markets.

Retailers that can successfully team up with their vendors can achieve a sustainable competitive advantage. There needs to be more than just a promise to buy and sell on a regular basis. Strategic relationships require trust, shared goals, strong communications, and a financial commitment.

KEY TERMS

buyback, *385*

chargeback, *384*

commercial bribery, *384*

cooperative advertising, *381*

copyright, *385*

counterfeit merchandise, *385*

diverted merchandise, *386*

duties, *390*

exclusive dealing agreements, *386*

free riding, *384*

gray-market goods, *386*

house brands, *373*

intellectual property, *385*

licensed brand, *374*

lift-out, *385*

manufacturer brands, *372*

manufacturer suggested retail price, *383*

markdown money, *379*

market weeks, *377*

national brands, *372*

own brands, *373*

partnering relationship, *394*

private-label brands, *373*

resale price maintenance, *383*

resident buying offices, *392*

retail exchanges, *392*

reverse auctions, *388*

slotting allowance, *384*

slotting fee, *384*

stocklift, *385*

store brands, *373*

strategic relationship, *394*

tariff, *390*

trade show, *378*

trademark, *385*

trust, *394*

tying contract, *387*

wholesale market, *377*

GET OUT AND DO IT!

1. **CONTINUING ASSIGNMENT** Go visit the retailer you selected for the continuing assignment and perform an audit of its national and private brands. Interview a manager to determine whether the percentage of private brands has increased or decreased over the past five years. Ask the manager to comment on the store's philosophy toward national versus private brands. On the basis of what you see and hear, assess its branding strategy.

2. **INTERNET EXERCISE** Go to the WorldWide Retail Exchange (www.wwre.org) and GlobalNetXchange.com (www.gnx.com). Evaluate their offerings. Write a recommendation to a retailer of your choice regarding which of these offerings the retailer should use. You can also recommend that it doesn't use any of the offerings.

3. **INTERNET EXERCISE** Go to the home page for the Private Label Manufacturers Association (PLMA) and read the "Market Profile" that can be found at http://www.plma.com/storeBrands/sbt05.html. What are Store Brand products? Who purchases Store Brands? Who makes Store Brands? What Store Brands are you purchasing on a regular basis?

4. **INTERNET EXERCISE** Read the feature article, "Changing the Face of Private Labels," written by Dale Buss from brandchannel.com about private-label cosmetics at Kohl's, available at http://www.brandchannel.com/features_effect.asp?pf_id=209. What are the major benefits from the retailer's perspective of offering an Estée Lauder–developed private-label brand of cosmetics in Kohl's department stores? Discuss why Estée Lauder is interested in developing a private-label brand of cosmetics based on the forces fueling retailer power and the interdependence between retail business partners introduced in Chapter 10, "Information Systems and Supply Chain Management."

5. **GO SHOPPING** Go to your favorite food store and look up the prices for the items in the following table. Be sure to select the same sized package for this price comparison of national brands and store brands.

	Raspberry Cereal Bars	Coffee	Macaroni & Cheese Mix	Tissues	Cola
National brand					
Store brand					

How much can consumers save by purchasing store brands of these products? How would you compare the percentage of savings on different categories of merchandise? How did the various grocery stores selected by the class compare in terms of price savings on their store brand versus the national brands?

DISCUSSION QUESTIONS AND PROBLEMS

1. Assume you have been hired to consult with The Gap on sourcing decisions for sportswear. What issues would you consider when deciding whether you should buy from Mexico or China or find a source within the United States?

2. What kinds of social courtesies or gifts (lunches, theater tickets, etc.) are appropriate for buyers to accept from vendors?

3. What are the advantages and disadvantages of national brands versus private-label brands? Does your favorite clothing store have a strong private-label brand strategy? Should it?

4. What is the potential benefit of retail exchanges, and what has prevented them from providing these benefits?

5. What factors are the advantages and disadvantages of developing partnering relationships with vendors?

6. Describe the growth of private-label store brands. How can retailers capitalize on this growing trend? What conditions in the external environment have made it possible for private-label brands to thrive?

7. What merchandise categories are important for private-label brands, and where do you expect expansion in the future?

8. What are national-brand manufacturers and suppliers doing to respond to the growth of private-label brands?

9. Select three retailers that each have a different brand strategy—one that sells only store brands, one that sells a mixture of store brands and national brands, and one that sells only national brands—and compare their retail mixes and target audience.

SUGGESTED READINGS

Ailawadi, Kusum, and Kevin Keller. "Understanding Retail Branding: Conceptual Insights and Research Priorities," *Journal of Retailing* 80 (2004), pp. 331–52.

Balto, David. "Recent Legal and Regulatory Developments in Slotting Allowances and Category Management," *Journal of Public Policy & Marketing* 21, no. 2 (Fall 2002), pp. 289–95.

Bradford, Kevin; Anne Stringfellow; and Barton Weitz. "Managing Conflict to Improve the Effectiveness of Retail Networks," *Journal of Retailing* 80 (2004), pp. 181–95.

Bush, Darren, and Betsy D. Gelb. "When Marketing Practices Raise Antitrust Concerns," *Sloan Management Review* 46, no. 4 (Summer 2005), pp. 73–81.

Byron, Ellen, and Teri Agins. "When Exclusivity Means Illegality; Stores' 'Exclusives' Are Routine—And Sometimes Flout the Law," *The Wall Street Journal*, January 6, 2005, p. A11.

Cellich, Claude, and Subhash Jain. *Global Business Negotiations: A Practical Guide*. Mason, OH: Thomson/South-Western, 2004.

Clodfelter, Richard. *Retail Buying: From Basics to Fashion*. 2nd ed. New York: Fairchild Publications, 2003.

Flanagan, Michael. "How Retailers Source," *Just—Style*, January 2005, pp. 17–33.

Hartman, Laura; Denis Arnold; and Richard Wokutch. *Rising Above Sweatshops: Innovative Approaches to Global Labor Challenges*. Westport, CT: Praeger, 2003.

Jap, Sandy. "Online Reverse Auctions: Issues, Themes, and Prospects for the Future," *Journal of the Academy of Marketing Science* 30, no. 4 (Fall 2002), pp. 13–23.

Varley, Rosemary. *Retail Product Management: Buying and Merchandising*. 2nd ed. New York: Routledge, 2005.

Watkins, Michael. *Breakthrough Business Negotiation: A Toolbox for Managers*. New York: John Wiley & Sons, 2002.

Wilkie, William; Debra Desrochers; and Gregory Gundlach. "Marketing Research and Public Policy: The Case of Slotting Fees," *Journal of Public Policy & Marketing* 21, no. 2 (Fall 2002), pp. 275–89.

Retail Pricing

EXECUTIVE BRIEFING

Bruce Peterson, Senior Vice President, GMM of
Perishables, Wal-Mart Supercenters

The pricing of perishable goods plays a major role in our supercenter strategy. It supports the overall image of the store. For example, bananas are one of the most popular items in our supercenters. When bananas are at a great price, our customers will realize that other products in the store, like blenders and Vanilla Wafers, are also at great prices. Offering products at low prices benefits both Wal-Mart and its customers.

Because Wal-Mart's strategy is to sell products at the lowest prices, we need to keep our produce prices low. But if we set our prices too low, then we will not meet our gross margin goals. We are able to offer lower prices and still make money because we work closely with our produce vendors. We set up contracts specifying the prices we will pay based on the time of year, availability of products, and the competition in different markets. To reduce inventory levels and make sure we have the freshest produce, we work closely with our vendors on collaborative planning, forecasting, and replenishment (CPFR). My interest in retail, specifically produce, started early when I was working at a grocery store as a bag boy in high school. At first I worked there to save up to buy a car, but as I got older, my part-time job turned into a career. Most of my experience in produce and retail was acquired when I worked as a buyer at an independent grocery store. I would go to a produce terminal (located in Detroit) and negotiate deals with vendors. Instead of just selling produce to me, they taught me about the business, such as when certain produce comes into season and what to sell it for.

I left the company and started my own produce wholesale company. Owning my own company prepared me for the position I hold today because working for Wal-Mart is like running your own business within a business. You're in charge of your department, making sure others are doing their job and, most important, sales goals are being reached.

CHAPTER 15

It is really a thrill when you make a great buy. One year I negotiated a great deal on apples from New Zealand. We were able to sell them for 69 cents a pound compared to $1.29 the previous year. Our sales increased from 4,000 boxes to 100,000 boxes. Not only did we have a huge increase in sales in the following year but we also helped our customers make a big saving.

The decisions examined in this textbook are directed toward facilitating exchanges between retailers and their customers. As discussed in Chapter 1, retailers offer a number of benefits to their customers, including making merchandise available to customers when they want it, at a convenient location, and in the quantities they want. In addition, retailers provide services such as the opportunity for customers to see and try out merchandise before buying it. In exchange for these benefits, customers pay money for the merchandise and services provided by retailers.

The importance of pricing decisions is growing because today's customers have more alternatives to choose from and are better informed about the alternatives available in the marketplace. Thus, they are in a better position to seek a good value when they buy merchandise and services. **Value** is the ratio of what customers receive (the perceived benefit of the products and services offered by the retailer) to what they have to pay for it.

$$\text{Value} = \frac{\text{Perceived Benefits}}{\text{Price}}$$

Thus, retailers can increase value and stimulate more sales (exchanges) by either increasing the perceived benefits offered or reducing the price. To some customers, a good value means simply paying the lowest price because other benefits offered by retailers are not important to them. Others are willing to pay extra for additional benefits as long as they believe they're getting their money's worth in terms of product quality or service.

If retailers set prices higher than the benefits they provide, sales and profits will decrease. In contrast, if retailers set prices too low, their sales might increase, but profits might decrease due to the lower profit margin. In addition to offering an attractive value to customers, retailers need to consider the value proposition offered by their competitors and legal restrictions related to pricing. Thus, setting the right price can be challenging.

The first section of this chapter reviews the factors retailers consider in setting retail prices. Then the actual process that retailers use to determine prices is described. The next section examines methods that retailers use to charge different prices over time based on changes in demand, different market segments, and even individual customers. After discussing the different pricing strategies used by retailers, the chapter concludes with some special issues in pricing, such as loss leaders, category and odd pricing, and the potential increase in price competition due to the Internet.

CONSIDERATIONS IN SETTING RETAIL PRICES

As illustrated in Exhibit 15–1, the four factors retailers consider in setting retail prices are (1) the price sensitivity of consumers, (2) the cost of the merchandise and services, (3) competition, and (4) legal restrictions.

Customer Price Sensitivity and Cost

Generally, as the price of a product increases, the sales for the product will decrease because fewer and fewer customer feel the product is a good value. The price sensitivity of customers determines how many units will be sold at different price levels. If customers in the target market are not very price sensitive, sales will not decrease significantly if the prices are increased. However, if customers are very price sensitive, sales will decrease significantly when prices increase.

One approach that can be used to measure the price sensitivity of customers is a price experiment. Consider the following situation: A movie theater chain wants to determine how many movie tickets will be sold at different price levels. It selects six theaters in the chain with very similar trading areas and sets prices at different levels in each of the theaters for a week. Assume that the variable cost per ticket, the royalty paid to the movie distributor, is $5.00 per ticket sold, and the fixed cost of operating the theater for a week, the cost for rent, labor and energy, is $8,000.

The results of this experiment are shown in Exhibit 15–2. Notice in Exhibit 15–2a that as prices increase, the fixed costs remain the same, sales and variable costs both decrease, but sales decrease at a faster rate than variable costs (Exhibit 15–2b). So the highest profit level occurs at a $7.00 price (Exhibit 15–2c). If the movie theater only considers customers' price sensitivity and cost in setting prices, it would set prices for theatres with these trading characteristics at $7.00 to maximize profits.

EXHIBIT 15–1

Considerations in Setting Retail Prices

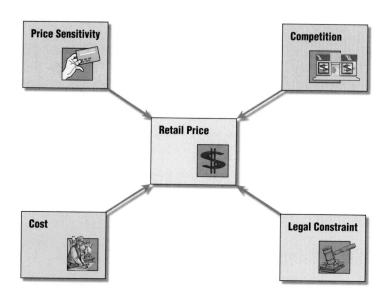

Results of Price Experiment **EXHIBIT 15–2**

Data from Price Experiment **EXHIBIT 15–2a**

Theater	Price	Quantity Sold	Column (1) × Column (2) Revenue	Column (2) × $5 Variable Cost per Ticket Variable cost	Fixed Cost	Column (3) – Column (4) – Column(5) Contribution to Profit
1	$6.00	9,502	$57,012	$47,510	$8,000	$1,502
2	6.50	6,429	41,789	32,145	8,000	1,644
3	7.00	5,350	37,450	26,750	8,000	2,700
4	7.50	4,051	30,383	20,255	8,000	2,128
5	8.00	2,873	22,984	14,365	8,000	619
6	8.50	2,121	18,029	10,605	8,000	−577

EXHIBIT 15–2b
Quantity Sold at Different Prices

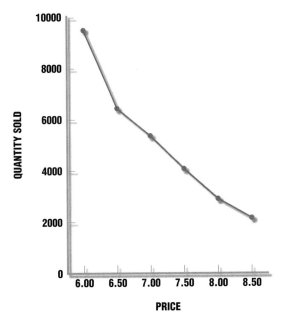

EXHIBIT 15–2c
Profit at Different Prices

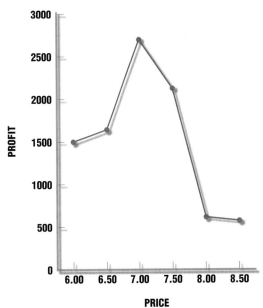

Price Elasticity A commonly used measure of price sensitivity is **price elasticity,** the percentage change in quantity sold divided by the percentage change in price.

$$\text{Elasticity} = \frac{\text{Percentage change in quantity sold}}{\text{Percentage change in price}}$$

Assume that a retailer originally priced a private-label DVD player at $90 and raised the price to $100. Prior to raising the price, the retailer was selling 1,500 units a week. When the priced was increased, sales dropped to 1,100 units per week. The calculation of the price elasticity is as follows:

$$\text{Elasticity} = \frac{\text{Percentage change in quantity sold}}{\text{Percentage change in price}}$$

$$= \frac{(\text{New quantity sold} - \text{Old quantity sold})/(\text{Old quantity sold})}{(\text{New price} - \text{Old price})/(\text{Old price})}$$

$$= \frac{(1100 - 1500)/1100}{(10 - 9)/9} = \frac{-0.2667}{.1111} = -2.4005$$

Because the quantity sold usually decreases when prices increase, price elasticity is a negative number.

The target market for a product is generally viewed to be price insensitive (referred to as inelastic) when its price elasticity is greater than −1—when a 1 percent decrease in price results in less than a 1 percent increase in quantity sold. The target market for a product is price sensitive (referred to as elastic) when the price elasticity is less than −1—when 1 percent decrease in price produces more than a 1 percent increase in quantity sold. The price elasticity for a product can be estimated by conducting an experiment as described previously or using statistical techniques to analyze how sales have changed in the past when prices changed.

A number of factors affect the price sensitivity for a product. First, the more substitutes a product or service has, the more likely it is to be price elastic (sensitive). For example, there are many alternatives for McDonald's sandwich meal, and thus, fast food prices are typically price elastic, but gasoline has almost no substitutes and is price inelastic (insensitive). Second, products and services that are necessities are price inelastic. Thus, medical care is price inelastic, whereas airline tickets for a vacation are price elastic. Third, products that are expensive relative to a consumer's income are price elastic. Thus, cars are price elastic, and books and movie tickets tend to be price inelastic. The estimated elasticities for some commonly purchased items are shown below.[2]

Product Class	Price Elasticity	
	Short Run	**Long Run**
Clothing	−0.90	−2.90
Wine	−0.88	−1.17
Jewelry and watches	−0.44	−0.67
Gasoline	−0.20	−0.60

Based on these estimates, a 1 percent decrease in the price of clothing would result in only a 0.90 percent increase in the quantity sold in the short run but 2.90 percent increase in the long run. So if you must have that new sweater today, you are much less responsive to a low price than if you can wait for the sweater to be on sale three months from now. In contrast, Americans aren't going to change their gasoline purchases much in the short or long run, regardless of slight price decreases or increases. However, these elasticity estimates are based on relatively small changes in prices and might be different for large price changes.

For products with price elasticities less than −1, the price that maximizes profits can be determined by the following formula:

$$\text{Profit-maximizing price} = \frac{\text{Price elasticity} \times \text{Cost}}{\text{Price elasticity} + 1}$$

So, if the private-label DVD player described in the preceding example cost $50, the profit-maximizing price would be:

$$\text{Profit-maximizing price} = \frac{\text{Price elasticity} \times \text{Cost}}{\text{Price elasticity} + 1}$$
$$= \frac{-2.4005 \times \$50}{-2.4005 + 1} = \$85.70$$

Competition

The previous discussion about setting price based on customer price sensitivity (elasticity) and cost ignores the effects of competitors' prices. For example, assume the movie theater chain that conducted the experiment had a $7.50 ticket price and, based on the results of the experiment, dropped its price to $7.00 to increase sales and profits. If the increased sales occurred, competitors would see a decline in their sales and react by dropping their prices to $7.00, and the experimenting theater then might not realize the sales and profit increase it anticipated.

Retailers can price above, below, or at parity with the competition. The chosen pricing policy must be consistent with the retailer's overall strategy and its relative market position. Consider, for instance, Wal-Mart and Tiffany and Co. Wal-Mart's overall strategy is to be the low-cost retailer for the merchandise it sells. It tries to price the products it sells below its competition. Tiffany, on the other hand, offers significant benefits to its customers beyond the merchandise. Its brand name and customer service assure customers that they will be satisfied with the jewelry they purchase. Due to the unique nature of Tiffany's offering, it is able to set prices higher than competitors.

Collecting and Using Competitive Price Data
Most retailers routinely collect price data about their competitors to see if they need to adjust their prices to remain competitive. Competitive price data are typically collected using store personnel, but pricing data also are available from business service providers.

A hypothetical example of such price comparison data is shown in Exhibit 15–3. In this example, CVS, the national drugstore chain, sets its prices generally above Winn-Dixie and Wal-Mart; however, pricing for shampoo, toothpaste, and shaving gel is very competitive. Similarly, Winn-Dixie, a grocery chain, is moderately priced with low prices on select items, like baby food. Wal-Mart is generally priced below its competitors but does not stock a full range of products.

Reducing Price Competition
Retailers attempt to reduce price competition by utilizing some of the branding strategies described in Chapter 14 to offer unique merchandise. For instance, they can develop lines of private-label merchandise, negotiate with national-brand manufacturers for exclusive distribution rights, or have vendors make unique products for them. Because the competition doesn't offer this merchandise, customers cannot make price comparisons easily.

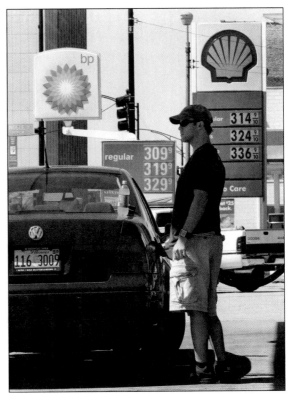

Historically, the price elasticity of gasoline has been greater than −1, so increases in price have not led to a proportional decrease in sales.

SKU	CVS	Winn-Dixie	Wal-Mart
Centrum Vitamins (130 tablets)	$9.49	$9.99	$8.26
Tylenol Liquid	6.49	4.69	5.47
Emfamil Liquid Baby Food	3.29	2.99	3.13
VO5 Shampoo	0.99	1.19	0.97
Pedialyte (1 liter)	5.79	5.29	
Colgate Toothpaste (6 oz.)	2.99	2.99	2.84
Duracell AA Batteries (4 pack)	4.79	3.49	3.24
9 Lives Canned Cat Food	1.49	1.29	0.98
Advil (50 caps)	5.99	5.59	
Edge Shaving Gel (7 oz.)	2.39	2.39	2.14
Competitive Price Index*	100%	91%	85%

EXHIBIT 15–3
Competitive Price Data

*Only common items are indexed.

Legal and Ethical Pricing Issues

In addition to customer price sensitivity, cost, and competition, retailers need to consider legal and ethical issues when setting prices. For example, pricing has been particularly difficult for Carrefour hypermarkets in France, where regulation prohibits how much it can lower its prices on branded merchandise. Carrefour has been hurt by competitors, such as two German chains, ALDI and Lidl, both of which sell private-label merchandise that is not subject to the French rules and thus can be priced more cheaply than Carrefour's products. Both of these retailers aggressively entered the French market, winning over many Carrefour shoppers.[3]

Some of these legal and ethical pricing issues are price discrimination, resale price maintenance, horizontal price fixing, predatory pricing, bait-and-switch tactics, and scanned versus posted prices.

Price Discrimination   **Price discrimination** by retailers occurs when a retailer charges different prices for the identical products and/or services sold to different customers. Price discrimination between retailers and their customers is generally legal.

Different customers typically receive different prices when buying products and services with coupons or meeting specified conditions, such as eating at a restaurant before 6:00 p.m. It is common for customers to negotiate for different prices when buying merchandise such as cars, jewelry, or collectibles. Women are often charged more for haircuts and dry cleaning, even though the costs of providing these services to women and men are about the same.[5] Some states have laws against retail price discrimination based on gender, race, or ethnicity.

How and why retailers engage in price discrimination is discussed later in the chapter. In many cases, customers are not aware that they are being charged different prices. However, if they become aware of this practice, they may feel they are being treated unfairly and be reluctant to patronize the retailer in the future.[6] For example, there was considerable negative reaction when Coca-Cola considered raising the price of soft drinks in vending machines on hot days.[7]

Predatory Pricing   **Predatory pricing** arises when a dominant retailer sets prices below its costs to drive competitive retailers out of business. Eventually, the predator hopes to raise prices when the competition is eliminated and earn back enough profits to compensate for its losses.

Some states have old statutes that declare it illegal to sell merchandise at unreasonably low prices, usually below their cost. However, a retailer generally may sell merchandise at any price so long as the motive isn't to destroy competition. For instance, independent retailers in small towns accuse Wal-Mart of selling goods below cost to drive them out of business, but Wal-Mart maintains that it hasn't violated the law because it didn't intend to hurt competitors. But it admits it has sold some products below cost, as do other retailers, to attract customers into the store in the hope that they will then buy other products during their visit.

Salons often engage in price discrimination by setting haircut prices for women higher than those for men. There are no federal laws prohibiting this practice, but some states have passed laws making it illegal.

Resale Price Maintenance   As discussed in Chapter 14, vendors often encourage retailers to sell their merchandise at a specific price, known as the manufacturer's suggested retail price (MSRP). Vendors set MSRP prices to reduce retail price competition among retailers, eliminate free riding, and stimulate retailers to provide complementary services. Vendors enforce MSRPs by withholding benefits such as cooperative advertising or even refusing to deliver merchandise to non-complying retailers. Although the legality of these practices has changed over time, they are now legal.

Horizontal Price Fixing   **Horizontal price fixing** involves agreements between retailers that are in direct competition with each other to set the same prices. This practice clearly reduces competition and is illegal. As a general rule of thumb, retailers should refrain from discussing prices or terms and conditions of sale with competitors. If buyers or store managers want to know competitors' prices, they can look at a competitor's advertisements, its Web sites, or its stores.

Bait-and-Switch Tactics   A **bait-and-switch** is an unlawful, deceptive practice that lures customers into a store by advertising a product at a lower-than-normal price (the bait) and then, once they are in the store, induces them to purchase a higher-priced model (the switch). Bait-and-switch can occur by having either inadequate inventory for the advertised product or salespeople disparage the quality of the advertised model and emphasize the superior performance of a higher-priced model. To avoid disappointing customers and risking problems with the Federal Trade Commission (FTC), the retailer needs to have sufficient inventory of advertised items and offer customers rain checks if stockouts occur.

Scanned versus Posted Prices   While many customers and regulators are concerned about price scanning accuracy, price scanning accuracy studies have usually found a high level of accuracy. In general, retailers lose money from scanning errors because the scanned price is below the posted price.[8] Periodic price audits are an essential component of good pricing practices. Price audits of a random sample of items should be done periodically to identify the extent and cause of scanning errors and develop procedures to minimize errors. Retailing View 15.1 describes how electronic shelf tags reduce scanning errors as well as operating costs.

REFACT

The average pricing error rate at retail stores using scanners is 3.86 percent. Undercharges represent 2.21 percent of the total errors, while overcharges represent 1.65 percent.[9]

Electronic Shelf Labels Reduce Costs   **RETAILING VIEW**   **15.1**

To reduce scanning errors as well as operating costs, retailers are beginning to replace paper shelf price labels with electronic shelf labels (ESL) that display prices on an LCD screen. The ESLs are linked to a central computer that uses radio signals to transmit price changes over a wireless network inside the store. The bar code scanners are also connected to the central computer, which updates prices on the scanners and ESLs simultaneously, helping ensure that the prices at both ends match.

With ESLs, prices can be changed instantly with a few keystrokes on the computer. Thus, retailers can respond quickly to

The use of this electronic shelf price tag enables retailers to change prices easily without incurring the labor cost needed to change conventional plastic or paper tags.

price changes by competitors or other market conditions. Thousands of labor hours needed to manually change prices are saved because with ESL technology, retailers don't have to send people out on the floor every time they have a sale.

Electronic shelf labels were developed more than 20 years ago, but the technology was too expensive to make it a cost-effective alternative to paper labels. Costs have come down dramatically in recent years. Five years ago, ESL units cost about $12 each, but the cost now is below $5.

Source: Randy Tucker, "Electronic Shelf Labels Update Easily," *Cincinnati Enquirer*, February 10, 2004, p. B3.

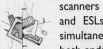

SETTING RETAIL PRICES

As described in the previous section, theoretically, retailers maximize their profits by setting prices on the basis of the price sensitivity of customers and the cost of merchandise. One limitation of just using price sensitivity and cost for setting prices is that it fails to consider the prices being charged by competitors. Another problem is that implementing this approach requires knowledge of the price sensitivity (price elasticity) of each item. Many retailers have to set prices for over 50,000 SKUs and make thousands of pricing decisions each month. From a practical perspective, they cannot conduct experiments or do statistical analyses to determine the price sensitivity for each item.

Thus, retailers typically set prices by marking up the item's cost to yield a profitable gross margin. Then these cost-based prices are adjusted on the basis of insights about customer price sensitivity and competitive pricing. The following section describes how retailers set prices solely on the basis of merchandise cost.

Retail Price and Markup

When setting prices based on merchandise cost, retailers start with the following equation:

Retail price = Cost of merchandise + Markup

The **markup** is the difference between the retail price and the cost of an item. Thus, if a sporting-goods retailer buys a tennis racket for $75 and sets the retail price at $125, the markup is $50. The appropriate markup is determined to cover all of the retailer's operating expenses (labor costs, rent, utilities, advertising, etc.) needed to sell the merchandise and produce a profit for the retailer. As discussed later in the chapter, retailers may price some merchandise below their costs and sell it at a loss because these low-priced items generate store traffic.

The **markup percentage** is the markup as a percentage of the retail price:

$$\text{Markup percentage} = \frac{\text{Retail price} - \text{Cost of merchandise}}{\text{Retail price}}$$

Thus, the markup percentage for the tennis racket is

$$\text{Markup percentage} = \frac{\$125 - \$75}{\$125} = 40\%$$

The retail price based on the cost and markup percentage is:

Retail price = Cost of merchandise + Markup

Retail price = Cost of merchandise + Retail price × Markup percentage

$$\text{Retail price} = \frac{\text{Cost of merchandise}}{1 - \text{Markup percentage (as a fraction)}}$$

Thus, if a buyer for an office supply category specialist purchases calculators at $14 and needs a 30 percent markup to meet the financial goals for the category, the retail price needs to be:

$$\text{Retail price} = \frac{\text{Cost}}{1 - \text{Markup percentage}} = \frac{\$14.00}{1 - 0.30} = \$20$$

Traditionally, apparel retailers used a 50 percent markup, referred to as **keystoning,** that set the retail price by simply doubling the cost. Retailing View 15.2 reviews the decision by Smith Drugstore to take a 0 percent markup on generic drugs.

Initial Markup and Maintained Markup

The previous discussion is based on the assumption that the retailer sells all items at an initially set price. However, retailers rarely sell all items at the initial price. They frequently reduce the price of items for special promotions or to get rid of excess inventory at the end of a season. In addition, discounts are given to employees, and some merchandise is lost to theft and accounting errors (inventory shrinkage). Factors that reduce the actual selling price from the initial sales price are called **reductions.** Thus, there is a difference between the initial and the maintained markup. The **initial markup** is the retail selling price initially set for the merchandise minus the cost of the merchandise, whereas the **maintained markup** is the actual sales realized for the merchandise minus its costs. Thus, the maintained margin is equivalent to the gross margin for the product.

The difference between initial and maintained markup is illustrated in Exhibit 15–4. The item illustrated costs $0.60, and the initial price for the item is $1.00, so the initial markup is $0.40, and the initial markup percentage is 40 percent. However, the average actual sale price for the item is $.90. The reductions are $0.10, so the maintained markup is $0.30, and the maintained markup percentage is 33 percent (0.30/0.90).

RETAILING VIEW 15.2

Ethics Determines the Markup at Smith Drugstore

Kaylei and Michael Mosier, owners of the 146-year-old Smith Drugstore in McKinney, Texas, made a decision that would change their lives and business: They weren't going to profit from the uninsured. Before their decision, the drugstore had a small but loyal base of customers because it offered free home delivery, credit accounts based on trust, and an old-fashioned cosmetics counter.

After newspapers across the state carried the story of their decision, their daily 100 calls turned into 1,000. "It changed our lives, obviously," Michael Mosier said. "We thought it would end, but it didn't. It's a good thing, but it's just overwhelming." The Mosiers added a computer and a second phone line, doubled their staff, started a Web site, and changed their business model. The customers from across the country, meanwhile, just keep coming.

The Mosiers' pricing decision highlights the price variability of generic drugs from store to store across the country. Drug companies make most of their profits on the brand-name medications that are patent protected, while pharmacies get high markups on generics. For customers with insurance,

Smith Drugstore in McKinney, Texas, made an ethical decision to charge fair pharmaceutical prices to the uninsured; the reaction from consumers across the country was dramatic.

the prices pharmacies can charge are largely fixed. But they have wide discretion when it comes to what to charge uninsured customers. A study of prescription drug prices found 1,000 percent markups on generic drugs in some cases, with some of the best prices at smaller, independent stores.

Source: Paul Meyer, "Drugstore's Ethics Are Drawing a Crowd," *Dallas Morning News,* January 29, 2005, p. B1. Reprinted with permission of the Dallas Morning News.

EXHIBIT 15–4
Difference between Initial Markup and Maintained Markup

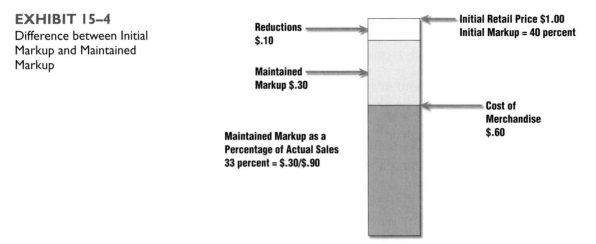

The relationship between the initial and the maintained markup percentage is:

$$\text{Initial markup percentage} = \frac{\begin{array}{c}\text{Maintained markup percentage} \\ \text{(as a percentage of planned} \\ \text{actual sales)} \end{array} + \begin{array}{c}\text{Percent reductions} \\ \text{(as a percentage of planned} \\ \text{actual sales)}\end{array}}{100\% + \begin{array}{c}\text{Percent reductions} \\ \text{(as a percentage of planned} \\ \text{actual sales)}\end{array}}$$

Thus, if the buyer setting the price for the item shown in Exhibit 15–4 planned on reductions of 10 percent of actual sales and wanted a maintained markup of 33 percent, the initial markup should be

$$\text{Initial markup percentage} = \frac{33\% + (\$0.10/\$0.90 = 11.111\%)}{100\% + 11.111\%} = 40\%$$

and the initial retail price should be

$$\text{Initial retail price} = \frac{\text{Cost}}{1 - \text{Initial markup percentage}} = \frac{\$0.60}{1 - 0.40} = \$1.00$$

Profit Impact of Setting a Retail Price: The Use of Break-Even Analysis

Retailers often want to know the number of units they need sell to begin making a profit. For example, a retailer might want to know:

- Break-even sales to cover a target profit.
- Break-even volume and dollars for a new product, product line, or department.
- Break-even sales change needed to cover a price change.

A useful analytical tool for making these assessments is a **break-even analysis,** an analysis that determines, on the basis of a consideration of fixed and variable costs, how much merchandise needs to be sold to achieve a break-even (zero) profit.

The formula for calculating the sales quantity needed to break even is:

$$\text{Break-even quantity} = \frac{\text{Total fixed costs}}{\text{Actual unit sales price} - \text{Unit variable cost}}$$

The following examples illustrate the use of this formula in determining the break-even volume of a new private-label product and the break-even change in volume needed to cover a price change.

Calculating Break-Even for a New Product   Hypothetically, PETsMART is considering the introduction of a new private-label, dry dog food targeting owners of older dogs. The cost of developing this dog food is $700,000, including salaries for the design team and testing the product. Because these costs don't change with the quantity of product that is produced and sold, they're known as **fixed costs.** PETsMART plans to sell the dog food for $12 a bag—the unit price. The **variable cost** is the retailer's expenses that vary directly with the quantity of product produced and sold. Variable costs often include direct labor and materials used in producing the product. PETsMART will be purchasing the product from a private-label manufacturer. Thus, the only variable cost is the dog food's cost, $5, from the private-label supplier. The **break-even point quantity** is the quantity at which total revenue equals total cost, and then profit occurs for additional sales.

$$\text{Break-even quantity} = \frac{\text{Fixed cost}}{\text{Actual unit sales price} - \text{Unit variable cost}}$$
$$= \frac{\$700,000}{\$12 - \$5} = 100,000 \text{ bags}$$

Thus, PETsMART needs to sell 100,000 bags of dog food to break even, or make zero profit, and for every additional bag sold, it will make $7 profit.

Now assume that PETsMART wants to make $100,000 profit from the new product line. The break-even quantity now becomes:

$$\text{Break-even quantity} = \frac{\text{Fixed cost}}{\text{Actual unit sales price} - \text{Unit variable cost}}$$
$$= \frac{\$700,000 + \$100,000}{\$12 - \$5} = 114,286 \text{ bags}$$

Calculating Break-Even Sales   A closely related issue to the calculation of a break-even point is determining how much unit sales would have to increase to make a profit from a price cut or how much sales would have to decline to make a price increase unprofitable. Continuing with the PETsMART example, assume the break-even quantity is 114,286 units based on the $700,000 fixed cost, the $100,000 profit, a selling price of $12, and a cost of $5. Now PETsMART is considering lowering the price of a bag of dog food to $10. How many units must it sell to break even if it lowers its selling price by 16.67 percent to $10? Using the formula,

$$\text{Break-even quantity} = \frac{\text{Fixed cost}}{\text{Actual unit sales price} - \text{Unit variable cost}}$$
$$= \frac{\$700,000 + \$100,000}{\$10 - \$5} = 160,000 \text{ bags}$$

So if PETsMART decreases its price by 16.67 percent from $12 to $10, unit sales must increase by 40 percent: (160,000 − 114,286)/114,286.

PRICE ADJUSTMENTS

The preceding section reviewed how retailers initially set prices on the basis of the merchandise cost and desired maintained margin. However, retailers adjust prices over time (markdowns) and for different customer segments (variable pricing).

Markdowns

Markdowns are price reductions or discounts from the initial retail price. This section examines why retailers take markdowns, how they optimize markdown decisions, how they reduce the amount of markdowns by working with vendors, how

REFACT

Marked-down goods, which accounted for just 8 percent of department store sales three decades ago, have climbed to around 20 percent of sales.[10]

The buyer for this merchandise category made a clearance markdown because the merchandise was selling at a significantly slower rate than planned.

they liquidate markdown merchandise, and the mechanics of taking markdowns.

Reasons for Taking Markdowns   Retailers' reasons for taking markdowns can be classified as either clearance (to dispose of merchandise) or promotional (to generate sales).

Clearance Markdowns   When merchandise is selling at a slower rate than planned, will become obsolete at the end of its season, or is priced higher than competitors' goods, buyers generally mark it down for clearance purposes. As discussed in Chapter 12, slow-selling merchandise decreases inventory turnover; prevents buyers from acquiring new, better selling merchandise; and can diminish the retailer's image for selling the most current styles and trends.

Markdowns are part of the cost of doing business, and thus, buyers plan for them. They tend to order more fashion merchandise than they forecast actually selling because they are more concerned about underordering and stocking out of a popular item before the end of the season than about overordering and having to discount excess merchandise at the end of the season. Stocking out of popular merchandise can have a detrimental effect on a fashion retailer's image, whereas discounting merchandise at the end of the season just reduces maintained markup.

Thus, a buyer's objective isn't to minimize markdowns. If markdowns are too low, the buyer is probably pricing the merchandise too low, not purchasing enough merchandise, or not taking enough risks with the merchandise being purchased. So buyers set the initial markup price high enough that, even after markdowns and other reductions have been taken, the planned maintained markup is still achieved.

Promotional Markdowns   Buyers also employ markdowns to promote merchandise and increase sales. Markdowns are taken to increase customer traffic flow. Retailers plan promotions in which they take markdowns for holidays, for special events, and as part of their overall promotional program. In fact, small portable appliances (such as toasters) are called *traffic appliances* because they're often sold at promotional or reduced prices to generate in-store traffic. Retailers hope that customers will purchase other products at regular prices while they're in the store. Another opportunity created by markdowns is to increase the sale of complementary products. For example, a supermarket's markdown on hot dog buns may be offset by increased demand for hot dogs, mustard, and relish—all sold at regular prices.

Optimizing Markdown Decisions   Retailers have traditionally created a set of arbitrary rules for taking markdowns.[11] One retailer, for instance, identifies markdown candidates when its weekly sell-through percentages fall below a certain value. Another retailer cuts prices on the basis of how long the merchandise has been in the store—marking products down by 20 percent after 8 weeks, then by 30 percent after 12 weeks, and finally by 50 percent after 16 weeks. Such a rules-based approach, however, is limited because it does not consider the sales generated by the merchandise at different price points and thus produces less-than-optimal profits.

Instead of relying on rules developed from averages, retailers can benefit significantly from merchandising optimization software. **Merchandising optimization software** is a set of algorithms that monitors merchandise sales and prices, determines the relationship between prices and sales generated, and then determines the optimal (most profitable) price and timing for markdowns.

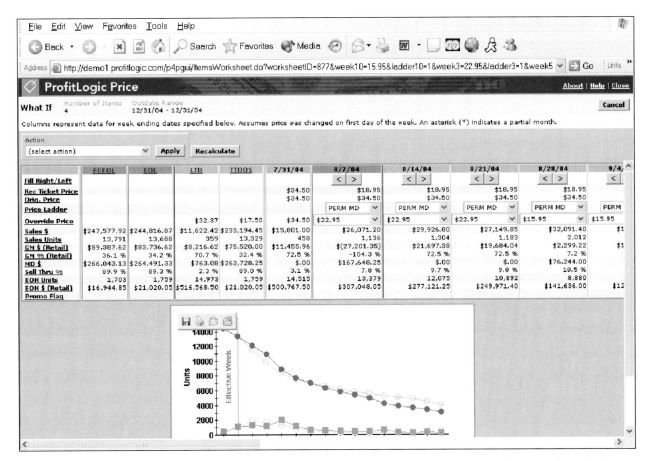

The output from the Oracle Retail markdown model indicates that the model's recommended markdown of $18.95 will result in more than $5,000 greater profit than the buyer's planned markdown of $22.95.

The optimization software works by continually updating its pricing forecasts on the basis of actual sales throughout the season and factoring in differences in price sensitivities. For example, the software recognizes that in early November, a winter item's sales are better than expected, so it delays taking a markdown that had been planned. Each week, as new sales data become available, it readjusts the forecasts to include the latest information. It computes literally thousands of scenarios for each item—a process that is too complicated and time consuming for buyers to do on their own. It then evaluates the outcomes on the basis of expected profits and other factors and selects the action that produces the best results.[12]

Bloomingdale's implemented markdown optimization in 40 percent of its apparel business across all stores, accounting for about 10 percent of its total sales. The software changed the mindset of its buyers. Buyers now take markdowns quicker, don't feel locked in to particular patterns, and don't think that every markdown has to be the same. By taking the first markdown when there is still customer demand, Bloomingdale's sells more units at a first markdown price and has fewer units selling at the second markdown price. In one instance, a buyer had planned to wait until after Christmas to take markdowns, but the software indicated that the buyer should start taking markdowns right after Thanksgiving. There was a great deal of uncertainty, but it worked. Bloomingdale's sold through the product before Christmas at a higher price than it had planned to run post-Christmas.[13]

Reducing the Amount of Markdowns by Working with Vendors   Retailers work closely with their vendor partners to coordinate deliveries and help share the financial burden of taking markdowns. Supply chain management systems (discussed in Chapter 10) reduce the lead time for receiving merchandise so that retailers can monitor changes in trends and customer demand more closely, thus reducing markdowns.

Vendors have a partnering relationship with their retailers and thus a vested interest in their success. Vendors that are knowledgeable about the market and competition can help with stock selections. Of course, a retailer must also trust its own taste and intuition; otherwise, its store will have the same merchandise as all other stores. As discussed in Chapter 14, buyers can often obtain markdown money—funds a vendor gives the retailer to cover lost gross margin dollars that result from markdowns and other merchandising issues.

Liquidating Markdown Merchandise   Even with the best planning, some merchandise may remain unsold at the end of a season. Retailers use one of five strategies to liquidate this unsold merchandise:

1. Sell the merchandise to another retailer.
2. Consolidate the unsold merchandise.
3. Place the remaining merchandise on an Internet auction site like eBay or have a special clearance location on its own Web site.
4. Give the merchandise to charity.
5. Carry the merchandise over to the next season.

Selling the unsold merchandise to another retailer has been very popular among retailers. For instance, off-price retailers such as TJX Corporation (owners of T.J. Maxx and Marshalls) and Bluefly.com purchase end-of-season merchandise from other retailers and sell it at deep discounts. However, this approach for liquidating unsold merchandise only enables retailers to recoup a small percentage of the merchandise's cost—often a mere 10 percent.

Markdown merchandise can be consolidated in a number of ways. First, the consolidation can be made into one or a few of the retailer's regular locations. Second, markdown merchandise can be consolidated into another retail chain or an outlet store under the same ownership. Saks Fifth Avenue (Off Fifth) and Neiman Marcus (Last Call Clearance Center) use this approach. Third, unsold merchandise can be shipped to a distribution center or rented space such as a convention center (Barney's of New York and J. Crew) for final sale. However, consolidation sales can be complex and expensive due to the extra transportation and record-keeping involved.

The Internet is increasingly useful for liquidating unsold merchandise. For example, an electronics store might partner with eBay to sell goods it has received from trade-ins. J. Crew and many others have separate areas of their Web sites for clearance merchandise.

Giving clearance merchandise to charities is a common practice. Charitable giving is always a good corporate practice. It is a way of giving back to the community and has strong public relations benefits. Also, the cost value of the merchandise can be deducted from income.

The final liquidation approach—to carry merchandise over to the next season—is used with relatively high-priced nonfashion merchandise, such as traditional men's clothing and furniture. Generally, however, it's not profitable carrying over merchandise because of excessive inventory carrying costs.

Variable Pricing and Price Discrimination

Retailers use a variety of techniques to maximize profits by charging different prices to different customers.[14]

Individualized Variable Pricing   Ideally, retailers would maximize their profits if they charged each customer as much as the customer was willing to pay. For instance, if a wealthy, price-insensitive customer wants to buy a new car battery, Autozone would like to price the battery at $200 but then price the same battery at $125 to make a sale to a more price-sensitive, lower-income customer. Charging each individual customer a different price based on their willingness to pay is called **first-degree price discrimination.**

Setting a selling price for this autographed baseball card using an auction is an example of first-degree price discrimination—the price is set by the customer with the highest willingness to pay for this baseball card.

Pricing merchandise through auction bidding is an example of first-degree price discrimination. A retailer offering a 1955 Mickey Mantle baseball card on eBay maximizes its profits because the customer with the highest willingness to pay bids and pays the highest price. Another example of retailers practicing first-degree price discrimination is when they allow customers to haggle over price, as described in Retailing View 15.3.

Although first-degree price discrimination is legal and widely used in some retail sectors, such as automobile and antique dealers, it is impractical in most retail stores. First, it is difficult to assess each customer's willingness to pay, and second, retailers cannot change the posted prices in stores as customers with different willingness to pay enter the store. In addition, customers might feel they are being treated unfairly if they realize that they are being charged a higher price than other customers.

Haggling for a Better Price   RETAILING VIEW   15.3

Out shopping a few weeks ago, Regina Ranonis was trying to decide between trendy low-heeled boots or a more conservative style. Then the salesman spoke up: If she would spring for both pairs, he would knock $270 off the total price.

Does this sound like the local flea market? It wasn't. An array of retailers is hoping to reel in sales by allowing haggling, or some form of it. While the practice isn't entirely new—and officially denied by most companies—good consumers say they're getting deals everywhere from Sunglass Hut to the trendy boutique Kenneth Cole. Big-name stores like Saks and Macy's say savvy shoppers who can cite competitors' prices may also find some wiggle room.

Many of the country's biggest retailers, from The Gap to Pottery Barn, say they're sticking to firm no-haggling policies. Many department stores use cash registers that won't accept unauthorized discount prices without managerial approval. Some even have video cameras not only to watch shoppers but also to make sure the staff isn't cutting sweetheart deals to their friends.

Some of the best negotiating territory is at franchises, where owners have the flexibility to operate more like mom-and-pop shops. But even at major department stores and small chains, a growing number of managers are now authorized to lower a price to meet the competition or throw in free alterations or delivery. Many stores take pains to insist that haggling is off limits, even as customers and sales associates say it goes on all the time. The policy is "Try not to come down in price too much, but don't let the business walk out."

Sources: Rick Popely, "For Some, Haggling Is Part of the Fun," *Knight Ridder Tribune Business News*, April 24, 2005, p. 1; Steve Burgess, "The Happy Haggler: Only the Meek Pay Retail," *BC Business*, November 2004, pp. 52–57; Teri Agins and Sarah Collins, "Retailers Hoping to Lift Holiday Sales Begin to Allow Customers to Haggle," *The Wall Street Journal*, November 16, 2001, p. B1.

However, first-degree price discrimination is possible when selling merchandise on the Internet. Retailers can assess each customer's willingness to pay by analyzing past purchase behavior and then serve up Web pages with unique pricing based on the customer's willingness to pay.[17]

Self-Selected Variable Pricing   An alternative approach for variable pricing is to offer the same price schedule to all customers but require that customers do something to get the lower price—something that discourages customers with a high willingness to pay to take advantage of the lower price. This approach is referred to as **second-degree price discrimination.** For example, restaurants often have early-bird specials, lower prices for meals served before 6:00 p.m. Anyone can take advantage of this discount; however, price-sensitive consumers are more likely to be attracted by the offer. Clearance markdowns, coupons and rebates, bundling, and multiunit pricing are other examples of this approach.

Clearance Markdowns for Fashion Merchandise   Clearance markdowns result in higher prices being charged at the beginning of the season than at the end of the season. Thus, fashion-conscious customers who have a high willingness to pay because they want to be the first to wear the latest fashions self-select to pay higher prices. More price-sensitive customers wait to buy the merchandise at the end of the season when prices are lower.

Coupons   **Coupons** offer a discount on the price of specific items when they're purchased. Coupons are issued by manufacturers and retailers in newspapers, on products, on the shelf, at the cash register, over the Internet, and through the mail. Retailers use coupons because they are thought to induce customers to try products for the first time, convert those first-time users to regular users, encourage large purchases, increase usage, and protect market share against competition.

Coupons are also considered a form of second-degree price discrimination because, in general, price-sensitive customers will expend the extra effort to collect and redeem coupons, while price-insensitive customers will not.

The evidence on couponing's overall profitability is mixed, depending on the product category.[18] Coupon promotions, like all temporary promotions, may be stealing sales from a future period without any net increase in sales. For instance, if a supermarket runs a coupon promotion on sugar, households may buy a large quantity of sugar and stockpile it for future use. Thus, unless the coupon is used mostly by new buyers, the net impact on sales will be negligible, and there will be a negative impact on profits by the amount of the redeemed coupons and cost of the coupon redemption procedures. Some believe that coupons annoy, alienate, and confuse consumers and therefore do little to increase store loyalty.[19] Customers see an ad for a supermarket with a headline reading "Double Coupons" but don't realize there might be conditions, such as a minimum purchase required, or that it may only apply to manufacturers' paper coupons.

Price Bundling   **Price bundling** is the practice of offering two or more different products or services for sale at one price. For instance, McDonald's offers a bundle of a sandwich, French fires, and a soft drink in a Value Meal® at a discount compared with buying the items individually. Price bundling is used to increase both unit and dollar sales by increasing the amount of merchandise bought on a store visit. The practice is also an example of second-degree price discrimination because it offers more price-sensitive customers a lower-priced alternative.

Multiple-Unit Pricing   **Multiple-unit pricing** or **quantity discounts** are similar to price bundling in that the lower total merchandise price increases sales, but the products or services are similar rather than different. For example, a convenience store may sell three liters of soda for $2.39 when the price per unit is 99 cents—a savings of 58 cents. Like price bundling, this variable pricing approach is used to increase sales volume. Depending on the type of product, however, customers may stockpile for use at a later time and simply shift sales in time.

Multiunit pricing is an example of second-degree price discrimination because customers who buy and consume more of a product are presumably more price sensitive and thus attracted by the lower prices if they buy more units.

Variable Pricing by Market Segment Retailers often charge different prices to different demographic market segments, a practice referred to as **third-degree price discrimination.** For example, movie theaters have lower ticket prices for seniors and college students, presumably because these segments are more price sensitive than other customers.

Another example of third-degree price discrimination is zone pricing. **Zone pricing** refers to the practice of charging different prices in different stores, markets, regions, or zones. Retailers generally use zone pricing to address different competitive situations in their various markets. For example, some multichannel retailers implement zone pricing by asking customers to enter their zip code before they are quoted a price. Food retailers often have up to four or five pricing zones in a single city. They'll have one zone if they're next to a Wal-Mart, and another zone if they're next to a less price-competitive regional chain. Prices can vary as much as 10 percent depending on the competition and the economic health of the neighborhood.[20] Drugstores frequently charge higher prices in poor urban areas and neighborhoods populated by elderly retirees, because customers in those areas tend to be relatively insensitive to price.[21] Third-degree price discrimination, when used in this manner to discriminate on the basis of income and age, is considered an unethical practice by many.

The preceding sections focus on how retailers set prices and then adjust them over time and for different market segments. The following sections examine the two prevalent pricing strategies used by retailers, pricing issues that confront services retailers, and special pricing techniques that retailers use.

PRICING STRATEGIES

Retailers use two basic retail pricing strategies: high/low pricing and everyday low pricing (EDLP). Each of these strategies and its advantages and disadvantages are discussed in this section.

High/Low Pricing

Retailers using a **high/low pricing** strategy frequently—often weekly—discount the initial prices for merchandise through frequent sales promotions. The sales undertaken by retailers have become more intense in recent years. In the past, fashion retailers would mark down merchandise at the end of a season; grocery and drugstores would have sales only when their vendors offered them special prices or when they were overstocked. Today, many retailers respond to increased competition and more value-conscious customers by increasing the frequency of sales.

Everyday Low Pricing

Many retailers, particularly supermarkets, home improvement centers, and discount stores, have adopted an **everyday-low-pricing (EDLP)** strategy. This strategy emphasizes the continuity of retail prices at a level somewhere between the regular nonsale price and the deep-discount sale price of high/low retailers. Although EDLP retailers embrace their consistent pricing strategy, they occasionally have sales, just not as frequently as their high/low competitors.

Even though Wal-Mart uses an everyday low pricing strategy (EDLP), it still offers sales for some merchandise.

The term *everyday low pricing* is somewhat misleading because low doesn't mean lowest. Although retailers using EDLP strive for low prices, they aren't always the lowest priced in the market. At any given time, a sale price at a high/low retailer may be the lowest price available in a market.

To reinforce their EDLP strategy, many retailers have adopted a **low price guarantee policy** that guarantees customers that they will have the lowest price in a market for products they sell. The guarantee usually promises to match or better any lower price found in the market and might include a provision to refund the difference between the seller's offer price and the lower price.

Advantages of the Pricing Strategies

The high/low pricing strategy has the following advantages:

- *Increases profits through price discrimination* High/low pricing allows retailers to charge higher prices to customers who are not price sensitive and are willing to pay the "high" price and lower prices to price-sensitive customers who will wait for the "low" sale price.
- *Sales create excitement* A "get them while they last" atmosphere often occurs during a sale. Sales draw a lot of customers, and a lot of customers create excitement. Some retailers augment low prices and advertising with special in-store activities like product demonstrations, giveaways, and celebrity appearances.
- *Sells merchandise* Sales allow retailers to get rid of slow-selling merchandise.

The EDLP approach has its own advantages, as follows:

- *Assures customers of low prices* Many customers are skeptical about initial retail prices. They have become conditioned to buying only on sale—the main characteristic of a high/low pricing strategy. The EDLP strategy lets customers know that they will get the same low prices every time they patronize the EDLP retailer. Customers don't have to read the ads and wait for items they want to go on sale.
- *Reduces advertising and operating expenses* The stable prices caused by EDLP limit the need for the weekly sale advertising used in the high/low strategy. In addition, EDLP retailers do not have to incur the labor costs of changing price tags and signs and putting up sales signs.
- *Reduces stockouts and improves inventory management* The EDLP approach reduces the large variations in demand caused by frequent sales with large markdowns. As a result, retailers can manage their inventories with more certainty. Fewer stockouts mean more satisfied customers, higher sales, and fewer rain checks. (**Rain checks** are given to customers when merchandise is out of stock; they're written promises to sell customers merchandise at the sale price when the merchandise arrives.) In addition, a more predictable customer demand pattern enables the retailer to improve inventory turnover by reducing the average inventory needed for special promotions and backup stock.

PRICING SERVICES

Additional challenges arise when pricing services due to (1) the need to match supply and demand and (2) the difficulties customer have in determining service quality.[22]

Matching Supply and Demand

Services are intangible and thus cannot be inventoried. When retailers are selling products, if the products don't sell one day, they can be stored and sold the next day. However, when a plane departs with empty seats or a play is performed with empty seats in the theater, the potential revenue from this unused capacity is lost forever. In addition, most services have limited capacity. For example, restaurants are limited in the number of customers that can be seated. Due to capacity constraints, services retailers might encounter situations when they cannot realize as many sales as they could make.

To maximize sales and profits, many services retailers engage in yield management.[23] **Yield management** is the practice of adjusting prices up or down in response to demand to control the sales generated. Airlines are the masters at yield management. Using sophisticated computer programs, they monitor the reservations and ticket sales for each flight and adjust prices according to capacity utilization. Prices are lowered on flights when sales are below forecasts and there is significant excess capacity. As ticket sales approach capacity, prices are increased.

Because air travel, like most services, cannot be inventoried, when this plane took off with empty seats, the opportunity to sell the seats was lost forever.

Other services retailers use less sophisticated approaches for matching supply and demand. For example, more people want to go to a restaurant for dinner or see a movie at 7:00 p.m. than at 5:00 p.m. Restaurants and movie theaters thus might not be able to satisfy the demand for their services at 7:00 p.m. but have excess capacity at 5:00 p.m. Thus, restaurants and movie theaters often price their services lower for customers who use them at 5:00 p.m. compared with 7:00 p.m. in an effort to shift demand from 7:00 p.m. to 5:00 p.m.

The time needed to provide a service can affect the service retailer's capacity for providing the service. Thus, services retailers need to increase prices and margins when the provision of the service is going to be restricted by capacity. For example, in restaurants, appetizers are often served while the main course is being prepared. Thus, serving appetizers does not lengthen the time customers spend in the restaurant or decrease the restaurant's capacity for serving customers. In contrast, desserts and coffee extend the time customers spend in the restaurant and reduce the restaurant's capacity to serve other customers. Thus, restaurants price desserts and coffee with a higher margin than they do appetizers. Retailing View 15.4 describes how Broadway theaters practice yield management.

REFACT

Yield management can increase revenues by 7 percent and increase net profit by as much as 100 percent.[24]

Determining Service Quality

Due to the intangibility of services, it is often difficult for customers to assess the quality of services. Thus, customers are likely to use price as an indicator of both service costs and quality.[25] Customers' use of price as an indicator of quality depends on several factors, one of which is the other information available to them. When service cues of quality are readily accessible, when brand names provide evidence of a company's reputation, or when the level of advertising communicates the company's belief in the brand, customers may prefer to use those cues instead of price. In other situations, however, such as when quality is hard to detect or quality or price varies a great deal within a class of services, consumers may believe that price is the best indicator of quality. Many of these conditions typify situations that face consumers when they purchase services.[26]

Another factor that increases the dependence on price as a quality indicator is the risk associated with a service purchase. In high-risk situations, many of which involve credence services such as medical treatment or legal consulting, the customer will look to price as a surrogate for quality.

Because customers depend on price as a cue of quality and because price sets expectations of quality, service prices must be determined carefully. In addition to being chosen to manage capacity, prices must be set to convey the appropriate quality signal. Pricing too low can lead to inaccurate inferences about the quality of the service. Pricing too high can set expectations that may be difficult to match in service delivery.

PRICING TECHNIQUES FOR INCREASING SALES

This section reviews three techniques used by retailers to increase sales. Each of these techniques—leader pricing, price lining, and odd pricing—takes advantage of the way customers process information.

Leader Pricing

Leader pricing involves a retailer pricing certain items lower than normal to increase customers' traffic flow or boost sales of complementary products. Some retailers call these products *loss leaders*. In a strict sense, loss leaders are sold below cost. But a product doesn't have to be sold below cost for the retailer to use a leader-pricing strategy.

The best items for leader pricing are frequently purchased products like white bread, milk, and eggs or well-known brand names like Coca-Cola and Pepsi Cola. Customers take note of ads for these products because they're purchased weekly. The retailer hopes consumers will also purchase their entire weekly grocery list while buying the loss leaders. Toys "R" Us has successfully used a leader-pricing strategy for disposable diapers. New parents get in the habit of shopping at Toys "R" Us when their children are infants and become loyal customers throughout their parenting period.

One problem with leader pricing is that is might attract shoppers, referred to as **cherry pickers,** who go from one store to another, buying only items that are on special. These shoppers are clearly unprofitable for retailers.[27]

15.4   **RETAILING VIEW**   How Much Did Your Ticket Cost?

Every night in New York, about 25,000 people, on average, attend Broadway shows. Ticket prices for Broadway shows have risen 31 percent since 1998, but theatergoers know that there are deals available through coupons, two-for-one deals, special prices for students, and the TKTS booth in Times Square.

A study of the tickets sold for plays found that customers paid 17 different prices. Some price variation was due to the quality of the seats—orchestra, mezzanine, balcony and so on—but most price differences were the result of

To maximize profits, Broadway theaters offer tickets unsold by the day of the performance at a discount from the TKTS kiosk in Times Square in New York.

various forms of discounting. The average difference of two randomly selected tickets chosen on a given night was about 40 percent of the average price paid.

Theaters use a variety of strategies to try to ensure that the seats are sold and sold at prices equivalent to what customers are willing to pay. Targeted direct mail coupons are often used when the play opens, while two-for-one tickets are introduced about halfway through the run.

The tickets sold at the TKTS booth in Times Square are typically the lower-quality orchestra seats. They sell at a fixed discount of 50 percent but are offered only for performances that day. Donald Trump doesn't wait in line at TKTS because people in his income bracket don't mind paying full price. But a lot of students, unemployed actors, and tourists in lower-income brackets use TKTS. The inconvenience of waiting in line at TKTS eliminates any price-insensitive customers willing to pay full price.

Sources: Hal Varian, "The Dynamics of Pricing Tickets for Broadway Shows," *New York Times,* January 13, 2005, p. B1; Ramin Setoodeh, "Neon Lights for Less," *Newsweek,* October 18, 2004, p. 78.

Price Lining

Retailers frequently offer a limited number of predetermined price points within a merchandise category. For instance, a tire store may offer tires at $69.99, $89.99, and $129.99 that reflect good, better, and best quality. This practice is referred to as **price lining.** Both customers and retailers can benefit from such a strategy for several reasons:

- Confusion that often arises from multiple price choices is essentially eliminated. The customer can choose the tire with the low, medium, or high price.
- From the retailer's perspective, the merchandising task is simplified. That is, all products within a certain price line are merchandised together. Furthermore, when going to market, the firm's buyers can select their purchases with the predetermined price lines in mind.
- Price lining can also give buyers greater flexibility. If a strict formula is used to establish the initial retail price (initial markup), there could be numerous price points. But with a price-lining strategy, some merchandise may be bought a little below or above the expected cost for a price line. Of course, price lining can also limit retail buyers' flexibility. They may be forced to pass up potentially profitable merchandise because it doesn't fit into a price line.
- Although many manufacturers and retailers are simplifying their product offerings to save distribution and inventory costs and make the choice simpler for consumers, price lining can be used to get customers to "trade up" to a more expensive model. Research indicates a tendency for people to choose the product in the middle of a price line. So, for example, if a camera store starts carrying a "super deluxe" model, customers will be more likely to purchase the model that was previously the most expensive. Retailers must decide whether it's more profitable to sell more expensive merchandise or save money by paring down their stock selection.[28]

Odd Pricing

Odd pricing refers to the practice of using a price that ends in an odd number, typically a 9. Odd pricing has a long history in retailing. In the nineteenth and early twentieth centuries, odd pricing was used to reduce losses due to employee theft. Because merchandise had an odd price, salespeople typically had to go to the cash register to give the customer change and record the sale, making it more difficult for salespeople to keep the customer's money. Odd pricing was also used to keep track of how many times an item had been marked down. After an initial price of $20, the first markdown would be $17.99, the second markdown $15.98, and so on.

The results of empirical studies in this area are mixed;[29] however, many retailers believe that odd pricing can increase profits. For example, the computerized pricing system at CVS Stores begins by applying the necessary markup to an item's cost. After that is completed, the program takes the pennies digit of the resulting price and raises it to the nearest 5 or 9. Wal-Mart takes a different approach to this fine tuning. The exact prices are determined by marking costs up by a fixed percent, thus producing a variety of price endings.[30]

Many retailers set prices to end in 9s because they believe customers will perceive the prices as lower than they actually are.

The theory behind odd pricing is an assumption that shoppers don't notice the last digit or digits of a price, so that a price of $2.99 is perceived as $2. An alternative theory is that 9 endings signal low prices. Thus, for products that are believed to be sensitive to price, many retailers will round the price down to the nearest nine to create a positive price image.

If, for example, the price would normally be $3.09, many retailers will lower the price to $2.99.

Research results suggest the following guidelines for making price-ending decisions:

- When the price sensitivity of the market is high, it is likely to be advantageous to raise or lower prices so that they end in high numbers such as 9.
- When the price sensitivity of the market is not especially high, the risks to the retailer's image of using 9 endings are likely to outweigh the benefits. In such cases, the use of even dollar prices and round number endings would be more appropriate.
- Many upscale retailers appeal to price-sensitive segments of the market through periodic discounting, which suggests the value of a combination strategy: Only break from a standard policy of round number endings to use 9 endings when communicating discounts and special offers.[31]

THE INTERNET AND PRICE COMPETITION

Retailers are concerned that the growth of electronic retailing will intensify price competition. Traditionally, price competition between store-based retailers offering the same merchandise was reduced by geography because consumers typically shop at the stores and malls closest to where they live and work. However, using the Internet, consumers can search for merchandise across the globe at a low cost. The number of stores that a consumer can visit to compare prices is no longer limited by physical distance.[32]

Using shopping bots like Bottomdollar.com, consumers can easily collect and compare prices for branded merchandise sold through an electronic retail channel.

Searching for the lowest prices is facilitated by shopping bots. **Shopping bots** or **search engines** are computer programs that search for and provide a

---

iPod mini 4GB 2nd Gen. MP3 Player - Blue (Apple-M9802LLA) - Bottomdollar.com - Shopping Compari - Microsoft Internet Explorer

File Edit View Favorites Tools Help

Address http://www1.bottomdollar.com/p_Apple_iPod_mini_4GB_2nd_Gen_MP3_Player_Blue,_6987615/search=MP3

COMPUTERS | PHOTOGRAHY | ELECTRONICS | HOME & GARDEN | MOVIES | VIDEO GAMES | JEWELRY & WATCHES | APPAREL | MORE

bottomdollar.com   September 22, 2005
                                                                    HOME

Search Electronics ▾ for MP3   Go

Home > Electronics > Portable Audio > MP3 Players   Add to Shopping List |

Apple iPod mini 4GB 2nd Gen. MP3 Player - Blue
(4GB Internal Hard Drive - SKU: M9802LLA)
Price Range: **$182.99 - $199.88** from 11 Sellers
Rebates & Special Offers: $100 Offer available

Description: Weighing in at just 3.6 ounces and smaller than many cell phones, iPod mini fits your lifestyle and your bag, whether it be cocktail purse or messenger duffle. The chic, matte anodized aluminum case resists stains and scratches, all the whi.... Read More

| Compare Prices | Product Details | User Reviews |

New (11 Sellers from $182.99)

Seller	Price	Tax & Shipping	Availability	Seller Rating
SHOP ⊕ **ebuyer** Featured Merchant MEMBER PROTECTED Merchant Info	$187.00	**Enter Zip Code** To View Shipping & Tax	In Stock	★★★★☆ 1440 Reviews
SHOP ⊕ **MacMall** Featured Merchant MEMBER PROTECTED Merchant Info	$194.00	Price + Shipping + Tax	In Stock	★★★★☆ 168 Reviews
SHOP ⊕ **dataVis.com** Featured Merchant MEMBER PROTECTED Merchant Info	$185.00 $100.00 Rebate	= BottomLinePrice	In Stock	★★★☆☆ 491 Reviews
SHOP ⊕ **PC Connection** Featured Merchant MEMBER PROTECTED Merchant Info	$199.88	[ ] Go (Enter Zip Code)	In Stock	★★★★★ 414 Reviews
SHOP ⊕ **TriState** MEMBER PROTECTED Merchant Info	$182.99		In Stock	★★★☆☆ 173 Reviews

Done   Internet

list of all Internet sites selling a product category or price of specific brands offered. To limit price comparisons, electronic retailers initially made it hard for customers to go from one Internet site to another. The electronic retailers used different interfaces so customers needed to learn how to search through the offerings at each new site they visited. In addition, some Internet retailers electronically prevented shopping bots from accessing their sites, collecting information about the products sold at the site, or using these collected data to compare the prices offered at different electronic retailing sites.[33] While these strategies made it more difficult to compare prices, they also made it more difficult to attract customers to Web sites. Although consumers shopping electronically can collect price information with little effort, they can get a lot of other information about the quality and performance of products at a low cost.

For instance, an electronic channel offering custom-made Oriental rugs can clearly show real differences in the patterns and materials used for construction. Electronic grocery services offered by Safeway (www.shop.safeway.com) and Albertson's (www.albertsons/shop) allow customers to sort cereals by nutritional content, thus making it easier to use that attribute in their decision making. The additional information about product quality might lead customers to pay more for high-quality products, thus decreasing the importance of price.[34]

Retailers using an electronic channel can reduce the emphasis on price by providing better services and information. Because of these services, customers might be willing to pay higher prices for the merchandise. For example, Amazon.com provides a customer with the table of contents and synopsis of a book, as well as reviews and comments by the author, or authors, and people who have read the book. When the customer finds an interesting book, Amazon's system is programmed to suggest other books by the same author or of the same genre. Finally, customers can tell Amazon about their favorite authors and subjects and then receive e-mails about new books that might be of interest. The classic response to the question, What are the three most important things in retailing? used to be "location, location, location." In the world of electronic retailing, the answer will be "information, information, information."[35]

SUMMARY

Setting prices is a critical decision in implementing a retail strategy because price is a critical component in customers' perceived value. In setting prices, retailers consider the price sensitivity of customers in their target market, the cost of the merchandise and services offered, competitive prices, and legal restrictions. Theoretically, retailers maximize their profits by setting prices on the basis of the price sensitivity of customers and the cost of merchandise. However, this approach does not consider the prices being charged by competitors. Another problem with attempting to set prices on the basis of customer price sensitivity is the implementation challenges associated with the large number of pricing decisions a retailer makes. Thus, retailers typically set prices by marking up the item's cost to yield a profitable maintained margin. Then these cost-based initial prices might be adjusted according to the retail buyer's insights about customer price sensitivity and competitive pricing.

Initial prices are adjusted over time (markdowns) and for different market segments (variable pricing). Retailers take markdowns to either dispose of merchandise or generate sales. Markdowns are part of the cost of doing business, and thus, buyers plan for them.

Retailers use a variety of techniques to maximize profits by charging different prices to different customers. These techniques include setting different prices for individual customers, providing an offering that enables customers to self-select the price they are willing to pay, and setting different prices according to customer demographics.

Retailers use two basic retail pricing strategies: everyday low pricing (EDLP) and high/low pricing. Each of these strategies has its advantages and disadvantages. The high/low strategy increases profits through price discrimination, creates excitement, and provides an opportunity to sell slow-moving merchandise. The EDLP approach assures customers of low prices, reduces advertising and operating expenses, reduces stockouts, and improves supply chain management.

Additional challenges arise when pricing services, due to the need to match supply and demand and the difficulties customers have in determining service quality. Retailers use yield management techniques to match supply and demand for services.

Finally, retailers use a variety of pricing techniques to stimulate sales, including price lining, leader pricing, and odd pricing.

KEY TERMS

bait-and-switch, *407*

break-even analysis, *410*

break-even point quantity, *411*

cherry picker, *420*

coupons, *416*

everyday low pricing (EDLP), *417*

first-degree price discrimination, *414*

fixed cost, *411*

high/low pricing, *417*

horizontal price fixing, *407*

initial markup, *409*

keystoning, *408*

leader pricing, *420*

low-price guarantee policy, *418*

maintained markup, *409*

markdowns, *411*

markup, *408*

markup percentage, *408*

merchandising optimization software, *412*

multiple-unit pricing, *416*

odd pricing, *421*

predatory pricing, *406*

price bundling, *416*

price discrimination, *406*

price elasticity, *403*

price lining, *421*

quantity discount, *416*

rain check, *418*

reductions, *409*

search engine, *422*

second-degree price discrimination, *416*

shopping bot, *422*

third-degree price discrimination, *417*

value, *401*

variable cost, *411*

yield management, *419*

zone pricing, *417*

GET OUT AND DO IT!

1. **CONTINUING ASSIGNEMNT** Go shopping at the retailer you have selected for the continuing assignment. Does the retailer use a high/low pricing or EDLP strategy? Ask the store manager how markdown decisions are made and how the store decides how much a markdown should be. What rule-based approaches does it use to make markdowns? Does the retailer use the techniques for stimulating sales such as price lining, leader pricing, and odd pricing? Are the prices on its Web site the same as in the store?

2. **INTERNET EXERCISE AND GO SHOPPING** Go to the Web sites for Bloomingdale's (www.bloomingdales.com), Dillard's (www.dillards.com), and a local department store. Which department store chains are using an EDLP strategy and which are using a high/low strategy? How can you tell?

3. **INTERNET EXERCISE** Price bundling is very common in the travel and vacation industry. Go to the Web site for Sandals (www.sandals.com) and see what you can get at an all-for-one, all-inclusive price.

4. **GO SHOPPING** Go to a supermarket that uses shelf pricing labels instead of labels on each item. Note each shelf label price. Buy 20 items. How many items were priced correctly? How many were under- and overpriced?

5. **GO SHOPPING** Go to three different types of stores and try to bargain your way down from the tagged price. Explain your experience. Was there any difference in your success rate as a result of the type of store or merchandise? Did you have better luck when you spoke to a manager?

6. **GO SHOPPING** Go to your favorite food store and your local Wal-Mart to find the prices for the market basket of goods at the bottom of the page. What was the total cost of the market basket at each store? How did the prices compare? Did Wal-Mart live up to its slogan of "Always lower prices"?

7. **WEB OLC EXERCISE** Go to the student side of the online learning center. Click on pricing and then on markdown model. Oracle Retail has provided you the opportunity to play buyer and test your analytical abilities for taking markdowns. You will be given the opportunity to make markdown decisions for several products over several weeks. You can either play this simulation game on your own or against your classmates.

Item	Size	Brand	Supermarket	Wal-Mart
Grocery			Price	Price
Ground coffee	11.5 oz can	Folgers		
Corn Flakes	18 oz box	Kellogg's		
Pet Supplies				
Puppy Chow	4.4 lb bag	Purina		
Cleaning				
Liquid laundry detergent	100 oz bottle	Gain		
Dryer sheets	80 count	Bounce		
Liquid dish detergent	25 oz bottle	Joy		
Health & Beauty				
Shampoo	12 oz bottle	Dove		
Toothpaste	4.2 oz tube	Colgate Total		

DISCUSSION QUESTIONS AND PROBLEMS

1. How does merchandising optimization software help buyers make better markdown decisions?

2. A simple examination of markdowns could lead us to believe that they should be taken only when a retailer wants to get rid of merchandise that's not selling. What other reasons could a retailer have to take markdowns?

3. Do you know any retailers that have violated any of the legal issues discussed in the this chapter? Explain your answer.

4. What is the difference in the pricing strategies of ebay.com, priceline.com, and staples.com? Which firm do you think will have the strongest position in the market in 10 years? Why?

Note: **For questions 5–9, you may use the student side of the online learning center. Click on pricing.**

5. A department's maintained markup is 38 percent, reductions are $560, and net sales are $28,000. What's the initial markup percentage?

6. Maintained markup is 39 percent, net sales are $52,000, and reductions are $2,500. What are the gross margin in dollars and the initial markup as a percentage? Explain why initial markup is greater than maintained markup.

7. The cost of a product is $150, markup is 50 percent, and markdown is 30 percent. What's the final selling price?

8. Manny Perez bought a tie for $9 and priced it to sell for $15. What was his markup on the tie?

9. Answer the following questions: *(a)* The Limited is planning a new line of leather jean jackets for fall. It plans to retail the jackets for $100. It is having the jackets produced in the Dominican Republic. Although The Limited does not own the factory, its product development and design costs are $400,000. The total cost of the jacket, including transportation to the stores, is $45. For this line to be successful, The Limited needs to make $900,000 profit. What is its break-even point in units and dollars? *(b)* The buyer has just found out that The Gap, one of The Limited's major competitors, is bringing out a similar jacket that will retail for $90. If The Limited wishes to match The Gap's price, how many units will it have to sell?

SUGGESTED READINGS

Darke, Peter, and Cindy Chung. "Effects of Pricing and Promotion on Consumer Perceptions: It Depends on How You Frame It," *Journal of Retailing* 81, no. 1 (2005) pp. 35–52.

Homburg, Christian; Wayne Hoyer; and Nicole Koschate. "Customers' Reactions to Price Increases: Do Customer Satisfaction and Perceived Motive Fairness Matter?" *Academy of Marketing Science* 33 (Winter 2005), pp. 36–50.

Levy, Michael; Dhruv Grewal; Praveen Kopalle; and James Hess. "Emerging Trends in Retail Pricing Practice: Implications for Research," *Journal of Retailing* 80, no. 3 (2004), p. xiii–xxi.

Monroe, Kent. *Pricing: Making Profitable Decisions.* 3rd ed. New York: McGraw-Hill, 2002.

Nagle, Thomas, and Reed Holden. *The Strategy and Tactics of Pricing: A Guide to Profitable Decisions.* Upper Saddle River, NJ: Prentice Hall, 2002.

Shankar, Venkatesh, and Ruth Bolton. "An Empirical Analysis of Determinants of Retailer Pricing Strategy," *Marketing Science* 23 (Winter 2004), pp. 28–50.

Shugan, Steven M., and Ramarao Desiraju. "Retail Product-Line Pricing Strategy When Costs and Products Change," *Journal of Retailing* 77 (Spring 2001), pp. 17–38.

Srivastava, Joydeep, and Nicholas Lurie. "Price-Matching Guarantees as Signals of Low Store Prices: Survey and Experimental Evidence," *Journal of Retailing* 80 (2004), p. 117.

Tsay, Andy A. "Managing Retail Channel Overstock: Markdown Money and Return Policies," *Journal of Retailing* 77 (Winter 2001), pp. 457–92.

Voss, Glenn, and Kathleen Seiders. "Exploring the Effect of Retail Sector and Firm Characteristics on Retail Price Promotion Strategy," *Journal of Retailing* 79 (2003), p. 37.

Xia, Lan; Kent Monroe; and Jennifer Cox. "The Price Is Unfair! A Conceptual Framework of Price Fairness Perceptions." *Journal of Marketing* 68 (October 2004), pp. 1–19.

Retail Communication Mix

EXECUTIVE BRIEFING
Lary Sinewitz, Executive Vice President,
BrandsMart USA

BrandsMart is the No. 1 discount retailer in South Florida of consumer appliances, electronics, and housewares, and we anticipate dominating the Atlanta market which we recently entered. Our mission is to deliver the best name-brand products to our customers at the lowest possible prices. We communicate this mission through the broad assortment of national brand products in our stores and our advertising.

Each of our stores contains thousands of products including televisions, all types of major appliances, audio, video, home theater, projection televisions, car stereo, small appliances, computers, cellular telephones, satellites, entertainment furniture, and thousands of accessories for your every need. For example, in our stores, you can find more than 100 large screen televisions, 80 camcorders, 200 refrigerators, 85 washers and dryers, 300 televisions, and 150 DVDs. This means our customers can take most products with them or choose to let our professional delivery and installation department deliver it to their homes.

Due to our scale, with over $125 million in sales for each location, we can offer this broad assortment at the lowest prices in our markets and we emphasize these low prices and broad assortments within our advertising. Each year we spend over $30 million on advertising. While we do some radio and TV advertising, most of our advertising is done through free standing inserts (FSIs) in newspapers. For example, we have 28 pages of advertising each week in the *Miami Herald* and another 28 pages in *El Nuevo Herald,* the newspaper targeting the Latino market. Advertising plays an important role in our business model. It attracts customers to our stores, which increases sales, creates greater scale economies, and allows us to lower costs and prices.

Each of our inserts features over 500 national products with our low prices prominently displayed. We use the same FSI advertising design format so that our customers can recognize a BrandsMart insert. For example, the first page of the FSI typically has over 50 different products featured from a GPX clock radio at $4.58 to a Sony 50-inch, LCD HDTV at $1698.88.

CHAPTER 16

QUESTIONS

How can retailers build brand equity for their stores and their private-label merchandise?

What are the strengths and weaknesses of the different methods for communicating with customers?

Why do retailers need to have an integrated marketing communication program?

What steps are involved in developing a communication program?

How do retailers establish a communication budget?

How can retailers use the different elements in a communication mix to alter customers' decision-making processes?

The weekly ads are also featured on our Web site, www.brandsmart.com. On the Web site, we provide product information and list all additional savings available through mail-in rebates from our suppliers.

We leverage our advertising budget with contributions from our vendors through their co-op advertising programs. However, some vendors require us to advertise their products at manufacturer-suggested retail prices even though we might be selling them at a lower price in our stores, so we tell our customers in our advertising and on our Web site that they may find even lower prices when they visit our stores.

The preceding chapters in this section on merchandise management described how retailers develop an assortment and merchandise budget plan and then buy and price merchandise. The next step in the retail management decision-making process is developing and implementing a communication program to build appealing brand images, attract customers to stores and Internet sites, and encourage those customers to buy merchandise. The communication program informs customers about the retailer as well as the merchandise and services it offers and plays a role in developing repeat visits and customer loyalty.

Communication programs can have both long- and short-term effects on a retailer's business. From a long-term perspective, communications programs can be used to create and maintain a strong, differentiated image of the retailer and its private-label brands. This image develops customer loyalty and creates a strategic advantage. Thus, brand image–building communication programs complement the objectives of a retailer's CRM program, as discussed in Chapter 11.

In addition, retailers frequently use communication programs to realize the short-term objective of increasing sales during a specified time period. For example, retailers often have sales during which some or all merchandise is priced at a discount for a short time. Supermarkets usually place weekly ads with coupons that can be used to save money on purchases made during the week.

The first part of this chapter examines the role of communication programs in building brand images. The second part of the chapter focuses on developing and implementing communication programs. The appendix includes more detailed material related to the implementation of advertising programs, including developing the ad message and selecting media for distributing the message.

Retail advertising can be used to achieve long-term objectives, such as building a brand image or short-term sales. The T.J. Maxx ad (left) supports a long-term objective by reinforcing the retailer's fashionable image, whereas the Payless ShoeSource ad (right) generates short-term sales through a special promotion.

USING COMMUNICATION PROGRAMS TO DEVELOP BRAND IMAGES AND BUILD CUSTOMER LOYALTY

A **brand** is a distinguishing name or symbol, such as a logo, that identifies the products or services offered by a seller and differentiates those products and services from the offerings of competitors.[1] In a retailing context, the name of the retailer is a brand that indicates to consumers the type of merchandise and services offered by that retailer. As we discussed in Chapter 14, some retailers develop private-label brands that are exclusively sold through their channels. In some cases, this private-label merchandise bears the retailer's name, such as Walgreens aspirin and Victoria's Secret lingerie. In other cases, special brand names are used, such as Federated Department Stores' INC apparel and JCPenney's Arizona jeans.

Value of Brand Image

Brands provide value to both customers and retailers. Brands convey information to consumers about the nature of the shopping experience—the retailer's mix—they will encounter when patronizing a retailer. They also affect the customers' confidence in their decisions to buy merchandise from a retailer. Finally, brands can enhance the customers' satisfaction with the merchandise and services they buy. Consumers feel different when wearing jewelry bought from Tiffany rather than from Zales or by staying at a Ritz-Carlton hotel rather than a Fairfield Inn.

The value that a brand image offers retailers is referred to as **brand equity.** Strong brand names can affect the customer's decision-making process, motivate repeat visits and purchases, and build loyalty. In addition, strong brand names enable retailers to charge higher prices and lower their marketing costs.

Customer loyalty to brands arises from heightened awareness of the brand and the emotional ties to it. For example, Chapter 4 discussed the need for retailers to be in a customer's consideration set. Some brands such as Wal-Mart and Sears are so well known by consumers that they typically appear in a consumer's consideration set. In addition, customers identify and have strong emotional relationships with some brands. For example, Target has an image of offering fashionable merchandise at bargain prices. As one retail consultant says, "Going to Target is a cool experience, and everybody now considers it cool to save money. On the other hand, is it cool to save at Kmart, at Wal-Mart? I don't think so. You walk into

Wal-Mart, and there are these big boxes of corn flakes. How ugly! How totally uncool!" Customers affectionately use the faux French pronunciation of "Tar-zhay" when referring to Target.[3] High brand awareness and strong emotional connections reduce the incentive of customers to switch to competing retailers.

A strong brand image also enables retailers to increase their margins. When retailers have high customer loyalty, they can engage in premium pricing and reduce their reliance on price promotions to attract customers. Brands with weaker images are forced to offer low prices and frequent sales to maintain their market share.

Finally, retailers with strong brand names can leverage their brands to introduce new retail concepts with only a limited amount of marketing effort. For example, The Gap has efficiently extended its brand to GapKids, GapBody, and babyGap, and Toys "R" Us extended its brand name to Kids "R" Us and Babies "R" Us.

As we discussed in Chapter 5, a strong brand name creates a strategic advantage that is very difficult for competitors to duplicate. Just think how hard it would be for Kmart to change its image to that of Wal-Mart or Target, the more successful discount store chains.

Building Brand Equity

The activities that a retailer needs to undertake to build the brand equity for its firm or its private-label merchandise are (1) create a high level of brand awareness, (2) develop favorable associations with the brand name, and (3) consistently reinforce the image of the brand.

Brand Awareness   **Brand awareness** is the ability of a potential customer to recognize or recall that the brand name is a type of retailer or product/service. Thus, brand awareness is the strength of the link between the brand name and the type of merchandise or service in the minds of customers.

There is a range of awareness, from aided recall to top-of-mind awareness. **Aided recall** is when consumers indicate they know the brand when the name is presented to them. **Top-of-mind awareness,** the highest level of awareness, occurs when consumers mention a specific brand name first when they are asked about the type of retailer, a merchandise category, or a type of service. For example, Best Buy has top-of-mind awareness if a consumer responds "Best Buy" when asked about retailers that sell consumer electronics. High top-of-mind awareness means that a retailer typically will be in the consideration set when customers decide to shop for a type of product or service.

Retailers build top-of-mind awareness by having memorable names; repeatedly exposing their name to customers through advertising, locations, and sponsorships; and using memorable symbols. Some brand names are easy to remember, such as the name Home Depot. Because "Home" is in its brand name, it probably is more memorable and closely associated with home improvements than the name Lowe's.[4]

By using these symbols, KFC and Taco Bell build awareness for their offerings and make it easier for consumers to recall their names and brand images.

Starbucks does very little advertising but has high awareness because of the large number of stores it has. Customers walk and drive by the stores on their way to and from work. The sheer number of stores provides substantial exposure to its brand.

Symbols involve visual images that typically are more easily recalled than words or phrases and thus are useful for building brand awareness. For example, the image of Colonel Sanders and the golden arches enhances the ability of customers to recall the names KFC and McDonald's.

Sponsorships of well-publicized events also can provide considerable exposure to a retailer's name and increase awareness. For example, watching the Macy's Thanksgiving Parade in New York City has become a holiday tradition. The Macy's brand name is now exposed to tens of millions of television viewers for several hours. In addition, newspaper articles are devoted to previewing the parade and describing it afterward.

REFACT

The first Macy's Thanksgiving Day Parade, held in 1924, was organized by a handful of volunteer, immigrant employees.[5]

Associations Building awareness is the first step in developing brand equity, but the value of the brand is largely based on the associations that customers make with the brand name. **Brand associations** are anything linked to or connected with the brand name in a consumer's memory. For example, some of the associations that consumers might have with McDonald's are golden arches, fast food, clean stores, hamburgers, French fries, Big Macs, and Ronald McDonald. In the case of McDonald's, these links are so strong that when a consumer thinks of fast food, hamburgers, or French fries, they also tend to think of McDonald's. These strong associations influence consumer buying behavior. For example, when consumers think about having their car serviced, Jiffy Lube might immediately come to mind, stimulating a visit to a Jiffy Lube service center.

Some common associations that retailers develop with their brand name are as follows:

1. *Merchandise category* The most common association is to link the retailer to a category of merchandise. For example, Office Depot would like to have consumers associate its name with office supplies. Then when a need for office supplies arises, consumers immediately think of Office Depot.

2. *Price/quality* Some retailers, such as Neiman Marcus, want to be associated with offering high prices and unique, high-fashion merchandise. Other retailers, such as Wal-Mart, want associations with low prices and good value.

16.1   **RETAILING VIEW**   L.L. Bean Celebrating the Outdoors

Leon Leonard Bean, an outdoorsman living in Freeport, Maine, founded L.L. Bean in 1912. The first product he sold through the mail was boots (The Maine Hunting Shoe) with waterproof rubber bottoms and lightweight leather tops. The boots provided significant benefits over heavyweight, all-leather boots in wet weather. However, the first pairs he sold had a stitching problem. Bean decided to refund each customer's money, which led to L.L. Bean's legendary "Guarantee of 100% Satisfaction." Some of the associations that L.L. Bean reinforces through its advertising and Web site, as well as other elements in its retail mix, are

- *Friendly*—L.L. Bean is comfortable and familiar, easy to approach.

- *Honest*—L.L. Bean is straightforward and honest. It would never mislead its customers. It provides factual information about its products.

- *Expertise*—L.L. Bean's employees are experts about their products and the outdoors. They'll do anything they can to help customers choose which product is best for them or

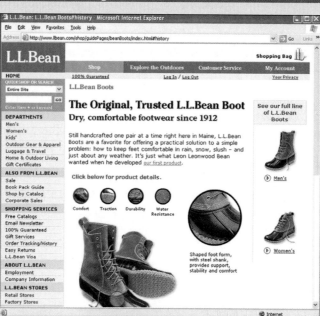

L.L. Bean uses its Web site to reinforce its image of offering expertise in practical, economical outdoor merchandise.

even help them find the best place to camp.

- *Practical and economical*—Building on its Yankee New England roots, L.L. Bean offers products that are functional, with nononsense features at fair prices. As Bean said, "I attribute our success to the fact that, to the best of my judgment, every article we offer for sale is practical for the purpose for which we recommend it."

These associations that L.L. Bean promotes might also result in the development of a less favorable set of impressions. For example, the association with its New England heritage may associate L.L. Bean, in some customers' minds, with old-fashioned and out-of-date merchandise and an antiquated way of doing business. The brand might also be viewed as very male oriented and not appealing to women or families.

Sources: Edward Murphy, "Portland, Maine–Based L.L. Bean Ranks High in Customer Loyalty," *Knight Ridder Tribune Business News*, April 8, 2005, p. 1; David Aaker and Erich Joachimsthaler, *Brand Leadership* (New York: Free Press, 2000), pp. 68–71; www.llbean.com.

3. *Specific attribute or benefit* A retailer can link its stores to attributes such as convenience (7-Eleven) or service (Nordstrom).

4. *Lifestyle or activity* Some retailers associate their name with a specific lifestyle or activity. For example, The Nature Company, a retailer offering books and equipment to study nature, is linked to a lifestyle of interacting with the environment. Electronic Boutique is associated with the home use of computer game software.

In turn, the **brand image** is a set of associations that are usually organized around some meaningful themes. Thus, the associations that a consumer might have about McDonald's might be organized into groups such as kids, service, and type of food. Retailing View 16.1 illustrates how L.L. Bean nurtures its brand image of selling high-quality, functional products and providing helpful service for outdoor living.

Consistent Reinforcement The retailer's brand image is developed and maintained through the retailer's communication program and other elements of the communication mix, such as its merchandise assortment and pricing, the design of its stores and Web site, and the customer service it offers. To develop a strong set of associations and a clearly defined brand image, retailers need to be consistent in portraying the same message to customers over time and across all of the elements of their retail mix.

Rather than creating unique communication programs for sales associates, retailers need to develop an **integrated marketing communication program**— a program that integrates all of the communication elements to deliver a comprehensive, consistent message. Without this coordination, the communication methods might work at cross-purposes. For example, the retailer's TV advertising campaign might attempt to build an image of exceptional customer service, but the firm's sales promotions might all emphasize low prices. If communication methods aren't used consistently, customers may become confused about the retailer's image and therefore not patronize the store.

For example, Abercrombie & Fitch (A&F) uses an integrated marketing communication program to reinforce its brand image, which is associated with fun-loving, independent, uninhibited teenagers and young adults. To stay on top of its target market's tastes and find ideas for new merchandise, A&F sends employees to college campuses each month to chat with students about what they play, wear, listen to, and read.

The stores have comfortable armchairs, designed to be gathering places for its customers. They are staffed by high-energy "brand reps" recruited from local campuses who dress in A&F clothes. Selling skills are not required. The brand reps just need to fit the company's brand image, wear its apparel, and have fun inside the store.

In addition, A&F's main promotional tool has been its controversial "magalog," a quarterly magazine/catalog crammed with product information, sexual imagery, and provocative articles. (A **magalog** is a combination of a magazine and catalog.) Large blowups of enticing photographs from the magalog appear in store displays.[6]

Abercrombie & Fitch uses its Web site as part of an integrated marketing communication program to reinforce its image, which is associated with attractive and stylish teenagers and young adults.

Providing a consistent image can be challenging for multichannel retailers. American Eagle Outfitter wants its home page at www.AE.com to have the same look and feel as the front windows of its stores. However, each channel has its own needs for image displays. Images used in its stores stress lifestyle connotations, but its online images need to provide more product images. Stores can rely on lifestyle images without highlighting product details because in-store shoppers can see and feel the actual products on display. In addition, images for in-store displays and ads often are difficult to fit within a 17-inch computer screen to effectively promote products online. To address these issues, American Eagle Outfitters considers the needs of all its channels early in the planning of its communication program.[7]

Extending the Brand Name

Retailers can leverage their brand names to support the growth strategies discussed in Chapter 5. For example, IKEA used its strong brand image to enter the U.S. home furnishing retail market successfully; Talbots introduced a Talbots Woman collection for women who wear sizes 12 to 18; and the Pottery Barn launched its Pottery Barn Kids catalog to target children. In other cases, retailers have pursued growth opportunities using a new and unrelated brand name. For example, The Gap used the brand name Old Navy for its off-the-mall value concept, and Sears named its new home store concept The Great Indoors.

There are pluses and minuses to extending a brand name to a new concept. An important benefit of extending the brand name is that minimal communication expenses are needed to create awareness and a brand image for the new concept. Customers will quickly transfer their awareness and associations about the original brand to the new concept. However, in some cases, the retailer might not want to have the original brand's associations connected with the new concept. For example, The Limited decided to invest in building a new and different brand image for Victoria's Secret rather than branding the new concept with a name like Limited Secret.

These issues also arise as a retailer expands internationally. Associations with the retailer's brands that are valued in one country may not be valued in another. For example, French consumers prefer to shop at supermarkets that offer good service and high-quality grocery products, whereas German shoppers prefer supermarkets that offer low prices and good value. Thus, a French supermarket retailer with a brand image of quality and service might not be able to leverage its image if it decides to enter the German market.[8]

Retailers communicate with customers through five vehicles: advertising, sales promotion, publicity, store atmosphere and visual merchandising, and personal selling. This chapter focuses on the first three of those vehicles in the communication mix. In large retail firms, these three communication mix elements are managed by the firm's marketing or advertising department and the buying organization. The other elements, store atmosphere and salespeople, are managed by store personnel and thus discussed in Section IV. The following sections of this chapter examine the methods that retailers use to communicate with their customers and how they plan and implement communication programs to build brand equity as well as short-term sales.

METHODS OF COMMUNICATING WITH CUSTOMERS

Exhibit 16–1 classifies the communication methods used by retailers. The classification is based on whether the methods are impersonal or personal and paid or unpaid.

Paid Impersonal Communications

Advertising, sales promotions, store atmosphere, and Web sites are examples of paid impersonal communications.

Advertising   **Advertising** is a form of paid communication to customers using impersonal mass media such as newspapers, TV, radio, direct mail, and the Internet.

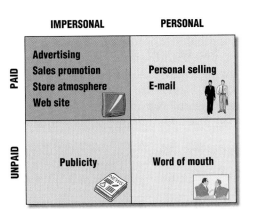

EXHIBIT 16–1
Communication Methods

Sales Promotions   **Sales promotions** offer extra value and incentives to customers to visit a store or purchase merchandise during a specific period of time. For example, Winkler's Diamonds, in Kansas City, Kansas, has a "repair promotion" twice a year. It sends out mailers to its customers offering free jewelry checkups and special discounts on repairs. "Once people are in the store, we show them things they haven't seen before or that complement something they have," says a spokesperson. "Many come in for a repair and walk out with a diamond bracelet."[10] The most common promotion is a sale. Other sales promotions involve special events, in-store demonstrations, coupons, and contests.

Some retailers use in-store demonstrations and offer free samples of merchandise to build excitement in the store and stimulate purchases. In department stores, fashion shows and cooking demonstrations draw customers to the store and encourage impulse purchases. Retailing View 16.2 describes a special promotion Wal-Mart offers in Germany to attract single shoppers.

Contests are promotional games of chance. They differ from price-off sales in that (1) only a few customers receive rewards and (2) winners are determined by luck. For example, fast-food restaurants frequently have contests associated with major films (such as *Star Wars*) or sports events (such as the Super Bowl).

REFACT

The Christmas story about Rudolph the Red-Nosed Reindeer was developed by a Montgomery Ward copywriter in 1939 for a store promotion.[11]

Attracting the Single Shopper   RETAILING VIEW   16.2

A photo on the singles' board, a glass of sparkling wine, and freshly shucked oysters coupled with the lowest priced milk in town? Now that's worth a visit to Wal-Mart. In Germany, singles shopping night is an effective promotion, boosting store traffic and sales. The Dortmund store launched its first singles' shopping event in fall 1993 at the suggestion of two workers who thought it might help an unmarried bakery worker at the store who complained about being too old for discos and too proud for Internet dating. Wal-Mart's German headquarters in Wuppertal decided to try singles' night nationally on February 13. It was so successful that now all 91 supercenters in Germany have a singles' night almost every week, and smaller stores have the event about once a month.

Singles' greeters meet customers at the doors with wine, hors d'oeuvres, and a table with romance-themed and singles-oriented merchandise (candles, wine, frozen dinners, DVDs). They take a picture of the single customer and post it on a singles' bulletin board, along with his or her age, interests, and qualities the customer is seeking in a prospective partner.

Carts with small red bows identify single shoppers. Women who arrive in groups are advised to split up, and shoppers fill out a lottery slip; the winner gets a candlelit dinner worth about $130.

Hundreds of couples have found each other at a singles' shopping night. The events have become such hits in Germany, increasing Friday night sales by 25 percent, that Wal-Mart has trademarked the name "Singles Shopping" to prevent competitors from using the term. Employees at the Dortmund store fight to work the Friday evening shifts, says Martina Busse, Wal-Mart district manager.

Sources: Shellee Fitzgerald, "Engaging the Single Shopper," *Canadian Grocer*, May 2005, pp. 59–63; Laura Heller, "Cracking the German Code Not So Easy This Time Around," *DSN Retailing Today*, December 13, 2004, pp. 55–56; Ann Zimmerman and Almut Schoenfeld, "Wal-Marts in Germany Redefine the Term 'Checkout Aisle,'" *The Wall Street Journal*, November 9, 2004, p. B1.

Albertson's holds special promotions in its stores, like Shrimp Fest, that are tied to neighborhood activities. These promotions increase store traffic.

REFACT

The first coupons were handwritten notes given out by Asa Chandler, an Atlanta druggist, offering customers a free glass of his new soft drink, Coca-Cola, in 1895.[12]

REFACT

American manufacturers offer more than $250 billion in coupons annually, with slightly more than 1 percent redeemed. Forty-six percent of U.S. retailers report offering some form of bonus coupon program.[13]

REFACT

Sixty-eight percent of national retailers run e-mail marketing programs, but only one-quarter of the retailers that send e-mails personalize the messages.[15]

Coupons offer a discount on the price of specific items when they're purchased at a store. Coupons are the most common promotional tool used by supermarkets. Retailers distribute them in their newspaper ads and through direct mail programs. For example, Publix, a Florida-based supermarket chain, targets promotions at affluent customers using a direct-mail piece that includes recipes for a gourmet meal with coupons to purchase the products needed to prepare it.

Manufacturers also distribute coupons for their products that can be used at retailers that stock the products. To attract customers, some supermarkets accept coupons distributed by competing retailers. Another technique is for a retailer to offer double or triple the value of coupons distributed by manufacturers.

Although sales promotions are effective at generating short-term interest among customers, they aren't very useful for building long-term loyalty. Customers who participate in the promotion might learn more about a store and return to it, but typically customers attracted by sales promotions are interested in the promoted merchandise, not the retailer. Unfortunately, when a specific promotion is effective for a retailer, competing retailers learn about it quickly and offer the same promotion, which prevents the innovating retailer from gaining any long-term advantage.

Store Atmosphere   The retail store itself provides paid, impersonal communications to its customers. **Store atmosphere** reflects the combination of the store's physical characteristics, such as its architecture, layout, signs and displays, colors, lighting, temperature, sounds, and smells, which together create an image in the customer's mind. The atmosphere communicates information about the store's service, its pricing, and the fashionability of its merchandise.[14] Chapter 18 discusses elements of store atmosphere further.

Web Site   Finally, retailers are increasing their emphasis on communicating with customers through their Web sites. Retailers use their Web sites to build their brand image; inform customers of store locations, special events, and the availability of merchandise in local stores; and sell merchandise and services. For example, in addition to selling merchandise, Office Depot's Web site has a business center with forms and worksheets used by businesses to comply with Occupational Safety and Health Act (OSHA) requirements, check job applicant records, estimate cash flow, and develop a sexual harassment policy; "how-to" tutorials for running a business; and local and national business news. By providing this information on its Web site, Office Depot reinforces its image as the essential source of products, services, and information for small businesses.

Paid Personal Communications

Retail salespeople are the primary vehicles for providing paid personal communications to customers. **Personal selling** is a communication process in which salespeople help customers satisfy their needs through face-to-face exchanges of information.

E-mail is another paid personal communication vehicle that involves sending messages over the Internet. Retailers use e-mail to inform customers of new merchandise, confirm the receipt of an order, and indicate when an order has been shipped. Some retailers send the same message to all of their customers, but they can also send a personalized message to each of their customers using the targeting capabilities of the Internet.

Unpaid Impersonal Communications

The primary method for generating unpaid impersonal communication is publicity. **Publicity** is communication through significant, unpaid presentations about the retailer, usually a news story, in impersonal media. Examples of publicity are newspaper and TV coverage of Home Depot's support of the Olympic Job Opportunities Program, which provides part-time jobs for athletes while they train for the Olympics. Retailing View 16.3 describes how Neiman Marcus creates a newsworthy event by offering unusual gifts in its annual Christmas catalog and builds its image of having unique merchandise.

Most communications are directed toward potential customers. Publicity, however, is often used to communicate with employees and investors. Favorable news stories generated by publicity can build employee morale and help improve employee performance. Much of the communication to employees is done through internal newsletters, magazines, bulletin board notices, handbooks, and inserts into pay envelopes. However, news about the retailer published in newspapers or broadcast over TV and radio can have a greater impact on employees than internally distributed information. Just like customers, employees place more

---

The Ultimate Gifts   RETAILING VIEW   16.3

The Neiman Marcus Christmas catalog is perhaps the nation's best-known retail catalog. Its reputation is largely due to its annual tradition of ultra-extravagant his-and-hers gifts. The Christmas catalog was first distributed in 1915 as a Christmas card inviting Neiman Marcus customers to visit the store during the holiday season. In the late 1950s, customers were asking Neiman Marcus about unique gifts and merchandise not available in the store or from other catalogs.

The first unique gift was a pair of vicuna coats offered in 1951. In 1959, the gift of a black angus steer, delivered on the hoof or in steaks, generated a lot of publicity and elevated the catalog to national prominence. The most expensive gift was a set of his-and-hers diamonds priced at $2 million. Most of these gifts are actually sold. A highly publicized chocolate

Monopoly set was purchased by Christie Hefner, president of Playboy Enterprises, for her father, Hugh Hefner, founder of *Playboy* magazine.

The 2004 Christmas catalog featured a $1.45 million his-and-hers bowling center and a 230-foot zeppelin. While sales of these items were limited, Neiman Marcus did sell 60 of its $125,000, limited-edition, Maserati Quattroporte cars; one set of $16,000 jeweled Mr. and Mrs. Potato Heads; and even a $20,000 custom suit of armor.

Sources: Joyce Smith, "Retailers Predict Gift Givers Will Open Their Wallets Wide," *Knight Ridder Tribune Business News,* November 12, 2004, p. 1; Heather Landy, "Gifts in Neiman Marcus Christmas Book to Appeal to Average, Wealthy Customers," *Knight Ridder Tribune Business News,* September 29, 2004, p. 1.

The extravagant gifts, like the $1.5 million private concert by Sir Elton John, in Neiman Marcus's 2005 Christmas catalog generate considerable free publicity for the retailer.

credibility on information provided by news media than on that generated by the retailer. Similarly, stockholders, the financial community, vendors, and government agencies are influenced by publicity generated by retailers.

Unpaid Personal Communications

Finally, retailers communicate with their customers through **word of mouth,** communication between people about a retailer.[16] For example, retailers attempt to encourage favorable word-of-mouth communication by establishing teen ambassadors composed of high school student leaders. These ambassadors are encouraged to tell their friends about the retailer and its merchandise. However, unfavorable word-of-mouth communication can seriously affect store performance.

Word-of-mouth communications are very effective, but retailers encounter difficulties in harnessing that power in a disciplined, strategic way. Several firms, such as BzzAgent LLC, are now providing a service to help firms generate word of mouth. When a company decides to use the service, BzzAgent searches its database for "agents" who match the demographic and psychographic profile of the client's target market. The "agents" then are offered a chance to sign up for a word-of-mouth campaign.

The volunteers receive a sample product and a training manual for buzz-creating strategies. These may include talking about the retailer to friends or e-mailing influential people on the retailer's behalf. Each time the agent completes an activity, he or she is expected to file a report describing the nature of the buzz and its effectiveness. BzzAgent coaches respond with encouragement and feedback about additional techniques. Although agents get to keep the new products and services they promote, and can earn points redeemable for extra rewards (typically, books, CDs, and promotional items) by filing detailed reports, the network was designed to discourage folks from signing up just to get freebies.

This approach for creating word of mouth costs about $85,000 to put 1,000 agents on a 12-week campaign, exclusive of product samples. But the results can be impressive. Rock Bottom Restaurants saw its sales grow by $1.2 million in one quarter after 400 members of its frequent-diner program became BzzAgents.[18]

Strengths and Weaknesses of Communication Methods

Exhibit 16–2 compares these communication methods in terms of control, flexibility, credibility, and cost.

Control   Retailers have more control when using paid versus unpaid methods. When using advertising, sales promotions, Web sites, e-mail, store atmosphere, and paid buzz agents, retailers determine the message's content, and for advertising, e-mail, and sales promotions, they control the time of its delivery. Because

EXHIBIT 16–2
Comparison of Communication Methods

	Control	Flexibility	Credibility	Cost
Paid impersonal				
Mass-media advertising	High	Lowest	Lowest	Modest
Direct mail	Highest	High	Low	Modest
Sales promotion	High	Low	N/A	Modest
Store atmosphere	High	Low	N/A	Modest
Web site	High	Modest	Low	Modest
Paid personal				
Salespeople	Modest	Highest	Low	Highest
E-mail	Highest	High	Low	Low
Unpaid impersonal				
Publicity	Low	Low	High	Low
Unpaid personal				
Word of mouth	Low	Low	High	Lowest

salespeople have their own style and might deliver different messages, retailers have less control over personal selling than other paid communication methods.

Retailers have very little control over the content or timing of publicity and word-of-mouth communications. Because unpaid communications are designed and delivered by people not employed by the retailer, they can communicate unfavorable as well as favorable information. For example, news coverage of a food poisoning incident at a restaurant or racial discrimination at a hotel can result in significant declines in sales.

Flexibility   Personal selling is the most flexible communication method, because salespeople can talk with each customer, discover his or her specific needs, and develop unique presentations. E-mails are also very flexible because they can be personalized to specific customer interests, and Web sites can be tailored to individual visitors. Other communication methods are less flexible. For example, ads deliver the same message to all customers.

Credibility   Because publicity and word of mouth are typically communicated by independent sources, their information is usually more credible than the information in paid communication sources. For example, customers tend to doubt claims made by salespeople and in ads because they know retailers are trying to promote their merchandise.

Recognizing that younger consumers have greater doubts about the credibility of advertising, The Gap has launched a Web site, www.watchmechange.com, to promote its apparel unobtrusively. Visitors to the site first create a computer likeness of themselves. The computer model does a strip tease, shedding its clothes down to the undergarments while dancing to disco music. Then the model goes into a dressing room and comes out, still dancing, in a new outfit that the viewer selects. The Gap doesn't advertise the Web site, and its logo flashes onscreen for only a few seconds. The site doesn't offer any clothes for purchase. But visitors can create an animated character and e-mail it to a friend; the tagline in the e-mail reads "Meet me in the back of Gap." The Gap plans that people will stumble onto the site and pass the word onto others—an advertising technique known as "viral marketing."[20]

Cost   Publicity and word of mouth are classified as unpaid communication methods, but retailers do incur costs to stimulate them. For example, Staples spends $5 million a year to name the Staples Center in Los Angeles, home of the NBA's Los Angeles Lakers. However, the local and national exposure offered by this sponsorship helped Staples successfully enter the California market and become a national office supply retailer.[21] Paid impersonal communications often are economical. For example, a full-page advertisement in the *Los Angeles Times* costs about two cents per person to deliver the message in the ad.

REFACT

Eighty-six percent of teens and young adults, ages 14 to 30 years, ranked word of mouth as the most credible source among nine information sources, and 46 percent said friends were their leading source of information about fashion merchandise.[19]

Lowe's sponsorship of a NASCAR racing team generates publicity and builds brand awareness, but this publicity could have an unfavorable effect if the racing team engaged in unsanctioned activities.

In contrast, personal selling, because of its flexibility, is more effective than advertising, but it is more costly. A 10-minute presentation by a retail salesperson paid $12 per hour costs the retailer $2—100 times more than exposing a customer to a newspaper, radio, or TV ad. While maintaining a Web site on a server is relatively inexpensive, it is costly to design, continuously update, and promote the site to attract visitors; however, e-mails can be sent to customers at low cost.

Due to the differences just described, communication methods differ in their effectiveness in performing communication tasks, as well as in different stages of the customer's decision-making process (see Chapter 4). Typically, advertising through mass media advertising is most effective for building awareness. Web sites, direct mail, and newspaper advertising are effective for conveying information about a retailer's offerings and prices. Personal selling and sales promotion are most effective at persuading customers to purchase merchandise. Mass media advertising, publicity, Web sites, and store atmosphere are most cost effective in building the retailer's brand image and encouraging repeat purchases and store loyalty.

PLANNING THE RETAIL COMMUNICATION PROGRAM

Exhibit 16–3 illustrates the four steps in developing and implementing a retail communication program: setting objectives, determining a budget, allocating the budget, and implementing and evaluating the mix. The following sections detail each of these steps.

Setting Objectives

Retailers establish objectives for their communication programs to provide (1) direction for people implementing the program and (2) a basis for evaluating its effectiveness. As discussed at the beginning of this chapter, some communication programs can have a long-term objective, such as creating or altering a retailer's brand image. Other communication programs focus on improving short-term performance, such as increasing store traffic on a specific weekend.

Communication Objectives   While retailers' overall objective is to generate long- and short-term sales and profits, they often use communication objectives rather than sales objectives to plan and evaluate their communication programs. **Communication objectives** are specific goals related to the retail communication mix's effect on the customer's decision-making process.

Exhibit 16–4 shows some hypothetical information about customers in the target market for a Safeway supermarket. This information illustrates the goals related to the stages in the consumer decision-making process outlined in Chapter 4. Note that 95 percent of the customers are aware of the store (the first stage in the

EXHIBIT 16–3   Steps in Developing a Retail Communication Program

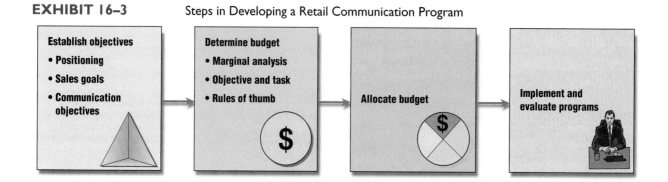

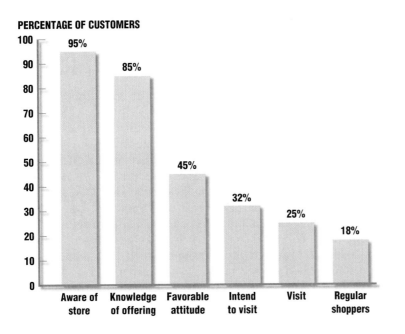

PERCENTAGE OF CUSTOMERS

decision-making process), and 85 percent know the type of merchandise it sells. But only 45 percent of the customers in the target market have a favorable attitude toward the store. Thirty-two percent intend to visit the store during the next few weeks; 25 percent actually visit the store during the next two weeks; and 18 percent regularly shop at the store.

In this hypothetical example, most people know about the store and its offering. The major problem confronting the Safeway supermarket is the big drop between knowledge and favorable attitudes. Thus, the store should develop a communication program with the objective of increasing the percentage of customers with a favorable attitude toward it.

To effectively implement and evaluate a communication program, its objectives must be clearly stated in quantitative terms. The target audience for the communication mix needs to be defined, along with the degree of change expected and the time period over which the change will be realized.

For example, a communication objective for a Safeway program might be to increase from 45 percent to 55 percent within three months the percentage of customers within a five-mile radius of the store who have a favorable attitude toward the store. This objective is clear and measurable. It indicates the task the program should address. The people who implement the program thus know what they're supposed to accomplish.

The communication objectives and approaches used by vendors and retailers differ, and these differences can lead to conflicts. Some of these points of conflict are

• *Long-term versus short-term goals* Most communications done by vendors are directed toward building a long-term image of their products. In contrast, most retailer communications are typically used to announce promotions and special sales that generate short-term revenues.

• *Product versus location* When vendors advertise their branded products, they don't care where the customer buys them. In contrast, retailers don't care what brands customers buy as long as they buy them in their store.

• *Geographic coverage* Because people tend to shop at stores near their homes or workplaces, most retailers use local newspapers, TV, and radio to target their communications. National retailers, however, increasingly are utilizing national media such as magazines and television, particularly for brand-building programs. In contrast, most vendors sell their brands nationally and thus tend to use national TV and magazines.

The "Spot the Dog" scavenger hunt was a comarketing program developed by Wal-Mart and Coppertone. The promotional program increased both Wal-Mart's and Coppertone's sales.

• *Breadth of merchandise* Typically, because vendors have a small number of products to promote, they can devote a lot of attention to developing consistent communication programs for each brand they make. Retailers have to develop communications programs that promote a much wider range of products.

Even though vendors and retailers have different goals, they frequently work together to develop mutually beneficial outcomes, as illustrated by Wal-Mart and Coppertone's sunscreen promotion program. The program was based on Little Miss Coppertone's losing her dog in a Wal-Mart store. For three months prior to the event, the program was promoted to sales associates through Wal-Mart's internal communication channels, including its satellite TV broadcasts, headquarters meetings, and sell sheets distributed to sales associates. On the day of the event, a scavenger hunt, Wal-Mart greeters wore "Spot the Dog" buttons and distributed game pieces to children and their parents. The game pieces described the scavenger hunt and encouraged customers to find clues located in different areas of the store—sun care, lawn and garden, and pet food. The pieces also promoted Coppertone's innovative rub-free sprays and offered a $2 Wal-Mart coupon for the products. **Shelf talkers**—signs on shelves providing information about the merchandise and its price—in each area provided answers to the clues. When all three answers were filled in, the customer turned in the game pieces for a free beach ball at the "Scavenger Hunt Center" in the store.

The comarketing promotion benefited both Wal-Mart and Coppertone. It built sun care customers' loyalty for Wal-Mart and Coppertone, kept customers in the Wal-Mart store longer and encouraged them to visit different areas of the store, and increased sunscreen sales for Wal-Mart and Coppertone. Almost 2,500 stores participated in the one-day event. Over 1.2 million prizes were delivered. Wal-Mart's sales of Coppertone sunscreen increased by 6 percent, and sales in other categories also increased.[22]

Setting the Communication Budget

The second step in developing a retail communication program is determining a budget (see Exhibit 16–3). The economically correct method for setting the communication budget is marginal analysis. Even though retailers usually don't have enough information to perform a complete marginal analysis, the method shows how managers should approach budget-setting programs. The marginal analysis method for setting a communication budget is the approach retailers should use when making all of their resource allocation decisions, including the number of locations in a geographic area (Chapter 8), the allocation of merchandise to stores (Chapter 14), the staffing of stores (Chapter 17), and the floor and shelf space devoted to merchandise categories (Chapter 18).

Marginal Analysis Method   **Marginal analysis** is based on the economic principle that firms should increase communication expenditures as long as each additional dollar spent generates more than a dollar of additional contribution. To illustrate marginal analysis, consider Diane West, owner manager of a specialty store selling women's business clothing. Exhibit 16–5 shows her analysis to determine how much she should spend next year on her communication program.

For 21 different communication expense levels (column 1), she estimates her store sales (column 2), gross margin (column 3), and other expenses (columns 4 and 5). Then she calculates the contribution, excluding expenses on communications (column 6), and the profit when the communication expenses are considered (column 7). To estimate the sales generated by different levels of communications, West can simply rely on her judgment and experience, or she might analyze past data to determine the relationship between communication expenses and sales.

Marginal Analysis for Setting Diane West's Communication Budget   **EXHIBIT 16–5**

Level	Communication expenses (1)	Sales (2)	Gross margin realized (3)	Rental expense (4)	Personnel expense (5)	Contribution before communication expenses (6) = (3) − (4) − (5)	Profit after communication expenses (7) = (6) − (1)	
1	$0	$240,000	$96,000	$44,000	$52,200	$ (200)	$ (200)	
2	5,000	280,000	112,000	48,000	53,400	10,600	5,600	
3	10,000	330,000	132,000	53,000	54,900	24,100	14,100	
4	15,000	380,000	152,000	58,000	56,400	37,600	22,600	
5	20,000	420,000	168,000	62,000	57,600	48,400	28,400	
6	25,000	460,000	184,000	66,000	58,800	59,200	34,200	
7	30,000	500,000	200,000	70,000	60,000	70,000	40,000	Last year
8	35,000	540,000	216,000	74,000	61,200	80,800	45,800	
9	40,000	570,000	228,000	77,000	62,100	88,900	48,900	
10	45,000	600,000	240,000	80,000	63,000	97,000	52,000	
11	50,000	625,000	250,000	82,500	63,750	103,750	53,750	
12	55,000	650,000	260,000	85,000	64,500	110,500	55,500	
13	60,000	670,000	268,000	87,000	65,100	115,900	55,900	
14	65,000	690,000	276,000	89,000	65,700	121,300	56,300	Best profit
15	70,000	705,000	282,000	90,500	66,150	125,350	55,350	
16	75,000	715,000	286,000	91,500	66,450	128,050	53,050	
17	80,000	725,000	290,000	92,500	66,750	130,750	50,750	
18	85,000	735,000	294,000	93,500	67,050	133,450	48,450	
19	90,000	745,000	298,000	94,500	67,350	136,150	46,150	
20	95,000	750,000	300,000	95,000	67,500	137,500	42,500	
21	100,000	750,000	300,000	95,000	67,500	137,500	37,500	

Historical data also provide information about the gross margin and other expenses as a percentage of sales.

Notice that at low levels of communication expenses, an additional $5,000 in communication expenses generates more than a $5,000 incremental contribution. For example, increasing the communication expense from $15,000 to $20,000 increases the contribution by $10,800 (or $48,400 − $37,600). When the communication expense reaches $65,000, further increases of $5,000 generate less than $5,000 in additional contributions. For example, increasing the budget from $65,000 to $70,000 generates only an additional $4,050 in contribution ($125,350 − $121,300).

In this example, West determines that the maximum profit would be generated with a communication expense budget of $65,000. But she notices that expense levels between $55,000 and $70,000 all result in about the same level of profit. Thus, West makes a conservative decision and establishes a $55,000 budget for her communication expenses.

In most cases, it's very hard to do a marginal analysis because managers don't know the relationship between communication expenses and sales. Note that the numbers in Exhibit 16–5 are simply West's estimates; they may not be accurate.

Sometimes retailers perform experiments to get a better idea of the relationship between communication expenses and sales. Say, for example, a catalog retailer selects several geographic areas in the United States with the same sales potential. The retailer then distributes 100,000 catalogs in the first area, 200,000 in the second area, and 300,000 in the third. Using the sales and costs for each distribution level, it could go through an analysis like the one in Exhibit 16–5 to determine the most profitable distribution level. (Chapter 15 described the use of experiments to determine the relationship between price and sales.)

EXHIBIT 16–6
Illustration of Objective-and-Task Method for Setting a Communication Budget

Objective: Increase the percentage of target market (working women living or working within 10 miles of our store) who know of our store's location and that it sells women's business attire from 25 percent to 50 percent over the next 12 months.	
Task: 480, 30–second radio spots during peak commuting hours (7:00 to 8:00 A.M. and 5:00 to 6:00 P.M.).	$12,300
Task: Sign with store name near entrance to mall.	4,500
Task: Display ad in the Yellow Pages.	500
Objective: Increase the percentage of target market who indicate that our store is their preferred store for buying their business wardrobe from 5 percent to 15 percent in 12 months.	
Task: Develop TV campaign to improve image and run 50, 30–second commercials.	$24,000
Task: Hold four "Dress for Success" seminars followed by a wine-and-cheese social.	8,000
Objective: Sell merchandise remaining at end of season.	
Task: Special event.	$6,000
Total budget	$55,300

Some other methods that retailers use to set communication budgets are the objective-and-task method and rules of thumb, which includes the affordable, percentage-of-sales, and competitive parity methods. These methods are less sophisticated than marginal analysis but easier to use.

Objective-and-Task Method   The **objective-and-task method** determines the budget required to undertake specific tasks to accomplish communication objectives. To use this method, the retailer first establishes a set of communication objectives, then determines the necessary tasks and their costs. The total of all costs incurred to undertake the tasks is the communication budget.

Exhibit 16–6 illustrates how Diane West uses the objective-and-task method to complement her marginal analysis. West establishes three objectives: to increase awareness of her store, to create a greater preference for her store among customers in her target market, and to promote the sale of merchandise remaining at the end of each season. The total communication budget she requires to achieve these objectives is $55,300.

In addition to defining her objectives and tasks, West rechecks the financial implications of the communication mix by projecting the income statement for next year using the communication budget (see Exhibit 16–7). This income statement includes an increase of $25,300 in communication expenses compared with last year. But West feels that this increase in the communication budget will boost annual sales from $500,000 to $650,000. Based on West's projections, the increase in communication expenses will raise store profits. The results of both the marginal analysis and the objective-and-task methods suggest a communication budget between $55,000 and $65,000.

Rule-of-Thumb Methods   In the previous two methods, the communication budget is set by estimating communication activities' effects on the firm's future sales or communication objectives. The **rule-of-thumb methods** discussed in this section use the opposite logic; they use past sales and communication activities to determine the present communication budget.[23]

EXHIBIT 16–7
Financial Implications of Increasing Communication Budget

	Last Year	Next Year
Sales	$500,000	$650,000
Gross margin (realized)	200,000	260,000
Rental, maintenance, etc.	70,000	85,000
Personnel	60,000	64,500
Communications	30,000	55,300
Profit	$ 40,000	$55,200

Affordable Budgeting Method   When using the **affordable budgeting method,** retailers first forecast their sales and expenses, excluding communication expenses, during the budgeting period. The difference between the forecast sales and expenses plus the desired profit is then budgeted for the communication mix. In other words, the affordable method sets the communication budget by determining what money is available after operating costs and profits are subtracted.

The major problem with the affordable method is that it assumes that the communication expenses don't stimulate sales and profit. Communication expenses are just a cost of business, like the cost of merchandise. When retailers use the affordable method, they typically cut "unnecessary" communication expenses if sales fall below the forecast rather than increase communication expenses to increase sales.

Percentage-of-Sales Method   The **percentage-of-sales method** sets the communication budget as a fixed percentage of forecast sales. Retailers use this method to determine the communication budget by forecasting sales during the budget period and applying a predetermined percentage to set the budget. The percentage may be the retailer's historical percentage or the average percentage used by similar retailers.

The problem with the percentage-of-sales method is that it assumes that the same percentage used in the past, or by competitors, is appropriate for the retailer. Consider a retailer that hasn't opened new stores in the past but plans to open many new stores in the current year. It must create customer awareness for these new stores, so the communication budget should be much larger in the current year than in the past.

Using the same percentage as competitors also may be inappropriate. For example, a retailer might have better locations than its competitors. Due to these locations, customers may already have a high awareness of the retailer's stores. Thus, the retailer may not need to spend as much on communications as competitors with poorer locations.

One advantage of both the percentage-of-sales method and the affordable method for determining a communication budget is that the retailer won't spend beyond its means. Since the level of spending is determined by sales, the budget will only go up when sales go up and the retailer generates more sales to pay for the additional communication expenses. When times are good, these methods work well because they allow the retailer to communicate more aggressively with customers. But when sales fall, communication expenses are cut, which may accelerate the sales decline.

Competitive Parity Method   Under the **competitive parity method,** the communication budget is set so that the retailer's share of communication expenses equals its share of the market. For example, consider a sporting goods store in a small town. To use the competitive parity method, the owner manager would first estimate the total amount spent on communications by all of the sporting goods retailers in town. Then the owner manager would estimate his or her store's market share for sporting goods and multiply that market share percentage by the sporting goods stores' total advertising expenses to set the budget. Assume that the owner manager's estimate of advertising for sporting goods by all stores is $5,000 and the estimate of his or her store's market share is 45 percent. On the basis of these estimates, the owner manager would set the store's communication budget at $2,250 to maintain competitive parity.

Like the other rule-of-thumb methods, the competitive parity method doesn't allow retailers to exploit the unique opportunities or problems they confront in a market. If all competitors used this method to set communication budgets, their market shares would stay about the same over time (assuming that the retailers develop equally effective campaigns).

REFACT

Supermarkets spend 1.1 percent of their annual sales revenue on advertising, while department store retailers spend 3.7 percent of sales, and women's apparel specialty retailers spend 4.7 percent of sales.[24]

Allocation of the Promotional Budget

After determining the size of the communication budget, the third step in the communication planning process is to allocate the budget (see Exhibit 16–3). In this step, the retailer decides how much of its budget to allocate to specific communication elements, merchandise categories, geographic regions, or long- and short-term objectives. For example, Dillard's must decide how much of its communication budget to spend in each area it has stores: Southeast, Mid-Atlantic, Southwest, Midwest, and West Coast. Michaels decides how much to allocate to merchandise associated with different crafts. The sporting goods store owner manager must decide how much of the store's $2,250 communication budget to spend on promoting the store's image versus generating sales during the year and how much to spend on advertising and special promotions.

Research indicates that allocation decisions are more important than the decision about the amount spent on communications.[25] In other words, retailers often can realize the same objectives by reducing the size of the communication budget but allocating it more effectively.

An easy way to make such allocation decisions is to spend about the same in each geographic region or for each merchandise category. But this allocation rule probably won't maximize profits because it ignores the possibility that communication programs might be more effective for some merchandise categories or for some regions than for others. Another approach is to use rules of thumb, such as basing allocations on the sales level or contributions for the merchandise category.

Allocation decisions, like budget-setting decisions, should use the principles of marginal analysis. The retailer should allocate the budget to areas that will yield the greatest return. This approach for allocating a budget is sometimes referred to as the **high-assay principle.** Consider a miner who can spend his time digging on two claims. The value of the gold on one claim is assayed at $20,000 per ton, while the assay value on the other claim is $10,000 per ton. Should the miner spend two-thirds of his time at the first mine and one-third of his time at the other mine? Of course not! The miner should spend all of his time mining the first claim until the assay value of the ore mined drops to $10,000 a ton, at which time he can divide his time equally between the claims.

Similarly, a retailer may find that its customers have a high awareness and very favorable attitude toward its women's clothing but not know much about its men's clothing. In this situation, a dollar spent on advertising men's clothing might generate more sales than a dollar spent on women's clothing, even though the sales of women's clothing is greater than the sales of men's clothing.

Planning, Implementing, and Evaluating Communication Programs—Three Illustrations

The final stage in developing a retail communication program is its implementation and evaluation (see Exhibit 16–3). This chapter's appendix discusses some specific issues in implementing advertising programs, including developing the message, selecting the media used for delivering the message, and determining the timing and frequency for presenting the message. This final section of the chapter illustrates the planning and evaluation process for three communication programs: an advertising campaign by a small specialty retailer, a sales promotion opportunity confronting a supermarket chain, and a communication program emphasizing direct marketing undertaken by a large retail chain.

Advertising Campaign   Hypothetically, imagine South Gate West is one of several specialty import home furnishing stores competing for upscale shoppers in Charleston, South Carolina. The store has the appearance of both a fine antique store and a traditional home furnishing shop, but most of its merchandise is new Asian imports.[26]

Harry Owens, the owner, realized his communication budget was considerably less than the budget of the local Pier 1 store. (Pier 1 is a large national chain that imports home furnishings.) He decided to concentrate his limited budget on a specific segment and use highly distinctive copy and art in his advertising. His target market was experienced, sophisticated consumers of housewares and home decorative items. His experience indicated the importance of personal selling for more seasoned shoppers because they (1) make large purchases and (2) seek considerable information before making a decision. Thus, Owens spent part of his communication budget on training his sales associates.

The advertising program Owens developed emphasized his store's distinctive image. He used the newspaper as his major vehicle. Competitive ads contained line drawings of furniture with prices. His ads emphasized imagery associated with Asian furniture by featuring off-the-beaten-path scenes of Asian countries with unusual art objects. This theme was also reflected in the store's atmosphere.

To evaluate his communication program, Owens needed to compare the results of his program with the objectives he developed during the first part of the planning process. To measure his campaign's effectiveness, he conducted an inexpensive tracking study. Telephone interviews were performed periodically with a representative sample of furniture customers in his store's trading area. Communication objectives were assessed using the following questions:

Communication Objectives	Questions
Awareness	What stores sell East Asian furniture?
Knowledge	Which stores would you rate outstanding on the following characteristics?
Attitude	On your next shopping trip for East Asian furniture, which store would you visit first?
Visit	Which of the following stores have you been to?

Here are the survey results for one year:

Communication Objective	Before Campaign	6 Months After	One Year After
Awareness (% mentioning store)	38%	46%	52%
Knowledge (% giving outstanding rating for sales assistance)	9	17	24
Attitude (% first choice)	13	15	19
Visit (% visited store)	8	15	19

The results show a steady increase in awareness, knowledge of the store, and choice of the store as a primary source of East Asian furniture. This research provides evidence that the advertising was conveying the intended message to the target audience.

Sales Promotion Opportunity   Many sales promotion opportunities undertaken by retailers are initiated by vendors. For example, Colgate-Palmolive might offer the following special promotion to Kroger: During a one-week period, Kroger can order Fab laundry detergent in the 48-ounce size at 15 cents below the standard wholesale price. However, if Kroger elects to buy Fab at the discounted price, the grocery chain must feature the 48-ounce container of Fab in its Thursday

The end-aisle display of Fab is part of a special Colgate-Palmolive promotion in which the supermarket bought Fab at a discount in exchange for the prominent display.

newspaper advertisement at $1.59 (20 cents off the typical retail price). In addition, Kroger must have an end-aisle display of Fab.

Before Kroger decides whether to accept such a trade promotion and then promote Fab to its customers, it needs to assess the promotion's impact on its profitability. Such a promotion may be effective for the vendor but not for the retailer.

To evaluate a trade promotion, the retailer considers

- The realized margin from the promotion.
- The cost of the additional inventory carried due to buying more than the normal amount.
- The potential increase in sales from the promoted merchandise.
- The potential loss suffered when customers switch to the promoted merchandise from more profitable private-label brands.
- The additional sales made to customers attracted to the store by the promotion.[27]

When Fab's price is reduced to $1.59, Kroger will sell more Fab than it normally does. But Kroger's margin on the Fab will be less because the required retail discount of 20 cents isn't offset by the wholesale discount of 15 cents. In addition, Kroger might suffer losses because the promotion encourages customers to buy Fab, which has a lower margin than Kroger's private-label detergent that those customers might have bought. Customers may even stockpile Fab, buying several boxes, which will reduce sales of Kroger's private-label detergent for some time after the special promotion ends. In contrast, the promotion may attract customers who don't normally shop at Kroger but who will visit to buy Fab at the discounted price. These customers might buy additional merchandise, providing a sales gain to the store that it wouldn't have realized if it hadn't promoted Fab.

Special Promotion Using a CRM/Campaign Management Tool   A national retailer with 1,600 store locations used its customer relationship management (CRM)/campaign management system to plan, design, evaluate, and implement a special Easter promotion.[28] The diagram of the system is shown in Exhibit 16–8. The retailer owns a customer database with purchase information, complemented with additional customer information acquired through external sources.

After an initial planning meeting, the retailer decided to use both direct-mail and e-mail communication channels with supporting in-store promotions and existing advertising. Customers would need to bring in a coupon to take advantage of the special promotion. The goal of the campaign was to generate a 10 percent increase in sales during the holiday period.

Using the campaign management system, the retailer examined a number of what-if scenarios, which enabled the team to chart the tasks, costs, and related deadlines to determine its projected return on investment (ROI). Initially, they wanted to target customers who had visited the stores and made a purchase within the last nine months. During the target market segmentation evaluation process, the team determined that the counts were too low and increased the target criteria to customer purchases within the last 12 months. According to this criterion, the communication program would be directed to 2.6 million customers. A review of past holiday promotion programs suggested a response rate of 2.5 percent.

Based on the 2.5 percent response rate for 2.6 million customers, the number of people projected to visit the stores was 65,000. The special promotion was a $49 item, but the average sale once people were in the store was $99. On the basis of

CRM/Campaign Management System **EXHIBIT 16–8**

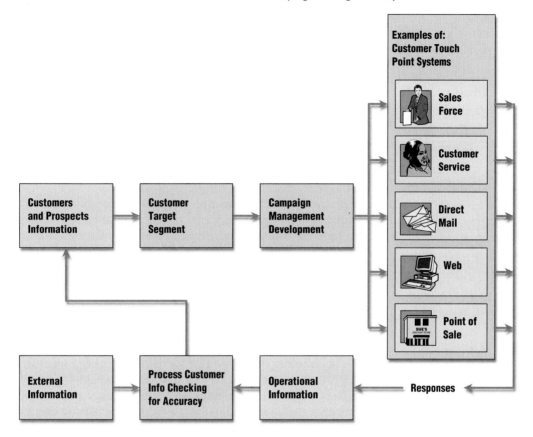

this information, the holiday event special promotion was targeted to generate gross sales between $3.1 million and $6.4 million.

The cost for each direct-mail piece was 65 cents, and the individual e-mails were 3 cents. To mail and e-mail 2.6 million customers, the cost was $1,768,000. In determining the product costs for the special promotion item, a 75 percent markup was used, and the campaign profit margin was projected to be between $600,000 and $3.1 million. The financial analysis developed by the planning tool is shown in Exhibit 16–9.

Once the what-if analysis was completed and the campaign plan was built with all of the details and responsibilities of each department, it was set into action. The action plan includes all the required steps in the campaign process, along with the

EXHIBIT 16–9
Financial Analysis of Special Easter Promotion

CAMPAIGN PLANNING FINANCIALS			
Target Market Count		**Campaign Costs**	
Records in 12-month period	2.6 million	Direct mail ($.65/piece)	$1,690,000
2.5 percent response rate		E-mail ($.03/e-mail)	$ 78,000
Project response count	65,000	Total cost	$1,768,000
Gross Revenue		**Net Revenue (less product cost of 25%)**	
Special promotion $49/each	$3,185,000	$2,388,750	
Average sale $99/each	$6,435,000	$4,826,250	
	Campaign Profitability		
	Special promotion	$620,750	
	Average sale	$3,058,250	

costs, responsibilities, and deadlines in the marketing production schedule. When the plan is put into production, all of the tasks are sent to the people responsible for completing them, so that deadlines and costs are tracked. Each department receives a series of tasks specific to that department's deliverables.

The creative department was assigned the responsibility of designing the direct-mail piece with the coupon. It also designed the e-mail piece with a print coupon. Once the design process was completed and approved, the artwork was sent to the print vendor for printing and the marketing department for e-mail distribution.

The database marketing department was responsible for sending the list of customers in the target market analysis (customers who had visited a store and made a purchase in the last 12 months) to the mail vendor. Each record in the customer database had a unique identifier so that the results of the campaign would be properly tracked and analyzed.

The store promotions department received its responsibility to make sure that the in-store promotional materials were consistent with the message in the campaign. Media services also received a task to verify consistency among all media with the campaign message.

During the entire campaign process, management's view of the financial information and campaign deliverables/deadline information was available. As the stores reported their customer sales, management's reports were automatically generated, and the response ROI was analyzed to determine if the marketing campaign was successful.

The information from all of the customer touch points was collected, processed, and added to the customer database. The successful campaign was then templated for future use, which will save the retailer time in the planning phase for the next holiday campaign. The matrix solution allowed management to optimize resources and manage deadlines and deliverables, thus increasing productivity, efficiency, and ROI.

SUMMARY

A communication program can be designed to achieve a variety of objectives for the retailer, such as building a brand image of the retailer in the customer's mind, increasing sales and store traffic, providing information about the retailer's location and offering, and announcing special activities.

Retailers communicate with customers through advertising, sales promotions, Web sites, store atmosphere, publicity, personal selling, e-mail, and word of mouth. These elements in the communication mix must be coordinated so customers have a clear, distinct image of the retailer and not be confused by conflicting information.

Many retailers use rules of thumb to determine the size of the promotion budget. Marginal analysis, the most appropriate method for determining how much must be spent to accomplish the retailer's objectives, should be used to determine whether the level of spending maximizes the profits that could be generated by the communication mix.

The largest portion of a retailer's communication budget is typically spent on advertising and sales promotions. A wide array of media can be used for advertising. Each medium has its pros and cons. Newspaper advertising is effective for announcing sales, whereas TV ads are useful for developing an image. Sales promotions are typically used to achieve short-term objectives, such as increasing store traffic over a weekend. Most sales promotions are supported in part by promotions offered to the retailer by its vendors. Publicity and word of mouth are typically low-cost communications, but they are very difficult for retailers to control.

KEY TERMS

advertising, *432*	brand equity, *428*	cost per thousand (CPM), *454*
affordable budgeting method, *443*	brand image, *431*	coupons, *434*
aided recall, *429*	communication objectives, *438*	coverage, *454*
brand, *428*	competitive parity method, *443*	cumulative reach, *454*
brand associations, *430*	contests, *433*	e-mail, *434*
brand awareness, *429*	cooperative (co-op) advertising, *451*	freestanding insert (FSI), *452*

GET OUT AND DO IT!

1. **CONTINUING ASSIGNMENT** Evaluate the communication activities undertaken by the retailer you selected for the continuing assignment. List all of the specific elements and information in the retailer's store and on its Web site that communicate the store's image and the merchandise it is offering to customers. What image does the retailer communicate through its store atmosphere, sales associates, Web site, and advertising? What are the associations it attempts to develop with its brand? Are the elements in its communication program consistent in terms of communicating the same image? Why or why not?

2. **GO SHOPPING** Look though the freestanding inserts (FSIs) in your Sunday newspaper. Evaluate the general use of FSIs and select the FSIs that you think are most effective. Why are these FSIs more effective than others?

3. **INTERNET EXERCISE** Retailers and manufacturers now deliver coupons through the Internet rather than by mail or in freestanding inserts. Go to www.coolsavings.com for coupons offered over the Internet. How does this coupon distribution system compare with more traditional distribution systems?

4. **INTERNET EXERCISE** Trader Joe's has an interesting retail concept: It's an off-price retailer selling gourmet food and wine. Go to www.traderjoes.com and see how the firm uses its Internet site to promote its retail offering. How effective do you think the site is in promoting the store and building its image?

5. **INTERNET EXERCISE** You can find more information about the use of radio as an advertising medium at the Radio Advertising Bureau site, www.rab.com. According to this information, what types of retail messages can be delivered most effectively by radio compared with other media?

6. **INTERNET EXERCISE** Go to the home page for Floorgraphics at www.floorgraphics.com/site/1_solution.html. Read about this in-store medium for communicating with shoppers. How does in-store advertising support the other elements of the communication mix? Have you seen floor ads in your own shopping experiences? Describe the store, aisle, and product/brand. Rate the effectiveness of this in-store communication tool.

7. **INTERNET EXERCISE** Read the *BusinessWeek* online article entitled, "How In-Store TVs Play to Shoppers," available at www.businessweek.com/bwdaily/dnflash/nov2004/nf20041122_9652.htm. How are retailers using TV as an in-store communication tool? What are the key advantages of implementing in-store TV in the communication mix?

DISCUSSION QUESTIONS AND PROBLEMS

1. How do brands benefit consumers? Retailers?

2. How can advertising, personal selling, and promotion complement one another in an integrated marketing communications program?

3. As a means of communicating with customers, how does advertising differ from publicity?

4. For which of the following growth opportunities do you think the retailer should use its brand name when pursuing the opportunity? Why? (*a*) McDonald's starts a new chain of restaurants to sell seafood in a sit-down environment competing with Red Lobster. (*b*) Sears starts a chain of stand-alone stores that sell just home appliances. (*c*) Blockbuster starts a chain of stores selling consumer electronics.

5. What factors should be considered in dividing up the advertising budget among a store's different merchandise areas? Which of the following should receive the highest advertising budget: fashionable women's clothing, men's underwear, women's hosiery, or kitchen appliances? Why?

6. Outline some elements in a communication program to achieve the following objectives: (*a*) Increase store loyalty by 20 percent. (*b*) Build awareness of the store by 10 percent. (*c*) Develop an image as a low-price retailer. How would you determine whether the communication program met the objective?

7. Retailers use TV advertising to build a brand image. Television advertisers have identified many types of

markets on the basis of the day, time, and type of show during which their ads may appear. During which days, times, and types of shows should retailers advertise fresh produce and meat, power drills, beer, and health club memberships? Why?

8. A retailer plans to open a new store near a university. It will specialize in collegiate merchandise such as tee-shirts, fraternity/sorority accessories, and sweatshirts. Develop an integrated communication program for the retailer. What specific advertising media should the new store use to capture the university market?

9. Cooperative (co-op) advertising is a good way for a retailer to extend an advertising budget. Why isn't it always in a retailer's best interests to rely extensively on co-op advertising?

10. What positive brand associations do customers have with retail brand names? Select Target, Sears, Tiffany, or your favorite retail store and complete the table below:

Retail Brand _____

Characteristic	Favorable Brand Associations
Merchandise category	
Price/quality	
Attribute/benefit	
Lifestyle/activity	

SUGGESTED READINGS

Aaker, David, and Erich Joachimsthaler. *Brand Leadership: Building Assets in an Information Economy.* New York: Free Press, 2000.

Belch, George, and Michael Belch. *Advertising and Promotion: An Integrated Marketing Communications Perspective.* 6th ed. New York: McGraw-Hill, 2004.

Grewal, Dhruv; Michael Levy; and Donald Lehmann. "Retail Branding and Customer Loyalty: An Overview," *Journal of Retailing* 80 (Winter 2004), pp. 249–53.

Hughes, Mark. *Buzzmarketing.* New York: Pennguin/Portfolio, 2005.

Kumar, V., and Srinivasan Swaminathan. "The Different Faces of Coupon Elasticity," *Journal of Retailing* 81, no. 1 (2005), pp. 1–14.

Mangleburg, Tamara; Patricia Doney; and Terry Bristol. "Shopping with friends and Teens' Susceptibility to Peer Influence," *Journal of Retailing* 80, no. 2 (2004), pp. 101–23.

Percy, Larry. *Strategic Advertising Management.* 2nd ed. Oxford: Oxford University Press, 2005.

Shimp, Terence A. *Advertising, Promotion and Supplemental Aspects of Integrated Marketing Communications.* 6th ed. Mason, OH: Thomson South-Western, 2003.

Smith, Steve. *How to Sell More Stuff: Promotional Marketing that Really Works.* Chicago: Dearborn Trade Publishers, 2005.

Tongeren, Michel van. *Retail Branding: From Stopping Power to Shopping Power.* Amsterdam: BIS EnfieldAirlift, 2003.

"What's in Store? Consumer Desires, Branding Concerns and Service Industries Shape Store-Design Trends," *Chain Store Age*, May 2002, pp. 114–17.

APPENDIX 16A   Implementing Retail Advertising Programs

Implementing an advertising program involves developing the message, choosing the specific media to convey the message, and determining the frequency and timing of the message. Each of these decisions is examined in this section.

DEVELOPING THE ADVERTISING MESSAGE

Most retail advertising messages have a short life and are designed for immediate impact. This immediacy calls for a copywriting style that grabs the reader's attention. Exhibit 16–10 outlines specific suggestions for developing local newspaper ads.[29]

Assistance in Advertising

Retailers get assistance in developing advertising campaigns from vendors through their co-op programs, advertising agencies, and media companies.

REFACT

The average consumer sees over 2,000 advertising messages per week.[30]

Suggestions for Developing Local Ads **EXHIBIT 16–10**

Have a dominant headline	The first question a consumer asks is, What's in it for me? Thus, retailers need to feature the principal benefit being offered in the headline along with a reason why the consumer should act immediately. The benefit can be expanded on in a subhead.
Use a dominant element	Ads should include a large picture or headline. Typically, photographs of real people attract more attention than drawings. Action photographs are effective in getting readers' attention.
Stick to a simple layout	The ad's layout should lead the reader's eye through the message from the headline to the illustration and then to the explanatory copy, price, and retailer's name and location. Complex elements, decorative borders, and many different typefaces distract the reader's attention from the retailer's message.
Provide a specific, complete presentation	Ad readers are looking for information that will help them decide whether to visit the store. The ad must contain all of the information pertinent to this decision, including the type of merchandise, brands, prices, sizes, and colors. Consumers are unlikely to make a special trip to the store on the basis of vague information. Broadcast ads, particularly radio ads, tend to be very creative but often leave the consumer thinking, Gee, that was a clever ad, but what was it advertising?
Use easily recognizable, distinct visuals	Consumers see countless ads each day. Thus, to get the consumers' attention, retailers must make their ads distinct from those of the competition. Ads with distinctive art, layout, design elements, or typeface generate higher readership.
Give the store's name and address	The store's name and location are the two most important aspects of a retail ad. If consumers don't know where to go to buy the advertised merchandise, the retailer won't make a sale. The retailer's name and location must be prominently displayed in print ads and repeated several times in broadcast ads.

Co-op Programs Co-op (cooperative) advertising is a program undertaken by a vendor. The vendor pays for part of the retailer's advertising but dictates some conditions. For example, Sony may have a co-op program that pays for half of a consumer electronics retailer's ads for Sony digital TVs.

Co-op advertising enables a retailer to increase its advertising budget. In the previous example, Best Buy only pays for half of its expenses for ads including Sony digital TVs. In addition to lowering costs, co-op advertising enables a small retailer to associate its name with well-known national brands and use attractive artwork created by the national brand.

Co-op advertising programs also are often used to support a vendor's effort to discourage retailers from discounting the vendor's products. For example, Estée Lauder might give its department store retailers 7 percent of sales for co-op advertising if the retailers agree not to advertise a price below its suggested retail price.

Co-op advertising has other drawbacks. First, vendors want the ads to feature their products, whereas retailers are more interested in featuring their store's name, location, and assortment of merchandise and services offered. This conflict in goals can reduce the effectiveness of co-op advertising from the retailer's perspective. In addition, ads developed by the vendor often are used by several competing retailers and may list the names and locations of all retailers offering their brands. Thus, co-op ads tend to blur any distinctions between retailers. Finally, restrictions the vendor places on the ads may further reduce their effectiveness for the retailer. For example, the vendor may restrict advertising to a period of time when the vendor's sales are depressed, but the retailer might not normally be advertising during this time frame.

Agencies Most large retailers have a department that creates advertising for sales and special events. Large retailers often use advertising agencies to develop ads for store image campaigns but develop promotional newspaper advertisements with their in-house staffs. Many small retailers use local agencies to plan and create all of their advertising. These local agencies are often more skilled in planning and executing advertising than the retailer's employees are. Agencies also work on other aspects of the

Simmons paid for part of this coop advertisement, enabling Back to Bed Sleep Centers to stretch its advertising budget and associate itself with a well-respected national brand.

EXHIBIT 16–11   Media Capabilities

Media	Targeting	Timeliness	Information Presentation Capacity	Life	Cost
Newspapers	Good	Good	Modest	Short	Modest
Magazines	Modest	Poor	Modest	Modest	High
Direct mail	Excellent	Modest	High	Short	Modest
Television	Modest	Modest	Low	Short	Modest
Radio	Modest	Good	Low	Short	Low
Internet					
Banner	Excellent	Excellent	Low	Modest	High
Web site	Excellent	Excellent	High	Long	Modest
E-mail	Excellent	Excellent	Modest	Short	Low
Outdoor billboards	Modest	Poor	Very low	Long	Modest
Shopping guides	Modest	Modest	Low	Modest	Low
Yellow Pages	Modest	Poor	Low	Long	Low

communication programs, such as contests, direct mail, and special promotions.

Media Companies   In addition to selling newspaper space and broadcast time, the advertising media offer services to local retailers, ranging from planning an advertising program to actually designing the ads. Media companies also do market research on their audiences and can provide information about shopping patterns in the local area.

CHOOSING THE MOST EFFECTIVE MEDIA

After developing the message, the next step is to decide what medium to use to communicate the message. The media used for retail advertising are newspapers, magazines, direct mail, radio, TV, outdoor billboards, the Internet, shopping guides, and the Yellow Pages. Exhibit 16–11 summarizes their characteristics.

Newspapers
Retailing and newspaper advertising grew up together over the past century. But the growth in retail newspaper advertising has slowed recently as retailers have begun using other media. Still, 16 of the nation's 25 largest newspaper advertisers are retailers.[31]

In addition to displaying ads with their editorial content, newspapers distribute freestanding inserts. A **freestanding insert (FSI),** also called a **preprint,** is an advertisement printed at the retailer's expense and distributed as an insert in the newspaper. Because newspapers are distributed in a well-defined local market area, they're effective at targeting retail advertising. Often the local market covered by a newspaper is similar to the market served by the retailer. Newspapers offer opportunities for small retailers to target their advertising by developing editions for different areas of a city. For example, the *Los Angeles Times* has 11 special editions for regions of southern California, including those for Ventura County, the desert cities, and San Diego County.

Newspapers also offer a quick response. There's only a short time between the deadline for receiving the advertisement and the time that the advertisement will appear. Thus, newspapers are useful for delivering messages on short notice.

Newspapers, like all print media, effectively convey a lot of detailed information. Readers can go through an advertisement at their own pace and refer back to part of the advertisement when they want. In addition, consumers can save the advertisement and take it to the store with them, which makes newspaper ads effective at conveying information about the prices of sale items. But newspaper ads aren't effective for showing merchandise, particularly when it's important to illustrate colors, because of the poor reproduction quality.

While newspapers are improving their printing facilities to provide better reproductions and color in ads, retailers continue to rely on preprints to get good reproduction quality. JCPenney uses FSIs extensively, distributing them to over 50 million newspaper readers weekly. However, FSIs are so popular that the insert from one retailer can be lost among the large number of inserts in the newspaper. Walgreens has reduced its FSIs from two to one a week because of the clutter and because it has found that young people don't read newspapers as much as their parents. However, Walgreens is trying to increase the effectiveness of its FSIs by streamlining the message and using a better grade of paper.

The life of a newspaper advertisement is short because the newspaper is usually discarded after it's read. In contrast, magazine advertising has a longer life since consumers tend to save magazines and read them several times during a week or month.

Finally, the cost of developing newspaper ads is very low. Newspaper ads can be developed by less experienced people and don't require expensive color photography or typesetting. However, the cost of delivering the message may be high if the newspaper's circulation is broader than the retailer's target market, which would require the retailer to pay for exposures that won't generate sales.

There are so many FSIs in local newspapers that it is difficult for a retailer to get consumers to notice its FSI.

Magazines

Retail magazine advertising is mostly done by national retailers such as Target and The Gap. But magazine advertising is increasing with the growth of local magazines and regional editions of national magazines. Retailers tend to use this medium for image advertising because the reproduction quality is high. Due to the lead time—the time between submitting the advertisement and publication—a major disadvantage of magazine advertising is that the timing is difficult to coordinate with special events and sales.

Direct Mail

Retailers frequently use data collected at POS terminals to target their advertising and sales promotions to specific customers using direct mail (see Chapter 11). For example, Neiman Marcus keeps a database of all purchases made by its credit card customers. With information about each customer's purchases, Neiman Marcus can target direct mail about a new perfume to customers with a history of purchasing such merchandise.

Retailers also can purchase a wide variety of lists for targeting consumers with specific demographic profiles, interests, and lifestyles. For example, a home furnishings store could buy a list of subscribers to *Architectural Digest* in its trading area and then mail information about home furnishings to those upscale consumers. Finally, many retailers encourage their salespeople to maintain a preferred customer list and use it to mail personalized invitations and notes. While direct mail can be very effective due to the ability to personalize the message, it's also costly. In addition, many consumers ignore direct-mail advertising and treat it as junk mail.

Television

Television commercials can be placed on a national network or local station. A local television commercial is called a **spot.** Retailers typically use TV for image advertising, to take advantage of the high reproduction quality and the opportunity to communicate through both visual images and sound. Television ads can also demonstrate product usage. For example, Walgreens' advertising campaign emphasizes its position as the leading national drugstore via the theme "The Pharmacy America Trusts."

REFACT

Americans spend 1,645 hours annually watching TV and only 175 hours a year reading newspapers.[32]

In addition to its high production costs, broadcast time for national TV advertising is expensive. Spots have relatively small audiences, but they may be economical for local retailers. To offset the high production costs, many vendors provide modular commercials, in which the retailer can insert its name or a "tag" after information about the vendor's merchandise.

Radio

Many retailers use radio advertising because messages can be targeted to a specific segment of the market.[33] Some radio stations' audiences are highly loyal to their announcers. When these announcers promote a retailer, listeners are impressed. The cost of developing and broadcasting radio commercials is quite low.

One disadvantage of radio advertising, however, is that listeners generally treat the radio broadcast as background, which limits the attention they give the message. As with all broadcast media, consumers must get the information from a radio commercial when it's broadcast. They can't refer back to the advertisement for information they didn't hear or remember.

Internet

Three uses of the Internet by retailers to communicate with customers are (1) banner ads and affiliate programs to generate awareness, (2) Web sites to provide information about merchandise and special events, and (3) e-mails to target messages.[34] Banner ads and affiliate programs are very effective for targeting communication, but they are not cost effective for building awareness. Using information from a visitor's navigation and purchase behavior and IP address, banner ads can be targeted to specific individuals. For example, Sportsline.com visitors who look at the box scores for Kansas City Royals baseball games are shown ads for Royals logo apparel and hats. DoubleClick, an Internet advertising agency, downloads different banner ads from its server to host Web sites on the basis of the information it has about the specific visitor. However, Internet advertising is not cost effective for building awareness because the large number of Web sites reduces the number of customers who might visit a site and see a particular ad.

Although the Internet is not effective for building awareness, it is an excellent vehicle for conveying information to customers. In addition to selling merchandise on a Web site, retailers can provide a wide array of information, ranging from store locations to the availability and pricing of merchandise in specific stores. The interactivity of the Internet gives customers the opportunity to quickly sift through a vast amount of information. For example, visitors to the Circuit City Web site can find detailed information about specific digital camera models

Sports Authority uses billboards to create awareness and remind customers to consider Sports Authority when they need sports equipment.

and generate a table to compare a select group of cameras on features important to the customer.

Finally, retailers can use the Internet to send e-mails to customers informing them of special events and new merchandise.

Outdoor Billboards

Billboards and other forms of outdoor advertising are effective vehicles for creating awareness and providing a very limited amount of information to a narrow audience. Thus, outdoor advertising has limited usefulness in providing information about sales. Outdoor advertising is typically used to remind customers about the retailer or to inform people in cars of nearby retail outlets.

Shopping Guides

Shopping guides are free papers delivered to all residents in a specific area. This medium is particularly useful for retailers that want to saturate a trading area. Shopping guides are cost effective and assure the local retailer of 100 percent coverage. In contrast, subscription newspapers typically offer only 30 to 50 percent coverage. An extension of the shopping guide concept is the coupon book or magazine. These media contain coupons offered by retailers for discounts. Shopping guides and coupon books make no pretense about providing news to consumers; they're simply delivery vehicles for ads and coupons.

Yellow Pages

The Yellow Pages are useful for retailers because they have a long life. The Yellow Pages are used as a reference by consumers who are definitely interested in making a purchase and seeking information.

Considerations in Selecting Media

To convey their message with the most impact to the most consumers in the target market at the lowest cost, retailers need to evaluate media in terms of coverage, reach, cost, and impact that they will deliver for advertising messages.

Coverage   **Coverage** refers to the number of potential customers in the retailer's target market that could be exposed to an advertisement in a given medium. For example, assume that the size of the target market is 100,000 customers. The local newspaper is distributed to 60 percent of the customers in the target market, 90 percent of the potential customers have a TV set that picks up the local station's signal, and 5 percent of the potential customers drive past a billboard. Thus, the coverage for newspaper advertising would be 60,000; for TV advertising, 90,000; and for the specific billboard, 5,000.

Reach   In contrast to coverage, **reach** is the actual number of customers in the target market exposed to an advertising medium. If on any given day, 60 percent of the potential customers who receive the newspaper actually read it, then the newspaper's reach would be 36,000 (or 60 percent of 60,000). Retailers often run an advertisement several times, in which case they calculate the **cumulative reach** for the sequence of ads. For example, if 60 percent of the potential customers receiving a newspaper read it each day, 93.6 percent (or 1 minus the probability of not reading the paper three times in a row [.40 × .40 × .40]) of the potential customers will read the newspaper at least one day over the three-day period in which the advertisement appears in the paper. Thus, the cumulative reach for running a newspaper advertisement for three days is 56,160 (or 93.6 percent × 60,000), which almost equals the newspaper's coverage. When evaluating Internet advertising opportunities, the measure used to assess reach is the number of unique visitors who access the Web page on which the advertisement is located.

Cost   The **cost per thousand (CPM)** measure is often used to compare media. Typically, CPM is calculated by dividing an ad's cost by its reach. Another approach for determining CPM is to divide the cost of several ads in a campaign by their cumulative reach. If in the previous example, one newspaper ad costs $500 and three ads cost $1,300, the CPM using simple reach is $13.89, or $500/(36,000/1,000). Using cumulative reach, the CPM is $23.15, or $1,300/(56,160/1,000). Note that the CPM might be higher using cumulative reach instead of simple reach, but the overall reach is also higher, and many potential customers will see the ad two or three times. Thus, CPM is a good method for comparing similarly sized ads in similar media, such as full-page ads in the *Los Angeles Times* and the *Orange County Register*. But CPM can be misleading when comparing the cost effectiveness of ads in different types of media, such as newspaper and TV. A TV ad may have a lower CPM than a newspaper ad, but the newspaper ad may be much more effective at achieving the ad's communication objectives, such as giving information about a sale.

Impact   **Impact** is an ad's effect on the audience. Due to their unique characteristics, different media are particularly effective at accomplishing different communication tasks. Exhibit 16–12 shows the effectiveness of various media for different communication tasks. Television is particularly effective at getting an audience's attention, demonstrating merchandise, changing attitudes, and announcing events.

Effectiveness of Media on Communication Objectives   **EXHIBIT 16–12**

Communication Task	Newspapers	Magazine	Direct Mail	TV	Radio	Web sites	E-Mail	Outdoor
Getting attention	Low	Medium	Medium	Medium	Low	Low	High	Medium
Identifying name	Medium	High	Low	Low	Low	Low	Medium	High
Announcing events	High	Low	High	High	Medium	Low	High	Low
Demonstrating merchandise	Low	Medium	High	High	Low	High	Low	Low
Providing information	Low	High	High	Low	Low	High	Medium	Lowest
Changing attitudes	High	Medium	High	High	Medium	High	Low	Low
Building brand image	Low	Medium	High	High	Low	High	Low	Low

Magazines are appropriate for emphasizing the quality and prestige of a store and its offering and providing detailed information to support quality claims. Newspapers are useful for providing price information and announcing events. Web sites are particularly effective for demonstrating merchandise and providing information. Outdoor advertising is most effective at promoting a retailer's name and location.

DETERMINING ADVERTISING FREQUENCY AND TIMING

The frequency and timing of ads determine how often and when customers will see the retailer's message.

Frequency

Frequency is how many times the potential customer is exposed to an ad. When assessing frequency for Internet advertising, it is typically assessed by measuring the number of times a Web page with the ad is downloaded during a visit to the site.

The appropriate frequency depends on the ad's objective. Typically, several exposures to an ad are required to influence a customer's buying behavior. Thus, campaigns directed toward changing purchase behavior rather than creating awareness emphasize frequency over reach. Ads announcing a sale are often seen and remembered after one exposure. Thus, sale ad campaigns emphasize reach over frequency.

Timing

Typically, an ad should appear on, or slightly precede, the days consumers are most likely to purchase merchandise. For example, if most consumers buy groceries Thursday through Sunday, then supermarkets should advertise on Thursday and Friday. Similarly, consumers often go shopping after they receive their paychecks at the middle and the end of the month. Thus, advertising should be concentrated at these times.

Store Management

Section IV focuses on the implementation issues associated with store management, including managing store employees and controlling costs (Chapter 17), presenting merchandise (Chapter 18), and providing customer service (Chapter 19).

Traditionally, the issues pertaining to merchandise management were considered the most important retail implementation decisions, and buying was considered the best career path for achieving senior retail management positions. Now, developing a strategic advantage through merchandise management is becoming more and more difficult. Competing stores often have similar assortments of national-brand merchandise.

Since customers can find the same assortments in a number of conveniently located retail outlets and through the Internet, store management issues have become a critical basis for developing strategic advantage. Retailers are increasing their emphasis on differentiating their offering from competitive offerings on the basis of the experience that customers have in the stores, including the service they get from store employees and the quality of the shopping environment.

Introduction to the World of Retailing → Retailing Strategy → Merchandise Management / Store Management

Managing the Store

Joyce Rivas (right) discusses the sales report with two assistant managers.

EXECUTIVE BRIEFING
Joyce Rivas, Store Manager, Walgreens

When I was a student at Florida International University in Miami, I majored in Health Administration because I wanted to pursue a career that involved helping people. I planned to work for a hospital when I graduated. While I was in college, I worked part-time at a Walgreens store as a pharmacist technician and discovered that working for Walgreens offered an opportunity to both help people with their health care problems and be involved in a dynamic and exciting business environment.

Walgreens has a strong set of corporate values that emphasizes providing outstanding customer service. Our pharmacists don't just fill prescriptions. They talk with customers about the medications that they are taking, answer questions, and try to address concerns customers might have.

I really like working in a store. I would be bored if I had to sit behind a desk all day. I need to walk around and talk with people. As a store manager, I interact with a lot of people—customers, store employees, people in our district office—and I do a lot of different things. In a single day, I will handle some personnel issues, help customer find what they need, decide on how to display some new merchandise, and review reports summarizing the financial performance of my store.

Being a store manager at Walgreens is like running your own business. The annual sales for my store, which employs 50 people, is over $15 million and I am responsible and rewarded for the store's performance. But the rewards I get are more than just money. I like to work with and help people. Walgreens is a great place to work because it cares about its customers and employees just like I do.

As the manager of this business, I try to create an environment in which my store employees feel that they are all part of a team working together to provide an attractive offering for our customers. I want all of my

CHAPTER 17

QUESTIONS

What are the responsibilities of store managers?

How should store managers recruit, select, motivate, train, and evaluate their employees?

How should store managers compensate their salespeople?

What legal and ethical issues must store managers consider in managing their employees?

What can store managers do to increase productivity and reduce costs?

How can store managers reduce inventory losses due to employee theft and shoplifting?

team members to learn more about how our store and company operates, develop their skills, and realize their potential. By working together and helping each other, we can all achieve our goals.

S tore managers are on the firing line in retailing. Due to their daily contact with customers, they have the best knowledge of customer needs and competitive activity. From this unique vantage point, store managers play an important role in formulating and executing retail strategies. Buyers can develop exciting merchandise assortments and procure them at low cost, but the retailer only realizes the benefits of the buyers' efforts when the merchandise is sold. Good merchandise doesn't sell itself. Store managers must make sure that the merchandise is presented effectively and offer services that stimulate and facilitate customer buying decisions.[1]

Even in national chains, store managers are treated as relatively independent managers of a business within the corporation. Some store managers are responsible for $150 million in annual sales and manage more than 1,000 employees. For example, James Nordstrom, former CEO of Nordstrom, told his store managers, "This is your business. Do your own thing. Don't listen to us in Seattle, listen to your customers. We give you permission to take care of your customers."[2]

The first portion of this chapter, in focusing on the management of store employees, complements the strategic human resource management issues discussed in Chapter 9. Whereas Chapter 9 examined the organization of the tasks performed by retailers and the general approaches for motivating retail employees and building their commitment to the firm, this chapter discusses how store managers implement the retailer's human resource strategy.

STORE MANAGEMENT RESPONSIBILITIES

The responsibilities of store managers are shown in Exhibit 17–1. These functions are divided into four major categories: managing employees, controlling costs, managing merchandise presentation, and providing customer service. Issues concerning the management of store employees and controlling costs are discussed in this chapter. Subsequent chapters examine the store manager's responsibilities in presenting and managing merchandise and providing customer service.

Store managers are responsible for increasing the productivity of two of the retailer's most important assets: the firm's investments in its employees and its real estate. Most of this chapter is devoted to increasing labor productivity, namely, the sales generated by each store employee, by effectively managing them through recruiting and selecting good employees, training them to be more effective, and motivating them to perform at high levels. Even though most of this chapter focuses on managing store employees, Retailing View 17.1 describes how retailers also are using technology to increase store labor productivity.

In addition to increasing labor productivity, store managers also affect their stores' profits by controlling costs. The major costs are compensation and benefits for employees. But store managers also need to control maintenance costs and inventory loss due to shoplifting and employee theft. These cost-control issues are discussed at the end of the chapter.

Exhibit 17–2 outlines the steps in the employee management process that affect store employees' productivity: (1) recruiting and selecting effective people, (2) improving their skills through socialization and training, (3) motivating them to perform at higher levels, (4) evaluating them and finally (5) compensating and rewarding them.[4] Store managers also need to develop employees who can assume more responsibility and be promoted to higher-level management positions. By developing subordinates, managers help both their firms and themselves. The firm benefits from having more effective managers, and the manager benefits because the firm has a qualified replacement when the manager is promoted.

EXHIBIT 17–1

Responsibilities of Store Managers

MANAGING STORE EMPLOYEES (Chapter 17)
Recruiting and selecting
Socializing and training
Motivating
Evaluating and providing constructive feedback
Rewarding and compensating

CONTROLLING COSTS (Chapter 17)
Increasing labor productivity
Reducing maintenance and energy costs
Reducing inventory losses

MANAGING MERCHANDISE
Displaying merchandise and maintaining visual standards (Chapter 18)
Working with buyers
    Suggesting new merchandise
    Buying merchandise
    Planning and managing special events
    Marking down merchandise

PROVIDING CUSTOMER SERVICE (Chapter 19)

Steps in the Process of Managing Store Employees **EXHIBIT 17–2**

| 1. Recruit and select employees | 2. Socialize and train new employees | 3. Motivate and manage employees to achieve store performance goals | 4. Evaluate employee performance and provide feedback | 5. Compensate and reward employees |

RECRUITING AND SELECTING STORE EMPLOYEES

The first step in the employee management process is recruiting and selecting employees. To recruit employees effectively, store managers need to undertake a job analysis, prepare a job description, find potential applicants with the desired capabilities, and screen the best candidates to interview. (Appendix 1A to Chapter 1

Retail Stores Are Going High Tech **RETAILING VIEW** 17.1

Men's Wearhouse has POS terminals that enable sales associates to quickly respond to customer requests. If the store is out of stock of a particular sports jacket size, there's no need for the sales associate to call other stores—the Internet-enabled POS terminal provides instant access to the inventory at every one of the chain's 700 stores. If a customer needs directions to another store, the associate can immediately link to Mapquest on the Internet. The POS terminals also reduce the time sales associates need to spend on returns and exchanges; fingerprint scanners connected to the terminals provide immediate recognition of the customer and access to the customer's purchase history. With the old system, employees had to go through several screens and passwords to handle returns. The fingerprint scanners also help the chain cut down on inventory losses due to employee theft. Now an associate cannot use another person's ID number to make a fraudulent transaction.

Many supermarket retailers are installing self-checkout lanes. This technology offers benefits to both retailers and their customers. Ninety percent of the cost of maintaining a checkout line is the cashier. Thus, eliminating the cashier can reduce costs and/or enable the store to open more checkout lanes. To limit potential theft in the self-checkout lanes, retailers are using various techniques. Some of these deterrents are psychological, such as displaying customers on a video screen as they scan their merchandise. In addition, an electronic scale beneath the shopping bags knows what's just been scanned and how much it's supposed to weigh. So if a shopper scans a candy bar while slipping a rib roast in the shopping bag, the system beeps and asks that the item be entered again.

Airlines also are getting a high return on their investment by using kiosks for self-check-ins. A typical airline kiosk costs about $10,000, compared with a salary for a customer service agent of $20,000–$40,000, plus benefits. Self-check-in systems pay for their $80,000 price tags after about 15 months. Many travelers prefer self-check-in systems because they are quicker than waiting for an agent.

Retailers increase labor productivity when they install self-checkout systems.

Self-service kiosks never call in sick or go on vacations. Thus, the workforce schedule also is simplified for managers.

Sources: Doug Desjardins, "Shoppers Tapping into High Tech," *DSN Retailing Today,* January 10, 2005, pp. 16–17; Amy Harmon, "More Consumers Reach Out to Touch the Screen," *New York Times,* November 17, 2003, p. A7; Suzanne Smalley, "Next Frontiers," *Newsweek,* April 29, 2002, p. 40.

described the recruiting and selection process from the perspective of people interested in pursuing retail careers and applying for management trainee positions.)

Job Analysis

The **job analysis** identifies essential activities and is used to determine the qualifications of potential employees. For example, retail salespeople's responsibilities vary from company to company and department to department within a store. Apparel salespeople work on an open floor and need to approach customers. Jewelry salespeople work behind a counter, so their customers approach them. Due to these differences, effective open-floor selling requires more aggressive behavior than does counter selling.

Managers can obtain the information needed for a job analysis by observing employees presently doing the job and determining the characteristics of exceptional performers. Exhibit 17–3 lists some questions that managers should consider in a job analysis for sales associates. Information collected in the job analysis then is used to prepare a job description.

Job Description

A **job description** includes (1) activities the employee needs to perform and (2) the performance expectations expressed in quantitative terms. The job description is a guideline for recruiting, selecting, training, and, eventually, evaluating employees.

Locating Prospective Employees

Staffing stores is becoming a critical problem because changing demographics are reducing the size of the labor pool. Some novel approaches being used by retailers to recruit applicants are

- *Look beyond the retail industry.* For example, a jewelry store owner recruited a waitress from a deli she frequented because the server was unflappable. Another jeweler hired a dance instructor whose artistic eye and charisma made her a very effective jewelry salesperson.
- *Use your employees as talent scouts.* Ask employees if they know someone you could hire or if they have recently encountered a particularly good salesperson when purchasing any item.

EXHIBIT 17–3
Questions for Undertaking a Job Analysis

- How many salespeople will be working in the department at the same time?
- Do the salespeople have to work together in dealing with customers?
- How many customers will the salesperson have to work with at one time?
- Will the salesperson be selling on an open floor or working behind the counter?
- How much and what type of product knowledge does the salesperson need?
- Does the salesperson need to sell the merchandise or just ring up the orders and provide information?
- Is the salesperson required to make appointments with customers and develop a loyal customer base?
- Does the salesperson have the authority to negotiate price or terms of the sale?
- Does the salesperson need to demonstrate the merchandise?
- Will the salesperson be expected to make add-on sales?
- Is the salesperson's appearance important? How should an effective salesperson look?
- Will the salesperson be required to perform merchandising activities such as stocking shelves and setting up displays?
- Whom will the salesperson report to?
- What compensation plan will the salesperson be working under?

• *Provide incentives for employee referrals.* At the Container Store, one of *Fortune Magazine*'s five best places to work, recruiting is part of everybody's job. Employees get $500 for every full-time hire and $200 for every part-timer. All employees, from stockers to managers, carry recruiting cards to pull out when chatting with customers. The program is so successful that the company often goes six to eight months without placing a single classified ad.[5]

• *Recruit minorities, immigrants, and older workers.* Retailers that aggressively pursue the growing number of Hispanic immigrants print application forms in English and Spanish. Prospective employees can bring a family member or friend to act as an interpreter during the interview. Training programs are developed for people who aren't familiar with U.S. business practices. For example, many foreign-born workers don't understand benefits like life insurance and are reluctant to report job-related injuries for fear of being fired. Borders, Home Depot, and Walgreens are working with the American Association of Retired Persons (AARP) to form the Workforce Initiative, which matches seniors with job openings at the companies. Retailing often is attractive to seniors because its wide range of store hours fits seniors' need for flexible work schedules. In addition, retailers often will pay health care benefits to part-time workers, an important consideration for seniors. Exclusively targeting seniors or minorities would violate antidiscrimination laws, but retailers can advertise in publications that are typically read by seniors, and the AARP Web site lists companies interested in hiring seniors, with links to the employment areas of those Web sites.[6]

• *Use your storefront creatively.* Retailers are going beyond posting a "Help Wanted" sign. A more effective sign might read "Thank you! Business is great. Because things are so good, we're hiring additional staff. Please stop in to discuss career opportunities."

Ads can be an effective method of locating prospective employees.

Screening Applicants to Interview

The screening process matches applicants' qualifications with the job description. Many retailers use automated prescreening programs as a low-cost method to identify qualified candidates. Applicants either interact with a Web-enabled store kiosk or call a toll-free telephone number; the applicants then answer some basic questions using the keyboard or telephone buttons in response to a computer program.

The questions are tailored to the retailer's specific needs and environment. For example, Hot Topics, a mall-based chain selling music-themed merchandise, asks, "Would you work in an environment where loud, alternative music is played?" The response time for answering the questions is monitored, and follow-up questions are asked when the answers are unusually slow. When applicants pass this automated prescreening, additional information is collected using application forms, reference checks, and tests.[7]

Application Forms   **Job application forms** contain information about the applicant's employment history, previous compensation, reasons for leaving his or her previous employment, education and training, personal health, and references. This information enables the manager to determine whether the applicant has the minimum qualifications and also provides information useful when interviewing the applicant.[8]

References   A good way to verify the information given on an application form is to contact the applicant's references. Contacting references is also helpful for collecting additional information from people who've worked with the applicant. In addition, store managers should check with former supervisors not listed as

REFACT

Wal-Mart receives over 4 million applicants a year, and many of them are customers.[9]

references. Due to potential legal problems, however, many companies have a policy of not commenting on prior employees.[10]

Store managers generally expect to hear favorable comments from an applicant's references or previous supervisors, even if they may not have thought highly of the applicant. One approach for reducing this positive bias is to ask the reference to rank the applicant relative to others in the same position. For example, the manager might ask, "How would you rate Pat's customer service skill in relation to other retail sales associates you have worked with?" Another approach is to use a positively toned scale ranging from "somewhat effective" to "extremely effective."

Testing   Intelligence, ability, personality, and interest tests can provide insights about potential employees. For example, intelligence tests yield data about the applicant's innate abilities and can be used to match applicants with job openings and develop training programs. However, tests must be scientifically and legally valid. They can only be used when the scores have been shown to be related to job performance. It is illegal to use tests that assess factors that are not job related or that discriminate against specific groups.

Due to potential losses from theft, many retailers require applicants to take drug tests. Some retailers also use tests to assess applicants' honesty and ethics. Paper-and-pencil honesty tests include questions to find out if an applicant has ever thought about stealing and if he or she believes other people steal ("What percentage of people take more than $1 from their employer?").

Realistic Job Preview   Turnover is reduced when applicants understand both the attractive and unattractive aspects of the job.[14] For example, PETsMART, a pet supply category specialist, shows each applicant a 10-minute video that begins with the advantages of being a company employee and continues with scenes of employees dealing with irate customers and cleaning up animal droppings. This type of job preview typically screens out 15 percent of the applicants who would most likely quit within three months if they were hired.

Selecting Applicants

After screening applicants, the selection process typically involves a personal interview. Because the interview is usually the critical factor in the hiring decision, the store manager needs to be well prepared and have complete control over the interview.

Preparation for the Interview   The objective of the interview is to gather relevant information, not simply to ask a lot of questions. The most widely used interview technique, called the *behavioral interview*, asks candidates how they have handled actual situations they have encountered in the past, especially those situations requiring the skills outlined in the job description. For example, applicants applying for a job requiring them to handle customer complaints would be asked to describe a situation in which they were confronted by someone who was angry with something they had done. Candidates might be asked to describe the situation, what they did, and the outcomes of their actions. These situations also can be used to interview references for the applicants.[15]

An effective approach to interviewing involves some planning by the managers but also allows some flexibility in questions selections. Managers should develop objectives for what they want to learn about the candidate. Each topic area covered in the interview starts with a broad question, such as "Tell me about your last job," which is designed to elicit a lengthy response. The broad opening question is followed by a sequence of more specific questions, such as "What did you learn from that job?" or "How many subordinates did you have?" Finally, managers need to avoid asking questions that are discriminatory.

Interviewing Questions **EXHIBIT 17–4**

EDUCATION

What were your most and least favorite subjects in college? Why?

What types of extracurricular activities did you participate in? Why did you select those activities?

If you had the opportunity to attend school all over again, what, if anything, would you do differently, Why?

How did you spend the summers during college?

Did you have any part-time jobs? Which of your part-time jobs did you find most interesting? What did you find most difficult about working and attending college at the same time? What advice would you give to someone who wanted to work and attend college at the same time?

What accomplishments are you most proud of?

PREVIOUS EXPERIENCE

What's your description of the ideal manager? Subordinate? Coworker?

What did you like most/least about your last job?

What kind of people do you find it difficult/easy to work with? Why?

What has been your greatest accomplishment during your career to date?

Describe a situation at your last job involving pressure. How did you handle it?

What were some duties on your last job that you found difficult?

Of all the jobs you've had, which did you find the most/least rewarding?

What is the most frustrating situation you've encountered in your career?

Why do you want to leave your present job?

What would you do if . . . ?

How would you handle . . . ?

What would you like to avoid in future jobs?

What do you consider your greatest strength/weakness?

What are your responsibilities in your present job?

Tell me about the people you hired on your last job. How did they work out? What about the people you fired?

What risks did you take in your last job, and what were the results of those risks?

Where do you see yourself in three years?

What kind of references will your previous employer give?

What do you do when you have trouble solving a problem?

QUESTIONS THAT SHOULD NOT BE ASKED PER EQUAL EMPLOYMENT OPPORTUNITY GUIDELINES

Do you have plans for having children/a family?

What are your marriage plans?

What does your husband/wife do?

What happens if your husband/wife gets transferred or needs to relocate?

Who will take care of your children while you're at work?

(Asked of men) How would you feel about working for a woman?

How old are you?

What is your date of birth?

How would you feel working for a person younger than you?

Where were you born?

Where were your parents born?

Do you have any handicaps?

As a handicapped person, what help are you going to need to do your work?

How severe is your handicap?

What's your religion?

What church do you attend?

Do you hold religious beliefs that would prevent you from working on certain days of the week?

Do you feel that your race/color will be a problem in your performing the job?

Are you of _____ heritage/race?

Managing the Interview   Exhibit 17–4 shows some questions the manager might ask. Here are some suggestions for questioning the applicant during the interview:

- Encourage long responses by asking questions like "What do you know about our company?" rather than "How familiar are you with our company?"

- Avoid asking questions that have multiple parts.

- Avoid asking leading questions like "Are you prepared to provide good customer service?"

- Be an active listener. Evaluate the information being presented and sort out the important comments from the unimportant ones. Some techniques for active listening include repeating or rephrasing information, summarizing the conversation, and tolerating silences.

Legal Considerations in Selecting and Hiring Store Employees

Heightened social awareness and government regulations emphasize the need to avoid discriminating against hiring the handicapped, women, minorities, and older workers. Title VII of the Civil Rights Act prohibits discrimination on the basis of race, national origin, sex, or religion in company personnel practices. Discrimination is specifically prohibited in the following human resource decisions: recruitment, hiring, discharge, layoff, discipline, promotion, compensation, and access to training. In 1972, the act was expanded by the **Equal Employment Opportunity Commission (EEOC)** to allow employees to sue employers that violate the law. Several major retailers have been successfully sued because they discriminated in hiring and promoting minorities and women.

Discrimination arises when a member of a protected class (women, minorities, etc.) is treated differently from nonmembers of that class (**disparate treatment**) or when an apparently neutral rule has an unjustified discriminatory effect (**disparate impact**). An example of disparate treatment is if a qualified woman does not receive a promotion given to a less qualified man. Disparate impact occurs when a retailer requires high school graduation for all its employees, thereby excluding a larger proportion of disadvantaged minorities, when at least some of the jobs (e.g., custodian) could be performed just as well by people who did not graduate from high school. In such cases, the retailer is required to prove the imposed qualification is actually needed to be able to perform the job. The **Age Discrimination and Employment Act** also makes it illegal to discriminate in hiring and termination decisions concerning people over the age of 40 years.

Finally, the **Americans with Disabilities Act (ADA)** opens up job opportunities for the disabled by requiring employees to provide accommodating work environments. A **disability** is defined as any physical or mental impairment that substantially limits one or more of an individual's major life activities or any condition that is regarded as being such an impairment. Although merely being HIV positive does not limit any life activities, it may be perceived as doing so and is therefore protected as a disability. Similarly, extreme obesity may be either actually limiting or perceived as such and be protected as long as the obese person can perform the duties of the job.

SOCIALIZING AND TRAINING NEW STORE EMPLOYEES

After hiring employees, the next step in developing effective employees (as Exhibit 17–2 shows) is introducing them to the firm and its policies. Retailers want the people they hire to become involved, committed contributors to the firm's successful performance. Moreover, newly hired employees want to learn about their job responsibilities and the company they've decided to join.

Socialization is the set of steps taken to transform new employees into effective, committed members of the firm. Socialization goes beyond simply orienting new employees to the firm. A principal objective of socialization is to develop a long-term relationship with new employees to increase productivity and reduce turnover costs.[16]

Orientation Programs

Orientation programs are critical in overcoming entry shock and socializing new employees.[18] Even the most knowledgeable and mature new employees encounter some surprises. College students who accept management trainee positions often are quite surprised by the differences between their student and employee roles. Retailing View 17.2 describes some of these differences.

Orientation programs can last from a few hours to several weeks. The orientation and training program for new salespeople might be limited to several hours during which the new salesperson learns the retailer's policies and procedures and how to use the POS terminal. Alternatively, the orientation program for management trainees might take several weeks. For example, Macy's Florida hires approximately 150 college students each year into its management training program. New trainees typically report to work at corporate headquarters in Miami. They're housed in a hotel for a four-week orientation during which they attend classes, meet company executives, and work on projects. After completing the orientation program, they begin their initial assignment as a department manager in a store or an assistant buyer.

Disney overhauled its orientation program to emphasize emotion rather than company policies and procedures. The new program begins with current employees, referred to as cast members, discussing their earliest memories of Disney, their visions of great service, and their understanding of teamwork. Then trainers relate "magic moments" they have witnessed to emphasize that insignificant actions can have a big impact on a guest. For example, a four-year-old trips and falls, spilling his box of popcorn. The boy cries, the mother is concerned, and a costumed cast member, barely breaking stride, picks up the empty box, takes it to the popcorn stand for a refill, presents it to the child, and goes on his way.

The orientation program is just one element in the overall training program. It needs to be accompanied by a systematic follow-up to ensure that any problems and concerns arising after the initial period are considered.

Training Store Employees

Effective training for new store employees includes both structured and on-the-job learning experiences.

Structured Program During the structured program, new employees are taught the basic skills and knowledge they'll need to do their job. For example, salespeople learn what the company policies are, how to use the point-of-sale terminal, and how to perform basic selling skills; stockroom employees learn procedures for receiving merchandise. This initial training might include lectures, audiovisual presentations, manuals, and correspondence distributed to the new employees. In large firms, structured training may be done at a central location (such as the corporate headquarters or district office) under the human resources department's direction.

In this structured training program, newly hired Men's Wearhouse salespeople learn about merchandise they will be selling.

Transition from Student to Management Trainee   **RETAILING VIEW**   17.2

Many students have some difficulty adjusting to the demands of their first full-time job, because student life and professional life are very different. Students typically "report" to three or four supervisors (professors), but the student selects new "supervisors" every four months. In contrast, management trainees have limited involvement, if any, in selecting the one supervisor they'll report to, often for several years.

Student life has fixed time cycles—one- to two-hour classes with a well-defined beginning and end. Retail managers, however, are involved in a variety of activities with varied time horizons, ranging from a five-minute interaction with a customer to season-long development and implementation of a merchandise budget.

The decisions students encounter differ dramatically from the decisions retail managers encounter. For example, business students might make several major decisions a day when they discuss cases in class. These decisions are made and implemented in one class period, and then a new set of decisions is made and implemented in the next class. In a retail environment, strategic decisions evolve over a long time period. Most decisions, such as those regarding merchandise buying and pricing, are made with incomplete information. The buyers in real life often lack the extensive information provided in many business cases studied in class. Finally, there are long periods of time when retail managers undertake mundane tasks associated with implementing decisions and no major issues are being considered. Students typically don't have these mundane tasks to perform.

Source: Professor Daniel Feldman, University of Georgia.

The initial structured program should be relatively short so new employees don't feel like they are simply back in school. Effective training programs bring new recruits up to speed as quickly as possible and then get them involved in doing the job for which they've been hired.

On-the-Job Training The next training phase emphasizes on-the-job training. New employees are assigned a job, given responsibilities, and coached by their supervisors. The best way to learn is to practice what is being taught. New employees learn by engaging in activities, making mistakes, and then learning how not to make those mistakes again. Information learned through classroom lectures tends to be forgotten quickly unless it's used soon after the lecture.[19]

For example, students can learn about developing a merchandise budget plan by reading Chapter 13 of this text or listening to a lecture. But they typically don't acquire all the necessary information or remember the information from these sources. The actual hands-on experience of making a plan and getting feedback provides more complete and lasting knowledge. Retailers' use of the Internet for training is described in Retailing View 17.3.

Analyzing Successes and Failures Every new employee makes mistakes. Store managers should provide an atmosphere in which salespeople try out different approaches for providing customer service and selling merchandise. Store

---

17.3 RETAILING VIEW E-Training in Virtual Classrooms

Training store employees is costly and challenging for retailers due to the high turnover rate. Every month some employees leave, new ones are hired, and the training process needs to start all over again. To increase training effectiveness, many retailers are using the Internet to train their store employees on customer service and product knowledge.

Some of the benefits of e-training are greater consistency compared with on-the-job training by different supervisors, lower costs due to interactive self-training and reduced travel costs, and the ability to organize and launch major marketing and service programs nationwide and respond rapidly to market opportunities. In addition, e-training has contributed to strengthening vendor relationships. For example, many vendors provide briefings on new products to Circuit City so that store associates can learn about new product features and benefits.

The JCPenney e-training system has one-way video with two-way audio and data exchange capability, which allows instructors to chat online with students during training programs. Along with the presentations from the instructors, the training includes pre- and postclass testing to measure comprehension levels. Instructors also can break students into groups in which they

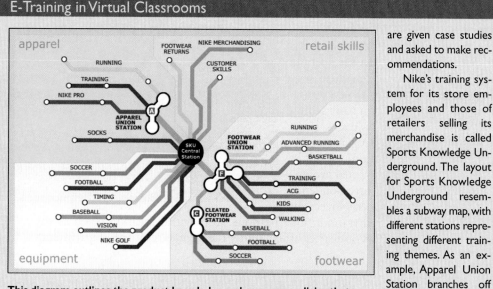

This diagram outlines the product knowledge and company policies that store employees can acquire using Nike's e-learning training solution, called **Sports Knowledge Underground.**

are given case studies and asked to make recommendations.

Nike's training system for its store employees and those of retailers selling its merchandise is called Sports Knowledge Underground. The layout for Sports Knowledge Underground resembles a subway map, with different stations representing different training themes. As an example, Apparel Union Station branches off into the apparel technologies line, the running products line, and the Nike Pro products line. The Cleated Footwear Station offers paths to football, whereas the Central Station offers such broad lines as customer skills. Each segment is three to seven minutes long and gives the associate the basic knowledge he or she needs about various products. As new products are introduced each season, the training is updated, and Nike customizes the program for each retailer if requested. When stores implement Sports Knowledge Underground, they see a 4–5 percent increase in sales.

Sources: Jessica Marquez, "Faced with High Turnover, Retailers Boot Up E-Learning Programs for Quick Training," *Workforce Management*, August 2005, pp. 74–75; Matthew Haeberle, "Virtual Classrooms," *Chain Store Age*, March 2003, pp. 68–69.

managers need to recognize that some of these new approaches are going to fail, and when they do, managers shouldn't criticize the individual salesperson. Instead, they should talk about the situation, analyze why the approach didn't work, and discuss how the salesperson could avoid the problem in the future. Similarly, managers should work with employees to help them understand and learn from their successes. For example, salespeople shouldn't consider a large, multiple-item sale to be simply due to luck. They should be encouraged to reflect on the sale, identify their key behaviors that facilitated the sale, and then remember these sales behaviors for future use.

It's important to help salespeople assign the right kinds of reasons for their performance. For example, some salespeople take credit for successes and blame the company, the buyers, or the merchandise for their failures. This tendency to avoid taking responsibility for failures doesn't encourage learning. When salespeople adopt this reasoning pattern, they aren't motivated to change their sales behavior because they don't take personal responsibility for losing a sale.

Managers can help salespeople constructively analyze their successes and failures by asking "why" questions that force them to analyze the reasons for effective and ineffective performance. To encourage learning, managers should get salespeople to recognize that they could have satisfied the customer if they had used a different approach or been more persistent. When salespeople accept such responsibility, they'll be motivated to search for ways to improve their sales skills.

MOTIVATING AND MANAGING STORE EMPLOYEES

After employees have received their initial training, managers need to work with them to help them meet their performance goals by being effective leaders and providing appropriate motivation (refer to Exhibit 17–2).

Leadership

Leadership is the process by which one person attempts to influence another to accomplish some goal or goals. Store managers are leaders of their group of employees. Managers use a variety of motivational techniques to increase productivity by helping employees achieve personal goals consistent with their firm's objectives.[20]

Leader Behaviors   Leaders engage in task performance and group maintenance behaviors. **Task performance behaviors** are the store manager's efforts at planning, organizing, motivating, evaluating, and coordinating store employees' activities. **Group maintenance behaviors** are activities store managers undertake to make sure that employees are satisfied and work well together. These activities include considering employees' needs, showing concern for their well-being, and creating a pleasant work environment.

Leader Decision Making   Store managers vary in how much they involve employees in making decisions. **Autocratic leaders** make all decisions on their own and then announce them to employees. They use the authority of their position to tell employees what to do. For example, an autocratic store manager determines who will work in each area of the store, when they'll take breaks, and what days they'll have off.

In contrast, a **democratic leader** seeks information and opinions from employees and bases his or her decisions on this information. Democratic store managers share their power and information with their employees. The democratic store manager asks employees where and when they want to work and makes schedules to accommodate those employee desires.

The manager of this Sandy Hill, Utah, Shopko store is a democratic leader who holds meetings to keep employees informed about company and store activities. He encourages them to make suggestions about improving store performance.

Leadership Styles   Store managers tend to develop a specific leadership style. They emphasize either task performance or group maintenance behaviors. They range from autocratic to democratic in their decision-making style.

After 80 years of research, psychologists have concluded there's no one best style. Effective managers use all styles, selecting the style most appropriate for each situation. For example, a store manager might be autocratic and relations oriented with an insecure new trainee but democratic and task oriented with an effective, experienced employee.

The previous discussion and most of this chapter describe specific behaviors, activities, and programs store managers use to influence their employees. But the greatest leaders and store managers go beyond influencing employee behaviors to change the beliefs, values, and needs of their employees. **Transformational leaders** get people to transcend their personal needs for the sake of the group or organization. They generate excitement and revitalize organizations.

Transformational store managers create this enthusiasm in their employees through their personal charisma. They are self-confident, have a clear vision that grabs employee attention, and communicate this vision through words and symbols. Finally, transformational leaders delegate challenging work to subordinates, have free and open communication with them, and provide personal mentoring to develop subordinates.[21]

Motivating Employees

Motivating employees to perform up to their potential may be store managers' most important but also frustrating task. The following hypothetical situation illustrates some issues pertaining to employee motivation and evaluation.

After getting an associate's degree at a local community college, Jim Taylor was hired for a sales position at a department store in San Jose's Eastridge Mall. The position offered firsthand knowledge of the firm's customers, managers, and policies. Taylor was told that if he did well in this assignment, he could become a management trainee.

His performance as a sales associate was average. After observing Taylor on the sales floor, his manager, Jennifer Chen, felt he was effective only when working with customers like himself: young, career-oriented men and women. To encourage Taylor to sell to other types of customers, Chen reduced his fixed salary and increased his commission rate. She also reviewed Taylor's performance goals with him.

Taylor now feels a lot of pressure to increase his sales level. He's beginning to dread coming to work in the morning and is thinking about getting out of retailing and working for a bank.

In this hypothetical situation, Chen focused on increasing Taylor's motivation by providing more incentive compensation. In discussing this illustration, we'll examine the appropriateness of this approach versus other approaches for improving Taylor's performance.

Setting Goals or Quotas

Employee performance improves when employees feel that (1) their efforts will enable them to achieve the goals set for them by their managers and (2) they'll receive rewards they value if they achieve their goals. Thus, managers can motivate employees by setting realistic goals and offering those rewards that employees want.[22]

For example, Jennifer Chen set specific selling goals for Jim Taylor when he started to work in her department. Taylor, like other store sales associates, has goals in five selling areas: sales per hour, average size of each sale, number of multiple-item (add-on) sales, number of preferred clients, and number of appointments made with preferred clients. (**Preferred clients** are customers whom salespeople communicate with regularly, send notes to about new merchandise and sales in the department, and make appointments with for special presentations of merchandise—the upper-tier customer discussed in Chapter 11.) In addition to selling goals, salespeople are evaluated on the overall department shrinkage due to stolen merchandise, the errors they make in using the POS terminal, and their contribution to maintaining the department's appearance.

Chen also designed a program for Taylor's development as a sales associate. The activities she outlined over the next six months required Taylor to attend classes to improve his selling skills. Chen needs to be careful in setting goals for Taylor though. If she sets the goals too high, he might become discouraged, feel the goals are unattainable, and, thus, not be motivated to work harder. However, if she sets the goals too low, Taylor can achieve them easily and won't be motivated to work to his full potential.

Rather than setting specific goals for each salesperson, this retailer uses the average performance for all salespeople as its goal. However, goals are most effective at motivating employees when they're based on the employee's experience and confidence. Experienced salespeople have confidence in their abilities and should have "stretch" goals (high goals that will make them work hard). New salespeople need lower goals that they have a good chance of achieving. The initial good experience of achieving and surpassing goals builds new salespeople's confidence and motivates them to improve their skills.[23] The use of rewards to motivate employees is discussed later in this chapter.

Maintaining Morale

Store morale is important in motivating employees. Typically, morale goes up when things are going well and employees are highly motivated. But when sales aren't going well, morale tends to decrease and employee motivation declines. Some approaches used to build morale are

• Storewide or department meetings prior to the store opening, during which managers pass along information about new merchandise and programs and solicit opinions and suggestions from employees.

• Educating employees about the firm's finances, setting achievable goals, and throwing a pizza party when the goals are met.

• Dividing the charity budget by the number of employees and inviting employees to suggest how their "share" should be used.

• Stickers that tell customers that this sandwich was "wrapped by Roger" or this dress was "dry cleaned by Sarah."

• Giving every employee a business card with the company mission printed on its back.

This Sears manager builds morale and motivates her sales associates by holding "ready meetings" before the store opens. At this meeting, the manager is discussing approaches for improving customer service.

For example, one store manager used real-time sales data collected in her firm's information system (see Chapter 10) to build excitement among her employees. On the first day of the Christmas season, she wrote $3,159 on a blackboard in the store. That was the store's sales during the first day of the Christmas season last year. She told her sales associates that beating that number was not enough; she wanted to see a 36 percent increase, the same sales increase the store achieved over the prior Christmas season.

By setting financial objectives and keeping sales associates informed of up-to-the-minute results, an eight-hour shift of clock watchers gets converted into an excited team of racers. All day, as customers come and go, sales associates take turns consulting the backroom computer that records sales from the store's POS terminals.

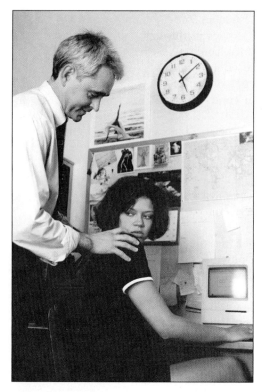

Store managers and coworkers must avoid behaviors that employees might interpret as sexual harassment.

Sexual Harassment

Sexual harassment is an important issue in terms of the productivity of the work environment. Managers must avoid and make sure that store employees avoid any actions that are, or can be interpreted as, sexual harassment. Otherwise, the retailer and the manager may be held liable for the harassment. The EEOC guidelines define **sexual harassment** as a form of gender discrimination, as follows:

> Unwelcome sexual advances, requests for sexual favors, and other verbal or physical conduct of a sexual nature constitutes sexual harassment when . . . submission to or rejection of such conduct by an individual is used as a basis for employment decisions affecting such individual, or . . . such conduct has the purpose or effect of unreasonably interfering with an individual's work performance or creating an intimidating, hostile, or offensive working environment.

An appropriate procedure for dealing with a sexual harassment allegation is outlined below:

Step 1: Establish and post an anti–sexual harassment policy, including a complaint procedure outside the normal supervisory channels. Supervisors are often accused of sexual harassment.

Step 2: If a complaint is made, always treat it seriously.

Step 3: Get information from the alleged victim. Ask questions like

- Tell me what happened. Who was involved?
- What did the harasser do and say?
- When did this happen? If this wasn't the first time, when has it happened before?
- Where did it happen?
- Were there any witnesses?
- Have you told anyone else about this or these instances?
- Has anyone else been the object of harassment?
- How did you react to the harasser's behavior?
- Would you care to speak with someone else: another member of management, the personnel department, or the company employment assistance plan person?

Step 4: Document the meeting with the alleged victim.

Step 5: Inform the human resource department or the next higher level of company management of the complaint and of the meeting with the alleged victim.[24]

EVALUATING STORE EMPLOYEES AND PROVIDING FEEDBACK

The fourth step in the management process (Exhibit 17–2) is evaluating and providing feedback to employees. The objective of the evaluation process is to identify those employees who are performing well and those who aren't. On the basis of the evaluation, high-performing employees should be rewarded and considered for positions of greater responsibility. Plans need to be developed to increase the productivity of those employees performing below expectations. Should poor performers be terminated? Do they need additional training? What kind of training do they need?

Who Should Do the Evaluation?

In large retail firms, the evaluation system is usually designed by the human resources department. But the evaluation itself should be done by the employee's immediate supervisor—the manager who works most closely with the employee. For example, in a discount store, the department manager is in the best position to observe a salesperson in action and understand the reasons for the salesperson's performance. The department manager also oversees the recommendations that come out of the evaluation process. Inexperienced supervisors are often assisted by a senior manager in evaluating employees.

How Often Should Evaluations Be Made?

Most retailers evaluate employees annually or semiannually. Feedback from evaluations is the most effective method for improving employee skills. Thus, evaluations should be done more frequently when managers are developing inexperienced employees' skills. However, frequent formal evaluations are time consuming for managers and may not give employees enough time to respond to suggestions before the next evaluation. Managers should supplement these formal evaluations with frequent informal ones. For example, Jennifer Chen should work with Jim Taylor informally and not wait for the formal six-month evaluation. The best time for Chen to provide this informal feedback is immediately after she has obtained, through observations or reports, positive or negative information about Taylor's performance.

Format for Evaluations

Evaluations are only meaningful if employees know what they're required to do, the expected level of performance, and how they'll be evaluated. Exhibit 17–5 shows a specialty retailer's criteria for evaluating sales associates.

Factors Used to Evaluate Sales Associates at a Specialty Store   **EXHIBIT 17–5**

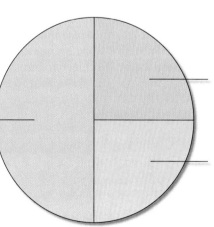

50%
SALES/CUSTOMER RELATIONS

1. Greeting. Approaches customers within 1 to 2 minutes with a smile and friendly manner. Uses open-ended questions.

2. Product knowledge. Demonstrates knowledge of product, fit, shrinkage, and price and can relay this information to the customer.

3. Suggests additional merchandise. Approaches customers at fitting room and cash/wrap areas.

4. Asks customers to buy and reinforces decisions. Lets customers know they've made a wise choice and thanks them.

25%
OPERATIONS

1. Store appearance. Demonstrates an eye for detail (color and finesse) in the areas of display, coordination of merchandise on tables, floor fixtures, and wall faceouts. Takes initiative in maintaining store presentation standards.

2. Loss prevention. Actively follows all loss prevention procedures.

3. Merchandise control and handling. Consistently achieves established requirements in price change activity, shipment processing, and inventory control.

4. Cash/wrap procedures. Accurately and efficiently follows all register policies and cash/wrap procedures.

25%
COMPLIANCE

1. Dress code and appearance. Complies with dress code. Appears neat and well groomed. Projects current fashionable store image.

2. Flexibility. Able to switch from one assignment to another, open to schedule adjustments. Shows initiative, awareness of store priorities and needs.

3. Working relations. Cooperates with other employees, willingly accepts direction and guidance from management. Communicates to management.

In this case, the employee's overall evaluation is based on subjective evaluations made by the store manager and assistant managers. It places equal weight on individual sales/customer relations activities and activities associated with overall store performance. By emphasizing overall store operations and performance, the assessment criteria motivate sales associates to work together as a team.

The criteria used at the department store to evaluate Jim Taylor are objective sales measures based on point-of-sale data, not subjective measures like those used by the specialty store. Exhibit 17–6 summarizes Taylor's formal six-month evaluation. The evaluation form lists results for various factors in terms of both what's considered average performance for company salespeople and Taylor's actual performance. His department has done better than average on shrinkage control, and he has done well on system errors and merchandise presentation. However, his sales performance is below average, even though he made more than the average number of presentations to preferred customers. These results suggest that Taylor's effort is good but his selling skills may need improvement.

Evaluation Errors

Managers can make evaluation errors by first forming an overall opinion of the employee's performance and then allowing this opinion to influence their ratings of each performance factor (haloing). For example, a store manager might feel a salesperson's overall performance is below average and then rate the salesperson below average on selling skills, punctuality, appearance, and stocking. When an overall evaluation casts such a halo on multiple aspects of a salesperson's performance, the evaluation is no longer useful for identifying specific areas that need improvement.

In making evaluations, managers are often unduly influenced by recent events (recency) and their evaluations of other salespeople (contrast). For example, a manager might remember a salesperson's poor performance with a customer the day before and forget the salesperson's outstanding performance over the past three months. Similarly, a manager might be unduly harsh in evaluating an average salesperson just after completing an evaluation of an outstanding salesperson. Finally, managers have a natural tendency to attribute performance (particularly poor performance) to the salesperson and not to the environment in which the salesperson is working. When making evaluations, managers tend to underemphasize effects of external factors such as merchandise on the department and competitors' actions.

The department store's evaluation of sales associates (Exhibit 17–6) avoids many of these potential biases because most of its ratings are based on objective data. In contrast, the specialty store evaluation (Exhibit 17–5) considers a wider range of activities but uses more subjective measures of performance. Because subjective information about specific skills, attitudes about the store and customers,

EXHIBIT 17–6
Summary of Jim Taylor's Six-Month Evaluation

	Average Performance for Sales Associates in Department	Actual Performance for Jim Taylor
Sales per hour	$75	$65
Average amount per transaction	$45	$35
Percentage multiple transactions	55%	55%
Number of preferred customers	115	125
Number of preferred customer appointments	95	120
Departmental shrinkage	2.00%	1.80%
Systems errors	10	2
Merchandise presentation (10-point scale)	5	8

interactions with coworkers, enthusiasm, and appearance aren't used in the department store's evaluation, performance on these factors might not have been explicitly communicated to Jim Taylor. The subjective characteristics in the specialty store evaluation are more prone to bias, but they also might be more helpful to salespeople as they try to improve their performance. To avoid bias when making subjective ratings, managers need to observe performance regularly, record their observations, avoid evaluating many salespeople at one time, and remain conscious of the various potential biases.

COMPENSATING AND REWARDING STORE EMPLOYEES

The fifth and final step in improving employee productivity in Exhibit 17–2 is compensating and rewarding employees. Store employees receive two types of rewards from their work: extrinsic and intrinsic. **Extrinsic rewards** are rewards provided by either the employee's manager or the firm, such as compensation, promotion, and recognition. **Intrinsic rewards** are rewards employees get personally from doing their job well. For example, salespeople often like to sell because they think it's challenging and fun. Of course, they want to be paid, but they also find it rewarding to help customers and make sales.[26]

Extrinsic Rewards

Managers can offer a variety of extrinsic rewards to motivate employees. However, store employees don't all seek the same rewards. For example, some salespeople want more compensation; others strive for a promotion in the company or public recognition of their performance. Jim Taylor wants a favorable evaluation from his manager so he can enter the management training program. Part-time salespeople often take a sales job to get out of the house and meet people. Their primary work objective isn't to make money.

Because of these different needs, managers may not be able to use the same rewards to motivate all employees. Large retailers, however, find it hard to develop unique reward programs for each individual. One response is to offer **à la carte plans** that give effective employees a choice of rewards for their good performance. For example, salespeople who achieve their goals could choose a cash bonus, extra days off, or a better discount on merchandise sold in the store. This type of compensation plan enables employees to select the rewards they want. Recognition is another important nonmonetary extrinsic reward for many employees. Although telling employees they've done a job well is appreciated, it's typically more rewarding for them when good performance is recognized publicly. In addition, public recognition can motivate all store employees, not just the star performers, because it demonstrates management's interest in rewarding employees.

Most managers focus on extrinsic rewards to motivate employees. For example, a store manager might provide additional compensation if a salesperson achieves a sales goal. However, an emphasis on extrinsic rewards can make employees lose sight of their job's intrinsic rewards. Employees can begin to feel that their only reason for working is to earn money and that the job isn't fun.

Public recognition programs make employees feel they are appreciated and motivate them to improve their performance. Marshalls stores that deliver exceptional customer service are recognized by the "All-Star Award," which includes a plaque to hang in the store.

Intrinsic Rewards

Note that Jennifer Chen tried to motivate Jim Taylor by using extrinsic rewards when she linked his compensation to how much he sold. This increased emphasis on financial rewards may be one reason Taylor now dreads coming to work in the morning. He might not think his job is fun anymore.

When employees find their jobs intrinsically rewarding, they're motivated to learn how to do them better. They act like a person playing a video game: The game itself is so interesting that the player gets rewards from just trying to master it. Charlene Rogers, manager of a Hot Topic store in Brea, California, described how the involvement of her employees is intrinsically rewarding: "Hot Topic buyers rely on my associates for input on trends that change quickly. The company encourages all of us to call the buyers after we come back from a club or a concert to fill them in on what people are wearing. Store associates feel appreciated. They crave responsibility."[27]

Another approach to making work fun is to hold contests with relatively small prizes. Contests are most effective when everyone has a chance to win. Contests in which the best salespeople always win aren't exciting and may even be demoralizing.

For example, consider a contest in which a playing card is given to salespeople for each men's suit they sell during a two-week period. At the end of two weeks, the best poker hand wins. This contest motivates all salespeople during the entire period of the contest. A salesperson who sells only four suits can win with four aces. Contests should be used to create excitement and make selling challenging for everyone, not to pay the best salespeople more money. Experienced employees often lose interest in their jobs because they no longer find them exciting or challenging. Extrinsic rewards, such as pay or promotion, might not be so attractive to them. They might be satisfied with their present income and job responsibilities.

More experienced employees can be motivated by intrinsic rewards presented as job enrichment. **Job enrichment** is the redesign of a job to include a greater range of tasks and responsibilities. For example, an experienced sales associate who has lost some interest in his or her job could be given responsibility for merchandising a particular area, training new salespeople, or planning and managing a special event.

Compensation Programs

The objectives of a compensation program are to attract and keep good employees, motivate them to undertake activities consistent with the retailer's objectives, and reward them for their effort. In developing a compensation program, the store manager must strike a balance between controlling labor costs and providing enough compensation to keep high-quality employees.

A compensation plan is most effective for motivating and retaining employees when the employees feel the plan is fair and that their compensation is related to their efforts. In general, simple plans are preferred to complex plans. Simple plans are easier to administer and employees have no trouble understanding them.

Types of Compensation Plans   Retail firms typically use one or more of the following compensation plans: straight salary, straight commission, salary plus commission, and quota–bonus.

With **straight salary compensation,** salespeople or managers receive a fixed amount of compensation for each hour or week they work. For example, a salesperson might be paid $8 per hour or a department manager $800 per week. This plan is easy for the employee to understand and for the store to administer. Under a straight salary plan, the retailer has flexibility in assigning salespeople to different activities and sales areas. For example, salaried salespeople will undertake nonselling activities, such as stocking shelves, and won't be upset if they're transferred from a high sales-volume department to a low sales-volume department.

The major disadvantage of the straight salary plan is employees' lack of immediate incentives to improve their productivity. They know their compensation won't change in the short run, whether they work hard or slack off. Another disadvantage for the retailer is that straight salary becomes a fixed cost the firm incurs even if sales decline.

Incentive compensation plans reward employees on the basis of their productivity. Many retailers now use incentives to motivate greater sales productivity by their employees. With some incentive plans, a salesperson's income is based entirely on commission—called a **straight commission.** For example, a salesperson might be paid a commission based on a percentage of sales made minus the merchandise returned. Normally, the percentage is the same for all merchandise sold (such as 7 percent). But some retailers use different percentages for different categories of merchandise (such as 4 percent for low-margin items and 10 percent for high-margin items). Different percentages provide additional incentives for salespeople to sell specific items. Typically, the compensation of salespeople selling high-priced items such as men's suits, appliances, and consumer electronics is based largely on their commissions.

Incentive plans also may include a fixed salary plus a commission on total sales or a commission on sales over quota. For example, a salesperson might receive a salary of $200 per week plus a commission of 2 percent on all sales over a quota of $50 per hour.

Incentive compensation plans are a powerful motivator for salespeople to sell merchandise, but they have a number of disadvantages. For example, it's hard to get salespeople who are compensated totally by commission to perform nonselling activities. Understandably, they're reluctant to spend time stocking shelves when they could be making money by selling. Also, salespeople will concentrate on the more expensive, fast-moving merchandise and neglect other merchandise. Sales incentives can also discourage salespeople from providing services to customers. Finally, salespeople compensated primarily by incentives don't develop loyalty to their employer. The employer doesn't guarantee them an income, so they feel no obligation to the firm. Retailing View 17.4 illustrates the adverse effects of basing too much of a store manager's incentives on controlling costs.

Under a straight commission plan, salespeople's incomes can fluctuate from week to week, depending on their sales. Because retail sales are seasonal, salespeople might earn most of their income during the Christmas season but much less during the summer months. To provide a more steady income for salespeople who are paid by high-incentive plans, some retailers offer a **drawing account.** With a drawing account, salespeople receive a weekly check based on their estimated annual income, and commissions earned are credited against the weekly payments. Periodically, the weekly draw is compared with the commission earned. If the draw exceeds the earned commissions, the salespeople return the excess money they've been paid, and their weekly draw is reduced. If the commissions earned exceed the draw, salespeople are paid the difference.

Quotas are often used with compensation plans. A **quota** is a target level used to motivate and evaluate performance. Examples might include sales per hour for salespeople or maintained margin and inventory turnover for buyers. For department store salespeople, selling quotas vary across departments due to differences in sales productivity levels.

A **quota–bonus plan** provides sales associates with a bonus when their performance exceeds their quota. A quota–bonus plan's effectiveness depends on setting reasonable, fair quotas, which can be hard. Usually, quotas are set at the same level for everyone in a department, but salespeople in the same department may have different abilities or face different selling environments. For example, in the men's department, salespeople in the suit area have much greater sales potential than salespeople in the accessories area. Newly hired salespeople might have a harder time achieving a quota than more experienced salespeople. Thus, a quota based on average productivity may be too high to motivate the new salesperson and too low to effectively motivate the experienced salesperson. Quotas should be developed for each salesperson on the basis of his or her experience and the nature of the store area in which he or she works.[28]

Group Incentives   To encourage employees in a department or store to work together, some retailers provide additional incentives based on the performance of the department or store as a whole. For example, salespeople might be paid a commission based on their individual sales and then receive additional compensation according to the amount of sales over plan, or quota, generated by all salespeople in the store. The group incentive encourages salespeople to work together in their nonselling activities and handling customers so the department sales target will be achieved.[29]

Designing the Compensation Program

A compensation program's two elements are the amount of compensation and the percentage of compensation based on incentives. Typically, market conditions determine the amount of compensation. When economic conditions are good and labor is scarce, retailers pay higher wages. Retailers that hire inexperienced salespeople pay lower wages than those that recruit experienced salespeople with good skills and abilities.

Incentive compensation is most effective when a salesperson's performance can be measured easily and precisely. It's difficult to measure individual performance when salespeople work in teams or must perform a lot of nonselling activities. Retailers can easily measure a salesperson's actual sales, but it's hard to measure their customer service or merchandising performance.

When the salesperson's activities have a great impact on sales, incentives can provide additional motivation. For example, salespeople who are simply cashiers have little effect on sales and thus shouldn't be compensated with incentives. However, incentives are appropriate for salespeople who provide a lot of information and assistance about complex products such as designer dresses or stereo systems.

17.4   RETAILING VIEW   Wal-Mart's Incentive for Store Managers Causes Problems

After finishing her 10:00 p.m. to 8:00 a.m. shift, Verette Richardson clocked out and was heading to her car when a Wal-Mart manager ordered her to turn around and straighten up the store's apparel department. She spent the next hour working unpaid, tidying racks of slacks and blouses and picking up hangers and clothes that had fallen to the floor. Other times after clocking out, she was ordered to round up shopping carts in the parking lot or rush to a cash register and start ringing up purchases without clocking in. Sometimes, she said, she worked for three hours before clocking in. She and 40 other current and former Wal-Mart workers interviewed say Wal-Mart forced or pressured its employees to work hours that were not recorded or paid.

Federal and state laws bar employers from making hourly employees work unpaid hours. Many current and former workers and managers said an intense focus on cost cutting had created an unofficial policy that encouraged managers to request or require off-the-clock work and avoid paying overtime. These practices have helped Wal-Mart control its costs, offer lower prices, and become the world's largest retailer.

In response, a Wal-Mart spokesperson said, "Off-the-clock work is an infrequent and isolated problem that is corrected whenever we become aware of it. It is Wal-Mart's policy to pay its employees properly for the hours they work." Managers who required or requested off-the-clock work were subject to disciplinary action, including dismissal.

Although company policy prohibits off-the-clock work, Wal-Mart has created a system of rewards that gives managers strong incentives to squeeze down labor costs by pegging their annual bonuses to the profits of individual stores. Many store managers have a base salary of $52,000, with bonuses often running $70,000–$150,000.

In response to the negative publicity associated with lawsuits alleging unfair labor practices, Wal-Mart has launched a communication program emphasizing its job creation and employee benefits. The campaign stresses that most of Wal-Mart's employees have benefits, and the average store employee earns twice the minimum wage. The advertising features predominantly Wal-Mart employees talking about the quality and positive aspects of their work life.

Sources: Katherine Bowers, "Wal-Mart Takes the Offensive," *WWD*, April 6, 2005, p. 2; Steven Greenhouse, "Suits Say Wal-Mart Forces Workers to Toil Off the Clock," *New York Times*, June 25, 2002, p. B16.

Incentives are less effective with inexperienced salespeople, who are less confident in their skills, because they inhibit learning and thereby can cause excessive stress.

Finally, compensation plans in which too much of the incentive is based on sales may not promote good customer service. Salespeople on commission become interested in selling anything they can to customers, but they aren't willing to spend time helping customers buy the merchandise they need. They tend to stay close to the cash register or the dressing room exits so they can ring up a sale for a customer who's ready to buy.

Setting the Commission Percentage   Assume that a specialty store manager wants to hire experienced salespeople. To get the type of person she wants, she feels she must pay $12 per hour, and her selling costs are budgeted at 8 percent of sales. With compensation of $12 per hour, salespeople need to sell $150 worth of merchandise per hour ($12 divided by 8 percent) for the store to keep within its sales cost budget. The manager believes the best compensation would be one-third salary and two-thirds commission, so she decides to offer a compensation plan of $4 per hour salary (33 percent of $12) and a 5.33 percent commission on sales. If salespeople sell $150 worth of merchandise per hour, they'll earn $12 per hour ($4 per hour in salary plus $150 multiplied by 5.33 percent, which equals $8 per hour in commission).

Legal Issues in Compensation

The **Fair Labor Standards Act** of 1938 set minimum wages, maximum hours, child labor standards, and overtime pay provisions. Enforcement of this law is particularly important to retailers because they hire many low-wage employees and teenagers and ask their employees to work long hours.

The **Equal Pay Act,** now enforced by the EEOC, prohibits unequal pay for men and women who perform equal work or work of comparable worth. Equal work means that the jobs require the same skills, effort, and responsibility and are performed in the same working environment. Comparable worth implies that men and women who perform different jobs of equal worth should be compensated the same. Differences in compensation are legal when compensation is determined by a seniority system, an incentive compensation plan, or market demand.

CONTROLLING COSTS

Labor scheduling and store maintenance offer two opportunities for reducing store operating expenses. Retailing View 17.5 describes how a convenience store chain reengineered its operations to reduce costs and increase customer service.

Labor Scheduling

Using store employees efficiently is an important and challenging problem. While store employees provide important customer service and merchandising functions that can increase sales, they also are the store's largest operating expense. **Labor scheduling** (determining the number of employees assigned to each area of the store) is difficult because of the multiple shifts and part-time workers needed to staff stores 12 hours a day, seven days a week. In addition, customer traffic varies greatly during the day and the week. Bad weather, holidays, and sales can dramatically alter normal shopping patterns and staffing needs.

Managers can spot obvious inefficiencies like long checkout lines and sales associates with nothing to do. But some inefficiencies are more subtle. For example, if 6 percent of a store's sales volume and 9 percent of the total labor hours occur between 2:00 and 3:00 p.m., the store might be overstaffed during this time period. Many stores use specially designed computer software to deal with the

REFACT

In France, the average number of hours worked annually is 1,568, compared with 1,976 in the United States. French workers have 253 paid hours off, compared with 160 hours for U.S. workers.[30]

complexities of labor scheduling. Labor schedulers can reduce store payroll costs between 2 and 5 percent without affecting store sales.[31]

Efficient labor scheduling requires more than POS sales data by day and time of day though. The manager also needs to know the traffic patterns and the impact of store employees on sales. For example, one store manager saw a downturn in sales during the hour before the store closed and considered reducing the level of staffing. However, when traffic counters were installed, the manager discovered that the number of customers in the store did not decline during the last open hour. The manager then realized that employees were forsaking customer service and spending time preparing to close the store. Rather than reducing the staff, the manager extended the work hours so sales associates would realize the sales potential during the last hour.

Labor scheduling is even more difficult in some European countries. For example, in France, a store manager works only 35 hours a week, rarely works at night or on weekends, and has six weeks of annual paid vacation. A store manager in the United States with similar responsibilities works 44 hours a week, including evening and weekend shifts; frequently brings work home at night; and spends some off-time shopping the competitors. Workers in France are guaranteed five weeks paid vacation by law. Most stores other than discount stores are closed during lunch and after 7:00 p.m. Few stores are open on Sunday. Store hours are even more restricted in Germany and Italy.

17.5 RETAILING VIEW Increasing Operating Efficiency

Sheetz, a convenience store chain with 310 stores based in Altoona, Pennsylvania, started a series of detailed studies to determine how store-level tasks could be performed more efficiently. It looked at everything from how the store managers closed out the day to how the staff emptied the trash. Two years after the company implemented the recommendations from the study, it had saved $5.1 million in payroll costs alone.

Sheetz, a Pennsylvania-based convenience store chain, reengineered its operations to reduce costs and increase customer service.

Sheetz found that store managers were taking three to four hours to close out their sales day. Each day, they had to fill out 40 computer screens of information and would spend an hour looking for a $5 error. Furthermore, the time spent on closing was affecting customer service. Managers would do the paperwork during the morning of the following day, the busiest traffic time, when they should have been out in the stores managing. When Sheetz reexamined these practices, it eliminated over 160,000 hours annually of time the store managers were spending on nonproductive administrative tasks.

Sheetz also found that a lot of the information being sent to store managers was of questionable value. There were too

many redundant reports. Thus, the 204 reports that had been available on the store managers' computers were reduced to 23.

Sheetz saved 55 employee hours per week per store by reexamining its labor scheduling. Prior to the study, staffing for stores was based on sales. However, this approach did not consider that some stores generate a lot of sales from labor-intensive activities such as food service, while others derive sales from labor-free pay-at-the-pump transactions (called *outside sales* by convenience store operators). Some tasks performed in the store were eliminated, and the company stopped tracking newspapers at the SKU level. On some newspapers, Sheetz only makes a two-cent margin. If store employees spend time receiving and tracking them by SKU, the firm loses money on each paper it sells.

Sources: Rick Romel, "Convenience Stores with a Little Extra," *Knight Ridder Tribune Business,* May 9, 2005, p. 1; "Stan Sheetz," *Chain Store Age,* February 2005, pp. 26–27; "Sheetz: Customer-Friendly, Technologically Superior," *Beverage Aisle,* March 15, 2002, p. 38.

Store Maintenance

Store maintenance entails the activities involved with managing the exterior and interior physical facilities associated with the store. The exterior facilities include the parking lot, entrances to the store, and signs on the outside of the store. The interior facilities include the walls, flooring, ceiling, and displays and signs. Store maintenance affects both the sales generated in the store and the cost of running the store. A store's cleanliness and neatness affect consumer perceptions of the quality of its merchandise, but maintenance is costly. For instance, floor maintenance for a 40,000 square foot home center runs about $10,000 a year. Poor maintenance shortens the useful life of air conditioning units, floors, and fixtures.

REDUCING INVENTORY SHRINKAGE

An important issue facing store management is reducing inventory losses due to employee theft, shoplifting, mistakes, inaccurate records, and vendor errors. Examples of employee mistakes are failing to ring up an item when it's sold and miscounting merchandise when it's received or during physical inventories. Inventory shrinkage due to vendor mistakes arises when vendor shipments contain less than the amount indicated on the packing slip.

Although shoplifting receives the most publicity, employee theft accounts for more inventory loss. A recent survey attributes 47 percent of inventory shrinkage to employee theft, 34 percent to shoplifting, 14 percent to mistakes and inaccurate records, and 5 percent to vendor errors.[32]

In developing a loss prevention program, retailers confront a trade-off between providing shopping convenience and a pleasant work environment on the one hand and, on the other hand, preventing losses due to shoplifting and employee theft. The key to an effective loss prevention program is determining the most effective way to protect merchandise while preserving an open, attractive store atmosphere and a feeling among employees that they are trusted. Loss prevention requires coordination among store management, visual merchandising, and store design.

Calculating Shrinkage

Shrinkage is the difference between the recorded value of inventory (at retail prices) based on merchandise bought and received and the value of the actual inventory (at retail prices) in stores and distribution centers divided by retail sales during the period. For example, if accounting records indicate inventory should be $1,500,000, the actual count of the inventory reveals $1,236,000, and sales were $4,225,000, the shrinkage is 6.7 percent [($1,500,000 − $1,236,000) ÷ $4,225,000]. Reducing shrinkage is an important store management issue. Retailers' annual loss from shrinkage is between 1 and 5 percent of sales. Every dollar of inventory shrinkage translates into a dollar of lost profit.

REFACT

Retailers lose more than $31 billion annually due to shrinkage.[33]

Detecting and Preventing Shoplifting

Losses due to shoplifting can be reduced by store design, employee training, and special security measures.

Store Design   Security issues need to be considered when placing merchandise near store entrances, delivery areas, and dressing rooms. For example, easily stolen merchandise such as jewelry and other small, expensive items should never be displayed near an entrance. By reducing the height of fixtures and maintaining open sight lines to entrances and exits, store employees can see customers in the store

EXHIBIT 17–7
Spotting Shoplifters

DON'T ASSUME THAT ALL SHOPLIFTERS ARE POORLY DRESSED
To avoid detection, professional shoplifters dress in the same manner as customers patronizing the store. Over 90 percent of all amateur shoplifters arrested have the cash, checks, or credit to purchase the merchandise they stole.

SPOT LOITERERS
Amateur shoplifters frequently loiter in areas as they build up the nerve to steal something. Professionals also spend time waiting for the right opportunity but less conspicuously than amateurs.

LOOK FOR GROUPS
Teenagers planning to shoplift often travel in groups. Some members of the group divert employees' attention while others take the merchandise. Professional shoplifters often work in pairs. One person takes the merchandise and passes it to a partner in the store's restroom, phone booths, or restaurant.

LOOK FOR PEOPLE WITH LOOSE CLOTHING
Shoplifters frequently hide stolen merchandise under loose-fitting clothing or in large shopping bags. People wearing a winter coat in the summer or a raincoat on a sunny day may be potential shoplifters.

WATCH THE EYES, HANDS, AND BODY
Professional shoplifters avoid looking at merchandise and concentrate on searching for store employees who might observe their activities. Shoplifters' movements might be unusual as they try to conceal merchandise.

and watch for shoplifters while providing better service. Dressing room entrances should be visible to store employees so they can easily observe customers entering and exiting with merchandise. Because cash wraps are always staffed, they should be near areas that theft is likely to occur. (**Cash wraps** are the places in a store where customers can buy their purchases and have them "wrapped"—placed in a bag.)[34]

Employee Training   Store employees can be the retailer's most effective tools against shoplifting. They should be trained to be aware, visible, and alert to potential shoplifting situations. Exhibit 17–7 outlines some rules for spotting shoplifters. Perhaps the best deterrent to shoplifting is an alert employee who is very visible.

Security Measures   Exhibit 17–8 describes retailers' use of security measures. Although over one-third of the sample for this survey were department and specialty apparel stores, overall, retailers have found some interesting

EXHIBIT 17–8
Use of Security Measures by Retailers

Security Measure	Percentage of Retailers Surveyed Using Security Measure
Live visible closed-circuit TV	82
Check approval screening systems	60
Cables, locks, and chains	52
EAS (electronic article surveillance) tags	50
Observation mirrors	49
Secured displays	48
Mystery and honesty shoppers	46
Uniformed guards	45
Secured display fixtures	45
Plain-clothes detectives	44
Simulated visible closed-circuit TV	37

SOURCE: Richard Hollinger and Lynn Langton, *2004 National Retail Security Survey Final Report.* (Gainesville, FL: Security Research Project, University of Florida, 2004), p. 22.

Retailers use EAS tags to reduce shoplifting. The price tags (left) contain a device that is deactivated when the merchandise is purchased. If a customer has not purchased the merchandise, an alarm is triggered when the stolen merchandise passes through sensor gates (right) at the store's exit.

approaches to deterring merchandise theft. Closed-circuit TV cameras can be monitored from a central location, but purchasing the equipment and hiring people to monitor the system can be expensive. Some retailers install nonoperating equipment that looks like a TV camera to provide a psychological deterrent to shoplifters but saves costs compared with purchasing real TV cameras. Department and specialty stores often chain expensive merchandise to fixtures. In addition, by placing one-way observation mirrors at key locations, retailers enable employees to observe a wide area of the store. Some retailers use mystery and honesty shoppers—people posing as real shoppers—to watch for employee and customer theft.

While these security measures reduce shoplifting, they can also make the shopping experience more unpleasant for honest customers. The atmosphere of a fashionable department store is diminished when guards, mirrors, and TV cameras are highly visible. Customers may find it hard to try on clothing secured with a lock and chain or an electronic tag. They can also be uncomfortable trying on clothing if they think they're secretly being watched via a surveillance monitor. Thus, when evaluating security measures, retailers need to balance the benefits of reducing shoplifting with the potential losses in sales.

Electronic article surveillance is a useful approach for reducing shrinkage with little effect on shopping behavior. With **electronic article surveillance (EAS) systems,** special tags are placed on merchandise. When the merchandise is purchased, the tags are deactivated by the POS scanner. If a shoplifter tries to steal the merchandise, the active tags are sensed when the shoplifter passes a detection device at the store exit, and an alarm is triggered.[35]

In addition, EAS tags do not affect shopping behavior because customers do not realize they're on the merchandise. Due to the effectiveness of tags in reducing shoplifting, retailers can increase sales by displaying theft-prone, expensive merchandise openly rather than behind a counter or in a locked enclosure.

Some large national retailers insist that vendors install EAS tags during the manufacturing process because the vendors can install the tags at a lower cost than the retailers can. In addition, retail-installed tags can be removed more easily by shoplifters. Vendors are reluctant to get involved with installing EAS tags because industry standards have not been adopted. Without such standards, a vendor would have to develop unique tags and merchandise for each retailer.

Prosecution   Many retailers have a policy of prosecuting all shoplifters. They feel a strictly enforced prosecution policy deters shoplifters. Some retailers also sue shoplifters in civil proceedings for restitution of the stolen merchandise and the time spent in the prosecution.

Reducing Employee Theft

The most effective approach for reducing employee theft and shoplifting is to create a trusting, supportive work environment. When employees feel they're respected members of a team, they identify their goals with the retailer's goals. Stealing from their employer thus becomes equivalent to stealing from themselves or their family, and they go out of their way to prevent others from stealing from the "family." Thus, retailers with a highly committed workforce and low turnover typically have low inventory shrinkage. Additional approaches for reducing employee theft are carefully screening employees, creating an atmosphere that encourages honesty and integrity, using security personnel, and establishing security policies and control systems.

Screening Prospective Employees   As mentioned previously, many retailers use paper-and-pencil honesty tests and undertake extensive reference checks to screen out potential employees with theft problems. A major problem related to employee theft is drug use. Some retailers now require prospective employees to submit to drug tests as a condition of employment. Employees with documented performance problems, an unusual number of accidents, or erratic time and attendance records are also tested. Unless they're involved in selling drugs, employees who test positive are often offered an opportunity to complete a company-paid drug program, submit to random testing in the future, and remain with the firm.

Using Security Personnel   In addition to uniformed guards, retailers use undercover shoppers to discourage and detect employee theft. These undercover security people pose as shoppers. They make sure salespeople ring up transactions accurately.

Establishing Security Policies and Control Systems   To control employee theft, retailers need to adopt policies relating to certain activities that may facilitate theft. Some of the most prevalent policies are

- Randomly search containers such as trash bins where stolen merchandise can be stored.
- Require store employees to enter and leave the store through designated entrances.
- Assign salespeople to specific POS terminals and require all transactions to be handled through those terminals.
- Restrict employee purchases to working hours.
- Provide customer receipts for all transactions.
- Have all refunds, returns, and discounts cosigned by a department or store manager.
- Change locks periodically and issue keys to authorized personnel only.
- Have a locker room where all employees' handbags, purses, packages, and coats must be checked before the employee leaves.

In addition, computer software is available to detect unusual activity at POS terminals. For example, a POS terminal where shortages are frequently reported or return activity is unusually high can be located, and then employees using the terminal can be monitored. Transactions can also be analyzed to identify employees who ring up a lot of no-receipt returns or void other employees' returns.

REFACT

A dishonest employee typically takes over $1,000 worth of goods and cash, whereas the average customer shoplifter takes $128 in merchandise.[36]

SUMMARY

Effective store management can have a significant impact on a retail firm's financial performance. Store managers increase profits by increasing labor productivity, decrease costs through labor deployment decisions, and reduce inventory loss by developing a dedicated workforce.

Increasing store employees' productivity is challenging because of the difficulties in recruiting, selecting, and motivating store employees.

Employees typically have a range of skills and seek a spectrum of rewards. Effective store managers need to motivate their employees to work hard and develop skills so they improve their productivity. To motivate employees, store managers need to understand what rewards each employee is seeking and then provide an opportunity for that employee to realize those rewards. Store managers must establish realistic goals for employees that are consistent with the store's goals and motivate each employee to achieve them.

Store managers also must control inventory losses due to employee theft, shoplifting, and clerical errors. Managers use a wide variety of methods to develop loss prevention programs, including security devices and employee screening during the selection process. However, the critical element of any loss prevention program is building employee loyalty to reduce employee interest in stealing and increase attention to shoplifting.

KEY TERMS

Age Discrimination and
   Employment Act, *466*
à la carte plan, *475*
Americans with Disabilities Act
   (ADA), *466*
autocratic leader, *469*
cash wraps, *482*
democratic leader, *469*
disability, *466*
discrimination, *466*
disparate impact, *466*
disparate treatment, *466*
drawing account, *477*
electronic article surveillance
   (EAS) system, *483*

Equal Employment Opportunity
   Commission (EEOC), *466*
Equal Pay Act, *479*
extrinsic reward, *475*
Fair Labor Standards
   Act, *479*
group maintenance
   behavior, *469*
incentive compensation
   plan, *477*
intrinsic reward, *475*
job analysis, *462*
job application form, *463*
job description, *462*
job enrichment, *476*

labor scheduling, *479*
leadership, *469*
preferred clients, *471*
quota, *477*
quota–bonus plan, *477*
sexual harassment, *472*
shrinkage, *481*
socialization, *466*
store maintenance, *481*
straight commission, *477*
straight salary compensation, *476*
task performance behavior, *469*
transformational leader, *470*

GET OUT AND DO IT!

1. **CONTINUING CASE ASSIGNMENT** Go to the store you have selected for the continuing case and meet with the person responsible for personnel scheduling. Report on the following:
   - Who is responsible for employee scheduling?
   - How far in advance is the schedule made?
   - How are breaks and lunch periods planned?
   - How are overtime hours determined?
   - On what is the total number of budgeted employee hours for each department based?
   - How is flexibility introduced into the schedule?
   - How are special requests for days off handled?

   - How are peak periods (hourly, days, or seasons) planned for?
   - What happens when an employee calls in sick at the last minute?

2. **CONTINUING CASE ASSIGNMENT** Go to the store you have selected for the continuing case and talk to the person responsible for human resource management to find out how sales associates are compensated and evaluated for job performance.
   - What are the criteria for evaluation?
   - How often are they evaluated?

- How much importance does the store attach to a buyer's or manager's merchandising skill versus his or her ability to work with people?
- For an associate, what action is taken if the person does not meet his or her sales goals? Can goals be adjusted? Can associates be moved to another area or type of function?
- Do salespeople have quotas? If they do, how are they set?
- Can sales associates make a commission? If yes, how does the commission system work? What are the advantages of a commission system? What are the disadvantages?
- If there is no commission system, are any incentive programs offered? Give an example of a specific program or project used by the store to boost employee morale and productivity.

3. **GO SHOPPING** Go to a store, observe the security measures in the store, and talk with a manager about the store's loss prevention program.
   - Are there surveillance cameras? Where are they located?
   - What is the store's policy against shoplifters?
   - What are the procedures for approaching a suspected shoplifter?

- How are shoplifters handled?
- How are sales associates and executives involved in the security programs?
- Is employee theft a problem? Elaborate.
- How is employee theft prevented in the store?
- How is shrinkage prevented in the store?
- How is customer service related to loss prevention in the store?

4. **INTERNET EXERCISE** Go to www.astd.org, the Web site for the American Society for Training and Development, and read one of the articles from the latest issue of *Training and Development*, a magazine published by the society. How would you suggest that a retailer use the information in this article to increase the effectiveness of its employees?

5. **INTERNET EXERCISE** St. Michaels Strategies (www.bmi.ca) sells systems that enable retailers to assess potential sales by counting the customers entering the stores and passing through specific areas. Kronos (www.kronos.com) is a leader in developing software for labor scheduling. Visit the homepages of these companies. What products and services are they selling? By looking at the comments in the discussion groups, decide what issues are of concern to retailers.

DISCUSSION QUESTIONS AND PROBLEMS

1. How do on-the-job training, Internet training, and classroom training differ? What are the benefits and limitations of each approach?

2. Give examples of a situation in which a manager of a McDonald's fast-food restaurant should utilize different leadership styles.

3. Job descriptions should be in writing so employees clearly understand what's expected of them. But what are the dangers of relying too heavily on written job descriptions?

4. Name some laws and regulations that affect the employee management process. Which do you believe are the easiest for retailers to adhere to? Which are violated the most often?

5. What's the difference between extrinsic and intrinsic rewards? What are the effects of these rewards on the behavior of retail employees? Under what conditions would you recommend that a retailer emphasize intrinsic rewards over extrinsic rewards?

6. Many large department stores, such as JCPenney, Sears, and Macy's, are changing their salespeople's reward system from a traditional salary to a commission-based system. What problems can incentive compensation systems cause? How can department managers avoid these problems?

7. When evaluating retail employees, some stores use a quantitative approach that relies on checklists and numerical scores similar to the form in Exhibit 17–6. Other stores use a more qualitative approach whereby less time is spent checking and adding and more time is devoted to discussing strengths and weaknesses in written form. Which is the best evaluation approach? Why?

8. What are the different methods for compensating employees? Discuss which methods you think would be best for compensating a sales associate, store manager, and buyer.

9. Is training more important for a small, independent retailer or a large national chain? Why? How does training differ between these two types of retailers?

10. Discuss how retailers can reduce shrinkage from shoplifting and employee theft.

11. Drugstore retailers, such as CVS, place diabetic test strips and perfume behind locked glass cabinets and nearly all over-the-counter medicines behind plexiglass panels. These efforts are designed to deter theft. How do these security measures impact honest customers?

SUGGESTED READINGS

Ackfeldt, Anna-Lena, and Leonard Coote. "A Study of Organizational Citizenship Behaviors in a Retail Setting," *Journal of Business Research* 58 (February 2005), pp. 151–63.

Bernardin, H. John. *Human Resource Management: An Experiential Approach*, 4th ed. Burr Ridge, IL: McGraw-Hill, 2006.

Cascio, Wayne, and Herman Aguinis. *Applied Psychology in Human Resource Management*, 6th ed. Upper Saddle River, NJ: Pearson/Prentice Hall, 2005.

Hendrie, James. "A Review of a Multiple Retailer's Labour Turnover," *International Journal of Retail & Distribution Management* 32 (2004), pp. 434–41.

Hollinger, Richard, and Lynn Langton. *2004 National Retail Security Survey Final Report.* Gainesville, FL: Security Research Project, University of Florida, 2004.

Hornsby, Jeffrey, and Donald Kuratko. *Frontline HR: A Handbook for the Emerging Manager.* Mason, OH: Thomson, 2005.

Manley, Anthony. *The Retail Loss Prevention Officer: The Fundamental Elements of Retail Security and Safety.* Upper Saddle River, NJ: Pearson/Prentice Hall, 2004.

Masters, Greg. "Retailers Cry for Help Wanted," *Retail Merchandiser,* October 2004, pp. 17–21.

Noe, Raymond; John Hollenbeck; Barry Gerhart; and Patrick Wright. *Fundamentals of Human Resource Management*, 2nd ed. Burr Ridge, IL: McGraw-Hill, 2006.

Podmoroff, Dianna. *How to Hire, Train & Keep the Best Employees for Your Small Business.* Ocala, FL: Atlantic Publishing. Group, 2005.

Rothstein, Mark. *Employment Law*, 3rd ed. St. Paul, MN: Thomson/West, 2005.

Shim, Soyeon; Robert Lusch; and Ellen Goldsberry. "Leadership Style Profiles of Retail Managers: Personal, Organizational and Managerial Characteristics," *International Journal of Retail and Distribution Management* 30 (2002), pp. 186–202.

Store Layout, Design, and Visual Merchandising

EXECUTIVE BRIEFING
Margot Myers, Manager, Retail In-Store Programs, U.S. Postal Service

Our 32,000 Post Offices offer a variety of products and services for consumers. In addition to core products (e.g., stamps, Express Mail, Priority Mail, etc.), we accept passport applications and sell shipping supplies, money orders, licensed products, and phone cards. These services generate more than $17 billion annual retail sales. However, our retail revenue has been threatened by the increased usage of e-mail and electronic funds transfers and the decline in first-class stamp sales.

My area is responsible for the "look and feel" of the retail space and the elements in that space that communicate with our customers. To improve our customers' experiences and increase our retail revenues, we are now expanding the use of in-store retail merchandising principles in our business. Two projects I am working on are standardizing the appearance of the retail space in our Post Offices and using digital signage to improve customer service.

Traditionally, the postmasters, our store managers, have focused more attention on mail delivery operations and not as much on the retail space. Thus, the retail space was often not consistently maintained and there was no standard for merchandising some of our products in Post Offices.

In our standardization program, we use Starbucks as a role model. Most Starbucks stores have different footprints, but each Starbucks store has a well-defined set of design elements—signage with the menu, a POS counter for placing orders, a pickup counter, displays of other merchandise for sale, tables and chairs, etc. When customers walk into any Starbucks around the world, they encounter a similar environment. Like Starbucks, our Post Offices do not have a standard footprint, but through our standardization efforts, our customers, just like Starbucks' customers, will also encounter a familiar environment when they walk into our Post Offices. They will see the

CHAPTER 18

QUESTIONS

What are the critical issues retailers consider in designing a store?

What are the advantages and disadvantages of alternative store layouts?

How is store floor space assigned to merchandise and departments?

What are the best techniques for merchandise presentation?

How exciting should a store be?

same design elements (service counters, point-of-sale displays, etc.) and the Offices will be a consistent, reliable retail environment.

The key benefit of digital signage in our environment is message flexibility. With digital signage, we can economically tailor the information we provide our customers in different Post Offices and at different times during the day. For example, the messaging displayed when the retail area is operating informs customers about the services we offer and helps them make purchase decisions before they get to the counter. When the retail space is closed, we can switch the messaging to inform customers about nearby offices with extended retail hours or to recommend usps.com as an alternate retail channel.

Before taking my present position, I worked for the Postal Service in public affairs and communications. While retail marketing is a different context, the principles of effectively communicating with customers through POP and store design are similar to those I used in my prior positions to communicate with the media and our employees.

Recognizing the significant impact of store environment on shopping behavior, retailers have devoted considerable resources to their store design and merchandise presentation. For example, Toys "R" Us spent $35 million to make its Times Square New York store "the ultimate toy store that is the personification of every kid's dream."

A well-designed store is like a good story,[1] with a beginning, middle, and end. The story begins at the entrance, which creates expectations and offers promises. As for the first impression, the storefront says, "I have low prices," or "I have the latest fashions," or "I'm easy to shop." Rather than launching right into "Here's what we've got to sell," the store entrance should entice, hint, and tease.

A single message at the entrance is the most effective approach for creating a positive store image. Customers need a few seconds to orient themselves when they enter the store. Thus, cluttering the entrance with a lot of products and signage can create confusion and an uncomfortable feeling for customers.

The middle of the story comes from inside the store. It starts off slow and builds to a crescendo. The store design leads customers on a journey through the store. Using lighting, signage, displays, and aisles, the design creates destinations and guides customers down a path of discovery. During this journey, the store engages shoppers by using design elements to relate the merchandise and services offered to their own needs.

Finally, the cash wrap or checkout counter is the story's climactic finale. It provides an opportunity for customers to quickly and easily purchase merchandise and conclude their store visit.

This chapter is part of the store management section because store managers are responsible for implementing the design and visual merchandising developed by specialists at the retailer's corporate headquarters. They adapt the prototype plans to the unique characteristics of their store and then make sure the image and experience provided by the design is consistent over time. However, as discussed in this chapter, store design and visual merchandising are also elements of a retailer's communication mix. Store design plays an important role in creating and reinforcing a retailer's brand image.

The chapter begins with a discussion of store design objectives. Next the three elements of store design—layout, signage, and feature areas—are discussed. Then the decisions about how much space to allocate to different merchandise categories and where the categories should be located in the store are reviewed. The chapter concludes with an examination of store design elements, such as the use of color, lighting, and music, that affect the customer's shopping experience.

STORE DESIGN OBJECTIVES

REFACT

Retailers remodel their stores every eight years on average.[2]

Some objectives for a store design are to (1) implement the retailer's strategy, (2) influence customer buying behavior, (3) provide flexibility, (4) control design and maintenance costs, and (5) meet legal requirements.

Store Design and Retail Strategy

The primary objective of a store design is to implement the retailer's strategy. The design must be consistent with and reinforce the retailer's strategy by meeting the needs of the target market and building a sustainable competitive advantage.[3] For instance, warehouse clubs, like Sam's or Costco, target customers that are very price sensitive. Thus, their stores have high ceilings with metal racks and concrete floors—design elements that signal low costs and reinforce a brand image of low prices.

Home improvement centers such as Lowe's and Home Depot initially targeted men who found the warehouse atmosphere supported their image of a person with a job to do. When Lowe's discovered that the majority of its sales were made to women, it redesigned its stores to be more attractive to women. It lowered the ceilings, increased the lighting, widened the aisles, and provided better signage— all design aspects appealing to women.[4]

By using a store design that incorporates bright lighting and softer colors, Lowe's provides a more appealing shopping environment for women.

In contrast, Recreational Equipment Inc. (REI) targets customers who seek the adventure of engaging in active outdoor activities such as rock climbing, kayaking, and hiking. Its stores are designed to appeal to these adventure seekers and support the retailer's image of expertise in providing outdoor equipment. For example, the Denver store has a large, steel-encased, freezer-like fixture in which shoppers can test winter parkas and sleeping bags. Mountain bikes can be tested on a rugged 318-foot trail that runs through the store's landscaped outdoor courtyard. Inside, shoppers can try out hiking boots on a footwear test track, compare bike lights and reflectors in an illuminator room, and test water purifiers in a ministream. The centerpiece of the store is a 45-foot, sculptured, indoor rock-climbing pinnacle offering a variety of climbing terrains, including routes specifically geared toward children.[5]

Flooring and shelving also affect the retailer's image. For example, stainless steel shelving creates an entirely different image than natural wood. Glass shelving creates an element of elegance and emphasizes the merchandise it displays and thus is often used to display expensive fashion accessories. Retailing View 18.1 describes how W hotels are designed to appeal to the company's target market.

Influence Customer Buying Behavior

A second design objective is to influence customer buying behavior. Specifically, retailers would like the store design to attract customers to the store; enable them to easily locate merchandise of interest; keep them in the store for a long time; motivate them to make unplanned, impulse purchases; and provide them with a satisfying shopping experience.

The influence of store design on buying behavior is increasing with the rise in two-income and single head-of-household families. Due to the limited time these families have, they are spending less time planning shopping trips and making

---

Hotels for Generation X Businesspeople   RETAILING VIEW   18.1

Starwood's W hotels are designed to appeal to Generation X businesspeople—its target market. Gen Xers prefer sleek, high-tech boutique hotels, whereas Baby Boomers, who grew up with Holiday Inns and Hiltons, care most about functional utility. They want a traditional look and setting that is warm, comforting, and relaxing. Boomers want to spend the evening sitting on their bed, eating from room service, and watching TV. Gen Xers want to cruise to the lobby and bars.

W is known for its stylish décor, funky bars and restaurants, and bustling nightlife, often set in the lobby. The hotel design features loft-like guest rooms, landscaped outdoor space for socializing day and night, and an energetic lounge scene.

Gen Xers are far more interested in technological features and less interested in traditional services, like concierge floors. Hotel chains targeting Gen Xers offer wireless Internet access and "grab and go," 24-hour pantries in their hotel lobbies. Some have installed iPod docking stations in guest rooms and sell CDs of hip-hop, electronica, and other types of music in their minibars.

To appeal to Gen Xers, W hotels host lifestyle events, called W Happenings, that offer film screenings, wine tastings, art previews, and celebrity book readings. Some W Happenings have included performances by Moby and the Wallflowers, DJ Chef (cooking and DJ classes), An Evening of Luxury (private photos of Jackie Onassis), and knitting sessions.

Style icon Diane von Furstenberg created exclusive DVF beauty and fashion "emergency kits" for W guestrooms and

The lobby of the Starwood W hotel in San Diego is designed to encourage social interactions between guests and thus appeal to Gen X travelers.

retail stores. The "survival kit" features a boxed set of mini lip glosses, mascara, and perfume from von Furstenberg's signature cosmetics line.

Sources: Jane Levere, "To Bed or to Bar?" *New York Times,* September 20, 2005, p. C1; Karyn Strauss and Derek Gale, "Lifestyle Brands Enter into Fashion-Oriented Retail Partnerships," *Hotels,* September 2005, p. 18.

more purchase decisions in stores. Recognizing the increasing importance of the store environment, consumer goods manufacturers are working with retailers and spending more on advertising, packaging, and market research to address what Procter & Gamble calls the consumer's "first moment of truth"—the three to seven seconds when a customer notices an item on a store shelf.[6]

For example, Procter & Gamble, as part of its relationship-building activities, works with supermarket retailers to locate its brands in positions that increase the brand's sales and the sales of adjacent brands. Its market research found that supermarket shoppers do not walk down one aisle then up the next. They often park their shopping carts at one end of an aisle, walk partway down the aisle to pick up a product, and return to their cart.[7] To encourage shoppers to see more of the products in each aisle, Procter & Gamble recommends that retailers put their best-selling brands, such as Tide laundry detergent and Campbell's soup, in the middle of the aisle.

Flexibility

Retailing is a very dynamic business. Merchandise that sold well today might not sell well tomorrow. Competitors might enter a market and cause existing retailers to change the mix of merchandise offered. As the merchandise mix changes, so must the space allocated to merchandise categories and the layout of the store change. Thus, store designers attempt to design stores with maximum flexibility. Flexibility can take two forms: the ability to physically move and store components and the ease with which components can be modified.

Most stores are designed with flexibility in mind. For instance, Wallace's Bookstores, one of the nation's largest operators of college bookstores, has an innovative concept with built-in merchandising and design flexibility called *flexsmart*. The format allows book stores to expand or contract their spaces to accommodate the seasonal fluctuations inherent in the college-bookstore business. College bookstores need to change their space allocations to accommodate the rush for textbooks at the beginning of each semester and the slower in-between periods. During the semester, the allocation of space to books or apparel can be increased or decreased by as much as 30 percent. The key to Wallace's flexibility lies in an innovative fixturing and wall system that is used to portion off the textbook area.[8] **Fixtures** are the equipment used to display merchandise.

Wallace bookstores are designed to be flexible. Metal frames on end caps swing open and shut, allowing the store to expand and contract the space devoted to different merchandise categories.

Cost

The fourth design objective is to control the cost of implementing the store design and maintain the store's appearance. For instance, the free-form design found in many specialty stores is much more costly to construct and maintain than a design involving rows of shelves in a discount store. But the free-form design also can encourage customers to explore more of the store and thus increase sales.

Certain types of lighting that highlight expensive jewelry and crystal use more electricity and thus lead to higher energy costs than rows of bare fluorescent bulbs. However, the more expensive lighting can make the merchandise look better and thus increase sales.

The store design can also affect labor costs and inventory shrinkage. Traditional department stores typically are organized into departments that are isolated from one another. This design provides an intimate and comfortable shopping experience that can result in more sales. However, the design prevents sales associates from observing and covering adjacent departments, which makes it necessary to have at least one sales associate permanently stationed in each department to provide customer service and prevent shoplifting.

Retailing View 18.2 describes Wal-Mart's environmentally sensitive prototype store that reduces energy costs and helps build Wal-Mart's image as a socially responsible retailer.

Legal Considerations

A critical objective in any store design or redesign decision is to be in compliance with the 1990 Americans with Disabilities Act (ADA).[9] This law protects people with disabilities from discrimination in employment, transportation, public

---

Wal-Mart's Eco-nomic Supercenter   RETAILING VIEW   18.2

Wal-Mart spent two years designing its supercenter in McKinney, Texas, to create a store that reduces the consumption of energy and natural resources. The design incorporates more than two dozen resource conservation and sustainable design technologies and is one of the "greenest" stores in the world. The store thus reflects Wal-Mart's efforts to consider the impact the company leaves on the environment.

The three main design objectives for the store were to (1) reduce the amount of energy and natural resources required to operate and maintain the store; (2) reduce the amount of raw materials needed to construct the facility; and (3) use, when appropriate, renewable materials to construct and maintain the facility. Although many of the design features reduce its impact on the environment, the store was expensive to build, and some of its elements make economic sense only if energy costs increase. Initial projections call for the energy used at the store to be 30–50 percent less, reducing the store's energy costs by $500,000 annually.

Some of its sustainable features are as follows:

* A wind turbine on top of the store produces enough energy to reduce the store's electricity consumption by 5 percent.

* A rainwater harvesting and treatment system provides 95 percent of the water needed for on-site irrigation and reduces demand on the local stormwater system.

* Standard Bermuda grass for landscaping has been eliminated in favor of native grasses that do not need irrigation or mowing.

* The store is 12 inches lower in height than a typical Supercenter. The height reduction means fewer building materials were needed, plus it reduces heating and cooling needs.

* Instead of fluorescent strips, LED lighting is used inside the grocery cases. The LEDs have a longer life span, produce less heat, use less energy, and provide better quality light.

* The main store area lighting uses high-output linear fluorescent lamps that, in combination with natural daylight and dimming controls, are expected to generate a lighting savings of 300,000 kwh a year.

* Heat generated by the building's refrigeration system is captured and redirected to heat the water used in the restroom

This ecofriendly Wal-Mart Supercenter incorporates resource conservation and sustainable design technologies that reduce operating costs and preserve natural resources.

sinks and to help heat the water used in the radiant floor-heating system beneath the entries and other areas.

* Cooking oil from the fryers and waste engine oil are burned in a bio-fuel boiler to generate heat that is directed into the heating, ventilation, and radiant floor-heating systems, conserving energy. The boiler generates heat to heat the building, reducing the demand for natural gas to operate mechanical equipment.

Sources: Marianne Wilson, "The Machine Goes Green," *Chain Store Age,* August 2005, pp. 110–12; Mike Troy, "New Wal-Mart Supercenter Has Eco-Nomic Upside," *DSN Retailing Today,* August 8, 2005, pp. 1–2.

accommodations, telecommunications, and the activities of state and local government. It affects store design because the act calls for "reasonable access" to merchandise and services in retail stores that were built before 1993. Stores built after 1993 must be fully accessible.

The Act also states that retailers should not have to incur "undue burdens" to comply with ADA requirements. While retailers are concerned about the needs of their disabled customers, they are also worried that making merchandise completely accessible to people in a wheelchair or a motorized cart will result in less space available to display merchandise and thus reduce sales. However, providing for wider aisles and more space around fixtures can result in a more pleasant shopping experience for able-bodied as well as disabled customers.

The ADA does not clearly define critical terms such as "reasonable access," "fully accessible," or "undue burden." So the actual ADA requirements are being defined through a series of court cases in which disabled plaintiffs have filed class-action suits against retailers.[10] Based on these court cases, retailers are typically required to (1) provide 32-inch-wide pathways in the main aisle, to bathrooms, fitting rooms, and elevators, and around most fixtures; (2) lower most cash wraps (checkout stations) and fixtures so they can be reached by a person in a wheelchair; and (3) make bathrooms and fitting rooms fully accessible. These accessibility requirements are somewhat relaxed for retailers in very small spaces and during peak sales periods such as the Christmas holidays.[11]

Design Trade-Offs

Typically, a store design cannot achieve all of these objectives, so managers need to make trade-offs among them. Although the design of an REI store compared with a Costco warehouse offers an exciting and entertaining environment for its customers, it is far more costly to build and maintain. In addition, the space devoted to the climbing wall and other experiential features in the REI store reduces the space that can be used to display merchandise that might encourage more impulse purchases.

Retailers often make trade-offs between stimulating impulse purchases and making it easy to buy products. For example, supermarkets place milk, a commonly purchased item, at the back of the store to make customers walk through the entire store and thus stimulate more impulse purchases. However, customers that are only interested in buying milk will find this placement inconvenient and may select the convenience store format when buying milk.

The trade-off between the ease of finding merchandise and providing an interesting shopping experience is determined by the customer's shopping needs. For example, supermarket shoppers typically want to minimize the time they spend shopping, so supermarkets emphasize the ease of locating merchandise. In contrast, department store shoppers are more likely to find shopping enjoyable and therefore be more willing to explore the store and browse for new merchandise. Thus, department store retailers can place more emphasis on encouraging exploration rather than ease of finding merchandise.

Another trade-off is the balance between giving customers adequate space in which to shop and productively using this scarce resource for merchandise. For example, some customers may be attracted to stores with wide aisles and fixtures whose primary purpose is to display rather than hold the merchandise. However, this type of design reduces the amount of merchandise that can be shown to the customer, which may also reduce the customer's chances of finding what he or she is looking for. Also, a store with lots of people creates a sense of excitement and, it is hoped, increases buying. But too many racks and displays in a store can cause customers to get confused or even lost. The issue of overcrowded display fixtures and merchandise is particularly important when retailers consider the special needs of the disabled.

STORE DESIGN

Retailers first need to determine the basic layout of the store. Then they use signage and other techniques to guide customers through the store and assist them in locating and finding information about merchandise. Finally, a variety of approaches are used to feature specific products.

Layouts

One method of encouraging customer exploration is to present them with a layout that facilitates a specific traffic pattern. Customers can be enticed to follow what amounts to a yellow brick road, as in *The Wizard of Oz.* For instance, Toys "R" Us uses a layout that almost forces customers to move through sections of inexpensive impulse-purchase products to get to larger, more expensive goods. It takes a strong-willed parent to navigate through the balloons and party favors without making a purchase. Retailers use three general types of store layout design: grid, racetrack, and free-form. Each of these layouts has advantages and disadvantages that are discussed later in this section.

Another method of helping customers move through the store is to provide interesting design elements. For example, antique stores have little nooks and crannies that entice shoppers to wander around. Off-price retailers intentionally create some degree of messiness so that people will be encouraged to look through the racks for bargains. These feature design elements are also discussed later in this section.

Grid Layout   The **grid layout,** illustrated in Exhibit 18–1, has parallel aisles with merchandise on shelves on both sides of the aisles. Cash registers are located at the entrances/exits of the stores.

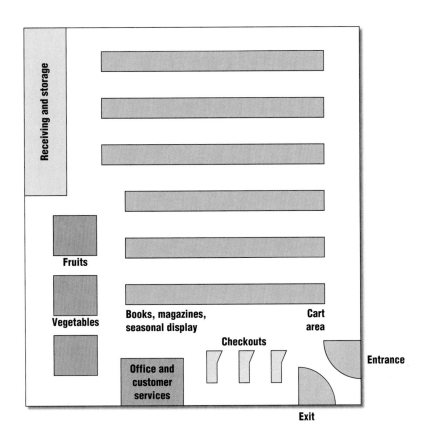

EXHIBIT 18–1
Grid Store Layout

A grid layout does not provide a visually exciting design, but it's well suited for shopping trips in which customers need to move throughout the entire store and easily locate products they want to buy. For instance, when customers do their weekly grocery shopping, they can weave in and out of the specific aisles, easily picking up their desired products every week. Since they know where everything is, they can minimize the time spent on a task that many don't especially enjoy. Thus, most supermarkets use a grid layout.

The grid layout is also cost efficient. There's less wasted space with the grid layout than with other layouts because the aisles are all the same width and designed to be just wide enough to accommodate shoppers and their carts. The use of shelves for merchandise enables more merchandise to be on the sales floor compared with other layouts. Finally, because the fixtures are generally standardized, the cost of the fixtures is low.

One problem with the grid layout is that customers typically aren't exposed to all of the merchandise in the store. This limitation generally isn't an issue in grocery stores, because most customers have a good notion of the types of products they are going to purchase before they enter the store. But other retailers, such as department stores, use a layout that pulls customers through stores and encourages them to explore and seek out new and interesting merchandise available in the store.

Racetrack Layout   The **racetrack layout,** also known as a **loop,** is a store layout that provides a major aisle that loops around the store to guide customer traffic around different departments within the store. Cash register stations are typically located in each department bordering the racetrack.

EXHIBIT 18–2   JCPenney Racetrack Layout at NorthPark Center in Dallas

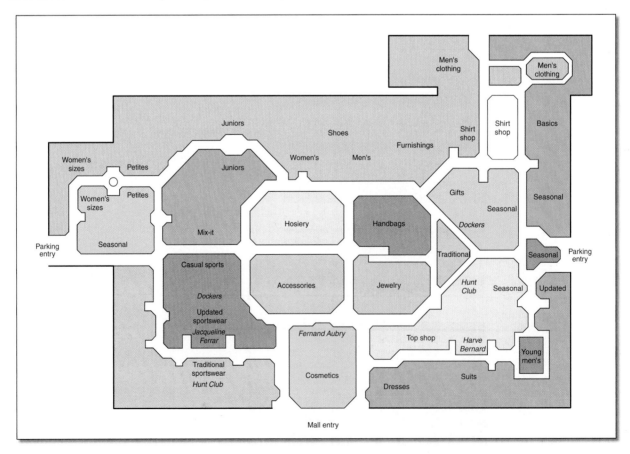

The racetrack layout facilitates the goal of getting customers to see the merchandise available in multiple departments and thus encourages impulse purchasing. As customers go around the racetrack, their eyes are forced to take different viewing angles rather than looking down one aisle, as in the grid design.

Exhibit 18–2 shows the layout of the JCPenney store in the North-Park Center in Dallas, Texas. Because the store has multiple entrances, the racetrack layout tends to place all departments on the main aisle by drawing customers through the store in a series of major and minor loops. To entice customers through the various departments, the design places some of the more popular departments, like juniors,

The racetrack layout of this Goody's store draws people through the store, exposing them to different site lines and encouraging impulse purchases.

toward the rear of the store. The newest items are featured on the aisles to draw customers into departments and around the loop.

To direct customers through the store, the aisles must be defined by a change in surface or color. For instance, the aisle flooring in the store is marble-like tile, while the department floors vary in material, texture, and color, depending on the desired ambiance.

Kohl's has modified the racetrack layout to increase shopper convenience. Conventional retail wisdom says store layouts should keep people shopping longer, but Kohl's management believes that their target market wants the convenience of easy access. So they actually try to shorten the shopping trip.

Kohl's stores, at 86,000 square feet, are about half the size of most department stores. Although management's objective is to help busy shoppers get in and out quickly, there is ample room to roam from department to department. A wide aisle that forms the racetrack provides room for shoppers with carts or families with children in tow. A middle aisle divides the track, serving as a shortcut for shoppers who don't need to finish the whole circuit. During clearance periods, Kohl's lines the track with markdown merchandise to get shoppers' attention. Cash register stations are located at the start and at the halfway point of the racetrack.[12]

Free-Form Layout   A **free-form layout,** also known as **boutique layout,** arranges fixtures and aisles in an asymmetric pattern (Exhibit 18–3). It provides an intimate, relaxing environment that facilitates shopping and browsing. This layout is typically used in small specialty stores or within the departments of large stores.

However, creating this pleasing shopping environment is costly. Because there is no well-defined traffic pattern, like the racetrack and grid layouts, customers aren't naturally drawn around the store, and personal selling becomes more important for providing guidance. In addition, the layout sacrifices some storage and display space to create the more spacious environment.

To illustrate a free-form boutique within a racetrack layout, consider the Bloomingdale's I.C.B. boutique in the picture on page 498. The designers' objective was to create a simple, clear space that draws customers into the area. Fixtures with the latest garments are placed along the perimeter of the boutique. Yet the flooring and lighting clearly delineate the area from adjacent departments

EXHIBIT 18–3
Free-Form Store Layout

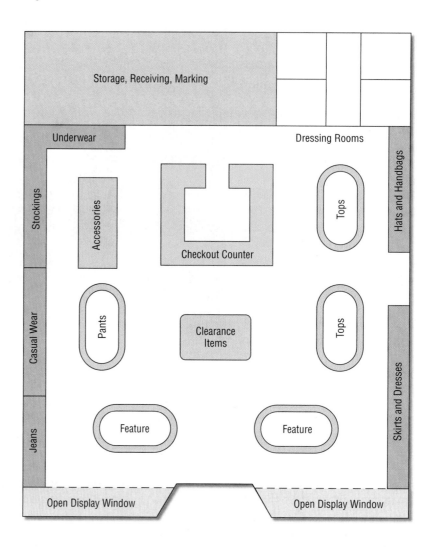

| Storage, Receiving, Marking |
Underwear	Dressing Rooms
Stockings	Accessories	Checkout Counter	Tops	Hats and Handbags
Casual Wear	Pants	Clearance Items	Tops	Skirts and Dresses
Jeans	Feature	Feature	
Open Display Window	Open Display Window

This department at a Bloomingdale's store places fixtures holding the latest styles along the perimeter of its boutique layout, drawing customers into the area. Flooring and lighting clearly delineate the boutiques from other areas of the store.

and the walkway. Retailing View 18.3 describes Diesel's unique approach to store layout.

Signage and Graphics

While the grid and racetrack layouts guide customers through the store, signage and graphics help customers locate specific products and departments, provide product information, and suggest items or special purchases. Graphics, such as photo panels, can add personality, beauty, and romance to the store's image.

Some of the uses of visual communications are:

- *Location.* Retailers use signage to identify the location of merchandise. Large stores often need to display directional signage to guide customers around the store and from one area to another. Hanging signs from the ceiling is often used to enhance their visibility. Larger stores, particularly stores with more than one level, also have a store guide. The location of this guide should be clearly visible from the entrance and the path to the guide clearly marked so that even the first-time customer can clearly see where to go.

- *Category signage.* Used within a particular department or sector of the store, category signs are usually smaller than directional signs. Their purpose is to identify types of products offered; they are usually located near the goods to which they refer.

- *Promotional signage.* This signage describing special offers may be displayed in windows to entice the customer into the store. For instance, value apparel stores for young women often display large posters in their windows of models wearing the items on special offer.

REFACT

Eighty-five percent of mall concourse traffic approaches stores from the side. However, almost all store window signage is designed for customers approaching the store head on.[13]

Diesel Breaks Store Design Rules   RETAILING VIEW   18.3

Diesel jeans stores are so confusing that they beg a question: Are they the worst designed stores, or is there method to their madness? Walking into a Diesel jeans store feels a lot like stumbling into a rave. Techno music pounds at a mind-rattling level. A television plays a videotape of a Japanese boxing match, inexplicably. There are no helpful signs pointing to the men's or women's departments and no obvious staff members in sight.

Customers who are industrious, or simply brave enough to reach the "denim bar"—Diesel's name for the counter separating shoppers from the wall of jeans at the back of the store—find themselves confronted by 35 different types of blue jeans costing $115 to $260 a pair. A placard intending to explain the various options looks like an organizational chart for a decent-sized federal agency.

Diesel jeans are a gas for the fashion-forward. Despite its high prices, Diesel prides itself on producing unusual yet modish men's and women's casual wear and a complementary store environment. Diesel's products are sold in over 80 countries through department stores and specialty retailers, as well as more than 50 company-owned stores.

Whereas apparel chains like Banana Republic and The Gap have standardized and simplified the layout of their stores in an effort to put customers at ease, Diesel's approach is based on the unconventional premise that the best customer is a disoriented one. The company intentionally designed an intimidating, user-unfriendly environment so that customers have to interact with the sales staff. Indeed, it is at just the moment

Diesel stores create a unique shopping environment by breaking the basic store design rules used by other retailers.

when a potential Diesel customer reaches a kind of shopping vertigo that members of the company's with-it staff make their move. Acting as salespeople-in-shining-armor, they rescue—or prey upon, depending on one's point of view—wayward shoppers.

Source: John Holusha, "A Shopping Destination for the Young and Hip," *New York Times*, August 29, 2004, p. 11; Warren St. John, "A Store Lures Guys Who Are Graduating from Chinos," *New York Times*, July 14, 2002, p. 9.

- *Point of sale.* These signs are placed near the merchandise they refer to so that customers know its price and other detailed information. Some of this information may already be on product labels or packaging. However, point-of-sale signage can quickly identify for the customer those aspects likely to be of greater interest, such as whether the product is on special offer.
- *Lifestyle images.* The retailer may use various images, such as pictures of people and places, to create moods that encourage customers to buy the products. These are part of the visual merchandising that the store uses.

Some suggestions for effectively using signage are discussed next:

- *Coordinate signs and graphics with the store's image.* Signs and graphics should act as a bridge between the merchandise and the retailer's target market. The colors and tone of the signs and graphics should complement the merchandise. For example, a formally worded, black-and-white, rectangular sign doesn't relate to a children's display as well as a red-and-yellow circus tent design does. Color combinations should appeal to specific target customers or highlight specific merchandise—primary colors for kids, hot vivid colors for teens, pastel shades for lingerie, bright hues for sportswear, and so forth. At The Athlete's Foot for Her, for instance, sliding graphic panels highlight the lifestyles of the target market while they display the product and conceal inventory.
- *Inform customers.* Informative signs and graphics make merchandise more desirable. For instance, The Athlete's Foot uses a series of freestanding prints to explain its five-step fitting process.[14] The process begins with a foot scanner, which ensures a perfect fit for each customer. Then after analyzing customers' activity levels, in-store personnel help them choose the right shoes and determine the best way to tie shoes to fit their feet.
- *Use signs and graphics as props.* Using signs or graphics that masquerade as props, or vice versa, is a great way to unify a theme and merchandise for an appealing overall presentation. For instance, Alphabet Soup, a small, Iowa-based chain of educational toy stores, uses lively graphics and props in a unifying theme that is consistent with the store's image.
- *Keep signs and graphics fresh.* Signs and graphics should be relevant to the items displayed and shouldn't be left in the store or in windows after displays are removed. New signs imply new merchandise.
- *Limit the text on signs.* Since a sign's main purpose is to catch attention and inform customers, the copy is important to its overall success. As a general rule, signs with too much copy won't be read. Customers must be able to quickly grasp the information on the sign as they walk through the store.
- *Use appropriate typefaces on signs.* Using the appropriate typeface is critical to a sign's success. Different typefaces impart different messages and moods. For instance, carefully done calligraphy in an Old English script provides a very different message than a hastily written price-reduction sign.

This sign identifies the location of the merchandise, is consistent with the store's image, and informs customers about a special promotion.

Digital Signage   Traditional print signage is typically developed and produced at corporate headquarters, distributed to stores, and installed by store employees or contractors.[15] Many retailers are beginning to replace traditional signage with digital signage systems. **Digital signage** is signs whose visual content is delivered digitally through a centrally managed and controlled network and displayed on a television monitor or flat-panel screen. The content delivered can range from entertaining video clips to simple displays of the price of merchandise.

Digital signage provides a number of benefits over traditional static signage. Due to their dynamic nature, digital signs are superior in attracting the attention of customers and having them recall the messages displayed. Digital signage also offers the opportunity to enhance a store's environment by displaying complex graphics and videos and providing an atmosphere that customers find appealing.

Digital signage also overcomes the time-to-message hurdle associated with traditional print signage. Changing market developments or events can immediately be incorporated into the digital sign. The ease and speed (flexibility) of content development and deployment of digital signage enables the content to be varied within and across stores at different times of the day or days of the week, such as reflecting different weather conditions.

Because the content is delivered digitally, it can easily be tailored to a store's market and changed during the week or even the day and hour. For example, Eddie Bauer analyzed its customer data warehouse and discovered that price-sensitive customers tended to shop in the mornings and that more brand-conscious customers tended to shop in the afternoon and evenings. Subsequently, it experimented with changing the content of its storefront digital signage. In the morning, the signage emphasized merchandise with lower price points and sale items. The merchandise at higher price points and brand image content was displayed later in the day. The result was targeted merchandising messaging to its customers. Messages thus can be targeted on the basis of demographics, merchandise location, store location, and location within a store.

The ability to control digital signage content centrally ensures that the retailer's strategy for communicating with its customers is properly executed systemwide. Digital signage thus eliminates the challenge facing retailers that send out static signage to stores announcing a special promotion or a new marketing initiative, namely, ensuring that the signage is installed in the right place at the right time.

Finally, digital signage eliminates the costs associated with printing, distributing, and installing static signage. In addition, it may decrease store labor costs while improving labor productivity. However, the drawback to using digital signage is the initial cost of the display devices and the system that supports the delivery of the signage.

Feature Areas

In addition to the layout and signage, customers are guided through stores by the placement of feature areas. **Feature areas** are those areas within a store designed to get the customers' attention. They include freestanding displays, end caps, promotional aisles or areas, windows, cash wrap or point-of-sale areas, and walls.

Freestanding Displays   **Freestanding displays** are fixtures or mannequins located on aisles designed primarily to attract customers' attention and bring them into a department. These fixtures often display and store the newest, most exciting merchandise in the department.

Cash Wraps   **Cash wraps,** also known as **point-of-purchase (POP) counters** or **checkout areas,** are places in the store where customers can purchase merchandise. Because many customers go to these areas and may wait in line to make a purchase, they are often used to display impulse items. For example, in supermarkets, batteries, candy, razors, and magazines are often shelved at the checkout counter.

Discount and extreme value retailers and category specialists use centralized checkouts at the front of their stores. But department stores have traditionally placed cash wraps off the main aisle within each department. Several department store chains, such as Kohl's, Sears, and JCPenney, are now switching to centralized cash wraps. By centralizing the checkout areas, these department stores increase customer convenience, reduce staff, and reduce customer complaints arising from slow or poor checkout service.[17]

REFACT

The average waiting time in a regular checkout lane in a grocery store is 3 minutes and 24 seconds. The average express checkout lane takes 3 minutes and 11 seconds.[16]

End Caps   **End caps** are displays located at the end of an aisle. Due to the high visibility of end caps, product sales are dramatically increased when the merchandise is featured on an end cap. Thus, retailers use end caps for higher margin, impulse merchandise. In the supermarket industry, vendors often negotiate for their products to be on end cap displays when offering special promotional prices.

Lowe's uses end caps to reinforce its brand image and theme of "Improving Home Improvement" by providing customers with easy-to-find product and project information in a consistent format. Its striking, 14-foot-tall end caps highlight a broad array of home products, including bath cabinetry and hardwood flooring.[19]

Lowe's uses end caps to reinforce its image of providing helpful information and a wide assortment of home improvement merchandise.

Promotional Aisle or Area   A **promotional aisle** or **area** is a space used to display merchandise that is being promoted. Walgreens, for instance, uses promotional aisles to sell seasonal merchandise, such as lawn and garden products in the summer and Christmas decorations in the fall. Albertsons supermarkets have a "10 for $10" aisle. From this promotional aisle, customers can purchase 10 selected items for $10. The products change each week and are highlighted in weekly grocery ads. Products can also be mixed, so that customers do not have to buy 10 of the same item. Apparel stores, like The Gap, often place their sale merchandise at the back of the store so customers must pass through the full-price merchandise to get to the sale merchandise.

Walls   Because retail floor space is often limited, many retailers increase their ability to store extra stock, display merchandise, and creatively present a message by utilizing wall space. Merchandise can be stored on shelving and racks and coordinated with displays, photographs, or graphics featuring the merchandise. At Niketown, for instance, a lot of merchandise is displayed relatively high on the wall. Not only does this allow the merchandise to "tell a story," it also helps customers feel more comfortable because they aren't crowded by racks or other people, and they can get a perspective on the merchandise by viewing it from a distance.

Windows   Although windows are external to the store, they can be an important component of the store layout. Window displays can help draw customers into the store. They provide a visual message about the type of merchandise offered in the store and the type of image the store wishes to portray.

Window displays should be tied to the merchandise and other displays in the store. For instance, if beach towels are displayed in a Bed, Bath & Beyond window, they should also be prominently displayed inside. Otherwise, the drawing power of the window display is lost. Finally, windows can be used to set the shopping mood for a season or holiday like Christmas or Valentine's Day.

SPACE MANAGEMENT

The space within stores and on the stores' shelves and fixtures is a scare resource. Space management involves two decisions involving this resource: (1) the allocation of store space to merchandise categories and brands and (2) the location of departments or merchandise categories in the store.

Space Allocated to Merchandise Categories

Some factors that retailers consider when deciding how much floor or shelf space to allocate to merchandise categories and brands are (1) the productivity of the allocated space, (2) the merchandise's inventory turnover, (3) impact on store sales, and (4) the display needs for the merchandise.

Space Productivity   A simple rule of thumb for allocating space is to allocate on the basis of the merchandise's sales. For example, if artificial plants represent 15 percent of the total expected sales for a hobby and craft retailer such as Michaels, then 15 percent of the store's space is allocated to artificial plants.

But, as the discussion of marginal analysis for advertising allocations in Chapter 16 indicates, retailers should allocate space to a merchandise category on the basis of its effect on the profitability of the entire store. In practice, this means that Michaels should add more space to the artificial plant section as long as the profitability of the additional space is greater that the profitability of the category from which space was taken away. In this condition, the additional space for artificial plants will increase the profitability of the entire store. However, at some point, it will be more profitable to not take away space from other categories.

Two commonly used measures of space productivity are **sales per square foot** and **sales per linear foot.** Apparel retailers that display most of their merchandise on freestanding fixtures typically measure space productivity as sales per square foot. In supermarkets, most merchandise is displayed on shelves. Because the shelves have approximately the same width, only the length, or linear dimension, sales per linear foot, is used to assess space productivity.

A more sophisticated productivity measure such as gross margin per square foot would consider the profits generated by the merchandise, not just the sales. Thus, if salty snacks generate $400 in gross margin per linear foot and canned soup only generates $300 per linear foot, more space should be allocated to salty snacks. However, factors other than marginal productivity need to be considered when making space allocation decisions.

Inventory Turnover   Inventory turnover affects space allocations in two ways. First, as discussed in Chapter 12, both inventory turnover and gross margin contribute to GMROI—a measure of the retailer's return on its merchandise inventory investment. Thus, merchandise categories with higher inventory turnover merit more space than merchandise categories with lower inventory turnover.

Second, the merchandise displayed on the shelf is depleted quicker for fast selling items with high inventory turnover. Thus, more space needs to be allocated to fast selling merchandise to minimize the need to frequently restock the shelf to reduce stockouts.

Impact on Store Sales   When allocating space to merchandise categories, retailers need to consider the allocation impact on the entire store. The objective of space management is to maximize the profitability of the store, not just a particular merchandise category or department. Thus supermarkets "overallocate" space to some low productivity categories such as milk because an extensive assortment in these categories attracts customers to the store and thus positively affects the sales of categories with higher GMROIs. Retailers might also overallocate space to categories purchased by their platinum customers, the customers with the highest lifetime value.

This supermarket allocates more shelf space to Pepperidge Farm Chocolate Chunk and Milano cookies because they have a higher sales rate and greater inventory turnover than other Pepperidge Farm cookies.

Display Considerations The physical limitations of the store and its fixtures affect space allocation. For example, the store planner needs to provide enough merchandise to fill an entire fixture dedicated to a particular item.

A retailer might decide that it wants to use a merchandise display as a form of promotion, as if to say, "We have a great assortment of this merchandise." For example, JCPenney has a very appealing offering of its private-label bath towels. To emphasize this offering, it might overallocate space for bath towels and present a wide range of colors.

Location of Merchandise Categories and Design Elements

As discussed previously, the store layout, signage, and feature areas can guide customers through the store. The location of merchandise categories also plays a role in how customers navigate through the store.[20]

By strategically placing impulse and demand/destination merchandise throughout the store, retailers increase the chances that customers will shop the entire store and that their attention will be focused on the merchandise that the retailer is most interested in selling—merchandise with a high GMROI. **Demand/destination merchandise** refers to products that customers have decided to buy before entering the store.

Introductory displays, including graphics, typically welcome and educate customers as they enter the store. The entry area is often referred to as the "decompression zone," because customers are making an adjustment to the new environment: taking off their sunglasses, closing their umbrellas, and developing a visual impression of the entire store.

Once customers pass through the decompression zone, they often turn right (in Western cultures) and observe the prices and quality of the first items they encounter. This area, referred to as the "strike zone," is critical because it creates the customer's first impression of the store's offering. Thus, retailers should display some of their most compelling merchandise in the strike zone.

After passing through the strike zone, the most heavily trafficked and viewed area is the right-hand side of the store. At this point in the journey through the store, customers have become accustomed to the environment, developed a first impression, and are ready to make purchase decisions. Thus, the right-hand side is a prime area for displaying high GMROI merchandise. For example, supermarkets typically locate the produce section in this area because produce appeals to the shoppers' senses. The smell of fresh fruits and vegetables gets a shopper's mouth watering, and the best grocery store customer is a hungry one.

Some additional implications for store design based on Envirosell's research findings are described in Retailing View 18.4.

Impulse Merchandise The prime store locations for selling merchandise are heavily trafficked areas such as the entrance, right side of the store, and areas near escalators and cash wraps. In multilevel stores, a space's value decreases the farther it is from the entry-level floor. Thus, **impulse products,** or products that are purchased without prior plans, like fragrances and cosmetics in department stores and magazines in supermarkets, are almost always located near the front of the store, where they're seen by everyone and may actually draw people into the store.

Demand Merchandise Demand merchandise and promotional merchandise are often placed in the back, left-hand corner of the store. Placing high-demand merchandise in this location pulls customers through the store, increasing the visibility of other products along the way. So supermarkets typically display items almost everyone buys—milk, eggs, butter, and bread—in the back, left-hand corner. In department stores, children's merchandise and furniture, as well as

Envirosell, a consulting firm in New York, has made a science out of determining the best ways to lay out a department or a store.[21] Although the firm utilizes lots of hidden video cameras and other high-tech equipment, its most important research tool is a piece of paper called a track sheet in the hands of people called trackers. Trackers follow shoppers and note everything they do. They also make inferences about consumer behavior on the basis of what they've observed. Examples of their quantitative research findings are found in Exhibits 18–4 and 18–5. Here are just a few of the things, in addition to the decompression and strike zones previously discussed, that they have learned:

* *Avoid the butt-brush effect.* The "butt-brush effect" was discovered at a New York City Bloomingdale's. The researchers taped shoppers attempting to reach the tie rack while negotiating an entrance during busy times. They noticed that after being bumped once or twice, most shoppers abandoned their search for neckwear. The conclusion: Shoppers don't like to shop when their personal space is invaded.

* *Place merchandise where customers can readily access it.* Toy store designers are, for the most part, still designing stores as if the customer were over five feet tall. Designers should be made to get down on their hands and knees (sitting on a skateboard also works quite well) and tour the store from a child's point of view.

* *Make information accessible.* Older shoppers often have a hard time reading the small print on the boxes and the prices. Thus, selective displays should take some of the information off the boxes and enlarge it with a simple 8″ X 8″ sign.

Source: http://www.envirosell.com; Paco Underhill, *Why We Buy: The Science of Shopping* (New York: Simon & Schuster, 2000).

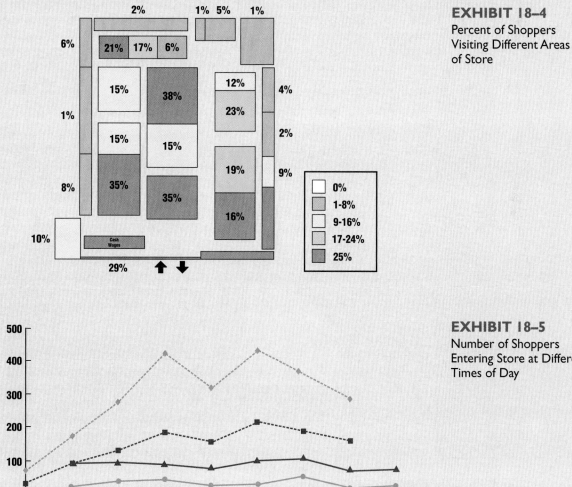

EXHIBIT 18–4
Percent of Shoppers Visiting Different Areas of Store

EXHIBIT 18–5
Number of Shoppers Entering Store at Different Times of Day

customer-service areas like beauty salons, credit offices, and photography studios, are demand or destination areas and thus located in lightly trafficked areas of the store.

Special Merchandise   Some merchandise categories involve a buying process that is best accomplished in a lightly trafficked area. For example, Steuben glass sculptures are unique, expensive art pieces that require thought and concentration for their purchase decision. Thus, Neiman Marcus locates this merchandise in a lightly trafficked area to minimize the distraction of customers contemplating a purchase. Similarly, women's lingerie is typically located in a remote area to offer a more private shopping experience.

Categories that require large amounts of floor space, like furniture, are often located in less desirable locations. Some categories, like curtains, need significant wall space, whereas others, like shoes, require accessible storage.

Adjacencies   Retailers often cluster complementary products together to facilitate multiple purchases. For example, men's dress shirts and ties will be located next to each other. On the basis of the market basket analyses described in Chapter 11, supermarkets locate some items in traditional areas and also adjacent to complementary items. For example, salsa is typically located with other condiments, next to corn chips in the salty snacks aisle, and in the Mexican section in the international aisle.

Location of Merchandise within a Category: The Use of Planograms

Retailers devote considerable attention to the location of specific SKUs within a category. For instance, supermarkets and drug stores place private-label brands to the right of national brands. Because Western consumers read from left to right, they will see the higher-priced national brand first and then see and purchase the lower-priced, higher margin, private-label item on the right. Produce departments in grocery stores are arranged so the first item most customers see are apples, because apples are the most popular produce item and thus can best initiate a buying pattern.

To determine where items should be located within a category or department, retailers generate maps known as planograms. A **planogram** is a diagram that shows how and where specific SKUs should be placed on retail shelves or displays to increase customer purchases. The locations can be illustrated using photographs, computer output, or artists' renderings (see planogram in Retailing View 18.5 on p. 507).

In developing the planogram, retailers need to make the category visually appealing, consider the manner in which customers shop (or the manner in which the retailer would like customers to shop), and achieve the retailer's strategic and financial objectives. There is an art and a science to planogramming. The art is in ensuring that the proper visual impact and presentation is maintained; the science is in the financial analysis portion. A planogrammer must be able to balance these two elements to create a planogram that is best for the store.

Technology for computer-generated planograms is quite sophisticated. On the basis of analyses of historical sales, gross margins, turnover, the sizes of product packaging for each SKU, and the retailer's design criteria, the software determines the optimal shelf space and location for each SKU. Advances in computer graphics and three-dimensional modeling allow planograms to be designed, tested with consumers, and changed, all in a "virtual" shopping environment.[22] Consumers can view merchandise on a computer screen that looks like a real store. They can "pick up" a package by touching its image on the monitor and turn the package so it can be examined from all sides. If they want the item, they can "purchase" it. The computer tracks the time spent shopping for and examining a particular product and the quantity purchased. Armed with this information, the retailer can test the effectiveness of different planograms.

Planograms are also useful for merchandise that doesn't fit nicely on shelves in a grocery or discount store. Most specialty apparel retailers provide their managers with photographs and diagrams of how merchandise should be displayed. Retailing View 18.5 describes how Marketmax's planogramming system automated Marks & Spencer's food business.

VISUAL MERCHANDISING

Visual merchandising is the presentation of a store and its merchandise in ways that will attract the attention of potential customers. This section examines issues related to the presentation of merchandise, and the following section explores more sensory aspects of the store's environment. This section begins with a review of the fixtures used to display merchandise and then discusses some merchandise presentation techniques.

Marks & Spencer Automates Planograms   RETAILING VIEW   18.5

Marks & Spencer is a large retailer of clothing, home goods, and high-quality food products in the United Kingdom. Its food business, specializing in high-quality convenience and fresh foods, such as sandwiches and take-home dinners, occupies a prominent position in the U.K. food retailing sector.

The retailer is continuously updating its product range with new products developed in conjunction with leading manufacturers of short-life food products. Until recently, this process has been labor intensive. For example, the adjustment of 50 displays in 50 stores requires 2,500 new individual planograms, unless some stores are exactly the same, which is not likely. It would take between 80 and 100 full-time planogrammers to implement weekly changes in its 310 stores.

The $4.2 billion retailer began looking for a planogramming system for its fresh food products. Store-specific space plans were necessary to reflect each store's individual needs.

Working with Marketmax, a division of SAS, the retailer was able to develop an automated planogramming system that could optimize weekly fresh food assortments to individual stores, as well as improve product layout and customer satisfaction.

The Marks & Spencer/Marketmax system calculates an optimal layout by determining how many shelf facings are needed for each SKU in each store. At the same time, the system maintains a consistent look but considers specific fixtures and store layouts.

By implementing automated space planning, Marks & Spencer has greatly increased the productivity of its centralized space planning team and gained control over store layout and product presentation. It can now do weekly plans with 20 planogrammers—and it does a much better job. Product placement is now more efficient and uniform throughout the chain, and customers can more easily find specific products. This ease is of particular importance to Marks & Spencer, as many of its customers shop in more than one of its stores.

Source: Communication with Marketmax.

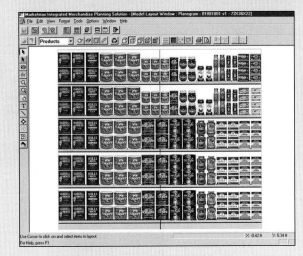

Marks & Spencer in the United Kingdom uses a planogram system developed by Marketmax to develop a layout that maximizes space productivity.

Fixtures

The primary purposes of fixtures are to efficiently hold and display merchandise. At the same time, they must help define areas of a store and encourage traffic flow. Fixtures must work in concert with other design elements, such as floor coverings and lighting, as well as the overall image of the store. For instance, in stores designed to convey a sense of tradition or history, customers automatically expect to see lots of wood rather than plastic or metal fixtures. Wood mixed with metal, acrylic, or stone changes the traditional orientation.

Fixtures come in an infinite variety of styles, colors, sizes, and textures, but only a few basic types are commonly used. For apparel, retailers utilize the straight rack, rounder, and four-way. The mainstay fixture for most other merchandise is the gondola.

The **straight rack** consists of a long pipe suspended from supports going to the floor or attached to a wall (Exhibit 18–6A). Although the straight rack can hold a lot of apparel, it's hard to feature specific styles or colors. All the customer can see is a sleeve or a pant leg. As a result, straight racks are often found in discount and off-price apparel stores.

A **rounder,** also known as a **bulk fixture** or **capacity fixture,** is a round fixture that sits on a pedestal (Exhibit 18–6B). Although smaller than the straight rack, it's designed to hold a maximum amount of merchandise. Because they're easy to move and efficiently store apparel, rounders are found in most types of apparel stores. But as with the straight rack, customers can't get a frontal view of the merchandise.

EXHIBIT 18–6
Four Fixture Types

(A) Straight rack.

(B) Rounder.

(C) Four-way.

(D) Gondola.

A **four-way fixture,** also known as a **feature fixture,** has two crossbars that sit perpendicular to each other on a pedestal (Exhibit 18–6C). This fixture holds a large amount of merchandise and allows the customer to view the entire garment. The four-way is harder to maintain properly than is the rounder or straight rack, however. All merchandise on an arm must be of a similar style and color, or the customer may become confused. Due to their superior display properties, four-way fixtures are commonly utilized by fashion-oriented apparel retailers.

Gondolas are extremely versatile (Exhibit 18–6D). They're used extensively, but not exclusively, in grocery and discount stores to display everything from canned foods to baseball gloves. Gondolas are also found displaying towels, sheets, and housewares in department stores. Folded apparel too can be efficiently displayed on gondolas, but because the items are folded, it's even harder for customers to view apparel on gondolas than on straight racks.

Presentation Techniques

Some presentation techniques are idea-oriented, style/item, color, price lining, vertical merchandising, tonnage merchandising, and frontage presentation.

Idea-Oriented Presentation   Some retailers use an **idea-oriented presentation**—a method of presenting merchandise based on a specific idea or the image of the store. Women's fashions, for instance, are often displayed to present an overall image or idea. Also, furniture is combined in room settings to give customers an idea of how it would look in their homes. Individual items are grouped to show customers how the items could be used and combined. This approach encourages the customer to make multiple complementary purchases.

Manufacturers with strong consumer demand are often merchandised together in the boutique layout described previously in this chapter. This technique is similar to the idea-oriented presentation in that merchandise made by the same vendor will tend to be coordinated. Some apparel manufacturers like Liz Claiborne and Jaeger coordinate both style and color to influence multiple purchases within the line and enhance the line's overall image.

REFACT

Fifty percent of women get their ideas for clothes from store displays or window shopping.[23]

Style/Item Presentation   Probably the most common technique of organizing stock is by style or item. Discount stores, grocery stores, hardware stores, and drugstores employ this method for nearly every category of merchandise, as do many apparel retailers. When customers look for a particular type of merchandise, such as sweaters, they expect to find all items in the same location.

Arranging items by size is a common method of organizing many types of merchandise, from nuts and bolts to apparel. Because the customer usually knows the desired size, it's easy to locate items organized in this manner.

Color Presentation   A bold merchandising technique is by color. For instance, in winter months, women's apparel stores may display all white cruisewear together to let customers know that the store is "the place" to purchase clothing for their winter vacation.

Price Lining   **Price lining** is when retailers offer a limited number of predetermined price points and/or price categories within another classification. This approach helps customers easily find merchandise at the price they wish to pay. For instance, men's dress shirts may be organized into three groups selling for $30, $45, and $60.

Vertical Merchandising   Another common way of organizing merchandise is **vertical merchandising.** Here, merchandise is presented vertically using walls and high gondolas. Customers shop much as they read a newspaper—from left to right, going down each column, top to bottom. Stores can effectively organize merchandise to follow the eye's natural movement. Retailers take advantage of this tendency in several ways. Many grocery stores put national brands at eye level and store brands on lower shelves because customers scan from eye level down. In addition, retailers often display merchandise in bold vertical bands of an item. For instance, you might see vertical columns of towels of the same color displayed in a department store or a vertical band of yellow-and-orange boxes of Tide detergent followed by a band of blue Cheer boxes in a supermarket.

Tonnage Merchandising   As the name implies, **tonnage merchandising** is a display technique in which large quantities of merchandise are displayed together. Customers have come to equate tonnage with low price, following the retail adage "stock it high and let it fly." Tonnage merchandising is therefore used to enhance and reinforce a store's price image. Using this display concept, the merchandise itself is the display. The retailer hopes customers will notice the merchandise and be drawn to it. For instance, before many holidays, grocery stores use an entire end of a gondola (i.e., an end cap) to display six-packs of Pepsi.

Frontal Presentation   Often, it's not possible to create effective displays and efficiently store items at the same time. But it's important to show as much of the merchandise as possible. One solution to this dilemma is the **frontal presentation,** a method of displaying merchandise in which the retailer exposes as much of the product as possible to catch the customer's eye. Book manufacturers, for instance, make great efforts to create eye-catching covers. But bookstores usually display books exposing only the spine. To create an effective display and break the monotony, book retailers often face an occasional cover out like a billboard to catch the customer's attention. A similar frontal presentation can be achieved on a rack of apparel by simply turning one item out to show the merchandise.

ATMOSPHERICS

Atmospherics refers to the design of an environment through visual communications, lighting, colors, music, and scent to stimulate customers' perceptual and emotional responses and ultimately to affect their purchase behavior.[24] Many retailers have discovered the subtle benefits of developing atmospherics that complement other aspects of the store design and the merchandise. Research has shown that it is important for these atmospheric elements to work together—for example, the right music with the right scent.[25]

Lighting

Good lighting in a store involves more than simply illuminating space. Lighting is used to highlight merchandise, sculpt space, and capture a mood or feeling that enhances the store's image. Lighting can also be used to downplay less attractive features that can't be changed. Having the appropriate lighting has been shown to positively influence customer shopping behavior.[26]

A good lighting system helps create a sense of excitement in the store. At the same time, lighting must provide an accurate color rendition of the merchandise. A green silk tie should look the same color in the store as at the customer's office. Similarly, lighting should compliment the customer. A department store's cosmetics area, for instance, requires more expensive lighting than the bare fluorescent lighting found in most grocery stores because it has to compliment the customer and make her skin look natural.

Highlighting Merchandise Another key use of lighting is called **popping the merchandise**—focusing spotlights on special feature areas and items. Using lighting to focus on strategic pockets of merchandise trains shoppers' eyes on the merchandise and draws customers strategically through the store. At Galleri Orrefors Kosta Boda on Manhattan's Madison Avenue, for example, limited and one-of-a-kind glass sculptures are highlighted with special lighting.

Mood Creation Traditionally, U.S. specialty and department stores have employed incandescent lighting sources to promote a warm and cozy ambience.[27] Overall lighting sources were reduced and accent lighting was pronounced to call attention to merchandise and displays. It was meant to feel like someone's home—dim lighting overall, with artwork and other areas of interest highlighted.

Galleri Orrefors Kosta Boda on New York's Madison Avenue uses special lighting to highlight its limited-production glass sculptures.

The European method of lighting can now be found in the most exclusive specialty stores of Rodeo Drive and Bal Harbour and even some department stores like Bloomingdale's.[28] European stores have long favored high light levels, cool colors, and little contrast or accent lighting. European lighting design has been more bold, stark, and minimal than in the United States, creating a very different mood and image than the softer incandescent lighting.

Downplay Features Lighting can hide errors and outmoded store designs. At Sentry Foods in Madison, Wisconsin, product lighting is very high compared with that in the rest of the store. The ceiling was intentionally kept dark to downplay an unsightly concrete ceiling.

Color

The creative use of color can enhance a retailer's image and help create a mood. Warm colors (red and yellow) produce excitement, whereas cool colors (blue and green) have a calming effect.[29]

Music

Like color and lighting, music can either add to or detract from a retailer's total atmospheric package.[30] Unlike other atmospheric elements, however, music can be easily changed. For example, a retailer with 1,000 stores across the United States wants to play jazzy music in the morning and adult contemporary in the afternoon, but just for stores on the East Coast. These selections are made because most of its morning shoppers are older, whereas the afternoon shoppers are more in the 35–40 year age range. For its West Coast stores, it wants modern rock in the morning and Caribbean beats in the afternoon. And in Texas, it's country music all day, every day.

Retailers can also use music to affect customers' behavior. Music can control the pace of store traffic, create an image, and attract or direct consumers' attention. For instance, Limited Too, a division of The Limited Group, has created a signature sound to appeal to its target market, 8- to 14-year-old girls. It uses a mix of hip hop, R&B, pop, and swing. The Disney Stores pipe in soundtracks from famous Disney movies that are tied directly to the merchandise.

REFACT

As people get older, their sense of smell decreases. Half of all people over age 65 and three-quarters over 80 years of age have almost no smell at all.[32]

Scent

Many buying decisions are based on emotions, and smell has a large impact on our emotions, such as happiness, hunger, disgust, and nostalgia—the same feelings marketers want to tap. Scent, in conjunction with music, has a positive impact on impulse buying behavior and customer satisfaction.[31] Scents that are neutral produce better perceptions of the store than no scent. Customers in scented stores think they spent less time in the store than subjects in unscented stores. Stores using scents may improve customers' subjective shopping experience by making them feel that they are spending less time examining merchandise or waiting for sales help or to check out.

How Exciting Should a Store Be?

Retailers such as REI, The Sharper Image, Bass Pro Shops, and Barnes & Noble attempt to create an entertaining shopping environment by viewing their stores as theatrical scenes: The floor and walls constitute the stage and scenery; the lighting, fixtures, and displays are the props; and the merchandise represents the performance. This creation of a theatrical experience in stores has resulted in the combination of retailing and entertainment. In contrast, retail chains such as Costco and Home Depot successfully use minimalist, warehouse-style shopping environments.

Does providing an exciting, entertaining store environment lead customers to patronize a store more frequently and spend more time and money during each visit? The answer to this question is: It depends.[33]

The impact of the store's environment depends on the customer's shopping goals. The two basic shopping goals are task completion, such as buying a new suit for a job interview, and recreation, such as spending a Saturday afternoon with a friend wandering through a mall. When customers are shopping to complete a task that they view as inherently unrewarding, they prefer to be in a soothing, calming environment—a simple atmosphere with slow music, dimmer lighting, and blue/green colors. However, when customers go shopping for fun, an inherently rewarding activity, they want to be in an exciting atmosphere—a complex environment with fast music, bright lighting, and red/yellow colors.

What does this mean for retailers? They must consider the typical shopping goals for their customers when designing their store environments. For example, grocery shopping is typically viewed as an unpleasant task, and thus, supermarkets should be designed in soothing colors and use slow background music. In contrast, shopping for fashion apparel is typically viewed as fun, so an arousing environment in apparel retail outlets will have a positive impact on the shopping behavior of their customers.

The level of excitement caused by the environment might vary across the store. For example, a consumer electronics retailer might create a low-arousal environment in the accessories area to accommodate customers who typically are task-oriented when shopping for these products, but then create a high-arousal environment in the home-entertainment centers that are typically visited by more pleasure-seeking shopping customers.

Finally, retailers might vary the nature of a Web site for customers depending on their shopping goals. For example, research suggests that Amazon should serve up complex, high-arousal Web sites with rich media to customers who indicate they are browsing but simpler, low-arousal sites to customers looking for a specific book.[34] Some parallels between store and Web site designs are drawn in the following section.

The Toys "R" Us store in New York's Times Square creates a very exciting store atmosphere.

WEB SITE DESIGN

In many, but not all, cases, good design principles that apply to a physical store can also be applied to a Web site.[35] Consider the following examples.

Simplicity Matters

A good store design allows shoppers to move freely, unencumbered by clutter. There is a fine line between providing customers with a good assortment and confusing them with too much merchandise.

Similarly in a Web site, it is not necessary to mention all the merchandise available at a site on each page. It is better to present a limited selection tailored to the customer's needs and then provide a few links to related merchandise and alternative assortments. It is also important to include a search engine feature on each page in case a customer gets lost. The search feature in the virtual world is similar to having sales associates readily available in the physical world. Also, less is more. Having a small number of standard links on every page makes it more likely that users will learn the navigation scheme for the site.

Getting Around

When a store is properly designed, customers should be able to find what they are looking for easily. The products that customers frequently purchase together are often displayed together. For example, umbrellas are displayed with raincoats, soft drinks with snack foods, and tomato sauce with pasta. One way to help customers get around a Web site is by using local links internal to the site. When establishing local links, Web sites should link:

- Products that are similar in price.
- Complementary products.
- Products that differ from the product shown on some important dimension (for example, a link to a color printer if the user is looking at a black-and-white printer).
- Different versions of the shown product (for example, the same blouse in yellow if the customer is viewing a red blouse).

Let Them See It

Stores are designed so customers can easily view the merchandise and read the signs. But in a store, if the lighting isn't good or a sign is too small to read, the customer can always move around to get a better view. Customers don't have this flexibility on the Internet. Web designers should assume that all potential viewers don't have perfect vision. They should strive for realistic colors and sharpness. Some retailers that use the Internet channel have developed interesting ways of viewing merchandise in multiple dimensions (see, for instance, www.landsend.com).

Blend the Web Site with the Store

It is important to visually reassure customers that they're going to have the same satisfactory experience on the Web site that they have in stores. So even if the electronic store is designed for navigation efficiency, there should still be some design elements that are common to both channels. For instance, though very different store types, www.tiffany.com and www.officedepot.com each have a similar look and feel to those of their stores.

Prioritize

Stores become annoying if everything jumps out at you as if to say, "Buy me! No buy me!" Other stores are so bland that the merchandise appears boring. Setting priorities for merchandise displays and locations is just as important on the

Web site as it is in a physical store. A common mistake on many Internet sites is that everything is too prominent: overuse of colors, animation, blinking, and graphics. If everything is equally prominent, then *nothing* is prominent. Being too bland is equally troublesome. The site should be designed to advise the customers and guide them to the most important or most promising choices, while ensuring their freedom to go anywhere they please. Like a newspaper, the most important items or categories should be given the bigger headlines and more prominent placement.

Type of Layout

Some stores are laid out to be functional, like supermarkets and discount stores. They use a grid design to make it easy to locate merchandise. Other stores, like department stores or bookstores, use a more relaxed layout to encourage browsing. The trick is to pick the appropriate layout that matches the typical motives of the shopper.

Here is where store layout and Web site layout differ. Although many higher-end multichannel retailers experimented with fancy and complex designs in their early years on the Internet, most have become much more simple and utilitarian than their bricks-and-mortar counterparts (see, for instance, www.polo.com, www.neimanmarcus.com, and www.bloomingdales.com). When shopping on the Web, customers are interested in speed, convenience, and ease of navigation, not necessarily fancy graphics.

Store designers also strive to make their stores different, to stand out in the crowd. A Web site, however, must strike the balance between keeping customers' interest and providing them with a comfort level based on convention. Users spend most of their time on *other* sites, so that's where they form their expectations about how most sites work. When trying to make a decision about Web site design, good designers look at the most visited sites on the Internet to see how they do it. If 90 percent or more of the big sites do things in a single way, then it is the de facto standard.

SUMMARY

Some objectives for a store design are to (1) implement the retailer's strategy, (2) influence customer buying behavior, (3) provide flexibility, (4) control design and maintenance costs, and (5) meet legal requirements. Typically, a store design cannot achieve all of these objectives, so managers make trade-offs between objectives, such as providing convenience versus encouraging exploration.

The basic elements in a design that guide customers through the store are the layout, signage, and features areas. A good store layout helps customers find and purchase merchandise. Several types of layouts commonly used by retailers are the grid, race track, and free-form. The grid design is best for stores in which customers are expected to explore the entire store, such as grocery stores and drugstores. Racetrack designs are more common in large upscale stores like department stores. Free-form designs are usually found in small specialty stores and within large stores' departments.

Signage and graphics help customers locate specific products and departments, provide product information, and suggest items or special purchases. In addition, graphics, such as photo panels, can enhance the store environment and the store's image. Digital signage has several advantages over traditional printed signage, but the initial fixed costs have made the adoption of this technology slow. Feature areas are areas within a store designed to get the customer's attention. They include freestanding displays, end caps, promotional aisles or areas, windows, cash wraps or point-of-sale areas, and walls.

Space management involves two decisions: (1) the allocation of store space to merchandise categories and brands and (2) the location of departments or merchandise categories in the store. Some factors that retailers consider when deciding how much floor or shelf space to allocate to merchandise categories and brands are (1) the productivity of the allocated space, (2) the merchandise's inventory turnover, (3) impact on store sales, and (4) the display needs for the merchandise. When evaluating the productivity of retail space, retailers generally use sales per square foot or sales per linear foot.

The location of merchandise categories also plays a role in how customers navigate through the store. By strategically placing impulse and demand/destination merchandise throughout the store, retailers can increase the chances that customers will shop the entire store and that their attention will be focused on the merchandise that the retailer is most interested in selling. In locating merchandise categories, retailers need to consider typical consumer shopping patterns.

Retailers utilize various forms of atmospherics—lighting, colors, music, and scent—to influence shopping behavior.

The use of these atmospherics can create a calming environment for task-oriented shoppers or an exciting environment for recreational shoppers.

Although a retailer's Web site is different than its physical store, in many but not all cases, good design principles that apply to a physical store space can also be applied to a Web site.

KEY TERMS

atmospherics, *510*
boutique layout, *497*
bulk fixture, *508*
capacity fixture, *508*
cash wrap, *501*
checkout area, *501*
demand/destination
  merchandise, *504*
digital signage, *500*
end cap, *502*
feature area, *501*
feature fixture, *509*

fixture, *492*
four-way fixture, *509*
free-form layout, *497*
freestanding display, *501*
frontal presentation, *510*
gondola, *509*
grid layout, *495*
idea-oriented presentation, *509*
impulse product, *504*
loop, *496*
planogram, *506*
point-of-purchase counter, *501*

popping the merchandise, *511*
price lining, *509*
promotional aisle or area, *502*
racetrack layout, *496*
rounder, *508*
sales per linear foot, *503*
sales per square foot, *503*
straight rack, *508*
tonnage merchandising, *510*
vertical merchandising, *510*
visual merchandising, *507*

GET OUT AND DO IT!

1. **CONTINUING EXERCISE** Go into the physical store location of the retailer you have chosen for the continuing exercise and evaluate the store layout, design, and visual merchandising techniques employed. Explain your answers to the following questions:
   (*a*) In general, are the store layout, design, and visual merchandising techniques used consistent with the exterior of the store and location?
   (*b*) Is the store's ambience consistent with the merchandise presented and the customer's expectations?
   (*c*) Does the store look like it needs to be redesigned?
   (*d*) To what extent are the store's layout, design, and merchandising techniques flexible?
   (*e*) Notice the lighting. Does it do a good job highlighting merchandise, structuring space, capturing a mood, and downplaying unwanted features?
   (*f*) How does the store utilize atmospheric elements like color, music, or scent? Are these uses appropriate given the store's target markets?
   (*g*) Are the fixtures consistent with the merchandise and the overall ambience of the store? Are they flexible?
   (*h*) Evaluate the store's signage. Does it do an effective job of selling merchandise?

   (*i*) Has the retailer used any theatrical effects to help sell merchandise?
   (*j*) Does the store layout help draw people through the store?
   (*k*) Has the retailer taken advantage of the opportunity to sell merchandise in feature areas?
   (*l*) Does the store make creative use of wall space?
   (*m*) What type of layout does the store use? Is it appropriate for the type of store? Would another type of layout be better?
   (*n*) Ask the store manager how the profitability of space is evaluated (e.g., profit per square foot). Is there a better approach?
   (*o*) Ask the store manager how space is assigned to merchandise. Critically evaluate the answer.
   (*p*) Ask the store manager if planograms are used. If so, try to determine what factors are considered when putting together a planogram.
   (*q*) Are departments in the most appropriate locations? Would you move any departments?
   (*r*) What method(s) has the retailer used to organize merchandise? Is this the best way? Suggest any appropriate changes.

2. **INTERNET EXERCISE** Go to your favorite multichannel retailer's Internet site. Evaluate its degree of simplicity, its ease of navigation, its readability, its use

of color, and its consistency with the image of its bricks-and-mortar store.

3. **INTERNET EXERCISE** Go to www.metirimensus. com (Apollo), and www.acnielsen.com (Spaceman). Evaluate their planogram programs. Which one would you choose?

4. **INTERNET EXERCISE** Go to http://www. visualstore.com/ and write a report on the latest trends in visual merchandising.

5. **INTERNET EXERCISE** Go to the home page for Perception Research Services at http://www. prsresearch.com/Index.htm. Read about its PSR Eye Tracking research. How can retailers use this information when making store layout and merchandise placement decisions?

DISCUSSION QUESTIONS AND PROBLEMS

1. One of the fastest growing sectors of the population is the over-60 age group. But these customers may have limitations in their vision, hearing, and movement. How can retailers develop store designs with the older population's needs in mind?

2. Assume you have been hired as a consultant to assess a local discount store's space productivity. What analytical tools would you use to assess the situation? What suggestions would you make to improve the store's space productivity?

3. What are the different types of design that can be used in a store layout? Why are some stores more suited for a particular type of layout than others?

4. Generally speaking, departments located near entrances, on major aisles, and on the main level of multilevel stores have the best profit-generating potential. What additional factors help determine the location of departments? Give examples of each factor.

5. A department store is building an addition. The merchandise manager for furniture is trying to convince the vice president to allot this new space to the furniture department. The merchandise manager for men's clothing is also trying to gain the space. What points should each manager use when presenting his or her rationale?

6. As a manager for a large department store, you are responsible for ADA compliance. But your performance evaluation is based on bottom-line profitability. How would you make sure your store is accessible to people in wheelchairs and at the same time not lose any sales?

7. Describe the ways in which designing a Web site is similar to and different from designing a store.

8. Why do supermarkets put candy, gum, and magazines at the front of the store?

9. What are the pros and cons for both centralized cash wraps and departmental cash wraps for stores such as JCPenney and Kohl's?

10. Most department store anchors place the cosmetics counters at the ground floor mall entrance. Explain why this is the preferred location in lieu of other potential locations.

11. If you were the manager of an apparel specialty store targeting men and women, how would you use information about sales per square foot for the various merchandise categories listed below when making merchandise location decisions within the retail space?

ICSS RESEARCH—MONTHLY MERCHANDISE INDEX, JUNE 2004 NON-ANCHOR MALL TENANTS	
Category	Sales per Square Foot
Women's apparel	$25
Women's accessories	$47
Men's apparel	$25
Children's apparel	$23
Women's shoes	$34
Men's shoes	$39
Children's shoes	$27

SUGGESTED READINGS

Baker, Julie; A. Parasuraman; Dhruv Grewal; and Glen Voss. "The Influence of Multiple Store Environment Cues on Perceived Merchandise Value and Patronage Intentions," *Journal of Marketing* 66 (April 2002), pp. 120–41.

Dean, Corrina. *Inspired Retail Space: Attract Customers, Build Branding, Increase Volume.* Rockport, ME: Rockport Publishers, 2005.

Diamond, Jay, and Ellen Diamond. *Contemporary Visual Merchandising and Environmental Design.* 3rd ed. Upper Saddle River, NJ: Prentice Hall, 2004.

Greely, Dave, and Joe Cataudella. *Creating Stores on the Web.* Atlanta: Peachpit Press, 1999.

Green, William R. *Retail Store: Design and Construction.* Universe, Incorporated, 2000.

Grewal, Dhruv; Julie Baker; Michael Levy; and Glenn Voss. "The Effects of Wait Expectations and Store Atmosphere Evaluations on Patronage Intentions in Service-intensive Retail Stores," *Journal of Retailing* 79, no. 4 (Fall 2003), pp. 259–68.

Kalchteva, Velitchka, and Barton Weitz. "How Exciting Should a Store Be?" *Journal of Marketing*, Winter 2006, pp. 34–62.

Lam, Shun Yin, and Avinandan Mukherjee. "The Effects of Merchandise Coordination and Juxtaposition on Consumers' Product Evaluation and Purchase Intention in Store-Based Retailing," *Journal of Retailing* 81, no. 3 (2005), pp. 231–45.

Mostaedi, Arian. *Cool Shops*. Singapore: Page One, 2004.

Reda, Susan. "Sign of the Times," *Stores*, June 2005, pp. 32–34.

Tucker, Johnny. *Retail Desire: Design, Display and Visual Merchandising*. Mies, Switzerland: Hove, 2003.

Underhill, Paco. *Why We Buy: The Science of Shopping*. New York: Simon & Schuster, 2000.

Wildrick, Rich. "Merchandising Strategies," *Chain Store Age*, Mid-December 2004, p. 100.

Customer Service

EXECUTIVE BRIEFING
Sybil Jackson,
Pet Director for PETsHOTEL^{SM}

I worked in the hospitality industry as a hotel operations manager before joining PETsMART. As manager for the grooming salon and pet hotel services we offer at our store, I strive to provide the level of customer service offered at five star hotels—service that is above and beyond the expectation of our pet parents.

PETsMART is the nation's leading retail supplier of products, services, and solutions for the lifetime needs of pets. We are a multi-channel retailer operating more than 700 pet superstores in the United States and Canada, a large pet supply catalog business, and the Internet's leading pet product Web site. While our stores offer the industry's broadest assortment of products, we are now focusing on providing services for pet parents. Nearly all of our stores have pet styling salons that offer safe, quality pet grooming services, from full-service styling to baths, toenail trimming and teeth cleaning. Many of our loca-

tions have veterinary hospitals inside the store. We also offer affordable education for puppies or adult dogs and are testing PETsHOTEL^{SM}, an innovative, high-quality pet boarding and day camp concept.

I have 40 people on my team. Some of them work behind the scenes providing grooming service, keeping the hotel rooms clean, and playing with the animals during their stay. Others, customer service representatives, interact with pet parents when they check their animals in. Providing outstanding customer service starts with hiring the right people. First and foremost, the people I hire must love animals and care about their well being. Then, for the customer representative positions, I look for people who are energetic and outgoing. When I hire for the behind-the-scenes jobs, I want them to have a realistic idea about what the job entails—the good and bad. While there are a lot of enjoyable parts of the job, they need to

CHAPTER 19

QUESTIONS

What services do retailers offer customers?

How can customer service build a competitive advantage?

How do customers evaluate a retailer's service?

What activities does a retailer have to undertake to provide high-quality customer service?

How can retailers recover from a service failure?

Suppose you are surfing the Internet for a digital camera. At www.realcheapcameras.com, a hypothetical site, you are asked to type in the name of the specific brand and model number you want. Then you are quoted a price with shipping charges and asked for your credit card number and a shipping address. In contrast, when you go to www.circuitcity.com, you can buy a specific digital camera, review the specifications for different cameras, or look through reviews by experts and other consumers of different cameras. You can then go to a store to see the cameras, get additional information about the cameras from a sales associate, and look at accessories, such as a carrying case and additional memory units. Circuit City is providing some valuable services to its customers—services customers cannot get from RealCheapCameras.com.

Customer service is the set of activities and programs undertaken by retailers to make the shopping experience more rewarding for their customers. These activities increase the value customers receive from the merchandise and services they purchase. Retailing View 19.1 describes some new health services being offered by drug and discount stores.

Some of these services are derived from the retailer's store design or Web site or from policies established by the retailer. However, this chapter focuses on some of the most important personalized services provided by sales associates interacting directly with customers.

> **REFACT**
> Shopping carts were first introduced in 1937 in a Humpty Dumpty store in Oklahoma City.[1]

The first section discusses retailers' opportunities to develop strategic advantages through customer service, followed by an examination of how retailers can take advantage of this opportunity by providing high-quality service.

> **REFACT**
> The word *service* is from the Latin term *servus*, meaning "slave."[2]

do unpleasant things like cleaning up after an animal messes up.

After hiring the right people, I motivate the employees on my team to provide outstanding service. I give them kudos when I see them doing something special. For example, this morning a customer came in to pick up her dog at 9:00 a.m. and decided, at the last minute, she wanted her dog to have a bath before she took her home. However, we did not have any bathers available. So the customer service representative, who is a trained and licensed groomer, rolled up her sleeves and gave the dog a bath herself. Her initiative showed me that she is a team player and cares about pleasing our customers, so I gave her a kudo on the spot—a $5 gift certificate at Starbucks.

STRATEGIC ADVANTAGE THROUGH CUSTOMER SERVICE

Nordstrom, Disney World, McDonald's, Amazon.com, and Marriott differentiate their retail offerings, build customer loyalty, and develop sustainable competitive advantages by providing excellent customer service. Good service keeps customers returning to a retailer and generates positive word-of-mouth communication, which attracts new customers.[3]

All employees of a retail firm and all elements of the retailing mix provide services that increase the value of merchandise. For example, employees in the distribution center contribute to customer service by making sure the merchandise is in stock. The employees responsible for store location and design contribute by increasing the customer's convenience in getting to the store and finding merchandise in the store.

Exhibit 19–1 lists some of the services provided by retailers. Most of these services furnish information about the retailer's offering and make it easier for customers to locate and buy products and services. Services such as alterations and the assembly of merchandise actually change merchandise to fit the needs of specific customers.

Providing high-quality service is difficult for retailers. Automated manufacturing makes the quality of most merchandise consistent from item to item. For example, all Super Twist Skil electric screwdrivers look alike and typically perform alike. But the quality of retail service can vary dramatically from store to store and from salesperson to salesperson within a store. It's hard for retailers to control the performance of employees who provide the service. A sales associate may provide good service to

---

19.1 RETAILING VIEW   Retailers Provide Health Care Services

To offer customers a one-stop provider for health care solutions, drug and discount store chains are opening in-store health clinics. These clinics offer customers fast access to routine medical services such as strep-throat tests, sports physicals, and flu shots. The clinics, which typically charge between $25 and $60 per visit, don't require an appointment and are open during pharmacy hours, including evenings and weekends. To keep costs down, they are staffed by nurse practitioners, who can legally treat patients and write prescriptions in most states. Third-party providers lease space in the stores and operate the clinics. (The drugstore chains must partner with outside companies because federal health care laws banning "self-referrals" prohibit pharmacy chains from running their own clinics.)

The clinics target a broad range of customers, from harried parents dropping by with sick children on the weekends to busy professionals ducking in for a prescription during work hours. Although the retailers don't profit directly from the new services, they anticipate that the clinics will increase sales when customers fill their prescriptions at the store pharmacy or pick up other items on their way out.

For example, 56-year-old Terri Whitesel, who runs a marketing consultancy in Minneapolis, had an allergic reaction to a bug bite last month. She dashed into a MinuteClinic at a Target in between meetings at work. "I didn't want to go to the doctor and sit around waiting with a bunch of people who are really sick," said Whitesel. The nurse practitioner was busy with another patient, but Whitesel wrote down her name, got a beeper at the check-in counter, and shopped for birthday cards until the nurse beeped her five minutes later. The entire visit took less than 15 minutes, and she wound up with a prescription for an anti-inflammatory drug.

Health insurers support the concept because the clinics promise considerable savings. Whereas a typical doctor visit for a basic illness costs an insurer about $110, a visit to one of the

To provide one-stop shopping solutions for its customers' health care needs, Rite Aid is adding these Take Care Clinics to its drugstores.

clinics usually costs under $60. Some of the clinics also use technology to increase the efficiency of care. When patients arrive, they check themselves in at a touch screen computer terminal, where they can swipe a credit card and enter basic information about their symptoms and family history. The patient's sign-in information is transmitted electronically to a computer terminal inside the treatment room where the nurses can enter additional information about the patient's symptoms and conditions as they talk with the patient. In one of the more novel uses of technology, the Take Care computer software program eventually will be involved in actually diagnosing illnesses.

Source: Jane Spencer, "Getting Your Health Care at Wal-Mart," *The Wall Street Journal*, October 5, 2005, p. D1. Used by permission of Dow Jones & Co., Inc. via the Copyright Clearance Center.

EXHIBIT 19-1
Services Offered by
Retailers

Acceptance of credit cards	Parking
Alterations of merchandise	Personal assistance in selecting
Assembly of merchandise	merchandise
ATM terminals	Personal shoppers
Bridal registry	Play areas for children
Check cashing	Presentations on how to use
Child-care facilities	merchandise
Credit	Provisions for customers with
Delivery to home or work	special needs (wheelchairs,
Demonstrations of merchandise	translators)
Display of merchandise	Repair services
Dressing rooms	Rest rooms
Extended store hours	Return privileges
Signage to locate and identity merchandise	Rooms for checking coats and
Facilities for shoppers with special needs	packages
(physically handicapped)	Shopping carts
Layaway plans	Special orders
Gift wrapping	Warranties

one customer and poor service to the next. In addition, most services provided by retailers are intangible; customers can't see or feel them. Clothing can be held and examined, but the assistance provided by a sales associate or an electronic agent can't. Intangibility makes it hard to provide and maintain high-quality service because retailers can't count, measure, or check service before it's delivered to customers.

The challenge of providing consistent high-quality service offers an opportunity for a retailer to develop a sustainable competitive advantage. For example, Nordstrom devotes much time and effort to developing an organizational culture that stimulates and supports excellent customer service. Competing department stores would like to offer the same level of service but find it hard to match Nordstrom's performance.[6]

REFACT

Seventy-three percent of consumers attribute their best customer service experience to store employees. Conversely, 81 percent of consumers attribute their worst customer service experience to employees.[5]

Customer Service Strategies

Customization and standardization are two approaches retailers use to develop a sustainable customer service advantage. Successful implementation of the customized approach relies on the performance of sales associates or the degree to which customer interactions can be customized using an electronic channel. The standardization approach relies more on policy, procedures, and store and Web site design and layout.[7]

The office supply category specialist (left) uses signage as part of its standardized approach for improving customer service, while Target's sales associates (right) use a customized approach to tailor their service to match the needs of their individual customers.

Customization Approach   The **customization approach** encourages service providers to tailor their service to meet each customer's personal needs. For example, sales associates in specialty stores help individual customers locate appropriate apparel and accessories. Some retailers have introduced a human element into their electronic channel. At Lands' End, customers can simply click on a button and chat—referred to as instant messaging—with a service provider. Lands' End was one of the first retailers to offer live chats with service representatives on its Web site. Sales representatives respond within 20 seconds when a customer clicks the "Help" button. Over 200 of Lands' End's 2,500 service representatives are dedicated to providing this service. Lands' End has found that the average order increases 8 percent when customers use the instant messaging service.[8]

Inspired by the Disney approach to customer service, Target launched its Guest Service program. Customers are treated as guests, with store employees as their hosts. Stock clerks are taught that helping guests isn't an intrusion on their work. Several employees, called guest ambassadors, roam the store looking for customers who need assistance. Employees are also empowered to make sure that guests have a satisfying experience in the store. If the shelf price isn't on an item, checkout clerks can take the customer's word about prices up to $20 so the guest doesn't have to wait for the clerk to check the price with someone on the floor.[9]

The customized approach typically results in most customers receiving superior service. But the service might be inconsistent because service delivery depends on the judgment and capabilities of the service providers. Some service providers are better than others, and even the best service providers can have a bad day. In addition, providing customized service is costly because it requires more well-trained service providers or complex computer software.

Standardization Approach   The **standardization approach** is based on establishing a set of rules and procedures and being sure that they are implemented consistently. By strict enforcement of these procedures, inconsistencies in the service are minimized. Through standardization, customers receive the same quality of food and service at McDonald's restaurants across the globe. The food may not be exactly what customers want, but it's consistent and served in a timely manner at a low cost.

Store or Web site design and layout also play an important role in the standardization approach. In many situations, customers don't need the services employees provide. They know what they want to buy, and their objective is to find it in the store and buy it quickly. In these situations, retailers offer good service by providing a layout and signs that enable customers to locate merchandise easily, having relevant information on display, and minimizing the time required to make a purchase.

Retailing View 19.2 shows how IKEA uses a standardized, self-service approach with some unique elements to attract customers expecting the traditional customized approach employed in furniture retailing.

Cost of Customer Service   As indicated previously, providing high-quality service, particularly customized service, can be very costly. For over 100 years, the Savoy Hotel in London maintained a special place in the hearts of the world's elite. Maids switch off vacuum cleaners when they greet guests entering the hallway in the morning. Each floor has it own waiter on duty from 7:00 a.m. to 3:00 p.m. Guests can get cotton sheets instead of the standard Irish linen sheets if they wish. Preferred fruits are added to the complimentary fruit bowl in each room. Rooms are personally furnished for customers who regularly have extended stays at the hotel. At times, the hotel staff moves the customers' furniture, including personal pictures, from storage into their rooms when they arrive.

But this high level of personal attention is very costly to provide. The Savoy employed three people for each of its 200 rooms, about double the average for a London hotel. These services resulted in annual losses, and the hotel was eventually sold to a corporation that eliminated some of the services.

In many cases, however, good customer service can actually reduce costs and increase profits. It costs much more to acquire a new customer than to generate repeat business from present customers. Thus, it costs a business much less to keep its existing customers satisfied and sell more merchandise to them than it does to sell to people who aren't buying from the business now.[10]

Retailers need to consider the costs and benefits of service policies. For example, many retailers are reconsidering their "no questions asked" return policy. Home Depot's policy was to take back all merchandise and give cash back. Now, if customers don't have a receipt, they can only get store credit. If they have a receipt, they can get cash back. Target now requires that customers have a receipt and return the merchandise in 90 days to get a credit. In addition, for some consumer electronics products, customers must pay a 15 percent restocking charge. Retailers are seeing too many big-screen TVs coming back the day after the Super Bowl and too many prom dresses coming back the day after prom night. However, the most significant contributor to the cost of returns are professionals that return stolen merchandise for cash.[11] The next section examines how customers evaluate service quality.

REFACT

Retailers lose nearly $30 billion, or 1.7 percent of sales, because of fraud, and roughly half of that may be related to bad returns.[12]

CUSTOMER EVALUATIONS OF SERVICE QUALITY

When customers evaluate retail service, they compare their perceptions of the service they receive with their expectations. Customers are satisfied when the perceived service meets or exceeds their expectations. They're dissatisfied when they feel the service falls below their expectations.[13]

Customer Service at IKEA   RETAILING VIEW   19.2

IKEA is a global furniture retailer based in Sweden. Its concept of service differs from that of the traditional furniture store. The typical furniture store has a showroom displaying some of the merchandise sold in the store. Complementing the inventory are books of fabric swatches, veneers, and alternative styles customers can order. Salespeople assist customers in going through the books. When the customer makes a selection, an order is placed with the factory, and the furniture is delivered to the customer's home in six to eight weeks. This system maximizes customization, but the costs are high.

In contrast, IKEA uses a self-service model based on extensive in-store displays. At information desks in the store, shoppers can pick up a map of the store, plus a pencil, order form, clipboard, and tape measure. After studying the catalog and displays, customers proceed to a self-service storage area and locate their selections using codes copied from the sales tags. Every product available is displayed in over 70 room-like settings throughout the 150,000 square foot warehouse store. Thus, customers don't need a decorator to help them picture how the furniture will go together. Adjacent to the display room is a warehouse with ready-to-assemble furniture in boxes that customers can pick up when they leave the store.

Although IKEA uses a "customers do it themselves" approach, it does offer some services that traditional furniture stores do not, such as in-store child-care centers and information about the quality of the furniture. Toddlers can be left in a

IKEA effectively uses a self-service method to provide customer service through signage and information in displays and on the merchandise.

supervised ballroom filled with 50,000 brightly colored plastic balls. There are changing rooms in each store, complete with bottle warmers and disposable diaper dispensers. Displays cover the quality of products in terms of design features and materials, with demonstrations of testing procedures.

Sources: John Kelly, "A Good Place by Design," *Washington Post*, December 23, 2004, p. C.13; Mike Duff, "Late-Blooming IKEA U.S. Wears 20 Well," *DSN Retailing Today*, September 6, 2004, pp. 6–9.

Role of Expectations

Customer expectations are based on a customer's knowledge and experiences.[14] For example, customers do not expect to get an immediate response to a letter or even a telephone call, but they expect to get a response to an e-mail the next time they turn on their computer.

Technology is dramatically changing the ways in which customers and firms interact. Customers now can interact with companies through automated voice response systems and place orders and check on delivery status through the Internet. But customers still expect dependable outcomes, easy access, responsive systems, flexibility, apologies, and compensation when things go wrong. In other words, they still want good service. But now they expect this level of service even when people are not involved.[15]

Expectations vary depending on the type of store. Customers expect a supermarket to provide convenient parking, be open from early morning to late evening, have a wide variety of fresh and packaged food that can be located easily, display products, and offer fast checkout. They don't expect the supermarket to have store employees stationed in the aisle to offer information about groceries or how to prepare meals. However, when these same customers shop in a specialty store, they expect the store to have knowledgeable salespeople who can provide information and assistance.

Because expectations aren't the same for all types of retailers, a customer may be satisfied with low levels of actual service in one store and dissatisfied with high service levels in another store. For example, customers have low service expectations for self-service retailers such as discount stores and supermarkets. Wal-Mart provides an unusual service for a discount store: An employee stands at the entrance to each store, greeting customers and answering questions. Because this service is unexpected in a discount store, customers evaluate Wal-Mart's service positively, even though the actual level of service is far below that provided by a typical specialty store.

Upscale, high-fashion department stores have many more salespeople available to answer questions and provide information than Wal-Mart does. But customer service expectations are also higher for department stores. If department store customers can't locate a salesperson quickly when they have questions or want to make a purchase, they're dissatisfied. When retailers provide unexpected services, they build a high level of customer satisfaction, referred to as **customer delight**.[17] Some examples of unexpected positive service experiences are

Wal-Mart employees greet customers when they enter the store and answer their questions. Because this service is unexpected in a discount store, it creates a favorable perception of Wal-Mart's customer service.

- A restaurant that sends customers who have had too much to drink home in a taxi and then delivers their cars in the morning.
- A men's store that sews numbered tags on each garment so the customer will know what goes together.
- A gift store that keeps track of important customer dates and suggests appropriate gifts.

Customer service expectations vary around the world. Although Germany's manufacturing capability is world renowned, its poor customer service is also well known. People wait years to have telephone service installed. Many restaurants do not accept credit cards, and customers who walk into stores near closing time often receive rude stares. Customers typically have to bag merchandise they buy themselves. Because Germans are unaccustomed to good service, they don't demand it. But as retailing becomes global and new foreign competitors enter, German retailers are becoming more concerned about how they service their customers.

In contrast, the Japanese expect excellent customer service. In the United States, it's said that "the customer is always right." In Japan, the equivalent expression is *okyakusama ha kamisama desu,* "the customer is God." When a customer comes back to a store to return merchandise, he or she is dealt with even more cordially than when the original purchase was made. Customer satisfaction isn't negotiable. The customer is never wrong. Even if the customer misused the product, retailers feel they were responsible for not telling the customer how to use it properly. The first person in the store who hears about the problem must take full responsibility for dealing with the customer, even if the problem involved another department.

This salesperson at a Kelo Department Store is providing the excellent personalized service that Japanese customers expect. The computer system scans the customer's feet and suggests shoes that will provide a good fit.

Perceived Service

Customers base their evaluations of store service on their perceptions. Although these perceptions are affected by the actual service provided, service, due to its intangibility, is often hard to evaluate accurately. Five customer service characteristics that customers use to evaluate service quality are reliability, assurance, tangibility, empathy, and responsiveness.[18] Some cues that customers use to assess these service characteristics include:

- *Reliability.* Accuracy of billing, meeting promised delivery dates.
- *Assurance (trust).* Guarantees and warranties, return policy.
- *Tangibility.* Appearance of store, salespeople.
- *Empathy.* Personalized service, receipts of notes and e-mails, recognition by name.
- *Responsiveness.* Returning calls and e-mails, giving prompt service.

Retailing View 19.3 describes how the Broadmoor Hotel maintains its five-star rating by focusing on these five service characteristics.

As Retailing View 19.3 indicates, employees can play an important role in customer perceptions of service quality. Customer evaluations of service quality are often based on the manner in which store employees provide the service, not just the outcome. Consider the following situation: A customer goes to return an electric toothbrush that isn't working properly to a store that has a no questions asked, money-back return policy. In one case, the employee asks the customer for a receipt, checks to see if the receipt shows the toothbrush was bought at the store, examines the toothbrush to see if it really doesn't work properly, completes some paperwork while the customer is waiting, and finally gives the customer the amount paid for the toothbrush in cash. In a second case, the store employee simply asks the customer how much he paid and gives him a cash refund. The two cases have the same outcome: The customer gets a cash refund. But the customer might be dissatisfied in the first case because the employee appeared not to trust the customer and took too much time providing the refund. In most situations, employees have a great effect on the process of providing services and thus on the customer's eventual satisfaction with the services.

REFACT

More than one-quarter of shoppers cite unsatisfactory service as more likely to drive them away from a store permanently than any other aspect of the shopping experience.[19]

THE GAPS MODEL FOR IMPROVING RETAIL SERVICE QUALITY

REFACT

Just 16 percent of traditional, retail store shoppers are extremely satisfied with their most recent customer service experience, whereas online shoppers are nearly three times as likely to be extremely satisfied with their online customer service experience (44 percent).[21]

The Gaps Model (Exhibit 19–2) indicates what retailers need to do to provide high-quality customer service.[20] When customers' expectations are greater than their perceptions of the delivered service, they are dissatisfied and feel the quality of the retailer's service is poor. Thus, retailers need to reduce the **service gap** (the difference between customers' expectations and perceptions of customer service) to improve customers' satisfaction with their service.

Four factors affect the service gap:

1. *Knowledge gap.* The difference between customer expectations and the retailer's perception of customer expectations.

2. *Standards gap.* The difference between the retailer's perceptions of customers' expectations and the customer service standards it sets.

3. *Delivery gap.* The difference between the retailer's service standards and the actual service provided to customers.

4. *Communication gap.* The difference between the actual service provided to customers and the service promised in the retailer's promotional program.

These four gaps add up to the service gap. The retailer's objective is to reduce the service gap by reducing each of the four gaps. Thus, the key to improving service quality is to (1) understand the level of service customers expect, (2) set standards for providing customer service, (3) implement programs for delivering service that meets the standards, and (4) undertake communication programs to

---

19.3   RETAILING VIEW   The Broadmoor Manages Service Quality for Five-Star Rating

Established in 1891 as a gambling casino and transformed into a "grand resort" in 1918, the Broadmoor, in Colorado Springs, Colorado, is one of the world's premier resorts. It has received a record 41 consecutive years of five-star ratings from the *Mobil Travel Guide.* Perry Goodbar, vice president of marketing for the Broadmoor, emphasizes, "It's the people who truly make this place special. Exceptional service quality begins with exceptional people." Some aspects of its service quality are as follows:

Reliability Every new Broadmoor employee, before ever encountering a customer, attends a two-and-a-half day orientation session and receives an employee handbook. Making and keeping promises to customers is a central part of this orientation. Employees are trained always to give an estimated time for service, whether it be room service, laundry service, or simply how long it will take to be seated at one of the resort's restaurants. When an employee makes a promise, he or she keeps that promise. Employees are trained to never guess if they don't know the answer to a question. Inaccurate information only frustrates customers. When an employee is unable to answer a question accurately, he or she immediately contacts someone who can.

Assurance The Broadmoor conveys trust by empowering its employees. An example of an employee empowerment policy is the service recovery program. If a guest problem arises, employees are given discretionary resources to rectify the problem or present the customer with something special to help mollify them. For example, if a meal is delivered and there's a mistake in the order or how it was prepared, a waiter can offer the guest a free item such as a dessert or, if the service

was well below expectations, simply take care of the bill. Managers then review expenses to understand the nature of the problem and help prevent it from occurring again.

Tangibility One of the greatest challenges for the Broadmoor in recent years has been updating rooms built in the early part of the twentieth century to meet the needs of twenty-first century visitors. To accomplish this, it spent $200 million between 1992 and 2002 in improvements for renovating rooms and adding a new outdoor pool complex.

Empathy One approach used to demonstrate empathy is personalizing communications. Employees are instructed to always address a guest by name, if possible. To accomplish this, employees are trained to listen and observe carefully to determine a guest's name. Subtle sources for this information include convention name tags, luggage ID tags, credit cards, or checks. In addition, all phones within the Broadmoor display a guest's room number and name on a screen.

Responsiveness Every employee is instructed to follow the HEART model of taking care of problems. First, employees must "Hear what a guest has to say." Second, they must "Empathize with them" and then "Apologize for the situation." Third, they must "Respond to the guest's needs" by "Taking action and following up."

Source: www.broadmoor.com (accessed October 9, 2005); Andrew J. Czaplewski, Eric M. Olson, and Stanley F. Slater, "Applying the RATER Model for Service Success: Five Service Attributes Can Help Maintain Five-Star Ratings," *Marketing Management,* January–February 2002, pp. 14–20.

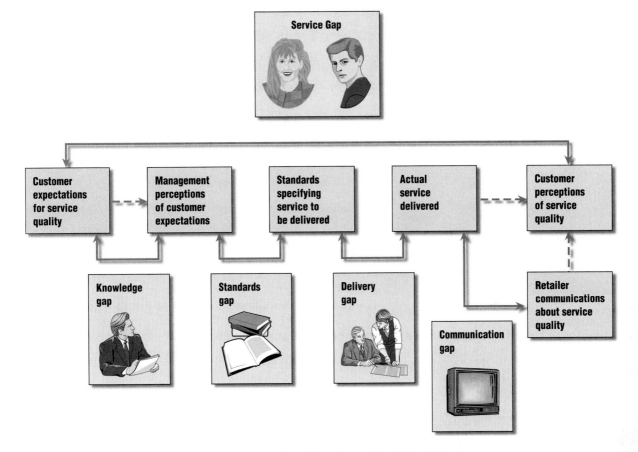

inform customers accurately about the service offered by the retailer. The following sections describe these gaps and methods for reducing them.

KNOWING WHAT CUSTOMERS WANT: THE KNOWLEDGE GAP

To close the **knowledge gap,** retailers need to do market research to know what customers want and then act on this research.

Researching Customer Expectations and Perceptions

The most critical step in providing good service is to know what the customer wants. Retailers often lack accurate information about what customers need and expect. This lack of information can result in poor decisions. For example, a supermarket might hire extra people to make sure the shelves are stocked so customers will always find what they want, but it may fail to realize that customers are most concerned about waiting in the checkout line. From the customer's perspective, the supermarket's service would improve if the extra employees were used to open more checkout lines rather than to stock shelves.

Retailers can reduce the knowledge gap and develop a better understanding of customer expectations by undertaking customer research, increasing interactions between retail managers and customers, and improving communication between managers and employees who provide customer service.

Market research also can be used to better understand customers' expectations and the quality of service provided by a retailer. Methods for obtaining this information range from comprehensive surveys to simply asking customers about the store's service.

REFACT

Eighty percent of Americans are willing to share personal information with companies if it means getting more personal service while shopping.[22]

The first step in providing good customer service is understanding customer expectations. This sales associate is conducting a survey in a mall to assess customer expectations.

Comprehensive Studies   Some retailers have established programs for assessing customers' expectations and service perceptions. For example, every year JCPenney sales associates pass out questionnaires to shoppers in each store and in malls. Shoppers are asked about the service and merchandise offered by JCPenney and by competing department stores in the mall. Over 50,000 completed questionnaires are collected and analyzed. Because the same questionnaire is used each year, JCPenney can track service performance, determine whether it is improving or declining, and identify opportunities for improving service quality. The annual customer service profile is so important to JCPenney that it is used as part of store managers' performance evaluations.

Gauging Satisfaction with Individual Transactions Another method for customer research is surveying customers immediately after a retail transaction has occurred. For example, Sears employees who deliver and assemble furniture in homes ask customers to complete a short survey describing how helpful, friendly, and professional the employees were. Airlines periodically ask passengers during a flight to evaluate the ticket-buying process, flight attendants, in-flight service, and gate agents.

Customer research on individual transactions provides up-to-date information about customers' expectations and perceptions. The research also indicates the retailer's interest in providing good service. Because the responses can be linked to a specific encounter, this research provides a method for rewarding employees who provide good service and correcting those who exhibit poor performance.

Customer Panels and Interviews   Rather than surveying many customers, retailers can use panels of 10–15 customers to gain insights into expectations and perceptions. For example, some store managers might meet once a month for an hour with a select group of customers who are asked to provide information about their experiences in the stores and offer suggestions for improving service. To reduce the knowledge gap, some supermarket managers go through the personal checks they receive each day and select customers who've made large and small purchases. They call these customers and ask them what they liked and didn't like about the store. With small purchasers, they probe to find out why the customers didn't buy more. Could they find everything they wanted? Did they get the assistance they expected from store employees?

Some retailers have consumer advisory boards composed of a cross-section of their preferred customers. Members of the board complete questionnaires three to four times a year on subjects like holiday shopping problems, in-store signage, and service quality. In exchange for their inputs, members receive gift certificates.

Interacting with Customers   Owner managers of small retail firms typically have daily contact with their customers and thus have accurate firsthand information about them. In large retail firms, managers often learn about customers through reports, so they may miss the rich information provided by direct contact with customers.

Stanley Marcus, founder of Neiman Marcus, felt managers could become addicted to numbers and neglect the merchandise and customers. He used suspenders as an example of how buyers could make poor decisions by only looking at the numbers. Originally, suspenders came in two sizes: short and long. By analyzing the numbers, buyers realized they could increase turnover by stocking one-size-only suspenders. The numbers looked good, but the store had a lot of dissatisfied customers. With only one size, short men's pants fell down, and the fit was uncomfortable for tall men. Said Marcus, "It comes back to the fact that the day is still only 24 hours long, and if you're a retailer, you've still got to spend some of those 24 hours with your customers and your products. You can't allow the computer to crowd them out as crucial sources of information."[23]

Customer Complaints   Complaints allow retailers to interact with their customers and acquire detailed information about their service and merchandise. Handling complaints is an inexpensive means to isolate and correct service problems.[24]

Catalog/electronic retailer L.L.Bean keeps track of all complaints and reasons for returned merchandise. These complaints and returns are summarized daily and given to customer service representatives so they can improve their service.

For example, a customer who returns a sweater might indicate the sweater was too large or the color tone differed from the picture in the catalog. With this information, customer service representatives can inform other customers who place an order for the sweater that it tends to be large and has a slightly different color than shown in the catalog. The information can also be used by buyers to improve vendor merchandise.

Although customer complaints can provide useful information, retailers can't rely solely on this source of market information. Typically, dissatisfied customers don't complain. To obtain better information about customer service, retailers need to encourage complaints and make it easy for customers to provide feedback about their problems. For example, some retailers set up a complaint desk in a convenient location where customers can get their problems heard and solved quickly.

REFACT

Only 39 percent of consumers surveyed say they would complain to the store manager if they received poor service.[25]

Using Technology   New, affordable information technology packages are enabling even small retailers to improve their customer service by maintaining and providing customer information to sales associates. The sales staff at Tina's Closet, a Lisle, Illinois-based women's apparel specialty store, uses a clienteling application with its customer database to track the buying history of its 15,000 customers and provide customer service. For example, when the store puts Bali bras on sale, it sends postcards to every customer who has bought one. The sales staff is provided with lists of customers who need to be contacted when the merchandise they have on hold is about to be put out for sale, their alterations are ready, or a new line of products is coming in from their favorite designer.[26]

Feedback from Store Employees   Salespeople and other employees in regular contact with customers often have a good understanding of customer service expectations and problems. This information can improve service quality only if the employees are encouraged to communicate their experiences to high-level managers who can act on it.

Some retailers regularly survey their employees, asking questions like,

1. What is the biggest problem you face in delivering high-quality service to your customers?

2. If you could make one change in the company to improve customer service, what would it be?

Using Customer Research

Collecting information about customer expectations and perceptions isn't enough. The knowledge gap is reduced only when retailers use this information to improve service. For example, store managers should review the suggestions and comments made by customers daily, summarize the information, and distribute it to store employees and managers.

Feedback on service performance needs to be provided to employees in a timely manner. Reporting the July service performance in December makes it hard for employees to reflect on the reason for the reported performance. Finally, feedback must be prominently presented so service providers are aware of their performance. For example, at Marriott, front-desk personnel's performance feedback is displayed behind the front desk, while restaurant personnel's performance feedback is displayed behind the door to the kitchen.

SETTING SERVICE STANDARDS: THE STANDARDS GAP

After retailers gather information about customer service expectations and perceptions, the next step is to use this information to set standards and develop systems for delivering high-quality service. Service standards should be based on customers' perceptions rather than internal operations. For example, a supermarket chain might set an operations standard of a warehouse delivery every day to each store. But frequent warehouse deliveries may not result in more merchandise on the shelves or improve customers' impressions of shopping convenience. To close the **standards gap,** retailers need to (1) commit their firms to providing high-quality service, (2) define the role of service providers, (3) set service goals, and (4) measure service performance.

Commitment to Service Quality

Service excellence occurs only when top management provides leadership and demonstrates commitment. Top management must be willing to accept the temporary difficulties and even the increased costs associated with improving service quality. This commitment needs to be demonstrated to the employees charged with providing the service. For example, a Lands' End poster prominently displays the following inscription for employees who process customer orders:

> What is a Customer? A Customer is the most important person in this office . . . in person or by mail. A Customer is not dependent on us . . . we are dependent on her. A customer is not an interruption in our work . . . she is the purpose of it. We are not doing her a favor by serving her . . . she is doing us a favor by giving us an opportunity to do so. A Customer is not someone to argue or match wits with.[27]

Top management's commitment sets service quality standards, but store managers are the key to achieving those standards. Store managers must see that their efforts to provide service quality are noticed and rewarded. Providing incentives based on service quality makes service an important personal goal, so rather than basing bonuses only on store sales and profit, part of store managers' bonuses should be determined by the level of service provided. For example, some retailers use the results of customer satisfaction studies to help determine bonuses.

Lands' End emphasizes its commitment to high-quality service by providing an unconditional guarantee and setting high standards for its employees.

Defining the Role of Service Providers

Managers can tell service providers that they need to provide excellent service but not clearly indicate what excellent service means. Without a clear definition of the retailer's expectations, service providers are directionless.

The Ritz-Carlton Hotel Company, winner of the Malcolm Baldrige National Quality Award, has its "Gold Standards" printed on a wallet-size card carried by all employees. The card contains the hotel's motto ("We Are Ladies and Gentlemen Serving Ladies and Gentlemen"), the three steps for high-quality service (warm and sincere greeting, anticipation and compliance with guests' needs, and fond farewell), and 20 basic rules for Ritz-Carlton employees, including

- Any employee who receives a complaint "owns" the complaint.
- Instant guest gratification will be ensured by all. React quickly to correct problems immediately.
- "Smile. We are on stage." Always maintain positive eye contact.
- Escort guests rather than giving directions to another area of the hotel.[28]

Setting Service Goals

To deliver consistent, high-quality service, retailers need to establish goals or standards to guide employees. Retailers often develop service goals based on their beliefs about the proper operation of the business rather than the customers' needs and expectations. For example, a retailer might set a goal that all monthly bills are to be mailed five days before the end of the month. This goal reduces the retailer's accounts receivable but offers no benefit to customers. Research undertaken by American Express showed that customer evaluations of its service were based on perceptions of timeliness, accuracy, and responsiveness. Management then established goals (such as responding to all questions about bills within 24 hours) related to these customer-based criteria.

Employees are motivated to achieve service goals when the goals are specific, measurable, and participatory in the sense that they participated in setting them. Vague goals—such as "Approach customers when they enter the selling area" or "Respond to e-mails as soon as possible"—don't fully specify what employees should do, nor do they offer an opportunity to assess employee performance. Better goals would be "All customers should be approached by a salesperson within 30 seconds after entering a selling area" or "All e-mails should be responded to within three hours." These goals are both specific and measurable.

Employee participation in setting service standards leads to better understanding and greater acceptance of the goals. Store employees resent and resist goals arbitrarily imposed on them by management. Chapter 17 says more about goal setting.

Measuring Service Performance

Retailers need to assess service quality continuously to ensure that goals will be achieved.[29] Many retailers conduct periodic customer surveys to assess service quality. Retailers also use mystery shoppers to assess their service quality. **Mystery shoppers** are professional shoppers who "shop" a store to determine the service provided by store employees and the presentation of merchandise in the store. Some retailers use their own employees as mystery shoppers, but most contract with an outside firm to provide the assessment. Information typically reported by the mystery shoppers includes (1) How long before a sales associate greeted you? (2) Did the sales associate act as if he or she wanted your business? and (3) Was the sales associate knowledgeable about the merchandise?

Retailers typically inform salespeople that they have "been shopped" and provide feedback from the mystery shopper's report. Some retailers offer rewards to sales associates who receive high marks and schedule follow-up visits to sales associates who get low evaluations.[30]

Toys "R" Us assesses customer satisfaction with checkout service by counting the number of abandoned shopping carts with merchandise left in the store because customers became impatient with the time required to make a purchase. After the firm noticed an alarming increase in abandoned carts, it developed a unique program to reduce customers' time in line waiting to pay. Cashiers' motions while ringing up and bagging merchandise were studied. On the basis of this research, the company developed a training program to show cashiers how to use their right hand to record purchases on the POS terminal and their left hand to push merchandise along the counter. Counters were redesigned with a slot lined with shopping bags in the middle of the counter. As the cashier pushes the merchandise along the counter, it drops into a bag. After the customer pays for the merchandise, the cashier simply lifts the bag from the slot and hands it to the customer, and a new bag pops into place.

To motivate cashiers to use the new system effectively, Toys "R" Us held competitions in each store, district, and region to select the fastest cashiers. Regional winners received a free vacation in New York City and participated in a competition at corporate headquarters to select a national champion.

REFACT

Two-thirds of the customers who put merchandise into an electronic shopping cart at a Web site do not complete the transaction.[31]

Giving Information and Training

Finally, store employees need to know about the retailer's service standards and the merchandise they offer, as well as their customers' needs. With this information, employees can answer customers' questions and suggest products. This knowledge also instills confidence and a sense of competence, which are needed to overcome service problems.

In addition, store employees need training in interpersonal skills. Dealing with customers is hard—particularly when they're upset or angry. All store employees, even those who work for retailers that provide excellent service, will encounter dissatisfied customers. Through training, employees can learn to provide better service and cope with the stress caused by disgruntled customers. Specific retail employees (salespeople and customer service representatives) are typically designated to interact with and provide service to customers. However, all retail employees should be prepared to deal with customers. For example, Walt Disney World provides four days of training for its maintenance workers, even though people can learn how to pick up trash and sweep streets in much less time. Disney has found that its customers are more likely to direct questions to maintenance people than to the clean-cut assistants wearing "ASK ME, I'M IN GUEST RELATIONS" buttons. Thus, Disney trains maintenance people to confidently handle the myriad of questions they'll be asked rather than responding, "Gee, I dunno. Ask her."[32]

MEETING AND EXCEEDING SERVICE STANDARDS: THE DELIVERY GAP

To reduce the **delivery gap** and provide service that exceeds standards, retailers must give service providers the necessary knowledge and skills, provide instrumental and emotional support, improve internal communications, reduce conflicts, and empower employees to act in the customers' and firm's best interests.[33] Retailing View 19.4 describes how chat rooms offered through an electronic channel enable customers to help the retailer provide services to others.

Providing Instrumental and Emotional Support

Service providers need to have the **instrumental support** (the appropriate systems and equipment) to deliver the service desired by customers. For example, a hotel chain installed a computer system to speed up the checkout process. But a study of the new system's effectiveness revealed that checkout time was not reduced because clerks had to wait to use the one stapler available to staple the customer's credit card and hotel bill receipts.

In addition to instrumental support, service providers need emotional support from their coworkers and supervisors. **Emotional support** involves demonstrating a concern for the well-being of others. Dealing with customer problems and maintaining a smile in difficult situations are psychologically demanding. Service providers need to be in a supportive, understanding atmosphere to deal with these demands effectively.[34] Retailing View 19.5 describes how Wing Zone reduces the emotional labor experienced by its service providers.

Improving Internal Communications

When providing customer service, store employees often must manage the conflict between customers' and the retail firm's needs.[35] For example, many retailers have a no questions asked return policy. Under such a policy, the retailer will provide a refund at the customer's request even if the merchandise wasn't purchased at the store or was clearly used improperly. When JCPenney inaugurated this policy, some employees refused to provide refunds on merchandise that had been worn or damaged by the customer. They were loyal JCPenney employees and didn't want customers to take advantage of their firm.

Retailers can reduce such conflicts by having clear guidelines and policies concerning service and by explaining the rationale for these policies. Once JCPenney employees recognized that the goodwill created by the no questions asked policy would generate more sales than losses due to customers abusing the policy, they implemented the policy enthusiastically.

Conflicts can also arise when retailers set goals inconsistent with the other behaviors expected from store employees. For example, if salespeople are expected to provide customer service, they should be evaluated on the service they provide, not just the sales they make.

Finally, conflicts can arise between different areas of the firm. An auto dealer with an excellent customer service reputation devotes considerable effort to reducing conflict by improving communication among its employees. The dealership holds a town hall meeting in which employees feel free to bring up service problems. For example, the receptionist discussed her frustration when she couldn't locate a sales rep for whom a customer had called. The customer finally said, "Well, I'll just take my business elsewhere." She used this example to emphasize that sales reps should tell her when they slip out to run an errand. Now no one forgets that the front desk is the nerve center of the dealership.

Empowering Store Employees

Empowerment means allowing employees at the firm's lowest levels to make important decisions regarding how service is provided to customers. When the employees responsible for providing service are authorized to make important

---

Retailers Use Customers to Deliver Service **RETAILING VIEW** 19.4

Retailers use message boards, chat rooms, and blogs on their Web sites to provide a valuable service by enabling customers to communicate with one another. Message boards are locations in an Internet site at which customers can post comments. Chat rooms are locations at which customers can engage in interactive, real-time, text-based discussions. For example, Tomboy Tools (www.tomboytools.com) sells tools designed for women and provides home improvement information for female do-it-yourselfers. Its Web site has chat room bulletin boards, called Tool Talk, on which customers can post home improvement questions to which other customers offer solutions. Blogs, short for Web logs, are public Web sites where users post informal journals of their thoughts, comments, and philosophies.

Authors and visitors to Amazon.com post comments and book reviews. Visitors to electronic travel retail sites frequently post messages inquiring about hotels, restaurants, and tourist attractions at places they will be visiting. Other customers who are familiar with the places respond to these inquiries with their suggestions. Many electronic retailers offer public chat rooms. At The Knot's site (www.theknot.com), people can enter a public chat room and have a real-time discussion about their experiences planning their weddings, seven days a week, 24 hours a day. In addition to the public chat room, The Knot also offers moderated chat rooms in which a staff member or well-known expert on an issue leads an electronic discussion at specific times during the day.

GourmetStation, an online retailer of prepared foods, created its blog, Delicious Destinations (www.gourmetstation.com), to post ideas about food, entertaining, gifts, and culture. A current posting details ways to serve salmon—whole or filet—and fun food discussions on topics such as the shapes of pasta, the history of tea, and setting a table. The initial goal was to build the brand with value-added content such as information about the

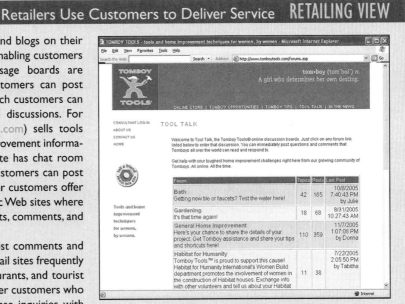

This message board at Tomboy Tools' Web site encourages customers to provide information to other customers.

region where food originates. It expects that people will appreciate the service and become repeat customers.

Blogs can help ease a shopper's fears when considering a purchase from an unknown retailer. The postings and responses from other customers give the prospective customer a glimpse of the retailer's practices and customer satisfaction. To be effective, however, retailers can't use the blogs as simply advertising tools. They must stress customer service as authentic to be successful.

Sources: Lorrie Grant, "Retailers Hope Shoppers Buy Blogs as the Place to Go," *USA Today*, August 24, 2005, p. D1; Andrea Coombes, "Hardware Shows Its Feminine Side," *Washington Post*, July 31, 2004, p. G.02; Kate Novack, "And the Bride Wore Lavender," *Time*, May 10, 2004, pp. C1–C4.

The Container Store uses the cartoon character Gumby to remind its employees that they need to be flexible and do whatever is necessary to assist customers and fellow employees.

REFACT

Trader Joe's, a gourmet supermarket chain, found that a change in its service policy that empowered employees to solve customer problems was accompanied by an increase in annual sales growth from 15 to 26 percent.[38]

decisions, service quality improves.[36] Retailing View 19.6 shows how an ice cream parlor empowers employees to be creative.

Nordstrom provides an overall objective—satisfy customer needs—and then encourages employees to do whatever is necessary to achieve the objective. For example, a Nordstrom department manager bought 12 dozen pairs of hosiery from a competitor in the mall when her stock was depleted because the new shipment was delayed. Even though Nordstrom lost money on this hosiery, management applauded her actions to make sure customers found hosiery when they came to the store looking for it. Empowering service providers with only a rule like "Use your best judgment" can cause chaos. At Nordstrom, department managers avoid abuses by coaching and training salespeople. They help salespeople understand what "Use your best judgment" means.

The Container Store also emphasizes the importance of flexibility, teamwork, and empowerment using the cartoon character Gumby. A six-foot Gumby character is prominently displayed at the entrance to the corporate headquarters, and small versions are on managers' desks. The frequent use of the phrase "We have to be Gumbylike" reinforces the corporate standard of doing whatever needs to be done to provide service for customers and help fellow employees complete tasks.[37] The Gumby cartoon character reinforces this point because it is so flexible it can bend over backwards, in much the same way that The Container Store employees bend over backwards to solve customer problems.

However, empowering service providers can be difficult. Some employees prefer to have the appropriate behaviors clearly defined for them. They don't want to spend the time learning how to make decisions or assume the risks of making mistakes. For example, a bank found that when it empowered its tellers, the tellers were frightened to make decisions about large sums of money. The bank had to develop decision guideposts and rules until tellers felt more comfortable.

In some cases, the benefits of empowering service providers may not justify the costs. For example, if a retailer uses a standardized service delivery approach like McDonald's, the cost of hiring, training, and supporting empowerment may not lead to consistent and superior service delivery. Also, studies have found that

19.5   RETAILING VIEW   Reducing the Emotional Labor of Service Providers

Robert Girau, a corporate manager for the Atlanta-based fast-food chain Wing Zone, just spent 30 minutes on the phone with an irate customer who hadn't received her order. "She said I was a liar," Girau says. She also threatened him. But Girau knew he had to keep his cool and try to solve the problem. "It was frustrating," he says. "No matter what the customer is saying, you [have to] try not to take it personally."

This experience describes the emotional labor that service providers experience when they have to manage their emotions on the job. While "the customer is always right" is a business mantra, employees on the receiving end of a service interaction gone wrong face incredible pressure to simply grin and bear it. Retailers need to be aware of how these stressful customer interactions affect the morale and performance of their service providers.

Matt Friedman, the CEO and cofounder of Wing Zone, understands the stress that angry customers can cause his employees, who take the majority of the company's food orders over the phone. Friedman says his entry-level employees, who are mostly college students, just don't have the experience

needed to handle these customers. Therefore, they've been trained to hand off overly demanding customers to the nearest manager right away. Wing Zone's managers then put the complaints back on the customers, asking them how they'd like the company to handle the problem. When both parties can't find some middle ground, managers refer the customer to the corporate office's toll-free number and Web site to file a formal complaint.

Girau, the point person at corporate headquarters for complaints that escalate, thinks the company's strategy works because the service providers know how to handle angry customers, managers understand what they can offer and are empowered to solve problems, and complaints with no easy solution can be routed up the organization. Having procedures to follow at the store level, Girau says, has made life easier for everyone.

Sources: Margaret Pressler, "The Customer Isn't Always Right; Retail Staff Say Shoppers' Behavior Is Going from Bad to Worse," *Washington Post*, March 24, 2002, p. H.05; Chris Penttila, "Touch Customer: Managing Abusive Customers," *Entrepreneur*, May 2001, pp. 5, 95.

empowerment is not embraced by employees in different cultures. For example, employees in Latin America expect their managers to possess all the information needed to make good business decisions. The role of employees is not to make business decisions; their job is to carry out the decisions of managers.[39]

Providing Incentives

As discussed in Chapter 17, many retailers use incentives, like paying commissions on sales, to motivate employees. But retailers have found that commissions on sales can decrease customer service and job satisfaction and motivate high-pressure selling, which leads to customer dissatisfaction. However, incentives can also be used effectively to improve customer service. For example, in one retail chain, managers distribute notes to store employees when they solve a customer's problem. The notes can then be converted into a cash bonus. This program was particularly effective because the reward was provided at about the same time the appropriate behavior occurred.

Developing Solutions to Service Problems

The previously discussed approaches for closing the service gap rely on informing, empowering, and motivating store personnel to provide better service. Retailers also use systems and technology to close the delivery gap.

Developing New Systems Finding ways to overcome service problems can improve customer satisfaction and, in some cases, reduce costs. For example, when customers complained about the long wait to check out, many hotels felt they couldn't do anything about the problem. Marriott, however, thought of a creative

---

Amy's Ice Cream Empowers Its Employees to Perform **RETAILING VIEW** 19.6

Amy's Ice Cream (a 10-store chain of premium ice cream shops in Austin, San Antonio, and Houston, Texas) sells terrific products and gives excellent service. But that's where the similarity to other scoop shops ends. Visit an Amy's store, and you'll see employees performing in a manner you won't forget. They juggle with their serving spades, toss scoops of ice cream to one another behind the counter, and break-dance on the freezer top. If there's a line out the door, they might pass out samples or offer free ice cream to any customer who'll sing or dance or recite a poem or mimic a barnyard animal or win a 60-second cone-eating contest.

Amy Miller, the founder and CEO, obviously sells entertainment along with ice cream. To provide this atmosphere, she has to hire the right people and get them to be inventive. To identify employees who'll take the initiative, she uses the "white paper bag" test. Instead of an application form, prospective employees get a plain white paper bag, along with the instructions to do anything they want with it and bring it back in a week. Those who just jot down a phone number will find that "Amy's isn't really for them," says Miller. But an applicant who produces "something unusual from a white paper bag tends to be an amusing person who would fit in with our environment." One job seeker turned his into an elaborate pop-up jack-in-the-box and became a scooper at the Westbank Market store. That store's former manager painted an intricate green-and-blue sphere resembling the earth atop a waffle cone on his bag.

Sources: Amy's Ice Creams, www.amysicecream.com/history/index.asp (accessed October 11, 2005); Tanya Rutledge, "Amy Miller, Sweet Success," *Austin Business Journal*, December 24, 2004, p. 16.

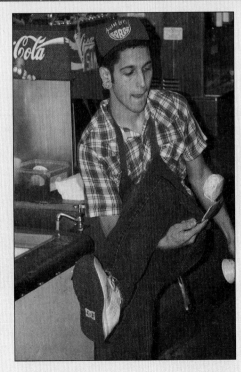

Amy's Ice Cream's employees are empowered to use their creativity to entertain customers and provide great customer service.

approach to address this service problem. It invented Express Checkout, a system in which a bill is left under the customer's door the morning before checkout; if the bill is accurate, the customer can check out by simply using the TV remote or calling the front desk and having the bill charged automatically to his or her credit card. Express Checkouts has been so successful that it has been adopted by many hotel chains.

Using Technology   Many retailers are installing kiosks with broadband Internet access in their stores. In addition to offering customers the opportunity to order merchandise not available in the store, kiosks can provide routine customer service, freeing employees to deal with more demanding customer requests and problems.[40] For example, customers can use kiosks to locate merchandise in the store and determine whether specific products, brands, and sizes are available. Kiosks can also be used to automate existing store services, such as gift registry management, rain checks, film drop-off, credit applications, and preordering service for bakeries and delicatessens.

Customers can use a kiosk to find more information about products and how they are used. For example, a Best Buy customer can use a kiosk to provide side-by-side comparisons of two VCRs and find more detailed information than is available from the shelf tag or a sales associate. The customer can also access evaluations of the models reported in *Consumer Reports.* The information provided by the kiosk could be tailored to specific customers through access to the retailer's customer database. For example, a customer who is considering a new set of speakers might not remember the preamplifier he or she purchased previously from Best Buy. This customer might not know whether the speakers are compatible with the preamplifier or what cables are needed to connect the new speakers. These concerns could be addressed by accessing the retailer's customer database through the kiosk. These types of applications could complement the efforts of salespeople and improve the service they can offer to customers.[42]

Retailers are also using hand-held scanners to provide customer service. At The Container Store in Manhattan, customers can register a credit card number at the front counter and get a wireless hand-held scanner. As they walk the aisles, they scan in the barcodes of desired items and then pay for the purchases when they are finished shopping. The items scanned are delivered to their homes the same day. The use of these hand-held scanners eliminates the need for customers to carry around bulky items in the store and transport them home. The physical and psychological limits on how much is purchased in a single trip are reduced, so the average customer purchase using this service is ten times greater than that of customers not using the service.[43]

Supermarkets also are equipping shopping carts with "intelligent shopping assistants," a device connected to the supermarket's customer database that hangs in the front compartment of a shopping cart and provides personalized information for shoppers. Customers can identify themselves by swiping their frequent-shopper card or putting a finger on a touchpad. Once they have logged in, a likely shopping list is displayed, based on their shopping history. As the customer selects and scans groceries, discounts and promotions are offered. The assistant device keeps a running total of that day's purchases and allows customers to order deli items without waiting in line, scan and bag their own groceries, and browse recipes.[44]

Retailers use technology to assist sales associates in providing customer service. This salesperson at Sam Dell Dodge reviews the cars in stock with a customer.

COMMUNICATING THE SERVICE PROMISE: THE COMMUNICATIONS GAP

The fourth factor leading to a customer service gap is the difference between the service promised by the retailer and the service actually delivered. Overstating the service offered raises customer expectations. Then, if the retailer doesn't follow through, expectations exceed perceived service, and customers are dissatisfied. For example, if a store advertises that a customer will always be greeted by a friendly, smiling sales associate, customers may be disappointed if this doesn't occur. Raising expectations too high might bring in more customers initially, but it can also create dissatisfaction and reduce repeat business. The **communications gap** can be reduced by making realistic commitments and managing customer expectations.

Realistic Commitments

Advertising programs are typically developed by the marketing department, whereas the store operations division delivers the service. Poor communication between these areas can result in a mismatch between an ad campaign's promises and the service the store can actually offer. This problem is illustrated by Holiday Inn's "No Surprises" ad campaign. Market research indicated hotel customers wanted greater reliability in lodging, so Holiday Inn's agency developed a campaign promising no unpleasant surprises. Even though hotel managers didn't feel they could meet the claims promised in the ads, top management accepted the campaign. The campaign raised customer expectations to an unrealistic level and gave customers who did confront an unpleasant surprise an additional reason to be angry. The campaign was discontinued soon after it started.

Managing Customer Expectations

How can a retailer communicate realistic service expectations without losing business to a competitor that makes inflated service claims? American Airlines' "Why Does It Seem Every Airline Flight Is Late?" ad campaign is an example of a communication program that addresses this issue. In print ads, American recognized its customers' frustration and explained some uncontrollable factors causing the problem: overcrowded airports, scheduling problems, and intense price competition. Then the ads described how American was improving the situation.

Information presented at the point of sale can be used to manage expectations. For example, theme parks and restaurants indicate the waiting time for an attraction or a table. Electronic retailers tell their customers if merchandise is in stock and when customers can expect to receive it. Providing accurate information can increase customer satisfaction even when customers must wait longer than desired.

Sometimes service problems are caused by customers. Customers may use an invalid credit card to pay for merchandise, not take time to try on a suit and have it altered properly, or use a product incorrectly because they fail to read the instructions. Communication programs also can inform customers about their role and responsibility in getting good service and give tips on how to get better service, such as the best times of the day to shop and the retailer's policies and procedures for handling problems.

SERVICE RECOVERY

The delivery of customer service is inherently inconsistent, so service failures are bound to arise. Rather than dwelling on negative aspects of customer problems, retailers should focus on the positive opportunities they generate. Service problems and complaints are an excellent source of information about the retailer's offering (its merchandise and service). Armed with this information, retailers can make changes to increase their customers' satisfaction.

Service problems also enable a retailer to demonstrate its commitment to providing high-quality customer service. By encouraging complaints and handling problems, a retailer has an opportunity to strengthen its relationship with its customers. Effective service recovery efforts significantly increase customer satisfaction, purchase intentions, and positive word of mouth. However, postrecovery satisfaction generally is less than the satisfaction level prior to the service failure.[45]

Most retailers have standard policies for handling problems. If a correctable problem is identified, such as defective merchandise, many retailers will make restitution on the spot and apologize for inconveniencing the customer. The retailer will offer replacement merchandise, a credit toward future purchases, or a cash refund.

In many cases, the cause of the problem may be hard to identify (did the salesperson really insult the customer?), uncorrectable (the store had to close due to bad weather), or a result of the customer's unusual expectations (the customer didn't like his haircut). In these cases, service recovery might be more difficult. The steps in effective service recovery are (1) listen to the customer, (2) provide a fair solution, and (3) resolve the problem quickly.[46]

Listening to Customers

Customers can become very emotional about their real or imaginary problems with a retailer. Often this emotional reaction can be reduced by simply giving customers a chance to get their complaints off their chests.

Store employees should allow customers to air their complaints without interruption. Interruptions can further irritate customers who may already be emotionally upset. It's very hard to reason with or satisfy an angry customer.

Customers want a sympathetic response to their complaints. Thus, store employees need to make it clear that they're happy the problem has been brought to their attention. Satisfactory solutions rarely arise when store employees have an antagonistic attitude or assume that the customer is trying to cheat the store.

Employees also need to listen carefully to determine what the customer perceives to be a fair solution. For example, a hotel employee might assume that a customer who's irritated about a long wait to check in will be satisfied with an apology. But the customer might be expecting to receive a free drink as compensation for the wait. A supermarket employee may brusquely offer a refund for spoiled fruit when the customer is also seeking an apology for the inconvenience of having to return to the store. Store employees shouldn't assume they know what the customer is complaining about or what solution the customer is seeking.[47]

This customer service representative is empowered to resolve the problems the customer has with a windbreaker purchased at the store.

Providing a Fair Solution

When confronted with a complaint, store employees need to focus on how they can get the customer back, not simply on how they can solve the problem. Favorable impressions arise when customers feel they've been dealt with fairly. When evaluating the resolution of their problems, customers compare how they were treated in relation to others with similar problems or in similar situations with other retail service providers. This comparison is based on observations of other customers with problems or information about complaint handling learned from reading books and talking with others. Customers' evaluations of complaint resolutions thus are based on distributive fairness and procedural fairness.[48]

Distributive Fairness   **Distributive fairness** is a customer's perception of the benefits received compared with their costs (inconvenience or loss). Customers want to get what they paid for, and their needs can affect the perceived correspondence between benefits and costs. For example, one customer might be satisfied with a rain check for a food processor that was advertised at a discounted price but sold out. This customer feels the low price for the food processor off-sets the inconvenience of returning to the store. But another customer may need the food processor immediately, so a rain check won't be adequate compensation for him. To satisfy this customer, the salesperson must locate a store that has the food processor and have it delivered to the customer's house.

Customers typically prefer tangible rather than intangible resolutions to their complaints. Customers may want to let off steam, but they also want to feel the re-tailer was responsive to their complaint. A low-cost reward, such as a free soft drink or a $1 discount, communicates more concern to the customer than a verbal apology. If providing tangible restitution isn't possible, the next best alternative is to let customers see that their complaints will have an effect in the future. This promise can be made by writing a note, in front of the customer, to a manager about the problem or writing to the customer about actions taken to prevent similar problems in the future.

Procedural Fairness   **Procedural fairness** is the perceived fairness of the process used to resolve complaints. Customers consider three questions when evaluating procedural fairness:

1. Did the employee collect information about the situation?

2. Was this information used to resolve the complaint?

3. Did the customer have some influence over the outcome?

Discontent with the procedures used to handle a complaint can overshadow the benefits of a positive outcome. For example, customers might be more satisfied with their refund for a clerk's mistake in ringing up groceries if they get a chance to talk about other problems they experienced in the store with the clerk.

Customers typically feel they're dealt with fairly when store employees follow company guidelines. Guidelines reduce variability in handling complaints and lead customers to believe they're being treated like everyone else. But rigid adherence to guidelines can have negative effects. Store employees need some flexibility in re-solving complaints, or customers may feel they had no influence on the resolution.

Resolving Problems Quickly

Customer satisfaction is affected by the time it takes to get an issue resolved. To respond to customers quickly, Smith & Hawken, a garden-supply mail-order com-pany, uses the telephone instead of the mail. The company feels that sending a letter is too time consuming and impersonal. Resolving complaints by phone can take minutes, whereas sending letters can take weeks.

As a general rule, store employees who deal with customers should be made as self-sufficient as possible to handle problems. Customers are more satisfied when the first person they contact can resolve a problem. When customers are referred to several different employees, they waste a lot of time repeating their story. Also, the chance of conflicting responses by store employees increases.

Retailers can minimize the time to resolve complaints by reducing the number of people the customer must contact, providing clear instructions, and speaking in the customer's language.

Giving Clear Instructions   Customers should be told clearly and precisely what they need to do to resolve a problem. When American Express cardholders ask to have an unused airline ticket removed from their bill, they're told immedi-ately that they must return the ticket to the airline or travel agency before a credit can be issued. Fast service often depends on providing clear instructions.

Speaking the Customer's Language   Customers can become annoyed when store employees use company jargon to describe a situation. To communicate clearly, store employees should use terms familiar to the customer. For example, a customer might be frustrated if a salesperson told her that the slacks in her size were located on a rounder to the right of the four-way.

Resolving customer complaints increases satisfaction. But when complaints are resolved too abruptly, customers might feel dissatisfied because they haven't received enough personal attention. Retailers must recognize the trade-off between resolving the problem quickly and taking time to listen to and show concern for the customer.

SUMMARY

Due to the inherent intangibility and inconsistency of services, providing high-quality customer service is challenging. However, customer service also provides an opportunity for retailers to develop a strategic advantage. Retailers use two basic strategies for providing customer service: the customized method and the standardized approach. The customized method relies primarily on sales associates. The standardized approach places more emphasis on developing appropriate rules, consistent procedures, and optimum store designs.

Customers evaluate customer service by comparing their perceptions of the service delivered with their expec-

tations. Thus, to improve service, retailers need to close the gaps between the service delivered and the customer's expectations. This gap may be reduced by knowing what customers expect, setting standards to provide the expected service, providing support so store employees can meet the standards, and realistically communicating the service offered to customers.

Due to inherent inconsistency, service failures are bound to arise. These lapses in service provide an opportunity for retailers to build even stronger relationships with their customers.

KEY TERMS

communications gap, *537*

customer delight, *524*

customer service, *519*

customization approach, *522*

delivery gap, *532*

distributive fairness, *538*

emotional support, *532*

empowerment, *533*

instrumental support, *532*

knowledge gap, *527*

mystery shopper, *531*

procedural fairness, *539*

service gap, *526*

standardization approach, *522*

standards gap, *530*

GET OUT AND DO IT!

1. **CONTINUING ASSIGNMENT** Go to a local store of the retailer you have selected for the continuing assignment and describe and evaluate the service it offers. What services are offered? Is the service customized or standardized? Ask the store manager if you can talk to some customers and employees. Choose customers who have made a purchase, customers who have not made a purchase, and customers with a problem (refund, exchange, or complaint). Talk with them about their experiences, write a report describing your conversations, and make suggestions for improving the store's customer service. Ask employees what the retailer does to assist and motivate them to provide good service.

2. **INTERNET EXERCISE** Bizrate (www.bizrate.com) is a company that collects information about consumer shopping experiences with electronic retailers. Go to

Bizrate's Web site and review the evaluations of different retailers that sell products electronically. How useful is this information to you? What could Bizrate do to make the information more useful?

3. **INTERNET EXERCISE** Visit the Lands' End Web site (www.landsend.com) and look for a shirt. How does the Web site help you locate the shirt that you might be interested in buying? How does customer service offered by the Web site compare to the service you would get at a specialty store like The Gap? A department store?

4. **GO SHOPPING** Go to a discount store such as Wal-Mart, a department store, and a specialty store to buy a pair of jeans. Compare and contrast the customer service you receive in the stores. Which store made it easiest to find the pair of jeans you would be interested in buying? Why?

DISCUSSION QUESTIONS AND PROBLEMS

1. For each of these services, give an example of a retailer for which providing the service is critical to its success, then give an example of a retailer for which providing the service is not critical: (a) personal shoppers, (b) home delivery, (c) money-back guarantees, and (d) credit.

2. Nordstrom and McDonald's are noted for their high-quality customer service, but their approaches to providing this quality service are different. Describe this difference. Why have the retailers elected to use these different approaches?

3. Is customer service more important for store-based or electronic retailers? Why?

4. Providing customer service can be very expensive for retailers. When are the costs for providing high-quality services justified? What types of retailers find it financially advantageous to provide high-quality customer service? What retailers can't justify providing high-quality service?

5. Assume you're the department manager for menswear in a local department store that emphasizes empowering its managers. A customer returns a dress shirt that's no longer in the package in which it was sold. The customer has no receipt, says that when he opened the package he found that the shirt was torn, and wants cash for the price at which the shirt is being sold now. The shirt was on sale last week when the customer claims to have bought it. What would you do?

6. Citibank found that chat rooms were not an important service for customers of its electronic banking offering. However, the Wedding Channel, an electronic retailer targeting couples about to get married, found that chat rooms were an important service for attracting its customers. Why did these retailers have different experiences with the use of chat rooms?

7. Gaps analysis provides a systematic method of examining a customer service program's effectiveness. Top management has told an information systems manager that customers are complaining about the long wait to pay for merchandise at the checkout station. How can the systems manager use gaps analysis to analyze this problem and suggest approaches for reducing this time?

8. How could an effective customer service strategy cut a retailer's costs?

9. Employees play a critical role in customer perceptions of quality service. If you were hiring salespeople, what characteristics would you look for to assess their ability to provide good customer service?

10. Consider a recent retail service experience, such as a haircut, doctor's appointment, dinner in a restaurant, bank transaction, or product repair (not an exhaustive list), and answer the questions below:
    (a) Describe an excellent service delivery experience.
    (b) What made this quality experience possible?
    (c) Describe a service delivery experience in which you did not receive the performance that you expected.
    (d) What were the problems encountered, and how could they have been resolved?

SUGGESTED READINGS

Clark, Moira, and Susan Baker. *Business Success Through Service.* Edinburgh: Butterworth-Heinemann, 2004.

Cook, Sarah. *Measuring Customer Service Effectiveness.* Burlington, VT: Gower Publishing, 2004.

Doane, Darryl, and Rose Slout. *The Customer Service Activity Book: 50 Activities for Inspiring Exceptional Service.* New York: American Management Association, 2005.

Evanschitzky, Heiner; Gopalkrishnan Iyer; Josef Hesse; and Dieter Ahlert. "E-Satisfaction: A Re-Examination," *Journal of Retailing* 80, no. 3 (2004), pp. 239–52.

Gomez, Miguel; Edward McLaughlin; and Dick Wittink. "Customer Satisfaction and Retail Sales Performance: An Empirical Investigation." *Journal of Retailing* 80, no. 4 (2004), pp. 265–82.

Gross, T. Scott. *Positively Outrageous Service: How to Delight and Astound Your Customers and Win Them for Life*, 2nd ed. Chicago: Dearborn Trade Publishing, 2004.

Homburg, Christian; Wayne Hoyer; and Martin Fassnacht. "Service Orientation of a Retailer's Business Strategy: Dimensions, Antecedents, and Performance Outcomes," *Journal of Marketing* 66 (October 2002), pp. 86–102.

Iacobucci, Dawn. "Services Marketing and Customer Service." In *Kellogg on Marketing*, ed. Dawn Iacobucci. New York: Wiley, 2001.

Korczynski, Marek. *Human Resource Management in Service Work.* New York: Palgrave, 2002.

Rayport, Jeffrey, and Bernard Jaworski. *Best Face Forward: Why Companies Must Improve Their Service Interfaces with Customers.* Boston, MA: Harvard Business School Press, 2005.

Spector, Robert, and Patrick McCarthy. *The Nordstrom Way to Customer Service Excellence.* Hoboken, NJ: John Wiley & Sons, 2005.

Cases

Case	1	2	3	4	5	6	7	8	9	10	11	12	13	14	15	16	17	18	19	C
1 Rainforest Café	P	S					S											S		
2 Build-A-Bear Workshop	P	P																		
3 WeddingChannel.com		S	P		S															
4 Chen Family Buys Bicycles				P																
5 Is Wal-Mart in *Vogue?*				P																
6 Value Retailers	S	S			P															
7 Ahold					P				S											
8 Teen/College Apparel Market	S	S			P											P				
9 Best Buy/Radio Shack					S	P														
10 Stephanie's Boutique							P													
11 Hutch								P												
12 Home Depot					S				P											
13 Wal-Mart's Image									P							S	S			
14 Avon			S		S				P											
15 A&F Hiring for Looks									P											
16 Lawson Sportswear										P										
17 Diverted Hair Care Products														P						
18 SaksFirst											P								S	
19 Men's Wearhouse					S							P	S	S					S	
20 Nolan's												P	S							
21 Hughe's												P								
22 McFadden's													P							
23 eBay		S	S		S										P					
24 How Much for a Good Smell?															P					
25 Promoting a Sale														P						
26 Enterprise					S											P	P		S	
27 Diamond in the Rough																P	P			
28 Borders																P	P			
29 Grocery Store Layout																	P	P		
30 Sephora			S		S												P	P	S	
31 Discmart																S		P	P	
32 Nordstrom						S			S									P	P	
33 Sustainable Development in the U.K.	S					S	S								S					C
34 Lindy's Bridal Shoppe						S	S						S				S			C
35 Starbucks					P											S	S			C
36 Yankee Candle															P					C
37 Interviewing for a Management Trainee Position	S								P								S			

P Primary Use
S Secondary Use
C Comprehensive

CASE 1   Rainforest Café: A Wild Place to Shop and Eat

 Steve Schussler opened the first Rainforest Café in the Mall of America, the largest enclosed mall in the world, in 1994. Before opening this unique retail store and theme restaurant, Schussler tested the concept for 12 years, eventually building a prototype in his Minneapolis home. It was not easy sharing a house with parrots, butterflies, tortoises, and tropical fish, but Schussler's creativity resulted in a highly profitable and fast-growing chain.

In 1996, the Rainforest Cafés (www.rainforestcafe.com), located in Chicago; Washington, DC; Fort Lauderdale, Florida; and Disney World in Orlando, Florida, in addition to the Mall of America in Minneapolis, Minnesota, generated $48.7 million in sales and $5.9 million in profits. They offer a unique and exciting atmosphere, with state-of-the-art décor and animatronics that recreate a tropical rain forest in 20,000 to 30,000 square feet. The cafés are divided into a restaurant seating 300 to 600 people and a retail store stocking 3,000 SKUs of unique merchandise.

Retail merchandise accounts for 30 percent of the revenues generated by the cafés. Most theme restaurants stock fewer than 20 SKUs. At Rainforest, the merchandise emphasizes eight proprietary jungle animals featured as animated characters in the restaurant. They include Bamba the gorilla, Cha Cha the tree frog, and Ozzie the orangutan. In addition to stuffed animals and toys, the characters are utilized on clothing and gifts and in animated films and children's books.

The menu features dishes such as Leaping Lizard Lettuce Wraps, Rasta Pasta, Seafood Galapagos, Jamaica Me Crazy, and Eye of the Ocelot (meatloaf topped with sautéed mushrooms on a bed of caramelized onions). The restaurants have live tropical birds and fish plus animated crocodiles and monkeys, trumpeting elephants, gorillas beating their chests, cascading waterfalls surrounded by cool mist, simulated thunder and lightning, continuous tropical rain storms, and huge mushroom canapés. As Schussler said, "Our cafés feature the sophistication of a Warner Brothers store with the animation of Disney."

Rainforest Cafés contribute to the local community through an outreach program. Over 300,000 schoolchildren visit the cafés each year to hear curators talk about the vanishing rain forests and endangered species. All coins dropped into the Wishing Pond and Parking Meter in the cafés are donated to causes involving endangered species and tropical deforestation.

Technology is used in the Rainforest Cafés to increase efficiency and profits. When a party enters the restaurant, the host (called a tour guide) enters the party's name in a computer, which prints a "passport" indicating the party's name, size, and estimated seating time. The party can then go shopping or sightseeing, knowing it will be ushered into the dining room within 5 to 10 minutes of the assigned seating time. When the party returns, the computer tells the "safari guide" the table at which the party will be seated. Tour and safari guides communicate with one another using headsets. This technology enables the Rainforest Cafés to turn tables five to six times a day compared with two to three turns in a typical restaurant.

The company expanded rapidly. By 2000, it had annual sales of $200 million but earned only $8 million in profits from 28 locations. Many of the locations were in regional malls rather than high-traffic entertainment centers at which the restaurants were initially located. As of 2005, Rainforest Café was the only restaurant concept at all three U.S. Disney locations. This restaurant can be found in 16 states and Canada, China, Mexico, and Europe.

After a protracted negotiation, Rainforest Café was acquired by Landry's Restaurant Inc. Landry's, which operates 300 restaurants in 36 states under the trade names Joe's Crab Shack, Landry's Seafood House, Crab House, Charley's Crab, Chart House, Rainforest Café, and Saltgrass Steak House, generated $1.2 billion in revenue in 2004. Tilman Fertitta, the founder and CEO of Landry's, explains his strategy for operating restaurants: "Our approach has always been simple. Put good concepts in good locations. Rainforest is a strong concept. The problem wasn't with sales. The worst stores do $5 million a year. That's very different from other eatertainment chains like Planet Hollywood and Hard Rock Café. The major problem was poor locations in shopping centers with high lease costs." Following the acquisition, Landry's closed a number of Rainforest's mall locations but opened up new locations in London's Piccadilly Circus, Euro Disney outside Paris, Niagara Falls, the MGM Grand Hotel and Casino in Las Vegas, and Fisherman's Wharf in San Francisco.

DISCUSSION QUESTIONS

1. What is Rainforest Café's retail offering and target market?
2. Were malls good locations for Rainforest Cafés? Why or why not? What would be the best location types?
3. Many retailers have tried to make their stores more entertaining. In a number of cases, these efforts have failed. What are the pros and cons of providing a lot of entertainment in a retail store or restaurant?

Source: This case was written by Barton Weitz, University of Florida.

CASE 2 Providing a Retail Experience: Build-A-Bear Workshop

 Today's consumers want good value, low prices, and convenience, but they also are attracted to a great shopping experience. Build-A-Bear Workshop, a chain with over 170 stores generating $300 million in annual sales, is a teddy-bear–themed entertainment retailer whose stores are playgrounds for children.

The stores are exactly what the name says: Customers, or builders, choose an unstuffed animal and, working with the retailer's staff, move through eight "creation stations" to build their own bear. At the first station, the Stuffiteria, children can pick fluff from bins marked "Love," "Hugs and Kisses," "Friendship," and "Kindness." The stuffing is sent through a long, clear tube and into a stuffing machine. A sales associate holds the bear to a small tube while the builder pumps a foot peddle. In seconds, the bear takes its form. Before the stitching, builders must insert a heart. The builders follow the sales associates' instructions and rub the heart between their hands to make it warm. They then close their eyes, make a wish, and kiss the heart before putting it inside the bear. After selecting a name and having it stitched on the bear, builders take their bears to the Fluff Me station, where they brush their bears on a "bathtub" that features spigots blowing air. Finally, they move to a computer station to create a birth certificate for their bear.

Bears are sent home in Club Condo boxes, which act as mini-houses complete with windows and doors. Besides adding value as playhouses, the boxes advertise Build-A-Bear to the child's friends. "[You] could buy a bear anywhere" says Maxine Clark, founder and Chief Executive Bear. "It's the experience that customers are looking for." The experience is depicted on the retailer's Web site, www.buildabear.com.

Customers pay about $25 for the basic bear, but they can also buy sound, clothing, and accessories for their bear. To keep the experience fresh, Build-A-Bear regularly introduces new and limited-edition animals. Clothes and accessories are also updated to reflect current trends. There are also in-store birthday parties and an official CD. To make sure that customers have a great experience every time they visit, all sales associates attend a three-week training program at "Bear University," and the firm offers incentive programs and bonuses. The inventory in the stores changes frequently, with different bear styles arriving weekly. Build-A-Bear stores also feature seasonal merchandise such as a King of the Grill bear for Father's Day and a Sweetheart bear for Valentine's Day.

REFACT

The origin of the teddy bear was a 1903 incident in which President Teddy Roosevelt refused to shoot a cub while bear hunting. The spared animal was thereafter referred to as the Teddy Bear.

DISCUSSION QUESTIONS

1. Is the Build-A-Bear concept a fad, or does it have staying power?
2. What can Build-A-Bear do to generate repeat visits to the store?

Source: This case was written by Barton Weitz, University of Florida.

CASE 3 WeddingChannel.com

Anne is sitting at her desk eating her lunch and surfing the Internet. For a few months, she has been preparing for her wedding, which will take place in less than a month. She found many helpful articles that gave her some good ideas. These articles also helped her face reality and change her childhood dreams of a white carriage pulled by a team of horses to a stretch limo. She gave up the Snow White wedding gown with a 15-foot train and has now settled on a sleek sheath gown.

In planning her big day, Anne used the help of WeddingChannel.com to make a checklist of what she needs to do. The Web site helped her organize a guest list, design and buy her invitations, set up a gift registry, and post some information for her friends about how she and Steven met. They met in college and are from different cities; therefore, they decided to have their wedding somewhere in between where their friends and family could meet. She used the resources provided on WeddingChannel.com to book the chapel and restaurant where the reception would be held.

Every year, $72 billion is spent on weddings in the United States. The average American wedding ceremony costs $22,000. The average age of brides is 24.5, while the average groom is 26.5 years of age. With these statistics, it is no wonder that WeddingChannel.com has become so popular. Its target market is 18 to 35 years. Approximately 48 percent of engaged couples plan to use the Internet to help plan their wedding. WeddingChannel.com's goal is to help couples make their special day easier to plan and save time finding up-to-date information.

WeddingChannel.com began on July 15, 1997. The venture has helped not only brides-to-be but also retailers.

Over $100 million was spent purchasing gifts through the site in 2003. WeddingChannel.com's patented registry system searches 1.5 million registries from its many retail partners, including Federated Department Stores (Macy's, Bloomingdale's, Burdines, Goldsmith's-Macy's, Lazarus-Macy's and Rich's-Macy's), Tiffany & Co., Crate and Barrel, Neiman Marcus, Williams-Sonoma, Pottery Barn, Recreational Equipment, Inc. (REI), JCPenney, and others.

With access to so many registered couples, WeddingChannel.com has an attractive market. "Consistently, our targeted marketing tactics have resulted in five times the average Internet response rate, providing the most effective platform for companies to build their brand messages during a significant life stage when brand loyalties are being developed," said Adam Berger, president and CEO of WeddingChannel.com. About 89 percent of all gift purchasers buy wedding gifts from a registry.

WeddingChannel.com is not only the largest bridal registry online, but it also provides a comprehensive site that couples can use to plan their wedding. WeddingChannel.com is a virtual community that provides services for couples who have many questions. Where do brides start first? Most start with finding the perfect dress. WeddingChannel.com offers over 20,000 styles of wedding gowns, including both designer brands and less expensive brands. It also provides a great way to sort through the many different styles by offering different buttons to select sleeve length, silhouette, length, and neckline. It even has a virtual model so the bride-to-be can see how she would look in a particular style of gown. The site also provides many interactive tools that help couples make a budget, guest list, wedding page, and registry. There are also many articles that range from finding a reception site to planning a dream honeymoon.

WeddingChannel.com is unique because it is a comprehensive destination for couples planning their wedding. This interactive Web page allows for couples to make a customized Internet page describing how they met, how they became engaged, their wedding party, and the theme/colors for the big day. Guests can go online and shop at the well-known stores associated with WeddingChannel.com and conveniently purchase exactly what the couple needs for their future together.

DISCUSSION QUESTIONS

1. What are the keys to making WeddingChannel.com a success from the perspective of the companies investing in it?
2. Why would a retailer want to invest in a virtual community like WeddingChannel.com?
3. Can you think of other retailers that might benefit from developing a virtual community?

Source: This case was written by Teresa Scott, University of Florida.

CASE 4   The Chen Family Buys Bicycles

The Chens live in Riverside, California, west of Los Angeles. Terry is a physics professor at the University of California, Riverside. His wife Cheryl is a volunteer, working 10 hours a week at the Crisis Center. They have two children: Judy, age 10, and Mark, age 8.

In February, Cheryl's parents sent her $100 to buy a bicycle for Judy's birthday. They bought Judy her first bike when she was five. Now they wanted to buy her a full-size bike for her eleventh birthday. Even though Cheryl's parents felt every child should have a bike, Cheryl didn't think Judy really wanted one. Judy and most of her friends didn't ride their bikes often, and she was afraid to ride to school because of traffic. So Cheryl decided to buy her the cheapest full-size bicycle she could find.

Since most of Judy's friends didn't have full-size bikes, she didn't know much about them and had no preferences for a brand or type. To learn more about the types available and their prices, Cheryl and Judy checked the JCPenney catalog. After looking through the catalog, Judy said the only thing she cared about was the color. She wanted a blue bike, blue being her favorite color.

Using the Yellow Pages, Cheryl called several local retail outlets selling bikes. To her surprise, she found that a local hardware store actually had the best price for a 26-inch bicycle, even lower than Toys "R" Us and Wal-Mart.

Cheryl drove to the hardware store, went straight to the toy department, and selected a blue bicycle before a salesperson approached her. She took the bike to the cash register and paid for it. After making the purchase, the Chens found out that the bike was cheap in all senses. The chrome plating on the wheels was very thin and rusted away in six months. Both tires split and had to be replaced.

A year later, Cheryl's grandparents sent another $100 for a bike for Mark. From their experience with Judy's bike, the Chens realized that the lowest-priced bike might not be the least expensive option in the long run. Mark is very active and somewhat careless, so the Chens wanted to buy a sturdy bike. Mark said he wanted a red, 21-speed, lightweight bike with an aluminum frame, cross-country tires, and a full reflector kit.

The Chens were concerned that Mark wouldn't maintain an expensive bike with all these features. When they saw an ad for a bicycle sale at Kmart, Cheryl and Terry went to the store with Mark. A salesperson approached them at an outdoor display of bikes and directed them to the sporting goods department inside the store. There they found row after row of red 10-speed bikes with minimal accessories—the type of bike Cheryl and Terry felt was ideal for Mark.

A salesperson approached them and tried to interest them in a more expensive bike. Terry dislikes salespeople trying to push something on him and interrupted her in mid-sentence. He said he wanted to look at the bikes on his own. With a little suggestion, Mark decided he wanted one of these bikes. His desire for accessories was satisfied when they bought a multifunction sports computer for the bike. After buying a bike for Mark, Terry decided he'd like a bike for himself to ride on weekends. Terry had ridden bikes since he was five; in graduate school, before he was married, he'd owned a 10-speed; and he frequently took 50-mile rides with friends. But he hadn't owned a bike since moving to Riverside 15 years ago.

Terry didn't know much about current types of bicycles. He bought a copy of *Bicycling* at a newsstand to see what was available. He also went to the library to read *Consumer Reports'* evaluation of road, mountain, and hybrid bikes. Based on this information, he decided he wanted a Serrato. It had all the features he wanted: a lightweight frame, durable construction, and a comfort sports saddle. When Terry called the discount stores and bicycle shops, he found they didn't carry the Serrato brand. He then decided he might not really need a bike. After all, he'd been without one for 15 years.

One day, after lunch, he was walking back to his office and saw a small bicycle shop. The shop was run down, with bicycle parts scattered across the floor. The owner, a young man in grease-covered shorts, was fixing a bike. As Terry was looking around, the owner approached him and asked him if he liked to bicycle. Terry said he used to but had given it up when he moved to Riverside. The owner said that was a shame because there were a lot of nice places to tour around Riverside.

As their conversation continued, Terry mentioned his interest in a Serrato and his disappointment in not finding a store in Riverside that sold them. The owner said that he could order a Serrato for Terry but that they weren't in inventory and delivery took between six and eight weeks. He suggested a Ross and showed Terry one he currently had in stock. Terry thought the $500 price was too high, but the owner convinced him to try it next weekend. They would ride together in the country. The owner and some of his friends took a 60-mile tour with Terry. Terry enjoyed the experience, recalling his college days. After the tour, Terry bought the Ross.

DISCUSSION QUESTIONS

1. Outline the decision-making process for each of the Chens' bicycle purchases.

2. Compare the different purchase processes for the three bikes. What stimulated each of them? What factors were considered in making the store choice decisions and purchase decisions?

3. Go to the student side of the Online Learning Center (OLC) and click on multiattribute model. Construct a multiattribute model for each purchase decision. How do the attributes considered and importance weights vary for each decision?

Source: This case was written by Barton Weitz, University of Florida.

CASE 5 Consumer Buying Behavior—Is Wal-Mart in *Vogue?*

The September 2005 issue of *Vogue* magazine contained eight pages of advertisements from the world's largest retailer, Wal-Mart. The other 792 pages contained advertisements from Ralph Lauren, The Gap, Saks Fifth Avenue, Dior, Estée Lauder, Gucci, Lancôme, St. John, Louis Vuitton, Bill Blass, Yves Saint Laurent, L'Oreal, Guess, Michael Kors, David Yurman, Clinique, Marc Jacobs, Burberry, Calvin Klein, Manolo Blahnik, Donna Karan, Paul Mitchell, Vera Wang, and Jimmy Choo, to name just a portion of the brands in this fall issue.

The ads from Wal-Mart feature real customers including a martial artist, a musician, a mom, students, a cake decorator, a professor of art, and a fundraiser. Each woman is shown with a "Her Style" profile, locating her Wal-Mart and indicating what she is wearing in the photograph from Wal-Mart and from her own closet. These ads are a departure from the smiley-faced, low-price–focused messages seen from Wal-Mart in the past.

Do Wal-Mart ads belong in *Vogue* magazine? To help answer this question, complete the diagram in Exhibit 1 by describing the characteristics and attributes of the Wal-Mart shopper and the *Vogue* magazine reader. Use the following segmentation bases to complete this exercise:

Demographic Gender, age, race, life stage, birth era, family size/stage, residence tenure (own/rent), marital status.

Geographic Region, city size, climate, metropolitan area, density (urban, suburban, rural).

Psychographic Personality, values, lifestyle, activities, interests, opinions.

Socioeconomic Income, education, occupation.

Benefits sought To meet customers' desires.

Usage Rate Purchase behavior (frequency), brand loyalty.

EXHIBIT 1
Overlap of Wal-Mart and *Vogue* Target Markets

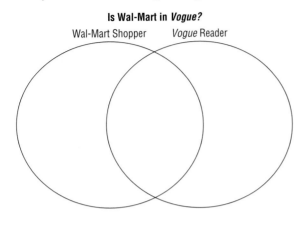

Is Wal-Mart in *Vogue?*

Wal-Mart Shopper   *Vogue* Reader

DISCUSSION QUESTIONS

1. Is there an overlap in these two consumer segments?
2. Can Wal-Mart change its image and appeal to an upscale shopper, or should it stick to loyal, cash-strapped customers?
3. Would you recommend that Wal-Mart purchase additional pages in *Vogue* magazine this year? Explain your rationale.

Source: This case was written by Hope Bober Corrigan, Loyola College in Maryland.

CASE 6   Dollar General and Family Dollar Cater to an Underserved Market Segment

Dollar General, headquartered in Goodlettsville, Tennessee, and Family Dollar, based in Mathews, North Carolina, are the two leading retailers in the fastest growing segment of the industry, referred to as extreme value retailing. In 2005, Dollar General had over 7,500 stores in 30 states with sales surpassing $7 billion. Its annual growth in sales has been above 20 percent for the last six years. Family Dollar, with 5,600 stores in 44 states, generated over $5 billion in sales in 2004. Both retailers are opening new stores at rates exceeding a store a day.

The extreme value retail format has become increasingly popular among a variety of customers, including rural and urban shoppers, low- to middle-income young families, ethnic groups, and older customers with fixed incomes. Consumers have come to trust both of these retailers to provide good quality merchandise at low prices without the hassle of crowds and lines. The breakdown by geographic segments is 25 percent rural, 33 percent urban, and 44 percent suburban. This distribution is about the same as the sales distribution for Wal-Mart and Kmart stores. About 25 percent of U.S. households shop at an extreme value retailer once a month.

Sometimes these firms are grouped under the category of dollar retailers—retailers that sell merchandise priced under one dollar. While Dollar General and Family Dollar keep their prices typically under $15, most of their merchandise is priced over a dollar. Family Dollar has multiple price points, whereas Dollar General prices its merchandise at even-dollar price points.

About 50 percent of the merchandise sold in the stores is consumables (pet supplies, food, paper, household cleaning and personal care products), with the remaining sales equally divided among basic clothing, hardware and seasonal merchandise, and home products. The percentage of consumable sales has been increasing over the past five years. Basic stock is supplemented with opportunistic buys of closeout/liquidation and impulse merchandise giving the impression of a changing merchandise mix in the stores.

Vendors are developing new products and packaging to meet the needs of these extreme value retailers. For example, Fruit of the Loom typically sells men's underwear in a nine-pack, but it offers small packs to value retailers. Procter & Gamble and Johnson Products also sell smaller sizes of hair care products with lower retail prices to extreme value retail chains.

Most of their locations are in the Southeast, where the companies are headquartered. The stores are small, 6,000 to 8,000 square feet, primarily located in small towns with populations under 40,000 and in suburban strip shopping centers. Because the stores are relatively small, it is easy to find good locations in almost any market the retailers choose to enter.

Initially, these extreme value retailers focused on low-income communities that were too small to support a large Wal-Mart or Kmart discount store. Residents of these towns appreciate the convenience of buying merchandise close to their homes rather than driving 30 minutes to a discount store in a larger town. Many of their customers walk to the stores. Not only are the stores closer to customers, but shoppers are able to park closer to the stores in uncrowded parking lots and avoid long checkout lines. With a small store, customers can get in easily, find what they are looking for, and get out in a few minutes. The average transaction is between $8 and $9. To maximize operating efficiencies, the retailers typically open a cluster of stores in a geographic area before entering a new area. Dollar General and Family Dollar are now opening stores in suburban strip shopping centers, using space that has been abandoned by drugstores that moved to stand-alone locations.

At one time, these extreme value retailers advertised sales using circulars. But both Dollar General and Family Dollar reduced their advertising expenses when they converted to an everyday low-pricing strategy. This cost saving allowed the retailers to pass even more savings on to their customers.

A recent Family Dollar annual report stated, "Supply chain efficiencies are vital to the success of any retailer, particularly one growing as fast as Family Dollar." Thus, Family Dollar and Dollar General are making significant investments in point-of-sale terminals, store-level inventory tracking systems, automated distribution centers, space allocation software, and replenishment systems to reduce stockouts and increase inventory turnover.

DISCUSSION QUESTIONS

1. What is the target market for extreme value retailers like Dollar General and Family Dollar?
2. Why are customers increasingly patronizing these extreme value retailer stores?
3. How do extreme value retailers make a profit when their prices and average transactions are so low?
4. Can extreme value retailers defend themselves against general merchandise discount retailers like Wal-Mart, or will Wal-Mart eventually drive them out of business? Why?

Source: This case was written by Valerie Bryan, University of Florida.

CASE 7   Ahold: The Biggest Supermarket Retailer You Have Never Heard Of

In 1887, 22-year-old Albert Heijn took over his father's small grocery store near Zaandam, West Holland. His strategy for growing the family business was to offer quality products with excellent customer service at the lowest prices. Now, 118 years later, Ahold (an abbreviation of Albert Heijn Holding) is the world's second-largest food retailer. It operates 1,600 stores in 27 countries, with 2003 sales greater than $56 billion. But its name is not on a single store it owns.

Ahold USA's retail operations comprise Stop & Shop, Giant-Landover, Giant-Carlisle, Tops, Bi-Lo, Bruno's, and Peapod. All six retail-operating companies are located along the U.S. eastern seaboard. The retail stores combined serve approximately 20 million customers every week, and Ahold USA employs over 170,000 people. Almost 60 percent of Ahold worldwide sales are generated in the United States.

 Ahold also operates under 26 different names in Europe, America, Asia, and Latin America. It uses 10 different formats for its stores, ranging from tiny gas station outlets in the Netherlands to 150,000-square-foot hypermarkets in northern Brazil. The company refers to its strategy as "multilocal, multiformat, multichannel." "Our culture is first and foremost the culture of the local operating company," says Cees van der Hoeven, Ahold's 54-year-old CEO. "What makes Ahold unique is that we're perceived by our customers as the local guy." Very few customers at a Bruno's supermarket in Alabama or a Disco store in Argentina realize that their store is part of a global retail giant headquartered in the Netherlands.

Wal-Mart and Carrefour, the first- and third-largest food retailers, use a different approach. From Paris to Shanghai, all Carrefour stores look the same and have identical layouts (to reach the deli counter, for example, you always turn left at the entrance). Wal-Mart also uses its name on most of its stores across the world. Three years ago, it acquired the Asada chain in the United

Kingdom and still operates the stores under the Asada name. But when it bought the Wertkauf chain and some Spar stores in Germany, it converted the stores to Wal-Marts. Their British and German stores are expected to conform to the cost-conscious, customer-oriented Wal-Mart culture.

Ahold is a food retailer. Food sales account for 90 percent of its revenues. Recognizing the lifestyle trend toward more out-of-home food consumption, Ahold is attempting to increase its share of the wallet through its acquisition of food-service companies. In contrast, Wal-Mart and Carrefour focus on operating larger supercenters or hypermarkets that offer general merchandise as well as food.

Another difference between Ahold and its major international competitors is its growth strategy. Although Wal-Mart has made some acquisitions, most of its international growth, and all of Carrefour's, has been internally generated. In contrast, Ahold has grown primarily through acquisitions. More than 50 percent of Ahold's revenue now comes from the U.S. supermarket chains it acquired. Its first acquisition in the United States, in 1977, was Bi-Lo, a South Carolina–based grocery store chain operating about 450 stores in South Carolina, Georgia, Tennessee, Florida, and Alabama. Then it acquired Stop & Shop, with 320 stores stretching from Massachusetts to eastern New Jersey; Giant Landover of Maryland in Maryland, Washington, Delaware, southern New Jersey, and northern Virginia; Giant Carlisle in Pennsylvania; Tops in New York; and Bruno in Alabama, the Florida Panhandle, and Mississippi. With 1,400 stores in the United States, Ahold is the largest food retailer in the eastern part of the country and the fourth biggest in the whole country, after Wal-Mart, Kroger, Safeway, and Albertson's.

In 1999, the company bought U.S. Foodservice, America's second-largest supplier of ready-made meals, prepared foods, and ingredients to restaurants, hotels, and other institutions. In 2000, Ahold acquired a majority stake in Peapod, one of the first Internet grocers. Peapod now operates out of Stop & Shop and Giant stores in the Boston, New York, and Washington, DC, areas, as well as on its own in its home base of Chicago. In 2001, Ahold acquired 56 stores and eight locations from Grand Union. No other European retailer has been as successful in entering the U.S. market as Ahold. For example, Carrefour opened two stores in suburban Philadelphia in the late 1980s but gave up quickly when it faced labor problems and the loyalty customers had to their local supermarket chains. The profit margin for Ahold's U.S. division is 5.7 percent, while the profit margin for the European division is only 3.9 percent of sales.

Van der Hoeven has a vision of a future in which Ahold's stores in Guatemala offer tips on pricing to their colleagues in the United States and the flooring for every Ahold supermarket from Boston to São Paulo is ordered from the same supplier. The payoff from this networked global juggernaut would be the ability to leverage its size to get rock-bottom prices from its vendors on everything from corn flakes to oranges. Meanwhile, Ahold's companies in Europe, America, Asia, and Latin America would lower their costs by using the same trucks, sharing the same accountants, and exchanging ideas over the corporate Intranet. But this global network would be invisible to the 20 million customers who pass through Ahold stores every week.

Ahold has yet to realize this vision. Although Ahold has centralized the procurement of fresh and chilled products across its six U.S. chains, only 5 percent of all merchandise in Ahold's stores is ordered on a cross-continental basis, about the same as Wal-Mart and Carrefour. Ahold's U.S. managers are just beginning to exchange best practices with their counterparts overseas. For example, Stop & Shop and Peapod are trying to improve their fulfillment accuracy by learning how Ahold's Scandinavian Internet home-delivery service has achieved its successes in performing these activities. However, Ahold's goal is to bring the same supply chain efficiencies achieved by Wal-Mart and Carrefour in general merchandise distribution to food distribution.

DISCUSSION QUESTIONS

1. What are the advantages and disadvantages of the growth strategies pursued by Ahold, Carrefour, and Wal-Mart?
2. Should Ahold use its name on all of its stores like Wal-Mart and Carrefour? Why or why not?
3. What are the advantages and disadvantages of Wal-Mart's and Carrefour's more centralized decision making compared with Ahold's decentralized decision making?

Source: This case was written by Barton Weitz, University of Florida.

CASE 8   Competitive Environment in the Teen/College Apparel Market

Jennifer Shaffer, a 17-year-old living in Newton, Massachusetts, used to shop at Abercrombie & Fitch (A&F) once a month. She thought the prices were high, but the brand name and image appealed to her. She says, "It's like I really had to have Abercrombie." Then an American Eagle (AE) store opened about 15 minutes from her home. Now she shops at the AE store about twice a month and rarely goes to the A&F store. "They look the same, and they're both really cute," she says. "But American Eagle's prices are a little cheaper."

Both A&F and AE are still growing into their present strategy of selling casual apparel to the teen/college market. When A&F was established as an outdoor sporting goods retailer over 100 years ago, it sold the highest quality hunting, fishing, and camping goods. A&F also outfitted some of the greatest explorations in the early part of the twentieth century, including Robert Perry's expedition to the North Pole and Theodore Roosevelt's trips to the Amazon and Africa.

Over time, its tweedy image became less attractive to consumers. The chain experienced a significant decline in sales and profits, and in 1977, it was forced to declare bankruptcy. The company, initially acquired by Oshman's

Sporting Goods, did not experience a turnaround until The Limited Inc. acquired it in 1988. Initially, The Limited positioned A&F as a tailored clothing store for men. In 1995, The Limited repositioned A&F to target both males and females in the teen and college market with an emphasis on casual American style and youth.

In 1999, The Limited sold A&F, which now operates as a separate company that operated 351 Abercrombie & Fitch stores, 167 abercrombie stores, 271 Hollister Co. stores, and 5 RUEHL stores at the end of May 2005. It operates e-commerce Web sites at www.abercrombie.com, www.abercrombiekids.com, and www.hollisterco.com.

American Eagle, though lacking the rich tradition of A&F, also was positioned as outfitter when it started in 1977. Initially offering apparel only for men, American Eagle shifted its focus to teens and college students in 1995. In 2000, it acquired two Canadian specialty retail chains—Bluenotes/Thriftys and Braemar. The Braemar locations were converted to American Eagle stores, whereas the Thriftys stores are being converted into Bluenotes stores, specialty stores that target a slightly younger, more urban teen demographic and that carry more denim merchandise. Today, American Eagle has 779

AE stores in 50 states, the District of Columbia, and Puerto Rico and 70 AE stores in Canada. It also operates via its Web business, www.ae.com.

Even though A&F and AE have evolved from their roots, there is still an outdoor, rugged aspect in their apparel. Both retail chains carry similar assortments of polos, pants, t-shirts, jeans, and sweaters. All the apparel and accessories carry the store's private-label brand. A lot of the merchandise is athletically inspired.

The rivalry between A&F and AE is intense; A&F even filed a lawsuit in 1998 in federal court accusing AE of copying its clothing styles and catalog. The courts found that though the designs were similar, there was nothing inherently distinctive in A&F's clothing designs that could be protected by a trademark. But the courts have ruled that Abercrombie's catalog design and image are worthy of trade dress protection. Trade dress is the overall image of a product used in its marketing or sales, composed of the nonfunctional elements of its design, packaging, or labeling (such as colors, package shape, or symbols).[1] However, the court also felt that AE's catalog had a different image that did not infringe upon the image of the A&F catalog.

It was the catalog and home page that first drew Jennifer to an A&F store a couple of years ago. She recalls going through the catalog and browsing the Web page with some girlfriends and looking at the muscular young men featured. "The guys in the magazine— that's what made us all go," she says. This young and sexy image is enhanced by store signage featuring scantily clad lacrosse players and young beachgoers. Abercrombie & Fitch has exploited this image by introducing a line of intimate apparel in 2001. Intimate apparel is now one of the best selling merchandise categories in the stores.

To reinforce its brand image and communicate with its target audience, AE teamed up with MTV to sponsor MTV Spring Break 2005. As a major sponsor, AE was the official apparel provider for the network's hottest annual event, broadcast from Cancun, Mexico, on March 18–20, 2005. American Eagle provided the wardrobe for the stars of *Dawson's Creek*, and it also has its apparel featured in various movies. While its commercials are less suggestive than those of A&F, its "Get Together" commercials feature college- and high-school–age teens dancing and then coming together and kissing.

[1]http://dictionary.reference.com/search?q=trade%20dress, accessed October 31, 2005.

Even though A&F devotes its advertising and marketing resources to reaching college-age consumers, many teenagers also patronize its stores. The company is concerned that the image of its stores will be negatively affected if they become a place for teenagers to hang out. The development of the Hollister chain is one of the approaches that A&F has taken to preserve the A&F image while catering to the growing teenage market

The Hollister stores are unique. Their target market consists of consumers ages 14 to 18 years. The merchandise in the stores is 20 to 30 percent less expensive than A&F's merchandise. The styling of the merchandise is also different, with brighter colors and larger logos. However, many teenagers fail to recognize the subtle differences. They contend that it is essentially the same merchandise except at lower prices.

Furthermore, Hollister stores are roughly 2,000 square feet smaller than A&F stores, and the store design is completely distinct. While A&F stores still convey an outdoor ruggedness in their décor, Hollister stores present a California beach–inspired theme. They want their customers to feel as though they are part of a beach party. This casual atmosphere provides young consumers with an enjoyable shopping experience. The décor in the stores inspires and evokes memories of hot summer days at any time of the year.

DISCUSSION QUESTIONS

1. What, if any, are the differences in A&F's and AE's retail strategy?
2. What are the brand images of A&F and AE? What words and phrases are associated with each retailer's brand name?
3. List other specialty apparel retailers that target the same customers as A&F and AE. How do these brands differentiate themselves in the competitive retail environment? Construct a product positioning map to illustrate.
4. Which retailer(s) has (have) the stronger competitive position? Why?

Source: This case was written by Kristina Pacca, University of Florida.

CASE 9   Radio Shack and Best Buy: Comparing Financial Performance

Both RadioShack and Best Buyer sell consumer electronic merchandise; however, the companies have different retail strategies. RadioShack targets three family-oriented customer segments: (1) active suburban families with teenage children, (2) urban "flash" consumers with preteen kids, and (3) "small-town values" families with children of all ages.

These three demographic groups represent 38 percent of the U.S. population and 46 percent of the consumer electronics market. Through its stores, kiosks, and Web site, RadioShack provides families with accessories, consumer electronic solutions, and proprietary novelty products.

The customers in its target markets are willing to pay a reasonable price in return for convenience, selection, and simplicity in their shopping experience. The company provides excellent customer service that provides solutions for families' home electronic needs, as emphasized in its "You've Got Questions. We've Got Answers," branding campaign.

RadioShack has over 5,000 stores in the United States, Puerto Rico, and the U.S. Virgin Islands. The stores, typically 2,500 square feet, are located in major malls and strip centers, as well as stand-alone locations. Each location carries a broad assortment of both private-label and national brand consumer electronics products. The product categories offered include mobile and wireless phones; direct-to-home satellite systems; computers and accessories; general and special purpose batteries; wire, cable, and connectivity products; digital cameras; radio-controlled cars and other toys; and satellite radios. In addition, RadioShack sells services provided by third parties, including cellular and PCS phone service, direct-to-home satellite activation, satellite radio service, and prepaid wireless airtime. The company also has a network of 2,000 dealers servicing smaller markets, operates 500 kiosks located in Sam's Club stores, and owns four manufacturing plants producing its private-label merchandise.

In contrast to RadioShack's specialty store format, Best Buy operates 700 category killer stores in the United States plus a Web site. The stores, averaging 42,000 square feet, are typically staffed by one general manager, four to five assistant managers, and 120 full- and part-time employees.

Best Buy's retail strategy focuses on bringing technology and consumers together in a retail environment that educates consumers on the features and benefits of technology and entertainment products. The stores offer merchandise in four product groups: consumer electronics,

EXHIBIT 1   Financial Data for Radio Shack and Best Buy

(all numbers in millions)	RADIO SHACK INCOME STATEMENT			BEST BUY INCOME STATEMENT		
	2004	2003	2002	2004	2003	2002
Net sales	$4,841	$4,649	$4,577	27,433	24,548	20,943
Cost of goods sold	2,407	2,334	2,339	20,938	18,677	15,998
Gross profit	2,434	2,315	2,238	6,495	5,871	4,945
Operating expenses Selling, general and administrative	1,775	1,740	1,729	5,053	4,567	3,935
Other expenses	101	92	83			
Total operating expenses	1,876	1,832	1,812	5,053	4,567	3,935
Net profit from operations	558	483	426	1,442	1,304	1,010
Number of employees	42,000	39,500	39,100	109,000	100,000	98,000
Selling space (square feet)	12,760,000	12,430,000	12,490,000	28,300,000	26,400,000	24,200,000
Growth in comparable store sales	3%	2%	−1%	4%	7%	3%

	RADIO SHACK BALANCE SHEET			BEST BUY BALANCE SHEET		
	2004	2003	2002	2004	2003	2002
Current assets						
Cash and equivalents	$438	$635	$447	$3,348	2,600	$1,914
Accounts receivable	241	182	208	375	343	312
Inventory	1,004	767	971	2,851	2,607	2,077
Other current assets	93	83	83	329	174	397
Total current assets	1,776	1,667	1,709	6,903	5,724	
Property, plant, equipment	652	513	422	2,464	2,244	3,089
Other assets	90	84	99	928	684	4,605
Total assets	2,518	2,264	2,230	10,295	8,652	7,694
Current liabilities	958	858	828	4,959	4,501	3,824
Long-term liabilities	637	618	672	887	729	1,140
Stockholder equity	923	788	730	4,449	3,422	2,730

SOURCE: SEC 10K filings at www.sec.gov.

home office, entertainment software, and appliances. Consumer electronics, the largest product group, consists of televisions, digital cameras, DVD players, digital camcorders, MP3 players, car stereos, home theater audio systems, mobile electronics, and accessories. The home office product group includes desktop and notebook computers, telephones, networking, and accessories. Entertainment software products include DVDs, video game hardware and software, CDs, computer software, and subscriptions. The appliances product group includes major appliances, as well as vacuums, small electrics, and housewares.

Best Buy also offers a variety of in-store and in-home services related to the merchandise offered within the four product groups. In-store services include computer setup, repair, and software installation, as well as the installation of mobile electronics. In-home services include computer setup, repair, software installation, and home networking, and the delivery and installation of appliances and home theater systems. Whereas services were not a significant part of its revenue in fiscal 2004, it feels that service revenues will become a more significant component of its business.

DISCUSSION QUESTIONS

1. Using Exhibit 2, construct strategic profit models for Radio Shack and Best Buy using data from the abbreviated income statements and balance sheets in Exhibit 1. You can do these calculations by hand or go to the student side of the Online Learning Center (OLC) and use the Strategic Profit Model Excel spreadsheet that is available. Click on Strategic Profit Model. Then click through to "Try it Yourself—the SPM Calculations." Click on "Spreadsheets: The Strategic Profit Model" at the lower left corner of your screen.

2. Explain, from a marketing perspective, why you would expect the gross margin percentage, expenses-to-sales ratio, net profit margin, inventory turnover, and asset turnover to be different for Radio Shack and Best Buy.

3. Assess which chain has better overall financial performance. Why?

Source: This case was written by Barton Weitz, University of Florida.

Strategic Profit Model   **EXHIBIT 2**

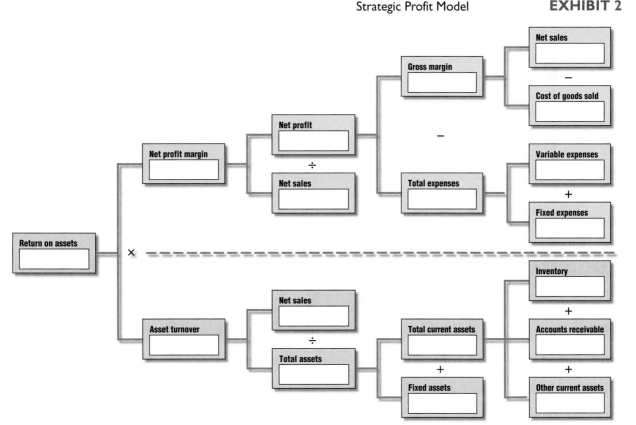

CASE 10 Stephanie's Boutique: Selecting a Store Location

Stephanie Wilson must decide where to open a ready-to-wear boutique she's been contemplating for several years. Now in her late 30s, she's been working in municipal government ever since leaving college, where she majored in fine arts. She's divorced with two children (ages five and eight) and wants her own business, at least partly to be able to spend more time with her children. She loves fashion, feels she has a flair for it, and has taken evening courses in fashion design and retail management. Recently, she heard about a plan to rehabilitate an old arcade building in the downtown section of her Midwestern city. This news crystallized her resolve to move now. She's considering three locations.

THE DOWNTOWN ARCADE

The city's central business district has been ailing for some time. The proposed arcade renovation is part of a master redevelopment plan, with a new department store and several office buildings already operating. Completion of the entire master plan is expected to take another six years.

Dating from 1912, the arcade building was once the center of downtown trade, but it's been vacant for the past 15 years. The proposed renovation includes a three-level shopping facility, low-rate garage with validated parking, and convention center complex. Forty shops are planned for the first (ground) floor, 28 more on the second, and a series of restaurants on the third.

The location Stephanie is considering is 900 feet square and situated near the main ground floor entrance. Rent is $20 per square foot, for an annual total of $18,000. If sales exceed $225,000, rent will be calculated at 8 percent of sales. She'll have to sign a three-year lease.

TENDERLOIN VILLAGE

The gentrified urban area of the city where Stephanie lives is nicknamed Tenderloin Village because of its lurid past. Today, however, the neat, well-kept brownstones and comfortable neighborhood make it feel like a trendy enclave. Many residents have done the remodeling work themselves and take great pride in their neighborhood.

About 20 small retailers are now in an area of the Village adjacent to the convention center complex. Most of them are vegetarian or nouveau cuisine restaurants. There are also three small women's specialty clothing stores.

The site available to Stephanie is on the Village's main street on the ground floor of an old house. Its space is also about 900 square feet. Rent is $15,000 annually with no coverage clause. The landlord knows Stephanie and will require a two-year lease.

APPLETREE MALL

This suburban mall has been open for eight years. A successful regional center, it has three department stores and 100 smaller shops just off a major interstate highway about eight miles from downtown. Of its nine women's clothing retailers, three are in a price category considerably higher than what Stephanie has in mind.

Appletree has captured the retail business in the city's southwest quadrant, though growth in that sector has slowed in the past year. Nevertheless, mall sales are still running 12 percent ahead of the previous year. Stephanie learned of plans to develop a second shopping center east of town, which would be about the same size and character as Appletree Mall. But groundbreaking is still 18 months away, and no renting agent has begun to enlist tenants.

The store available to Stephanie in Appletree is two doors from the local department store chain's mall outlet. At 1,200 square feet, it's slightly larger than the other two possibilities. But it's long and narrow—24 feet in front by 50 feet deep. Rent is $24 per square foot ($28,800 annually). In addition, on sales that exceed $411,500, rent is 7 percent of sales. There's an additional charge of 1 percent of sales to cover common-area maintenance and mall promotions. The mall's five-year lease includes an escape clause if sales don't reach $411,500 after two years.

DISCUSSION QUESTIONS

1. Give the pluses and minuses of each location.
2. What type of store would be most appropriate for each location?
3. If you were Stephanie, which location would you choose? Why?

Source: This case was prepared by Professor David Ehrlich, Marymount University.

CASE 11 Hutch: Locating a New Store

In June, after returning from a trip to the Bahamas, Dale Abell, vice president of new business development for the Hutch Corporation, began a search for a good location to open a new store. After a preliminary search, Abell narrowed the choice to two locations, both in Georgia. He now faces the difficult task of thoroughly analyzing each location and determining which will be the site of the next store.

COMPANY BACKGROUND

The Hutch store chain was founded in 1952 by John Henry Hutchison, a musician and extremely successful insurance salesman. Hutchison established the headquarters in Richmond, Virginia, where both the executive offices and one of two warehouse distribution centers are located. Hutch currently operates 350 popularly priced women's clothing stores throughout the Southeast and Midwest. Manufacturers ship all goods to these distribution centers. They are delivered floor-ready, in that the vendor has attached price labels, UPC identifying codes, and source tags for security purposes and placed appropriate merchandise on hangers. Once at the distribution centers, the merchandise is consolidated for reshipment to the stores. Some staple merchandise, such as hosiery, is stored at these distribution centers. All Hutch stores are located within 400 miles of a distribution center. This way, as Abell explains, "A truck driver can deliver to every location in two days."

Hutch Fashions

Hutch Fashions is considered one of the leading popular priced women's fashion apparel chains in the Southeast. The stores carry trendy apparel selections in juniors', misses', and women's sizes, all at popular prices. The chain offers a complementary array of accessories in addition to its main features of dresses, coats, and sportswear. Located mainly in strip centers and malls, these shops typically require 4,000 to 5,000 square feet.

Hutch Extra

Hutch Extra stores are primarily located in strip centers and malls. They bear a strong resemblance to Hutch Fashions. The difference is that Hutch Extra stores require less space (from 2,000 to 3,000 square feet) and cater to women requiring large and half-size apparel. (Women who wear half-sizes require a larger size but are not tall enough to wear a standard large size. In other words, a size 18 1/2 is the same as size 18 except that it is cut for a shorter woman.)

Hutch Fashions* Hutch Extra

Although Hutch Fashions and Hutch Extra stores selectively appear as separate entries, the corporate goal is to position both as a single entity. The combination store emerged in 1986 and is now used for all new stores. The Hutch Fashions* Hutch Extra combination occupies a combined space of 6,000 to 7,000 square feet, with separate entrances for each entity. A partial wall separates the two frontal areas of the store but allows for a combined checkout/customer service area in the rear. These stores are primarily located in strip centers and can occasionally be found in malls (Exhibit 1 shows a typical layout).

MARKETING STRATEGY

Customers

Hutch's target market is women between the ages of 18 and 40 years who are in the lower–middle to middle-income range. Abell explains, "We don't cater to any specific ethnic group, only to women who like to wear the latest fashions."

Product/Price

Hutch positions merchandise and price levels between the mass merchandisers and the department stores. You won't find any bluelight specials or designer boutiques in a Hutch store. By avoiding direct competition for customers with the large discounters (Kmart and Wal-Mart) and the high-fashion department stores and specialty shops, Hutch has secured a comfortable niche for itself. "Our products must be priced at a level where our customers perceive our products to be elegant and fashionable but not too expensive," notes Abell.

Location

Hutch stores are located throughout the Southeast and Midwest and must be within a 400-mile radius of a Hutch distribution center. Within this geographic area, Hutch stores are located in communities with a population range of 10,000 to 50,000 and a trade area of 50,000 to 150,000. These locations are characterized by a large concentration of people in the low- to middle-income brackets who work in agriculture and industry.

Hutch stores are primarily located in strip malls or strip centers—generally ones anchored by either a regional or national discount store (Wal-Mart or Target). In addition, these centers contain a mix of several nationally recognized and popular local tenants. Hutch stores are primarily located adjacent to the center's anchor. Mall locations must be on the main corridor, as close to "center court," as economics (rent) will allow. Abell remarked, "We don't care if it's the only center in the region. If the

EXHIBIT 1
Layout of Hutch Fashions* Hutch Extra Store

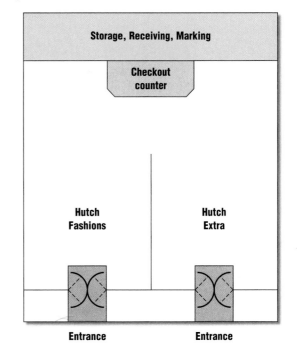

only space available is at the end of the mall, we won't go in there. Our plan is to be a complement to the anchor and to feed off the traffic coming to it. We may have a reputation for being picky and having one of the toughest lease agreements in the business, but it's one of the main reasons for our continued success."

DATA SOURCES

Abell is using several reports generated by Claritas to help him decide which location to choose for the next Hutch store. He has chosen reports that describe the 10-mile ring around each of the proposed locations. Exhibits 2

EXHIBIT 2

Population and Competitive Profile, 10-Mile Ring from Centers of Dalton and Hinesville, Georgia

		Dalton	Hinesville
Population	2005 projection	93,182	64,195
	1999 estimate	87,293	57,945
	1990 Census	79,420	49,853
	1980 Census	71,373	34,125
	% change, 1990–96	9.9%	16.2%
	% change, 1980–90	11.3%	46.1%
	In group quarters (military base) 1996	.9%	11.2%
Household	2005 projection	35,570	20,010
	1999 estimate	33,140	17,541
	1990 Census	29,340	14,061
	1980 Census	24,302	8,557
	% change, 1990–96	12.9%	24.7%
	% change, 1980–90	20.7%	64.3%
Families	1996 estimate	24,347	14,277
Race, 1999	White	92.0%	54.1%
	Black	4.9%	38.3%
	American Indian	0.2%	0.5%
	Asian or Pacific Islander	0.6%	3.1%
	Other	2.3%	4.0%
Age, 1999	0–20	31.2%	40.2%
	21–44	37.1%	47.0%
	45–64	21.7%	9.2%
	65+	9.9%	3.4%
	Median age, 1996	33.7	23.9
	Male	32.5	23.6
	Female	35.0	24.6
Household size, 1999	1 person	21.0%	15.2%
	2 persons	32.3%	26.6%
	3–4 persons	38.1%	45.7%
	5+ persons	8.7%	12.6%
Income, 1999	Median household income	$30,516	$23,686
	Average household income	$40,397	$28,677
Sex (% male)		49.1%	55.8%
Education, 1999	Population age 25+	49,298	22,455
	No high school diploma	41.0%	15.5%
	High school only	28.6%	41.2%
	College, 1–3 years	19.1%	29.7%
	College, 4+ years	11.3%	13.5%
Industry	Manufacturing: nondurable goods	42.3%	7.2%
	Retail trade	12.6%	23.3%
	Professional and related services	13.3%	21.4%
	Public administration	2.2%	20.0%
Retail sales (000)	Total	$706,209	$172,802
	General merchandise stores Apparel stores	$26,634	$9,339
Retail establishments	General merchandise stores	12	3
	Women's apparel stores	21	8

and 3 summarize these reports. They contain detailed population, household, race, income, education, and employment data plus figures on retail sales and number of establishments. The reports also provide information about women's apparel sales and give a market index that estimates the annual per-person spending potential for the trade area divided by the national average (see Exhibit 3). Dalton's 99 index means that the spending

potential for women's clothing is slightly lower than the national average of 100. Finally, Abell is using Claritas/UDS's PRIZM lifestyle reports. These reports contain numeric figures and percentages on the population, households, families, sex, age, household size, and ownership of housing. An excerpt from the report is given in Exhibit 4. Some of the cluster group names are described in Exhibit 5.

EXHIBIT 3

Sales Potential Index for Women's Apparel

	Area Sales ($ mil.)	Area Sales per Capita	U.S. Sales per Capita	Index (area sales ÷ U.S. sales)
Dalton	$18.01	$206.26	$207.65	99
Hinesville	$8.97	$154.74	$207.65	75

PRIZM Neighborhood Clusters   **EXHIBIT 4**

Prizm Cluster	Population, 1999	Percentage of Population	Prizm Cluster	Population, 1999	Percentage of Population
Dalton			**Mines & mills**	7,694	8.8
Big fish, small pond	4,727	5.4%	Back country folks	4,293	4.9
New homesteaders	6,030	6.9			
Red, white, & blues	31,123	35.7	**Hinesville**		
Shotguns & pickups	8,881	10.2	Military quarters	45,127	77.9
Rural industrial	12,757	14.6	Scrub pine flats	3,476	6.0

PRIZM Lifestyle Clusters   **EXHIBIT 5**

Big Fish, Small Pond

Small-town executive families; upper-middle incomes; age groups 35–44, 45–54; predominantly white. This group is married, family-oriented, and conservative. Their neighborhoods are older. Best described as captains of local industry, they invest in their homes and clubs and vacation by car in the United States.

Rural Industrial

Low-income, blue-collar families; lower-middle incomes; age groups <24, 25–34; predominantly white, high Hispanic. Nonunion labor found in this cluster, which is comprised of hundreds of blue-collar mill towns on American's rural backroads.

Mines & Mills

Older families; mine and mill towns; poor; age groups 55–64, 65+; predominantly white. Down the Appalachians, across the Ozarks to Arizona, and up the Missouri, this cluster is exactly as its name implies. This older, mostly single population with a few children lives in the midst of scenic splendor.

Shotguns & Pickups

Rural blue-collar workers and families; middle income; age groups 35–44, 45–54; predominantly white. This cluster is found in the Northeast, the Southeast, and the Great Lakes and Piedmont industrial regions. They are in blue-collar jobs; most are married with school-age kids. They are churchgoers who also enjoy bowling, hunting, sewing, and attending car races.

Back Country Folks

Older farm families; lower-middle income; age groups 55–64, 65+; predominantly white. This cluster is centered in the eastern uplands along a wide path from the Pennsylvania Poconos to the Arkansas Ozarks. Anyone who visits their playground in Branson, Missouri, or Gatlinburg, Tennessee, can attest that these are the most

blue-collar neighborhoods in America. Centered in the Bible Belt, many back country folks are hooked on Christianity and country music.

Scrub Pine Flats

Older African-American farm families; poor; age groups 55–64, 65+; predominantly black. This cluster is found mainly in the coastal flatlands of the Atlantic and Gulf states from the James to the Mississippi rivers. These humid, sleepy rural communities, with a mix of blacks and whites, live in a seemingly timeless, agrarian rhythm.

New Homesteaders

Young middle-class families; middle income; age groups 35–44, 45–54; predominantly white. This cluster is above-average for college education. Executives and professionals work in local service fields such as administration, communications, health, and retail. Most are married; the young have children, the elders do not. Life is homespun with a focus on crafts, camping, and sports.

Red, White, & Blues

Small-town blue-collar families; middle income; age groups 35–54, 55–64; predominantly white, with skilled workers primarily employed in mining, milling, manufacturing, and construction. Geocentered in the Appalachians, Great Lakes industrial region, and western highlands, these folks love the outdoors.

Military Quarters

GIs and surrounding off-base families; lower-middle income; age groups under 24, 25–34; ethnically diverse. Since this cluster depicts military life with personnel living in group quarters, its demographics are wholly atypical because they are located on or near military bases. Racially integrated and with the highest index for adults under 35, "Military Quarters" like fast cars, bars, and action sports.

THE POTENTIAL LOCATIONS

Dalton

Dalton produces most of the carpeting in the United States. Consequently, the carpet mills are the major employers in Dalton. Stain Master carpeting has been putting a strain on the city's water supply. Stain Master is said to require seven times the amount of water as regular carpeting and is rapidly becoming the largest proportion of carpeting produced. Expressing concern over market viability, Abell said, "If the Dalton area were ever to experience a severe drought, the carpet mills would be forced to drastically reduce production. The ensuing layoffs could put half the population on unemployment."

The proposed site for the new store is the Whitfield Square shopping center located off the main highway approximately two miles from the center of town (see Exhibit 6). After meeting with the developer, Abell was pleased with several aspects of the strip center. He learned that the center has good visibility from the highway, will be anchored by both Wal-Mart and Kroger (a large grocery chain), and has ample parking. Abell is also reasonably pleased with the available location within the center, which is one spot away from Wal-Mart. However, he was displeased with the presence of two large outparcels in front of the center that would reduce the number of parking spaces and direct visibility of the center. (An outparcel is a freestanding structure at the front of a mall, commonly a fast-food outlet, a bank, or a gas station.) Other tenants in the center include a nationally recognized shoe store, a beauty salon, two popular restaurants (Chinese and Mexican), and McSpeedy's Pizza at the end of the center, and a Century 21 real estate training school in the middle.

Hinesville

Like Dalton, Hinesville has one major employer, the Fort Stuart army base. Abell recalls that popular-priced stores generally do very well in military towns. Additionally, Fort Stuart is a rapid-deployment force base. Since the United States currently is involved in a number of international activities, Abell is concerned with a comment by a Hinesville native; "If these guys have to ship out, this place will be a ghost town." The location under consideration is the Target Plaza at the junction of State Route 119 and U.S. Highway 82 (see Exhibit 7). The center is anchored by Target and a grocery store that is part of a popular eastern chain. The two anchors are located side by side in the middle of the center. The spot available in the center is a 6,800-square-foot combination of three smaller units immediately adjacent to Target. Other tenants in the center include a bookstore, a waterbed store, a shoe store, an electronics retailer, a yogurt store, a video store, and a movie theater.

DISCUSSION QUESTIONS

1. How do the people living in the trade areas compare with Hutch's target customer?
2. How do the proposed locations, including the cities, tenant mix, and the locations within the malls, fit with Hutch's location requirements?
3. Which location would you select? Why?

Source: This case was written by Michael Levy, Babson College.

EXHIBIT 6
Whitfield Square
Shopping Center,
Dalton, Georgia

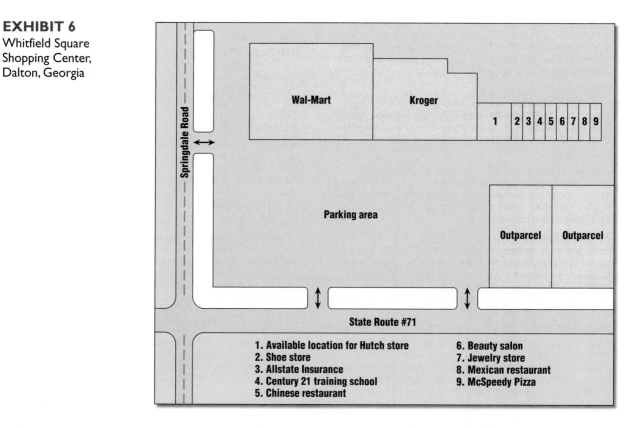

1. Available location for Hutch store
2. Shoe store
3. Allstate Insurance
4. Century 21 training school
5. Chinese restaurant
6. Beauty salon
7. Jewelry store
8. Mexican restaurant
9. McSpeedy Pizza

EXHIBIT 7
Target Plaza, Hinesville, Georgia

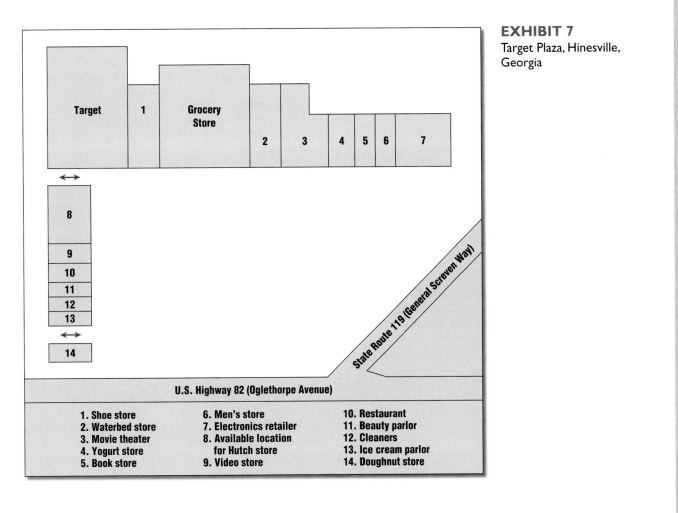

1. Shoe store
2. Waterbed store
3. Movie theater
4. Yogurt store
5. Book store
6. Men's store
7. Electronics retailer
8. Available location for Hutch store
9. Video store
10. Restaurant
11. Beauty parlor
12. Cleaners
13. Ice cream parlor
14. Doughnut store

CASE 12   Home Depot Changes Directions

Founded in Atlanta, Georgia, Home Depot has grown into the world's largest home improvement specialty retailer and the second-largest retailer in the United States. Twenty years of consistent growth is quite an achievement for any retailer; however, due to this growth, Home Depot is a much different company than it was when it was founded by Bernard Marcus and Arthur Blank in 1978. Changes in the company, put into motion by the new CEO, Bob Nardelli, shook up the way Home Depot does business.

HISTORY AND CULTURE OF THE COMPANY

During Home Depot's first 20 years, Bernard Marcus was CEO. In 1997, Arthur Blank succeeded his partner's place at the top of the company. In founding Home Depot, the partnership of Marcus and Blank revolutionized home improvement shopping by creating a different kind of store.

Warehouse is a better term for the stores' layout; each location stocks large volumes of goods that enable the company to compete by maintaining low prices. Because Home Depot's primary customer is the individual homeowner or small contractor, the stores also offer knowledgeable customer service to assist those in need of a little direction. In fact, the company took this service further by offering how-to clinics and longer four-week courses in its Home Depot University to educate customers about various home improvement projects, such as laying tile and caulking bathrooms. Thus, Home Depot effectively combined the strategies of low price and high service, not commonly seen in retailing.

Home Depot's "do-it-yourself" slogan was not just aimed at customers. This philosophy was fostered by the founders and trickled down through the entire company. Home Depot grew, not as a part of a complex plan, but as a result of a good business idea, good people, and some experimentation with new projects such as the Expo home decorating stores. Home Depot's corporate structure was very decentralized; many typical corporate policies were nonexistent in the firm. Each store manager was also a do-it-yourselfer and had a significant amount of control in making decisions pertaining to such areas as merchandising, advertising, and inventory selection for a particular area. Thus, Home Depot stores tended to be less homogeneous in their merchandise offerings than many other national retail chains.

But this decentralization of decision making allows managers to feel a stronger sense of ownership in a store's business. Associates of the company demonstrate a great deal of loyalty and pride in the company. Many store associates are hired with strong background experience in home improvement and are able to pass their knowledge along to customers. By building an enthusiastic staff, Home Depot has been able to deliver its promise of exceptional customer service.

FINDING A NEW LEADER

In 1999, with well over 900 stores, a market share of 24 percent, and several growth initiatives, Home Depot exuded success. However, historical success and future success are different concepts. Home Depot's board of directors was becoming increasingly unhappy. The company's performance at the time was faltering with a sharp drop in stock price in October 2000. After disputes about strategy, stores, and people, Home Depot's directors finally took action and so set out to find a leader capable, in their view, of continuing the firm's growth in sales and profits.

The board found their man in Bob Nardelli. At the time, Nardelli was vying for Jack Welch's position as CEO of GE but lost the battle to Jeff Immelt. Although he was passed up by GE, Bob Nardelli's career has been impressive, to say the least. From playing football at Western Illinois University to starting as a manufacturing engineer at GE, Nardelli's attitude was one of persistence and relentless hard work. Nardelli managed to work up through GE to the position of manufacturing Vice President, left to join the equipment maker Case as an executive vice president, and then returned to GE to run the Canadian appliance business. He then continued to prove himself at GE as the head of GE Transportation and CEO of GE Power Systems. Throughout his career at GE, Nardelli was recognized for his ability to improve operations and execute, but unfortunately, he was not viewed as a strong strategic leader. Believing he was finally in the right position to succeed Welch, Nardelli was very disappointed at the announcement of Immelt's appointment. Home Depot quickly snatched Nardelli up, placing him as CEO of Home Depot in December 2000. Nardelli redirected his energy into a mission to develop Home Depot.

CHANGES AT HOME DEPOT

Since Nardelli took the lead at Home Depot, the company has experienced significant changes. Home Depot is shifting toward a more centralized organization, one that can more efficiently handle the operations of a 1,400-store company in Canada, Mexico, and the United States.

For example, buying, once handled by nine regional offices, is now located at corporate headquarters in Atlanta. The company as a whole benefits from consolidation; buyers can get larger quantities of goods at lower costs, but how does this affect the do-it-yourself store manager? Nardelli, always a relentless workaholic, expects those around him to have the same attitude by holding frequent meetings and treating weekends like any other day of business.

Although a "can do, will do" atmosphere is necessary to implement Nardelli's plans, the hasty shift from laid-back to no-nonsense is creating some anxiety within the organization. In the first 19 months of his office, Nardelli lost 24 of 39 senior officers and has brought in several new faces, many from outside the retail industry. One newcomer, recruited by the new CEO, is Dennis Donovan from GE. Nardelli, believing in Donovan's efficiency, has made him an exceptionally high-paid chief of human resources.

Changes are not just affecting Home Depot's associates. In the past, Home Depot's customer return policy was simply to give cash back, no matter what. Although this was fantastic customer service, without receipt restrictions, abuse of the policy was out of control. Home Depot will now save close to $10 million annually with a new return policy of only store credit without a receipt.

Nardelli is applying the GE mindset, one characterized by strict measurement emphasizing efficiency, to his new company. Home Depot is now using GE's Six Sigma quality control method and quickly increasing the company's use of the Internet. Another new focus is that on associate training and evaluation. Pre-Nardelli, Home Depot had 157 different associate appraisal forms. All 295,000 associates are now reviewed using just two different forms.

These changes do not mean that the company is less interested in developing its people; in fact, Nardelli is trying to create an environment that will best highlight individual's abilities. At Home Depot's headquarters in Atlanta, the company is forming a leadership institute offering courses on leadership, merchandising, store planning, financial operations, and Six Sigma to executives with high potential. Nardelli wants a "coaching environment" that promotes succession planning and avoids the recent incident of having to hire a CEO from outside the company. Despite Nardelli's efforts, the market has not been kind to Home Depot. In Nardelli's first six months, the stock price rose from $39 to $53 but then curiously fell 10 percent after a first quarter announcement of 35 percent profits growth. Quarterly earnings continue to grow as in the past, but unfortunately, Home Depot's stock price is not reflecting this trend.

COMPETITION AND GROWTH POTENTIAL

As Home Depot struggles with its own growing pains, the company must also consider the ever-increasing competition from Lowe's. By placing stores in directly competing areas and growing at a faster rate than Home Depot,

Can Wal-Mart Improve Its Company Image?　CASE 13

561

Lowe's is definitely a factor in future planning. Lowe's best advantage is that its stores are designed with less of a "warehouse" feel, having wider aisles and better lighting. Store appearance may not be a crucial factor, but it is definitely a differentiating feature for a female shopper. And women are increasingly doing a greater percentage of home improvement shopping. Home Depot is trying to address this issue by cleaning up and modernizing its store look with lower shelving and different product mixes.

Extending its already strong business targeted at individual customers, Home Depot is now opening several professional stores for contractors, developers, and superintendent or maintenance people. The firm is also looking to expand through purchases of European home improvement companies.

DISCUSSION QUESTIONS

1. What is the best way for the Home Depot to continue to grow?
2. Can Home Depot maintain its current market position with its new policies and increasing competition?
3. Will more efficient operations and increased centralization be effective in streamlining Home Depot's business?
4. How might the shifts in corporate culture affect executives, management, and associates?

Source: This case was written by Cynthia Wongsuwan, University of Florida.

CASE 13　Can Wal-Mart Improve Its Company Image?

BACKGROUND FROM THE COMPANY

The company Sam Walton built has become the world's number one retailer. The organization has grown in a variety of retail formats, including Wal-Mart Stores, Supercenters, Sam's Clubs, Neighborhood Markets, online, and internationally. Wal-Mart operated units in the following countries as of April 2005:

Country	Number of Stores	Country	Number of Stores
Argentina	11	South Korea	16
Brazil	151	Mexico	700
Canada	261	Puerto Rico	54
China	45	United Kingdom	286
Germany	89	United States	3,719

As Wal-Mart has grown, it has also become a large job creator. According to the company home page, "more than 1.2 million Associates work at Wal-Mart in the U.S. The majority of Wal-Mart's hourly store associates in the U.S. work full-time. That's well above the 20–40 percent typically found in the retail industry. We are a leading employer of Hispanic Americans, with more than 139,000 Hispanic associates. Wal-Mart is one of the leading employers of African Americans, with more than 208,000 African-American associates. More than 220,000 of our associates are 55 or older. We project we will create positions for more than 100,000 new jobs in 2005."

WAL-MART FACES CRITICISM

Over the years, Wal-Mart has had its share of negative press about its labor and management practices. As a large company and employer, Wal-Mart has grown to expect attention and criticism. Some of the key areas of concern include discriminating against women, resisting unions, paying lower wages and offering fewer benefits, purchasing merchandise from China, employing contractors who hire illegal immigrants, and growing too rapidly. Constructive criticism has helped Wal-Mart improve its operations; however, the company takes issue when the criticism becomes an unwarranted attack that tarnishes their reputation.

ADVERTISING CAMPAIGN TO IMPROVE CORPORATE IMAGE

To reverse negative criticism and improve its public image, Wal-Mart launched an informative Web page, http://www.walmartfacts.com/Default.aspx; had key high-ranking executives appear for interviews on ABC, CNN, Fox, and CNBC; and took out full-page advertising in over 100 newspapers. Wal-Mart is proactively fighting back against critics and special interest groups to dispel myths about its employment and business practices.

To tell the Wal-Mart story and clear up misperceptions, the Web page contains company news and press releases, illustrates community impact and involvement programs, describes employee benefits and wages, and explains the status of current lawsuits facing the organization. This noncommercial Web page also summarizes Wal-Mart's diversity and equal employment opportunity policies, international operations, employee promotion strategies, charitable giving, and merchandise sourcing. An important

562

objective of the Web site is to help associates, consumers, reporters, and investors learn about the company.

To reach the mass media and take control of its image, Wal-Mart's Chief Executive Officer, H. Lee Scott, appeared on many networks including ABC, CNN, Fox, and CNBC for interviews. As part of this promotional campaign to show Wal-Mart in a positive light, he also granted interviews with *USA Today* and the Associated Press.

Wal-Mart put a full-page ad in more that 100 newspapers including the *New York Times* and *The Wall Street Journal* on January 13, 2005. The ads contained a five-paragraph letter from CEO Scott in response to misinformation about Wal-Mart. To set the record straight, the national print ads stated that the average wage for full-time hourly workers at Wal-Mart is $9.68, which is almost twice the federal minimum wage of $5.15 per hour.

DISCUSSION QUESTIONS

1. Can this type of advertising campaign improve Wal-Mart's image in the eyes of associates, consumers, investors, and the press?
2. What else could Wal-Mart do to improve its reputation?
3. Go to Wal-Mart Stores home page at http://www.walmartstores.com and click on College Recruiting. Explore what this page has to offer. If a Wal-Mart recruiter came to your campus, would you consider Wal-Mart as an employer? Why or why not?

Source: This case was written by Hope Bober Corrigan, Loyola College in Maryland.

CASE 14   Avon Embraces Diversity

Women have always played an important role at Avon, the largest cosmetics firm in the United States. Mrs. P. F. E. Albee of Winchester, New Hampshire, pioneered the company's now-famous direct-selling method. Women have been selling Avon since 1886—34 years before women in the United States won the right to vote! Today, with sales representatives numbering three and a half million, Avon products are sold in 143 countries around the world.

Although most of Avon's employees and customers are women, until recently, the company has been run by men. However, a series of poor strategic decisions in the 1980s led the company to aggressively increase the number of women and minorities in its executive ranks. This decision to increase diversity among its managers was a major factor in Avon's improved financial performance.

Now Avon is recognized as a leader in management diversity. It has more women in management positions (86 percent) than any other Fortune 500 company. Half of the members of its Board of Directors are women. The company has undertaken a number of programs to ensure that women and minorities have opportunities for development and advancement. In the United States and elsewhere, Avon has internal networks of associates, including a parents' network, a Hispanic network, a black professional association, an Asian network, and a gay and lesbian network. The networks act as liaisons between associates and management to bring their voice to critical issues that affect the workplace and the marketplace.

Avon's problems started in the 1970s when its top management team, composed of all men, tried to change the firm's strategy. The management first ignored its own marketing research indicating that more women were entering the workforce and seeking professional careers, that cosmetic needs would change, and that new approaches for selling products to them were needed. Then sales growth slowed, and the company reacted by seeking growth through unrelated diversifications. Fi-nally, as the firm was on the brink of bankruptcy, a new top management team was brought in. Led by CEO Jim Preston, Avon refocused itself on its roots and began to again market cosmetics to a female, but very different, market.

Preston realized that Avon's customers needed to be represented in senior management. He enacted policies to quickly promote more women into higher-level positions. In addition, Preston shifted the firm's organization culture to be more accommodating of all its employees. For example, the firm dropped its season-ticket purchases to Knicks and Yankees games and replaced them with season tickets for the New York City Ballet and the New York Philharmonic. Avon has also turned to foreign markets for additional growth. Preston credits several key female executives for championing the international push and making sure that it was done right. Now many new managers come from international operations.

Preston's vision is reflected in Avon's senior management. Andrea Jung is Chairman of the Board and Chief Executive Officer, and Susan Kropf is President and Chief Operating Officer. Half of the members of the executive committee, the senior management of the firm, are women. Clearly, Avon is a firm that has changed its own culture and that appreciates the power of diversity and multiculturalism.

The new management team has launched a number of growth initiatives building on Avon's strong brand name and distribution channel through its customer representative network. Avon is the world's leading direct seller of beauty and related products, with $6.8 billion in annual revenues. Avon product lines include such recognizable brand names as Avon Color, Anew, Skin-So-Soft, Avon Solutions, Advance Techniques Hair Care, Avon Naturals, Mark, and Avon Wellness. Avon also markets an extensive line of fashion jewelry and apparel. More information about Avon and its products can be found on the company's Web site at http://www.avoncompany.com.

Recently, Avon representatives in North America sold more than 40 million lipsticks, making Avon the number one seller of lipstick in the mass market. Avon's brand Anew is the number one line of anti-aging skin care products in the world. The Advance Techniques hair care line offers high performance hair products for every hair type, age group, and ethnic background to accommodate a diverse, worldwide consumer base.

Avon Wellness promotes a balanced, healthy lifestyle for women and their families and includes nutritional supplements, a weight management line, and therapeutic products. In 2005, Avon partnered with the fitness phenomenon Curves, an international fitness franchise, to help women look and feel their best. Through this partnership, Avon Wellness will offer an array of Curves-branded fitness and healthy eating accessories.

For the first time in its 119-year history, Avon began focusing on the needs and desires of men by offering grooming products and accessories in one catalog. The Men's Catalog offers a wide variety of skin care products for men.

Finally, Avon is using technology to support the efforts of its 4.9 million independent sales representatives. An electronic ordering system allows the representatives to run their businesses more efficiently and improve order processing accuracy. Avon representatives use the Internet to manage their business electronically. In the United States, Avon representatives use an online marketing tool called youravon.com. The site helps representatives build their own Avon business by enabling them to sell online through their own personalized Web pages, developed in partnership with Avon. Avon e-representatives are able to promote special products, target specific groups of customers, place and track orders online, and capitalize on e-mail to share product information, selling tips, and marketing incentives.

DISCUSSION QUESTIONS

1. Why is Avon so committed to diversity?
2. Why don't more retailers follow Avon's lead?
3. How has increasing diversity been beneficial to Avon as it develops new strategies?
4. Evaluate the new opportunities that Avon is pursuing.

Source: This case was written by Barton Weitz, University of Florida.

CASE 15   Abercrombie & Fitch: Hiring for Looks

Clothing retailer Abercrombie & Fitch often recruited on college campuses and in the mall to find attractive young people and then urged them to apply for jobs. This company, known for building an attractive workforce, did so by aggressively hiring pretty young women and handsome young men to match their all-American brand image. Abercrombie & Fitch refers to these great-looking sales associates as brand ambassadors. They project the retailer's brand and make the store a better experience for customers.

Is seeking good-looking employees a necessary trend in the retail industry? Is hiring an attractive sales force a smart and necessary practice to differentiate the store in the competitive retail environment? Do salespeople need to mirror the images seen in the retailer's catalog and home page? Does all-American mean thin, tall, and white with blonde hair and blue eyes? If the store has great-looking college students working in the store, will others want to shop there? How important are retail experience and ability versus a pretty face?

In seeking good-looking employees, companies are risking lawsuits for discriminatory hiring practices. Hiring attractive people is not illegal, but discrimination on the basis of age, gender, race, national origin, disability, or ethnicity is. Employers may establish and enforce grooming and appearance standards. Exceptions to Title VII are possible if the employer can prove that one of the protected characteristics is a bona fide occupational qualification.

In 2003, Abercrombie & Fitch was named in two class-action lawsuits alleging discriminatory hiring practices. Black, Asian, and Latino plaintiffs alleged that they were denied sales associate positions. These workers were directed to low-visibility jobs in the stock room or maintenance department.

Abercrombie & Fitch did not admit guilt and denies that it engaged in any discriminatory practices but settled these cases for $40 million distributed to several thousand minority and female plaintiffs. The company agreed to appoint a vice president for diversity, use benchmarks, train all hiring managers, and hire 25 diversity recruits in an attempt to alter its white, all-American image and more accurately reflect the applicant pool in its stores. The settlement also calls for Abercrombie & Fitch to increase diversity in its promotional materials.

DISCUSSION QUESTIONS

1. Why would Abercrombie & Fitch want to hire employees with a certain look?
2. From a business perspective, do you think this is a good idea? What about from an ethical perspective or a legal perspective?

Source: This case was written by Hope Bober Corrigan, Loyola College in Maryland.

CASE 16 Lawson Sportswear

"We need to have vendors who can take this burden off of us," said Clifton Morris, Lawson Sportswear inventory manager. "We have had a sales increase of 20 percent over the last two years and my people can't keep up with it anymore."

Keith Lawson, general manager of Lawson Sportswear, reviewed the colorful chart showing the sales trend and replied, "I never thought I would have to complain about a sales increase, but it is obvious that the sales are well beyond our control. Something has to be done, and that is why we are meeting today."

Lawson Sportswear was founded by George Lawson in 1963 in a major southwestern metropolitan area. For five years, Lawson Sportswear has been successful in the sportswear market. In 1995, George Lawson retired, and his son, Keith Lawson, was appointed general manager. From the beginning, Keith Lawson has been a real go-getter. Recently completing his MBA, he has wasted no time in locating new markets for Lawson Sportswear. He immediately contacted two major universities and gained four-year exclusive contracts for apparel purchases made by the sports teams of their athletic departments. Soon after, Lawson Sportswear became popular among students. This growing demand for the company's products motivated Lawson to open two more retail stores. During the fall of 2006, sales had increased beyond expectations. Although the company achieved a successful reputation in the marketplace, sales growth has generated major problems.

In the beginning, operations were fairly smooth, and the company's inventory control department updated most of its procedures. Morris emphasized the crucial role of routinization in the overall inventory maintenance process to keep up with the increasing turnover. The sales increase was 20 percent, not 12 percent, as had been forecast for 2006. It was this increase that initiated a series of problems in the inventory control department. To temporarily alleviate the backlog, Lawson authorized Morris to lease an additional warehouse (see the replenishment level for July 2006 in Exhibit 1). It was decided that a maximum of 16 percent of the total inventory carrying costs were going to be dedicated to the off-premise inventory.

Worrying about not being able to meet demand on time, Morris met with suppliers and asked them to provide more timely delivery schedules to Lawson Sportswear. When he stated that the company was not going to tolerate any reasons for future delays, two major suppliers expressed their concerns about his lack of flexibility and requested price concessions. They simply indicated that Morris's demand had to be supported by providing cash or reducing quantity discounts. Morris ignored these comments and indicated how serious he really was by stating that Lawson Sportswear could always find new suppliers. By the end of a long discussion, arguments were beyond the manageable point, and the two large suppliers decided to quit dealing with the company.

EXHIBIT 1

Sales for Lawson Sportswear 2006

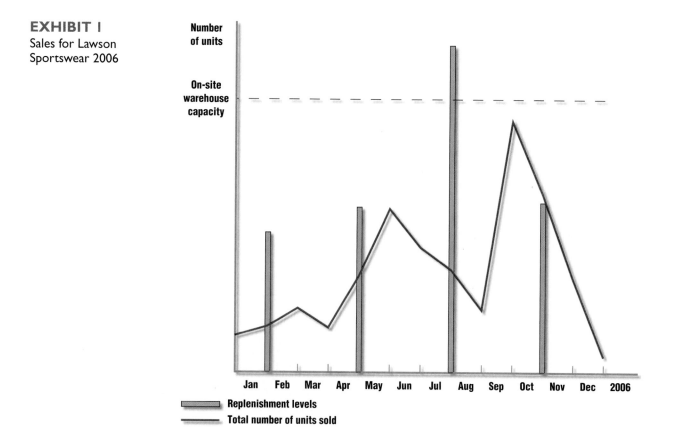

Legend:
- Replenishment levels
- Total number of units sold

After the meeting, Morris received a memo from Lawson. Lawson was very concerned about the potential reactions of the rest of the vendors. He stated in his memo that since Lawson Sportswear was continuously growing, it was expected to present a more supportive attitude to its suppliers. He expressed his belief that the company needed a cohesive atmosphere with the rest of the channel members, especially its vendors.

During the next six months, Morris had limited success in locating one or more large suppliers that would be able to deliver the products to Lawson Sportswear on a timely basis. Faced with growing demand from the surrounding high schools, he had to accumulate excess stock to avoid possible shortages. At the end of the six-month period, a memo from the accounting department of the company indicated the financial significance of the problem. In his memo, accounting manager Roger Noles simply addressed the high costs of inventory maintenance/security functions (for details, see Exhibit 2). He advised finding a substitute inventory policy to lower these cost figures. Specifically, he stated that the rental cost for the additional warehouse had leveled off at 16 percent, well beyond the maximum.

Keith Lawson immediately scheduled a meeting and asked the top managers to come up with alternative plans to eliminate this problem.

"I should have never let those suppliers quit," said Morris. "It had a negative effect on our image, and now we all see the results."

"It's too late to worry about that," admonished Lawson. "Instead, we have to come up with a strategy to meet the demand effectively without increasing our costs to the detriment of profits. You realize that the university contracts will expire at the end of the year."

"That's the crucial fact," said Noles. "We simply cannot afford to stock up beyond the current level; it is just too expensive. It is well beyond the funds we have had even from the increased sales."

"In other words, the elimination of the excess inventory is necessary. Who are the vendors that we have at the moment?" asked Lawson.

"There are only three suppliers remaining after the last meeting," replied Morris. "They are fairly small businesses, but we've been dealing with them for quite some time. They have been successful in keeping up with us, and the details of their operations are summarized in their report."

"It seems like we have a good selection here," said Lawson, after looking at the report in front of him. "If they mostly work with us, we should be able to influence the future direction in their operations. In other words, it should not be difficult to convince them that they need to

	2007 (forecast)	2006	2005
Net sales	$165,000	$120,000	$100,000
Cost of sales			
Beginning inventory	7,000	6,000	4,000
Purchases (net)	140,000	92,000	62,000
	147,000	98,000	66,000
Ending inventory	9,000	7,000	6,000
	138,000	91,000	61,000
Gross profit	27,000	29,000	39,000
Expenses			
Stock maintenance	7,500	5,250	750
Rent	2,500	1,250	250
Insurance	4,500	3,500	1,500
Interest	4,500	2,500	1,000
Selling	3,500	2,500	2,000
Promotion	7,500	5,500	4,000
Supplies	2,750	1,500	250
Miscellaneous	2,250	1,500	250
	35,000	23,500	10,000
Net profit from operations	(8,000)	5,500	29,000
Other income			
Dividends	925	750	450
Interest	825	600	350
Miscellaneous	650	400	200
	2,400	1,750	1,000
Net profit before taxes	(5,600)	7,250	130,000
Provision for income taxes	1,008	1,305	8,100
Net profit after taxes	(4,592)	5,945	21,900

EXHIBIT 2
Comparative Statement of Profit and Loss for Years Ended December 31

upgrade their deliveries in such a way that we can eliminate our excess inventory."

"That would cut down the rental costs that we incur from the additional warehouse," said Noles.

"Obviously!" Lawson replied impatiently. "We will probably need to provide those vendors with a comprehensive support program. If we can convert the floor space of the warehouse from storage to sales, we will have additional funds in retail operations. We can invest a portion of these funds in supporting our vendors and improve our image by forming a cohesive network with them. Of course, there will be a limit to this support. After all, it will be expensive for us to make the transition, too. Therefore, I would like you to come up with an analysis of converting the existing system to a more efficient one. I would like to know what we can do and how we can do it. To be very honest, gentlemen, I do not want to increase the sales if we do not know how to handle that increase."

DISCUSSION QUESTIONS

1. How might Lawson change its supply chain to be more efficient?
2. What problems would Lawson have implementing these changes with vendors?

Source: This case was prepared by S. Alton Erdem, University of Minnesota–Duluth.

CASE 17   Salon-Only Hair Care Products Found Outside the Salon

High-end, salon-only hair care products have been showing up on the shelves at grocery stores, discounters, and drugstores. Premium brands such as Nexxus, Paul Mitchell, Redken, Rusk, and Sebastian are clearly marked with "For Sale in Professional Salons Only." However, these brands are being sold through mass-market chains in addition to the exclusive salon-only channel. This practice is known as diverting products from the intended channel of distribution.

Is this practice illegal? Currently there is no legislation prohibiting mass retailers from selling premium brands. Because a strong gray market exists for professional hair care products, drug chains, discounters, and food retailers offer salon-only brands in the same health and beauty aisles as the mass-market hair care brands. These high-demand hair care lines are also available through online retail sites.

When beauty supply distributors or wholesalers break contractual agreements with manufacturers, the makers of salon-only brands lose millions of dollars and risk their exclusive brand image and reputation when their products are sold in stores. Improperly diverted hair care products are estimated to be valued at up to $800 million of the industry's $29 billion in annual sales.

On the Paul Mitchell Web site (www.paulmitchell.com), the company is reminding customers to fight against the manufacturing, distribution, and retailing of counterfeit products through its Product Control Campaign. This education program is designed to warn customers of the possible danger of purchasing the Paul Mitchell brand from intermediaries other than professional salons. The risks associated with purchasing diverted products include possible tampering, expiration, contamination, or substitution.

DISCUSSION QUESTIONS

1. How do customers, manufacturers, salons, and retailers react to the practice of diverting "salon-only" products to discounters, drug chains, and grocery stores?
2. Will the education campaign launched by Paul Mitchell change where consumers shop for professional hair care products? Explain your rationale.

Source: This case was written by Hope Bober Corrigan, Loyola College in Maryland.

CASE 18   SaksFirst Builds Customer Relationships

It's Wednesday afternoon, and as usual, Gwendolyn has a fitting room ready for Mrs. Johnson. She has picked out some of the new items in Mrs. Johnson's size that came in the previous week. She has everything from scarves to jewelry to shoes ready to go along with the outfits.

"Good evening, Mrs. Johnson. So how was your birthday?" Gwen asked.

"It was wonderful. My husband took me to Italy. Thank you for the card."

"I pulled some new items for you to try on," Gwendolyn said.

"Thank you, Gwen. You are the best!" replied Mrs. Johnson.

The reason Mrs. Johnson has such a friendly relationship with Gwen is because Mrs. Johnson is a regular customer and a SaksFirst member.

Saks Fifth Avenue started in the early twentieth century. Saks is considered the epitome of class, style, and luxury. When customers go to Saks, they receive excellent customer service; when they join SaksFirst—started in 1994—they also receive a lot of additional benefits. Saks-First is a preferred customer program that helps facilitate more personal customer–sales associate relationships.

To become a member, a customer has to have a Saks Fifth Avenue credit card, and once she or he spends at least $1,000 dollars a year, the customer is automatically enrolled. For every dollar spent, the customer will receive a reward point. At the end of the year, preferred customers receive 2, 4, or 6 percent in bonus points based on how much they charged that year above $5,000 at Saks.

SaksFirst customers receive many exclusive benefits. The tangible benefits include the points, rewards, and discounts. Customers also receive complimentary shipping and delivery for catalog and online orders, advance notice of sale events, the SaksFirst newsletter, catalogs, promotions and giveaways, double- and triple-point events, and double points on their birthdays. The intangible benefits include recognition and preferential treatment.

For the retailer, the main purpose of the SaksFirst program is to promote excellent customer service. The better the relationship between the customer and the sales associates, the more money loyal customers will spend. Every year there is a triple-point event in the first week of November. That one-day event accounts for the highest volume sales day of the year, higher than the day after Thanksgiving or Christmas Eve. Knowing this, the company understands the importance of the preferred program.

The SaksFirst program can also be used by sales associates as a selling tool. If a customer is uneasy about purchasing large-ticket items, the sales associate can remind the member of the bonus certificate that will return a percentage of the cost. Sales associates are motivated to enroll as many of their customers as they can because they are given incentives such as "lottery tickets" that are redeemed for cash.

DISCUSSION QUESTIONS

1. How does SaksFirst build loyalty for Saks Fifth Avenue versus other upscale retailers (such as Nordstrom)?
2. How effective is the SaksFirst program in developing customer loyalty?
3. Whom should Saks target the SaksFirst program toward?
4. Is the SaksFirst program worth what it spends giving back to customers?

Source: Case prepared by Teresa Scott, University of Florida.

CASE 19 Men's Wearhouse: Adding Complementary Merchandise and Services to Bring Customers Value

Men's Wearhouse, Inc., is one of the largest discount men's apparel companies in North America. The first location of this men's specialty store was opened in August 1973 in a strip shopping center near Houston, Texas. Thirty years later, Men's Wearhouse operates 693 stores in 44 states in America and 10 provinces in Canada under the Men's Wearhouse, K&G, and Moores brand names.

MERCHANDISE

Men's Wearhouse sells high-quality men's clothing at prices 20 to 30 percent lower than department stores. This retailer specializes in suits and other tailored business apparel. Other merchandise offered includes dress shirts, slacks, sports jackets, and sweaters. As many businesses moved to a more casual dress code, Men's Wearhouse responded by increasing the casual business clothing selections in its stores. This retailer offers both national branded attire and its own private-label brands. Men's Wearhouse also sells accessories such as ties, belts, and shoes. In 1994, the company successfully added Big-and-Tall sizes to its product offerings.

LOCATION

Men's Wearhouse stores are located in strip shopping centers adjacent to residential areas. This proximity to the shopper's home is a benefit for customers who must visit the store twice, once to select a suit and a second time to pick up the garment after it has been altered. Locating outside of malls in strip shopping centers allows for a generous store size (between 4,000 and 4,500 square feet) while still controlling costs associated with rent. Executives at Men's Wearhouse also observed that men prefer to stay away from a crowded mall when shopping for clothing.

PROMOTION

Men's Wearhouse uses a variety of media to inform and remind customers about its stores, merchandise, and sales events. The company's founder, Chairman, and CEO, George Zimmer, is the gravelly voiced spokesperson featured in both television and radio advertisements espousing the company's memorable tag line, "You're going to like the way you look. I guarantee it."

SERVICES

Men's Wearhouse is known for having a well-trained sales staff that can assist customers with their wardrobe selection. In addition to helpful sales associates, each tailored item can be brought back to the store for free pressing when needed. All stores have an in-house tailor to make the necessary alterations to ensure the desired fit for each garment. Another service offered at Men's Wearhouse is the Perfect Fit Credit Card loyalty program. This frequent shopper program lets repeat customers charge their purchases, earn points toward discount coupons, and save 5 percent on all purchases placed on the card.

GROWTH STRATEGIES

One of the most profitable additions to the services provided by Men's Wearhouse is the tuxedo rental business. Men's formalwear has been offered since 1999 in the United States and represented $51 million in sales in 2003. This service offering has been so strong that it encouraged the company to expand the floor space in the stores, move into the dry cleaning arena, and begin a test for women's bridal wear.

Because tuxedos need to be dry cleaned between each prom and wedding party, Men's Wearhouse quickly saw the importance of acquiring a dry cleaning chain and expanding into this business. Currently, the $7 billion dry cleaning industry is comprised primarily of small, single-facility, family-owned operations.

To launch the women's formalwear concept, Men's Wearhouse is test marketing two locations of its new bridal shop, Bride and Joy, in California. These stores will offer convenient shopping for the women in the bridal party including the bride, bride's maids, and the mother of the bride. The test stores will be located next door to Men's Wearhouses in approximately 3,000 square foot stores.

DISCUSSION QUESTIONS

1. Men's Wearhouse successfully added tuxedo rental to its merchandise offerings in 1999. Now this retailer plans to add women's bridal wear and the service of dry cleaning. List the pros and cons for each of these growth strategies.

2. What other merchandise and services could Men's Wearhouse add to reach a new segment of the market, benefit customers, and grow its business?

Source: This case was written by Hope Bober Corrigan, Loyola College in Maryland.

CASE 20   Nolan's Finest Foods: Category Management

Nolan's Finest Foods is a full-service retailer that offers shoppers the convenience of one-stop shopping at its high-end, food-and-drug combo stores in the San Francisco Bay area. The chain features a variety of high-quality products at competitive prices but uses promotional pricing as well. Historically, Nolan's has enjoyed great success in its markets and led the region for several years. However, on this winter morning, Roberto Ignacio, the director of strategic planning, had a more immediate concern. The wire services had reported a few weeks ago that the Valumart grocery chain had announced plans for the construction of 10 new food-and-drug combo centers throughout Nolan's markets. After poring over current research and financial results, Ignacio had decided to examine category management as a defense against the encroachment of Valumart.

To date, Nolan's did not have any experience with category management. A decision was also made to pilot test category management in some categories before implementing a systemwide rollout. One of the categories chosen for the test was shampoo. Ignacio's immediate assignment was to review the product category and report back to management with an initial recommendation. As Ignacio looked out of his window at the scenic sunset over the San Francisco Bay, he reviewed the events of the past few weeks and the information that he had obtained on the shampoo category. He had several third-party reports (Exhibits 1, 2, and 3) that provided background information about national trends in the shampoo category and trends in supermarkets. Another report (Exhibit 4) provided him with information on how Nolan's shampoo sales compared to the rest of the market.

However, these reports did not provide Ignacio with information about how Nolan's stacked up against the competition in terms of its assortment and pricing. After

EXHIBIT 1
Total U.S. Supermarket Dynamics: Shampoo

52 Weeks	# Active SKUs	% New SKUs	# SKUs Handled	SKU Dollar Velocity
Category	1,974	15%	235	$1.64
Brands	1,714	16	229	1.65
Private label	241	12	5	1.33
Generic	19	—	1	1.00

EXHIBIT 2
Shampoo Dollar Share

Trade Channel	12 Months Last Year	12 Months This Year
Food	51.7%	50.5%
Drug	25.6	25.0
Mass merchant	22.7	24.5

EXHIBIT 3
Shampoo Growth

Trade Channel	Dollar Sales % Change versus a Year Ago
Food	0.9%
Drug	4.2
Mass merchant	8.1

EXHIBIT 4
Dollar Sales: Percent Change versus a Year Ago

	MARKET		NOLAN'S FINEST	
	13 Weeks	52 Weeks	13 Weeks	52 Weeks
Total dollar sales	+.1	+1.2	−10.6	−4.5
HBA department	+1.5	+4.2	−8.5	−4.3
Shampoo category	−3.5	+.7	−19.6	−9.7

EXHIBIT 5
Competitive Price Comparison for Shampoo: Counts of Items Showing Differences from the Base Zone (Nolan's Finest Foods)

	Nolan's	Food #1	Mass Merch.	Chain Drug	Food #2
Competition is higher	0	87	0	101	0
Competition is same	103	0	0	0	59
Competition is lower	0	16	103	2	44
Competition does not carry	0	0	0	0	0

some checking around, Ignacio found that he could order reports from third-party vendors that would provide him with an analysis of Nolan's and the competition in terms of product mix and pricing. He placed an urgent order for these analyses, which arrived this morning through courier (Exhibits 5, 6, and 7).

Here are explanations of a few terms in the analyses:

SKU dollar velocity	Revenue per SKU per store per week
HBA	Health and beauty aids
Market	All food stores
Remaining market	All food stores excluding Nolan's

As Ignacio headed for the water cooler, feeling upbeat in the thought that he had a handle on the shampoo category, he ran into Hal Jeffreys, a longtime veteran at Nolan's and vice president of information systems. Knowing that

Jeffreys had at one time managed health and beauty aids at Nolan's, Ignacio mentioned his review of the shampoo category and the category management initiative. Jeffreys responded that for years he had a simple approach for category management. He would begin by generating a list of slow sellers in the category and then try to replace these slow sellers with new products or increase the shelf space for existing products. With the new information systems that Nolan's had installed in the past year, generating a slow seller list was very easy. To prove his point, Jeffreys walked back with Ignacio to his office and, using his PC, generated a slow seller report for the shampoo category (Exhibit 8).

Brand Importance Report for Shampoo: Nolan's Foods versus Remaining Market for 13 Weeks   **EXHIBIT 6**

Description	Chain Sales	Chain Rank	Rem. Mkt. Rank	Rem. Mkt. Sales	Chain Mkt. Share	Chain Category Impt.	Rem. Mkt. Cat. Impt.
Clean & Soft	$108,826	1	1	$512,345	17.5%	14.5	13.0
1st Impressions	77,672	2	3	370,341	17.3	10.3	9.4
Mane Tame	64,446	3	4	244,160	20.9	8.6	6.2
Bargain Bubbles	56,864	4	2	433,300	11.6	7.6	11.0
Silky Style	43,198	5	6	147,773	22.6	5.8	3.7
Elegance	30,869	6	5	181,075	14.6	4.1	4.6

Product Mix Summary Report: Shampoo Dollar Sales—13 Weeks   **EXHIBIT 7**

	Clean & Soft	1st Impressions	Mane Tame	Bargain Bubbles	Silky Style	Elegance	Private Label
Items carried							
Nolan's	25	25	15	21	13	5	7
Rem. mkt.	25	39	28	42	20	16	28
Sizes carried							
Nolan's	6	6	6	2	4	1	4
Rem. mkt.	7	10	11	3	5	4	6
Types carried							
Nolan's	6	7	6	19	4	5	6
Rem. mkt.	6	10	8	32	5	7	21

EXHIBIT 8   Slow Seller Report: Shampoo for Nolan's Foods, 13 Weeks versus a Year Ago

Item	Chain Sales	Chain Mkt. Shr.	Chain Subcat Impt.	Rem. Mkt. Growth	Chain Growth	Chain Avg. % Stores Selling
Golden JJB Lq T 3 oz.	$ 3	9.9%	.0	−51.2-	−50.0	0%
1st Imprs. DF ND Lot. 11 oz.	10	.7	.0	−59.4	−99.4	0
Gentle GLD Lq. 11 oz.	11	100.0	.0	−100.0	9.6	0
Golden AV Lq. T 3 oz.	12	22.4	.0	13.2	−69.2	1
Suds PB Lq. 8 oz.	14	6	.0	107.1	2.9	0
Silky Style X-B Lq. 18 oz.	14	1.6	.0	−65.6	−99.5	0

"See, technology has made this a real cinch," said Jeffreys and wondered aloud whether the expense and effort of category management would produce net improvements over and above this very simple "knock off the slow seller" approach. "I'll try to come to your presentation tomorrow," said Jeffreys as he left Ignacio's office.

As Jeffreys left his office, Ignacio sank back into his chair with a knot in his stomach. He felt that he had jumped the gun in thinking that he had a handle on the shampoo category. Things seemed to be more complicated than they had appeared earlier in the day. Ignacio wondered whether the shampoo category seemed so difficult because it was the first attempt at category management. In any case, his immediate concern was to prepare for his presentation tomorrow. Since Hal Jeffreys would be in the audience, he knew that he would have to address the "knock out the slow sellers" perspective.

DISCUSSION QUESTIONS

1. What are the national sales trends in the shampoo category?
2. What are the differences in shampoo sales trends at Nolan's compared with national trends?
3. What would be causing these differences?
4. Suggest a plan of action.

Source: This case was written by Professor Kirthi Kalyanam, Retail Management Institute, Santa Clara University. © Dr. Kirthi Kalyanam.

CASE 21   Developing a Buying Plan for Hughe's

A well-established, medium-size department store in the Midwest, Hughe's reflects consumers' needs by featuring popular names in fashion for the individual consumer, family, and home. It tries to offer a distinctive, wide assortment of quality merchandise with personalized customer service. The many customer services include personal shoppers; credit through in-house charge, American Express, and Visa; and an interior design studio. Hughe's pricing policy permits it to draw customers from several income brackets. Moderate-income consumers seeking value and fashion-predictable soft goods are target customers, as are upscale customers with a special interest in fashion.

The department store is implementing new marketing strategies to prepare for continuing growth and expansion. Hughe's merchandising philosophy is to attract the discerning middle-market customer who comprises 70 percent of the population as well as sophisticated fashion-conscious consumers who expect to buy high-quality, brand-name merchandise at competitive prices.

One portion of Hughe's buying staff is responsible for the Oriental rug department within home furnishings. The open-to-buy figure for this classification within the home furnishings division will be based on last year's sales history (Exhibit 1).

EXHIBIT I

Last Year's Fall/Winter Sales Results for Oriental Rugs

Sales volume	$120,000			
Markup	51.5%			
Size	Percentage of Sales		Fabrication	Percentage of Sales
3′ × 5′	20%		Silk	15%
4′ × 6′	40		Cotton	25
6′ × 9′	15		Wool	60
8′ × 10′	10			
9′ × 12′	15			

EXHIBIT 2
Ghuman's Wholesale Price List

Size	FABRICATION		
	Silk	Wool	Cotton
3 × 5′	$400	$250	—
4 × 6′	700	500	$200
6 × 9′	850	700	275
8 × 10′	1,200	1,000	350
9 × 12′	1,400	1,300	500

Colors: Background colors available are navy, burgundy, black, and cream.

Quantities required for purchase: No minimum orders required.

Payment plan: Payment can be made in American dollars or Indian rupees. Letter of credit needs to be established prior to market trip.

Delivery: Air freight—10 to 14 days delivery time; cost is usually 25 percent of total order.

Ocean freight—39 days plus inland time is necessary; cost is usually 8–10 percent of total order.

Customer loyalty: Loyalty to customers is exceptional. Damaged shipments can be returned. Ghuman's philosophy is to help the retailers obtain a profit on their product lines.

It has been projected that a 15 percent increase over last year's sales volume can be attained due to Oriental rugs' continued popularity. This year's open-to-buy for fall/winter will be $66,200.

The buying staff will be making its purchases for fall/winter in Amritsar, India, a city known for top-quality carpets. Ghuman Export Private, Ltd., of Amritsar, Punjab, India, is the manufacturer the buyers will contact. Exhibit 2 shows information about Ghuman to use in the decision-making process.

DISCUSSION QUESTION

1. Work up a buying plan to use when buying from Ghuman's. Decide how to distribute the allotted open-to-buy dollars among the available sizes, colors, and fabrications. Since it's an overseas manufacturer, consider additional costs such as duty and shipping, which also need to be covered by the allocated open-to-buy dollars.

This case was prepared by Professor Ann Fairhurst, Indiana University.

CASE 22   McFadden's Department Store: Preparation of a Merchandise Budget Plan

McFadden's Department Store has been a profitable family-owned business since its beginning in 1910. Last year's sales volume was $180 million. More recently, however, many of its departments have been losing ground to national stores moving into the area. To complicate this problem, the National Retail Federation (NRF) predicts a recession. The NRF estimates a 6.5 percent drop in sales in the coming year for the Pacific Coast, where McFadden's operates.

Department 121 has one of the more profitable departments in the store, maintaining a gross margin of 55 percent. Its basic merchandise is young men's clothing. Last year, sales reached $2,780,750 for the July–December season. The highest sales period is the back to-school period in August, when autumn fashions are supported by strong promotional advertising. Reductions (including markdowns, discounts to employees, and shrinkages) typically run 20 percent of sales. The percentages of reductions are spread throughout the season as follows:

July	August	September	October	November	December
10	20	15	10	10	35

By month, the percentage of annual sales for Department 121 within this six-month period had been distributed as follows:

	July	August	September	October	November	December
2002	3.5	10.1	9.2	6.4	4.8	9.1
2003	3.5	10.3	9.5	6.8	5.3	8.8
2004	3.5	10.5	9.6	6.2	5.5	8.2
2005	3.0	10.3	9.8	6.6	5.5	8.0

A pre-Christmas sale has been planned in an attempt to counterbalance the slackened sales period following the first of the year. The buyer has decided to bring in some new merchandise for the sale to go along with the remaining fall fashion merchandise. The buyer expects that this will increase December's percentage of annual sales to 30 percent above what it would be without the sale. Top management has emphasized that the department should achieve a gross margin return on investment (GMROI) of 250 percent. Forecasted ending stock level in December is $758,000.

Additional information is available on the historical stock-to-sales ratio for this type of department. This information is taken from a similar department in another store that happens to have a lower average stock-to-sales ratio:

July	August	September	October	November	December
3.0	1.9	2.1	2.4	2.5	2.2

DISCUSSION QUESTION

1. Your task is to prepare a merchandise budget plan. You may do the plan by hand by using the form in Exhibit 1, or you may prepare the plan using the Excel spreadsheet on the student side of the Online Learning Center (OLC). You will have to prepare some intermediate calculations before inputting your answers onto the spreadsheet. Click on the Merchandise Management Module. Click through the exercises until you get to "The Calculation Section." You can access an Excel-based six-month merchandise budget plan by clicking on the link "merchandise budget". Plug in the numbers from the case. On a separate sheet of paper, explain how you determined the sales forecast, percentage of sales per month, and the monthly stock-to-sales ratios.

Source: This case was prepared by Michael Levy, Babson College, and Harold Koenig, Oregon State University.

EXHIBIT 1   Form for Merchandise Budget Plan

McFadden's Merchandise Budget

Planning Data

SALES FORECAST $ _____

Planned GMROI = (Gross Margin / Net Sales) × (Net Sales / Inventory Costs)

$ \text{Planned GMROI} = \dfrac{\$}{\$} \times \dfrac{\$}{\$} $

(Sales / Inventory Costs) × (100% − GM%) = Inventory Turnover

[X] × [%] = [X]

12 ÷ Inventory Turnover = B.O.M. Stock/Sales

÷ [X] = [X]

Forecasted Ending Inventory $ [   ]

The Plan

Markdowns [%] [$]
Discounts + [%] [$]
Shortages + [%] [$]
Total Reductions [%] [$]

		Jan	Feb	Mar	Apr	May	Jun	Jul	Aug	Sept	Oct	Nov	Dec	Total (Average)	Remarks
% Distribution of Sales by Month	1													100.0%	History/Projection
Monthly Sales	2														Step (1) × Net Sales
% Distribution of Reductions/Mo	3													100.0%	History/Projection
Monthly Reductions	4														Step (3) × Net Sales
B.O.M. Stock/Sales Ratios	5														Adjusted by Mo. Sales Fluctuations
B.O.M. Stock ($000)	6													(Forecasted End Inventory)	Step (2) × Step (5)
E.O.M. Stock ($000)	7														EOM Jan = BOM Feb
Monthly Additions to Stock ($000)	8														Steps 2 + 4 + 7−6 Sales + Reductions + EOM−BOM

CASE 23   eBay

The concept for eBay was born during a conversation between Pierre Omidyar and his wife, an avid Pez collector. (She currently has a collection of more than 400 dispensers.) She commented to Pierre how great it would be if she were able to collect Pez dispensers and interact with other collectors over the Internet. As an early Internet enthusiast, Pierre felt that many people like his wife needed a place to buy and sell unique items and meet other users with similar interests. He started eBay in 1995 to fulfill this need.

Luckily for Pierre Omidyar, he was living in Silicon Valley when he got the idea for eBay. If Omidyar's family had been living in France, his idea never would have gotten off the ground. It's not a lack of venture capital or

Internet audience in France that would have stopped him; it was the law at that time. Under French regulations, only a few certified auctioneers are allowed to operate, so eBay could not have been opened for business in its founder's homeland back in 1995. Ten years later, eBay operated auctions in Argentina, Australia, Austria, Belgium, Brazil, Canada, China, France, Germany, Hong Kong, India, Ireland, Italy, Korea, Malaysia, Mexico, Netherlands, New Zealand, Philippines, Poland, Singapore, Spain, Sweden, Switzerland, Taiwan, and the United Kingdom.

OFFERING TO CUSTOMERS

Most retailers follow the business-to-consumer sales model. eBay pioneered online person-to-person trading, also known as the consumer-to-consumer sales model, by developing a Web-based community in which buyers and sellers are brought together. Initially, most of the items auctioned were collectibles such as antiques, coins, stamps, and memorabilia.

Many of the sellers on eBay are small entrepreneurial businesses that use the site as a sales channel. By 2003, most of the merchandise available on eBay had shifted from collectibles to practical items, such as power drills and computers. Now big businesses such as Disney and Sun Microsystems have discovered eBay. Retailers, manufacturers, and liquidators are using the site to unload returned merchandise, refurbished merchandise, and used products.

The eBay service permits sellers to list items for sale and enables buyers to bid on items of interest. All eBay users can browse through listed items in a fully automated, topically arranged, intuitive, and easy-to-use online service that is available 24 hours a day, seven days a week. However, even with automated bidding features, participating in an online auction requires more effort than buying fixed-price goods, and once the auction is over, most buyers have to send a check or money order and then get the merchandise up to two weeks later. Buyers have the option to purchase items in an auction-style format or at a fixed price through a feature called Buy It Now.

More than 500 million items are listed for sale each year. From Civil War to *Star Wars* items, from Beanie Babies to fine antiques, chances are that you'll find it among eBay's 45,000 categories of merchandise from 254,000 online sellers. "If you can't sell it on eBay, you might as well open up the window and throw it out in the backyard because it ain't worth a damn," says Bob Watts, an antique dealer in Fairfield, Virginia. The Web site has over 135 million registered users worldwide.

People spend more time on eBay than any other online site, making it the most popular shopping destination on the Internet. Users often refer to eBay as a community— a group of people with similar interests. For example, Dr. Michael Levitt by day is a distinguished medical researcher at the Minneapolis Veterans Medical Center, but by night, he is an eBay warrior. Levitt is a collector of antique California Perfume Company bottles. Every night he logs on to eBay to see if anything new is being offered. He has purchased hundreds of bottles through eBay sim-

EXHIBIT 1
Financial Overview for eBay

	2004	2003	2002	2001	2000
Net revenues ($ mil)	3,271	2,165	1,214	748	431
Net income ($ mil)	778	442	250	90	48
Employees	8,100	6,200	4,000	2,500	1,927
Net profit margin	23.8%	20.4%	20.6%	12.1%	11.2%

ply because it's the most convenient way to connect with sellers.

The Web site requires that all new sellers have a credit card on file, insurance, authentication, and escrow accounts. Buyers and sellers can check the "reputation" of anyone using eBay. A Feedback Forum is provided, through which eBay users can leave comments about their buying and selling experiences. If you're a bidder, you can check your seller's Feedback Profile before you place a bid to learn about the seller's reputation with previous buyers. If you're a seller, you can do the same with your bidders.

BUSINESS MODEL

Unlike most e-commerce companies, eBay has been profitable from the very beginning. Exhibit 1 contains net revenues, net income, employees, and net profit margin figures from 2000 to 2005. Most of the company's revenues come from fees and commissions (between 1.25 and 5.0 percent of the sale price) associated with online and traditional offline auction services. Online revenues come from placement and success fees paid by sellers; eBay does not charge fees to buyers. Sellers pay a nominal placement fee, and by paying additional fees, they can have items featured in various ways. Sellers also pay a success fee based on the final purchase price. Online advertising on eBay has not made significant contributions to net revenues, and no significant revenue from advertising is expected in the near future. Additional revenues come from auction-related services, including bidder registration fees and appraisal and authentication.

Its online business model is significantly different from electronic retailers. Because individual sellers, rather than eBay, sell the items listed, the company has no procurement, carrying, or shipping costs and no inventory risk. The company's expenses are just personnel, advertising and promotion, and depreciation on the site's hardware and software.

COMPETITION

Due to the popularity of auctions with consumers, a number of e-businesses have entered the market. Some competing Internet auctions offering a broad range of products are Amazon.com, Yahoo!, uBid, and Overstock.com. In addition to these multicategory sites, there are vertical auction sites specializing in a single category of merchandise such as stamps or baseball cards.

Perhaps the most significant competitor is Amazon. com, which launched an auction site in 1999. Amazon has a well-known and highly regarded brand name and substantial traffic on its Web site. (Amazon is the most widely known e-business, with eBay ranking third in brand awareness.) When Amazon launched its auction site, it offered some unique benefits to customers, including a no-deductible, no-haggle, no third-party money-back guarantee for purchases up to $250 and a feature called Going, Going, Gone that extends the auction for 10 minutes if a bid is made in the last 10 minutes before closing. On eBay, it is common for items to be picked off in the closing minutes by vigilant consumers who make the last bid.

Amazon is known for the usability of its site. In response to Amazon's entry, eBay took steps to make buying and selling easier. It now offers a Personal Shopper program that searches out specified products and My eBay, which gives user information about current eBay activities, including bidding, selling, account balances, favorite categories, and recent feedback.

Finally, some Internet businesses have arisen that simply search and display summary information from many auction sites to enable comparison shopping. However, eBay sued one such site and has used technology to block access of another site to prevent them from gathering and displaying eBay auction data.

DISCUSSION QUESTIONS

1. What are the advantages and disadvantages from the buyer's and seller's perspectives of purchasing merchandise through Internet auctions like eBay?
2. Will a significant amount of retail sales be made through Internet auctions like eBay in the future? Why or why not?
3. What are eBay's competitive advantages? Will it be able to withstand the competition from other auction sites like Yahoo! and Amazon's auctions?

Source: This case was written by Barton Weitz, University of Florida.

CASE 24   How Much for a Good Smell?

BACKGROUND INFORMATION

For the past two Christmas seasons, Courtney's, an upscale gift store, has carried a sweet-smelling potpourri in a plastic bag with an attractive ribbon. Heavily scented with cloves, the mixture gives a pleasant holiday aroma to any room, including the store.

Two years ago, the mixture cost $4.50 a bag. Courtney's (the only store in town that carried it) sold 300 pieces for $9.50. Courtney's supply ran out 10 days before Christmas, and it was too late to get any more.

Last year, the manufacturer raised the price to $5.00, so Courtney's raised its retail price to $9.95. Even though the markup was lower than the previous year, the store owner felt there was "magic" in the $10 price. As before, the store had a complete sellout, this time five days before Christmas. Sales last year were 600 units.

This year, the wholesale price has gone up to $5.50, and store personnel are trying to determine the correct retail price. The owner once again wants to hold the price at $10 ($9.95), but the buyer disagrees: "It's my job to push for the highest possible markup wherever I can. This item is a sure seller, as we're still the only store around with it, and we had some unsatisfied demand last year. I think we should mark it $12.50, which will improve the markup to 56 percent. Staying at $10 will penalize us unnecessarily,

especially considering the markup would be even lower than last year. Even if we run into price resistance, we'll only have to sell 480 to maintain the same dollar volume."

The owner demurs, saying, "This scent is part of our store's ambiance. It acts as a draw to get people into the store, and its pleasant smell keeps them in a free-spending state of mind. I think we should keep the price at $9.95, despite the poorer markup. And if we can sell many more at this price, we'll realize the same dollar gross margin as last year. I think we should buy 1,000. Furthermore, if people see us raising a familiar item's price 25 percent, they might wonder whether our other prices are fair."

DISCUSSION QUESTIONS

1. What prices caused Courtney's charge?
2. Which price would result in the highest profit?
3. What other factors should Courtney's consider?
4. What price would you charge, and how many units would you order?

Source: This case was written by Professor David Ehrlich, Marymount University.

CASE 25   Promoting a Sale

A consumer electronic chain in the Washington, DC, area is planning a big sale in its suburban Virginia warehouse over the three-day President's Day weekend (Saturday through Monday). On sale will be nearly $2 million worth of consumer electronic products, 50 percent of the merchandise sold in the store. The company hopes to realize

at least $900,000 in sales during the three days. In the retailer's past experience, the first day's sales were 50 percent of the total. The second day's were 35 percent, and the last day's, 15 percent. One of every two customers who came made a purchase.

It's known further that large numbers of people always flock to such sales, some driving as far as 50 miles. They come from all economic levels, but all are confirmed bargain hunters. You're the assistant to the general merchandise manager, who has asked you to plan the event's marketing campaign. You have the following information:

1. A full-page *Washington Post* ad costs $10,000, a half page ad costs $6,000, and a quarter-page ad costs $3,500. To get the maximum value from a newspaper campaign, it's company policy to always run two ads (not necessarily the same size) for such events.

2. The local northern Virginia paper is printed weekly and distributed free to some 15,000 households. It costs $700 for a full page and $400 for a half page ad.

3. To get adequate TV coverage, at least three channels must be used, with a minimum of eight 30-second spots on each at $500 per spot, spread over three or more days. Producing a TV spot costs $3,000.

4. The store has contracts with three radio stations. One appeals to a broad general audience aged 25 to 34 years. One is popular with the 18-to-25 group. A classical music station has a small but wealthy audience. Minimum costs

for a saturation radio campaign, including production, on the three stations are $8,000, $5,000, and $3,000, respectively.

5. To produce and mail a full-color flyer to the store's 80,000 charge customers costs $10,000. When the company used such a mailing piece before, about 3 percent responded.

DISCUSSION QUESTIONS

1. Knowing that the company wants a mixed-media ad campaign to support this event, prepare an ad plan for the general merchandise manager that costs no more than $40,000.
2. Work out the daily scheduling of all advertising.
3. Work out the dollars to be devoted to each medium.
4. Justify your plan.

Source: This case was prepared by David Ehrlich, Marymount University.

CASE 26   Enterprise Builds on People

When most people think of car rental firms, they think of Hertz, Alamo, Budget or Avis, but Enterprise is the largest and most profitable car rental business in North America. The company operates 700,000 rental and fleet vehicles worldwide and has annual revenues of $7.4 billion. In 2005, Enterprise was listed as number 16 on the *Forbes* "500 Largest Private Companies in America" list. Enterprise operates in the United States, Canada, Germany, Ireland, and the United Kingdom.

In 1957, Jack Taylor started Enterprise with a unique strategy. Most car rental firms targeted business and leisure travel customers who arrived at an airport and needed to rent a car for local transportation. Taylor decided to target a different segment—individuals whose own cars are being repaired, who are driving on vacation, hauling home improvement materials, providing an extra vehicle for an out-of-town guest, or, for some other reason, simply need an extra car for a few days.

The traditional car rental companies have to charge relatively high daily rates because their locations in or near airports are expensive. In addition, their business customers are price insensitive because their companies pay for the rental expenses. Whereas the airport location is convenient for customers traveling by air, this location is inconvenient for people seeking a replacement car while their car is in the shop. Although Enterprise has airport locations, it also has rental offices in downtown and suburban areas, near where its target market lives and works. The firm provides local pickup and delivery service in most areas.

Enterprise's human resource strategy is a key to its success. The firm hires college graduates for its management

trainee positions because it feels that a college degree demonstrates intelligence and motivation. Rather than recruiting the best students, it focuses on hiring people who were athletes or officers of social organizations, such as fraternities, sororities, and clubs, because they typically have the good interpersonal skills needed to effectively deal with Enterprise's customers.

Jack Taylor's growth strategy was based on providing high-quality, personalized service so that customers would return to Enterprise when they needed to rent a car again. But operating managers were compensated on the basis of sales growth initially, not customer satisfaction. So service quality declined.

The first step Enterprise took to improve customer service was to develop a customer satisfaction measure. The questionnaire, called the Enterprise Service Quality Index, was developed on the basis of input from the operating managers. Thus, the managers felt ownership of the measurement tool. As the index gained legitimacy, Enterprise made a big deal about it. It posted the scores for each location prominently in its monthly operating reports—right next to the net profit numbers that determined managers' pay. The operating managers were able to track how they were doing, and how all their peers were doing, because all of the locations were ranked.

To increase the motivation of managers and improve the service at their location, Enterprise announced that managers could be promoted only if their customer satisfaction scores were above the company average. Then it demonstrated that it would abide by this policy by failing to promote some star performers who had achieved good growth and profit numbers but had below-average satisfaction scores.

To provide a high level of service, new employees generally work long, grueling hours for what many see as relatively low pay. They, like all Enterprise managers, are expected to jump in and help wash or vacuum cars when the agency gets backed up. But all this hard work can pay off. The firm does not hire outsiders for other than entry-level jobs. At Enterprise, every position is filled by promoting someone already inside the company. Thus, Enterprise employees know that if they work hard and do their best, they may very well succeed in moving up the corporate ladder and earn a significant income.

DISCUSSION QUESTIONS

1. What are the pros and cons of Enterprise's human resource management strategy?
2. Would you want to work for Enterprise? Why or why not?
3. How does its human resource strategy complement the quality of customer service delivered by its representatives?

Source: This case was written by Barton Weitz, University of Florida.

CASE 27   Diamond in the Rough

BACKGROUND INFORMATION

Ruth Diamond, president of Diamond Furriers, was concerned that sales in her store appeared to have flattened out and was considering establishing a different method of compensating her salespeople.

Diamond was located in an affluent suburb of Nashville, Tennessee. Ruth's father had founded the company 40 years earlier, and she had grown up working in the business. After his retirement in 1980, she moved the store into an upscale shopping mall not far from its previous location, and sales had boomed almost immediately, rising to just over $1 million in five years. However, once it had reached that sales volume, it remained there for the next three years, making Ruth wonder whether her salespeople had sufficient incentive to sell more aggressively.

Diamond's staff was all women, ranging in age from 27 to 58. There were four full-timers and four part-timers (20 hours a week), all of whom had at least three years of experience in the store. All of them were paid at the same hourly rate, which was $10; there was also a liberal health benefit plan. Employee morale was excellent, and the entire staff displayed strong personal loyalty to Mrs. Diamond.

The store was open 78 hours a week, which meant that there was nearly always a minimum staff of three on the floor, rising to six at peak periods. Diamond's merchandise consisted exclusively of fur coats and jackets, ranging in price from $750 to more than $5,000. The average unit sale was about $2,000. Full-timers' annual sales averaged about $160,000, and the part-timers' were a little over half of that.

Mrs. Diamond's concern about sales transcended her appreciation for her people's loyalty. She had asked them, for example, to maintain customer files and call their customers when the new styles came in. While some of them had been more diligent about this than others, none of them appeared to want to be especially aggressive about promoting sales.

So she began to investigate commission systems and discussed them with some of her contacts in the trade. All suggested lowering the salespeople's base pay and installing either a fixed or a variable commission rate system.

One idea was to lower the base hourly rate from $10 to $7 and let them make up the difference through a 4 percent commission on all sales, to be paid monthly. Such an arrangement would allow them all to earn the same as they currently did.

However, she realized that such a system would provide no incentive to sell the higher-priced furs, which she recognized might be a way to improve overall sales. So she considered offering to pay 3 percent on items priced below $2,000 and 5 percent on all those above.

Either of these systems would require considerable extra bookkeeping. Returns would have to be deducted from commissions. And she was also concerned that disputes might arise among her people from time to time over who had actually made the sale. So she conceived of a third alternative, which was to leave the hourly rates the same but pay a flat bonus of 4 percent of all sales over $1 million, and divide it among the people on the basis of the proportion of hours each had actually worked. This "commission" would be paid annually, in the form of a Christmas bonus.

DISCUSSION QUESTIONS

1. What are the advantages and disadvantages of the various alternatives Ruth Diamond is considering?
2. Do you have any other suggestions for improving the store's sales?
3. What would you recommend? Why?

Source: This case was prepared by Professor David Ehrlich, Marymount University.

CASE 28 Borders Bookstore: A Merchandise Display Problem

Michael Chaim, general manager of the Borders Bookstore in Madison, Wisconsin, was proud of his store. Located in a city that has one of the highest levels of book purchases per capita, Chaim felt Borders' selection, services, and location near the 40,000-student university served the community well. Even with competitive pressure from the newly opened Barnes & Noble on the west side of town, his bookstore/café was often a busy place.

Chaim was taken aback when an article in a widely read alternative newspaper criticized the bookstore's merchandise arrangement as being prejudiced. The store carries a large selection of literature and poetry, but it separates some specialty categories, such as African American literature, gay and lesbian literature, and feminist literature, from the general literature and poetry sections. In part, this arrangement reflects Borders' college town roots in Ann Arbor, Michigan, where specialty collections were established to match course offerings.

The article described this arrangement as "ghettoizing" authors who were not white males, though some female authors were in the general literature and poetry sections. The article and some follow-up letters to the newspaper's editor derided Borders for the few "nontraditional" authors who made it into the general literature collection.

They felt that these African American, homosexual, Native American, and other nontraditional writers probably would not have been separated from the general collection had the management known the literature better. While Madison is known as a very liberal community, Chaim thought the accusation was unfair. He strongly believed that he was doing his customers a service in highlighting authors and literary genres that might be overlooked in a large, nondifferentiated collection. More immediately, he knew that he should respond to the article's accusations.

DISCUSSION QUESTIONS

1. Although Chaim has several options, one is to duplicate the titles that could be shelved in either the general literature section or in a specialty collection. What are the advantages and disadvantages of this tactic?

2. The Borders store described in this case is in a college town. How should the merchandise be arranged in a different location, such as a suburban residential location or a more urban setting?

Source: This case was prepared by Jan Owens, University of Wisconsin, and Parkside.

CASE 29 Fresh Ideas in Grocery Store Layout

Research conducted by faculty at the Wharton School at the University of Pennsylvania tracked and studied consumers' behavior as they were food shopping. The study was conducted at a West Coast supermarket where the bottoms of grocery carts were equipped with radio frequency identification (RFID) devices that allowed the travel pattern of individual shoppers to be recorded. The RFID tags helped to track how long customers spent shopping, where they went in the store, and how many items they purchased.

The results of the study showed that shoppers move through the store in a different way than retailers had expected. People do not weave sequentially up and down through every aisle but instead move in a clockwise direction, stick to the perimeter of the store, and skip entire sections. Therefore, many customers never see merchandise in the center of the aisle, and end-of-aisle displays are especially important promotional tools.

More time should be spent on store layout in the grocery store industry to meet shoppers' needs and purchasing patterns. Customers are making more quick trips to the food store. They are deciding what to serve for dinner on the way home from work and only purchasing what they need for the next day or two. The once-per-week stock-up trip, which takes 55 minutes or more, accounts for only 10 percent of all grocery store visits.

Based on the Food Marketing Institute's annual "U.S. Grocery Shopper Trends" report, Americans go to food stores on average 2.2 times a week. Nearly two-thirds of shoppers visit the grocery store three or four times per week. On average, each U.S. household spends $92.50 per week at the food store. More than half of those surveyed shop multiple channels, including discounters and warehouse clubs for groceries. The report also found that 54 percent of shoppers make a list. Lastly, younger shoppers felt that self-checkout is an important feature when selecting a food store.

Grocery retailers have seen the following key trends affecting the industry, which call for related improvements in the store:

- Time-strapped customers—grouping items together, offering meal solutions, and improving checkout for speed and convenience.
- Competition for customer loyalty—offering bonus programs and private-label brands.
- Increased pressure from discounters—differentiating the store on benefits other than price.
- Growing interest in nutrition—providing heath information, fresh produce and meat, and organic options.
- Internet shopping—giving technologically savvy shoppers the opportunity to place orders and shop online.

DISCUSSION QUESTIONS

1. How is the supermarket that you shop at most frequently laid out? Describe the store's entry, departments around the perimeter, dry goods, frozen foods, special displays, and checkout.

2. Based on the information in the case and your own shopping behavior, what store layout and design features would improve the supermarket and make the experience more enjoyable and convenient for shoppers and more profitable for retailers?

Source: This case was written by Hope Bober Corrigan, Loyola College in Maryland.

CASE 30 Sephora

Sephora, a division of Moet Hennessy Louis Vuitton (LVMH), is an innovative retail concept from France that is changing the way cosmetics are sold. Sephora dares to be different in its store design and product offerings. In fact, it defines the fashion retail concept to give its customers what they want: "freedom, beauty, and pleasure." Some of Sephora's product offerings include hair care, makeup, fragrances, bath and body, skin care, and Sephora's own private-label brand of beauty products. There is no doubt that every woman can find the products that she desires at Sephora to pamper herself like a queen.

Sephora takes beauty offerings in a new, exciting direction, allowing the customer to choose her own level of service. The customer may opt for "an individual experience and reflection to detailed expert advice," whether that is in Sephora's store locations or on its highly interactive Web site. Sephora has been taking the U.S. market by storm ever since it arrived in mid-1998 with its first two store locations in New York and Miami. Its flagship store that encompasses 21,000 square feet opened in Rockefeller Center in New York City in October 1999. Now, Sephora operates approximately 515 stores in 14 countries worldwide, with an expanding base of over 95 stores across North America. Sephora opened its first Canadian store in Toronto in 2004.

Most fashion-oriented cosmetics are sold in department stores. The scent and cosmetics area in department stores consists of areas devoted to the products made by each manufacturer. Salespeople specializing in a specific line stand behind a counter and assist customers in selecting merchandise.

Sephora represents "the future of beauty," so it is no surprise that its store designs are a reflection of what to expect in the future. It lures customers into its stores with a bright red carpet that immediately induces excitement and an intrigue that cannot be matched. Once the customers enter the store, they are surrounded by what Sephora likes to call "the temple of beauty." An extraordinary assortment of products is arranged alphabetically and by category along the walls of the store. Customers are encouraged to sample the beauty products on their own from self-serve modules. The stores sell a tremendous variety of brands, including new lines, best sellers, classics, and an exclusive Sephora collection.

Sephora has a strong presence throughout the United States; however, it also has stores located in Canada, Czech Republic, England, France, Greece, Italy, Luxembourg, Monaco, Spain, Poland, Portugal, Romania, Russia, and Turkey. The company decided to pull out of Japan and Germany because of financial concerns, unable to sell to Japanese and German consumers with its unique retail concept.

Sephora offers its cosmetic products online. There has been much speculation in recent years that beauty products cannot be displayed properly on a two-dimensional Web page. Many other retailers have attempted to make the transition, but they have been unsuccessful time and time again. On the other hand, Sephora has managed to set itself apart from other retailers once again by making it work while still yielding a profit. Sephora offers over 250 classic and emerging brands, some that consumers have a difficult time finding in department stores, such as Philosophy, Bare Escentuals, and Lip Fusion.

Women have been making purchases on the Sephora Web site because they cannot find these products in their hometown malls. To many customers' dismay, Sephora stores are not located in every regional mall across the country. For these customers, Sephora.com represents a one-stop shop for all of their beauty needs. They know that they can find the brands they love at a reasonable price with no hassles. What else can a person ask for?

Even though Sephora is the world's largest beauty retailer, it still recognizes the importance of giving back to the community. It has joined forces with Operation Smile, which provides reconstructive facial surgery for young children in developing countries and the United States, to provide kids with a greater sense of confidence so that they can live a more normal life. It committed itself to help improve the lives of children around the world. This joint effort allows children who would not normally be able to afford surgical procedures get the help that they deserve to feel like a regular kid. The children have no reason to be self-conscious anymore because they are beautiful on the inside and outside. Sephora continues to make a difference by getting involved in the community even through its daily operations. Even though some women do not believe in the art of makeup, it is essential to recognize that it does allow many other women to feel more confident about their looks on a daily basis, and this contribution, in itself, is truly irreplaceable.

DISCUSSION QUESTIONS

1. Describe Sephora's target market.
2. Why do women prefer the self-service environment of Sephora rather than the service-oriented environment in department store cosmetic areas?
3. Explain why was Sephora was unsuccessful in Japan and Germany when it has been so successful in other foreign countries.
4. How can a beauty retailer make a successful transition to online selling? What makes Sephora's online site so successful?

Source: This case was written by Kristina Pacca, University of Florida.

CASE 31 A Stockout at Discmart: Will Substitution Lead to Salvation?

Robert Honda, the manager of a Discmart store (a discount retailer similar to Target and Wal-Mart) in Cupertino, California, was surveying the Sunday morning activity at his store. Shoppers were bustling around with carts; some had children in tow. In the front side of the store, a steady stream of shoppers were heading through the checkout counters. Almost all the cash registers that he could see from his vantage point were open and active. The line in front of register 7 was longer than the other lines, but other than that things seemed to be going quite smoothly.

The intercom beeped and interrupted his thoughts. A delivery truck had just arrived at the rear of the store. The driver wanted to know which loading dock to use to unload merchandise. Honda decided to inspect the available space before directing the driver to a specific loading dock. As he passed the cash registers on his way to the rear of the store, he noticed that the line at register 7 had gotten a little bit longer. The light over the register was flashing, indicating that the customer service associate (CSA) had requested assistance. (At Discmart, all frontline personnel who interact with customers are called CSAs.) As he passed by the register, he could not help overhearing the exchange between what seemed to be a somewhat irate customer and the CSA. The customer was demanding that another item should be substituted for an item that was on sale but currently out of stock, and the CSA was explaining the store policy to the customer. Normally, during a busy time like this, Honda would have tried to help the CSA resolve the situation, but he knew that the truck driver was waiting to unload merchandise that was needed right away on the floor. Hence, he quickly walked to the rear of the store.

After assigning the truck to a docking bay for unloading, Honda headed back toward the front of the store. On the way back, he ducked into the breakroom to get a Coke and noticed that Sally Johnson, the CSA who was at register 7, was on a break. Sally had been on the Discmart team for about a year and was considered a very capable employee who always kept the store's interests at heart.

Robert: Hi Sally, I noticed that you had quite a line in front of your register earlier today.

Sally: Hi Robert. Yes, I had a very irate customer, and it took us a while to resolve the issue.

Robert: Oh really! What was he irate about?

Sally: We are out of stock on the 100-ounce Tide Liquid Detergent that was advertised in our flyer and was on sale at 20 percent off. I offered the customer a rain check or the same discount on the same size of another brand, but he kept insisting that he wanted us to substitute a 200-ounce container of Tide Liquid Detergent at the same discount. Apparently, Joe Chang [the assistant manager] had told the customer that we would substitute the 200-ounce size.

Robert: Did you point out to the customer that our sale prices are valid only while supplies last?

Sally: I did mention this to him, but he thought it was strange that we ran out of stock on the morning of the first day of the sale.

Robert: Well, I guess you should have gone ahead and given him what he wanted.

Sally: As you know, our point-of-sale systems allow me to make adjustments only on designated items. Since the 200-ounce sizes were not designated as substitutes, I had to request a supervisor to help me.

Robert: I am glad that you got it resolved.

Sally: Well, the customer got tired of waiting for the supervisor, who was busy helping another customer, so he decided to take a rain check instead. He seemed quite dissatisfied with the whole episode and mentioned that we should stop running these TV ads claiming that we are always in stock and that we guarantee satisfaction.

Robert: I do hate it when they run these ad campaigns and we have to take the heat on the floor, trying to figure out what those cowboys in marketing promised the customer.

Sally: Well, my break is nearly over. I have to get back.

Honda pondered the encounter that Johnson had with the customer. He wondered whether to discuss this issue with Joe Chang. He remembered talking to him about inventory policies a couple of days ago. Chang had indicated that their current inventory levels were fairly high and that any further increases would be hard to justify from a financial perspective. He mentioned some market research that had surveyed a random sample of customers who had redeemed rain checks. The results of the survey indicated that customers by and large were satisfied with Discmart's rain check procedures. Based on this finding, Chang had argued that current inventory levels, supplemented with a rain check policy, would keep customers satisfied.

Source: This case was prepared by Dr. Kirthi Kalyanam, Retail Management Institute, Santa Clara University. © Dr. Kirthi Kalyanam.

CASE 32   Customer Service and Relationship Management at Nordstrom

Nordstrom's unwavering customer-focused philosophy traces its roots to founder Johan Nordstrom's values. Johan Nordstrom believed in people and realized that consistently exceeding their expectations led to success and a good conscience. He built his organization around a customer-oriented philosophy. The organization focuses on people, and its policies and selections are designed to satisfy people. As simple as this philosophy sounds, few of Nordstrom's competitors have truly been able to grasp it.

A FOCUS ON PEOPLE

Nordstrom employees treat customers like royalty. Employees are instructed to do whatever is in the customer's best interest. Customer delight drives the values of the company. Customers are taken seriously and are at the heart of the business. Customers are even at the top of the Nordstrom's so-called organization chart, which is an inverted pyramid. Following customers from the top of the inverted pyramid are the salespeople, department managers, and general managers. Finally, at the bottom is the board of directors. All lower levels work toward supporting the salespeople, who in turn work to serve the customer.

Employee incentives are tied to customer service. Salespeople are given personalized business cards to help them build relationships with customers. Uniquely, salespeople are not tied to their respective departments but to the customer. Salespeople can travel from department to department within the store to assist their customer, if that is needed. For example, a Nordstrom salesperson assisting a woman shopping for business apparel helps her shop for suits, blouses, shoes, hosiery, and accessories. The salesperson becomes the "personal shopper" of the customer to show her merchandise and provide fashion expertise. This is also conducive to the building of a long-term relationship with the customer, as over time, the salesperson understands the customer's fashion sense and personality.

The opportunity to sell across departments enables salespeople to maximize sales and commissions while providing superior customer service. As noted on a *60 Minutes* segment, "[Nordstrom's service is] not service like it used to be, but service that never was."

Despite the obsession with customer service at Nordstrom, ironically, the "customer comes second." Nordstrom understands that customers will be treated well by its employees only if the employees themselves are treated well by the company. Nordstrom employees are treated almost like the extended Nordstrom family, and employee satisfaction is a closely watched business variable.

Nordstrom is known for promoting employees from within its ranks. The fundamental traits of a successful Nordstrom salesperson (such as a commitment to excellence and customer service) are the same traits emphasized in successful Nordstrom executives.

Nordstrom hires people with a positive attitude, a sense of ownership, initiative, heroism, and the ability to handle high expectations. This sense of ownership is reflected in Nordstrom's low rate of shrinkage. Shrinkage, or loss due to theft and record-keeping errors, at Nordstrom is under 1.5 percent of sales, roughly half the industry average. The low shrinkage can be attributed in large part to the diligence of salespeople caring for the merchandise as if it were their own.

Employees at all levels are treated like businesspeople and empowered to make independent decisions. They are given the latitude to do whatever they believe is the right thing, with the customers' best interests at heart. All employees are given the tools and authority to do whatever is necessary to satisfy customers, and management almost always backs subordinates' decisions.

In summary, Nordstrom's product is its people. The loyal Nordstrom shopper goes to Nordstrom for the service received—not necessarily the products. Of course, Nordstrom does offer quality merchandise, but that is secondary for many customers.

CUSTOMER-FOCUSED POLICIES

One of the most famous examples of Nordstrom's customer service occurred in 1975 when a Nordstrom salesperson gladly took back a set of used automobile tires and gave the customer a refund, even though Nordstrom had never sold tires! The customer had purchased the tires from a Northern Commercial Company store, whose retail space Nordstrom had since acquired. Not wanting the customer to leave the Nordstrom store unhappy, the salesperson refunded the price of the tires.

Nordstrom's policies focus on the concept of the "Lifetime Value of the Customer." Although little money is made on the first sale, when the lifetime value of a customer is calculated, the positive dollar amount of a loyal customer is staggering. The lifetime value of a customer is the sum of all sales generated from that customer, directly or indirectly. To keep its customers for a "lifetime," Nordstrom employees go to incredible lengths. In a Nordstrom store in Seattle, a customer wanted to buy a pair of brand-name slacks that had gone on sale. The store was out of her size, and the salesperson was unable to locate a pair at other Nordstrom stores. Knowing that the same slacks were available at a competitor nearby, the sales clerk went to the rival, purchased the slacks at full price using petty cash from her department, and sold the slacks to the customer at Nordstrom's sale price. Although this sale resulted in an immediate loss for the store, the investment in promoting the loyalty of the happy customer went a long way.

Nordstrom's employees try to "Never Say No" to the customer. Nordstrom has an unconditional return policy. If a customer is not completely satisfied, he or she can return the new and generally even heavily used merchandise at any time for a full refund. Ironically, this is not a company policy; rather, it is implemented at the discretion of the salesperson to maximize customer satisfaction. Nordstrom's advice to its employees is simply, "Use good judgment in all situations." Employees are given the freedom, support, and resources to make the best decisions to enhance customer satisfaction. The cost of Nordstrom's high service, such as its return policy, coupled with its competitive pricing would, on the surface, seem to cut into profit margins. This cost, however, is recouped through increased sales from repeat customers, rare markdowns, and, if necessary, the "squeezing" of suppliers.

Nordstrom's up-channel policies also focus on maximizing customer satisfaction. According to former CEO Bruce Nordstrom, "[Vendors] know that we are liberal with our customers. And if you're going to do business with us, then there should be a liberal influence on their return policies. If somebody has worn a shoe and it doesn't wear satisfactorily for them, and we think that person is being honest about it, then we will send it back." Nordstrom realizes some customers will abuse the unconditional return policy, but Nordstrom refuses to impose that abuse back onto their vendors. Here again, the rule of "doing what is right" comes into play.

Nordstrom's merchandising and purchasing policies are also extremely customer focused. A full selection of merchandise in a wide variety of sizes is seen as a measure of customer service. An average Nordstrom store carries roughly 150,000 pairs of shoes with a variety of sizes, widths, colors, and models. Typical shoe sizes for women range from 2 1/2 to 14, in widths of A to EEE. Nordstrom is fanatical about stocking only high-quality merchandise. Once when the upper parts of some women's shoes were separating from the soles, *every* shoe from that delivery was shipped back to the manufacturer.

DISCUSSION QUESTIONS

1. What steps does Nordstrom take to implement its strategy of providing outstanding customer service?
2. How do these activities enable Nordstrom to reduce the gaps between perceived service and customer expectations, as described in Chapter 19?
3. What are the pros and cons of Nordstrom's approach to developing a competitive advantage through customer service?

Source: This case was written by Alicia Lueddemann, the Management Mind Group, and Sunil Erevelles, University of North Carolina, Charlotte.

CASE 33   Retailers and Sustainable Development in the U.K.

INTRODUCTION

 During the past decade, the concept of sustainable development has moved steadily up the United Kingdom's political agenda. The U.K. government has set out its Sustainable Development Strategy in "Securing the Future" (HM Government 2005) whose ambitious aim is "to enable all people throughout the world to satisfy their basic needs and enjoy a better quality of life without compromising the quality of life of future generations." Within this strategy there is a clear recognition that "retailers both shape the sustainability of their supply chains and determine the range of products and services available to consumers" and "have a role to play in cutting down on energy use, water use and waste in their operations."

 Many of the United Kingdom's large retailers recognize the impacts they have on the environment, the economy, and society and are increasingly interested in addressing sustainability issues and communicating their commitment to sustainability to their shareholders and the general public. The retail industry within the United Kingdom has become increasingly concentrated, and the number of independent retailers has declined. This concentration has increased the power of large retailers in channel relationships and brought them into direct contact with a large number, and often a wide cross-section, of customers. The former gives the large retailers greater power over many aspects of their buying relationships with their suppliers, whereas the latter keeps them well attuned to consumer buying behavior and allows them to develop sophisticated marketing strategies. It is these large retailers that have the greatest impacts on the environment, the economy, and society and that could have the dominant role to play in encouraging more sustainable patterns of production and consumption.

RETAILING AND THE ENVIRONMENT

Large U.K. retailers are addressing a range of environmental issues including energy consumption and emissions, raw material usage, water consumption, waste, the volume of packaging, recycling, genetically modified foods, and the use of chemicals. The U.K. grocery retailer Tesco, for example, has been investing in a range of energy-saving schemes and reduced energy consumption per square foot of sales space by some 23 percent between 2001 and 2005. The company participates in the U.K.'s Emissions Trading Scheme and is committed to making an absolute reduction of 74,000 tons of greenhouse gases over five years at a control group of 188 stores. The bulk of the company's emissions into the atmosphere come from its trucking fleet. Thus, the company is focusing on increasing the number of product cases delivered per gallon of fuel consumed.

In a similar vein, the John Lewis Partnership, operators of John Lewis department stores and Waitrose supermarkets in the United Kingdom, faces challenges in its truck delivery fleet associated with customer demands for more stores, longer opening hours, and home deliveries for online shopping. The company reported a small reduction in its commercial vehicle mileage and emissions, a 44 percent increase in backhauled journeys that utilize the transport fleet more fully, and the fitting of Continuously Regenerating Taps, which help significantly reduce carbon monoxide and hydrocarbon emissions, on many of its vehicles.

John Lewis also has developed a sustainable timber policy designed to ensure that all timber used in the course of its business is sourced with the least possible damage to the natural environment. The company sells a broader range of furniture than the majority of its competitors and uses some 30 different species of tropical hardwoods from over 100 suppliers. Keeping track of sources of timber is a major task, but the company is concentrating its sourcing policy on timber from countries such as Indonesia and the Central African Republic, where the risk of illegal practices or poor forest management is considered to be greatest.

Marks & Spencer, the U.K.-based department and grocery store chain, recognizes that chemicals are used in the production of every product sold within its stores but has particularly focused its attention on pesticides, polyvinyl chloride (PVC), and dyeing. The company has sought to balance the need for sufficient quantities of high-quality food against environmental concerns and set for itself two sets of goals pertaining to fresh fruit, vegetables, potatoes, and salads. It has committed to use the minimum amounts of pesticides and banned or replaced 79 pesticides. Some 99 percent of PVC packaging, the disposal of which releases chemicals that cause environmental concerns, had been replaced by 2002. By 2004, 73 percent of its food merchandise was residue free.

Dixons, a large consumer electronics chain in the United Kingdom, addresses the problem that disposal of waste places a significant burden on the environment. It has adopted measures to segregate waste materials for recycling in an attempt to reduce this burden and reports some success in encouraging its suppliers to use less packaging. The company also has a system for compacting waste materials for collection by recyclers and is continuing to develop both internal services and those available to customers for the recycling and safe disposal of products and their associate consumables. During 2003/2004, Dixons was the first major retailer in the United Kingdom to introduce 100 percent recycled plastic carrier bags.

Many of the leading retailers in the United Kingdom are committed to recycling programs. Several have also begun to introduce recycling units at their stores for customer use. At some Tesco stores, customers can recycle plastic bottles and jars, tins, glass bottles, cardboard, textiles, and CDs. The retail industry also generates an enormous amount of packaging, which customers dispose of domestically. Many retailers are now seeking to redesign and simplify their packaging to reduce costs and packaging waste for customers; a growing number have also introduced degradable plastic shopping bags in their stores.

RETAILING AND THE ECONOMY

The United Kingdom's large retailers make a major contribution to the economy through the employment opportunities they create and the wages and salaries their employees earn, the dividends they pay their shareholders, the profits they retain to fund future growth, and the taxes they generate for the government. In 2004–2005, Tesco, for example, reported employing a workforce of 366,000 people, paying them £3,534 million in salaries and wages, reinvesting £779 million back into the business, and paying £587 million to its shareholders. At the same time, the leading retailers have a wider range of economic impacts, and more retailers are addressing some of the sustainability agendas associated with these impacts. These include urban regeneration, the sourcing of local foods, and the vitality of urban areas. Tesco is focusing on opening stores in some of the United Kingdom's most deprived areas and claims success in its "regeneration partnerships," which focus on training and employing staff who have been out of work for years, older people who are unemployed, and young people who may never have worked.

John Lewis recognizes the importance that retail development can have on the current and future vitality of towns and city centers. The company completed extensive renovations in Edinburgh, Nottingham, and central London and has announced new department stores in Cardiff and Leicester and relocations in Cambridge, Liverpool, and Sheffield. It argues that many of its recent and proposed retail developments are key components in the regeneration of town and city centers.

Within many parts of the United Kingdom, growing concern has been expressed about the decline of local shopping areas within many large towns and cities, the market towns within rural areas, and the growth of out-of-town superstores selling an increasingly diverse range of products and services. The large retailers recognize these concerns but argue that they bring new investment and create jobs, thus stimulating local economies. However, urban residents do not always believe that large retailers are contributing to rural sustainability.

National supermarket chain retailers are increasing their commitment to source and stock locally produced foods. Somerfield, for example, has a long-established policy of sourcing local and regional foods that enable its customers to support producers in their own areas. The company stocks over 2,000 local lines, and some lamb, pork, and beef products identify the actual farm of origin.

Many large retailers have increased their awareness of, and vigilance in, sourcing and ethical sourcing policies. Such policies embrace both economic and social dimensions. Marks & Spencer, for example, established a set of global sourcing principles in 1999, which noted supplier requirements relating, for example, to working hours and conditions, rates of pay, terms of employment, and minimum age of employment. All Marks & Spencer's 2,000 direct suppliers of finished goods are expected to meet these principles, and in 2004–2005, the company worked with human rights groups in India, Morocco, Sri Lanka, and Indonesia in an attempt to improve the working and living conditions of people working in associated manufacturing plants.

More specifically, a growing number of U.K. retailers are taking a growing interest in "Fair Trade," which seeks to ensure that producers receive an adequate return on their input of skill, labor, and resources. The Co-op is widely regarded as the United Kingdom's leading Fair Trade food retailer. It stocks a range of coffees, teas, cakes, chocolate, fruit juices, fruit, and wine. While many retailers are committed to ethical trading schemes, initiatives, and Fair Trade, they must grapple with the complexities caused by purchasing from sources in very distant countries and those with unstable or inhospitable governments and regulations.

RETAILING AND SOCIETY

Many U.K. retailers are also addressing issues related to their impact on society at large and on the communities within which they operate. These issues include both training and staff development, diversity, health, safety, and education issues for both retail employees and their customers.

All the large retailers are committed to attracting and retaining a culturally and socially diverse workforce, emphasizing recruiting the best people and meeting the needs of the communities in which they trade. These commitments are strengthened by the provision of flexible working arrangements and respecting the balance between life and work. Training and development is also a major theme.

J.Sainsbury, another U.K. food retailer with interests in financial services, for example, provides a range of different types of training including courses, job shadowing, mentoring, qualifications, and self-development books and videos. All employees have access to "Learning@Sainsbury's" via the company Intranet, which offers information on Sainsbury's behaviours, operational training, and the company's program of qualifications and learning library. ASDA, another grocery chain owned by Wal-Mart, reports having invested about $14 million in 15 "Stores of Learning" (SOL), which provide training for new and existing managers. The SOLs have provided training for almost 4,000 managers, and the company reports that posttraining evaluations suggest that SOL-trained managers are outperforming their trading targets by significant margins.

John Lewis offers its employees a dedicated occupational health advisory service. Within each of its stores, the health advisory team performs routine health checks and workplace risk assessments; provides advice on diets, healthy eating, and exercise; and offers subsidized physiotherapy and podia-

try services. The company has also introduced an electronic accident reporting system for all its employees. This system enables each store to report accidents immediately and then monitor the employee's progress until he or she returns to work. The system also allows the company to analyze accident causes and severity, either locally or across the entire business, and develop appropriate preventative measures.

Many large retailers are also taking a growing interest in providing healthy lifestyle alternatives for their customers. Some food retailers have launched "healthy living" ranges of products, containing reduced fat, salt, and sugar contents. J.Sainsbury first introduced health labeling on its own brand products in 1994. In 2004, the company developed its "Wheel of Health," which uses the so-called traffic light approach to show at a glance how much fat, saturated fat, calories, sugar, and salt are in each serving. The colors indicate whether each of these elements makes a low, medium, or high contribution to the recommended daily intake for an average adult. The company also reports that it highlights the nutritional benefits of some foods on packaging and the extension of its "5-a-day logo," which indicates the number of fruit or vegetable portions a pack or serving contains. More generally, the company also reports making healthier choices available in all its price ranges, including its Basics, for which it believes price may be a higher priority for customers than nutrition, as well as its support for a number of initiatives designed to encourage children to eat more healthily and be more active.

Source: This case was written by Peter Jones (pjones@glos.ac.uk), Daphne Comfort, and David Hillier. Peter Jones and Daphne Comfort work in the Business School at the University of Gloucestershire, and David Hillier is Head of Geography at the University of Glamorgan.

References

HM Government, "Securing the Future," Cm.6467, 2005, http:www.sustainable-development.gov.uk/publications/uk-strategy-2005.htm.

P. N. Stearns, "Stages of Consumerism: Recent Work on the Issues of Periodization," *Journal of Modern History* 69, pp. 102–17.

World Commission on Environment and Development, *From One Earth to One World: An Overview* (Oxford: Oxford University Press, 1987).

CASE 34   Lindy's Bridal Shoppe

Located in Lake City (population 80,000), Lindy's Bridal Shoppe, a small bridal store, sells bridal gowns, prom gowns, accessories, and silk flowers. It also rents men's formal wear and performs various alteration services.

Lindy Armstrong, age 33, has owned the store since its founding in March 1997. She's married to a high school teacher and is the mother of three young children. A former nurse, she found the demands of hospital schedules left too little time for her young family. An energetic, active woman with many interests, she wanted to continue to work but also have time with her children.

The silk flowers market enabled Lindy to combine an in-home career with child rearing. She started Lindy's Silk Flowers with $75 of flower inventory in Vernon, a small town of about 10,000 people 10 miles from Lake City. Working out of her home, she depended on word-of-mouth communication among her customers, mainly brides, to bring in business. As Lindy's Silk Flowers prospered, a room was added onto the house to provide more space for the business. Lindy was still making all the flowers herself. Her flower-making schedule kept her extremely busy. Long hours were the norm.

Lindy was approached by a young photographer named Dan Morgan, who proposed establishing a one-stop bridal shop. In this new business, Dan would provide photography, Lindy would provide silk flowers, and another partner, Karen Ross (who had expertise in the bridal market), would provide gowns and accessories. The new store would be located in Vernon in a rented structure. Shortly before the store was to open, Dan and Karen decided not to become partners, and Lindy became the sole owner. She knew nothing about the bridal business. Having no merchandise or equipment, Lindy was drawn to an ad announcing that a bridal store in a major city was going out of business. She immediately called and arranged to meet the owner. Subsequently, she bought all his stock (mannequins, racks, and carpet) for $4,000. The owner also gave her a crash course in the bridal business.

From March 1997 to December 2005, Lindy owned and operated a bridal gown and silk flowers store named Lindy's Bridal Shoppe in Vernon. The location was chosen primarily because it was close to her home. While Vernon is a very small town, Lindy felt that location was not a critical factor in her store's success. She maintained that people would travel some distance to make a purchase as important as a bridal gown. Rent was $250 per month plus utilities. Parking was a problem.

During this period, Lindy's Bridal Shoppe grew. Bridal gowns and accessories as well as prom dresses sold well. As the time approached for Lindy to renew her lease, she wondered about the importance of location. A move to Lake City might be advisable. A much larger town than Vernon, Lake City is the site of a state university. Lindy decided to move.

GENERAL BUSINESS DESCRIPTION

The majority of Lindy's Bridal Shoppe's current sales are made to individuals who order bridal gowns from the rack or from the catalogs of three major suppliers. At the time of the order, the customer pays a deposit, usually half of the purchase price. The balance is due in 30 days. Lindy would like payment in full at the time of ordering regardless of the delivery date, but payment is often delayed until delivery. Once ordered, a gown must be taken and the bill paid when delivered.

No tuxedos are carried in the store, so customers must order from catalogs. Fitting jackets and shoes are provided to help patrons size their purchases. Lindy's Bridal Shoppe rents its men's formal wear from suppliers. Payment from the customer is due on delivery.

Certain times of the year see more formal events than others. Many school proms are held during late April and May, and June, July, and August are big months for weddings. Since traditional dates for weddings are followed less and less closely, Lindy believes that the business is becoming less seasonal, though January and February are quite slow.

PROMOTION PRACTICES

Lindy's Bridal Shoppe engages in various promotional activities but is constrained by limited finances. The firm has no operating budget, which prevents any formal appropriation for advertising expenses.

Newspaper ads constitute the primary promotional medium, though radio is occasionally used. Ads for prom dresses are run only during prom season. These ads usually feature a photograph of a local high school student in a Lindy's Bridal Shoppe gown plus a brief description of the student's activities.

Other promotional activities include bridal shows at a local mall. Lindy feels these have been very successful, though they're a lot of work. A recent prom show in a local high school used students as models, which proved to be an excellent way to stimulate sales. Lindy hopes to go into several other area high schools during the next prom season, though this expansion will demand much planning.

PERSONNEL

Lindy, the sole owner and also the manager of the firm, finds it hard to maintain a capable workforce. A small company, Lindy's Bridal Shoppe can't offer premium salaries for its few positions. There's one full-time salesperson. The part-time staff includes a salesperson, alterations person, bookkeeper, and custodian.

Lindy handles all the paperwork. Her responsibilities include paying bills, ordering merchandise and supplies, hiring and firing personnel, fitting customers, and selling various items. She makes all the major decisions that directly affect the firm's operations. She also makes all the silk flowers herself. It's time consuming, but she isn't satisfied with how anyone else makes them.

MERCHANDISE OFFERINGS

Lindy's Bridal Shoppe's major product lines are new wedding, prom, and party gowns. No used gowns are sold. Discontinued styles or gowns that have been on the rack for a year are sold at reduced prices, primarily because discoloration is a major problem. Gowns tend to yellow after hanging on the racks for a year.

A wide variety of accessories are provided. Lindy believes it's important that her customers not have to go anywhere else for them. These accessories include shoes, veils, headpieces, jewelry, and foundations. Slips may be rented instead of purchased. One room of Lindy's Bridal Shoppe is used only to prepare silk flowers.

SERVICE OFFERINGS

Lindy's Bridal Shoppe's major service offering is fitting and alteration. Most gowns must be altered, for which there's a nominal charge. Lindy feels that personal attention and personal service set her apart from her competitors. Emphasizing customer satisfaction, she works hard to please each customer. This isn't always easy. Customers can be picky, and it takes time to deal with unhappy people.

LOCATION

Lindy's Bridal Shoppe is located at the end of Lake City's main through street. Initially Lindy didn't think location was important to her bridal store's success, but she's changed her mind. Whereas business was good in Vernon, it's booming in Lake City. Vehicular traffic is high, and there's adequate, if not excess, parking.

Lindy's Bridal Shoppe has a 12-year lease. Rent ($1,800 per month) includes heat and water, but Lindy's Bridal Shoppe must pay for interior decoration. The physical facility is generally attractive, with open and inviting interior display areas. But some areas both inside and outside the store have an unfinished look.

Some storage areas require doors or screens to enhance the interior's appearance. The fitting room ceilings are unfinished, and the carpeting inside the front door may be unsafe. One other interior problem is insufficient space; there seems to be inadequate space for supporting activities such as flower preparation, customer fittings, and merchandise storage, which gives the store a cluttered look.

Several external problems exist. The signs are ineffective, and there's a strong glare on the front windows, which detracts from the effectiveness of the overall appearance and interior window displays. The parking lot needs minor maintenance: Parking lines should be painted, and curbs must be repaired. Much should be done to add color and atmosphere through basic landscaping.

COMPETITION

Lindy's Bridal Shoppe is the only bridal shop in Lake City. Lindy believes she has four main competitors. Whitney's Bridal Shoppe is 30 miles from Lake City; Ender's Brides, a new shop with a good operation, is in Spartan City, 50 miles away; Carole's is a large, established bridal shop in Smithtown, 70 miles distant; and Gowns-n-Such is in Andersonville, 75 miles away. A new store in Yorktown (15 miles away) is selling used gowns and discontinued styles at very reduced prices. Lindy watches this new- and used-gown store closely.

Some of her potential customers are buying wedding gowns from electronic retailers such as The Knot (www.theknot.com) and the Wedding Channel (www.weddingchannel.com). Although these electronic retailers already are making significant sales in her trading area, Lindy is concerned that some of the services offered by these electronic retailers (such as gift registries, e-mail notices, wedding planning, and wedding picture displays) will attract more of her customers.

FINANCIAL CONSIDERATIONS

Basic financial information includes

1. Markup: 50 percent.
2. 2006 sales: $200,000 (estimated).
3. Average inventory: $70,000.
4. Turnover: 3.0 (approximately).
5. Annual expenses: rent $19,200, labor $24,000, utilities $7,000, supplies $12,000, equipment $4,000, and miscellaneous $4,000.
6. Estimated total costs ($200,000 sales): $170,200.
7. Implied profit including owner's salary: $29,800.
8. Capital invested (equipment, $8,000; inventory, $70,000): $78,000.
9. ROI: $5,800/$78,000 = 7.4 percent. (Assume owner salary of $24,000 per year.)

THE FUTURE

Lindy Armstrong is uncertain about the future. She enjoys the business but feels that she's working very hard and not making much money. During all the years of Lindy's Bridal Shoppe's operation, she hasn't taken a salary. She works 60 hours or more a week. Business is excellent and growing, but she's tired. She has even discussed selling the business and returning to nursing.

DISCUSSION QUESTIONS

1. Could Lindy change the emphasis of her merchandise mix to increase her sales?
2. Which products should have more emphasis? Which should have less?
3. What personnel decisions must Lindy face to improve her business?
4. How could someone like Lindy Armstrong balance the demands of her family and her business?
5. If one of Lindy's competitors were to offer her $150,000 for her business, should she sell?

Source: This case was prepared by Linda F. Felicetti and Joseph P. Grunewald, Clarion University of Pennsylvania.

CASE 35 Starbucks Coffee Company

 Starbucks is the leading retailer of specialty coffee beverages and beans and related food and merchandise. Its annual sales for 2005 were $5.3 billion, with a profit of $392 million. Starbucks owns and operates more than 5,200 retail stores and has licensed an additional 2,800 airport and shopping center stores in 30 countries.

In addition to its direct retailing activities, Starbucks has formed strategic alliances with Dreyer's Grand Ice Cream, Kraft Foods, Barnes & Noble Booksellers, Jim Beam, United Airlines, and PepsiCo to expand its product and distribution portfolios. Howard Schultz, chairman and CEO, and his senior management team were focusing on how to sustain its phenomenal growth and maintain Starbucks' market leadership position.

THE COFFEE MARKET

The commercial market for coffee began in AD 1000 when Arab traders brought the coffee tree from its native Ethiopia to the Middle East. Over the next 200 years, coffee drinking spread through the Arab world and was eventually introduced in Europe in the 1500s by Italian traders. By 1650, coffee houses emerged as popular meeting places in England and France. Well-known public figures would frequent London coffee houses to discuss political and literary issues.

Coffee consumption flourished in the mid-twentieth century, aided by developments in manufacturing and cultivation. By 1940, large coffee processors such as Nestlé (Hills Bros. brand), Kraft General Foods (Maxwell House), and Procter & Gamble (Folgers) developed instant and decaffeinated coffee varieties in addition to their staple regular ground. Supermarkets emerged as the primary distribution channel for traditional coffee sales.

In the late 1980s, per capita coffee consumption fell slowly and steadily as consumers turned to soft drinks, bottled water, juices, and iced teas. The three major manufacturers—Procter & Gamble, Nestlé, and Kraft—fought for market share in a stagnant market. All of the major coffee brands were unprofitable. In an effort to regain profitability, the majors decreased their historically high expenditures on image advertising, increased the use of robusta beans (as opposed to high-quality arabica beans) to further reduce costs, and converted from 16-ounce cans to 13-ounce cans, claiming that the contents produced the same amount of coffee. Coupons and in-store promotions dominated manufacturer marketing plans as price warfare continued.

THE STARBUCKS COFFEE COMPANY: BACKGROUND

Inspiration for the present Starbucks concept came to Howard Schultz when he went to Italy on a buying trip in 1983. While wandering through the ancient piazzas of Milan, Schultz took particular note of the many cheerful espresso bars and cafes he passed. Italians, he felt, had captured the true romance of the beverage. Coffee drinking was an integral part of the Italian culture. Italians started their day at the espresso bar and returned there later on. "There's such a strong sense of community in those coffee bars," he mused. "People come together every single day and in many cases they don't even know each other's names. In Italy, coffee is the conduit to the social experience."

Schultz realized that Americans lacked the opportunity to savor a good cup of coffee while engaging in good conversation in a relaxed atmosphere. He returned to the United States convinced that Americans would find the Italian coffee house culture attractive. In 1987, Schultz bought Starbucks.

THE INITIAL YEARS
Retail Offering
Starbucks offers more than a cup of coffee. Scott Bedbury, the VP of marketing, elaborates:

> Our product is not just that which resides in the cup. The product is the store and the service you get in the store. We need to help people appreciate at a higher level why that coffee break feels the way it does, why it's worth the time it takes to prepare a good cup of coffee. I like to think that Starbucks is not so much *food* for thought, but *brewed* for thought. Coffee has for centuries been for thought. I have sometimes thought to myself, "Get out of this chair. You hit the wall." It's that private time for me between 2 and 3 p.m. when I walk down the Commons area here and make myself an Americano and think something through. I think that's maybe what Starbucks has to offer people: that safe harbor, that place to kind of make sense of the world. In the long run, what distinguishes us from our competitors, what is the most enduring competitive advantage we have, is that we are able to give our customers an experience at the store level . . . better than any competitor out there, even the small ones. Starbucks should be a place, an experience, tied up in inspired thought.

Although designs vary in any particular store to match the local market, the typical Starbucks store works around a planned mix of organic and manufactured components: light wood tones at the counters and signage areas, brown bags, polished dark marble countertops, glass shelves, thin modern white track lighting, and pure white cups. Even the logo delivers the double organic/modern message: The Starbucks icon is earthy looking, yet rendered in a modern abstract form, in black and white with a band of color around the center only. The colors of the lamps, walls, and tables mimic coffee tones, from green (raw beans) to light and darker browns. Special package and cup designs are coordinated to create livelier, more colorful tones around holidays. Starbucks also keeps its look lively with rotating in-store variations based on timely themes.

Starbucks stores are spacious so that customers can wander around the store, drinking their coffee and considering the purchase of coffee paraphernalia ranging from coffee beans to brushes for cleaning coffee grinders to $1,000 home cappuccino machines. Retail sales are composed of coffee beverages (58 percent), whole bean coffee by the pound (17 percent), food items (16 percent), and coffee-related equipment (9 percent). Although coffee beverages are standardized across outlets, food offerings vary from store to store.

At Starbucks, espresso is brewed precisely 18 to 23 seconds and thrown away if it is not served within 10 seconds of brewing. Coffee beans are donated to charities seven days after coming out of their vacuum-sealed packs. Drip coffee is thrown away if it is not served within an hour of making it. Throughout the store, there exists a keen attention to aroma: Employees are not allowed to wear colognes, stores use no scented cleaning products, and smoking is *verboten*.

Human Resource Management

The company, recognizing that its frontline employees are critical to providing "the perfect cup," has built an organizational culture based on two principles: (1) strict standards for how coffee should be prepared and delivered to customers and (2) a laid-back, supportive, and empowering attitude toward its employees.

All new hires, referred to as partners, go through a 24-hour training program that instills a sense of purpose, commitment, and enthusiasm for the job. New employees are treated with the dignity and respect that goes along with their title as *baristas* (Italian for bartender). To emphasize their responsibility in pleasing customers, baristas are presented with scenarios describing customers complaining about beans that were ground incorrectly. The preferred response, baristas learn, is to replace the beans on the spot without checking with the manager or questioning the complaint. Baristas learn to customize each espresso drink, explain the origins of different coffees, and claim to be able to distinguish Sumatran from Ethiopian coffees by the way it "flows over the tongue."

Holding on to their motivated, well-trained employees is important, so all are eligible for health benefits and a stock option plan called "Bean Stock." Each employee is awarded stock options worth 12 percent of his or her annual base pay. (Starbucks now allows options at 14 percent of base pay in light of "good profits.") Employees are also given a free pound of coffee each week and a 30 percent discount on all retail offerings. Baristas know about and are encouraged to apply for promotion to store management positions. Every quarter the company has open meetings at which company news, corporate values, and financial performance data are presented and discussed.

Due to the training, empowerment, benefits, and growth opportunities, Starbucks' turnover is only 60 percent, considerably less than the 150 to 200 percent turnover at other firms in the food service business. "We treat our employees like true partners and our customers like stars," comments Schultz.

And stars they are. The average Starbucks customer visits the store 18 times a month; 10 percent visit twice a day. "I don't know of any retailer or restaurant chain that has that kind of loyalty," Schultz says.

Location Strategy

Starbucks' retail expansion strategy was sequential, based on conquering one area of a city or region at a time. Centralized cities served as hubs or regional centers for rollout expansion into nearby markets (e.g., Chicago as a hub for the Midwest). "Clustering" was also central to the strategy—major markets were saturated with stores before new markets were entered. For example, there were over 100 Starbucks outlets in the Seattle area before the company expanded to a new region. Having several stores in close proximity to one another generally increased overall revenues, though slowed growth in comparable store sales in saturated markets suggested sales came at the expense of some cannibalization of existing businesses.

Traffic was the major determinant in selecting cities and locations. "We want to be in highly visible locations," senior VP of real estate Jim Rubin explains, "with access to customers that value quality and great coffee. You want a store in the path of people's weekly shopping experience, their route to work, their way home from a movie. You want to be America's porch that no longer exists."

PHASE II GROWTH STRATEGY

Product Strategy

Starbucks has introduced a number of new products designed to capitalize on the company's strong brand name. "My plan is to bring the company and consequently the brand closer to consumers and to help unlock a greater potential for the brand while keeping its soul and integrity intact," explains Bedbury.

- *Blue Note Blend.* Blue Note Blend was introduced in conjunction with Capitol Records and its Blue Note label for jazz. "The combination of jazz music and coffees was consistent with the atmosphere of Starbucks," explained Bedbury.
- *Frappuccino.* The Frappuccino beverage is a sweet, cold, creamy drink that combines milk, coffee, and ice. The product was very successful when introduced to cafés in 1995, so Starbucks entered a joint venture with PepsiCo to bottle a ready-to-drink (RTD) version. Frappuccino coffee drinks come in six varieties (Mocha, Decaf Mocha, Vanilla, Coffee, Caramel, and Mocha Lite) and are available at convenience or grocery stores.
- *MAZAGRAN.* MAZAGRAN is a carbonated coffee RTD beverage. The product is manufactured, bottled, and distributed by PepsiCo, but Starbucks shared in the R&D and set flavor standards.
- *Dreyer's Grand Ice Cream.* Dreyer's Grand Ice Cream agreed to produce a line of premium ice cream products flavored with Starbucks coffee. The first products in this line, five coffee-flavored gourmet ice creams, were sold under the Starbucks name and distributed through supermarket outlets. Starbucks ice cream is the leading brand of gourmet coffee ice cream on the market. The ice cream is available in the following flavors: Java Chip Big, Mud Pie, Coffee Almond Fudge, Coffee Fudge Brownie, Low Fat Latte, Classic Coffee, and Caramel Cappuccino Swirl. Frozen Frappuccino ice cream bar novelties are available in three varieties: Mocha, Java Fudge, and Caffe Vanilla.
- *Kraft and supermarkets.* Through an agreement with Kraft, the company also sells its branded coffee beans through supermarkets, which command 80 percent of all coffee sales and generate nearly $3 billion in sales annually. The company designed a line of specialty coffees just

for supermarkets and opened Starbucks-operated kiosks in selected grocery chains. Kraft manages all distribution, marketing, advertising, and promotions for Starbucks' whole bean and ground coffee in grocery and mass-merchandise stores. By the end of fiscal year 2001, the company's whole bean and ground coffees were available throughout the United States in approximately 18,000 supermarkets.

• *Jim Beam.* Through a partnership with Jim Beam, a Starbucks coffee liqueur was developed.

Distribution Strategy

Several alternative channels had already been established, including the sale of whole beans through Nordstrom department stores and the sale of coffee by the cup in the cafés of Barnes & Noble bookstores. Additional channels under consideration or in place include distribution through service providers like Holland America Cruise Lines, United Airlines, and Sheraton and Westin Hotels.

In addition to company-operated stores, Starbucks has entered into licensing and joint venture agreements involving 2,800 stores in North America plus outlets in 15 countries, including Saudi Arabia, Switzerland, Israel, Japan, Taiwan, China, New Zealand, and South Korea.

Communication Strategy

Starbucks historically invested very little in advertising—less than $100 million in its entire history. Explains Bedbury, "Our brand is at its best in the store."

DISCUSSION QUESTIONS

1. What is Starbucks' retail strategy? What is its target market, and how does it try to develop an advantage over its competition?

2. Describe Starbucks' retail mix: location, merchandise assortment, pricing, advertising and promotion, store design and visual merchandising, customer service, and personal selling. How does its retail mix support its strategy?

3. What factors in the environment provided the opportunity for Starbucks to develop a new, successful retail chain? What demand and supply conditions prevailed in the U.S. coffee market when Howard Schultz purchased Starbucks in 1987? What insight did Schultz have that other players in the coffee market did not possess?

4. What were the principal drivers behind Starbucks' success in the marketplace? What does the Starbucks brand mean to consumers? How have the growth opportunities that Starbucks has pursued affected the value of its brand name?

5. What are the major challenges facing Starbucks as it goes forward? Is the brand advantage sustainable going forward? Can Starbucks defend its position against other specialty coffee retailers?

Source: This case was written by Susan Fournier, Boston University, and Barton Weitz, University of Florida.

CASE 36   New Product Development at Yankee Candle Company

COMPANY OVERVIEW

Yankee Candle Company, Inc. (YCC), is a leading manufacturer, wholesaler, and retailer of premium scented candles in the $55 billion giftware industry. Gross sales (wholesale and retail combined) were $554 million in 2004. YCC has maintained steady growth since its inception in 1969, displaying impressive sales performance. Exhibit 1 lists the revenue, net income, net profit margin, and number of employees for the company from 2000 to 2004.

Yankee Candle products and accessory items are distributed through a network of 15,600 wholesale customers operating gift stores (e.g., Hallmark) nationwide, an expanding retail base of 366 company-owned stores in 42 states, a mail-order catalog, a Web site (www.yankeecandle.com), and a growing network of European retailers. Headquartered in Whately, Massachusetts, YCC employs 5,500 people nationwide. Its flagship store in South Deerfield is the second-largest tourist destination in Massachusetts, attracting over 2.5 million visitors annually.

EXHIBIT I
Historical Financials for Yankee Candle Company

Year	Revenue ($ mil.)	Net Income ($ mil.)	Net Profit Margin	Number of Employees
2004	554.2	82.7	14.9%	4,200
2003	508.6	74.8	14.7	3,800
2002	444.8	64.0	14.4	3,500
2001	379.8	43.3	11.4	3,000
2000	338.8	43.6	12.9	3,000

CORE PRODUCT LINES

The two core product lines for YCC are scented candles and candle accessories. The premium-quality scented candles are offered in over 125 fragrances. All candles are produced on site at the Whately facility. Candles are manufactured with strict quality control standards to ensure a true scent, long burn time, and consistency of fragrance over the life of the candle. Candles are available in clear or frosted glass Housewarmer jars, Sampler votive candles, wax potpourri Tarts, pillars, tapers, Cocktail Candles, and tea lights.

Coordinating candle accessory products include jar toppers (decorative lids for the Housewarmer jar candles); taper holders; pillar and jar bases; matching jar shades, plates, and sleeves; votive holders; and tea-light holders. One additional accessory product line, "Car Jars," is an assortment of air fresheners in the shape of the Housewarmer jar designed to hang from a car/truck rear view mirror. Go to the Yankee Candle home page to look at their full line of product offerings at http://www.yankeecandle.com.

NEW PRODUCT DEVELOPMENT ACTIVITY AT YANKEE CANDLE

Clearly, new product development is a key activity for members of the YCC management team. A core committee meets weekly to discuss new product ideas, strategies, and other marketing-related issues. This six-person team is composed of senior vice presidents, vice presidents, directors, and buyers from three key functional areas: marketing, retailing, and wholesaling.

New product ideas are discussed in a "roundtable" format. Ideas come from the core committee team members and sources outside the team (e.g., other YCC employees, wholesale customers, retail customers, suppliers). Ideas typically surface in response to industry trends, observations from trade shows, and information in syndicated marketing research reports purchased by YCC. One notable idea that became a successful product is the Car Jar. On the basis of prior discussions with Robert Nelson, manager of the testing lab at YCC, a supplier representative presented the idea for the Car Jar to the core committee. The product development team gave the representative some latitude to explore the idea, and he came back with a finished prototype. YCC endorsed the idea, and it is now a successful line for the company.

The core committee regularly discusses upcoming seasonal additions to the line as new products. For example, for the 2001 holiday season (Christmas, Hanukah), YCC offered candles in three new fragrances (Starry Night, Icicles, and Poinsettia) to complement the four established fragrances (Nutcracker, Peace on Earth, Holiday Spirit, and Christmas Wish).

THE NEW PRODUCT DEVELOPMENT PROCESS FOR COUNTRY CLASSICS

A new product line, Country Classics (CC), was successfully launched in June 2000 and remains a strong performer for YCC. Briefly, CC is a line of candles and accessories decorated with the artwork of folk artist, Warren Kimble. A unique aspect of the CC line is the introduction of candles in an additional type of container, a ceramic crock, and a host of non-candle kitchen and home decorating products (e.g., clocks, coaster/trivet set, picture frames). The process to launch the CC line is described next using a new product development framework.

Stage 1: Idea Generation

The core committee began consideration of CC in late 1999 when Gail Flood, Senior VP Retailing, brought in samples of Kimble's artwork and proposed a joint product/marketing effort. She began thinking of licensing possibilities after seeing two Kimble patterns on dinnerware in a Kitchen Etc. store in Boston. After an initial positive reaction, Erin O'Connor, Director New Product Package Design, and her staff developed concept boards pairing Kimble artwork with YCC fragrances. The core committee continued to discuss particular fragrance options and artwork pairings during December 1999.

Stage 2: Screening

In early January 2000, the idea for CC was refined; Chuck Murphy, Senior Retail Buyer, worked with counterparts in purchasing/operations to gather pricing information regarding production of the candles from candle, glass, and fragrance suppliers, among others. Information on licensing arrangements between YCC and the Warren Kimble organization was obtained by John Cummo, VP Marketing, and his staff. Additional team members joined the core committee at some of the weekly meetings to discuss CC for the purpose of screening this particular new idea. These additional team members included Tom Sweeney, Senior Candle Buyer, Retail; Robert Nelson, Director of Product Testing; and Jane Tate, Production/Manufacturing Manager.

By mid-January 2000, the core committee felt that CC was a feasible idea for a new product line. One additional screening activity was to bring in five managers of YCC retail stores in the eastern Massachusetts area to get their opinions about the concept. The retail managers were in agreement that the "look" of the Kimble folk art was a strong complement to the general YCC image. Harlen Kent, VP Wholesaling, and Sean Gillespie, Director of Wholesaling, coordinated a similar meeting of several prominent wholesale customers in the Massachusetts area to get their evaluations and reactions to the CC concept.

Stage 3: Product Development

After a presentation to senior management in late January, the core committee moved forward to begin converting the CC concept into a reality. Robert Nelson and his staff in the testing lab worked closely with members of the core committee to develop 10 fragrances for pairing with 10 chosen pieces of Kimble artwork. Representatives from manufacturing, along with Jane Tate, began to plan production runs for the chosen fragrance/candle products. Gail Flood and her staff finalized the licensing arrangement details with Warren Kimble. A prototype candle was developed by mid-February 2000.

Stage 4: Product/Market Testing

Product testing activity included a limited production run so that candle prototypes could be tested in a lab setting for quality control variables such as burn time, fragrance dispersion, and fragrance quality. Quality control testing was completed by mid-March 2000.

Next, a limited production run was manufactured for shipment to the Deerfield store, plus 10 New England area retail stores in a limited market test. The product was available in test market stores on April 1, 2000. Product sales were monitored, and the retail managers were contacted often to report on consumer reaction to the CC products. Consumer response was extremely favorable; the limited inventory was sold within four weeks of delivery to the stores, exceeding the expectations of the core committee.

Stage 5: Business Analysis

The development process for CC was not as sequential. The business analysis activity was conducted at about the same time as the product prototype development (Stage 3). New team members from the operations side of YCC entered to conduct a feasibility analysis for CC. Jennifer Flynn, Business Analyst Leader, worked with the core committee to complete the financial projections for CC. Financial projections were based on demand for Warren Kimble merchandise, current market information from syndicated research reports, and past YCC sales history data.

Stage 6: Commercialization

The limited test market was judged successful based on the level of sales achieved compared with expectations. "The CC situation is like all our new product decisions. We go to test market with a target sales goal in mind. If a new product meets the goal and we feel good about it, we go with it; if it doesn't meet the target, we probably won't go forward," said the YCC VP of marketing, John Cummo. YCC introduced CC to its wholesalers and made the initial line of 10 fragrances available in its retail stores on June 23, 2000.

As the CC line was taken to commercial rollout in June 2000, an unusual thing happened. One member of the core committee saw a decorative, three-dimensional, resin-based lid for a glass jar at a giftware trade show. A vendor was quickly secured, the licensing with Warren Kimble was put into place, and coordinating Jar Toppers were offered in the retail stores shortly after the June 23 rollout. Although this part of the product line was an afterthought, the flexibility demonstrated by the YCC core committee and other members of the firm made it possible to get this complementary item into the market quickly.

Sales of the CC line represented another success for YCC, according to its 2000 Annual Report. As with other YCC lines, CC is constantly being scrutinized and updated. Two new fragrances, Sage and Citrus and Fruit Basket, were introduced along with matching jar toppers in March 2001.

NEW PRODUCT STRATEGY AND TRENDS: WHAT'S ON THE HORIZON FOR YANKEE CANDLE?

Craig Rydin, CEO, summarized YCC's market situation at present: "The combination of our brand strength, breadth of product offering, and new product development and merchandising initiatives have enabled us to continue to generate very strong growth and market share gains." But it is clear that YCC is not resting on its laurels. First quarter results for fiscal 2005 show sales up 12 percent and earnings per share up 10 percent.

So where does YCC go from here? New product development continues at a fast pace for the company. Fragrances recently added to the line include Balsam and Cedar, Peppermint Cocoa, Hot Buttered Rum, Jack Frost, and Snow Angels for the winter season. Room perfume was introduced with spring scents including Ginger and Green Tea, Rain Washed, and Sweet Pea. These perfumes match the candle scents and are an ideal gift. During the fall season, Macintosh and Peach and Pineapple Citrus scents were added to the Housewarmer candle collection, as well as potpourri, room spray, and the Car Jars. For summer, Yankee Candle added Cocktail Candles that come in Apple Martini, Mandarin Mimosa, and Strawberry Daiquiri scents. These candles are 6 oz. in size and sell for $12.99.

DISCUSSION QUESTIONS

1. How was the new product development process for Country Classics cross-functional?

2. What are the strengths of YCC's approach to new product development?

3. What are some weaknesses of YCC's approach to new product development?

4. What other new products would you recommend for the company to introduce that would appeal to its target audience of women from 20 to 60 years of age that would be complementary to existing product lines and the Yankee Candle brand?

Source: This case was written by Elizabeth J. Wilson, Suffolk University. The author gratefully acknowledges the Sawyer School of Management, Suffolk University, and the Carroll School of Management, Boston College, for support in preparation of this case.

CASE 37 Interviewing for a Management Trainee Position

1. Assume the role of the college recruiter for a national retail chain that is reviewing resumes to select candidates to interview for a management trainee position. Which of the three resumes on the following pages do you think are effective? Ineffective? Why? Which would you select to interview? Why?

2. Update your resume and prepare for an interview for a manager training program with a large lumber and building supply retailer. This full-time position promises rapid advancement upon completion of the training period. A college degree and experience in retail, sales, and marketing are preferred. The base pay is between $28,000 and $34,000 per year plus a bonus of up to $7,000. This retailer promotes from within, and a new manager trainee can become a store manager within 2 to 3 years, with an earning potential of $100,000 or more. The benefits package is generous, including medical/hospitalization/dental/disability/life/insurance, 401k plan, profit sharing, awards and incentives, paid vacations, and holidays. Your resume should include your contact information, education and training, skills, experience and accomplishments, and honors and awards.

3. Roleplay a practice interview for this position. Pairs of students should read each other's resumes and then spend 20 to 30 minutes on each side of the interview. One student should be the human resource manager screening applicants, and the other person should be the candidate for the manager training program. Here are some questions to use in the role-playing scenario:

- Why are you applying for this position?
- What are your strengths and weaknesses for this position?
- Why should this organization consider you for this position?
- Why are you interested in working for this company?
- What are your career goals for the next five to ten years?
- Describe your skills when working in a team setting.
- What questions do you have about the company?

Source: This case was written by Cecelia Schulz, University of Florida.

Martin L. Cox

xxxx@ufl.edu, (xxx) 3xx-xxxx
123 Your Street, Apt. 301
Gainesville, Florida 32605

OBJECTIVE
Seeking a marketing internship utilizing leadership experience, strong work ethic, and interpersonal skills with a focus in product planning.

EDUCATION

Bachelor of Science in Business Administration	May 2006
University of Florida, Gainesville, Florida	GPA 3.69
Major in Marketing	

LEADERSHIP
Student Government

Theatre Nights Chair	Jan. 2005-Present
Emerging Leaders Conference Executive Assistant	Sept. 2004-Present
Student Integrity Court Justice	May 2004-Present
Banquet Cabinet Assistant Director	May 2004-Present
Innovate Party House Representative	Jan. 2004-April 2004
Homecoming Supper Staff	Oct. 2003, 2004 Pan-Hellenic Council
Assistant Director of Jr. Pan-Hellenic	Dec. 2003-Present
Jr. Pan-Hellenic Executive VP Int. Relations	Sept. 2003-Jan. 2004 Tri-Delta
Philanthropy	Triple Play
Intramural Soccer-Captain	Oct. 2003, 2004
Intramural Basketball-Captain	Sept. 2004-Present
Member since Aug. 2003	Jan. 2004-Present

HONORS

Savant UF Leadership Honorary	Oct. 2004-Present
Sandra Day O'Connor Pre-Law Society	Sept. 2004-Present
Alpha Lambda Delta Honor Society	Inducted March 2004
Phi Eta Sigma Honor Society	Inducted March 2004

COMMUNITY SERVICE

Mentor to Freshmen Students for SG Mentor/Mentee	Sept. 2004-Present
Basketball On Wheels Volunteer	Sept. 2004-Present
Dance Marathon Dancer	Jan. 2004-March 2004
After School Gators Volunteer	Jan. 2004-April 2004
Pillows for Patriots Service Project Volunteer	Sept. 2003-Dec. 2003

WORK EXPERIENCE

Senior Customer Service Associate, Video-R-Us, Tampa, FL	Jan. 2002-Aug. 2003
Secretarial Assistant, Law Firm, Mount Dora, FL	June-Aug. 2002

References available upon request.

Tina Acosta
123 Your Street #335
Gainesville, FL 32608
(727) xxx-xxxx
lxxx@ufl.edu

OBJECTIVE

To integrate my financial and business background with my creative and artistic skills in a fast-paced industry

EDUCATION

University of Florida
Warrington College of Business
Bachelor of Science in Finance
Minor in Spanish
Graduation: May 2006
GPA: 3.73

International Baccalaureate Program
St. Petersburg High School
Focus in Theatre, English, and History
Graduation 2002
GPA: 4.0

RELEVANT CLASSES

Retail Management, Study Abroad in Spain, Business Finance, Managerial Accounting, Problem Solving Using Computer Software, Debt and Money Markets

EXPERIENCE

Abercrombie and Fitch—Gainesville, FL   Brand Representative (October 2004-Present)
- Oversaw customer service on the sales floor
- Maintained and updated the sales floor design
- Handled purchases and returns at the register
- Prepared shipments and the floor for an internal audit
- Promoted the brand name for the women's fashion line

Olive Garden—St. Petersburg, FL   Server (April 2003-August 2003)
- Used a computerized food and beverage ordering system
- Maintained the management's expectations through customer service
- Interacted with customers
- Memorized an extensive menu and recommended foods satisfying customer's needs while maximizing the restaurant's profits

Sacino's Formalwear—St. Petersburg, FL   Sales Representative (August 2001-August 2002)
- Managed incoming and outgoing shipment responsibilities
- Organized financial paperwork
- Oversaw customer service on the sales floor
- Headed the formal wear department for young women

SKILLS

Proficient in Spanish
Office XP: Word-Document Formatting, Letters, Tables, Flyers, and Macros
        Excel-Spreadsheets, Formulas, and Graph Database Analysis, Functions, and Simples Macros
        PowerPoint-Professional Presentations

HONORS

Third place in the preliminary competition for the University of Florida's Center for
    Entrepreneurship and Innovation
Florida's Bright Futures Scholar
University of Florida Dean's List Student 2003

Richard Kates
xxxxxx@ufl.edu

123 Your Street. #164	123 8th Ave N
Gainesville, Florida 32608	Tampa, Florida 33713
(352) xxx-xxxx	(813) xxx-xxxx

Objective	Seeking an internship for the summer of 2006 utilizing marketing, management, and organizational abilities, as well as interpersonal skills.
Education	**Marketing Major** May 2006 University of Florida Gainesville, Florida Minor in Mass Communications and Minor in Entrepreneurship GPA 3.7
Experience	**Entrepreneur/CEO,** Long River PC, LLC August 2002 to Tampa, FL Present -Helped create and manage a new software company based in South Florida. -Helped develop revolutionary program that will aid the visually impaired. Researched and developed multiple original non-disclosure as well as non-compete agreements. -Responsible for hiring, funding, managing, and controlling progress of almost a dozen private software engineers. Reported to and allocated funds of angel investors. **Server,** Carraba's April 2004 to Gainesville, Florida Present -Help train new employees through shadowing and demonstration. -Serve over 70 guests per day, and ensure customer satisfaction and attentiveness. -Multiple top sales, as well as winner of "Perfect Check" contest. **Usher/Security/Technician,** Ben Hill Griffin Stadium August 2002 to Gainesville, Florida August 2004 **Pool/Health Club Attendant,** Don Cesar Resort May 2001 to St. Petersburg, Florida August 2003
Leadership	**Executive Board Member, Varsity Tennis Team. Social Chair** University of Florida August 2003 to Present Organized, planned, and financed all Tennis Team social events. In charge of planning large events, gatherings at home and away meets, coordinating the activities of over 60 members. **Executive Board Member, Fisher School of Accounting** University of Florida January 2004 to May 2004 Aided in revision and draft of new official Fisher School of Accounting Council's by-laws. Drafted a new 5 year program for the expansion and direction of the new Fisher School including member growth, activities, graduate prerequisites, and facility uses. **CHAMPS Mentoring Volunteer Program** Gainesville Florida January 2004 to Present Met with an "at risk" elementary school student 2 hours per week each semester to spend quality time encouraging the child's healthy growth and development.
Affiliations	**Phi Eta Sigma Honor Society,** Member active 2002 to present **Florida Tennis Team,** Fall 2002 to Spring 2004. Varsity Fall 2003 to Spring 2004 **Team Florida Cycling,** Spring 2004 to present **Student Alumni Association Member,** Fall 2003 to present **American Marketing Association,** Member Fall 2004 **International Business Society,** Fall 2004 **Business Administration College Council,** Fall 2004 Member-at-Large **The Entrepreneurs Club,** Fall 2004
Skills	Computer-Fluent in Microsoft Word, Excel, PowerPoint, Explorer, and Media Player, Fluent-Spanish
References	Available upon request.

GLOSSARY

ABC analysis An analysis that rank orders SKUs by a profitability measure to determine which items should never be out of stock, which should be allowed to be out of stock occasionally, and which should be deleted from the stock selection.

accessibility (1) The degree to which customers can easily get into and out of a shopping center; (2) ability of the retailer to deliver the appropriate retail mix to customers in the segment.

accessories Merchandise in apparel, department, and specialty stores used to complement apparel outfits. Examples include gloves, hosiery, handbags, jewelry, handkerchiefs, and scarves.

accordion theory A cyclical theory of retailer evolution suggesting that changes in retail institutions are explained in terms of depth versus breadth of assortment. Retail institutions cycle from high-depth/low-breadth to low-depth/ high-breadth stores and back again.

account opener A premium or special promotion item offered to induce the opening of a new account, especially in financial institutions and stores operating on an installment credit basis.

accounts payable The amount of money owed to vendors, primarily for merchandise inventory.

accounts receivable The amount of money due to the retailer from selling merchandise on credit.

actionability Criteria for evaluating a market segment scheme indicating what the retailer should do to satisfy its needs.

activity-based costing (ABC) A financial management tool in which all major activities within a cost center are identified, calculated, and then charged to cost objects, such as stores, product categories, product lines, specific products, customers, and suppliers.

adaptive selling An approach to personal selling in which selling behaviors are altered on the basis of information about the customer and the buying situation.

additional markup An increase in retail price after and in addition to an original markup.

additional markup cancellation The percentage by which the retail price is lowered after a markup is taken.

additional markup percentage The addition of a further markup to the original markup as a percentage of net sales.

add-on selling Selling additional new products and services to existing customers, such as a bank encouraging a customer with a checking account to apply for a home improvement loan from the bank.

administered vertical marketing system A form of vertical marketing system designed to control a line or classification of merchandise as opposed to an entire store's operation. Such systems involve the development of comprehensive programs for specified lines of merchandise. Vertically aligned companies—manufacturers or wholesalers—even though in non-ownership positions, may work together to reduce the total systems cost of such activities as advertising, transportation, and data processing. See also *contractual vertical marketing system* and *corporate vertical marketing system.*

advanced shipping notice (ASN) An electronic document received by the retailer's computer from a supplier in advance of a shipment.

advertising Paid communications delivered to customers through nonpersonal mass media such as newspapers, television, radio, direct mail, and the Internet.

advertising manager A retail manager who manages advertising activities such as determining the advertising budget, allocating the budget, developing ads, selecting media, and monitoring advertising effectiveness.

advertising reach The percentage of customers in the target market exposed to an ad at least once.

affinity marketing Marketing activities that enable consumers to express their identification with an organization. An example is offering credit cards tied to reference groups like the consumer's university or an NFL team.

affordable budgeting method A budgeting method in which a retailer first sets a budget for every element of the retail mix except promotion and then allocates the leftover funds to a promotional budget.

Age Discrimination and Employment Act A federal act that makes it illegal to discriminate in hiring and termination decisions concerning people between the ages of 40 and 70 years.

agent (1) A business unit that negotiates purchases, sales, or both but does not take title to the goods in which it deals; (2) a person who represents the principal (who, in the case of retailing, is the store or merchant) and acts under authority, whether in buying or in bringing the principal into business relations with third parties.

aging The length of time merchandise has been in stock.

aided recall When consumers indicate they know the brand when the name is presented to them.

à la carte plans An employee reward program giving employees a choice of rewards and thus tailoring the rewards to the desires of individual employees.

allocator Position in merchandise management responsible for allocating merchandise and tailoring the assortment in several categories for specific stores in a geographic area.

alteration costs Expenses incurred to change the appearance or fit, to assemble, or to repair merchandise.

alternative dispute resolution A provision included in a contract between retailer and vendor to help avoid litigation in the case of a dispute. Can include methods of settling the dispute that the parties agree on, such as mediation, arbitration, or med-arb.

Americans with Disabilities Act (ADA) A federal civil rights law that protects people with disabilities from discrimination in employment, transportation, public accommodations, telecommunications, and the activities of state and local government.

analog approach A method of trade area analysis also known as the *similar store* or *mapping* approach. The analysis is divided into four steps: (1) describing the current trade areas through the technique of customer spotting; (2) plotting the customers on a map; (3) defining the primary, secondary, and tertiary area zones; and (4) matching the characteristics of stores in the trade areas with the potential new store to estimate its sales potential.

anchor store A large, well-known retail operation located in a shopping center or Internet mall and serving as an attracting force for consumers to the center.

ancillary services Services such as layaway, gift wrap, and credit that are not directly related to the actual sale of a specific product within the store.

anticipation discount A discount offered by a vendor to a retailer in addition to the cash discount or dating, if the retailer pays the invoice before the end of the cash discount period.

anticompetitive leasing arrangement A lease that limits the type and amount of competition a particular retailer faces within a trading area.

antitrust legislation A set of laws directed at preventing unreasonable restraint of trade or unfair trade practices. Aim is to foster a competitive environment. See also *restraint of trade*.

application form A form used to collect information on a job applicant's education, employment experience, hobbies, and references.

arbitration Used in the case of a dispute between retailer and vendor that involves the appointment of an neutral party—the arbitrator—who considers the arguments of both sides and then makes a decision that is usually agreed on in advance as binding.

artificial barriers In site evaluations for accessibility, barriers such as railroad tracks, major highways, or parks.

asset management path One of the two paths in the strategic profit model affecting a retailer's return on assets.

assets Economic resources, such as inventory or store fixtures, owned or controlled by an enterprise as a result of past transactions or events.

asset turnover Net sales divided by total assets.

assortment The number of SKUs within a merchandise category. Also called *depth of merchandise*.

assortment plan A list of merchandise that indicates in very general terms what should be carried in a particular merchandise category.

atmospherics The design of an environment through visual communications, lighting, colors, music, and scent to stimulate customers' perceptual and emotional responses and ultimately to affect their purchase behavior.

auction A market in which goods are sold to the highest bidder; usually well publicized in advance or held at specific times that are well known in the trade. Auctions are becoming very popular over the Internet.

autocratic leader A manager who makes all decisions on his or her own and then announces them to employees.

automatic reordering system A system for ordering staple merchandise in which an automatic reorder is generated by a computer on the basis of a perpetual inventory system and reorder point calculations.

average BOM stock-to-sales ratio The number of months in the period divided by planned inventory turnover for the period.

average inventory The sum of inventory on hand at several periods in time divided by the number of periods.

Baby Boomer The generational cohort of people born between 1946 and 1964.

back order A part of an order that the vendor has not filled completely and that the vendor intends to ship as soon as the goods in question are available.

backup stock The inventory used to guard against going out of stock when demand exceeds forecasts or merchandise is delayed. Also called *safety stock* or *buffer stock*.

backward integration A form of vertical integration in which a retailer owns some or all of its suppliers.

bait-and-switch An unlawful deceptive practice that lures customers into a store by advertising a product at lower than usual prices (the bait), then inducing the customers to switch to a higher-price model (the switch).

balance sheet The summary of a retailer's financial resources and claims against the resources at a particular date; indicates the relationship between assets, liabilities, and owners' equity.

bank card Credit card issued by a bank, such as Visa and MasterCard.

bar code See *Universal Product Code (UPC)*.

bargain branding A branding strategy that targets a price-sensitive segment by offering a no-frills product at a discount price.

bargaining power of vendors A characteristic of a market in which retailers are so dependent on large, important vendors that their profits are adversely affected.

barriers to entry Conditions in a retail market that make it difficult for firms to enter the market.

base stock See *cycle stock*.

basic merchandise See *staple merchandise*.

basic stock list The descriptive and record-keeping function of an inventory control system; includes the stock number, item description, number of units on hand and on order, and sales for the previous periods.

basic stock method An inventory management method used to determine the beginning-of-month (BOM) inventory by considering both the forecast sales for the month and the safety stock.

benchmarking The practice of evaluating performance by comparing one retailer's performance with that of other retailers using a similar retail strategy.

benefits The customer's specific needs that are satisfied when the customer buys a product.

benefit segmentation A method of segmenting a retail market on the basis of similar benefits sought in merchandise or services.

black market The availability of merchandise at a high price when it is difficult or impossible to purchase under normal market circumstances; commonly involves illegal transactions.

block group A collection of adjacent census blocks that contain between 300 and 3,000 people that is the smallest unit for the sample data.

blog A public Web site where users post informal journals of their thoughts, comments, and philosophies.

blue laws Laws prohibiting retailers from being open two consecutive days of the weekend—ostensibly to allow employees a day of rest or religious observance. Most states no longer have blue laws.

bonus Additional compensation awarded periodically, based on a subjective evaluation of the employee's performance.

book inventory system See *retail inventory method.*

bottom-up planning When goals are set at the bottom of the organization and filter up through the operating levels.

boutique (1) Departments in a store designed to resemble small, self-contained stores; (2) a relatively small specialty store.

boutique layout See *free-form layout.*

brand A distinguishing name or symbol (such as a logo, design, symbol, or trademark) that identifies the products or services offered by a seller and differentiates those products and services from the offerings of competitors.

brand association Anything linked to or connected with the brand name in a consumer's memory.

brand awareness The ability of a potential customer to recognize or recall that a particular brand name belongs to a retailer or product/service.

brand building The design and implementation of a retail communication program to create an image in the customer's mind of the retailer relative to its competitors. Also called *positioning.*

brand equity The value that brand image offers retailers.

brand image Set of associations consumers have about a brand that are usually organized around some meaningful themes.

brand loyalty Indicates customers like and consistently buy a specific brand in a product category. They are reluctant to switch to other brands if their favorite brand isn't available.

breadth of merchandise See *variety.*

break-even analysis A technique that evaluates the relationship between total revenue and total cost to determine profitability at various sales levels.

break-even point The quantity at which total revenue equals total cost and beyond which profit occurs.

breaking bulk A function performed by retailers or wholesalers in which they receive large quantities of merchandise and sell them in smaller quantities.

breaking sizes Running out of stock on particular sizes.

broker A middleman that serves as a go-between for the buyer or seller; assumes no title risks, does not usually have physical custody of products, and is not looked upon as a permanent representative of either the buyer or seller.

buffer stock Merchandise inventory used as a safety cushion for cycle stock so the retailer won't run out of stock if demand exceeds the sales forecast. Also called *safety stock.*

building codes Legal restrictions describing the size and type of building, signs, type of parking lot, and so on that can be used at a particular location.

bulk fixture See *rounder.*

bullwhip effect. The buildup of inventory in an uncoordinated channel.

buyback A strategy vendors and retailers use to get products into retail stores, either when a retailer allows a vendor to create space for goods by "buying back" a competitor's inventory and removing it from a retailer's system or when the retailer forces a vendor to buy back slow-moving merchandise.

buyer Person in a retailing organization responsible for the purchase and profitability of a merchandise category. Similar to *category manager.*

buyer's market Market occurring in economic conditions that favor the position of the retail buyer (or merchandiser) rather than the vendor; in other words, economic conditions are such that the retailer can demand and usually get concessions from suppliers in terms of price, delivery, and other market advantages. Opposite of a *seller's market.*

buyer's report Information on the velocity of sales, availability of inventory, amount of order, inventory turnover, forecast sales, and, most important, the quantity that should be ordered for each SKU.

buying behavior The activities customers undertake when purchasing a good or service.

buying calendar A plan of a store buyer's market activities, generally covering a six-month merchandising season based on a selling calendar that indicates planned promotional events.

buying committee A committee that has the authority for final judgment and decision making on such matters as adding or eliminating new products.

buying power The customer's financial resources available for making purchases.

buying process The stages customers go through to purchase merchandise or services.

buying situation segmentation A method of segmenting a retail market based on customer needs in a specific buying situation, such as a fill-in shopping trip versus a weekly shopping trip.

buzz Genuine, street-level excitement about a hot new product.

call system A system of equalizing sales among salespersons—for example, some stores rotate salespeople, giving each an equal opportunity to meet customers.

capacity fixture See *rounder.*

career path The set of positions to which management employees are promoted within a particular organization as their careers progress.

cash Money on hand.

cash discounts Reductions in the invoice cost that the vendor allows the retailer for paying the invoice prior to the end of the discount period.

cash wraps The places in a store where customers can purchase merchandise and have it "wrapped"—placed in a bag.

catalog retailer A nonstore retailer that communicates directly with customers using catalogs sent through the mail.

catalog retailing Nonstore retail format in which the retail offering is communicated to a customer through a catalog.

category An assortment of items (SKUs) the customer sees as reasonable substitutes for one another.

category captain A supplier that forms an alliance with a retailer to help gain consumer insight, satisfy consumer needs, and improve the performance and profit potential across the entire category.

category killer A discount retailer that offers a narrow but deep assortment of merchandise in a category and thus dominates the category from the customers' perspective. Also called a *category specialist*.

category life cycle A merchandise category's sales pattern over time.

category management The process of managing a retail business with the objective of maximizing the sales and profits of a category.

category manager See *buyer*.

category specialist See *category killer*.

caveat emptor Latin term for "let the buyer beware."

census block An area bounded on all sides by visible (roads, rivers, etc.) and/or invisible (county, state boundaries) features that is the smallest geographic entity for which census data are available.

census tracts Subdivisions of a Metropolitan Statistical Area (MSA), with an average population of 4,000.

central business district (CBD) The traditional downtown business area of a city or town.

centralization The degree to which authority for making retail decisions is delegated to corporate managers rather than to geographically dispersed regional, district, and store management.

centralized buying A situation in which a retailer makes all purchase decisions at one location, typically the firm's headquarters.

central market See *market*.

central place A center of retailing activity such as a town or city.

central place theory Christaller's theory of retail location suggesting that retailers tend to locate in a central place. As more retailers locate together, more customers are attracted to the central place. See also *central place*.

chain discount A number of different discounts taken sequentially from the suggested retail price.

chargeback A practice used by retailers in which they deduct money from the amount they owe a vendor.

chat room Location in an Internet site at which customers can engage in interactive, real-time, text-based discussions.

checking The process of going through goods upon receipt to make sure that they arrived undamaged and that the merchandise received matches the merchandise ordered.

checkout areas See *cash wraps*.

cherry picking Customers visiting a store and buying only merchandise sold at big discounts or buying only the best styles or colors.

classic A merchandise category that has both a high level and a long duration of acceptance.

classification A group of items or SKUs for the same type of merchandise, such as pants (as opposed to jackets or suits), supplied by different vendors.

classification dominance An assortment so broad that customers should be able to satisfy all of their consumption needs for a particular category by visiting one retailer.

classification merchandising Divisions of departments into related types of merchandise for reporting and control purposes.

Clayton Act (1914) An act passed as a response to the deficiencies of the Sherman Act; it specifically prohibits price discrimination, tying arrangements, and exclusive dealing contracts that have the effect of limiting free trade, and it provides for damages to parties injured as a result of violations of the act.

clearance sale An end-of-season sale to make room for new goods; also pushing the sale of slow-moving, shopworn, and demonstration model goods.

closeout (1) An offer at a reduced price to sell a group of slow-moving or incomplete stock; (2) an incomplete assortment, the remainder of a line of merchandise that is to be discontinued and so is offered at a low price to ensure immediate sale.

closeout retailer Off-price retailer that sells a broad but inconsistent assortment of general merchandise as well as apparel and soft home goods, obtained through retail liquidations and bankruptcy proceedings.

cocooning A term that describes a behavioral pattern of consumers who increasingly turn to the nice, safe, familiar environment of their homes to spend their limited leisure time.

COD (cash on delivery) Purchase terms in which payment for a product is collected at the time of delivery.

collaboration, planning, forecasting, and replenishment (CPFR) A collaborative inventory management system in which a retailer shares information with vendors. CPFR software uses data to construct a computer-generated replenishment forecast that is shared by the retailer and vendor before it's executed.

commercial bribery A vendor's offer of money or gifts to a retailer's employee for the purpose of influencing purchasing decisions.

commission Compensation based on a fixed formula, such as percentage of sales.

committee buying The situation whenever the buying decision is made by a group of people rather than by a single buyer. A multiunit operation is usually the type of firm that uses this procedure.

common stock The type of stock most frequently issued by corporations. Owners of common stock usually have voting rights in the retail corporation.

communication gap The difference between the actual service provided to customers and the service promised in the retailer's promotion program. This factor is one of the four factors identified by the Gaps model for improving service quality.

communication objectives Specific goals for a communication program related to the effects of the communication program on the customer's decision-making process.

community centers See *neighborhood centers*.

comparative price advertising A common retailing practice that compares the price of merchandise offered for sale with a higher "regular" price or a manufacturer's list price.

comparison shopping A market research method in which retailers shop at competitive stores, comparing the merchandise, pricing, visual display, and service to their own offering.

compatibility The degree to which the fashion is consistent with existing norms, values, and behaviors.

compensation Monetary payments including salary, commission, and bonuses; also, paid vacations, health and insurance benefits, and a retirement plan.

competition-oriented pricing A pricing method in which a retailer uses competitors' prices, rather than demand or cost considerations, as guides.

competitive parity method An approach for setting a promotion budget so that the retailer's share of promotion expenses is equal to its market share.

competitive rivalry The frequency and intensity of reactions to actions undertaken by competitors.

competitor analysis An examination of the strategic direction that competitors are likely to pursue and their ability to successfully implement their strategy.

composite segmentation A method of segmenting a retail market using multiple variables, including benefits sought, lifestyles, and demographics.

computerized checkout See *point-of-sale (POS) terminal.*

conditional sales agreement An agreement that passes title of goods to the consumer, conditional on full payment.

conditions of sale See *terms of sale.*

conflict of interest A situation in which a decision maker's personal interest influences or has the potential to influence his or her professional decision.

congestion The amount of crowding of either cars or people.

consideration set The set of alternatives the customer evaluates when making a merchandise selection.

consignment goods Items not paid for by the retailer until they are sold. The retailer can return unsold merchandise; however, the retailer does not take title until final sale is made.

consortium exchange A retail exchange that is owned by several firms within one industry.

consumer cooperative Customers own and operate this type of retail establishment. Customers have ownership shares and share in the store's profits through price reductions or dividends.

Consumer Goods Pricing Act (1975) The statute that repealed all resale price maintenance laws and made it possible for retailers to sell products below suggested retail prices.

consumerism The activities of government, business, and independent organizations designed to protect individuals from practices that infringe on their rights as consumers.

contest Promotional activity in which customers compete for rewards through games of chance. Contests can also be used to motivate retail employees.

contract distribution service company Firm that performs all of the distribution functions for retailers or vendors, including transportation to the contract company's distribution center, merchandise processing, storage, and transportation to retailers.

contractual vertical marketing system A form of vertical marketing system in which independent firms at different levels in the channel operate contractually to obtain the economies and market impacts that could not be obtained by unilateral action. Under this system, the identity of the individual firm and its autonomy of operations remain intact. See also *administered vertical marketing system* and *corporate vertical marketing system.*

contribution margin Gross margin less any expense that can be directly assigned to the merchandise.

convenience center A shopping center that typically includes such stores as a convenience market, a dry cleaner, or a liquor store.

convenience goods Products that the consumer is not willing to spend the effort to evaluate prior to purchase, such as milk or bread.

convenience store A store that provides a limited variety and assortment of merchandise at a convenient location in a 2,000- to 3,000-square-foot store with speedy checkout.

conventional supermarket A self-service food store that offers groceries, meat, and produce with limited sales of nonfood items, such as health and beauty aids and general merchandise.

conversion rates Percentage of consumers who buy the product after viewing it.

cookies Computer text files that identify visitors when they return to a Web site.

coop advertising Enables a retailer to associate its name with well-known national brands and use attractive art work created by the national brand. Also a method a retailer uses to share the cost of advertising with a vendor.

cooperative (co-op) advertising A program undertaken by a vendor in which the vendor agrees to pay all or part of a promotion for its products.

cooperative buying When a group of independent retailers work together to make large purchases from a single supplier.

copy The text in an advertisement.

copycat branding A branding strategy that imitates the manufacturer brand in appearance and trade dress but generally is perceived as lower quality and is offered at a lower price.

copyright A regulation that protects original works of authors, painters, sculptors, musicians, and others who produce works of artistic or intellectual merit.

core assortment A relatively large proportion of the total assortment that is carried by each store in the chain, regardless of size.

corporate vertical marketing system A form of vertical marketing system in which all of the functions from production to distribution are at least partially owned and controlled by a single enterprise. Corporate systems typically operate manufacturing plants, warehouse facilities, and retail outlets. See also *administered vertical marketing system* and *contractual vertical marketing system.*

corporation A firm that is formally incorporated under state law and is a different legal entity from stockholders and employees.

cost code The item cost information indicated on price tickets in code. A common method of coding is the use of letters from an easily remembered word or expression with nonrepeating letters corresponding to numerals. For example, y o u n g b l a d e 1 2 3 4 5 6 7 8 9 0.

cost complement Used in the cost method of accounting, the percentage of net sales represented by the cost of goods sold.

cost method of accounting A method in which retailers record the cost of every item on an accounting sheet or include a cost code on the price tag or merchandise container. When a physical inventory is conducted, the cost of each item must be determined, the quantity in stock is counted, and the total inventory value at cost is calculated. See *retail inventory method.*

cost multiplier Used in the cost method of accounting, the cumulative markup multiplied by 100 percent minus cumulative markup percentage.

cost-oriented method A method for determining the retail price by adding a fixed percentage to the cost of the merchandise; also known as *cost-plus pricing.*

cost per thousand (CPM) A measure that is often used to compare media. CPM is calculated by dividing an ad's cost by its reach.

counterfeit merchandise Goods that are made and sold without permission of the owner of a trademark, a copyright, or a patented invention that is legally protected in the country where it is marketed.

coupons Documents that entitle the holder to a reduced price or X cents off the actual price of a product or service.

courtesy days The days on which stores extend to loyalty club customers the privilege of making purchases at sale prices in advance of public sale.

coverage The theoretical number of potential customers in the retailer's target market that could be exposed to an ad in a given medium.

credit Money placed at a consumer's disposal by a retailer, financial or other institution. For purchases made on credit, payment is due in the future.

credit limit The quantitative limit that indicates the maximum amount of credit that may be allowed to be outstanding on each individual customer account.

cross-docking distribution area An area in a distribution center in which merchandise is delivered to one side of the facility by vendors, is unloaded, and is immediately reloaded onto trucks that deliver merchandise to the stores. With cross-docking, merchandise spends very little time in the warehouse.

cross-selling When sales associates in one department attempt to sell complementary merchandise from other departments to their customers.

cross-shopping A pattern of buying both premium and low-priced merchandise or patronizing expensive, status-oriented retailers and price-oriented retailers.

culture The meaning and values shared by most members of a society.

cumulative attraction The principle that a cluster of similar and complementary retailing activities will generally have greater drawing power than isolated stores that engage in the same retailing activities.

cumulative markup Used in the cost method of accounting, the average percentage markup for the period; the total retail price minus cost divided by retail price.

cumulative quantity discounts Discounts earned by retailers when purchasing certain quantities over a specified period of time.

cumulative reach The cumulative number of potential customers that would see an ad that runs several times.

current assets Cash or any assets that can normally be converted into cash within one year.

current liabilities Debts that are expected to be paid in less than one year.

customer allowance An additional price reduction given to the customer.

customer buying process The stages a customer goes through in purchasing a good or service. Stages include need recognition, information search, evaluation and choice of alternatives, purchase, and postpurchase evaluation.

customer database See *data warehouse.*

customer delight A high level of customer satisfaction created by retailers providing greatly unexpected services.

customer loyalty Customers' commitment to shopping at a store.

customer relationship management (CRM) A business philosophy and set of strategies, programs, and systems that focuses on identifying and building loyalty with a retailer's most valued customers.

customer returns The value of merchandise that customers return because it is damaged, doesn't fit, and so forth.

customer service The set of retail activities that increase the value customers receive when they shop and purchase merchandise.

customer service department The department in a retail organization that handles customer inquiries and complaints.

customer spotting A technique used in trade area analysis that "spots" (locates) residences of customers for a store or shopping center.

customization approach An approach used by retailers to provide customer service that is tailored to meet each customer's personal needs.

cycle stock The inventory that goes up and down due to the replenishment process. Also known as *base stock.*

cyclical theories Theories of institutional change based on the premise that retail institutions change on the basis of cycles. See also *wheel of retailing* and *accordion theory.*

database retailing The development and implementation of retailing programs to build store loyalty utilizing a computerized file (data warehouse) of customer profiles and purchase patterns.

data mining Technique used to identify patterns in data found in data warehouses, typically patterns that the analyst is unaware of prior to searching through the data.

data warehouse The coordinated and periodic copying of data from various sources, both inside and outside the enterprise, into an environment ready for analytical and informational processing. It contains all of the data the firm has collected about its customers and is the foundation for subsequent CRM activities.

dating A series of options that tells retailers when discounts can be taken from vendors and when the full invoice amount is due.

deal period A limited time period allowed by manufacturers for retailers to purchase merchandise at a special price.

debit card A card that resembles a credit card but allows the retailer to automatically subtract payments from a customer's checking account at the time of sale.

decentralization When authority for retail decisions is made at lower levels in the organization.

deceptive advertising Any advertisement that contains a false statement or misrepresents a product or service.

decile analysis A method of identifying customers in a CRM program that breaks customers into ten deciles based on their LTV (lifetime value). When using decile analysis, the top 10 percent of the customers would be the most valued group.

deferred billing An arrangement that enables customers to buy merchandise and not pay for it for several months, with no interest charge.

delivery gap The difference between the retailer's service standards and the actual service provided to customers. This factor is one of the four factors identified by the Gaps model for improving service quality.

demalling The activity of revitalizing a mall by demolishing a mall's small shops, scrapping its common space and food courts, enlarging the sites once occupied by department stores, and adding more entrances into the parking lot.

demand/destination area Department or area in a store in which demand for the products or services offered is created before customers get to their destination.

demand/destination merchandise Products that customers have decided to buy before entering the store.

demand-oriented method A method of setting prices based on what the customers would expect or be willing to pay.

democratic leader A store manager who seeks information and opinions from employees and bases decisions on this information.

demographics Vital statistics about populations such as age, sex, and income.

demographic segmentation A method of segmenting a retail market that groups consumers on the basis of easily measured, objective characteristics such as age, gender, income, and education.

department A segment of a store with merchandise that represents a group of classifications the consumer views as being complementary.

departmentalization An organizational design in which employees are grouped into departments that perform specific activities to achieve operating efficiencies through specialization.

department store A retailer that carries a wide variety and deep assortment, offers considerable customer services, and is organized into separate departments for displaying merchandise.

depth interview An unstructured personal interview in which the interviewer uses extensive probing to get individual respondents to talk in detail about a subject.

depth of merchandise See *assortment*.

deseasonalized demand The forecast demand without the influence of seasonality.

destination store A retail store in which the merchandise, selection, presentation, pricing, or other unique feature acts as a magnet for customers.

dialectic theory An evolutionary theory based on the premise that retail institutions evolve. The theory suggests that new retail formats emerge by adopting characteristics from other forms of retailers in much the same way that a child is the product of the pooled genes of two very different parents.

digital signage Signs whose visual content is delivered digitally through a centrally managed and controlled network and displayed on a television monitor or flat panel screen.

direct investment The investment and ownership by a retail firm of a division or subsidiary that builds and operates stores in a foreign country.

direct-mail catalog retailer A retailer offering merchandise or services through catalogs mailed directly to customers.

direct-mail retailer A nonstore retailer that communicates directly with customers using mail brochures and pamphlets to sell a specific product or service to customers at one point in time.

direct marketing A form of nonstore retailing in which customers are exposed to merchandise through print or electronic media and then purchase the merchandise by telephone, mail, or over the Internet.

direct product profitability (DPP) The profit associated with each category or unit of merchandise. DPP is equal to the per-unit gross margin less all variable costs associated with the merchandise such as procurement, distribution, sales, and the cost of carrying the assets.

direct-response advertising Advertisements on TV and radio that describe products and provide an opportunity for customers to order them.

direct retailing See *nonstore retailing*.

direct selling A retail format in which a salesperson, frequently an independent distributor, contacts a customer directly in a convenient location (either at a customer's home or at work), demonstrates merchandise benefits, takes an order, and delivers the merchandise to the customer.

disability Any physical or mental impairment that substantially limits one or more of an individual's major life activities or any condition that is regarded as being such an impairment.

disclosure of confidential information An unethical situation in which a retail employee discloses proprietary or confidential information about the firm's business to anyone outside the firm.

discount A reduction in the original retail price granted to store employees as a special benefit or to customers under certain circumstances.

discount-oriented center See *promotional center*.

discount store A general merchandise retailer that offers a wide variety of merchandise, limited service, and low prices.

discrimination An illegal action of a company or its managers when a member of a protected class (women, minorities, etc.) is treated differently from nonmembers of that class (see *disparate treatment*) or when an apparently neutral rule has an unjustified discriminatory effect (see *disparate impact*).

disintermediation When a manufacturer sells directly to consumers, thus competing directly with its retailers.

disparate impact The case of discrimination when an apparently neutral rule has an unjustified discriminatory effect, such as if a retailer requires high school graduation for all its employees, thereby excluding a larger proportion of disdvantaged minorities, when at least some of the jobs (e.g., custodian) could be performed just as well by people who did not graduate from high school.

disparate treatment The case of discrimination when members of a protected class are treated differently from nonmembers of that class—if a qualified woman (protected class), for example, does not receive a promotion given to a lesser qualified man.

dispatcher A person who coordinates deliveries from the vendor to the distribution center or stores or from the distribution center to stores.

display stock Merchandise placed on various display fixtures for customers to examine.

distribution See *logistics*.

distribution center A warehouse that receives merchandise from multiple vendors and distributes it to multiple stores.

distribution channel A set of firms that facilitate the movement of products from the point of production to the point of sale to the ultimate consumer.

distribution intensity The number of retailers carrying a particular category.

distributive fairness A customer's perception of the benefits received compared to their costs (inconvenience or loss) when resolving a complaint.

distributive justice Arises when outcomes received are viewed as fair with respect to outcomes received by others.

diversification opportunity A strategic investment opportunity that involves an entirely new retail format directed toward a market segment not presently being served.

diversionary pricing A practice sometimes used by retailers in which low price is stated for one or a few goods or services (emphasized in promotion) to give the illusion that the retailer's prices are all low.

diverted merchandise Merchandise that is diverted from its legitimate channel of distribution; similar to *gray-market merchandise* except there need not be distribution across international boundaries.

diverter A firm that buys diverted merchandise from retailers and manufacturers and then resells the merchandise to other retailers. See *diverted merchandise*.

double coupon A retail promotion that allows the customer to double the face value of a coupon.

drawing account A method of sales compensation in which salespeople receive a weekly check based on their estimated annual income.

drugstore Specialty retail store that concentrates on pharmaceuticals and health and personal grooming merchandise.

duty See *tariff*.

economic order quantity (EOQ) The order quantity that minimizes the total cost of processing orders and holding inventory.

efficient customer response (ECR) The set of programs supermarket chains have undertaken to manage inventory and increase inventory turnover.

80–20 rule A general management principle where 80 percent of the sales or profits come from 20 percent of the customers.

electronic agent Computer program that locates and selects alternatives based on some predetermined characteristics.

electronic article surveillance system (EAS) A loss prevention system in which special tags placed on merchandise in retail stores are deactivated when the merchandise is purchased. The tags are used to discourage shoplifting.

electronic data interchange (EDI) The computer-to-computer exchange of business documents from retailer to vendor and back.

electronic retailing A retail format in which the retailers communicate with customers and offer products and services for sale over the Internet.

e-mail A paid personal communication vehicle that involves sending messages over the Internet.

emotional support Supporting retail service providers with the understanding and positive regard to enable them to deal with the emotional stress created by disgruntled customers.

employee discount A discount from retail price offered by most retailers to employees.

employee productivity Output generated by employee activities. One measure of employee productivity is the retailer's sales or profit divided by its employee costs.

employee turnover The number of employees occupying a set of positions during a period (usually a year) divided by the number of positions.

empowerment The process of managers sharing power and decision-making authority with employees.

empty nest A stage in a family life cycle where children have grown up and left home.

empty nester Household where all children are grown and have left home.

end cap Display fixture located at the end of an aisle.

end-of-month (EOM) dating A method of dating in which the discount period starts at the end of the month in which the invoice is dated (except when the invoice is dated the 25th or later).

energy management The coordination of heating, air conditioning, and lighting to improve efficiencies and reduce energy costs.

environmental apparel Merchandise produced with few or no harmful effects on the environment.

Equal Employment Opportunity Commission (EEOC) A federal commission that was established for the purpose of taking legal action against employers that violate Title VII of the Civil Rights Act. Title VII prohibits discrimination in company personnel practices.

Equal Pay Act A federal act enforced by the Equal Employment Opportunity Commission that prohibits unequal pay for men and women who perform equal work or work of comparable worth.

escape clause A clause in a lease that allows the retailer to terminate its lease if sales don't reach a certain level after a specified number of years or if a specific cotenant in the center terminates its lease.

e-tailing See *electronic retailing.*

ethics A system or code of conduct based on universal moral duties and obligations that indicate how one should behave.

evaluation of alternatives The stage in the buying process in which the customer compares the benefits offered by various retailers.

everyday low pricing (EDLP) A pricing strategy that stresses continuity of retail prices at a level somewhere between the regular nonsale price and the deep-discount sale price of the retailer's competitors.

evolutionary theories Theories of institutional change based on the premise that retail institutions evolve. See *dialectic theory* and *natural selection.*

exclusive dealing agreement Restriction a manufacturer or wholesaler places on a retailer to carry only its products and no competing vendors' products.

exclusive geographical territory A policy in which only one retailer in a certain territory is allowed to sell a particular brand.

exclusive use clause A clause in a lease that prohibits the landlord from leasing to retailers selling competing products.

executive training program (ETP) A training program for retail supervisors, managers, and executives.

expenses Costs incurred in the normal course of doing business to generate revenues.

experiment A research method in which a variable is manipulated under controlled conditions.

expert system Computer program that incorporates knowledge of experts in a particular field. Expert systems are used to aid in decision making and problem solving.

exponential smoothing A sales forecasting technique in which sales in previous time periods are weighted to develop a forecast for future periods.

express warranty A guarantee supplied by either the retailer or the manufacturer that details the terms of the warranty in simple, easily understood language so customers know what is and what is not covered by the warranty.

extended problem solving A buying process in which customers spend considerable time at each stage of the decision-making process because the decision is important and they have limited knowledge of alternatives.

external sources of information Information provided by the media and other people.

extra dating A discount offered by a vendor in which the retailer receives extra time to pay the invoice and still take the cash discount.

extranet A collaborative network that uses Internet technology to link businesses with their suppliers, customers, or other businesses.

extreme value food retailers See *limited assortment supermarkets.*

extreme value retailers Small, full-line discount stores that offer a limited merchandise assortment at very low prices.

extrinsic reward Reward (such as money, promotion, or recognition) given to employees by their manager or the firm.

factoring A specialized financial function whereby manufacturers, wholesalers, or retailers sell accounts receivable to financial institutions, including factors or banks.

factory outlet Outlet store owned by a manufacturer.

fad A merchandise category that generates a lot of sales for a relatively short time—often less than a season.

Fair Labor Standards Act A federal law, enacted in 1938, that sets minimum wages, maximum hours, child labor standards, and overtime pay provisions.

fair trade laws See *resale price maintenance laws.*

fashion A type of product or a way of behaving that is temporarily adopted by a large member of consumers because the product, service, or behavior is considered to be socially appropriate for the time and place.

fashion merchandise Category of merchandise that typically lasts several seasons, and sales can vary dramatically from one season to the next.

fashion/specialty center A shopping center that is composed mainly of upscale apparel shops, boutiques, and gift shops carrying selected fashions or unique merchandise of high quality and price.

feature area Area designed to get the customer's attention that includes end caps, promotional aisles or areas, freestanding fixtures and mannequins that introduce a soft goods department, windows, and point-of-sale areas.

feature fixture See *four-way fixture.*

features The qualities or characteristics of a product that provide benefits to customers.

Federal Trade Commission Act (1914) The congressional act that created the Federal Trade Commission (FTC) and gave it the power to enforce federal trade laws.

fill rate The percentage of an order that is shipped by the vendor.

financial leverage A financial measure based on the relationship between the retailer's liabilities and owners' equity that indicates financial stability of the firm.

first-degree price discrimination Charging customers different prices on the basis of their willingness to pay.

fixed assets Assets that require more than a year to convert to cash.

fixed costs Costs that are stable and don't change with the quantity of product produced and sold.

fixed expenses Expenses that remain constant for a given period of time regardless of the sales volume.

fixed-rate lease A lease that requires the retailer to pay a fixed amount per month over the life of the lease.

fixtures The equipment used to display merchandise.

flattening the organization A reduction in the number of management levels.

flexible pricing A pricing strategy that allows consumers to bargain over selling prices.

flextime A job scheduling system that enables employees to choose the times they work.

floor-ready merchandise Merchandise received at the store ready to be sold, without the need for any additional preparation by retail employees.

FOB (free-on-board) destination A term of sale designating that the shipper owns the merchandise until it is delivered to the retailer and is therefore responsible for transportation and any damage claims.

FOB (free-on-board) origin A term of sale designating that the retailer takes ownership of the merchandise at the point of origin and is therefore responsible for transportation and any damage claims.

focus group A marketing research technique in which a small group of respondents is interviewed by a moderator using a loosely structured format.

forward buy An opportunity to purchase at an extra discount more merchandise than the retailer normally needs to fill demand.

forward integration A form of vertical integration in which a manufacturer owns wholesalers or retailers.

four-way fixture A fixture with two cross-bars that sit perpendicular to each other on a pedestal.

franchisee The owner of an individual store in a franchise agreement.

franchising A contractual agreement between a franchisor and a franchisee that allows the franchisee to operate a retail outlet using a name and format developed and supported by the franchisor.

franchisor The owner of a franchise in a franchise agreement.

free-form layout A store design, used primarily in small specialty stores or within the boutiques of large stores, that arranges fixtures and aisles asymmetrically. Also called *boutique layout*.

free riding A situation in which a retailer, such as a discount store, takes more than its fair share of the benefits derived by another retailer's promotional or service efforts but does not incur its fair share of the costs and is thus able to sell the merchandise at a lower price.

freestanding fixture Fixtures and mannequins located on aisles that are designed primarily to get customers' attention and bring them into a department.

freestanding insert (FSI) An ad printed at a retailer's expense and distributed as a freestanding insert in the newspaper. Also called a *preprint*.

freestanding site A retail location that is not connected to other retailers.

free trade zone A special area within a country that can be used for warehousing, packaging, inspection, labeling, exhibition, assembly, fabrication, or transshipment of imports without being subject to that country's tariffs.

freight collect When the retailer pays the freight.

freight forwarders Companies that purchase transport services. They then consolidate small shipments from a number of shippers into large shipments that move at a lower freight rate.

freight prepaid When the freight is paid by the vendor.

frequency The number of times a potential customer is exposed to an ad.

frequent shopper program A reward and communication program used by a retailer to encourage continued purchases from the retailer's best customers. See *loyalty program*.

fringe trade area See *tertiary zone*.

frontal presentation A method of displaying merchandise in which the retailer exposes as much of the product as possible to catch the customer's eye.

full-line discount store Retailers that offer a broad variety of merchandise, limited service, and low prices.

full-line forcing When a supplier requires a retailer to carry the supplier's full line of products if the retailer wants to carry any part of that line.

full warranty A guarantee provided by either the retailer or manufacturer to repair or replace merchandise without charge and within a reasonable amount of time in the event of a defect.

functional discount See *trade discount*.

functional needs The needs satisfied by a product or service that are directly related to its performance.

functional product grouping Categorizing and displaying merchandise by common end uses.

functional relationships A series of one-time market exchanges linked together over time.

future dating A method of dating that allows the buyer additional time to take advantage of the cash discount or to pay the net amount of the invoice.

Gaps model A conceptual model that indicates what retailers need to do to provide high-quality customer service. When customers' expectations are greater than their perceptions of the delivered service, customers are dissatisfied and feel the quality of the retailer's service is poor. Thus, retailers need to reduce the service gap—the difference between customers' expectations and perceptions of customer service to improve customers' satisfaction with their service.

general merchandise catalog retailers Nonstore retailers that offer a broad variety of merchandise in catalogs that are periodically mailed to their customers.

generational cohort People within the same generation who have similar purchase behaviors because they have shared experiences and are in the same stage of life.

Generation X The generational cohort of people born between 1965 and 1976.

Generation Y The generational cohort of people born between 1977 and 1995.

generic brand Unbranded, unadvertised merchandise found mainly in drug, grocery, and discount stores.

gentrification A process in which old buildings are torn down or restored to create new offices, housing developments, and retailers.

geodemographic segmentation A market segmentation system that uses both geographic and demographic characteristics to classify consumers.

geographic information system (GIS) A computerized system that enables analysts to visualize information about their customers' demographics, buying behavior, and other data in a map format.

geographic segmentation Segmentation of potential customers by where they live. A retail market can be segmented by countries, states, cities, and neighborhoods.

glass ceiling An invisible barrier that makes it difficult for minorities and women to be promoted beyond a certain level.

gondola An island type of self-service counter with tiers of shelves, bins, or pegs.

graduated lease A lease that requires rent to increase by a fixed amount over a specified period of time.

gray-market goods Merchandise that possesses a valid U.S. registered trademark and is made by a foreign manufacturer but is imported into the United States without permission of the U.S. trademark owner.

green marketing A strategic focus by retailers and their vendors to supply customers with environmentally friendly merchandise.

greeter A retail employee who greets customers as they enter a store and who provides information or assistance.

grid layout A store design, typically used by grocery stores, in which merchandise is displayed on long gondolas in aisles with a repetitive pattern.

gross margin The difference between the price the customer pays for merchandise and the cost of the merchandise (the price the retailer paid the supplier of the merchandise). More specifically, gross margin is net sales minus cost of goods sold.

gross margin return on investment (GMROI) Gross margin dollars divided by average (cost) inventory.

gross profit See *gross margin.*

gross sales The total dollar revenues received from the sales of merchandise and services.

group maintenance behaviors Activities store managers undertake to make sure that employees are satisfied and work well together.

habitual decision making A purchase decision involving little or no conscious effort.

hedonic needs Needs motivating consumers to go shopping for pleasure.

high-assay principle A resource allocation principle emphasizing allocating marketing expenditures on the basis of marginal return.

high/low pricing A strategy in which retailers offer prices that are sometimes above their competition's everyday low price, but they use advertising to promote frequent sales.

home improvement center A category specialist offering equipment and material used by do-it-yourselfers and construction contractors to make home improvements.

horizontal price fixing An agreement between retailers in direct competition with each other to charge the same prices.

house brand See *generic brand.*

Huff's gravity model A trade area analysis model used to determine the probability that a customer residing in a particular area will shop at a particular store or shopping center.

human resource management Management of a retailer's employees.

hype Artificially generated word of mouth, manufactured by public relations people.

hypermarket Large (100,000–300,000 square feet) combination food (60–70 percent) and general merchandise (30–40 percent) retailer.

idea-oriented presentation A method of presenting merchandise based on a specific idea or the image of the store.

identifiability A criteria for evaluating market segments in which retailers must be able to identify the customers in a target segment for the segmentation scheme to be effective. By identifying the segment, it allows retailers to determine (1) the segment's size and (2) with whom the retailer should communicate when promoting its retail offering.

illegal discrimination The actions of a company or its managers that result in number of a protected class being treated unfairly and differently than others.

impact An ad's effect on the audience.

implied warranty of merchantability A guarantee that accompanies all merchandise sold by a retailer, assuring customers that the merchandise is up to standards for the ordinary purposes for which such goods are used.

impulse buying A buying decision made by customers on the spot after seeing the merchandise.

impulse merchandise See *impulse products.*

impulse products Products that are purchased by customers without prior plans. These products are almost always located near the front of the store, where they're seen by everyone and may actually draw people into the store.

impulse purchase An unplanned purchase by a customer.

incentive compensation plan A compensation plan that rewards employees on the basis of their productivity.

income statement A summary of the financial performance of a firm for a certain period of time.

independent exchange A retail exchange owned by a third party that provides the electronic platform to perform the exchange functions.

infomercials TV programs, typically 30 minutes long, that mix entertainment with product demonstrations and solicit orders placed by telephone from consumers.

information search The stage in the buying process in which a customer seeks additional information to satisfy a need.

infringement Unauthorized use of a registered trademark.

ingress/egress The means of entering/exiting the parking lot of a retail site.

in-house credit system See *proprietary store credit card system.*

initial markup The retail selling price initially placed on the merchandise less the cost of goods sold.

inner city Typically a high-density urban area consisting of apartment buildings populated primarily by ethnic groups.

input measure A performance measure used to assess the amount of resources or money used by the retailer to achieve outputs.

installment credit plan A plan that enables consumers to pay their total purchase price (less down payment) in equal installment payments over a specified time period.

institutional advertisement An advertisement that emphasizes the retailer's name and positioning rather than specific merchandise or prices.

in-store kiosk Spaces located within stores containing a computer connected to the store's central offices or the Internet.

instrumental support Support for retail service providers such as appropriate systems and equipment to deliver the service desired by customers.

integrated marketing communication (IMC) program The strategic integration of multiple communication methods to form a comprehensive, consistent message.

intellectual property Property that is intangible and created by intellectual (mental) effort as opposed to physical effort.

intelligent agent A computer program that locates and selects alternatives based on some predetermined characteristics.

interactive electronic retailing A system in which a retailer transmits data and graphics over cable or telephone lines to a consumer's TV or computer terminal.

interest The amount charged by a financial institution to borrow money.

internal sources of information Information in a customer's memory such as names, images, and past experiences with different stores.

Internet A worldwide network of computers linked to facilitate communications among individuals, companies, and organizations.

Internet retailing See *electronic retailing*.

intertype competition Competition between retailers that sell similar merchandise using different formats, such as discount and department stores.

intranet A secure communication system that takes place within one company.

intratype competition Competition between the same type of retailers (e.g., Kroger versus Safeway).

intrinsic rewards Nonmonetary rewards employees get from doing their jobs.

inventory Goods or merchandise available for resale.

inventory management The process of acquiring and maintaining a proper assortment of merchandise while keeping ordering, shipping, handling, and other related costs in check.

inventory shrinkage See *shrinkage*.

inventory turnover Net sales divided by average retail inventory; used to evaluate how effectively managers utilize their investment in inventory.

invoice cost The actual amount due for the merchandise after both trade and quantity discounts are taken.

job analysis Identifying essential activities and determining the qualifications employees need to perform them effectively.

job application form A form a job applicant completes that contains information about the applicant's employment history, previous compensation, reasons for leaving previous employment, education and training, personal health, and references.

job description A description of the activities the employee needs to perform and the firm's performance expectations.

job enrichment The redesign of a job to include a greater range of tasks and responsibilities.

job sharing When two or more employees voluntarily are responsible for a job that was previously held by one person.

joint venture In the case of global expansion, an entity formed when the entering retailer pools its resources with a local retailer to form a new company in which ownership, control, and profits are shared. More generally, any business venture in which two or more firms pool resources to form a new business entity.

junk bond Bond that offers investors a higher-risk/higher-yield investment than conventional bonds.

key items The items that are in greatest demand. Also referred to as best sellers or "A" items (in the case of an ABC analysis).

keystone method A method of setting retail prices in which retailers simply double the cost of the merchandise to obtain the original retail selling price.

kickback See *commercial bribery*.

kiosk A small selling space offering a limited merchandise assortment.

knockoff A copy of the latest styles displayed at designer fashion shows and sold in exclusive specialty stores. These copies are sold at lower prices through retailers targeting a broader market.

knowledge gap The difference between customer expectations and the retailer's perception of customer expectations. This factor is one of four identified by the Gaps model for improving service quality.

labor scheduling The process of determining the number of employees assigned to each area of the store at each hour the store is open.

layaway A method of deferred payment in which merchandise is held by the store for the customer until it is completely paid for.

leader pricing A pricing strategy in which certain items are priced lower than normal to increase the traffic flow of customers or to increase the sale of complementary products.

leadership The process by which a person attempts to influence another to accomplish some goal or goals.

lead time The amount of time between recognition that an order needs to be placed and the point at which the merchandise arrives in the store and is ready for sale.

leased department An area in a retail store leased or rented to an independent company. The leaseholder is typically responsible for all retail mix decisions involved in operating the department and pays the store a percentage of its sales as rent.

lessee The party signing the lease.

lessor The party owning a property that is for rent.

less-than-carload (LCL) The transportation rate that applies to less-than-full carload shipments.

level of support See *service level*.

liabilities Obligations of a retail enterprise to pay cash or other economic resources in return for past, present, or future benefits.

licensed brand Brand for which the licensor (owner of a well-known name) enters a contractual arrangement with a licensee (a retailer or third party). The licensee either manufactures or contracts with a manufacturer to produce the licensed product and pays a royalty to the licensor.

lifestyle Refers to how people live, how they spend their time and money, what activities they pursue, and their attitudes and opinions about the world they live in.

lifestyle center A shopping center with an outdoor traditional streetscape layout with sit-down restaurants and a conglomeration of specialty retailers.

lifestyle segmentation A method of segmenting a retail market based on how consumers live, how they spend their time and money, what activities they pursue, and their attitudes and opinions about the world they live in.

lifetime customer value (LTV) The expected contribution from the customer to the retailer's profits over his or her entire relationship with the retailer.

lift-out See *buyback*.

limited assortment supermarkets A supermarket offering a limited number of SKUs.

limited problem solving A purchase decision process involving a moderate amount of effort and time. Customers engage in this type of buying process when they have some prior experience with the product or service and their risk is moderate.

limited warranty A type of guarantee in which any limitations must be stated conspicuously so that customers are not misled.

local links A way to help customers get around a Web site on the Internet by using links that are internal to the Web site.

logistics Part of the supply chain process that plans, implements, and controls the efficient, effective flow and storage of goods, services, and related information from the point of origin to the point of consumption to meet customers' requirements.

long-term liabilities Debts that will be paid after one year.

loop layout See *racetrack layout*.

loss leader An item priced near or below cost to attract customer traffic into the store.

low-price guarantee policy A policy that guarantees that the retailer will have the lowest possible price for a product or group of products and usually promises to match or better any lower price found in the local market.

loyalty program A program set up to reward customers with incentives such as discounts on purchases, free food, gifts, or even cruises or trips in return for their repeated business.

magalog Combination of magazine and catalog.

mail-order retailer See *direct-mail catalog retailer*.

Main Street The central business district located in the traditional shopping area of smaller towns, or a secondary business district in a suburb or within a larger city.

maintained markup The amount of markup the retailer wishes to maintain on a particular category of merchandise; net sales minus cost of goods sold.

maintenance-increase-recoupment lease A provision of a lease that can be used with either a percentage or straight lease. This type of lease allows the landlord to increase the rent if insurance, property taxes, or utility bills increase beyond a certain point.

mall A shopping center with a pedestrian focus where customers park in outlying areas and walk to the stores.

management by objectives A popular method for linking the goals of a firm to goals for each employee and providing information to employees about their role.

managing diversity A set of human resource management programs designed to realize the benefits of a diverse workforce.

manufacturer brand A line of products designed, produced, and marketed by a vendor. Also called a *national brand*.

manufacturer's agent An agent who generally operates on an extended contractual basis, often sells within an exclusive territory, handles noncompeting but related lines of goods, and possesses limited authority with regard to prices and terms of sale.

manufacturer's outlet store A discount retail store owned and operated by a manufacturer.

manufacturer's suggested retail price (MSRP) The lowest price specified by a manufacturer at which a retailer can sell the manufacturer's product.

maquiladoras Manufacturing plants in Mexico that make goods and parts or process food for export to the United States.

marginal analysis A method of analysis used in setting a promotional budget or allocating retail space, based on the economic principle that firms should increase expenditures as long as each additional dollar spent generates more than a dollar of additional contribution.

markdown The percentage reduction in the initial retail price.

markdown cancellation The percentage increase in the retail price after a markdown is taken.

markdown money Funds provided by a vendor to a retailer to cover decreased gross margin from markdowns and other merchandising issues.

market A group of vendors in a concentrated geographic location or even under one roof or over the Internet; also known as a *central market*.

market attractiveness/competitive position matrix A method for analyzing opportunities that explicitly considers the capabilities of the retailer and the attractiveness of retail markets.

market basket analysis Specific type of data analysis that focuses on the composition of the basket (or bundle) of products purchased by a household during a single shopping occasion.

market development See *market penetration opportunity*.

market expansion opportunity A strategic investment opportunity that employs the existing retailing format in new market segments.

marketing segmentation The process of dividing a retail market into homogeneous groups. See *retail market segment*.

market penetration opportunity An investment opportunity strategy that focuses on increasing sales to present customers using the present retailing format.

market research The systematic collection and analysis of information about a retail market.

market share A retailer's sales divided by the sales of all competitors within the same market.

market week See *trade show*.

markup The increase in the retail price of an item after the initial markup percentage has been applied but before the item is placed on the selling floor.

markup percentage The markup as a percent of retail price.

marquee A sign used to display a store's name or logo.

mass customization The production of individually customized products at costs similar to mass-produced products.

mass-market theory A theory of how fashion spreads that suggests that each social class has its own fashion leaders who play a key role in their own social networks. Fashion information trickles across social classes rather than down from the upper classes to the lower classes.

Mazur plan A method of retail organization in which all retail activities fall into four functional areas: merchandising, publicity, store management, and accounting and control.

med-arb Used in the case of a dispute between retailer and vendor that involves an initial attempt at mediation followed by binding arbitration if the mediation is unsuccessful. See *mediation* and *arbitration*.

media coverage The theoretical number of potential customers in a retailer's market who could be exposed to an ad.

mediation Used in the case of a dispute between retailer and vendor that involves selecting a neutral party—the mediator—to assist the parties in reaching a mutually agreeable settlement.

memorandum purchases Items not paid for by a retailer until they are sold. The retailer can return unsold merchandise; however, the retailer takes title on delivery and is responsible for damages. See *consignment goods*.

mentoring program The assigning of higher-level managers to help lower-level managers learn the firm's values and meet other senior executives.

merchandise budget plan A plan used by buyers to determine how much money to spend in each month on a particular fashion merchandise category, given the firm's sales forecast, inventory turnover, and profit goals.

merchandise category See *category*.

merchandise classification See *classification*.

merchandise group A group within an organization managed by the senior vice presidents of merchandise and responsible for several departments.

merchandise kiosks Small, temporary selling spaces typically located in the walkways of enclosed malls, airports, train stations, or office building lobbies.

merchandise management The process by which a retailer attempts to offer the right quantity of the right merchandise in the right place at the right time while meeting the company's financial goal.

merchandise show See *trade show*.

merchandising See *merchandise management*.

merchandising optimization software Set of algorithms (computer programs) that monitors merchandise sales, promotions, competitors' actions, and other factors to determine the optimal (most profitable) price and timing for merchandising activities, especially markdowns.

merchandising planner A retail employee responsible for allocating merchandise and tailoring the assortment in several categories for specific stores in a geographic area.

message board Location in an Internet site at which customers can post comments.

Metropolitan Statistical Area (MSA) A city with 50,000 or more inhabitants or an urbanized area of at least 50,000 inhabitants and a total MSA population of at least 100,000 (75,000 in New England).

metro renters One of ESRI's Community Tapestry segmentation scheme clusters. Young, well-educated singles beginning their professional careers in the largest cities, such as New York, Chicago, and Los Angeles.

micropolitan statistical area A city with only 10,000 inhabitants in its core urban area.

mission statement A broad description of the scope of activities a business plans to undertake.

mixed-use development (MXD) Development that combines several uses in one complex—for example, shopping center, office tower, hotel, residential complex, civic center, and convention center.

model stock list A list of fashion merchandise that indicates in very general terms (product lines, colors, and size distributions) what should be carried in a particular merchandise category; also known as a model stock plan.

monthly additions to stock The amount to be ordered for delivery in each month, given the firm's turnover and sales objectives.

months of supply The amount of inventory on hand at the beginning of the month expressed in terms of the time it will take to sell. A six-month supply means it will take six months for the merchandise to sell. A six-month supply is equivalent to an inventory turnover of two.

multiattribute attitude model A model of customer decision making based on the notion that customers see a retailer or a product as a collection of attributes or characteristics. The model can also be used for evaluating a retailer, product, or vendor. The model uses a weighted average score based on the importance of various issues and performance on those issues.

multichannel retailer Retailer that sells merchandise or services through more than one channel.

multilevel direct selling A form of direct selling in which people sell directly to customers, serve as master distributors, and recruit other people to become distributors in their network. The master distributors either buy merchandise from the firm and resell it to their distributors or receive a commission on all merchandise purchased by the distributors in their network.

multilevel network A retail format in which people serve as master distributors, recruiting other people to become distributors in their network.

multiple-unit pricing Practice of offering two or more similar products or services for sale at one price. Also known as *quantity discounts*.

mystery shopper Professional shopper who "shops" a store to assess the service provided by store employees.

national brand See *manufacturer brand*.

natural barrier A barrier, such as a river or mountain, that impacts accessibility to a site.

natural selection A theory of retail evolution that argues that those institutions best able to adapt to changes in customers, technology, competition, and legal environments have the greatest chance for success.

needs The basic psychological forces that motivate customers to act.

negligence A product liability suit that occurs if a retailer or a retail employee fails to exercise the care that a prudent person usually would.

negotiation An interaction between two or more parties to reach an agreement.

neighborhood center A shopping center that includes a supermarket, drugstore, home improvement center, or variety store. Neighborhood centers often include small stores, such as apparel, shoe, camera, and other shopping goods stores.

net invoice price The net value of the invoice or the total invoice minus all other discounts.

net lease A lease that requires all maintenance expenses such as heat, insurance, and interior repairs to be paid by the retailer.

net profit A measure of the overall performance of a firm; revenues (sales) minus expenses and losses for the period.

net profit margin Profit a firm makes divided by its net sales.

net sales The total number of dollars received by a retailer after all refunds have been paid to customers for returned merchandise.

network direct selling See *multilevel direct selling*.

net worth See *owners' equity*.

never-out list A list of key items or best sellers that are separately planned and controlled. These items account for large sales volume and are stocked in a manner so they are always available. These are "A" items in an ABC analysis.

noncumulative quantity discount Discount offered to retailers as an incentive to purchase more merchandise on a single order.

nondurable Perishable product consumed in one or a few uses.

nonstore retailing A form of retailing to ultimate consumers that is not store-based. Nonstore retailing is conducted through the Internet, vending machines, mail, direct selling, and direct marketing.

North American Industry Classification System (NAICS) Classification of retail firms into a hierarchical set of six-digit codes based on the types of products and services they produce and sell.

notes payable Current liabilities representing principal and interest the retailer owes to financial institutions (banks) that are due and payable in less than a year.

objective-and-task method A method for setting a promotion budget in which the retailer first establishes a set of communication objectives and then determines the necessary tasks and their costs.

observability The degree to which a new fashion is visible and easily communicated to others in a social group.

observation A type of market research in which customer behavior is observed and recorded.

odd pricing The practice of ending prices with an odd number (such as 69 cents) or just under a round number (such as $98 instead of $100).

off-price retailer A retailer that offers an inconsistent assortment of brand-name, fashion-oriented soft goods at low prices.

off-the-job training Training conducted in centralized classrooms away from the employee's work environment.

omnicenter A combination of mall, lifestyle, and power center components in a unified, open-air layout.

one hundred percent location The retail site in a major business district or mall that has the greatest exposure to a retail store's target market customers.

one-price policy A policy that, at a given time, all customers pay the same price for any given item of merchandise.

one-price retailer A store that offers all merchandise at a single fixed price.

1-to-1 retailing Developing retail programs for small groups or individual customers.

online chat A customer service offering that provides customers with an opportunity to click a button at anytime and have an instant messaging, e-mail, or voice conversation with a customer service representative.

online rataling See *electronic retailing*.

on-the-job training A decentralized approach in which job training occurs in the work environment where employees perform their jobs.

open-to-buy The plan that keeps track of how much is spent in each month and how much is left to spend.

operating expenses Costs, other than the cost of merchandise, incurred in the normal course of doing business, such as salaries for sales associates and managers, advertising, utilities, office supplies, and rent.

opinion leader Person whose attitudes, opinions, preferences, and actions influence those of others.

opportunity cost of capital The rate available on the next best use of the capital invested in the project at hand. The opportunity cost should be no lower than the rate at which a firm borrows funds, since one alternative is to pay back borrowed money. It can be higher, however, depending on the range of other opportunities available. Typically, the opportunity cost rises with investment risk.

optical character recognition (OCR) An industrywide classification system for coding information onto merchandise; enables retailers to record information on each SKU when it is sold and transmit the information to a computer.

opt in A customer privacy issue prevalent in the European Union. Takes the perspective that consumers "own" their personal information. Retailers must get consumers to explicitly agree to share this personal information.

option credit account A revolving account that allows partial payments without interest charges if a bill is paid in full when due.

option-term revolving credit A credit arrangement that offers customers two payment options: (1) pay the full amount within a specified number of days and avoid any finance charges or (2) make a minimum payment and be assessed finance charges on the unpaid balance.

opt out A customer privacy issue prevalent in the United States. Takes the perspective that personal information is generally viewed as being in the public domain and retailers can use it in any way they desire. Consumers must explicitly tell retailers not to use their personal information.

order form When signed by both parties, a legally binding contract specifying the terms and conditions under which a purchase transaction is to be conducted.

order point The amount of inventory below which the quantity available shouldn't go or the item will be out of stock before the next order arrives.

organization chart A graphic that displays the reporting relationships within a firm.

organization culture A firm's set of values, traditions, and customs that guide employee behavior.

organization structure A plan that identifies the activities to be performed by specific employees and determines the lines of authority and responsibility in the firm.

outlet center Typically stores owned by retail chains or manufacturers that sell excess and out-of-season merchandise at reduced prices.

outlet store Off-price retailer owned by a manufacturer or a department or specialty store chain.

outparcel A building or kiosk that is in the parking lot of a shopping center but isn't physically attached to a shopping center.

output measure Measure that assesses the results of retailers' investment decisions.

outshopping Customers shopping in other areas because their needs are not being met locally.

outsourcing Obtaining a service from outside the company that had previously been done by the firm itself.

overstored trade area An area having so many stores selling a specific good or service that some stores will fail.

own brand See *private-label brand.*

owners' equity The amount of assets belonging to the owners of the retail firm after all obligations (liabilities) have been met; also known as *net worth* and *stockholders' equity.*

pallet A platform, usually made of wood, that provides stable support for several cartons. Pallets are used to help move and store merchandise.

parallel branding A branding strategy that represents a private label that closely imitates the trade dress (packaging) and product attributes of leading manufacturer brands but with a clearly articulated "invitation to compare" in its merchandising approach and on its product label.

parasite store A store that does not create its own traffic and whose trade area is determined by the dominant retailer in the shopping center or retail area.

partnering relationship See *strategic relationship.*

party plan system Salespeople encourage people to act as hosts and invite friends or coworkers to a "party" at which the merchandise is demonstrated. The host or hostess receives a gift or commission for arranging the meeting.

patent A law that gives the owner of a patent control over the right to make, sell, and use a product for a period of 17 years (14 years for a design).

penetration A low-pricing strategy for newly introduced products or categories.

percentage lease A lease in which rent is based on a percentage of sales.

percentage lease with specified maximum A lease that pays the lessor, or landlord, a percentage of sales up to a maximum amount.

percentage lease with specified minimum The retailer must pay a minimum rent no matter how low sales are.

percentage-of-sales method A method for setting a promotion budget based on a fixed percentage of forecast sales.

periodic reordering system An inventory management system in which the review time is a fixed period (e.g., two weeks), but the order quantity can vary.

perpetual book inventory See *retail inventory method.*

perpetual ordering system The stock level is monitored perpetually and a fixed quantity is purchased when the inventory available reaches a prescribed level.

personal selling A communication process in which salespeople assist customers in satisfying their needs through face-to-face exchange of information.

physical inventory A method of gathering stock information by using an actual physical count and inspection of the merchandise items.

pick ticket A document that tells the order filler how much of each item to get from the storage area.

pilferage The stealing of a store's merchandise. See also *shoplifting.*

planners Employees in merchandise management responsible for the financial planning and analysis of the merchandise category and, in some cases, the allocation of merchandise to stores.

planogram A diagram created from photographs, computer output, or artists' renderings that illustrates exactly where every SKU should be placed.

point-of-purchase (POP) area See *point-of-sale area.*

point-of-sale area An area where the customer waits at checkout. This area can be the most valuable piece of real estate in the store, because the customer is almost held captive in that spot.

point-of-sale (POS) terminal A cash register that can electronically scan a UPC code with a laser and electronically record a sale; also known as *computerized checkout.*

polygon Trade area whose boundaries conform to streets and other map features rather than being concentric circles.

popping the merchandise Focusing spotlights on special feature areas and items.

population density The number of people per unit area (usually square mile) who live within a geographic area.

positioning The design and implementation of a retail mix to create in the customer's mind an image of the retailer relative to its competitors. Also called *brand building.*

postpurchase evaluation The evaluation of merchandise or services after the customer has purchased and consumed them.

poverty of time A condition in which greater affluence results in less, rather than more, free time because the alternatives competing for customers' time increase.

power center Shopping center that is dominated by several large anchors, including discount stores (Target), off-price stores (Marshalls), warehouse clubs (Costco), or category specialists such as Home Depot, Office Depot, Circuit City, Sports Authority, Best Buy, and Toys "R" Us.

power perimeter The areas around the outside walls of supermarket that have fresh merchandise categories.

power retailer See *category killer* or *category specialist.*

power shopping center An open-air shopping center with the majority of space leased to several well-known anchor retail tenants—category specialists.

predatory pricing A method for establishing merchandise prices for the purpose of driving competition from the marketplace.

preferred client High-purchasing customers salespeople communicate with regularly, send notes to about new merchandise and sales in the department, and make appointments with for special presentations of merchandise.

premarking Marking of the price by the manufacturer or other supplier before goods are shipped to a retail store. Also called *prepricing.*

premium branding A branding strategy that offers the consumer a private label at a comparable manufacturer-brand quality, usually with a modest price savings.

premium merchandise Offered at a reduced price, or free, as an incentive for a customer to make a purchase.

prepricing See *premarking.*

preprint An advertisement printed at the retailer's expense and distributed as a freestanding insert in a newspaper. Also called a *freestanding insert (FSI).*

press conference A meeting with representatives of the news media that is called by a retailer.

press release A statement of facts or opinions that the retailer would like to see published by the news media.

prestige pricing A system of pricing based on the assumption that consumers will not buy goods and services at prices they feel are too low.

price bundling The practice of offering two or more different products or services for sale at one price.

price comparison A comparison of the price of merchandise offered for sale with a higher "regular" price or a manufacturer's list price.

price discrimination An illegal practice in which a vendor sells the same product to two or more customers at different prices. See *first-degree price discrimination* and *second-degree price discrimination.*

price elasticity of demand A measure of the effect a price change has on consumer demand; percentage change in demand divided by percentage change in price.

price fixing An illegal pricing activity in which several marketing channel members establish a fixed retail selling price for a product line within a market area. See *vertical price fixing* and *horizontal price fixing.*

price lining A pricing policy in which a retailer offers a limited number of predetermined price points within a classification.

pricing experiment An experiment in which a retailer actually changes the price of an item in a systematic manner to observe changes in customers' purchases or purchase intentions.

primary data Marketing research information collected through surveys, observations, and experiments to address a problem confronting a retailer.

primary trade area The geographic area from which a store or shopping center derives 50 to 70 percent of its customers.

private exchanges Exchanges that are operated for the exclusive use of a single firm.

private-label brands Products developed and marketed by a retailer and only available for sale by that retailer. Also called *store brands.*

private-label store credit card system A system in which credit cards have the store's name on them, but the accounts receivable are sold to a financial institution.

PRIZM (potential rating index for zip markets) A database combining census data, nationwide consumer surveys, and interviews with hundreds of people across the country into a geodemographic segmentation system.

procedural fairness The perceived fairness of the process used to resolve customer complaints.

procedural justice An employee's perception of fairness (how he or she is treated) that is based on the process used to determine the outcome.

product attributes Characteristics of a product that affect customer evaluations.

product availability A measurement of the percentage of demand for a particular SKU that is satisfied.

productivity measure The ratio of an output to an input determining how effectively a firm uses a resource.

product liability A tort (or wrong) that occurs when an injury results from the use of a product.

product line A group of related products.

profitability A company's ability to generate revenues in excess of the costs incurred in producing those revenues.

profit margin Net profit after taxes divided by net sales.

profit margin management path One of two paths to increasing return on assets.

prohibited use clause A clause in a lease that keeps a landlord from leasing to certain kinds of tenants.

promotion Activities undertaken by a retailer to provide consumers with information about a retailer's store, its image, and its retail mix.

promotional aisle Area aisle or area of a store designed to get the customer's attention. An example might be a special "trim-the-tree" department that seems to magically appear right after Thanksgiving every year for the Christmas holidays.

promotional allowance An allowance given by vendors to retailers to compensate the latter for money spent in advertising a particular item.

promotional area A feature area in a store in which merchandise on sale is displayed.

promotional center A type of specialty shopping center that contains one or more discount stores plus smaller retail tenants. Also called *discount-oriented center.*

promotional department store A department store that concentrates on apparel and sells a substantial portion of its merchandise on weekly promotion.

promotional stock A retailer's stock of goods offered at an unusually attractive price in order to obtain sales volume; it often represents special purchases from vendors.

promotion from within A staffing policy that involves hiring new employees only for positions at the lowest level in the job hierarchy and then promoting employees for openings at higher levels in the hierarchy.

promotion mix A communication program made up of advertising, sales promotions, Web sites, store atmosphere, publicity, personal selling, and word of mouth.

proprietary EDI systems Data exchange systems that are developed primarily by large retailers for the purpose of exchanging data with their vendors.

proprietary store credit card system A system in which credit cards have the store's name on them and the accounts receivable are administered by the retailer; also known as *in-house credit system*.

providing assortments A function performed by retailers that enables customers to choose from a selection of brands, designs, sizes, and prices at one location.

psychographics Refers to how people live, how they spend their time and money, what activities they pursue, and their attitudes and opinions about the world they live in.

psychological needs Needs associated with the personal gratification that customers get from shopping or from purchasing and owning a product.

publicity Communications through significant unpaid presentations about the retailer (usually a news story) in impersonal media.

public warehouse Warehouse that is owned and operated by a third party.

puffing An advertising or personal selling practice in which a retailer simply exaggerates the benefits or quality of a product in very broad terms.

pull supply chain Strategy in which orders for merchandise are generated at the store level on the basis of demand data captured by point-of-sale terminals.

purchase visibility curve A display technique in which the retailer tilts low shelves so more merchandise is in direct view.

push money (PM) An incentive for retail salespeople provided by a vendor to promote, or push, a particular product; also known as *spiff*.

push supply chain Strategy in which merchandise is allocated to stores on the basis of historical demand, the inventory position at the distribution center, and the stores' needs.

pyramid scheme When the firm and its program are designed to sell merchandise and services to other distributors rather than to end users.

quantity discount The policy of granting lower prices for higher quantities. Also known as *multiple-unit pricing*.

quick response (QR) delivery system System designed to reduce the lead time for receiving merchandise, thereby lowering inventory investment, improving customer service levels, and reducing distribution expenses; also known as a just-in-time inventory management system.

quota Target level used to motivate and evaluate performance.

quota–bonus plan Compensation plan that has a performance goal or objective established to evaluate employee performance, such as sales per hour for salespeople and maintained margin and turnover for buyers.

racetrack layout A type of store layout that provides a major aisle to facilitate customer traffic that has access to the store's multiple entrances. Also known as a *loop layout*.

radio frequency identification device (RFID) A technology that allows an object or person to be identified at a distance using radio waves.

rain check When sale merchandise is out of stock, a written promise to customers to sell them that merchandise at the sale price when it arrives.

reach The actual number of customers in the target market exposed to an advertising medium. See *advertising reach*.

rebate Money returned to the buyer in the form of cash based on a portion of the purchase price.

receipt of goods (ROG) dating A dating policy in which the cash discount period starts on the day the merchandise is received.

receiving The process of filling out paperwork to record the receipt of merchandise that arrives at a store or distribution center.

recruitment Activity performed by a retailer to generate job applicants.

reductions Includes three things: markdowns, discounts to employees and customers, and inventory shrinkage due to shoplifting, breakage, or loss.

reference group One or more people whom a person uses as a basis of comparison for his or her beliefs, feelings, and behaviors.

reference price A price point in the consumer's memory for a good or service that can consist of the price last paid, the price most frequently paid, or the average of all prices customers have paid for similar offerings. A benchmark for what consumers believe the "real" price of the merchandise should be.

refusal to deal A legal issue in which either a vendor or a retailer reserves the right to deal or refuse to deal with anyone it chooses.

region In retail location analysis, refers to part of the country, a particular city, or Metropolitan Statistical Area (MSA).

regression analysis A statistical approach for evaluating retail locations based on the assumption that factors that affect the sales of existing stores in a chain will have the same impact on stores located at new sites being considered.

Reilly's law A model used in trade area analysis to define the relative ability of two cities to attract customers from the area between them.

related diversification opportunity A diversification opportunity strategy in which the retailer's present offering and market share something in common with the market and format being considered.

relational partnership Long-term business relationship in which the buyer and vendor have a close, trusting interpersonal relationship.

remarking The practice of changing the price label or identification tag on merchandise due to price changes, lost or mutilated tickets, or customer returns.

reorder point The stock level at which a new order is placed.

resale price maintenance laws Laws enacted in the early 1900s to curb vertical price fixing. These laws were designed to help protect small retailers by prohibiting retailers from selling below manufacturer's suggested retail price. Also called *fair trade laws*. In 1975, these laws were repealed by the Consumer Goods Pricing Act.

resale price management (RPM) A requirement imposed by a vendor that a retailer cannot sell an item for less than the specific price (the manufacturer's suggested retail price).

resident buying office An organization located in a major buying center that provides services to help retailers buy merchandise.

restraint of trade Any contract that tends to eliminate or stifle competition, create a monopoly, artificially maintain prices, or otherwise hamper or obstruct the course of trade and commerce as it would be carried on if left to the control of natural forces; also known as unfair trade practices.

retail audit See *situation audit*.

retail chain A firm that consists of multiple retail units under common ownership and usually has some centralization of decision making in defining and implementing its strategy.

retailer A business that sells products and services to consumers for their personal or family use.

retail exchanges Electronic marketplaces operated by organizations that facilitate the buying and selling of merchandise using the Internet.

retail format The retailers' type of retail mix (nature of merchandise and services offered, pricing policy, advertising and promotion program, approach to store design and visual merchandising, and typical location).

retail format development opportunity An investment opportunity strategy in which a retailer offers a new retail format—a format involving a different retail mix—to the same target market.

retail information system System that provides the information needed by retail managers by collecting, organizing, and storing relevant data continuously and directing the information to the appropriate managers.

retailing A set of business activities that adds value to the products and services sold to consumers for their personal or family use.

retailing concept A management orientation that holds that the key task of a retailer is to determine the needs and wants of its target markets and direct the firm toward satisfying those needs and wants more effectively and efficiently than competitors do.

retail inventory method (RIM) An accounting procedure whose objectives are to maintain a perpetual or book inventory in retail dollar amounts and to maintain records that make it possible to determine the cost value of the inventory at any time without taking a physical inventory; also known as *book inventory system* or *perpetual book inventory*.

retail market A group of consumers with similar needs (a market segment) and a group of retailers using a similar retail format to satisfy those consumer needs.

retail market segment A group of customers whose needs will be satisfied by the same retail offering because they have similar needs and go through similar buying processes.

retail mix The combination of factors used by a retailer to satisfy customer needs and influence their purchase decisions; includes merchandise and services offered, pricing, advertising and promotions, store design and location, and visual merchandising.

retail-sponsored cooperative An organization owned and operated by small, independent retailers to improve operating efficiency and buying power. Typically, the retail-sponsored cooperative operates a wholesale buying and distribution system and requires its members to concentrate their purchases from the cooperative wholesale operation.

retail strategy A statement that indicates (1) the target market toward which a retailer plans to commit its resources, (2) the nature of the retail offering that the retailer plans to use to satisfy the needs of the target market, and (3) the bases upon which the retailer will attempt to build a sustainable competitive advantage over competitors.

retained earnings The portion of owners' equity that has accumulated over time through profits but has not been paid out in dividends to owners.

return on assets Net profit after taxes divided by total assets.

return on owners' equity Net profit after taxes divided by owners' equity; also known as return on net worth.

reverse auction Auction conducted by retailer buyers. Known as a *reverse auction* because there is one buyer and many potential sellers. In reverse auctions, retail buyers provide a specification for what they want to a group of potential vendors. The competing vendors then bid down the price at which they are willing to sell until the buyer accepts a bid.

reverse logistics A flow back of merchandise through the channel, from the customer to the store, distribution center, and vendor, for customer returns.

review time The period of time between reviews of a line for purchase decisions.

revolving credit A consumer credit plan that combines the convenience of a continuous charge account and the privileges of installment payment.

RFM (recency, frequency, monetary) analysis Often used by catalog retailers and direct marketers, a scheme for segmenting customers on the basis of how recently they have made a purchase, how frequently they make purchases, and how much they have bought.

ribbon center See *strip center*.

road condition Includes the age, number of lanes, number of stoplights, congestion, and general state of repair of roads in a trade area.

road pattern A consideration used in measuring the accessibility of a retail location from major arteries, freeways, or roads.

Robinson-Patman Act (1946) The Congressional act that revised Section 2 of the Clayton Act and specifically prohibits certain types of price discrimination.

rounder A round fixture that sits on a pedestal. Smaller than the straight rack, it is designed to hold a maximum amount of merchandise. Also known as a *bulk* or *capacity fixture*.

routine decision making See *habitual decision making*.

rule-of-thumb method A type of approach for setting a promotion budget that uses past sales and communication activity to determine the present communications budget.

safety stock See *buffer stock.*

sale-leaseback The practice in which retailers build new stores and sell them to real estate investors who then lease the buildings back to the retailers on a long-term basis.

sales associate The same as a salesperson. The term is used to recognize the importance and professional nature of the sales function and avoids the negative image sometimes linked with the term "salesperson."

sales consultant See *sales associate.*

sales per cubic foot A measure of space productivity appropriate for stores such as wholesale clubs that use multiple layers of merchandise.

sales per linear foot A measure of space productivity used when most merchandise is displayed on multiple shelves of long gondolas, such as in grocery stores.

sales per square foot A measure of space productivity used by most retailers since rent and land purchases are assessed on a per-square-foot basis.

sales promotions Paid impersonal communication activities that offer extra value and incentives to customers to visit a store or purchase merchandise during a specific period of time.

same store sales growth The sales growth in stores that have been open for over one year.

satisfaction A postconsumption evaluation of the degree to which a store or product meets or exceeds customer expectations.

saturated trade area A trade area that offers customers a good selection of goods and services, while allowing competing retailers to make good profits.

scale economies Cost advantages due to the size of a retailer.

scanning The process in point-of-sale systems wherein the input into the terminal is accomplished by passing a coded ticket over a reader or having a hand-held wand pass over the ticket.

scrambled merchandising An offering of merchandise not typically associated with the store type, such as clothing in a drugstore.

search engines Computer programs that simply search for and provide a listing of all Internet sites selling a product category or brand with the price of the merchandise offered. Also called *shopping bots.*

seasonal discount Discount offered as an incentive to retailers to place orders for merchandise in advance of the normal buying season.

seasonal merchandise Inventory whose sales fluctuate dramatically according to the time of the year.

secondary data Market research information previously gathered for purposes other than solving the current problem under investigation.

secondary trade area The geographic area of secondary importance in terms of customer sales, generating about 20 percent of a store's sales.

second-degree price discrimination Charging different prices to different people on the basis of the nature of the offering.

security An operating unit within a retail organization that is responsible for protecting merchandise and other assets from pilferage (internal or external). Those working in security may be employees or outside agency people.

security policy Set of rules that apply to activities in the computer and communications resources that belong to an organization.

self-analysis An internally focused examination of a business's strengths and weaknesses.

self-service retailer A retailer that offers minimal customer service.

selling agent An agent who operates on an extended contractual basis; the agent sells all of a specified line of merchandise or the entire output of the principal and usually has full authority with regard to prices, terms, and other conditions of sale. The agent occasionally renders financial aid to the principal.

selling process A set of activities that salespeople undertake to facilitate the customer's buying decision.

selling space The area set aside for displays of merchandise, interactions between sales personnel and customers, demonstrations, and so on.

sell-through analysis A comparison of actual and planned sales to determine whether early markdowns are required or more merchandise is needed to satisfy demand.

seniors The generational cohort of people born before 1946.

service gap The difference between customers' expectations and perceptions of customer service to improve customers' satisfaction with their service.

service level A measure used in inventory management to define the level of support or level of product availability; the number of items sold divided by the number of items demanded. Service level should not be confused with customer service. Compare *customer service.*

services retailer Organization that offers consumers services rather than merchandise. Examples include banks, hospital, health spas, doctors, legal clinics, entertainment firms, and universities.

sexual harassment Unwelcome sexual advances, requests for sexual favors, or other verbal or physical conduct with sexual elements.

share of wallet The percentage of total purchases made by a customer in a store.

shelf talkers Signs on the shelf providing information about the merchandise and its price.

Sherman Antitrust Act (1890) An act protecting small businesses and consumers from large corporations by outlawing any person, corporation, or association from engaging in activities that restrain trade or commerce.

shoplifting The act of stealing merchandise from a store by employees, customers, or people posing as customers.

shopping bots See *search engines.*

shopping center A group of retail and other commercial establishments that is planned, developed, owned, and managed as a single property.

shopping goods Products for which consumers will spend time comparing alternatives.

shopping guide Free paper delivered to all residents in a specific area.

shopping mall Enclosed, climate-controlled, lighted shopping centers with retail stores on one or both sides of an enclosed walkway.

shortage See *shrinkage*.

shrinkage An inventory reduction that is caused by shoplifting by employees or customers, by merchandise being misplaced or damaged, or by poor bookkeeping.

situation audit An analysis of the opportunities and threats in the retail environment and the strengths and weaknesses of the retail business relative to its competitors.

skimming A high-pricing strategy for newly introduced categories or products.

SKU See *stockkeeping unit*.

sliding scale A part of some leases that stipulates how much the percentage of sales paid as rent will decrease as sales go up.

slotting allowance Fee paid by a vendor for space in a retail store. Also called *slotting fee*.

slotting fee See *slotting allowance*.

socialization The steps taken to transform new employees into effective, committed members of the firm.

sole proprietorship An arrangement in which an unincorporated retail firm is owned by one person.

span of control The number of subordinates reporting to a manager.

specialization The organizational structure in which employees are typically responsible for only one or two tasks rather than performing all tasks. This approach enables employees to develop expertise and increase productivity.

specialty catalog retailer A nonstore retailer that focuses on specific categories of merchandise, such as fruit (Harry and David), gardening tools (Smith & Hawken), or seeds and plants (Burpee).

specialty department store A store with a department store format that focuses primarily on apparel and soft home goods (such as Neiman Marcus or Saks Fifth Avenue).

specialty product A product which the customer will expend considerable effort to buy.

specialty shopping Shopping experiences when consumers know what they want and will not accept a substitute.

specialty store A type of store concentrating on a limited number of complementary merchandise categories and providing a high level of service.

spending potential index (SPI) Compares the average expenditure in a particular area for a product to the amount spent on that product nationally.

spiff See *push money*.

split shipment A vendor ships part of a shipment to a retailer and back orders the remainder because the entire shipment could not be shipped at the same time.

spot A local television commercial.

spot check Used particularly in receiving operations when goods come in for reshipping to branch stores in packing cartons. Certain cartons are opened in the receiving area of the central distribution point and spot-checked for quality and quantity.

spotting technique See *analog approach*.

staging area Area in which merchandise is accumulated from different parts of the distribution center and prepared for shipment to stores.

standardization approach An approach used by retailers to provide customer service by using a set of rules and procedures so that all customers consistently receive the same service.

standards gap The difference between the retailer's perceptions of customers' expectations and the customer service standards it sets. This factor is one of four factors identified by the Gaps model for improving service quality.

staple merchandise Inventory that has continuous demand by customers over an extended period of time. Also known as *basic merchandise*.

stockholders' equity See *owners' equity*.

stockkeeping unit (SKU) The smallest unit available for keeping inventory control. In soft goods merchandise, an SKU usually means a size, color, and style.

stocklift See *buyback*.

stockout A situation occurring when an SKU that a customer wants is not available.

stock overage The amount by which a retail book inventory figure exceeds a physical ending inventory.

stock-to-sales ratio Specifies the amount of inventory that should be on hand at the beginning of the month to support the sales forecast and maintain the inventory turnover objective. The beginning-of-month (BOM) inventory divided by sales for the month. The average stock-to-sales ratio is 12 divided by planned inventory turnover. This ratio is an integral component of the merchandise budget plan.

store atmosphere The combination of the store's physical characteristics (such as architecture, layout, signs and displays, colors, lighting, temperature, sounds, and smells), which together create an image in the customers' mind. See *atmospherics*.

store brand See *private-label brand*.

store image The way a store is defined in a shopper's mind. The store image is based on the store's physical characteristics, its retail mix, and a set of psychological attributes.

store loyalty A condition in which customers like and habitually visit the same store to purchase a type of merchandise.

store maintenance The activities involved with managing the exterior and interior physical facilities associated with the store.

straight commission A form of salesperson's compensation in which the amount paid is based on a percentage of sales made minus merchandise returned.

straight lease A type of lease in which the retailer pays a fixed amount per month over the life of the lease.

straight rack A type of fixture that consists of a long pipe suspended with supports going to the floor or attached to a wall.

straight salary compensation A compensation plan in which salespeople or managers receive a fixed amount of compensation for each hour or week they work.

strategic alliance Collaborative relationship between independent firms. For example, a foreign retailer might enter an international market through direct investment but develop an alliance with a local firm to perform logistical and warehousing activities.

strategic profit model (SPM) A tool used for planning a retailer's financial strategy based on both margin management (net profit margin) and asset management (asset turnover). Using the SPM, a retailer's objective is to achieve a target return on assets.

strategic relationship Long-term relationship in which partners make significant investments to improve both parties' profitability.

strategic retail planning process The steps a retailer goes through to develop a strategic retail plan. It describes how retailers select target market segments, determine the appropriate retail format, and build sustainable competitive advantages.

strengths and weaknesses analysis A critical aspect of the situation audit in which a retailer determines its unique capabilities—its strengths and weaknesses relative to its competition.

strict product liability A product liability suit in which the injury to the customer may not have been intentional or under the retailer's control.

strip center A shopping center that usually has parking directly in front of the stores and does not have enclosed walkways linking the stores.

style The characteristic or distinctive form, outline, or shape of a product.

subculture A distinctive group of people within a culture. Members of a subculture share some customs and norms with the overall society but also have some unique perspectives.

subculture theory A theory of how fashion spreads that suggests that subcultures of mostly young and less affluent consumers, such as motorcycle riders and urban rappers, have started fashions for such things as colorful fabrics, t-shirts, sneakers, jeans, black leather jackets, and surplus military clothing.

subjective employee evaluation Assessment of employee performance based on a supervisor's ratings rather than on objective measures such as sales per hour.

supercenter Large store (150,000 to 220,000 square feet) combining a discount store with a supermarket.

superregional center Shopping center that is similar to a regional center, but because of its larger size, it has more anchors and a deeper selection of merchandise, and it draws from a larger population base.

superstore A large supermarket between 20,000 and 50,000 square feet in size.

supply chain management The integration of business processes from end user through original suppliers that provides products, services, and information that add value for customers.

survey A method of data collection, using telephone, personal interview, mail, or any combination thereof.

sustainable competitive advantage A distinct competency of a retailer relative to its competitors that can be maintained over a considerable time period.

sweepstakes A promotion in which customers win prizes based on chance.

target market The market segment(s) toward which the retailer plans to focus its resources and retail mix.

tariff A tax placed by a government upon imports. Also known as *duty*.

task performance behaviors Planning, organizing, motivating, evaluating, and coordinating store employees' activities.

television home shopping A retail format in which customers watch a TV program demonstrating merchandise and then place orders for the merchandise by phone.

terms of purchase Conditions in a purchase agreement with a vendor that include the type(s) of discounts available and responsibility for transportation costs.

terms of sale Conditions in a sales contract with customers including such issues as charges for alterations, delivery, or gift wrapping or the store's exchange policies.

tertiary trade area The outermost ring of a trade area; includes customers who occasionally shop at the store or shopping center.

theme/festival center A shopping center that typically employs a unifying theme that is carried out by the individual shops in their architectural design and, to an extent, their merchandise.

third-degree price discrimination Charging different prices to different demographic market segments.

third-party logistics company Firm that facilitates the movement of merchandise from manufacturer to retailer but is independently owned.

thrift store A retail format offering used merchandise.

ticketing and marking Procedures for making price labels and placing them on the merchandise.

tie-in An approach used to attract attention to a store's offering by associating the offering with an event.

tonnage merchandising A display technique in which large quantities of merchandise are displayed together.

top-down planning One side of the process of developing an overall retail strategy where goals are set at the top of the organization and filter down through the operating levels.

top-of-mind awareness The highest level of brand awareness; arises when consumers mention a brand name first when they are asked about a type of retailer, a merchandise category, or a type of service.

trade area A geographic sector that contains potential customers for a particular retailer or shopping center.

trade discount Reduction in a retailer's suggested retail price granted to wholesalers and retailers; also known as a *functional discount*.

trade dress A product's physical appearance, including its size, shape, color, design, and texture. For instance, the shape and color of a Coca-Cola bottle is its trade dress.

trademark Any mark, work, picture, or design associated with a particular line of merchandise or product.

trade show A temporary concentration of vendors that provides retailers opportunities to place orders and view what is available in the marketplace; also known as a *merchandise show* or *market week*.

traditional distribution center Warehouse in which merchandise is unloaded from trucks and placed on racks or shelves for storage.

traditional strip center A shopping center that is designed to provide convenience shopping for the day-to-day needs of consumers in their immediate neighborhood.

traffic appliance Small portable appliance.

traffic flow The balance between a substantial number of cars and not so many that congestion impedes access to the store.

transformational leader A leader who gets people to transcend their personal needs for the sake of realizing the group goal.

transportation cost The expense a retailer incurs if it pays the cost of shipping merchandise from the vendor to the stores.

travel time contours Used in trade area analysis to define the rings around a particular site based on travel time instead of distances.

trialability The costs and commitment required to initially adopt a fashion.

trickle-down theory A theory of how fashion spreads that suggests that the fashion leaders are consumers with the highest social status—wealthy, well-educated consumers. After they adopt a fashion, the fashion trickles down to consumers in lower social classes. When the fashion is accepted in the lowest social class, it is no longer acceptable to the fashion leaders in the highest social class.

triple-coupon promotion A retail promotion that allows the customer triple the face value of the coupon.

trust A belief that a partner is honest (reliable, stands by its word, sincere, fulfills obligations) and benevolent (concerned about the other party's welfare).

tying contract An agreement between a vendor and a retailer requiring the retailer to take a product it does not necessarily desire (the tied product) to ensure that it can buy a product it does desire (the tying product).

ultimate consumers Individuals who purchase goods and services for their own personal use or for use by members of their household.

undercover shopper Person hired by or working for a retailer who poses as a customer to observe the activities and performance of employees.

understored trade area An area that has too few stores selling a specific good or service to satisfy the needs of the population.

unit pricing The practice of expressing price in terms of both the total price of an item and the price per unit of measure.

Universal Product Code (UPC) The black-and-white bar code found on most merchandise; used to collect sales information at the point of sale using computer terminals that read the code. This information is transmitted computer to computer to buyers, distribution centers, and then to vendors, who in turn quickly ship replenishment merchandise.

unrelated diversification Diversification in which there is no commonality between the present business and the new business.

UPC See *Universal Product Code.*

URL (uniform resource locator) The standard for a page on the World Wide Web (e.g., www.nrf.org).

utilitarian needs Needs motivating consumers to go shopping to accomplish a specific task.

value Relationship of what a customer gets (goods/services) to what he or she has to pay for it.

values of lifestyle survey (VALS2) A tool used to categorize customers into eight lifestyle segments. Based on responses to surveys conducted by SRI Consulting Business Intelligence.

variable costs Costs that vary with the level of sales and can be applied directly to the decision in question.

variable pricing Charging different prices in different stores, markets, or zones.

variety The number of different merchandise categories within a store or department.

vending machine retailing A nonstore format in which merchandise or services are stored in a machine and dispensed to customers when they deposit cash or use a credit card.

vendor Any firm from which a retailer obtains merchandise.

vendor-managed inventory (VMI) An approach for improving supply chain efficiency in which the vendor is responsible for maintaining the retailer's inventory levels in each of its stores.

vertical integration An example of diversification by retailers involving investments by retailers in wholesaling or manufacturing merchandise.

vertical merchandising A method whereby merchandise is organized to follow the eye's natural up-and-down movement.

vertical price fixing Agreements to fix prices between parties at different levels of the same marketing channel (for example, retailers and their vendors).

virtual community A network of people who seek information, products, and services and communicate with one another about specific issues.

virtual mall A group of retailers and service providers that can be accessed over the Internet at one location.

visibility Customers' ability to see the store and enter the parking lot safely.

visual communications The act of providing information to customers through graphics, signs, and theatrical effects—both in the store and in windows—to help boost sales by providing information on products and suggesting items or special purchases.

visual merchandising The presentation of a store and its merchandise in ways that will attract the attention of potential customers.

want book Information collected by retail salespeople to record out-of-stock or requested merchandise.

warehouse club A retailer that offers a limited assortment of food and general merchandise with little service and low prices to ultimate consumers and small businesses.

weeks of supply An inventory management method most similar to the stock-to-sales method. The difference is that everything is expressed in weeks rather than months.

wheel of retailing A cyclical theory of retail evolution whose premise is that retailing institutions evolve from low-price/service to higher-price/service operations.

wholesale market A concentration of vendors within a specific geographic location, perhaps even under one roof or over the Internet.

wholesaler A merchant establishment operated by a concern that is primarily engaged in buying, taking title to, usually storing, and physically handling goods in large quantities, and reselling the goods (usually in smaller quantities) to retailers or industrial or business users.

wholesale-sponsored voluntary cooperative group An organization operated by a wholesaler offering a merchandising program to small, independent retailers on a voluntary basis.

word of mouth Communications among people about a retailer.

yield management The practice of adjusting prices up or down in response to demand to control sales generated.

zone pricing Charging different prices for the same merchandise in different geographic locations to be competitive in local markets.

zoning The regulation of the construction and use of buildings in certain areas of a municipality.

Chapter 1

1. Laurie Sullivan, "Wal-Mart's Way," *InformationWeek*, September 24, 2004.

2. Jim Fredrick, "Winning Combini: The Rise of 7-Eleven Is a Welcome Victory for Corporate Japan," *TimeAsia*, August 11, 2003, http://www.time.com/time/asia/2003/cool_japan/711.html, accessed on April 19, 2004; David Bell and Hal Hogan, *7-Eleven, Inc.* (Harvard Business School Press: Boston, 2004).

3. Mike Troy, "In-Sourcing the Role of the Middleman," *DSN/Retailing Today*, December 13, 2004, p. 27.

4. For a more detailed discussion of distribution channels, see Louis W. Stern, Adel I. El-Ansary, Erin Anderson, and Anne T. Coughlan, *Marketing Channels* (Englewood Cliffs, NJ: Prentice Hall, 2002).

5. *Retail Industry Indicators*, Washington, DC: National Retail Foundation, August 2004, p. 7.

6. Ibid., p. 33.

7. Christina Almeida, "Luxury Stores Prove There's More to Vegas," *Boston Globe*, December 17, 2004, p. B1.

8. *Retail Industry Indicators*, p. 17.

9. "2004 Global Powers of Retailing," *Stores*, January 2004, pp. G1–45.

10. www.forbes.com/billionaires, accessed on April 19, 2004.

11. "Jeff Bezos: The Wizard of Web Retailing," *BusinessWeek*, December 2004, p. 13.

12. Susan Caminiti, "Will Old Navy Fill the Gap?" *Fortune*, March 18, 1996, pp. 59–64; Amy Merrick, "Retail Legend Leaves The Gap," *The Wall Street Journal*, May 22, 2002, p. B1.

13. Ibid., Caminiti, p. 60.

14. Jack Hayes, "Dave Thomas, Founder, Wendy's International," *Nation's Restaurant News*, August 23, 2004, p. 62; Gregg Cebrzynski, "'Mr. Wendy' Shines as Wendy's Spokesman Even Though He's Not," *Nation's Restaurant News*, March 15, 2004, p. 14.

15. Louise Kramer, "Pioneer of the Year: David Thomas," *Nation's Restaurant News*, October 9, 1995, p. 152.

16. "Rating the Stores," *Consumer Reports*, November 1994, p. 714.

17. Bill Hare, *Celebration of Fools: An Inside Look at the Rise and Fall of JCPenney* (New York: AMACOM, 2004); Debbie Howell, "JCPenney Chooses Outsider as Chief Exec," *DSN Retailing Today*, November 8, p. 1; Maria Halkias, "JCPenney Reports Good Start for Five Year Strategy," *Knight Ridder Tribune Business News*, April 9, 2004, p. 1; Cora Daniels, "JCPenney Dresses Up," *Fortune*, June 9, 2003, p. 127; JCPenney 100th Anniversary," *Chain Store Age*, June 2002, pp. 48–51.

18. Dan Scheraga, "Penney's Net Advantage," *Chain Store Age*, September 2000, pp. 114–18.

19. Daniel McGinn, "The Green Machine," *Newsweek*, March 21, 2005, pp. 43–47; Charles Fishman, "The Anarchist's Cookbook," *Fast Company*, July 2004, pp. 70–79; Julia Boorstin, "No Preservatives, No Unions, Lots of Dough," *Fortune*, September 15, 2003, pp. 127–31.

20. eBrain Market Research, http://www.ebrain.org/, accessed on April 22, 2004.

21. Whole Foods Market, "Declaration of Interdependence," company philosophy, www.wholefoodsmarket.com/company/declaration.html, accessed on April 24, 2004.

22. Bruce Horovitz, "A Whole New Ballgame in Grocery Shopping," *USA TODAY*, March 9, 2005, p. A1.

23. *Retail Industry Indicators*, p. 24.

Chapter 2

1. *Retail Industry Indicators*, Washington, DC: NRF Foundation, August 2004, p. 7.

2. Netflix Fun Facts, http://www.netflix.com/PressRoom?id=5206, accessed on April 9, 2005.

3. *Industry Outlook: Food Channel*, Columbus, OH: Retail Forward, February 2004.

4. *Language of the Food Industry* (Washington, DC: Food Marketing Institute, 1998).

5. Ibid., p. 16

6. "Roaring 20's Ends in Depression," *Chain Store Age Executive*, June 1994, p. 49.

7. Teresa Lindeman, "'Limited Assortment' Grocery Stores Battle Supermarkets in Pennsylvania," *Knight Ridder Tribune Business News*, October 17, 2004, p. 1.

8. Tim Tripplet, "More U.S. Grocers Turning to ECR to Cut Waste," *Marketing News*, September 12, 1994, pp. 3–6.

9. Susan Reda, "Supermarket Slugfest," *Stores*, February 2005, pp. 30–33; Thomas Lee, "Supermarkets Try a Fresh Approach," *Minneapolis Star Tribune* April 4, 2005, p. C.1.

10. Walter Nicholls, "Destination Supermarket: The Growing Attraction of Dining In, with the Eggplant Close," *Washington Post*, January 12, 2005, p. F01.

11. *Industry Outlook: Food Channel*, p. 31.

12. Ibid.

13. John Dolen, "Far and Away from Miami, Lake Worth Latin Supermarket Thrives," *Fort Lauderdale Sun Sentinel*, July 5, 2004, p. B1.

14. Private Label Manufacturers Homepage, http://www.plma.com, accessed on April 10, 2005.

15. *FDM Shopper Update*, Columbus, OH: Retail Forward, February 2004, p. 4.

16. *Industry Outlook: Warehouse Clubs*, Columbus, OH: Retail Forward, October 2004, p. 12.

17. *Industry Outlook: Convenience Stores*, Columbus, OH: Retail Forward, January 2005, p. 5.

18. "A Short History of the Convenience Store Industry," www.cstorecentral.com, accessed on April 9, 2005.

19. Thaddeus Herrick, "Discounters Gain as Price of Gas Rises," *The Wall Street Journal*, April 7, 2005, p. D1.

20. Bernard Simon, "Going Beyond Mere Convenience," *New York Times*, October 19, 2003, p. B1.

21. Paula Ward, "Sheetz Family Brings Its Own Meaning to 'Convenience Store,'" *Pittsburgh Post-Gazette*, March 13, 2005, p. B1.

22. David Moin, "Department Stores: The Issues," *WWD Infotracs*, June 1997, pp. 4–6.

23. *Industry Outlook: Department Stores*, Columbus, OH: Retail Forward, February 2004, p. 3.

24. Phillip Marineau, "Fitting In: In Bow to Retailer's New Clout, Levi Strauss Makes Alterations," *The Wall Street Journal*, June 17, 2004, p. A1

25. *Industry Outlook: Department Stores*, pp. 20–32.

26. Emily Scardino, "Mid-Tiers Coming Back into Favor: Basics Take a Backseat to Fashion," *DSN Retailing Today*, July 5, 2004, p. 41.

27. *Industry Outlook: Mass Channel*, Columbus, OH: Retail Forward, April 2004, p. 3.

28. http://www.hbc.com/hbc/history/, accessed on April 12, 2005.

29. *Industry Outlook: Mass Channel*, p. 22.

30. Steven Vames, "Hot Topics Aims to Stay Ahead of Teen Trends," *The Wall Street Journal*, January 28, 2004, p. A1.

31. *IRI Times & Trends*, December 30, 2004.

32. *Industry Outlook: Drug Channel*, Columbus, OH: Retail Forward, August 2004.

33. Susan Reda, "Redefining Pharmacy's Role," *Stores*, April 1997, pp. 34–36.

34. "Lowe's Widens Its Growth Focus," *National Home Center News*, September 8, 1997, p. 7.

35. http://www.homedepot.com/HDUS/EN_US/corporate/about/didyouknow.shtml, accessed on April 10, 2005.

36. "Dollar Formats Continue Food Expansion," *DSN Retailing Today*, July 19, 2004, p. 10.

37. "Extreme Value Store Shopper," *DSN Retailing Today*, January 5, 2004, p. 4.

38. Allen Salkin, "Bargain-Hunting in a BMW: The Lure of 99 Cents," *New York Times*, December 7, 2004, p. G3.

39. "Back to the Future," *New York Times Magazine*, April 6, 1997, pp. 48–49.

40. *Statistical Factbook 2004* (Washington, DC: Direct Marketing Association, 2004), p. 29.

41. Richard S. Hodgson, "It's Still the 'Catalog Age,'" *Catalog Age*, June 1, 2001.

42. *Statistical Factbook 2004*, p. 65.

43. Ibid., p. 61.

44. "Internet Generates 13 Percent of Catalog Sales," *Retail Industry*, January 2002, http://retailindustry.about.com/library/bl/q2/bl_dma060401b.htm, accessed on April 13, 2005.

45. Mark Del Franco, "Penney Redesigns Its Big Book," *Catalog Age*, January 16, 2002.

46. www.usaa.com/cp-aboutusaa.asp, accessed on April 13, 2005.

47. www.dsa.org/research/numbers.htm, accessed on April 12, 2005.

48. http://inventors.about.com/library/inventors/blvendingmachine.htm, accessed on April 13, 2005.

49. Elliot Maras, "State of Vending Industry Report," *Automated Merchandiser*, August 2002, p. 44.

50. Rachael Persando, "Why the Vending Difference?" *Northwest Nikkei*, September 10, 2003, p. 1; "Japanese Retailing—Marketplace Is Alive and Kicking," *Retail Week*, April 27, 2001, p. 16.

51. Keith Reed, "Office Supplies, Snacks on the Side for Those in a Hurry, Staples Offers Vending Machines," *Boston Globe*, April 22, 2004, p. c2.

52. www.zoots.com, accessed on April 14, 2005.

53. Valarie Zeithaml, A. Parasuraman, and Leonard Berry, "Problems and Strategies in Services Marketing," *Journal of Marketing* 49 (Spring 1985), pp. 33–46; Stephen W. Brown and Mary Jo Bitner, "Services Marketing," *AMA Management Handbook*, 3rd ed. (New York: AMACOM Books, 1994), pp. 15-5–15-15.

Chapter 3

1. *FDM Outlook to 2008*. Columbus, OH: Retail Forward, 2004, p. 9.

2. Bob Tedeschi, "Online Travel Firms Try Real People," *New York Times*, January 17, 2005, p. B1.

3. "Aligning Retail Technologies with Growth Strategies," Retail Forward 2004 Strategic Outlook Conference.

4. William Wilkie and Peter R. Dickson, "Consumer Information Search and Shopping Behavior," working paper, Management Science Institute, Cambridge, MA, 1985.

5. "Survey of Retail Payment Systems," *Chain Store Age*, December 1999, p. 4A.

6. David Moin, "Getting Personal," *Women's Wear Daily Internet Supplement*, May 2000, pp. 10–17.

7. Susan Kuchinskas, "A Decade of E-Commerce," October 18, 2004, http://www.Intyernetnews.com, accessed on April 29, 2005.

8. Rob McGann, "Holiday Visits to Retail Sites Up 24 Percent over 2003," December 15, 2004, http://www.clickz.com/stats, accessed on April 28, 2005.

9. Jared Sandberg, "It Isn't Entertainment That Makes the Web Shine: It's Dull Data," *The Wall Street Journal*, July 20, 1998, pp. A1, A6.

10. James Peltier, John Schibrowsky, and John Davis, "Using Attitudinal and Descriptive Database Information to Understand Interactive Buyer–Seller Relationships," *Journal of Interactive Marketing* 12 (Summer 1998), pp. 32–45; John Eighmey, "Adding Value in the Information Age: Uses and Gratifications of Sales on the World-Wide Web," *Journal of Business Research* 41 (March 1998), pp. 34–45.

11. Phil Patton, "Buy Here, and We'll Teach You What You Like," *New York Times*, Electronic Commerce Special Section, September 22, 1999, p. 5; Pattie Maes, "Smart Commerce: The Future of Intelligent Agents in Cyberspace," *Journal of Interactive Marketing* 3 (Summer 1999), pp. 66–76.

12. Wilkie and Dickson.

13. Rachel Ledford, "The Connected Customer," *E-Retailing Intelligence Update* (Columbus, OH: Retail Forward, December 2001), p. 6.

14. Jacques Nantel, "My Virtual Model: Virtual Reality Comes to Fashion," *Journal of Interactive Marketing* (Summer 2004), p. 73.

15. Ledford, p. 3.

16. Jim Fuquay, "Online Travel Sites Need to Expand Offerings to Stay Relevant, Say Experts," *Knight Ridder Tribune Business News*, March 2, 2005, p. 1.

17. Anthony Boright, "Banking on the Web," *Marketing Magazine*, March 7, 2005, p. 26.

18. Patrica Sabatini, "Shopping Online Can Be Just Fine If You Take Basic Security Steps," *Knight Ridder Tribune Business News*, November 24, 2004, p. 1.

19. Valerie Seckler, "E-Tailing Sales: Data Privacy Is Seen as Key," *WWD*, August 25, 1999, p. 5.

20. Debby Garboto, "Best Buy Enhances the Image of Digital Kiosks," *Retail Merchandiser*, August 2004, p. 8.

21. For more information on approaches for increasing share of wallet, see Tom Osten, *Customer Share Marketing* (Upper Saddle River, NJ: Prentice Hall, 2002).

22. Lynda Hyde, "Multi-channel Integration," Columbus, OH: Price Waterhouse Coopers, 2001.

23. Wendy Moe and Peter Fader, "Capturing Evolving Visit Behavior in Clickstream Data," *Journal of Interactive Marketing* (Winter 2004), pp. 5–16.

24. Marco Vriens and Michael Grigsby, "Building Profitable Online Customer-Brand Relationships," *Marketing Management*, November–December 2001, pp. 34–36.

25. George Anders, "Virtual Reality: Web Firms Go on Warehouse Building Boom," *The Wall Street Journal*, September 8, 1999, pp. B1, B9.

26. Faye Brookman, "Drugstores Face New Rival," *WWD*, March 5, 1999, p. 16.

27. James Frederick, "Walgreens Gears for Opening of Its Own Internet Pharmacy," *Drug Store News*, July 19, 1999, pp. CP1–CP4; "State of the Industry: Drug Stores: Chain Drug Stores Provide Rx for Whole Health," *Chain Store Age*, State of the Industry Supplement, August 1999, pp. A21–A24.

28. Ellen Neuborne, "Happy Returns: How to Deal with Rejected Web Purchases," *BusinessWeek*, October 8, 2001, p. SB12.

29. "Integrating Multiple Channels," *Chain Store Age Executive*, August 2001, p. A24.

30. Stacy Forster, "When One Hand Doesn't Know What the Other Hand Is Doing, Customers Notice. And They Aren't Pleased," *The Wall Street Journal*, March 22, 2004, p. B1.

Chapter 4

1. For a detailed discussion of customer behavior, see J. Paul Peter and Jerry C. Olson, *Consumer Behavior and Marketing Strategy*, 7th ed. (New York: McGraw-Hill, 2005); Michael R. Solomon, *Consumer Behavior: Buying, Having, and Being*, 6th ed. (Upper Saddle River, NJ: Prentice Hall, 2005).

2. *Shopper Update–Softgoods*, Columbus, OH: Retail Forward, May 2004, p. 3.

3. Barry Babin, William Darden, and Mitch Griffin, "Work and/or Fun: Measuring Hedonic and Utilitarian Shopping Value," *Journal of Consumer Research* 20 (March 1994), pp. 644–56.

4. Anthony Cox, Dena Cox, and Ronald Anderson, "Reassessing the Pleasures of Store Shopping," *Journal of Business Research* 58 (March 2005), pp. 250–65; Leslie Stoel, Vanessa Wickcliffe, and Kyu Lee, "Attribute Beliefs and Spending as Antecedents to Shopping Value," *Journal of Business Research*, 57 (October 2004), pp. 1067–78; Mark Arnold and Kristy Reynolds, "Hedonic Shopping Motives," *Journal of Retailing* 79, no. 2 (2003), pp. 77–93.

5. Stephen Grove and Raymond Fisk, "The Impact of Other Customers on Service Experiences: A Critical Incident Examination of Getting Along," *Journal of Retailing* 73 (Spring 1997), pp. 63–86; Dale Duhan, Scott Johnson, James Wilcox, and Gilbert Harrell, "Influence on Consumer Use of Word-of-Mouth Recommendation Sources," *Journal of the Academy of Marketing Science* 25 (Fall 1997), pp. 283–95; Kenneth Evans, Tim Christiansen, and James Gill, "The Impact of Social Influence and Role Expectations on Shopping Center Patronage Intentions," *Journal of the Academy of Marketing Science* 24 (Summer 1996), pp. 208–18; Yong-Soon Kang and Nancy Ridgeway, "The Importance of Consumer Market Interactions as a Form of Social Support for Elderly Consumers," *Journal of Public Policy & Marketing* 15 (Spring 1996), pp. 108–17.

6. Harn Luomala and Martti Laaksonene, "A Qualitative Exploration of Mood-Regulatory Self-Gift Behaviors," *Journal of Economic Psychology*, 20 (April 1999), pp. 147–83; David Mick and Corinne Faure, "Consumer Self-Gifts in Achievement Contexts: The Role of Outcomes, Attributions, Emotions, and Deservingness," *International Journal of Research in Marketing*, 15 (October 1998), pp. 293–308; David Mick, Michelle DeMoss, and Ronald Faber, "A Projective Study of Motivations and Meanings of Self-Gift," *Journal of Retailing*, 68 (Summer 1992), pp. 112–44.

7. "Crossover Jeans Customers Shop at Macy's Today, Wal-Mart Tomorrow," *DNR*, August 21, 2000, p. 74; Myra Stark, "Confessions of a Cross-Shopper," *Brandweek*, July 12, 1999, pp. 16–17; Lisa Vincenti, "Fashion-Forward Discounters Score," *HFN*, July 20, 1998, pp. 9, 59; Michelle Morganosky, "Retail Market Structure Change: Implications for Retailers and Consumers," *International Journal of Retail & Distribution Management* 25 (August 1997), pp. 269–84.

8. Philip Titus and Peter Everett, "The Consumer Retail Search Process: A Conceptual Model and Research Agenda," *Journal of the Academy of Marketing Science* 23 (Spring 1995), pp. 106–19; Paul Bloom and James Pailin, "Using Information Situations to Guide Marketing Strategy," *Journal of Consumer Marketing* 12 (Spring 1995), pp. 19–28.

9. Sanjay Putrevu and Brian T. Ratchford, "A Model of Search Behavior with an Application to Grocery Shopping," *Journal of Retailing* 73 (Winter 1997), pp. 463–87; Sridhar Moorthy, Brian Ratchford, and Debabrata Talukdar, "Consumer Information Search Revisited: Theory and Empirical Analysis," *Journal of Consumer Research* 23 (March 1997), pp. 263–78; Jeffrey Schmidt and Richard Prend, "A Proposed Model of Consumer External Information Search," *Journal of the Academy of Marketing Sciences* 24 (Summer 1996), pp. 246–56.

10. Arch Woodside and Eva Thelen, "Accessing Memory and Customer Choice: Benefit-to-Store Retrieval Models that Predict Purchase," *Marketing & Research Today* 24 (November 1996), pp. 260–88.

11. Jean Halliday, "Survey: New-Vehicle Online Research Climbs," *Automotive News*, October 25, 2004, p. 22J.

12. Ugur Yavas, "A Multi-Attribute Approach to Understanding Shopper Segments," *International Journal of Retail & Distribution Management* 31, no. 11/12 (2003), pp. 541–49; Richard Lutz, "Changing Brands Attitudes through Modification of Cognitive Structure," *Journal of Consumer Research* 1 (1975), pp. 49–59.

13. Patrich Van Kenhove, Walter Van Waterschoot, and Kristoff De Wulf, "The Impact of Task Definition on Store-Attribute Saliences and Store Choice," *Journal of Retailing* 75 (Spring 1999), pp. 125–36.

14. William L. Wilkie and Edgar D. Pessimier, "Issues in Marketing's Use of Multi-Attribute Attitude Models," *Journal of Marketing Research* (November 1973), pp. 428–41; Richard J. Lutz and James R. Bettman, "Multi-Attribute Models in Marketing: A Bicentennial Review," in *Consumer and Industrial Buying Behavior*, eds. A. G. Woodside, J. N. Sheth, and P. D. Bennett (New York: Elsevier–North Holland, 1977), pp. 13–50.

15. Pat West, P. Brockett, and Linda Golden, "A Comparative Analysis of Neural Networks and Statistical Methods for Predicting Consumer Choice," *Marketing Science* 16, no. 4 (1997), pp. 370–91.

16. David Bell, Tech-Hua Ho, and Christopher Tang, "Determining Where to Stop: Fixed and Variable Costs of Shopping," *Journal of Marketing Research* 35 (August 1998), pp. 352–70.

17. Richard Brand and Joseph Cronin, "Consumer-Specific Determinants of the Size of Retail Choice Sets: An Empirical

Comparison of Physical Good and Service Providers," *Journal of Services Marketing* 11 (January–February 1997), pp. 19–39; Ronald LeBlanc and L. W. Turley, "Retail Influence on Evoked Set Formation and Final Choice of Shopping Goods," *International Journal of Retail & Distribution Management* 22 (1994), pp. 10–17.

18. Wayne D. Hoyer and Steven Brown, "Effects of Brand Awareness of Choice for a Common, Repeat-Purchase Product," *Journal of Consumer Research* (September 1990), pp. 141–49.

19. Itamar Simonson, "The Effect of Product Assortment on Buyer Preferences," *Journal of Retailing* 75 (Fall 1999), pp. 347–70; Susan M. Broniarczyk, Wayne D. Hoyer, and Leigh McAlister, "Consumers' Perceptions of the Assortment Offered in a Grocery Category: The Impact of Item Reduction," *Journal of Marketing Research* 35 (May 1998), pp. 166–77.

20. Pallavi Gogoi, "I Am Woman, Hear Me Shop," *Business-Week*, February 14, 2005, p. 23.

21. Peter N. Child, Suzanne Heywood, and Michael Kliger, "Do Retail Brands Travel?" *McKinsey Quarterly*, no. 1 (2002), pp. 25–34.

22. Richard J. Lutz, "Changing Brand Attitudes through Modification of Cognitive Structure," *Journal of Consumer Research* 1 (March 1975), pp. 49–59.

23. Roger Bennett, "Queues, Customer Characteristics and Policies for Managing Waiting-Lines in Supermarkets," *International Journal of Retail & Distribution Management* 26 (February 1998), pp. 78–86; M. Kostecki, "Waiting Lines as a Marketing Issue," *European Management Journal* 14, no. 3 (1996), pp. 295–303; M. K. Hui and D. K. Tsi, "What to Tell Consumers in Waits of Different Lengths: An Integrative Model of Service Evaluation," *Journal of Marketing* 60, no. 2 (1996), pp. 81–90; K. L. Katz, B. M. Larson, and R. C. Larson, "Prescriptions for Waiting in Line Blues: Entertain, Enlighten, and Enrage," *Sloan Management Review* 32, no. 4 (1991), pp. 44–53; S. Taylor, "The Effects of Filled Waiting Time and Service Provider Control over the Delay on Evaluation of Service," *Journal of the Academy of Marketing Science* 23 (1995), pp. 38–48.

24. Tom Lueker, "Abandonment Surveys Help Boost Sales," *Marketing News*, November 24, 2003, p. 6.

25. Sandra Kennedy, "Keeping Customers Happy," *Chain Store Age*, February 2005, p. 24; Heiner Evanschitzky, Gopalkrishnan Iyer, Josef Hesse, and Dieter Ahlert, "E-satisfaction: A Re-examination," *Journal of Retailing* 80, no. 3 (2004), p. 239–52; Emin Babakus, Carol Bienstock, and James Van Scotter, "Linking Perceived Quality and Customer Satisfaction to Store Traffic and Revenue Growth," *Decision Sciences* 35 (Fall, 2004), pp. 713–38; Jarrad Dunning, Anthony Pecotich, and Aron O'Cass, "What Happens When Things Go Wrong? Retail Sales Explanations and Their Effects," *Psychology & Marketing* (July 2004), pp. 553–68; Richard Oliver, Roland Rust, and Sajeev Varki, "Customer Delight: Foundations, Findings, and Managerial Insights," *Journal of Retailing* 73 (Fall 1997), pp. 311–36.

26. Jacqueline Kacen and Julie Lee, "The Influence of Culture on Consumer Impulsive Buying Behavior," *Journal of Consumer Psychology* 12, no. 20 (2002), pp. 163–77.

27. "The Urge to Splurge," *Chain Store Age*, February 2004, pp. 64–65; Roy Baumeister and David Mick, "Yielding to Temptation: Self-Control Failure, Impulsive Purchasing, and Consumer Behavior," *Journal of Consumer Research* 28 (March 2002), pp. 670–77; Seounmi Youn and Ronald Faber, "The Dimensional Structure of Consumer Buying Impulsivity: Measurement and Validation," *Advances in Consumer Research* 29, no. 1 (2002), p. 280; Angela Hausman, "A Multi-Method Investigation of Consumer Motivations in Impulse Buying Behavior," *Journal of Consumer Marketing* 17, no. 4/5 (2000), pp. 403–20.

28. Sharon Beatty and M. Elizabeth Ferrell, "Impulse Buying: Modeling Its Precursors," *Journal of Retailing* 74 (Summer 1998), pp. 169–91.

29. Joel Urbany, Peter Dickson, and Rosemary Kalapurakai, "Price Search in the Retail Grocery Market," *Journal of Marketing* 60 (April 1996), pp. 91–111; Peter Dickson and Alan Sawyer, "The Price Knowledge and Search of Supermarket Shoppers," *Journal of Marketing* 55, no. 3 (July 1991), pp. 49–59.

30. Debbie Howell, "National Brands Feel the Pressure," *DSN Retailing Today*, October 25, 2004, pp. 22–28.

31. Michael Belch, Kathleen A. Krentler, and Laura Willis-Flurry, "Teen Internet Mavens: Influence in Family Decision Making," *Journal of Business Research* 58 (May 2005), pp. 569–92; Laura Flurry and Alvin Burns, "Children's Influence in Purchase Decisions: A Social Power Theory Approach," *Journal of Business Research* 58 (May 2005), pp. 593–617; Michael Belch, A. Midol, and Laura Willis, "Family Decision at the Turn of the Century: Has the Changing Structure of Households Impacted the Family Decision-Making Process?" *Journal Of Consumer Behavior* 2 (December 2002), pp. P111–25.

32. "Changing Decision Dynamics," *Nation's Restaurant News*, May 5, 2004, p. 20.

33. Joanne Kaufman, "Youth Must Be Served (Especially on Vacation)," *New York Times*, February 13, 2005, p. 5.3.

34. David Ackerman and Gerald Tellis, "Can Culture Affect Prices? A Cross-Cultural Study of Shopping and Retail Prices," *Journal of Retailing* 77 (Spring 2001), pp. 57–63; Aaron Ahuvia and Nancy Wong, "The Effect of Cultural Orientation in Luxury Consumption," in *Advances in Consumer Research*, vol. 25, eds. Eric J. Arnould and Linda M. Scott (Ann Arbor MI: Association for Consumer Research, 1998), pp. 29–32.

35. Ibid.

36. Soyeon Shim and Mary Ann Eastwick, "The Hierarchical Influence of Personal Values on Mall Shopping Attitudes and Behaviors," *Journal of Retailing* 74 (Spring 1998), pp. 139–60.

37. Cyndee Miller, "Top Marketers Take a Bolder Approach in Targeting Gays," *Marketing News*, July 4, 1994, pp. 1–2.

38. *Twenty Trends for 2010: Retailing in an Age of Uncertainty*. Columbus, OH; Retail Forward, 2003, p. 8.

39. Michael J. Weiss, *The Clustered World* (Boston: Little, Brown, 2000).

40. VALS1, the original lifestyle survey, assessed general values and lifestyles. The VALS2 survey focuses more on values and lifestyles related to consumer behavior and thus has more commercial applications.

41. Unmesh Kher, "Who Will Buy It?" *Time*, March 14, 2005, p. 35; Gary McWilliams, "Minding the Store," *The Wall Street Journal*, November 8, 2004. p. A.1

42. For additional information about fashion and the fashion industry, see Giannino Malossi, ed., *The Style Engine: Spectacle, Identity, Design and Business: How the Fashion Industry Uses Style to Create Wealth* (New York: Monacelli Press, 1998); Jeannette Jarnow and Kitty G. Dickerson, *Inside the Fashion Business*, 6th ed. (Upper Saddle River, NJ: Merrill, 1997); Mike Easey, ed., *Fashion Marketing* (Oxford, England: Blackwell, 1995).

43. Tina Cassidy, "How Fashions That Models Wear in Milan or Paris Find Their Way to a Mall Near You," *Boston Globe*, March 14, 2002, p. D1.

44. "The Fashion Innovators," *WWD*, March 20, 1997, p. 2.

45. http://www.hottopic.com/About us, accessed on May 6, 2005.

Chapter 5

1. See David Aaker, *Strategic Market Management*, 7th ed. (New York: Wiley, 2004); A. Coskun Samli, *Up Against the Retail Giants: Targeting Weakness, Gaining an Edge* (Mason, OH: Thomson, 2004).

2. Roger Evered, "So What Is Strategy?" *Long Range Planning* 16 (Fall 1983), p. 120.

3. Michael Porter, *On Competition* (Boston: Harvard Business School Press, 1998); Michael Porter, "What Is Strategy?" *Harvard Business Review*, November–December 1996, pp. 61–78.

4. Bridget Finn and Gary Heavin, "How to Grow a Chain That's Already Everywhere," *Business 2.0*, March 2005, p. 52; Clarke Canfield, "No-Frills Fitness Club Takes Its Alternative Routine to Small Towns, *Los Angeles Times*, November 26, 2004. p. C.4.

5. Todd Benson, "Courting the Poor, a Retailer Rises to No. 3 in Brazil," *New York Times*, July 14, 2004.

6. Tracie Rozhon, "A Big Middle-Age Demand for Not So Revealing but Still Stylish," *New York Times*, April 7, 2004, p. C1.

7. http://www.savealot.com, accessed April 7, 2005.

8. Anthony Boardman and Aidan Vining, "Defining Your Business Using Product-Customer Matrices," *Long Range Planning* 29 (February 1996), pp. 38–48.

9. Morten Hansen and Nitin Nohria, "How to Build Collaborative Advantage," *MIT Sloan Management Review* 46 (Fall 2004), pp. 22–28; Jeffrey Dyer and Harbir Singh, "The Relational View: Cooperative Strategy and Sources of Interorganizational Competitive Advantage," *Academy of Management Review* 23 (October 1998), pp. 660–80; Cynthia Montgomery, "Creating Corporate Advantage," *Harvard Business Review*, May–June 1998, pp. 71–80; Shelby Hunt and Robert Morgan, "The Comparative Advantage Theory of Competition," *Journal of Marketing* 59 (April 1995), pp. 1–15; Kathleen Conner and C. K. Prahalad, "A Resource-Based Theory of the Firm: Knowledge versus Opportunism," *Organizational Science* 7 (September–October 1996), pp. 477–501.

10. Gerrard Macintosh and Lawrence Lockshin, "Retail Relationships and Store Loyalty: A Multi-Level Perspective," *International Journal of Research in Marketing* 14 (1997), pp. 487–97.

11. Jo Marney, "Bringing Consumers Back for More," *Marketing Magazine*, September 10, 2001, p. 33; Kathleen Seiders and Douglas Tigert, "Impact of Market Entry and Competitive Structure on Store Switching/Store Loyalty," *International Review of Retail, Distribution and Consumer Research* 7, no. 3 (1997), pp. 234–56; Niren Sirohi, Edward McLaughlin, and Dick Wittink, "A Model of Consumer Perceptions and Store Loyalty Intentions for a Supermarket Retailer," *Journal of Retailing* 74 (June 1998), pp. 223–47.

12. http://www.llbean.com/customerService/aboutLLBean/guarantee.html?feat=gn, accessed April 25, 2005.

13. Robert Morgan, Carolyn Strong, and Tony Mcguinness, "Product-Market Positioning and Prospector Strategy: An Analysis of Strategic Patterns from the Resource-Based Perspective," *European Journal Of Marketing* 10 (2003), pp. 1409–40; Richard Czerniawski and Michael Maloney,

Creating Brand Loyalty: The Management of Power Positioning and Really Great Advertising (New York: AMACOM, 1999); S. Chandrasekhar, Vinod Sawhney, Rafique Malik, S. Ramesh Kumar, and Pranab Dutta, "The Case of Brand Positioning," *Business Today*, June 7, 1999, pp. 131–40; Bernard Schmitt, Alex Simonson, and Joshua Marcus, "Managing Corporate Image and Identity," *Long Range Planning* 28 (October 1995), pp. 82–92; Tim Ambler, "Category Management Is Best Deployed for Brand Positioning," *Marketing*, November 29, 2001, p. 18; Harriet Marsh, "Why New Look Must Take Stock," *Marketing*, March 29, 2001, p. 17.

14. David Lei and John Slocum Jr., "Strategic and Organizational Requirements for Competitive Advantage," *Academy of Management Executive*, February 2005, pp. 31–46.

15. "Competitive Advantage through Supply-Chain Innovation," *Logistics & Transport Focus*, December 2004, pp. 56–59; "Competitive Advantage Lies in Systems Efficiencies," *Chain Store Age*, August 2002, pp. 74–76.

16. Kerrie Brïdson and Jody Evans, "The Secret to a Fashion Advantage Is Brand Orientation," *International Journal of Retail & Distribution Management* 32, 8/9 (2004), pp. 403–20.

17. "Store Brands Today," Private Label Manufacturers Association Homepage, http://www.plma.com, accessed April 21, 2005.

18. Stephan Wagner and Jean Johnson, "Configuring and Managing Strategic Supplier Portfolios," *Industrial Marketing Management*, November 2004, pp. 717–31; S. Shaw and J. Gibbs, "Procurement Strategies of Small Retailers Faced with Uncertainty: An Analysis of Channel Choice and Behaviour," *International Review of Retail, Distribution and Consumer Research* 9, no. 1 (1999), pp. 61–75.

19. "Global Brands Face Up to International Retailing," *Marketing Week*, October 26, 2000, p. 32.

20. Tim Matanovich, "Know Your Service Strategy," *Marketing Management*, July/August 2004, pp. 14–16; Mary Jo Bitner, "Self-Service Technologies: What Do Customers Expect?" *Marketing Management*, Spring 2001; Mary Jo Bitner, Steven W. Brown, and Matthew L. Meuter, "Technology Infusion in Service Encounters," *Journal of the Academy of Marketing Science* 28 (March 2000); Mary Jo Bitner and Valerie Zeithaml, *Services Marketing*, 2nd ed. (Burr Ridge, IL: McGraw-Hill/Irwin, 1999); Leonard Berry, "Relationship Marketing of Services Growing Interest: Emerging Perspectives," *Journal of the Academy of Marketing Science* 23 (Fall 1995), pp. 236–45; Mary Jo Bitner, "Building Service Relationships: It's All about Promises," *Journal of the Academy of Marketing Science* 23 (Fall 1995), pp. 246–51.

21. William Werthar and Jeffrey Kerr, "The Shifting Sands of Competitive Advantage," *Business Horizon* 38 (May–June 1995), pp. 11–17.

22. *Growth Mining: The New Retail Imperative for Retailers*. Columbus, OH: Retail Forward, May 2004; Susan Mudambi, "A Topology of Strategic Choice in Retailing," *International Journal of Retail & Distribution Management* 22 (1994), pp. 22–25.

23. Ian Murphy, "Marketers Ponder P-O-P in Stores of the Future," *Marketing News*, May 26, 1997, p. 2.

24. Ross Tucker, "Hollister Helps A&F Rebound," *WWD*, May 12, 2004, p. 22; Kristin Young, "Ramping Up at Hollister," *WWD*, April 23, 2003, p. 8.

25. Alan Field, "Extending Their Reach," *Journal of Commerce* 5, no. 49 (1948), pp. 38–41.

26. Stephanie Armour, "These People Do Make House Calls—And Business Is . . . " *USA Today*, January 17, 2005, p. A1.

27. Anita McGahan, "Sustaining Superior Profits: Customer and Supplier Relationships," *Harvard Business Online*, http://harvardbusinessonline.hbsp.harvard.edu, March 1, 1999, pp. 1–7; Randolph Beard, "Regulation, Vertical Integration and Sabotage," *Journal of Industrial Economics* 49, no. 3 (2001), pp. 319–33.

28. Rebecca Mead, "Brooks Brothers a Go-Go," *New Yorker Magazine*, March 22, 1999, p. 88.

29. "2005 Global Powers of Retailing," *Stores*, January 2005, p. G11; Jay McIntosh and Julie Kunkel, "Top 100 Global Retailers," *Chain Store Age*, December 2004, pp. 76–78.

30. "2005 Global Powers of Retailing."

31. "Going Global," *DSN Retailing Today*, December 14, 2005, pp. 19–24; Tim Craig, "Merchants Without Borders," *DSN Retailing Today*, July 5, 2004, p. 16.

32. Elisabeth Rosenthal, "Buicks, Starbucks and Fried Chicken. Still China?" *New York Times*, February 25, 2002. http://www.NYTimes.com.

33. This section is adapted from "Winning Moves on a Global Chessboard: Wal-Mart and Costco in a Global Context," Goldman Sachs Investment Research, May 12, 2000.

34. Lisa Penaloza and Mary Gilly, "Marketer Acculturation: The Changer and the Changed," *Journal of Marketing* 63 (Summer 1999), pp. 84–95.

35. Shirley Leung, " It's a Grande-Latte World," *The Wall Street Journal*, December 15, 2003, p. A1.

36. See Enrico Colla and Marc Dupuis, "Research and Managerial Issues on Global Retail Competition: Carrefour/Wal-Mart," *International Journal of Retail & Distribution Management* 30 (2002), pp. 103–12.

37. Diana Farrell, Jaana Remes, and Heiner Schulz, "The Truth about Foreign Direct Investment in Emerging Markets," *McKinsey Quarterly* 1, no. 1 (2004), pp. 24–36.

38. Jean-Pierre Jeannet and H. David Hennessey, *Global Marketing Strategies*, 6th ed. (Boston: Houghton Mifflin, 2004); "What's the Best Way to Set Up Shop?" *Chain Store Age Global Retailing Supplement*, December 1997, pp. 32–35.

39. http://www.marksandspencer.com, accessed May 1, 2005.

40. Donald Lehman and Russell Winer, *Analysis for Marketing Planning*, 6th ed. (Burr Ridge, IL: McGraw-Hill/Irwin, 2004); Aaker, *Strategic Market Management*.

41. Andrew Campbell, "Mission Statements," *Long Range Planning* 30 (December 1997), pp. 931–33.

42. Alfred Rappaport, *Creating Shareholder Value: The New Standard for Business Performance* (New York: Wiley, 1988).

43. See Linda Gatley and David Clutterbuck, "Superdrug Crafts a Mission Statement," *International Journal of Retail & Distribution Management* 26 (October–November 1998), pp. 10–11, for an interesting example of the process used by a U.K. drugstore chain to develop a mission statement.

44. Aaker, *Strategic Market Management*.

45. http://www.catofashions.com, accessed May 3, 2005.

46. Michael Porter, "Strategy and the Internet," *Harvard Business Review*, March 2001, pp. 63–78; Michael Porter, *Competitive Strategy* (New York: Free Press, 1980).

47. Naomi Aoki, "Brooks Brothers Trying to Reach Out to New Customers," *Knight Ridder Tribune Business News*. November 12, 2003, p. 1; Teri Agins, "Media & Marketing—Advertising: Brooks Brothers Tailors Campaign; Ads Aim to Renew Luster, But Slumping Men's Line Will Present a Challenge, *The Wall Street Journal* (Eastern edition), August 18, 2003, p. B.5.

48. Cindy Guier, "Cosmic Bowling Strikes at Whole New Audience," *Amusement Business*, May 18, 1998, pp. 20–24.

49. See Aaker, *Strategic Market Management*, ch. 7. Another matrix that is often used in strategic planning is the Boston Consulting Group (BCG) market growth/market share matrix. Rather than considering all of the factors that determine market attractiveness and competitive position, the BCG matrix focuses on just two factors: market growth and market share. Research indicates that concentrating on these two factors may result in poor strategic decisions. See Robin Wensley, "Strategic Marketing: Betas, Boxes, and Basics," *Journal of Marketing* 45 (Summer 1981), pp. 173–82, for a critical analysis of these approaches.

Chapter 6

1. Robert Kaplan and David Norton, "How Strategy Maps Frame an Organization's Objectives," *Financial Executive*, March/April 2004, pp. 40–46.

2. Patrick Dunne and Robert Lusch, *Retailing*, 5th ed. (Mason, OH: Southwest, 2000) pp. 39–40.

3. "Diversity at McDonald's: A Way of Life," *Nation's Restaurant News*, January 2005, pp. 92–95.

4. 2004 Federated Fact 2004, p. 24.

5. http://www.costco.com/Images/Content/Misc/PDF/Costco-Story04.pdf, accessed May 1, 2005.

6. "Wal-Mart Still Retail's Greatest Market Challenge," *Progressive Grocer*, May 6, 2005, p. 1.

7. James Surowiecki, "The Most Devasting Retailer in the World," *The New Yorker*, September 18, 2000, p. 74.

8. Although the use of asset turnover presented here is helpful for gaining an appreciation of the performance ratio, capital budgeting or present value analyses are more appropriate for determining the long-term return of a fixed asset.

9. http://www.bizstats.com/inventory.htm, accessed May 3, 2005.

10. Ibid.

11. http://www.bizstats.com/emprodretail.htm, accessed May 5, 2005.

12. "Productivity Growth and the Retail Sector," *FRBSF Economic Letter*, 2004–37, December 17, 2004, p. 2.

13. http://www.fmi.org/facts_figs/superfact.htm, accessed May 5, 2005.

14. "Top Self-Checkout Retail Segments," *Supermarket News*, December 27, 2004, p. 28.

Chapter 7

1. http://www.icsc.org/srch/sct/sct0405/by_the_numbers_042005.pdf, accessed on May 23, 2005.

2. Doug Desjardins, "Sears, JCPenney Push Off-Mall Stores West," *DSN Retailing Today*, November 22, 2004, pp. 4–5; Kortney Stringer, "Abandoning the Mall; To Attract Busy Customers, Department-Store Chains Open Stand-Alone Outposts," *The Wall Street Journal*, March 24, 2004, p. B1.

3. Bill Levine, "The Store Stands Alone," *Chain Store Age*, April 1998, pp. 107–8.

4. Sharon Rosenberg, "Retail Kiosks Hot This Holiday Season at Miami-Area Shopping Malls," *Knight Ridder Tribune Business News*, December 19, 2004, p. 1.

5. Cushman and Wakefield report, March 2005, http://www.cushmanwakefield.com, accessed on May 23, 2005.

6. Sarah Raper, "Gap's Tour de Force," *WWD*, July 1, 1999, p. 3.

7. Association of Town Center Management, http://www.atcm.org, accessed on May 22, 2005.

8. International Downtown Association, http://ida-downtown. org, accessed on May 24, 2005.

9. Sally Patten, "Pressure on High Street 'Set to Grow,'" *Financial Times*, February 26, 2001; Sarah Ellison and Christopher Rhoads, "Already Hurting, European Retailers Hold Their Breath—Confidence and Consumption Were Already Weakening," *The Wall Street Journal*, September 24, 2001, p. 25; Dana Milbank, "Guarded by Greenbelts, Europe's Town Centers Thrive," *The Wall Street Journal*, May 3, 1995, pp. B1, B9.

10. Frank Green, "Core Values; Retailers Moving into Inner-City Areas Find that It's Just Good Business," *San Diego Union-Tribune*, November 18, 2001.

11. Personal communication, Cynthia Cohen, CEO, Strategic Mindshare, April 2002.

12. Morris Newman, " A Onetime Industrial Field Now Sprouting Storefronts," *New York Times*, January 7, 2004, p. C1.

13. James Goodno, Paul Van Buskirk, and Carleton Ryffell, "Rethinking Retail," *Planning*, November 2004, pp. 10–16; Connie Robbins Gentry, "Building a Downtown," *Chain Store Age*, March 2004, p. 123.

14. "Best of Best," *NREI*, July 2004, p. 44.

15. *The SCORE: Shopping Center Operations, Revenues, and Expenses*. New York: International Council of Shopping Centers, 2004.

16. John McCloud, "The World Beckons American Retail," *Shopping Center World*, May 1998, pp. 23–34.

17. http://www.quirksworld.com, accessed on May 25, 2005.

18. "Back to the Future," *New York Times Magazine*, April 6, 1997, pp. 48–49.

19. Stephen Metcalf, "Destination: Megamall," *TRAVEL + LEISURE*, April 2004, p. 60.

20. Kevin Kenyon, "Mall of America Turns Trash into Cash," *Shopping Centers Today*, October 1997, pp. 5–6.

21. "Mall-Based Stores Losing Market Share," *Chain Store Age*, August 2004, p. 33. Research conducted by New Canaan, CT-based Customer Growth Partners.

22. *The SCORE.*

23. Dean Starkman, "Making 'Sick' Malls Better," *The Wall Street Journal*, January 21, 2004, p. B1.

24. *The SCORE.*

25. Laura Williams-Tracy, "Mall Eyes Completion of $100 Million Makeover," *Charlotte Business Journal*, March 5, 2004, p. 30.

26. Connie Gentry, "Adding Life to Aging Centers," *Chain Store Age*, February 2005, pp. 135–36; Mark Hequet, "Makeover Time," *Retail Traffic*, February 2005, pp. 38–44.

27. Matt Valley, "The Remalling of America," *National Real Estate Investor*, May 2002, pp. 18–23.

28. "R.I. Reform School to Be Lifestyle Center," *Shopping Centers Today*, July 2004.

29. Presentation by Michael P. Kercheval, President and CEO, International Council of Shopping Centers at Executive Advisory Board Meeting for the Miller Center for Retailing Education and Research, University of Florida, October 2004.

30. Terry Pristin, "Merger Seen as Sign Outlet Malls Are Not Just a Niche," *New York Times*, October 13, 2004, p. C6.

31. Ray A. Smith, "Outlet Centers in the U.S. Turn Upmarket in Amenities," *The Wall Street Journal*, June 8, 2002, p. B11.

32. Izumi Yuasa, "Gotemba, Japan, Outlet's Cheap Brand Goods Are Explosively Popular," *Knight Ridder Tribune Business News*, October 15, 2004, p. 1.

33. Debra Hazel, "Omnicenters Blend Aspects of Malls and Power and Lifestyle Centers," *ICSC.org*, March 21, 2005.

34. Joe Gose, "Country Club Plaza Rides Again," *Reed Business Information*, September 2001.

35. Terry Pristin, "Retail Experience at the Airport," *New York Times*, July 2, 2003.

36. "Airport 2000," *VM & SD*, December 2000, pp. 40, 42, 44. Research attributed to Aviation Consumer Action Project.

37. "Resorts Generate Lucrative Retail Revenues," *Chain Store Age*, June 2000, pp. 150–53.

38. Sheila Muto, "A Frappuccino with Your X-Ray? Hospitals Turn to Retail Stores to Lure Staff and Cash," *The Wall Street Journal*, November 7, 2001.

Chapter 8

1. U.S. Burea of Census, http://www.census.gov/population/ www/estimates/metroarea.html.

2. Ibid.

3. "Company Profile," *Hoovers Online*, June 2002, www. hoovers.com.

4. Milford Prewitt, "Chains Tap Inner-City Locations as Golden Opportunities," *Nation's Restaurant News*, August 30, 2004, pp. 1–2.

5. Mike Duff, "Wal-Mart Stores Inc.," *DSN Retailing Today*, February 28, 2005, p. 44; Don Longo, "Wal-Mart Says Cannibalization Is Good," *Retail Merchandiser*, January 2005, p. 14.

6. Shirley Leung, "Secrets of My Success: What Separates the Profitable from the Unprofitable Franchisee? It's Often the Small Stuff," *The Wall Street Journal*, December 15, 2003, p. R4.

7. Connie Robbins, "Small Chains with Big Growth Plans," *Chain Store Age*, March 2005, pp. 121–24.

8. Karen A. Machleit, Sevgin A. Eroglu, and Susan Powell Mantel, "Perceived Retail Crowding and Shopping Satisfaction: What Modifies This Relationship?" *Journal of Consumer Psychology* 9, no. 1 (2000), p. 29.

9. Cherie Jacobs, "'Cumulative Attraction' Draws Lowe's, Home Depot Locations Together," *Knight Ridder Tribune Business News*, April 2003, p. 1.

10. Gene Marcial, "Having a Ball with Party City," *BusinessWeek Online*, April 16, 2002.

11. *Census 2000 Basics*. Washington, DC: U.S. Census Bureau, September 2002.

12. Ibid.

13. http://geography.about.com/.

14. Connie Gentry, "Science Validates Art," *Chain Store Age*, April 2005, pp. 83–4.

15. http://www.esribis.com/pdfs/ctsegments.pdf.

16. David L. Huff, "Defining and Estimating a Trade Area," *Journal of Marketing* 28 (1964), pp. 34–38; David L. Huff and William Black, "The Huff Model in Retrospect," *Applied Geographic Studies* 1, no. 2 (1997), pp. 22–34.

17. Tammy Drezner and Zvi Dressner, "Validating the Gravity-Based Competitive Location Model Using Inferred Attractiveness," *Annals of Operations Research* 111 (March 2002), pp. 227–41.

Chapter 9

1. Susan Jackson and Randall Schuler, *Managing Human Resources Through Strategic Relationships*, 8th ed. (Mason, OH: Southwestern, 2003), p. 5.

2. *Merchandising and Operations Cost Report* (New York: Fairchild Publications, 1999).

3. Anthony Rucci, Steven Kirn, and Richard T. Quinn, "The Employee–Customer–Profit Chain at Sears," *Harvard Business Review*, January–February 1998, pp. 82–97.

4. Jeffrey Pfeffer, *The Human Equation* (Boston: Harvard Business School Press, 1998), pp. 26–28.

5. *Retailing Indicators* (Washington, DC: National Retailer Federation Foundation, August 2004), p. 18.

6. Ibid., p. 23.

7. Paul Harris, "Boomer vs. Echo Boomer: The Work War?" *T+D*, May 2005, pp. 44–49.

8. Milt Freudenheim, "More Help Wanted: Older Workers Please Apply," *New York Times*, March 23, 2005, p. C3; Thomas Stewart, "Older and Wiser," *Harvard Business Review*, March 2004, p. 10.

9. Don Longo, "In China, Local and Multinational Retailers Share Problems," *Retail Merchandiser*, September 2003, pp. 10–11.

10. Betty Jane Punnett, *International Perspectives on Organizational Behavior and Human Resource Management* (Armonk, NY: M.E. Sharpe, 2004); Pawan S. Budhwar and Yaw A. Debrah, eds., *Human Resource Management in Developing Countries* (London & New York: Routledge, 2001).

11. Matt Moffett and Geraldo Samor, "In Brazil, Ticket of Red Tape Spoils Recipe for Growth," *The Wall Street Journal*, May 24, 2005, p. A1.

12. Catherine Fredman, "HR Takes Center Stage," *Chief Executive*, November 2003, pp. 36–42.

13. *Census of Retail Trade* (Washington, DC: U.S. Department of Commerce, Bureau of the Census, 1999), p. 15.

14. "Business Antiquities," *The Wall Street Journal*, November 17, 1999, p. B1.

15. Paul M. Mazur, *Principles of Organization Applied to Modern Retailing* (New York: Harper & Brothers, 1927).

16. "Saturday Morning Fever," *The Economist*, December 8, 2001, p. 30.

17. Jay Barney, "An Interview with William Ouchi," *Academy of Management Executive*, November 2004, pp. 108–17; William Ouchi, "A Conceptual Framework for the Design of Organizational Control Mechanisms," *Management Science* 25 (September 1979), pp. 833–49.

18. Jackson and Schuler, *Managing Human Resources*, p. 405.

19. Ibid., p. 525.

20. Jeffrey Pfeffer, "Sins of Commission Performance-Based Pay Isn't Just for CEOs and Salespeople Anymore. But Short-Term Rewards Could Be Costly in the Long Run," *Business 2.0*, May 2004, pp. 56–61; Jeffrey Pfeffer, "Six Dangerous Myths about Pay," *Harvard Business Review*, May–June 1998, pp. 109–29.

21. Donna McAleese and Owen Hargie, "Five Guiding Principles of Culture Management: A Synthesis of Best Practice," *Journal of Communication Management* 9 (2004), pp. 155–65: Beverly Kaye and Betsy Jacobson, "True Tales and Tall Tales: The Power of Organizational Storytelling," *Training & Development* (March 1999), pp. 44–51; Nancy L. Breuer, "The Power of Storytelling," *Workforce*, December 1998, pp. 36–42.

22. D. Roth, "My Job at Container Store," *Fortune*, January 10, 2000, p. 75.

23. This section is based on Chapter 3 in Jeffrey Pfeffer, *The Human Equation* (Boston: Harvard Business School Press, 1998).

24. "Fact Sheet: Turnover, 2005," www.epg.org.

25. Gary Dessler, "How to Earn Your Employees' Commitment," *Academy of Management Executive* 13 (May 1999), pp. 58–59; Deb McCusker, "Loyalty in the Eyes of Employers and Employees," *Workforce*, November 1998, pp. 23–28; David L. Stum, "Five Ingredients for an Employee Retention Formula," *HR Focus*, September 1998, pp. S9–S11.

26. Shari Caudron, "How HR Drives Profits: Academic Research and Real-World Experience Show How HR Practices Affect the Bottom Line," *Workforce*, December 2001, pp. 26–30; "HR's New Role: Creating Value," *HR Focus*, January 2000, pp. 1–4.

27. "State of the Industry Operational Management," *Chain Store Age*, August 1, 1998, p. 17A.

28. Jackson and Schuler, *Managing Human Resources*, p. 19.

29. Catherine Yang, "Low-Wage Lessons," *BusinessWeek*, November 11, 1996, pp. 108–16.

30. Gretchen Weber, "Preserving the Counter Culture," *Workforce Management*, February 2005, p. 32.

31. Yahya Melhem, "The Antecedents of Customer-Contact Employees' Empowerment," *Employee Relations* 26 (2004), pp. 72–78.

32. Jackson and Schuler, *Managing Human Resources*, p. 141.

33. "Why Going Back to the Floor Ensures Execs Stay in Touch," *Retail Week*, November 16, 2001, p. 31.

34. Shankar Ganesan and Barton Weitz, "The Impact of Staffing Policies on Retail Buyer Job Attitudes and Behaviors," *Journal of Retailing*, Spring 1996, pp. 231–45.

35. Charlotte Huff, "With Flextime, Less Can Be More," *Workforce Management*, May 2005, pp. 65–69; Joe Mullich, "Giving Employees Something They Can't Buy With A Bonus Check," *Workforce Management*, July 2004, pp. 66–68.

36. Glenda Strachan, John Burgess, and Anne Sullivan, "Affirmative Action or Managing Diversity: What is the Future of Equal Opportunity Policies in Organizations?" *Women in Management Review* 18 (2004), pp. 196–205; R. Roosevelt Thomas, "From Affirmative Action to Diversity," *Harvard Business Review*, March–April 1990, pp. 107–17.

37. Doug Daft, "Managing Diversity," *Executive Excellence*, June 2002, pp. 6–7; "Diversity Programs Become Valuable Tools for Increased Profitability," *Black Enterprise*, July 1998, pp. 120–21.

38. Stephanie Payne and Ann Hoffman, "A Longitudinal Examination on the Influence of Mentoring on Organizational Commitment and Turnover," *Academy of Management Journal* 46 (February 2005), pp. 158–68.

39. "80 Most Influential People in Sales and Marketing," *Sales & Marketing Management*, October 1998, p. 78.

40. Dina Berta, "NAFE Survey: Women Must Start at Bottom Line to Reach Top Posts," *Nation's Restaurant News*, February 9, 2004, pp. 16–17; Tony Wilbert, "Women Climbing Corporate Ladder at Home Depot," *The Atlanta Journal*, February 3, 2004, p. B1; Ann Zimmerman, "Federal Judge Will Consider Wal-Mart Suit for Class Action," *The Wall Street Journal*, September 23, 2003, p. B2; Linda Wirth, *Breaking through the Glass Ceiling: Women in Management* (Washington DC: International Labor Office, 2001).

41. Ann Zimmerman, "Big Retailers Face Overtime Suits as Bosses Do More 'Hourly' Work," *The Wall Street Journal*, May 26, 2004, p. B1.

42. Andrew Galvin, "Grocers, Union Still Smarting a Year After Strike," *Knight Ridder Tribune Business News*, March 12, 2005, p. 1; Harold Meyerson, "What Wal-Mart Has Wrought," *The Washington Post*, March 5, 2004, p. A.23.

43. Ken Clark, "Ready or Not, Here Comes OSHA," *Chain Store Age*, March 1, 2001, p. 94.

44. Bill Sanderson, "Retailers Warned to Manage Sexual Harassment," *Retail World*, April 12–23, 2004, p. 23.

45. A. Colquitt, "On the Dimensionality of Organizational Justice: A Construct Validation of a Measure," *Journal of Applied Psychology* 86 (2001), pp. 386–400.

46. Denise Power, "Penney's Human Resources Goes Self-Service," *WWD*, June 23, 1999, p. 13.

47. Mary Wagner, "Don't Call Us," *Internet Retailer*, June 2002, pp. 8–9.

Chapter 10

1. http://www.ediuniversity.com/glossary/.

2. Walter Zinn and Peter Liu, "Consumer Response to Retail Stockouts," *Journal of Business Logistics* 22 (2001), pp. 49–72.

3. Just-food.com, "Retailers, Manufacturers Lose Out Through Poor Availability," July 2, 2003.

4. Joseph Tarnowski, "Data Mining at Meijer," *Retail Merchandiser*, June 2003, p. 1.

5. Just-food.com, "Retailers, Manufacturers."

6. JP Morgan study reported in Malcon Buxton, "How New Technology Can Give Small and Mid-Sized Retailers a Lift Against Larger Foes," www.line56.com, May 31, 2005.

7. Food Marketing Institute study reported in Buxton, www.line56.com.

8. http://www.uc-council.org/glossary/index.cfm; Steve Lohr, "Bar Code Détente: U.S. Finally Adds One More Digit," *New York Times*, July 12, 2004, p. C3.

9. Constance Hays, "What Wal-Mart Knows about Customers' Habits," *New York Times*, November 14, 2004, p. C1.

10. See Jean Murphy, "Supply-Chain Management Plays Strategic Role at Grocery Retailer," www.gisc.com, March 2005.

11. "Bar Codes Change the Way Retailers Stocked, Priced Products," *Boston Globe*, June 29, 2004, p. C1.

12. "Action Plan to Accelerate Trading Partner Electronic Collaboration," *ATKearney*, September 2003, pp. 1–15.

13. Tom Zeller Jr., "The Scramble to Protect Personal Information," *New York Times*, June 9, 2005, p. B1.

14. "You'll Be Upgrading: Big Retailers Want Tech-Savvy Vendors," *BusinessWeek*, March 14, 2005, www.businessweek.com.

15. W. Masuchun, S. Davis, and J. Patterson, "Comparison of Push and Pull Control Strategies for Supply Network Management in a Make-to-Stock Environment," *International Journal of Production Research* 42, no. 20, (2004), pp. 4401–20.

16. Presented at the annual business meeting, Council of Logistics Management, Anaheim, CA, October 1998. The definition is posted on CLM's home page, www.CLM1.org.

17. Alan Goldstein, "Logistics Goes High-Tech to Figure Demand in Dallas Area," *Knight Ridder Tribune Business News*, April 21, 2002, p. 1.

18. "ProFlowers Streamlines Floral Business," *DSN Retailing Today*, May 9, 2005, p. 29.

19. Eugene Gilligan, "From Shore to Store," *Journal of Commerce*, March 22, 2004, p. 1.

20. See Arnold Maltz and Nichole Denoratius, *Warehousing: The Evolution Continues* (Oakbrook, IL: Warehousing Education and Research Council, 2004), www.werc.com.

21. Susan Reda, "Crossdocking: Can Supermarkets Catch Up?" *Stores Online*, November 9, 2001, www.stores.org.

22. Jan Hammond and Kristin Kohler, "In the Virtual Dressing Room Returns Are a Real Problem," *HBS Working Knowledge*, www.hbsworkingknowledge.hbs.edu, April 15, 2002.

23. "Returns Don't Need to Cost So Much," *Internet Retailer*, www.internetretailer.com, May 23, 2002.

24. "Auctioning Returned Goods Online Is Tougher than Anticipated, Genco Says," Internetretailer.com, May 23, 2002; "Sears Nets Greater Return by Moving Surplus Inventory to Online Auctions," Internetretailer.com, March 2002.

25. James R. Stock and Douglas Lambert, *Strategic Logistics Management*, 4th ed. (New York: McGraw-Hill, 2000).

26. "Chain Reaction: Managing a Supply Chain Is Becoming a Bit Like Rocket Science," *The Economist*, January 31, 2002, pp. 34–40; and Hau Lee, V. Padmanabhan, and Seungjin Whang, "The Bullwhip Effect in Supply Chains," *Sloan Management Review*, Spring 1997, pp. 93–102.

27. Matthias Holweg, Stephen Disney, Jan Holmstrom, and Johanna Smaros, "Supply Chain Collaboration: Making Sense of the Strategy Continuum," *European Management Journal* 23 (April 2005), pp. 170–81.

28. Susan Kulp, Hau Lee, and Elie Ofek, "Manufacturer Benefits from Information Integration with Retail Customers," *Management Science* 50 (April 2004), pp. 431–45.

29. Kurt Salmon Associates, *Efficient Consumer Response: Enhancing Customer Value in the Grocery Industry* (Washington, DC: The Food Marketing Institute, 1993).

30. "Wanted: Skilled Marketing Analysts," *DSN Retailing Today*, February 28, 2005, Supplement, pp. 13–16; "Competitive Advantage Lies in Systems Efficiencies," *Chain Store Age*, August 2002, p. 74.

31. http://www.usnet03.uc-council.org/glossary/.

32. Andres Angulo, Heather Nachtmann, and Matthew A. Waller, "Supply Chain Information Sharing in a Vendor Managed Inventory Partnership," *Journal of Business Logistics* 25 (2004), pp. 101–20.

33. Gabriel Kahn, "Made to Measure: Invisible Supplier Has Penneys Shirts All Buttoned Up" *The Wall Street Journal*, September 11, 2003, p. A1.

34. Terrance Pohlen and Thomas Goldsby, "VMI and SMI Program," *Journal of Physical Distribution & Logistics Management* 33 (2003), pp. 565–82; S. Disney and D. Towell, "The Effect of Vendor Managed Inventory (VMI) Dynamics on the Bullwhip Effect in Supply Chains," *International Journal of Production Economics*, August 2003, pp. 199–216.

35. http://www.ediuniversity.com/glossary; Mark Barratt, "Positioning the Role of Collaborative Planning in Grocery Supply Chains," *International Journal of Logistics Management* 14 (2003), pp. 53–67.

36. Liz Parks, "Transforming the Supply Chain with Technology," *Drug Store News*, July 19, 1999, p. 10.

37. Tom Pisello, "Does RFID Equal ROI?" *ROI Insider Newsletter*, May 12, 2004, Alinean Corporation, www.alinean.com/.

Chapter 11

1. Lillie Guyer, "Best Marketing Tool? It's Loyalty," *Automotive News* 79, no. 6122 (November 2004), p. 30; Fredrick Reichfeld, *The Loyalty Effect* (Cambridge, MA: Harvard Business School Press, 1996).

2. "Measuring Value," *1-to-1 Marketing*, June 2003, p. 13.

3. Matthew Budman, "Customer Loyalty: Are You Satisfying the Right Ones?" *Across the Board* 42, no. 2 (March/April 2005), pp. 51–52.

4. Sandra Yin, "Chronic Shoppers," *American Demographics* 25, no. 10 (2004), p. 13.

5. Paul Gauvreau, "Making Customers Feel Special Brings Loyalty," *Pharmacy Post* 11, no. 10 (October 2003), p. 40; Anna S. Mattila, "Emotional Bonding and Restaurant Loyalty," *Cornell Hotel and Restaurant Administration Quarterly*, December 2001, pp. 73–80; Susan Fournier, Susan Dobscha, and David Glen Mick, "Preventing the Premature Death of Relationship Marketing," *Harvard Business Review*, January–February 1998, pp. 42–50.

6. Joseph Tarnowski, "Touch of Class," *Progressive Grocer* 84, no. 8 (May 15, 2005), pp. 16–19.

7. Author's personal experience, 2004.

8. Amy Wong and Akrik Sohal, "A Critical Incident Approach to the Examination of Customer Relationship Management in Retail Chain: An Exploratory Study," *Qualitative Market Research* 6, no. 4 (2003), pp. 248–62.

9. Mark Albright, "Peddling Prestige," *St. Petersburg Times*, August 22, 2001, p. 8E.

10. Amy C. Edmondson, "Mitchells/Richards," *Harvard Business School Publications*, Case Number 9-604-010, December 2003.

11. Laurie Sullivan, "Car Dealers Rev CRM to Manage Net Leads," *Information Week*, September 13, 2004, p. 40.

12. Personal communication with stores, June 15, 2005.

13. *Marketing News*, August 15, 2004, p. 3.

14. Joseph A. Bellizzi and Terry Bristol, "An Assessment of Supermarket Loyalty Cards in One Major US Market," *Journal of Consumer Marketing* 21, no. 2 (2004), pp. 144–54.

15. Suzanne Vita Palazzo, "House of Cards: Frequent Shopper Programs Must Give Customers Reason to Value Their Shopping Experience if They're to be Anything More than Price Vehicles," *Grocery Headquarters* 71, no. 5 (2005), p. 53.

16. "Biometric Buying," *Toronto Star*, www.thestar.com, accessed June 23, 2005.

17. Jay Fitzgerald, "BJ's to Tighten Security in Wake of Cyberthefts," *The Boston Herald*, July 17, 2005; Mark Jewell, "BJ's Agrees to Audits," *BusinessWeek Online*, June 17, 2005.

18. Martha Neil, "Thinking Globally," *ABA Journal* 91 (2005), p. 62.

19. Rick Whiting, "Wary Customers Don't Trust Businesses to Protect Privacy," *InformationWeek* 902 (2002), p. 34; Tiffany Barnett White, "Consumer Disclosure and Disclosure Avoidance: A Motivational Framework," *Journal of Consumer Psychology* 14, no. 1&2 (2004), pp. 41–51; George Milne, "Privacy and Ethical Issues in Database/Interactive Marketing and Public Policy: A Research Framework and Overview of the Special Issue," *Journal of Public Policy & Marketing* 19 (Spring 2000), pp. 1–7.

20. *Marketing News*, August 15, 2004, p. 3.

21. Junko Yoshida, "Sounding the Alarm as Big Brother goes Digital," *Electronic Engineering Times*, April 4, 2005, pp. 1–2; Orin S. Kerr, "The Fourth Amendment and New Technologies: Constitutional Myths and the Case for Caution," *Michigan Law Review* 102, no. 5 (March 2004), pp. 801–89; Mary Culnan, "Protecting Privacy Online: Is Self-Regulation Working?" *Journal of Public Policy & Marketing* 19 (Spring 2000), pp. 20–26.

22. "Fact Sheet: Privacy and Your Health Information," www.hhs.gov/ocr/hipaa, accessed June 22, 2005.

23. Katherine Macklem, "Protecting Privacy," *Maclean's* 114, no. 3 (January 19, 2004), p. 34.

24. H. Jeff Smith, "Information Privacy and Marketing: What the U.S. Should (and Shouldn't) Learn from Europe," *California Management Review* 43, no. 2 (Winter 2001), pp. 8–34.

25. Bob Evans, "Protecting Customer Data Is Good Business," *InformationWeek*, May 9, 2005, p. 82; Christopher Robertson and Ravi Sarathy, "Digital Privacy: A Pragmatic Guide for Senior Managers Charged with Developing a Strategic Policy for Handling Privacy Issues," *Business Horizons* 45 (January–February 2002), pp. 2–6.

26. Jill Dyche, *The CRM Handbook* (Upper Saddle River, NJ: Addison-Wesley, 2002), pp. 134–35.

27. Frank Badillo, *Retail Perspectives in Customer Relationship Management* (Columbus, OH: Retail Forward, 2001), p. 25.

28. "Retailers Plan to Invest in CRM in 2002," *CyberAtlas*, January 23, 2002, www.cyberatlas.internet.com.

29. Valarie Zeithaml, Roland Rust, and Katherine Lemon, "The Customer Pyramid: Creating and Serving Profitable Customers," *California Management Review* 43 (Summer 2001), p. 124.

30. V. Kumar and Denish Shah, "Building and Sustaining Profitable Customer Loyalty for the 21st Century," *Journal of Retailing* 80, no. 4 (2004), pp. 317–30; see Werner Reinartz and V. Kumar, "On the Profitability of Long-Life Customers in a Noncontractual Setting: An Empirical Investigation and Implications for Marketing," *Journal of Marketing* 64 (October 2000), pp. 17–33, for an examination of programs designed to develop long-term relationships.

31. Frank Badillo, *Customer Relationship Management* (Columbus, OH: Retail Forward, 2001); Stephan Butscher, *Customer Clubs and Loyalty Programmes* (Aldershot, Hampshire: Ashgate Publishing, Limited, 2002).

32. Badillo, *Customer Relationship Management.*

33. James Cigliano, Margaret Georgladis, Darren Pleasance, and Susan Whalley, "The Price of Loyalty," *McKinsey Quarterly* 4 (2000), p. 73.

34. Stephanie M. Noble and Joanna Phillips, "Relationship Hindrance: Why Would Consumers Not Want a Relationship with a Retailer?" *Journal of Retailing* 80, no. 4 (Winter 2004), pp. 289–303.

35. "At Sentry Foods, a Changing of the Card," *Chain Store Age* 81, no. 5 (May 2005).

36. Kate Fitzgerald, "Grocery Cards Get an Extra Scan," *Credit Card Management* 16, no. 13 (March 2004), p. 34.

37. Edmondson, "Mitchells/Richards."

38. Ed McKinley, "Custom-Fit Solutions," *Stores*, June 2005, p. 23.

39. "Amazon.com Knows, Predicts Shopping Habits," *Associated Press*, March 28, 2005.

40. Roland Rust, Valarie Zeithaml, and Katherine Lemon, *Driving Customer Equity* (New York: Free Press, 2002), ch. 13; Zeithaml, Rust, and Lemon, "The Customer Pyramid."

41. David Pinto, "The Shopping Buddy," *Mass Market Retailers*, October 8, 2003.

42. Robert C. Blattberg, Gary Getz, and Jacquelyn S. Thomas, *Customer Equity: Building and Managing Relationships as Valuable Assets* (Boston: Harvard Business School Press, 2001), pp. 112–15; "Oprah on Oprah Perfectionist," *Newsweek International*, January 8, 2001, pp. 33–35.

43. Rust, Zeithaml, and Lemon, *Driving Customer Equity*, ch. 13.
44. "Retail IT 2001," *Chain Store Age*, October 1, 2001, p. 24.

Chapter 12

1. *Consumer Marketing at Retail 2004: Category Management Benchmarking Study* (Wilton, CT: Cannondale Associates, 2004).
2. Brandon Copple, "Shelf-Determination," Forbes.com, April 15, 2002.
3. *Consumer Marketing at Retail 2004.*
4. Ibid.
5. Laurie Russo, "Category Management Still a Delicate Balance," *Beverage Industry*, June 2004, p. 72.
6. Debra Desrochers, Gregory Gundlach, and Albert Foer, "Analysis of Antitrust Challenges to Category Captain Arrangements," *Journal of Public Policy & Marketing*, 22 (Fall 2003), pp. 201–16; David Balto, "Recent Legal and Regulatory Developments in Slotting Allowances and Category Management," *Journal of Public Policy & Marketing* 21 (Fall 2002), pp. 289–95.
7. Daniel J. Sweeney, "Improving the Profitability of Retail Merchandising Decisions," *Journal of Marketing*, January 1973, pp. 60–68.
8. Walter S. Mossberg, "Palm's New Hand-Held Goes Mano a Mano with BlackBerry," *The Wall Street Journal*, January 31, 2002, p. B1.
9. Martin Letscher, "How to Tell Fads from Trends," *American Demographics*, December 1994, pp. 38–45.
10. Teri Agins and Kathryn Kranhold, "Coat Peddlers Are Using Forecasters to Beat the Heat," *The Wall Street Journal*, February 18, 1999, pp. B1, B13.
11. James Curtis,"The Weather Effect," *Marketing*, July 17, 2003, p. 22.
12. Suzanne Osborn, "Stop, Look and Listen," *Chain Store Age*, May 2000, p. 40.
13. www.donagar.com.
14. Robin Givha, "Paper Rocks Hipsters: 20 Years of Cool Hunting," *Washington Post*, September 24, 2004, p. C2.
15. Connie Robbins Gentry, "Success for Sears and CVS," *Chain Store Age*, August 2003, p. 83.
16. Richard A. Kreuger and Mary Anne Casey, *Focus Groups*, 3rd ed. (Thousand Oaks, CA: Sage Publications: April 2000).
17. Ramarao Desiraju and Steven Shugan, "Strategic Service Pricing and Yield Management," *Journal of Marketing* 63 (Winter 1999), pp. 44–64; Jeffrey McGill and Garret Van Ryzin, "Revenue Management: Research Overview and Prospects," *Transportation Science* 23 (May 1999), pp. 233–56.
18. Steven Shugan and Jinhong Xie, "Advance Selling for Services," *California Management Review* 46 (Spring 2004), pp. 37–45.
19. Barbara Kahn and Brian Wansink, "The Influence of Assortment Structure on Perceived Variety and Consumption Quantities," *Journal of Consumer Research*, March 2004, pp. 519–34; Peter Boatwright and Joseph C. Nunes, "Reducing Assortment: An Attribute-Based Approach," *Journal of Marketing* 65 (July 2001), pp. 50–63.

Chapter 13

1. "Inventory Management 2003: An Overview," *Chain Store Age*, December 2003, p. 3A.
2. Maggie Overfelt, "No More Fowl-Ups," *FSB: Fortune Small Business*, May 2005, pp. 65–67.
3. "Robbery, Employee Theft, Leading Causes of Supermarket Losses," *Chain Store Age*, August 1998, p. 84; based on the Food Marketing Institute's annual security survey.
4. Murali Mantrala, "Allocating Marketing Resources," in *Handbook of Marketing*, Barton Weitz and Robin Wensley, eds. (London: Sage Publications, 2002).

Chapter 14

1. "The Best Global Brands," *BusinessWeek*, August 2, 2004, p. 15.
2. "European Private Label Numbers," Private Label Manufacturers Association, January 2002.
3. www.federated-fds.com/home.asp, accessed August 2, 2005.
4. Robin Rusch, "Private-Labels: Does Branding Matter?" Brandchannel.com, May 13, 2002, www.brandchannel.com/; features-effect.asp?id=94, based on research by John Stanley of John Stanley Associates.
5. "Private-Label Preferred?" www.retailindustry.about.com, June 15, 2005.
6. Greg Saitz,"Retailers Improve Quality of Their Own Brands, while Increasing Profit Margin," *New Jersey Star Ledger*, August 17, 2004, p. B1.
7. Stuart Elliott, "Breaching the Barriers between Name Brands and Private-Labels," *New York Times*, October 20, 2004, p. C4.
8. Mark Bergen, Shantanu Dutta, and Steven Shugan, "Branded Variants: A Retail Perspective," *Journal of Marketing Research*, February 1996, pp. 9–20.
9. Rusch, "Private-Labels: Does Branding Matter?"
10. John Stanley, "Brands versus Private-Labels," *About Retailing Industry Newsletter*, www.retailindustry.about.com, January 2, 2002.
11. www.fashioncenter.com.
12. www.dallasmarketcenter.com.
13. Ibid.
14. www.mccormickplace.com.
15. These guidelines are based on Roger Fisher and William Ury, *Getting to Yes* (New York: Penguin, 1981).
16. Paul Stancil, "Still Crazy after All These Years: Understanding the Robinson-Patman Act Today," *Business Law Today*, September/October 2004, pp. 34–44.
17. Michelle Nichols, "When Customers Want Kickbacks," *BusinessWeek*, May 6, 2005, p. 30; Tracie Rozhon, "Stores and Vendors Take Their Haggling over Payment to Court," *New York Times*, May 17, 2005, p. B1.
18. Robin Givhan, "The Grim Reality of the Bottom Line," *The Washington Post*, May 27, 2005, p. C02.
19. Paul Bloom, Gregory Gundlach, and Joseph Cannon, "Slotting Allowances and Fees: Schools of Thought and the Views of Practicing Managers," *Journal of Marketing* 64, no. 2 (April 2000), pp. 92–108; Ramarao Desiraju, "New Product Introductions, Slotting Allowances, and Retailer Discretion," *Journal of Retailing* 77, no. 3 (Fall 2001), pp. 335–58.
20. *Sebao Inc. v. GB Unic. SA*, 1999 E.T.M.R. 681.
21. Irvine Clarke III and Margaret Owens, "Trademark Rights in Gray Markets," *International Marketing Review* 17, no. 2/3 (2000), p. 272.
22. *In re Toys R Us Antitrust Litigation*, 191 F.R.D. 347 (E.D.N.Y. 2000).
23. Carlye Adler, "Soft Branding," *FSB: Fortune Small Business*, September 2004, pp. 79–83.
24. Bruce Fox, "Arizona Chain Pioneers Reverse Auctions for Grocery Buying," *Stores*, January 2002, pp. 62–64.

25. Sandy Jap, "Online Reverse Auctions: Issues, Themes, and Prospects for the Future," *Journal of the Academy of Marketing Science* 30, no. 4 (Fall 2002), pp. 13–26; M. L. Emiliani, "Business-to-Business Online Auctions: Key Issues for Purchasing Process Improvement," *Supply Chain Management: An International Journal* 5, no. 4 (2000), pp. 176–86.

26. Richard Wise and David Morrison, "Beyond the Exchange: The Future of B2B," *Harvard Business Review*, November–December 2000, pp. 86–96.

27. David Barboza, "In Roaring China, Sweaters Are West of Socks City," *New York Times*, December 24, 2004, p. C2.

28. Ted Fishman, "The Chinese Century," *New York Times Magazine*, July 4, 2004, p. 26.

29. Personal communication, David Gunter, director of corporate communications, Coldwater Creek, July 2002.

30. Steven Greenhouse, "18 Major Retailers and Apparel Makers Are Accused of Using Sweatshops," *New York Times*, January 14, 1999, p. A9.

31. Cheryl Dahle, "Gap; New Look: The See-Through," *Fast Company*, September 2004, pp. 69–70.

32. Dan Scheraga, "Collaboration Evolves," *Chain Store Age*, July 2005, p. 58.

33. Janet Adamy, "Retail Exchanges Plan Merger to Vie with Wal-Mart," *The Wall Street Journal*, April 26, 2005, p. B7.

34. Barton Weitz and Sandy Jap, "Relationship Marketing and Distribution Channels," *Journal of the Academy of Marketing Sciences* 23 (Fall 1995), pp. 305–20; F. Robert Dwyer, Paul Shurr, and Sejo Oh, "Developing Buyer–Seller Relationships," *Journal of Marketing* 51 (April 1987), pp. 11–27.

35. Nirmalya Kumar, "The Power of Trust in Manufacturer–Retailer Relationships," *Harvard Business Review*, November–December 1996, pp. 92–106.

36. Erin Anderson and Anne Coughlan, "Structure, Governance, and Relationship Management," in *Handbook of Marketing*, eds. B. Weitz and R. Wensley (London: Sage, 2002), pp. 223–47.

37. Erin Anderson and Barton Weitz, "The Use of Pledges to Build and Sustain Commitment in Distribution Channels," *Journal of Marketing Research* 29 (February 1992), pp. 18–34.

38. Jim Yardley, "Vendorville," *New York Times Magazine*, March 8, 1998, p. 62.

39. Anderson and Weitz, "The Use of Pledges."

Chapter 15

1. "Survey Reveals Shoppers' Peeves," *Chain Store Age*, May 2000, p. 54.

2. Roger Kerin, Steven Hartley, Eric Berkowitz, and William Rudelius, *Marketing*, 8th ed. (New York: McGraw-Hill, 2005).

3. Robert Matthews, "With Profit Falling, Carrefour Rethinks Strategy," *The Wall Street Journal*, March 11, 2005, p. B3.

4. Ted Bridis, "Customers in Dark about Retail Pricing," *Houston Chronicle*, June 1, 2005, p. B3.

5. Frances Cerra Whittelsey and Marcia Carroll, *Why Women Pay More* (New York: New Press, 1995).

6. Donald Lehmann, "Perceptions of Price Fairness Influence Consumer Behavior," *Marketing News*, October 15, 2004, p. 52.

7. David Leonhardt, "Why Variable Pricing Fails at the Vending Machine," *The Wall Street Journal*, June 27, 2005, p. B1.

8. Richard Clodfelter, "Price Strategy and Practice: An Examination of Pricing Accuracy at Retail Stores that Use Scanners," *Journal of Product and Brand Management* 13 (2004), pp. 269–83.

9. Ibid.

10. Amy Merrick, "Priced to Move: Retailers Try to Get Leg Up on Markdowns with New Software," *The Wall Street Journal*, August 7, 2001, p. A1.

11. Michael Levy, Dhruv Grewal, Praveen K. Kopalle, and James D. Hess, "Emerging Trends in Retail Pricing Practice: Implications for Research," *Journal of Retailing* 80, no. 3 (2004), pp. xiii–xxi; Marc Millstein, "Banking on Optimization," *WWD*, January 12, 2005, p. 12B; Dan Scheraga, "Pricing to Sell," *Chain Store Age*, March 2004, p. 52; Scott Friend and Patricia Walker, "Welcome to the New World of Merchandising," *Harvard Business Review*, November 2001, pp. 133–41.

12. Murali Mantrala and Surya Rao, "A Decision-Support System That Helps Retailers Decide Order Quantities and Markdowns for Fashion Goods," *Interfaces*, May/June 2001, Part 2, pp. S146–63.

13. Liz Parks, "Bloomie's Revamps Buyers' Culture," *Stores*, December 2004, pp. 35–38.

14. Carl Shapiro, Carol Shapiro, and Hal R. Varian, *Information Rules: A Strategic Guide to the Network Economy* (Boston, MA: Harvard Business School Publishing, 1998).

15. "Levi Strauss Reacquires a Pair of Jeans, at Markup," *The Wall Street Journal*, May 29, 2001, p. B13A.

16. "80 Most Influential People in Sales and Marketing," *Sales & Marketing Management*, October 1998, p. 78.

17. "What Consumers—and Retailers—Should Know about Dynamic Pricing," *Knowledge @ Wharton*, July 13, 2005.

18. Dillip Soman, "Does Holding on to a Product Result in Increased Consumption Rates?" *Advances in Consumer Research* 24 (1997), pp. 33–35; Brian Wansink, "Do We Use More When We Buy More? The Effects of Stockpiling on Product Consumption," *Advances in Consumer Research* 25 (1998), pp. 21–22; Valerie S. Folkes, Ingrid M. Martin, and Kamal Gupta, "When to Say When: Effects of Supply on Usage," *Journal of Consumer Research* 20, no. 3 (December 1992), pp. 467–77.

19. Tony Lisanti, "The Almighty Coupon, Redux," *Discount Store News*, September 21, 1998, p. 13.

20. Dan Scheraga, "One Price Doesn't Fit All," *Chain Store Age*, March 2001, pp. 104–5.

21. Ibid.

22. Valarie A. Zeithaml and Mary Jo Bitner, *Services Marketing: Integrating Customer Focus across the Firm*, 4th ed. (New York: McGraw-Hill, 2005).

23. Barry Berman, "Applying Yield Management Pricing to Your Service Business," *Business Horizons* 48 (March/April 2005), pp. 169–82; and Ramao Desiraju and Steven Shugan, "Strategic Service Pricing and Yield Management," *Journal of Marketing* 63 (January 1999), pp. 44–56.

24. Howard Marmorstein, Jeanne Rossome, and Dan Sarel, "Unleashing the Power of Yield Management in the Internet Era: Opportunities and Challenges," *California Management Review* 45 (Spring 2003,), pp. 147–67.

25. Glenn Voss, A. Parasuraman, and Dhruv Grewal, "The Roles of Price, Performance and Expectations in Determining Satisfaction in Service Exchanges," *Journal of Marketing* 62, no. 4 (October 1998), pp. 46–61; Dhruv Grewal, Jerry Gotlieb, and Howard Marmorstein, "The Moderating Effects of Contextual Cues on the Relationship between Price and Post-Purchase Perceived Quality," *Journal of Business and Psychology* 14, no. 4 (Summer 2000), pp. 579–91.

26. Dhruv Grewal, Kent B. Monroe, and R. Krishnan, "The Effects of Price Comparison Advertising on Buyers' Perceptions of Acquisition Value and Transaction Value," *Journal of Marketing* 137, no. 3 (April 1998), pp. 16–59.

27. Edward Fox and Stephen Hoch, "Cherry Pickers," *Retail Navigator* (Gainesville, FL: Miller Center for Retailing Education and Research, September 2004).

28. Itamar Simonson, "Shoppers Easily Influenced Choices," *New York Times*, November 6, 1994, p. 311; based on research by Itamar Simonson and Amos Tversky, www.nytimes.com.

29. This discussion has been going on for at least 70 years; see Louis Bader and James De Weinland, "Do Odd Prices Earn Money?" *Journal of Retailing* 8 (1932), pp. 102–4. For recent research in this area, see Robert Schindler and Rajesh Chandrashekaran, "Influence of Price Endings on Price Recall: A By-Digit Analysis," *Journal of Product and Brand Management* 7, no. 13, (2004), pp. 514–35; Eric Anderson and Duncan Simester, "Effects of $9 Price Endings on Retail Sales: Evidence from Field Experiments," *Quantitative Marketing and Economics*, March 2003, pp. 93–110; Mark Striving, "Price-Endings When Prices Signal Quality," *Management Science* 12, no. 46 (2000), pp. 1617–29.

30. Robert Schindler, "Fine Tuning a Retail Price," *Retail Navigator* (Gainesville, FL: Miller Center for Retailing Education and Research, April 2004).

31. Ibid.

32. Michelle Rafter, "Cheap, Cheaper, Cheapest," *The Industry Standard*, January 11, 1999, pp. 50–52; George Anders, "Comparison Shopping Is the Web's Virtue—Unless You're a Seller," *The Wall Street Journal*, July 23, 1998, pp. A1, A8.

33. Rebecca Quick, "Web's Robot Shoppers Don't Roam Free," *The Wall Street Journal*, September 3, 1998, pp. B1, B8.

34. John Lynch Jr. and Daniel Arliey, "Wine Online: Search Costs and Competition on Price, Quality and Distribution," *Marketing Science* 19, no. 1 (2000), pp. 83–103.

35. Xing Pan, Brian Ratchford, and Venkatesh Sankar, "Why Aren't the Prices for the Same Items the Same at Me.com and You.com? Drivers of Price Dispersion among E-Tailers," working paper, Robert H. Smith Business School, University of Maryland, 2001; Erik Brynjolfsson and Michael Smith, "Frictionless Commerce? A Comparison of Internet and Conventional Retailer," *Management Science* 46, no. 4 (April 2000), pp. 563–85.

Chapter 16

1. David Aaker, *Managing Brand Equity* (New York: Free Press, 1991), p. 7.

2. Linda Hyde and Elaine Pollack, *What's in a Name?* (Columbus, OH: Retail Forward, Inc., June 1999), p. 9.

3. Laura Heller, "Target Pumps Chic into HBC—And Mass Never Looked Better," *DSN Retailing Today*, June 7, 2004, pp. 18–19; Mike Duff, "Home Epitomizes Cheap Chic," *DSN Retailing Today*, April 7, 2003, p. 35; Shelly Branch, "How Target Got Hot: Hip Goods and Hipper Ads Are Luring the MTV and BMW Crowds into the Big Box," *Fortune*, May 24, 1999, pp. 169–70.

4. Debby Garbato Stankevich, "What's in a Name?" *Retail Merchandiser*, April 2001, p. 59.

5. "History in the Making: A Look at 16 Campaigns that Helped Redefine Promotion Marketing," *Promo*, March 2002, p. 23.

6. Tracie Rozhon, "Abercrombie & Fitch May Be Cool. But Cool Only Goes So Far," *New York Times*, July 13, 2004, p. C1; Jennifer Bayot, "The Teenage Market: Young, Hip and Looking for a Bargain," *New York Times*, December 1, 2003, p. C8.

7. "Integrating Online and Store Images Pays Off for American Eagle," Internetretailer.com, August 3, 2005.

8. Peter Childs, Suzanne Heywood, and Michael Kliger, "Do Retail Brands Travel?" *McKinsey Quarterly* 1 (2001), pp. 12–16.

9. "100 Leading National Advertisers," *Advertising Age*, Supplement, June 27, 2005, p. S1–S10.

10. William Shuster, "Retailing in Tough Times: The Power of Promotions," *Jewelers Circular Keystone*, April 1, 2002, p. 70.

11. "The Man Who Created Rudolph from an Idea That Almost Didn't Fly," *Chicago Tribune*, December 13, 1990, p. 1C.

12. Ibid.

13. "Coupon Usage Increases," *Progressive Grocer*, August 31, 2004, p. 1.

14. Julie Baker, A. Parasuraman, Dhruv Grewal, and Glenn Voss, "The Influence of Multiple Store Environment Cues on Perceived Merchandise Value and Patronage Intentions," *Journal of Marketing* 66 (April 2002), pp. 120–41; Dhruv Grewal, Julie Baker, Michael Levy, and Glenn B. Voss, "Wait Expectations, Store Atmosphere and Store Patronage Intentions," *Journal of Retailing* 79, no. 4 (2003), pp. 259–68; Sevgin Eroglu, Karen Machleit, and Jean-Charles Chebat, "The Interaction of Retail Density and Music Tempo: Effects on Shopper Responses," *Psychology & Marketing*, July 2005, pp. 577–59.

15. Enid Burns, "The State of Retail E-Mail," www.clickz.com/stats/sectors/email/, accessed May 25, 2005.

16. Tom Brown, Thomas Barry, Peter Dacin, and Richard Gunst, "Spreading the Word: Investigating Antecedents of Consumers' Positive Word-of-Mouth Intentions and Behaviors in a Retailing Context," *Journal of the Academy of Marketing Science* 33 (Spring 2005), pp. 123–39; and Terace Paridon, "Retail Opinion Sharing: Conceptualization and Measurement," *Journal of Retailing & Consumer Services* 11 (March 2004), pp. 87–94.

17. Frederick Reichheld, "Loyalty-Based Management," *Harvard Business Review*, March–April 1993, p. 65.

18. Linda Tischler, "WhaT's ThE Buzz?" *Fast Company*, May 2004, pp. 76–77.

19. Valerie Seckler, "Buzz Brightens as TV Spots Fade," *WWD*, June 29, 2005, p. 13.

20. Amy Merrick, "Gap Deploys 'Viral' Online Ad to Pump Up Sales," *The Wall Street Journal*, August 10, 2005, p. B1.

21. Ken Clark, "Play Ball," *Chain Store Age*, July 2002, p. 39.

22. George Belch and Michael Belch, *Advertising and Promotion*, 5th ed. (New York: McGraw-Hill, 2001), p. 531.

23. Leonard Lodish, *Advertisers and Promotion Challenge: Vaguely Right or Precisely Wrong* (New York: Oxford University Press, 1986).

24. Belch and Belch, *Advertising and Promotion*, pp. 227–28.

25. Murali Mantralla, "Allocating Marketing Resources," in *Handbook of Marketing*, ed. Barton Weitz and Robin Wensely (London: Sage, 2002), pp. 409–35.

26. This example was adapted by William R. Swinyard, professor of business management, Brigham Young University, from the "Overseas Airlines Service" case.

27. Ronald Curhan and Robert Kopp, "Obtaining Retailer Support for Trade Deals: Key Success Factors," *Journal of Advertising Research* 27 (December 1987–January 1988), pp. 51–60.

28. This illustration was provided by Kathy Perry, senior vice president, Matrix Technology Group, Inc., www.mxtg.net.

29. Donald Ziccardi and David Moin, *Master Minding the Store: Advertising, Sales Promotion, and the New Marketing Reality* (New York: Wiley, 1997).

30. Gary Witkin, "Effective Use of Retail Data Bases," *Direct Marketing*, December 1995, pp. 32–35.

31. "100 Leading National Advertisers."

32. Tony Case, "A Rocky Road Predicted for Newspaper Advertising," *Editor and Publisher*, September 23, 1995, p. 27.

33. "Maximizing the Potential of Audio Advertising," *Chain Store Age*, March 1995, p. B13.

34. Susan Reda, "Retailers Use Affiliate Programs to Drive Internet Traffic and Sales," *Stores*, May 1998, pp. 46–49; Greg Notess, "Intricacies of Advertisement Information on the Web," *Online Magazine*, November 1999, pp. 79–81; "Retooling for Interactivity," *Response*, November 1999, pp. 28–31.

Chapter 17

1. Christopher Manton-Jones, "Workforce Management: The Last Great Differentiator For Retailers?" *European Retail Digest*, Autumn 2003, pp. 66–70.

2. Seth Lubovek, "Don't Listen to the Boss, Listen to the Customers," *Forbes*, December 4, 1995, pp. 45–46.

3. *Food Marketing Industry Speaks*, Washington, DC: Food Marketing Institute, 2004. http://www.fmi.org/facts_figs/MarketingCosts.pdf.

4. H. John Bernardin, *Human Resource Management: An Experiential Approach*, 4th ed. (Burr Ridge, IL: McGraw-Hill, 2006); Raymond Noe, John Hollenbeck, Barry Gerhart, and Patrick Wright, *Fundamentals of Human Resource Management*, 2nd ed. (Burr Ridge, IL: McGraw-Hill, 2006).

5. Vicki Powers, "Finding Workers Who Fit the Container Store Built a Booming Business for Neatniks Who Turned Out to Be Their Best Employees," *Business 2.0*, November 2004, p. 74.

6. Lauri Giesen, "Seniors' Moment," *Stores*, June 2005, p. 80.

7. Lauri Giesen, "Pre-Screening Drafts Best Players," *Stores*, May 2005, p. 124; Debby Stankevich, "Retailers Focus on Optimizing Technology," *Retailer Merchandiser*, March 2002, pp. 55–58.

8. Sarah Fister, "Separating Liars from Hires," *Training*, July 1999, pp. 22–24.

9. Susan Jackson and Randall Schuler, *Managing Human Resources: Through Strategic Relationships*, 8th ed. (Mason, OH: South-Western, 2003), p. 328.

10. Jane Bahls, "Available upon Request," *HR Magazine*, January 1999, pp. S2–S7.

11. Jackson and Schuler, *Managing Human Resources*, p. 330.

12. Richard Hollinger and Lynn Langton, *2004 National Retail Security Survey Final Report* (Gainesville, FL: Security Research Project, University of Florida, 2004), p. 3.

13. John McKinnon, "Retailers Beware!" *Florida Trend*, June 1996, pp. 20–21.

14. Hiram Barksdale, Jr., Danny Bellenger, James Boles, and Thomas Brashear, "The Impact of Realistic Job Previews and Perceptions of Training on Sales Force Performance and Continuance Commitment: A Longitudinal Test," *Journal of Personal Selling & Sales Management* 23 (Spring 2003), pp. 125–40.

15. Paul Taylor, "Providing Structure to Interviews and Reference Checks," *Workforce*, Workforce Tools Supplement, May 1999, pp. S11–S55; Allen Huffcutt and David Woehr, "Further Analysis of Employment Interview Validity: A Quantitative Evaluation of Interviewer-Related Structuring Methods," *Journal of Organizational Behavior* 20 (July 1999), pp. 549–56.

16. Daniel Cable and Charles Parson, "Socialization Tactics and Person-Organization Fit," *Personnel Psychology* 54 (Spring 2001), pp. 1–24; Cheri Young and Craig Lundberg, "Creating a First Day on the Job," *Cornell Hotel and Restaurant Administration Journal*, December 1996, pp. 26–29.

17. Mya Frazier, "Help Wanted," *Chain Store Age*, April 2005, pp. 37–40.

18. Keith Rollag, "The Impact of Relative Tenure on Newcomer Socialization Dynamics," *Journal of Organizational Behavior* 25 (November 2004), pp. 853–73; John Wanous and Arnon Rechers, "New Employee Orientation Program," *Human Resource Management Review* 10 (Winter 2000), pp. 435–52; Charlotte Garvey, "The Whirlwind of a New Job," *HR Magazine* 46 (June 2001), pp. 110–16.

19. Bert Versloot, Jan Jong, and Jo Thijssen, "Organisational Context of Structured on-the-Job Training," *International Journal of Training and Development* 5 (March 2001), pp. 2–23.

20. Chris Roebuck, *Effective Leadership* (New York: AMACOM, 1999); John Kotter, *John Kotter on What Leaders Really Do* (Boston: Harvard Business School Press, 1999).

21. John Sparks and Joseph Schenk, "Explaining the Effects of Transformation Leadership," *Journal of Organizational Behavior* 22 (December 2001), pp. 849–68; Vicki Goodwin, J. C. Wofford, and J. Lee Whittington, "A Theoretical and Empirical Extension to the Transformational Leadership Construct," *Journal of Organizational Behavior* 22 (November 2001), pp. 759–72.

22. Gerard Seijts, "Setting Goals," *Ivey Business Journal*, January–February 2001, pp. 40–45.

23. Deborah Gibbons and Laurie Weingart, "Can I Do It? Will I Try? Personal Efficacy, Assigned Goals, and Performance Norms as Motivators of Individual Performance," *Journal of Applied Social Psychology* 31 (March 2001), pp. 624–49.

24. Professor Ross Petty and John Farr, "Sexual Harassment: Handling the 'He-Said-She-Said' Hot Potato," *Chain Store Age*, April 1998, pp. 56–59.

25. Mark Albright, "Hiring the Right Person," *St. Petersburg Times*, March 25, 2002, p. 8E.

26. Carol Sansone and Judith M. Harackiewicz, *Intrinsic and Extrinsic Motivation: The Search for Optimal Motivation and Performance* (San Diego: Academic Press, 2000).

27. "Front Lines," *Chain Store Age*, September 1, 2001, p. 38.

28. David Good and Charles Schwepker, "Sales Quotas: Critical Interpretations and Implications," *Review of Business* 22 (Spring–Summer 2001), pp. 32–37.

29. Todd Zenger and C. R. Marshall, "Determinants of Incentive Intensity in Group-Based Rewards," *Academy of Management Journal* 43 (April 2000), pp. 149–63.

30. Lisa Girion, "Working Longer?" *Los Angeles Times*, September 10, 2000, p. G1.

31. Dan Scheraga, "Handling Manpower by the Hour," *Chain Store Age*, August 1, 2000, pp. 51–54.

32. Hollinger and Langton, *2004 National Retail Security Survey*, p. 6.

33. Ibid., p. 3.

34. Marianne Wilson, "Building in Security," *Chain Store Age*, November 2001, pp. 129–30.

35. "Combating Shrink at the Source," *Chain Store Age*, December 2000, p. 152.

36. Timothy Henderson, "Loss Prevention Software Aids in Retail Fight against Costly Employee Theft," *Stores*, March 2001, pp. 68–72.

Chapter 18

1. Raymond Burke, "Exploring Shopability," *Chain Store Age*, September 2005, p. 58; Mitchell Mauk, "The Store as Story," *VM & SD*, October 2000, pp. 23, 25.

2. "Growing Pains," *Chain Store Age*, August 2005, p. 31A.

3. M. Joseph Sirgy, Dhruv Grewal, and Tamara Mangleburg, "Retail Environment, Self-Congruity, and Retail Patronage: An Integrative Model and a Research Agenda," *Journal of Business Research* 49, no. 2 (August 2000), pp. 127–38.

4. Lisa Eckelbecker, "Female Persuasion; Lowe's, Others Learn How to Design Stores with Women Shoppers in Mind," *Worcester Telegram & Gazette*, February 13, 2005, p. E.1.

5. Marianne Wilson, "Peak Experience," *Chain Store Age*, June 2000, pp. 144–45.

6. Emily Nelson and Sarah Ellison, "Shelf Promotion," *The Wall Street Journal*, September 21, 2005, p. A.1.

7. Candy Sagon, "Move It Along, Please," *Washington Post*, June 8, 2005, p. F01.

8. "College Bookstore Gets Smart," *Chain Store Age*, September 2000, p. 160.

9. Marianne Wilson, "Retailers Hit Hard by ADA," *Chain Store Age*, August 2003, p. 136; Stacey Menzel Baker and Carol Kaufman-Scarborough, "Marketing and Public Accommodation: A Retrospective on Title III of the Americans with Disabilities Act," *Journal of Public Policy & Marketing* 20, no. 2 (Fall 2001), pp. 297–304; Carol Kaufman-Scarborough, "Reasonable Access for Mobility-Disabled Persons Is More than Widening the Door," *Journal of Retailing* 75, no. 4 (Winter 1999), pp. 479–508; Carol Kaufman-Scarborough, "Sharing the Experience of Mobility-Disabled Consumers: Building Understanding through the Use of Ethnographic Research Methods," *Journal of Contemporary Ethnography* 30, no. 4 (August 2001), pp. 430–65.

10. Marianne Wilson, "ADA: Open to Interpretation," *Chain Store Age*, July 2002, p. 110.

11. Michael Barbaro, "Department Stores Settle Disability Lawsuit," *The Washington Post*, February 9, 2005, p. E.02.

12. Calmetta Coleman, "Kohl's Retail Racetrack," *The Wall Street Journal*, March 1, 2001, pp. B1, B6.

13. Craig Childress, "The Signing of America," *American Christmas Tree Journal*, October 2002, pp. 12–14.

14. "Five Easy Steps," *VM&SD*, June 2000, pp. 42–43.

15. This section is based on Steven Keith Platt, Kingshuck Sinha, and Barton Weitz, *Implications for Retail Adoption of Digital Signage Systems* (Chicago, IL: Platt Retail Institute, 2004).

16. Craig Childress, "Supermarkets Coming to Their Senses, All Five of Them," *Progressive Grocer*, June 4, 2004, p. 23.

17. Doris Hajewski, "JCPenney Now Hot on Kohl's Heels, Retail Industry Watchers Say," *Knight Ridder Tribune Business News*, November 7, 2004, p. 1.

18. Michael Applebaum, "More Eyeballs at Checkout," *Brandweek*, June 27–July 4, 2005, p. 54.

19. "Fixtures Improve Shopping Experience," *Chain Store Age*, July 2003, p. 78.

20. Ron Bond, "The Art and Science of Retail Displays," *Entrepreneur.com*, August 15, 2005.

21. Paco Underhill, *Why We Buy: The Science of Shopping* (New York: Simon & Schuster, 2000).

22. Raymond R. Burke, "Virtual Shopping: Breakthrough in Marketing Research," *Harvard Business Review*, March–April 1996, pp. 120–34.

23. "The Need for Speed," *WWD*, November 5, 1998, p. 2.

24. The concept of atmospherics was introduced by Philip Kotler, "Atmosphere as a Marketing Tool," *Journal of Retailing* 49 (Winter 1973), pp. 48–64. The definition is adapted from Richard Yalch and Eric Spangenberg, "Effects of Store Music on Shopping Behavior," *Journal of Service Marketing* 4, no. 1 (Winter 1990), pp. 31–39.

25. Anna S. Mattila and Jochen Wirtz, "Congruency of Scent and Music as a Driver of In-Store Evaluations and Behavior," *Journal of Retailing* 77, no. 2 (Summer 2001), pp. 273–89.

26. Teresa A. Summers and Paulette R. Hebert, "Shedding Some Light on Store Atmospherics; Influence of Illumination on Consumer Behavior," *Journal of Business Research* 54, no. 2 (November 2001), pp. 145–50.

27. Susan Franke, "Architects, Experts Say Proper Design Can Propel Shoppers into Stores," *Pittsburgh Business Times*, July 12, 2002, p. 8.

28. Earl Print, "Euro Lighting," *VM&SD*, May 1999, pp. 38, 40.

29. Malaika Brengman and Maggie Geuens, "The Four Dimensional Impact of Color on Shopper's Emotions," *Advances in Consumer Research* 31 (2003), pp. 122–25; Barry Babin, David Hardesty, and Tracy Suter, "Color and Shopping Intentions: The Intervening Effect of Price Fairness and Perceived Affect," *Journal of Business Research* 56 (July 2003), pp. 541–55.

30. Nicole Bailey and Charles S. Areni, "When a Few Minutes Sound like a Lifetime: Does Atmospheric Music Expand or Contract Perceived Time?" *Journal of Retailing* (Forthcoming); Sevgin Eroglu, Karen Machleit, and Jean-Charles Chebat, "The Interaction of Retail Density and Music Tempo: Effects on Shopper Responses," *Psychology & Marketing* 22 (July 2005), pp. 577–90; and Michael Morrison and Michael Beverland, "In Search of the Right In-Store Music," *Business Horizons* 46 (November/December 2003), pp. 77–87.

31. Jean-Charles Chebat and Richard Michon, "Impact of Ambient Odors on Mall Shoppers' Emotions, Cognition, and Spending: A Test of Competitive Causal Theories," *Journal of Business Research* 56 (July 2003), pp. 529–45.

32. Cathleen McCarthy, "Aromatic Merchandising: Leading Customers by the Nose," *Visual Merchandising and Store Design*, April 1992, pp. 85–87.

33. Velitchka Kalchteva and Barton Weitz, "How Exciting Should a Store Be?" *Journal of Marketing*, Winter 2006, pp. 34–62.

34. Ibid.

35. Adapted from Jacob Nielsen, Alertbox, www.useit.com; "Communicating with Your Customers on the Web," Harvard Management Communication Letter, article reprint no. COOO8A, 2000.

Chapter 19

1. "Retailers Join the War Effort," *Chain Store Age*, June 1994, p. 15.

2. Murray Raphael, "Tell Me What You Want and the Answer Is Yes," *Direct Marketing*, October 1996, p. 22.

3. Valarie Zeithaml, Leonard Berry, and A. Parasuraman, "The Behavioral Consequences of Service Quality," *Journal of Marketing* 60 (April 1996), pp. 31–46.

4. "Driving Customers Away," *Chain Store Age*, June 2001, p. 39.

5. James Fitzsimmons and Mona Fitzsimmons, *Service Development: Creating Memorable Experiences* (Thousand Oaks, CA: Sage Publications, 2000); Suzanne Barry Osborn, "Is Your Customer Being SERVED?" *Chain Store Age*, November 1, 2000, p. 52.

6. Robert Spector and Patrick McCarthy, *The Nordstrom Way: The Inside Story of America's #1 Customer Service Company*, 3d ed. (New York: John Wiley, 2005).

7. G. Odekerken-Schroder, K. De Wulf, H. Kasper, M. Kleijnen, J. Hoekstra, and H. Commandeur, "The Impact of Quality on Store Loyalty: A Contingency Approach," *Total Quality Management* 12 (May 2001), pp. 307–22; Benjamin Schneider and David Bowen, *Winning the Service Game* (Boston: Harvard Business School Press, 1995).

8. Paul Lima, "Instant Gratification," *Profit*, April 2002, p. 56.

9. "Combining Class with Mass," *MMR*, January 8, 2001, p. 12; "Workers Are Seeking Employers of Choice," *Chain Store Age*, October 1998, pp. 72, 74.

10. Sunil Gupta, Donald Lehmann, and Jennifer Stuart, "Valuing Customers," *Journal of Marketing Research* 41 (February 2004), pp. 7–19.

11. Ariana Eunjung Cha, "Finding Fewer Happy Returns," *The Washington Post*, November 7, 2004, p. A.01; Sandra Baker, "Retailers Get Stingier with Merchandise-Return Policies," *Knight Ridder Tribune Business News*, December 5, 2002, p. 1.

12. Cha, "Finding Fewer Happy Returns."

13. A. Parsuraman and Valarie Zeithaml, "Understanding and Improving Service Quality: A Literature Review and Research Agenda," in *Handbook of Marketing*, eds. B. Weitz and R. Wensley (London: Sage, 2002); Praveen Kopalle and Donald Lehmann, "Strategic Management of Expectations: The Role of Disconfirmation Sensitivity and Perfectionism," *Journal of Marketing Research* 38 (August 2001), pp. 386–401.

14. Kenneth Clow, David Kurtz, John Ozment, and Beng Soo Ong, "The Antecedents of Consumer Expectations of Services: An Empirical Study across Four Industries," *Journal of Services Marketing* 11 (May–June 1997), pp. 230–48; Ann Marie Thompson and Peter Kaminski, "Psychographic and Lifestyle Antecedents of Service Quality Expectations," *Journal of Services Marketing* 7 (1993), pp. 53–61.

15. Mary Jo Bitner, "Self-Service Technologies: What Do Customers Expect? In This High-Tech World, Customers Haven't Changed—They Still Want Good Service," *Marketing Management*, Spring 2001, pp. 10–15.

16. Todd Beck, "Want Loyal Customers? Don't Stop at Satisfaction," *Customer Inter@ction Solutions*, February 2005, pp. 36–49.

17. Timothy Keiningham and Terry Vavra, *The Customer Delight Principle* (Chicago: American Marketing Association, 2002).

18. Parasuraman and Zeithaml, "Understanding and Improving Service Quality."

19. Valerie Seckler, "The Shopping Experience: Service Is Key," *WWD*, August 10, 2005, p. 10.

20. The following discussion of the Gaps model and its implications is based on Deon Nel and Leyland Pitt, "Service Quality in a Retail Environment: Closing the Gaps," *Journal of General Management* 18 (Spring 1993), pp. 37–57; Valarie Zeithaml, A. Parasuraman, and Leonard Berry, *Delivering Quality Customer Service* (New York: The Free Press, 1990);

Valarie Zeithaml, Leonard Berry, and A. Parasuraman, "Communication and Control Processes in the Delivery of Service Quality," *Journal of Marketing* 52 (April 1988), pp. 35–48.

21. Linda Abu-Shalback Zid, "Another Satisfied Customer," *Marketing Management*, March/April 2005, p. 5.

22. http://retailindustry.about.com, April 4, 2001.

23. "Merchant Prince: Stanley Marcus," *Inc.*, June 1987, pp. 41–44.

24. Christian Homburg and Andreas Fürst, "How Organizational Complaint Handling Drives Customer Loyalty: An Analysis of the Mechanistic and the Organic Approach," *Journal of Marketing* 69 (July 2005), pp. 95–107; Moshe Davidow, "Organizational Responses to Customer Complaints: What Works and What Doesn't," *Journal of Service Research* 5 (February 2003), pp. 225–51; U. Chapman and George Argyros, "An Investigation into Whether Complaining Can Cause Increased Consumer Satisfaction," *Journal of Consumer Marketing* 17 (2000), pp. 9–19.

25. "Driving Customers Away," *Chain Store Age*, June 2001, p. 39.

26. Staci Kusterbeck, "Clienteling: Retailers Get Up Close and Personal with Customers," *Apparel*, May 2005, pp. 38–42.

27. www.andsend.com.

28. Paul Hemp, "My Week as a Room-Service Waiter at the Ritz," *Harvard Business Review*, June 2002, pp. 50–62; Len Berry, *On Great Customer Service* (New York: Free Press, 1995), pp. 73–74.

29. See Chuck Chakrapani, *How to Measure Service Quality and Customer Satisfaction: The Informal Field Guide for Tools and Techniques* (Chicago: American Marketing Association, 1998).

30. Emily Le Coz, "Mystery Shoppers Help Businesses Improve Customer Service," *Knight Ridder Tribune Business News*, April 25, 2005, p. 1.

31. Moria Cotlier, "Adieu to Abandon Carts," *Catalog Age*, October 2001, p. 39.

32. Disney Institute and Michael Eisner, *Be Our Guest: Perfecting the Art of Customer Service* (New York: Disney Editions, 2001).

33. See Jim Poisant, *Creating and Sustaining a Superior Customer Service Organization: A Book about Taking Care of the People Who Take Care of the Customers* (Westport, CT: Quorum Books, 2002); "People-Focused HR Policies Seen as Vital to Customer Service Improvement," *Store*, January 2001, p. 60; Michael Brady and J. Joseph Cronin, "Customer Orientation: Effects on Customer Service Perceptions and Outcome Behaviors," *Journal of Service Research*, February 2001, pp. 241–51; Michael Hartline, James Maxham III, and Daryl McKee, "Corridors of Influence in the Dissemination of Customer-Oriented Strategy to Customer Contact Service Employees," *Journal of Marketing* 64 (April 2000), pp. 25–41.

34. Alicia Grandey and Analea Brauburger, "The Emotion Regulation behind the Customer Service Smile," in *Emotions in the Workplace: Understanding the Structure and Role of Emotions in Organizational Behavior*, eds. R. Lord, R. Klimoski, and R. Kanfer (San Francisco: Jossey-Bass, 2002); Mara Adelman and Aaron Ahuvia, "Social Support in the Service Sector: The Antecedents, Processes, and Consequences of Social Support in an Introductory Service," *Journal of Business Research* 32 (March 1995), pp. 273–82.

35. Mark Johlke and Dale Duhan, "Supervisor Communication Practices and Service Employee Job Outcomes," *Journal of Service Research*, November 2000, pp. 154–65.

36. Conrad Lashley, *Empowerment: HR Strategies for Service Excellence* (Boston: Butterworth/Heinemann, 2001).

37. Daniel Roth, "My Job at the Container Store," *Fortune*, January 10, 2000, p. 76.

38. Alan Randolph and Marshall Sashkin, "Can Organizational Empowerment Work in Multinational Settings?" *Academy of Management Executive* 16 (February 2002), pp. 102–16.

39. Ibid.; Graham Bradley and Beverly Sparks, "Customer Reactions to Staff Empowerment: Mediators and Moderators," *Group and Organization Management* 26 (March 2001), pp. 53–68.

40. Jennifer Rowley and Frances Slack, "Kiosks in Retailing: The Quiet Revolution," *International Journal of Retail & Distribution Management* 31, no. 6/7 (2003), pp. 329–40.

41. Tammy Joyner, "More Businesses Telling Customers: Do It Yourself," *The Atlanta Journal-Constitution*, August 10, 2003, p. B2.

42. Sandra Guy, "Stores Juggle Service with High-Tech Savvy," *Chicago Sun-Times*, July 1, 2002, p. B12; Julie Clark, "The Importance of Kiosks in Retail Has Grown," *Display and Design Ideas*, September 2001, p. 18; Ken Clark, "Confused about Kiosks," *Chain Store Age*, November 1, 2000, p. 96.

43. Scott Donaton, "Check It Out: Hand-Held Scanners Will Change the Way You Shop," *Advertising Age*, August 29, 2005, p. 15; Michelle Higgins, "Grocery Shopping Enters a New Age," *The Wall Street Journal*, March 30, 2004, p. D4.

44. Shia Kapos, "High-Tech Shopping Lists Guide Grocery Shoppers," *Chicago Tribune*, June 20, 2005, p. C1.

45. Tom DeWitt and Michael Brady, "Rethinking Service Recovery Strategies," *Journal of Service Research* 6 (November 2003), pp. 193–209; James Maxham, "Service Recovery's Influence on Consumer Satisfaction, Positive Word-of-Mouth, and Purchase Intentions," *Journal of Business Research*, October 2001, pp. 11–24; Michael McCollough, Leonard Berry, and Manjit Yadav, "An Empirical Investigation of Customer Satisfaction after Service Failure and Recovery," *Journal of Service Research*, November 2000, pp. 121–37.

46. "Correcting Store Blunders Seen as Key Customer Service Opportunity," *Stores*, January 2001, pp. 60–64; Stephen W. Brown, "Practicing Best-in-Class Service Recovery: Forward-Thinking Firms Leverage Service Recovery to Increase Loyalty and Profits," *Marketing Management*, Summer 2000, pp. 8–10.

47. Ko de Ruyter and Martin Wetsel, "The Impact of Perceived Listening Behavior in Voice-to-Voice Service Encounters," *Journal of Service Research*, February 2000, pp. 276–84.

48. Hooman Estelami, "Competitive and Procedural Determinants of Delight and Disappointment in Consumer Complaint Outcomes," *Journal of Service Research*, February 2000, pp. 285–300.

CREDITS

Chapter 1

2 © Gideon Menel/CORBIS; 4 Courtesy of Jim Wright; 6 Courtesy 7-Eleven Japan Co., Ltd.; 8 © Todd Buchanan; 9 AP Photo/ Home Depot, Denis Poroy; 13 © Neil Beer/Getty Images/DIL; 14 Mark Richards; 14 © Steven Pumphrey; 15 © Dan Lamont/ CORBIS; 17 Courtesy of Blockbuster Inc.; 17 Courtesy of Netflix.; 20 Courtesy of JCPenney Company, Inc.; 20 Courtesy of JCPenney Company, Inc.; 22 © Bob Daemmrich/The Image Works; 27 Courtesy of James McClain; 28 Courtesy of Debbie Harvey

Chapter 2

32 Courtesy of Maxine Clark; 36 Courtesy of Netflix; 37 © Peter Southwick; 37 Courtesy Toys 'R Us; 41 Courtesy of ALDI; 42 Courtesy Eatzi's Market & Bakery; 44 Courtesy Costco; 47 Courtesy of Kohl's Department Stores; 49 Courtesy of Sephora USA LLC; 49 © Getty Images; 51 Courtesy of Bass Pro Shops; 52 Courtesy of Dollar General; 55 © Michael J. Hruby; 57 Courtesy Penzoil-Quaker State; 61 © PG/Magnum Photos; 62 © Cesar Rubio, 2003, Courtesy of Elephant Pharmacy

Chapter 3

68 Courtesy of Ken Hicks; 70 Courtesy of REI; 72 Courtesy of Office Depot; 74 Courtesy of WeddingChannel.com; 75 Courtesy of Venus USA; 78 Courtesy of Coach Inc.; 79 Courtesy of Lands' End; 83 © Susan Van Etten/PhotoEdit; 87 Courtesy of Talbots

Chapter 4

92 Courtesy of Andrea Learned; 95 © Jeff Greenberg/Index Stock; 95 © Jeff Baker; 96 © BananaStock/SuperStock; 99 Courtesy of Autobytel Inc.; 103 © Joel W. Rogers/CORBIS; 104 © Michael Newman/PhotoEdit; 106 © LWA-Sharie Kennedy/CORBIS; 107 © Jeff Greenberg/Unicorn Stock Photos; 109 Courtesy Costco; 109 © Tony Anderson/Getty Images; 110 Courtesy 7-Eleven Japan Co., Ltd.; 113 © Don Mason/CORBIS; 117 © Getty Images; 122 © Getty Images; 122 © Getty Images

Chapter 5

124 © Walter Hodges/CORBIS; 126 Courtesy of Jim Cossin; 128 Courtesy of Curves International; 134 Courtesy of Harry Rosen Inc.; 135 © Rob Crandall/The Image Works; 136 © Getty Images; 137 Courtesy of The Container Store; 139 Courtesy of Foot Locker Inc.; 141 © Najilah Feanny/CORBIS; 143 AP Photo/Chien-min Chung; 148 Courtesy of Dave Umber/Umber's Ace Hardware; 152 Courtesy of Brunswick Indoor Recreation Group; 152 Courtesy of Brunswick Indoor Recreation Group

Chapter 6

158 Courtesy of Bill Moran; 161 © Michael Newman/PhotoEdit; 163 Courtesy of Macy's; 164 Courtesy of Costco Wholesale Corporation; 170 © Jeff Greenberg/PhotoEdit; 170 Courtesy of Costco Wholesale Corporation; 179 AP Photo/Gregory Smith

Chapter 7

184 Courtesy of Michael Allen; 187 © Getty Images; 187 Courtesy Galleria at Roseville; 188 AP/Wide World Photos; 189 © Nik Wheeler/CORBIS; 191 © David Young-Wolff/PhotoEdit; 193 Courtesy West Edmonton Mall; 195 Courtesy of General Growth Properties, Inc.; 196 Photo provided by the ICSC. Used with permission of Aspen Grove Lifestyle Center; 197 Courtesy of Phipps Plaza; 199 Courtesy of Borders Group, Inc.; 200 Bill Serne/St. Petersburg Times; 200 Courtesy of Beall's Inc.; 202 © Dion Ogust/The Image Works

Chapter 8

206 Courtesy of Scott Jennerich; 210 © Tom Ianuzzi/Mercury Pictures; 212 © Michael J. Hruby; 214 © Keri Johnson; 215 Courtesy Outlet Centres International; 219 Courtesy of Talbots; 219 Courtesy of Talbots; 227 Courtesy of The Edward Beiner Group; 227 Courtesy of The Edward Beiner Group

Chapter 9

236 Courtesy of Shelley Hollock; 238 Courtesy of The Men's Wearhouse; 243 Courtesy of PETsMART; 250 © Jon Riley/ Getty Images; 253 © Steven Pumphrey; 255 Courtesy of IKEA; 256 © Michael Newman/PhotoEdit; 258 © Stone/Getty Images; 261 © Getty Images

Chapter 10

266 Courtesy of Jim LaBounty; 270 © Getty Images; 277 Courtesy of Dreyer's Grand Ice Cream; 279 © Charles Gupton/Getty Images; 280 Courtesy of Walmart; 280 Courtesy of Walmart; 281 © David Strickland; 287 © James Leynse/CORBIS

Chapter 11

292 Courtesy of Bari Harlam; 295 Courtesy of Neiman Marcus Group, Inc.; 297 AP Photo/Tribune Newspapers, Darryl Webb; 298 © Michael J. Hruby; 307 © 2005 Amazon.com, Inc. All Rights Reserved.; 308 Courtesy of MarineMax, Inc.; 309 Courtesy of Cuesol, Inc.; 309 Courtesy of JCPenney Company, Inc.

Chapter 12

314 © Annie Engel/zefa/CORBIS; 316 Courtesy of Natalie Kaplan; 318 © Ryan McVay/Getty Images; 320 © Mark E. Gibson/CORBIS; 326 © Getty Images; 327 © Annie Reynolds/ PhotoLink/Getty Images; 329 © Time Life Pictures/Getty Images; 331 © Getty Images; 332 © Getty Images; 333 Courtesy of Fashion Information Ltd., www.Trendzine.com; 337 Courtesy of dELiAs; 339 Courtesy of Fleming Company, Inc.

Chapter 13

344 Courtesy of Bill Lucas; 346 Courtesy of Office Depot; 348 Courtesy of Lowe's; 352 © Tony Freeman/PhotoEdit; 354 © Vic Bider/PhotoEdit; 359 © Geri Engberg/The Image Works; 362 © Kenneth Lambert/AP Wide World Photos

Chapter 14

370 Courtesy of Jennifer O'Neill; 372 © Barbara Norman; 373 © ELDER NEVILLE/CORBIS SYGMA; 375 © Bill Aron/PhotoEdit; 376 © Getty Images; 378 Courtesy of the Consumer Electronics Association; 379 © Rolf Bruderer/CORBIS; 380 © Jim Sugar/Corbis; 382 © Royalty-Free/Corbis; 384 Courtesy of Audio Classics, Ltd.; 385 © Getty Images; 389 Courtesy of William Alcorn; 390 © Paula Bronstein/Liaison Agency; 393 Courtesy of GlobalNetXchange International

Chapter 15

400 Courtesy of Bruce Peterson; 405 © Getty Images; 406 © Myrleen Ferguson Cate/PhotoEdit; 407 NCR Corporation; 409 Kaylei A. Mosier; 412 © The Image Works; 413 Courtesy of ProfitLogic;. 415 These materials have been reproduced with the permission of eBay Inc. © EBAY INC., ALL RIGHTS RESERVED.; 417 © Dennis McDonald/PhotoEdit; 419 © Jeff Greenberg/PhotoEdit; 420 AP Photo/Mary Altaffer; 421 © Mary Kate Denny/PhotoEdit; 422 Courtesy of Price-Grabber.com

Chapter 16

426 Courtesy of Larry Sinewitz; **428** Courtesy of The TJX Companies, Inc.; **428** Courtesy of Payless ShoeSource; **429** Courtesy Taco Bell; **429** Courtesy KFC Corporation; **430** Courtesy of L.L. Bean Inc.; **431** Abercrombie & Fitch; **434** Courtesy Albertson's Inc.; **435** Courtesy of Neiman Marcus Group, Inc.; **435** Courtesy of Neiman Marcus Group, Inc.; **437** Courtesy of Lowe's; **440** "Coppertone & Wal-Mart 'Spot the Dog' Scavenger Hunt Promotion," DVC, Morristown, NJ; **446** © Bonnie Kamin/PhotoEdit; **451** Courtesy of Back to Bed Sleep Centers; **453** © M. Hruby; **454** © M. Hruby

Chapter 17

456 © Shannon Stapleton/Reuters/CORBIS; **458** © Tom Stack; **461** AP Photo/Shelly Mays/The Tennessean; **463** Courtesy of The TJX Companies, Inc.; **467** © Jay Freis/Image Bank; **468** Courtesy of Nike, Inc.; **470** Courtesy of ShopKo Stores, Inc.; **471** Courtesy Sears Roebuck & Co.; **472** © Jack Star/PhotoLink; **475** Courtesy of The TJX Companies, Inc.; **480** Courtesy of Sheetz, Inc.; **483** Courtesy of Checkpoint Systems, Inc.; **483** Courtesy of Checkpoint Systems, Inc.

Chapter 18

488 Courtesy of Margot Myers; **490** Courtesy of Lowe's; **491** Courtesy of Starwood Hotels; **492** © Laszlo Regos/Laszlo Regos Photography; **493** © JEFF MITCHELL/Reuters/Corbis; **497** © T. Whitney Cox; **498** © Paul Warchol/Warchol Photography; **499** © Douglas A. Salin—http://www.dougsalin.com; **500** Courtesy of Xstream Solutions, Inc., http://www.xstreamsolutions.com; **502** Courtesy of Lowe's; **503** © Tom Carter/PhotoEdit; **507** Courtesy Marketmax, Inc.; **507** Courtesy Marketmax, Inc.; **508** © Sharon Hoogstraten; **508** © Sharon Hoogstraten; **508** © Sharon Hoogstraten; **508** © Sharon Hoogstraten; **511** © Scott Francis; **512** Courtesy Chain Store Age

Chapter 19

518 © Michael Newman/PhotoEdit; **520** © Craig Mitchelldyer/Mitchelldyer Photography; **521** Miller/Zell; **521** Discount Store News; **523** © Getty Images; **524** © McINTYRE PHOTOGRAPHY; **525** © Hironori Miyata/Fujifotos/The Image Works; **528** © Stock Boston; **530** © Rick Armstrong; **533** Courtesy of Tomboy Tools, Inc.; **534** Courtesy of The Container Store; **535** Courtesy of Amy's Ice Cream; **536** © Dick Blume/The Image Works

Cases

542 © Robert Essel NYC/CORBIS

co.com/ www.searsholdings.com/ www.aldifoods.com/ www.i

reens.com www.lowes.com www.itoyokado.iyg.co.jp/ www.te

ww.americanexpress.com www.edeka.de www.e-leclerc.fr ww

v.autonation.com www.mcdonalds.com www.publix.com/ ww

rated-fds.com www.loews.com/ www.morrisons.co.uk/ www.

aizegroup.com www.tjx.com www.marksandspencer.com ww

ww.winndixie.com/ www.otto.nl www.toysrusinc.com/ www.c

ed.com www.marriott.com www.yum.com/ www.boots.com

ww.johnlewis.com/ www.bjs.com/ www.lesechos.fr/ www.nor

ww.metcash.com/ www.coxenterprises.com www.barnesandno

motive.com/ www.hm.com/ www.footlocker-inc.com/ www.fa

ww.radioshack.com/ www.longs.com/ www.harrahs.com/ ww

www.rossstores.com/ www.hrblock.com/ www.bordersgroup

ww.nytco.com/ www.walmart.com/ www.carrefour.com www

w.ahold.com/ www.costco.com/ www.searsholdings.com/ ww

nney.com www.walgreens.com www.lowes.com www.itoyoka

ww.tiaa-cref.org www.americanexpress.com www.edeka.de w

www.autonation.com www.mcdonalds.com www.publix.com/

rated-fds.com www.loews.com/ www.morrisons.co.uk/ www.

aizegroup.com www.tjx.com www.marksandspencer.com ww

ww.winndixie.com/ www.otto.nl www.toysrusinc.com/ www.c

ed.com www.marriott.com www.yum.com/ www.boots.com